Exploring Employee Relations

Exploring Employee Relations

Second Edition

Mike Leat

AMSTERDAM • BOSTON • HEIDELBERG • LONDON • NEW YORK • OXFORD
PARIS • SAN DIEGO • SAN FRANCISCO • SINGAPORE • SYDNEY • TOKYO
Butterworth-Heinemann is an imprint of Elsevier

Butterworth-Heinemann is an imprint of Elsevier
Linacre House, Jordan Hill, Oxford OX2 8DP, UK
30 Corporate Drive, Suite 400, Burlington, MA 01803 USA

First edition 2001
Second edition 2007

British Library Cataloguing in Publication Data
A catalogue record for this book is available from the British Library

Library of Congress Cataloguing in Publication Data
A catalogue record for this book is available from the Library of Congress

ISBN-13: 978-0-7506-6939-9
ISBN-10: 0-7506-6939-X

For information on all Butterworth-Heinemann publications visit
our web site at http://books.elsevier.com

Typeset by Charon Tec Ltd (A Macmillan Company), Chennai, India
www.charontec.com
Printed and bound in Great Britain

07 08 09 10 11   10 9 8 7 6 5 4 3 2 1

Contents

Preface

This second edition of *Exploring Employee Relations* has been substantially rewritten whilst maintaining the same basic structure, as is outlined at the end of Chapter 1. The focus of the book is upon the employment relationship and the conflicts inherent within it. However, all employment relationships exist within, and are influenced by, a range of different contexts which, in this work, we address in parts; the international or global, the national and the organizational.

In this edition I have endeavoured to make the work more international and generic in its focus while maintaining sufficient material on the UK to satisfy what is likely to be the dominant market. The content then is consistent with the view that employee relations are both organization and nation specific but that at both the organizational and national level the actors, processes and outcomes are becoming more and more influenced by developments in the wider international and global environment.

In addition to reworking the content, a chapter on negotiating has been added in this edition and the material on equal opportunities has been incorporated into other chapters, those on demography and labour force developments, the European Union and on government.

The style of the work is still intended to be student friendly with activities at the end of each chapter which enable the reader to develop their analytical and critical thinking skills as well as to test their knowledge and understanding of the content. However, the book no longer contains answers to the activities, these will be available to tutors on a password protected site.

The intended audience are those who for whatever reason find themselves confronted for the first time with a module or study programme on employee or industrial relations and the author envisages that the book is suitable for those studying at undergraduate, postgraduate and professional levels, a particular eye has been kept upon the requirements of personnel practitioners studying for the CIPD professional education scheme.

In addition the book contains a fairly extensive bibliography, glossary and detailed list of contents.

I would like to thank all those colleagues and students who collectively and over more years than I care to detail have contributed to the development of the author's views and understandings as reflected in the text. Thanks are also expressed to all those authors and copyright holders who have given their permission to reproduce material.

Part One

Introduction

Chapter 1

Employee relations and the employment relationship

Introduction

'Employee relations' is a term that has only in relatively recent years become commonly used to indicate a particular area of subject matter. Prior to this it is likely that you would have found the term 'industrial relations' in more common use. The question of whether there are genuine differences attached to the meanings and uses of these two terms forms part of the discussion in this chapter. Also we examine briefly the issues of the nature of the employment relationship, whether it is characterized by conflict or consensus, the significance of perspective and the relevance of expectations, interests and the notion of a psychological contract. You are also introduced to the questions of what constitutes good industrial or employee relations, what does quality mean, what does it look like and, perhaps even more relevant, whether we can actually measure it in any meaningful sense. The relevance of perspective to that debate is also illustrated. Finally in this chapter we introduce the notion of an industrial relations system and its limitations as a theory of industrial relations and, in this context, outline a framework which centres upon the employment relationship and which also provides an explanation for the structure and contents of this book.

Learning objectives

After studying this chapter you will be able to:

- Discuss the main differences of view as to the subject matter of both employee and industrial relations and the differences between them.
- Identify the relevance of contexts to the employment relationship.
- Explain the concept and relevance of a psychological contract.
- Analyse the employment relationship in terms of the form of power available to employers and the nature of employee involvement.
- Examine the nature of the employment relationship in terms of compliance or commitment.
- Distinguish between the notions of employee involvement and commitment.
- Demonstrate the significance of perspective to our understanding of the employment relationship.
- Decide whether you think the employment relationship is essentially a conflictual one.
- Examine the meaning of quality in employee relations and explain the relevance of perspective.
- Discuss the appropriateness of the many possible indicators of the quality of employee relations and the relevance of perspective.
- Critically examine the notion of an industrial relations system.

Definitions of employee relations

There are debates and differences of view as to the meaning of each of the two terms, employee and industrial relations. Some people argue that there are identifiable differences between them, that there are differences of a substantive nature which justify the use and maintenance of each term, while others argue that the concepts and phenomena described are to all intents and purposes interchangeable.

Blyton and Turnbull (1994: 7–9) discuss this in explaining why they have chosen to use the term 'employee' as opposed to 'industrial'. They begin by arguing that they see no hard and fast distinction between the two, the difference being in the tendency of each to focus the subject inside different boundaries, but in reviewing various contributions to the debate they do state some of the more common views.

They point out that **industrial relations**:

- became inevitably associated with trade unions, collective bargaining and industrial action;
- had too strong a tendency to view the world of work as synonymous with the heavy extractive and manufacturing sectors of employment, sectors which were dominated by male manual workers working full-time and which are in decline in nearly all developed economies.

Using the term **employee relations** enables them to adopt a broader canvas and to:

- encompass the now dominant service sector which, in many developed countries, now employs more than 70 per cent of the workforce, and the changes in the composition of the labour force such as more women working and more part-time, temporary and fixed-term contracts;
- include non-union as well as union scenarios and relationships.

Nevertheless, Blyton and Turnbull do not go as far as some others in that they choose to continue to focus their study of employee relations upon the **collective** aspects of the employment relationship. They suggest that in this they are maintaining a distinction between employee relations and those other areas of study: personnel management and human resource management (HRM), each of which, they suggest, focuses upon the individual as opposed to the collective elements of the relationship.

Marchington and Wilkinson (1996: 223) also discuss this 'difference' and they suggest that the term employee relations has emerged for three main reasons:

1 Usage, fashion and slippage.
2 It is increasingly used by personnel practitioners to describe that part of personnel and development concerned with the regulation of relations (collective and individual) between employer and employee.
3 There are actual and real differences of focus, with employee relations tending to focus upon management and management issues alone and on contemporary rather than historical practices; the way things are as opposed to the way things were.

Marchington and Wilkinson have chosen to use the term employee relations principally for the second of these three reasons, though they also acknowledge that they use the terms interchangeably.

A comparison of these two views indicates that both seek to argue that use of the term **employee relations** makes it easier to encompass change in the employment relationship, its environment and in the make up of the labour force, and both explanations would appear to allow the term **employee relations** to encompass union and non-union relations.

However, where Blyton and Turnbull are keen to maintain a collective focus and see this as the basis of a continuing distinction between employee relations and both personnel and HRM in which, they suggest, the focus is upon the individual and the individual employment relationship, Marchington and Wilkinson see employee relations encompassing both individual and collective relations.

Another point of difference is that Marchington and Wilkinson seem to endow the term employee relations with a managerial focus, suggesting as they do that there is a tendency for the subject matter of employee relations to be dominated by a concern with managerial issues and a managerial perspective rather than being concerned with all parties and interests in the employment relationship.

Arguably, another point of similarity is that both views tend to see employee relations as a wider concept than industrial relations, and the former can encompass the latter.

The managerial focus identified by Marchington and Wilkinson is also adopted by Gennard and Judge (2002) in their text for the Chartered Institute of Personnel and Development (CIPD), the professional body for personnel and HRM practitioners in the UK. In seeking to explain what employee relations is they state the following:

> Employee relations is a study of the rules, regulations and agreements by which employees are managed both as individuals and as a collective group, the priority given to the individual as opposed to the collective relationship varying from company to company depending upon the values of management. As such it is concerned with how to gain people's commitment to the achievement of an organization's business goals and objectives in a number of different situations ...

Here we have the subject matter being defined to include both collective and individual dimensions of the employment relationship, a managerial focus is adopted and they go further and spell out what they perceive to be the purpose or objective of management in its dealings with both individuals and collectives. They also suggest that it is management that determines the priority given to the individual or collective relationship.

What is clear from this brief discussion of a number of different definitions and perspectives is that it is the employment relationship that is at the core or heart of the subject. In this text I use the term to encompass both individual and collective dimensions, union and non-union relationships, the changing nature of work and the employment relationship, and the wider contexts within which the employment relationship occurs. I do not take a managerial perspective or standpoint but do examine the management of employee relations.

The employment relationship

In this section we examine some of the more important issues and debates surrounding the employment relationship. In particular we examine the concept of a psychological contract, the importance of values, the interests of the parties and the extent to which the employment relationship is characterized by compliance or commitment, conflict and/or cooperation, the relevance of perspective and the notion of control of the labour process.

No employment relationship occurs in a vacuum and it is important to realize that there is a range of contexts within which it occurs and which, to varying degrees, impinge upon the relationship. One of these is the legal context and at the level of the individual, there is a legally enforceable contract between employee and employer. It has also been suggested that the employment relationship can be perceived as a psychological contract.

A psychological contract: interests and expectations

Schein (1988) is largely responsible for this notion of a psychological contract and his suggestion was that between employer and employee there exists an implicit contractual relationship which is derived from a series of assumptions on the part of employer and employee about the nature of their relationship. These assumptions may not be legally enforceable but they constitute a set of reciprocal arrangements and form the basis for a series of expectations which may have a considerable degree of moral force.

The main assumptions are:

- that employees will be treated fairly and honestly;
- that the relationship should be characterized by a concern for equity and justice and that this would require the communication of sufficient information about changes and developments;

- that employee loyalty to the employer would be reciprocated with a degree of employment and job security;
- that employees' input would be recognized and valued by the employer.

Underlying this notion of a psychological contract we can also detect assumptions about what people look for in terms of returns and satisfactions from work and, indeed, there is an element of prescription in that Schein can be interpreted as specifying the way in which employees should be treated.

In this particular instance it is pretty clear that these underlying assumptions are essentially consistent with the sets of individual needs identified many years ago by American researchers such as Roethlisberger and Dickson (1939), Maslow (1943) and Herzberg (1966) and which encompass equity and justice, security and safety, recognition of worth and input and self-fulfillment. This model of a psychological contract, where fulfilled, provided the means for employees to derive intrinsic as well as extrinsic satisfactions and rewards from their work.

The notion of a psychological contract has been extended in recent years to encompass a wider range of expectations of both parties to the relationship; these, to some extent, can be perceived not only as expectations but also as the respective interests of the parties.

Gennard and Judge 2002, in discussing the psychological contract and employees' and employers' interests, suggest that, in addition to a reward package representing the monetary and extrinsic aspect of the relationship, employees may have the following expectations:

- Security of employment
- Social relations and sociable atmosphere
- Potential for advancement
- Access to training and development
- To be treated as a human being rather than as a commodity
- Job satisfaction and empowerment regarding their job
- Family friendly/work life balance conditions of work
- Fair and consistent treatment
- Some influence over their day-to-day operations but also at a policy level (often the term 'voice' is used in this context).

They also suggest that, in return for the reward package offered, employers have the following implicit expectations of employees:

- Functional, task, flexibility
- Minimum standards of competence
- A willingness to change
- Ability to work as a member of a team
- Commitment to achieving organizational objectives

■ Capability to take initiative
■ The talent to give discretionary effort.

As noted above this set of mutual expectations which are implicit in nature, plus the issue of monetary reward, can be seen to be indicative of the differences of interests between employer and employee.

The question of whether employees and employers have common or mutual interests is fundamental to the subject matter of the perspectives section later in this chapter. However, the issue is one over which there is debate and disagreement, generally those adopting a managerial focus or whose interests are managerial tending to argue that employers and employees have a self-enlightened and mutual interest at least in reconciling their differences. Gennard and Judge argue that there are obvious costs of failure to both parties which can be simplified as: organizations won't make profit, won't be successful and employees won't have a job or income.

Blyton and Turnbull (2004) take the alternative view and argue that the interdependence of labour and capital should not be mistaken for common interests and they also suggest that common interests cannot be assumed, or willed, or managed into existence.

In addition, examining this concept of a psychological contract also brings home the importance of values in and to the employment relationship. Equity, justice, dignity and trust are among the values often argued to be fundamental to the effectiveness of the employment relationship and to the achievement of the organizations objectives.

There is certainly some evidence from the UK that employees do seek from work the rewards implied by the expectations forming the psychological contract, though it has to be acknowledged that the extent of the expectations are likely to vary between employees.

Whether these expectations are being satisfied has been the subject of much research activity. For example Guest and Conway (1999) found that the psychological contract remained healthy, with about two-thirds of those surveyed feeling that their employers had substantially kept their promises and commitments to them.

The 1998 Workplace Employee Relations Survey (WERS) addressed this issue as part of an attempt to ascertain the extent to which employees in the UK were satisfied with their job/work. They compiled a measure of job satisfaction which took into account employees' satisfaction with four different components of their overall reward package incorporating both intrinsic and extrinsic factors. The intrinsic factors can be seen to reflect components of the psychological contract above:

■ influence (the level of autonomy and control) over the job;
■ a sense of achievement derived from meeting the challenge presented by work;

■ respect from managers in terms of recognition for a job well done.

The fourth component of the measure was pay.

The conclusions of the researchers were that, overall, a majority of employees were satisfied (54 per cent), however:

■ employees tended to be least satisfied with pay;
■ managers tended to be more satisfied than other occupational groups;
■ older workers tended to be more satisfied than younger workers;
■ part-time workers were more satisfied than full-time workers.

The researchers comment that 'a significant minority of employees feel that the overall deal they have – their implicit or psychological contract – is a poor one'. Other findings relevant to this concept are that 65 per cent of the employees surveyed said they felt a loyalty to the organization that they worked for and job satisfaction levels appear to be positively associated with employees feeling that they are consulted about change in the workplace. They also found a positive association between job satisfaction and employee commitment.

The WERS 2004 also pursued the question of job satisfaction and used a wider range of criteria or expectations, again incorporating both intrinsic and extrinsic components of the overall reward package (**Table 1.1**).

The authors report that employee job satisfaction varied markedly across the eight items, being highest with respect to 'the work itself',

Table 1.1
Job satisfaction

	Percentage of employees				
	Very satisfied	Satisfied	Neither	Dissatisfied	Very dissatisfied
Sense of achievement	18	52	19	8	3
Scope for using initiative	20	52	18	8	3
Influence over job	12	45	28	11	3
Training	11	40	26	16	7
Pay	4	31	24	28	13
Job security	13	50	22	11	5
Work itself	17	55	19	7	3
Involvement in decision making	8	30	39	17	6

Base: All employees in workplaces with 10 or more employees.
Figures are weighted and based on responses from at least 21,024 employees.
Source: Inside the Workplace First Findings from the WERS 2004.

'scope for using own initiative' and 'sense of achievement'. It was lowest in respect of 'involvement in decision making' and pay. The other items were; training, job security and influence over the job.

They also report that 27 per cent of employees were 'satisfied' or 'very satisfied' on seven or eight items, 23 per cent were satisfied on less than three items, while 51 per cent expressed a mixture of satisfaction and dissatisfaction across the eight measures.

As noted above, three of the job satisfaction questions were also asked in 1998 – those relating to influence, pay and sense of achievement. Whilst satisfaction with influence and pay has remained unchanged since 1998, there has been an increase in the percentage of workers satisfied with the sense of achievement they get from work (from 64 per cent in 1998 to 70 per cent in 2004).

The WERS 2004 findings demonstrate that a majority of the respondents were satisfied with the rewards received in relation to their expectations regarding six out of the eight components. Observers will no doubt argue that this demonstrates that for many employees their implicit or psychological contract with their employer is healthy, they are satisfied and this implies that their expectations are being met. However, as noted above, it is important that we remember that these findings tell us nothing about the level of employees' expectations.

A different perspective on these issues has been provided by research conducted for the ESRC Future of Work Programme and in particular by the Working in Britain in 2000 Survey (WIB2000S). Taylor (2002) in reviewing the evidence collected through this survey concluded that:

> Todays world of work is much less satisfying to employees than the one they were experiencing 10 years ago. It has also grown more stressful for all categories of employee without exception.

In particular, the survey found that there had been a decline in satisfaction with the hours that the employee was required to work and the amount of work that had to be accomplished. Employees were also less satisfied with their pay, job prospects and training. Taylor also comments that the findings indicate that there has been significant deterioration in employees' feelings of personal commitment to the company employing them.

Forms of attachment, compliance and commitment

Compliance

Central to an understanding of the employment relationship is the question of employee attachment or involvement, how it is achieved and what the nature of the relationship is.

Some years ago Etzioni (1975) suggested that employees were engaged with, attached to or involved with employing organizations in a number of different ways and with differing degrees of intensity and this still has relevance today. He used the term compliance rather than attachment and divided compliance into two elements: the form of power wielded by the employer to achieve control and the nature of the employee's involvement.

Etzioni identified three different sources and forms of power that could be utilized by employers and three different forms of involvement.

The sources and forms of power were named: coercive, remunerative and normative, and the forms of involvement were named: alienative, calculative and moral.

The three different forms of involvement can be perceived to represent different degrees of negative or positive feelings towards the employing organization with alienative the most negative and moral the most positive.

Each form of power can in theory be combined with each form of involvement and together this provides the possibility of nine different combinations of power and involvement and nine different types of compliance.

Etzioni suggested that there were three ideal or congruent combinations of these two elements that were more effective than the others. For example, if the nature of the employee's involvement with work was essentially calculative, instrumental or extrinsic, then the ideal or matching form of power the employer should use would be remunerative. Where the nature of the employee's involvement is alienative or highly negative, the appropriate form of power may well be coercive. If the nature of the employee's involvement was highly positive or moral, meaning that they identify with or share the values and purposes of the organization, then the ideal form of power the employer should use would be normative, implying the allocation or withholding of symbolic rewards such as prestige and recognition.

However, these days the term 'compliance' is not perceived as encompassing a range of forms of attachment, as was the case with Etzioni's use of the term. It is used as a comparative descriptor of a form of attachment that is less positive and intense than commitment, a form of attachment commonly achieved and maintained through the administration of rules and bureaucratic controls. In this latter context compliance results in reactive behaviour and a concern with rights and rules.

Commitment

In terms of the Etzioni model or typology the term 'commitment' refers to moral involvement, employees positively identifying with and sharing the values and purposes of the organization. It describes the kind of attachment that we tend to associate with membership of voluntary associations or perhaps with employment in public-sector service and caring organizations such as the National Health Service, rather than with membership of the more common private-sector and profit-making employing organizations.

Commitment is portrayed as an internalized belief leading to constructive proactivity by employees; it leads to employees 'going one step further' (Legge, 1995: 174).

Both here and with compliance above, assumptions are being made between forms of attachment and consequential behaviour and it may well be that the form of attachment between employees and the organization is discernible from observable behaviour.

It has also been suggested that distinctions can sometimes be drawn between attitudinal and behavioural commitment:

- ■ Attitudinal commitment is the form depicted above and which would be compatible with Etzioni's moral involvement: commitment in terms of a sharing of values and attitudes, a psychological bond to an organization, an affective attachment.
- ■ Behavioural commitment is demonstrated by a willingness to exert effort beyond the requirements of contract and/or by a desire to remain a member of an organization.

It has been suggested that Japanese organizations often demonstrate employment relationships that are high commitment, with employees demonstrating both an affective bond with the organization and the desire to remain, a desire traditionally reciprocated by management pursuing policies of lifetime employment whereby employees are recruited direct from their studies with both the opportunity and expectation that they will spend the whole of their working lives with the one employer.

Mowday *et al.* (1982) have suggested that there may well be a reciprocal relationship between these two forms, with attitudes influencing behaviour and *vice versa*. An assumption of such a relationship underlies much of the interest in the concept of commitment in recent years. However, care is needed here in that, whilst it may be that the extra effort or desire to remain with the organization are indications that the individual does have positive attitudinal commitment to it, there are other possible explanations such as there being little or no alternative employment available.

Commitment of an attitudinal nature has been at the centre of much of the prescriptive literature on HRM over the last few decades, from Beer *et al.* (1984) onwards, and in terms of the UK literature perhaps most famously by Guest (1987) who identified employee commitment as one of four outcomes that HRM should try to develop, but not for its own sake. Employee commitment became a desirable HRM outcome because of an assumption that attitudinal commitment would yield certain specified and desirable behaviours and, through these, certain desirable organizational outcomes, such as better quality of product or service, or lower labour turnover, or greater efficiency. These issues are examined in more depth in **Chapter 8**.

Employers have been exhorted by academics, popular and otherwise, and by politicians to pursue measures and policies aimed at securing this commitment and, in their turn, employers have exhorted their employees to take on and share the organization's objectives and values, often emphasizing as they did so their view that employee and employer interests were essentially the same. On this issue, we noted earlier the views of Gennard and Judge, who see securing employee commitment as the purpose of the management of employee relations, though they do not refer to attitudinal commitment as such. They refer to a commitment to the achievement of the organization's objectives rather than to the objectives themselves. Alternative perceptions of the nature of the employment relationship and the realism of this view are pursued in the following sections on conflict and perspective.

It is not difficult to perceive the attractions to management of this concept. Implicit in this attractiveness is an assumed relationship between commitment and desired behaviours and, in particular, that committed employees will work harder, be more productive and innovative and exhibit a greater concern with the quality of their output and customer satisfaction. These assumptions also underlie much of the clamour from employers and politicians in recent years for employees to be more involved in their organizations.

Unfortunately we have further confusion around the meanings attached to words. The use of the word 'involvement' here does not denote a range of forms of attachment on the part of employees, as was the case in the Etzioni typology. Here, the term is used more narrowly to describe initiatives and techniques that make the employee feel more a part of the organization, as for example might be achieved by and through effective communications policies or through the organization of social events and clubs.

Employee involvement (EI) initiatives have become popular in the UK, primarily because it is assumed that EI initiatives will encourage employees to be more content and satisfied in their work; it is assumed that this will yield employee commitment, and satisfied and committed employees are harder working, etc. In the context of the pressures for organizations to be more productive and competitive, and if you believe that helping employees to feel more a part of the organization will encourage them to work harder, then such initiatives are justified.

In addition to commitment being a prescribed desirable outcome of the softer HRM models there has been much debate about how it is to be achieved (see **Chapter 8**). There is a degree of coincidence between measures thought to enhance employee satisfaction, involvement and commitment; in other words, the same measures hopefully will achieve all of these objectives. Examples include teamworking, team-briefing, quality circles and problem-solving groups, the advent of development-led appraisal, multi-skilling and job rotation, enlargement and enrichment programmes. The increased frequency and incidence of practices of this kind have often implied and required changes in the way that employees are managed, the mechanisms used, the way work is organized and, consequently, the nature of the employment relationship.

In **Chapters 2** and **8** we come across many of these initiatives and innovations again, in **Chapter 2** we examine the nature of work and work organization and in **Chapter 8** we examine EI initiatives and the pursuit of employee commitment.

However, the popularity of these initiatives among management seems to have occurred in the absence of conclusive evidence of the relationships between involvement, commitment and improved performance that have been assumed.

The 1998 WERS findings confirmed that many organizations say they are using a range of the techniques and programmes commonly seen as encouraging EI (and thereby commitment) and, as was noted earlier, there was evidence that a majority of employee respondents expressed themselves both satisfied and committed. The findings lent support to a belief in an association between the measures designed to engender employee commitment and levels of job satisfaction but not to the belief that satisfied workers are more productive.

In the WERS 1998 survey commitment was measured by the employees' responses to questions concerned with whether they shared the goals and values of the organization, their sense of loyalty to the employer and whether they were proud to tell people who they worked for. Referring back again to the Etzioni typology, the notion of commitment pursued by the WERS research seems to be attitudinal and close to the notion of moral involvement, the sharing of objectives and values.

The ESRC WIB2000S also examined the issue of employee commitment. There are similarities with the WERS survey questions in that the respondents were asked to agree or disagree with four different statements. The first of these was concerned to test employee pride in the organization they worked for, another tested willingness to go beyond contract, and the other two were both concerned with the respondents desire to stay with the organization. Arguably, this survey demonstrates an interest in behavioural more than attitudinal commitment and these differences of focus between the two major surveys may go some way towards explaining differences in outcomes, as noted earlier, Taylor's conclusion in relation to the evidence of this survey was that there had been little advance in any sense of organizational commitment by workers.

It is worth pointing out that some of the literature treats the terms 'employee involvement' and 'employee participation' synonymously, whereas others insist upon a conceptual difference and we return to this in **Chapter 9**, concerning employee relations processes.

Conflict, cooperation and perspectives

In addition to the debates referred to above about the nature of the employment relationship in terms of forms of attachment and the means by which management achieve control, there has also been considerable debate about the extent to which the fundamental nature of the employment relationship is one of, and is characterized by, conflict or cooperation and indeed what the fundamental conflicts may be about. Central to this debate is the issue of perspective, or frame of reference.

Students should be aware that conflict in this context refers to difference and is not to be regarded as synonymous with or be confused with industrial action. Often, in the media and elsewhere, the term 'industrial conflict' is used as an alternative description for strikes and other industrial action; this is not the intention here. Industrial action is unlikely unless there is conflict and so it is reasonable to view such action as a symptom of conflict, but conflict exists in many situations without it resulting in industrial action and there are many other potential symptoms such as poor performance, absenteeism, high stress and anxiety levels and labour turnover.

Students also often have difficulty with this notion of **perspective** and tend to confuse it with a system or form of organization so that, for example, they talk and write about 'unitaristic' organizations. It is important to appreciate that a perspective is an approach or way of looking at something, not the thing itself. We each have values and views and these have been determined through the process of socialization and informed by our experience. The perspective that we each have will mean that we approach issues, concepts and events with a particular orientation that will influence our interpretation and understanding of what we see and experience. Our view and understanding of the nature of employing organizations and the employment relationship will be subject to these influences.

Fox (1966) used the term 'frame of reference' and this may help in enabling you to understand the nature of a perspective. Initially Fox identified two particular and relevant frames of reference, the unitarist and pluralist. Subsequently and additionally a third, radical or Marxist, variant has been distinguished and contrasted with the others. These are not the only perspectives on the fundamental nature of the employment relationship and on whether it is characterized by conflict: Nicholls

(1999) adds a feminist perspective which perceives capitalism and employee relations in terms of patriarchy and male domination of women. However, these three main perspectives do represent distinctly different viewpoints on these issues and are indicators of the range of potential perspectives.

Unitarism

This perspective perceives employing organizations as peopled by individuals and groups that have common interests, objectives and values, and that are harmonious and integrated. Management's right to manage is legitimate and rational and management (representing the organization and the interests of capital) should be the single focus of employee loyalty as well as the sole source of legitimate authority within the organization. Unsurprisingly, therefore, this perspective tends to be associated with, and is often promoted by, management since it supports management's interests. Frequently this perspective has been characterized as the 'Team' or 'One big happy family' approach.

From the unitarist perspective conflict between labour and management is viewed as being both unnecessary and avoidable. Where conflict does occur it is argued that this is not because it is inherent to the capitalist system or even because groups have legitimate differences between their aspirations and interests; it occurs because of poor communication, because the parties to the relationship lack understanding of the extent to which their interests are coincident, because the conflict has been deliberately created by saboteurs or because individual personalities clash. The perspective argues that conflict is irrational and pathological and that it should not occur; if and where it does, management has the legitimate right to manage, to control, where necessary to subordinate, labour; employees owe loyalty and therefore conflict resolution ought not to be an issue.

In this context the employment relationship is likely to be perceived to be characterized by cooperation rather than by conflict, with management or other representatives of capital adopting autocratic or paternalist approaches to the exercising of their authority. Cooperation between the interests of capital and labour should be normal in this scenario.

Managements holding this perspective will often try to persuade their employees that they do not need a trade union to represent them and that management will look after them; indeed these managements often try to create circumstances at work which tend to reinforce this message. Examples of companies in which this attitude has dominated would certainly include big names such as Marks and Spencer, IBM and Hewlett Packard. Management style in organizations in which this management perspective dominates tends to be perceived as being on a continuum between the extremes of autocracy and paternalism.

Pluralism

This perspective assumes that employing organizations are made up of individuals and groups with different interests, values and objectives. Each group is likely to develop its own leadership and source of loyalty. The various interests and objectives of one group are likely to conflict with those of others and, while this will include the interests of labour versus the interests of capital, conflict will not be exclusive to these interests. It is common, for example, that there are conflicts within organizations between different groups of employees and between different management functions as well as between labour and capital. We must not assume that all employees have the same interests and expectations, nor indeed that all managers do. For example, it is not unusual for the finance function within an organization to come into conflict with other functions or departments over issues such as the determination of budgets and expenditure plans, and it is not uncommon for groups of employees to come into conflict over issues such as the 'ownership' of particular work or tasks and the rates of pay received by each of the groups. These latter conflicts arguably used to be more common than they are these days given technological change and the spread of flexible working, multi-skilling and teamworking, but they do still occur. One of the major arguments against the introduction of a minimum wage is that it may well provoke conflicts between groups of employees, with those lowest paid appearing to benefit as the minimum rate of pay is higher than their current earnings, whereas those on higher rates of pay are unaffected and this can lead to conflicts between groups of employees over the maintenance, or not, of existing pay differentials.

In the context of this perspective, management is likely to be confronted by a workforce which does not necessarily accept its right to manage and who owe loyalty to other sources and interests. Management has a very different role in this context: the task facing it is not to exercise a unilateral right to manage, whether this takes an autocratic or paternalistic form; the emphasis is now upon securing the agreement of the other interests to decisions. As Flanders (1970: 172) put it: 'the paradox, whose truth managements have found it difficult to accept, is that they can only regain control by sharing it'.

Management's job, therefore, is not to try and insist upon a right to manage unilaterally but to manage and resolve the conflict and to do this via mechanisms that emphasize the achievement of consensus and that involve representation and participation from the various interests concerned. In this sense conflict becomes institutionalized.

This is a perspective which argues that the greatest potential lies in joint approaches to conflict resolution. Pluralists tend to assume a rough equality of bargaining power between the parties and that the outcome will be a negotiated order and stability.

Collective bargaining is one possible mechanism and, in this context, the formation of trade unions is a realistic and rational response on the part of the labour resource, since they, through their collective strength, are able to provide employees with a counter to the otherwise unfettered power of the employer. The absence of collective organization on the part of the workforce leaves it weak and open to exploitation.

Radical/Marxist

From this perspective organizations employing labour do so only in order to exploit it. The purpose of capitalism according to Marxists is to make surplus value/profit from the employment of resources in the labour process, and it is in this sense that it is argued that labour is exploited, since this surplus value accumulates to capital (rather than to labour). Profit is made from employing labour for a price less than the value of its product.

The labour process is the term used to describe the process whereby labour is added to capital and technology to produce goods and services which are then exchanged for others. It is the process through which labour potential is converted into actual.

This perspective also views industrial organizations as microcosms of the wider society and the frictions in that wider society are likely also to be reflected and present in the organization. Underlying the Marxist perspective is an assumption that power in capitalist society is weighted in favour of the owners of capital, the means of production and not with the owners and sellers of the labour resource. This is a perspective that uncompromisingly predicts a fundamental and continuing conflict of interest between labour and capital and the conflict is likely to be about who should control the labour process as well as about the price of labour. Such conflict is inevitable and, unlike in the pluralist perspective, is not amenable to resolution through mechanisms which emphasize compromise and sharing of power. This is a perspective which does not accept the conclusion of Flanders quoted above.

The nature and depth of this endemic conflict is such that compromise and resolution via peaceful means is not a realistic option. If labour compromises it will inevitably do so on capital's terms and therefore to its own disadvantage; collective bargaining in the context of this perspective is to be avoided since it is a means by which capital secures a continuation of the status quo. The negotiation of order results in a compromise that is unsatisfactory to both parties. The only means by which this capitalist status quo can be overcome is through thoroughgoing revolution and the replacement of control by capital with control by labour, the replacement of capitalism with a dictatorship by the proletariat; the long-term solution is in the overthrow of the capitalist system. In this struggle trade unions are to be expected and are desirable as the armies of the working class in what will inevitably be a class war leading to the creation of a socialist economy.

It is important to realize and remember that these three perspectives are 'ideal types' and that organizational reality may well reflect a hybrid of perspectives. Of the three viewpoints, the unitarist tends to be the most popular with employers and governments and other interests that have a liberal and individualist ideology, whereas the pluralist tends to be the most common among employee representatives and governments of a liberal collectivist (or corporatist) persuasion. The Marxist or radical approach is relatively unpopular, especially since the decline of Communist states such as the USSR, and uncommon in the UK. However, there are other European countries in which it has a stronger presence and tradition, such as in France and Italy where there are still relatively strong Marxist trade union confederations and political alliances. In the mid-1990s France experienced a number of large-scale and militant strikes and other forms of industrial action; these were partly a protest against right-wing government policies and also partly a Marxist response to the global pressures upon business to be more and more competitive, more and more efficient.

Edwards (1995: 15) argues a realistic compromise that none of these ideal types can be relied upon exclusively and that the employment relationship is accurately and realistically perceived as one characterized by both conflict and cooperation. In this he expresses similar conclusions to those of Gospel and Palmer (1993) who in their introductory chapter argue that 'Conflict and cooperation therefore coexist within organizations ... Cooperation and conflict must both be expected'. Edwards characterizes the employment relationship as one of **structured antagonism**, a relationship that is both contradictory and antagonistic. The contradiction is due to management needing both to control the labour resource and also to tap into and release its creativity, and it is inevitably antagonistic because employers have to exploit labour in order to create surplus value and thereby profit. It is this deeper antagonism or conflict of interest that needs to be structured in order to facilitate the day-to-day production of goods and services through the labour process. He suggests that cooperation may have benefits for employees and, indeed, that the parties may share some interests, but this should not disguise the fact that ultimately the purpose of employing labour is to exploit it.

The balance of bargaining power

In discussing these perspectives we have alluded to perceptions regarding the equality or not of bargaining power in the employment relationship. This is an issue that is significant in determining not only the approaches to managing employee relations and the outcomes that are often described as the rules (see later section on the industrial relations system), but it also influences the employees' approach and the nature of their involvement with the employing organization. We examine this concept and the influences upon it in **Chapter 9** on Employee Relations Processes.

A legal contract and the relevance of ideology

As already noted, the employment relationship does not occur in a vacuum. There are several different contexts which provide the backdrop and within which the interests of labour and capital are reconciled. Amongst others there are economic and business contexts, demographic and labour force contexts, cultural, legal, political, ideological and technical contexts and we deal with the majority of these in various of the later chapters in this text. (See also the final sections of this chapter where we discuss the notion of an industrial relations system and develop a framework for studying the subject and for the structure of this text.)

There is a legal environment and dimension to the employment relationship (see **Chapter 5**). As a unit of labour is hired, a legally binding contract is created; the terms of the contract may be the product of individual or collective agreement, derived from works rules, custom and practice, or they may be determined legislatively. Governments have taken different approaches to the question of regulation of this relationship depending in large measure upon their beliefs regarding the efficiency and effectiveness of the market and the value of competition as a mechanism for coordinating business activity. There is therefore an ideological dimension to the context within which the employment relationship exists in any particular country at any given time. We return to this in **Chapter 5** concerning the role of government and the legislative context.

The quality of employee relations

This notion of quality is one that has bothered analysts for some time, since there is a lack of satisfactory indicators; the quantitative indicator most commonly used or referred to is that of the incidence of strikes.

As a measure of quality this has a number of drawbacks since peace can be bought by employers giving in to the demands of employees and, in such circumstances, it might be difficult to justify the assertion that relations are good. As with other possible quantitative indicators, such as labour turnover or absenteeism rates, or rates of Foreign Direct Investment (FDI), into the country, it may be that they do indeed give some measure of quality but it may also be that they indicate some other phenomenon entirely. For example, as in Japan where taking such action has generally been perceived to imply a loss of face for both employer and employee, the relative absence of strikes in such circumstances is reflective of cultural phenomena rather than the quality of employee relations. Another example may be where the rate of unemployment in an economy is high and the degree of employment security low, an absence of strike action and/or low labour turnover rates may be indicative of fear on the part of the employee rather than of good employee relations.

Nevertheless, this particular measure (the rate and incidence of strike action) is commonly used as an indicator of quality in international and comparative work and many comparative texts contain chapters comparing the strike statistics in one country with those of another and from which implications are drawn about relative quality. It is interesting that these works commonly detail not only about the shortcomings of this as a measure but also about the difficulties of ensuring that like is compared with like, since countries tend to collect data differently and indeed apply different parameters on the data. An example of this may be that in some countries the minimum duration or numbers involved may be very different from those used elsewhere as the threshold above which strikes are counted and below which they are not.

Governments and the media tend to use this particular measure and in the UK over the last 20 years it has been common for the government to point to the decrease in the incidence of strikes and days lost through strike action as evidence of an improvement in the quality of employee relations. To some extent this is understandable since the figures tend to be available and the audience may well be a largely uncritical one.

The taking of strike action depends upon factors such as:

- it being allowed or facilitated by the law;
- culture–value systems and attitudes;
- the existence and power of effective collective employee organizations;
- the degree of employment security afforded employees;
- the potential costs to the employees;
- the availability of other means by which employees can both demonstrate and purge their dissatisfaction.

So we can see that a low incidence of strike activity may have relatively little to do with the quality of employee relations; it may simply be the result of such action being outlawed and/or employees finding alternative means of venting their frustrations or mitigating their dissatisfaction, such as absenteeism, labour turnover, working to rule, withdrawing cooperation or banning overtime, each of which may also be indicators of quality.

Once again we can trace the relevance of perspective. As implied earlier, it isn't only the difficulty of knowing whether what you are actually measuring is or is not what you want to measure; there is also the problem that perceptions of 'good' can vary quite considerably from one person to another and between the various interests and actors. If we return to our three stereotypes of perspective, the unitarist, the pluralist and the radical/Marxist, we can identify for each what might constitute 'good' and thereby illustrate some of the range of viewpoints on this matter.

Unitarist

The unitarists are likely to see peace, as indicated by the absence of overt conflict behaviour, as evidence of good employee relations. They are also likely to view as evidence of good employee relations management control/prerogative, the absence of alternative sources of employee loyalty within the organization, and the effective use of labour as indicated by rising productivity and diminishing unit costs.

Pluralist

The pluralist is likely to concentrate upon the existence of effective mechanisms for conflict resolution as evidence of good employee relations. These mechanisms should be joint, demonstrating management's recognition of and willingness to resolve conflict through shared decision making and compromise. Employees with this perspective are also likely to refer to the existence and recognition of effective trade unions as additional criteria to be met if employee relations are to be considered good.

Radical/Marxist

The Marxist is much more likely to be concerned with issues of control of the labour process. Shared decision making through agreed procedures are much less likely to be accepted as evidence of good employee relations since the Marxist viewpoint is likely to see these mechanisms as means through which management secures the maintenance of the status quo. Industrial peace is also likely to be viewed negatively since, on the one hand it is probably evidence that management has secured effective control and, on the other, this viewpoint is one that promotes the belief that revolution is necessary to wrest control from the owners of capital and the trade unions are to be the armies of the working classes in this struggle.

Evidence of the relevance of interests and that actors may view circumstances differently is illustrated by the responses of managers and employees to questions in the WERS 1998 and 2004 concerning the quality of employee relations in the workplace. The results indicate that employees' ratings of management–employee relations were generally lower or more negative than those of management. In 2004 93 per cent (88 per cent in 1998) of managers rated the relations as either good or very good, compared with 60 per cent (56 per cent in 1998) of employees. Comparing employees' perceptions to those of their employers in 2004, employees had poorer perceptions of relations than management in half of all cases (51 per cent), whereas management ratings were worse than the employee's in only 13 per cent of cases.

An industrial relations system

We move on now to examine one of the most important contributions to the study of industrial relations (and subsequently employee relations since the former is encompassed by the latter), which is the notion of an industrial relations system as devised by J.T. Dunlop in 1958.

Many would argue that this constitutes the major American contribution to the literature and theory of industrial relations. Dunlop thought that he was developing a general theory of industrial relations when he devised this notion of an industrial relations system, which he saw as a subsystem on its own rather than as part of a wider economic system, though it will partially overlap and interact with the economic and political systems.

Within the Industrial Relations subsystem Dunlop identifies a range of Inputs, Processes and Outputs.

Outputs

For Dunlop, the **outputs** or **outcomes** of the system are a body of both **procedural and substantive rules**, which together govern the actors at the workplace, and the purpose of the system framework is to facilitate the analysis and explanation of these rules, their formulation and administration.

The distinction between procedural and substantive rules is one that students often find difficult. Substantive rules are outcomes such as rates of pay or hours of work and it is important to realize that the procedural rules referred to as an output of the system comprise both the rules governing the determination of the substantive rules, the 'how' that explains rule determination, as well as the procedures governing the application of the rules in particular situations. These procedures can be seen as the rules of governance, the rules created (by different processes) to govern the interaction of the parties engaged in the rule-making process as well as to determine and act as a point of reference for decisions concerning the application of substantive rules.

An example of the first type of procedure might be a recognition and negotiating procedure agreed between employer and employee representatives that spells out the detail of how the parties will interact with a view to the joint determination of rates of pay, hours of work, etc. Such a procedure may include details about not only who is to participate in the negotiations but also when and where it is to take place. There may be a number of stages agreed, so that if the parties fail to agree initially it is clear how the matter is to be progressed without the need for either party to apply sanctions on the other. Commonly such procedures will also lay out a number of options for dealing with the matter if the parties cannot agree among themselves, such as provision for referral to conciliation or arbitration (see **Chapter 5**, section on Advisory, Conciliation and Arbitration Service (ACAS), for the distinction between these two processes).

An example of the second type of procedural rule might be agreed procedures governing the detailed application of an agreed increase in pay (substantive) in and to a complex grading system and also encompassing procedures to deal with grievances and appeals raised as a result of the application of the pay increase. The substantive rule in this example would be the increase in the rates: this is the matter of substance.

While the rules are the outcomes of the system, they are also the product of a range of inputs and the utilization of particular processes for the determination of the rules and for the resolution of conflict. There are considerable varieties of processes available and they vary from one country or scenario to another, as do the precise nature of the environmental contexts, combination of actors and ideology that Dunlop identifies as making up the inputs to the system.

Inputs

Dunlop perceived three types of independent variable falling into this category, **actors**, **contexts** and **ideology**. Each of these needs a little explanation and elaboration.

Actors

There are three main actors in the system:

- A hierarchy of non-managerial employees and their representative collective institutions, the trade unions and similar associations, which may be competitive with each other.
- A hierarchy of managers and their representatives which will encompass managerial and employers associations.
- Various third-party agencies, including government agencies, for example in the UK the ACAS or in America the National Labour Relations Board (NLRB).

Each of these are dealt with at some length in later chapters.

Contexts

There are also three main areas of environmental context:

- *Technology*: The technological context has significant implications for and impact upon the interactions within the system and the outcomes; for example, the technology available at any one time will impact upon the production process and the organization of work in turn influencing the nature of skills, quantity and location of labour demanded.
- *Market or budgetary influences*: Product markets are particularly important to the interactions and outcomes. Recent years have demonstrated this with many arguing increased international competition in product markets as one of the major influences in the drive for flexibility of labour and the development of models of the flexible firm.

The locus and distribution of power in the wider society, outside but impinging upon the industrial relations system. An example might be the power afforded the owners of capital relative to labour. Having said that, it is also the case that the distribution of power outside the system tends to be reflected in the system. It is suggested that this distribution of power will have a particular impact upon the state's third-party agencies. An example may be that after a long period of uninterrupted rule by one particular political party it is likely that the power distribution reflected by and in this dominance will also be reflected in the make up and disposition of the hierarchies of such agencies.

Ideology

The third category of input identified by Dunlop is ideology, by which is meant a collection of assumptions, values, beliefs and ideas that, shared by all the parties, will have the effect of binding the system together and rendering it stable. The hallmark of a mature industrial relations system is that the ideologies held by the main actors are sufficiently congruent to serve the purpose of allowing common ideas to emerge about the role and place of the actors within the system.

The most commonly quoted illustration of this is the assertion that, at the time that Dunlop was writing, there was in the UK an ideology of 'voluntarism' that fitted this stereotype. The voluntarism ideology was essentially that the employees and managers and their respective representative institutions should be left to resolve problems, difficulties and conflicts on their own without the intervention of government and, particularly, without the intervention of the law. At the time, this view/belief was shared by all three main actors and presumably Dunlop would have cited the UK as an example of a mature system. Subsequent events illustrate that mature and stable systems do not necessarily remain stable in the face of changing beliefs and values. Other nations might well have mature systems in which there is such a shared ideology but of course the dominant ideas and beliefs may be different as we see in **Chapter 5**. There are, for example, countries within Europe, Holland and Germany amongst others, where the dominant and shared ideology is corporatism and this has led to genuine social and economic partnership with a substantial role for government and legislative regulation as well as for bargaining.

Processes

As with any system the inputs are converted into the outputs through some process or other. Dunlop identified a number of processes through which this might happen and, at the time that he was writing, the dominant process in the UK, USA and other developed countries was collective bargaining, a process through which the parties seek to resolve conflict and determine jointly agreed rules, both substantive and procedural. Other processes that might apply include the unilateral determination by either of the main actors, management and employees, the use of third parties either through the process known as conciliation or that known as arbitration, or the government might intervene and determine rules via the mechanism of legislation.

Criticisms of the Dunlop model

The Dunlop system has been widely criticized. Dunlop appears to have thought that he was devising a general theory of industrial relations and much of the criticism of him and his systems model has been grounded in assertions of failure in this respect; that is that he did not produce such a theory since the model lacks analytical rigour and does not facilitate the analysis and explanation of industrial relations in a dynamic context, but is merely a description and the organization of facts. Another specific but related criticism is that therefore the model is too static.

Further criticisms have been made that: the systems approach tends to reinforce the status quo through its uncritical approach to the existing relationships and interactions and, perhaps most importantly, to the existing disposition of power within society and in the employment relationship. Those of a radical persuasion are most likely to be critical on these grounds. The system as devised and depicted by Dunlop is consistent with the pluralist perspective in that it tends to emphasize the joint resolution of conflict through the determination and application of agreed procedures and the achievement of consensus, the outcomes being further rules geared towards the perpetuation of the status quo rather than the radical and revolutionary change favoured by the radical perspective. The whole emphasis of the Dunlop position is the achievement of stability and maturity through shared values/ideologies, whereas the emphasis of the radical position is upon change and, where appropriate, radical and revolutionary change.

One of the common current uses of the Dunlop model is as a framework which facilitates analysis, description and comparison; in particular students and others find it a useful template or checklist for the analysis and comparison of different companies, industries or countries.

A framework for studying employee relations

What is proposed in this section is not intended as a theory of employee relations but a framework in which we can locate the various actors and influences which should provide the newcomer to the subject with an idea of the content and focus of the study of employee relations. This framework also provides the reader with a convenient guide to and picture of the contents of this text and how it is structured.

At the centre of the framework (**Figure 1.1**) is the employment relationship. There are many different dimensions to this relationship. We have already noted that it is a relationship between buyers and sellers of labour capacity; it is therefore an economic exchange. We have also noted that the relationship is contractual and that it has both a psychological and legal dimension to it: both a legally enforceable and a psychological contract. It is also a relationship which tends to be relatively continuous and traditionally, though less so these days, was open ended. It is also a power and authority relationship with the employee agreeing to an element of subordination to the authority of the employer, and in

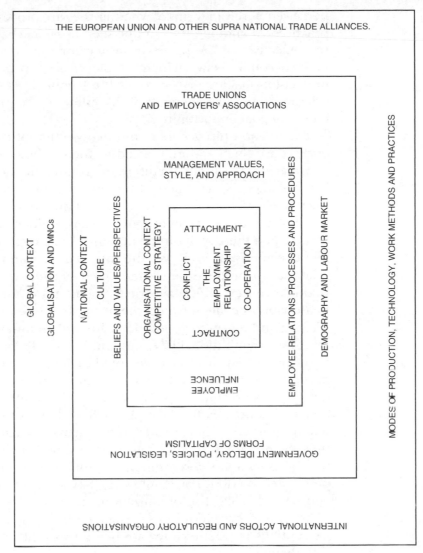

Figure 1.1
Employee relations
framework.

this context it is also an asymmetrical relationship since the employer has the greater power. The nature of the relationship is variously perceived; for example, some see it as a relationship dominated by the inherent conflicts of interest between the parties whereas others perceive it as a relationship that is, or at least should be, dominated by cooperation. It is also a relationship that is secured through different modes and forms of involvement and attachment, ranging from an alienative to a moral involvement and from compliance to commitment as the base for the ongoing attachment of the parties.

The employment relationship and the interaction between the parties can be seen to produce a number of different employee relations outcomes within the organization. At one level, these outcomes can be perceived purely in terms of whether they are processes, procedures or practices. At another, they can be seen to be mechanisms for securing the objectives of the parties whether, for example, this be the resolution of conflict between them, employee participation and involvement in decision making or control of the labour process, the handling of grievances and management of discipline or the pursuit and achievement of equal opportunities.

The relationship occurs within many different contexts and is variously constrained and influenced by them. These contexts can be differentiated on a number of different grounds and here we differentiate between international, national and organizational contexts. Throughout the framework there are two-way interactions between the various layers of context, the international context exerts influence upon the national context and thereby upon the organizational context and the employment relationship itself, yet the interactions within the employment relationship produce outcomes which become a part of the organizational context which may then impact upon the national context. Reasonably one might expect the strength or intensity of the outwardly directed influences to be less than those of an inward direction.

At the organizational level influences include the values and beliefs of the parties which, as we have noted earlier, are likely to influence the parties' expectations and their perceptions of their interests and the nature of the relationship. These are likely to influence management style and approach, for example such as their attitudes towards trade unionism, whether they are prepared to share power and control, whether they are prepared to enter into mechanisms for the joint determination of issues and the resolution of conflict, and their preferences for personnel or HRM. For employees, they are likely to determine their approach to collective organization, the nature of their attachment, whether they have a right to participate in decision making and their perceptions of whether they are being treated fairly, consistently and with dignity.

At the level of the organization, decisions will be taken about the production and competitive strategies to be pursued, about the way in which work is organized, the labour force required and the distribution of work between primary and secondary labour markets. All of these will have implications for the parties to the employment relationship and the interactions between them.

Outside the organization there are two levels of context, the international and national. At the national level we have the influence of the values, beliefs and attitudes that can be perceived as constituting the national culture. At this level also we have the nature of the dominant form of economic activity, government and its ideology, and the policies and priorities pursued by government in its role as economic regulator. The government also has an influential role in the determination of the legal context. Additionally, at this level of context we have to consider the structure of industrial and economic activity, the composition and structure of the labour force, demographic circumstances and trends, the distribution of power in society and the history and traditions of the country. The supply of labour will be influenced by the nature of the dominant education and training regimes. Employers and trades unions also function at this level pursuing their own objectives but also engaging with government in order to exert influence and achieve certain specific outcomes.

Outside the level of the nation there are several influential international contexts. Perhaps the most important of these is associated with global capital, its objectives and its activities, encompassing the multi-national enterprise and its ability to invest and locate around the world. We also have nation states forming supra-national trading blocs and alliances and for the UK and other member states, the European Union (EU) forms an important element of the international context. There are also international associations and federations of employers and employee organizations and there is at least one influential international regulatory organization, the International Labour Organization (ILO). Last, but by no means least, are the influence of modes of production, technology and technological change with their implications for the way in which is organized and the day-to-day experience of people at work.

The remainder of the text is structured in parts consistent with this framework, so that we work from the outside in, from the international to the national to the organizational. Inevitably it is impossible to be comprehensive but the contents chosen do reflect the author's perceptions of relative importance. Choices have also had to be made where to include some of the material and it has to be acknowledged that there are alternative approaches to structuring a text such as this. For example, I have chosen to examine the nature and organization of work as part of the international context, others might argue that it would be more appropriate at an organizational level. Similarly, I examine managing employee relations as part of the organizational context whereas others might argue that given debates about the development of a global model of high commitment, high performance HRM it might be more appropriate to study it as part of the international context. It is, therefore, a matter of judgement and the structure of this text reflect those of the author.

Summary

So far we have examined different interpretations and meanings attached to the term 'employee relations' and in so doing have touched upon differences between employee and industrial relations.

You have learned that the employment relationship does not occur in a vacuum and indeed that there are various different contexts together comprising the overall environment. You have also been introduced to the notion of a psychological contract between employee and employer and the range of different interests and expectations of the parties.

The employment relationship is characterized by a range of potential and different forms of attachment, some of which may imply employee commitment to the values of the organization and some of which acknowledge more instrumental or calculative motives.

There are also differing perspectives upon this relationship and in particular we have examined three, each of which has implications for the way in which the issues of conflict and/or cooperation between labour and capital are perceived. Integral to this is the question of whether these two sets of interests can coincide.

The quality of employee relations is difficult to determine and the criteria by which it may be assessed are influenced by perspective.

We have examined the notion of an industrial relations system and the various criticisms of it and have proposed a framework for studying the subject which centres upon the employment relationship and provides the structure for this text.

Activities to test understanding

Activity 1

Re-read the material concerned with Etzioni's typology and then apply it to some of your own experiences. Think of some of the organizations (not necessarily work organizations) to which you have been or are attached and try and identify in your own mind the nature of the compliance relationship in each case. Try also to decide whether the form of compliance is one of those that Etzioni argued were congruent and effective.

Activity 2

Re-read the accounts of the three perspectives which are examined in this chapter and then answer the following:

1 Which of the three perspectives perceive conflict as something that is inevitable within employing organizations?
2 What are the implications of each of the perspectives for the appropriate means through which conflict is to be resolved?
3 If there is an inherent and inevitable conflict between the interests of employees and employers, what is the nature and root of that conflict?

Activity 3

It is important to realize your own views and values and therefore your own perspective on the employment relationship and so take a few more minutes now to think through which of the viewpoints referred to above as perspectives seem to you to be the more realistic and with which you find yourself agreeing. Don't worry if you find yourself in agreement with elements of differing perspectives. As we said earlier, the three perspectives are somewhat idealized and hybrid viewpoints are common. Write down now what you think.

Activity 4

Re-examine the subsections on commitment, perspective and conflict and work out for yourself whether there is any coincidence between the notion of employee commitment when prescribed as a desirable HRM outcome and the three perspectives detailed.

Activity 5

1 Determine for yourself the criteria you might consider acceptable as an indicator of the quality of employee relations and write them down.
2 Now write a short essay in which you discuss the arguments for and against the suggestion that strike statistics are an adequate/ appropriate measure/indicator of the quality of employee relations.

Activity 6

Think about the systems model and write down the advantages and value of the model. Having done this you should then write another list in which you identify the limitations or disadvantages.

References

Beer, M., Spector, B., Lawrence, P.R., Quinn Mills, D. and Walton, R., 1984. *Managing Human Assets*. Free Press, New York.

Blyton, P. and Turnbull, P., 1994. *The Dynamics of Employee Relations*. Macmillan, Basingstoke.

Blyton, P. and Turnbull, P., 2004. *The Dynamics of Employee Relations*. 3rd Edition. Macmillan, Basingstoke.

Cully, M., O'Reilly, A., Millward, N., Forth, J., Woodland, S., Dix, G. and Bryson, A., 1998. *The Workplace Employee Relations Survey: First Findings*. DTI, ACAS, ESRC, PSI.

Dunlop, J.T., 1958. *An Industrial Relations System*. Holt, New York.

Edwards, P., 1995. The employment relationship. In Edwards, P. (ed.), *Industrial Relations: Theory and Practice in Britain*. Blackwell, Oxford.

Etzioni, A., 1975. *A Comparative Analysis of Complex Organizations*. Free Press, New York.

Flanders, A., 1970. *Management and Unions*. Faber, London.

Fox, A., 1966. *Industrial Sociology and Industrial Relations*. Royal Commission Research Paper No. 3. HMSO, London.

Gennard, J. and Judge, G., 2002. *Employee Relations*. CIPD, London.

Gospel, H. and Palmer, G., 1993. *British Industrial Relations*, 2nd Edition. Routledge, London.

Guest, D., 1987. Human resource management and industrial relations. *Journal of Management Studies* 24(5): 503–521.

Guest, D. and Conway, N., 1999. *Fairness at Work and the Psychological Contract*. IPD, London.

Herzberg, F., 1966. *Work and the Nature of Man*. World Publishing, Cleveland, Ohio.

Kersley, B., Alpin, C., Forth, J., Bryson, A., Bewley, H., Dix, G. and Oxenbridge, S., 2005. *Inside the Workplace First Findings from the 2004 Workplace Employment Relations Survey (WERS 2004)*.

Legge, K. 1995. *Human Resource Management: Rhetorics and Realities*. Macmillan, Basingstoke.

Marchington, M. and Wilkinson, A., 1996. *Core Personnel and Development*. IPD, London.

Maslow, A. 1943. A theory of human motivation. *Psychological Review* 50: 370–396.

Mowday, R.T., Steers, R.M. and Porter, L.W., 1982. *Employee–Organization Linkages: The Psychology of Commitment, Absenteeism and Turnover*. Academic Press, New York.

Nicholls, P. 1999. Context and theory in employee relations. In Hollinshead, G., Nicholls, P. and Tailby, S. (eds), *Employee Relations*. Financial Times, Pitman, London.

Roethlisberger, F.J. and Dickson, W.J., 1939. *Management and the Worker*. Harvard University Press, Cambridge, Mass.

Schein, E., 1988. *Organizational Psychology*. Prentice Hall, Englewood Cliffs, NJ.

Taylor, R., 2002. *Britain's World of Work – Myths and Realities*. ESRC, Swindon.

Part Two

The Global Context

Chapter 2

The nature of work

Introduction

In **Chapter 1** we examined the nature of the employment relationship. In this chapter we examine the nature of work, how it is organized and how it has changed in recent years. We examine the scale and nature of recent developments, perceptions of their impact, the inter-relationship between the nature of work and the employment relationship, and associated developments.

It seems reasonable enough to assume that there will be some degree of inter-relationship between the nature of work and the nature of the employment relationship. Certainly it has been argued in recent years that the information technology revolution and new globally competitive product markets have impacted significantly upon the nature and organization of work and that these developments have been accompanied by identifiable and common change in the nature of the employment relationship.

We pay particular attention to the recently popular thesis that organizations need to be flexible, need to be able to compete on the grounds of quality and need a labour force that is committed if they are to compete in the new global marketplace. Guest's (1987; see **Chapter 8**) normative model or theory of human resource management (HRM) identifies, and in some respects prescribes, quality, flexibility and commitment as desirable outcomes. It is argued that these competitive imperatives have imposed upon companies and thereby their workforce new forms of work organization and new work practices.

We examine models of the flexible firm and **flexible specialization** and we look also at the influence of Japanese companies, their approaches and practices. In examining these 'developments' you should try to bear in mind their relevance for the issues that we examined in the first chapter, that is, whether these new forms of work organization, assuming that they exist, impact upon the employment relationship and if so, how. We will return therefore to the issues of commitment or compliance and job satisfaction.

Where appropriate we utilize recent survey evidence from the UK to examine the extent to which the various developments in the organization of work and their presumed consequences for the labour resource actually appear to have both been implemented and occurred. As we see in **Chapters 5 and 8** both Government and employers in the UK have been amongst the greatest proponents of the advantages of flexibility and the pursuit of high commitment Human Resource strategies.

In order to contextualize our discussion of new forms of work organization and practices we start with a brief introduction to the form of production system and work organization that supposedly dominated in Western economies for much of the 20th century, this being the system characterized by mass production and often referred to as Fordist. In describing this form of system we must identify the underlying principles which owe much to the work of F.W. Taylor (1911) and which are frequently collectively referred to as Taylorism and 'scientific management'.

Learning objectives

After studying this chapter you will be able to:

- Identify the principles of Taylorism and assess the extent to which particular work situations demonstrate them.
- Distinguish between Fordist and a number of other production regimes.
- Assess the relevance of the principles of scientific management to production strategies at the end of the 20th century.

- Identify the main features of the flexible firm model, apply the model to work situations and examine whether the features of the model do or might apply.
- Distinguish between a number of different forms of job design/re-design and how each may contribute to the goals of quality and commitment.
- Define the concepts of total quality management, just-in-time and lean production and assess how each might contribute to the goals of quality and commitment.
- Assess and discuss the implications of changing systems of work organization for employees and for the employment relationship.

Taylorism, scientific management and Fordism

It is often suggested that, prior to the intervention of Taylor, work was typified by the craftsman exercising his skills in the conception and planning of a job as well as in its execution. This no doubt presents a somewhat idealized view; however, for the purposes of contrasting pre- and post-Taylorist scenarios it is useful. Taylor's great contribution was to attempt to apply the principles of scientific analysis to work and its organization. He placed great emphasis upon measurement and time and conceived the idea that there was a 'one best way' of organizing work, one way that would yield greater efficiencies in terms of time and costs than any other. He assumed that the nature of man's motivation was essentially instrumental, that man could and would be motivated by the prospect of earning more. Armed with these beliefs Taylor began the process of measurement and experimentation that led to the development of the means whereby the labour process could be designed and so organized to facilitate the efficient mass production of standardized products. This was achieved through the design and fragmentation of work into a large number of small tasks, each of which required very little skill and were performed by units of labour on a repetitive basis. Each of the tasks was to be as simple as possible and the belief was that with experience labour would become more and more proficient at the individual constituents of the process and efficiency would improve almost without end. Responsibility for the design, planning, organizing and control of the process of production was to be divorced from the labour engaged in the production process and performed by others. This contributed in large measure to the development of the management functions, and formed a basis for the development of a managerial elite or cadre.

Where possible, the machine, the technology, should control the pace of the production and, as labour became more and more proficient, the speed of the machine could be increased and the rate of production enhanced. As long as pay was linked to performance or output, the labour would accept these conditions since they would be content providing they earned more. Labour would also become cheaper if it were possible to break down jobs into a number of smaller tasks which could be performed repetitively, since it would be possible to use largely unskilled units that required relatively little training to perform the simplified tasks.

The effectiveness of these principles was enhanced further by the technological developments that facilitated the emergence of the conveyer belt and assembly line. It was when all these came together that capital really had the opportunity to engage in mass production.

One of the major disciples and champions of these techniques and principles was Henry Ford, the automobile manufacturer, and it is because of this that such production systems have often been referred to as **Fordist**. The development of large-scale manufacture facilitated by the work of Taylor must be seen as part of the process of industrialization and urbanization that has characterized developing economies in the 20th century. Large-scale manufacture required plenty of labour and, in the early days, that labour had to live close to the place of work, given the absence of quick and cheap transport.

Mass production of standardized products also requires mass markets for standardized products and the labour employed in the resulting factories became part of these markets as their own living standards improved. In the post-war period there was a fit between the pursuit of full employment as an economic policy priority and the creation of the necessary mass markets for the output of these production systems.

In the industrial and employment circumstances created by mass production trades unions also eventually flourished. Large numbers of semi-skilled and unskilled labour were employed on fragmented and standardized tasks, the pace of work was controlled by the technology, the working conditions were often noisy and dangerous and the collective common interests of the employees were apparent. Pressures were generated for the standardization of terms and conditions of employment. Logistically, trades unions have tended to revel in circumstances of this kind.

Fordist production systems have been criticized for their effect upon the nature of work and their implications for the labour resource. Chief among the critics was probably Braverman (1974). It is alleged that such systems have caused a general de-skilling of the labour force, a degradation and cheapening of the labour resource and that they have been influential in the exploitation of labour and its input into the labour process. In terms of the radical perspective, these 20th-century mass-production strategies and processes have facilitated capital's control over both the labour process and the price of labour. Braverman argued that the process of de-skilling and degradation was as applicable to non-manual clerical and administrative tasks and their labour as it was to manual production work.

It has been suggested that the accuracy of Braverman's assertion can be seen in many call centres where the phone is the machine and employees are programmed to perform highly standardized procedures often according to a specific script and they are required to deal with so many calls per minute or hour, all of these being combined with a continual monitoring of their performance facilitated by the new computer-based information and telecommunication technologies. The technology enables the monitoring of the length of calls, completion times and whether calls lead to sales, this information then being used to support performance-based pay systems. In such systems employees have little or no control over their work and they are in turn often subject to very tight control by management. It has been alleged that systems of this kind produce high stress levels and low satisfaction amongst employees and that this results in high rates of sickness absence, labour turnover and low quality.

We have already noted in **Chapter 1** Taylor's (2002) conclusions on the findings of the Working in Britain in 2000 Survey (WIB2000S) that the world of work is much less satisfying and more stressful than it was in the early 1990s. He also concludes that most people feel that they are working much harder in intensity and suggests that the conclusions reached by Gallie and White (1998) in relation to the 1992 survey apply also to the 2000 survey, in particular, in this context, the conclusion that: 'The structures of control of work performance are being modified, but control remains pervasive and possibly more intense in the pressures it brings to bear on work effort.'

Supiot (2001) summarized the Fordist model as one characterized by mass employment of male breadwinners, standard hours and an employment relationship characterized by employee subordination and disciplinary control. These were the conditions and consequences that encouraged governments in Europe to develop the traditional European social model encompassing welfare capitalism and a regulatory system of labour law. The latter provides protection and security to labour, prevents its impoverishment, provides the opportunity for employee participation in decision making and enables the maintenance of social stability and cohesion.

The Braverman critique of Fordist production systems and its implications for the labour resource has itself been subject to criticism, in particular that it is both an over-simplification and inaccurate to suggest the dominant concern of management is the exploitation of labour and the creation of surplus value through processes designed to de-skill and degrade.

Disadvantages of Fordism and the emergence of post-Fordism

We have already mentioned some of the disadvantages of Fordist systems, that they tend to result in bored, dissatisfied and alienated labour forces, but there are other problems associated with mature Fordism which are arguably inherent. These systems require massive investment in plant and technology to facilitate the production of large numbers of standard items relatively cheaply and, once installed, this plant and equipment is relatively fixed and inflexible. It is not common for these production systems to be amenable to change and, of course, the labour also tends to be relatively fixed in terms of what workers can do.

The advantages of Fordist systems when confronted with mass markets for standardized products become disadvantages the moment that the mass markets disappear or the product must be changed; both the technology and the labour tend to be highly specialized. The massive fixed overheads generated by these systems also pose problems if competition emerges from parts of the world where labour and other materials may be cheaper. Arguably the greatest threat to the viability of these systems occurs if and when customers changes their requirements; for example when they decide that they want something a little different from the man next door, they develop a desire for customization. As living standards improve it seems that people tend to become more discriminating and less prepared to have the same as everyone else; they not only want something different but also something better.

Other disadvantages emerge from the degree of specialization and the separation of tasks and functions. Unskilled and semi-skilled workers engaged in the production process are not required, or able, to exercise control over quality and the technology also often does not lend itself to inspection prior to the end of the process; so this function is either not performed or performed by expensive specialist quality inspection and control functions. As the size of the operation increases there is also a tendency for the overhead element, owing to the employment of specialist management and administration, to become a greater burden.

In response to these disadvantages the appropriateness of Fordism as the dominant form for organizing production has been questioned and a number of post-Fordist strategies and systems have emerged. The increasing demand by customers for customization and quality, allied to competition on both price and quality from developing economies, has encouraged employers to vary the nature of production systems to something which is more flexible and in which quality can more easily and cheaply be achieved.

Flexibility in this context needs to include both the technology and the labour and, in the latter case, the flexibility requirement may apply to both the quantity and qualitative capacity of the labour input. The demand for large quantities of relatively unskilled labour characteristic of Fordist systems has been at least partially replaced by a demand for labour that is multiskilled and flexible, that is familiar with the new technologies and does not need external supervision. This form of labour flexibility is commonly termed functional flexibility and this can be contrasted with the concept of numerical flexibility which we return to later in this chapter.

Flexible specialization

This production paradigm has been presented as the solution to the problems associated with Fordism in the new international economic world order, given the change in product markets towards customization and away from mass markets and given the new technological possibilities. It has been suggested that flexible specialization can be seen as the re-emergence of the traditional 19th century craft production regime. The essence of the paradigm is the use of general-purpose technology and multiskilled and adaptable labour in the production of a range of semi-customized and changing products for niche markets. In contrast to Fordist systems this paradigm allows employers to produce efficiently small batches of products which enable them to satisfy demand for high quality customized goods. This new system would enable smaller firms to compete successfully as economies of scale were replaced by economies of scope.

These systems bring advantages to labour in that jobs become enlarged or enriched, see later section, and employment becomes more secure since the new requirement for skilled and adaptable labour meant that it is no longer so easy for employers to replace existing labour from the external labour market. In this context labour becomes an asset that needs to be retained and developed. It is also suggested that employers need to develop commitment within the labour force in order to motivate and retain workers and that this would lead to the development of new participatory mechanisms through which employees could contribute to decision making and which replace the traditional hierarchical and technological modes of control.

Critics of this thesis have argued that it overstates some of the disadvantages of Fordism, in particular the inflexibility of Fordist production regimes, the flexibility of the new production regimes and the benefits to employees. They have pointed out that, as in the reference to call centres above, the new production and information technologies greatly enhance management's ability to control and monitor employee performance from a distance.

Critics have also focussed on the implementation of this and other new initiatives alleging that they have often been implemented in an incoherent and piecemeal fashion with the result that much of their potential may not have been realized and their objectives often not achieved.

We examine some of the specific changes to work organization that are argued to be management's response to the new production and market realities later in this chapter. But before we do it is necessary to examine the model of the flexible firm devised in the early 1980s and which has achieved prominence both as an analytical tool and as a blueprint for the way forward for firms in these new contexts.

The flexible firm

By the early 1980s the developments outlined above, allied to changes in the political and regulatory environments, had encouraged developments in the organization of work and the demand for labour summed up in the model of the 'flexible firm' that was devised by Atkinson (1984). This model became an ideal, a blueprint, in Western economies, for the successful firm of the latter decades of the 20th century and into the 21st century. It constitutes a form of organization which satisfies the requirements of the employer in the context of newly global and competitive markets but it is arguable the extent to which it is a model of organization which provides much scope for the satisfaction of employee needs, such as needs for security, recognition, relationships, high earnings or self-actualization identified by and associated with the work of motivation theorists such as Maslow (1943) and Herzberg (1966).

The essence of the model is the distinction drawn and highlighted between core and peripheral workers and the primary and secondary labour markets. It was also a model or blueprint which pointed up the distinctions between different dimensions of flexibility, functional and numerical. In this context, functional means a flexibility of task and/or skill, the ability to do different things. The core group of workers needs to be functionally flexible and numerical flexibility is primarily derived from the selective use of labour in the secondary labour markets. These two categories of flexibility are often also referred to as internal and external flexibility and external flexibility or rigidity is a reflection of the labour market in the country in which the business is located. The UK and America are characterized as labour markets that are flexible or deregulated whereas the majority of European markets would be characterized as rigid.

It is entirely possible that these two categories of flexibility become alternatives, for example in countries where labour markets are flexible or deregulated it is relatively easy and cheap for the necessary functional and numerical flexibility to be achieved externally through the use of the secondary labour markets. However, in labour markets which are rigid and regulated this is unlikely to be an option and employers may therefore have to pay much more attention to achieving flexibility and competitiveness internally through the training and development of the core labour force and through more innovative approaches to the organization of work.

Returning to Atkinson's model, the core group of workers benefits from security of employment and demand for the skills it possesses, and the organization might invest in the training and development of this group. Again, though, we do need to bear in mind that there are temptations for employers to try and achieve both functional and numerical flexibility from their core workers and perhaps, in particular, to achieve this through a more flexible approach to the hours actually worked so that their core workers work some form of flexi-hours to cope with fluctuations in demand. Contracts may stipulate a certain number of hours to be worked per week, per month or per year, but the precise distribution of when these hours are worked is at management's discretion, thereby enabling them to satisfy variations in demand through using labour flexibly.

Consistent with the model and an external labour market that is flexible is the practice of outsourcing services and activities so that the service is bought in from the external market thereby reducing the size of the core labour force. The impact of this practice in many organizations, both private and public, is to reduce significantly the number of employees in the core groups, with many individuals previously in the core group being shifted into peripheral and external service provision and contracting categories. We do need to bear in mind that while there may be little or no security in the external market there may be both high levels of skill and good pay; the providers of many professional services fall into this category.

In the peripheral groups, both first and second, where the emphasis is upon numerical rather than task flexibility, labour may be given the status of employees but this labour is likely to be both less skilled and more vulnerable than that in the core group. The part-time, temporary and relatively unskilled are likely to be used just as any other resource and effectively discarded when no longer required. It is extremely unlikely that the workers in this group would be developed by the employer and, of course, many of them will not have the means to finance their own development.

Marchington and Wilkinson (1996: 30) identified a number of reservations and concerns about the flexible firm model:

1   They cite the views of Pollert (1988) that the flexible firm model has the tendency to fuse together description, prediction and prescription into what becomes a self-fulfilling prophecy. Writings on the subject tend to veer between describing flexible practices in the workplace, predicting that the model is the

ideal design for the future and prescribing that, if organizations want to be successful in the future, this is the model that they should take as the blueprint. They also point out Legge's (1995) concerns that in the UK the model has been 'talked up' because it was consistent with the UK government ideology concerning the efficiency of the market, the need for markets therefore to be deregulated and organizations to be lean.

2   They note the doubts expressed by commentators and analysts that flexibility, particularly functional flexibility, is as common or extensive as the proponents of the model and deregulation would have us believe (see also Geary, 2003). They refer to a number of surveys that had indicated that the introduction of flexibility in terms of **working practices** was not as extensive as some proponents might lead us to believe, and comment that there are often gaps between the rhetoric and the reality.

3   They point out that there are reasons to doubt the benefits claimed for flexibility and they suggest that there may well be costs that are not realized or acknowledged. They cite studies that have cast doubts on the productivity, attendance rates, levels of commitment, quality of work and loyalty of employees employed on a flexible basis. They also note that core workers may well be disaffected by witnessing events around them, particularly when they see friends and colleagues losing their jobs through rationalization and redundancy caused for example by decisions to outsource or offshore functions and jobs. We discuss in more detail in **Chapter 3** the increasingly frequent practice of exporting or offshoring to developing countries such as China and India jobs and functions previously the preserve of core employees. It is suggested that in such circumstances core worker commitment and feelings of security may well be damaged and that the nature of their attachment to the organization may revert from commitment to compliance.

We have already begun to voice concerns or reservations about the value to, and impact of, the flexible firm for and upon workers: if you are in the core you may well benefit but outside the core life may be very unpredictable, characterized by uncertainty and high levels of anxiety and stress.

Survey evidence in the UK

The UK 1998 Workplace Employment Relations Survey (WERS), Cully *et al.* (1999), investigated the issue of workplace flexibility and distinguished between numerical and functional flexibility.

On functional flexibility the 1998 WERS findings are consistent with the criticisms made above, they did not find functional flexibility was widespread. They found negative associations between the proportion of employees trained to be functionally flexible (internal flexibility) and the use of non-standard workers, particularly the use of temporary agency workers (external flexibility). As noted earlier, this may imply that companies tend to use one or the other and that, given the relatively flexible external market, firms in the UK tend not to make use of internal flexibility. When this internal rigidity is combined with a relative lack of investment in training and development, as in the UK, it is likely that progress towards functional and skill flexibility will be slow (see Geary, 2003).

The WERS 2004 survey pursued the training of staff to be functionally flexible and found that 66 per cent of workplaces had trained at least some staff to be functionally flexible (69 per cent in 1998). In most cases (88 per cent) at least some of those trained in this way were undertaking jobs other than their own at least once a week. However, where functional flexibility training had been undertaken a comparison with the situation in 1998 showed that it was less embedded in 2004 than it had been in 1998. In 2004 19 per cent (29 per cent in 1998) of workplaces had trained at least three-fifths (60 per cent) of core employees to be functionally flexible.

In respect to the utilization of new information technologies at work Taylor (2002) concludes from the results of the WIB2000S that the demand for more complex multiskilling is increasing.

In relation to numerical flexibility the WERS 1998 sought information on:

- the contracting-out of particular services
- the current use of particular forms of non-standard contracts
- the variation in their use over the preceding 5 years.

The findings were that around 90 per cent of workplaces contract out at least one service, the average figure was four services. The most popular included:

- building maintenance
- cleaning
- transporting documents or goods
- training
- security.

The incidence of this practice did not seem to vary much between the private and public sectors but in the public sector it was more likely that catering would be contracted out. In the private sector, it was more likely that recruitment and security would be contracted out.

One-third of the managers interviewed said that, 5 years previously, the services now contracted out would have been performed by employees of the organization and, of these workplaces, one-third were using contractors of whom at least some were former employees. This latter development was considerably more common in the public sector than in the private sector and was, presumably, the product of the process known as compulsory competitive tendering (CCT) (see discussion in **Chapter 5**).

In examining non-standard employment (temporary or agency staff, fixed-term contractors and part-time) the WERS 1998 findings indicated that there was evidence of an increase in their use over the preceding 5 years, with the greatest increase occurring in the use of part-time employees and contractors. However, overall, the incidence of the use of these forms of employment was not as great as one might have imagined. The evidence did seem to confirm an increasing use of professionals as temporary staff and on fixed-term contracts.

The 2004 WERS found that 83 per cent (79 per cent in 1998) of workplaces had part-time employees and in 30 per cent of all workplaces part-time employees accounted for more than half of the workforce. Women made up the totality of the part-time workforce in 44 per cent of workplaces that employed part-time staff. The proportion of workplaces using temporary or fixed-term contracts had remained relatively stable (30 per cent in 2004 compared with 32 per cent in 1998).

They also found that the use of temporary agency staff, although less prevalent than fixed-term contracts, had also remained relatively stable with 17 per cent (18 per cent in 1998) of all workplaces employing 'temps'.

Echoing the findings of the WERS surveys, the WIB2000S found no significant evidence that jobs had become more transitory and uncertain. The WIB2000S found that 92 per cent of workers held permanent employment contracts in 2000 compared with 88 per cent in 1992 and that the proportion of workers on both temporary and fixed-term contracts had actually fallen between 1992 and 2000. However, as noted in **Chapter 1** there was evidence of declining employee satisfaction with their hours of work and in 2000 46 per cent of men said that they frequently worked more hours than their basic week, a possible indication that employers are indeed pursuing numerical flexibility through the hours worked by their core employees.

The evidence then suggests that some multiskilling has taken place along with some outsourcing of services, there is use of secondary labour markets and atypical contracts, yet the practices associated with both functional and numerical flexibility are not as widespread as might have been expected.

Other competitive production strategies

Consistent with the work that casts doubt upon the extensiveness of the replacement of Fordism with post-Fordist production regimes such as flexible specialization and the introduction of the flexible firm model is the work of Regini (1995) who found that a range of competitive and production strategies were being adopted by managements in Europe and that by no means all of these were consistent with the models of post-Fordist production that emphasize competition on the basis of quality, product differentiation and customization, and flexibility of response.

In all, Regini identifies five ideal types of strategy, each of which can be seen to embody a different pattern of human resource utilization, only some of which are similar to that depicted in the models of flexibility referred to above. These are:

1   **Diversified quality production**. Here, the intent is to compete on both quality and product diversification thereby avoiding competition on price with low-wage economies. Often this takes the form of a high level of customization of the product and requires the kind of labour resource that is a mix of high and broad-based skills, that is adaptive, willing and able to learn new tasks rapidly and is capable itself of contributing to innovation and product development.

2   **Flexible mass production**. The strategy is to mass-produce a number of different goods thereby competing in a number of different markets and to do so on price if necessary. Production can be extensively automated and the organization tends to require a mix of labour, low and unskilled at the production end and highly skilled middle-management, marketing, sales and technical staff.

3   **Flexible specialization**. Here the emphasis is upon the organization's ability to adapt to changes in demand and Regini suggests that this strategy is more common amongst small firms. The requirements of labour include both functional and numerical flexibility allied to broadly based social and interactive skills.

4   **Neo Fordist**. The suggestion is that, even in the developed economies of Europe in the late 20th century and in an era supposedly post-Fordist, there are in fact still in existence many firms that operate in a largely traditional Fordist fashion, relying upon Taylorist techniques of organizing production and work practices with the traditional emphasis upon the fragmentation of the work and the de-skilling of the labour input. The requirement of such systems is for labour that is unskilled and is not required to be functionally flexible. We have already noted

the potential for such systems to be applied in the service sector as well as in manufacturing.

5   **Traditional small firm**. These organizations seek to compete on price but not through obtaining the economies that may come from scale and mass production; they can compete only by keeping down their costs, including their labour costs. Many survive only because they operate in product markets that make few demands upon the skills of the labour resource thereby enabling the employment of cheap unskilled labour.

Each of these competitive and production strategies imposes its own demand features upon the labour market in terms of types, levels and mixes of skill and only some require labour that is flexible.

Having discussed developments and change in terms of competitive production strategies and the model of the flexible firm it is time to look more closely at some of the more common specific changes in work organization and practices/techniques that it is alleged have been at the forefront of attempts by organizations both to address the disadvantages of Fordism and also enable companies to compete in the international markets of the late 20th and early 21st centuries.

Job re-design and the search for commitment, flexibility and quality

In most instances, as has been noted earlier, changes to working practices and the way in which work is organized and jobs designed have been introduced and motivated by the desire to compete more effectively. It is important that we do not forget that this has often been perceived in terms of reducing labour costs by cutting down the quantity and quality of labour input, a process which technological innovation and development has often assisted. We must not forget, as the work of Regini clearly suggests, that the nature of change and response to market pressures has by no means always been to try and achieve HR outcomes such as commitment, quality and labour flexibility. Competition continues on the basis of price as well as on the quality of the product.

Nevertheless, in this section we are concerned to identify and describe some of the major developments in the arena of work and its nature and design; the more interesting innovations have tended to be introduced in order, ostensibly, to achieve one or more of these desirable HR outcomes.

Some organizations have pursued change in job design and working practices oriented towards enhancing the intrinsic satisfactions that employees derive from their experience at work, assuming both that they have such needs and that satisfied employees will contribute more to the organization. Some of these schemes have been directed at adding variety and scope for achievement while others have been more concerned to enhance employee involvement or participation in the task-related decision-making process.

Evidence from the UK

There certainly is evidence that employees do seek these rewards from work, see the discussion of the expectations incorporated in the psychological contract, and the results of the 2004 WERS in **Chapter 1**. The WERS 2004 respondents exhibited the greatest levels of satisfaction with 'the work itself', 'scope for using own initiative' and 'sense of achievement'.

Whether designing work to give employees the opportunity to gain these intrinsic satisfactions then results in higher levels of **commitment** is another matter, despite the fact that many such schemes, and perhaps those associated with Japanization (which we examine in the next section) more than others, have been referred to as High Commitment Management.

As noted earlier (**Chapter 1**), commitment is a concept that is difficult to measure and attitudinal commitment more so than behavioural commitment. There may be a relationship between them so that measuring behaviour may give an indication of attitudinal commitment but this is by no means certain and, in any event, whether you believe that it is realistic to envisage employees sharing the values and objectives of their employing organization will depend in part upon your perspective (see **Chapter 1**) and their (the employees) needs.

It is also important to realize that designing jobs and work processes so as to facilitate employees achieving intrinsic satisfactions may yield more satisfied and even more productive employees, but only if their other needs are also being met.

Evidence from the UK

The WERS 1998 (see **Chapter 1**) demonstrated that employees consider extrinsic factors such as pay, working conditions and job security to be equally as important as the intrinsic satisfactions and presumably employers seeking a satisfied workforce need to design the wider context of work to facilitate the satisfaction of these needs too. The WERS 1998 data indicated that pay may be a potent source of dissatisfaction and it may well be that what some would argue was a relatively low overall satisfaction level (54 per cent) can be ascribed in part to this dissatisfaction with an extrinsic feature of the job. The 2004 WERS probed satisfaction with a wider range of components of jobs and found that it was lowest in respect of pay, training and 'involvement in decision making'.

The most common of the experiments in job design falling into this category are: job rotation, job enlargement and job enrichment, which we examine in this section and the creation of autonomous (or semi-autonomous) teams which we look at in the following section on Japanization.

Job rotation

The essence of this mechanism is the simple rotation of employees between jobs of a similar skill level so as to alleviate boredom. The employee still only undertakes one job at a time. One might automatically think of assembly line production systems as lending themselves to this kind of re-design but there are other circumstances in which this can be practised; the obvious danger is that you simply swap one boring job for another that is equally as boring.

Job enlargement

This is where tasks of a similar skill level and nature to the existing job are added so that the job is enlarged in a horizontal sense. The level of responsibility remains the same but the number of tasks being undertaken increases. This widening of the job can relieve the repetitiveness of a highly fragmented and specialized process and thereby arguably yield benefits for the employee in terms of interest and boredom relief. However, the counter view is that you may actually make the situation worse, in that with one repetitive and boring task employees may become so proficient that they can effectively switch off and obtain relief; with two or more such tasks it may require sufficient concentration to prevent this relief-giving escape and thereby breed resentment and even more dissatisfaction.

Job enrichment

Here the enlarging of the job is vertical rather than horizontal so that responsibility is added to the job; for example, a production operator may also be given the responsibility for inspecting quality, ordering materials, devising and implementing maintenance schedules on the machinery or possibly even responsibility of a supervisory nature. Commonly, enrichment of this kind occurs when organizations are seeking to de-layer or reduce the number of different skill and responsibility levels within the organization. It is sometimes suggested that reductions in the number of tiers of management may provide opportunities for enlargement of this nature in the jobs lower down.

In each of these mechanisms a measure of functional flexibility is achieved, even if it is not the major motivation or prime objective. Whether this functional flexibility equates to multiskilling rather than multitasking is a moot point and undoubtedly varies. Similarly, as indicated above, it is questionable whether these experiments in job design also result in the provision of opportunities for greater intrinsic satisfaction, employee involvement and employee commitment.

Japanization? quality, involvement and commitment as competitive advantage

Throughout the 1980s and 90s there were many companies in Europe and America that sought to achieve the competitive success which they associated with Japanese companies and the Japanese model of HRM. It has been suggested that American MNCs exported Taylorism and Fordism to the rest of the world and that Japanese MNCs have exported the lean production model emphasizing flexibility, minimizing waste, and quality, and this applies to labour as well as to the other production resources. Integral to this model is the continuous search for improvement that pervades all aspects of the organization's activity and recognizes their interdependence, a system of apparent consensual decision making and an emphasis upon employee involvement in and commitment to the organization's objectives.

European and American organizations have therefore been keen to introduce a range of new working methods and philosophies which they associate with Japanese organizations and their success: that is, quality circles (QCs) and other problem-solving groups; cell or teamworking; total quality management (TQM) processes; just-in-time (JIT) and lean production. All of these have implications for the nature of work and the employment relationship, terms and conditions of employment and the traditions and practice of employee relations.

Some analysts (e.g. Eaton, 2000) have suggested that the significance of these Japanese approaches and in particular their concern to minimize waste, search for continuous improvement and emphasize quality and flexibility in machine and labour usage have resulted in a new paradigm or mode of production, referred to as lean production and associated in particular with Toyota, which has replaced Fordism as the dominant mode of production in the developed world.

In the remainder of this section attention is given to the nature of the more common of these 'methods and techniques' and the different views that exist, some positive and some negative, as to their impact upon employees and employee relations.

The quality circle: problem-solving group

Probably the most famous technique associated with 'Japanization', it became popular in the UK and some other parts of Europe in the 1970s and 1980s. The popularity of this concept in Europe was linked to the perceived need for European manufacturers to compete on the grounds of nil-defects. QCs are intended to contribute to the process of reducing defects and the need for repair. They comprise relatively small numbers of employees (six to ten) meeting voluntarily on a regular basis to identify, examine and resolve quality or other operational problems concerned with their own work and immediate environment. Their remit may be primarily to deal with quality problems but they are commonly also expected both to devise ways of reducing costs and means for improving the design of work. These groups rarely have the authority to implement their own recommendations and, as the problems are resolved, there is a danger that there may be a loss of momentum. Generally they are centred on a particular part of the production process. The formation and active and successful operation of such groups is not quite as easy as it may at first seem and experience has tended to reinforce the view that these groups need to be both guided and led; it is quite common for the participants also to need training and some access to resources. As with many of the other mechanisms referred to here, it is important that management is seen to take note and implement at least some of the recommendations of such groups; the effective continuation of problem-solving groups, whether QCs or others, tends to depend upon evidence that their work is valued.

The success of QCs has been the subject of debate over the years, with some commentators acting as protagonists and others openly critical. They certainly have been introduced into hundreds of companies and some success was claimed in terms of quality improvements and improvements in job satisfaction and employee involvement.

Much of the criticism of the adoption and application of the concept in Europe has focused upon ambiguity about the true purpose of such schemes, with the view being expressed by some (Batstone and Gourley, 1986) that the true purpose of these experiments was not so much to secure improvements in quality and employee involvement, and thereby employee satisfaction, as to provide a means whereby management was able to circumvent and bypass the traditional collective mechanisms of industrial relations and develop a more individual relationship with employees. In Japan, with its very different culture and industrial relations traditions, these were not issues.

Another explanation for the relative lack of success and longevity of the original form of QCs was that, because they were voluntary, they gave the impression that a concern for quality improvement was voluntary and therefore not crucial to the success of the organization. As time went by and the degree of conviction that quality was integral to competitive advantage increased, alternative and more comprehensive approaches were required.

Evidence from UK

The 2004 WERS found that 21 per cent (16 per cent in 1998) of workplaces had groups of non-managerial employees that met to solve specific problems or discuss aspects of performance or quality. Larger workplaces were less likely than smaller workplaces to involve most of their non-managerial employees in problem-solving groups.

The WIB2000S also found that there had been an increase in the use of QCs over the period 1992–2000.

Teamworking

Mueller *et al.*, 2000 has defined teamworking as, 'a group of employees, normally between 3 and 15, who meet regularly in order to work independently on fulfilling a particular task'.

In practice, the nature of teams and teamworking varies enormously on a range of different criteria and there is a considerable body of literature concerned to identify the factors critical for team success as well as the different types of teams.

For example, Greenberg and Baron (1996) concluded that teams could be categorized according to four major dimensions. These dimensions are: purpose; the length of time that the team is operational; the degree of autonomy; and whether the teams extend across organizational functions or not. Hayes (1997) concentrated on function or purpose and differentiated: (1) production or service teams; (2) action or negotiation teams; (3) project and development teams and (4) advice and involvement teams.

Banker *et al.* (1996) adopted a different approach and categorized team types according to autonomy, ranging from low to high, though they also incorporate other of the dimensions used by those above. The types identified are: traditional work groups, QCs, semi-autonomous work groups, self-managing teams and self-designing teams. Traditional work groups perform the production activities without any management responsibility. In QCs, as noted above, membership should be voluntary and the members are drawn from a particular department with a responsibility for making suggestions without authority to make decisions. Semi-autonomous work groups consist of members who manage major production activities, while others perform support activities like maintenance. Self-managing teams consist of a group of individuals with control over their tasks. Self-designing teams are similar to self-managing teams but with control over the design of the team. They point out that there is a difference between teams having a measure of autonomy and teams being self-managing, the latter being identified as a particular and separate category or type.

In sum, therefore, common dimensions used to differentiate types of team are: purpose, nature of membership, including whether the team membership is cross-functional, and the degree and nature of autonomy allowed to the team.

Teamworking is integral to the Japanese system and tends to comprise work or production teams and teams with quality control and other problem-solving roles. There has been considerable debate surrounding the degree of autonomy of teams in the context of Japanization.

What is clear is that the introduction of teamworking in the west has taken all the various forms referred to above and it is also clear that teamworking may provide employees with greater autonomy, greater variety through multiskilling, greater involvement and that it may lead to greater employee satisfaction and commitment. As Womack *et al.*, 1990 claimed, it is the dynamic work team that emerges at the heart of the lean factory, skills are upgraded and employees are empowered, employees become committed to defect free output and the search for continuous improvement. The alternative view is that teams in lean production environments are given relatively little autonomy and that the pressures of continuous improvement lead to standardization, rationalization and stress. Multitasking is the order of the day rather than multiskilling and jobs are enlarged rather than enriched. Employees attachment is secured through compliance mechanisms rather than commitment and employees are certainly not empowered in any meaningful sense.

Much of the debate in the west about the extension of teamworking has focused upon the assertions by many managements that they have introduced some form of autonomous teamworking as part of a high commitment management programme associated with Japanization.

Evidence from the UK

The WERS 2004 data indicated that 72 per cent of workplaces had at least some core employees in formally designated teams. They conclude that, though the incidence and operation of teamworking had changed little since 1998, where it was in place it was usually embedded among staff and 80 per cent of workplaces with teamworking extended it to at least three-fifths of core employees.

However, teams did not always have full autonomy. In 83 per cent of workplaces with teamworking, teams were given responsibility for specific products and services and in 61 per cent they could jointly decide how work was done, however, in only 6 per cent of workplaces were the teams allowed to appoint their own team leaders.

There was also evidence that employees viewed greater levels of autonomy positively and those working in teams with greater autonomy were more satisfied with the amount of influence they had over their jobs than team-workers who were given limited freedom or responsibility.

The WIB2000S also found evidence to question the extent to which teams are autonomous given that, while 71 per cent of men (41 per cent in 1992) and 56 per cent of women said that they worked in some form of team or group, 92 per cent of all workers said that their work was covered by a supervisor.

There is, then, clear evidence that the incidence of teamworking has increased and that the dominant form of team is a work, product or service team. There are questions concerning the extent to which these teams are fully autonomous.

Total quality management

The essence of the approach is a comprehensive and continuous search for improvement, the production of goods and services with 'zero defects', which involves most employees and knows few boundaries in terms of organizational activity; as noted above it was the advent of this approach that probably contributed to the demise of the more partial QCs. In many respects it is an approach that seeks/needs to generate a culture of quality throughout the organization.

The driver for this attention to TQM should be the customer and this should include internal as well as external customers. Internally customers are the employees involved in the next stage of the process; they may be the next individuals or team in the assembly process, the next person to receive a report or the recipient of advice from a service function internal to the organization such as the line manager who has asked the personnel officer for advice on whether it would be fair to dismiss someone in a particular set of circumstances.

The focus of improvements in quality should be on the employees doing the job and a fear of failure should be replaced with a search for failure: if people are blamed for failure they are unlikely to take risks, they are unlikely to search for failures and put them right but are more likely to try and hide them.

As noted already, the formation of cells or teams and the devolution of some additional responsibilities to these semi-autonomous teams are commonly part of this overall approach, as may be the formation of QCs and other problem-solving groups concerned with issues of wider impact than can be dealt with by a QC. These other groups may be cross-functional.

The customer-driven nature of such initiatives and programmes and the implications for employees are illustrated in the 'Guiding Principles' governing a programme initiated within Ford in the UK and quoted in Storey (1992: 57):

- quality comes first
- customers are the focus of everything we do
- continuous improvement is essential to our success
- employee involvement is our way of life
- dealers and suppliers are our partners
- integrity is never compromised.

TQM programmes then are likely to include an emphasis upon employee involvement as the means through which the search for continuous improvement is to be achieved.

Just-in-time

The essence of the JIT approach and appropriate systems is to eliminate waste and superficially this may have little to do with either flexibility or quality. However, there are interdependent relationships between these concepts and systems.

The basic theory of JIT is that, at all stages of the production of a good or the provision of a service, consideration should be given to minimizing the time between the product or raw material being needed and its acquisition. Systems should be designed which result in the final product being produced just before it is required in the marketplace, sub-assemblies are produced just before final assembly and bought components are acquired just before they are needed. This enables the company to respond more quickly to market demand and it confirms demand as the driver of the production process. This contrasts with traditional Fordist systems in which vast quantities of standardized products are made and may be stockpiled until they are sold.

In JIT systems the production time is reduced to a minimum, the various contributions to the final product are performed and acquired at the last reasonable moment and the likelihood is that the system will be geared towards and capable of satisfying the demand for relatively small batches of differentiated goods and services. It is a system, therefore, which places an emphasis upon both quality and flexibility. The materials, labour and sub-assembly processes have to be of the right quality and a premium is placed upon this by the shortness of the timescale; if materials are only acquired just before they are needed, they have to be of the desired quality or else the system fails. In the 1998 WERS survey in the UK, 29 per cent of the workplaces surveyed indicated that they had a JIT system of inventory control in place.

If the object is to respond to market demand and to undertake relatively short production runs, given that the demand in the market is for customized or variated products, then both labour and machinery must be flexible. Quality, ideally TQM and flexibility are crucial to the effective operation of these schemes and they are very vulnerable to failure or shortcomings in either.

These organizational and technical systems give purchasers considerable power. For example, big companies such as Toyota, Ford, BT, etc. which are likely to be the major customer of any supplier of components, can exert great pressure upon the supplier to deliver on time a product of the desired quality.

From an employee relations perspective these systems place an emphasis upon trust and cooperation since the relationship between management and employees is one of high dependency as the system operates without stocks at both ends of the process.

These same constraints place similar pressures upon the efficiency and effectiveness of the entire system and arguably act as the impetus for the application of continuous improvement, the approaches that are the basis of TQM.

Both TQM and JIT imply comprehensive change within organizations, the emphasis of the former is upon cultural change whereas the latter is more directly concerned with organizational and technical systems. There is, however, likely to be an inter-relationship since massive change such as is associated with the introduction of JIT is likely to imply cultural change as a pre-requisite to its successful implementation.

In a sense these schemes have been dealt with in an order reflecting an increasing degree of re-design of traditional systems and work practices, the changes in the latter being of a more fundamental and profound nature than in the earlier ones. However, it would be unwise to overestimate the frequency with which these more profound experiments have been tried in a coherent fashion.

The more profound the re-design, the greater is the impact upon employees, management and the employment relationship. In theory it would seem that an enhancement of employee flexibility and autonomy is integral to many of these initiatives and changes of this kind are likely to have implications for management style, the degree of control that management remains able to exert and the mechanisms through which they seek to do so.

Incidence and impact of the new approaches to the organization of work: perceptions and conclusions

In this chapter we have examined a number of the new approaches to the organization of work, each of which can be seen to be variously concerned to achieve competitiveness in what is referred to as the post-Fordist era. In particular, we have examined the approaches associated with flexible specialization, the flexible firm, job re-design and Japanization. As noted above, some, if not all, of these approaches imply fairly fundamental and comprehensive change to traditional ways of working.

In this section we examine the differing views regarding their impact on the employment relationship and workers' experience of work. Various claims have been made in this respect of the advantages of these various schemes and approaches and commonly it is argued that they variously provide employees with more involvement, autonomy, influence in the decision-making process regarding the organization and undertaking of the task, control and job satisfaction, and that they also have the advantage of producing a more committed workforce. There are of course also alternative viewpoints about the effect that these changes have had.

The supporters of the various schemes are likely to claim that: compliance is being replaced with/by commitment; conflict by cooperation; dissatisfaction and alienation with satisfaction; rigidity with flexibility and variety; and control with involvement, autonomy and discretion.

Critics of these new approaches, perhaps particularly if they have a radical perspective, are likely to argue that changes are being introduced that are motivated by management's and capital's desire for increased competitiveness, productivity and profit and that they result in:

- The intensification of labour use and exploitation.
- The intensification of management control through means that utilize the new information technologies and peer surveillance as well as the never-ending search for faults and the apportionment of blame.
- Unacceptable levels of stress, anxiety and insecurity for labour.

What is presented as employee involvement and participation is in fact no more than a sham designed to give employees the opportunity to acquiesce to pre-ordained management decisions.

The more neutral observers are more likely to ask:

- Whether the claims made by the supporters of the new approaches are realistic and being realized?
- Whether change is being introduced in a coherent fashion by managements that truly understand the implications of what they are doing?
- What other effects the schemes may have?
- Whether any of these other effects or implications may be consistent with or counter productive to the claims made for the programmes?

So we have very different interpretations of the impact of these changes upon the nature of work and the employment relationship.

It is very difficult to ascertain which of these viewpoints may be closest to the 'truth' of the nature of the post-Fordist employment relationship. It has to be acknowledged that there are always likely to be factors specific to particular workplaces, and managements, that influence employee experiences and perceptions of the effects of the introduction of new approaches to work organization.

Evidence from UK

A number of surveys have been conducted in the UK over the years, some of which have given credence to the critical viewpoint of these initiatives. For example, Undy and Kessler (1995) conducted a survey which lends support to those who argue that the new techniques result in intensification, exploitation and stress. Geary (1995), in his review of the evidence and assessment of the impact of these new work structures upon employees' working lives, presented a fairly depressing picture of the extent to which these working lives have in any real sense been improved. He concluded that the dominant impacts included:

- Increased stress and effort levels.
- Little significant upskilling, with task specialization and gendered divisions of work remaining pretty much as they were.
- Little increase in employees' control of the work process and its organization, managements having remained opposed to extending employees' autonomy and to any other moves that might impair their ability to define the content of acceptable work behaviour.

- More assertive managements that have been successful in gaining greater control over the labour process.
- Little or no lasting impact upon employees' commitment to the organization and its objectives and no significant improvements in the extent to which employees trust their managements.
- No change in the fundamentally conflictual nature of the employment relationship.

Another survey, Burchell *et al.* (1999) found that anxiety and stress had risen in both public and private sectors and this was linked to increased concerns about job security and work intensification resulting from the increased pressures to achieve competitiveness and consequential reductions in staffing levels. More than 60 per cent of the employees surveyed argued that the pace of work and the effort that they have to put into their work had increased over the preceding 5 years. The biggest increase in insecurity was among professional workers and this was consistent with the findings in an earlier survey (Felstead *et al.*, 1998) that managers and professionals were experiencing significant increases in both job and employment insecurity. The Cambridge researchers also found that there was a lack of trust among workers and a sense of a loss of control over the pace of work. Interesting in the light of the discussion earlier (**Chapter 1**) on perspectives and the issue of conflict between the interests of employees and employers was the finding that only 26 per cent of workers surveyed felt that employees and employers were on the same side and 44 per cent felt that management could be expected to look after employees' best interests 'only a little' or 'not at all'. Both of these latter surveys make it clear that there is a negative association between insecurity, stress and anxiety and general mental and physical health and well being and also that stress and anxiety are demotivating.

Heery and Salmon (2000) also found that workers are experiencing greater levels of insecurity and stress.

Supiot (2001) also adds to these findings in his analysis of Fordism and post-Fordism in Europe and concludes that Fordism is being replaced by a mode of production which emphasizes: increasingly flexible, fragmented and individual working arrangements, increased labour insecurity, more frequent career breaks and periods of unemployment and retraining and an increased use of outsourcing and subcontracting.

Yet if we examine the 2004 WERS data and that from the WIB2000S we do obtain some alternative insights.

The evidence from both surveys suggests that some multiskilling or tasking has taken place along with some outsourcing of services, there is use of secondary labour markets and atypical contracts, yet the practices associated with both functional and numerical flexibility are not as widespread as might have been expected.

Echoing the findings of the WERS surveys the WIB2000S found no significant evidence that jobs had become more transitory and uncertain. Taylor (2002) concludes that the shift away from permanent and full-time jobs is exaggerated and the overwhelming majority of workers do not feel insecure in their jobs.

There is clear evidence that the incidence of teamworking has increased though WIB2000S found evidence to question the extent to which teams are autonomous and the vast majority of employees said that their work was covered by a supervisor.

Taylor (2002), in commenting on the survey results concerning autonomy and control over the job, concludes that there had been little significant change in the extent to which workers are supervised and that most workers find their jobs are still under the control of management. The survey provides important evidence to suggest that while a trend exists to greater freedom for the worker on the job (e.g. concerning the task, how work is performed and the pace of work), the degree of control and surveillance by management has also increased.

There was evidence that employees viewed greater levels of autonomy positively and those working in teams with greater autonomy were more satisfied with the amount of influence they had over their jobs than team-workers who were given limited freedom or responsibility. However, there was also evidence that 56 per cent of all workers said they did not want more say over their work (WIB2000S).

We have already noted, that the WERS 2004 data gave results indicating that a majority of employees expressed satisfaction with: the sense of achievement that they obtain at work; their scope for initiative; their influence over the job; training; their job security; and also with the work itself. Satisfaction was lowest in respect of pay, training and 'involvement in decision-making'.

However, the WIB2000S found evidence of declining employee satisfaction with their hours of work, possibly the product of work intensification and the practice of using the hours worked by core employees to achieve numerical flexibility. Taylor (2002) concludes that the world of work is much less satisfying to employees than the one they were experiencing 10 years ago, employees' satisfaction in every facet of their job had declined since 1992. It has also grown more stressful for all categories of employees. Most people say they are working much harder in intensity and clocking on for more hours than in the recent past. He suggests the disgruntled manager has joined the disgruntled manual worker, at least in complaints about the long hours culture.

However, the WERS 2004 also asked a question in which the respondents were asked to indicate the frequency with which they experienced a range of feelings or emotional states which the researchers encompass in the term 'job-related well being'. From the results it would be fair to summarize the responses as indicating that relatively few employees (less than 20 per cent in each case) feel tense, worried or uneasy either most or all of the time, whereas, 38 per cent, 33 per cent and 26 per cent respectively say they feel content, calm and relaxed either most or all of the time. There is certainly no evidence to support contentions that overall employees' feelings of well being at work are poor. The researchers also conclude that job-related well being is higher in small workplaces and small organizations than in larger ones and among employees who are not union members, but falls with increased education and is U-shaped with respect to age.

Taylor also concludes that there was little evidence that enlightened HRM techniques are being translated into practical measures ensuring the growth of more high commitment workplaces. There was evidence of a significant deterioration in workers having any sense of personal commitment to the company that employs them. He asserts that, in most enterprises, it was hard to discern the advance of any coherent HRM agenda.

Summary

Overall we have sought to identify and describe some of the more important changes to working practices, the nature and organization of work and the nature of the employment relationship in the latter years of the 20th century and early years of the 21st century. In particular we have considered forms of job re-design and some of the innovations which have been attributed to the impact of Japanese companies in Europe and which are associated with the concept of Japanization culminating in the suggestion that lean production is the new dominant model of production in the developed world. These changes have in most cases been motivated by the desire of companies to be efficient and competitive in the global market. There is a degree of inter-relationship between them and we need to bear in mind that change tends to be prompted, in this case by the radical changes ongoing in the global marketplace and the imperative that companies must be competitive. The initiatives have often been presented as changes geared to obtaining greater labour flexibility, greater job satisfaction, employee involvement and commitment; however, the evidence that these objectives are actually achieved is varied. It is important to be aware and bear in mind the fact that an assessment of the motives for and impact of these developments is inevitably influenced by the perspective of the observer and perceptions of whether the employment relationship is one characterized by conflict or cooperation, or both.

Activities to test understanding

Activity 1

To ensure that you understand the differences between Fordist and post-Fordist devise for yourself lists of the main characteristics of each. To help, you could compare the regimes on the grounds of:

- the type of products that each system might be appropriate for
- the type of labour required
- the nature of the technology implied.

Activity 2

Look back at the model of the flexible firm and compile lists of the advantages and disadvantages from both the employer/manager and employee/labour viewpoints.

Activity 3

Examine each of the competitive production strategies identified by Regini and in each case identify whether there is a requirement for the labour resource to be flexible, whether this flexibility is of a functional or numerical nature and comment upon the appropriateness of the flexible firm model to each of these production scenarios.

Activity 4

Take another look at each of job rotation, job enlargement and job enrichment and work out for yourself the extent to which each is consistent with the assumptions underlying the principles of Taylorism.

Activity 5

How do each of the 'techniques' associated with Japanization contribute to the achievement of quality and commitment?

References

Atkinson, J., 1984. Manpower strategies for the flexible organization. *Personnel Management* August, pp. 28–31.

Banker, R., Field, J., Schroeder, R. and Sinha, K., 1996. Impact of work teams on manufacturing performance: a longitudinal field study. *Academy of Management Journal* 39(4): 867–890.

Batstone, E. and Gourley, S., 1986. *Unions, Unemployment and Innovation.* Blackwell, Oxford.

Braverman, H., 1974. *Labour and Monopoly Capital.* Monthly Review Press, New York.

Burchell, B., Day, D., Hudson, M., Lapido, D., Mankelow, R., Nolan, J., Reed, H., Wichert, I. and Wilkinson, F., 1999. *Job Insecurity and Work Intensification.* Joseph Rowntree Foundation, London.

Cully, M., Woodland, S., O'Reilly, A. and Dix, G., 1999. *Britain at Work as Depicted by the 1998 Workplace Employee Relations Survey.* Routledge, London.

Eaton, J., 2000. *Comparative Employment Relations.* Polity Press, Cambridge.

Felstead, A., Burchall, B. and Green, F., 1998. Insecurity at Work. *New Economy* 5(3): 180–184.

Gallie, D. and White, M., 1998. *Restructuring the Employment Relationship.* Oxford University Press, Oxford, p. 316.

Geary, J., 2003. New forms of work organisation: still limited, still controlled, but still welcome? In Edwards, P. (ed.), *Industrial Relations: Theory and Practice*, 2nd Edition. Blackwell, Oxford, pp. 338–678.

Geary, J.F., 1995. Work practices: the structure of work. In Edwards, P. (ed.), *Industrial Relations: Theory and Practice in Britain.* Blackwell, Oxford.

Greenberg, J. and Baron, R.A., 1996. *Behavior in Organizations: Understanding and Managing the Human Side of Work*, 6th Edition. Prentice-Hall, New Jersey.

Guest, D., 1987. Human resource management and industrial relations. *Journal of Management Studies* 24(5): 503–521.

Hayes, N., 1997. *Successful Team Management.* International Thomson Business Press, London.

Heery, E. and Salmon, J. (eds). 2000. *The Insecure Workforce.* Routledge, London.

Herzberg, F., 1966. *Work and the Nature of Man.* World Publishing, Cleveland, Ohio.

Kersley, B., Alpin, C., Forth, J., Bryson, A., Bewley, H., Dix, G. and Oxenbridge, S., 2005. *Inside the Workplace First Findings from the 2004 Workplace Employment Relations Survey (WERS 2004).*

Legge, K., 1995. *Human Resource Management: Rhetorics and Realities.* Macmillan, Basingstoke.

Marchington, M. and Wilkinson, A., 1996. *Core Personnel and Development.* IPD, London.

Maslow, A., 1943. A theory of human motivation. *Psychological Review* 50: 370–396.

Mueller, F., Procter, S. and Buchanan, D., 2000. Team working in its context: antecedents, nature and dimensions. *Human relations* 53(11): 1387–1424.

Pollert, A., 1988. The flexible firm: fixation or fact. *Work, Employment and Society* 2(3): 281–306.

Regini, M., 1995. Firms and institutions: the demand for skills and their social production in Europe. *European Journal of Industrial Relations* 1(2): 191–202.

Storey, J., 1992. Developments in the Management of Human Resources, Blackwell, Oxford.

Supiot, A., 2001. Beyond Employment – Changes in Work and the Future of Labour Law in Europe. Oxford University Press, Oxford, p. 245.

Taylor, F.W., 1911. *Principles of Scientific Management.* Harper, New York.

Taylor, R., 2002. *Britain's World of Work – Myths and Realities.* ESRC, Swindon.

Undy, R. and Kessler, I., 1995. The changing nature of the employment relationship. Presentation to the IPD national conference.

Womack, J., Jones, D. and Roos, D., 1990. *The Machine that Changed the World.* Rawson Associates, New York.

Chapter 3

Globalization, multinational corporations and employee relations

Introduction

The latter part of the 20th century and the beginning of the 21st century witnessed a massive expansion in the extent to which business has become international and associated with this huge increase in the number of employing organizations that have either become, or are part of, a multinational. Employee relations within any national context have as a consequence become subject to a much broader and international range of influences.

This chapter falls into two main parts, the first of which is concerned primarily with establishing the meaning of the term globalization, the scale of international business and the significance of the Multinational Corporation (MNC) in these processes, some of the characteristics and stages of development of the modern MNC, including the reasons why companies become MNCs, and some of the more influential models or typologies. We also in this first part identify national culture as an important contextual influence and identify some of the more common benefits claimed for, and criticisms made of, MNCs and the internationalization of business.

In the second part of the chapter the relationship between the MNC and employee relations is examined further. A number of main themes are addressed including:

- the importance of headquarters (HQ) approach, mindset and strategic decisions, etc.;
- the relevance of national contextual differences upon the activities and organization of MNCs' employee relations policies and practices;
- the impact that MNCs from economically successful countries can have upon employee relations within national systems and indeed internationally;
- the attitudes of MNCs towards trade unions and the trade union response;
- the question of whether and how MNCs diffuse employment relations policies and practices internally across national borders;
- international trade unionism and their perceptions of globalization;
- the role played by some of the supranational regulatory organizations in seeking to influence the employee relations policies and practices of MNCs and the arguments surrounding the issue of minimum labour standards.

Learning objectives

After studying this chapter you will be able to:

- Identify and explain the benefits of the internationalization of business.
- Understand and explain the constituents of globalization and potential consequences for labour of both globalization and FDI.
- Explain and discuss the options open to MNCs in the approach they adopt to managing employee relations in different national systems.
- Appreciate that potentially there is a two-way interaction between MNCs and national systems.
- Discuss the influences for and the prospects of the convergence of employee relations within MNCs and across national borders.

- Identify and discuss the difficulties faced by the trades unions and other regulatory bodies in influencing the employee relations strategies of MNCs.
- Identify and discuss the arguments for and against the need to regulate the employee relations activities of MNCs.

Globalization and the internationalization of business

There are a number of different dimensions and components to the internationalization of business:

- a significant expansion of international trade;
- the liberalization of trade across national borders through the removal of tariff barriers, the extension of free trade agreements, for example the European Union (EU), and North Atlantic Free Trade Agreement (NAFTA), and the proposed free trade area including China, Japan, South Korea and Association of Southeast Asian Nations (ASEAN);
- development of more global product markets and enhanced pressures of international competition;
- the cross-national integration of production within MNCs;
- an expansion in the number and influence of MNCs through joint ventures, cross-national acquisitions and mergers or foreign direct investment (FDI);
- an international division of labour.

This globalization or internationalization of business has been significantly enabled by the development and use of new technologies, particularly in the arena of information transfer and communications. Also the increase in the size and extent of free trade agreements incorporating the free movement of capital inevitably facilitates cross-border investment of all kinds.

The term Globalization has become increasingly used to describe both this process of internationalization and its outcomes. There are numerous different definitions of this term and the range of these definitions is illustrated by those of Ohmae (1990); Walters (1995) and Needle (2000).

Ohmae defines it in terms of the emergence of: a borderless world or interlinked economy in which globalized

- production chains
- product markets
- corporate structures and
- financial flows

would, to all intents and purposes, make the nation state and national boundaries largely irrelevant.

Walters (1995) has a different emphasis and focuses on social and cultural dimensions:

> A social process in which the constraints of geography on social and cultural arrangements recede and in which people become increasingly aware they are receding. (p. 3)

Needle (2000) also introduces the notion of political convergence:

> Globalization is a process in which the world appears to be converging economically, politically and culturally. (p. 45)

Undoubtedly MNCs play an active and influential, some would say dominant, role in driving this process of globalization and internationalization.

From the perspective of the interests of labour and the impact upon employee relations, Hyman (1999) suggests that it is the cross-national integration of production within MNCs that poses the biggest threat, given their ability to move operations across frontiers if confronted with a disliked regulatory regime or to take advantage of differences in labour supply, costs, etc.

An example of an integrated production chain might be how Ford Motor Company has organized its engine production within Europe with different engines being developed and built in plants in several countries. The manufacture and acquisition of other components and assembly of the finished car are undertaken elsewhere within the Ford Europe complex.

Hyman (1999) cites an International Labour Organization (ILO) review of the state of labour movements worldwide which suggests that there are three main elements of globalization that may be perceived to be particularly threatening to both employees and their representatives and also to national systems of employment regulation:

- the internationalization of financial markets;
- the liberalization of trade across national boundaries which has facilitated the shift of low-skilled manufacturing from the developed to the developing countries; and
- the growing ability of MNCs to use the 'exit option' as a means of avoiding unwanted regulation or to threaten governments and employees in order to obtain beneficial regulation or tax incentives, development grants, etc.

We look in a later section at the options that MNCs may have when seeking to influence government or trade unions and also at whether trade unions show signs of being able to counter such initiatives.

The definitions of globalization above and their emphasis upon convergence raises also the issue of whether national employee relations systems, comprising a range of regulations and traditional approaches and practices, are also converging. We noted in the previous chapter that technological developments and the activities and influences of MNCs can impact the nature of work, job design and work systems and thereby have impacts for employee relations. We revisit and extend our consideration of these issues in the second part of this chapter.

The advantages of the internationalization of business

The internationalization of business is commonly claimed to yield a number of benefits:

- It enhances the availability of goods and services, even the largest of countries has limited resources and natural advantages, such as minerals or climate, and the development of international trade enables consumers to have access to a wider range of goods and services, goods and services that might well not be available otherwise.
- It is also argued that internationalization enables products and services to be produced most cheaply, the availability of resources and input costs vary from one location to another and where individuals, firms or countries specialize in the production of goods and services at which they are the most efficient then there are benefits to be obtained for everyone.
- Where companies invest in foreign countries in order to take advantage of input cost differentials there is the potential for knowledge and technology transfer to the long-term advantage of the recipient country.
- Given the above consumers gain from a wider range of products and at a lower cost, incomes rise and wealth is created and this fuels further consumption.
- Higher profits provide scope for further investment in research and the development of new technologies.
- Jobs are created in activities in which there is comparative advantage and
- As wealth and incomes rise governments gain greater tax receipts which enables them to invest further in social and public services and infrastructure thereby enhancing the populations health, welfare and levels of educational attainment.

Multinational corporations

Definition

There are many organizations which trade internationally but which do not fall into the category of an MNC. Also, many terms are used to refer to multinational organizations including **global**, **transnational** and **international** as well as **multinational**. Some observers (e.g. Bartlett and Ghoshal, 1989) have sought to assign specific meanings to each of these and to distinguish between them. However, in this chapter we will use the term 'multinational' as the generic.

The simplest of definitions is:

> MNCs are enterprises which in more than one country own or control production or service facilities and activities that add value (Leat, 1999 p. 96).

A more comprehensive definition is given by the United Nations Conference on Trade and Development (UNCTAD) when they define Transnational organizations as: 'Transnational corporations' (TNCs) comprise parent enterprises and their foreign affiliates: a parent enterprise is defined as one that controls assets of another entity or entities in a country or countries other than its home country, usually by owning a capital stake. An equity capital stake of at least 10 per cent is normally considered as a threshold for the control of assets in this context.

It is the dimension of ownership and control of value-adding activity in more than one country that sets the MNC apart from the organization which simply trades internationally or which enters into strategic and international alliances or partnerships which do not involve these elements of ownership and control.

The distinction between organizations trading internationally and those that fall within the definition of an MNC was demonstrated by Wilkins (1970), who suggested that it was possible to identify four typical stages in the development of American MNCs:

1   The US concern sold items abroad through independent agents or, on occasion, filled orders directly from abroad.
2   The company appointed a salaried export manager and/or acquired an existing export agency and its contacts. This stage might also involve the appointment of independent agencies in foreign countries to represent the company. The foreign agent would sell on its own account or handle shipments on consignment.
3   The company either installed one or more salaried representatives, a sales branch or a distribution subsidiary abroad, or it purchased a formerly independent agent located in a foreign

country. At this point, for the first time, the company made a foreign investment; *it is only at this point that the company becomes an MNC.*

4   A finishing, assembly or manufacturing plant might be built abroad to fill the needs of a foreign market.

In recent years the mechanisms for achieving international expansion have more commonly included:

Takeovers, mergers, joint ventures, international networking/alliances. Hofstede (1997) identified five means of international expansion:

- Greenfield start
- Foreign takeover
- International merger
- Foreign joint venture and
- Partial cooperation with foreign partner.

Where the outcome is at least a share in ownership and control then we can say that the resulting organization would be an MNC, but where there is not this sharing then we may have an organization which is internationally active but is not an MNC.

This element of ownership or control tends to bring with it the challenge of managing human resources and employee relations in different national contexts and poses for the organization's management problems associated with international human resource management.

International human resource management is commonly defined in terms of the management of human resources **within** MNCs.

Scale and nature of multinational activity and FDI

In their World Investment Report for 2004, UNCTAD (2005) estimated that there were some 70,000 TNCs with 690,000 affiliates. They had estimated that employment in foreign affiliates had been in the region of 54 million people in 2003, UNCTAD (2004). The latter years of the 20th century had seen annual growth rates in FDI and the value of cross-border M and As approaching 50 per cent per year. The early years of the 21st century witnessed a significant slow down in these rates of growth; in particular there was a big drop in the value of cross-border mergers and acquisitions (M and As), which, UNCTAD (2004) suggested was due to a number of factors:

- Slow economic growth in most parts of the world.
- Dim prospects for recovery in the short term.
- Falling stock market valuations.

- Lower corporate profitability.
- A slowdown in the pace of corporate restructuring.

However, they also identified signs of a recovery at the beginning of 2004 which they ascribed to higher economic growth in the main home and host countries, improved corporate profitability and higher stock valuations.

This recovery is confirmed in UNCTAD's World Investment Report for 2004. Overview (UNCTAD, 2005, p. 1):

> 2004 saw a slight rebound in global FDI after 3 years of declining flows. At $648 billion, world FDI *inflows* were 2 per cent higher in 2004 than in 2003. Inflows to developing countries surged by 40 per cent, to $233 billion, but developed countries as a group experienced a 14 per cent drop in their inward FDI.

And they suggest the following explanation and outlook:

> Many factors help to explain why the growth of FDI was particularly pronounced in developing countries in 2004. Intense competitive pressures in many industries are leading firms to explore new ways of improving their competitiveness. Some of these ways are by expanding operations in the fast-growing markets of emerging economies to boost sales, and by rationalizing production activities with a view to reaping economies of scale and lowering production costs. Higher prices for many commodities have further stimulated FDI to countries that are rich in natural resources such as oil and minerals. In some developed as well as developing countries, increased inflows in 2004 were linked to an upturn in cross-border merger and acquisition (M&A) activity. Greenfield FDI continued to rise for the third consecutive year in 2004. Provided economic growth is maintained, the prospects for a further increase in global FDI flows in 2005 are promising.

It has been estimated that 80 per cent of world trade is attributable to MNCs and all FDI and it is accepted that there is a close association between the growth in the number and activity of MNCs and FDI.

As noted in the previous section FDI can take a number of forms, the most significant being the total or partial acquisition of existing operations in other countries, which may themselves already be operating as an MNC, or the establishment of a completely new operation in another country, commonly referred to as investment of a greenfield nature. It is the acquisition of interests in existing operations through merger and amalgamation that seems to be largely responsible for the massive rate of increase in FDI in the late 1990s. The European Commission (1999: 125) points out that much (perhaps as much as 80 per cent) of FDI takes the form of a change in the ownership of existing assets from resident to non-resident and, in particular, in the ownership of shares in companies rather than some form of tangible asset.

Reasons for investing abroad, becoming MNCs and locational determinants

Ghertman and Allen (1984) suggested the following reasons why companies decide to establish their own manufacturing or extraction units in foreign countries:

1   In certain industries there are production limits in any one factory. These may be due to the perishability of the product or, for example, its weight and the transportation costs involved. Examples would be in industries such as the production of milk derivatives or liquid gas. It is not advisable to build huge factories in these industries since the economies of scale in production are not sufficient to offset higher transport or wastage costs. It is far better to set up new factories in the countries where the customers are based. In contrast, in other industries like chemicals or steelmaking, it is possible to make such economies of scale that a large production unit in a single country is justified on the grounds of profitability.

2   Local governments often prefer to have the MNCs invest in their countries rather than export to them. There are benefits in terms of local employment and an outflow of foreign currency can be avoided, resulting in a better trade balance for the host country.

3   Within MNCs, local managements obviously prefer the parent company to set up a manufacturing plant in the host country because this makes the subsidiary more important within the group and at the same time facilitates relations with the host country.

4   Production in only one country leaves the company open to risks of war, nationalization or confiscation, or vulnerable to increases in duties or the establishment of import quotas or fluctuations in rates of exchange. Similarly, strikes in a single factory could halt sales to several countries at the same time.

Barrell and Pain (1997) take a somewhat different approach and have suggested that cross-border production activity takes place for a number of reasons:

■   Market size.
■   Cost differentials: relatively low production costs (incorporating the impact of real exchange rates) are an incentive.
■   The role played by knowledge-based firm-specific assets. This term refers to assets such as managerial or marketing skills or reputation (including such factors as brand images) and/or process or product innovations that are firm specific and may

be patented. Barrell and Pain suggest that such assets give economies of scale at the level of the firm rather than at the level of the plant and this may enable single-firm multi-plant operations (some overseas) to have a cost advantage over the alternative of two single-plant firms. They also suggest that innovating companies, in possession of patents, are more likely to invest overseas themselves than to license others in foreign markets to provide the product or service.

■ To improve market access and bypass trade barriers such as those that surround the EU. There are potentially great advantages to the organization if it sets up a production or service facility within such a free trade area since it gives access to the whole of the new market and avoids the tariffs and other barriers that confront products and services from outside.

In the specific EU context, Barrell and Pain argue that the fact that the UK is a net outward investor within Europe and elsewhere casts doubt upon the supposed attractiveness of low labour costs and deregulated labour markets. They suggest that once an organization has decided to invest within the EU in order to obtain the benefits referred to above, then the decisions regarding the precise location of the investment within the EU are influenced by national or regional variables such as:

■ Corporate tax burdens.
■ The skills and training, the quality of the labour force.
■ The quality of the infrastructure.
■ Language and cultural factors.
■ The cost of labour: the more high-tech the operation, the less do labour costs play a significant part in the investment and location decision.

Individual national regimes and infrastructure are therefore relevant at this stage.

Traxler and Woitech (2000) conducted an analysis of the impact of national labour market regimes in Western Europe on the investment decisions of US MNCs in the period 1981–1992. Their underlying hypothesis was that, given that there are significant differences between these national labour markets in terms both of material labour standards and the extent to which regimes constrain employer prerogative or control, one might expect the MNC to adopt an opportunistic approach and 'regime shop' resulting in investment in those regimes that were beneficial in terms of lower material standards and the least amount of restriction upon managerial prerogative. Their analysis, however, does not support this hypothesis and they conclude that investors neither attributed high priority to labour market regimes in their location or investment decisions nor did they pursue coherent strategies regarding these regimes. Nevertheless, while other factors such as those mentioned above play an important role in guiding investment decisions, Traxler and Woitech do also comment that internationalization and the threat of regime shopping can put pressure on regimes' labour standards and upon governments to deregulate in order to compete for investment.

FDI: advantages and disadvantages

Governments and the citizens of a country can demonstrate different attitudes towards the proposition of an MNC setting up in that country or acquiring ownership of a home-country company; some countries, for example Japan, have been particularly resistant to the notion whereas others have been much more open. However, in the world of increasingly free trade, global markets and electronic communication and commerce, it has become more difficult for countries to resist the mobility of capital and the influence of foreign-owned MNCs.

Governments often encourage foreign-owned MNCs to set up a production or service facilities in their country and it is possible to identify a number of common reasons why such investment may be welcomed. It is usually anticipated that the investment will:

■ create jobs and improve the working conditions, living standards and prospects of those in the local labour market;
■ have a beneficial impact upon wages in the local labour market;
■ assist with the necessary process of industrialization in undeveloped countries;
■ assist the host country's development through the process of technology and knowledge transfer and thereby boost the productivity of local manufacturers or suppliers;
■ generate tax revenues and foreign exchange receipts for the host-country government.

There is a tendency to assume that any such investment will have a positive effect upon employment levels and other terms and conditions of employment in the host or receiving country; however, it is important to be careful in assessing this impact. In assessing the impact upon jobs what matters are the net employment effects and these are determined through the combined effect of several factors, including:

■ direct job creation, dependent upon the scale of the investment and its nature in terms of the capital–labour mix in the production process;
■ indirect job creation, dependent upon factors such as whether the company buys supplies and services from the host-country market or whether it imports them;

■ the Trojan horse, or displacement effect of the investment: does this investment displace other local producers and suppliers? If the new investment simply displaces existing investment, then the net effect upon jobs may be nothing like what one might initially expect. This is equally applicable to the impact of FDI when it is no more than a change in the ownership of existing assets.

FDI which takes the form of a merger with or acquisition of a going concern may have no beneficial impact upon employment at all and indeed it may in the long-term lead to employment decline as activities and structures are rationalized and reorganized on a European or wider international basis. Similarly, attracting investment may in the first instance create jobs, but, even where this investment has been attracted by substantial amounts of government aid there is little likelihood that the jobs created will be any less susceptible to market pressures.

Within multinational trade alliances and markets, such as the EU, an additional potential complication to these calculations is that investment in one country may have beneficial net effects upon employment there at the expense of employment in one of the other member states. Within the EU there have been instances of this occurring, and the concept referred to as *social dumping* encapsulates these concerns. One of the major concerns associated with the creation of the single market, and subsequent enlargements of the EU and the implementation of the principle of freedom of movement of capital and labour, was that capital was very much more mobile than labour and that consequently capital would be relocated within the market to those areas, regions and countries where the costs of production were the cheapest and the degree of labour market regulation the lowest. This would result in jobs being created in one area, such as Poland, Hungary or the Czech Republic where labour and other production costs are relatively cheap and where effective labour market regulation is limited, at the expense of employment levels in places such as Germany and France. The UK, with a government that was keen to create flexible and deregulated labour markets and which saw lower labour costs and enhanced employer prerogative or control as a source of competitive advantage, was also seen as a potential beneficiary.

While the UK, with its relatively deregulated labour market, skilled and flexible labour force was seen to be a potential beneficiary of such developments within the EU, this deregulation has arguably also facilitated the relocation from the UK of both manufacturing and service sector jobs to other countries both within and outside the EU where cost advantages were available. Within the EU manufacturing activity has been relocated to the new member states and outside the EU both manufacturing and service sector activity has been relocated to China and other countries in the far east and to India. An example of the latter being the outsourcing of call centre activity to India where English speaking graduates are available and willing to take the newly created jobs at a fraction of the costs that would be incurred if the activities remained within the UK.

We noted earlier the conclusions of Traxler and Woitech that labour standards and regulatory regimes had not been the prime influences upon US investment into Europe during the 1980s and early 1990s but they also noted the potential for MNCs to use the threat of regime shopping to encourage competition between regimes for and in order to keep such investment, particularly when it is job creating investment.

The arguments in favour of governments encouraging inward FDI to boost wages and productivity in the local labour market have also been questioned. Wakelin *et al.* (1999) found that during the period 1991–1996 foreign-owned firms operating in the UK did tend to have a positive productivity gap over home-country firms and that they tended to pay higher wages. However, they also found no evidence that the arrival of foreign firms had a generally beneficial impact upon productivity levels and growth and upon wage levels in local firms in the same sectors.

Over the years there has been much criticism of the activities of MNCs and they have often been accused of exploiting and damaging the countries in which they have invested by:

- causing massive environmental damage through their extraction and exploitation of raw materials and their cynical attitudes towards the land and agriculture;
- distorting and destroying traditional cultures and
- cynically exploiting host-country labour.

Other allegations have also been made.

- While MNCs claim to be investing capital and technology in Third World countries, many extract a large outflow of capital and never relinquish control of their technology.
- They are able to create artificially low profits in high-tax countries and high profits in low tax countries by 'transfer pricing'. These techniques can also be used in negotiations with trade unions, whereby a plant may be shown to be 'unprofitable' by the use of creative accounting and a harder bargain may be driven.
- Their great global size enables them to interfere in the political affairs of smaller host countries.
- Having been attracted to regions or countries offering financial inducements such as investment grants, tax concessions, training grants and cheap labour, it is not unknown for the MNC to uproot and depart when these inducements are no longer available. This phenomenon is known as the 'runaway

firm' and if that firm is the main employer in the region, the whole community suffers when the company withdraws.

■ In times of high unemployment national governments are particularly prone to seek to attract MNCs to invest and this gives the MNC considerable bargaining power to persuade both governments and employees and their representatives to make concessions.

■ By dint of widespread and glamorous advertizing and promotion, their products often swamp locally produced goods and put local manufacturers out of business.

Allegations concerning the exploitation of labour in the host or undeveloped countries have increased in recent years and there have been a number of exposes of global firms such as Nike, Gap and Adidas. Allegations have been made that the contractors used by these organizations to manufacture their products pay very low wages, employ children, that the employees are subject to harassment and bullying and on occasion violence, that they are compelled to work very long hours, that they are not allowed breaks, that the health and safety concerns of the workers are not being addressed and that they are not allowed to form or join trades unions to protect their interests. The term sweatshops is often used to describe these operations. An alternative view sometimes expressed is that jobs on these terms are better than no job at all and that while conditions and wage rates may seem poor to us in the west, they are complying with the labour standards and regulations in the countries concerned. It is this kind of behaviour on the part of MNCs and their contractors that encourage the argument that the activities of MNCs should be regulated and that free trade agreements should contain minimum labour standards, much like the social dimension of the EU. We return to this later.

Another example of labour in the host country being exploited by the MNC might be if the company takes advantage of low employment levels in a region to force down the price of labour and the value of other terms and conditions of employment. Labour is forced to make concessions in order that the investment is attracted. Once established, the company is often able to continue with such practices by threatening to leave or shift production to other sites where labour is more compliant, examples of the 'exit options' referred to earlier. Again, different labour groups are forced into making concessions in order to keep work.

An MNC practice which achieved a degree of notoriety in the UK in the 1980s, probably not warranted by the frequency of the practice, was to force a number of trade unions effectively to bid against each other for recognition rights in greenfield investment sites. The practice of promoting competition for members among two or three trade unions had some severe repercussions within the trade union movement and the Electricians Union (Electrical, Electronic, Telecommunication and Plumbing Union: EEPTU) was expelled from the Trades Union Congress (TUC) as a consequence of the internal conflict that was caused by a few companies pursuing policies of such a nature.

The benefits of such investment may be positive for employment levels and for terms and conditions of employment in the host country but they may be negative if the MNC has a strong enough bargaining position and if it chooses to use that power to force concessions from the labour force.

One of the criticisms commonly made of the massive increase of FDI in recent years has been that, though it may be good for the recipient countries, developed countries may lose out. Where the FDI represents a relocation of investment, assets and activities from a high-cost or developed country to a developing one, the downside in the developed economy is that there is a loss of employment.

However, FDI from developed to developing countries can create or maintain employment in the home country in a number of ways.

- It may be that the FDI is to create marketing or servicing functions for the home made product, thereby creating demand in the host country for the product of the home country and thereby creating employment.
- The FDI may create demand in the home country for capital goods and services.
- The FDI may be geared towards the production of low cost components which are then transported to the home country for final assembly.

MNC: approaches to the management of employee relations

MNCs have a number of choices when it comes to deciding how to manage their overseas subsidiaries. In part their response to this dilemma will be conditioned by factors such as the industry in which they operate and their particular organizational or structural form, and this is likely to also be related to the stage of development which the MNC has reached. Additionally these decisions will be influenced by the mindset of the crucial HQ staff and this in part is likely to be a product of the culture and traditions of the country in which the company originated. Schuler *et al.* (2002) have characterized this dilemma as being between the need to integrate and differentiate, the need to be and to think global perhaps at the same time as acting locally.

Do they try and pursue the same policies and practices in all their operations irrespective of location, in effect exporting the home-country approach which has been successful? At least this will enable a degree of strategic integration and consistency within the company and between the various units. Or do they pursue policies and practices which are more adaptive and local, thereby securing compliance with the requirements of local regimes and the expectations of employees in each of the various subsidiaries?

These questions and issues have occupied many academics over the years, with much research being undertaken to establish the relative significance of host- and home-country influences upon the management of employee relations in any particular subsidiary.

Another related area of interest has centred upon the question of convergence and whether it is possible to identify a set of employee relations policies and practices emerging as a model of best practice and upon which this convergence is based and which at least partially is being driven by MNCs.

Against this are those who argue that the strength of the influence of local traditions, institutions and cultures in particular national regimes and business systems and which will mitigate convergent influences. The deregulation of national labour markets in response to the pressures of international competition and the drive to liberalize trade are likely to reduce the effect of these national influences as barriers to convergence.

There have also been debates about how culture specific particular practices may be and whether they can actually and meaningfully be transferred to other cultures, the culture free viewpoint.

In this context we can examine a particular typology of MNC approaches associated with Perlmutter.

Perlmutter (1969) devised a typology of MNCs and their approach to the management of their overseas operations and this typology can be usefully applied to the management of employee relations. Each approach can be seen to be linked to particular beliefs about how operations and relationships should be conducted and what matters in life and to some extent each approach can be examined in the context of whether it reflects and facilitates a desire on the part of the MNC HQ to control activity in its subsidiaries. We can identify four major approaches to the management of overseas subsidiaries: ethnocentric, polycentric, regiocentric and geocentric.

Ethnocentric

The values, culture and strategic decisions are determined by the outlook of the parent company, which gives very little power or autonomy to the overseas subsidiaries. Subsidiaries are largely managed and controlled by expatriates or former HQ staff and locals have very little input into the way things are carried out in their own country. Lines of communication are often one way as directives are issued by HQ. The host-country subsidiary has a tactical rather than strategic role to play and is dominated by the concerns and culture of the parent company. It is often suggested that this commonly represents the first stage in the development of the MNC and that only after time has elapsed will management at the centre be prepared to move in an alternative direction. Many Japanese and American companies have been accused over the years of trying to introduce employee relations policies and practices that may work at home but that are inconsistent with the traditions of other countries. This approach is sometimes characterized as a belief at the centre of the organization that the ways of the home country are not only the best but also the only way of proceeding.

The danger of this approach for companies is that they will take insufficient notice of the traditions and practices that contribute to the host-country regime, that the employees in the subsidiary will not share the same values and beliefs and so they will not conform to the home-country stereotype.

Home-country attitudes and practices may just not work very well elsewhere. An obvious example of the kinds of issues that can arise would be an American company, typically anti-trade union, setting up a subsidiary in Sweden and trying to avoid the recognition of trade unions and joint decision making that are typical of the Swedish employee relations regime.

Polycentric

Here much more notice is taken of local conditions, values and systems. The subsidiary is likely to be managed by a home-country national and regarded as an autonomous business unit. Key decisions, financial investment and overall strategic goals are still determined at HQ but this approach demonstrates an awareness that countries vary considerably and therefore local managers are most likely to have an understanding of the requirements of the local regulatory regime. This approach is much more likely to facilitate the maintenance of policies and practices in the field of employee relations that are consistent with the culture and regulatory regime of the host country.

However, we do also need to bear in mind that adopting a polycentric approach to the management of employee relations can pose problems for the MNC in terms of internal consistency in the way that employees in different countries are treated, their terms and conditions of employment and general management of the employment relationship, and also in terms of consistency between the policies and strategies determined and pursued at the centre and what may be going on at the local level. An example of the latter may be an overseas subsidiary which signs an agreement with a trade union about job security for its members that may then prove an embarrassment to the corporate HQ which is planning a down-sizing or cost-cutting exercise.

Regiocentric and geocentric

Here subsidiaries and functions may be organized on a regional or some other geographic basis, such as a worldwide or global one, that is not con-strained by national boundaries of either the home country or of the par-ticular country in which activities are being conducted. Control of both staff and decisions are carried out on a regional or other geographical basis, and there will be a tendency for managers to be appointed either from within the particular region or, in the case of geocentric, with no specific country or even region-of-origin dimension to the appointment at all: the best person available is appointed wherever they may be from.

It is companies conforming to one of these latter structures that are perhaps more truly international or global and one would expect the approach to employee relations to be less likely to be conditioned by any particular national culture or regulatory regime, though aspects of national regulatory regimes may have to be complied with. In such com-panies one might expect the development of region- or worldwide approaches to employee relations policies and practices. It is also com-panies of this form that are perhaps most likely to pose the threat to national systems that some commentators see as the consequence of globalization.

Schulten (1996) has discussed the development of Eurocentric approaches by companies, the development of structures and the organ-ization of value-adding activities in and on Europe as a region. However, in the area of employee relations there can only be a partial Eurocentric approach given that we cannot yet talk about a single European labour market. Variations in regulatory regimes persist despite the influence of the EU social dimension – see **Chapter 4** on the EU – and some effort has to be put in to complying with the requirements of particular national labour markets. However, if progressive deregulation of European labour markets occurs, we might expect the steady development of company-wide Eurocentric approaches to an expanding number of working prac-tices and terms and conditions of employment.

Both Hendry (1994) and Edwards *et al.* (1996) caution against too rigid or exclusive an interpretation of models such as Perlmutter's and make the point that it is quite possible to come across companies that present a combination of these approaches, a hybrid, for example a regiocentric approach to the organization and control of some areas of activity combined with polycentric or ethnocentric approaches in other areas.

As far as employee relations are concerned it does seem that there is greater importance attached to the pursuit of essentially polycentric approaches; certainly a number of researchers have, over the years, pointed up the value of a polycentric approach to the management of employee relations within MNCs. These include Schregle (1981) who asserted that 'industrial relations phenomena are a very faithful expression of the society in which they operate' and Prahalad and Doz (1987) who asserted that 'The lack of familiarity of MNC managers with local industrial and political conditions has sometimes needlessly worsened conflict that a local firm would have been likely to resolve'. Dowling and Schuler (1990) also emphasized the point that employee relations (ER) are so diverse across national borders that it is imperative that MNCs employ a polycentric approach when appointing ER managers.

Such a polycentric approach to the management of ER is also consistent with 'societal effect theory' (Maurice *et al.*, 1980). This implies that specific national cultures and national social systems impact upon and condition the organizational practices of foreign-owned subsidiaries, thereby explaining both the absence of a universal convergence of organization structures and a continuing existence of national diversity.

However, the utilization of a predominantly polycentric approach to employee relations is certainly not universal and MNCs often continue to adopt partially ethnocentric approaches with an influence of country of origin in some of the employee relations practices pursued. This is perhaps particularly the case in respect of attitudes towards the recognition of trades unions and involving employees and their representatives jointly in decision making. An example might be an American MNC operating in say Germany where there are legal requirements for employees to be able to participate in decision making and where the emphasis is upon collective participation. The American MNC might try to diffuse the influence of the collective arrangements by instituting alongside the collective arrangements additional arrangements emphasizing individual involvement.

The factors conditioning these approaches include both the mindset of HQ, which as we noted earlier is likely to reflect the culture and tradition of the home country, and the strength and flexibility of the institutions and regulatory regimes in the host country. Where regulation in the host country is weak the incoming MNC has greater freedom to pursue the policies and practices that it wishes and in such circumstances it may well be that they choose to operate using the policies and practices that they know from the home country. However, there are other factors influencing these decisions and research has indicated that amongst the factors encouraging an ethnocentric approach are:

■ Poor performance owing to labour relations problems; where a particular subsidiary has labour relations problems there is a greater likelihood that the MNC HQ will attempt to introduce parent–country labour relations practices aimed at reducing industrial unrest or increasing productivity.

- The relative size of home and foreign markets; where the home market is relatively large there is a greater tendency for the centre to treat the subsidiary as an extension of domestic operations and subject it to central control and ethnocentricity. Lack of a large home market is a strong incentive to adapt to host-country institutions and norms, a polycentric approach. American and European MNCs can be contrasted in this respect since the American market is generally much greater than any of the countries in which they have subsidiaries, whereas the reverse tends to be true for European MNCs, it is the latter that have generally shown greater willingness to pursue adaptive approaches to employee relations.

- If the investment is of a greenfield nature; investments of this kind provide a greater opportunity for the MNC to export home practices and approaches, whereas if the investment consists of acquiring a going concern there are likely to be many more problems associated with the introduction of foreign practices, the greater the embeddedness of the existing operation in a particular national system, the greater is the disruption caused by seeking to introduce foreign, home country, practices.

- The perceived success of home-country practices; as noted in an earlier section, the success of Japanese companies in the latter part of the 20th century encouraged many Japanese concerns to seek to adopt ethnocentric approaches to their overseas operations, as well as encouraging many non-Japanese companies to copy them. Earlier in the century it was American MNCs that exported Fordism to the rest of the world.

- The degree of cultural distance; the closer the countries are in terms of culture and tradition, the greater the likelihood that the MNC may seek to employ an ethnocentric approach.

Nevertheless, it does seem that polycentricity has been the favoured approach to ER of MNCs an approach through which the company is able to deal flexibly and responsively with local circumstance, traditions and culture and comply with local and national regulatory regimes. Remember, however, that we did note earlier that MNCs may seek to locate their activities in the least regulated labour markets (see the discussion of Social Dumping earlier).

Brewster *et al.* (2000) in their study of employee relations practices in large companies in 25 different countries concluded that employee relations practices had stubbornly retained their national distinctions. These conclusions are supported by O'Hagan *et al.* (2005) who assert that industrial relations practices in international firms are still rooted at the national level and that the host-country thesis is still the most convincing, though it must be noted that their conclusions relate to research that has a predominantly European focus.

However, if, as noted in the earlier section on Globalization, the world is converging, and if it is converging on a deregulatory basis so that national systems as well as trade become less regulated, we may well expect the policies and practices used by MNCs to manage employee relations to become more similar and less representative of either home- or host-country influence. In this context we may well see the development of more genuinely regiocentric or geocentric approaches based on the policies and practices that appear to be consistent with best practice, high performance and adding value, or alternatively with cost minimization.

The discussion so far has assumed that MNCs are able to diffuse practices internally across national borders. To some extent each of the approaches, other than a purely adaptive or polycentric one, assumes that such diffusion is possible, irrespective of whether it is a diffusion of those practices identified as best practice and associated with high performance or whether it is the diffusion of practices geared towards cost minimization. It is worth bearing in mind that diffusion itself implies a desire to control and reflects at least some centralization of decision making.

One way in which it has been argued that MNCs can secure an effective diffusion is through the practice known as concession bargaining. This practice relies upon management being able to encourage competition for work within the company, between locations and groups of employees. This exerts a downward pressure on terms and conditions of employment, and hence costs, as employees compete against each other for the available work resulting in a 'negative convergence' in which all subsidiaries are caught in a race to undermine existing social standards and the result is the negative convergence of labour relations at a low level of social regulation.

In their study of the European automotive industry, Mueller and Purcell (1992) found that 'management systematically played one subsidiary against another to introduce nightshifts and to extend operating time in capital intensive areas (gear box and engine production, press shops). After the first subsidiary agreed to a relaxation of existing working time regulations, a kind of 'domino-effect' was set in motion. Sooner or later, all the other subsidiaries followed the same pattern'. In this situation a phenomenon called 'information asymmetry' occurs. Information is not uniformly available, so local negotiators threatened with social dumping may not be in a position to check the figures of other subsidiaries.

Concession bargaining is a mechanism through which labour flexibility and cost and waste minimization may be achieved. However, another model of diffusion is linked to the best practice alternative.

Here management search out and implement across the organization instances and practices that fall into this category. It has been suggested that this is most likely to occur in organizations that are actively and continuously seeking to improve quality and searching for a more productive and innovative production model.

Edwards *et al.* (1999) argue that diffusion within MNCs is the product of a combination of structural factors and internal political processes. They assert that diffusion is not a universal tendency and is promoted or retarded by four structural factors which they identify as significant and which echo much of the earlier discussion. The four structural factors are:

- Country of origin
- The degree of production integration
- The extent to which companies are structured along global lines and
- The nature of the product market.

There is a degree of interaction between these structural influences. For example the nature of the product market, whether consumer tastes are homogeneous across national borders or competition in the market is international, influences the extent to which it is realistic or desirable to integrate production activities and management structures internationally. Where consumer tastes are common and the company is engaged in the production of a product that can be sold across national boundaries, it is easier for the company to integrate production internationally, sometimes in product divisions, and where the MNC has taken the opportunity of such circumstances to structure management internationally, the greater is the potential for the MNC to diffuse employment practices throughout the organization or product specific division. On the other hand, if consumer tastes differ across national boundaries and competition is national, it is more likely that production and management structures will be nation specific and it will probably be less relevant and more difficult for the organization to diffuse employment practices.

The research also highlighted the significance of company growth profiles in that, where the company has grown through the creation of Greenfield sites rather than through the acquisition of going concerns, it is easier to diffuse employment practices.

However, they suggest that whether or not diffusion actually occurs, even in organizations where the appropriate structural factors are present, is also dependent upon the strategic choices of the actors within the organization, the location and use of power and the existence of what they refer to as 'networking within hierarchy'. Local managements may be able to resist diffusion in markets that are local and central management may be able to encourage diffusion through encouraging internal competition between plants for investment whereby diffusion is one of the factors taken into account in determining where investment should be undertaken and by ensuring that management promotion is linked to the implementation of diffusion. The greater the degree of management networking between plants, often underpinned by central management strategies of this latter kind, the greater is the potential for diffusion.

They assert that it is the interaction of both structural and political factors that shape the nature and extent of diffusion or internal convergence, with networking, for example, being more likely in highly integrated and cohesive organizations.

MNCs and the trade unions

Whilst trades unions may well welcome inward investment and the jobs that are either protected or created as a result, they have long feared the size, growth and spread of MNCs, not only because of their apparent preference for avoiding union recognition where they can (see below) but also because even where the MNC recognizes trades unions for collective bargaining there are various strategies which the MNC can adopt in order to counter the influence of the trade union and any action that it may decide to take. One of the disadvantages confronting the trades unions is that they are organized nationally and we discuss in subsequent sections the weakness of trade union organization at an international level.

As Kennedy (1980), Dowling *et al.* (1999) and others have pointed out the MNC may:

- have formidable financial resources, which may enable them to absorb losses in a particular foreign subsidiary that is in dispute with a national union and still show a profit on overall worldwide operations;
- well have alternative sources of supply, and this may take the form of an explicit 'dual sourcing' policy to reduce the vulnerability of the corporation to a strike by a national union;
- be able to move production temporarily to facilities in other countries, and there is also the permanent threat of closure of facilities in a particular country or region, what has come to be known as the 'exit option';
- be able to hide from the unions by centralizing decision making at a remote corporate HQ so that it is actually physically difficult for the trade union to find and deal with the real decision makers in the company;
- have the capacity to stage an 'investment strike' whereby the MNC refuses to invest any additional funds in a plant, thus ensuring that the plant will become obsolete and economically

uncompetitive, which can be used as a threat to achieve compliance;

■ be able to exert considerable pressures upon governments to regulate or deregulate in their favour especially when there are jobs to be lost or gained as a result of the MNC decision;

■ use one or more of the above to persuade the union into competitive or concession bargaining whereby material labour standards or labour flexibilities in terms of working practices are conceded in return for promises of job security, possibly in competition with employees in a subsidiary in another country.

The ability of the MNC to use these strategies depends in part upon the structure of the organization and the extent to which production is integrated; for example, if the structure is that of a multi-domestic, it might be quite easy to source demand in the national market concerned from another country; if, however, the union represents employees who are the sole producers of a particular component in what is a European or global production chain, then the power of the union is that much greater and the ability of the MNC to counter the threat that much less.

As is noted in the later chapter on trades unions, trades union membership in many developed economies has been in decline in the last years of the 20th century continuing into the 21st century. Among the reasons for this are the internationalization of business and the activities and approaches of MNCs both of which can be seen to contribute to **the international division of labour** whereby high volume, low-tech manufacture and assembly has been exported to developing countries, where labour and other production costs are lower and where the regulatory regime may be much less constraining upon managerial control and therefore preferable to the employer.

Trade union membership has declined as the industries and trades in which trades unions were traditionally strong have declined. This may be the result of trades, and in some instances sectors, becoming obsolete or redundant as a result of technological advance and/or changing patterns of demand or it may be due to the inability of producers and suppliers in the developed economies to compete with low cost competition from developing countries. MNCs are influential here in that they are often instrumental in the exporting of work from developed to developing economies: sometimes they may transfer work from one of their own plants in the developed world to another of their own but much lower cost plant in a developing economy; sometimes they may contract out work previously undertaken in the developed world to contractors in developing countries. Examples might include a Japanese MNC shifting the production of low-tech high-volume television sets from one of its plants in the UK to a newly acquired plant in Eastern Europe, or it might be a US MNC fashion clothes retailer deciding to contract the manufacture and assembly of its garments to companies in Cambodia and Indonesia rather than to contractors in the UK or USA.

From the perspective of the trades unions, matters have been made worse in the developed economies because many of the new jobs created have been in new industries in the service sector where there is not the tradition of trades unionism and where employers are often unwilling to recognize unions for bargaining purposes, and indeed to be fair where the trades unions have not distinguished themselves with their approach and ability to organize.

The membership lost in the developed world has not in the main been replaced by increasing membership in the developing economies to which much of the production has been exported. Fledgling trades union movements almost always need support from government, if only in terms of the creation of a regulatory regime in which individuals have the right to form and join trades unions and to take action to protect their interests (see later section on international trades unionism and regulation of the activities of MNCs). Often MNCs encourage the absence of such a regulatory regime through their willingness or not to invest in the country and in their own attitudes towards recognizing unions for bargaining purposes.

MNC attitudes towards trade unionism

Dowling *et al.* (1999) in examining MNC relations with trades unions noted that antipathy towards and a desire to avoid trades unions was deeply ingrained in American managers' value systems and that an MNC's initial mindset is an important factor in shaping its position regarding trade unions and employee relations. In earlier research Hamill (1983) had investigated the employee relations practices and preferences of 84 US-owned and 50 UK-owned MNCs operating in three different industries in the UK and had concluded that the US MNCs were less likely to recognize trades unions.

Edwards *et al.*'s (1996) research included 101 MNCs of which 58 were UK-owned and 43 foreign-owned and amongst their conclusions were the following:

- The prospects for trade union recognition appear to diminish as globalism advances. Over half of the UK and just under half of the European respondents asserted that it was their general policy to avoid bargaining with trade unions.
- Where companies were organized on multi-domestic lines, 40 per cent avoided unions whereas the figure for those companies dominated by global organization rose to 63 per cent.
- Avoiding unions also seemed to be associated with a strategic emphasis upon market penetration and the existence of

advanced organizational systems of management development, a mechanism through which contacts and culture can be reinforced.

■ The avoidance of trade unions was something that many of the companies would choose to do but it was not of sufficient importance in most of the companies that they would base location decisions on this factor alone.

■ If nation state governments or the EU strengthen the rights of labour and trade unions, it is unlikely to cause an immediate flight of capital from the country or region concerned.

There are of course rational reasons why employers might prefer to avoid trades unions if they can, two of the more important of which are that the existence and recognition of trades unions inevitably implies some limits upon what might otherwise be unfettered managerial prerogatives, control, and of course that the purpose of trades unions includes raising the living standards of employees and many managements see this purely in terms of trade unions raising costs and thereby harming competitiveness. Alternative views that trade unions may be a source of innovation and enhanced efficiency tend often to carry less weight.

The influence of trades unions on MNCs

Dowling and Schuler (1990) suggested that trade unions may have the ability to constrain the choices of MNCs in three main ways:

1 By influencing wage levels.
2 By limiting employment level variation.
3 By hindering global integration.

They suggested that labour costs, although decreasing in significance, still play a major part in determining cost competitiveness, though the impact is likely to be greater in low tech operations where labour costs as a proportion of total costs are likely to be the greatest. However, any influence that unions do have on wage levels is potentially significant and may influence employment levels. Dowling and Schuler (1990) further state that the ability of unions to restrict hours of work and patterns of employment may have a more serious effect on profitability than spiralling labour costs.

Trades unions in Europe have traditionally had significant input into the political process, and national regulatory systems are inevitably the product of interaction at this political level. Many countries have legislation that specifies a minimum wage or prohibits redundancies or changes in working practices unless the company can show that structural conditions make these labour losses unavoidable. Often such procedures are long and drawn out and involve the employer in high redundancy costs.

Payments for involuntary redundancy in some countries can be substantial, especially when compared to the USA.

The ability of trades unions to influence the policies and activities of MNCs will also to some extent depend upon the structure of the MNC and the extent and manner of integration of the production chain. For example where the company relies upon a single group of employees or site for essential components without which the following stages of production cannot take place then the group of employees and their trade unions have enhanced bargaining power. JIT production techniques offer the same opportunities. This strength may however, only be a short-term benefit since the company may rearrange in order to minimize such possibilities. Where the actions of employees in one country affect the interests of those in another country cross-national cooperation rather than competition between different national trade union movements becomes important. If, as in the case of Hoover closing down its operations in France and shifting them to Scotland a few years ago, the unions in the recipient country accept the new production arrangements there is very little that the unions in the country in which operations are closed can do.

Dowling and Schuler (1990) observed that 'many MNCs make a conscious decision not to integrate and rationalize their operations to the most effective degree, because to do so could cause industrial and political problems'. They use as an example Prahalad and Doz's (1987) description of General Motors' (GM) sub-optimization of integration. The latter alleged that in the early 1980s GM made substantial investments in Germany (matching its new investments in Austria and Spain) at the demand of the German Metalworkers Union (IG Metal – one of the largest industrial unions in the western world) in order to foster good labour relations in Germany. They conclude:

> Union influence thus not only delays the rationalization and integration of MNC's manufacturing networks and increases the cost of such adjustments (not so much in the visible severance payments and 'golden handshake' provisions as through economic losses incurred in the meantime), but also, at least in such industries as automobiles, permanently reduces the efficiency of the integrated MNC network. Therefore, treating labour relations as incidental and relegating them to the specialists in the various countries is inappropriate. In the same way as government policies need to be integrated into strategic choices, so do labour relations. (p. 102)

However, recent developments that have enhanced the power and influence of MNCs and diminished the power of both the trade union movement (see e.g. the developing international division of labour above) and national governments to control and limit their activities cast serious doubts upon the abilities of trade unions to continue to influence the objectives and activities of MNCs in the ways and to the extent that is suggested in these earlier studies. The research findings of Edwards *et al.*

would tend to confirm that the influence of the unions upon MNCs diminishes the more the MNCs move along the road of global integration and adopt a global orientation.

Ietto-Gillies (1997) argues that TNCs derive power from their multi-national interests, which they can wield against uni-nationals, governments, labour organizations and consumers and that there is a need to try to reverse this trend and give countervailing power to these other players. He suggests that governments should use their control over the quality of both the physical infrastructure and the labour force as bargaining weapons to give support to those players that do not themselves have transnational power.

Trade union responses

At a fairly early stage it became apparent that effective opposition to the power of the MNC demanded from the worldwide trade union movement cooperation and organization. However, this has not proved to be an easy objective to achieve.

Study of trade union movements in different countries demonstrates the diversity of trade unions: their membership bases, their structures, their objectives and orientations and their political affiliations differ substantially both within and between countries (see Hollinshead and Leat (1995) for a comparison of trade union movements in a number of countries on these and other criteria).

There are many countries in which various union factions and confederations exist and in which effective cooperation on a national scale has been largely unattainable (France and Italy are examples of this in Europe), let alone cooperation on an international scale. In some respects the decline of communism as practised in the Soviet bloc has helped the process of integration and cooperation in the past decade as confederations that viewed the Communists as their political and ideological allies have been forced to reappraise their objectives and organization.

It is also important to bear in mind that when dealing with MNCs, unions may have conflicting national interests. When one country is suffering an economic downturn, trade union officials may put national interests – the interests of their own constituency – before those of international worker solidarity. An example of this occurred in the early 1970s, when the Ford Motor Company, exasperated by the labour climate in its UK plants, decided to make no further investment in them and the media at the time hinted darkly that Ford was about to pull out of the UK and make further investments in the Netherlands. The UK unions were highly critical of Ford but the unions in the Netherlands made no attempt to express solidarity with them. In fact, they expressed full support for the Netherlands businesspeople who were trying to woo Ford away from the UK.

While the leaders may appreciate the imperative of effective international organization to combat the power of the MNC, the individual members of these national unions and confederations, who at the end of the day are the constituency that has to be satisfied for the union officials to keep their jobs and in order to attract and retain members, are predominantly concerned with their own interest and the interests of their colleagues at a national level.

The primacy of national interests is also demonstrated by the following interview: Milne (1991), in an interview with the German IG Metall leader at Ford, Wilfred Kuckelkorn, indicates that there are still significant difficulties facing joint union action: Kuckelkorn says:

> 'We want the British unions to win a 35-hour week and they will get practical solidarity from Germany, including overtime bans and working to rule'. But with another breath Kuckelkorn rejects out of hand any thought of joint European collective bargaining with Ford: 'the national unions cannot accept European negotiations. If you take away the power of the national unions they will go down'.

There is relatively little evidence of change in this respect and a number of studies (Hyman, 1999; Hancke, 2000; Traxler and Woitech, 2000) continue to point up the fact that trades unions, especially within Europe, continue to adopt essentially national or local strategies and indeed that they cooperate often with governments in the pursuit of competitive strategies to attract or retain investment.

Attempts are being made to consolidate international trade union links and to mount worldwide campaigns against global capitalism but the current lack of coherence and coordination does provide MNCs with the opportunity to continue to engage in strategies which effectively pit unions and their members in one country against those in another country and to engage in competitive and concession bargaining. In addition to creating discord between trade unionists across national boundaries, these strategies can also be used to drive down material labour standards.

Nevertheless, there have been instances over the years of spontaneous and *ad hoc* international trade union solidarity and activity against particular multinationals. An example of this latter form of cooperation was in 1997 over the decision of Renault to close one of its more productive plants in Belgium in favour of the retention of plants in France. This was made worse by the revelation at the time that the company was seeking grants and other forms of assistance from both the Spanish government and the European Commission to build a new plant in Spain. This occasioned marches and demonstrations of support involving union members and delegations from Belgium, France, Germany, Italy, Spain, the UK, the Netherlands, Portugal, Greece and Austria, but to no avail. Renault demonstrated the power of the MNC to exercise its autonomy and ignore the views of the international trade union movement as represented and also to ignore the requirements of the EU Directive that provides employee representatives with rights to prior consultation in the event of collective redundancies.

International Trade Union Organization

International Trade Union Organizations exist at the global, regional and sectoral levels and there has been a great deal of debate over the years concerned with how these might best be organized and coordinated and as noted above one of the continuing obstacles to such coordination in pursuit of effective action at an international level remains the predominance of the movement's essentially national orientations. The international confederations and unions that do exist are made up of national unions and union confederations; some are general in that they welcome affiliation and membership from all industries and occupations, whereas some are sector specific.

Global Unions

The International Confederation of Free Trade Unions (ICFTU)

On a global level, transnational union organizations have tended to be aligned with political and ideological interests. That is to say, in the West, ICFTU emerged, with its counterpart in the Communist bloc being the World Federation of Trade Unions (WFTU). There is also a smaller Christian-based World Confederation of Labour (WCL).

The ICFTU has been the most influential of these organizations and this has been perpetuated by the impact upon the WFTU of the break-up of the Soviet bloc.

The ICFTU was set up in 1949 and in the early years of the 21st century had 234 affiliated organizations in 152 countries and territories on all five continents, with a membership of 148 million.

It has three major regional organizations, APRO for Asia and the Pacific, AFRO for Africa and ORIT for the Americas. It also maintains close links with the European Trade Union Confederation (ETUC) (which includes all ICFTU European affiliates) and 10 Global Union Federations, which link together national unions from a particular industry or occupational group at international level.

It is a Confederation of national trade union centres and confederations, each of which links together the trade unions of that particular country. Membership is open to bona fide trade union organizations that are independent of outside influence and have a democratic structure.

The ICFTU cooperates closely with the International Labour Organization and has contacts with the International Monetary Fund, the World Bank and the World Trade Organization (WTO).

Traditionally the ICFTU has been concerned with issues such as:

- The respect for and defence of trade union and workers' rights.
- The eradication of forced and child labour.
- The promotion of equal rights for working women.
- The environment.
- Education programmes for trade unionists all over the world.
- Encouraging the organization of young workers.

The five main ICFTU priorities are for the early part of the 21st century were:

- Employment and international labour standards.
- Tackling the multinationals.
- Trade union rights.
- Equality, women, race and migrants.
- Trade union organization and recruitment.

In recent years the ICFTU has become particularly concerned with the impact of globalization and the activities of MNCs for labour, a core theme in this chapter, and has been campaigning with other organizations to ensure that core labour standards expressed as a workers' rights clause are included in trade agreements brokered by, and the procedures of, organizations such as the WTO.

At the 4-yearly ICFTU conference in South Africa in 2000 and in a document addressing the future of the trade union movement, there was fairly trenchant criticism of the impact of globalization and justification of the role of free trade unions.

'Our vision is vastly different to the limitless free-for-all and destructive exploitation, which characterize the era of globalization directed by the unbridled greed and power of the free market. The rights of working people to express their solidarity and advance their interests have been subjected to relentless attack and erosion, as power has been concentrated in the hands of a privileged few. Yet workers around the world continue to fight for their rights, often against tremendous odds. The free trade union movement remains the most powerful democratic and representative global force for social justice and democracy.'

They express their concern that the globalization of the world economy through increased trade and foreign investment by multinational companies (MNCs) is exacerbating income inequality and undermining democratic decision making by national governments and argue that discrimination and gross exploitation at the workplace in violation of fundamental workers' rights have increasingly become part of global commerce. Often the victims are young and unorganized female workers in export processing zones (EPZs) which advertize the absence of trade union rights to attract investment.

Often it is assumed that the only abuses of labour occur in developing countries but this would appear not to be the case and the ICFTU have pointed out that gender discrimination and child labour are still significant issues in developed economies within the EU.

Exhibit

Social Dimensions of Globalization: ICFTU submission to first meeting of ILO World Commission on Globalization (25–26 March 2002)

The downside to globalization

The ratio of average incomes in the world's twenty richest countries to those of the world's poorest has risen from a ratio of twenty to one in 1960 to about forty to one nowadays. As the United Nations Development Programme (UNDP) noted recently, some 66 countries ranging across every corner of the globe are poorer now than a decade ago.

Such inequity leads to appalling contrasts. For example, in Europe $50 billion are spent on cigarettes annually. According to United Nations figures, providing all developing countries, for 1 year, with basic health and education as well as water, sanitation and nutrition, would cost much less than that.

More than 10 million children in developing countries still die every year from preventable diseases that their industrialized country counterparts rarely face.

And a World Bank study has shown that inequality between people within countries rose for most of the second half of the 20th century, particularly in the years after 1987.

The period of increasing globalization has also been associated with seriously adverse effects of trade liberalization on women. In many developing countries, traditional agricultural products, mainly produced by women, have been unable to compete with imported goods when trade barriers have been reduced. This has resulted also in decreased food security.

The expansion of EPZs and clothing, textiles and light manufacturing industries in developing countries over recent decades has generally been based on low-wage female labour working in unacceptably bad conditions and without any protection of their right to organize into trade unions.

On average, 80 per cent of the workers in EPZs are women. Their average wage can be half of what men get. Some countries even boast about the fact that they employ women workers in advertizing aimed at attracting foreign investment, pointing out that not only are the women cheap, but they are also supposedly more docile and less likely to become trade union activists. Many companies have been only too happy to take advantage.

That exploitation of women is but one example of the links we have so often seen between globalization and the violation of basic workers' rights over the past 20 years or more.

Rather than trade providing increased resources for improving living and working conditions, it has all too often resulted in governments actually reducing workers' rights in order to minimize labour costs. All the standards included in the ILO Declaration on Fundamental Principles and Rights at Work have been under attack in consequence.

The countries worst affected are those developing countries genuinely seeking to protect workers' human rights and raise basic living standards, for these are the countries most vulnerable at the margin to being forced out of the world market.

This phenomenon is worsening. The update in 2000 by the OECD of its 1996 report on 'Trade and Labour Standards' noted that the number of EPZs in the world had risen from some 500 zones at the time the 1996 study was written to about 850 zones – not counting China's special economic zones – in 1999.

There are many differences between EPZs around the world but they tend to have one over-riding characteristic. In almost all zones, trade unions are not tolerated. In some cases, this is due to special exceptions to national laws so that freedom of association cannot be exercised in the zones. In many cases, it is not so much the law but simply the reality that trade union officers are physically prevented from entering the plants or even from entering into the zones at all. The consequences of the lack of union representation can be seen in poor and often dangerous working conditions and low wages.

Furthermore, at least 15 million children are working in export production in sectors like mining, garments and textiles, shoe production, agriculture, carpet making, footballs and even production of surgical instruments.

A minority of countries is prepared to tolerate child labour in the belief that it will give them a competitive edge. But any short-term gain they obtain will easily be outweighed by the long-term damage being done a country's skills base by putting its children in factories rather than in classrooms. In other words, today's child labourers are tomorrow's unskilled and unemployed young workers.

Tens of millions of workers are also engaged today in forced labour – otherwise known as a contemporary form of slavery. That includes countries like Burma, where hundreds of thousands of indigenous people, supervised by armed guards, work on railways and pipelines for foreign companies such as TOTAL-Fina-Elf, UNOCAL and Premier Oil.

It is in order to prevent such extremes of exploitation which derive from global trade and investment that action is needed to construct a more humane global economy. This requires system-wide follow-up throughout the international institutions, including UN agencies, the IMF, the World Bank and the WTO.

The organization is aware that there have been criticisms of the failure of the international trade union movement to combat the activities of the MNCs effectively. They stress the role to be played by the Global Union Federations at sector level (see below) and within individual MNCs and the need for the trades unions to cooperate within MNCs to ensure a dialogue with management at the highest possible corporate level.

They feel that there is a growing awareness and concern among consumers and particularly the young about the working conditions of the people who make the products they buy which can be tapped into in order to encourage MNCs to take these matters seriously. As was noted earlier, there have been a number of exposes concerning precisely these issues and the activities of companies such as Nike and Gap.

Formation of ITUC

The International Trade Union Confederation (ITUC) was formed on the 1st November 2006 and the ICFTU ceased to exist. The new ITUC will comprise the affiliated organizations of the former ICFTU and WCL together with eight other national trade union organizations that will for the first time affiliate to a global body.

The formation of this new Confederation is a sign of the international trade union movement adapting in order to strengthen its capacity to fight for workers rights in the era of globalization. The motivation for the formation of the new confederation is indicated in the comments of Guy Ryder, the former General Secretary of the ICFTU. 'The creation of the ITUC will solidify the trade union movement's capacity at the national and international levels. Stronger, we will exert more influence on companies, governments and the international financial and trade institutions. The founding of the ITUC is an integral part of the process of uniting the power of trade unionism," he added.

International Trade Secretariats and Global Union Federations

In some industrial sectors there is a long history of attempts to build international links and organization. In 1864, the first International Workingmen's Association brought together in London a mix of Socialists and trade unionists. The 1890s saw international organizations founded by industrial sectors such as dockers, steel workers, miners, engineers and garment workers. By 1914, 28 international bodies (latter known as International Trade Secretariats, ITS) were in operation.

The ITS have the primary responsibility for dealing with global companies. They are the major instruments for workers to come together at international level inside enterprises and industries. The ICFTU works in partnership with ITS in many areas including efforts to strengthen international trade union solidarity and build global social partnership. These ITS are now more commonly known as Global Union Federations and at the beginning of the 21st century there were 10 such sectoral federations.

Over the years, the global union federations, as have the ICFTU, have argued the case for a social dimension to globalization and have established an ongoing social dialogue with a number of multinational enterprises in their sectors or industries. These discussions have led to a wide range of formal and informal agreements and understandings. They include regular contacts through well-established communication channels as well as, in some cases, formal framework agreements.

A framework agreement is an agreement negotiated between a multinational company and a global union federation concerning the international activities of that company. The main purpose of a framework agreement is to establish a formal ongoing relationship between the multinational company and the global union federation which can solve problems and work in the interests of both parties. The contents of these agreements tend to be limited to broad principles and minimum provisions and rights.

Union Network International (UNI), as an example, has negotiated a number of framework agreements including with Telefonica, Carrefour and OTE and has also produced a Charter for call centres which sets out the Union's views as to the minimum employment standards that call centre operators should adhere to and also argues the business case for operators to comply with the standards set out in the charter. Whether businesses will commit to the Charter and implement its provisions is an open question. UNI has nearly 1000 affiliated unions in 140 countries around the world, representing more than 15 million members in sectors including commerce, finance, telecoms, post, IT and white collar, graphical, property services, media and entertainment, electricity, social insurance and private health care, tourism, hair and beauty.

Exhibit

UNI Call Centre Charter

The 'UNI Call Centre Charter' is a set of broad principles relating to the call centre industry. The aim of the charter is to set a reasonable industry standard and identify those call centres that are committed to the key principles embodied in that standard.

Call centres that commit to the 'UNI Call Centre Charter' will be publicly acknowledged on the UNI web site, by UNI's affiliates and in the industry. This will make them attractive to clients, business partners, potential employees, employment agencies, the community and their customers.

Meeting the minimum standards as provided in the 'UNI Call Centre Minimum Standards' will be a guide to call centres as to whether they meet the 'UNI Call Centre Charter' principles. This will assist in defining a standard acceptable to the industry and rewarding those call centres that are investing in their staff and customers. In addition, it will provide a guide to customer service professionals as to what the standard should be and which prospective employers meet it.

UNI believes that the competitive advantage of call centres signatory to the 'UNI Call Centre Charter' should be the skill of their staff and professionalism of their operations. This is both advantageous to customer service professionals and the call centre industry:

Key principles of the 'UNI Call Centre Charter':

- Provision of minimum workplace conditions pay and benefits as outlined in the 'UNI Call Centre Minimum Standards';
- Performance targets to be based on providing high-quality customer service and not solely on quantity of calls taken or made;
- Increased training and development that
  Provides employees with skills and product training to facilitate the development of meaningful careers and quality service for our customers;
  Provides broad based, portable and accredited training and skills development;
- Priority to retaining and re-training existing staff in the event that new technologies or products that require new skills or qualifications are being introduced;
- Work organization that enables communication of changes in company policy and product developments prior to implementation so that employees can increasingly participate in key decisions regarding improvements to the provision of customer service;
- Issues to be considered when locating a call centre should not be based on costs only but instead on other key operational requirements such as:
  Being close to one's customer base
  Demand for skilled and multilingual staff and
  Access to a competitive telecommunications infrastructure
- Provide sufficient staffing level to ensure that
  There are enough staff to effectively handle customer requirements;
  Employees are able to attend training and staff meetings;
  Backfilling of leave and other absences;
  Employees are able to manage work, family and community responsibilities.
- Respect for core labour standards as set in the ILO Declaration on Fundamental Principles and Rights at Work

UNI Call Centre Minimum Standards

1 General

- Written working contract/terms of employment
- National legislation and agreements shall be respected, trying wherever reasonably possible to create stable employment
- Managers and supervisors to support the employee's commitment to quality customer service, including providing all employees with adequate support and advice and a flexible approach to performance reviews

2 Health and safety

- *Ventilation, lighting and heating*
- Light, ventilation, air filtering and heating systems need to be designed to cope with continued occupation, also at night-time
- *Ergonomic design of telephone and computer equipment, chairs and desks in order to avoid back strain and repetitive strain injury*
- Training on how to sit, work and use the equipment safely/advise by ergonomic consultant/adjustable work station and equipment (headset, ear piece, etc.)
- *Protection for workers using visual display units in order to avoid eyestrain and voice and hearing loss*
- Employer to assess the risks of working with visual display units
- European directive on display screen equipment
- Ten minute screen breaks at least every 2 hours
- *Work-related stress and bullying*
- Staff should spend no more than about 60–70 per cent actually taking calls
- Performance targets based on providing high-quality customer service and not solely on quantity of calls taken or made
- Protection from violence at work (abusive callers)
- *General*
- Dedicated space for breaks
- Food and drink provision, also for night workers
- Adequate toilets and washing facilities
- (Non-)Smoking policy
- First aid provision and employee security, especially if staff are arriving for work or leaving work very late at night (large percentage of the call centre staff may be women, who are more vulnerable to attack)

3 Working time and workload

- Maximum 40 working hours per week
- Rest period of 12 hours every working day and 48 hours continuous break every 7 days
- Flexible working hours can benefit employees as well as management, but must be introduced by agreement
- Call centre staff need to have influence over the hours and shifts which they are asked to work (child care!!)
- Shift rosters should be drawn up with adequate notice to staff
- Employees must have flexibility in the arrangement of working hours to ensure that they can lead normal, active social lives
- Employees must have the ability to take time off away from work, for example for care for dependants
- Staffing levels sufficient to ensure
- there are enough staff to effectively handle customer requirements
- employees are able to attend training and staff meetings

- backfilling of leave and other absences
- employees are able to manage work, family and community responsibilities

4 Surveillance, electronic monitoring and privacy

- Monitoring may only be allowed when the purpose is known and acceptable
- The collected data may only be used for that purpose
- The employee must know that he/she is being monitored or can be monitored
- Listening in may only occur incidentally and not continuously
- The employee must be allowed access to the registered data and be able to correct inaccuracies
- Tapings must be destroyed after a certain period

5 Pay and benefits

- Link pay levels to demonstrable skills
- Direct pay comparisons with 'traditional' employees and clear pay levels/structures in order to avoid high staff turnover
- Extra premia payments for working evenings, weekends or public holidays
- Bonus payments no more than 10 per cent of gross wages
- Paid holidays according to national law, but at least 4 weeks per year
- Holiday pay at least what the call centre employee earned on average over the last 12 weeks before the holiday and include overtime and regular bonuses
- Sick pay
- Maternity and paternity pay/leave
- Two month's notice of dismissal
- Statutory redundancy pay after 1 year of employment

6 Equal opportunities and training

- Regular, broad based, portable and accredited training and skills development for all employees
- Priority to retaining and re-training of existing staff in the event of introduction of new technologies or products that require new skills or qualifications
- Provide employees with the tools to resolve, as far as practicable, a customer's concern in the one call
- Provide employees with skills and product training to facilitate the development of meaningful careers and quality service for our customers

7 Workers representation

- Right to form and join trade unions
- Right of trade unions to represent workers in
- Collective bargaining
- Settlement of disputes
- Negotiations and consultations in all matters affecting jobs and training
- Workers representatives not be discriminated against and full access to all workplaces necessary to enable them to carry out their representation functions. Negotiation of specific collective workplace agreement that meets the particular needs of the company
- Communication of changes in company policy and product developments prior to implementation so that the employees have input into the decision-making process
- Right of free access by employees, trade unions and works councils to corporate email, so that information can be exchanged and communication being established
- Right of free access to the internet to enable them to access trade union websites and other information relevant to their rights at work.

The ETUC

The most influential international trade union organization within Europe is undoubtedly the ETUC. Membership is not confined to federations from member states of the EU and early in 2004 ETUC represents 78 national trade union centres from 34 countries and 11 European industry federations with a represented membership totalling more than 60 million.

The ETUC has long been accustomed to lobbying and representing the views of its members on a wide variety of issues within the EU such as:

- gender equality;
- employee participation;
- protection of employees rights in the event of plant closure or transfer of ownership;
- Health and safety at work and also
- broader issues of social and macro economic policy.

However, the ETUC is a diverse organization and it would be wrong to give the impression that there is much cohesion within the movement; yet again we need to bear in mind that the members have national as well as international objectives. The size, nature, traditions and interests of the many union confederations and unions in membership vary considerably, as do their autonomy and authority in respect of their own membership.

The ETUC has been designated by the EU Commission as the representative social partner of European employees and it is in this role that it is likely to have its greatest effect and impact upon the regulatory environment for both MNCs and employees in Europe. The treaties agreed at Maastricht in 1991 and at Amsterdam in 1997 provide an extension of the role and the influence of the Social Partners, in particular via the Social Agreement procedures. As a social partner more detail is given on the ETUC and its role within the EU in the **later chapter** on the EU.

International regulation and control of MNCs activities

We have noted earlier that there are various grounds for and perspectives on the issue of the need to regulate MNCs and we should certainly not believe that all MNCs are bad employers or that they pursue strategies aimed at the exploitation of their employees in the pursuit of competitive advantage and profit; nevertheless we also need to recognize that the competitive pressures upon managements can be great and that there are views such as those of the ICFTU earlier which stress the regulation imperative.

It is now questionable whether effective regulation is really possible but nevertheless several international organizations have tried to address this issue, although with varying degrees of influence. These include the International Chambers of Commerce in 1972 and the Organization for Economic Cooperation and Development in 1975 revised in 2000. Both these organizations have produced codes of conduct and guidelines seeking to regulate the activities of MNCs in the area of employment and employee relations.

The OECD Guidelines for Multinational Enterprises (2000) are addressed to the adhering governments, 33 at the time that they were issued, and these governments are charged with the responsibility of promoting the guidelines to MNCs operating in their territory; they also have a responsibility to try and resolve disputes that may arise. Nevertheless the guidelines are voluntary in nature and, of course, the adherent governments do not include the developing countries and export zones where the problems are arguably the greatest.

The OECD guidelines recommend that MNCs should contribute to the effective abolition of child labour and all forms of forced or compulsory labour and not discriminate against their employees on the grounds of race, colour, sex, religion, political opinion, national extraction or social origin. They also recommend that MNCs should seek to provide a healthy and safe working environment and employ and train local people with a view to raising skill levels in the host country. MNCs are also urged to provide terms and condition of employment no less favourable than those offered by comparable host-country employers. There are also a series of recommendations generally encouraging MNCs to respect the right of their employees to be represented by trades unions, to engage in collective bargaining on employment conditions and to facilitate employee participation through the provision of information and opportunities for consultation. MNCs are exhorted not to use threats to relocate their activities to influence negotiations. Where operational decisions might have the effect of involving collective layoffs or dismissals MNCs are encouraged to provide reasonable notice and to seek to mitigate these adverse effects.

The ILO

The ILO has been the most active in seeking to establish global standards for the employment and treatment of labour at work.

Established in 1919, the ILO became a part of the United Nations, which itself emerged from the League of Nations (see **Chapter 18** of Hollinshead and Leat (1995) for a detailed account of the origin, development and initiatives of the ILO). The ILO has been influential in setting world standards in Health and Safety and in industrial relations and did issue a Code in 1977 which was concerned with the social policy of

MNCs. This was amended in 2000 and gives guidance to both member state governments and individual MNCs on issues including:

- employment, including equality of opportunity and treatment and the promotion and security of employment;
- training;
- working conditions, including wages and benefits, minimum working age and health and safety;
- industrial relations including freedom of association, collective bargaining, consultation and dealing with grievances and disputes.

Most recently attention has tended to centre on regulation through the insertion of minimum labour standards into international arrangements and agreements allowing trade liberalization, such as those associated with the WTO, NAFTA and membership of the EU. It was noted in the previous section on the ICFTU that this is perceived as a prime objective as a mechanism for ensuring that labour is not cynically exploited by MNCs in the pursuit of competitive advantage in the global marketplace. Those in favour of regulation, in addition to the concern that labour should be treated with decency and respect, also tend to argue that labour standards in the developed world can only be protected if those in the poorest and developing countries are protected, an expression of a fear of a global downward convergence of labour and living standards if markets and MNCs are allowed to operate freely and without regulation. It is also argued that if the international trade system already has rules in respect of intellectual property rights, market access and subsidies, why not labour and environmental standards?

Nevertheless there are also fears among the developing countries that what at first sight appear to be altruistic concerns on the part of trades unions and others in the developed world hide motives that have more to do with the protection of jobs in the developed world than with the protection and raising of labour standards in the developing world. The essence of their concern is that by raising standards in developing countries costs will be raised and this will make those countries less attractive as homes for international investment.

The labour standards that are envisaged in this context tend to centre on the protection of certain fundamental human rights at work and are reflected in the ILO's core labour conventions. The ILO has identified 8 conventions (Nos. 29, 87, 98, 100, 105, 111, 138 and 182) which it considers to be fundamental, not just in the preservation of human rights and dignity at work but also as prerequisites for further action in improving both individual and collective conditions of work. These are concerned with:

- employees having rights to organize and to join free trades unions in order to protect their interests;

- these unions being free to engage in collective bargaining on terms and conditions of employment without public interference;
- employees being free from forced or compulsory labour and such labour being abolished;
- workers being free from discrimination and entitled to equality of treatment and remuneration irrespective of race, colour, sex, religion and political opinion;
- putting a ban on child labour below compulsory school end age;
- banning slavery and child prostitution;
- workers having rights to occupational health and safety.

However means for the effective policing and enforcement of any such rights or minimum standards are currently lacking. Membership of the ILO is voluntary and agreeing to abide by such conventions is also voluntary. Even where governments agree to abide by a convention but then do not, there is very little that the ILO and its members can do about it.

It is even more difficult to police and regulate the activities of individual MNCs effectively. Associations of countries in free trade arrangements such as in the EU may have greater success if they have the ability to hurt the MNC financially, for example by refusing entry and thereby imposing tariff barriers upon the MNCs' products and services, or denying tax benefits, or alternatively by legislating so that non-compliance brings court action and the possibility of the imposition of substantial fines. Even in this latter instance, the pressure to comply is diminished by the length of time that the legal process is likely to take and the possibility that the MNC may relocate to another country with the negative consequences on employment that this may bring. Nevertheless, if the market is big enough and if the threat of financial loss is great enough, there is at least the prospect of having an influence.

If attempts to introduce minimum labour standards into the WTO arrangements and procedures did succeed then there would be a greater chance of success in influencing the activities of MNCs since it would also be in the interests of those MNCs abiding by the rules to ensure effective policing and enforcement, through the courts if necessary.

However, we are left with the perhaps unpalatable conclusion that, for the foreseeable future, effective regulation of the employment and human resource management policies of MNCs are largely left to the efforts of individual governments and their respective legal codes and national level trade union organization. As we have seen earlier, MNCs have a powerful array of weapons with which they can exert pressure upon both governments and trade unions in any one country and the evidence suggests that, when the chips are down, governments and national trade union organization have pursued essentially national strategies, even within the EU.

Summary

In this chapter we have examined the concept of globalization, the benefits to be derived from the internationalization of business and the scale and nature of multinational activity and FDI. The increasing liberalization of international trade has been accompanied by a significant expansion of the activities and complexity of MNCs which now combine multinational ownership with control over multinational value-adding activities.

We have noted that MNCs have a range of options when it comes to deciding how to manage employees and employee relations in foreign-based subsidiaries. Traditionally, MNCs appear to have adopted either an ethnocentric or polycentric approach to the management of employee relations in their various subsidiaries; in countries where there is significant regulation of the labour market and the employment relationship it is difficult for the MNC to pursue anything other than a partially polycentric approach. We noted research evidence concluding that industrial relations practices in international firms are still rooted at the national level and that the host-country thesis is still the most convincing. However, as liberalization and deregulation continue, in combination threatening the exclusivity of national systems, there will be greater scope for the MNC to develop its own Eurocentric or geocentric approach which is company specific and crosses national borders. We have also noted the possibility that MNCs might be driving a global convergence of employee relations practices which may be based on either a best practice, high performance value adding or least cost model.

The trade unions and other regulatory authorities have not so far demonstrated effectiveness at countering or influencing the activities of MNCs and there is no good reason to imagine at this stage that this will change in the foreseeable future. MNCs are able to organize their activities in such a way as to render effective opposition by unions at a national level difficult and cross-national cooperation between trade unions has not been common. There are a number of ways in which the MNC can thwart or frustrate the activities and objectives of the trade unions. The liberalization of trade across national borders and within free trade areas has enhanced the ability of the MNC to frustrate the interests of its employees if that is what it wants to do. Most recently attempts at regulating the employment and employee regulations activities of MNCs have tended to centre on the insertion of minimum labour standards into free trade agreements and the standards commonly identified in this context are the ILO core labour conventions.

Activities to test understanding

Activity 1

Try to answer briefly the following questions without re-reading the text.

1 What are the benefits of the internationalization of business?
2 What distinguishes an MNC from companies that simply trade internationally?
3 What do you understand by the term 'the exit option' and why is it important?
4 What do you understand by the term Globalization?

Activity 2

Examine the potential employment consequences in the home country of outward FDI.

Activity 3

Identify the potential advantages and disadvantages to labour of inward FDI.

Activity 4

One form of MNC activity and organization is sometimes referred to as the multi-domestic. This is characterized by the subsidiary in each country being pretty much a replica of the home-country operation and therefore similar to it. Usually this would mean that the whole product or service is supplied, manufactured and assembled within the country in which it is sold. The MNC is made up of a number of reasonably self-contained subsidiaries, each supplying a particular national market, with little or no internal transfer of knowledge, expertise, service or product between them. Think through and outline the strengths and weaknesses of this form of organization with respect to the bargaining power of the trade unions taking action in one of the subsidiaries.

Activity 5

1 MNCs have choices in their approach to the management of employee relations in their foreign subsidiaries. What is the essence of the difference between a polycentric approach and an ethnocentric approach?
2 List three strategies which an MNC may use to frustrate the interests of employees organized on a national basis.

> **Activity 6**
>
> Summarize the ICFTU view of the consequences of globalization for labour.

References

Barrell, R. and Pain, N., 1997. EU: an attractive investment. Being part of the EU is good for FDI and being out of EMU may be bad. *New Economy* 4(1): 50–54.

Bartlett, C.A. and Ghoshal, S., 1989. *Managing Across Borders: The Transnational Solution*. Harvard Business School Press, Boston, Mass.

Brewster, C., Mayrhofer, W. and Morley, M. (eds), 2000. *New Challenges for European Human Resource Management*. Palgrave Macmillan, Basingstoke.

Dowling, P. and Schuler, R., 1990. *International Dimensions of Human Resource Management*. PWS, Kent.

Dowling, P., Welch, D. and Schuler, R., 1999. *International Human Resource Management*. South Case Western, Cincinnati.

Edwards, P., Marginson, P., Armstrong, P. and Purcell, J., 1996. Towards the transnational company? The global structure and organization of multinational firms. In Crompton, R., Gallie, D. and Purcell, K. (eds), *Changing Forms of Employment*. Routledge, London.

Edwards, T., Rees, C. and Coller, X., 1999. Structure, politics and the diffusion of employment practices in multinationals. *European Journal of Industrial Relations* 5(3) November: 286–306.

European Commission 1999. *Employment in Europe 1998.*

Ghertman, M. and Allen, M., 1984. *An Introduction to the Multinationals*. Macmillan, Basingstoke.

Hamill, J., 1983. The labour relations practices of foreign owned and indigenous firms. *Employee Relations* 5(1): 14–16.

Hancke, B., 2000. European works councils and the industrial restructuring in the European motor industry. *European Journal of Industrial Relations* 6(1): 35–59.

Hendry, C., 1994. *Human Resource Strategies for International Growth*. Routledge, London.

Hofstede, G., 1991. *Cultures and Organisations. Software of the Mind*. McGraw Hill. New York.

Hollinshead, G. and Leat, M., 1995. *Human Resource Management: An International and Comparative Perspective on the Employment Relationship*. Pitman, London.

Hyman, R., 1999. National industrial relations systems and transitional challenges: an essay in review. *European Journal of Industrial Relations* 5(1): 90–110.

Ietto-Gillies, G., 1997. Working with the big guys: hostility to transnationals must be replaced by co-operation. *New Economy* 4(1): 12–16.

Kennedy, T., 1980. *European Labour Relations*. Lexington Books.

Leat, M., 1999. Multi-nationals and employee relations. In Hollinshead, G., Nicholls, P. and Tailby, S. (eds), *Employee Relations*. Financial Times Pitman Publishing.

Maurice, M., Silvestre, J.-J. and Sellier, F., 1980. Societal differences in organizing manufacturing units: a comparison of France, West Germany and Great Britain. *Organizational Studies* 1: 59–86.

Milne, S., 1991. Germany 37, Britain 39, *The Guardian,* 25 October.

Mueller, F. and Purcell, J., 1992. The Europeanisation of manufacturing and the decentralisation of bargaining: multinational management strategies in the European automobile industry. *International Journal of Human Resource Management* 3(1).

Needle, D., 2000. *Business in Context,* 3rd Edition. Thomson Learning, London.

O'Hagan, E., Gunnigle, P. and Morley, M., 2005. Issues in the management of industrial relations in international firms. In Scullion, H. and Linehan, M. (eds), *International Human Resource Management – A critical Text.* Palgrave Macmillan, Basingstoke.

Ohmae, K., 1990. *The Borderless World: Power and Strategy in the Interlinked Economy.* Harper, New York.

Perlmutter, H., 1969. The tortuous evolution of the multi-national corporation. *Columbus Journal of World Business* 4(1): 9–18.

Prahalad, C.K. and Doz, Y.L., 1987. *The Multinational Mission.* Free Press, New York.

Schregle, J., 1981. Comparative industrial relations: pitfalls and potential. *International Labour Review* 120(1).

Schuler, R., Budwhar, P. and Florkowski, G., 2002. International Human Resource management: review and critique. *International Journal of Management Reviews* 4(1): 41–70.

Schulten, T., 1996. European Works Councils: prospects of a new system of European industrial relations. *European Journal of Industrial Relations* 2(3): 303–324.

Traxler, F. and Woitech, B., 2000. Transnational investment and national labour market regimes: a case of regime shopping. *European Journal of Industrial Relations* 6(2) July: 141–159.

UNCTAD 1999. UNCTAD Report on World Investment 1998. New York, United Nations.

UNCTAD 2004. World Investment Report 2003. New York, United Nations.

UNCTAD 2005. World Investment Report for 2004. Overview. New York, United Nations.

Wakelin, K., Girma, S. and Greenaway, D., 1999. *Wages, Productivity and Foreign Ownership in UK Manufacturing.* Centre for Research on Globalization and Labour Markets. University of Nottingham: Centre for Research on Globalisation and Labour Markets.

Walters, M., 1995. Globalisation. Routledge, London.

Wilkins, M., 1970. *The Emergence of the Multinational Enterprise.* Cambridge University Press, Cambridge.

Chapter 4

The European Union

Introduction

In this chapter we are concerned predominantly with what is called the social dimension of the European Union (EU). We have already discussed the process of globalization and the views of those who think that international free trade agreements and supra-national alliances should encompass a core set of minimum labour standards in order to ensure that free trade does not result in the exploitation of labour, which in comparison with capital and goods and services is relatively immobile. We have also examined the potential for multinational corporations (MNCs) to locate and relocate their activities in order to take advantage of least cost production and regulatory regimes and to use their power to persuade both governments and labour movements to give concessions in order both to attract and retain investment and jobs.

The EU is an example of a trading bloc, a single market containing 25 different nation states, which has sought to balance the advantages to business with a set of minimum labour standards, protections and guidelines, which together comprise a significant part of the social dimension of the EU. These standards and protections have often been given legal force and impact upon the national employee relations systems of each of the member states. As such the EU may well act as a guide to other trading blocs in the world as they develop.

At the heart of the EU is a single market for goods, services and capital and in theory for labour. However, while labour has the right to be mobile within the Union the reality is that cross-border mobility is relatively rare and at best the union is made up of a number of national and sectoral labour markets with national trade union movements and national governments' agendas still dominated by the interests of their national constituencies and therefore subject to pressure from the activities of multinational capital.

It is in this context that the EU has enacted a core set of minimum rights for labour (obligations for employers) and sought to ensure that labour as an interest group has a role in the policy-making and legislative process as a social partner. This approach is consistent with the traditions of most of the member states prior to enlargement in 2004 and, so far, this regulatory or social protectionist perspective has dominated the Union's decision making. It would be fair to depict the EU as an example of a Coordinated Market Economy (CME) rather than a Liberal Market Economy (LME) (see **Chapter 5**). However, there is a deregulationist lobby within the Union, comprised mainly of business interests and one or two governments with different traditions and perspectives such as the UK.

There are different trajectories or paths available for the future development of the social dimension of the Union. The deregulated approach represented by the creation of the single market and calls for labour market flexibility may be extended further in order to facilitate change and international competitiveness. Alternatively, there may be an extension of social regulation at the level of the Union which results in a more extensive common floor of employee rights, protections and constraints upon the autonomy of managements in order to ensure that change and competitiveness are not achieved at the expense of labour. It is important that you realize that labour comprises a very large proportion of the overall population of the Union and coordinated effectively has the potential to exert massive influence upon the futures of political leaders at both the national and Union levels. Either path or trajectory is possible and both could result in a greater degree of convergence in the employee relations systems and practices within the member states and across national borders: the one base of convergence being deregulation and the other a greater measure of social protectionism than currently exists within the Union as a whole. We discuss these issues further later in the chapter.

The importance of creating a Union that connects with and appeals to its citizens was demonstrated in 2005 when, in a referendum, the French electorate rejected the newly agreed Constitution for the Union. It was suggested at the time that at least one of the reasons for the rejection was the belief by many French citizens that the Constitution would provide far too many benefits for business at the expense of the traditional social model much valued in France and much of mainland Europe (see the discussion of Fordism and its consequences in **Chapter 2**).

As noted above the chapter is mainly concerned with the content of the social dimension as it impacts upon the employment relationship, the management of employee relations and the participation of labour in decision making. However, before we address these issues it is necessary to identify and examine briefly the major institutions and their roles and responsibilities, these include the social partners and their roles in the decision-making processes. Then we examine the social dimension and in particular focus on the elements of this dimension that impact employee influence, the organization of working time, the prevention of discrimination and provision of equal opportunities and working conditions.

At the beginning of 2006 there was considerable doubt about the future of the Constitution agreed by the member state governments in 2004. As noted above, the Constitution was subject to ratification by each member state and at the time of writing two member states had rejected the Constitution. The content of the chapter refers to the pre-Constitution situation, but where appropriate we identify features of the Constitution that might make a significant impact if eventually adopted.

Learning objectives

After studying this chapter you will be able to:

- Understand the structure and role of the main EU institutions, including the social partners.
- Explain the motivations behind, and the arguments for and against, the need for a social dimension.
- Understand the relevance of the Treaties and competence.
- Discuss the main initiatives, the arguments for and against, and analyse their impact.

History and membership of the EU

The EU started life in 1957 as the European Economic Community (EEC), with six members; Germany, France, Italy, the Netherlands, Belgium and Luxembourg, later became the European Community (EC) and in 1993 became the European Union (EU) with the ratification of the treaty changes agreed at Maastricht in 1991.

Perhaps inevitably there is a tendency to see the EU as an organization primarily concerned with economic and trading matters but these were not the only reasons for the formation of the EEC and are not the only justifications for membership and the subsequent enlargement. A strong motivation for the original members was the desire to prevent further war within Europe and also to halt the spread of Communism. It was felt that nations bound together in economic and trading terms would be less likely to go to war with each other and, in particular, this was the concern of Germany and France which have a long history of conflict between them.

Since 2004 the Union has comprised 25 member states. The six founding member states have subsequently been joined by: UK, Ireland and Denmark in 1973, Greece in 1981, Spain, Portugal and Austria in 1986, Sweden and Finland in 1995 and Poland, Czech Republic, Hungary, Slovenia, Estonia, Cyprus, Slovakia, Latvia, Lithuania and Malta all joined in the single largest enlargement in 2004. Other countries keen to join are Bulgaria, Romania and Turkey.

Aspirant members are required to satisfy a range of conditions prior to membership. These can be separated into:

- *Political criteria*: Article 6 of the Treaty of the European Union spells these out 'The Union is founded on the principles of liberty, democracy, respect for human rights and fundamental freedoms and the rule of law'.
- *Economic criteria*: which were spelt out at the Copenhagen Summit in 1993 and can be summarized as the existence of a functioning market economy and the capacity to withstand competitive pressure and market forces within the Union.
- *Additional criteria and obligations of membership*: The Copenhagen European Council indicated that membership requires 'the ability to take on the obligations of membership, including adherence to the aims of political, economic and monetary union'. This is sometimes referred to as the 'acquis communitaire'.

The criteria for membership are not universally popular and have been criticized for being too biased in favour of the requirements of business and capital rather than those of the Union's citizens (see the comments about the French citizens' rejection of the Constitution earlier). One of the critical suggestions for improving this perceived imbalance was for a Charter of core or fundamental rights, duties and obligations, acceptance of which would form the base for membership as well as forming the base upon which the EU might become a citizens' Europe, a Europe consistent with the principles and traditions of social democracy and not dominated by the single market and the interests of business. Somewhat ironically the Constitution agreed in 2004, but subject to ratification by member states, included such a Charter of Fundamental Rights, this being the Charter proclaimed at the Heads of Government summit meeting at Nice in 2000 (see later section).

Institutions

There are four main Union institutions: the **European Commission,** hereafter referred to as the Commission, the **Council of the European Union** (often also known as the **Council of Ministers**) and hereafter referred to as the Council, the **European Parliament** (EP) and the **Court of Justice of the European Communities** (ECJ). The main roles of each of these institutions and the relationship between them are indicated in **Figure 4.1**.

Historically the Council has been the single decision maker when it came to determining policy and adopting legislation, but in the last

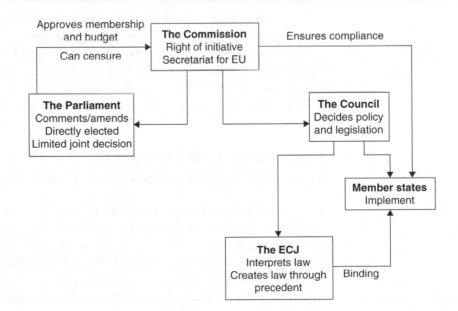

Figure 4.1
The role and relationships of the major institutions.

decade of the 20th century and early years of the 21st century there was a change in the distribution of power in these areas with the thrust of the change being in the direction of allowing the Parliament a greater role with the adoption of a new decision-making process called the Co-decision procedure (see later). This co-decision process has now become the default mechanism with other processes being used only in respect of certain specific areas of subject matter.

The Commission

The Commission is politically independent and represents and upholds the interests of the EU as a whole.

The European Commission has four main roles:

1   To propose legislation to Parliament and the Council, the right of initiative.
2   To manage and implement EU policies and the budget.
3   To enforce European law (jointly with the Court of Justice).
4   To represent the European Union on the international stage, for example by negotiating agreements between the EU and other countries.

The term 'Commission' is used in two senses. First, it refers to the Members of the Commission: that is, the team ('college') of men and women appointed by the member states and Parliament to run the institution and take its decisions, each member state being able to appoint one commissioner. Second, the term 'Commission' refers to the institution itself and to its staff.

The Commission remains politically answerable to Parliament, which has the power to dismiss it by adopting a motion of censure.

The Commission will propose action at EU level only if it believes that a problem cannot be solved more efficiently by national, regional or local action. This principle of dealing with things at the lowest possible level is called the 'subsidiarity principle' (see later section).

The Council of the European Union (the Council of Ministers and the European Council)

The Council is an intergovernmental body. Whenever it sits the membership is made up of representatives of the national governments of all the member states. The meetings of the Council tend to be subject based and the national government representatives are normally the members of those governments with specific responsibilities for the subject matter under discussion, so that as an example when the Council meets as a Social Affairs Council it will be comprised of the representatives of the member state governments with those particular responsibilities. The Council, therefore, is not a directly elected body and the members are not accountable to any particular constituency of electors, but only to their own member state governments.

The council has a number of roles. As noted above, for many years the Council was the legislature of the Union, with the Parliament having only a consultative role; however, much legislation is now adopted jointly by the Council and the Parliament through the Co-decision procedure. As a rule legislation is only adopted after proposals have been made by the Commission. The most common voting procedure in Council is 'qualified majority voting' (QMV). This means that, for a proposal to be adopted, it needs the support of a specified minimum number of votes. (The details of the votes available to each member state are given in **Figure 4.2.**)

From 1 November 2004, the number of votes each country can cast (including the new member states) is given in **Figure 4.2**.

However, in some particularly sensitive areas such as common foreign and security policy (CFSP), taxation, asylum and immigration policy, Council decisions have to be unanimous. In other words, each member state has the power of veto in these areas.

From 1 November 2004, a qualified majority will be reached:

- if a majority of member states (in some cases a two-thirds majority) approve and
- if a minimum of votes is cast in favour which is 72.3 per cent (232 votes) of the total (roughly the same share as under the previous system).

In addition, a member state may ask for confirmation that the votes in favour represent at least 62 per cent of the total population of the Union. If this is found not to be the case, the decision will not be adopted.

In addition to the legislative role the Council also has responsibility for: co-ordinating the economic policies of member states, approving

Figure 4.2
The details of the votes available to each member state.

Germany, France, Italy and the United Kingdom	29
Spain and Poland	27
The Netherlands	13
Belgium, Czech Republic, Greece, Hungary and Portugal	12
Austria and Sweden	10
Denmark, Ireland, Lithuania, Slovakia and Finland	7
Cyprus, Estonia, Latvia, Luxembourg and Slovenia	4
Malta	3
Total	321

the EU budget jointly with the Parliament, facilitating intergovernmental cooperation on foreign and security policy and in relation to certain categories of cross border criminal activities.

The Parliament

Parliament is the only one of the main institutions to be comprised of directly elected representatives and it has three main roles:

1   It shares with the Council the **power to legislate**. The fact that it is a directly elected body helps guarantee the democratic legitimacy of European law.
2   It exercises **democratic supervision** over all EU institutions, and in particular the Commission. It has the power to approve or reject the nomination of Commissioners, and it has the right to censure the Commission as a whole.
3   It shares with the Council **authority over the EU budget** and can therefore influence EU spending. At the end of the procedure, it adopts or rejects the budget in its entirety.

Each member state has the right to elect a specified number of Members of the European Parliament (MEPs), as indicated in **Figure 4.3**. The allocation of seats in the parliament is intended to be roughly proportional on population grounds. Though elected by electors in and on behalf of a particular member state, the MEPs tend to ally themselves in multinational political groupings. They are not sent to the Parliament with a brief to look after the interests of the particular member state from which they come.

Number of seats per country (in alphabetical order according to the country's name in its own language).

Country	Seats	Country	Seats
Belgium	24	Lithuania	13
Czech Republic	24	Luxembourg	6
Denmark	14	Hungary	24
Germany	99	Malta	5
Estonia	6	The Netherlands	27
Greece	24	Austria	18
Spain	54	Poland	54
France	78	Portugal	24
Ireland	13	Slovenia	7
Italy	78	Slovakia	14
Cyprus	6	Finland	14
Latvia	9	Sweden	19
		United Kingdom	78
		TOTAL	**732**

Figure 4.3

The Court of Justice of the European Communities

The ECJ is the final arbiter of European Community/Union law. It is the Court of Last Resort. It tends to deal with two different categories of case.

1 Cases that are concerned with matters of EU-level significance such as a member state alleging that the Council or the Commission has acted improperly or unlawfully, or where the Commission is seeking to ensure that a member state complies with EU legislation or where one member state is in legal dispute with another.
2 Cases that commence within individual member states but require the ECJ's final decision on what the law means or how and when it should apply.

Associated with the ECJ is the *Court of First Instance* (CFI). This was established by the Single European Act (SEA) of 1986 and was intended to help speed up the judicial process in cases brought by private parties. The scope of the CFI's jurisdiction was extended by the Maastricht Treaty and now the court can hear cases brought by private parties in all areas or fields. Appeal from the CFI is to the ECJ.

Other institutions

In addition to the three main EU institutions above there are several others that are relevant to the subject matter of employee relations. In particular, there are the organizations known as the 'social partners'. We have already discussed one of these, the ETUC in **Chapter 3**.

The social partners

At EU level the **social partners** participate in a process known as the **social dialogue.** This process occurs most publicly at the level of the Union itself and this level is now known as the cross-industry social dialogue. At this level the dialogue is between the **European Trade Union Confederation** (ETUC), representing the labour movement at EU level and the employers' associations: the **Union of Industrial and Employers Confederations of Europe** (UNICE), which represents primarily private-sector employers, and the **European Centre of Public Enterprises** (CEEP), representing primarily public-sector employer interests.

The European Trade Union Confederation (ETUC)

It has long been the view of the Commission that the internal market and the deregulation implied by and in its creation would only be possible with the support/acquiescence of European labour. It is therefore necessary that the labour movement within the EU has a voice and it is in this context that the Commission has been supportive of the ETUC, both politically and financially. However, as was intimated earlier in **Chapter 3**, the organization has not always easily been able to formulate a coherent approach to particular issues and there is always potential for conflict between the member federations, given their different national agendas and interests.

The nature and traditions of the many union confederations in membership vary considerably as also do their autonomy and authority in respect of their own membership. Turner (1996) took a relatively optimistic view of the future of the ETUC despite acknowledging that in many respects the development of structures at such a transnational level seemed to be at odds with the trends towards the decentralization of decision making and collective bargaining. However, he does also point out that the development of an effective labour movement at this EU level needs, in addition to the structures, transnational rank and file protest and he thought this most likely to occur in protest at some specific EU-level policy, although it is difficult to conceive what such a policy might be.

Below the level of the EU there are various sectoral (industry) federations, many of them affiliated to the ETUC, that are active in a social dialogue at a sectoral level with employers in their respective industries and which also often provide the employee representative mechanism in discussions at the level of the individual MNC.

Employers' organizations

UNICE was formed in 1958 and represents employers from 27 different countries.

At the level of the EU the organization wants to be influential representing a particular interest to the legislators and policy makers but, unlike the ETUC, it was not keen to become involved with the Commission and ETUC in policy making as a social partner and it is even less keen to become involved in any EU-level bargaining arrangements with the ETUC. To some extent this is no doubt due to the fact that it does not have a mandate to act in this way, and it and the ETUC do not have compatible structures.

Among its priorities the emphasis is upon international competitiveness, full employment, multilateral trade agreements and minimum regulation. Social policies should be based on economic realities and structural reforms (lower taxation, more efficient public services and more flexible labour markets), innovation and life-long learning in order to meet the challenges of the information and learning society.

CEEP Membership tends to be comprised of individual employers rather than federations and the geographic spread of the members of this organization is much smaller than that of either of the other two above, since full membership is only open to organizations from within the Union. As with UNICE, the direction of the organization's activities is primarily to represent its members' interests to the policy makers and legislators and, like UNICE, the preference of the membership would be not to participate in the process of social dialogue and social policy formulation in a direct way.

The UK

Within the UK the Social Partners at a national level are the Trades Union Congress (TUC) (see **Chapter 7**) and the Confederation of British Industry (CBI) although they have not traditionally been referred to in these terms. In the past the TUC was very sceptical of the UK's membership of the EU and of the regulatory initiatives taken at an EU level. However, in the latter part of the 1980s and early 1990s, it became one of the more avid supporters of the whole European project, perceiving it as one of its best chances of obtaining and retaining employment and social protection(s) for its members in the face of successive attempts by UK governments to deregulate and minimize such protection.

The CBI also tended to support the EU concept, although for different reasons – those associated with the prospects for business to be derived from the creation of a single market and in the 1990s from monetary union. Both of these UK partners are active members of the appropriate organizations at the level of the EU.

Legislative forms and decision-making processes

Legislation adopted at EU level takes precedence over national legislation and in the case of conflict or inconsistency between them it is the EU legislation that takes precedence. EU legislation cannot be countermanded at the level of the individual member state. As noted above, new entrants to the Union have to accept the *acquis communitaire* – the existing body of laws and regulations.

Legislative forms

Legislation within the Union can be adopted using a range of different mechanisms and instruments.

Regulations

These are relatively rare but, once adopted, they are applicable directly and generally throughout the EU; they are immediately binding on member states and individuals and do not require any action at member state level to render them effective. The Council can empower the Commission to make regulations.

Directives

Most of the legislation so far adopted in the field of employee relations has been adopted using this form of instrument. A directive is not immediately applicable, and requires some action at member state level for it to be given effect, though this action need not be legislative (implementation can, for example, be through agreement by the social partners).

Normally a directive specifies the objective to be achieved and the date by which it should be achieved, usually referred to as the implementation date, but leaves the precise means of achieving the objective to the individual member states. However, states cannot avoid implementing unwelcome directives because, once the implementation date is reached and irrespective of the progress made at national level towards implementation, the directive becomes the law within the Union. There are further rules with respect to organizations in the public sector or which are 'Emanations of the State', since directives generally become applicable to and in such organizations upon adoption rather than at the specified implementation date.

Decisions

These can be made by the Council and, in some instances, by the Commission and once made they are binding on the parties that sought the decision in the first place. They do not automatically have general effect.

There are several non-legally binding instruments that can be used such as **Recommendations**, **Communications**, **Codes of Conduct or Practice** and **Opinions**. These are often used when one or more of the main institutions wants to exert influence but either knows that they will not gain sufficient support for the proposal to be adopted as legislation or that they do not really have the competence to act. Competence in this sense is provided by the Treaties agreed by the member states. If the Treaty does not provide for the Union institutions to act in a certain field of activity then it and they cannot lawfully do so.

Decision-making processes

The decision-making procedures used within the Union have developed considerably since the adoption of the Single European Act in 1986.

Initially and until quite recently the Council was the sole legis-lature and decisions had to be reached unanimously, meaning in effect that any single member state government could veto legisla-tive proposals and prevent all the other member states doing some-thing which they collectively wished. Now the situation has changed as it had to do as the size of the Union grew. It is reasonably possible to obtain unanimity when there are only six member states but as the Union grew to a Union of 15 in the mid 1990s and to one of 25 in 2004, insisting upon unanimity became a recipe for stagnation; some would say paralysis.

Consequently, new processes and rules have been introduced which have resulted in sharing of the legislature role with Parliament and also the introduction of QMV (see above). There are still areas of sub-ject matter where unanimity is required but QMV has become the norm, and there are still areas of subject matter not subject to the co-decision procedure but again co-decision has become the norm. Details of the QMV voting requirements have been referred to already and the co-decision procedure is complex, providing for a number of readings and positions to be adopted with fairly detailed rules regard-ing how disagreements between the Council and Parliament are to be resolved and including provision for conciliation between the parties under the auspices of the Commission. The bottom line is that, if the Parliament and Council are unable to reach an agreed position, then the proposal can not be adopted.

One of the distinctive features of the Treaty provisions in respect of legislation in the Social field is the procedure which was originated in a protocol to the Treaty agreed at Maastricht in 1991 and which became known as the Social protocol or Agreement procedure. This procedure is embodied in Articles 138 and 139 of the EC Treaty (see **Figure 4.4**). In essence the procedure provides for the social partners to come to an agreement at EU or Sectoral level which they can ask the Commission to propose to the Council as draft legislation. Depending on the subject matter, the proposal would be subject to adoption via either QMV or Unanimity.

The essence of these arrangements is that the social partners have to be consulted on both the direction and content of Commission pro-posals for action in the social policy field. Having been consulted, the social partners can ask for the opportunity to reach an agreement on the issue between themselves. If such an agreement is reached, there are two possible options with respect to its implementation:

1   The first is to leave it to the parties at national level, presum-ably through some form of implementation arrangements agreed between the partners and possibly with government at national level giving legal effect to the arrangements

Article 138

1 The Commission shall have the task of promoting the consultation of management and labour at Community level, and shall take any relevant measure to facilitate their dialogue by ensuring balanced support for the parties.
2 To this end, before submitting proposals in the social policy field, the Commission shall consult management and labour on the possible direction of Community action.
3 If, after such consultation, the Commission considers Community action advisable, it shall consult management and labour on the content of the envisaged proposal. Management and labour shall forward to the Commission an opinion or, where appropriate, a recommendation.
4 On the occasion of such consultation, management and labour may inform the Commission of their wish to initiate the process provided for in Article 139. The duration of the procedure shall not exceed nine months, unless the management and labour concerned and the Commission decide jointly to extend it.

Article 139

1 Should management and labour so desire, the dialogue between them at Community level may lead to contractual relations, including agreements.
2 Agreements concluded at Community level shall be implemented either in accordance with the procedures and practices specific to management and labour and the Member States or, at the joint request of the signatory parties, by a Council decision on a proposal from the Commission.

Figure 4.4
The Social Agreement Procedure – Articles 138 and 139 of the EC Treaty.

agreed by the national-level partners. Some member states have a tradition of dealing with employee relations matters this way.

2 The second provides for the partners to request jointly that the Commission makes a proposal to the Council that the agreement be given legal effect.

The intention is that any such agreements reached between the social partners should take the form of frameworks or agreements on principle, the details to be worked out at individual member state level.

A number of Directives have been adopted subsequent to the social partners reaching such an agreement, and these include:

- the Directive on Parental Leave, 1996/34/EC;
- the Directive on equality between the rights of part-time and full-time workers, 1997/81/EC and
- the Directive on Fixed Term Work,1999/70/EC.

While some agreements have been reached, the partners have also failed to reach agreement on a number of occasions and on other occasions have declined the opportunity even to try to reach agreement. As noted earlier the employers associations have been much more reluctant to enter into this process than have the ETUC.

Subsidiarity

One of the debates that simmered throughout the 1980s and early 1990s concerned the question of whether and when action should be taken at the level of the EU compared with the level of the nation state (or lower such as local or regional levels). The UK governments of the time were at the centre of these debates and generally they took the view that action at the EU level should be a measure of last resort and linked the debate to the issue of national sovereignty. Other interests, with perhaps greater ambitions for the creation of EU-wide systems, and those keen on Europe becoming a Union much more like the United States of America, tended to argue for more and wider and deeper action at the EU level.

The debate resulted in a restatement of the principle in Article 3b of the Treaty agreed at Maastricht:

> In areas which do not fall within its exclusive competence, the Community shall take action, in accordance with the principle of subsidiarity, only if and in so far as the objectives of the proposed action cannot be achieved by the member states and can therefore, by reason of the scale or effects of the proposed action, be better achieved by the Community. Any action by the Community shall not go beyond what is necessary to achieve the objectives of this Treaty.

The implication is clear: the Commission and the EU should seek to act only when it is clear that the objectives cannot be achieved at the level of each of the member states *and* that they can be better achieved through action at the centre.

This restatement of the principle and its enunciation is significant in that it both indicates a shift of intent away from the production, through Union-level interventions and upward harmonization, of Union-wide and convergent systems, and a greater willingness to try to achieve common objectives while retaining national and diverse traditions and practices.

The meaning and application of this principle was further developed in the Amsterdam Treaty with a new Protocol on subsidiarity which cites three criteria for judging whether the condition above has been fulfilled:

1 Does the action have transnational aspects that cannot be satisfactorily regulated by member states?
2 Would action by member states or lack of action conflict with the requirements of the Treaty?
3 Would action at Community level produce clear benefits?

As we note later in the section on employee participation, the Institutions and member states have concluded that action at the level of the Union is necessary if the objective is to regulate the transnational activities of MNCs. Consequently action has been taken at the level of the Union in order to ensure that employees of an MNC in one member state have rights to be informed and consulted about decisions and developments likely to affect their interests but which may be made or occur in another member state. Examples of such decisions might include decisions taken in one member state to close down plants and make employees redundant in another member state.

Social policy: the social dimension

In the context of the EU, social policy and the social dimension encompass matters that relate to the employment relationship and employee relations as well as to more general areas of social protection.

The development of the social dimension has been the subject of much debate and disagreement over the years with different perspectives as to the need for and desirability of interventionary action and regulation at the level of the EU.

These debates and disagreements about the need for and desirability of regulation and socially protective legislation were given a particular impetus by the decision in 1986 to create the single market. It was recognized at the outset by its architects that the creation of a single market and the process of economic integration would inevitably create some dislocation of industry and employment and a need for restructuring – that there would be losers as well as winners.

The single market concept required the removal of the barriers to the free movement of capital, goods, services and labour, and this resulted in fears that without legislative regulation, support for and protection of employees and other minorities, the forces of multinational capital free of restriction upon movement, acquisition and the location of investment would seek to maximize profit and locate and relocate to those regulatory regimes within the Union in which costs and restrictions were least (they would engage in 'regime shopping').

While this might result in lower costs, greater competitiveness and greater profits, there would be an impact upon jobs and living standards, especially if the process resulted in relocation of investment within the Union. Jobs might be created in one area such as Spain or Portugal at the expense of employment levels, living standards and wealth creation in places such as Germany and France. Such consequences are often referred to as Social Dumping.

Concern about social dumping tended to be greatest in those countries with the most developed labour standards and correspondingly highest labour costs.

The direct employment effects were likely to be only part of the problem and there were additional concerns that this in turn could lead to significant disruptive effects upon:

- Existing patterns, terms and conditions of employment.
- The distribution of income and wealth, poverty and social cohesion, both within individual countries and the Union as a whole.
- Equality of opportunities and pay between the sexes.
- The relative wealth and well-being of each of the member states.

The UK, with a government that was keen to create flexible and deregulated labour markets and which saw lower labour costs and the absence of social protection as a source of competitive advantage, was seen as a potential beneficiary.

In the main the debate has been between:

- Those who considered that intervention and regulation would be necessary in order to cushion these effects and to promote the restructuring and more efficient use of labour that was both necessary and an inevitable consequence of the further economic integration envisaged in the creation of the single market.
- Those who take the view that while integration might have these effects, the solution was to leave the market to cope and that to intervene would simply prevent the adjustment mechanisms of the market working effectively. Circumstances justifying intervention should be limited to those in which the intervention itself contributed to the process of market integration.

As Hall (1994) explained, the Commission and most of the member states have viewed the social dimension as:

> an important vehicle for securing the support of the European labour movement for the single market project and for enhancing the 'social acceptability' of the consequent economic restructuring ... the human face of the EC.

Those in favour of the creation of a social dimension to the single market argued that the way forward was to create a measure of Union-wide commonality in labour market regulation and social protection, the creation of what has often been referred to as a level playing field. The idea was that a floor of minimum employment rights and protections across the whole of the Union would be the best way of ensuring that the worst excesses of liberalism of capital mobility and free trade would be checked. It was thought that the danger of MNCs shopping between different regulatory regimes and locating activities in those which are the most favourable (cheapest and least regulated) would be minimized.

An early indication of the rights and obligations that would form at least the base of a social dimension was given in the Community Charter of the Fundamental Social Rights of Workers (usually known as the Social Charter) being presented for adoption to a meeting of the Council in Dec. 1989. The charter was not adopted due to the refusal of the UK government which exercised its right of veto. However, action has been taken to implement rights and protections in some of the areas specified, but these had to be adopted as individual initiatives (see later sections).

However, the New Labour government elected in the UK in 1997 agreed to Treaty amendments at the Amsterdam summit council which effectively gave the Social Charter a kind of quasi legal status by allowing it to be referred to in the Preamble and allowing a statement that member states were committed to giving effect to its contents.

The contents of the charter are incorporated in **Figure 4.5**. These same differences of perspective about the need for a social dimension can be seen to inform deliberations within the EU on solutions to the problems of unemployment and international competitiveness. The Commission and the European labour movements have tended to argue the case for the protection of those in employment and the regulation of the labour market to ensure social justice, with employers and other interests arguing the case that economic performance in Europe, including job creation, is actually being undermined by excessive intervention and regulation leading to labour market inflexibility.

Hall (1994) points out that the leading proponent of the view that an extensive EU social policy/dimension would damage competitiveness since it would raise employment costs and reduce labour market flexibility was the UK Conservative government. This was a consistent position after its election in 1979 and was demonstrated by its opposition to a number of individual proposals, in addition to its refusal to adopt the Social Charter in 1989 and to agree to the Maastricht Treaty in 1991 until the Social Chapter was removed from the draft.

These different perspectives can also be seen to inform and underpin the different traditions and regulatory systems in the member states.

Different traditions and systems

Gold (1993) adopts Teague's (1989) distinction between the social protectionist and the deregulatory perspectives. The social protectionist perspective encompasses the Socialist, Social Democrat and Christian Democrat philosophies, all of which, though to varying degrees and with different priorities, accept the principle of intervention and the need for government to regulate the labour market, insist upon minimum

The rights proposed and incorporated in the Charter fell into 12 main sections:

1 Freedom of movement of labour, including the removal of obstacles arising from the non-recognition of diplomas and equivalent occupational qualifications

2 Employment and remuneration, including the rights to fair and equitable wages thereby enabling a decent standard of living

3 Improvement of living and working conditions, specific reference was made to working hours, weekly rest periods and annual leave, temporary, fixed-term and part-time contracts

4 Social protection, here the terms used are adequate and sufficient

5 Freedom of association and collective bargaining. Both workers and employers should have a right to form and join, or not, associations for the defence of their economic and social interests. The associations should have the right to negotiate and conclude collective agreements and the right to take collective action including strike action. Conciliation, arbitration and mediation should be encouraged. This section also refers to improvement of the dialogue between the social partners at European level

6 Vocational training, all workers should have the right of access to such training and retraining throughout their working life

7 Equal treatment for men and women should be assured and equal opportunities should be developed. Particular mention is made of equality of access to employment, remuneration, working conditions, social protection, education, vocational training and career development. Mention was also made of measures to facilitate both men and women reconciling their work and family lives/obligations

8 Information, consultation and participation of workers, with particular reference to organizations with establishments or companies in two or more member states. In particular these rights should apply in cases of technological change having major implications for the workforce in terms of working conditions and/or work organization, where restructuring or mergers also have an impact upon the employment of workers and in cases of collective redundancy procedures

9 Health, protection and safety at the workplace. Specific mention is also made of training, information and consultation

10 Protection of children and adolescents, they should receive equitable remuneration, be protected from working below a certain age and their development, vocational training and access to employment needs should be met. There should also be limits on the duration of such work and on working at night. There should also be an entitlement to initial vocational training upon leaving full-time education

11 Elderly persons upon retirement should have an entitlement to a decent standard of living

12 Disabled persons should be entitled to measures aimed at improving their social and professional integration and in particular to vocational training, ergonomics, accessibility and mobility.

Figure 4.5
The Social Charter.

employee rights and promote social justice. This perspective, shared by the majority of the political groups within the EU and also crucially by influential groups within the Commission, can be contrasted with that of the UK Conservative governments between 1979 and 1997 and arguably also that of the New Labour government elected in 1997, which has been portrayed as an essentially deregulatory approach. In terms of philosophy or ideology, the UK governments between 1979 and 1997 can be characterized as liberal individualist, putting their faith in:

- the process of individual exchange, initiative and enterprise;
- the operation of market forces;
- deregulation of the labour market and the employment relationship including the removal of employee protection;
- a very determined effort to reduce the power and influence of the trade unions.

Hall (1994) and Gold(1993) both sought to locate the regulatory systems in the EU in one of the following three categories:

1 *The Roman–German system:* Here the state plays a crucial role in industrial relations. In these systems there is a core of fundamental rights and freedoms guaranteed by the constitution and it is these that constitute the base of national industrial relations. It is common in such systems for there to be quite extensive legal regulation of areas such as working time and the rights of employees to be represented and the mechanisms of that representation. Germany, France, the Netherlands, Belgium and Italy are quoted as being in this category/tradition.

2 *The Anglo-Irish system:* Here the role of the state is more limited and there is a much less extensive set of legislatively created and supported basic rights and protections. Governments in these countries have traditionally left more to the parties themselves and stepped in to regulate and protect only when necessary to defend either the national interest and/or the interests of certain vulnerable minorities, such as children. These systems have been referred to as voluntarist. Both the UK and Ireland were located in this category.

3 *The Nordic system:* Prior to the enlargement of the EU in 1995 only Denmark fell into this category, although as Gold (1993) points out, the other Scandinavian countries that were part of this enlargement, Sweden and Finland, also share this tradition. The difference between this system and the Anglo-Irish group is in the degree of emphasis and reliance placed on and in the collective agreement. It is suggested that in these countries more emphasis is placed upon the basic agreement freely entered into, usually at national or sectoral level, by both employer and trade union and it is this that provides the central element of the industrial relations system. The state has intervened to regulate only at the request of the parties.

The Commission has traditionally pursued policies and taken initiatives consistent with the Roman–German tradition and there is plenty of recent evidence that this is still the inclination of the Commission Directorates with responsibility for social affairs (see next section). The debate on unemployment, which has occupied the member states, Commission and other interests substantially since the early 1990s, illustrates these preferences, with the Commission often arguing that while it may be desirable to reduce the regulation of the labour market and labour costs so as to encourage employment, this should not be achieved at the expense of social justice and the weakest and poorest members of the EU.

However, it is also clear that there are other interests within the Commission – for example, those with responsibility for industry and competition policy – that are distancing themselves from the traditions of the Roman–German system of regulation and social protection and becoming more willing to countenance deregulation as a necessary response to the pressures of international competition and the need to enhance flexibility in terms of response to the market and labour usage. These same pressures are also leading some member state governments with Roman–German traditions to investigate ways in which existing systems of labour market regulation and social protection may be eased in order to facilitate job creation and enhance international competitiveness.

Social policy: the Treaties

Competence

As we have noted earlier the ability of the Union to adopt laws and take initiatives is limited to what is provided for in the Treaties. Treaties and amendments to them have to be agreed by all member states in some form of meeting of the Council and there is also usually a requirement for some element of ratification at national level. Over the years since the Treaty of Rome in 1957, which was the founding treaty, there have been a number of revisions and amendments and the Amsterdam Treaty agreement in 1997, consolidated at Nice in 2000, clarified the specific competences of the Union in the Social Policy field (see **Figure 4.6**).

However, the Charter of the Fundamental Rights of the Union which was proclaimed at the intergovernmental conference at Nice in 2000 may well be significant in extending individual rights within the Union. There has been considerable debate about the legal status of this Charter and in particular whether it does create legally enforceable individual rights.

Certainly the Commission and some member states have argued that individuals will be able to rely on the charter in cases where they

TITLE XI

SOCIAL POLICY, EDUCATION, VOCATIONAL TRAINING AND YOUTH

CHAPTER 1

SOCIAL PROVISIONS

Article 136

The Community and the Member States, having in mind fundamental social rights such as those set out in the European Social Charter signed at Turin on 18 October 1961 and in the 1989 Community Charter of the Fundamental Social Rights of Workers, shall have as their objectives the promotion of employment, improved living and working conditions, so as to make possible their harmonisation while the improvement is being maintained, proper social protection, dialogue between management and labour, the development of human resources with a view to lasting high employment and the combating of exclusion.

To this end the Community and the Member States shall implement measures which take account of the diverse forms of national practices, in particular in the field of contractual relations, and the need to maintain the competitiveness of the Community economy.

They believe that such a development will ensue not only from the functioning of the common market, which will favour the harmonisation of social systems, but also from the procedures provided for in this Treaty and from the approximation of provisions laid down by law, regulation or administrative action.

Article 137 (*)

1   With a view to achieving the objectives of Article 136, the Community shall support and complement the activities of the Member States in the following fields:
   (a)   improvement in particular of the working environment to protect workers' health and safety;
   (b)   working conditions;
   (c)   social security and social protection of workers;
   (d)   protection of workers where their employment contract is terminated;
   (e)   the information and consultation of workers;
   (f)   representation and collective defence of the interests of workers and employers, including co-determination, subject to paragraph 5;
   (g)   conditions of employment for third-country nationals legally residing in Community territory;
   (h)   the integration of persons excluded from the labour market, without prejudice to Article 150;
   (i)   equality between men and women with regard to labour market opportunities and treatment at work;
   (j)   the combating of social exclusion;
   (k)   the modernisation of social protection systems without prejudice to point (c).

Note:
The following paragraphs in this chapter detail that action in relation to paragraph 1(c), (d), (f) and (g) must be taken unanimously whereas action in relation to the other paragraphs can be taken using qualified Majority Voting and the Co-decision procedure.

Paragraph 5. of Article 137 further specifies that: 'The provisions of this article shall not apply to pay, the right of association, the right to strike or the right to impose lock-outs.'

Unanimity is also to apply to action taken under the new Article 13 of this Treaty which for the first time gave the Union competence to take action in respect of: appropriate action to combat discrimination based on sex, racial or ethnic origin, religion or belief, disability, age or sexual orientation.

Figure 4.6

The objectives and competence of the Union re Social Policy as per the Treaty agreed at Nice in 2000. This is often referred to as the Social Chapter.

feel that any of their individual rights within it are being challenged by EU laws or decisions by the EU institutions and indeed that the ECJ will draw inspiration from the Charter when confronted with difficult decisions as to whether Union law challenges fundamental human rights.

The 50 rights spelt out in the Charter are grouped into six headings: dignity, freedom, equality, solidarity, citizens' rights and justice.

Only some of the rights included in the Charter agreed in 2000 at Nice are relevant to the contents of this programme and they are included in **Figure 4.7**.

In this section we have reviewed the arguments for and against a social dimension to the EU, the impetus given it by the decision to create a single market embodied within The Single European Act, and the competences which have been agreed and incorporated within the various Treaty agreements and amendments. Most recently these competences have been restated within the Constitution for Europe agreed in 2004 and this incorporates The **Charter of Fundamental Rights** but at the time of writing this is subject to ratification at member state level. If the Constitution is eventually ratified, it is possible that the Charter will have a significant effect in extending individual legally enforceable rights, though the effect will vary according to the current position in individual member states. It is notable that some of the potentially more contentious rights have been qualified by reference to phrases such as: 'in accordance with Community law and national laws and practices'.

Main initiatives

Within the competence provided by the Treaties the EU has taken a number of legislative initiatives relevant to the subject matter of employee relations. It is not possible or necessary to examine all of these and in this section we concentrate upon those that have been taken to:

- enhance employee participation;
- provide employees with protection from being coerced into working very long hours; provide minimum rights in relation to breaks between spells of work and to ensure minimum holiday entitlements;
- ensure equality of treatment and in the case of the sexes equality of pay.

So far there has been relatively little intervention in or interference with the established procedures and processes of collective interaction and conflict resolution in individual member states and in many cases,

Figure 4.7

Charter of Fundamental Rights of the Union.

Article 5
Prohibition of slavery and forced labour
1. No one shall be held in slavery or servitude.
2. No one shall be required to perform **forced or compulsory labour.**
3. Trafficking in human beings is prohibited.

Article 12
Freedom of assembly and of association
1. Everyone has the **right to freedom of peaceful assembly and to freedom of association at all levels, in particular in political, trade union and civic matters, which implies the right of everyone to form and to join trade unions for the protection of his or her interests.**

Article 15
Freedom to choose an occupation and right to engage in work
1. Everyone has **the right to engage in work** and to pursue a freely chosen or accepted occupation.
2. Every citizen of the Union has the freedom to seek employment, to work, to exercise the right of establishment and to provide services in any Member State.
3. Nationals of third countries who are authorised to work in the territories of the Member States are entitled to working conditions equivalent to those of citizens of the Union.

Article 21
Non-discrimination
1. **Any discrimination based on any ground such as sex, race, colour, ethnic or social origin, genetic features, language, religion or belief, political or any other opinion, membership of a national minority, property, birth, disability, age or sexual orientation shall be prohibited.**
2. Within the scope of application of the Treaty establishing the European Community and of the Treaty on European Union, and without prejudice to the special provisions of those Treaties, any discrimination on grounds of nationality shall be prohibited.

Article 23
Equality between men and women
  Equality between men and women must be ensured in all areas, including employment, work and pay. The principle of equality shall not prevent the maintenance or adoption of measures providing for specific advantages in favour of the under-represented sex.

Article 27
Workers' right to information and consultation within the undertaking
  Workers or their representatives must, at the appropriate levels, be guaranteed information and consultation in good time in the cases and under the conditions provided for by Community law and national laws and practices.

Article 28
Right of collective bargaining and action
  Workers and employers, or their respective organisations, have, in accordance with Community law and national laws and practices, the right to negotiate and conclude collective agreements at the appropriate levels and, in cases of conflicts of interest, to take collective action to defend their interests, including strike action.

Article 29
Right of access to placement services
  Everyone has the right of access to a free placement service.

Article 30
Protection in the event of unjustified dismissal
  Every worker has the right to protection against unjustified dismissal, in accordance with Community law and national laws and practices.

Article 31
Fair and just working conditions
1. Every worker has the right to working conditions which respect his or her health, safety and dignity.
2. Every worker has the right to limitation of maximum working hours, to daily and weekly rest periods and to an annual period of paid leave.

Article 32
Prohibition of child labour and protection of young people at work
  The employment of children is prohibited. The minimum age of admission to employment may not be lower than the minimum school-leaving age, without prejudice to such rules as may be more favourable to young people and except for limited derogations.
  Young people admitted to work must have working conditions appropriate to their age and be protected against economic exploitation and any work likely to harm their safety, health or physical, mental, moral or social development or to interfere with their education.

Article 33
Family and professional life
1. The family shall enjoy legal, economic and social protection.
2. To reconcile family and professional life, everyone shall have the right to protection from dismissal for a reason connected with maternity and the right to paid maternity leave and to parental leave following the birth or adoption of a child.

Figure 4.7
(*Continued*)

as noted above the EU has taken initiatives which specify the objectives to be achieved but which also emphasize that these objectives should be achieved in a manner consistent with national laws and practices.

However, the area of employee participation is one in which it is arguable that some member states, perhaps particularly the UK, have been required to introduce rights for employees and their representatives and obligations upon employers which do impact traditional procedures and processes of collective interaction and conflict resolution. We have noted earlier in this chapter that there are different regulatory traditions and regimes in the various member states and it is arguable that Union initiatives in this area are associated with the values and beliefs that underpin the Roman–German model and notions of a stakeholding democracy.

Employee participation

There is a history stretching back to the 1970s of EU initiatives of various kinds designed to provide legislatively supportable rights for employees and their representatives to participate more in the activities and decision-making processes of their employing organization. In the main, these initiatives have been concerned to promote participation of a representative and downward communication/consultative nature, though some of the earlier initiatives were more ambitious but were not adopted.

Some initiatives have sought to encourage participation across a range of strategic and financial/business issues, whereas others have been targeted at particular issues and events such as providing employees with rights to information and consultation in circumstances such as the Transfer of Ownership of the employing undertaking or in the event of there being a need to introduce collective redundancies.

Commission initiatives can be seen as:

- An expression of the desire for and belief in a community founded on consensus and harmony underpinned by a belief in equity and democracy, participation rights providing a counter to the otherwise unfettered rights of capital.
- An expression of the belief that providing employees with the right to participate will, through the utilization of their knowledge, skill, problem-solving capacity and innovation, provide organizations and economies with the competitive advantage necessary.
- A contribution to the quality of working life.
- A means by which the increasing autonomy and influence of multinational companies might be countered or at the least mitigated.

So there are moral, political, social, economic and rational justifications for the initiatives taken and the policies proposed and the Commission believes that greater employee participation has the potential to deliver benefits for employees, employers, national economies and the economy and social fabric of the Union as a whole.

The views and intentions of the Commission, and it must be said that these are shared by many of the member states, can be detected from the Commission's 1997 consultative Green Paper *Partnership for a New Organization of Work*, which is concerned with issues of employee participation and involvement. The authors of this document argue the desirability of 'A new balance of regulatory powers between the State and the social partners, in particular in the areas connected with the internal management of firms'. and 'the need to review and strengthen the existing arrangements for workers' involvement in their companies'.

In recent years also the Commission and some of the member states have become more supportive of schemes designed to give employees a financial stake in the ownership and/or performance of their employing organization.

In the remainder of this section we concentrate upon initiatives in respect of information and consultation rights in respect of collective redundancies, transfers of undertakings, within Community-scale undertakings, at a national level and also with respect to encouraging employees' financial participation in their employing organization.

Collective redundancies

There have been three different Directives on this subject, the most recent being Council Directive 98/59/EC; earlier directives were numbers

75/129 and 92/56. The first two numbers indicate the year of adoption, so we can see that legislation on this issue dates back to 1975.

Here the motivations for the measure can be seen to have been several. The directive is a reflection of the moral imperative that employees have a right to be informed of and involved in decisions regarding their job security and standard of living. There is also the political dimension in that, if the labour movement's support for the concept of a single market was ever to be obtained, it was not going to be obtained in a legislative and economic context in which business can arbitrarily decide to close and relocate activities (possibly into another member state) thereby causing potentially large numbers of employees to be made redundant, without employees even having the legal right to be informed in advance. It is also a reflection of concerns that emerged as early as the 1970s about the activities of Multinationals and their ability to make decisions in one country that threaten the jobs and livelihood of employees in another country without informing and consulting with the employees to be affected and their representatives. By giving employees and their representatives a legal right to be consulted in advance, there is also the opportunity for alternatives to be considered and explored and the opportunity for the ingenuity, knowledge and skill of the workforce to be brought to bear on the problem.

For the purposes of the Directive, 'collective redundancies' means dismissals effected by an employer for one or more reasons not related to the individual workers concerned where, according to the choice of the member states, the number of redundancies is:

1. either, over a period of 30 days:
   - at least 10 in establishments normally employing more than 20 and less than 100 workers;
   - at least 10 per cent of the number of workers in establishments normally employing at least 100 but less than 300 workers;
   - at least 30 in establishments normally employing 300 workers or more;
2. or, over a period of 90 days, at least 20, whatever the number of workers normally employed in the establishments in question.

The directive(s) specify that workers representatives should be given in writing all relevant information including:

- the reasons for the projected redundancies;
- the number of categories of workers to be made redundant;
- the number and categories of workers normally employed;
- the period over which the projected redundancies are to be effected;

- the criteria proposed for the selection of the workers to be made redundant;
- the method for calculating any redundancy payments other than those arising out of national legislation and/or practice.

The consultation should take place before the redundancies take effect and should take place at the workplace where the redundancies are to occur even if the decision has been taken elsewhere, including in another member state, and the consultation should involve local management. The object of the consultation should be to **agree** on ways of avoiding or mitigating the number of redundancies and their consequences and companies are required to consult in good time to enable agreement to be reached.

The Directive does not define the term Worker Representative and this is left to be decided at national level in accordance with national traditions.

Despite the intentions of the Commission and Member States a number of issues have arisen over the years which apply to this and some other directives:

- How it is possible to ensure that the parties actually consult with a view to reaching agreement.
- How consultation at a local level with local management can significantly impact decisions made by a controlling undertaking in another part of the world.
- The effectiveness of sanctions that can be imposed upon organizations that do not comply with the requirements of the Directive. The nature of the judicial process inevitably means that such sanctions are likely to be determined long after the event and are likely to be of relatively little use to those employees who lost their jobs and livelihoods.

Also, and as noted earlier in **Chapter 3**, large MNCs can be very resistant to pressures from within particular regimes given that they may well be able to satisfy the requirements of that particular market from sources outside the jurisdiction of the government concerned and given that the movement of capital is relatively easy and MNCs can have a relatively powerful armoury of means of exerting pressure and wielding influence.

The transfers of undertakings

Here again there have been a number of Directives, the latest of which is Council Directive 2001/23/EC on the approximation of the laws of the Member States relating to the safeguarding of employees' rights in the event of transfers of undertakings, businesses or parts of undertakings or businesses.

This Directive has replaced earlier Directives in this area which were also known, perhaps more meaningfully, as the Acquired Rights Directives. The purpose of the Directive is primarily concerned with the protection of employees' rights and terms and conditions of employment on the sale or transfer of the undertaking or business that employs them. As the introduction to the Directive puts it:

> Economic trends are bringing in their wake, at both national and Community level, changes in the structure of undertakings, through transfers of undertakings, businesses or parts of undertakings or businesses to other employers as a result of legal transfers or mergers. It is necessary to provide for the protection of employees in the event of a change of employer, in particular, to ensure that their rights are safeguarded.

However, as part of the strategy for ensuring that these acquired rights are protected, the directive also provides employees of both the transferee and transferor and their representatives with rights to be both informed and consulted and that the consultation should be 'in good time' and again with the intention of reaching agreement.

They should be informed and consulted on:

- the date or proposed date of the transfer;
- the reasons for the transfer;
- the legal, economic and social implications of the transfer for the employees;
- any measures envisaged in relation to the employees.

The transferor must give such information to the representatives of his employees in good time, before the transfer is carried out.

The transferee must give such information to the representatives of his employees in good time, and in any event before his employees are directly affected by the transfer as regards their conditions of work and employment.

However, there is no obligation upon the entity acquiring the undertaking to have any contact at all with the employees employed by the undertaking being acquired prior to the acquisition.

In this instance, unlike the Directive(s) considered in the section above, employees are not excluded from the protection of the Directive solely because they are working part-time, or are employed on fixed-term or temporary contracts of employment and it is the intention of the Directive that pension and survivor benefits are protected as are terms and conditions of employment of those currently in employment and who are affected by the transfer.

The obligations imposed by the Directive are to apply irrespective of whether the decision resulting in the transfer is taken by the employer or an undertaking controlling the employer.

Over the years there have been numerous debates and court cases concerned to define 'undertaking' and in particular in the UK there were debates concerning the question of whether the earlier Directives applied to undertakings in the public sector, with successive UK governments arguing for many years in the 1980s and 1990s that they did not. These issues have now at least been partially resolved with and by the definition of scope in the Directive which states:

Article 1

(c) This Directive shall apply to public and private undertakings engaged in economic activities whether or not they are operating for gain. An administrative reorganisation of public administrative authorities, or the transfer of administrative functions between public administrative authorities, is not a transfer within the meaning of this Directive.

Where there are no representatives of the employees affected, and this is through no fault of their own, the employees themselves should be given the same information. Employers therefore are not able to circumvent the rights to information simply by virtue of there being no elected employee representatives as might for example be the case in undertakings where trades unions are not recognized for collective bargaining purposes and/or there are no union members.

THE UK

The original directives on Collective Redundancies and Transfers of Undertakings were implemented in the UK by a Labour government keen to help the unions in their battle with staff associations and in increasing their membership. The implementing legislation in the UK only made reference to information and consultation for recognized trade unions, not 'employee representatives' as in the directive. The failure of the legislation to refer to employee representatives meant that as trade union membership and recognition declined in the 1980s–1990s, (see **Chapter 7**) fewer employers had any legal obligation to inform and consult on these issues. As the EU authorities were made more and more aware of the deficiencies of the implementing legislation in the UK, pressure grew for the law in the UK to be amended. In June of 1994 the ECJ ruled that the requirements of the directives did apply to non-unionized workplaces, that the UK interpretation was incorrect and that non-unionized employees were being deprived by the UK implementing legislation.

The situation was remedied by the Collective Redundancy and Transfer of Undertakings (Amendment) Regulations 1995 (effective 1 March 1996).

The law in the UK now requires that UK employers:

- Choose whether to consult with a recognized and independent trade union or with elected representatives of the employees that are affected by the events in question.
- Give elected employee representatives similar rights and protections as would be enjoyed by the representatives of an independent recognized trade union.
- Consult 'in good time' and not at 'the earliest opportunity' as was the prior terminology.

However, these new regulations do not define 'elected representative' and do not appear to require employers to inform their employees that they are entitled to elect representatives for the purposes of this consultation.

The European Works Council Directive 94/45/EC

Originally this Directive, adopted in 1994, was not applicable in the UK because it was adopted using the procedures agreed at Maastricht in 1991 from which the UK had excluded themselves. However, after the election of a Labour government in 1997, the Directive was extended to the UK by Directive 97/74/EC.

It must be remembered that the Directive is aimed only at transnational or Community-scale undertakings and should be viewed as a response to Commission, labour movement and some member state concerns about the autonomy and power of the multinational to take decisions in one member state that affect employees in one or more other member states without the employees or their representatives being at all involved in the decision-making process.

The intention of the Directive is to ensure that all employees in the same Community-scale undertaking/group are both properly and equally informed and consulted about such decisions. The Directive was in part therefore a response to the increase in the number and scale of multinational activities and undertakings that accompanied and followed the creation of the single market, their ability to divert capital investment from one member state to another, and the absence of alternative employee representative arrangements and structures at corporate level.

The Directive applies to 'Community-Scale Undertakings' and for the purposes of the Directive 'Community-scale' has two labour force size dimensions. A Community-scale undertaking is one:

1   That employs at least 1000 employees in member states covered by the Directive.
2   Employs at least 150 in each of two such member states.

Both of these workforce size criteria have to be satisfied and the calculations are to be based on the average labour force over the preceding 2 years. This is a Directive that is consistent with the principle of subsidiarity (see earlier) since it is only at EU level that action could effectively be taken, although whether you think such action necessary is another issue.

The Directive applies to companies of any nationality. There is no requirement that the company/undertaking be domiciled in one of the member states, and once covered by the Directive, all of an undertaking's establishments within the member states should be covered by the one procedure.

While the Directive contains reference to a model EWC that may in certain circumstances be imposed within an undertaking, this was perceived to be an action of last resort and the Directive contains two Articles (6 and 13) which allow for the parties to agree voluntarily arrangements consistent with their own preferences and different national traditions and practices as long as certain minimum requirements are satisfied. Article 13 agreements refer to agreements made between the adoption and implementation of the Directive and Article 6 agreements are agreements reached voluntarily but after the implementation of the Directive.

The imposition of the mandatory model form of EWC may be the product of companies and employee representatives trying but failing to agree voluntary arrangements, or as the product of one party, likely to be the employer, refusing even to enter into such negotiations, or not taking the matter seriously.

The directive places the onus upon the employer to ensure that it is complied with. The model EWC that can be imposed in an organization clearly indicates what was in the mind of the legislators and the main points of what is referred to as the specified or mandatory model are summarized in **Figure 4.8**.

At the time of the Directive being adopted there was a great deal of debate about the likely consequences, with concerns being expressed by the various interested parties on a number of different dimensions:

- Trade unions felt that they might be damaged by it since there is no requirement that the unions be involved in the Works Council; they might be bypassed by employers encouraging employees not to include the union.
- Employers have argued that the directive is unnecessary, that it will be expensive to operate, be time consuming, damage efficiency and that, more importantly, there will be threats to their business secrets and thereby their competitiveness.
- Employees and trade unions had concerns that once again the requirement in the directive is only of an 'inform and consult'

The main points of the specified/mandatory model of an EWC are:

(i)   The EWC must have between 3 and 30 members.

(ii) The EWC should be comprised of employees of the undertaking or group elected or appointed by them and in accordance with the national legislation or practice.

(iii) The competence of the EWC should be limited to information and consultation on matters concerning the undertaking or group as a whole or at least establishments or undertakings in two different member states.

(iv) The composition of the EWC should include at least one member from each member state in which the undertaking or group has an establishment with the remaining membership determined on proportionate grounds.

(v)   Such an EWC is to be reviewed after 4 years and the parties may choose to allow it to continue or to negotiate an alternative.

(vi) The EWC has the right to an annual meeting with central management to be informed and consulted on the basis of a written report provided by management and concerned with the progress of the business of the Community Scale undertaking or ... group of undertakings and its prospects.

The **subject matter** of the meeting is then detailed as:

• the structure of the business;
• economic and financial situation;
• the probable development of the business and of production and sales;
• the situation and probable trend of employment;
• investments and substantial changes concerning organization;
• introduction of new working methods or production processes;
• transfers of production;
• mergers, cut backs or closures of undertakings, establishments or important parts thereof; and
• collective redundancies.

Figure 4.8
Mandatory model
of an EWC.

form rather than something approaching more genuine joint determination or co-decision (see **Chapter 9**).

■ Other union concerns were that the EWC employee representatives might become isolated both from their own national constituencies and from the wider labour movement and that they might lack the expertise to understand and be able to discuss and challenge the information given and the position adopted by management.

■ Another union concern was that the EWC might effectively be captured by management relying upon their expertise and power effectively to negate the challenge that the EWC might pose to managerial control.

In addition to these concerns, analysts and commentators have debated among themselves what the impact of the directive was likely to be upon employee relations in Europe. For example whether:

■ The directive would harm or hinder the Europeanization of employee relations, whether it would encourage the development of European-wide systems, both within each of the companies to which the directive applies and/or on a wider dimension between national systems.

- ■ The EWC would provide the base required for the trade unions to acquire knowledge and expertise from each other and would result in stronger cross-national links on the union side, thereby enhancing their ability to mobilize their resources effectively to combat the interests of capital.

- ■ The concept of the EWC would present Europe with a new model for the resolution of conflict and/or the achievement of partnership and would provide a template for the development of structures at a national level, and/or whether companies would be forced to comply at Euro level then begin to comply also at national level.

- ■ It would just be another means whereby an illusion of participation is created but without the autonomy of management being fundamentally challenged.

- ■ The directive would harm or hinder prospects for Euro-wide collective bargaining.

- ■ The directive would lead to the development of new formal and informal relationships between management and employees that would in themselves create a more favourable climate for the management of employee relations and the resolution of conflict.

The impact of the Directive

The most authoritative figures on the number of companies covered by the Directive and on the number of EWCs created are those compiled by the European Trade Union Institute (ETUI), which estimates that the number of companies falling within the scope of the EWCs Directive rose to 2169 in 2004, largely due to the enlargement of the EU in 2004. However, the number of companies in which EWCs were operating in 2004 was only roughly a third of this total at nearly 750.

For a number of years prior to 2004 the ETUC had been lobbying the Commission for amendments to the Directive to rectify what they saw as weaknesses in the original legislation, and in 2004 the Commission opened up consultations with the social partners about 'how best to ensure that the potential of EWCs to promote constructive and fruitful transnational social dialogue' can be 'fully realized', including the possible revision of the EWCs Directive. In the main the employers' organizations were reluctant to countenance further regulation and have consistently argued that improvements in the operation of the information and consultation requirements were best left to the parties to work out between themselves at company level.

The ETUC has identified a number of areas in which they would like to see amendments and enhanced rights and in some instances these reflect concerns expressed at the time the original legislation was adopted; these areas included:

- 'Improved definitions of information and consultation', reflecting the corresponding provisions in the more recent information and consultation Directive at national level, (see next section).
- The fact that the Directive should specify that information and consultation must take place in good time and before decisions are taken, and that EWCs should have the right to draw up their own proposals in time for them to be taken into account by management before decisions are taken.
- The guaranteed participation of representatives of the sectoral European trade union federations in both special negotiating bodies and EWCs.
- Their particular concerns about the implications of company restructuring, mergers and amalgamations, for both the role and shape of EWCs, and the need for a more closely specified procedure for renegotiating agreements in such circumstances.
- The ETUC's desire to see: a right to training for EWC members; a shorter period for EWC negotiations; stronger sanctions; measures to prevent abuses of confidentiality requirements; improved access to experts; guaranteed access for EWC members to company sites; and the right to preparatory and follow-up meetings of employee EWC members.

A substantial body of research evidence has now been accumulated on the impact of the Directive. The research undertaken tends to be a mix of examining data bases of EWC agreements and seeking to determine trends and a more detailed observation of the creation and functioning of the works councils in particular sectors or companies. The evidence is so far mixed. Hyman (2000) reviewed much of the evidence and noted that there were examples of managements not taking the EWC seriously and employee representatives not enhancing transnational cooperation but rather using the information and consultation obtained through participation in the EWC to fight national battles for investment and jobs within the organization. Alternatively, there are more optimistic scenarios in which, despite initial scepticism and lack of trust between employee representatives, this changed over time and the various employee representatives began to cooperate effectively to their mutual advantage. Hyman concluded that three points seem to deserve emphasis:

1   There is enormous diversity of experience rather than a standard model, there is evidence of some national and some sector specific influences.

2   The institutions are evolving; there is learning to be derived for all parties; some seem to be evolving and becoming stronger whereas others are not. Much more research needs to be undertaken to try and determine why some grow stronger and are successes and why others appear not to.

3   An EWC that develops internal cohesion and strategic vision can make an impact; again there is a need for much more research into the hows and whys of this.

More recently (2004) the European Industrial Relations Observatory (EIRO) has reviewed the research evidence and there is certainly evidence that at least some of the fears and criticisms of the Unions do appear to have been well founded. The picture is definitely a mixed one with both good and bad, however, there is evidence in many companies that information and consultation does take place only after the decision has been taken and that the consultation focuses on the implementation of those decisions, rather than upon the decision itself. There is also evidence that the practice of EWCs is largely confined to information provision, and in some instances, EWCs would appear not even to be informed, let alone consulted, about transnational management decisions. Other evidence suggests that in many companies there is little or no contact between employee representatives, or with management, between annual meetings.

However, there are examples of good practice and others have developed a more active and influential role involving, to varying degrees, ongoing contact and activity between employee representatives and regular liaison with management. Some EWCs have been able to exert a measure of influence over management decision making and even engage in the negotiation of agreements, evidence that may support the potential claimed at the outset that the EWC might lead to the creation of collective bargaining at a transnational level.

A study of EWCs in eight UK- and US-based companies Marginson *et al.*, (2004) found that the capacity of EWCs to influence the outcome of transnational management decision making was fundamentally conditioned by the nature of companies' business operations and the degree to which they are internationalized.

The impact of the EWC on management decision making was found to be greatest in single-business companies whose operations are spread across countries and where production and other activities are integrated across European borders. No EWC impact on management decision making was evident in multi-business companies whose operations tended to be concentrated in one country and/or where there was little or no cross-border integration of production.

Management structure and management attitude are also both important. How far EWCs are 'active' rather than 'symbolic' was facilitated or constrained by whether there was a European-level management structure which actually corresponded to the EWC. Where there was a close 'fit' there was a greater likelihood that the EWC would be able to influence management decisions. Similarly, where the attitude of management was positive towards the potential of the EWC input, there was a greater likelihood that the EWC would be able to influence decision making.

Judgements as to whether the Directive has been a success or failure inevitably depends upon your interest.

Trade union fears that they would be marginalized, do not appear to have been well founded. In the main, the agreements that have been reached have included the active involvement of trades unions and their officials, many providing for the active involvement of trades union officials as members of the EWC or with rights to attend and observe proceedings. However, there is much evidence to support their concern that the Directive would not result in genuine consultation prior to decisions being taken, that managements would provide information only, that consultation would be concerned with the implementation of decisions already taken and that management prerogative would not be seriously impaired. The picture with regard to whether EWCs have facilitated closer cooperation between employee representatives from different national regimes is inconclusive and there is evidence of national agendas and interests continuing to dominate.

On management's side there would appear to be little evidence of breaches of confidentiality but they continue to resist further regulation aimed at requiring more genuine consultation in good time so that the EWC can make informed and constructive contributions to the decision-making process. They continue to argue that decision making needs to be undertaken more quickly than would be allowed by such a requirement.

If we look at the numbers of EWCs created as a proportion of the total covered, then we might conclude that 10 years after the adoption of the Directive a rate of about a third is not indicative of success.

As for whether the EWC is contributing to the development of European wide collective bargaining within undertakings, there would be appear to be very little evidence to support the contention that it would. There will inevitably be instances where within the EWC a form of *ad hoc* bargaining may occur on particular issues but systematic developments in this direction seem unlikely in the short to medium term. The development of transnational or European-wide collective bargaining within individual MNCs has to overcome a number of obstacles, the first and possibly most significant of which is the general opposition or lack of interest of the management of the company; there is as yet little evidence to suggest that outside one or two sectors MNC employers/ managers have any interest at all in such a development. In fact, the tendency is for them to prefer a situation in which they can engage in concession and competitive bargaining with their separate workforces member state by member state. Another obstacle is the inability or lack of willingness of the trades unions from different member states to adopt an effective European dimension to their outlook. It still seems that the unions adopt a national perspective first and foremost, thereby facilitating the ability of the employer to engage in competitive bargaining, playing employees in one country off against those in another. Ultimately, the ability of the trades unions to exert pressure upon the management of the company depends upon their ability to organize effective employee action across the company.

Information and consultation at a national level

Directive 2002/14/ establishing a general framework for informing and consulting employees

As noted in the preceding section, subsequent to the Directive concerning the creation of EWCs, the EU has adopted legislation requiring similar arrangements to be established within employing organizations that are not community scale and which may only operate within a particular national context. This directive was adopted in 2002 and the effective date for implementation is 2005. We discuss the implementation of this directive within the UK in **Chapter 9**. We have also noted above that some of the amendments that the ETUC wish to see in the EWC directive are informed by specific aspects of this new directive, particularly regarding definitions of information and consultation, the requirement to inform and consult in good time, and indeed also the objectives of the information and consultation process.

The Directive applies, to:

    (a)   undertakings employing at least 50 employees in any one member state or

    (b)   establishments employing at least 20 employees in any one member state.

In this context 'undertaking' means a public or private undertaking carrying out an economic activity, whether or not operating for gain and 'establishment' means a unit of business where an economic activity is carried out on an ongoing basis with human and material resources. However, the legislation provides for transitional provisions to be adopted by member states allowing them to phase in the requirements (something the UK government has taken advantage of) over a period of time.

The transitional provisions allow a member state may limit the application of the national provisions to:

    (a)   undertakings employing at least 150 employees or establishments employing at least 100 employees until 23 March 2007;

    (b)   undertakings employing at least 100 employees or establishments employing at least 50 employees during the year following the date above.

In effect member states have the opportunity to delay the application of the Directive to undertakings of 50 and establishments of 20 until after March 2008.

The perceived advantages, to the employees, the employing organization and to society, of informing and consulting employees and their representatives are stated in the purposes of the directive as being to enhance:

- mutual trust
- risk anticipation
- flexibility of work organization
- identification of training needs
- employee awareness of the need for change
- employment and employability
- employee involvement
- increased competitiveness.

The definitions of information and consultation incorporated within this Directive are more specific than in the EWC directive and meet some of the criticisms made of that Directive.

For the purposes of this Directive:

> *Information* means transmission by the employer to the employees' representatives of data in order to enable them to acquaint themselves with the subject matter and to examine it; information shall be given at such time, in such fashion and with such content as are appropriate to enable, in particular, employees' representatives to conduct an adequate study and, where necessary, prepare for consultation.
>
> *Consultation* means the exchange of views and establishment of dialogue between the employees' representatives and the employer and the Directive further specifies that consultation shall take place:

(a) ensuring that the timing, method and content are appropriate;

(b) at the relevant level of management depending on the subject;

(c) on the basis of information supplied by the employer and the opinion which the employees' representatives are entitled to formulate;

(d) in such a way as to enable employees' representatives to meet the employer and obtain a response, and the reasons for that response, to any opinion they might formulate;

(e) with a view to reaching an agreement on decisions likely to lead to substantial changes in work organization or in contractual relations.

Of these the last is perhaps the most interesting and implies that, with respect to decisions that might lead to substantial changes to work organization or in contractual relations, the process is intended to result in co-decision or joint decision making. Clearly there is considerable scope for different interpretations of this particular stipulation and it seems that the requirement stops short of providing employees with a right to co-decision or of veto; the requirement is not that agreement is reached but that the parties enter into the process with the intention of reaching agreement. Presumably if agreement is not reached, the employer would still be able to proceed as long as the other requirements have also been met. Presumably also it will not always be easy to ascertain with certainty whether a particular party did genuinely intend to reach agreement and it is not difficult to envisage disagreements between the parties on this issue.

This particular category of subject matter is one of three specified in the Directive which states that:

Information and consultation shall cover:

(a)   Information on the recent and probable development of activities and economic situation note it is information only in respect of this subject matter.

(b)   Information and consultation on the situation, structure and probable development of employment and on any anticipatory measures envisaged, in particular where there is a threat to employment.

(c)   Information and consultation on decisions likely to lead to substantial changes in work organization or in contractual relations (this is the only category to which the requirement referred to above to inform and consult with a view to reaching agreement applies).

In the context of this Directive the term employees representatives is to be determined according to national laws and practices, in other words no particular definition is being imposed, and clearly whether these are trades union representatives will depend on both national arrangements and circumstances within particular undertakings.

Other significant components of the Directive provide some protections for employers regarding the disclosure of sensitive information and the Directive provides employers with the right to not inform and consult where this would seriously damage the undertaking.

The Directive does not specify any particular mechanism for the achievement of the necessary information and consultation but it does also specify that both employer and the employees' representatives should work in a spirit of cooperation taking into account the interests both of the undertaking or establishment and of the employees.

Clearly the directive will have different implications for member states dependent upon whether national laws and practices already require some form of information and consultation within undertakings. Member states such as the UK where there have been no such general requirements are likely to find the Directive more of a challenge than others.

Council Directive 2001/86/EC supplementing the Statute for a European Company with regard to the involvement of employees

The Statute for the European Company, an idea that can be traced back to the mid 1970s, will make it possible for a company to be set up within the territory of the Community in the form of a public limited-liability company, with the Latin name 'Societas Europaea' (SE).

The rules relating to employee involvement in the SE are the subject of the Directive whose provisions seek to ensure that in all cases of such a company being created there should be procedures established for the information and consultation of workers at transnational level. As with the EWC Directive, and given the diversity of practice and tradition within the member states, the emphasis is upon the parties themselves agreeing these procedures but there is a fall back position and this is incorporated in an Annexe to the Directive.

There was concern that the creation of an SE should not provide the opportunity for the disappearance or reduction of practices of employee involvement existing within the companies participating in the establishment of an SE. When rights to participate exist within one or more of the companies establishing an SE, those rights will be preserved through their transfer to the SE unless the parties involved decide otherwise within a Special Negotiating Body, which brings together the employees' representatives of all companies concerned.

The requirements of the EWC Directive are in general not to apply to SEs once created, though where there is a failure to agree between the parties on the transnational arrangements for information and consultation in the SE they may continue to apply.

The Directive also seeks to protect the confidentiality of information given to and acquired by employee representatives and to enable the participation in agreeing the new arrangements of trade union officials as well as employees of the companies concerned. Employee representative participating in the arrangements within an SE should also be afforded protection against discrimination and the application of sanctions by the company including dismissal.

The Directive in Article 2 incorporates some interesting definitions of the terms involvement, information, consultation and participation:

(h)   'involvement of employees' means any mechanism, including information, consultation and participation, through which employees' representatives may exercise an influence on decisions to be taken within the company;

(i)   'information' means the informing of the body representative of the employees ... in a manner and with a content which allows the employees' representatives to undertake an in-depth assessment of the possible impact and, where appropriate, prepare consultations with the competent organ of the SE;

(j)   'consultation' means the establishment of dialogue and exchange of views between the body representative of the employees and/or the employees' representatives and the competent organ of the SE, at a time, in a manner and with a content which allows the employees' representatives, on the basis of information provided, to express an opinion on measures envisaged by the competent organ which may be taken into account in the decision-making process within the SE;

(k)   'participation' means the influence of the body representative of the employees and/or the employees' representatives in the affairs of a company by way of:
  – the right to elect or appoint some of the members of the company's supervisory or administrative organ, or
  – the right to recommend and/or oppose the appointment of some or all of the members of the company's supervisory or administrative organ.

The use of the term involvement as the generic and participation to refer only to a form of influence exerted at board level seems odd to say the least and is inconsistent with pretty well all of the literature on employee participation which would generally include consultation, works councils, collective bargaining and a wide range of direct mechanisms as means through which employee participation can be achieved.

Part 2 of the annexe or standard rules, which might be imposed upon companies in certain circumstances such as when the parties are unable to agree on appropriate arrangements, give an indication of the areas of subject matter that employee representatives should be informed and consulted on:

'the representative body shall have the right to be informed and consulted and, for that purpose, to meet with the competent organ of the SE at least once a year, on the basis of regular reports drawn up by the competent organ, on the progress of the business of the SE and its prospects.

The meeting shall relate in particular to the structure, economic and financial situation, the probable development of the business and of production and sales, the situation and probable trend of employment, investments, and substantial changes concerning organization, introduction of new working methods or production processes, transfers of production, mergers, cut-backs or closures of undertakings, establishments or important parts thereof, and collective redundancies.

(c)   Where there are exceptional circumstances affecting the employees' interests to a considerable extent, particularly in the event of relocations, transfers, the closure of establishments or undertakings or collective redundancies, the representative body shall have the right to be informed.

Financial participation

The Commission has sought to encourage the development of both profit and equity sharing arrangements. In 1992 the Council adopted a non-binding Recommendation 92/443 on Equity Sharing and Financial Participation, which encourages member states themselves to promote such schemes via the creation of sympathetic legal and fiscal environments and regimes, and provides advice on the issues and criteria that those seeking to encourage and introduce such arrangements should consider. More recently, the Commission has sought to relaunch the debate on encouraging such schemes with the publication in July 2001 of a staff working paper in which they identify the agenda as:

- identifying the general principles underpinning national policies;
- addressing the transnational barriers; these relate essentially to tax, the social and cultural environment, and (differing) social security contributions;
- establishing a series of Community measures to improve understanding of the different financial participation systems.

In the main, the attraction of these schemes is in the belief, supported by some evidence, that there is an association between employee financial participation and increases in productivity. The Commission in its recent working paper confirms that: 'worker participation in company profits is associated with higher productivity levels in every case, regardless of methods, model specification and data used. The development of financial participation schemes is strongly influenced by government action, particularly when tax incentives are made available.' Recent governments in the UK have supported these schemes and provided a favourable tax regime to encourage their take-up.

The Organization of working time

Directives on the Adaptation of Working Time, 93/104, 2000/34 and 2003/88

The original Directive was adopted in 1993 and the most recent Directive consolidates the two earlier Directives into one.

The Directives have been adopted as being predominantly concerned with the protection of workers' health and safety and have therefore been adopted by QMV. The UK challenged the adoption of the original Directive as a health and safety issue but the challenge was rejected by the ECJ. A range of occupations was originally exempted from the Directive, but these have now all been brought within the remit of the Directive by Directive 2000/34. The UK government was also instrumental in securing a degree of flexibility within the Directive allowing for the voluntary variation of the maximum hours provisions either by collective bargaining or by individual agreement.

Briefly, the Directive's key provisions are as follows:

- *Rest period*: Workers are entitled to a minimum daily rest period of 11 consecutive hours per 24-hour period.
- *Breaks*: Every worker is entitled to a rest break where the working day is longer than 6 hours.
- *Weekly rest period*: An uninterrupted rest period of 24 hours is required for each 7-day period, plus the 11 hours daily rest referred to above.
- *Maximum weekly working time*: The average working time for each 7-day period, including overtime, must not exceed 48 hours. For the calculation of the average the Directive allows a reference period of 4 months, from which periods of annual leave and sick leave have to be excluded. However, workers are able to agree to 'opt out' of the maximum weekly working time. The UK is the only member state currently making general use of this possibility.
- *Four weeks' paid annual leave*: Workers are entitled to paid annual leave of at least 4 weeks and the replacement of the leave by an allowance in lieu is prohibited.
- *Night work*: The normal hours of work for night workers should not exceed an average of 8 hours in any 24-hour period. The notion of 'normal hours of work' includes overtime. Other important provisions on night work relate to a free health assessment for night workers, the transfer from night work to day work in certain circumstances and notification by employers of the use of night workers.

The feeling in the UK at the time that the Directive eventually became applicable, October 1998, was that the greatest benefit to employees would be in the area of annual paid holiday entitlement. The UK Labour Force Survey 1996 estimated that there were as many as 2.7 million full-time workers with less than 4 weeks' holiday entitlement per year, with 1.8 million entitled to less than 3 weeks.

Over the years since the Directive was adopted a number of issues have arisen including difficulties concerning the appropriate treatment of on-call hours and the implementation in the UK of the rules regarding the individual opt out allied to the need to keep adequate records of individuals' working time. At the time of writing the Commission had issued proposals for amendments to the Directive that would distinguish between active and inactive on-call hours and they had also expressed concerns regarding the widespread practice in the UK of employers getting employees to sign an opt out clause or agreement as part of their contract of employment. The concerns were primarily about the extent to which employees could genuinely be said to be exercising freedom of choice, one of the safeguards in the Directive, in agreeing to an opt out if they are being required to sign at the time that they are offered employment. There is evidence that the number of people in the UK who have agreed to opt out is considerably greater than the number who regularly work above the 48-hour threshold, again raising concerns that employers are requiring employees to agree to an opt out as standard practice and not on a genuine as needed basis. There are a number of common reasons why the opt out is used; it is because:

- people habitually work more than 48 hours and want to continue to be able to do so;
- the reference period for calculating the 48-hour week does not make it possible to respond to the flexibility needs of undertakings, and it can be extended to 1 year only by collective agreement;
- it minimizes administrative constraints.

Long hours working in the UK

The EIRO reports that approximately 4 million people, or 16 per cent of the UK workforce, currently work more than 48 hours per week, compared with 3.3 million (or 15 per cent) at the beginning of the 1990s and the UK was the only Member State where weekly working time had increased over the decade preceding 2003. The number of people working over 55 hours per week had increased to 1.5 million. Among those declaring that they work more than 48 hours, 65 per cent say that they work over 50 hours, 54 per cent over 52 hours and 38 per cent over 55 hours.

However, the EIRO reports that in a document sent to the Commission in April 2003 by the UK government, the percentage of people stating that they habitually work more than 48 hours had been constantly falling since 1999, albeit slowly, although the trend in the preceding period was upwards below. The coincidence of this decline with the

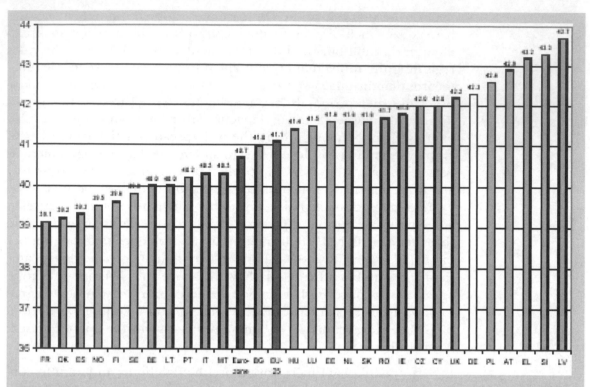

Figure 4.9
Number of hours actually worked per week for full-time employed people, EU-25 (*Source*: Eurostat, LFS).

implementation of the Directive in the UK in late 1998 has led some observers to the tentative conclusion that it was the Directive that was responsible for the decline.

The 2004 WERS found that 11 per cent of employees (not only full-time employees as in **Figure 4.9** above) usually worked more than 48 hours a week. Working long hours was less common amongst women than men, even when only full-time workers were considered.

The survey also found that 54 per cent of employees had not worked in excess of 48 hours a week over the previous year and 10 per cent of employees had worked more than 48 hours a week every week over the previous 12 months. Employees tended to work more than 48 hours a week with greater frequency in the private sector, and in workplaces without a recognized union.

It is also worth remembering that the WIB2000S found that there was significant dissatisfaction with the number of hours that employees had to work (see **Chapter 2**).

Comparisons of working time within the EU, see **Figure 4.9** show that at the end of 2004 the UK average at 42.3 hours per week for full-time employees is higher than the EU average but is by no means the highest.

The source of the details in this section is 'Working time – developments in EU and national regulation' produced by the EIRO in 2004.

There are different views concerning the desirability of long hours working and the need for regulation. Employers and their representative organizations may well be in favour of long hours working as a means of enhancing output and service provision at what, in the short term at least, might seem to be least cost, especially if the additional hours are worked without extra pay as is the case with many professions and higher skilled white collar and knowledge workers. They are also likely to argue that there are individual freedoms and preferences at stake and that, in order to be able to compete in the international market place with companies located in countries where there is no such regulation, they need the flexibility of long hours working as and when it is required. We certainly cannot assume that all long hours working is the product of coercion by the employer; working long hours may well be the expression of individual preferences.

However, against this must be set the effects of long hours working on health, safety, the commission of errors, the incidence of accidents and, over time, there will be cumulative effects of tiredness upon both quality and quantity of performance.

In addition there are significant adverse consequences of long hours working upon the quality of life and, in particular, upon the reconciliation of work and family life. The social consequences of long hours working can be significant with largely still unknown effects upon marriage and the care and upbringing of children and their behaviour.

Those in favour of regulation and the imposition of limits upon long hours working tend to use all the above consequences as arguments in their favour. Additionally in parts of the EU, France in particular, there is a belief that in limiting the hours worked by each individual you create the potential for the creation of more jobs and the employment of more people, unfortunately an argument for which there is relatively little statistical support. We have also noted in **Chapter 2** that rigidity in external labour markets may well act as a catalyst encouraging the pursuit of innovation and flexibility in the internal labour market. Arguments in favour of regulation are also likely to emphasize the dependence and market weakness of the individual, reflected somewhat in the concerns about the way the opt out is being used in the UK (see above), a weakness that has been heightened by the decline of trades union membership and the influence and incidence of collective bargaining.

Equality

The promotion of equality and the prevention of discrimination have long been objectives of the EU. Since the original Treaty of Rome in 1957 the Union has had the competence to act in the area of equal pay between the sexes and, subsequently, it was decided that the Union also had an implied competence in the area of equality of treatment between the sexes on the grounds that this constituted a fundamental human right. Directives were adopted on the subjects of equality of pay and treatment between the sexes in the mid 1970s, Equal Pay in 1975 (75/117) and Equal Treatment in 1976 (76/207). However, it was not until 1997 with agreement on the Amsterdam treaty, see earlier, that the Union assumed competence to take action in a range of other areas or grounds upon which discrimination may occur. The new Article 13 agreed at Amsterdam has been a significant milestone in the development of EU legislation to combat discrimination and three Article 13 Directives have been adopted:

1   Council Directive 2000/43/EC implementing the principle of equal treatment between persons irrespective of racial or ethnic origin, known as the *Racial Equality Directive.*
2   Council Directive 2000/78/EC establishing a general framework for equal treatment in employment and occupation on the grounds of religion or belief, disability, age or sexual orientation, known as the *Employment Equality Directive*
3   Directive 2002/73/EC of the European Parliament and of the Council amending Council Directive 76/207/EEC on the implementation of the principle of equal treatment for men and women as regards access to employment, vocational training and promotion, and working conditions also known as the *Gender Equality Directive.*

Before looking at these Directives in any detail it is worth pointing out that in the area of sex equality, and after 30 years of legislative intervention, there are still significant gender gaps in terms of pay and participation in the labour force. We examine labour force participation in **Chapter 6** where we also examine some of the main causes of gender inequality in employment. As for pay, the gap varies according to sector and type of occupation as well as between countries.

The overall picture is presented in a Commission report early in 2004 entitled 'Gender equality: slow progress in closing gender gap hampering EU competitiveness' the Commission reports that:

Progress has been made in the EU on narrowing the gender gap, but remains slow ... significant gender gaps remain, especially in the labour market. Failure to address this could hamper the EU's attempt to reach the targets set at the Lisbon Council in 2000, such as reaching a 60% employment rate for women in the EU by 2010.

Women's employment rate is rising, having leaped from less than 50 in the early 1990s to 55.6% now ... In paid labour, a 17.2 gap exists between men and women's employment rates in the EU15 (72.8% and 55.6% respectively in 2002). The unemployment gender gap is 1.8%. Women remain the majority of those working part-time, with some 34% of women employees working part-time in the EU15 (men account for just 7%).

Once in a post, women can expect to earn less than their male counterparts. The gender pay gap is 16% in the EU. Women are also 3% more likely to fall into poverty than men. The gender pay gap may also act as a disincentive for women to enter the labour market, depriving it of their human capital.

In education, women represent 55% of graduates throughout the EU and outnumber men in secondary and tertiary education. Consequently, more women are taking up managerial and professional posts. Progress has also been made in gender mainstreaming in certain policy areas, especially research, external relations and development cooperation.

But more effort is needed to address the remaining inequalities.

More attention also needs to be paid to making the care of children a shared duty between men and women. While some progress has been made in working towards the childcare targets set out at the Barcelona summit in 2003 (providing childcare for 90% of children between 3 years old and mandatory school age by 2010), focus still needs to be given to reconciling family and work life.

Labour market gaps persist despite women's advances in education. Choices of subjects remain gender stereotyped, with women accounting for just 21% of those graduating in engineering, building and construction and only 20.6% of engineering, manufacturing or construction PhDs.

In the key area of decision making, women still lag significantly behind men. Just 25.4% of parliamentary seats in the EU are occupied by women. They also account for just 30% of managerial positions.

The picture is one of gradual and slow improvement with a great deal to be done if equality of pay and treatment is to be achieved.

Updated statistics at the end of 2004 demonstrate the continuing and gradual improvement with the EU 15 employment rates for men and women being 72.8 per cent and 57.2 per cent respectively bringing the gender gap down to 15.6 per cent.

Article 13 Directives

In its 2004 Report on equality and Non-discrimination the Commission summarizes the main points of the Racial Equality and Employment Equality Directives (see **Figure 4.10**).

It is worth pointing out that both Directives include pay as an area of treatment where discrimination on one of the grounds concerned is unlawful. In addition, both Directives provide for some areas of exception and where it might be permissible to discriminate lawfully as well as preserving the right for positive action in accordance with the principle enunciated in Article 141(4) of the treaty agreed at Amsterdam (see later section on positive action).

Main features of the Racial Equality and Employment Equality Directives
The Directives are intended to establish a minimum level of legal protection against discrimination throughout the European Union. It is open to national governments to introduce more favourable provisions but they cannot reduce the level of protection if this is already higher than the minimum required.

SCOPE
The Directives cover everyone living or working in the EU. The Directives outlaw discrimination on grounds of racial or ethnic origin and on grounds of religion and belief, disability, age and sexual orientation, in respect of:

- access to employment and self-employment as well as to opportunities for promotion
- access to vocational guidance and training at all levels as well as work experience
- employment and working conditions, including dismissals and pay
- membership of trade unions and professional bodies and access to any benefits they provide

The Racial Equality Directive further prohibits discrimination in respect of:

- social security and health care
- social advantages, such as free prescriptions, housing benefits and concessions of various kinds
- education
- access to goods and services available to the public, including housing

FORMS OF DISCRIMINATION
The Directives outlaw the following forms of discrimination:

- **direct discrimination,** which arises where a person is treated less favourably than another is, has been or would be treated on any of the grounds covered by the Directives;
- **indirect discrimination,** which arises where an apparently neutral provision, criterion or practice, whether intentionally or not, puts people of a particular racial or ethnic origin, religion or belief, disability, age or sexual orientation at a particular disadvantage compared with others. If it has this effect, the provision, criterion or practice will constitute discrimination unless it is objectively justified by a legitimate aim and the means of achieving that aim are appropriate and necessary;
- **harassment,** which arises when unwanted conduct related to any of the grounds covered by the Directives takes place with the purpose or effect of violating the dignity of a person and of creating an intimidating, hostile, degrading, humiliating or offensive environment.

The Directives also ban instructions to discriminate and victimization (or retaliation against those complaining about or giving evidence of discrimination).

REMEDIES AND SANCTIONS
Victims of discrimination should have access to administrative or judicial procedures, including conciliation where appropriate, to enforce their right to equal treatment. Bodies with a legitimate interest in ensuring that the provisions of the Directives are complied with (such as trade unions or representative organizations) must be given the right to support victims of discrimination in any proceedings. Those responsible for discrimination should face sanctions which are effective, proportionate and dissuasive (in the sense of deterring discriminatory behaviour).

BURDEN OF PROOF
Once someone who considers that they have not been treated equally establishes facts from which it may be presumed that discrimination has occurred, it is then for the person accused of discrimination to prove that there has been no breach of the principle of equal treatment.

EQUALITY BODY
The Racial Equality Directive requires a specialized body to be designated in each Member State to promote equal treatment in relation to race or ethnic origin. These bodies must provide independent assistance to victims of discrimination to pursue their complaints, conduct independent surveys, publish independent reports and make recommendations.

Figure 4.10
The main features of the Racial Equality and Employment Equality Directives.

ACCOMMODATING PEOPLE WITH DISABILITIES
Employers are required to take appropriate measures, where necessary, to enable a person with a disability to have access to, participate or advance in employment, or to undergo training, unless such measures impose a disproportionate burden on the employer.

DISSEMINATION OF INFORMATION
Governments have an obligation to make people aware, by all appropriate means, of the provisions of the legislation and the right which they have to be treated equally as a result.

Figure 4.10
(*Continued*)

Genuine occupational requirements and other exceptions

The Directives allow member states to provide for discrimination to be lawful in a number of circumstances which include grounds related to a genuine occupational requirement or qualification. Treatment based on a characteristic covered by the Directives shall not constitute discrimination where, by reason of the nature of the particular occupational activities concerned or of the context in which they are carried out, such a characteristic constitutes a genuine and determining occupational requirement, provided that the objective is legitimate and the requirement is proportionate.

The Employment Equality Directive allows for lawful differences of treatment on a number of the specific grounds covered by the Directive, specifically on grounds of age, religion and disability. So that, for example in the case of occupational activities, it will remain lawful for churches to treat people differently on the grounds of their religion where by reason of the nature of these activities, or of the context in which they are carried out, a person's religion or belief constitutes a genuine, legitimate and justified occupational requirement.

In the case of age the member states may provide that differences of treatment on grounds of age shall not constitute discrimination in certain specific circumstances such as:

- the setting of special conditions on access to employment and vocational training; employment and occupation, including dismissal and remuneration conditions;
- for young people and older workers in order to promote their vocational integration or ensure their protection.

Interestingly, there is also provision for member states to allow for the fixing of a maximum age for recruitment which is based on the training requirements of the post in question or the need for a reasonable period of employment before retirement. Member states may also provide that the fixing of ages for admission to occupational social security schemes or for entitlement to retirement or invalidity benefits is lawful, provided this does not result in discrimination on the grounds of sex.

The Directive is without prejudice to national provisions laying down retirement ages.

With respect to disability, the Directive points out that the provision of measures to accommodate the needs of disabled people at the workplace plays an important role in combating discrimination on grounds of disability, for example adapting premises and equipment, patterns of working time, the distribution of tasks or the provision of training. However, without prejudice to the obligation to provide reasonable accommodation for people with disabilities, the Directive is careful to specify that it does not require the recruitment, promotion, maintenance in employment or training of an individual who is not competent, capable and available to perform the essential functions of the post concerned or to undergo the relevant training or integration of resources. The Directive acknowledges that the measures necessary to accommodate the needs of disabled people may impose a disproportionate burden in which case they may be excused; however, the Directive stipulates that in determining whether the measures in question give rise to a disproportionate burden, account should be taken in particular of the financial and other costs entailed, the scale and financial resources of the organization or undertaking and the possibility of obtaining public funding or any other assistance.

Positive action

This particular issue achieved an unwelcome notoriety as a result of an ECJ decision in 1995 in the Kalanke case. One of the regional governments in Germany was pursuing a recruitment, selection and promotion policy that gave automatic priority to women who, it was felt, were underrepresented. Automatic preference was given to women as long as they had the same qualifications as any men also competing for the job. The ECJ found that rules and procedures which give one sex **absolute** and **unconditional** priority goes beyond promoting equal treatment or opportunities and oversteps the lawful provisions for positive action. The ECJ found that to **guarantee** women priority went too far.

Concern over this judgement led the member states to incorporate into the treaty agreed at Amsterdam in 1997 a new **Article 141(4)** which states:

'With a view to ensuring full equality in practice between men and women in working life, the principle of equal treatment shall not prevent any member state from maintaining or adopting measures providing for specific advantages in order to make it easier for the *underrepresented sex* to pursue a vocational activity or to prevent or compensate for disadvantages in professional careers.'

It seems therefore that positive action giving one sex **absolute** and **unconditional** priority is unlawful but, as long as the positive action consists of measures such as targets in terms of quotas and time limits, which express a preference but which also allow for exception, then it should remain lawful.

Gender Equality Directive

This Directive amends the earlier Directive on Equal Treatment (76/207).

The 1976 Directive introduced the overarching principle that equal treatment means that there should be no discrimination whatsoever on the grounds of sex either directly or indirectly by reference in particular to marital or family status.

The Directive specifically applied to:

- the conditions, including selection criteria, for access to all jobs or posts at all levels of the hierarchy;
- access to all types and all levels of vocational guidance, basic and advanced vocational training and retraining;
- working conditions, including conditions governing dismissal; men and women should be guaranteed the same conditions.

Exceptions were allowed for occupational activities for which the sex of the worker constitutes a determining factor.

There was also provision for positive action (for women only) in respect of measures to remove existing inequalities which affect women's opportunities in the areas covered by the Directive.

Employees were also granted some protection against victimization and specifically against dismissal by the employer as a reaction to a complaint by individuals seeking to enforce their rights under the terms of the Directive.

Over the years following the Directive, many issues arose and the ECJ was active in interpreting the law in respect of many areas of doubt and made decisions which in some instances led to the adoption of additional legislation such as the Directive concerning the rights of part-time workers (see below).

Amendments introduced by the 2002 Directive

The amended version of the Directive gives a definition of sexual harassment, which the Directive determines to be a form of discrimination and therefore unlawful, and which is taken to mean a situation:

> where any form of unwanted verbal, non-verbal or physical conduct of a sexual nature occurs, with the purpose or effect of violating the dignity

of a person, in particular when creating an intimidating, hostile, degrading, humiliating or offensive environment.

Additionally, employers are encouraged to take preventive measures against sexual harassment and to provide employees with appropriate information on equal treatment for women and men in the workplace.

The new Directive makes it clear that a woman on maternity leave must be given protection and will be entitled, after her period of leave, to return to her job or to an equivalent post on terms and conditions which are no less favourable, and to benefit from any improvement in working conditions to which she would have been entitled during her absence.

The Directive also brings a number of definitions and interpretations into line with those in the two earlier Article 13 Directives. These include:

- harassment;
- positive action (as per Article 14194) of the Amsterdam treaty;
- the exception in respect of genuine occupational requirements;
- the definitions of direct and indirect discrimination;
- pay is included as an area of treatment covered by the Directive.

In addition to the original Directive on Equal Treatment and these new Article 13 Directives, there have been a number of Directives adopted to deal with particular issues related to equal treatment between the sexes. These include the following.

Council Directive 97/81/EC concerning the Framework Agreement on Part-Time Work concluded by UNICE, CEEP and the ETUC

The reason why this is treated as an equality between the sexes directive relates to a number of decisions by the ECJ which determined that, because the vast majority of part-time workers were women, to discriminate against part-time workers in terms of rights to redundancy payments, rights to join an occupational pension scheme and rights to claim unfair dismissal was indirect sex discrimination.

The main provisions of the Directive 97/81 on equality for part-time workers are that:

- those with an employment contract or relationship for less than normal hours compared with a full-time worker should be entitled to equality of treatment on a pro-rata basis;
- employees should not be discriminated against solely on the grounds that they work part-time rather than full-time.

In addition to enhancing the equality of treatment of part-time workers, this Directive is also concerned to facilitate the development of part-time work.

*Council Directive 1999/70/EC concerning the Framework Agreement
on fixed-term work concluded by ETUC, UNICE and CEEP*

In this instance fixed term is defined as:

'fixed-term worker' means a person having an employment contract or
relationship entered into directly between an employer and a worker
where the end of the employment contract or relationship is determined by objective conditions such as reaching a specific date, completing a specific task, or the occurrence of a specific event.

The main purpose of the directive is to ensure that:

In respect of employment conditions, fixed-term workers shall not be
treated in a less favourable manner than comparable permanent workers solely because they have a fixed-term contract or relation unless different treatment is justified on objective grounds.

Specific mention is made in the Directive to both opportunities to
be informed of and apply for permanent positions as they arise and of
access to training opportunities.

Directive on Parental Leave (96/34)

The main provisions are:

- that both parents should be entitled to three months' unpaid
  leave after the birth or adoption of a child, the leave to be
  taken before the eighth birthday of the child;
- protection from dismissal for asking for parental leave;
- protection of the right to return to work after the leave;
- provision for additional time off in urgent family circumstances such as sickness and accident.

In the case of these framework agreements and directives, many of the
details were deliberately left for determination at national level.

Equal Pay

The new Article 13 directives all include pay as one of the aspects of
employment on which discrimination is unlawful. However, as noted earlier a Directive on Equal Pay between the sexes was adopted first in 1975
(75/117), competence for this Directive being based on the original treaty.

The relevant article is now Article 141 (ex Article 119) of the EC
Treaty which states:

1 Each member state shall ensure that the principle of equal
   pay for male and female workers for equal work or work of equal
   value is applied.

2   For the purpose of this Article, 'pay' means the ordinary basic or minimum wage or salary and any other consideration, whether in cash or in kind, which the worker receives directly or indirectly, in respect of his employment, from his employer.

Equal pay without discrimination based on sex means:

(a)   that pay for the same work at piece rates shall be calculated on the basis of the same unit of measurement;

(b)   that pay for work at time rates shall be the same for the same job.

The original Article 119 failed to define equal work adequately, and the Directive adopted in 1975 sought to deal with issues of equal work and work of equal value, though it must be said that it did not achieve much success on this front and once again the ECJ have had a significant role to play in seeking to define and deal with these and associated issues satisfactorily.

There are several difficulties associated with the concept of value. First, the criterion of value to be used has to be decided, and this can itself concentrate upon either inputs or outputs. For example, the criterion could be:

- the effort, skill and responsibility put into the work;
- the content of the work;
- a measure of the value of the output;
- a mix of these.

Job evaluation and classification schemes tend to be based upon a mix of input and content rather than upon output.

Despite the fact that the Directive specified in Article 1 that job classification systems should be based on the same criteria for men and women and designed so that they exclude any discrimination on grounds of sex, there are still many unresolved dilemmas in this area. There have been many criticisms over the years that traditional and existing schemes often did demonstrate a bias in favour of the jobs that were 'male' as opposed to 'female', emphasizing more or awarding more points to the characteristics associated with and forming part of the male jobs.

The Commission sought to address some of the remaining problems concerning the meaning, measurement and application of this principle of equal pay for work of equal value via a Memorandum (94/6); pursuant to that it has issued a Code of Practice on the Implementation of Equal Pay for Work of Equal Value for Women and Men COM (96) 336.

The Code aims to eliminate sexual discrimination whenever pay structures are based on job classification and evaluation systems, and made two main proposals:

1   That negotiators at all levels should carry out an analysis of the remuneration system and evaluate the data required to detect sexual discrimination in pay structures so that it becomes possible to devise remedies.
2   That a plan for follow-up should be drawn up and implemented so that sexual discrimination is eliminated.

Interestingly, the Code states quite clearly that the prime responsibility for the avoidance of discrimination rests with the employers.

Well-intentioned though the Code of Practice and the Commission are, it should be remembered that interventions of this kind are subject to the dangers that the greater the degree of the discrimination or wage/earnings gap, the greater may be the employment impact of the interventions directed at narrowing or eliminating that gap, and the greater the extent of occupational segregation, the smaller will be the impact of the equal value interventions.

Other issues that have emerged concern the question of indirect discrimination such as payment systems and arrangements that attached pay to the possession of longevity of continuous service, the completion of specified training and an ability to work flexible hours.

There is then a long history of the EU taking initiatives to encourage equality between the sexes and much more recently competence has been taken to take initiatives to encourage equality and outlaw discrimination on a much wider group of categories or grounds. However, it must be acknowledged that progress towards achieving equality in practice has been slow. The new Article 13 has provided the opportunity for new Directives to be adopted and we have seen that the legislation in the various areas of equality and non-discrimination is much more uniform and encompasses similar definitions of issues such as direct and indirect discrimination and harassment. The legislators have also sought to retain both the possibility of positive action to aid the achievement of equality and exemptions where appropriate and legitimate.

There is a moral imperative to the outlawing of discrimination on most of the grounds now encompassed but we should not lose sight of the additional motives for seeking to outlaw such discrimination which are linked to the need for the Union as a whole to increase rates of economic activity in response to the demographic trends identified in **Chapter 6** and their implications. As we see in this later chapter, there is a need to enhance labour force participation and, to the extent that inactivity is a product of discrimination and/or the absence of equality of opportunities and pay, the new legislative interventions and accompanying measures geared towards the active promotion of equality should over time provide at least a partial solution.

The Europeanization of social protection and employee relations

We have noted in an earlier chapter that the process which we have labelled globalization and which is being driven by the interests of capital, the activities of MNCs and the widening and extending of international free trade arrangements may well be influential in securing a convergence of employee relations arrangements, activities and outcomes. In this chapter we are more concerned with the influence of the social dimension of the single market but we must not forget that the creation and extension of the social dimension that has been the subject matter of this chapter has and is taking place within this wider environment and contextual influences. Indeed, as we have noted, to some extent particular initiatives have been taken specifically to counter some of these global developments.

There has been much debate over the years as to whether the social dimension of the EU might lead to a convergence of systems of social protection and employee relations within the EU. To some extent the evidence presented in the preceding sections of this chapter indicates a gradual extension of the social dimension, incorporating both the creation of minimum individual rights for employees which are the same across the Union and an emphasis upon the information and consultation of employees and their representatives on a widening range of subject matter and in a widening range of organizational contexts. The treaties have also been amended to facilitate the EU taking initiatives on a widening range of social and employment issues. Set against these pressures that are arguably convergent in their direction and impact are others that may be perceived to mitigate these effects; for example, most of the recent initiatives have left many details for resolution at national level and in accordance with national traditions and practices. At the same time there are crucial areas in which the Union still either has no competence or where initiatives would require unanimity such as regarding trade union rights, collective bargaining, the right to take strike action, wage regulation and the protection of employees in circumstances of contract termination. So, at best, we are looking at a limited convergence. Convergence can, of course, be in both positive and negative directions: convergence can be upon an improved standard or upon a lower standard and while the EU tends to include in its initiatives protections against a negative convergence or worsening of rights or other terms and conditions of employment in member states, many MNCs seem to prefer a situation in which they can beat down terms and conditions of employment through competitive bargaining, a form of negative convergence.

If convergence is the objective, then this can be achieved through mechanisms other than those used by the EU institutions, the creation of rights and the imposition of particular procedural requirements. It can also be achieved through the free operation of market forces within an ever-growing single market. However, the interests of multinational capital would seem likely to ensure that such convergence would be downward in its direction as, confronted by international competition, they try to compete by forcing down costs including labour costs and the costs of social protection. Member state governments with high unemployment can also be tempted by the attractions of deregulation and lower employment costs. As we have noted, one of the motives for the creation of a minimum floor of social and employment rights within the EU is precisely to protect labour from these downward pressures and a situation in which member states are competing with one another for investment and jobs at the expense of labour standards.

Enlargement of the Union ought not to lead to any weakening of the existing levels of social protection since the aspirant members have to accept the existing acquis communitaire. However, in reality there are grave concerns that MNCs will use the lower living standards and labour costs prevailing in the aspirant member countries to export jobs to these countries and to force down labour and social protection costs in the existing member states and, in particular, in those member states bordering those included in the enlargement. It is concerns of this kind which prompted the Austrian and German governments to ask for restrictions upon inward labour mobility from those countries in Eastern Europe on their borders for a period of time after their accession into membership. They are concerned that jobs will be exported and that labour will flood into their countries, thereby exerting downward pressures upon wages and levels of social protection.

There is then evidence of an embryonic and very partial EU model of minimum employment rights and procedures relating to employee participation, but with many of the details left to the member states to determine in accordance with local national traditions and practices. At the same time there is considerable pressure for a weakening of regulation and social protection in order to facilitate company competitiveness and employment. Both may result in greater convergence within the EU but such convergence is likely to be in opposite directions.

Summary

In this chapter we have briefly examined the main institutions and decision-making processes of the European Union, but the emphasis has been upon the social dimension of the Union, the arguments and debates about its necessity and impact, the measures taken and their consequences.

The emphasis in the Union so far has been upon economic and monetary integration, the creation of single markets in capital, goods, services and labour, and the creation of a single currency. The social dimension of the Union is relatively underdeveloped in comparison.

The institutions of the Union and the member states are increasingly seeking to take decisions utilizing processes that provide the opportunity for majority, as opposed to unanimous, decisions and involve the social partners in the process. The Social Dialogue has developed and the Social Agreement procedures between the social partners have now yielded a number of framework agreements which have been given legal effect as Directives. The co-decision procedure at last provides a limited degree of additional influence for the EP. The extension of QMV to more of the EU's competence in the social arena and the widening of this competence, in particular the new Article 13 agreed at Amsterdam, both augur well for further widening and deepening of the Social Dimension. Also the Constitution agreed in 2004, but yet to be ratified, may extend the social rights of EU citizens if the Charter of Fundamental Rights comes to have legal effect.

Whilst in these contexts the future for the Social Dimension may look brighter, some would argue that so far the influence of the EU in the social and employment field has been relatively limited; even in the areas where there has been the most activity, it can be argued that the impact has been disappointing.

It seems as if the debates and arguments between those opposed to regulation and the statutory protection of workers and those arguing its necessity will continue and there are clear signs that the traditional social protection model that has been a defining characteristic of European systems is under threat, an argument used by many to explain the French rejection of the Constitution in 2005.

Activities to test understanding

Activity 1

Try to answer the following short answer questions without re-reading the text.

1 Which of the central institutions has the right of initiative?
2 Which of the central institutions has the role of adopting legislation?
3 What is the difference between a directive and a regulation?
4 How does the ECJ create the law?
5 What is the *acquis communitaire*?

6 What are the roles of the European Parliament?
7 Who are the social partners?

Activity 2

Outline the principle of subsidiarity, why is it important?

Activity 3

Outline the arguments for and against a Social Dimension to the Single market/union.

Activity 4

Explain the relationship between regime shopping and social dumping and why there is concern about the latter.

Activity 5

Why do you think the social protocol or social agreement procedure was so abhorrent to the 1991 government in the UK that they vetoed its inclusion in the Treaty agreed at Maastricht?

Activity 6

1 The Commission thinks employee participation is desirable. What are their reasons?
2 What do you think are the main reservations on the part of management?

Activity 7

Outline the main arguments in favour of regulating working time.

Activity 8

Explain the relevance of whether the working time directive was properly a health and safety issue.

Activity 9

Try to think through the difference between positive action and positive discrimination and write it down in your own words.

Activity 10

Explain the thinking behind the introduction of the Part-Time Workers Directive as an equality issue.

References

European Commission, 2004. Report on equality and non-discrimination.

European Commission, 2004. Gender equality: slow progress in closing gender gap hampering EU competitiveness.

European Industrial Relations Observatory 2004. Developments in European Works Councils.

European Industrial Relations Observatory 2004. Working time – developments in EU and national regulation.

Gold, M., 1993. Overview of the social dimension. In Gold, M. (ed.), *The Social Dimension – Employment Policy in the European Community.* Macmillan, Basingstoke.

Hall, M., 1994. Industrial Relations and the Social Dimension of European Integration: Before and after Maastricht. In Hyman, R. and Ferner, A. (eds), *New Frontiers in European Industrial Relations.* Blackwell, Oxford.

Hyman, R. (2000) Editorial. *European Journal of Industrial Relations* 6(1): 5–7.

Kersley, B., Alpin, C., Forth, J., Bryson, A., Bewley, H., Dix, G. and Oxenbridge, S., 2005. *Inside the Workplace First Findings from the 2004 Workplace Employment Relations Survey (WERS 2004).*

Marginson, P., Hall, M., Hoffmann, A. and Müller, T., 2004. The Impact of European Works Councils on management decision-making in UK and US-based multinationals: a case study comparison. *British Journal of Industrial Relations* 42(2): 209–234.

Teague, P., 1989. *The European Community: The Social Dimension.* Kogan Page, London.

Turner, L., 1996. The Europeanization of labour: structure before action. *European Journal of Industrial Relations* 2(3): 325–344.

Directives and other EU instruments

- Community Charter of the Fundamental Social Rights of Workers (The Social Charter) 1989.
- Council Directive 97/80/EC of 15 December 1997 on the burden of proof in cases of discrimination based on sex.
- Council Directive 97/81/EC concerning the Framework Agreement on Part-Time Work concluded by UNICE, CEEP and the ETUC.
- Council Directive 98/59/EC on the approximation of the laws of the member states relating to collective redundancies and consolidating The Directive on Collective Redundancies (75/129 extended by 92/56).
- Council Directive 1999/63/EC concerning the agreement on the organization of working time of seafarers concluded by the European Community Shipowners Association(ECSA) and the federation of Transport Workers Unions in the European Union (FST).

- Council Directive 1999/70/EC concerning the Framework Agreement on fixed term work concluded by ETUC, UNICE and CEEP.
- Council Directive 2000/34/EC of the European Parliament and the Council of 22 June 2000 amending Council Directive 93/104/EC concerning certain aspects of the organization of working time to cover sectors and activities excluded from that Directive.
- Council Directive 2000/43/EC of 29 June 2000 implementing the principle of equal treatment between persons irrespective of racial or ethnic origin.
- Council Directive 2000/78/EC of 27 November 2000 establishing a general framework for equal treatment in employment and occupation on the grounds of religion or belief, disability, age or sexual orientation.
- Council Directive 2001/23/EC of 12 March 2001 on the approximation of the laws of the Member States relating to the safeguarding of employees' rights in the event of transfers of undertakings, businesses or parts of undertakings or businesses.
- Council Directive 2001/86/EC supplementing the Statute for a European Company with regard to the involvement of employees.
- Council Recommendation 92/443 on Equity Sharing and Financial Participation. PEPPER I.
- Directive on Collective Redundancies 75/129 extended by 92/56.
- Directive on the Transfer of Undertakings 77/187.
- Directive on the Protection of Pregnant Workers: The Tenth Daughter Directive 92/85.
- Directive on the Adaptation of Working Time 93/104.
- Directive on the Establishment of a European Works Council or a Procedure in Community Scale Undertakings and Community Scale Groups of Undertakings for the Purposes of Informing and Consulting Employees 94/45.
- Directive on Parental Leave (96/34). Introduced pursuant to an agreement between the Social Partners in accordance with Article 2.2 of the Social Policy Agreement.
- Directive 2002/14/ establishing a general framework for informing and consulting employees.
- Directive 2002/73/EC of the European Parliament and of the Council amending Council Directive 76/207/EEC on the implementation of the principle of equal treatment for men and women as regards access to employment, vocational training and promotion, and working conditions also known as the Gender Equality Directive.

- Equal Pay Directive 75/117.
- Equal Treatment Directive 76/207.
- Code of Practice on the Implementation of Equal Pay for Work of Equal Value for Women and Men COM (96) 336.
- PEPPER II: *Promotion of Participation by Employed Persons in Profits and Enterprise Results (Including Equity Participation) in Member States* COM (96) 697.
- Green (Consultative) Paper, *Partnership for a New Organisation of Work* COM (97) 128.

Part Three

The National Context

Chapter 5

The role of government

Introduction

At the national level, government is one of the major influences upon the particular form of business system, variety of capitalism, institutional and regulatory regime within which national systems of industrial or employee relations exist.

In recent years there has been an awakening of interest in identifying and explaining the emergence and persistence of different national business systems and varieties of capitalism and in examining whether any particular variant has advantages in terms of economic performance.

A number of different typologies have been developed among which is that associated with Hall and Soskice (2001) which distinguishes between liberal market economies (LMEs) and coordinated market economies (CMEs). Among the determinants of which variety of capitalism exists within any country is the role of the state and, in particular, whether the state has encouraged market or non-market forms of coordination and regulation. A key feature that distinguishes these two broad types of market economy is the presence or absence of external institutions beyond the market mechanism for the regulation of the labour market and thereby the relationships between capital and labour. In LMEs the economic actors will have greater autonomy and it is likely that the interests and power of capital will dominate, relationships between labour and capital will be voluntary, self-regulating and constrained only by the market. In CMEs the economic actors will have less autonomy and the interests of capital are less likely to dominate, the relationships between capital and labour will be regulated by social institutions external to the market, there will be less emphasis upon self-regulation and more emphasis upon the integration of the various interests into the regulatory process and the decisions of the economic actors will be subject to broader collective and moral concerns.

Whether government as part of the state encourages market or non-market forms of regulation will be dependent in part upon beliefs and values. We noted in the earlier chapter on the EU that there are differences of regulatory regime between the member states and, in essence, we can note that the UK is an example of a predominantly LME, whereas, despite the differences between them, the remaining member states all to some extent exhibit the characteristics of CMEs. These member states all have business and employee relations systems which have been influenced by the belief that individual market relations should respect underlying social and moral values, hence the use of terms such as 'social market economy' and 'social' or 'welfare' capitalism.

Attitudes towards the desirability of market or non-market forms of regulation are likely to be reflected in:

- the economic policies pursued, including labour market policies, and the economic environment deemed to be desirable;
- approaches towards public versus private ownership;
- approaches towards the legislative support for or constraint of the employment relationship and the interactions between the employee relations actors or social partners;
- approaches towards whether the actors should be left to resolve their own differences voluntarily and through the market or whether to provide dispute resolution facilities and assistance;
- perceptions of an appropriate distribution of power between them;
- their willingness to enter into a political exchange with the other actors.

The potential significance of the role government plays can be detected from the comments by Blyton and Turnbull (1998) who assert 'the influence of the modern state permeates every aspect of people's working and non-working lives', by Kochan *et al.* (1986) who suggest government values and choices, with respect to macroeconomic and social policy, influence both the processes and outcomes of employee relations and by Crouch (1982: 146) who points out that government is the only one of the main actors able to change the rules unilaterally.

Government then is able to exert a significant influence upon the macroeconomic, labour market, political and legal contexts within which employee relations in any country occur and is therefore able to influence significantly the relative bargaining power of the actors. It may also be a major actor in any system as an employer and as an exemplar of good practice.

For the purposes of this chapter, we examine these issues through the roles performed by government as economic policy maker and manager, as legislator and provider of dispute resolution facilities, and as an employer. **In each case we use the UK as an example of the state's impact upon employee** relations.

However, before examining each of these roles in turn, we discuss one of the main typologies of ideology and its relevance to forms of capitalism.

Learning objectives

After studying this chapter you will be able to:

- understand and explain the main constituents of liberalism and corporatism and their relevance for the policies pursued by government and whether nation states have LMEs or CMEs;
- explain the roles through which government impacts upon employee relations;
- analyse the impact of government policies on the bargaining power of the main actors;
- understand and explain the different implications of Keynesian and Monetarist prescriptions for the conduct of economic and labour market policy;
- understand how governments can influence the nature of the employment relationship and employee relations through their role as legislator;
- understand the different government approaches towards the public sector and how it can use its role as employer to influence employee relations in both public and private sectors;
- understand how governments might assist with dispute resolution and the differences between conciliation and arbitration.

Ideologies and political approaches

Liberalism

Liberalism is the term given to the ideology or set of beliefs which perceives the market as the basis for regulation. The market is perceived as an efficient mechanism for allocating resources including labour and the individual seller of labour is perceived as being able to look after his own interest in the marketplace. The individual is perceived to be rational and to have a rough equality of bargaining power in the marketplace with the buyer. The terms of the employment relationship are determined through the process of individual exchange in the marketplace. This ideology is sometimes also referred to as the laisser-faire or free market ideology. It is an ideology that focuses upon individualism and efficiency. Governments with this viewpoint are unlikely to perceive a need to intervene to ensure social justice or to protect employees from exploitation, there will probably be little support for trades unions who will be perceived as sources of imperfection in the marketplace, and they are likely to protect capital's property rights and management's prerogative. It is also an ideology inconsistent with government playing a role as the provider of goods and services. **The USA is the stereotypical example of a country within which governments have consistently adopted such a set of beliefs.**

A variant on this liberalist, laisser-faire theme is the ideology known as liberal collectivism. Here there is a recognition and acceptance that employees do not as individuals have a rough equality of bargaining power with employers in the market and that therefore employees may need some measure of protection and collective strength in their activities in the marketplace if labour is not to be exploited. Trades unions therefore are recognized as legitimate agents acting on behalf of individuals with their labour to sell. Nevertheless, in the context of this ideology, the parties, employers and trades unions will still be perceived as able to look after their own interests in the marketplace and there is likely to be relatively little intervention by government to ensure alternatives to what is still predominantly a market-based system. Terms and conditions of employment are likely to be the product of freely entered into collective bargaining and it is these collective agreements that regulate the economic elements of the employment relationship, with non-economic aspects of the employment relationship still likely to be the preserve of management. Sometimes the term voluntarism has been used to describe such systems. The dominant concern is still with efficiency but there is a greater measure of concern also with fairness and issues of social justice. Government may intervene to support a rough balance of power between employers and trades unions and also to ensure public access to certain categories of goods and services through public ownership and provision; examples of such intervention would include utilities such as water and the provision of health care and education. Examples of countries where this form of ideology has predominated would include a number of the Scandinavian countries (see the chapter on the EU, **Chapter 4**).

The UK

Within Europe it is the UK which has best exhibited these two approaches, the liberal collectivist view characterized post-war governments of both main political parties and underpinned the post-war consensus that had facilitated the emergence and development of a system of industrial relations at the core of which was free collective bargaining and which was known as **voluntarism**. This voluntarism has also been characterized as a system based in mutual autonomy, a system of industrial self-government. Flanders (1974: 352–70) identified the key features of voluntarism as encompassing a general desire that wages and other terms and conditions of employment be determined by the parties through the process of free or voluntary collective bargaining rather than by state regulation and that the agreements arrived at should not be legally binding except in as much as they constituted terms in the individual employment contract (see later section in this chapter on the contract of employment). Amongst developed economies the UK is unusual in this respect, that collective agreements freely entered into are not legally binding, whereas similar agreements entered into by individuals are commonly legally enforceable as contracts (see also **Chapter 9** in which we examine collective bargaining).

The election in 1979 of a Conservative government heralded the return of an approach which had more in common with the liberal individualist ideology and which pursued policies emphasizing individual exchange and contract and a reduction in the power and influence of trades unions and in the encouragement given to free collective bargaining. This government perceived trades unions as a source of imperfection or distortion in the market, the balance of power was perceived to have shifted in favour of the unions at the expense of the employer and the unions were perceived to have succeeded in raising wages above the market rate thereby being a source of price inflation.

The liberal collectivist post-war consensus had also been accompanied by the creation of the welfare state and a significant increase in the public ownership and provision of many goods and services. The return to a more liberal individualist approach was also accompanied by a reversal of this policy with much of the public sector being returned to private ownership and the market mechanism reintroduced. Efficiency once again became the dominant concern rather than social justice or fairness, **and it is arguable, as we see below, that the pursuit of efficiency inevitably leads to greater inequality and a lack of social justice**.

Corporatism

Corporatism is an ideology which has a very different perception of the consequences of allowing the market to operate freely. The belief is that liberal systems in which decision making is both competitive and decentralized are inevitably inefficient, disruptive and, perhaps most concerning for government, unpredictable and uncontrollable. Additionally these liberal decision-making processes are quite capable of resulting in inequalities, unfairness and waste. It is the responsibility of government to protect individuals from the social injustice that inevitably results from the operation of free market systems.

Consequently, governments with this set of beliefs seek to introduce:

■ decision-making mechanisms which serve to integrate the interests of capital, labour and government, usually through some process of exchange or bargaining;
■ political institutions which facilitate tripartite discussion and decision making, particularly with respect to economic, industrial and social policies, such as the pursuit of economic growth, full employment and price stability.

Government then seeks to play an active role mediating the interests of capital and labour and in partnership with these competing interest groups, directing the activities of the still privately owned enterprises.

It is an approach which emphasizes the interdependence of the various interest groups and the notion of partnership, rather than encouraging competition between them, and which of course provides government with a greater capacity to influence and control compared with a decentralized market mechanism.

In some countries such as Germany, the Netherlands, Sweden and Australia with lengthy corporatist traditions, it has been quite common for the partnership to be emphasized by the use of the term 'social partners' when referring to the representatives of capital and labour and, indeed, this is the term used within the EU (see **Chapter 4**). Commonly, representatives of capital and labour participate with government representatives in a tripartite administration of the mechanisms established to achieve the agreed policy objectives. However, it is also the case that in the last decades of the 20th century some of these countries have begun to witness a shift in the dominant political value system away from that which underpins corporatism towards liberalism and in particular its implications for regulation of the labour market and the role and scale of the public sector.

Typically corporatism in developed and democratic societies is of a voluntary and bargained nature where the various parties willingly participate in the process and where the outcomes are the product of bargaining between them. Examples might be a temporary agreement whereby the non-governmental interest groups agree to moderate their demands for wage or price increases in return for concessions from the other parties which might take the form of increased social security benefits, enhanced co-determination rights for employees or renewed commitments by both government and employers to full employment. For employers, the concessions might involve investment allowances, tax allowances or reductions in company taxation. There is a massive range of social, economic and industrial objectives that can be pursued through such arrangements.

The UK

I have asserted above that the dominant ideologies of governments in the UK have been liberalist; however, it can also be argued that in the mid-1970s the UK had a government which sought to determine economic, social and industrial policies in a manner that was consistent with a form of bargained **corporatism**, rather than liberal collectivism.

When a Labour government was elected in 1974 a Social Contract was agreed with both the Confederation of British Industry (CBI), representing the employers and with the Trades Union Congress (TUC), representing the trade unions (see **Chapter 7**). In this tripartite agreement the unions agreed with the others that they would exercise wage restraint in return for the employers' exercising restraint on price increases and the government giving them both a more active and influential role in economic and industrial policy making and in the regulatory institutions. The unions also sought a code of individual and protective employment rights, positive rights, as well as an extension of trade union immunities (see below). The unions obtained a measure of success in this respect and, during the first 2 years of this government and its corporatist experiment, the degree of legal regulation of the employment relationship was significantly enhanced through the enactment of three major pieces of trade union and employee-friendly legislation (the Trade Unions and Labour Relations Act of 1974 (TULRA), the Health and Safety at Work Act 1974 (HASAW), and the Employment Protection Act of 1975 (EPA)).

Advisory, Conciliation and Arbitration Service (ACAS) was also created in this period with a governing council that was made up in equal shares of trade union representatives, employer representatives and independent experts. Perhaps unfortunately, the experiment did not last as each of the parties began to perceive that the others were not delivering their part of the deal. This is consistent with the comments of Keller (1991) who pointed out that the participants are likely to continue as such only as long as they are satisfied with the outcomes and it is quite common for such arrangements to break up or fall into disrepair.

A corporatist approach to government and to policy making then provides for a more interventionist role for the government in terms and conditions of employment and for legal regulation of the employment relationship in general. Certainly it implied the cessation of free collective bargaining as evidenced by various attempts in these years to apply both bargained and coercive incomes policies.

Government and the economy

We noted in the introduction to this chapter that governments are influential in determining the form of economy in a particular country and we contrasted two simple stereotypes of the LME, in which governments pursue an essentially non-interventionist approach, and the CME in which governments adopt an interventionist imperative.

Governments can have a range of economic objectives and their ideology is likely to influence the objectives they choose to pursue, the priorities attached to them and the methods used to achieve them. To some extent all governments have the same economic objectives in that they all tend to pursue the objectives of full employment, price stability, economic growth and a balance of trade surplus. However, the priorities attached to each will vary.

Our interest is not so much in the economics of the subject but in the implications of the various priority options for employee relations and, in particular, the implications for the relative bargaining power of the various interests associated with capital and labour and for the specific policies pursued in relation to the labour market. The bargaining power of the parties can be influenced by the policies government pursues in relation to employment, interest and exchange rates, inflation and taxation.

In this section we examine the simple stereotypes of Keynesian style demand management approaches and those associated with monetarism and their respective implications for the bargaining power of the parties to the employment relationship. We then focus on different labour market options with a particular emphasis upon active versus passive approaches.

Keynesian approaches

Keynesian approaches are commonly associated with the pursuit of full employment as a priority and the management of aggregate demand or spending power within the economy in order to achieve this objective. Aggregate demand can be influenced by government in a number of ways.

For example, government can raise or reduce taxation, it can raise or reduce interest rates and it can increase or decrease public expenditure and its own borrowing requirements. If the rate of unemployment rises, government can seek to expand demand for labour through a range of options: it can reduce personal and corporate taxes thereby increasing spending power and demand; it can reduce interest rates thereby stimulating spending power and investment or it can increase its own spending. If the policy options chosen are successful and both demand and employment rise, the bargaining power of labour relative to capital is enhanced and may well result in inflationary wage increases being secured as employers compete for labour. Developments of this kind can then result in declining labour productivity and a worsening competitive scenario for the goods and services as their unit cost rises.

If the pursuit of full employment results in rising prices and declining productivity and competitiveness, there will be a temptation for government to reallocate priorities so that it limits price inflation by going into reverse and taking steps to reduce aggregate demand which then, over time, will have the effect of reducing demand for labour and hence employment. The Keynesian prescription for such an eventuality was to step in directly and seek to influence both wage rates and prices through some form of compulsory or bargained prices and incomes policy, such as through the Social Contract referred to above. You stimulate demand and employment and then counter the effects upon wages and prices by direct controls which will limit the unwanted effects upon productivity. Both wage and price inflation will be controlled and the negative effects upon competitiveness will be mitigated. The difficulties with such policies is in making them work and this will in part depend upon the willingness and ability of both employers and trades unions to deliver the agreement, or on the public authorities to police and enforce the policy limits.

You should bear in mind that the Keynesian approach and its concern with the pursuit of full employment were in part a response to the great depression and mass unemployment of the late 1920s and early 1930s.

Monetarism

Monetarism can mean different things to different people but here we deal only with the simple stereotype. The policy priorities associated with the pursuit of monetarist approaches tend to be price stability and international competitiveness, rather than full employment. It is an approach to the economy which is arguably less interventionist and which at its core believes in the efficiency of the market and is essentially laisser-faire in its approach to the market. Where governments with this view intervene, it is likely to be to remove regulation and barriers to the operation of market forces rather than to create them.

The emphasis of monetarism tends to be on influencing supply rather than demand. The essence of this view is that if increases in demand, purchasing power, are outstripping increases in the supply of goods and services, this will result in inflationary pressures on both prices and wages as the price is bid up within the market in order to ration the goods and services that are effectively in short supply. This approach is often characterized as one that sees too much money (purchasing power) chasing too few goods and services.

The solution is not to manage the aggregate level of demand but to influence the supply side of the markets, in particular to increase the productive capacity of the economy to produce goods and services and exert controls on the supply of money or purchasing power. It is referred to as monetarism precisely because of this focus upon money supply as well as upon enhancing productive capacity. It is argued that the supply of money can be influenced through a range of techniques including interest rates, public expenditure and by direct controls. It is true that if you succeed in influencing purchasing power through supply-side measures, you are using supply-side initiatives to influence demand, so to some extent even monetarism is an approach that seeks to influence the aggregate level of demand in the economy in order to attain the specific objective of price stability.

Measures to improve productive capacity might include:

- creating incentives to work, for example by reducing levels of social protection and benefits;
- stimulating investment in productive capacity, for example by reducing interest rates but also by measures such as removing planning barriers;
- stimulating private enterprise; there are many ways in which this can be done, for example by providing grants and incentives to self-employment and the creation of businesses and again the removal of restrictive bureaucratic and legal requirements;
- improving the quality of labour supply, for example through encouraging training and retraining and through encouraging people to remain in education for longer;
- deregulating labour markets, here the emphasis is likely to be upon removing barriers to both hiring and firing, for example reducing protections against unfair dismissal and redundancies and relaxing bureaucratic requirements linked to the employment of labour and perhaps particularly the use of temporary, fixed-term and part-time employment contracts coupled with the removal or relaxation of restrictions upon hours of work;
- reducing corporate taxes;

- the privatization of public-sector activities on the assumption that private-sector organizations are more responsive to the market and have an incentive to enhance their productive capacity and ability to compete.

As can be seen above, many of the potential initiatives associated with the monetarist approach are measures taken to influence the supply side of the labour market, enhancing both the quality and quantity of labour supply at the same time as easing restrictions upon effective demand.

In recent years concerns with unemployment have dominated much of the activity of governments in Europe, particularly Germany, France, Italy and Spain. Many member states in the EU have been trying to reconcile social protection and labour market regulation with a need to reduce unemployment and retain competitiveness in international markets. They have in many instances been unwilling or unable to adopt stereotypical laisser-faire or monetarist approaches but have become increasingly interested in trying to address unemployment through supply-side initiatives. The diagnosis has tended to focus on the quality rather than the quantity of labour supply including skill level and type and in particular the mismatch between the skills, or lack of them, of the unemployed and those required in the expanding sectors of the economy and by those employers that are creating jobs and recruiting.

The solution is perceived to be available through a mix of supply-side initiatives and active labour market policies geared towards:

- the improvement of the quality of the labour force;
- ensuring that the skills which people have are the skills which are needed in the economy;
- improving the services which are concerned with job search and skills matching.

The terms passive and active have been used to distinguish the approaches to the labour market traditionally associated with CMEs and the Keynesian approach from those associated with LMEs and an emphasis upon supply-side initiatives and deregulation.

Passive policies tend to emphasize protection of both those employed and unemployed and in the context of unemployment passive policies are geared towards making unemployment bearable through, for example:

- improved unemployment benefits/social security payments;
- generous redundancy schemes and pay;
- generous approaches to early retirements not linked to health.

In this respect, some argue that passive policies actually encourage unemployment.

Active approaches on the other hand have tended to focus on different objectives such as job creation and making it easier for those out of work to find alternative employment through measures such as:

- encouraging job creation through some form of employer subsidy or business start-up scheme;
- providing additional training opportunities;
- improvement of the public job search and matching arrangements.

Policy makers in Europe are grappling with many dilemmas. On the one hand, they are reluctant to renounce the traditions of social protection, large public sectors, regulated labour markets and comfortable unemployment associated with CMEs and an essentially Keynesian approach. On the other, they are confronted with high unemployment, slow growth and high proportionate public expenditure. Their labour markets are characterized by labour inflexibility, skill shortages, disincentives to economic activity and job creation, yet they need to improve productive capacity, economic growth and their international competitiveness. It is in this context that some at least, **encouraged by the success of more liberal economies such as the USA and the UK**, have started to move selectively in the direction of a more LME approach in which labour markets are deregulated and social protection curtailed.

As we noted in the previous chapter on the EU (**Chapter 4**), these dilemmas are mirrored in the debates surrounding the need for and desirability of a social dimension.

The UK

The approach of governments in the UK over the last quarter of the 20th century exemplifies these different policy approaches. As noted earlier, it is arguable whether the approach of the Labour government elected in 1974 was corporatist or liberal collectivist; certainly the consensus of governments of both main political parties was essentially Keynesian in the post-war period up to the early to mid-1970s. There was agreement that governments had a responsibility to try to ensure full employment and there was consensus that this could best be achieved through the expansionary management of aggregate demand within the economy in accordance with the prescriptions of Keynes. Also in line with the Keynesian approach, there was a commitment to social protection. A range of mechanisms was available for use to stimulate demand, including fiscal and monetary instruments; that is, taxation and government borrowing provided the resources for public expenditure and interest rates and the exchange rate could also be used to manage the level of demand.

Demand management policies and instruments can, of course, also be used to achieve the objective of low inflation or price stability. The instruments are used to damp down or choke off demand on the assumption that this would reduce inflationary pressures in the economy, beneficially influence a nation's international competitiveness and thereby achieve growth via exports. Demand management, then, was variously used to expand demand in times of economic slump or recession and to damp down demand and thereby combat inflationary pressures.

Throughout the 1950s and 1960s unemployment and inflation were both relatively low, as producers in the UK were confronted with friendly market conditions around the world. However, and after the inflationary impact of the oil price rises of 1973–1974, by the mid-1970s not only had inflation risen to all-time post-war highs (in excess of 20 per cent per annum) but unemployment was also rising, a combination referred to as 'stagflation'. Government's attempts to control inflation through corporatist approaches and prices and incomes policies failed and eventually it had to approach the International Monetary Fund (IMF) for a loan to cover an expanding balance of payments deficit and public-sector borrowing requirement (PSBR), this latter in part the product of higher social security bills as unemployment rose and partly the product of high pay increases in the public sector as the unions fought to keep up with inflation.

The IMF insisted that the UK government change tack as far as economic policy was concerned, stating that what was needed was the implementation of monetarist policies giving priority to the control of inflation, public expenditure (including public-sector wages) and the PSBR, and thereby the country's international competitiveness. The instruments of the new way were to use the government's ability to control the supply of money into the economy and public expenditure and, if necessary, short-term unemployment was to be allowed to rise as the trade-off for low inflation. These essentially supply-side policies had a demand effect which was deflationary rather than expansionist.

The Conservative government elected in 1979 was firmly committed to implementing policies similar to those required by the IMF and to do so vigorously; priority was to be given to the control of inflation. The underpinning ideology was liberalist and essentially individual. The market was to be allowed to reign, including the labour market where there was also a conviction that institutional deregulation (see below for some examples), also often referred to in terms of institutional or regulatory flexibility, was essential in order to encourage enterprise and employment. Social protection was to be reduced (thereby also reducing public expenditure) as an incentive for the unemployed and disadvantaged to accept responsibility for their own fate and wherever possible obtain work; enterprise was to be encouraged and industries and companies that could not compete were to be allowed to founder. The bargaining power of the trades unions was also to be addressed. As noted earlier, it was felt that Keynesian type policies giving priority to full employment and public expenditure had resulted in a situation in which the activities of the unions were seen to be inflationary, the labour shortages enabling them to bid wage rates up above the market rate. It was felt that while the new economic priorities and approach would, over time, redress the balance of power, this was to be supported also by a legislative programme (see later) that would gradually make it more difficult for the unions to take effective industrial action and governmental support and encouragement for collective bargaining was to diminish. Government also determined to use their control over the public sector to provide an example to the private sector in how to combat the power of the unions (see later).

So the government operated a mix of:

1 laisser-faire policies towards markets;
2 controls on money supply and public expenditure, supply-side initiatives which also had an indirect and deflationary impact upon demand;
3 policies geared towards reforming labour market institutions and regulations and through which they:
    • limited the bargaining power of the trades unions;
    • eliminated the remnants of minimum wage protection through the Wages Councils;
    • made it more difficult for employees to gain entitlement to legislative protection and/or compensation from arbitrary action by the employer, for example through unfair dismissal proceedings and redundancy pay;
    • made it easier and cheaper for employers to hire and fire;
    • amended restrictions upon hours of work and the use of certain atypical contracts;
    • removed some of the restrictions upon the employment of cheap labour such as immigrants and children.

These policies had an immediate impact in the labour market and, over a relatively short period, 1979–1981, unemployment doubled from 1.14 million (4.7 per cent) to 2.3 million (9.4 per cent) and by 1986 it had reached over 3 million (11.4 per cent), most of this in manufacturing industries. Employment in manufacturing industries declined by over 2 million between 1979 and 1987. In the early 1990s the UK again experienced a massive recession during which unemployment rose again close to the 3 million mark and there was another substantial erosion of employment in manufacturing.

Labour market and labour force statistics are included in **Chapter 6**.

The Labour government elected in 1997 has continued with an approach to economic management rooted in the liberal ideology of market freedom and competition. It has pursued economic policies concerned to achieve economic stability, control over interest rates was given to the Bank of England who were given the task of using interest rates to achieve price stability, and at least initially a tight grip was maintained over public expenditure.

There have been few interventions aimed at reviving the level of social protection or labour market regulation associated with the pre-1979 period. Some measure of encouragement of collective bargaining was provided by the new legislative rights to trade union recognition, but there has been no widespread encouragement of free collective bargaining, labour market flexibility remained an objective and in the public sector a tight grip has been maintained on public-sector pay. There has been concern to continue with active supply-side policies aimed at encouraging enterprise and job creation, enhancing the quality of the labour force through continuance in education and programmes aimed at improving the employability of the unemployed, providing incentives to economic activity through continuing restrictions on the receipt of unemployment and disability benefits combined with exhortations to the inactive that they have a duty to be economically active.

For the first years of this administration, the UK economy was indeed relatively stable with low levels of price inflation, arguably facilitated by global competitive pressures, historically low interest rates and low levels of unemployment. However, this was accompanied by relatively low levels of social protection, wages, public expenditure and productivity.

As the administration proceeded towards a third term of office commitments were given to increased levels of investment in public-sector services such as education and health. These commitments and their implications for public expenditure and PSBR were greeted with criticism from international agencies such as the IMF.

In this section we have briefly examined the role of government as economic manager. We began by briefly outlining the stereotypes of Keynesian and Monetarist approaches with the former giving priority to full employment, government intervention and market regulation, and demand management and the latter to price stability, a reliance on the market mechanism and the use of supply-side initiatives. To some extent the debate was overtaken by global developments which have tended to squeeze inflationary pressures out of developed economies at the same time as they enhanced concerns about levels of employment, employ-ability and job creation. As the 20th century came to a close many developed economies were more concerned about high unemployment than price stability and whether the prescriptions associated with lib-eral regimes of deregulation and market flexibility represented the best route to achieving greater employment and employability, in add-ition to their concerns about the social justice consequences of such policies. In this context there was a resurgence of interest in what might be referred to as neo-Keynesian approaches in which it was argued that, with inflation having been effectively forced out of the global economy by competition, the recipe for reducing unemploy-ment should now emphasize faster rates of economic growth and that this can be influenced by governments through policies encouraging an expansion of demand rather than through supply-side measures or institutional deregulation.

In the summer of 1999, the OECD added some credibility to this alter-native view in its annual Employment Outlook (1999), in which it asserted that it could find no direct link between either tough regulations giving employees job security or levels of trade union membership and strength, and the overall incidence of high unemployment. It acknow-ledged that regulatory flexibility may assist the speed with which labour markets respond to changing patterns of demand and that inflexibility and trade union strength may protect insiders at the expense of out-siders, making it more difficult for those not in employment to break into employment. This may mean that once in work it is likely that indi-viduals are relatively protected, but once out of work, once they become outsiders, the period of unemployment is likely to be longer. This report points out that, without an adequate level of demand within the economy, there is nothing for the flexible labour market to respond to. So economic growth and demand for labour are the driv-ers of employment expansion with a deregulated and institutionally flexible labour market facilitating the speed and ease with which the labour market responds **but there must be demand for it to respond to. Supply-side policies may enhance individual employability and the quality of labour supply, but of themselves they are unlikely to cre-ate jobs.**

Examples of the kind of expansionary demand-side initiatives that might be acceptable are:

1   increased public expenditure on infrastructure schemes which stimulate demand for labour;
2   other schemes directed at job creation in the public sector and geared towards the employment of the young- or long-term unemployed, as in the creation of community work and welfare programmes;

3   schemes that encourage employers to employ more labour
by making the employment of labour cheaper, for example
by government reducing the non-wage cost of employment
such as employers' national insurance and social security
contributions.

In its 2004 Employment Outlook the OECD also provides some caution-
ary advice to governments pursuing full employment though labour market deregulation, supply-side initiatives and competition. They suggest
that pursuing more and better jobs needs to be combined with other
social objectives, in particular adequate social protection, a better reconciliation of work and family life and labour market outcomes that do not
enhance inequality. They point out that there is a need for some measure of income and employment security, that reducing entitlements to
benefits for the unemployed can result in poverty and that the use of
more flexible working arrangements can have undesirable consequences
for balancing work and non-work life and responsibilities.

Government as legislator and the legal context

We have already noted that the beliefs and values of governments influence the priorities and policies pursued in the economic sphere and that
these encompass attitudes towards the efficiency and effectiveness of the
market as a mechanism for determining the allocation of resources
between different uses but they also include evaluations of the social
acceptability of market outcomes. Liberal individualists are likely to
believe in the capacity of individuals to look after their own interests in
the marketplace, entering into individual and contractual relationships
with employers for the sale of their labour and the terms upon which
the exchange takes place. Liberal collectivists are likely to believe in the
efficiency and effectiveness of the market mechanism but acknowledge
that market outcomes associated with individualism are likely to favour
the employer given the balance of bargaining power and so they are
likely to encourage freely entered collective organization and collective
determination of the terms of the employment contract. They may also
identify particular groups within society who need additional protection
in order to prevent their exploitation and it may be that the only way in
which such protection can be provided is through legislation. Corpo-
ratists have a much more critical view of the efficiency and effectiveness
of the market mechanism and the desirability and social acceptability of
unregulated market outcomes. They are likely to perceive the market
as a source of inefficiency, waste and inequality, outcomes which are
unacceptable and which require that the employment relationship is
regulated. This latter may be the product of collective, integrative and
tripartite decision making or it may be achieved through legislative

intervention. We have already noted the corporatist traditions of many European countries and many of these countries are characterized by extensive welfare systems and comprehensive systems of labour law which have been introduced in order to protect labour from the economic dependence and exploitation that would, in their view, be the product of laisser-faire market liberalism.

Labour or employment law then may have a number of objectives, for example it may:

- seek to protect the weak from exploitation;
- determine the terms and conditions of employment;
- encourage and regulate both individual and collective relationships including the application of sanctions by one or more parties on the other;
- encourage particular forms of behaviour;
- promote particular processes for the determination of the terms of the employment relationship;
- establish minimum rights and obligations;
- remedy inbalances of bargaining power;
- promote certain social values and objectives such as fairness, equality and democracy.

The above is not intended to be an exhaustive list of the possible objectives of legislative intervention into and regulation of the employment relationship and the relationships between the parties, but it does illustrate that the content and purpose can be very varied.

The need for and future development of labour law in Europe was examined in the Supiot report presented to the European Commission in 1998. This report examines changes in the nature of work and in the labour market with a view to determining whether a regulatory body of labour law was still necessary in Europe and, if so, what the directions in which it needed to be developed were.

The authors take as the framework for their analysis of change a Fordist model of work and employment balanced by the traditional European social model encompassing welfare capitalism and a regulatory system of labour law which:

- provides protection and security to labour,
- prevents its impoverishment,
- provides the opportunity for participation;
- enables the maintenance of social stability and cohesion.

In the view of the authors, the regulatory regime should be reformulated so as to ensure maintenance of four main democratic requirements:

- individual security,
- freedom in terms of worker protection against dependence,

- equality,
- collective rights guaranteeing participation.

It is arguable that none of these objectives are likely to be achieved in a national system characterized by a liberal approach.

Specific suggestions include:

- the extension of labour law from being concerned primarily with employees to cover all kinds of contracts involving the performance of work for others,
- extending legal regulation to facilitate the reconciliation of family and work life but also to facilitate women's participation in the labour force with an emphasis upon maintaining the legality of positive action,
- the possibility of introducing requirements for mandatory collective bargaining.

One of the problems with examining this subject is that the nature and extent of legislative intervention do vary considerably from country to country; another of the difficulties is associated with structuring the examination, given that there are various options and approaches in the literature.

Gennard and Judge 2002 for example adopt Kahn–Freund's typology which focuses on the functions of the law and which distinguishes the auxiliary, regulatory and restrictive functions:

- The auxiliary function is where the law is designed to promote particular forms of behaviour such as collective bargaining or the information and consultation of employees.
- The regulatory function results in legislation which tends to be protective in nature and which provides individual rights as a mechanism for regulating the behaviour of management towards their workers or trades unions towards their members, so that individuals may be given rights not to be treated unfairly.
- The restrictive function is where the law effectively seeks to determine the rules within which relationships are conducted, so that governments might legislate in order to limit the circumstances in which the parties can lawfully apply sanctions against each other.

Others (Hollinshead and Leat, 1995) have argued the case for distinguishing between legislation aimed at protecting the interests and rights or freedoms of the parties compared with legislation primarily concerned with regulating the relationships between them, providing a legal framework within which the parties interact and pursue the resolution of the conflicts between them.

Yet another is that of Dickens and Hall (1995) who focus on sets of relationships and who have sought to distinguish between legislation concerned to regulate:

- employer–worker relations,
- employer–union relations,
- union–member relations.

Another approach has been taken by Willey and Morris (2003), who again focus on purpose or objective and distinguish between law concerned to:

- regulate the individual employment relationship, including the contract of employment;
- achieve the particular social objectives of equality of opportunity and non-discrimination;
- encourage and regulate collective representation;
- provide a legislative framework for the collective processes of employment relations;
- regulate what they refer to as industrial conflict by which they mean both individual and collective industrial action.

There appears to be little disagreement about the scope and subject matter of the legislative context as it may impact employee relations and it clearly encompasses:

- the individual employer–employee relationship, the terms and conditions of that relationship and the creation of individual rights, freedoms and obligations;
- collective association, interactions and processes, and industrial action;
- the promotion of certain socially desirable objectives such as equality and non-discrimination.

As noted in the introduction to this chapter, we are going to focus on the **UK as an exemplar of the state's impact upon employee relations. The UK is** a country with long traditions of liberalism and voluntarism now operating within a legislative context at the European level which is derived from very different traditions. We intend to adopt an essentially threefold structural approach as above. It must also be remembered that this work is not primarily a legal text and therefore only an outline of the context is envisaged.

The legislative context in the UK

The individual employment relationship

One of the characteristics of the UK context is that there are legal distinctions between employees, workers and the self-employed. We have already noted above that the Supiot report suggests that labour law be extended to encompass all categories of workers and not only those that fall within the definition of employee. We also note elsewhere (**Chapter 10**) that legislation in the UK is increasingly being extended to encompass workers, for example the right to be accompanied at disciplinary and grievance hearings. Minimum wage legislation and the working time regulations also apply to workers but the distinction remains in other areas such as the provisions relating to the protection of employees from unfair dismissal. Generally employment law does not extend to include the self-employed.

The status of employee is determined by whether a contract of employment exists between the parties. Tests of whether a contract is a contract of employment include:

- the degree of control exercised by the employer and whether there is an obligation on the employer to provide work;
- whether wages are paid;
- the integration of the person into the business, who bears the risk and who provides the tools for the performance of the work;
- the extent to which there is an obligation on the person to work;
- whether the relationship is continuous;
- whether the employer deducts income tax and national insurance contributions.

In deciding cases the courts will make a judgement on the balance of the evidence and no one of these characteristics is likely to be sufficient in itself.

Where there is a contract of employment it is legally enforceable; however, there are a number of issues and questions surrounding the contents and form of the contract.

For example:

- Does the contract have to be in writing and do the parties have to sign it? what constitutes the contract?
- Where do the terms of the contract emanate from and do they all have to be expressed clearly and agreed between the parties?
- Do the rights granted to individual employees by statute form part of the contract and, if so, how?
- Can the terms of collective agreements between employers and trade unions form part of the contract and, if this is so, what other sources might there be?

Some of these questions can be answered quite easily and clearly; however, some of them are also difficult to answer clearly.

Contracts do not have to be in writing and signed; the contract exists whether written or not; they do not have to be expressly agreed by the parties in their entirety though some of the terms may be; the employer is legally obliged in most cases to give the employee a written statement detailing some of the main particulars of the contract (these are spelt out in Section 1 of the Employment Rights Act 1996, see below) but this document rarely is sufficiently comprehensive for it to constitute the contract. Yes, many of the statutory rights do constitute part of the contract and in the main these will be assumed to be incorporated into the contract even though they may not be the subject of discussion or agreement between the parties; in fact, the parties may not even know of them. Other sources of terms implied and incorporated into the contract may be custom and practice, collective agreements, common law rights and duties, staff handbooks and various other documentary sources.

The Section 1 (Employment Rights Act 1996) statement

The requirement for employers to give their employees written details of some of the main particulars of the terms of their employment contract dates from the Contracts of Employment Act 1963, revised subsequently and, as noted above, the current state of the law in this area is contained in the 1996 Act.

The Section 1 statement should give employees written details of the following:

- Names of employer and employee;
- Date of commencement of continuous employment;
- Rate of pay and frequency of payment;
- Hours of work;
- Holidays and holiday pay;
- Matters concerning sickness and sick pay;
- Pension rights and arrangements;
- Indication of job title;
- Notice to be given and received;
- Details of grievance and disciplinary rules, procedures and arrangements;
- Place of work;
- Details of collective agreements that directly affect the contract and the names of the parties that made them.

In some instances the requirement to provide these details can be satisfied by a reference in the statement to other documents where the details may be found, for example in relation to the details of sickness and pension rights and grievance and disciplinary procedures.

This statement should be given to employees within the first 8 weeks of their employment. The written statement is not the contract and has no direct legal force at all, though employees can make a complaint to an Employment Tribunal (the new name for Industrial Tribunal) if they are not provided with these details. We noted above that the terms of a contract may be expressed or implied and, where expressed, this may be done in writing or orally. The Section 1 statement is usually the best evidence of the express terms of the contract.

Implied terms

The implied terms of a contract are in the main implied either from statute or from the decisions of the courts over the years as what is known as the common law duties and obligations of the parties were developed. Terms implied from these sources apply in general to all contracts of employment but, again, these are not the only sources of implied terms. Terms may be implied from custom and practice in a particular organization or they may be implied from the conduct of the parties. In these latter cases the implied terms are likely to be more specific to the contracts of a particular group of employees, or indeed to a particular individual contract.

There are now, after the developments of the last 30 years, a whole range of statutory rights and obligations which, to all intents and purposes, constitute implied terms of the contract. They exist as terms of the contract of employment without their being expressed in the contract or indeed in the statement given to employees. Examples would be in the following areas:

- written statement,
- maternity pay and leave,
- minimum wages,
- minimum notice periods,
- redundancy pay,
- not to be unfairly dismissed,
- time off for public activities and duties,
- health and safety responsibilities,
- equal pay,
- not to be discriminated against,
- data protection.

Very rarely would these rights be written into even the most comprehensive of Section 1 statements or a document purporting to be the contract, but they are nevertheless there as rights and obligations of the parties to the employment relationship.

The other major source of implied terms is from **common law** (**Figure 5.1**). This represents the decisions of the judiciary over the centuries and to some extent what they have decided to be both custom and practice and fair and reasonable. Specifically we can say that

Employees have a duty to

- provide faithful service which would include a duty not to commit theft or fraud;
- be willing and available to work;
- exercise reasonable care in the performance of that work;
- not wilfully to disrupt the employers undertaking;
- obey reasonable orders;
- work for the employer in the employer's time;
- respect trade secrets and not disclose sensitive and confidential information.

Employers have a duty to

- treat the employee with mutual trust, confidence and respect;
- pay the agreed wages;
- provide the opportunity for the wages to be earned. It is a moot point as to whether there is an obligation to provide work, but failure to satisfy this requirement is likely to require some payment in lieu of the opportunity to work and thereby earn the agreed wages;
- take reasonable care to ensure their employees' safety and to indemnify them for injury or loss, or expense, incurred.

Figure 5.1

Duties of employers and employees.

from this source the employee and employer each has a number of obligations and rights.

We noted earlier that terms could be implied from **custom and practice**. Here, the test to be satisfied is whether the custom or practice is 'reasonable, certain and notorious'; in other words, do the courts consider it reasonable?

- In the context of what might be normal in that industry?
- Is it capable of relatively precise definition?
- Did the parties know about it?

Where the courts conclude that the answers to these questions are positive, then it is likely that they will take the view that the custom or practice does constitute a term of the contract.

As we see there is a complex legal context to the employment relationship and to the behaviour of the parties and their representatives or agents. This context derives from a number of different sources, only some of which can be said to be outcomes of direct government intervention.

Since contracts are supposed to be agreed between the parties, unilateral variation of the terms of the contract is likely to be considered by the courts as breach of contract, though this may depend upon the terms of the contract itself; for example, the contract may provide the employer with rights to vary certain terms such as location or working hours. Where employers want to vary the contract, but are unable to obtain the agreement of the employee, it is possible for them to give the appropriate notice of termination of the contract and to invite the employee to agree to a new contract containing the new terms. Termination in this context may well be considered by the courts as a dismissal and, depending upon the circumstances, such a dismissal may be fair.

Trades unions and collective processes

Trade unions

Over the last 25 years of the 20th century and into the new millennium the voluntarist traditions of the UK were rejected, particularly by Conservative governments between 1979 and 1997, and there has been a considerable amount of legislative intervention and regulation of trades unions, their activities and their relationship with their members. Much of the detail is contained within **Figure 5.2** but it is impossible for us to examine this in this work; suffice to say that during this period the rights and freedoms of the trades unions were significantly curtailed.

The election of a Labour government in 1997 did not appear to herald a return to the legal situation as it was prior to 1979. The new government has made it quite clear that the trade union movement is not to be treated any more favourably than are the interests of business. There were a number of commitments made, for example:

- to reintroduce a statutory means by which trade unions could obtain recognition for collective bargaining from employers given evidence of adequate support levels;
- to introduce a minimum wage;
- to sign up to the social chapter of the EU Treaty as amended at the Amsterdam summit in the summer of 1997 (see **Chapter 4**);
- to end the requirement for a 3-yearly renewal of check-off arrangements
- for some protection for lawful strikers against unfair dismissal.

However, there was no general commitment to repeal the legislation of the preceding 18 years or to alter radically the balance of the legal context surrounding the employment relationship.

Trades unions are generally permitted to exist, to seek to regulate the employment relationship with employers through negotiation and to take industrial action in pursuit of a legitimate trade dispute. There are legal definitions of what constitutes a trade dispute and secondary and political action is excluded. As long as certain legislatively prescribed procedures have been complied with, they are also protected from civil actions being taken against them in respect of the damage caused by such action provided they have complied with the law. These protections are generally referred to in terms of trade union immunities. In the main these rights and protections only apply to trades unions that have been determined by the Certification Officer to be independent. Independence in this context refers to their not being under the domination or control of an employer. Most of the legislation relating to trades unions and their status, what they can do and cannot do, definitions of trade dispute, the procedures that have to be complied with for industrial action to be lawful are contained within the Trade Union and

The Employment Act 1980

- repealed the statutory procedure through which unions could obtain recognition;
- restrictions on the closed shop, people were to be given the right not to join on grounds of deeply held personal convictions, and any new closed shop was required to demonstrate an 80 per cent support level (or 85 per cent of those voting);
- repealed procedures whereby the CAC could extend collective agreements within industries to companies and groups of workers not currently covered;
- secondary picketing was outlawed and new legal requirements for picketing to be lawful;
- gave employers legal remedies against secondary action and picketing;
- public funds were made available to unions to encourage them to hold postal ballots for electing officers and before important policy decisions;
- employees' unfair dismissal rights were significantly reduced, as were rights to maternity leave and reinstatement, the relevant qualifying periods being increased from 6 months.

The Employment Act 1982

- continued the fight against the closed shop by requiring periodic ballots on all existing arrangements;
- tightened the definition of a trade dispute and reduced the scope of issues upon which trade unions could lawfully take industrial action and thereby retain their immunities from being sued in respect of loss suffered by others as a result. Excluded from the scope of lawful action were secondary and political actions;
- became lawful to dismiss strikers selectively after a specified period of strike activity.

The Trades Union Act 1984

- pre-strike ballots became a legal prerequisite for strike action to be lawful;
- union executive committee members (voting) had to submit themselves to periodic re-election (at least every 5 years);
- unions wishing to have a political fund should have this approved by the membership in a secret ballot at least every 10 years.

The Wages Act 1986

- removed young persons (those under 21 years of age) from the protection of the Wages Councils and also reduced the scope of the Councils' activities.

The Sex Discrimination Act 1986

- restrictions on (protection of) women's working hours were removed.

The Employment Act 1988

- gave trade union members the right not to be disciplined for not taking part in lawful industrial action and the right to take legal action against the union if that industrial action was taken without the appropriate secret ballot;
- established a new role of Commissioner for the Rights of Trade Union Members (CROTUM);
- all senior union officials (all National Executive Committee (NEC) members irrespective of whether they held the right to vote or not) were to be chosen by secret ballot;
- the post-entry closed shop was finally rendered unenforceable.

The Employment Act 1989

- repealed laws protecting young people through the regulation of the hours they could work and their working conditions;
- limited trade union officers' rights to time off for trade union activities;
- exempted small firms from the requirement that they should have written disciplinary procedures.

The Employment Act 1990

- effectively made the closed shop inoperable, action in support could not now be lawful and refusal of employment on grounds related to union membership (pre-entry) was also unlawful;

Figure 5.2
The extent and nature of legislative interventions in the UK over the past 25 years.

- employers were given greater freedom to dismiss employees taking unofficial industrial action;
- rendered unlawful any industrial action taken in support of employees dismissed for taking unofficial action;
- balloting requirements on the taking of lawful industrial action were tightened up; generally made much more difficult to take lawful secondary action.

The Trades Union Reform and Employment Rights (TURER) Act 1993

- Wages Councils were finally abolished;
- employees were given a right to belong to any union of their choice, thereby undermining long-standing jurisdictional and no-poaching agreements within the TUC-affiliated union movement;
- employers were given the responsibility of ensuring that individuals authorize deduction of union dues from their pay (check-off agreements) at least once every 3 years, thereby posing a threat to union finances;
- role of ACAS was diminished by removing from it the responsibility to encourage the extension of collective bargaining;
- the Transfer of Undertakings Regulations (1981) which protect employees job rights and terms and conditions in such circumstances were amended (in accordance with EU requirements) to include public-sector transfers;
- employees were given further protections from being penalized for undertaking legitimate health and safety activities;
- employees, through their representatives, were given information and consultation rights in the event of collective redundancy;
- subject to the receipt of qualified legal advice, employees were given rights to conclude agreements with their employers by which they opt out of their statutory rights regarding termination of employment and sexual and racial discrimination;
- it became lawful for employers to offer inducements to employees to switch to individual contracts, including inducements to opt out of collective bargaining and/or leave a trade union. Arguably for the first time it became lawful to pay non-union members more than union members;
- the traditional tripartite nature of industrial tribunals potentially weakened by allowing certain cases to be heard by the Chair alone with just one lay member;
- unions were required to give the employer at least 7 days' notice of their intention to hold the necessary ballot and/or take industrial action;
- citizens were given the right to take legal action in cases of unlawful industrial action affecting the supply of goods and services;
- various provisions were introduced concerning trade union amalgamation ballots, political funds and other union financial matters;
- employees were now to be given a more detailed written statement of the main particulars or terms of their contract of employment.

Employment Rights Act 1996

- in the main a consolidation of existing rights.

The Employment Relations Act 1999

- employees and their trade unions were given limited rights to force an employer to recognize the union for the purposes of collective bargaining, given evidence of majority membership or adequate support levels in some form of ballot;
- disputes on these provisions to be decided by the CAC;
- there were some amendments to the procedural rules on trade union ballots in respect of taking industrial action;
- a requirement was introduced for employers to consult recognized trade unions on training plans and policies;
- the dismissal of strikers would be unlawful for the first 8 weeks of lawful action;
- workers (not employees) were given the right to be accompanied by a trade union official or fellow worker at disciplinary and grievance hearings, irrespective of whether the union is recognized;

Figure 5.2
(Continued)

- employees were given the right not to be unfairly dismissed after the completion of 1 year of continuous employment (2 years before);
- the limit was raised on the size of financial award available to employees in the event of unfair dismissal;
- the waiver of unfair dismissal rights was prohibited in fixed-term contracts;
- maternity leave rights were extended to 18 weeks (40 weeks after 1 year of continuous service);
- effect was given to the European directive on parental leave but the rights were to unpaid leave;
- the European directive on equality for part-time workers was given effect.

Employment Act 2002

- introduced the requirement for all employers to have minimum (standard) internal disciplinary and grievance procedures;
- removed the 20-employee threshold on the requirement for employers to provide information on disciplinary and grievance procedures in the statement of main particulars;
- altered the way unfair dismissals were to be judged so that, provided the minimum standards set out in the Act were met and the dismissal was otherwise fair, procedural shortcomings could be disregarded;
- provided for efficient, swifter delivery of tribunal services through practice directions, management of weak cases, revision of the costs regime and mandatory tribunal forms; implemented the EC directive on fixed-term work which prevents pay and pension discrimination against fixed-term employees;
- limited the use of successive fixed-term contracts to ensure that people were not on a string of contracts in what was really a permanent job;
- introduced a new statutory right to time off for trade union learning representatives (ULRs) to ensure that they were adequately trained to carry out their duties;
- introduced an equal pay questionnaire in employment tribunal equal pay cases.

Employment Relations Act 2004

- measures were introduced to tackle the intimidation of workers during recognition and derecognition ballots by introducing rules which define improper campaigning activity by employers and unions and by clarifying what 'reasonable access' unions have to the workers in the bargaining unit;
- measures were introduced to improve the operation of the statutory recognition procedure. For example, the Act clarified issues surrounding the determination of the appropriate bargaining unit and the 'topics' for collective bargaining; it allowed unions to communicate with workers at an earlier stage in the process, and clarified and built upon the current legislation relating to the supply of information to the CAC and ACAS; provisions were introduced to increase employees' protection against being dismissed when taking official, lawfully organized industrial action, the 'protected period' was extended from 8 to 12 weeks and 'lock out' days were exempted from the 12-week protected period;
- the Act defined more closely the actions which employers and unions should undertake when taking reasonable procedural steps to resolve industrial disputes;
- it introduced measures to simplify the law on industrial action ballots and ballot notices;
- measures were taken to widen the ability of unions to expel or exclude racist activists and others whose political behaviour is incompatible with trade union membership;
- the Secretary of State was given the power to make funds available to independent trade unions and federations of trade unions to modernize their operations;
- the role of the companion in grievance and disciplinary hearings was clarified; the Secretary of State was given the power to make regulations to introduce the EU directive on information and consultation in the workplace;
- measures were taken to improve the enforcement regime of the national minimum wage;
- the Secretary of State was given the power to allow the inclusion of non-postal methods of balloting in statutory union elections and ballots.

Figure 5.2
(Continued)

Labour Relations Consolidation Act (TULRCA) of 1992. In addition, independent trades unions have a number of legislatively prescribed rights; for example, to information of assistance in collective bargaining and to take advantage of the statutory recognition procedures (Employment Relations Act 1999).

Trade union representatives as employee representatives also have rights to information and consultation on a range of subject matter and at various organizational levels as detailed in the chapter on the EU. It is important that we remember that EU legislation almost always grants rights to employee representatives and not to trade union representatives only. Where trades unions are recognized for collective bargaining, the trade union representatives also have rights to time off with pay in order to enable them to undertake legitimate trades union activities and to undergo training for their roles. Both trade union and non-union employee representatives generally have legal protection against being victimized or dismissed for undertaking their role.

Trade union members

Individuals generally have a right to join or not join a trade union and not to be discriminated against on the grounds of their union membership or non-membership. This right applies to employment, selection for redundancy, dismissal or other forms of disciplinary action and it is also unlawful for an employer to take such action to try and prevent or deter an individual from becoming a union member or to compel an individual to become a member of a particular union. Individuals again generally have a right not to be excluded from membership of a union and not to be expelled from membership except in certain permitted circumstances.

In the 1980s the Conservative government enacted legislation to compel unions to give their members certain rights in relation to the governance and administration of their trades unions, union members therefore have rights to elect in a secret postal ballot the members of the principal executive committee of the union and also to take part in a ballot on the establishment or continuance of a political fund.

Union members also have rights to take part in a secret ballot before the union takes organized industrial action against an employer, and the action must be in contemplation or furtherance of a trade dispute.

Collective bargaining

Generally, collective bargaining in the UK is freely entered into and the agreements made are not legally binding. There are legal definitions of both collective bargaining and collective agreements and they both relate to a range of specified subject matters which include both procedural and substantive matters such as terms and conditions of employment, discipline and grievance procedures and the machinery for negotiation and consultation.

It is worth pointing out that, whilst the agreements are not themselves legally binding, the contents can obtain a degree of legal force through the contract of employment, collective agreements being one of the sources of implied terms of the contract.

There is now statutory procedure which can be used by trades unions to force employers to recognize a trade union for collective bargaining, introduced in the **Employment Relations Act of 1999** and intended to encourage employers to enter into voluntary arrangements.

This new legislation applies only to independent trades unions and is quite complex, with a number of stages and final decisions on disputes to be taken by the Central Arbitration Committee (CAC), part of ACAS.

The initial claim is to be made by the trade union and in it they have to specify the workers for whom recognition is sought, the bargaining unit.

If the union can establish that it has majority membership in the unit specified, then recognition is relatively automatic, though the employer can appeal to the CAC for a secret ballot on grounds such as it being good for employee relations or their belief that a substantial minority of the workers in the proposed unit do not want recognition.

Where the union does not have a majority in membership, they should have at least 10 per cent membership and be able to demonstrate majority support as indicated for example by results of survey or petition.

The original application to the employer has to be in writing.

Once the claim is received by the employer, they have a number of possible options. They can of course agree to recognize and enter into discussions with a view to coming to an agreement. Alternatively, they can contest the claim in which case the union can make an application to the CAC to resolve the issue.

If this happens, the CAC has the power to decide the bargaining unit and to conduct a ballot of the workers in the unit. If such a ballot is conducted and the union gets a majority of those voting in favour and these constitute at least 40 per cent of the proposed unit, then the CAC will order that the employer recognize and if necessary impose a collective bargaining procedure, the subject matter to include hours, pay, workload allocation and discipline.

The trades unions have complained about the fact that small employers are excluded from the coverage of the legislation and that they have to obtain support in a ballot of at least 40 per cent of those entitled to vote. They have also argued against the opportunity that an employer has to circumvent the intention of the legislation by concluding a prior agreement with a staff association or non-independent union.

Information and consultation

The laws in the UK regarding requirements for employers to provide information and engage in consultation with employee representatives all pretty much derive from EU legislation, discussed in the earlier chapter on the EU (**Chapter 4**) and also in the subsequent chapter looking at employee relations processes (**Chapter 9**). Suffice to say that there are legislative requirements to inform and consult with regard to health and safety, transfers of undertakings, collective redundancies, in community scale undertakings and from 2005 onwards in undertakings at a national level. In this latter case the chapter on employee relations processes examines in some detail the implementing regulations for the UK.

Industrial action

We have noted earlier that unions can take lawful industrial action as long as it is in contemplation or furtherance of a trade dispute and the legislative procedural requirements have been complied with, part of which relate to the holding of a ballot of the members involved. If these conditions are satisfied, then the union will be protected from being sued. However, if the action is unlawful, and this includes unofficial action, then the immunities will no longer apply and those who suffer loss or damage as a result of the action may well be able to sue the union. This latter possibility is, of course, a very strong incentive for the unions to comply with the law part of which may involve the union leaders repudiating unofficial action.

Individuals taking part in industrial action may well be in breach of their contract of employment, definitely the case where the individual is engaged in strike action. Those taking part in lawful strike action are protected from fair dismissal for the first 8 weeks of the strike, but after that the employer can dismiss the strikers and employ alternative labour.

The extent and nature of legislative interventions in the UK over the last 20 years of the 20th century and into the new millennium can be seen from **Figure 5.2** in which we list the major Acts of Parliament concerning the employment relationship and the parties to it which have been adopted since 1979 and in which we briefly outline the major initiatives taken by each.

The law on discrimination and equality

The law in the UK with regard to the issues of discrimination and equality has to a very large extent been influenced by the UK's membership of the EU. We have noted in the previous chapter how the scope of the EU's competence in this field was expanded by agreement at the Amsterdam Council meeting in 1997 and we have noted the new Article 13

Directives which have been adopted since then and which are to be given effect in the UK as in all other member states. Prior to the adoption of the Article 13 Directives, the EU had already adopted legislation on equal opportunities and equal pay with regard to sex, and had sought to render unlawful discrimination against part-time and fixed-term workers. Prior to the Article 13 Directives being adopted, the UK had legislation seeking to secure equality of treatment and prevent discrimination on the grounds of race and disability; the former, as with legislation relating to equality on the grounds of sex, had been adopted back in the 1970s. The legislation on disability had been adopted in the UK in 1995.

The law in the UK either does or will include provisions relating to issues covered in the new Article 13 Directives concerning:

- direct and indirect discrimination,
- objective justification and genuine occupational qualifications,
- the burden of proof,
- victimization,
- positive action.

Government as employer

The size and nature of the public sector is inevitably linked to the dominant notions that government has about the kind of society it considers desirable, its economic and social objectives and priorities and its beliefs and judgements about how these may be best achieved. Within this will be government's ideas about what the public sector is for. It is likely that countries in which government has an essentially liberal ideology will have a relatively small public sector, with government leaving the provision of goods and services to the private sector, whereas countries in which government adopts an essentially corporatist approach are likely to have a significantly greater public sector with many services and goods being provided through state-owned undertakings.

Having said that, there is always likely to be a public sector comprised of the various national, regional and local government administrative functions and operations so that the public sector tends to be made up of government administrative agencies and staff at various levels as well as organizations acting as providers of utilities, goods and services.

There are also different degrees to which government might want to own and operate the various activities that might make up the public sector directly. Full nationalization tends to imply that the state will both own and run the activity with overall policy being determined by politicians and operations being handled by a state appointed board. Alternatively, the government might take a different and more commercial approach whereby they retain majority ownership and control but give both policy and operations over to a board appointed by government with an expectation that the undertaking will operate in an essentially private-sector manner, or government might take the view that the undertaking should be placed in the private sector but with a regulator appointed by government and with responsibilities in areas of quality of service provision and price.

Whatever the form of public-sector government chooses it is in a position to influence employee relations within it.

Frequently governments have sought to act as model employers, employers of best practice setting an example to the private sector. What constitutes 'best practice' of course varies according to the perspective of government and the traditions and culture prevalent in the country concerned, and it is quite likely to extend into procedures and practices as well as substantive terms and conditions of employment. Public-sector organizations, because of the dominant influence of central or local government in policy determination and decision making, often exhibit centralized decision-making processes and many of the other features of bureaucracies.

It is also common for management and staff in public-sector organizations, particularly those employed in the public and welfare services, to exhibit relatively high degrees of commitment to the values, objectives and activities of the 'service'. This commitment, however, can be diminished or enhanced by the management styles as well as by the human resource policies and practices pursued. Some governments have used their control of funding in the public sector to encourage particular approaches and styles. The UK is perhaps the best example of this in recent years, where public-sector managements have been encouraged to pursue efficiency and performance and to take responsibility for wage determination locally rather than relying, as is traditional, on national level bargaining.

Public-sector trade unionism is often higher than that in the private sector and one of the reasons for this is that, whether as a model employer or not, governments have often encouraged trade union membership and collective bargaining. Having said that, it is also common for trade union membership and/or collective bargaining to be discouraged, if not against the law, in certain selected public-sector activities such as defence, the armed forces and the police service. In particularly sensitive areas such as these, it is relatively common for industrial action by employees to be unlawful and governments often use the national interest and employer prerogative as the justification for such discouragement or illegality. As an alternative to free collective bargaining and the ability to take industrial action, government might insist on compulsory conciliation and/or arbitration as the means of resolving disputes. Public-sector employees may also be excluded from some legislative rights provided to employees in the private sector.

In the civil, welfare and public service areas, terms and conditions of employment are often determined, either unilaterally or jointly, using some form of mechanism that seeks to compare them with those applicable in 'similar' private-sector organizations or employment categories. Through its control of funding, government can also apply various forms of incomes policy to its own employees, and often does so as an example to the private sector. It is therefore quite common for these public-sector employees to be continually seeking to 'catch up' with terms and conditions prevailing elsewhere, although it is also the case in some systems that 'non-wage benefits', perhaps particularly security of employment and retirement provisions, are better than those available in the private sector and in this respect at least the employees are privileged.

Public-sector employees are vulnerable to governmental change, particularly if the perspective of an incoming government is of a liberalist nature. Privatization, exposure to market forces and public expenditure cuts obviously contain the potential for insecurity of employment, but they also frequently herald imperatives for cultural change within the organizations that remain.

The UK

Pre-1979

As we have detailed in earlier sections of this chapter the election of a Conservative government in 1979 constituted something of a watershed and this is also the case with regard to the role and scale of the public sector and to the management of employee relations within the sector.

Most analysts appear to agree that, prior to 1979 and perhaps with the exception of rates of pay, the public sector set an example to the private sector with respect to the employment and management of human resources and industrial relations, the example set being consistent with both liberal collectivist and pluralist notions and perspectives. Trade union membership and recognition were encouraged and terms and conditions of employment were determined jointly through collective bargaining at national level. The systems of industrial relations were formal, constitutional with an emphasis upon agreed procedures, and centralized.

At local level, the role of personnel management, and to some extent also union representatives, was essentially that of administering and interpreting the national agreements, some of which were both enormous and enormously complex. Black and Upchurch (1999) quote the example of the Civil Service Pay and Conditions of Service Code as containing 11,500 paragraphs of regulations from major pay scales down to 'daily pedal cycle allowances'.

In most instances also there were procedural agreements in place in respect of grievances and appeals against decisions made locally which ensured that final decisions were taken at the centre, in many ways resembling judicial processes that provide for appeal to the highest court in the land. Decisions made at the centre in this way also tended to constitute binding precedent for the practitioners at local level and were often promulgated as such in newsletters and other communications by both sets of parties to these central institutions.

Terms and conditions of employment, with the exception of pay, were generally better than those in the private sector, especially in areas such as job security, pension rights, entitlements to sickness leave and pay, holiday entitlements, working hours and the limitations upon management prerogative imposed through the emphasis upon joint decision making and consultation. In the main, pay was determined through collective bargaining but the scope available to the bargainers was limited. The base for pay determination tended to be derived from comparisons made with the rates being paid in the private sector for similar skills or jobs. It was always a catching-up process in that the rates agreed for the forthcoming year tended to reflect the rates already being paid in the private sector. This did not pose too much of a problem whilst inflation was low but as inflation increased in the 1970s (in 1974/1975 it reached 24 per cent) the issue of public-sector pay became a major one, not helped by successive governments seeking to exert a moderating influence upon rates of pay in the private sector by restraining pay in the public sector. Employees and their union representatives began to feel that they were the subject of what these days might be referred to as a 'double whammy' with public-sector pay lagging behind private-sector rates and then, whenever government wanted to exert downward pressures on private-sector rates, it would impose restraint in the public sector so that public-sector rates were perceived to fall further behind. The culmination of these policies and dissatisfactions with pay policy in the public sector was the 'winter of discontent' of 1978–1979 and the subsequent election of a Conservative government. During this pre-1979 period the emphasis in the public sector was upon service provision.

Post-1979

The late 1970s and early 1980s represent the high point of the size of the public sector, at least as measured by the numbers employed. In 1979 some 7.4 million people were employed and this constituted almost 30 per cent of the total working population; by 1997 this had declined to around 5 million and 20 per cent of the working population. The first 5 years of Labour government after 1997 showed an overall increase of 350,000 over 1997 and the total was 5.3 million in 2002, about 19 per cent of the total working population. The vast majority of the decrease in public-sector employment over the period 1979–2002 had occurred in the public corporations sector, which includes the nationalized industries, from in excess of 1.75 million to less than 400,000 in 2002.

The decline in public-sector employment has been the product of a number of influences and initiatives by government; this includes a radical programme of denationalization or privatization, allied to policies of severe financial stringency in those sectors remaining where managers have been required to achieve successive cost efficiencies and savings year on year with government using a policy of **cash limits** and its ability to control public-sector borrowing as levers to achieve these objectives. Inevitably, labour costs have been in the forefront of the attack on costs.

In addition to the privatization of many undertakings, the government used other measures to commercialize the public sector. It sought to separate the role of purchaser from provider, with the purchasing role remaining within the public sector but with provision being in the private sector. For example, local authorities, acting as purchasers, were encouraged to put the provision of the service out for competitive tender to organizations in the private sector, the contract for the provision of the specified service in terms of quantity, frequency and quality then being awarded to the cheapest tender, or bid.

In the health service, also, we saw a separation between purchasing and providing achieved through giving health authorities the purchasing role and forcing the providers, the hospitals, doctors, etc. into separate organizations: health service trusts (which have remained part of the public sector) which were able to compete with one another for contracts to provide services. Again the opportunity was also given for private-sector organizations to enter into this competitive process.

The Conservative government elected in 1979 was firmly of the view that the trade union movement was too powerful and a source of imperfection and rigidity in the labour market. Additionally, the public sector was too big, it took too large a share of the nation's resources, it was inefficient, insufficiently responsive to the needs of society – not market responsive, employees were far too protected and too comfortable and management was weak.

The incoming government therefore began a programme of initiatives geared towards achieving the objectives of reducing the size of the public sector and the burden of public expenditure, making the public sector more market responsive and efficient and reducing the power of the unions, the unions in the public sector being singled out as of particular concern given their size and their ability to resist government policy initiatives. It was public-sector unions, in particular in the coal mining industry, that had been at the root of the defeat of the previous Conservative government in 1974 and it was the public-sector unions, particularly in local government, that had been in the fore-front of resistance to the Labour governments' incomes policies in the late 1970s and the ensuing troubles in the winter of 1978–1979.

Public-sector management were also exhorted by government to stand up to their employees and in particular their unions, to re-exert their authority and prerogative, and government often refused to allow dis-putes to go to arbitration (see later section on ACAS). Government has used its ultimate control over funding to encourage public-sector man-agements to introduce changes to work practices and payment schemes, the most common example in recent years probably being some elem-ent of individual performance-related pay. They have also used their control of funding to influence and contain rates of wage increase indirectly, making use of the cash limits mechanism to encourage the directly involved parties to confront a trade-off between employment, efficiency and wage rates.

The emphasis placed upon performance-related pay is reflective of initiatives whereby managements were also encouraged to introduce into the public sector a greater emphasis upon performance and per-formance measurement. Business units and cost centres were created with the emphasis being upon cost reduction and measures of output per unit of financial input, rather than the tradition of service and effectiveness.

Initiatives were also deliberately taken to bring into the public-sector managers from the private sector in the belief that they would be more in tune with and more adept at achieving what the government wanted.

Where organizations were created anew, even though they remained in the public sector, for example the NHS Trusts, they were required by government to develop their own terms, conditions and contracts of employment and employee relations policies and procedures. One of the government's intentions in doing this was to fragment employee relations in the public sector, to force a decentralization of employee relations, break up the centralized determination of terms and condi-tions and the highly structured and bureaucratic procedures referred to earlier which, it was felt (by government), contributed significantly to the power of the public-sector unions.

It was also firmly part of the government agenda to force pay deter-mination down to a local level because it was thought that the national determination of pay inevitably led to rates that were far higher than would otherwise have been necessary to attract labour in many local labour markets, this in turn forcing up rates for other labour in those same local labour markets as other employers competed for that labour.

By and large, public-sector employees have the same or equivalent employment rights and protections as those in the private sector, although some groups have had their freedom to join a trade union and rights to be represented arbitrarily removed. This happened in 1984 to GCHQ employees, GCHQ being a highly sensitive national security establishment, teachers also having their collective bargaining rights removed from them by the Remuneration of Teachers Act 1987. Perhaps more important still was the belief/determination of the government to argue that the Transfers of Undertakings Regulations 1981 did not apply to the public sector (see **Chapter 4** on the EU).

Throughout the 1980s and into the 1990s the government refused to acknowledge the relevance of the directive to those in the public sector, to operations that it itself controlled. It is difficult to escape the conclusion that the reason for this was because it saw the requirements of the directive as undermining its desire to reduce costs in the public sector by forcing service provision into the private sector where employees could be paid less and where they would have worse terms and conditions of employment. This was a particular issue where local authorities were being forced to put service provision out to tender and where contracts were being won on the basis that the service would be provided more cheaply. Government was finally forced to accept that it had not implemented the directive appropriately and non-commercial organizations were brought into the scope of the regulations in the Trades Union Reform and Employment Rights (TURER) Act 1993.

From the perspective of the employees and their representatives, all of these initiatives had a number of significant implications. Employees were in many instances confronted fairly suddenly with significant cultural change and with insecurity; many were actually made redundant either prior to privatization or subsequent to it. Many public-sector employees were quite suddenly confronted by a management with a different agenda; service provision was no longer as important as cost reduction, performance measurement and efficiency. Employees were also confronted with new ways of working and with initiatives such as performance appraisal. Whereas in the past employees and their representatives had recourse to appeal, grievance and dispute procedures outside the organization, they found these avenues cut off and they were confronted with a more assertive and influential local management, even though that local management was often quite inexperienced in employee relations matters.

These changes also confronted the unions with resourcing issues since, as employment declined so did union membership, and as this declined so did their income. However, at the same time as income was declining, the unions were in many cases being forced to deal with a much larger number of organizations at a local level rather than with the one body at national level. Not surprisingly, the unions fought hard to resist the government's wish to decentralize and localize employee relations in the public sector, with some eventual success, for example within the health service and education.

The public sector has seen pro-rata more overt industrial conflict over the last two and a half decades than has been the case in the private sector and this would appear, in part at least, to be a response to the changes that government have sought to introduce and to the government's determination to succeed, and if this meant standing up to the unions and resisting strike action, then so be it. The most famous instance of this determination was the strike in the coal industry in 1984–1985, but there have been many other instances of attempted resistance in the civil service, the health service, by teachers in schools and further education, in local authorities, on the railways and even by ambulance workers and firefighters.

There is no doubt that significant changes have been introduced into the public sector with considerable impact upon employees and employee relations. This change was introduced by a government pursuing confrontational and competitive policies and approaches.

In the face of such a concerted and significant series of initiatives to change employee relations in the public sector, it is perhaps surprising that trade union membership is still considerably higher than in the private sector (see **Chapter 7** on trade unions) and the unions have managed to resist the drive for localization of bargaining and the determination of terms and conditions to a much greater extent than one might have expected, with main terms and conditions still determined at national level in sectors such as the NHS and education.

Picking up on the discussion in the first chapter regarding the difference between employee and industrial relations, Black and Upchurch (1999) suggest that the framework in much of the public sector is still indicative of industrial relations rather than employee relations.

The election of a Labour government in 1997 brought some change in the policies adopted towards the public sector. Early commitments to maintain the previous governments' spending plans have been relaxed and there has been some expansion of both health and education. Yet privatization has not been abandoned and government's insistence that capital projects should be funded through private finance, as an alternative to public expenditure, is perceived by many employees and the trades unions as privatization by another name.

This government seems just as keen on setting performance targets and in tying pay increases to performance, change or modernization, as it likes to refer to it. In many sectors, perhaps most notably with the firefighters, the government has been determined to try and change traditional and outmoded working practices in the pursuit of greater flexibilities and unit cost reductions. It has shown itself willing to stand firm against what it perceived to be outdated and selfish behaviour on the part of the workers.

There is still a belief that the public sector is full of inefficiency, that considerable cost savings are waiting to be achieved and that businessmen from the private sector are more likely to achieve these efficiencies than are those in the public sector, though there may be little evidence to support this belief.

There is some evidence that this government is not so intent upon pursuing the decentralization of the determination of basic pay and other terms and conditions of employment and the fragmentation of collective bargaining. However, there is little evidence to suggest that the government is concerned to improve terms and conditions of employment in the public sector and it is still the case that many public-sector workers have low pay and poor working conditions.

Public-sector workers tend to be surrounded by performance targets, many of which relate to achieving best value and customer satisfaction; these constitute twin pressures on public-sector workers and no doubt have some role in the low levels of employee satisfaction and morale often reported. Certainly the public sector that many workers joined, a sector concerned with service and quality of provision and care, and where employee relations were firmly pluralist in nature with leading edge terms and conditions of employment is not the same as the public sector that these workers now experience, one which they perceive to be concerned with cost reduction and the ruthless pursuit of efficiency savings, where terms and conditions of employment have worsened, where pressure is much greater and where management do not seem to share the traditional value system.

The state and dispute resolution

We noted in the introduction to this chapter that attitudes towards the desirability of market versus non-market forms of regulation would influence whether the state relied upon the parties resolving their own disputes through the exercise of market power or whether they would require or provide facilities for the resolution of such disputes through some form of non-market mechanism. In this particular context it is relatively common for governments of a corporatist, and possibly liberal collectivist, persuasion to require or encourage the parties to take advantage of opportunities for conciliation, arbitration or mediation by an independent third party as an alternative to resorting to industrial action to exert further pressure upon the other party or to the judicial process in the case of the dispute concerning a statutory or other legal right. These disputes can be either collective or individual, but we should remember that non-liberal approaches perceive individual workers to be at a significant disadvantage in their relationship with the employer if the resolution of disputes is left to the market. In some countries, government establishes and funds organizations to undertake this role.

In the UK an independent but largely government funded body, ACAS, performs these roles.

Advisory, Conciliation and Arbitration Service

ACAS was created in 1974 by the incoming Labour government which had the agreement with the unions and employers that we have referred to earlier as the Social Contract. At the level of the governing council, ACAS was an example of the tripartite approach we have associated with a corporatist ideology; however, it was given a formal role emphasizing the improvement of industrial relations through the extension of collective bargaining and through encouraging the voluntary development and reform of collective bargaining machinery. In this context, the organization can be seen to be reflective of the traditional liberal collectivist perspectives and preferences of the parties. Given the inclinations of the Conservative governments from 1979 onwards, it is surprising that the formal requirement to encourage collective bargaining was not actually removed until 1993 in the TURER Act.

What services does ACAS provide?

As its name suggests, ACAS has always had a role in dispute resolution, both individual and collective, and it has always provided a mix of conciliation, advisory and information services and arbitration and this continues. It has also over the years produced a number of Codes of Practice to be taken into account by the employment tribunals and other levels of the judicial system, the Code of Practice on Grievance and Disciplinary Procedures being one of them (see **Chapter 10**):

- **Arbitration** is where the parties involved ask a third party to **decide**, much like a judge, an issue or dispute between them which they cannot themselves resolve and they agree to abide by the outcome.
- **Conciliation** is where in the event of a dispute between the parties, they both ask a third party to **help** them come to an agreement. These disputes may concern an individual employee or a group.
- **Mediation** is somewhere between the two processes above and consists of a third party coming up with **recommendations** to the parties on how the dispute might be resolved.

By far the majority of the ACAS caseload is concerned with conciliating in individual disputes where the individual feels that one or more

Table 5.1

Individual conciliation caseload by subject

All jurisdictions						
Nature of claim	**2005/2006**		**2004/2005**		**2003/2004**	
	Number	**%**	**Number**	**%**	**Number**	**%**
Unfair dismissal	**44,397**	**23.1**	42,459	28.8	47,682	27.0
Wages Act	**33,175**	**17.3**	36,785	25	40,928	23.2
Breach of contract	**25,761**	**13.4**	21,030	14.3	28,471	16.1
Redundancy pay	**6,818**	**3.6**	6,427	4.4	8,707	4.9
Sex discrimination	**12,984**	**6.8**	10,813	7.3	13,778	7.8
Race discrimination	**4,112**	**2.1**	3,277	2.2	3,418	1.9
Disability discrimination	**4,529**	**2.4**	4,730	3.2	5,490	3.1
Working time	**34,365**	**17.9**	3,255	2.2	7,506	4.3
Equal pay	**14,147**	**7.4**	7,586	5.1	3,073	1.8
National minimum wage	**371**	**0.2**	432	0.3	569	0.3
Flexible working	**237**	**0.1**	240	0.2	201	0.1
Other	**10,989**	**5.7**	10,384	7.0	16,682	9.4
Total	**191,885**		**147,418**		**176,505**	

Source: ACAS Annual Report for 2004.

statutory rights has been infringed and there might be a legitimate claim to an employment tribunal. **Table 5.1** shows how large this caseload is with some 176,000 cases being dealt with in the year 2003–2004. ACAS has a statutory responsibility to promote a settlement in many of these disputes. **Table 5.1** shows the individual conciliation caseload by subject. Of these cases, ACAS manages to reduce the number that actually progress to a tribunal hearing by about three-quarters.

These figures do appear to indicate an enormous number of individuals alleging that an employer or some other party, another employee or a trade union, had infringed one or more of their legal rights with regard to work. It seems reasonable to assume that the increase over the years in the numbers of these cases is a response to the increased number of statutory rights acquired by employees in recent years, but it is also possible that it is a reflection of people both becoming more aware of their rights and being increasingly willing to exercise them.

The number of collective disputes in which ACAS conciliates is much lower and in the same year the number of such collective conciliations was 1245 and ACAS claims a success rate in such cases of over 90 per cent. Arbitration in collective disputes was 69 in the year in question. When ACAS arranges arbitration in such cases it has a panel of independent arbitrators from which one or more are picked to deal with the case in question.

ACAS' role has developed and changed over its first 30 years of existence and now its mission is to 'improve organizations and working life through better employment relations'. It feels that it can best do this through focusing on five main themes:

1 workplace effectiveness and productivity,
2 supporting smaller businesses,
3 individuals and working life,
4 equality and diversity,
5 managing change in the public sector.

ACAS claims in its annual report for 2004 that all of its services aim to make workplaces more effective – from good practice advice and training to in-depth projects with individual organizations. It has developed its own model of an effective workplace which can be seen as a statement of best practice. This model suggests that effective workplaces typically have at least some of the following:

- ambitions, goals and plans that employees are familiar with and understand;
- managers who genuinely listen to and consider their employees' views so everyone is actively involved in making important decisions;
- people who feel valued so they can talk confidently about their work and learn from both successes and mistakes;
- everyone treated fairly and valued for their differences;
- work organization that encourages initiative, innovation and people working together;
- an understanding that people have interests and responsibilities outside work so they can openly discuss ways of working that suit personal needs and the needs of the business;
- a pay and reward system that is clear, fair and consistent;
- a safe and healthy place to work;
- as much employment security as possible;
- a culture where everyone is encouraged to learn new skills so that they can look forward to further employment either in their present workplace or elsewhere;
- a good working relationship between management and employee representatives that in turn helps build trust throughout the business;
- procedures for dealing with disciplinary matters, grievances and disputes that managers and employees know about and use fairly.

ACAS emphasizes the role of communication and consultation with employees and state that, where relationships are not running smoothly, it often finds poor communication is one of the main causes.

There are distinct similarities between this model and the elements of the psychological contract which Gennard and Judge (2002) and others have identified as the expectations of the parties (see **Chapter 1**). This model emphasizes fairness and equity, trust, family-friendly conditions of work, employees having a measure of influence over day-to-day operations, a culture emphasizing training and development and potential, job security, being valued as a person as well as an employee, effective communication and consultation, the ability to work with others, the capability to take initiative and cope with change and a culture in which taking initiative is valued.

There are also significant similarities between this ACAS model of the effective workplace and the advice given in the literature concerning how to ensure that workers are committed to the success of the organization (see **Chapter 8**).

Summary

In this chapter we have examined the various roles or ways in which government at a national level forms part of the context in which employee relations are conducted. In the main we have concentrated upon the four functions or roles: as economic manager, as legislator, employer and its role in dispute resolution.

In all of these areas attention has been paid to demonstrate the relevance of ideology, values and beliefs, to the policies and strategies pursued. In particular, we examined the ideological approaches known as liberalism and corporatism and the relevance of these approaches to whether nation states have a predominantly LME or CME.

In exemplifying these roles and influences, we focus on developments in the UK over the last quarter of the 20th century and the early years of the new millennium. In the context of the influence of government upon employee relations in the UK, it seems clear that 1979 and the election of a Conservative government constitute watersheds. Analysts may argue as to whether economic policy or the new legislative framework were the more influential but there is little disagreement that profound change was signalled by this event. Economic policy was driven by a conviction that competitiveness on the world stage was linked to the achievement of control over inflation, that this control was to be achieved through supply-side measures rather then through the management of aggregate demand and that unemployment was a price worth paying. Trade union power had to be diminished, management had to reclaim its authority and the regulations and institutions of the labour market and social protection had to be reformed.

In the public sector, it signalled the end of a dominant concern with service provision and equity, social welfarism and the beginnings of a period of management by confrontation, deteriorating employee terms and conditions of employment and greater insecurity and a determined drive to decentralize and localize the determination of terms and conditions of employment and the conduct of employee relations. This was to be accompanied by a drive for efficiencies and economies with the emphasis upon performance and output productivity per unit of input.

The election of a Labour government in 1997 has not signalled a return to the pre-1979 situation, though there has been some encouragement of collective bargaining, the introduction of a minimum wage, some extension of employee protection and some expansion of the public sector in service areas such as education and health. However economic policies have been geared towards achieving stability and international competitiveness through a continuing reliance upon essentially deregulated product markets with some active initiatives on the supply side of the labour market to enhance the quality of the labour force and to encourage employability. Pressure on the economically inactive has been maintained, with benefit policies geared towards incentivizing work.

In the final section of the chapter, we examined the role that government can play towards the resolution of disputes, including the role of ACAS, the trends in and distribution of its workload and its recently devised model of an effective workplace. A model that has distinct similarities with modern perceptions of the psychological contract and also with notions of how to secure a committed workforce.

Activities to test understanding

Activity 1

Think about the ideological stereotypes detailed here and think through the implications of each for the role of government in employee relations.

Activity 2

Which of the Ideologies is consistent with market and non-market-based systems of regulation?

Activity 3

Briefly explain how the different approaches of monetarism and Keynesianism influence the bargaining power of the parties to employee relations.

Activity 4

Why is the OECD concerned by the pursuit of full employment through market-based and supply-side approaches?

Activity 5

Look back over the text concerning the legal context and in particular **Figure 5.2**, and work out for yourself the *major* elements of the legal framework in the UK regarding:

- the framework for collective relationships and interactions,
- the relationship of the individual trade union member with his trade union.

Activity 6

Explain the meaning of the term 'implied' with regard to the terms of a contract of employment and identify the main sources of such implied terms.

Activity 7

Read again the section on the industrial/employee relations systems in the UK public sector before and after 1979, pick out the main elements and contrast them.

Activity 8

Explain the difference between arbitration and conciliation.

Activity 9

One or other of the parties are often reluctant to allow a dispute to go to arbitration and in the UK the incidence of arbitration is less than the incidence of conciliation. Why do you think this is?

References

ACAS 2004 Annual Report for 2004.

Black, J. and Upchurch, M., 1999. Public sector employment. In Hollinshead, G., Nicholls, P. and Tailby, S. (eds), *Employee Relations*. Financial Times Pitman Publishing, London.

Blyton, P. and Turnbull, P., 1998. *The Dynamics of Employee Relations*, 2nd Edition. Macmillan, Basingstoke.

Crouch, C., 1982. *The Politics of Industrial Relations*, 2nd Edition. Fontana, London.

Dickens, L. and Hall, M., 1995. The state: labour law and industrial relations. In Edwards, P. (ed), 1995. Industrial and Relations: Theory and Practice in Britain. Blackwell, Oxford.

Flanders, A., 1974. The tradition of Voluntarism. *British Journal of Industrial Relations*. 12(3): 352–70.

Gennard, J. and Judge, G., 2002. *Employee Relations*. CIPD, London.

Hall, P.A. and Soskice, D., 2001. *Varieties of Capitalism: The Institutional Foundations of Comparative Advantage*. Oxford University Press, Oxford.

Hollinshead, G. and Leat, M., 1995. *Human Resource Management: An International and Comparative Perspective on the Employment Relationship*. Financial Times Pitman, London.

Keller, B.K., 1991. The role of the state as corporate actor in industrial relations systems. In Adams, R.J. (ed.), *Comparative Industrial Relations, Contemporary Research and Theory*. Harper Collins, New York, p. 83.

Kochan, T.A., Katz, H.C. and McKersie, R.B. 1986. *The Transformation of American Industrial Relations*. Basic Books, New York.

OECD, 1999. *Annual Employment Outlook*.

OECD, 2004. *Annual Employment Outlook*.

Supiot, A., 2001. *Beyond Employment-Changes in Work and the Future of Labour Law in Europe*. Oxford University Press, Oxford.

Willey, B. and Morris, H., 2003. Regulating the employment relationship. In Hollinshead, G., Nicholls, P. and Tailby, S. (eds), *Employee Relations*. Financial Times Pitman, London.

UK Acts of Parliament

The Contracts of Employment Act 1963
The Industrial Training Act 1964
The Redundancy Payments Act 1965
The Trades Disputes Act 1965
The Race Relations Act 1968
The Equal Pay Act 1970
The Industrial Relations Act 1971
The Trade Unions and Labour Relations Act 1974
The Health and Safety at Work Act 1974
The Sex Discrimination Act 1975
The Employment Protection Act 1975
The Employment Protection (Consolidation) Act 1978
The Employment Act 1980
The Transfers of Undertakings Regulations 1981
The Employment Act 1982
The Trades Union Act 1984
The Wages Act 1986
The Sex Discrimination Act 1986

The Remuneration of Teachers Act 1987
The Employment Act 1988
The Employment Act 1989
The Employment Act 1990
The Trades Union and Labour Relations Consolidation Act 1992.
The Trades Union Reform and Employment Rights (TURER) Act 1993
The Employment Rights Act 1996
The Employment Relations Act 1999
The Employment Act 2002
The Employment Relations Act 2004.

Chapter 6

Demography, labour force and market characteristics and trends

Introduction

I noted in **Chapter 2** that the dominant model of employment associated with Fordism which was characterized by the mass employment of male breadwinners, working full time and with continuity of employment and career was being replaced with something much more flexible, fragmented and unstable, with employees experiencing much more frequent career breaks, unemployment and greater insecurity. I also noted in the context of the model of the flexible firm that numerical flexibility was increasingly being achieved through the utilization of peripheral and secondary groups taking in temporary and agency workers, subcontracting and self-employment. It is against this background that we examine in this chapter the relevance of demographic developments and labour market and labour force developments and trends.

It was also pointed out in **Chapter 3** that no national labour market exists in isolation from international developments and the process of globalization and expansion of international free-trade arrangements has contributed to the exporting of traditional manufacturing activities to the developing world, resulting in implications for the value of traditional skills and the job security of employees in the developed countries and also for the distribution of employment by sector and the availability and nature of jobs. Many countries within the developed world have experienced persistent unemployment and, proportionately, employment in the services sector continues to increase.

It has also been noted in earlier chapters on the European Union (EU) and the role of the State that the pursuit of different policy objectives and the use of particular instruments are likely to have differential implications for labour markets and the make up of the labour force. Governments are able to influence economic growth rates, the distribution of income and wealth, the nature and availability of employment, the extent to which labour markets are regulated and employees protected, the nature of employment contracts and the economic activity participation rates of different groups within the population.

The relevance of these developments for employee relations is, of course, that they impact upon the bargaining power (see **Chapter 9**) of the various parties and influence the nature of the employment relationship and the terms and conditions of employment.

In this chapter I examine:

■ demographic developments;
■ trends in labour force participation with a particular emphasis upon gender and age group;
■ the incidence of part-time employment;
■ the experience of unemployment with particular focus upon gender, youth and long-term unemployment;
■ trends in the sectoral distribution of employment;
■ factors influencing female participation;
■ the influence of educational attainment levels on labour force participation and unemployment.

These issues and trends are examined in the context of data for the OECD member states and those in the EU 15. Again we use the UK as an example though I will point out where there are important international differences. The UK is a member of both the OECD and the EU 15 and we identify relevant developments in the UK in a series of boxes as we deal with each of the various topics.

Learning objectives

After studying this Chapter you will be able to:

- Identify and explain the main demographic trends, in particular the phenomenon of an ageing population and workforce, and the implications for future labour supply.

- Analyse and discuss a range of labour force participation and labour market trends with a particular focus on trends by gender and age group.
- Identify and explain trends in part-time working.
- Discuss and explain trends in unemployment with particular focus on variations according to gender, age and length of unemployment.
- Understand and discuss the range of social, cultural, economic and other influences upon female participation in the labour force.
- Discuss the relationship between educational attainment levels and employability by gender.

Demography

There are two main demographic trends visible in developed countries over the latter part of the 20th century and extending into the 21st. These are declining birth and mortality rates which, in combination, are resulting both in an ageing population and an ageing workforce. The proportion of the population under 15 is declining and the proportion of the population over current retirement ages is increasing. As can be seen in **Table 6.1** in which a comparison is made between the situation in 1960 and that in 2000, it is clear that, while there are country by country variations, there is a consistency to these trends in OECD countries. While the proportion of the population that is of working age has not yet started to decline, a continuation of these trends will eventually result in that happening. Inevitably, as these trends work their way through, the workforce will age and the potential workforce, given current retirement ages, will decline. As is pointed out in another OECD working paper of 2004:

> In the face of the substantial ageing of population expected to occur in OECD countries over coming decades, policies that boost labour-force participation attract considerable interest. There remain large cross-country divergences in participation rates that are largely accounted for by differences in participation of specific groups, in particular prime-age women, older workers and also youth. This suggests that policies targeting these groups could have important effects.

Table 6.1

Main Demographic Trends: OECD countries.

DEMOGRAPHY													
	Total area (000 sq. km)	Population Thousands		Per sq. km	Growth rate	Age structure % of total population						Foreign population[1] % of total population	
						Under 15		15–64		65 and over			
		2000	1990	2000	2000/ 1999	2000	1990	2000	1990	2000	1990	2000	1990
				%									
Australia	7 687	19 157	17 065	2	1.2	20.5	30.2	67.2	61.3	12.3	8.5	23.6	22.3[c]	Australia
Austria	84	8 110	7 718	97	0.2	16.7	22.0	67.8	65.8	15.5	12.2	9.3	5.9	Austria
Belgium	31	10 251	9 967	338	0.2	17.6[a]	23.5	65.5[a]	64.5	16.6[a]	12.0	8.8[a]	9.1	Belgium
Canada	9 976	30 750	27 701	3	0.8	19.1	33.7	68.4	68.7	12.5	7.8	17.4[i]	16.1[c]	Canada
Czech Republic	79	10 272	10 362	130	−0.1	16.4	25.4	69.8	64.4	13.8	10.2	2.0	0.4[b]	Czech Republic
Denmark	43	5 340	5 141	124	0.3	18.5	25.2	66.7	64.2	14.8	10.8	4.8	3.1	Denmark
Finland	338	5 181	4 986	15	0.2	18.1	30.4	66.9	62.3	15.0	7.3	1.8	0.5	Finland
France	549	58 892	56 709	108	0.5	18.8	26.4	65.1	62.0	16.1	11.8	5.6[a]	6.3	France
Germany	357	82 205	63 254[c]	230	0.1	15.3	21.3[c]	67.5	67.8[c]	17.2	10.8[c]	8.9	8.4	Germany
Greece	132	10 543	10 089	80	0.2	15.5[b]	28.1	67.5[b]	65.8	16.7[b]	8.1	..	..	Greece
Hungary	93	10 024	10 365	108	−0.4	17.0	..	68.4	..	14.7	..	1.3[a]	1.3[i]	Hungary
Iceland	103	281	255	3	1.4	23.3	34.8	65.1	57.1	11.6	8.1	..	..	Iceland
Ireland	70	3 787	3 503	54	1.1	21.8	30.5	67.0	58.6	11.2	10.9	3.3	2.3	Ireland
Italy	301	57 189	56 737	190	0.2	14.5	23.4[d]	67.8	67.8[a]	17.7	9.0	2.4	1.4	Italy
Japan	378	126 926	123 611	338	0.2	14.8	30.2	67.9	64.1	17.3	5.7	1.3	0.9	Japan
Korea	99	47 275	42 869	478	0.9	21.6	42.3	71.2	54.8	7.1	2.9	0.4	0.1	Korea
Luxembourg	3	439	384	169	1.4	19.0	21.4	66.7	67.9	14.3	10.8	37.3	29.4	Luxembourg
Mexico	1 996	97 379	81 250	49	−0.2	33.7	..	61.0	..	5.3	..	0.5	0.4	Mexico
The Netherlands	41	15 926	14 947	390	0.7	18.8	30.0	67.8	61.0	13.6	9.0	4.1[a]	4.6	The Netherlands
New Zealand	269	3 831	3 363	14	0.5	22.9	32.9	65.3	58.5	11.8	8.7	24.2	..	New Zealand
Norway	324	4 491	4 241	14	0.8	20.0	25.9	64.8	63.2	15.2	10.9	4.1	3.4	Norway
Poland	313	38 646	38 119	124	0.0	19.2	33.5	68.6	60.8	12.2	5.8	0.1[a]	..	Poland
Portugal	92	10 008	9 873	108	0.2	17.0	..	67.9	..	15.1	..	2.1	1.1	Portugal
Slovak Republic	49	5 401	5 298	110	0.1	19.5	..	69.1	..	11.4	..	0.5	0.2[k]	Slovak Republic
Spain	505	39 466	38 851	78	0.1	15.0	27.3	68.1	64.5	16.8	8.2	2.2	0.7	Spain
Sweden	450	8 872	8 559	20	0.2	18.4	22.4	64.3	65.9	17.3	11.8	5.4	5.6	Sweden
Switzerland	41	7 184	6 712	174	0.6	16.8	23.5	67.4	66.3	15.8	10.2	12.3	16.3	Switzerland
Turkey	781	67 461	56 203	88	2.5	30.0	41.2	64.6	55.1	5.4	3.7	..	..	Turkey
United Kingdom	245	59 766	57 561	244	0.4	19.1[a]	23.3	65.0[a]	64.9	15.6[a]	11.7	4.0	3.2	United Kingdom
United States	9 372	275 372	249 973	29	0.9	21.3	31.0	66.1	59.7	12.6	9.2	10.4	7.9	United States
G7[2]	21 178	691 100	635 546	33	0.5	18.3	27.9	66.6	63.0	15.0	9.0	..	..	G7[2]
EU-15[2]	3 240	375 974	348 279	116	0.3	16.8	23.6	66.7	63.2	16.4	10.1	..	..	EU-15[2]
OECD Total[2]	34 800	1 120 423	1 015 300	32	0.6	20.4	28.6	66.4	61.6	13.2	8.5	..	..	OECD Total[2]

Notes
.. not available
[1] Data for Australia, Canada, Mexico, New Zealand and the US relate to the proportion of foreign-born persons in total population.
[2] Area totals include only countries for which data are shown in the table.
[a] 1999.

[b] 1998.
[c] Former West Germany only.
[d] Under 14.
[e] 14–64.
[f] 1996.
[g] 1991.
[h] 1992.

[i] 1994.
[k] 1993.

Sources: Labour Force Statistics 1980–2000, OECD, Paris, 2001; Trends in International Migration, OECD, Paris, 2002.

Source: OECD in Figures. 2002.

and the authors conclude that

> the combined effect of possible reforms targeting prime-age women, older workers and youth might suffice to stabilize the average participation rate in OECD countries over the next 25 years but will be insufficient to offset the additional reduction of participation likely to be caused by demographic changes beyond 2025 (Burniaux *et al.*, 2004).

There are then concerns about the impact of these demographic changes upon the quantitative adequacy of the labour force in developed countries in the future and this poses threats to economic growth and to living standards. In addition to the impact of declining birth rates, enhanced participation of the below 25 groups in full-time education (see later) is likely to exacerbate the problem. The authors of the OECD report suggest that medium-term solutions may be achieved through policies aimed at enhancing participation rates of certain groups, particularly they imply the need to enhance the labour force participation rates of working age women, older workers and youth. The need to address the female participation rate is enhanced by the fact that in many countries the life expectancy of women is greater than that for men. The UK is an example of this with life expectancy for women being 5 years or so more than for men. Perhaps more pertinent, however, is that in the UK mortality rates for men are substantially greater than for women in pre-pensionable age ranges, an example being the 50–64 age group in which mortality rates for men are some 60 per cent greater than for women.

However, longer-term solutions may require other measures, one of which may be increased immigration and another might be raised retirement ages, so that people retire later. The latter solution has the additional benefit of reducing the pension burden on the state together with it also being consistent with moves within Europe to outlaw discrimination on the grounds of age.

There are various explanations of these demographic trends. The decline in mortality rates tends to be associated with medical advances, expansion of health care facilities and a generally healthier diet and lifestyle as countries develop; together these are resulting in people living longer and average life expectancy rising. Declining birth rates are often explained in terms of more women and men choosing not to marry and have children at all, women and men marrying later and having children later, and married couples having fewer children by choice. Social attitudes have changed, educational opportunities for women and opportunities for women to work and have careers have grown and people are more able to plan parenthood through various medical advances.

An alternative way of examining the impact of these demographic phenomena is to examine what are referred to as dependency ratios. The dependency ratio is a measure of the population over the age of 65 as a percentage of the labour force.

In **Figure 6.1** we can see the ratios for OECD member states comparing the position in 2000 with that projected for 2020.

The dependency ratio (right panel of the table) is projected to exceed 50 per cent in Hungary, France, Italy and Japan by 2020. This means that, for each elderly person, there will be only two persons in the labour force.

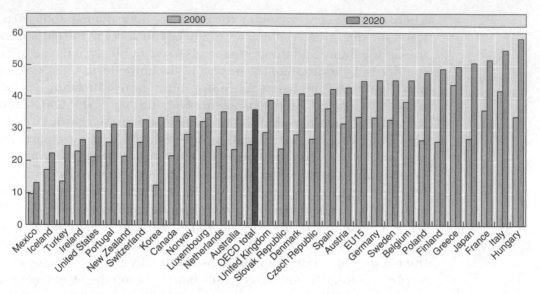

Figure 6.1
Ratio of the population aged 65 and over to the labour force (*Source: OECD Factbook 2006 – Economic, Environmental and Social Statistics*).

The lowest dependency ratios, under 30 per cent, are projected for Mexico, Iceland, Turkey and Ireland.

Labour force participation

Labour force participation rates are a measure of the proportion of the population of working age who are economically active; this is a wider measure than employment rates since it includes those who are economically active and not only those in employment.

The *OECD Employment Outlook 2005* provides information on labour force participation rates for 30 different countries and for both the EU 15 and total OECD. It is clear from these data that over the period 1990–2004 labour force participation had increased both for the EU 15 (from 67.3 to 70.8 per cent) and for the total OECD (from 69.3 to 70.1 per cent). There are, however, variations between the individual countries with rates in 2004 ranging from a low of 51.5 per cent in Turkey to 85.5 per cent in Iceland. Of the 30 countries included in the data only Hungary, Poland, Denmark, Finland, Sweden, Turkey, the UK and the USA had experienced declines in participation rates over the period covered. The picture then is one of generally increasing participation rates; however, both the EU 15 and total OECD rates indicate that some 30 per cent of the working age population were not economically active.

Labour force participation by gender

However, when the data are separated into gender rates, a somewhat different picture emerges; participation rates for men for the EU 15 (from 79.9 per cent in 1990 to 78.8 per cent in 2004) and for the total OECD (from 82.3 per cent in 1990 to 80.3 per cent in 2004) both show a decline. There are again variations between countries with lows in 2004 of 67.2 per cent in Hungary and 70.4 per cent in Poland and highs of 89.1 per cent in Iceland and 88.0 per cent in Switzerland. The trend picture in individual countries is more mixed with 10 of the 27 countries for which there were complete data over the period showing increased male participation rates.

Given that the general trends identified so far are increasing participation rates overall but declining male participation rates, it is no surprise to discover that female participation rates have been increasing over the period 1990–2004. For the EU 15 the rate has increased from 54.7 to 62.8 per cent and for the total OECD from 56.6 to 60.1 per cent. In the EU 15 the difference in male and female participation rates is 16 per cent and for the total OECD 20.2 per cent. It is evident straightaway why the OECD includes working age women as one of the major potential sources of increase in labour supply, despite the increases that have already occurred. Again there are considerable country variations with Turkey having the lowest female participation rate of 27.0 per cent and a high of 81.8 per cent in Iceland. If we look at the gap between male and female rates in individual countries, by far the biggest is Turkey where the gap is 49.1 per cent whilst the smallest gap is in Finland at 3.5 per cent. Of the 27 countries for which there are complete data only 6 show a decrease in female participation rates over the period, these being Sweden, Finland, Hungary, Poland, Denmark, and surprisingly, also Turkey.

There is a mix of social, cultural, religious, institutional, economic and other reasons to explain these country variations. Nevertheless, the overall trends are clear, increasing participation rates for the populations as a whole with the increase in female participation rates generally more than making up for the decrease in male rates. Despite this there are still significant differences in total, and in the majority of countries, between male and female participation rates with the rates for females being substantially lower than for men.

It is difficult to obtain comparable data for some of the developing economies such as China and India, however, the ILO (2003) indicates that for 1995 the labour force participation rate in China was 85.4 per cent, with the gap between male and female rates being a little under 10 per cent at 90.1 per cent for men and 80.4 per cent for women. The picture in India in the same year was very different with a total participation rate of 66.4 per cent and the gap between the male and female rates exceeding 40 per cent at 87.6 per cent for men and 43.6 per cent for women.

The UK

Labour force participation in the UK actually decreased slightly over the period 1990–2004, from 77.8 per cent in 1990 to 76.2 per cent in 2004; nevertheless the participation rate in the UK is significantly above the EU and total OECD averages. Male participation rates declined from 88.3 to 83.1 per cent and female participation rates increased from 67.3 to 69.6 per cent; these rates again are above the averages for the EU 15 and the total OECD and the gap between the gender rates is lower than the averages at 13.5 per cent. These participation rates are amongst the highest in the countries for which data are presented and suggest that there is somewhat less scope in the UK for increasing labour supply by increasing participation rates than is the case in many other countries.

Labour force participation by age group

In addition to working age women, other categories of the population identified earlier as providing scope for enhancing labour supply were older workers and youth. The same OECD source also provides data on these issues. The working age population is separated into three age ranges, 15–24, 25–54 and 55–64. Participation rates for these three age groups are strikingly different; in 2004, EU 15 and total OECD rates for the younger group were 48.2 and 49.9 per cent, both lower than the respective figures for 1990. For the middle age group the participation rates for EU 15 and total OECD were 83.9 and 80.6 per cent, both higher than in 1990 and for the older group the rates were 44.6 and 53.1 per cent and again these were both higher than in 1990. Overall trends then were declining participation among the young, possibly a reflection of people in this age range staying on longer in education and training, and increasing participation among both the other age groups. Nevertheless, there is considerable scope for enhancing labour force participation among both the youngest and oldest of these groups, and perhaps particularly within the EU among the 55 and over group.

If we examine the gender rates for the same age groups, we see gender gaps of less than 10 per cent in the youngest group in both EU 15 and total OECD, and between 17 and 23 per cent in the other age groups, the gaps in the EU are smaller than in the total OECD. The trends are the same for both sexes in the two younger groups; decreasing participation among the youngest group and increasing participation among the middle group; however, in the older group the participation rate for men has declined marginally whereas among women it has increased quite substantially and it is the increased participation of women in this older group that explains the overall increase among the 55+ group. Despite this increase, the participation rates for women in the oldest group are only 34.5 per cent in the EU 15 and 42.2 per cent in the total OECD.

The UK

Labour force participation among the younger group is substantially higher in the UK than are the EU 15 and total OECD averages above. In 2004, 67.4 per cent of this group in the UK were economically active. Participation among the middle group was slightly higher at 83.8 per cent and at 58 per cent participation among the oldest group was also higher. Similar overall trends were also detectable with decreasing participation among the youngest group and increasing participation among the oldest group, however, in the UK there had been a marginal decline in participation in the middle-age group.

The gender-based data show a gap in favour of men in each of the age groups, but it is narrowest in the youngest group (5.6 per cent) and increases further with each of the older groups, so that in the 55+ group the gender gap is 19.7 per cent. The participation rate for men has declined over the period 1990–2004 in all three age groups, though in the oldest of the groups the decline is marginal at 0.1 per cent and this hides steady increases in the last 3–4 years. For women there has been a decline in the youngest group but in both the other age groups the trend has been for increasing participation. As noted above, the participation rates in the UK tend to be relatively high in comparison with most of the other countries.

Part-time employment

One of the explanations often given for the increasing female participation rates that have been noted above is an expansion in the opportunities for part-time employment. Given that it is still very much the case that women perform the major caring and homekeeping roles within families, it seems logical that an expansion of opportunities for people to work part time is likely to benefit women disproportionately in their desire to be economically active.

The OECD also (see **Table 6.2**) provides evidence on the incidence and composition of part-time employment.

Trends over the period of 1994–2005 show that part-time employment as a proportion of total employment has been increasing; in the EU 15 the increase was from 14.6 to 18.1 per cent and in the total OECD it was from 11.6 to 15.4 per cent. There are again considerable variations between countries with the Netherlands having the highest proportion at 35.7 per cent in 2005 and a number of the East European

Table 6.2
Incidence and composition of part-time employment[a]
Percentages

	Part-time employment as a proportion of total employment					Women's share in part-time employment				
	1994	2002	2003	2004	2005	1994	2002	2003	2004	2005
Australia[b,c]	24.4	27.5	27.9	27.1	27.3	69.6	67.0	67.2	67.1	68.3
Austria	..	13.6	13.6	15.5	16.2	..	87.6	87.3	86.9	83.8
Belgium	14.6	17.2	17.7	18.3	18.1	81.8	80.1	81.0	80.6	80.8
Canada	18.9	18.8	18.9	18.5	18.3	68.9	68.8	68.8	68.8	68.6
Czech Republic	3.6	2.9	3.2	3.1	3.3	67.7	73.4	71.9	72.9	72.8
Denmark	17.3	16.2	15.8	17.5	18.0	69.4	66.2	64.2	64.5	64.1
Finland	8.9	11.0	11.3	11.3	11.2	62.8	64.6	63.5	63.3	63.6
France	13.8	13.7	12.9	13.3	13.6	78.6	79.5	80.2	80.7	79.1
Germany	13.5	18.8	19.6	20.1	21.8	87.1	83.7	83.3	82.8	81.4
Greece	7.8	5.6	5.6	6.0	6.1	59.1	67.3	68.3	68.7	69.6
Hungary	..	2.6	3.2	3.3	3.2	..	69.9	69.0	67.7	70.5
Iceland	22.6	20.1	..	..	..	78.3	73.1	..	..	..
Ireland	13.5	18.1	18.8	18.7	18.6	70.3	77.1	76.7	78.8	79.1
Italy	10.0	11.9	12.0	14.9	14.7	72.6	74.4	74.7	76.1	78.0
Japan[b,d]	21.4	25.1	26.0	25.5	25.8	67.6	67.0	66.7	67.4	67.7
Korea[b]	4.5	7.6	7.7	8.4	9.0	61.3	58.3	59.4	59.0	57.9
Luxembourg	10.7	12.6	13.3	13.3	14.0	88.6	89.1	92.9	91.7	92.9
Mexico	..	13.5	13.4	15.1	..	..	65.6	65.7	65.1	..
The Netherlands	28.9	33.9	34.6	35.0	35.7	76.8	75.4	76.1	76.0	76.3
New Zealand	21.0	22.6	22.3	22.0	21.7	76.1	72.9	73.7	73.6	74.8
Norway	21.5	20.6	21.0	21.1	20.8	80.6	76.2	75.2	74.1	74.6
Poland	..	11.7	11.5	12.0	11.7	..	65.0	66.2	65.7	66.5
Portugal	9.5	9.7	10.0	9.6	9.8	71.3	67.6	68.2	67.0	67.9
Slovak Republic	2.7	1.6	2.3	2.7	2.6	72.0	66.1	69.1	73.0	69.2
Spain	6.4	7.7	8.0	8.5	11.4	75.5	80.1	80.6	80.9	78.0
Sweden	15.8	13.8	14.1	14.4	..	76.8	71.8	70.8	69.5	..
Switzerland[c]	23.2	24.8	25.1	24.9	25.1	83.3	82.8	82.2	82.1	82.7
Turkey	9.1	6.6	6.0	6.7	5.8	60.5	58.3	56.9	58.8	59.4
United Kingdom	22.4	23.4	23.8	24.1	23.6	82.7	79.2	77.8	77.8	77.3
United States[e]	14.2	13.1	13.2	13.2	12.8	68.4	68.3	68.8	68.3	68.4
EU-15[f]	14.6	16.4	16.6	17.4	18.1	80.1	78.9	78.6	78.6	78.3
EU-19[f]	14.1	15.3	15.5	16.2	16.8	79.9	78.0	77.9	77.8	77.6
OECD Europe[f]	13.8	14.7	14.8	15.4	15.8	78.6	77.3	77.1	77.1	77.0
Total OECD[f]	11.6	14.6	14.8	15.2	15.4	73.9	72.3	72.3	72.2	72.9

[a] Part-time employment refers to persons who usually work less than 30 hours per week in their main job. Data include only persons declaring usual hours.
[b] Data are based on actual hours worked.
[c] Part-time employment based on hours worked at all jobs.
[d] Less than 35 hours per week.
[e] Data are for wage and salary workers only.
[f] For above countries only.
Sources and definitions: OECD database on Labour Force Statistics (see URLs at the beginning of the Annex). For Austria, Belgium, Denmark, France, Germany, Greece, Ireland, Italy, Luxembourg, the Netherlands, Portugal, Spain and the United Kingdom, data are from the European Union Labour Force Survey. See OECD (1997). "Definition of Part-time Work for the Purpose of International Comparisons". Labour Market and Social Policy Occasional Paper No. 22 available on Internet (www.oecd.org/els/workingpapers).
Statlink:http://dx.doi.org/10.1787/606732285655

countries having rates below 5 per cent, including the Slovak Republic and the Czech Republic. Within Europe, Turkey, Portugal, Hungary and Greece also have rates of part-time employment below 10 per cent.

Women's share of this part-time employment tends to be high, in 2005 the EU 15 share being 78.3 per cent and the total OECD share being 72.9 per cent. In both these cases, however, women's share of the total part-time employment decreased between 1994 and 2005 as the proportion of part-time male employment increased. However, in every country women do dominate the part-time work market, the lowest share being 57.9 per cent in Korea.

General trends then are that part-time work is increasing. While women dominate part-time working, there is evidence also that the proportion of male employment that is part time is increasing.

The UK

In the UK the proportion of total employment that is part time was relatively high at 23.6 per cent in 2005 and had increased over the period from 22.4 per cent. Women's share of this part-time employment was close to the averages given above at 77.3 per cent but had decreased from 82.7 per cent in 1994. Part-time employment constituted 39.3 per cent of total employment for women in 2005. The proportion of part-time male employment had increased over the period from 5.3 to 10.0 per cent.

The increasing incidence of the use of part-time contracts and the female domination of this form of employment is further demonstrated by the 2004 WERS data. The survey found that a large majority (83 per cent) of workplaces had part-time employees, up from 79 per cent in 1998, and in 30 per cent of all workplaces part-time employees accounted for more than half of the workforce. Women constituted all of the part-time workforce in 44 per cent of workplaces which employed part-time staff.

Unemployment

It was mentioned at the outset of this chapter that the continuity of employment and career associated with the Fordist model of employment was being replaced by a regime in which unemployment and insecurity were more commonplace. In this section we are concerned with the issue of unemployment and it is important to realize that there are different definitions of unemployment; the one used in this section, and for comparative purposes, conforms to ILO guidelines and is derived from data obtained through labour force surveys. As

1. The relatively simple measure of the difference between the supply of and demand for labour in a price-adjusting market, with the excess supply comprising active searchers and the excess demand represented by unfilled vacancies;
2. A measure of immediately available workers willing to accept market clearing wages;
3. The difference between employment levels at a market clearing equilibrium wage and employment at the prevailing market wage where the latter is greater;
4. What is often referred to as the claimant count which takes into account those registered as unemployed and claiming unemployment and related benefits.

The main weakness of series based on claimants for benefits is that it excludes people who are not working, not entitled to benefits but who might like to work, for example people who have taken early retirement and are in receipt of an occupational pension but below state retirement age. It also excludes many women who are married, not working, would like to, but do not register as unemployed and are not entitled to receipt of benefit.

Figure 6.2
The other definitions of unemployment.

such, the figures are not limited to those actually unemployed and claiming unemployment benefits.

These surveys generally seek to ascertain by means of survey the numbers of people:

(a) without work, by which is meant both paid employment and self-employment;

(b) who are available for/to work;

(c) who are actively seeking work, specific evidence of which may be required.

These are then expressed as a percentage of total labour force, including members of the armed forces.

For example, in the UK the LFS treats as unemployed those people without a job who were available to start work in the 2 weeks following the survey interview and who had either looked for work in the 4 weeks prior to the interview or were waiting to start a job that they had already obtained. However, there are also problems with the LFS data since they are estimates projected from the survey results and they tend to ignore those who are homeless: it is a household survey!

The cost of unemployment tends to be measured in terms of production foregone or lost and the costs of maintaining people in the state of unemployment. However, we need also to keep in mind that there are emotional, personal and social costs that are much more difficult to quantify.

There are other definitions of unemployment. These are listed in **Figure 6.2**.

Gross standardized unemployment rates: 1990–2005

Unemployment rates inevitably vary between countries, the genders and age groups and in Europe; in particular over the latter part of the

Table 6.3

Standardized unemployment rates in 27 OCED Countries

As a percentage of civilian labour force												
	1990	1994	1995	1996	1997	1998	1999	2000	2001	2002	2003	2004	2005
Australia	6.7	9.5	8.2	8.2	8.3	7.7	6.9	6.3	6.8	6.4	6.1	5.5	5.1
Austria	..	3.8	3.9	4.3	4.4	4.5	4.0	3.6	3.6	4.2	4.3	4.9	5.2
Belgium	6.6	9.8	9.7	9.5	9.2	9.3	8.5	6.9	6.6	7.5	8.2	8.4	8.4
Canada	8.1	10.4	9.5	9.6	9.1	8.3	7.6	6.8	7.2	7.7	7.6	7.2	6.8
Czech Republic	..	4.4	4.1	3.9	4.8	6.4	8.6	8.7	8.0	7.3	7.8	8.3	7.9
Denmark	7.2	7.7	6.8	6.3	5.3	4.9	5.1	4.4	4.5	4.6	5.4	5.5	4.8
Finland	3.2	16.8	15.2	14.6	12.7	11.3	10.2	9.8	9.1	9.1	9.0	8.9	8.4
France	8.5	11.7	11.1	11.6	11.5	11.1	10.5	9.1	8.4	8.9	9.5	9.6	9.5
Germany[a]	4.8	8.3	8.0	8.6	9.2	8.8	7.9	7.2	7.4	8.2	9.1	9.5	9.5
Greece	6.3	8.9	9.1	9.7	9.6	11.1	12.0	11.3	10.8	10.3	9.7	10.5	9.8
Hungary	..	11.0	10.4	9.6	9.0	8.4	6.9	6.4	5.7	5.8	5.9	6.1	7.2
Ireland	13.4	14.3	12.3	11.7	9.9	7.5	5.7	4.3	4.0	4.5	4.7	4.5	4.3
Italy	8.9	10.6	11.2	11.2	11.2	11.3	11.0	10.1	9.1	8.6	8.4	8.0	7.7
Japan	2.1	2.9	3.2	3.4	3.4	4.1	4.7	4.7	5.0	5.4	5.3	4.7	4.4
Korea	2.4	2.5	2.1	2.0	2.6	7.0	6.6	4.4	4.0	3.3	3.6	3.7	3.7
Luxembourg	1.7	3.2	2.9	2.9	2.7	2.7	2.4	2.3	2.1	2.8	3.7	4.8	5.3
The Netherlands	5.9	6.8	6.6	6.0	4.9	3.8	3.2	2.8	2.2	2.8	3.7	4.6	4.8
New Zealand	7.8	8.1	6.3	6.1	6.6	7.4	6.8	6.0	5.3	5.2	4.6	3.9	3.7
Norway	5.8	6.0	5.5	4.8	4.0	3.2	3.3	3.4	3.6	3.9	4.5	4.4	4.6
Poland	..	14.4	13.3	12.3	10.9	10.2	13.4	16.1	18.2	19.9	19.6	19.0	17.8
Portugal	4.8	6.9	7.3	7.3	6.8	5.1	4.5	4.0	4.0	5.0	6.3	6.7	7.6
Slovak Republic	..	13.7	13.1	11.3	11.9	12.6	16.3	18.8	19.3	18.7	17.6	18.2	16.4
Spain	13.0	19.5	18.4	17.8	16.7	15.0	12.5	11.1	10.3	11.1	11.1	10.6	9.2
Sweden	1.7	9.4	8.8	9.6	9.9	8.2	6.7	5.6	4.9	4.9	5.6	6.4	..
Switzerland	..	3.9	3.5	3.9	4.2	3.6	3.0	2.7	2.6	3.2	4.2	4.4	4.5
United Kingdom	6.9	9.3	8.5	7.9	6.8	6.1	5.9	5.4	5.0	5.1	4.9	4.7	4.7
United States	5.6	6.1	5.6	5.4	4.9	4.5	4.2	4.0	4.7	5.8	6.0	5.5	5.1
EU-15[b]	8.1	10.5	10.1	10.2	9.9	9.3	8.6	7.7	7.3	7.7	8.0	8.1	7.9
OECD Europe[b]	8.0	10.5	10.1	10.0	9.7	9.2	8.9	8.4	8.2	8.6	8.9	8.9	8.6
Total OECD[b]	6.1	7.7	7.3	7.2	6.9	6.9	6.7	6.2	6.4	6.9	7.1	6.9	6.6

[a] For 1990, the data refer to western Germany, subsequent data concern the whole of Germany.

[b] For above countries only.

Note: In so far as possible the data have been adjusted to ensure comparability over time and to conform to the guidelines of the International Labour Office. All series are benchmarked to labour-force survey-based estimates. In countries with annual surveys, monthly estimates are obtained by interpolation/extrapolation and by incorporating trends in administrative data, where available. The annual figures are then calculated by averaging the monthly estimates (for both unemployed and the labour force). For countries with monthly or quarterly estimates, the annual estimates are obtained by averaging monthly or quarterly, respectively. For several countries, the adjustment procedure used is similar to that of the Bureau of Labor Statistics, US Department of Labor. For EU countries, the procedures are similar to those used in deriving the Comparable Unemployment Rates (CURs) of the Statistical Office of the European Communities. Minor differences may appear mainly because of various methods of calculating and applying adjustment factors, and because EU estimates are based on the civilian labour force. For a fuller description, please refer to the following URL www.oecd.org/etd.

Sources: OECD (2006), OECD Main Economic Indicators, May, Paris.

Statlink:http://dx.doi.org/442538841646

20th century there were concerns about the overall rates of unemployment, youth unemployment and also long-term unemployment.

The OECD provides information on these issues (see **Table 6.3**).

Over the period 1990–2005 the EU 15 average rate of unemployment varied between 7.3 and 10.5 per cent whereas for the total OECD it varied between 6.1 and 7.7 per cent. Of the countries for which complete data were available Greece had the highest rate in 2005 of 9.8 per cent. The rates for the UK varied between 10.0 per cent in 1993 and 4.7 per cent in 2005. Individual country rates are influenced by international events and developments but they are also influenced by the economic, labour market and social policies pursued by the respective governments discussed earlier in **Chapter 5**. To some extent the rate of unemployment represents also a measure of immediately available labour supply though we do need to bear in mind that the rate is a purely quantitative measure of availability and takes no account of the nature and location of demand.

Data for developing economies are generally limited, where data are available they tend to be limited to unemployment in urban areas and therefore only partial in coverage. As economies begin the process of industrialization jobs tend to be created in manufacturing activity and there are job losses in the agricultural sector. Many developing economies also have relatively high birth rates and a relatively young and undereducated population. One of the tasks often confronted by governments in such circumstances is securing sufficient job creation to employ the new workers entering the labour force for the first time every year as well as providing the job opportunities for those leaving agriculture and moving to the cities in search of work and a better standard of living. A further complication often is posed by the need for industries and, perhaps particularly the public sector, to become more efficient driven by the influence of incoming multinational enterprises (MNEs), the influence of new technologies and the need for home-owned organizations to compete internationally. Public sectors in many developing economies are sources of significant underemployment and it is common for public sector jobs to be lost as industrialization progresses and the country opens up to the influences associated with globalization.

Even countries such as China, where economic growth rates have been running at around 7 per cent per year in the early years of the 21st century, have experienced rising unemployment, with official figures indicating an increase from 3.1 per cent in 1999–2000 to 4 per cent in 2002 with a government commitment to keep the figure below 4.7 per cent in 2004. Informed observers have suggested that these figures are underestimates of the real unemployment situation and that accurate figures might well be two or three times greater.

Gender unemployment rates: 1990–2004

A comparison of the gender unemployment rates shows that, in both the EU 15 and total OECD, unemployment rates for men tend to be lower than for women; however, the gap has narrowed over the period. In 1990 the EU 15 rates were 10.9 per cent for women and 6.7 per cent for men and by 2004 these rates were 9.1 and 7.5 per cent; for the total OECD the rates at the beginning of the period were 7.3 for women and 5.7 per cent for men; by the end of the period the rates were 7.2 and 6.7 per cent. In the EU 15 the rate for women had declined considerably and the male rate had risen by a relatively small amount. However, in the OECD, the narrowing of the gap had resulted from an increase in unemployment for men and a slight decrease for women.

The UK

Unusually, in the UK the rate of unemployment for women had consistently been lower than for men. At the beginning of the period 1990–2004 the rates were 6.6 per cent for women and 7.1 per cent for men and by the end of the period the rates were 4.3 and 5.0 per cent; both rates had declined but the gap between women and men had actually widened in favour of women. As in the EU 15, the rate of unemployment for women had declined considerably whilst the rate for men had declined but not to the same extent.

Unemployment by age group: 1990–2004

When we look at unemployment rates by age group, there is marked consistency in that for both the EU 15 and total OECD and throughout the period, the rates of unemployment are highest among the youngest age group (15–24) and lowest in the oldest age group (55–64), this latter perhaps not surprising since we must remember that the rate includes only those actually seeking work and one would expect many in the older age group who are not economically active to have taken early retirement. It is also the case that the young unemployed tend to have little or no skills of a vocational kind and little or no relevant work experience. It is of note that in the EU 15 the rate of unemployment among the youngest group had declined over the period whereas in the total OECD it had increased. It is clear from the data that some countries have particularly severe problems with youth unemployment; for example, Spain, the Slovak Republic, Poland, Italy, Greece, Finland, the Czech Republic and France all had unemployment rates for this youngest group above 20 per cent.

When we undertake a gender comparison for this younger age group, we find that in the EU 15 trends over the period were markedly different with the unemployment rate for men increasing over the period from

14.2 to 15.3 per cent and the rate for women decreasing from 18.8 to 16.0 per cent. In the total OECD the rates for both men and women in this youngest group had increased over the period but the rate of increase for men was considerably greater than for women (from 15.2 to 17.9 per cent compared with 12.8 to 13.1 per cent).

The UK

In the UK the rate of unemployment for the younger group was consistently greater than for the other groups and had increased over the period from 10.1 to 10.9 per cent. Over the period under review (1990–2004) the gap between the rates for this group and the other age groups had widened as the rates for both the other groups had decreased. The rate for women was consistently lower than for men and the gap had narrowed in favour of men from (from 2.1 per cent in 1990 to 1.9 per cent in 2004).

Long-term unemployment

The reasons for someone to be unemployed are many and amongst them may be that they are looking for their first job, it may be that they have left a job from choice and already have one to go to and the length of their unemployment may be relatively short, or it may be that they are unemployed because the company they worked for has ceased trading, or there is no longer a demand for the product of their labour, or because the particular skills that they have are no longer required due to technological advances and innovation. In these later cases it is likely that the period of unemployment will be longer and indeed that in order to find a new job the individual may have to learn new skills or move location. We tend to refer to these forms of unemployment as either technological or structural whereas the more temporary forms tend to be referred to as frictional. All economies are dynamic and demand for labour changes over time. It is important that there are pools of labour supply ready to fill vacancies and jobs as they are created. It has been argued that if all unemployment was frictional then you really have full employment.

It is then structural and long-term unemployment that constitutes the bigger problem for economies and for governments. Structural unemployment, by its nature, is likely to pose more of a problem in developed economies as the demand for traditional products and skills declines and ceases in the face of new product development and technical innovation which may for example replace labour with computers. The impact of these developments is exacerbated when traditional roles such as manufacture are exported to developing economies because of the economies in production cost which can be obtained and which are necessary in the face of international competition in the era of free trade. Long-term unemployment also creates the greater social and emotional costs and problems for the individuals and in some cases, the communities that suffer it. It is also the case that the longer people are unemployed, the more difficult it becomes for them to obtain employment. Their skills and experience have a declining value the longer they are out of work. Their employability declines.

It is often also argued that there is a greater propensity to long-term unemployment where labour markets are regulated and employees legally protected. In essence, the greater the costs of employment and the greater the difficulties and costs of making employees redundant, the less inclined will employers be to employ people.

We would therefore expect the incidence and burden of long-term unemployment to be greater in developed economies with regulated labour markets.

The OECD source already used above provides data which essentially support this supposition. The incidence of long-term unemployment in the EU 15 being considerably greater than for the total OECD. In the EU 15 the proportion of those unemployed who had been unemployed for more than 6 months exceeded 60 per cent throughout the period 1990–2004 and the proportion of the total that had been unemployed for more than 12 months exceeded 40 per cent throughout. The total OECD figures are substantially lower throughout the period averaging out around 45 and 30 per cent, respectively. Comparison with the USA is interesting in that while a developed economy it is also renowned as having an unregulated labour market, little social protection and a reputation for being extremely effective at job creation. In the USA the comparable figures were 10.0 and 5.5 per cent in 1990 and 21.9 and 12.7 per cent in 2004. The gap has narrowed but is still substantial.

The UK

In the UK the incidence of long-term unemployment has reduced substantially over the period. In 1990, the figures were 50.3 and 34.4 per cent and by 2004 these had improved to 38.8 and 21.4 per cent, worse than in the USA but substantially better than in the EU 15 as a whole.

As noted already, individual country experiences differ with regard to unemployment and national governments are able to influence these rates through a mix of economic and social policies. Nevertheless it is possible to draw some general conclusions from the data. First, unemployment in the EU has been greater than in the total OECD but by the end of the period in question the gap had narrowed. Unemployment rates for women have traditionally been greater than for men but the gap has narrowed and particularly in the EU 15 the rate for women had declined considerably over the period. The youngest age group tends to experience much higher rates of unemployment than the higher age groups but again, while this is true for both men and women, there were considerable changes during the period under review so that by the end of the period the rates of unemployment in this age group were higher for men than for women and in the EU 15 in particular the rate for women had decreased considerably. Long-term unemployment is more of a problem in Europe than in the OECD as a whole and there has been relatively little improvement in the figures over the period. Comparisons with the USA are striking with the proportion of the unemployed who are unemployed for 12 months or more being approximately a quarter that in the EU 15.

Employment by sector

It appears that one of the characteristics of developed economies is the sectoral shift in employment from agriculture and industry into the service sector, trends that are likely to be enhanced by the opening up of developed economy markets to agricultural products from the developing world and by the shifting of manufacture in the opposite direction. **Table 6.4** shows this development for the EU 15 over the period 1993–2004. In 1993 the proportions of total employment employed in the various sectors were 5.3, 28.2 and 66.5 per cent, respectively. By 2004 these figures were 3.9, 24.3 and 71.9 per cent. The table also demonstrates that the sectoral distribution of employment varies between the genders with greater proportions of men employed in agriculture and industry and a greater proportion of women employed in the service sector. In 2004 for the EU 15 as a whole, 85.1 per cent of women in employment were in the service sector compared with 61.2 per cent of men. Despite these gender differences the trends for men and women are both in the same direction as for the combined sectoral distribution of employment.

The UK

The sectoral distribution of employment in the UK demonstrates the same trends as for the EU as a whole; however, the UK economy seems to be further along the road of the shift into service sector employment and in the domination of service sector employment for women. In 2004, 91.6 per cent of women in employment were in the service sector compared with 72.0 per cent of men, the combined figure being 81.3 per cent.

Table 6.4

Key employment indicators European Union of 15 Member States (EU-15)

All

All	1993	1994	1995	1996	1997	1998	1999	2000	2001	2002	2003	2004
1. Total population (000)	363,415	364,791	365,962	367,055	367,997	368,347	369,731	370,902	373,067	374,831	376,407	378,066
2. Population aged 15–64 (000)	244,081	244,783	245,359	246,161	246,691	247,576	248,364	248,387	249,436	250,392	251,339	251,947
3. Total employment (000)	154,476	154,365	155,627	156,473	157,924	160,795	163,646	166,935	169,249	170,342	170,933	172,127
4. Population in employment aged 15–64	146,632	146,392	147,394	148,358	149,723	152,118	155,369	157,530	159,763	160,760	161,687	163,077
5. Employment rate (% population aged 15–64)	60.1	59.8	60.1	60.3	60.7	61.4	62.6	63.4	64.0	64.2	64.3	64.7
6. Employment rate (% population aged 15–24)	39.5	38.1	37.5	36.9	37.2	38.2	39.6	40.5	40.9	40.6	39.9	40.0
7. Employment rate (% population aged 25–54)	73.0	72.9	73.2	73.5	73.9	74.6	75.7	76.5	77.0	77.1	77.1	77.6
8. Employment rate (% population aged 55–64)	35.7	35.7	36.0	36.3	36.4	36.6	37.1	37.8	38.8	40.2	41.7	42.5
9. FTE employment rate (% population aged 15–64)	:	:	55.6	55.5	55.7	56.3	57.2	58.0	58.6	58.8	58.7	58.5
10. Self-employed (% total employment)	16.2	16.2	16.1	15.9	15.7	15.5	15.1	14.9	14.7	14.6	14.8	14.9
11. Part-time employment (% total employment)	14.8	15.4	15.8	16.3	16.7	17.3	17.5	17.7	17.9	18.1	18.5	19.4
12. Fixed-term contracts (% total employment)	11.0	11.5	12.0	12.0	12.4	13.0	13.4	13.7	13.5	13.1	13.1	13.6
13. Employment in services (% total employment)	66.5	67.2	67.6	68.2	68.6	68.9	69.5	70.1	70.5	71.1	71.5	71.9
14. Employment in industry (% total employment)	28.2	27.7	27.5	27.0	26.7	26.5	26.1	25.7	25.4	24.9	24.6	24.3
15. Employment in agriculture (% total employment)	5.3	5.1	4.9	4.7	4.7	4.5	4.4	4.2	4.1	4.0	3.9	3.9
16. Activity rate (% population aged 15–64)	67.1	67.2	67.2	67.7	67.9	68.3	68.9	69.2	69.2	69.7	70.1	70.6
17. Activity rate (% of population aged 15–24)	49.8	48.6	47.5	47.0	47.0	47.4	48.2	48.2	47.8	47.8	47.5	47.6
18. Activity rate (% of population aged 25–54)	80.1	80.4	80.5	81.1	81.3	81.7	82.2	82.4	82.3	82.8	83.1	83.7
19. Activity rate (% of population aged 55–64)	38.7	38.9	39.1	39.8	40.1	40.1	40.3	40.8	41.5	42.9	44.5	45.5
20. Total unemployment (000)	16,721	17,398	16,849	17,064	16,728	15,914	14,789	13,440	12,842	13,632	14,418	14,681
21. Unemployment-rate (% labour force 15+)	10.0	10.4	10.0	10.1	9.8	9.3	8.5	7.6	7.2	7.6	8.0	8.1
22. Youth unemployment rate (% labour force 15–24)	21.4	21.8	21.0	21.2	20.6	19.0	17.1	15.3	15.1	15.6	16.3	16.6
23. Long term unemployment rate (% labour force)	4.4	5.0	4.9	4.9	4.8	4.4	3.9	3.4	3.1	3.1	3.3	3.4
24. Youth unemployment ratio (% population aged 15–24)	10.3	10.5	10.0	10.2	9.7	9.2	8.5	7.7	6.9	7.2	7.6	7.6

Male

Male	1993	1994	1995	1996	1997	1998	1999	2000	2001	2002	2003	2004
1. Total population (000)	176,763	177,562	178,230	178,831	179,352	179,733	180,524	180,781	182,005	182,988	183,852	184,682
2. Population aged 15–64	121,624	122,062	122,388	122,877	123,214	123,812	124,240	123,917	124,526	125,034	125,533	125,837
3. Total employment (000)	91,175	90,880	91,406	91,481	92,101	93,434	94,475	95,698	96,608	96,639	96,624	96,755
4. Population in employment aged 15–64	86,338	85,931	86,312	86,473	87,043	88,222	89,574	90,156	91,021	91,034	91,203	91,427
5. Employment rate (% population aged 15–64)	71.0	70.4	70.5	70.4	70.6	71.2	72.1	72.8	73.1	72.8	72.7	72.7
6. Employment rate (% population aged 15–24)	42.8	41.3	41.0	40.3	40.7	41.7	43.1	43.9	44.3	43.6	42.8	42.9
7. Employment rate (% population aged 25–54)	85.7	85.2	85.4	85.2	85.3	85.8	86.6	87.2	87.3	86.8	86.5	86.4
8. Employment rate (% population aged 55–64)	48.0	47.5	47.2	47.3	47.2	47.4	47.4	48.0	48.9	50.1	51.6	52.2
9. FTE employment rate (% population aged 15–64)	:	:	69.3	68.9	69.1	69.7	70.4	71.1	71.5	71.2	70.7	70.4
10. Self-employed (% total employment)	18.6	18.7	18.7	18.7	18.5	18.3	18.0	17.8	17.6	17.7	17.9	18.1
11. Part-time employment (% total employment)	4.5	4.9	5.2	5.4	5.7	6.0	6.1	6.1	6.2	6.6	6.7	7.2
12. Fixed-term contracts (% total employment)	10.0	10.7	11.3	11.2	11.7	12.3	12.7	12.8	12.5	12.2	12.2	12.9
13. Employment in services (% total employment)	56.8	57.6	57.9	58.4	58.7	59.0	59.4	59.9	60.2	60.7	61.0	61.2
14. Employment in industry (% total employment)	37.3	36.7	36.6	36.2	36.0	35.8	35.4	35.1	34.9	34.5	34.3	34.1
15. Employment in agriculture (% total employment)	5.9	5.7	5.5	5.4	5.3	5.2	5.1	5.0	4.9	4.8	4.7	4.7
16. Activity rate (% population aged 15–64)	78.5	78.2	77.8	77.9	70.0	78.1	78.3	78.3	78.3	78.4	78.6	78.6
17. Activity rate (% of population aged 15–24)	53.5	52.2	51.0	50.6	50.5	51.0	51.7	51.6	51.4	51.2	50.9	50.9
18. Activity rate (% of population aged 25–54)	93.0	92.9	92.7	92.7	92.6	92.6	92.7	92.7	92.4	92.4	92.4	92.4
19. Activity rate (% of population aged 55–64)	52.2	51.8	51.4	51.8	51.8	51.7	51.5	51.6	52.2	53.4	55.1	55.0
20. Total unemployment (000)	8528	8819	8348	8400	8177	7626	7003	6207	6122	6638	7091	7201
21. Unemployment rate (% labour force 15+)	8.8	9.1	8.6	8.7	8.4	7.8	7.1	6.4	6.1	6.6	7.0	7.1
22. Youth unemployment rate (% labour force 15–24)	19.8	20.1	18.8	19.2	18.4	17.0	15.2	13.7	13.6	14.7	15.9	16.0
23. Long-term unemployment rate (% labour force)	3.6	4.1	4.1	4.1	4.0	3.6	3.2	2.8	2.5	2.6	2.8	3.0
24. Youth unemployment ratio (% population aged 15–24)	10.7	10.8	10.0	10.3	9.8	9.3	8.5	7.7	7.1	7.6	8.1	8.0

Female

Female	1993	1994	1995	1996	1997	1998	1999	2000	2001	2002	2003	2004
1. Total population (000)	186,646	187,224	187,727	188,222	188,644	188,613	189,206	190,121	191,062	191,843	192,555	193,384
2. Population aged 15–64	122,460	122,723	122,973	123,286	123,479	123,764	124,123	124,469	124,910	125,358	125,805	126,110
3. Total employment (000)	63,301	63,486	64,221	64,992	65,823	67,361	69,171	71,237	72,641	73,703	74,309	75,372
4. Population in employment aged 15–64	60,295	60,464	61,083	61,886	62,682	63,898	65,796	67,375	68,742	69,726	70,484	71,650
5. Employment rate (% population aged 15–64)	49.2	49.3	49.7	50.2	50.8	51.6	53.0	54.1	55.0	55.6	56.0	56.8
6. Employment rate (% population aged 15–24)	36.2	34.9	34.0	33.4	33.7	34.7	36.0	36.9	37.4	37.5	37.0	37.0
7. Employment rate (% population aged 25–54)	60.2	60.4	61.0	61.8	62.3	63.2	64.7	65.8	66.7	67.3	67.7	68.8
8. Employment rate (% population aged 55–64)	24.2	24.7	25.3	25.8	26.1	26.3	27.2	28.0	29.1	30.7	32.2	33.2
9. FTE employment rate (% population aged 15–64)	:	:	42.3	42.5	42.8	43.2	44.3	45.4	46.2	46.8	47.1	47.0
10. Self-employed (% total employment)	12.7	12.6	12.4	12.1	11.9	11.7	11.3	11.0	10.8	10.6	10.7	10.8
11. Part-time employment (% total employment)	29.6	30.4	31.0	31.5	32.2	33.0	33.2	33.2	33.3	33.3	33.9	35.1
12. Fixed-term contracts (% total employment)	12.2	12.6	13.0	12.9	13.4	13.8	14.4	14.7	14.6	14.3	14.1	14.4
13. Employment in services (% total employment)	80.0	80.5	81.0	81.6	82.0	82.3	82.9	83.3	83.7	84.3	84.7	85.1
14. Employment in industry (% total employment)	15.5	15.2	15.0	14.6	14.3	14.1	13.7	13.5	13.2	12.7	12.4	12.1
15. Employment in agriculture (% total employment)	4.5	4.3	4.1	3.8	3.7	3.6	3.4	3.2	3.1	3.0	2.9	2.8
16. Activity rate (% population aged 15–64)	55.9	56.3	56.6	57.4	57.9	58.6	59.5	60.0	60.2	61.0	61.6	62.5
17. Activity rate (% of population aged 15–24)	46.1	45.0	44.0	43.4	43.4	43.8	44.6	44.7	44.2	44.3	44.0	44.2
18. Activity rate (% of population aged 25–54)	67.0	67.8	68.3	69.4	70.0	70.7	71.6	72.1	72.3	73.1	73.8	75.0
19. Activity rate (% of population aged 55–64)	26.0	26.7	27.1	28.4	28.9	28.9	29.6	30.3	31.1	32.8	34.3	35.5
20. Total unemployment (000)	8193	8579	8501	8578	8550	8289	7737	7077	6719	6994	7327	7480
21. Unemployment rate (% labour force 15+)	11.7	12.2	12.0	11.9	11.8	11.2	10.3	9.3	8.7	8.9	9.2	9.3
22. Youth unemployment rate (% labour force 15–24)	23.1	23.7	23.5	23.5	23.0	21.3	19.3	17.1	16.8	16.7	16.9	17.3
23. Long term unemployment rate (% labour force)	5.5	6.1	6.1	6.0	5.9	5.4	4.8	4.2	3.8	3.7	3.9	4.0
24. Youth unemployment ratio (% population aged 15–24)	9.9	10.1	10.0	10.0	9.7	9.1	8.5	7.8	6.8	6.8	7.0	7.3

Source: Eurostat, EU Labour Force Survey and National Accounts.

Factors influencing female participation in the labour force

Throughout this chapter we have examined the differential experience in terms of labour force participation and unemployment of the genders, without considering in any depth the factors that explain and account for these differences. In this section therefore we examine the major explanations.

Socialization and stereotypes

As we grow up in a particular society, we acquire values and attitudes which influence both our perceptions of others and our behaviour. These values and attitudes are acquired or learned from others, they tend to be shared and they provide a base upon which group cohesion is developed. As they provide a base for the formation and reinforcement of groups, they also provide a base upon which groups are distinguished from each other; each group having a shared set of values and attitudes which are, to some extent, distinct from those of other groups. We then tend to develop stereotypes of these other distinct groups which, of course, may or may not be accurate and which we tend to ascribe to all members of that group as if they were one and which, as noted above, are likely to include perceptions of appropriate and acceptable roles, including work roles, for members of the other group.

In this context, men and women are likely to be in different groups and one outcome is likely to be sexual or gender stereotyping.

In his work on cultures Hofstede (1991) refers to culture as: 'collective programming of the mind which distinguishes the members of one group or category of people from another' (p. 5), and asserts that 'The (mental) programming starts within the family; continues within the neighbourhood, at school, in youth groups, at the workplace, and in the living community' (p. 4). In elaborating upon this notion of culture he suggests that in any society:

> there is a men's culture and a different women's culture and that women are often not considered suitable for jobs traditionally filled by men, not because they are technically unable to perform the jobs but because they don't carry the symbols, do not correspond to the hero images, do not participate in the rituals or foster the values dominant in the men's culture; and vice versa.

In discussing gender roles within societies Hofstede suggests that stereotypically men are supposed to be assertive, tough and competitive, whereas women are supposed to be more concerned with taking care of the home, the children and people in general; the contrast is between the achieving male and the caring female. There are differences between societies in the degree to which these gender roles are separated and in the degree to which the attitudes and behaviour of the sexes actually conform to them. Nevertheless, his work does suggest that there are common and pervasive sexual stereotypes. He identifies a number of attitudes and behaviours that might be considered as symptoms or indicators of the extent to which a particular society is structured in a manner in which these dominant sexual and gender stereotypes prevail. Indicators of consistency with the dominant stereotype might be:

- boys and girls studying different subjects at school and dominant social values that favour competition, the achievement of success and a concern with materialism

whereas indicators of a society in which the dominant gender stereotypes are less prevalent might include:

- boys being taught that it is okay for them to cry and the dominant values include caring and a concern for equality and the quality of working life.

We have noted in earlier sections the variable female participation rates in different countries and it is likely that at least in part this is due to differences in culture and social norms and values concerning the appropriate role for women in a particular society and also appropriate work roles, occupations and sectors.

Economic explanations

Female participation rates also have economic explanations. We have noted earlier that some women never enter the labour market and in some societies there is very little investment in female human capital in terms of education and training. Where this is the case, it is also likely that those women who do enter the labour market are likely to do so in relatively unskilled and less valuable roles, thereby earning lower rates of pay. Where women have lower levels of educational and skills attainment, we should expect this to be the outcome of a competitive and efficient market. Women earn less because their labour is worth less.

A relative lack of investment in education and skills training for women may be the product of discrimination but it may also be the product of perfectly rational decision making. For example, in the case of women it may be rational for families to invest less in education and training for women and concentrate their scarce resources in investment in the human capital of husbands and sons. Why? There may be an expectation that women will experience discontinuous employment because of:

- their role in childbirth;
- the absence of adequate and convenient childcare facilities;
- dominant social attitudes and social customs with regard to the distribution of family responsibilities and which frown upon mothers working.

We noted above that outcomes and workplace experience may be the product of tastes, and tastes may result in discrimination against particular categories of labour. Becker (1957) saw discrimination as a taste of the employer, which is itself the result of prejudice. There are profit consequences for employers who discriminate in this way, they may not be willing to employ labour whose marginal product is greater than the wage that would have to be paid and in this sense they can be perceived to be willing to pay a price to exercise and practise their prejudices. A further consequence of such a policy on the part of the employer is that competition in the labour market is restricted and the categories of labour that have preferential status gain or earn a wage that is higher than it would be if the categories of labour that are discriminated against were active competition for the work available.

A further consequence of such discrimination on the part of employers is a segmented labour market in which there are categories of labour that do not compete with one another even though there may be competition within each segment. Under competitive conditions such discrimination would be removed by employers not prepared to pay the price of discriminating. They would be more efficient and their costs would be lower.

A further explanation of employers' willingness to discriminate may be in their unwillingness to upset their existing labour force and employment structures. For example, if insiders are racist or unwilling for whatever reason to work with women, it is unlikely the employers will voluntarily make decisions on hiring that threaten existing relationships. In this scenario outsiders are doomed to remain so and therefore must remain within the secondary employment sectors characterized by poorer terms and conditions of employment, fewer opportunities, less training and investment, less security and lower expectations. The inequality and discrimination practised in such firms also then tend to confirm existing stereotypes and inequality and discrimination are perpetuated.

So, one might argue differential workplace experiences and outcomes in terms of participation (and pay) may be the product of the market working efficiently and effectively, reflecting differences in educational and skills attainment. However, you might also argue that they may also be the product of employers being willing to pay the price of their own prejudices or they may be the product of employers being unwilling to upset their existing workforce.

The Marxist analysis of the consequences of capitalism suggests that not only does capitalism result in the exploitation of labour, it also results in male domination and exploitation of women who serve the interests of capital by providing a cheap way of ensuring that the well being of the labour resource (men) is taken care of and that the next generation of labour is produced and raised. Additionally, the Marxist analysis suggests that certain sections of the population of working age constitute a 'reserve army of labour' and women and their treatment in the labour market can be viewed in these terms. What this means is that they constitute a pool of labour that will be drawn into the labour market only periodically and in periods of tight labour supply. Marxists might point to the treatment of women in the two World Wars of the 20th century. In these circumstances, special measures were taken and facilities provided to enable the reserve army to work but as soon as they are no longer required, they were effectively returned to reserve status; to employ a sporting analogy, they are on the bench and to be used only in emergency.

This frame of mind and attitude may result in crèches and family-friendly work practices when labour supply is insufficient and also in gender being a criterion for selection for redundancy when necessary; the reserve army is quickly returned to the bench when no longer needed. Associated with this analysis is the notion that women only work for pin money, that the main breadwinner is the male in the household, that the female's earnings are not really necessary and so they do not have to be paid so much.

Other explanations of differential participation, treatment and outcome

So far we have mentioned the acquisition of values and attitudes that may result in stereotyping, the productivity and value of the labour that is affected by educational and skills attainment, employers' and insider employees' preferences and prejudices and the influence of expectations of discrimination. In addition to these there are several other partial explanations and influences.

Opportunity for and participation of female labour may also be a product of the nature of the technological environment. The increase in opportunities and participation in recent decades may be a reflection of technological change, de-emphasizing the strength aspects of much work and emphasizing attributes and abilities allegedly possessed by women to a greater extent than men.

The degree and nature of regulation in the labour market may also have a negative impact upon female participation rates as well as upon labour market outcomes and it has been suggested that regulations such as those imposing:

- a minimum wage, which should narrow wage gaps and attract more females into the market;
- employment rights for part-time and other atypical contract workers that are equivalent on a pro rata basis to those provided for full-time workers;
- employment rights for pregnant workers, the right to return, the right to maternity leave and pay, the right not to be dismissed when pregnant, etc.

All work to the detriment of the demand for female labour and therefore the opportunities available.

Another viewpoint is that since managements have demonstrated a considerable capacity to circumvent regulations geared towards the achievement of greater equality of opportunity, treatment and outcome, there is no reason to imagine that further regulation will have the desired impact. Also, where demand is significantly influenced by prejudicial attitudes on the part of employers and they have demonstrated their willingness to pay the price of prejudice, it is unlikely that the passage of legislation will have much impact; it is notoriously difficult to change values and attitudes through the passage of legislation.

So far we have skirted around the issue of childbirth and its implications as an explanation of differential opportunities and participation. We have implied that the impact of childbirth as a source of discontinuity of employment may influence decisions regarding investment in human capital, education and training; we have referred to the relevance of dominant social attitudes regarding the role of women in child rearing; lifetime working patterns for women do tend to show a decline in labour force participation associated with childbirth, which is then partially redeemed as the children grow up; and we have discussed the potential impact of regulation geared towards ensuring that pregnant women are not discriminated against simply because they are or are liable to become pregnant.

However, associated with this are the issues of childcare and the availability and cost of childcare facilities. Those countries in Europe that have high female participation rates tend also to have plentiful childcare provision in the right place and at an affordable price, in many cases involving considerable amounts of state or employer subsidy. A particularly good example of the relevance of availability of affordable childcare occurred with the reunification of East and West Germany at the beginning of the 1990s. The collapse of the state childcare service in the East after reunification certainly contributed to a rapid and marked decline in the ability of women to take up work outside the home and female unemployment soared.

Additionally, the number of children that a woman has, the age of the youngest child and whether the family is a two-parent family appear to be influential factors.

The discontinuity of employment associated with the female role in childbirth tends also to affect detrimentally opportunities for career advancement and also labour market outcomes in terms of pay. This is particularly likely to be the case where salary scales are incremental with length of service.

Educational attainment and labour force participation

There has been an increased degree of research activity into the relationship between educational attainment levels and employment in recent years. In the UK this research has been fuelled in part by debates about the merits, demerits and impact of changes introduced by government to the funding of higher and further education and the drive to ensure that the consumers of education pay a greater proportion of the costs. Consumers need to be assured that the costs are outweighed by the benefits and one of the assumed benefits is that educational attainment enhances employability. However, there are other motives for this interest and concern and these include:

- the perceived need for a more highly educated and skilled labour force to facilitate adaptation to and assimilation of technological change and changes in working practices;
- enhancement of a country's competitiveness;
- concerns about the role of education and training in achieving greater equality of opportunities;
- decline in the demand for unskilled labour.

The OECD Employment Outlook 2005 again provides data on the relationship between educational attainment levels and labour force participation and unemployment rates.

For both the EU 15 and total OECD labour force participation rates increase with level of educational attainment and unemployment rates decrease with educational attainment level, this is the case for both men and women.

For both the EU 15 and total OECD the lowest participation rate and highest unemployment rate is among those women with less than an upper secondary education and the gender gap in participation rates for this group is greater than for any other (2004 figures are: EU 15 men 76 per cent, women 51.2 per cent participation, total OECD men 75.0 per cent, women 50.7 per cent participation). The level of educational attainment appears to have a much greater impact on labour force participation of women than it does for men. The particularly low participation rates of this group of women may well be explained by many of them never entering the labour force at all and/or because they do not reenter the labour force after childbirth, though it may also be that the demand for relatively unskilled labour has held up more in the agriculture and industry sectors than in services (see above).

Nevertheless we can conclude that:

- there is a generally positive relationship between educational attainment levels and the ability to find and remain in employment;
- many women with low educational attainment may not enter the labour market at all;
- the less well-educated men and women are more likely to be unemployed;
- the relationship between level of educational attainment and propensity to be unemployed is more marked for women.

The UK

In the UK the same positive relationship between educational attainment level and labour force participation is discernible and even more marked than in the EU 15 and total OECD with the participation rate of the least educated group being lower and the rate for the most well-educated group being higher than in the EU or OECD. Consistent with the data on unemployment in the UK, above, the highest rate of unemployment is among the male group who have less than upper secondary education and this contrasts with the experience of both the EU 15 and total OECD. The participation rate for women in the least educated group is slightly higher than in either the EU 15 or OECD but the participation rate for men in this educational category is substantially lower in the UK and, at least in part, this may be a reflection of the relatively lower rates of employment in agriculture and industry in the UK.

Summary

In this chapter we have examined demographic and labour force trends within OECD member states and the EU 15.

There are two main demographic trends, a declining birth rate and declining mortality rates resulting in average age and life expectancy increasing. Women will continue to have an advantage over men in terms of life expectancy. These have already and are going to have a significant impact upon the age distribution of the population and the population of working age. The shift will be in the direction of the older age groups. While the proportion of the population that is of working age has not yet started to decline, a continuation of these trends will eventually result in that happening. Inevitably, as these trends work their way through, the workforce will age and the potential workforce, given current retirement ages, will decline. Certain medium-term solutions were identified, particularly the need to enhance the labour force participation rates of working age women, older workers and youth.

With respect to labour force participation we noted that participation rates for the populations as a whole have been increasing with the increase in female participation rates generally more than making up for the decrease in male rates. Despite this there are still significant differences between male and female participation rates in the EU and total OECD, and in the majority of countries, with the rates for females being substantially lower than for men.

We examined labour force participation by age group and concluded that the overall trends were declining participation among the young, possibly a reflection of people in this age range staying on longer in education and training, and increasing participation among both the other and older age groups. Nevertheless, there is considerable scope for enhancing labour force participation among both the youngest and oldest of these groups, and perhaps particularly within the EU among the 55 years and over group.

The incidence of part-time work is increasing; women dominate part-time working but there is evidence also that the proportion of male employment that is part time is increasing.

In examining unemployment we discovered that:

- Unemployment in the EU has been greater than in the total OECD but the gap has narrowed.
- Unemployment rates for women have traditionally been greater than for men but again the gap has narrowed with the female rate declining considerably.
- The youngest age group tends to experience much higher rates of unemployment than the higher age groups but again, while this is true for both men and women, there were considerable changes during the period under review so that by the end of the period the rates of unemployment in this age group were higher for men than for women and in the EU 15 in particular, the rate for women had decreased considerably.
- Long-term unemployment is more of a problem in Europe than in the OECD as a whole and there has been relatively little recent improvement.

The shift from employment in agriculture and industry continues as does the female dominance of employment in the service sector.

We also discussed in some depth the various explanations for existing patterns of female participation and concluded that there was a mix of cultural, social, economic, technological, regulatory and 'other' explanations.

Finally we examined the relationship between level of educational attainment and both labour force participation and unemployment and concluded that:

- there is a generally positive relationship between educational attainment levels and the ability to find and remain in employment;
- many women with low educational attainment may not enter the labour market at all;
- the less well-educated men and women are more likely to be unemployed;
- the relationship between level of educational attainment and propensity to be unemployed is more marked for women.

Activities to test understanding

Activity 1

Look at **Table 6.4**. The table gives a whole range of statistics for the EU 15 between 1993 and 2004.
Identify and comment upon:

- the trends that can be identified concerning the proportions of each sex working part time;
- trends in the employment rates for each sex;
- how these combine to provide FTE employment rates.

Activity 2

1 In the section on demography two major trends were identified. What were they?
2 What are the explanations for these trends?
3 What are the implications of these trends for the composition of the labour force?
4 What are the policy recommendations for seeking to alleviate these implications?

Activity 3

It is often suggested that long-term unemployment poses problems that are more intractable than those caused by frictional unemployment. Why is this?

Activity 4

Take a few moments now to think through how and why regulation aimed at helping women gain equality of opportunity and treatment may have the opposite effect.

Activity 5

Without going back to the text try to recall the main differences between the people included in each of (1) the claimant unemployment count and (2) LFS unemployment data. What are the strengths and weaknesses of each series?

Activity 6

1 For what reasons might employers choose to employ more expensive male labour when adequate cheaper female labour is available?
2 What do we mean by the process of socialization and why is it relevant to female participation in the labour force?

References

Burniaux, J.-M., Duval, R., and Jaumotte, F., 2004. *Coping with ageing: a dynamic approach to quantify the impact of alternative policy options on future labour supply in OECD countries.* Economics department working papers no. 371. OECD.

Becker, G., 1957. *The Economics of Discrimination.* The University of Chicago Press, Chicago, IL.

European Commission, 2005. *Employment in Europe, 2004.*

Hofstede, G., 1991. *Cultures and Organizations: Software of the Mind.* McGraw-Hill, New York.

ILO., 2003–2004. *Key Indicators of the Labour Market 2003.* Geneva.

OECD. *Employment outlook 2006.*

OECD. *Employment outlook 2005.*

OECD. *Employment outlook 2004.*

OECD Factbook 2006 – Economic, Environmental and Social Statistics.

OECD. *OECD in Figures, 2002.*

Chapter 7

Trade unions

Introduction

In earlier chapters of this text we have noted that, in the context of the Dunlop model, trade unions are one of the major actors in the system and as such they participate in the determination of the rules that are the outputs of the system. This participation may be through the process known as collective bargaining with employers, the second set of actors, which we examine later in **Chapter 9**, or it may be through exerting influence upon government, the third major actor, in order to achieve particular desired outcomes. We have already examined in **Chapter 6** how government, through its economic, industrial and legislative policies, can influence the environment within which employee relations are conducted and the bargaining power of the other parties.

Trade unions exist in order both to protect and further the interests of their members but, like other interest groups and institutions in society, they have to operate within contexts that constrain their freedom and their power and ability to pursue their interests selfishly and, of course, they have to interact with other interest groups and achieve an accommodation, commonly requiring compromise. Trade unions, therefore, generally pursue their objectives through the process of representation, to employers, other trade unions and to government and in doing so have been characterized as acting as agents for their members.

We have also in **Chapter 3** pointed out that there are levels of international trade union organization, but that these are predominantly made up of national trade union confederations with national constituencies and agendas and that the priority given to these latter interests has often made genuinely effective international representation of the interests of labour problematic. The labour movement has an international agenda but the only conclusion that can be drawn so far is that this international agenda is subservient to the interests of trade union members at a national or local level when it comes to issues such as job creation or protection, or protection of existing labour standards or terms and conditions of employment.

In the later chapter on managing employee relations at the level of the firm, we examine the issue of managing with or without trades unions as one dimension of management's strategy towards the management of employee relations.

In this chapter we are concerned with trades unions within a national context, what they are, why people join them, what their objectives may be, how they are organized and structured, membership trends, trade union recognition, the challenges that confront them and some of the survival strategies that the unions have available. There is both a comparative and generic dimension to some of the material.

Learning objectives

After studying this chapter you will be able to:

- define a trade union and discuss the reasons for and conditions in which they emerge and why individuals join them;
- identify and analyse the objectives of trade unions in the context of a distinction between business and welfare movements and the factors that may explain national variations;
- understand how structures vary and the differential nature of membership policies;
- explain how and why unions are regarded as democratic in terms of their internal organization and government, and identify and discuss various criteria by which the degree of democracy may be determined;
- understand membership trends and discuss reasons for these trends;
- understand the importance of trade union recognition;
- assess some of the debates about what the unions should do now to ensure their survival in the 21st century.

Definitions

There is no single and universally accepted definition of a trade union. Each country tends to use a definition peculiar to that country and which is sometimes enshrined in the law. The variations in definition make international comparison of trade union membership levels difficult and we return to this later. Nevertheless, it is possible to identify common strands to these definitions in terms of membership and purpose. Generally trades (or labour) unions are defined by reference to their membership being comprised of either workers or employees. There are exceptions however. For example, in Hong Kong there are both employee and employer trades unions. Often also the definition refers to the union having among its purposes the negotiation or regulation of basic terms and conditions of employment. An example of such a definition is the Australian definition which defines a trade union as:

> consisting predominantly of employees, the principal activities of which include the negotiation of rates of pay, and conditions of employment for its members.

The legal definition in the UK dates from the Trade Union and Labour Relations Act 1974 and states that a trade union is:

> an organization, whether permanent or temporary, which consists wholly or mainly of workers of one or more descriptions and is an organization whose principal purposes include the regulation of relations between workers of that description and employers or employers' associations.

These definitions are relatively narrow in terms of purpose and many trades unions in Europe have traditionally pursued objectives much wider than the regulation or joint determination of the terms and conditions and employment of their members. An example of a definition which indicates such wider purposes is that of Salamon (1992) who suggests that a trade union is:

> any organization, whose membership consists of employees, which seeks to organize and represent their interests both in the workplace and society and, in particular, seeks to regulate their employment relationship through the direct process of collective bargaining with management.

Although we cannot go much further with the question of definition, the essential elements have already been identified. Nevertheless, it is important to realize that even within countries, let alone across national borders, trades unions can differ considerably in terms of whom they allow into membership and their objectives. We pursue these issues further later in this chapter.

In the UK

We have already noted the legal definition of a trade union, but in the UK considerable importance is also attached to the question of whether the trade union is independent from the influence and control of an employer. The legal rights and immunities which trade unions enjoy are linked to their obtaining from the Certification Officer (CO) confirmation that they are indeed independent in this respect. The CO was given this role by the Employment Protection Act 1976. The linking of rights and immunities to independence encouraged many employee organizations which had previously been regarded as either staff or professional associations, and indeed in many instances had proudly proclaimed that they were not a trade union, to seek a certificate of independence as a trade union. Others entered into merger or other amalgamation arrangements with organizations already confirmed as independent trade unions.

The UK

Staff associations

Staff associations often act like trade unions in that they seek to determine with the employer the terms and conditions of employment of their members but they are often not independent of the employer, variously relying upon him/her for facilities and/or finance. Membership of a staff association is usually limited to the employees of one organization and in this respect they may appear to resemble the enterprise unions that are characteristic of Japan. In many instances they have been established with the considerable help and encouragement of the employer, sometimes in the hope that the staff association will prevent the spread of trade unionism within the company and that they will be easier to deal with than would a trade union.

Almost always the membership of staff associations has been dominated by white-collar as opposed to manual or blue-collar workers. Over the years there have been many examples of conflict between staff associations and trade unions. The banking, insurance and finance sector appears to have been particularly prone to the establishment of staff associations though, as noted above, over the years many of the associations formed have subsequently become trade unions in their own right or have been merged into other trade unions.

In some organizations in recent years managements have demonstrated a resurgence of interest in the establishment of a staff association as a preferable alternative to an independent trade union. This has sometimes occurred in conjunction with management derecognition of an independent trade union and the creation of alternative consultation arrangements with white-collar staff, such as a company council. Some of the privatized utilities sought to take advantage of their newfound independence from the public sector (where the employee relations traditions were consistent with a pluralist perspective and the joint resolution of conflict and determination of substantive and procedural outcomes) to create new arrangements of this kind, South West Water being an example. From the employee viewpoint however, staff associations, house unions and company councils all appear to suffer the same potential disadvantages associated with being reliant upon the employer for funds and facilities, not being able to derive support, strength, expertise and resources from a wider membership base or from membership of the wider trade union movement and being inherently vulnerable to pressure from the employer not to damage the organization's competitive position, not to rock the boat.

The activists in these associations and arrangements are potentially vulnerable to pressure from the employer, given that they rely upon the employer for their security of employment and career progression and they have no external support. Trade unions are also likely to argue that the staff association member suffers in comparison because the activists are not likely to have had the training or developed the expertise in protecting and progressing the interests of their members that a trade union representative has.

Managements with a unitarist perspective are likely to see trade unions as unnecessary and an illegitimate intrusion into the workplace, as organizations which lay an unwarranted claim upon the loyalty of employees, a loyalty which should be solely owed to the organization. In such a context it is likely that, given the opportunity, management will opt for a staff association or staff or company council arrangement rather than trade unionism. The former are all in-house arrangements and management is likely to feel that they provide much less opportunity for the conflict of loyalty which management perceives as the inevitable consequence of employee membership of a trade union.

Why trade unions and why do people join?

As Braverman (1974), among many others, has pointed out, the logic of capitalism is that the labour resource is subject to exploitation as surplus value is created through the labour process and accumulates to capital. In unregulated labour markets, individual sellers or units of labour resource are relatively weak participants in the process of market exchange between buyer and seller; they have relatively little bargaining power. Yet the same individuals in combination and through concerted action to control supply to the market are able to enhance their bargaining power significantly and exert a greater influence upon market outcomes. It is this market weakness of individuals and the strength derived from association and collective action that is at the root of trade unionism, and it is probably the case that trades unions tend to be formed in the first instance for primarily economic reasons. This analysis of inequality in the process of exchange between buyer and seller in the marketplace can be extended to encompass the employment relationship as a whole. However, having formed themselves into collectives, employees have not stopped at seeking to influence market price and, as we see in the next section, trade union objectives often transcend this initial market dimension, seeking, for example, to exert a wider control over the work environment and the labour process and, in some instances, to transform the nature of society. We have seen in the earlier chapter on globalization (**Chapter 3**) that people are not necessarily free to form and join trades unions in all countries and much of the work of organizations such as the International Labour Organization and International Confederation of Free Trade Unions (ILO and ICFTU, respectively) is geared towards achieving this right in a wider range of countries. One of the fundamental prerequisites for the formation of trades unions is that they are not outlawed or banned and that initiators are protected effectively from victimization. The history of trades unionism in many different countries demonstrates that employers and governments have often sought to combat what they perceive as a threat by outlawing or suppressing them, avoiding or refusing to recognize their right to take part in collective bargaining.

The inherent relative weakness of the individual seller of labour when contrasted with the relative strength of the corporate buyer may well be at the root of trade union organization, but we must not assume that this is necessarily the prime motivation for people when they decide to join an existing trade union. It is important to bear in mind that for many trade union members, availability and visibility in the workplace is a crucial prerequisite to membership. This highlights the importance of recognition for collective bargaining purposes. Where employer attitudes are favourable, where unions are recognized and seen by potential members to be effective participants in regulating the employment relationship, it is likely that recruiting members become easier.

However, other motives or reasons why people join trades unions may include:

- having values and political beliefs that coincide with those of the union movement. In countries such as France and Italy there are significant religious dimensions to the trade union movements and people would join the union that represented people sharing their religious beliefs;

■ some element of compulsion, whether this be the product of some form of agreement or legislation stipulating union membership as a condition for obtaining or retaining a specific employment, or the product of peer pressure;

■ a moral concern that those who benefit should in some sense pay the price by joining. It is usual for benefits or improvements obtained by trade unions to be extended to all in the appropriate bargaining unit, irrespective of trade union membership;

■ a belief that individual benefit will be derived from membership, either because, unlike the previous point, beneficial terms and conditions of employment are limited to trade union members only, or because the individual believes that the union's capacity to obtain or win benefits will be enhanced by his/her membership;

■ the image of unionism at the time, including both public opinion and individual perceptions of the role being played by trade unions and their leaders;

■ for protection, security and/or representation. Undoubtedly, many individuals join trade unions for one or more of these reasons. For example, it may be that they are primarily concerned with the risk of unemployment or threats posed to their standard of living by rising prices and feel that they will gain some measure of individual protection as a product of union membership. Alternatively, they may be attracted by the belief that the union will represent them as individuals in any grievance, disciplinary or dismissal proceedings and, if necessary, before a court of law;

■ so that they can benefit from facilities and services offered by the union, such as:

(a) retirement and sickness benefits and facilities;

(b) a range of financial and other membership services such as are offered by many other voluntary organizations and which may well include discounted rates and prices from various goods and service providers – mortgages, pensions, loans, credit cards, insurance, car rentals, etc. Many commentators and others over recent years have argued that the development of services of this nature should be deliberately undertaken as a means of encouraging people to join, as a recruitment attraction, and a number of trade union leaders have argued that the unions need to change their attitude towards their members so that they regard and treat them as customers rather than as troops that can be marshalled to fight industrial battles. In the UK there has been considerable debate within the union movement as to the relative merits of what are referred to as the organizing and servicing approaches (see later);

(c) unemployment services and benefits. Some trade unions act as recruitment and selection consultants for employers providing them with names of unemployed members, or it may be that the union circulates job vacancy information to its members, or that the union participates in some way in the administration of state financial unemployment and/or social security benefits;

(d) education and training opportunities, facilities and schemes;

■ for career reasons, either because they seek a career within the union as an official or because they consider that experience as a union official may open up other career avenues, such as in management. It is by no means unusual for trade union officials who have shown themselves to be competent to be offered management opportunities.

Those given above are the main reasons why people join a trade union rather than why they join a particular union. In many instances, which union to join is prescribed by the structure of the union movement in any one country and we revisit this point later in the chapter.

The objectives of trade unions

So far in this chapter we have examined what trades unions are, why they emerge and why workers join them. In this section we look further into what their objectives are. We have already alluded to the fact that trades unions emerge for primarily economic reasons concerned to rectify the unequal balance of power within the labour market and the employment relationship between individual sellers and buyers of labour, and we have mentioned that, whilst this may be the primary reason for their emergence, many trades unions have objectives wider than the workplace and participation in the regulation of terms and conditions of employment.

It has become common to distinguish trade unions and national trade union movements according to whether they have pursued essentially 'business' or 'political/welfare' objectives. 'Business' movements tend to be apolitical, not too interested in the pursuit of particular 'class' interests, and very much concerned with and focused on the provision and protection of improved benefits and services to their members at their place of work. These benefits and services may well include aspects of job control and these movements often have craft origins and traditions. Movements in this category have tended to emphasize collective bargaining at the level of the enterprise and the use of the strike as their preferred mechanism for resolving conflicts and achieving control. Conflictual and cooperative approaches and relationships are both consistent with these objectives, since 'business' unions often accept that the interests of their members are closely interwoven with the success of the enterprise. Unions and movements of this type are often referred to as being predominantly concerned with the bread and butter issues of employee relations and they are sometimes criticized for being essentially defensive or reactive, concerned to protect what they have managed to achieve in the interest of their members rather than initiate, promote or even accommodate change.

'Political' or 'welfare' movements do tend to pursue particular class interests, do have political or religious affiliations, do seek to transform society for the benefit of their members and, in particular, attempt to influence economic, legal and social policy so as to protect and further their members' interests. It is not uncommon for such movements to mobilize their membership in such a way that fundamental change is achieved, if necessary outside the framework of the existing political system. Industrial action to achieve political and social change is consistent with this approach. These 'political' movements are commonly affiliated to and/or sponsored by political or religious groups (e.g. the Communist party and the Catholic Church). Given the nature of their dominant objectives, movements in this group have often not given priority to the development of effective bargaining or other influencing mechanisms at the level of the firm or in the workplace. Criticisms of these movements tend to centre on the absence of a concern with the bread and butter issues of terms and conditions of employment within the workplace and for their members. They are also criticized for being involved in issues and activities that ought not to concern them, that they should not have political affiliations and should not seek to influence government and the policies pursued.

There are then significant differences of view as to what are legitimate objectives for trades unions in much the same way as there are fundamental differences of view concerning what might constitute legitimate means or methods for achieving them. There seems little dispute over the legitimacy of trade unions having as objectives the protecting and furthering of the interests of their members in the workplace and in relation to terms and conditions of employment. However, there are many who take the view that the pursuit of objectives outside the workplace is not a legitimate arena for trade unions. The alternative view might be that, since terms and conditions of employment, the nature of the employment relationship and the overall well-being and interests of its members are subject to so many external constraints, it is incumbent upon the trade union movement to seek to influence, possibly even control, that external environment.

Somewhere between these two extremes of business and political unions are those movements, perhaps best exemplified by those in some of the Northern European and Scandinavian countries, which have become social partners in neo- and bargained corporatist arrangements. These movements have been concerned to protect and further the interests of their members, but not primarily through activity at the level of the enterprise or through class-based and militant action aimed at transforming society. They have pursued the interests of their members predominantly through discussion, negotiation and concerted action at national level with the other main corporate actors – the employers and the state. Normally, these movements see their interests as being consistent with the achievement of national economic and social objectives such as full employment, price stability, income and wealth redistribution and economic growth. Inevitably, if these arrangements are to flourish, the other parties must be sympathetic and, perhaps most importantly, such arrangements must be consistent with the ideology of government (see **Chapter 5**).

As we shall see, US and Japanese unions have been considered to fit most closely the mould of 'business' unions, concentrating their efforts on the improvement of terms and conditions of employment within the enterprise, and accepting as inevitable the broader economic and political system. In France and Italy, however, the union movements have tended towards the 'political' type, seeking change centrally through political affiliation and pressure, on occasion mobilizing the membership into industrial action aimed at achieving specific political objectives. In both countries, the union movements are fragmented on both political and religious lines; they have tended to place low importance on workplace activity and, in France particularly, there has been a neglect of collective bargaining and a reliance on legislation as the mechanism through which employees' terms and conditions of employment are regulated.

Clearly, there is scope for variation within countries, as is evidenced by the fragmentation within France and Italy. Also changes can occur over time: thus in the US, unions have become increasingly involved in campaigning in the political sphere for favourable legislation, whereas there is some evidence that in continental Europe, the 'rank and file' are becoming more 'instrumental' in their approach and rejecting the 'political' orientation of their leaderships in favour of a greater business orientation. We do need to acknowledge that the objectives of trades unions are, at least in part, likely to reflect the society within which they exist and as this changes so may their objectives.

Similarly we should point out that the objectives being pursued are likely to have implications for the means used to achieve them. If the concern is bread and butter workplace issues then expect the unions to seek to use means that work at that level, the obvious examples in this case being collective bargaining with workplace management and, if they need to exert pressure through threatening or taking industrial action, it is likely to be confined to that same workplace. If, however, the objectives are to secure particular economic, social or legislative policies at a national level, then we must expect the unions to seek to exert influence at that same level, through political affiliation and lobbying and even possibly through the calling of a national strike.

The UK

Traditionally the union movement in the UK has encompassed both business and welfare or political objectives as can be detected from the list of objectives that were prepared by the Trades Union Congress (TUC, see later) and presented to the Royal Commission on Trade Unions and Employers Associations (Donovan) in 1965. This listed 10 main objectives which are paraphrased here and are not in any priority order:

1 improved terms of employment;
2 improved working conditions including the physical environment;
3 security of both employment and income;
4 industrial democracy;
5 full employment;
6 fair(er) shares in national income and wealth;
7 improved social security;
8 the public control and planning of industry;
9 a voice in government;
10 improved public and social services.

Only the first four of these could be regarded as being concerned with the kind of bread and butter issues that are associated with business unionism.

It should also be borne in mind that the Labour Party was created by the trade union movement as its political arm or wing and, even today, the trade union movement is a major financier of the Labour Party.

If we regard business and political as the extreme stereotypes of trade union movement distinguished by objectives then it would be fair to say that the movement in the UK has traditionally been towards the political or welfare end of an intervening spectrum. It always had the normal business objectives and operated at the level of the firm, but it also always had the political, social dimension to it and sought to operate and influence at the national level.

Recent decades have, however, witnessed a shifting of this position in the direction of business unionism, ties with the Labour Party have become strained and loosened. It is alleged that members, confronted by technological and structural change, by the competitive pressures of globalization, by inflation, recession and unemployment, all of which variously threaten jobs and living standards, have tended to take a more instrumental approach to union membership with an enhanced emphasis on what the union can do for them at the workplace and particularly in terms of job protection and security. It has also been argued that there have been changes in dominant values and social attitudes in the direction of individualism and instrumentalism. The debate within the UK movement has been between servicing and organizing approaches, the new realists and the traditionalists. The drive to recruit new and more members (see later) is itself evidence of this shift.

We also need to bear in mind that governments within the UK over the period since 1979 have gradually and cumulatively altered the rules of the game in favour of the employer and have encouraged the union movement towards business unionism through legislative changes which, for example, have made it unlawful for trades unions to take industrial action in respect of anything other than a trade dispute between workers and their own employer. Secondary action in support of colleagues employed by another employer and strikes in support of wider social or political objectives are now unlawful.

More recently the New Labour government elected in 1997 has been encouraging unions and employers to think in terms of partnership. Partnership in this context encompasses both talking to government and employers' associations at a national level in order to achieve objectives such as securing inward investment, and promoting training and equal opportunities and the conclusion of partnership agreements at the level of the firm or workplace. Partnership in this latter context does not relate to partnership in terms of ownership or control so much as recognizing that through partnership or cooperation business objectives can more readily be achieved. Unions are being encouraged to focus their energies and attention on facilitating the achievement of business objectives through the acceptance of change and enhanced employee flexibility, in return for trade union recognition, guarantees on job security and a greater focus on quality of work life issues.

Factors influencing objectives/orientation

Explanations of these variations in the orientation and objectives of union movements are inevitably complex and numerous. We explain

below some of the factors and variables that seem to have been significant in contributing to the development of objectives.

- The nature of the society before and in the early years of industrialization. Where societies had traditions of feudalism or
  where, as in Australia, there were other specific historical circumstances, it seems much more common for union movements to have emerged with a 'class' dimension and with social
  change and transformation as an objective.
- The attitudes of government and employers. Where governments were sympathetic to trade unionism and where there were
  political affiliations, union movements seem to have been
  encouraged to seek a central role and pursue the interests of
  their members politically and consensually. Where employers
  were anti-union and strongly resisted union recognition,
  unions tend to have been encouraged to concentrate their
  activity at the level of the firm and to concern themselves with
  'bread and butter' issues.
- Social homogeneity certainly favours the development of broad
  class-based movements, as compared with heterogeneous
  societies in which there are numerous and diverse interests
  and value systems.
- Cultural characteristics may well be relevant, for example, using
  Hofstede's (1991) typology of cultural dimensions, whether a
  society emphasizes individualism or collectivism, masculinity
  or femininity may influence the orientation and objectives
  of trades unionism. Certainly the enterprise-based, business-
  orientated union movement in Japan is consistent with the cultural dimensions identified by Hofstede, and the solidaristic
  policies and objectives pursued by the Dutch and Swedish
  movements over many years seem consistent with an emphasis
  on egalitarianism.
- The prosperity of the population has also been proposed as
  an explanation, the argument being that the more prosperous workers were, the more likely they were to be content with
  the social status quo and hence incline towards business
  unionism.
- The speed or pace of industrial and/or technological change
  and development. Again, the argument is that the faster the
  rate of change, the greater the likelihood that unions would
  be forced to concentrate on job-related issues at or near to the
  workplace.

The issue of whether unions are predominantly concerned with the
pursuit of business objectives at the level of the firm, or with exerting
political influence on a national basis, evidently also has a bearing on

how they structure themselves internally and how power is distributed at different levels of union organization.

Trade union structure

In this section we are concerned with how trade union movements are structured rather than how an individual union may be structured internally. Commonly trade unions have been classified by virtue of their membership base. Often they are distinguished by whether membership is job centred or not. Is the union that an individual can join determined predominantly by the job that he/she is doing, or by some other factor? In some countries, such as Japan, the dominant basis for organization is employment by a particular company. In others, such as Germany, the dominant basis is employment in a particular industry. In yet others, such as France and Italy, the membership base is essentially ideological or religious and the unions are general. Job-centred structures tend to focus on the possession of a particular skill or qualification or employment in a specific occupation. In some systems, there are trade unions of a general nature which recruit across trades, occupations and industries, but without the religious or political affiliations of those in France or Italy. It is common, therefore, in the literature to find unions being described as:

- company or enterprise, membership is limited to employees of the company; craft or skill, where membership is open only to those who possess a particular skill and where entry into the skill is often controlled by the union through formal apprenticeship schemes;
- occupational, there is similarity with the craft type, membership is open to those practising a particular profession or occupation such as teaching or being a doctor;
- industrial, here membership is limited to those working in a particular industry such as mining or railways;
- general, here there are theoretically no boundaries to recruitment and membership, anyone doing any job can be a member, though in practice there often are industrial or occupational boundaries to membership.

The process of industrial and labour force evolution in response to changing tastes, new technology and production systems and international competition has had significant consequences for the internal structures of some movements. The decline in demand for the products of particular skills, occupations and industries (and the emergence of new ones) has rendered the traditional structures inappropriate and many craft and some occupational and industrial unions have ceased to be viable as separate entities. Sometimes they have simply ceased to operate, but in many cases such decline has been accommodated by mergers and amalgamations and, where this has happened, there has been a consequential reduction in the numbers of trade unions.

An alternative classification system that is still concerned with membership base is a simple distinction between whether unions are pursuing open or closed membership strategies (Turner, 1962); job-centred unions tend towards being closed in this context with membership limited to those with particular skills, etc.

Membership base is only one dimension of structure. Trade unions and movements vary also on other dimensions of organization. One such dimension is concerned with level: are unions organized at a local, regional or national level and what is the level at which decision making is concentrated or focused? Often we seek to distinguish between those unions and movements in which the dominance, focus or emphasis is centralized as opposed to decentralized.

Another important structural dimension is concerned with the extent to which movements are unified or fragmented. For example, in some countries, movements are fragmented in that there are large numbers of unions, but nevertheless the movement is unified by experience, or by ideology and purpose, and represented by one 'peak' confederation at national level. Other national movements may comprise a relatively small number of independent unions but the movement is nevertheless fragmented at national level with a number of confederations differentiated on ideological, religious or some other ground. For example the UK, USA and Germany have the one peak association acting as the national voice for the movement as a whole, whereas in France and Italy there are several such associations, each with a particular religious or political affiliation.

Trade unions are secondary organizations in structural terms, being to some extent reflective of the way in which the other corporate actors and environment have structured industry and the labour force. Employers have usually formed employees into groups of one kind or another before trade unions are in a position to structure themselves. This is not to say that the unions can exert no influence or choice in these structural matters; they can and do, but they rarely have a green field in which to decide. There are certain factors that can be readily identified as providing the context within which employers and government make their decisions with respect to the structure of industry and the workforce, these being, perhaps primarily, the nature and availability of technology and production systems, and the nature and extent of international competition and consumer demand. In recent years, there is evidence of considerable and rapid global change in these contexts and, as we have noted above, the consequential pressures on the structure of industry and the workforce also constitute pressures on the structure of the trade union movement.

If we were to compile a list of the factors that influence trades union structures, we would have to include:

- the structure of industry and the labour force,
- the attitudes and objectives of employers,
- the objectives and orientations of the unions themselves,
- technology and production regimes,
- the beliefs and approach of government,
- the nature of product markets and the extent of competition.

These factors in combination will have an influence upon initial structures but, as they change, they will continue to exert pressures upon the structure of the trade union movement within any national system.

The UK

The union movement in the UK emerged initially in the middle of the 19th century amongst skilled craft workers, and it was not until towards the end of the 19th century that unions emerged to look after the interests of semi- and unskilled manual workers and it was well into the 20th century before unions began to be formed to represent the interests of white-collar and public-sector employees. Trade unions in the UK have traditionally been job centred in terms of membership base. The union movement and its structure was not planned, it emerged and developed in response to the emergence and development of industry and more recently the public and service sectors and as new categories and groups of employees felt the need for representation. The absence of coordination and planning in the early years resulted in a movement that was characterized by large numbers of relatively small unions often in competition with one another as their membership bases and ambitions overlapped. In 1920 the number of trades unions in the UK reached its peak at approximately 1400. The later decades of the 20th century have been decades of rationalization; however, this has itself often been opportunistic and we do not necessarily have a structure any more coherent than before. In the early part of the 21st century, the number of unions has declined to 193 in 2005 (see **Table 7.2**), down from 475 in 1979 (see **Table 7.1**).

The recent decline in the number of unions has largely been the product of rationalization through the mechanisms of amalgamation and merger, whereby two or more unions agree to join together to form one. There was something of a merger frenzy in the 1980s with 149 occurring between 1980 and 1991. Mergers and amalgamations occur for many reasons and in recent years many have occurred in response to the problems, both financial and organizational, caused by declining membership, rapid industrial restructuring and the decline of many of the traditional industries and skills that provided the core of trade union membership, and the need to gain both organizational and financial economies of scale to be financially viable.

As a consequence, the UK now has a trade union movement which is much more concentrated with a small number of very large unions accounting for the vast majority of

Table 7.1
Number of trade unions and membership; Great Britain,
1975–2002

Year	Membership (millions)	Unions
1975	11.7	446
1976	12.1	484
1977	12.7	436
1978	13.1	455
1979	13.2	475
1980	12.6	467
1981	12.3	482
1982	11.7	456
1983	11.3	432
1984	11.1	400
1985	10.8	391
1986	10.6	374
1987	10.5	344
1988	10.4	326
1989	10.0	319
1990	9.8	306
1991	9.5	291
1992	8.9	305
1993	8.7	297
1994	8.2	273
1995	8.0	260
1996	7.9	255
1997	7.8	252
1998	7.9	238
1999	7.9	237
2000	7.8	226
2001	7.8	216
2002	7.7	213

Source: Annual Reports of the Certification officer.

trade union members. **Table 7.2** shows that in 2005 the nine largest trade unions, each with a membership in excess of 250,000, accounted for 74 percent of all union members. Of the total of 193 trades unions 138 had a membership of less than 5000.

It becomes increasingly difficult to classify these large unions in terms other than whether they are essentially open or closed in relation to their membership base. Some might be classified as traditionally general (the GMB and TGWU) or occupational (teaching, nursing) but in the main they are hybrids, being the product of mergers between unions representing workers in different trades and working in different industrial sectors.

Table 7.2
Trades unions, numbers and size, accounting periods ending between October 2004 and September 2005.

Number of members	Number of unions	Membership	Number of unions		Membership of all unions	
			Per cent	Cumulative per cent	Per cent	Cumulative per cent
Under 100	34	733	17.6	17.6	0.0	0.0
100–499	40	11,186	20.7	38.3	0.1	0.2
500–999	18	12,452	9.3	47.7	0.2	0.3
1,000–2,499	25	41,167	13.0	60.6	0.6	0.9
2,500–4,999	21	76,140	10.9	71.5	1.0	1.9
5,000–9,999	11	86,140	5.7	77.2	1.2	3.0
10,000–14,999	4	46,494	2.1	79.3	0.6	3.7
15,000–24,999	8	141,436	4.1	83.4	1.9	5.6
25,000–49,999	15	530,626	7.8	91.2	7.1	12.7
50,000–99,999	3	197,441	1.6	92.7	2.6	15.3
100,000–249,999	5	788,549	2.6	95.3	10.6	25.9
250,000 and over	9	5,540,636	4.7	100.0	74.1	100.0
Total	193	7,473,000	100	100	100	100

Source: Annual Reports of the CO for 2004–2005, June 2006.

The TUC

The trade union movement in the UK has been relatively unusual in that it has developed without the plethora of national-level federations that characterize many European movements. The TUC, formed in 1868, is the single peak association for the trade union movement as a whole in the UK, though not all trades unions are members or affiliates. At the beginning of the 21st century, the TUC had in membership a minority of the total number of individual trades unions. However, these include the larger unions and the TUC affiliated unions accounted for approximately 80 percent of the total trade union membership in the UK.

Initially, the formation and existence of the TUC was to provide the labour movement with a collective voice in discussions with government and to represent the views of the trade union movement as a whole on issues of concern. This role remains but has become more international as the TUC represents the views of the UK movement within international trade union confederations such as the ICFTU and ETUC (European Trade Union Confederation) and to international organizations such as the ILO. There still are close links between the Labour Party and the TUC but they are weaker than they were even though the union movement is still a major funder of the political party.

The TUC has other important roles:

1 It is concerned with the prevention and, if necessary, resolution of inter-union conflicts. In the main these disputes tend to occur either over jurisdictional or membership

issues, who represents who and whether one union has been poaching members from another, or over demarcation matters, who has a 'right' to particular work. The incidence of such disputes has diminished in recent years as the trade union movement has rationalized itself and as the structure of the industrial landscape has changed. What might in the past have been inter-union disputes have sometimes become intra-union disputes as the consequence of mergers and amalgamations. Nevertheless, the role remains and decisions are made by an internal disputes committee with affiliates bound by the decision.

There were concerns at the end of the 20th century that the new legislative regulations regarding trade union recognition which came into force in the year 2000 might create increased dangers of competition between unions as they compete to do deals with employers. In response to this the TUC issued a consultative document to its members in the spring of 1999 entitled 'British Trade Unionism – the Millennial Challenge' in which it sought to address the issues both of avoiding and dealing with disputes that do arise.

2 Substantial educational, advisory and informational roles are also performed and provided for affiliates.

3 There is also a policing role to ensure that affiliates do not act in a manner that is inconsistent with general policies and principles agreed by the general Council or Congress.

4 Generally the TUC does not engage in collective bargaining with employers or employers' associations. It can become involved in industrial disputes between an affiliated union and an employer but only in circumstances where it is asked to by the affiliate and then it performs what is essentially a conciliation role.

Internal government and democracy

Trade unions are voluntary bodies which, in the main, people join because they want to. They are also generally intended to be democratic organizations. However, there are various different definitions, models and perspectives of democracy.

In many respects the simplest definition is that commonly associated with the American President Abraham Lincoln, who talked of government of the people by the people and for the people. In relatively small organizations or units it is possible to achieve this objective through the direct participation of all the 'people'. However, as the size of the unit to be governed increases it becomes more difficult to achieve efficient and effective government if decisions have to be taken by all the members and so there is a tendency for the organization to develop mechanisms that rely upon the election or appointment of representatives to act on behalf of a number of ordinary members. This is often referred to as the representative or parliamentary model of democracy and is contrasted with the direct or participatory model. Democracy in this context then can be measured by factors such as the extent to which decision making is decentralized and the extent to which members can and do participate in the formulation of policy and in the organization's government. Also it may be suggested that the greater the decentralization of decision making the greater are the checks upon the union leadership and the less opportunity they have to give effect to Michels' fears (see below).

Many years ago Michels (1966) developed his 'Iron Law Of Oligarchy', whereby it is argued that increasing size, the need for administrative efficiency and organizational effectiveness would inevitably lead in organizations such as trade unions to a concentration of power into the hands of an elite or oligarchy. This elite was likely to be in position because of its skill, knowledge and expertise, which it was then able to use, if it chose, to pursue its own interests as well as, indeed possibly instead of, the interests of the membership as a whole. The longer this elite is in power the greater is the likelihood that the leadership will become distanced and divorced from the membership. Such a situation has obvious dangers for the maintenance of democracy within the union.

We might therefore suggest that large, centralized and efficient organizations are less likely to achieve internal democracy easily, whereas organizations that are relatively small and local, or large but with effective decentralized decision-making mechanisms are likely to find it easier to achieve internal democracy.

Similarly, evidence of any widespread rank-and-file dissatisfaction with the objectives or policies being pursued by union leaders might be indicative of a lack of internal democracy as might low levels of membership participation at meetings and in elections of officers and representatives on policy-making bodies.

Examples of other criteria of democracy might variously include:

- the existence of opposition factions within the union and whether they are provided with equal facilities to get their message across to the members, especially prior to elections for membership of the various internal decision-making bodies;
- the degree of debate and discussion within the union and the presence of mechanisms facilitating this;
- the closeness of election results, the assumption being that landslide victories might be indicative of an absence of democracy;
- the participation and representation of particular factions or groups in the activities of the union and in the decision-making process; examples usually quoted are the participation of ethnic minority groups and women in the affairs of the union.

The UK

In **Figure 7.1** we outline a stereotype of how unions tend to be structured for the purpose of internal government and how the activities of the union are organized.

The figure demonstrates that policy and decision making begin at the bottom of the organization with the members who elect an individual to represent them in discussions and negotiations with management at the place of work. Normally these 'lay' representatives are called shop stewards and they remain employees of the employing organization and not employees of the union. These shop stewards then represent their members at the lowest level of official organization within the union, the branch. Depending upon the size of the workplace and the concentration of members, the branch may be either geographically or workplace based. Whichever base is used for determining the branch network, and it is quite common to have a mix within the same union, decisions of the branch are fed up through the hierarchy of the union organization through trade, district or regional arrangements to the annual or biannual conference of the union as a whole. Commonly the branch members will elect the members of the district or trade committees and these, in turn, elect or nominate representatives to the next level of union management, including the delegates to the national conference.

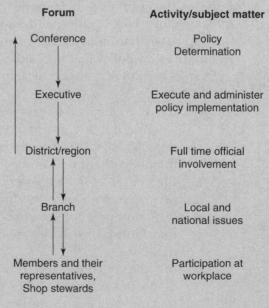

Forum	Activity/subject matter
Conference	Policy Determination
Executive	Execute and administer policy implementation
District/region	Full time official involvement
Branch	Local and national issues
Members and their representatives, Shop stewards	Participation at workplace

Figure 7.1
Internal government of a union.

It is this national conference that is the policy-making body for the union. Since an annual or biannual conference of delegates from the branches or districts cannot, in practice, be responsible for the day-to-day operations of the union and for the execution of the policies determined, trade unions tend to devise some form of executive committee arrangements.

Usually the executive committee of the union is comprised of a mix of senior elected representatives and full-time paid officials and, in addition to executing the wishes of the conference, they are likely also, in practice, to be in a position to amend or determine policy between conferences as events unfold. On really major issues the union may convene a special or extraordinary conference to determine a particular policy stance. You will find those who argue that the reality usually is that the executive committee is the real seat of power within a union and that this is the major policy-making forum rather than the formal position which allocates that role to the conference.

Since legislation in the Trade Union Act 1984, the members of the executive committee must be elected via a secret postal ballot of the members at least once in every 5 years. This applies to the principal paid and full-time officials of the union as well as to the other members.

One of the advantages of these arrangements has been that unions have been able to operate relatively cheaply, relying upon the unpaid shop stewards to undertake a great deal of the servicing of members at the level of the workplace. Full-time officers of the union commonly only become involved in servicing members and furthering their interests above the level of the branch. McIlroy (1995: 39) estimated that in the 1960s the ratio of full-time officers to members was somewhere near 1:4000.

The Conservative government elected in 1979 was of the view that the union movement as a whole had too much power and, as a corollary to this, there was a feeling that the unions were being led by militant unrepresentative minorities who took advantage of the absence of democratic accountability within the unions to pursue their own, often political, ends at the expense of the interests of the members. Whether this was the case or not, the new government determined, in their terms, to return the unions to their members, to bring democracy back to the union movement.

To this end the government adopted a number of measures to encourage membership participation in the election of senior union officials and members of the executive committee and in decisions concerning the taking of industrial action (Trade Union Act 1984) primarily through the enforcement of a requirement for secret postal ballots and direct democracy, but at a distance. This approach suggests that the government adhered to the parliamentary model of democracy. They also took a number of measures aimed at diminishing the power of the union in regard to the rights of members; for example, employees were given the right to belong to any union of their choice (Trades Union Reform and Employment Right Act 1993), restrictions were imposed upon the right of the union to discipline and expel members found guilty of strike breaking (Employment Act 1988) and additional rights were granted for members to examine the financial affairs of the union.

Critics of these legislative measures have pointed out that they reflected a concern with only one or two of the dimensions of democracy and that there are others which were not addressed.

Trade union membership

Problems of measurement

It is not easy to make cross-national comparisons of trade union membership owing to a number of problems associated with measurement. First, there are some differences in definition as to what constitutes a trade union. In the USA, for example, professional associations may not define themselves as trade unions, although they are involved in collective bargaining. However, in the UK it is possible for an organization to engage in collective bargaining but not be included as a trade union because it has not applied for a certificate of independence. Second, the source of the figures varies from country to country, and in some cases may be suspect. In many instances, for example, the sources of data are the unions themselves and there is obvious potential for these to be under- or overstated. It is also the case that national statistics on trade union membership may not be very meaningful, given that in some countries (e.g. Germany, France and the Netherlands) many non-unionized employees are by law covered by the terms of collective agreements, and that in others, membership may include retired or unemployed members, as in the Netherlands and Italy. The most meaningful measurement is that of trade union membership density, the proportion of potential members who actually are members; but even here comparisons can be difficult because the definitions of 'potential' or 'eligible' are not the same. In some statistical series, potential will simply be the total actually in employment; in others, it is the total plus those registered unemployed, while in others the self-employed are also included in the potential calculation.

Table 7.3
EIRO crude density figures for 2003 for 25 European countries.

- over 90 per cent in Romania
- 80–89 per cent in Belgium, Denmark, Finland and Sweden
- 70–79 per cent in Italy and Norway
- 60–69 per cent in Cyprus and Malta
- 50–59 per cent in Luxembourg
- 40–49 per cent in Austria and Slovenia
- 30–39 per cent in Hungary, Ireland and Portugal
- 20–29 per cent in Bulgaria, Germany, Greece, the Netherlands, Slovakia and the UK
- 10–19 per cent in Estonia, Latvia, Poland and Spain

Source: EIRO on-line. Trade Union Membership 1993–2003, p. 14.

The European Industrial Relations Observatory (EIRO) conducted a study of the available data from 26 European countries (1993–2003), and despite the fact that they argue that the data only enable the calculation of crude density rates they were able to derive the important conclusion that trade union density appeared to have declined between 1993 and 2003 in all but one of the countries (Malta) for which they could obtain data covering the 10-year period (20 in all). The scale of the decline varied considerably with falls in excess of 30 per cent in central and eastern European states but of no more than 15 per cent in other countries. The data also demonstrate significant variations in trade union membership density from one country to another (see **Table 7.3**); for example, density exceeded 80 per cent in Belgium, Denmark, Sweden and Finland, but was below 20 per cent in Poland and Spain and below 30 per cent in Germany, Greece, the Netherlands and the UK. They also concluded that in the 14 countries for which the data were available, female density exceeded male density in half the countries, with the reverse being the case in the others.

Another source of data on trade union membership and density is the ILO (**Table 7.4**). However, the data available from this source calculates density as the total trade union membership as a percentage of the total in paid employment and is very far from comprehensive. It is a source of information for a number of countries that are not in Europe and again demonstrates a pattern of both considerable variation between countries and general decline in membership density.

Reasons for variations

Despite the difficulties of measurement and comparison referred to above, there has nevertheless been a long history of attempts at

Table 7.4
ILO data on trade union density per cent.

Country	1980	1990	2003
Australia	55	40.5	23
Canada	37.6	35.7	30 (1999)
China	82	90.8	90.3 (2000)
India		21.2 (1992)	
Japan	30.8	25.2	20.2 (2002)
Taiwan		43.3	38.3
USA	20.1 (1983)	16.1	12.9

Adapted and derived from Statistics of Trade Union Membership. Data for 47 countries taken mainly from national statistical publications, November 2004. ILO Bureau of Statistics (unpublished).

explaining variations: over time, between industrial and labour force sectors and between countries. This interest has partly been fuelled by assumptions that trade union membership levels positively correlate with their bargaining power in dealings with employers and also with their political influence with governments.

Early explanations tended to assert relatively simple business cycle–membership relationships, linking changes over time to factors such as the rate of change in prices, unemployment and the rate of increase in money wages. Union membership would grow in the upswing of the business cycle because there would be greater pressure from employees for concessions from employers, who would be in a better position and more willing to make those concessions. The opposite trends would be discernible in periods of downswing.

There is wide acceptance that within countries cyclical variables account for a significant proportion of year-on-year fluctuations. Over a longer period, membership may vary as trade union organization availability varies in response to changes in the structure of industry occasioned by structural changes in demand, international competition and technological innovation. The socio-political, legal and institutional framework in a country, which is partially the product of the strategic choices that are made by the main actors (employers, trade unions and government) within the framework, will also influence levels of union organization and membership, and changes in this framework may explain long-term variations.

However, when it comes to explaining cross-national variations in union membership, there are at least two quite different views. One argues that there is a need to encompass country characteristics such as size, industrial and economic concentration and societal homogeneity, and the indirect influence they exert through their effects on the national actors, their strategic choices, structures and institutions. The other view argues that the crucial explanation of these cross-national variations is not national characteristics, institutions, strategic decisions, etc.; it is the strength and effectiveness of local union organization and activity. The former view notes that local organization and availability are important to membership levels, but sees this as a product of the more dominant and important national characteristics, institutions, choices, etc.; whereas the latter view rejects these national explanations as mistaken and argues that local organization is the dominant variable.

The UK

The high point of trade union membership in the UK was in 1979, when membership exceeded 13 million (see **Table 7.1**) and density exceeded 50 per cent. Excess of 5 million members were lost between 1979 and 1995–1996 since when the total membership has been relatively stable varying between a total of 7.5 and 7.9 million. In 2004–2005 the total membership was 7.47 million according to the CO returns (**Table 7.2**); however, this figure excluded some 86,000 members from the Association of University Teachers and Community, the overall total would therefore appear to be close to 7.56 million.

In the UK there are two main series of data on trade union membership, one provided by the CO who derives figures from the information presented to him by the trade unions themselves who are required to provide annual returns. The other series is derived by estimating from the Labour Force Survey (LFS) data. The LFS compiles information from a sample of those in employment in a particular reference week and this series tends to produce lower figures than the CO data. The CO membership count includes all members of unions having their head office in Great Britain, including those members in Northern Ireland, the Irish Republic and 'elsewhere abroad'. These figures may also include union members who are unemployed or retired and if a person was a member of two unions, he/she would be included twice in the CO data.

The LFS data are much more detailed, though the time series is not so long, and for the rest of this section we use data from the LFS.

From the tables presented we are able to draw a number of conclusions concerning the trends and characteristics of trade union membership in the UK in recent years.

Table 7.5 shows that trade union density has continued to decline amongst male employees (period 1995–2005) but that density amongst females has been more stable and is now greater than for male. If we look at the overall membership figures, whilst there has been relative stability over the period with year-on-year fluctuations in both directions, it also shows that membership amongst men has declined pretty consistently whereas membership amongst women has increased pretty consistently. This may, of course, be no more than a reflection of the increasing participation of women in the labour force.

Table 7.5

Trade union membership and density for the UK, autumn 1995–2005

	In employment[a]		Employees[b]	
	Members[c]	Density	Members[c]	Density
People				
Autumn 1995	7,070	29.0	6,791	32.6
Autumn 1996	6,918	28.4	6,631	31.7
Autumn 1997	6,911	27.5	6,643	30.6
Autumn 1998	6,890	27.2	6,640	30.1
Autumn 1999	6,911	27.2	6,622	29.8
Autumn 2000	6,924	27.2	6,636	29.7
Autumn 2001	6,846	26.8	6,558	29.3
Autumn 2002	6,840	26.6	6,577	29.2
Autumn 2003	6,820	26.6	6,524	29.3
Autumn 2004	6,784	26.0	6,513	28.8
Autumn 2005	6,677	26.2	6,394	29.0
Change from 1995	−393	−2.8	−397	−3.6
Change from 2004	−107	+0.2	−119	+0.2
Male				
Autumn 1995	3,936	29.9	3,727	35.3
Autumn 1996	3,797	28.8	3,579	33.6
Autumn 1997	3,788	27.8	3,600	32.4
Autumn 1998	3,730	27.3	3,545	31.4
Autumn 1999	3,730	27.3	3,526	31.1
Autumn 2000	3,652	26.7	3,457	30.4
Autumn 2001	3,636	26.6	3,426	30.1
Autumn 2002	3,531	25.8	3,354	29.4
Autumn 2003	3,500	25.5	3,297	29.4
Autumn 2004	3,432	24.7	3,243	28.5
Autumn 2005	3,331	24.6	3,122	28.2
Change from 1995	−605	−5.3	−605	−7.1
Change from 2004	−101	−0.1	−121	−0.3
Female				
Autumn 1995	3,134	28.0	3,064	29.9
Autumn 1996	3,121	27.9	3,051	29.7
Autumn 1997	3,124	27.0	3,043	28.7
Autumn 1998	3,160	27.0	3,100	28.7
Autumn 1999	3,181	27.1	3,100	28.5
Autumn 2000	3,273	27.7	3,180	29.1
Autumn 2001	3,210	27.0	3,132	28.4
Autumn 2002	3,307	27.6	3,223	29.0
Autumn 2003	3,320	27.8	3,227	29.3
Autumn 2004	3,353	27.6	3,269	29.1
Autumn 2005	3,346	28.1	3,272	29.9
Change from 1995	+212	+0.1	+208	0.0
Change from 2004	−7	+0.5	+3	+0.8

Thousands not seasonally adjusted.
Source: Labour Force Survey, Office for National Statistics.
[a] Excludes members of the armed forces, unpaid family workers and those on college-based schemes.
[b] Excludes members of the armed forces.
[c] Those who did not report their union status on a pro-rata basis are no longer allocated. Note the figures for male and female may not sum to the total due to rounding.
Derived from DTI website with © Crown.

Table 7.6 shows that trade union membership density is significantly greater in the public sector compared with the private sector. For 2005 the private-sector UK density rate was 17.2 per cent compared with an equivalent figure for the public sector of 58.6 per cent. Actual membership has fallen in the private sector whereas in the public sector it has increased; again employment in the public sector was expanding in the first years of the 21st century.

Table 7.7 demonstrates a number of features of the distribution of trade union membership among employees in the UK in 2005. Density is higher among full-time employees, there are considerable variations according to age with older employees demonstrating higher rates and the density rate of only 9.9 per cent among the under 25 years being a particular cause for concern to the trades unions. Workplace size appears also to be of significance since density in smaller workplaces is much lower than it is in workplaces employing more than 50. Logistically it is much more difficult for trades unions to organize and effectively represent employees in smaller workplaces. From the perspective of occupation, the highest rates of trade union membership density are among the professional and associated occupations, a particular phenomenon amongst female employees. Density is greater among managerial and supervisory employees than among the non-managerial category, and again this is more marked among female employees than among males. In looking more closely at the data for particular industries, it shows, as one would expect, much higher rates in those industries dominating the public sector and in industries which were once part of the public sector such as electricity, gas and water supply. There are some sectors with particularly low density, hotels and restaurants, retail and wholesale trades, and real estate and business services.

Table 7.8 provides data on a range of other variables and demonstrates that density is much higher among those with a higher-level education and this is particularly the case among women. There are variations according to ethnicity and the relationship between length of service and trade union membership would appear to be positive. Finally the data demonstrates that the highest rates of density are among those earning between £25 and £50,000 p.a.

Table 7.9 is also interesting in that it demonstrates the scale of what is referred to as the union wage premium and, while this has been declining, it is nevertheless substantial and particularly so in the public sector. Having said that, the gap in the private sector was still 8.1 per cent in 2005 and this provides ammunition for trades unions to argue the benefits of union membership and, of course, for employers to try and resist trade union membership and recognition among their labour force.

Additional information was obtained in the 1998 Workplace Employee Relations Survey (WERS) which is based on information from employers and this indicates that overall trade union density was 36 per cent. The data confirmed that there are positive associations between both trade union recognition and membership density and size of workplace. They also confirm that the attitude of management appears influential with regard to both union membership density and recognition; where managers are in favour of union membership, the density figure is 62 per cent and the rate of recognition is 94 per cent.

Table 7.6

Trade union membership and density for private and public sector employees[a] for the UK and Great Britain, autumn 1993–2005

	UK[b]		Great Britain	
	Members (ODD's)[b]	Density (per cent)	Members (ODD's)[b]	Density (per cent)
Private sector				
Autumn 1993	–	–	3,400	24.0
Autumn 1994	–	–	3,294	22.8
Autumn 1995	3,221	21.6	3,143	21.5
Autumn 1996	3,148	20.9	3,064	20.7
Autumn 1997	3,173	19.9	3,099	19.8
Autumn 1998	3,178	19.5	3,095	19.3
Autumn 1999	3,155	19.3	3,072	19.2
Autumn 2000	3,081	18.8	2,999	18.8
Autumn 2001	3,073	18.6	2,978	18.5
Autumn 2002	3,005	18.2	2,917	18.1
Autumn 2003	2,936	18.2	2,858	18.1
Autumn 2004	2,794	17.2	2,718	17.1
Autumn 2005	2,702	17.2	2,625	17.1
Change from 1995	−519	−4.4	−775	−4.4
Change from 2004	−92	0.0	−93	0.0
Public sector				
Autumn 1993	–	–	3,013	64.4
Autumn 1994	–	–	3,481	63.6
Autumn 1995	3,542	61.5	3,425	61.4
Autumn 1996	3,454	61.1	3,342	60.9
Autumn 1997	3,454	60.9	3,325	60.8
Autumn 1998	3,452	61.0	3,326	60.6
Autumn 1999	3,457	59.9	3,340	59.8
Autumn 2000	3,543	60.2	3,419	60.0
Autumn 2001	3,474	59.3	3,343	59.0
Autumn 2002	3,558	59.7	3,406	59.3
Autumn 2003	3,575	59.1	3,436	58.8
Autumn 2004	3,713	58.8	3,572	58.4
Autumn 2005	3,686	58.6	3,541	58.2
Change from 1995	+144	−2.9	+528	−6.2
Change from 2004	−27	−0.2	−31	−0.2

Source: Labour Force Survey, Office for National Statistics.
[a] Excludes members of armed forces.
[b] Those who did not report their union status on a pro-rata basis are no longer allocated. Note the figures public/private sector may not sum to the total due to rounding and the fact that some respondents may not have answered the question.
– Data only available from 1995 in the UK.
Derived from DTI website with © Crown.

Table 7.7
Trade union density for UK employees[a] by selected characteristics, autumn 2005

	All	Sex		Status (per cent)	
		Men	Women	Full-time	Part-time
All employees	29.0	28.2	29.9	31.7	21.5
Age band					
16–24	9.9	10.1	9.6	13.2	3.8
25–34	25.2	22.5	28.2	26.0	21.8
35–49	34.2	33.3	35	36.1	28.2
50 plus	34.5	35.9	35.2	40.2	25.3
Workplace size					
Less than 50	18.7	15.7	21.3	26.8	14.5
50 or more	38.5	38.3	38.8	40.0	32.2
Sector					
Private	17.2	20.0	13.5	19.5	10.1
Public	58.6	61.4	57.1	64.3	45.1
Occupation					
Managers and senior officials	18.9	17.0	22.3	19.1	16.4
Professional occupations	49.3	38.8	61.8	48.9	51.4
Associate professional and technical	42.2	36.6	47.3	41.0	47.7
Administrative and secretarial occupations	24.7	31.6	23	27.5	19.5
Skilled trades occupations	24.7	24.8	24.4	25.8	10.8
Personal service occupations	29.9	37.7	28.5	33.3	25.6
Sales and customer service occupations	11.6	8.7	12.8	14.4	9.6
Process, plant and machine operatives	34.2	35.7	25	36.7	10.8
Elementary occupations	20.9	25.4	15.7	28.4	12.1
Managerial status					
Manager	31.0	25.5	38.8	30.6	34.5
Foreman or supervisor	37.3	34.2	40.5	37.7	35.2
Non-manager	26.4	28.1	25.0	30.7	18.3
Industry					
Agriculture, forestry and fishing	8.5	9.9	*	9.8	*
Mining and quarrying	21.2	24.2	*	22.1	*
Manufacturing	24.8	27.7	16.2	26.2	8.9
Electricity, gas and water supply	47.0	50.8	38.4	48.7	*
Construction	15.7	16.9	9.3	16.7	*
Wholesale and retail trade	11.0	10.8	11.3	12.1	9.5
Hotels and restaurants	4.2	2.8	5.2	4.7	3.6
Transport and communication	42.2	47.4	27.4	45.0	23.3
Financial intermediation	24.4	19.8	28.5	22.7	32.9
Real estate and business services	10.1	11.2	8.7	10.8	7.0
Public administration	57.1	58.9	55.4	58.7	50.3
Education	56.0	60.9	54.3	66.6	38.4
Health	44.2	49.5	42.9	49.0	35.7
Other services	19.3	24.0	14.9	23.9	10.6

Source: Labour Force Survey, Office for National Statistics.
[a] Excludes members of the armed forces
* Sample size too small to provide a reliable estimate.
Derived from DTI website with © Crown.

Table 7.8

Trade union density for UK employees[a] by further characteristics, autumn 2005

	All	Sex		Status (per cent)	
		Men	Women	Full-time	Part-time
All employees	29.0	28.2	29.9	31.7	21.5
Ethnic group					
White	29.2	28.5	30.0	31.8	22.0
Mixed	25.6	22.1	28.9	28.0	*
Asian or Asian British	25.7	25.3	26.4	29.7	13.5
Black or Black British	30.1	27.3	32.6	33.7	17.0
Chinese and other ethnic groups	21.1	20.8	21.3	25.3	*
Flexible working status					
Flexitime	39.5	37.0	41.5	41.9	30.9
Annualized hours contract	41.6	42.2	41.0	44.8	31.2
Term-time working	53.1	67.7	50.6	72.2	35.8
Job sharing	40.5	*	42.1	*	41.1
4.5-day week/9-day fortnight	37.3	40.1	32.5	38.5	*
Zero hours contract	13.9	*	*	*	*
Work mainly at home/same grounds	12.5	15.5	10.5	17.7	*
Highest qualification					
Degree or equivalent	37.8	30.6	45.5	37.6	38.4
Other higher education	43.2	34.5	50.0	43.5	42.5
A-level or equivalent	25.9	28.0	22.6	29.3	15.2
GCSE or equivalent	23.5	25.5	22.1	27.0	16.3
Other qualifications	23.6	26.0	21.0	25.8	17.9
No qualifications	22.0	25.4	18.8	26.9	13.8
Dependent children					
No dependent children	29.2	28.1	30.3	31.2	21.0
Dependent children under 6	26.4	24.7	28.3	26.8	25.6
Dependent children 6 or over	29.3	29.4	29.2	34.1	20.9
Length of service					
Less than 1 year	11.4	11.4	11.5	13.6	6.9
One to 2 years	17.1	15.7	18.5	19.6	11.4
Two to 5 years	23.4	22.2	24.6	25.8	16.7
Five to 10 years	30.5	28.6	32.4	31.6	27.3
Ten to 20 years	43.2	40.1	46.3	44.3	39.7
20 years or more	58.2	57.4	59.5	60.4	48.3
Permanent or temporary status					
Permanent	29.6	28.9	30.5	32.2	21.9
Temporary	18.3	15.6	20.7	19.2	17.3
Weekly earnings in main job					
Less than £250	16.1	11.7	17.9	15.4	16.5
£250–499	33.9	30.5	38.3	32.3	52.1
£500–999	41.1	36.5	51.6	41.3	34.6
£1000 and above	19.0	18.9	19.3	19.1	*

Source: Labour Force Survey, Office for National Statistics.
[a] Excludes members of the armed forces.
* Sample size too small to provide a reliable estimate.
Derived from DTI website with © Crown.

Table 7.9
Average hourly earnings by trade union membership and sector, UK employees[a], autumn 1995–2005

	All employees (£)	Union membership		Union wage premium* (%)
		Member (£)	Non-member (£)	
All employees				
Autumn 1995	7.12	8.25	6.55	26.0
Autumn 1996	7.33	8.31	6.87	21.0
Autumn 1997	7.51	8.49	7.10	19.6
Autumn 1998	7.91	8.87	7.49	18.4
Autumn 1999	8.25	9.16	7.86	16.5
Autumn 2000	8.75	9.75	8.32	17.2
Autumn 2001	9.28	10.32	8.86	16.5
Autumn 2002	9.62	10.67	9.19	16.1
Autumn 2003	9.89	11.06	9.40	17.7
Autumn 2004	10.21	11.38	9.72	17.1
Autumn 2005	10.69	11.98	10.19	17.6
Change from 1995	3.57	3.73	3.64	n/a
Change from 2004	0.48	0.60	0.47	n/a
Change from 2004	+4.7%	+5.3%	+4.8%	n/a
Private sector				
Autumn 1995	6.68	7.34	6.49	13.1
Autumn 1996	7.02	7.63	6.86	11.2
Autumn 1997	7.19	7.86	7.06	11.3
Autumn 1998	7.59	8.17	7.45	9.7
Autumn 1999	8.03	8.53	7.90	8.0
Autumn 2000	8.49	9.06	8.35	8.5
Autumn 2001	9.04	9.51	8.93	6.5
Autumn 2002	9.32	9.71	9.23	5.2
Autumn 2003	9.57	10.20	9.42	8.3
Autumn 2004	9.80	10.29	9.69	6.2
Autumn 2005	10.29	10.97	10.15	8.1
Change from 1995	3.61	3.63	3.66	n/a
Change from 2004	1.21	0.68	0.46	n/a
Change from 2004	+5.0%	+6.6%	+4.7%	n/a
Public sector				
Autumn 1995	8.30	9.10	6.93	31.3
Autumn 1996	8.21	8.93	7.05	26.7
Autumn 1997	8.44	9.10	7.38	23.3
Autumn 1998	8.87	9.52	7.82	21.7
Autumn 1999	8.93	9.76	7.66	27.4
Autumn 2000	9.51	10.40	8.16	27.5
Autumn 2001	10.02	11.04	8.54	29.3
Autumn 2002	10.48	11.52	8.94	28.9
Autumn 2003	10.81	11.78	9.32	26.4
Autumn 2004	11.31	12.26	9.94	23.3
Autumn 2005	11.80	12.75	10.43	22.2
Change from 1995	3.50	3.65	3.50	n/a
Change from 2004	0.49	0.49	0.49	n/a
Change from 2004	+4.3%	+4.0%	+4.9%	n/a

Source: Labour Force Survey, Office for National Statistics.
[a] Excludes members of the armed forces.
* Percentage difference in average hourly earnings of union members compared with non-union employees in the same sector.
Derived from DTI website with © Crown.

The WERS in 2004 (see **Table 7.10**) also collected data on trade union membership from two sources and this data confirms the wide variation in density between the private (22 per cent) and public sectors (64 per cent).

The survey data also demonstrates the strong association between union density and management attitudes towards membership. The two characteristics are, of course, linked as management support for union membership is much more prevalent in the public sector than in the private sector, but the survey team assert that the association between membership density and management attitudes was just as strong among private-sector workplaces. Where managers were in favour of trade unions, density was 60 per cent compared with only 5 per cent where they were not in favour.

Findings from the survey of employees indicated that one-third (34 per cent) of all employees in workplaces with 10 or more employees were union members.

Almost two-thirds of workplaces (64 per cent) had no union members and union members made up a majority of the workforce in only one-sixth (18 per cent) of all workplaces. The earlier WERS 1998 had shown 57 per cent of workplaces had no union members and union members made up the majority of the workforce in 22 per cent of workplaces.

Inevitably, many researchers and commentators have sought to explain the reasons and causes of the long-term decline in both trade union membership and density in the UK since 1979. What has become clear is that there is no one explanatory variable

Table 7.10

Union presence, by sector of ownership and management attitudes

	Aggregate union density	No union members	Union density of 50 per cent or more	Recognized unions
	Per cent of employees	Per cent of workplaces	Per cent of workplaces	Per cent of workplaces
All workplaces	34	64	18	30
Sector of ownership				
Private	22	77	8	16
Public	64	7	62	90
Management attitude towards union membership				
In favour	60	8	58	84
Neutral	22	76	9	17
Not in favour	5	93	1	4

Base: All employees in workplaces with 10 or more employees (column 1) and all workplaces with 10 or more employees (columns 2–4).

Figures are weighted and based on responses from 21,540 employees (column 1) and 1,973 managers columns 2–4).

Source: Inside the Workplace. First Findings from the 2004 Workplace Employment Relations Survey (WERS 2004).

and that a number of developments can be argued to have contributed. Among these are:

- the macroeconomic climate, macroeconomic policy, recession and unemployment especially in the 1980s and early 1990s when the decline was most rapid;
- the gradual but nevertheless substantial legislative attack upon the trade unions that was mounted by the Conservative Party whilst in government between 1979 and 1997. This encompassed the removal of legal rights to recognition and the encouragement of collective bargaining, limits upon picketing and secondary action, the eventual outlawing of the closed shop, the removal of the ability of trade unions to discipline members for not taking part in lawful industrial action, the development of increasingly strict constraints upon the unions' freedom to take industrial action and the creation of a legal right to not be a member of a trade union;
- the determination of the Conservative government to stand firm against trades unions, particularly in the public sector;
- reduction in the size of the public sector;
- change in the structure of industry, the decline of manufacturing and extractive industries, the growth of the service sector;
- both an ageing population and the increased participation of women in the labour force (though the data presented above would arguably not support such an explanation);
- the attitudes of employers, their resistance to sharing employer prerogative and their opportunism in taking advantage of the circumstances created by the above (see the evidence from the 2004 WERS above);
- employer reaction to the need to become more competitive in the global market and perhaps, particularly, their desire to introduce greater flexibility to working practices and their use of labour;
- changes in values and culture in the UK reflected perhaps most obviously in the emphasis given to enterprise and individualism;
- the unions themselves, their failure to present the case in favour of trade unionism adequately and the attitudes and behaviour of both leaders and members.

Trade union recognition

We have mentioned the term trade union recognition on a number of occasions in this text without as yet really explaining what we mean. Generally, when we talk about it we mean that the employer has agreed to recognize, or accept, one or several trades unions for the purposes of representing employees and their interests in collective bargaining over a range of terms and conditions of employment. The range of issues that management is willing to bargain over will vary from one employer to another and over time.

Recognition is crucial for trades unions to be effective and for them to be perceived as effective by members and potential members. In an earlier section of this chapter we identified visibility and achievement as important influences upon membership, so that the trade union needs to be recognized and active to recruit members; but how can it gain recognition? Many employers take the view that they might be prepared to enter into a recognition agreement with a union but want evidence that the union has the support of the employees and that a substantial proportion of them are in membership. It is difficult for unions to recruit members in workplaces where they are not recognized since employees may be concerned with potential dismissal or other form of victimization if they join the union before it is recognized.

It is also important that we bear in mind that there are lots of reasons why employers and managements may want to resist the influence of trades unionism and collective bargaining. As we note elsewhere, recognizing unions for collective bargaining means that the employer is willing to share control and decision making even if the range of subject matter is narrow. Many managements prefer to retain their autonomy and right to make decisions, to determine terms and conditions of employment themselves and to inform and consult only when and if they want to. Many of the reasons why managements resist unionism are associated with the unitarist perspective outlined in **Chapter 1** and a willingness to recognize and bargain implies that management have a pluralist perspective. Having said that, there are many managements that do realize the benefits of having effective and well supported trades unions in the workplace.

The history of trades unionism is littered with examples of bloody conflicts between employers and employees when the latter have sought representation by and recognition of a trade union. It is in part a response to this potential that in many countries there are legislative supports for trades unions and mechanisms through which they are able to force their employer to recognize and bargain. Generally, the union may have to demonstrate a particular level of support before it can trigger the legislative mechanism and there are lots of other issues that may be covered by the relevant legislation; for example, the union might have to demonstrate that it has the support required possibly by stating who the members are, possibly through some form of balloting. There are questions about how the bargaining unit is to be determined: is it to be the union itself or the employer or an agreement between them, and if they cannot agree, does it go to a third party? How is the subject matter that is to be bargained over to be determined, with the same options? Should the employer have a right to veto a particular union, or to choose the union, or should this be the prerogative of the employees? How can employers be prevented from victimizing those employees perceived to be activists? How can employees be protected? All of these are issues that are variously covered by legislation where it exists.

The UK

It was noted earlier that one of the legislative changes (Employment Act 1980) introduced by the Conservative governments of the 1980s constituted a removal of the rights and mechanisms that the trade unions had available throughout the 1970s to enforce recognition upon employers for the purposes of collective bargaining, even in the face of employer opposition.

As we have noted above, 1979 was the high point of trade union membership since when there has been a decline both in trade union membership and the incidence of collective bargaining over even the most basic of terms and conditions of employment and pay.

The scale of this decline is indicated in the 1984–2004 WERS data which indicate a continuing decline in the proportion of workplaces where one or more unions are recognized for collective bargaining purposes. The 2004 data indicates that among workplaces with 25 or more employees, the incidence of recognition remained stable at around two-fifths (39 per cent in 2004, compared with 41 per cent in 1998 and down from 80 per cent plus in the early 1980s). The authors of the 2004 WERS First Findings assert that the continual decline in the rate of recognition seen among this group over the 1980s and 1990s, therefore, appears to have been arrested. However, if we include all workplaces the recognition rate is only 30 per cent in 2004 (see **Table 7.10** above) and these employ 50 per cent of all employees.

According to the WERS 2004 survey, most of the decline in recognition in recent years had been in the smaller workplaces, only 18 per cent of workplaces with 10–24 employees recognized unions in 2004, compared with 28 per cent 6 years earlier. We note later the concerns of the TUC with regard to obtaining recognition in the smaller workplaces.

Table 7.10 also demonstrates the substantial difference in recognition rates between public (90 per cent) and private sectors (16 per cent).

The LFS data in **Table 7.11** shows that from 1999 to autumn 2005 there has been an overall decrease in the number of employees saying that their pay is affected by collective agreements, though there had been an increase in the public sector where employment has been increasing; nonetheless, in percentage terms the public sector has seen a decline. In the private sector there has been both an actual and percentage decline. The LFS data in Table 7.11 indicate that in the Autumn of 2005 48.1 per cent of employees worked in a workplace where there was a union presence and this is close to the WERS 2004 finding that 50 per cent of employees were employed in workplaces where there was trade union recognition.

Overall this data does not provide evidence which might be indicative of any widespread increase in recognition of trades unions for collective bargaining purposes since the enactment of the new provisions in the Employment Relations Act 1999 (see below).

It would be easy to assume that the decline in trade union recognition, demonstrated in the WERS data, was the result of planned and deliberate derecognition by employers, taking the opportunity afforded by the new economic, political and legislative climate of the 1980s and 1990s to rid themselves of an unwelcome representative of their employees and a challenge to their authority and autonomy. While this undoubtedly did happen in some cases, and perhaps particularly in industries such as newspapers and the media,

Table 7.11

Trade union presence and coverage of collective agreements for UK employees[a], autumn 1996–2005[c]

	Trade unions present in workplace		Employee's pay affected by collective agreement	
	Number (000's)[a]	Per cent	Number (000's)[b]	Per cent
All employees				
Autumn 1996	11,144	50.3	8,243	37.2
Autumn 1997	11,105	48.9	8,198	36.1
Autumn 1998	11,130	48.0	8,177	35.3
Autumn 1999	11,439	48.7	7,274	36.2
Autumn 2000	11,684	49.1	7,269	36.3
Autumn 2001	11,611	48.3	7,215	35.7
Autumn 2002	11,769	48.6	7,273	35.7
Autumn 2003	11,759	48.8	7,236	36.0
Autumn 2004	11,664	48.4	7,225	35.0
Autumn 2005	10,614	48.1	7,054	35.3
Private sector				
Autumn 1996	5,723	35.3	3,762	23.4
Autumn 1997	5,787	34.2	3,755	22.3
Autumn 1998	5,791	33.2	3,744	21.6
Autumn 1999	6,110	34.9	3,421	23.1
Autumn 2000	6,223	35.2	3,350	22.7
Autumn 2001	6,126	34.3	3,316	22.4
Autumn 2002	6,155	34.3	3,212	21.6
Autumn 2003	6,079	34.4	3,222	22.1
Autumn 2004	5,995	34.2	3,042	20.5
Autumn 2005	5,147	32.8	2,967	20.9
Public sector				
Autumn 1996	5,421	89.6	4,482	74.7
Autumn 1997	5,318	89.2	4,442	75.0
Autumn 1998	5,340	89.5	4,433	75.0
Autumn 1999	5,329	87.9	3,853	73.0
Autumn 2000	5,461	87.7	3,934	73.5
Autumn 2001	5,483	88.0	3,889	72.5
Autumn 2002	5,614	88.2	4,062	73.8
Autumn 2003	5,660	87.4	4,015	72.2
Autumn 2004	5,669	84.7	4,183	71.6
Autumn 2005	5,455	86.8	4,080	71.0

Source: Labour Force Survey, Office for National Statistics.

[a] Excludes members of the armed forces.

[b] These figures have been revised from last year's publication and no longer allocate those who did not report their union status on a pro-rata basis. Note the figures for private/public sector may not sum to the total due to rounding and non-response.

[c] The line breaks under autumn 1998 represent a break in the trade union question. See technical notes for more details.

Derived from DTI website with © Crown.

it would seem from research that the incidence of such positive derecognition strategies was not in fact large.

Claydon (1996) concluded from his review of incidents of derecognition over a decade or more that it was possible to identify two general approaches to derecognition:

- **reactive**: representing a management response to a weakening of trade union power within the organization usually owing to one or more changes in the organization's industrial relations environment rather than it being the result of purposive action by management;
- **purposive**: reflective of long-term effort by management to eliminate unionized industrial relations from the organization.

There have been debates about the nature of the relationship between declining trade union membership density and derecognition with two views expressed, one being that weaker unions reduce the perceived need and incentive for management to derecognize; the other, which appears to be borne out more by the evidence, is that there is a positive relationship between the two, that is that as unions become weaker they become less able to fight derecognition and, in such circumstances, managements are more likely to take their opportunity and derecognize.

Claydon tends to favour this second view and further suggests that unions should be wary of entering into what are referred to as cooperative relationships with employers since there is little or no evidence to suggest that such an approach dissuades managements from pursuing policies aimed at derecognition. There are potentially important implications here for the new 'partnership' approach being advocated by the TUC (see the later section on trade union survival strategies).

In the UK formal recognition by the employer is additionally important in that recognition is essential for access to the protections, rights and immunities that are afforded the unions by the law. It is therefore not surprising that union leaders argued that it is crucial for the effectiveness and survival of the movement that they be granted a legal right to recognition from hostile and reluctant employers and appropriate mechanisms of enforcement. It is equally understandable that employers and their organizations and representatives should in many cases resist the introduction of such a right.

The new Labour government elected in 1997 did listen to these pleas from the trades unions and in the Employment Relations Act of 1999, a new set of provisions and rights was introduced. However, the trades unions were unhappy with a number of elements of the new law. They were concerned at the exemptions for small firms, the proportion of a workforce or bargaining unit that would need to vote in favour for the right to be triggered, and who it was that would have the right to determine the bargaining unit: the electorate or constituency in electoral terms. The TUC has continued to argue that the small-firm exemption should be ended and pointed out in a report late in 2003 that:

- there were 5.4 million employees working for establishments with less than 19 staff and therefore not covered by the law;
- 21.8 per cent of the UK workforce was employed in the small-firm sector;
- female workers are more likely than male to be denied a voice by the small-firm exemption, as almost a third of UK women employees (compared to just over a quarter of men, 26 per cent) work there.

The TUC General Secretary said: 'Once again UK workers find themselves getting a raw deal compared to workers in the rest of Europe. As a result of the changes in recognition law 3 years ago, thousands of UK workers in medium-sized and large firms now have a union to speak for them at work. There is no logical reason to continue to deny the same rights to 6 million others just because they work for small employers. The Government has paid too much attention to the irrational fears of the small business lobby'.

The TUC have also highlighted what they refer to as an increase in the incidence of bullying and intimidation by employers aimed at persuading employees not to vote in favour of union representation. The TUC stated that in 2002–2003 (Trade Union Trends Recognition Survey 2003),

> we saw for the first time a number of high-profile examples of companies using US style union-busting techniques to pressure staff not to choose union representation in a recognition ballot. Tactics included special anti-union publications, videos, one-on-one briefings and all-staff letters to persuade employees that a union voice would damage the company and increase the likelihood of redundancies and outsourcing.

However, in the report for 2003–2004 they report that only in three cases did the employer resort to unfair labour practices.

The impact of the 1999 legislation can be detected from the TUC's annual Trade Union Trends Recognition Surveys. The data in **Table 7.12** shows the number of new recognition agreements made over the period 1995–2004.

The evidence suggests that both in the year leading up to, and in the early years after, the new legislation many new recognition agreements were made, but after this the task of persuading employers to enter into new arrangements voluntarily became more difficult. This may be no more than might be expected as the softer targets were dealt with first. In the report for 2003–2004 the TUC comments that:

> Following a surge in recognition deals immediately after the legislation came into effect in 2000 deals are now stabilising. The current level reflects, in part, the difficulty of establishing

Table 7.12
New recognition agreements, 1995–2004

Period	Number of new deals
July 1995 to June 1996	108
July 1996 to July 1997	82
July 1997 to November 1998	89 (17 months)
December 1998 to October 1999	75 (11 months)
November 1999 to October 2000	159
November 2000 to October 2001	450 (plus 20 through the CAC)
November 2001 to October 2002	282 (plus 24 through the CAC)
November 2002 to October 2003	137 (plus 29 through the CAC)
November 2003 to October 2004	154 (plus 25 through the CAC)

Source: TUC Trade Union Trends Recognition Survey 2005.

a presence in new and smaller workplaces nevertheless the increase on the previous year is a sign of some success.

They also note that the average number of employees covered by each deal had declined from 471 in 2002–2003 to 154 in 2003–2004. As for the content of the agreements the TUC report that for the year 2003–2004:

> Over 90 per cent of deals provided for collective bargaining over pay, hours and holidays – up from 80 per cent last year. Just under three quarters (73%) had collective representation on grievance and disciplinary issues, down on the 77 per cent in last year's survey. Over three quarters (78%) covered bargaining or consultation over training and learning and at 42 per cent the trend towards more bargaining on pensions continues to grow. Over half of deals included the right for employees to be informed and consulted over an organisation's activities and economic situation.

A different perspective on the impact of the new legislation is provided by Moore *et al.* (2005) who conducted a survey of employers where new voluntary recognition agreements had been entered into between 1998 and 2002. They found that the statutory recognition procedure had encouraged the extension of recognition into new organizations, but in the main in sectors with trade union organization traditions.

The vast majority of employers reported that new trade union recognition agreements had led to the development of positive relationships with trade union representatives with three-quarters of employers regarding their relationships with both workplace representatives and full time officers as either good or very good. The majority of employers (85 per cent) also thought that their relationships with employees in the bargaining unit were either good or very good.

Employers had entered into discussions with trade unions over a range of issues, with active negotiations over pay. There were clear differences between employers' reports of the nature of discussions with the union and what was set out in the written recognition agreements. With the exception of annual pay bargaining, employers were more likely to see the nature of the discussions in terms of consultation or information sharing than negotiation, especially when it came to discussing the 'noncore' issues of pensions, equal opportunities and training.

Challenges and responses

We have noted in earlier chapters several developments that pose threats and challenges to trades unions in many different countries, though what follows is not intended as an exhaustive list. The era of international trade and investment, new technologies, production systems and methods of working, the ageing labour force, the emergence of new industries and occupations, the decline of manufacturing and extractive industries and continuing expansion of the service sector, the entry into the labour force of new types of worker, pressures for labour flexibility and cost reduction to facilitate competition with developing countries, the new ability of Multinational Corporations (MNCs) to relocate functions and activities, pressures upon governments to relax regulation of the labour market, attitudinal and cultural change, new management initiatives, relatively low rates of economic growth and job creation, all pose threats and challenges. They pose threats to jobs and trade union membership levels, terms and conditions of employment, and challenge the trades unions to devise new membership strategies, reassess structures, priorities and objectives, and devise new approaches and strategies in their dealings with employers and governments.

These challenges vary in their impact from country to country as have the responses of trades unions. Unions in particular countries have also faced challenges that are specific to their own national environment and, of course, any particular challenge may have more impact for some unions than for others.

It is not possible to examine a range of different countries in order to identify the trade union response, and in this instance we concentrate upon the UK. However it is important that we recognize that the responses of the union movement in the UK are not necessarily typical and that, as in all other countries, the union movement has faced specific challenges.

The UK

Survival strategies

Over the last 20 years of the 20th century, the union movement in the UK was confronted by a hostile environment and a number of major challenges. It is debatable whether the election of a New Labour Government in 1997 has significantly altered this situation though there have been some welcome interventions concerning trade union recognition...

Among the challenges were:

- a hostile government determined to reduce the unions' power and influence and which pursued a radical legislative programme geared towards the achievement of this objective;
- economic recessions encompassing the highest rates of unemployment since the early 1930s;
- increasing internationalization of business and the concentration of economic power in fewer and stronger hands, often remote from local management;

- technological development and change on a scale and at a rate not previously encountered, which had major implications for the demand for traditional skills and products;
- industrial restructuring resulting in new industries, new companies, new types of employee, and a massive expansion of the service sector within which the trades unions had little or no tradition;
- cultural change in which traditional values of collectivism and solidarity have been threatened by a government- and employer-inspired emphasis upon individualism and enterprise;
- new management initiatives emphasizing managerial control and employee involvement as individuals and on management's terms;
- significant membership decline with consequent major effects for the financial strength of the movement and for the services that can be provided for members;
- decline in the incidence and scope of collective bargaining.

The above list is not exhaustive and not intended to be in any order of importance. It is also important to appreciate that there are inter-relationships between many of these developments and forces for change.

Not surprisingly, and after an initial period in the 1980s when it is alleged that union leaders were unable to appreciate the scale and permanence of what was happening around them, these developments have forced the unions to debate what they could and should now do and it is on these major debates that we concentrate for the rest of this section.

In the main the debates revolved around:

- the objectives that the unions should pursue and the priorities attached to them;
- how to stop the membership and financial haemorrhage;
- securing the election of a friendlier government;
- the (new) strategies, towards employers and government, that might provide hope of improved relationships.

New objectives and priorities

In the context of these debates we have seen the emergence of the New Realists, who have been characterized as in opposition to the Traditionalists. This has been seen as a debate between those, on the one hand, who believe the time has come to adopt different objectives, to emphasize activity and achievement in the workplace and more cooperative approaches such as are embodied in the notion of partnership agreements, and the Traditionalists on the other, who retain a belief in the essentially conflictual nature of the employment relationship, the original objectives of the movement and who are willing, where necessary, to utilize adversarial means. For the moment at least it would seem that the New Realists have won the day.

Indeed it is arguable that relatively few of the objectives considered central to trade unionism in the UK in the 1960s (see earlier section of this chapter on the objectives of trade unions) would be considered central today.

In 1994 the TUC re-launched itself and in so doing addressed the issue of trade union objectives in a changed environment. The re-launch confirmed a new and different focus, which it has been argued is so fundamental that the movement in the UK no longer sits squarely within the social or political movement category referred to earlier. This re-launch of the TUC was proof of a shift in the direction of business unionism and workplace-based objectives.

In the TUC General Council Report for 1995, and in discussion of the re-launch, emphasis was given to:

- 'priorities rooted firmly in the world of work'

though reference was also made to:

- 'full employment remains our central objective',
- to the union movement seeking to influence all the main political parties.

The trade unions argue that they are being realistic in amending their objectives and perhaps particularly their priorities, that they are responding to the new economic, legal, political, social and cultural reality and that they are doing so against a background of considerable decline. It is in this context that the terms New Realism and New Unionism were devised and applied.

The minority traditional wing, in addition to considering that the original objectives should be pursued, also argue that in responding to the New Reality by becoming more workplace-oriented and less concerned to achieve a transformation of and a more egalitarian society, the movement is in fact demeaning its history and itself as well as contributing to its long-term marginalization.

Servicing or organizing approaches to recruitment and halting membership decline

As noted above, the debates over survival strategies have not only been concerned with the matter of objectives and their relative priority, there has also been considerable attention paid both to the question of how to halt the loss of membership and how to recruit more members. Depending upon their membership base and policies, trade unions have been confronted often with quite different membership environments over the last two decades and those with an open membership approach have tended to fair better than those that restricted their membership to people in a particular trade, occupation or industry. These latter are more vulnerable when the trade, industry or occupation is in decline. It is also the case that labour market and industrial trends which have seen a greater proportion of women working, a greater proportion of the labour force working part time and flexibly (see **Chapter 6**) and a continuing enhancement of the service and small-firm sectors, have also posed particular problems for the union movement in the UK, which has not traditionally shown itself to be adept at recruiting and retaining members in these and other groups and sectors. The dominant membership of the union movement in the UK has been white males in manufacturing and extractive industry.

However, despite the different circumstances and environments confronting individual unions there has also been a more general discussion within the movement on the respective efficacy of the organizing and servicing approaches to enhancing union membership, each of which implies a different perspective on why people join unions and what they want from their union membership.

The servicing model of union membership is also associated often with the New Realism referred to above. It is a model that perceives union members as individuals who will be attracted into membership by the range and value of the services which the union offers to them. It is a model that has been equated with private-sector organizations such as the RAC and insurance companies. In the light of this approach we have seen many trade unions expanding the range of membership services to include credit cards, discounts agreed with providers of various services, insurance and mortgage facilities. The opponents of this approach argue that it overestimates the extent to which workers in the UK have bought into the new individualist and enterprise culture and they cite research which demonstrates that protection and representation at work are still the dominant reasons why people join trade unions (Whitston and Waddington, 1994; Waddington and Whitston, 1995, 1997).

As noted above, the alternative approach to the servicing model is referred to as the organizing model and this approach is more consistent with the traditional notions of collectivism, self-help and democratic organization. Recruitment and membership enhancement in this model are bottom-up activities and in a sense are less important than building a new form of participative unionism. Blyton

Service model
- Union is seen as external – a third party
- Union official tells members how 'the union' will solve their problems
- Union relies on employer to provide lists of workers' names to union official
- Union relies on employer for workplace access
- Hard selling of union membership
- Union sold on basis of services and insurance protection
- Reliance on full-time officials to recruit and to solve problems
- Aim is to recruit only – to sign on the dotted line – not to organize
- Workers blame 'the union' when it can't get results
- Officers resent members for not coming to meetings or participating in activities. Members complain they pay fees and the union does nothing
- Management acts – union reacts – always on the defensive

Organizing model
- Members own the campaign to unionize their workplace
- Members generate own issues and organize to solve them together
- Names and information are provided by workers to union themselves
- Initial organizing can be done outside work – in coffee bars, pubs or at members' homes
- First recruiting steps are to establish contacts, find natural leaders, uncover issues
- Workers empowered to find solutions themselves through education and mutual support
- Workers encouraged to build the union through one-to-one organizing and to solve problems themselves
- Recruitment and organizing are integrated
- Members share decisions and solve problems together with union leaders – share responsibility
- Members identify with the union and contribute. An attack on the union is seen as an attack on themselves
- Union has its own agenda, is pro-active, keeps management off balance; members are involved

Figure 7.2
Two models of trade unionism (*Source*: IDS Focus No. 91, autumn 1999, p. 10).

and Turnbull (2004) characterize this difference as the difference between the union member who asks what the union will do for him (servicing) and another who asks what we can achieve with the union (organizing). They also provide evidence of a number of cases in which it would appear that the organizing approach works.

Figure 7.2 shows in tabular form the main features of each of the two models.

In the mid-1990s it appeared that the New Realists and the servicing model may have been in the ascendant, but there is also evidence of significant minority support for the alternative viewpoints and model and it seems unlikely that these debates have been concluded. In 1997/1998 the TUC gave additional impetus to the organizing model with the creation of its 'organizing academy' geared towards the training of new organizers. The emphasis is upon recruitment of new members and upon organization rather than upon servicing existing members.

Securing the election of a friendlier government

A friendlier government was always perceived as a potential, if partial, solution to the problems confronting the union movement in the 1980s and 1990s, at least to the extent that it might repeal the most damaging elements of the legislative environment created during the period after 1979 (see **Chapter 5**). The election of New Labour in May 1997 meant that to some extent this objective had been achieved though this new government was clearly not going to return to the pre-1979 legislative environment and promised the union movement fairness but not favours. We have referred earlier to the new legislation on trade union recognition for collective bargaining purposes and it was anticipated by many that it would become easier for unions to recruit members against the background of this legislative right. However, the legislation that was adopted left much to be desired as far as the unions were concerned, and the TUC has campaigned subsequently for change to the legislation to make it easier for them to satisfy the legislative requirements; in particular they were unhappy with the exclusion of firms with less than 20 workers and the requirement that, in a ballot, the union needed to demonstrate both a majority of those voting in favour as well as 40 per cent of the eligible workforce.

There has been a number of other initiatives such as the decision to implement EU social legislation fully, the promotion and provision of funding to support workplace partnerships and a number of legislative initiatives which could be perceived as a partial return on the union movement's investment in campaigning for and financing the election of the new Labour government. Critics would argue that in many cases the government has implemented EU legislation grudgingly and that this promotion of partnership is evidence of the government's concern to promote business interests rather than those of employees. There have also been well publicized and continuing disagreements between the unions and the government. The Fire Brigade Union was highly critical of the government's role in the firefighters dispute in 2002–2003 and some unions have refused to continue to fund the labour party.

The new government may have been friendlier to the trades unions than the governments of the 1980s and early 1990s but the relationship remained uneasy.

New strategies towards employers

Partnership and Partnership agreements

The TUC has been a supporter of partnership and has been instrumental in encouraging trades unions and employers to enter into workplace agreements.

This development has been associated with the New Unionism and, for the unions, this model of partnership seems to imply 'working together', with management at the level of the firm or workplace to achieve what are referred to as common objectives such as fairness and competitiveness and, at a national level, talking with government and employers' associations to achieve objectives such as attracting inward investment and promoting training and equal opportunities. The overarching objective of the new TUC and its members in the early part of the 21st century would seem to be the achievement of full and fair employment and to do so where possible through partnership with both employers and government.

Inevitably partnership agreements are likely to vary with the particular circumstances of the company concerned. Among the best-known early partnership agreements were those at Tesco, Littlewoods, Legal and General and Barclays and the participants to these agreements asserted that they were central elements in the companies' efforts to transform the nature of employee relations.

The Tesco agreement has been widely publicized as an example of such agreements. The agreement provided for a company-wide system of staff forums comprised of union and non-union representatives who meet with management to discuss and, where possible, agree upon a wide range of issues including matters of pay. This is combined with a payment scheme that provides for workers to receive shares in the company and overall the forums appear to adopt a joint problem-solving approach to the resolution of issues raised. After the agreement was reached, there was a significant increase in trade union membership within the company, and it was argued that this was a reflection of workers seeing management and the union actively cooperating to resolve problems.

While the current emphasis may be upon cooperation and responsibility, many of the trade unions seem ready to retain the ability and willingness to be militant if partnership does not work and this puts into a less favourable perspective the willingness of some unions to sign away their rights to take militant action in return for compulsory arbitration.

The TUC would appear to see the content of a model partnership agreement containing enhanced labour flexibility and commitment to the success of the organization from the employees and union in return for trade union recognition for collective bargaining over wages, greater information and consultation, guarantees on job security and an enhanced focus upon training, employee development and the quality of working life from management.

However, there is continuing tension between those in the union movement who actively support responsible partnership and those who believe in the need for aggressive recruitment and organizing.

In conclusion, the future of the trade unions in the UK appears to be dependent upon them:

- finding ways of attracting new workers in new companies and industries into membership;
- encouraging a more positive attitude amongst managers towards recognizing them as legitimate and constructive representatives of their workforce;
- being willing to enter into new types of arrangements with employers which, amongst others, have the objectives of facilitating change and adding value to the employing organization;
- coming to terms with the new individualism underpinned by new individual legislative rights, individual contracts and payments systems, and developing approaches which enable individuals to see the union as a source of individual protection and representation.

Summary

Trade unions are one of the major actors in the employee relations system. We have examined a number of definitions, why they emerge, why people tend to join and also what appear to be the factors that facilitate membership.

We explained the different objectives that unions may have and in particular the difference between and relevance of the distinction between political and business unionism. In examining structures, we identified the relevance of membership base and also discussed the issue of internal government and democracy, paying particular attention to the range of factors that may be used as criteria for assessing the extent to which unions are or are not democratic.

We examined the question of levels of trade union membership and how it varies from one country to another and over time and what the various explanatory variables may be; particular attention was paid to the issue of decline and also to the relevance and importance of the question of trade union recognition.

Finally, in the context of the challenges confronting the trade union movements in many developed countries, we examined some of the debates that have been ongoing about how best to secure the survival and future of trades unionism. It became apparent when examining these debates that central to them are differing perceptions concerning:

- appropriate and legitimate objectives;
- the reasons why people join and their expectations from membership;
- the need to identify and enter new markets;
- the nature of an appropriate relationship with employers .

Activities to test understanding

Activity 1

Consider the factors that might explain a change in the nature and objectives of trades unionism in the UK, in the direction of business unionism.

Activity 2

Without going back to the text try and remember why trades unions emerge.

Activity 3

What are the essential conditions necessary for trades unions to form and operate effectively?

Activity 4

If job-centred unions pursue membership policies which are closed what about general, enterprise and industrial unions?

Activity 5

Without going back to look at the text try and remember as many factors that influence trade union structure as you can.

Activity 6

Read the material on democracy again and
1 identify the two main models of democracy and briefly distinguish between them
2 devise a list of the factors that would appear in the light of the above discussion both to encourage and/or frustrate democracy within the union movement.

Activity 7

What are the two main schools of thought explaining the variations in trade union membership from one country to another?

Activity 8

Examine the data presented in **Tables 7.7** and **7.8** and identify for yourself the areas and categories of employee and employment where there might be the greatest scope for unions to recruit members.

Activity 9

Why is it so important that trades unions have a legal mechanism to enforce recognition?

Activity 10

Have another look at the list of objectives specified by the TUC in their evidence to the Donovan Commission included earlier in this chapter and think which of them might be realistic for the trade union movement to pursue actively today.

Also, and separately, ask yourself two other questions connected with this list: first, which of the 10 objectives you consider to be legitimate and second, which other objectives might you include in such a list today?

References

Annual Reports of the Certification Officer.

Blyton, P. and Turnbull, P., 2004. *The Dynamics of Employee Relations*, 3rd Edition. Macmillan, Basingstoke.

Braverman, H., 1974. *Labour and Monopoly Capital*. Monthly Review Press, New York.

Claydon, T., 1996. Union derecognition: a re-examination. In Beardwell, I. (ed.), *Contemporary Industrial Relations: A Critical Analysis*. OUP, Oxford.

Cully, M., O'Reilly, A., Millward, N., Forth, J., Woodland, S., Dix, G. and Bryson, A., 1998. *The Workplace Employee Relations Survey: First Findings*. DTI, ACAS, ESRC, PSI.

EIRO Online 2004. *Trade Union Membership 1993–2003*.

Grainger, H., 2006. *Trade Union Membership 2005*. DTI.

Hofstede, G., 1991. *Cultures and Organisations. Software of the Mind*. McGraw Hill, London.

ILO Bureau of Statistics. *Statistics of Trade Union Membership*. Data for 47 countries taken mainly from national statistical publications. November 2004 (unpublished).

Kersley, B., Alpin, C., Forth, J., Bryson, A., Bewley, H., Dix, G. and Oxenbridge, S. *Inside the Workplace. First Findings from the 2004 Workplace Employment Relations Survey (WERS 2004)*.

McIlroy, J., 1995. *Trades Unions in Britain Today*. Manchester University Press, Manchester.

Michels, R., 1966. *Political Parties*. Free Press, New York.

Moore, S., McKay, S. and Bewley, H., 2005. The content of new voluntary trade union recognition agreements 1998–2002. Volume 2 – *Findings from the Survey of Employers*. Employment Relations Research Series. No. 43. DTI.

Salamon, M., 1992. *Industrial Relations*, 2nd Edition. Prentice Hall, Englewood Cliffs, NJ.

TUC, 1995. *General Council Report for 1995*.

TUC, 1999. *British Trade Unionism – the Millennial Challenge*.

TUC, 2003. *Trade Union Trends Recognition Survey*.

TUC, 2005. *Trade Union Trends Recognition Survey 2004–2005*.

Turner, H.A., 1962. *Trade Union Growth, Structure and Policy*. Allen and Unwin, London.

Waddington, J. and Whitston, C., 1995. Trade unions: growth, structure and policy. In Edwards, P. (ed.), *Industrial Relations Theory and Practice in Britain*. Blackwell, Oxford, pp. 151–202.

Waddington, J. and Whitston, C., 1997. Why do people join trade unions in a period of membership decline? *British Journal of Industrial Relations*, December.

Whitston, C. and Waddington, J., 1994. Why join a union? *New Statesman and Society*, pp. 36–38.

Part Four

Organizational Context: Processes, Policies and Procedures

Chapter 8

Managing employee relations

Introduction

There are several different approaches to the management of employee relations and these differ from one country to another, depending upon the labour market institutions, history, traditions and culture of the country. It is impossible to examine all the different approaches and in earlier modules we have pointed out the influence of technology and dominant production regimes at the international level, different forms of capitalism, the role of governments as legislators, economic policy makers and employers, and demographic and labour force developments at the national level. The dominant values and beliefs within a country that make up its culture are also significant influences upon the expectations and behaviour of both employees and management. These expectations influence the nature of the psychological contract and the employment relationship and, within this context, certain management approaches will be regarded as legitimate whereas others are not. We noted in **Chapter 7** that they tend to confront particular pressures to adopt a locally sensitive, polycentric approach to the management of human resources and employee relations, an indication that there is a nation specific dimension to the management of employee relations. The management of employee relations takes place at an organizational level but within specific national and international contexts.

To exemplify the significance of culture for the management of employee relations we only have to look at the work of Hofstede and Trompenaars. These researchers have each undertaken substantial studies of dominant work-related values, beliefs and expectations in a wide range of different countries and they have concluded that these vary substantially across national borders and have implications for:

- Managements beliefs and expectations regarding their right to make decisions, whether they have the right to do this on their own or whether there is an expectation that employees will be involved in the decision-making process.
- Whether an autocratic, paternalistic or democratic management style will work best.
- Whether the emphasis within organizations should be on the task or the people, their well being and their development.
- Whether employees and managements are predominantly individualistic in their orientation and interests, pursuing their own self interest, or whether collectivism in terms of perceptions of belonging to a work group or to an organizational family dominates.
- Whether managements seek to treat employees as individuals, emphasizing individual performance and contract and resisting the joint and collective determination of terms and conditions of employment.
- Whether employees are likely to seek intrinsic or extrinsic rewards and satisfactions: is there a strong work ethic or do people expect to work to live rather than live to work? Is money the major reward which employees seek from work?
- Whether there are expectations that work and non-work life are to kept separate or whether they are expected to merge into each other.
- Whether people are comfortable with uncertainty and ambiguity, with decisions being made on an *ad hoc* basis, or have a preference for rules and procedures governing both employee and management action.

The above is not intended to be an exhaustive list of the implications of differences in national cultures for approaches to the management of employee relations but we can see that these differences do have significant implications for: management objectives and style, decision-making processes, dealing with differences of interest and conflict, the importance attached to having and following procedures, employee involvement and participation, employees feelings towards work and their employing organization and the nature of their attachment, compliance or commitment, appropriate reward policies, attitudes towards trade unions as representatives of employee interests and as participants in the decision-making processes.

In this and following modules we address a number of these issues, including management objectives and styles, the pursuit of commitment from employees and managing with and without trades unions. In subsequent modules, we examine conflict resolving and decision-making processes and employee participation, disciplinary, grievance and equal opportunities procedures.

As noted above, it is impossible to examine the management of employee relations at the level of the organization in a range of different country contexts. We have chosen to address these issues in the context of the emergence of Human Resource Management and the pursuit of employee commitment. There are various different models and debates which have accompanied this emergence with implications for management objectives and styles and attitudes towards trades unions. The issues raised in the following discussion are of wider international relevance.

There are several typologies of style, some of which distinguish between styles on the grounds of the implied attitudes to trade unionism and the sharing of decision making implied by recognition of trade unions. We examine two of the more acclaimed typologies and some of the implications of managing employee relations, both with and without trade unions.

Learning objectives

After studying this chapter you will be able to:

- Explain differences between Personnel Management (PM) and Human Resource Management (HRM) and the specific implications for the management of employee relations.
- Discuss the nature of management objectives in respect of employee relations.
- Identify and describe the variety of managerial styles and explanatory models.
- Explain why the more recent models seek to encompass individualism and collectivism and the dynamic nature of style.

- Identify and analyse the features of the external environment and the organizational characteristics that act as constraining influences upon the styles adopted by senior management.
- Identify the advantages and disadvantages of managing with and without trade unions.
- Understand and be able to advise on the pursuit of employee commitment with particular emphasis upon Employee Involvement mechanisms and the conditions necessary for their effective implementation.
- Understand the employee relations roles of employers associations and the influences upon their emergence.

HRM: What is it?

The concept which we now depict as Human Resource Management, of which there is arguably more than one version, emerged in the USA in the early 1980s. It is suggested that the emergence of this new model was driven by realization that the management of human resources might have more to contribute to organizational success if it had a more strategic focus and involvement with business strategy and if it could succeed in achieving a workforce highly committed to the success of the organization. HR specialists would develop a role with a policy and strategic focus through which a form of strategic integration of both business and HR strategy would be achieved and the responsibility for the day-to-day management of human resources and employee relations would be devolved to line management.

It emerged in a political and economic climate and business system dominated by belief in the principles and efficiency of the free market and with a particular set of dominant work-related values. We noted earlier in **Chapter 3**, that amongst the debates concerning the HRM policies and practices of MNCs were those concerned with; the relative influence on their behaviour of home and host country values and systems, the extent to which approaches and practices developed in one national system are transferable to another, and whether there is evidence of convergence on any particular model or system. These debates are also relevant here since the question arises as to whether the concept of HRM which emerged from the USA in the early 1980s is appropriate to other systems and cultures. We also mentioned the concept of cultural distance and, given that the US culture and the culture of the UK are close to one another, it is really no surprise that it was a model that soon found support in the UK especially since at the time the UK had a government committed to the same beliefs and principles and which was waging an ideological and legislative onslaught on the trade unions and the traditional pluralist institutions. The question of how appropriate the model is to other cultures and business systems has been the subject of much debate amongst academics concerned with International and Comparative HRM – see for example Brewster and Hegewisch (1994), Hollinshead and Leat (1995), and Schuler *et al.* (2002).

Commonly before the emergence of HRM, the management of employee relations was the preserve of specialists in Personnel Management (see **Exhibit 8.1**). The implications of the adoption of the HRM model are that the day-to-day management of employee relations should be devolved to line management.

Exhibit 8.1

History and Nature of Personnel Management in the UK

One thing we can say at the outset is that the management of industrial relations was perceived to be very firmly core to the 'territory' of Personnel Management. Personnel Management emerged towards the end of the 19th century out of the concern of some few employers for the welfare of their employees and their appointment of predominantly female welfare officers. As the years went by, the scope and range of the activities and responsibilities of Personnel Management expanded but this welfare tradition remained strong if not central. These early welfare workers were given a dual role, representing the interests and views of the employer and management to the employees but also representing the views and interests of employees to the other members of management. These appointments and the role afforded them are indicative of a pluralist approach in that different interests are being recognized. However, the motives of Christian charity and paternalism of these early employers were by no means wholly altruistic since there was clearly a recognition on their part that healthy and fit employees would be more productive.

Personnel Management's responsibilities for the management of industrial relations really took hold in the 1950s as the trade union movement increased in size and influence. The post-World War II boom created enormous demand for UK manufactured goods and the more widespread adoption of mass production techniques to satisfy these new mass markets created circumstances in which there was relatively full employment and it was relatively easy for the trades unions to recruit members and represent them. As labour became a relatively scarce resource its bargaining power increased, along with its determination to achieve a better deal. Companies found themselves in need of skilled and adept negotiators who could form relationships with the trade unions and develop with them the joint mechanisms necessary to ensure efficient and effective resolution of this conflict. The personnel practitioners tended to acquire this role and over a period of time they became the accepted and largely acceptable face of management in this new industrial relations arena. In addition to seeking consensus and acting for management in the negotiations to resolve conflicts, the personnel practitioner also became the administrator and in a sense the custodian of the implementation of the agreements that were jointly achieved.

This new role and influence, however, also brought with it a number of ambiguities and dilemmas. As personnel practitioners became responsible for negotiating, administering and implementing agreements on terms and conditions of employment, tensions emerged between them and line management some of whom felt that their own role and influence in the management of employees was being usurped. There were tensions and uncertainties as to who was responsible for what and whether the role of the personnel practitioner was to be an essentially advisory one or indeed whether they were to have executive responsibilities in areas such as the determination of terms and conditions of employment and the handling of discipline and grievances. In a very real sense there was the possibility of a split occurring between the personnel practitioner and other members of management who often regarded the personnel function as not really part of management at all but as some sort of intermediary between management and the employees and an intermediary that often seemed to have different values and interests from those of management, a degree of sympathy and empathy with the interests and intrinsic welfare of the employees that, in managements' eyes, somehow set the personnel function and its members apart.

As Torrington (1989) pointed out

> ... personnel management is directed mainly at the employees of an organization; ... personnel managers are never totally identified with management interests, as they become ineffective when not able to understand and articulate the views and values of the employees. To some extent the personnel manager is always a mediator between them and us.

As competition and the economic environment became tougher and government and employers began to look for scapegoats for the UK's economic woe and failures, the trade unions, and to some extent the personnel function, became demonized. These new pressures heightened the potential for conflict between the competitive organizational need for efficiency in the use of labour and the personnel function's traditional concerns for justice and equity in the treatment of employees, principles which elsewhere in this work are identified as underpinning good practice in the management of employee relations and which are core to the employees side of the psychological contract.

Personnel practitioners began to look for new roles that would indicate the coincidence of their interests with other members of management and management functions and it was in this context that there was further emphasis placed upon the personnel function's responsibility for manpower planning, organizational design and development. It was also against this background that the concept of HRM emerged from the USA with its different set of underpinning values, priorities and imperatives. To some personnel practitioners this appeared as a source of potential salvation; to others, it was a threat to their traditions, values and role.

In sum, Personnel Management emerged out of paternalism and a concern for employees' physical welfare and issues of social justice; later this became a concern for the intrinsic health and welfare of the employee. As the 20th century progressed and the imperatives of the environment changed and developed, it acquired other roles, but it was and is a function that suffers from tensions and ambiguities both internally and between itself and other management functions.

The notion that HRM must be fully involved in strategy formulation at a business level and that the HR specialist should have the responsibility for formulating employee relations strategy is supported by several of the attempts at the definition of HRM that have been made. One that is often quoted is that of Armstrong (1995) who argues that HRM is concerned with managements' needs for human resources to be provided and deployed and that it is, 'a strategic approach to the acquisition, development and management of an organization's human resources'.

This notion of HRM representing a strategic approach has been popular, since it tends to support the claim by HRM specialists that the function needs to be integrated fully into the formulation of corporate strategy and that it therefore must be represented fully at the highest decision-making levels of the organization. In other words, it is a definition that adds weight and importance to the function and the contribution that it can make to the success of the organization.

Guest (1989) has expanded on this by asserting that what is more important is the input to this strategic concern. In other words, what is needed is not just the capacity to think strategically but some distinctive view of the strategic direction that should be pursued. It is this direction that constitutes the distinctive feature of HRM.

It was at this point that Guest developed his framework or model of HRM in which he asserts/prescribes the direction that HRM should pursue and in this sense his and other models of HRM are prescriptive rather than explanatory. For him the objectives of HRM were/should be:

1   integration of strategy, attitudes and behaviour;
2   commitment of employees to the goals and values of the organization (an example of normative or attitudinal commitment);
3   flexibility in terms of organizational and work structures and employees, all of which facilitates innovation;
4   quality in terms of the staff employed, the management of them, their performance and in terms of the output of employee activity.

In 1987 Guest had already suggested that HRM and PM could be distinguished by the form of attachment emphasized and the nature of the employment relationship. In the case of PM it was a relationship where the form of attachment was one of compliance and the psychological contract was one emphasizing a fair day's work for a fair day's pay. Whereas, with HRM, the form of attachment characterizing the employment relationship was a moral or normative commitment with a psychological contract emphasizing reciprocal commitment (**Figure 8.1**).

HRM policies	Human resource outcomes	Organizational outcomes
Organization/ job design		**High** Job performance
Management of change	Strategic integration	**High** Problem-solving Change
Recruitment, selection/ socialization	Commitment	Innovation
Appraisal, training development	Flexibility adaptability	**High** Cost-effectiveness
Reward systems		
Communication	Quality	**Low** Turnover Absence Grievances

Leadership/culture/strategy

Figure 8.1
A theory of HRM
(*Source*: Guest
(1989) p. 49).

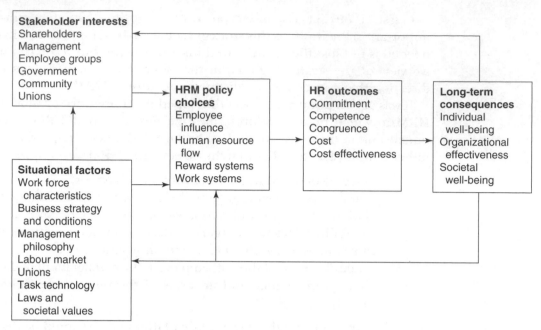

Figure 8.2
Map of the HRM territory (*Source:* Beer *et al.* (1984)).

Guest's model has much in common with the model of Beer *et al.* (1984). See **Figure 8.2** which the authors described as a model that is also a map of the territory.

This model also identifies specific HR outcomes:

- high commitment of employees to organizational goals and
- high individual performance leading to cost effectiveness.

Which are similar to those identified by Guest but there are also differences in that the Beer *et al.* model recognizes specifically that employees are stakeholders in the organization. Some would argue that the underpinnings contain elements of pluralism in that the model at least recognizes the existence of different interests in the organization. The possibility of conflict between these different stakeholders' interests, particularly between the interests of employees and employers, is recognized and emphasis placed upon the need for these to be resolved to the satisfaction of both (all) parties through processes resulting in trade-offs.

A feature of this model is that, in identifying the areas in which HRM policy decisions need to be made, it does spell out what the subject matter of HRM consists of (see **Figure 8.3**).

Human resource flows
- Into, through and out of the organization, to include:
  - recruitment and selection;
  - appraisal and assessment;
  - development;
  - promotion;
  - transfer and placement;
  - termination.

Reward systems
- To attract, motivate and retain labour and to include:
  - pay systems;
  - motivation;
  - other benefits.

Employee influence
- Employee participation and employee relations to include:
  - trade unions and collective bargaining;
  - the issue of managerial prerogative;
  - other participatory mechanisms such as works councils etc.

Work systems
- The organization of work and work practices to include:
  - job design;
  - the nature of the technology and issues of workpace and the source of control, the machine, management or the employee;
  - the flexibility of labour and technology.

Managing change

Communications which should be goal directed

Figure 8.3
The subject matter of HRM. Adapted from Beer *et al.* (1984) and Guest (1989).

In the context of this model, there is no doubt that the management of employee relations is part of the HRM territory.

One of the most significant contributions to our understanding of HRM was made by Storey (1987, 1989) who suggested that there were different forms of HRM. He distinguished between 'hard' and 'soft' versions or forms of HRM; to some extent these can be distinguished by the value they place upon the human resource. Both are strategic in that they stress the integration of HR policy and strategy with that of the business. Rather than viewing these stereotypes as two distinct choices, it is better to regard them as opposite ends of a spectrum, with the hard stereotype at one end and the soft at the other and with lots of varied and mixed positions between.

The hard version of HRM is driven by the strategic objectives of the organization and labour is perceived in the same terms as any other resource, something to be acquired, deployed, developed if necessary for the achievement of organizational objectives, used and then disposed of.

At the other extreme of the spectrum is the approach referred to as Soft HRM which sees human resources as potent sources of innovation and competitive advantage, as valued assets rather than as variable costs and a business expense, where the employees are involved in the organization through various communications mechanisms and the outcome is a labour force highly motivated, competent, flexible and committed to the values and goals of the organization.

In each case the underpinning values are unitarist and individualist and the objectives are performance oriented, but the two stereotypes reflect different views of how best to achieve these objectives, different views on the nature of man and what might motivate him. The soft version rests largely upon beliefs consistent with the theories of man and motivation associated with people such as Maslow (1943), McGregor (1960) and Herzberg (1966), beliefs that man can be motivated by recognition, achievement and involvement and that leadership style is an important influence upon motivation and performance.

The two stereotypes are also arguably reflective of different market realities and production strategies. For example, short-term cost reduction may be the competitive imperative and, in such circumstances, it might be inevitable that a hard variant is pursued, whereas in an organization with a much longer time horizon, and where the source of competitive advantage is knowledge, innovation, and quality, it might be realistic to pursue a set of policies and practices more akin to the soft variant.

Critics of HRM have argued that the Storey stereotypes do not so much represent the range of HRM in action as the difference between the rhetoric and the reality (Legge, 1989), with the hard version of HRM representing the reality and the soft version the rhetoric; it sounds good but you can not find it in action.

HRM in practice: evidence from UK

On this topic and in looking predominantly at the UK, Storey 2001, tends to agree that it is difficult to find organizations utilizing comprehensive and coherent soft HRM in which the various elements of policy and practice are linked together into a meaningful strategic whole. Nevertheless, there is plentiful evidence of management adopting a piecemeal approach with elements of the whole being used. The WERS 1998 evidence found that about a third of organizations were accredited investors in people and both the 1998 and 2004 WERS confirmed that many organizations were utilizing performance appraisal and communications mechanisms to involve employees and obtain their commitment – see later section on employee involvement. Nevertheless, the overwhelming conclusion was of piecemeal approaches or no attempt to introduce the soft version of HRM at all (**Figure 8.4**).

Dimension	PM	HRM
Perspective	Pluralist	Unitarist
Level of trust	Low	High
Attachment	Compliance	Commitment
Terms of contract	Collective agreement	Individual
Psychological contract	Fair day's work for fair day's pay	Reciprocal commitment
Time horizon	Short term	Long term
Approach	Reactive *ad hoc*	Proactive, strategic
Conflict	Institutionalized	De-emphasized/denied
Communication	Restricted/indirect	Individual and direct
Responsibility	Centralized, specialist	Devolved, line manager
Focus on needs of	Employees	Management

Figure 8.4
A selective comparison between HRM and PM. Adapted from Guest (1987) and Storey (1992).

HRM and implications for employee relations

As we discussed in **Chapter 1** of this text, the development and adoption of the term 'employee relations' rather than 'industrial relations' is itself symptomatic of the influence that HRM has had upon the nature and management of the employment relationship, the former encompassing individualism and non-union relationships, the latter associated with collectivism and decision making involving trade unions. We have already noted in the discussion of HRM above that it tends towards unitarism, managerial prerogative, individualism and communications schemes directed at employees and seeking to obtain their involvement in and commitment to the organization and that it is anti-trade union.

However, it is important to distinguish between the two versions that we have identified.

The **soft** versions of HRM are consistent, for example, with:

- direct employee-oriented communications mechanisms as a means of achieving greater employee involvement, itself perceived as a means of achieving high employee commitment rather than compliance (see later in this module);
- quality of working life (QWL) changes in the design and organization of work (referred to in **Chapter 2**) which tends to assume that employees will be motivated by schemes such as job enlargement, etc.;
- the introduction of Japanese methods: quality circles (QCs), total quality management (TQM), just-in-time (JIT), and the drive for quality employees and quality output;
- a decline in trade union membership, recognition, participation in decision making and influence and a decline of collectivism;

Page

Exploring Employee Relations

- an emphasis upon the employment relationship as being characterized by cooperation rather than conflict and, in particular, partnership approaches;
- some of the more paternalist management styles referred to later in this module;
- an emphasis upon individual contract and labour flexibility as depicted in the model of the flexible firm;
- continuing emphasis upon managerial prerogative.

The **harder** versions are consistent with:

- enforced trade union derecognition and a refusal to grant recognition for purposes of collective bargaining;
- authoritarian and autocratic management styles;
- enforced flexibility such as zero hours contracts and/or enforced working of long hours or the deliberate avoidance of employees statutory rights;
- the minimization of costs, low rates of pay and poor working conditions;
- a continuation of the process of deskilling and degradation;
- management policies that discriminate and exploit.

In both instances, hard and soft, management is unwilling to share or give up control of the labour process.

In examining the particular interface between HRM and trades unions, Guest 1995 identified four potential policy options:

1 *New realism*: combines both HRM and collective approaches to employee relations. There are joint approaches emphasizing mutuality with direct employee communications coexisting with systems of union representation. However doubts have been expressed about the long-term viability of robust trade unionism in a context of enthusiastic HRM.
2 *Traditional collectivism*: this is the continuation of traditional pluralist and collective industrial relations and with no attempt on the part of management to introduce HRM.
3 *Individualized HRM*: here we have HRM with no trades unions and no collective dimension to the conduct of employee relations.
4 *The black hole*: no soft HRM and no collective employee relations. Often this approach is associated with cost cutting strategies and an extreme version of hard HRM.

In the remaining sections of this chapter, we look at managerial objectives and styles of managing employee relations, including the management of employee relations in a non-union environment. We identify a number of the objectives that management may have in its conduct of employee relations with a particular emphasis upon achieving employee commitment, a strategy that has become strongly associated with HRM and achieving competitive advantage. Objectives and style are often interrelated and the one may dictate the other; the pursuit of particular objectives may necessitate, or at the least imply, the use of a particular and appropriate style.

Management's objectives

Management's employee relations objectives, or at least some of them, have been alluded to both in this and earlier previous modules. For example, in examining definitions of employee relations and the nature of the employment relationship it became clear that some analysts think that the prime management objective is to buy labour at the lowest price while others see the dominant objective as attaining control over the labour process. In this chapter we have already identified a number of objectives associated with the different versions of HRM. However, it is not always easy to establish employer/management objectives, one reason being that often they are not written down anywhere. Nevertheless, there is a range of possibilities that are reasonably common, many of which can be seen to be driven by the need to be competitive as well as by considerations that may have more to do with values and beliefs.

Marchington and Wilkinson (1996) identified (parentheses this author's):

- Reducing unit labour costs, not just wages.
- Increasing labour productivity (this has potential for overlap with the above).
- Minimizing disruption and the incidence of overt conflict (this term is often used to distinguish conflict that results in action, and which is therefore visible, from conflict which exists but which, for many reasons, may remain hidden or is latent).
- Achieving greater stability by channelling discontent through agreed procedures, something we pursue in more detail in later modules.
- Increasing employee cooperation and commitment so as to increase the likely acceptance of change and enhance productive efficiency (this is something we return to later in this module).

Marchington and Wilkinson (1996) comment that some analysts would argue that all of these objectives are subservient to the prime objective of control over the labour process.

There are other objectives not mentioned above, amongst which might be a determination to reduce the influence of and possibly rid the organization of trade unions and joint or shared decision making, thereby re-asserting managerial prerogative and reinserting management as the single legitimate focus of employee loyalty. It is unclear the extent to which this has been an explicit and actual objective of management in the UK over the last 15–20 years but there is certainly evidence that it has happened (see box).

Trends in the influence of trade unionism in the UK

Successive WIRS and WERS surveys and Labour Force Surveys have provided evidence of the following trends, see Modules 7 and 9:

- a significant reduction in the number of workplaces in which trade unions were recognized for collective bargaining purposes;
- a decline in trade union membership figures;
- a decline in the number of workplaces in which wages and other terms and conditions of employment were determined jointly through the collective bargaining process.

The 1998 **and 2004 WERS** associate trade union density and union recognition in organizations with the attitudes of management in these organizations and there are clear relationships, so much so that in relation to the 1998 survey the analysts assert that 'these figures suggest that anti-union sentiments on the part of employers provide a considerable hurdle to overcome if unions are to win members and recognition'.

The data confirm no causal relationships but, where management is generally favourably disposed towards trade unions, the WERS 2004 indicate that 84 per cent (94 per cent – 1998) of the organizations do recognize a trade union. However, where management are not in favour of trade unions, only 4 per cent (9 per cent – 1998) of workplaces recognize a trade union.

Another objective may be to create an employee relations environment in which employees are able to satisfy their needs at work and achieve enhanced fulfilment. We noted in **Chapter 2** that it is claimed that this philosophy has been at the root of many of the experiments in job re-design over the last 20 years or so. Yet other objectives may be specifically oriented towards the achievement of labour flexibility, both functional and temporal.

There is then quite a wide range of outcomes which may constitute the employee relations objectives of management and these may well vary over time and be either helped or hindered by the environment, economic, political and cultural. Which of these are pursued by employers, and with what priority, at any particular moment will be dependent upon a whole range of factors and influences.

Depending upon your perspective you may perceive some or all of these objectives contributing to an improvement in the **quality** of employee relations or indeed to a deterioration of quality (see **Chapter 1**).

Managerial style(s)

Early models of managerial styles and approaches to the management of the employment relationship and employee relations are reflective of the distinction drawn above between the unitarist and pluralist perspectives. Fox (1974) made the first really significant contribution to this debate by identifying four styles, each of which could be located in terms of these frames of reference or perspective. This contribution by Fox has, in many respects, formed the base for subsequent amendments and contributions, so that the latter work of Purcell and Sisson (1983), Purcell and Gray (1986), Purcell (1987) and Purcell and Ahlstrand (1989, 1994) can all be seen to be derived from and are adaptations of Fox's original model.

Before proceeding to look at some of this work, it is important that we seek to define our terms. The definition of style or approach that seems to have the greatest degree of credibility currently is that of Purcell (1987). He suggests that by 'style' is implied: 'the existence of a distinctive set of guiding principles, written or otherwise, which set parameters to and signposts for management action in the way employees are treated and particular events are handled'.

As noted in the first module, managerial style forms part of the organizational context within which the employment relationship is managed and employee relations occur. It is clear that management has some discretion in the style that it adopts and many have argued the styles adopted to be a consequence of the preferences of and strategic choices made by management, though there are also undoubtedly some environmental and other constraints upon this choice.

Culture and ideology are two such environmental constraints each of which, it is argued, explain in some measure national differences in dominant style. To this one can also add the institutional arrangements in any particular national system. A couple of simplified examples may demonstrate the importance of these contextual features.

The dominant style of employee relations management in Japan might be classified as paternalist authoritarian, reflecting the dominance of the Confucian culture with its emphasis upon obedience, the ordering of relationships according to status and the importance of family and responsibility. In this context management is afforded the opportunity to exercise its authority in a benevolent fashion, which it does, and certainly not conceding its authority and responsibility to employees or indeed to the trade unions. Employees are given the opportunity, and are obliged by their membership of the organization family, to:

- contribute to the family or group well being;
- take part in quality circles and contribute to continuous improvement;
- take part in other forums which provide ideas and solutions to problems which are then filtered as they rise up through the various layers of the hierarchy.

They are also expected to demonstrate their commitment to the family, put in long hours and form and join trade unions contained within the organization.

In contrast, and given that it is difficult to talk as if there is only one culture in the USA, it is common for the dominant characteristics of the American culture to be presented as one that emphasizes competition, individualism and individual achievement and reward and, in this context, there is no substantial tradition in the USA of managements favouring trade union-based employee relations systems and styles. Where possible, managements have tended to pursue policies of outright opposition or, alternatively, the more sophisticated paternalist approach whereby they seek to create work environments which encourage the employees to believe that they do not need a trade union. Employees do not feel the loyalty to the organization that is characteristic of Japan and they are much less likely to participate voluntarily in processes geared to achieving benefits for the organization unless there is also something in it for them.

You should by now have realized that in this context we are not dealing with individuals' preferences and style of managing; it is the approach that has been determined at a corporate level, or which is adopted, demonstrated and encouraged by senior management, that is our concern. However, we do also need to bear in mind that there will be variations within organizations and the model preferred and selected at the level of senior management may well not be the style actually adopted throughout the whole organization. It is quite common to find discrepancy between the policy or strategy espoused at an organizational level and that practised on the shop-floor.

Look now at **Figure 8.5**, which reproduces the amended model of Purcell and Gray (1986) depicting and describing five ideal or pure types of style used by managements in managing employee relations. In each case the figure also indicates the interrelationship between style and the expected role of central personnel management. It is no accident that each of the styles depicted in this figure are expressive of particular attitudes towards trade unions and the recognition of them for collective bargaining purposes.

It has been noted already above that some features of the external environment (culture and ideology) can be seen to act as constraining

Title	Description	Most likely to occur in these circumstances	Expected role of central personnel management
Traditional	Labour is viewed as a factor of production, and employee subordination is assumed to be part of the 'natural order' of the employment relationship. Fear of outside union interference. Unionization opposed or unions kept at arm's length.	Small owner-managed companies (or franchise operations). Product markets often highly competitive with the firm having a low share leading to emphasis on cost-control and low profit margins.	For personnel specialists.
Sophisticated human relations or paternalists	Employees (excluding short-term contract or sub-contract labour) viewed as the company's most valuable resource. Above-average pay. Internal labour-market structures with promotion ladders are common with periodic attitude surveys used to harness employees' views. Emphasis is placed on flexible reward structures. Employee appraisal systems linked to merit awards, internal grievance, disciplinary and consultative procedures, and extensive networks and methods of communication. The aim is to inculcate employee loyalty, commitment and dependency. As a by-product these companies seek to make it unnecessary or unattractive for staff to unionize.	American-owned single-industry, larger financially successful firms with a high market share in growth industries (electronics/finance sector).	Strong central personnel departments developing policies to be adopted in all areas of the company.
Sophisticated modems: Consultative	Similar to the sophisticated human resource companies that unions are recognized. The attempt is made to build 'constructive' relationships with the trade unions and incorporate them into the organizational fabric. Broad-ranging discussions are held with extensive information provided to the unions on a whole range of decisions and plans, including aspects of strategic management, but the 'right of last say' rests with management. Emphasis is also placed on techniques designed to enhance individual employee commitment to the firm and the need to change (share option schemes, profit sharing, briefing or cascade information systems, joint working parties, quality or productivity circles/councils).	British/Japanese-owned single-industry companies which are large and economically successful, often with a large market share. Companies with relatively low labour costs (process industries) often adopt this style	Central personnel departments produce policy guidelines or precepts providing advice and central direction when required.
Constitutional	Somewhat similar to the traditionalists in basic value structures but unions have been recognized for some time and accepted as inevitable. Employee relations policies centre on the need for stability,	Single-industry companies with mass production or large-batch production requiring a large unit of operation. Labour costs	Relatively strong emphasis on the central personnel auditing/control function.

Figure 8.5
Five styles of industrial relations management.

Title	Description	Most likely to occur in these circumstances	Expected role of central personnel management
	control and the institutionalization of conflict. Management prerogatives are defended through highly specific collective agreements, and careful attention is paid to the administration of agreements at the point of production. The importance of management control is emphasized, with the aim of minimizing or neutralizing union constraints on both operational (line) and strategic (corporate) management.	form a significant proportion of total costs. Product-market conditions are often highly competitive.	
Standard modems: Opportunistic	The approach to employee relations is pragmatic. Trade unions are recognized in some or all parts of the business, often inherited with company acquisition. Employee relations are viewed as the responsibility of operational management at unit and/or division level. The importance attached to employee-relations policies changes in the light of circumstances. When union power is high and product and labour markets buoyant. or when legislative needs dictate, negotiation and consultation is emphasized. Fashionable employee-relations techniques are adopted over short periods as panaceas. When union power is low, or product markers become unfavourable or major technical change threatens existing practices, unions are 'rolled back', and management seeks to regain its prerogatives. There can be marked differences of approach between establishments or divisions and between various levels in the hierarchy.	Most common in conglomerate multi-product companies which grew by acquisition and diversification, especially in the engineering and heavy manufacturing industries with long traditions of unionization.	Relatively weak central personnel departments with Personnel specialists at operating-unit level having a fire-fighting role, reacting to union claims and the impact of labour legislation. The personnel function tends to have a chequered history: sometimes strong, sometimes weak.

Source: J. Purcell and A. Gray (1986) 'Corporate personnel departments and the management of industrial relations: two case studies in ambiguity'. *Journal of Management Studies.* March pp. 214–215.

Figure 8.5
(*Continued*)

influences upon the styles adopted by senior management, though it is difficult to know the extent to which management preferences and the approach adopted are in practice constrained.

In your study of the figure above you have just identified a range of other contextual influences and constraints, most of which can be organized into one or more of the categories identified by Marchington and Wilkinson (1996):

- the product market;
- technology;

■   the labour market;
■   the social, legal and political environment and institutions.

There is also a series of organizational variables which may well have an impact and we have already mentioned some of these such as size and ownership; others might include organizational structure and the degree of centralization.

You may want to look again at the outline framework for studying employee relations at the end of **Chapter 1 (Figure 1.1).**

Product market

Marchington and Wilkinson (1996) suggest that there are subdivisions to this category of external environmental influence: orientation, intensity of competition and the rate of change in the size of the market. By orientation they mean the nature of the customer served by it, such as whether the customer is domestic or business, whether the product is subject to fashion and associated change or whether the product is sold on the basis of its quality or durability.

An example of how the nature of the product market may influence or constrain management style may be derived from comparing a company operating in a fiercely competitive, fashion-based and therefore potentially volatile market, where the competition is on price rather than quality, with one that is dealing with a stable product in a growing and not very competitive market where the competition is on quality rather than price. One would expect these circumstances and constraints to contribute to the two companies adopting quite different styles, notwithstanding the preferences of the senior managers themselves.

Technology

Technology can affect management style also in a number of ways; it in part determines the requirement for labour, the type and quantity, the value added and thereby the price at which it is profitable to hire. It also has a potentially significant impact upon labour productivity and the proportion of total costs attributable to labour. The rate of technical change influences change within the organization, changing job descriptions and the career prospects of individuals and groups.

The labour market

There are some reasonably predictable labour market influences and constraints, such as the level of unemployment, the supply of labour available both in terms of quantity and, in many cases, more importantly the quality, skill levels and mix. Other labour market factors might include the presence of trade unions and their policies with respect to exerting an influence over the labour supply. Unions have often been criticized for seeking to control the supply of labour and thereby influence the price at which that labour may be hired.

Social, legal and political environment

A prime example of the potential influence of these factors for management style can be seen in the UK over the last two decades of the 20th century, in particular linked to the election of a Conservative government in 1979. It is not possible here to do more than touch the surface of the scale and nature of the impact of this change in the political and subsequently also the legal and social environments (but see **Chapter 5**). Suffice it to say that many analysts have documented the attack upon the trade union movement, the rejection of tripartism and the search for consensus, the increased emphasis upon labour market deregulation and labour flexibility, the re-assertion in the public sector of management's right to manage and the concentration upon cost efficiency. These and other developments have facilitated approaches and styles very different from the bargained constitutional style (see **Figure 8.6**) which arguably dominated the public sector and manufacturing industry prior to this change in political climate.

We have noted in the first section of this chapter that the popularity and adoption of HRM rather than the more traditional PM has itself been encouraged by some of these same environmental and contextual developments.

Criticisms and developments

Criticisms of the Purcell and Gray model (**Figure 8.5**) and other early models devised in the UK included the assertion that the models did not facilitate identification and recognition of the tendency of many managements to distinguish between and treat differently employees as individuals and employees gathered together into collective organizations.

It was suggested that in some organizations management adopted different approaches and styles to each of these two scenarios. Purcell (1987) made the first significant attempt to devise a model that recognized this reality and this has been adapted and developed subsequently by Sisson (1989) and Purcell and Ahlstrand (1989, 1994), though it should be noted that the research upon which this was based is concerned with multi-divisional organizations (M-form companies) and we

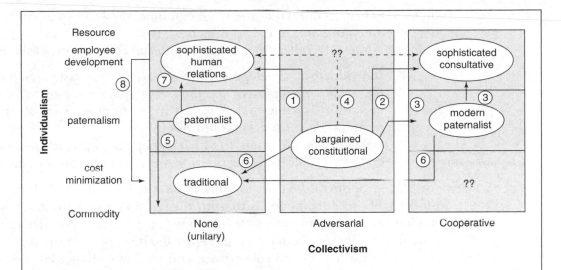

1 Employees encouraged to sign new individual contracts and union recognition for collective bargaining purposes withdrawn. New work practices, recruitment, selection, appraisal, and training initiatives implemented in accordance with 'soft' HRM and employee development policies.

2 Co-operative, consultative relations with trade unions/works councils/company councils developed alongside the introduction of employee development-type politics.

3 Co-operative, consultative relations initiated with unions as a prelude to subsequent initiatives in employee development. The new relationship with unions is often triggered by a crisis in the competitive position of the firm such that choice is forced. Competitive analysis reveals that the strength of the major firms in the market is based in part on employee development policies.

4 Unstable conditions exist as unions are bypassed in the change programme to introduce employee development policies. Subsequently either union membership declines and recognition is withdrawn, or both unions and management 'learn' to modify their behaviour to each other to emphasize partnership, or initiatives fail and the bargained constitutional pattern is reinforced.

5 Growing competition, falling profit margins, and declining market share force a reappraisal of employment policies leading to the introduction of cost minimization, reduction in job security, and reduced employee benefits. Or new entrants to the market base their competitive advantage on cheaper labour.

6 A new tough regime is introduced often triggered by a change in ownership, competitive tendering, subcontracting or acquisition. Union recognition is withdrawn and cost minimization policies reinforced, with employees working under worse conditions.

7 Emphasis placed on employee productivity achieved through employee development policies and technical change, based on realization that it is desirable to encourage employees to use diagnostic skills and their knowledge for the benefit of the business and to satisfy customers. Usually associated with reduction in numbers employed and thus rapid, early rises in productivity. The difficulty is to sustain this.

8 Rapidly falling market share in a depressed or mature market leading to substantial loss of profitability forces a major reappraisal of employment policies. These are often justified on the grounds of temporary expediency but, once implemented, are difficult to escape from. A change in top management is often a precursor to the abandonment of the employee development policies, and substantial cuts in employee investment. Often triggered by the arrival of low-cost entrants to the market and a slow response by the firm, leading to crisis and draconian action.

Figure 8.6

Movements in management style in employee relations. Source: Purcell and Ahlstrand 1994 pp. 209–210.

do need to bear in mind that size is a factor that may well explain differences between organizational approach or style.

In this context Purcell defines individualism and collectivism as follows:

- **Individualism**: the degree of weight attached to issues such as the welfare of employees and their development – note that this definition is somewhat different from the way in which the term has been used so far in this module.
- **Collectivism**: the extent to which management provide for and embrace employee collective organization and representation.

Another criticism of the early models, which the Purcell and Ahlstrand model seeks to encompass, is that no recognition was made in these models of managements' style changing over time, the dynamic dimension. The matrix depicted in **Figure 8.6** incorporates the dimensions of individualism and collectivism and provides a base that can be used to plot changes in style as they occur over time. The arrows on the figure indicate a range of movements over time which, in some respects, can be seen to represent stereotypes of arguably common trends in changing managerial styles in recent years and these are identified in the accompanying notes to the figure.

It is also sometimes possible to use this matrix as a base for distinguishing espoused style from the reality of employee experience so that, for example, many employees in the UK public sector might well argue that, through the late 1980s and early 1990s, managements have been espousing a style consistent with high levels of individualism and low collectivism ('Sophisticated human relations' in the matrix). Yet the employees' experience has been closer to a style consistent with low individualism and low collectivism ('Traditional' in the matrix), where the dominant concern appears to have been with cost-cutting and by-passing or derecognizing the trade unions. Some would see this latter in terms of a shift towards an approach consistent with the unitarist model or paradigm.

The employees in such circumstances are likely to be confused in the first instance by their management appearing to say one thing and do something else but, after a while the impact upon employees is quite likely to involve a loss of trust and development of a degree of cynicism. Employees in this context, as in the one above, are likely to perceive that a different style altogether should be adopted, either a return to the bargained constitutionalist style which, prior to the 1980s, was the norm in the public sector in the UK, or movement in the direction of the sophisticated consultative. In both cases employees would be expressing a preference for a style that encompasses employee collective organization.

In this section we have examined some of the several models of managerial style and we have emphasized the impact that external contexts and environments may have upon the style chosen by management and also that which is appropriate. Certainly some of the literature infers that an analysis of context can be used to establish whether the style used is appropriate or whether some other would be more consistent with the contextual circumstances. Nevertheless, it is important to realize that the ultimate discretion is with management and it may well be that for reasons of their own managements choose to operate with an approach to employee relations which is not appropriate in the context of the above analysis.

Managing with or without unions?

Trade unions are the subject matter of the previous module; however, before we proceed in a section concentrating upon managing without unions, it is important at least to consider whether there are any advantages for management and the organization in recognizing and working with the trade unions. After all, we can't assume that all employers who do manage employee relations with trade unions do so against their will and that they are in a real sense dragged kicking and screaming to the negotiating table.

Advantages of managing with trade unions

Freeman and Medoff (1984) highlighted one of the advantages of recognizing and dealing with trade unions, that they provide an effective mechanism through which the two groups can communicate with each other. This is often referred to as the 'voice' argument and some organizations which have found themselves in a new position of not dealing with trade unions have discovered after a while that there are problems in communicating with employees, a role that was often effectively performed by the unions. Effective direct communications from management to employee may be relatively straightforward but obtaining employee views in the absence of a trade union may not be (see following section for some of the techniques that may facilitate this).

Trade unions are often also useful to management as a mechanism through which employee discipline and fairness and equity of treatment can be achieved; indeed managements have been known to rely on the trade unions to exert discipline over employees, their members. However, perhaps the greatest advantages to management lie in the opportunity unions provide to create and operate effective conflict resolution mechanisms and grievance procedures without having to deal with each employee as an individual. Decisions and procedures that are the product of agreement with the trade unions are also invested with a useful degree of legitimacy as far as the workforce is concerned and, where they have been arrived at through processes which have involved the trade union, it is much more difficult for the employees not to comply with the agreement.

We have noted in **Chapter 7** that in recent years in the UK there has been an increased willingness for employers and unions to agree partnership arrangements. These emphasize the joint interests of the parties in the success of the business and provide a role for the unions in a range of problem-solving activities facilitating the utilization, in the interests of the company, of the knowledge and expertise of the workforce.

There is a degree of coincidence between the objectives of these agreements and the more prescriptive models of HRM referred to earlier. If the active participation of the labour force in the resolution of problems, the pursuit of quality and enhanced employee commitment and flexibility can all be obtained by management in return for recognizing the union, then this does make the prospect of managing with trade unions much less threatening, especially if, in return, the management achieves a single union, a no strike deal and retains its autonomy to decide issues in the event of a failure to reach agreed solutions. It should be noted that trade unions are an integral part of many Japanese organizations and that they can play a crucial role in achieving consensus and in securing change.

To some extent the models referred to in earlier sections do provide information on a range of reasons and circumstances that may explain managements' seeking to manage employee relations without trade unions; managements have in many cases taken advantage of opportunities to do so. There are some pretty obvious reasons why managers might prefer to avoid trade unions and paramount among them probably are reasons associated with the issues of autonomy and control, the belief that as management they should have the right and need to be able to manage unilaterally and also that employees should be loyal to the company rather than to some external organization. Cast your mind back to the unitarist perspective dealt with in the first module. In this perspective trade unions are perceived as unnecessary and as a challenge to the natural autonomy and authority of management. They also complicate and lengthen the decision-making process, no matter that the time might be well spent if it results in better decisions and if, once made, the decisions acquire legitimacy with the workforce and are more easily implemented.

Looking back at the Purcell and Ahlstrand (1994) matrix (**Figure 8.6**) and the material on hard and soft versions of HRM, it is clear that low collectivism or non-unionism takes different forms, occurs for different motives and may have good as well as bad consequences for employees. The emphasis upon the individual, as opposed to the collective, may be:

- Primarily developmental, with the employer anxious to invest in the labour resource.

- Paternalistic and beneficial to labour through the provision of benefits and treatment that is directed at convincing the employees that they can have no need for the union, that the union has no significant role since management is doing for the employees everything and more that the union would normally be expected to do.
- Upon the treatment of labour just as any other resource, to be acquired, used and disposed of at the least cost, a strictly utilitarian approach.

Organizations in this category may be relatively small and pursuing a competitive strategy which incorporates a strong element of price competition, hence the pressure upon costs. Many such organizations are also characterized by a lack of personnel procedures and personnel expertise. From the viewpoint of the employee, attitudes of government and other regulatory agencies and institutions to the responsibilities of small employers towards their employees have not been helpful. Throughout Europe the small employer tends to be protected from regulation on the grounds that it imposes financial and administrative burdens that would be sufficiently significant to damage business prospects and therefore harm the prospects for job creation and employment generally.

Unfortunately, it is often the case that it is the employees of small firms who are in most need of protection and least likely to be represented by a trade union. For logistical reasons alone trade unions find it most difficult to organize and effectively represent employees in small firms and locations where few are employed.

Evidence from the UK

The findings from the 1998 WERS confirmed that the incidence of trade union recognition tended to be positively associated with the number of employees; the percentage of workplaces in which trade unions were recognized increased from 39 per cent in workplaces employing less than 50, to 78 per cent in workplaces employing 500 plus. The WERS 2004 data also confirm this positive relationship, with recognition in only 18 per cent (28 per cent – 1998) of workplaces with 10–24 employees compared with 39 per cent in workplaces with 25 or more employees (41 per cent – 1998).

In addition to the typologies of style that we have already looked at there have been some attempts to devise models encompassing differences of style in non-union organizations, for example Guest and Hoque (1994) and McLoughlin and Gourlay (1994). We look here at the model devised by Guest and Hoque but, before doing so, try the next activity.

Guest and Hoque devised a fourfold typology of non-union firms and their policies/strategies/styles towards employee relations. Each of the four tends to represent a stereotype and you should realize that many firms will exhibit a mix of characteristics that do not conform with one particular type; they may partially fit in one category, demonstrating some of the characteristics but not all of them. The typology demonstrates the range of characteristics that have been found.

They have used the terms 'the good', 'the bad', 'the ugly' and 'the lucky' to depict the four styles or types of non-union firm. The first of these, the **good**, would exhibit the following characteristics in their pure form:

- They are often large employers with a clear strategy for managing people and often an emphasis upon staff as their most valuable asset, their source of competitive advantage.
- They often operate union substitution policies and provide an attractive alternative, part of which is the motive for being a market leader on pay and benefits.
- They are likely to afford a high priority to recruitment, selection and induction as a means of identifying and inducing 'right' attitudes and norms.
- They place stress on training and development and upon information sharing through mechanisms such as team briefing.
- They will try to demonstrate their commitment to providing secure and satisfying work.
- They may well operate single-status policies, ostensibly treating all employees the same with little if any discrimination between categories of staff.
- They may well also operate individualized payment schemes often linked to performance appraisal, thereby, they argue, rewarding best those who contribute the most.

A number of household name firms fit into this category, or at least they would claim to do so, and these would probably include Marks and Spencer, IBM, and Hewlett Packard. You may well know others that fit. Depending partially upon perspective and partially upon experience, organizations of this kind are sometimes criticized for presenting an illusion to their employees and being manipulative.

Very far removed from the good are the **bad and the ugly**. In both cases we are describing sweat-shop type conditions. The difference between these two is not so much in the actual terms and conditions of employment and the management of employees, these are likely to be very similar, the difference tends to lie in whether or not it is a deliberate policy to deprive employees of their rights and manipulate and exploit them (the ugly) or not (the bad). Guest and Hoque suggest that firms falling into this category are often suppliers to larger organizations, sometimes locked into contracts that put them under pressure on quality and delivery, which also puts them under extreme pressure to minimize costs and waste. Just-in-Time systems may well generate the conditions in which suppliers are confronted by these pressures. We noted in the earlier **Chapter 3** that the international trade union movement and others argue that these are conditions confronting employees in many contracting companies in the developing world but they exist in the developed world as well.

Characteristics of the 'bad' employer include:

- low pay;
- no fringe or welfare benefits;
- personalized rather than formal relationships, often a reliance upon personal exhortations and cajoling;
- an authoritarian management style;
- few if any procedures in areas such as discipline, employee grievances or equal opportunities, and little if any health and safety protection, monitoring or inspection and quite commonly hazardous working conditions;
- a harsh disciplinary regime and a hostility towards trade unions;
- little dissemination of information.

The last of the four categories is the **lucky**. Here Guest and Hoque are describing those firms which exhibit little sophistication but which also demonstrate no deliberate attempt to manage by fear and union suppression. The overall impression with these firms is that they are essentially opportunist, pragmatic and reactive. There is little planning, few if any policies or procedures, low pay and poor benefits and, probably more by luck than judgement, no trade union presence. It is a form that can perhaps best be described by the term 'ad-hocery'.

Employee involvement and the pursuit of employee commitment

In earlier sections of this chapter we have noted that employee commitment is an objective management may seek to pursue and that it is included as a desirable outcome in some of the models of HRM. We also noted in **Chapter 1** that the employment relationship may be characterized by a number of different forms of attachment and that employee commitment was amongst these. Also in **Chapter 1** we discussed different forms of employee commitment, distinguishing between attitudinal and behavioural and we noted that for some observers and analysts securing employee commitment to achieving the objectives of the organization was the primary purpose of the management of employee relations. In this context the quality of in an organization's employee relations might be measured by the degree of commitment demonstrated by employees though this is, of course, a management perspective. We have also noted that the attraction to management of securing employee commitment is that there is an assumption that if employees are committed to the achievement of organizational objectives, they will work harder, be more productive and innovative and exhibit a greater concern with the quality of their output and customer satisfaction.

What we need to do now is examine the mechanisms through which management might seek to secure greater employee commitment. In this context we concentrate upon Employee Involvement (EI) initiatives as the means through which commitment may be sought.

Before we go any further it is also important that in examining EI initiatives designed to achieve employee commitment, we distinguish these processes and mechanisms from those that we examine in the next chapter which are representative in nature and designed to facilitate both employee participation and the resolution of conflict between the interests of employees and employers.

In this context we use the term employee participation to refer to processes which provide employees, usually through representatives, with the opportunity to participate in decision making and thereby in the control and management of the assets, activities and direction of the enterprise.

Some analysts and observers take the view that, for all practical purposes, the terms employee participation and employee involvement (EI) can be treated as synonymous; others, and the author of this text would fall into this camp, argue that, while there may be overlap between them, the concepts and mechanisms are different and can and should be distinguished from each other.

Some EI initiatives (**Figure 8.7**) may provide employees with the opportunity to participate but many of the initiatives associated with EI do no more than provide information, managements' hope being that through the provision of this information employees will feel more involved in and with the enterprise.

Marchington *et al.* (1992) use the term 'employee involvement' to indicate the range of managerially inspired, designed and initiated processes at the level of the firm which 'are intended to improve communications with employees, to generate greater commitment, and enhance employee contributions to the organization'. Management motives in the introduction of such initiatives are clearly instrumental in nature and the objectives as specified do not include employee participation in decision making and control.

As Poole and Mansfield (1992) discovered, 'Managers appear to support most employee involvement practices so long as these do not radically affect their control function within the firm. In other words they tend to prefer a unitary rather than a pluralist approach to employee

Marchington and Wilkinson (1996) in drawing upon the literature, much of which is their own, conclude that EI initiatives can usefully be located into four main categories.

Downward communication

The principal purpose of these schemes, and there are many means available to management, is to educate and persuade employees of the value and merit of management initiatives and to inform about the performance of the organization or unit. Some organizations seek to reinforce their desired culture through this kind of mechanism.

Team Briefing is perhaps the best known initiative and regarded commonly as symptomatic of EI but there are other popular initiatives, including house journals and newspapers; **the use of e-mail, company intranets** and video is also becoming more popular.

Team briefing is a system of regular communication of information approved by senior management which is cascaded down the organization via line managers, with each manager informing the people reporting to him or her. The emphasis should be on information relevant to the people receiving it and team briefing can be a mechanism through which two-way communication occurs with employee responses and views being fed back up the line to senior management.

The WERS 2004 asked about the incidence of a range of methods of downward communication between managers and employees. There was widespread use of meetings, in the form of team briefings or meetings with the whole workforce – 91 per cent of all organizations. The use of noticeboards (74 per cent) to communicate with employees and the systematic use of the management chain or cascading of information were also very common (64 per cent). Also used, but to a lesser extent, were regular newsletters to all employees, e-mail and the company intranet.

The issues commonly discussed at meetings, including team briefing, included production issues, future plans, work organization, training and health and safety. Most of these meetings also allow time for employees to raise questions or make comments.

Upward problem solving

Here employees are commonly involved in task-oriented issues and problems, and either individually or as a group, are invited to examine and propose remedies for work problems. The best known of these techniques is the quality circle (see **Chapter 2**); others include attitude surveys and suggestion schemes. Management is seeking to use the knowledge and experience of employees and the assumption is that employees will not only contribute to the resolution of problems but also that they will feel more involved and, as such, the quality circle yields other benefits of enhanced commitment, productivity and quality, etc. For these schemes to have a positive benefit in terms of employee commitment, it is important that employees see action being taken in response to the problems or solutions that they identify.

The WERS 2004 found that 30 per cent of all workplaces operated a suggestion scheme (31 per cent in 1998), 21 per cent of workplaces had some non-managerial employees participating in problem-solving groups and 42 per cent of workplaces had conducted a staff attitude survey in the previous 2 years of which approximately 80 per cent made the results available, in written form, to the employees that took part in the survey.

Task participation

Many of these schemes can be seen to derive from, and are consistent with, the ideas of the QWL movement, the essence of which is that employees derive satisfaction from manageable variety and complexity; such tasks provide intrinsic satisfactions and opportunities for self-fulfilment and self-actualization and that satisfied employees are likely to be more productive, etc.

This form of EI then encompasses schemes such as job re-design, job enrichment, rotation and enlargement (see **Chapter 2**). It is also suggested that TQM (see **Chapter 2**) fits into this category with employees being encouraged to apply their knowledge of work processes and tasks in the context of achieving continuous improvement and innovation.

Financial involvement

There are various means by which employees can participate in the financial performance of the company. It may be through some form of bonus scheme linked to performance or it may be that they are encouraged to participate in the ownership of the organization through share holding; these schemes often go under the banner of Employee Share Ownership Schemes (ESOPs). It is assumed that employees with some form of financial stake in the organization over and above their salary or wage will work harder and be more productive.

As share holders, employees can, in theory, participate in decision making at a corporate level. However, in practice there have been very few schemes that provided employees with a sufficiently large stake in the ownership to enable them, even collectively, to exert a significant influence.

The WERS 2004 data show that 37 per cent of private sector workplaces gave profit-related payments or bonuses and 21 per cent (15 per cent in 1998) operated an employee share scheme.

Figure 8.7

Employee involvement (EI) initiatives and their frequency in the UK.

participation in decision making'. Even though the intentions may have nothing to do with employee participation, as we have defined it above, let alone democracy, it can be that a measure of enhanced participation is one of the outcomes, which is why we say that there may be overlap between the two notions. This is pursued further in the following module.

The central role given in Marchington's definition to the generation of greater employee commitment, as noted above, locates EI as encompassing a set of practices and intentions that are consistent with models of HRM such as those of Beer *et al.* (1984) and Guest (1989), which prescriptively place organizational commitment at the centre of the outcomes that should be achieved as a result of HRM initiatives.

EI processes are generally directed at individuals or work groups and tend to involve employees at this level. Generally they do not include a role for trade unions and it is sometimes suspected and/or alleged that the objectives for initiating the processes include the desire to bypass or weaken the trade unions by establishing that employees are valued for themselves and that the trade unions are not needed, that they are an anachronism.

In advocating the use of EI initiatives to generate greater employee commitment to the objectives and success of the organization, Gennard and Judge (2002) argue that it is imperative that management also demonstrates commitment to employees in terms of job security, single-status terms and conditions of employment, access to training and retraining and the provision of a healthy and safe working environment. This once again emphasizes the reciprocity of concepts such as trust and commitment; you can only expect to achieve either from your employees if it is reciprocated by management.

Selecting and implementing EI schemes and practices

When management has decided that it wishes to introduce employee involvement mechanisms in order to achieve one or more of the perceived advantages, it is important that managers are fully committed to it. They must not assume that practices which they have seen achieving results elsewhere will necessarily be appropriate to their own organization and workforce. It is also important that schemes are selected and introduced as part of a coherent and consistent strategy, after thorough analysis and evaluation and not as a piecemeal attempt to resolve a crisis. There are no one-size-fits-all panaceas. Generally a mix of methods will be more successful than any one mechanism and it is important that the strategy for securing greater employee commitment should be both horizontally and vertically integrated; this means that the mix of methods and initiatives should be consistent with one another and that they should all be consistent with and integral to the business strategy.

It is also advisable that, if the organization recognizes trades unions, they should be involved in agreeing the arrangements. If employees feel some joint ownership of the schemes introduced, there is a greater likelihood that they will feel a commitment to making them work. If the unions are involved, it will minimize the risk that they perceive the EI mechanisms, with their individual, non-union focus, as a threat to their own position within the organization and to their members.

Where the arrangements provide for employees to input their views, as for example in quality circles or other problem-solving activities, it is important that they have the opportunity to do this before decisions are taken and, of course, they need to be confident that management listens to the views expressed and considers the solutions identified. Failure on the part of management to ensure this can very quickly lead to the situation in which the schemes fall into disrepute and employees stop taking the schemes seriously.

Management also needs to consider seriously whether the particular schemes require skills and abilities that the participants do not currently have and, if this is the case, appropriate education and training needs to be implemented in order to ensure that the maximum benefit is obtained by the organization. Common skills required of participants in EI schemes include communication, presentation, persuasive and problem-solving skills.

Because EI costs money, of course the management of the organization need to be confident that the benefits to be derived will outweigh the costs, but often there needs to be investment before the benefits can be obtained. Management must therefore be willing and able to commit resource to the implementation of EI. There is likely to be training to be undertaken but it must also be remembered that communication and the engagement of staff in problem-solving costs both time and money and this may take the form of lost wages and output.

Management also needs to be aware that it is more difficult to introduce effective EI into a poor employee relations climate. We mentioned above the crucial nature of the reciprocity of trust and commitment. Trust is perhaps particularly important in that (for schemes to work) employees must feel that the climate is one of openness and honesty and that if they express views which can be implied as criticism of management decisions or abilities that this will be taken in the spirit intended and as a means of achieving improvements. If employees are afraid that expressing such views may result in disciplinary action or victimization, that their promotion prospects may be negatively impacted, then they will not be honest and the potential benefits for the organization will not be achieved.

It should be remembered that seeking employee views or giving employees a role in decisions concerning the task and how it is undertaken can often be perceived by first line and middle management as a threat to their position and authority as well as a source of potential criticism of their ability. These lower level managers also need to be reassured that they will not suffer; for schemes to work, they also need to be committed to the introduction and implementation of EI.

Finally, it is important that management sets up systems for monitoring and reviewing the arrangements and their effectiveness. Are they yielding the benefits that were anticipated and are they cost effective?

Legal requirements in the UK

There are no legal requirements on employers to introduce EI schemes of the kind discussed in the section, though, as we discuss elsewhere, there are some legal requirements for employers to inform and consult employees and their representatives on a range of specified subject matter.

However, companies employing more than 250 employees are required in their annual Directors report to report on the action they may have taken to introduce, maintain or develop arrangements for:

- informing and consulting employees on matters of concern to them as employees;
- achieving a common awareness on the part of employees of the financial and economic factors affecting the performance of the company;
- encouraging employees' financial participation in the company;
- consulting employees and their representatives on a regular basis on decisions likely to affect their interests.

Source: Companies Act 1989.

Employers associations

There is a tendency for students and others to think that the only collective organizations involved as actors or participants in employee relations are the trade unions and this is not so. Employers also form and join collective associations and these form part of the national and international context within which employee relations in an organization are conducted. Outside the UK these two forms of collectives are often referred to as the social partners and we have examined the role of the Social Partners at the level of the EU in **Chapter 4**.

In this section we examine these developments in the context of the historical emergence of and roles performed by employers associations, we examine why employers associations were formed, why employers join, the apparent dichotomy involved in such collaboration by parties that normally compete with one another, the relevance of multi-employer collective bargaining and its decline and what the prospects appear to be for the associations that remain.

However, before going any further we must point out that in this book we are concerned only with those associations that have an employee relations role, they may have a trade role as well but it is the employee relations role that concerns us. There are many trade and other associations of employers, chambers of commerce, rotary clubs, etc. that do not have such a role and these do not constitute employers associations for the purposes of this book.

Why employers form associations and their main roles

It might seem strange that employers form and join collective associations and that they act collaboratively within them given that in a capitalist system employers as producers and sellers of products and services in the same industry or area are commonly in competition with one another. There are a number of explanations for this and a brief consideration of these reasons also illustrates some of the more important roles of such organizations.

A study by the Commission on Industrial Relations in the UK (1972) suggested that:

> Employers organise for the economic purpose of influencing wage determination to their advantage and combine as a countervailing force to trade union organisation and as a defence against such trade union tactics as 'picking off' individual employers. p. 5.

Organization in these terms is initially a reactive or defensive measure, the employers form and join in response to the presence and activities of trade unions who will themselves seek to influence wage determination to their own advantage. When confronted with employers in a trade, sector or geographical area that are not organized it is possible for the union to decide which of the employers is in the weakest position and/or can afford to pay employees the most and to seek to negotiate an agreement with this single employer which they then seek to extend to the rest.

However, employers organize not only to prevent the bidding up of wages by the unions but also to stop particular employers gaining a competitive advantage by the undercutting of wages.

It is the desire to control and stabilize wages that in this instance encourages the formation of associations and their involvement in collective bargaining.

There are other reasons, the desire for stability and order has also encouraged many organizations to formulate and agree procedures and mechanisms external to the employing entity for the resolution of grievances and disputes.

The externalization of responsibility for the determination of terms and conditions of employment and the regulation of the employment relationship and resolution of grievances, etc. enabled companies to avoid the expense and hassle of employing its own expertise and dealing with their own industrial relations problems.

This externalization was criticized in the UK by the Donovan Commission Report in 1968 as being one of the reasons why informal systems of industrial relations had emerged in companies, one of the main 'problems' at the time. Employers were criticized for having abrogated their responsibilities and were encouraged to grasp the nettle and take responsibility for the conduct and management of industrial relations, to bring them back inside the employing organization.

In addition to these regulatory roles employers organizations, like trade unions, also provide advisory services to their members and represent their interests to other organizations and interest groups. Increasingly employers associations, especially those with a national constituency, also represent the interests of their members at an international level. They act as pressure groups. We noted earlier the increasing influence and more influential roles being performed by the social partners at the level of the EU.

It has been suggested that as the regulatory role of employers organizations has declined the priority attached to these other roles has been enhanced.

Other factors that are held to encourage the formation of employers organizations relate to the homogeneity of the product and labour markets, the extent to which the employers are producing the same product and require the same labour, and the extent to which employers are using the same technologies, in short the degree of common interest. The argument is that the greater the commonality of interest the greater are the chances and prospects of an employers organization being formed and being effective.

Hollinshead and Leat (1995) also point out the significance of the profile of the state as a factor influencing organization. Governments favouring corporatist structures and non-market coordination are likely to encourage the formation of collectives representing the interests of employers and employees whereas those favouring market freedom and a non-interventionist role for government are unlikely to provide such encouragement.

Hollinshead and Leat also provide information on the variations in organization, structure and purpose in a range of different countries.

The UK

In the UK the definition usually used is the legal one in TULR(C)A 1992, which states that an employers association:

> consists wholly or mainly of employers or individual owners of undertakings of one or more descriptions and whose principal purposes include the regulation of relations between employers of that description ... and workers or trade unions ...

In the UK the fate of employers associations since 1980 has in many ways mirrored that of the trade unions, numbers and membership have declined and they have been forced to appraise the services they offer their members and the reasons for their existence. This has encouraged the development of new and alternative roles as well as a refocussing and prioritizing of their functions. As companies internalized the regulation of terms and conditions of employment, subsequent to the recommendations of the Donovan Commission, they had a greater need for employee relations advice. These same recommendations are also credited with a measure of the responsibility for the subsequent decline in multi-employer bargaining and with the decline in the number and influence of employers organizations.

The retreat from voluntarism on the part of governments since the 1960s has also had an impact, as the volume and frequency of legislative intervention has increased so has the need of employing organizations for advice on their legal rights, responsibilities and obligations.

As one might expect it is the smaller employer that has the greatest need for these services, large and Multi-national employers are usually well able to look after their own interests in these arenas.

The climate created in 1979 and subsequently by the election of a Conservative government antagonistic to the trade unions and determined to reduce their influence, allied to their determination to pursue different economic priorities, also contributed to the decline in the bargaining role of employers associations and to the subsequent decline in numbers and members. The potency of the threat that the unions posed to an individual employer receded as did their ability to take effective action.

The decline in the number of employers associations in the UK can be detected from the Annual Reports of the Certification Officer. The report for 2006 lists 83 such associations at end of March 2006. This compares with 340 in 1979.

Summary

In this chapter we have focussed upon the emergence and development of HRM and its implications for the management of employee relations, noting in particular the emphasis that it tends to place upon the achievement of employee commitment. We have also distinguished between the hard and soft versions of HRM. Employee commitment is only one of a number of objectives that management may pursue through its management of employee relations and we have identified a number of others, noting that some argue that the dominant one may be control over the labour process. Management has a number of styles it may adopt; there are a number of models and the later ones try to encompass both individualism and collectivism and acknowledge the dynamic nature of style. You have also been made aware that some features of the external environment act as constraining influences upon the styles adopted by senior management.

One of the choices that management has in managing employee relations is to do so with or without trades unions and we have examined some of the advantages and disadvantages of each as well as identifying a number of different forms of managing without trades unions.

We also examined EI schemes designed to achieve employee commitment with the emphasis upon the steps management need to take and the conditions necessary for the effective implementation of such schemes.

Finally we examined briefly the employee relations roles of employer associations and the influences upon their formation. We also identified the significant decline in numbers in the UK and how the associations remaining have adapted to new circumstances so that now they provide an essentially advisory and representative role in contrast to their earlier active involvement in collective bargaining and the regulation of terms and conditions of employment.

Activities to test understanding

Activity 1

Take a look back at the material distinguishing soft and hard versions of HRM and try to work out for yourself where the following might fit on the spectrum:

- Personnel Management
- the models of Guest (1989) and Beer *et al.* (1984).

Activity 2

Look back at the various production strategies identified by Regini in **Chapter 2** and consider which of the varieties of HRM, hard or soft, would be appropriate in each scenario.

Activity 3

Drawing upon the material in this chapter and your reading of earlier chapters devise a list of what you think might be the employee relations objectives of employees.

Activity 4

Figure 8.5 indicates that the style adopted is a function of a range of circumstances and contexts. Make a list of those you can identify as relevant.

Activity 5

Look again at the material on HRM and PM and decide which of the styles in the Purcell and Ahlstrand matrix (**Figure 8.6**) seem to be consistent with the concept of HRM and its implications for the management of employee relations.

Activity 6

In the discussion of the impact that various external contexts and features may have upon management's choice of style in the management of employee relations, a number of comparisons were suggested. Consider each of the examples below and indicate in each case which style you think would be appropriate. You can use the Purcell and Ahlstrand model as the base for your answers:

1 Product market:
    (a) Fiercely price competitive and fashion-based.
    (b) Stable market not very competitive and with competition on quality rather than on price.
2 Technology:
    (a) long production run, capital intensive, low labour requirement and low labour cost per unit of process technology.
    (b) Small batch, multi-skilled, flexible specialization, relatively high labour costs.
3 Trades Unions:
    (a) Strong entrenched unions and a shortage of skills.
    (b) Trade union-free with plentiful supplies of skills.

Activity 7

Try to answer briefly the following questions without looking back at the text.

1 Identify some of the environmental constraints upon managerial styles.
2 What have been the major criticisms of early style models?
3 Make a list of the advantages of managing with trades unions.

Activity 8

Devise a profile of the kind of organization that is perhaps most likely to be non-union.

Activity 9

Identify the steps management should take and conditions necessary for the successful and effective implementation of EI.

References

Armstrong, M., 1995. *Personnel Management Practice*, 5th Edition. Kogan Page, London.

Beer, M., Spector, B., Lawrence, P.R., Quinn Mills, D. and Walton. R.E., 1984. *Managing Human Assets*. Free Press, New York.

Brewster, C. and Hegewisch, A. (eds), 1994. *Policy and Practice in European Human Resource Management*. Price Waterhouse/Cranfield Survey, Routledge, London.

Fox, A., 1974. *Beyond Contract*. Faber and Faber, London.

Freeman, R. and Medoff, J., 1984. *What do Trade Unions Do?* Basic Books, New York.

Gennard, J. and Judge, G., 2002. *Employee Relations*. CIPD, London.

Guest, D., 1995. Human resource management, trade unions and industrial relations. In Storey, J. (ed.), *Human Resource Management: A Critical Text*. Routledge, London.

Guest, D. and Hoque, K., 1994. The good, the bad and the ugly: employment relations in new non-union workplaces. *Human Resource Management Journal* 5(1): 1–14.

Guest, D., 1987. Human resource management and industrial relations. *Journal of Management Studies* 24(5): 503–521.

Guest, D., 1989. Human resource management: its implications for industrial relations and trade unions. In Storey, J. (ed.), *New Perspectives on Human Resource Management*. Routledge, London.

Herzberg, F., 1966. *Work and the Nature of Man.* World Publishing, Cleveland, Ohio.

Hofstede, G., 1991. *Cultures and Organisations: Software of the Mind.* McGraw Hill, London.

Hofstede, G., 1997. *Cultures and Organisations: Software of the Mind.* McGraw Hill, London.

Hollinshead, G. and Leat, M., 1995. *Human Resource Management: An International and Comparative Perspective on the Employment Relationship.* Pitman, London.

Kersley, B., Alpin, C., Forth, J., Bryson, A., Bewley, H., Dix, G. and Oxenbridge, S., 2005. *Inside the Workplace First Findings from the 2004 Workplace Employment Relations Survey (WERS 2004).*

Legge, K., 1989. Human resource management: a critical analysis. In Storey, J. (ed.), *New Perspectives on Human Resource Management.* Routledge, London.

Marchington, M. *et al.*, 1992. Recent Developments in Employee Involvement, Employment Department Research Series No. 1, London: HMSO.

Marchington, M. and Wilkinson, A., 1996. *Core Personnel and Development.* IPD, London.

Maslow, A., 1943. A theory of human motivation. *Psychological Review* 50: 370-396.

McGregor, D., 1960. *The Human Side of Enterprise.* McGraw Hill, New York.

McLoughlin, I. and Gourlay, S., 1994. *Enterprise Without Unions.* OUP, Oxford.

Poole, M. and Mansfield, R., 1992. Managers' attitudes to human resource management: rhetoric and reality. In Blyton, P. and Turnbull, P. (eds), *Reassessing Human Resource Management.* Sage, London.

Purcell, J. and Ahlstrand, B., 1989. The impact of corporate strategy and the management of employee relations in the multi-divisional company. *British Journal of Industrial Relations* 27(3): 397–417.

Purcell, J. and Ahlstrand, B., 1994. *Human Resource Management in the Multi-Divisional Company,* Oxford.

Purcell, J. and Gray, A., 1986. Corporate personnel departments and the management of industrial relations: two case studies in the management of ambiguity. *Journal of Management Studies* 23(2).

Purcell, J. and Sisson, K., 1983. Strategies and practice in the management of industrial relations. In Bain, G.S. (ed.), *Industrial Relations in Britain.* Blackwell, Oxford.

Regini, M., 1995. Firms and institutions: the demand for skills and their social production in Europe. *European Journal of Industrial Relations* 1(2): 191–202.

Schuler, R., Budwhar, P. and Florkowski, G., 2002. International human resource management: review and critique. *International Journal of Management Reviews.* 4(1): 41–70.

Storey, J. (ed.), 1989. *New Perspectives on Human Resource Management.* Routledge, London.

Storey, J., 1987. Developments in the management of human resources: an interim report. Warwick Papers In Industrial Relations No. 17, IRRU, School of Industrial and Business Studies, University of Warwick, November.

Storey, J. (ed.), 2001. *Human Resource Management; A Critical Text*, 2nd Edition. Thomson Learning, London.

Torrington, D., 1989. HRM and the personnel function. In Storey, J. (ed.), *New Perspectives on Human Resource Management*. Routledge, London.

Trompenaars, F., 1993. *Riding the Waves of Culture – Understanding Cultural Diversity in Business*. Economist Books, London.

Chapter 9

Employee relations processes

Introduction

In the first chapter we concluded that at the heart of the subject matter of employee relations was the employment relationship and the interactions of the various parties to that relationship. These interactions may be between individuals, employee and employer, or between collective organizations representing and acting as agents for individuals or, indeed, a mix of the two, an individual interacting with an organization. In this chapter we focus on some of these collective interactions.

We pointed out that there were different perspectives on and debates surrounding the nature of the employment relationship and that these would influence the perceived purpose of these interactions. In particular, we looked at different viewpoints on the issue of whether the interests of employees and employers coincide or conflict and the implications of these viewpoints both for individual and collective interactions. Academic viewpoints on this issue tend towards the view that there are probably elements of both, the relationship being characterized by both conflict and mutuality. If this is the case then the interactions are likely to serve a number of purposes including resolving conflicts between the parties as well as cooperation in pursuing mutual objectives. The interactions may be adversarial or cooperative in nature and form and it may be useful to refer again to Edwards' (1995) term 'structured antagonism' which he uses to characterize the relationship.

Whatever the perceived purpose of the interactions and the nature of the relationship, decision making may be unilateral, one of the parties makes the decision, or it may be joint, the parties make the decision together. Where the decisions are made by only one of the parties, the process leading up to that decision-making point may still be participative in that the other parties may have an opportunity to input their view, with this view being listened to and taken into account, prior to the decision being made. We noted in the previous chapter that, even where managements are seeking to introduce Employee Involvement (EI) schemes such as quality circles (QCs) and suggestion schemes, it is important that employees perceive management to be listening and that they do so before decisions are made. Truly joint decision making is where the parties make the decision together and where the decision is quite likely to take the form of an agreement.

However, you should not make the mistake of assuming that joint decisions are inevitably the product of cooperation or that it can only happen in a cooperative framework. Many joint decisions are the outcome of adversarial relations, are reached through a process of negotiation and are the product of compromises being made on all sides. The relative bargaining power of the parties to the interaction will have significant implications for the agreements arrived at through such a process.

The subject matter of this chapter is the main collective processes through which employee relations are regulated, conflicts are resolved and mutual interests pursued. The outcome of the process may be substantive terms and conditions of employment, such as rates of pay and hours of work, or it may be a new or revised policy or procedure for dealing with an issue such as equal opportunities or managing discipline and ensuring fairness and equity for all employees, or it may be concerned to establish the rules and conventions that will govern the actual interaction of the parties, how this should work and what their respective rights and obligations are to be in particular sets of circumstances.

Some of the processes can be wide ranging in terms of the subject matter dealt with, whereas others may be devised and intended to deal with specific issues. In examining these processes we will consider them in terms of whether they provide employees, usually through representatives, with opportunities to participate in decision making and thereby in the control and management of the assets, activities and direction of the enterprise.

The first section of the chapter examines the notion of employee participation and thereby provides a backdrop to the later consideration of:

- whether the processes do or do not provide employees with genuine participative opportunities;
- whether they are adversarial or cooperative in nature;
- whether they result in unilateral or joint decision making.

In addition to producing the kind of traditional substantive or procedural outcomes referred to above, the parties to these processes may perceive them as means of achieving other objectives and outcomes such as:

- enhanced EI;
- greater commitment on the part of employees to the goals and values of the organization as specified by management;
- greater employee satisfaction and motivation;
- production or service outcomes such as greater productivity or enhanced quality.

In a number of the preceding modules, including the last one, we have examined a number of initiatives and practices that some analysts would consider participative, such as: team briefing, QCs, problem-solving groups, team working and total quality management (TQM) and we are not going to examine these again. In this chapter the main focus is upon collective bargaining and joint consultation, the concept of bargaining power, the factors that may influence it and its relevance to the outcomes of employee relations processes.

In the following chapter we examine some of the specific policy and procedural outcomes of these processes.

Learning objectives

After studying this chapter you will be able to:

- discuss the concept of employee participation and the participatory potential of various employee relations processes;
- identify and distinguish the range of employee relations processes by which conflict may be resolved;
- explain the meaning and nature of collective bargaining;
- distinguish different models of joint consultation focusing upon the purposes of management and the degree of employee participation facilitated by them;
- understand the concept of bargaining power and how the balance of bargaining power influences bargaining outcomes.

Employee participation

Forms and paradigms

In capitalist systems, ownership tends to confer upon the owners the right to direct and control the assets and activities of the organization, and the legal system supports this distribution of power. Owners often appoint managers as their agents and it is these managers who claim the right to decide unilaterally, resting their claim upon their appointment as the agent of the owner(s) and also increasingly upon their expertise in performing these functions.

Employee participation, therefore, wherever and to the extent that it occurs, implies some diminution of these rights, some erosion of management's ability to decide issues unilaterally without consulting or paying any attention to the views or wishes of the labour force, a group who are after all one of the major stakeholders in the enterprise, its success and its future. Employee participation, therefore, implies an erosion of the traditional master–servant relationship.

Direct and indirect

Some forms of participation are direct and others indirect, the difference being in whether it is the employee him or herself that participates in the decision making or whether this participation is achieved through representatives.

Direct participation is logistically difficult on issues other than those that affect only a relatively small number of employees. Examples of decisions that may lend themselves to determination through direct participation might be decisions concerning workgroup matters such as the allocation of work, output quality or job redesign where the group members make the decision between themselves. It is in this kind of activity that EI initiatives may be participative. Decisions of a wider or more strategic nature are much more likely to be made through indirect or representative participatory mechanisms.

If we briefly examine some of the literature on the topic of employee participation and attempts at definition, we once again become aware that there are different perceptions of what the term means and thereby the extent to which processes are participative. For example, Walker (1974) argues that worker participation in management occurs when workers take part in 'the authority and managerial functions of the enterprise' indicating, as noted above, an erosion of managerial prerogative and change in the balance of power.

Some would see this as a relatively narrow definition and Strauss (1979) refers to three different participation models, each being distinguished on the dimension of the depth or the degree of workers' influence or control over management. Here, management relates primarily to the function rather than the people but inevitably there is a relationship between the two:

- **Consultative participation**: gives workers and/or their representatives the right (or opportunity) to be informed, to give a view or to raise objections but, crucially, the right to decide remains with management, their prerogative remains intact.
- **Co-management**: employees share the right to decide; they have joint decision-making powers with management and this may well translate into an effective right of veto, the consent of both parties being required before action can be taken.
- **Self-management by workers**: describes a scenario in which it is the employees either directly or through representatives that alone have the role of decision making; this may be by virtue of the employees being the owners of the enterprise.

Part of the value of this concern with the depth or degree of influence or control is that it points up the significance of **power**, the ability to influence and there are many potential sources of power and many influences upon them.

Traditionally employees and their representative associations have sought to gain power first of all through membership numbers and strength and then through a collective control over the supply of labour and thereby the job. Examples of the latter may be the pace of work, the degree of fragmentation, issues of quality and quality assurance and the allocation of work. Having obtained the power it has to be effectively exerted if employee objectives are to be realized and in the UK, the USA and many of the countries in the EU, the mechanism used to exert this power has most commonly been collective bargaining (which we examine in a subsequent section).

Both employees and employers sometimes resort to the use of industrial action and the imposition of sanctions upon the employer/employee as part of this power-based process.

In either event the depth of participation achieved through collective bargaining is likely to be a function, at least in part, of the relative power of the parties. Power is a factor in determining both the nature and extent of employee participation in any particular organization, country or time.

Further evidence of the range of definitions and interpretations can be detected from the work of Marchington *et al.* (1992). In this work they identify what they refer to as four paradigms or models of participation, each of which is distinguished on the basis of motive as well as on outcome in terms of the redistribution of power, and each of which can be seen to rest upon different underlying assumptions. The four paradigms are:

1   The control/labour process paradigm which perceives employee participation to result in a transfer of control of the labour process from management to employees.

2   The cooperation/industrial relations paradigm which links participation with conflict resolution, cooperation and with efficiency. Underpinning assumptions include a plurality of interests within organizations, conflict between them and the need to reconcile that conflict. Collective bargaining and consultation are perceived to be mechanisms through which employees can participate, conflict can be efficiently resolved and cooperation may also be enhanced.

3   The satisfaction/quality of working life (QWL) paradigm which assumes a link between employee participation and job satisfaction, the assumption being that enhanced participation leads to enhanced satisfaction. This is a notion that has much in common with initiatives and practices which focus upon job design and self-control of the task and immediate task environment. The participation envisaged in this paradigm is job- or task-centred with employees deriving satisfaction from an expansion or enrichment of their role, yielding them greater responsibility and authority. We are not looking here at a model that implies an erosion of managerial authority or autonomy, or indeed one that has much to do with reconciling inherent conflicts of interests.

4   The commitment/human resource management (HRM) paradigm, in which positive relationships are perceived to exist between employee participation and employee commitment to the objectives and values of the enterprise, and between such commitment and enhanced performance and productivity. Committed employees work harder and are more productive. We examined the pursuit of employee commitment in the preceding module.

We noted above that capitalist systems tend to support the rights and interests of employers and managers before those of the employees. Some of the arguments in favour of greater employee participation through employee relations processes such as collective bargaining, as well as through other methods, rest upon notions of morality and democracy; that as major stakeholders in the success of the enterprise employees have a moral right to participate in the managerial function, decision making and control. In the context of this argument, employee participation is a reflection of political democracy, that the governed have the right to exercise some control over those in authority. This is not a view that sits comfortably with the view that businesses are not democracies and that management should be allowed to exercise their expertise on behalf of shareholder value.

Continuum of participation

As noted above, in some instances employee participation will extend to joint decision making but in most, this is not what happens; management retains the right or ability to make the decision unilaterally, but employees play a participative role prior to the decision being made.

If we concentrate for a moment on this issue and if we view the various processes in terms of the extent to which they provide the participants with a full or partial share in decision making and therefore in control, it is possible to devise a continuum of participation (see **Figure 9.1**). This shows that at either end there is no sharing, only unilateral decision making or complete autonomy for one of the actors and none for the other. Terms commonly used for each of these extreme positions are managerial prerogative, where management has complete autonomy, and workers control where there is no participation by management/employer. In between these extremes lies a range of mechanisms and processes, each of which can be seen to demonstrate/exhibit different combinations of employee and employer autonomy and thereby different degrees of employee participation. As you can see from the figure, there are different forms of consultation and each implies a different degree of employee participation.

We have included in the figure, for the purposes of comparison, a couple of EI initiatives or processes which some might argue are participative but which in this context are demonstrably not. They may result in greater variety and satisfaction for employees, they may result in more information and greater EI but they are not participatory in the sense of providing employees with the opportunity to participate in decision making.

Which decisions?

We have been talking about participation in decision making without yet addressing the important issue of 'which decisions?'. 'Which areas of subject matter are we concerned with?' Perhaps inevitably there is a wide range of subject matter over which rights to autonomy are claimed by each side and there is often little consensus.

Many would argue that business decisions such as those concerning investment, location, expansion, competitive strategy, production systems and the technology to be employed should be the preserve of

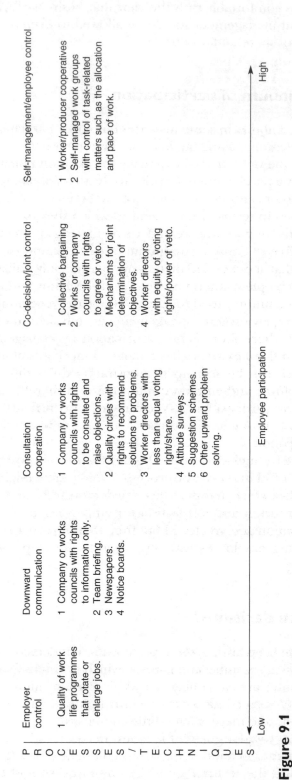

Figure 9.1

Continuum illustrating degree of depth of employee participation in decision making/control. Adapted from Leat (1998).

management. When it comes to issues specific to the management of labour, again many would suggest that management should retain prerogative over matters such as hiring and firing, promotions, transfers, discipline and the implementation of existing rules.

It is worth pointing out that in other countries within the EU, and perhaps particularly in Germany, there are very different traditions and many decisions are actually subject to employee assent through the mechanism of the works council – (see below). What this means in reality is that the works council has the ability, enshrined in legislation, to veto proposals in certain areas; if the employee representatives comprising the works council do not assent to the proposal it cannot proceed.

Another interesting dimension of the situation in Germany is that the works council also has other legal rights, on some issues to be consulted and on others to be informed, and this distinction is indicative of different degrees and forms of employee participation to which we also return later in this section.

Works Councils in Germany then have a range of legal rights, to co-decision making or co-determination on some issues, information and consultation on others and to information only on yet others. In each of these cases the degree or depth of participation can be perceived to be different and we have located each of them in **Figure 9.1** in order to illustrate this.

There is no similar tradition of works councils with legislatively conferred rights in the UK, though as we noted in the earlier chapter on the European Union, employees and their representatives do have legislatively supported rights to be given information and consulted in certain specific situations, for example when the ownership of an undertaking is to be transferred and when there is a likelihood of collective redundancies, another example of rights being linked to particular areas of subject matter.

Rights to participate are by no means always the product of legislative intervention and it is common for what we tend to call the scope of collective bargaining and joint consultation (see next sections) to itself be the product of bargaining between the parties.

There are then no easy solutions to the question of whether employees should participate, what the nature or degree or depth of the participation should be or indeed to the question of the scope of that participation. Sometimes employers will seek employee participation, for example in relation to task or quality issues; sometimes employees will fight for it and secure it through bargaining or exercising their power in some other way; sometimes it will result from legislative intervention. We pursue this issue of scope in the next sections on collective bargaining and consultation; however, you may find it useful to seek to distinguish between 'How?' and 'What?' decisions, with management arguably more willing to grant employees a degree of autonomy or influence in decisions concerned with the How than with the What. The distinction here is between being able to determine the objectives (the What), for example production targets in terms of both quantity and quality, and decisions relating to the How in terms of the means of organizing, allocating and inspecting work so as to achieve the objectives set.

Collective bargaining

There are several definitions of collective bargaining, each slightly different (see **Figure 9.2**).

The essence of the process is that employees and/or their representatives, and employers and/or their representatives negotiate with one another with a view to reaching an agreement on a range of issues. The scope and range of the possible subject matter is very wide and can encompass pretty well anything that concerns work and the employment relationship: terms and conditions of employment and working conditions are certainly encompassed. The process need not be formal and it is a fallacy to assume that collective bargaining only occurs within the confines of formal institutional arrangements. Experienced practitioners on both sides will usually readily acknowledge the value and frequency of informal negotiations and the agreements arrived at.

The single feature of the process that sets it aside from other joint employee relations processes is the intention to reach agreement. When parties enter into and engage in collective bargaining, they are overtly or tacitly agreeing to share the decision making on the particular

---

The International Labour Office (1986, Convention No. 154) defines collective bargaining as encompassing:

> all negotiations between employers (or employers' organizations) and workers' organizations for the purpose of determining relations between them.

Gospel and Palmer (1993: 15) describe it as

> a process by which trades unions and similar associations representing groups of employees, negotiate with employers or their representatives with the object of reaching collective agreements.

Salamon (1992: 309) defines it as a

> method of determining terms and conditions of employment which utilises the process of negotiation and agreement between representatives of management and employees.

Figure 9.2

issue, with the outcome to be subject to agreement. If there is not this intention to reach agreement, then the process is not collective bargaining. Central also is the willingness to move and compromise, the willingness to negotiate. It is then a process that has as its intended outcomes jointly agreed decisions.

Students sometimes make the mistake of thinking that collective bargaining is the only employee relations process or scenario in which negotiations occur. This is not the case and it is quite common for management and employees and their respective representatives to negotiate in other circumstances, such as when an individual grievance is heard.

Collective bargaining as a process occurs for a number of reasons, one of which is the mutual dependence of the parties to the employment relationship; each of the parties needs the other and it is this mutual need that encourages them to try and reach agreement and resolve conflicts through negotiations. Each has something that the other needs and wants; for example, the employee has his labour to sell and the employer needs to acquire and use that labour in the production or delivery of goods and services. However, the employee needs to try and obtain the best possible price for his labour whereas the employer's interest is to pay as little as possible for the labour resource.

Collective bargaining varies on a range of different dimensions, whether they are legally enforceable, (in many countries they are whereas the UK is unusual in that they are not), the scope of the bargaining, the level at which it takes place and the nature of the bargaining, by which we mean whether it is predominantly adversarial or cooperative. In this section we concentrate mainly on the dimensions of scope and level; however, before doing so we will briefly address the issue of nature.

In the UK there is a tradition of adversarial, rather than cooperative, bargaining in which each party seeks to exert pressure upon the other in order to persuade them to move towards a compromise position. It is for this reason that the process is sometimes referred to as being power based and the concept of bargaining power (see later) is integral to the process and to an understanding of the outcomes. Collective bargaining has also been distinguished according to whether it is distributive or integrative. Distributive bargaining tends to be adversarial in nature as the parties negotiate shares of a relatively fixed resource whereas integrative bargaining tends to be more cooperative as the parties seek to find solutions to problems and through cooperation to expand the resource available. Perspectives which emphasize the common interests of employees and employers are likely also to emphasize a form of bargaining in which the parties seek to cooperate, in which they work together in partnership for their mutual benefit. Those perspectives which perceive the interests of employees and employers to be in conflict are more likely to countenance approaches which are more adversarial, where one party tends to win or gain at the expense of the other. In the UK in recent years a lot of emphasis has been put by government and other interested parties on the non-adversarial, partnership, approach. We noted earlier in **Chapter 8** that there had been considerable emphasis upon seeking committed employees through EI programmes and the cooperative, partnership approach to collective bargaining is much more consistent with this than are adversarial forms of bargaining.

Bargaining scope

The range of subject matter which may be the subject of collective bargaining can be wide or narrow. Often the scope of bargaining is described as being either pay or non-pay issues. Non-pay issues might include:

- physical working conditions;
- staffing levels;
- the size of redundancy payments, the numbers to be made redundant;
- working hours;
- the introduction of change;
- a range of procedures including bargaining arrangements, discipline and grievance, redundancy and what to do in the event of a failure to agree.

You will remember that in **Chapter 1** we examined the concept of an industrial relations system where the outcomes are identified as being both substantive and procedural and, while this distinction is not precisely the same as that between pay and non-pay, there are similarities, with substantive issues being interpreted as factors upon which it is possible to put a price.

The initial stimulus for collective bargaining tends to come from the trade unions rather than employers and in the first instance bargaining tends to be concerned with pay and related issues. However, it is commonly not long before the parties realize that they need to agree between themselves just how they are going to conduct the bargaining on the basis of:

- what is to be acceptable or not in terms of the behaviour of the parties;
- what rights and obligations they are to have to each other;
- whether industrial action is to be allowed;
- what constraints are to be imposed upon the use of industrial action;
- how often they are to meet;
- whether the agreements reached are to be legally binding and for a fixed term?

These procedural issues and agreements can be seen as the parties determining for themselves the rules within which they will operate and it is this which has encouraged the view that collective bargaining is at heart a rule-making process, the rules providing part of the context within which the parties to the employment relationship interact with each other. A process that in part results in a system, voluntarily agreed and implemented, of industrial governance, they form their own rules and conventions to govern their relationship.

In discussing this, Farnham and Pimlott (1995) suggest that 'Underlying the concept of collective bargaining as a process of industrial governance is the principle that those who are integral to the running of the enterprise should have some voice in determining the decisions of most concern to them'. Again, as mentioned above, we are confronted by the political and moral dimensions of employee participation.

As the area of subject matter (sometimes you will find the term 'scope' used in this context) that is subject to joint determination through collective bargaining expands, so also does the participation of the employees, through their trade union, in the management of the enterprise. As the scope of collective bargaining expands, the area of managerial prerogative should logically diminish.

Bargaining level

You must also beware of thinking that collective bargaining only occurs at one level within any particular industry, sector or organization. It is common in many countries and industries for bargaining to occur at a number of different levels and for the bargaining at each particular level to deal with different subject matter, so that within one industry you might have:

- Bargaining at the level of the industry that dealt with certain subject matter, such as minimum rates of pay or national levels of holiday entitlement.
- Bargaining at the level of the firm where other subjects are dealt with; an example in this context might be the firm's occupational pension scheme or particular shift work pattern or, indeed, the interpretation and implementation of the national level agreement.
- Bargaining at the level of the division or at the level of the workplace where other matters might be dealt with, such as enhancements to national terms and conditions of employment to enable the firm to compete in the local labour market and the implications of the introduction of new working methods or technology.

It is not uncommon to find procedures being agreed at national level which seek to determine how issues are to be dealt with at the various possible lower levels.

In the era of globalization and increasing international competition combined with the new production regimes emphasizing labour flexibility and the pursuit of continuous improvement and the need for an increased speed of decision making within organizations, employers and some governments have expressed a preference for reducing the extent and scope of multi-employer bargaining, for example, at a national or sectoral level. There are many reasons why employers and government may prefer to decentralize the level at which collective bargaining takes place:

1   To achieve a greater congruence with the level of business decision making. There has been a significant decentralization of this process also, a response often to the need to be more flexible and more responsive to the requirements of the customer. It can also be perceived as an aid to the creation of a divisional or subsidiary identity.

2   To facilitate the introduction of local pay bargaining, national level pay bargaining may well result in rates in a local labour market which are higher than they need to be to attract the requisite labour and so decentralization in such a context is perceived as a way of reducing costs. An example of this has occurred in the UK public sector with successive governments in the 1980s and 1990s convinced that local pay bargaining would result in a lower overall pay bill.

3   Contrary to 1 above, to actually separate the levels of collective bargaining and business decision making, thereby giving management more freedom to act. If decisions to invest and locate are taken at corporate level it might be preferable to keep the unions away from this level so that they find it difficult to apply pressure at the appropriate level and time. This is sometimes known as a process of institutional separation.

4   To enhance management control or influence over the bargaining outcomes; in a system of multi-employer bargaining, individual employers can exert little influence over the outcomes. The additional strength provided by employers combining together to combat strong trade union movements is much less necessary when the strength and influence of trade unions decline as they have in many developed countries as traditional trade union strongholds in manufacturing and extractive industries have declined in significance and the new service sector industries have grown.

Decentralization does not only occur from multi-employer to single employer bargaining; it may also occur within organizations. Purcell

(1989) produced an interesting catalogue of the issues that management should consider when deciding whether to decentralize collective bargaining or not and there are many combinations of circumstances. It is clear from his analysis that there are no common recipes for success; in some circumstances centralization at the level of the company may be the beneficial solution; in others it would be decentralization to lower levels within the company. He produced something akin to a checklist that management could use if it was considering decentralization. He suggests that prior to making a decision on the issue management should consider:

1　the impact upon existing procedures and arrangements;
2　the role, structure and staffing of the personnel function;
3　the role of the first line supervisor and the impact of decentralized bargaining upon it;
4　the impact upon the representatives of the trade unions, the shop stewards and the full-time officials;
5　the impact of decentralization upon the integration of policy, strategy and practice;
6　the impact of the change upon consistency across the company.

We noted in the earlier chapter on MNCs that international trades unions are keen to develop bargaining structures within MNCs which are international but we also noted that there has so far been relatively little success. Efforts to achieve this objective being hampered by the difficulties the unions themselves have in coordinating their activities across national borders and, of course, resistance from the companies themselves. This resistance may be for a number of reasons, for example:

■　they may be pursuing polycentric approaches to employee relations in different subsidiaries;
■　they may also want to continue to be able to play one subsidiary off against another so that they can squeeze concessions out of workers;
■　they may be concerned to decentralize bargaining for the reasons specified above.

Experience in the UK

We have noted in the chapter looking at ideology and the roles of government (**Chapter 5**) that collective bargaining was supported as part of the voluntarist tradition as the process that provided the means through which employees could collectively seek to remedy the imbalance of power between employer and individual employee normally seen to exist in favour of employers (capital) in the labour market.

The tradition in the UK prior to 1980 was of main terms and conditions of employment being determined through collective bargaining and at a national or multi-employer level .The Donovan Commission Report (1968) had criticized employers in the private sector for abdicating their responsibilities for the conduct of industrial relations within their own companies and it had recommended a greater incidence of bargaining at the level of the firm, otherwise and commonly referred to as single employer bargaining.

We noted earlier in **Chapter 7** on trade unions, that the WERS 2004 data indicates that the percentage of all workplaces in which a trade union was recognized for the purposes of collective bargaining had declined from 66 per cent in 1984 to 30 per cent in 2004. It also shows that collective bargaining has continued to decline as a mechanism for the determination of pay.

The percentage of workplaces engaging in any collective bargaining over pay fell from 30 per cent in 1998 to 22 per cent in 2004. The decline was largely confined to the private sector, where the incidence fell from 17 per cent in 1998 to 11 per cent of workplaces in 2004. In the public sector the incidence of collective bargaining has remained broadly constant, with 77 per cent of public-sector workplaces using collective bargaining in 2004 compared with 79 per cent in 1998.

The WERS 2004 data also shows that the proportion of employees who have their pay set through collective bargaining has also declined. In 2004, 35 per cent (38 per cent in 1998) of employees had their pay set through collective bargaining. The decline was largely accounted for by a rise in the percentage of employees whose pay was set by management (up from 49 to 57 per cent). However, the picture differed markedly across sectors of the economy. In private manufacturing, 34 per cent of employees had their pay set through collective bargaining in 2004, (43 per cent in 1998). It also fell a little in private services – from 20 to 18 per cent. However, it rose in the public sector from 66 to 75 per cent. These figures are close to those obtained through the Labour Force Survey – see table … in the chapter on trades unions.

We noted earlier, that the scope of collective bargaining can be either wide or narrow and the trend in the UK over recent years has definitely been in the direction of a narrowing of this scope and a widening of the area of unilateral determination by management.

The WERS 2004 also investigated the joint regulation of a range of other terms and conditions of employment. Managers were asked whether they normally negotiated with, consulted, or informed union or non-union representatives over 12 terms and conditions of employment, including pay – see **Figure 9.3**.

The extent of the unilateral determination of terms and conditions of employment in the UK in the early part of the 21st century is dramatically illustrated by the data obtained. In two-thirds of workplaces (67 per cent) management did not inform, consult or negotiate with employees on any of the 12 listed items. Management were most likely to negotiate over pay, followed by hours and holidays, and least likely to negotiate over staffing plans, training and staff selection.

The crucial role played by trades unions in encouraging management to engage in joint decision making is still clearly visible in the **Figure 9.3**. The figures in brackets are the equivalents for workplaces where there are recognized trade unions. In the absence of a recognized union, management on average only negotiated, consulted or informed employees on one of the 12 items. In unionized workplaces, managers negotiated, consulted or informed employees on an average of nine items.

Table 7 Joint regulation of terms and conditions[a,b]

	% of workplaces			
	Nothing	*Inform*	*Consult*	*Negotiate*
Issue				
Pay	70(16)	6(10)	5(13)	18(61)
Hours	71(18)	5(10)	8(20)	16(53)
Holidays	71(19)	9(17)	5(13)	15(52)
Pensions	73(22)	11(25)	6(16)	10(36)
Staff selection	78(42)	10(26)	9(23)	3(9)
Training	75(36)	10(24)	13(31)	3(9)
Grievance procedure	69(15)	9(20)	14(36)	9(28)
Disciplinary procedure	69(15)	9(21)	13(35)	8(29)
Staffing plans	75(33)	11(26)	12(34)	3(7)
Equal opportunities	72(22)	10(23)	14(40)	5(15)
Health and safety	69(17)	9(19)	17(49)	5(15)
Performance appraisal	75(33)	9(20)	12(33)	4(14)

Base: All workplaces with 10 or more employees.
Figures are weighted and based on responses from at least 2007 managers.
Notes:
[a] Managerial respondent was asked 'whether management normally negotiates, consults informs or does not involve unions' on 12 items. Also asked with respect to non-union employee representatives.
[b] Figures in parentheses relate to workplaces with recognized trades unions and are based on responses from at least 1004 managers.

Figure 9.3
Trade unions in joint decision making (*Source*: WERS 2004).

The scale of the decline in the proportions of workplaces in which trades unions are recognized for collective bargaining and in which there is any collective bargaining over pay and other terms and conditions of employment, combined with the increase in the proportions of workplaces where there is no trade union presence (see chapter on trades unions), raises serious doubts about the ability of the unions in the UK to retrieve their role as collective bargaining institutions. We noted in the chapter on trades unions that the new legislative provisions regarding trade union recognition may have contributed to a relative stabilization but that there is little, if any, evidence of a reversal of the trends of the last 25 years.

In addition, it is clear that there has been a decentralization of bargaining from multi-employer to enterprise level, the 1998 WERS again confirming this trend with the proportion of employees covered by multi-employer bargaining declining from 82 to 39 per cent over the period 1984 to 1998.

There are also significant differences in both the extent and level of bargaining between the various sectors within the economy. Collective bargaining is still at its most extensive within the public sector and it still occurs at a national level in this sector to a greater extent than in other sectors. Manufacturing industry runs second to the public sector and the service sector demonstrates the least reliance upon collective bargaining for the determination of terms and conditions of employment and it is least likely to demonstrate national or multi-employer bargaining.

In addition to a shift from multi-employer to single employer bargaining, there has been a shift downwards within large companies from bargaining at the level of the firm to bargaining at the level of the division or other business unit, region or establishment: a decentralization within organizations as well as decentralization from multi-employer to single employer. This decentralization has been much more common in the private sector and, despite the open desire of government to achieve a measure of decentralization within the public sector, here it has been much less successful, partially because the unions have generally opposed the proposals.

We noted in the earlier chapter on trade unions (**Chapter 7**) that the union movement in the UK has been engaged in a change of direction in terms of its objectives and its approach and that there has been a formal shift by the Trades Union Congress (TUC) in the direction of cooperation and the conclusion of partnership agreements. It is possible that such agreements may include a diminished or even negligible role for collective bargaining and its replacement by some form of consultation arrangement.

Joint consultation

There are different perceptions about the nature of joint consultation, what it is and what it should be. There are different versions and the parties may well have different motives, objectives and very different expectations of the outcomes. Managers will often consult with employees on an individual basis or collectively but outside formal joint consultative machinery, for example within the aegis of a team briefing. Our concern here is with the formal joint consultative machinery and the nature of the process. In examining the nature of the process, Farnham and Pimlott (1995) distinguish between:

1 **Pseudo-consultation**, which refers to the process whereby management or union is doing no more than passing information without giving the other party the opportunity to comment or without listening genuinely to the comments that are made. Commonly manageme3nt is communicating a decision that is already firmly made. The intention is often not to consult but to give the impression that you are. In such circumstances the process cannot be regarded as one in which employees and their representatives are given the opportunity to participate in decision making.

2 **Classical consultation**, which describes the process when employees representatives are given information, often in the form of proposals or intentions, and asked for their views. When received, the views are considered prior to the decision being made. While the process differs from collective bargaining in that there is no commitment even of a moral nature that the process should end in agreement, it is nevertheless in such genuine circumstances possible for the employees' views to influence the decision eventually made and for the process therefore to be classified as a participative one. There is no obligation on either side that goes beyond listening and considering. Management does not give up any of its prerogative in entering into this process, it retains the right to decide the issue unilaterally, though there is the risk that the process will fall into disrepute if management is not seen over a period of time to take note at least sometimes of the views expressed and on occasion to modify its position prior to taking the decision.

3 **Integrative consultation**, which is described as a mechanism for furthering employee participation in management and is presented as a process of joint decision making on a range of subject matter that is wider than the norm for collective bar gaining. The process is commonly much more like a process of joint problem solving.

Marchington (1988) has identified four different models or faces of joint consultation and this typology is useful in that it identifies purpose and motive as variables. The four faces are the:

1   **Non-union model**, which is very similar to the pseudo form of consultation described above and has as its objective the prevention of unionism in the workplace by appearing to give employee representatives a role in decision making but generally the process is little more than educative.
2   **Competitive model**, where the intention is to create a process that competes with collective bargaining and thereby reduces the perceived value and need for collective bargaining.
3   **Adjunct model**, where intent is to distinguish collective bargaining from joint consultation by emphasizing and contrasting the high trust and open interactions of this process with collective bargaining, which tends to be less open and trusting and again it is argued that problem solving is common to this model.
4   **Marginal model**, where the intention is to keep employee representatives busy in the joint consultative machinery but at a low level, thereby hopefully dissipating any pressure that may have developed for more meaningful relations within either consultation or bargaining machinery.

Joint consultation is a process that includes the works council. Works councils have not been common in the UK but are common in many countries within the rest of the EU.

Works councils can take a number of forms and there is no one blueprint. The term is used in some countries in Europe to apply to groups of employee representatives only who meet together as the works council and also the council may then meet with management. In other countries the term 'works council' refers to the joint meeting of management and employee representatives and the council in these systems comprises both management and employee representatives. In a number of EU countries there are legal rights to form a works council, for that council to meet with management on a regular basis and for the meeting to have an agenda that is itself legally prescribed. It is also possible for the councils to have different legal rights in terms of the right to information, consultation and the right to agree or veto proposals, depending upon the subject matter under discussion.

Though there are pressures for change the system that has dominated the post-War period in Germany (see **Figure 9.4**) is an example of one which is legally underpinned and which has traditionally encompassed these three sets of rights. Which right applies is dependent upon the subject matter.

Whilst not common perhaps there are examples of joint consultative arrangements in companies in the UK that also differentiate the rights of the employee representatives according to the subject matter. The

The works council is the established and legislatively supported mechanism for achieving employee participation within the workplace.

The Works Constitution Acts of 1952 and 1972 constitute the major supporting legislation, although works councils have a history going back to World War I. This legislation, in addition to requiring the establishment of works councils, also regulates the subject matter and nature of their role.

The works councils are not trade union bodies, the members of the council being elected from amongst employees with no requirement that they are trade union members.

The role of the councils varies according to the nature of the subject matter. Three distinct roles are identifiable, that is, the right to give consent, the right to consultation and the right to information.

The right to consent covers a range of economic and personnel issues including discipline, overtime and holiday allocations and schedules, payment systems, piecework rates, safety, welfare, employee performance, the pace of work, working environment, staff selection and training.

Rights to information and consultation relate to a range of production and business matters, although when it comes to business performance and prospects, the rights are limited to those of information only.

Overall, the role of the works council is to look after and protect the interests and safety of employees and, in this respect in particular, it has a monitoring role in respect of company compliance with appropriate legislation.

The nature of the relationship between the main actors is a traditionally consensual one and this is supported by the legislative requirement that they work together in a spirit of mutual trust and for their mutual benefit.

Figure 9.4
Works Councils in Germany. Adapted from Hollinshead and Leat (1995), pp. 192–3.

following is an extract from the first section of an agreement in a manufacturing operation in the UK:

Function of the JCC.

1.1　For employee representatives and the Company's management to convey and discuss any legitimate concerns relating to performance efficiency, operating conditions and facts, and the general conditions of employment.

1.2　To receive, from the Company's management, information on the company's current trading position and future prospects.

This particular Company also requires that employee representatives agree in writing that they will abide by a secrecy agreement safeguarding company information.

Collective bargaining tends to be between recognized trade unions and employers' representatives. Joint consultation may involve trade unions representing the employees but it is also quite common for the process of consultation, even within formal structures, to include as representatives of the employees individual employees elected by their peers or selected and appointed by management.

We noted above the disputes in the early 1990s between the UK government and the EC as to whether the legislation implementing the directives concerned with the requirement for employers to consult on matters relating to collective redundancies and the transfer of an undertaking should specify employee representatives (the directives) or trade union officials (the UK legislation).

Joint consultation in the UK

Joint consultation in its formal guise has not been as popular in the UK as elsewhere in Europe and it has not been as common as collective bargaining.

Nevertheless, evidence from the WERS 2004 suggests that it is not only collective bargaining which is in decline in the UK. When examining the incidence of formal joint consultative arrangements, they found that Joint Consultative Committees (JCC) were present in only 14 per cent (20 per cent in 1998) of workplaces with 10 or more employees in 2004. A further 25 per cent (27 per cent in 1998) of workplaces did not have a workplace-level committee, but had a consultative forum that operated at a higher level in the organization.

Workplace-level JCC were much more common in larger workplaces and overall 42 per cent (46 per cent in 1998) of all employees worked in a workplace with a workplace-level JCC.

The survey also probed the topics discussed at these formal meetings and, in relation to the committee that dealt with the widest range of issues, the findings were:

- future plans (81 per cent);
- work organization (81 per cent);
- employment issues (78 per cent);
- production issues (71 per cent);
- financial issues (65 per cent).

Employment and financial issues were each more likely to have been discussed if trade union representatives sat on the committee compared with committees comprised wholly of non-union representatives.

These WERS 2004 findings, and those reported earlier on the joint regulation of terms and conditions of employment, have implications for the introduction of the new legislative requirements detailed in **Figure 9.5** below.

It would seem fair to conclude that, in the absence of a statutory requirement, employers in the UK do not believe in the value of either informing or consulting with their employees and their representatives, whether this be in formal or informal arrangements.

This lack of apparent enthusiasm for voluntarily entering into information and consultative arrangements with their employees highlights both the need for the new legislation detailed below in **Figure 9.5** and the scale of the difficulties that may be experienced in making them work.

However, it must be remembered that there are other mechanisms through which management may seek to consult employees, such as attitude surveys, team briefings, QCs and suggestion schemes.

Who will be affected?

The Regulations will give employees in larger undertakings – those with 50 or more employees – rights to be informed and consulted on a regular basis about issues in the business they work for.

The Regulations will apply to undertakings with:

150+ employees from April 2005;
100+ employees from April 2007 and
50+ employees from April 2008.

The Regulations will apply to public and private undertakings which carry out an 'economic activity' whether or not operating for profit. This covers companies, partnerships, cooperatives, mutuals, building societies, friendly societies, associations, trade unions, charities and individuals who are employers, if they carry out an economic activity. It may also cover schools, colleges, universities, NHS trusts, and central and local Government bodies, again, if they carry out an economic activity. The precise scope of the terms 'undertaking' and 'economic activity' will ultimately be for the courts to decide.

Overview of the Regulations

The legislation is triggered when a valid employee request to negotiate an Information and Consultation (I&C) agreement is made, or an employer starts the process on his own initiative. The agreement must set out how the employer will inform and consult employees or their representatives on an on-going basis. The Regulations will also provide for the retention of pre-existing agreements which have workforce support. Where the parties fail to negotiate an agreement the Regulations will allow for standard I&C provisions to be applied. The Regulations are designed to minimize the potential for disputes arising throughout the process but, where these do occur and cannot be settled, will provide for the Central Arbitration Committee to resolve them.

Key aspects of the Information and Consultation Regulations

Within the general process there are a number of important steps. Some of the more significant are listed below.

* An employee request to negotiate an I&C agreement must be made by at least 10 per cent of the employees in the undertaking (*subject to a minimum of 15 and a maximum of 2500 employees*).
* Upon receipt of a valid request an employer must negotiate an agreement **unless there is a valid pre-existing agreement in place** (see below).
* There is a 3-year moratorium on employee requests where: (1) a negotiated agreement is already in force, or (2) the standard I&C provisions apply, or (3) an earlier employee request to negotiate a new I&C agreement in place of a pre-existing agreement was not endorsed by the workforce in a ballot.
* Employers must initiate negotiations for an agreement no later than 3 months after a valid request is made. During this 3-month period the employer must make arrangements for the appointment or election of employee negotiating representatives.
* All negotiated agreements must:
  (i)   set out the circumstances in which employers will inform and consult their employees;
  (ii) provide either for employee I&C representatives or for information and consultation directly with employees (or both);
  (iii) be in writing and dated;

Figure 9.5

Regulations for the implementation of the EC Directive on Information and Consultation at a national level in the UK.

- cover all the employees of the undertaking;
  - (v) be signed by the employer and
  - (vi) be approved by the employees.
- More detailed issues such as method, subject matter, frequency and timing of information and consultation arrangements will be for the parties to agree.
- Agreements may cover more than one undertaking or make provision for different arrangements within different parts of an undertaking.
- The standard I&C provisions in the Regulations will apply where an employer fails to initiate negotiations following a valid employee request or where negotiations fail to lead to an agreement. The Regulations will allow for employers and I&C representatives to come to a different negotiated agreement at anytime after the standard provisions are applied.
- Where the standard I&C provisions apply, employee I&C representatives are to be elected and the employer must inform and consult in the way set out in the Regulations, namely:

Information on:
(i) recent and probable development of the undertaking's activities and economic situation; and

Information and **consultation** on:
(ii) the situation, structure and probable development of employment within the undertaking and, in particular, on any anticipatory measures envisaged where there is a threat to employment within the undertaking; and

Information and **consultation with a view to reaching agreement** on:
(iii) decisions likely to lead to substantial changes in work organization or in contractual relations.

- Decisions in category *(iii)* above will include decisions on collective redundancies and business transfers – areas which are already covered by existing legal obligations to consult employee representatives. However, employers will not need to consult on these matters under the standard I&C provisions where they notify I&C representatives, on a case-by-case basis, that they will be consulting under the legislation on collective redundancies or business transfers. Employers may wish to include a provision addressing this issue in any negotiated agreement.

Employers may, on confidentiality grounds, restrict information provided to employee representatives in the legitimate interests of the undertaking. They may also withhold information from them altogether where its disclosure would be prejudicial to, or seriously harm the functioning of the undertaking.

In the case of a negotiated agreement under the Regulations, or where the standard I&C provisions have been applied, complaints of failure to abide by the agreement or the standard provisions may be brought to the Central Arbitration Committee.

Pre-existing agreements

As a general rule, when a valid employee request is made, the employer will come under an obligation to enter into negotiations for an I&C agreement with representatives of the employees. However, there is an important exception where employers already have in place one or more pre-existing I&C agreements. Pre-existing agreements must meet certain criteria to be valid – these are that they should be: (1) in writing, (2) cover all the employees in the undertaking, (3) set out how the employer will inform and communicate with the employees and (4) be approved by the employees (further details below).

Figure 9.5
(*Continued*)

In these circumstances, where a valid employee request to negotiate a new agreement is made, employers may ballot the workforce to ascertain whether it endorses the request by employees. This exception only applies if fewer than 40 per cent of employees in the undertaking make the request. Where 40 per cent or more of the employees make the request, employers may not hold a ballot to determine whether the workforce endorses it – the obligation to negotiate a new agreement will apply. Where a ballot is held, and 40 per cent of the workforce *and* a majority of those who vote, endorses the employee request, the employer would come under the obligation to negotiate a new agreement. Where fewer than 40 per cent of the workforce *or* a minority of those voting endorses the employee request, the employer would not be under an obligation to negotiate a new agreement, and a 3-year moratorium on further employee requests would begin. Where a pre-existing agreement covers employees in more than one undertaking, employers may hold a single ballot of the employees in the undertakings covered by the agreement. Before holding a ballot to endorse an employee request, employers must inform the employees within 1 month of the request that they intend to do so. They must then wait 21 days before holding the ballot, in case employees wish to challenge the validity of the pre-existing agreement(s).

Figure 9.5
(*Continued*)

As noted in the earlier section the responsibility to encourage collective bargaining has been removed from ACAS' legislatively prescribed role and it has shown a preference for encouraging cooperation and partnership. As part of this it has been keen to promote the benefits, as it perceives them, of joint problem solving and joint consultation, **though the success of their efforts may be questioned given the findings presented above**.

In many countries within Europe there is a legal requirement that employers consult with employee representatives on specified subject matter and at specified intervals. In the UK the only legal requirements have been for consultation with employee representatives in cases of collective redundancy, in the event of a Transfer of Undertaking and on matters relating to health and safety; in each case this was the product of EU legislation rather than the result of the wishes of employers and the government.

In many respects the attitude of government in the UK does not appear to have changed significantly with the election of New Labour in 1997. They are implementing the EU Directive on Information and Consultation at a national level (Directive 2002/14/EC) with effect from April 2005 but are taking advantage of various phasing in options which mean that undertakings employing between 50 and 100 employees will not have to comply with the information and consultation requirements of the Directive until April 2008. As can be seen from **Figure 9.5** the regulations identify different rights and obligations, similar to the distinctions in the German system identified above and demonstrated in the continuum of participation earlier (**Figure 9.1**). Employees and their representatives are going to be entitled to be informed only on some issues, informed and consulted on others, and informed and consulted with a view to reaching agreement on others.

Level

Joint consultation, like collective bargaining, can occur at a number of different levels within organizations. The subject matter of the consultation will probably vary from one level to another, with consultation at the level of the company much more likely to be on issues of company-wide significance, whereas consultation at the level of the workplace or workgroup is more likely to address issues more relevant to these levels.

It was noted earlier that the European Works Council (EWC) Directive applies at the level of the company, or at least the European headquarters of the organization, and we have also already indicated the nature of the process, information and consultation, and the range of mandatory subject matter (see **Chapter 4**). You should be aware that the EWC Directive was motivated by the desire to extend these rights to employees and their representatives but also by an awareness on the part of the EC and many of the member states that it was necessary to try to limit the otherwise unfettered power of the multinational to locate where it chooses and, if the mood takes it, to go regime shopping and play one member state off against another.

Joint consultation then can take a number of forms, be introduced for a range of different motives, cover a range of different subject matter, occur at different levels, be trade union based or not and where the form incorporates the intention to try and reach agreement it can come very close to collective bargaining. However, in general it is not a process through which management loses its right to make decisions. Increasingly for those countries that are members of the EU the requirement to undertake information and consultation is becoming legally prescribed and regulated and underpinning this is a belief not only that employees have a right to be informed and consulted on specific subject matter but also that employees have expertise and knowledge which can itself inform better decisions. **This viewpoint would not appear to be one that is shared by many employers and managers in the UK.**

Bargaining power

The concept of the balance of bargaining power is integral to an understanding of the outcomes of employee relations processes, terms and conditions of employment and the processes through which these are determined. Individuals join trade unions in order to enhance their bargaining power and in the past employers joined employers associations and engaged in multi-employer bargaining in order to combat the influence of strong trades unions. The concept is relevant to an understanding of outcomes whether it be individual bargaining or collective. We noted earlier (**Chapter 5**) that one aspect of the different ideologies examined concerned beliefs about whether individual suppliers of labour and buyers had a rough equality of bargaining power or not in their exchanges in the labour market.

The balance of bargaining power is influenced by both external and internal contexts. Externally, the balance is likely to be influenced by economic, legal and technological environments. In the economic environment the balance is affected by factors such as the level of employment and the rate of economic growth; where unemployment is high the bargaining power of employees will be weaker given that there are alternative supplies of labour; where economic growth is strong and there is strong demand for labour, the bargaining power of employees will be stronger and that of employers weaker. Similarly, if governments legislate in a manner which provides employees and their trades unions with legal rights to force employers into trade union recognition and collective bargaining, then the bargaining power of workers is enhanced, whereas, if they legislate to make trades unions illegal or to limit their ability to take industrial action, then the bargaining power of employers will be greater.

Technology and technological change also have a significant impact. Many traditional trades and sectors of industry have declined in the face of new technologies, and as this happens, the bargaining power of those employees and their trades unions declines. Conversely, where technological change creates new skills and jobs for which there may be a relatively scarce labour supply, the bargaining power of employees with those skills is enhanced.

We noted also in **Chapter 3** how the development of free trade agreements has enhanced the bargaining power of employers in relation to their employees in developed countries as the MNCs have been able to export jobs to the developing world where labour is cheaper and use the threat of this to squeeze concessions out of their labour in developed countries.

At the level of the organization, there are other factors that influence the balance. Here it becomes a matter of whether either of the parties can inflict costs on the other. For example, if a particular group of workers occupy a strategic role in the production process, then they are able to inflict considerable costs on the employer if they withdraw their labour; this is particularly the case if there is no readily available alternative labour supply. The implementation of particular modes of production can also have the same effect; for example, if companies use a just-in-time (JIT) system, the absence of inventory makes it more difficult for employers to withstand disruption and continue supply. Other factors of a more ephemeral nature can also influence bargaining power, such as perceptions of power and influence. History also plays a part; if one of the parties has used its power before and was successful, it will feel that it has strong cards to play; where the previous experience was unproductive, then they are less likely to repeat the experience thus enhancing the power of the other.

Summary

In this chapter we have established that there is a range of employee relations processes and that the various schemes and processes imply different degrees of employer autonomy and employee participation in management decision making. The point was made that employer autonomy or prerogative and employee participation are in some respects opposite sides of the same coin, in that enhancement of the latter tends to occasion an erosion of the former.

We introduced the notion of a continuum of participation and located a range of different processes within it.

We have examined the processes known as collective bargaining and joint consultation, their nature and scope, the levels at which they can operate and the experience of decline in the UK. We have contrasted joint consultation with collective bargaining and have noted that there are different models of joint consultation which focus upon both the purposes of management and the degree of participation. We have also examined the concept of bargaining power and its relevance to the outcomes of employee relations.

Activities to test understanding

Activity 1

1 Which of the Marchington *et al.* (1992) paradigms seem to you to be consistent with the notion of participation as defined by Walker?
2 Try to work out whether Strauss' concept of employee participation and its forms or types fit with or are the same as Marchington *et al.*'s models and, if so, which?

Activity 2

Have another look at the four paradigms of participation identified by Marchington *et al.* (1992) and try and work out for yourself whether any of them are more consistent with notions of EI (see **Chapter 8**) than participation.

Activity 3

1 Think back to **Chapter 8**, section on 'Managerial style(s)', and try to identify the style(s) that would be consistent with managers pursuing EI initiatives.

2 With which of the main perspectives discussed in **Chapter 1** does
   the EI concept fit?

Activity 4

Look at the following list of subjects and ask yourself in each case
whether you think employees should control or take part in the particular area of decision making.

 1 Organizational structure
 2 Economic and financial state of company
 3 Probable developments in the business, production and sales
 4 Employment situation and trends
 5 Investment plans
 6 Organizational change
 7 Working methods and processes
 8 Transfers of production
 9 Mergers
10 Cutbacks and closures
11 Collective redundancies
12 Employee transfers, promotions and dismissals
13 Payment schemes and other substantive terms and conditions of
    employment
14 Allocation and pace of work
16 Discipline.

Activity 5

Look at the three definitions of collective bargaining in **Figure 9.2**
and identify the common elements of the definitions and also how
they differ.

Activity 6

We noted that collective bargaining has been the dominant process
in the UK and, indeed, it is also the case that it is the dominant process
in many of the other countries in Europe. The structures may be different but the process has been common. What do you think may be
the minimum requirements for collective bargaining to develop and
continue?

Activity 7

In an earlier chapter (**Chapter 1**) we looked at the issue and relevance
of perspective and we looked in some detail at three particular perspectives. Think back now to your understanding of those three perspectives and try and work out for yourself how each might view the
process of collective bargaining.

Activity 8

Take a look back at the material on joint consultation and collective bargaining and write down what you think it is that differentiates them.

Activity 9

Short answer questions:

1 What are the differences between employee participation and EI?
2 Which processes have gained in popularity in recent years and which have declined?

References

Donovan Commission Report, 1968. *The Report of the Royal Commission on Trade Unions and Employers Associations.* Command 3623, HMSO, London.

Edwards, P., 1995. The employment relationship. In Edwards, P. (ed.), *Industrial Relations: Theory and Practice in Britain.* Blackwell, Oxford.

Farnham, D. and Pimlott, J., 1995. *Understanding Industrial Relations*, 5th Edition. Cassell, London.

Gospel, H. and Palmer, G., 1993. *British Industrial Relations.* Routledge, London.

Kersley, B., Alpin, C., Forth, J., Bryson, A., Bewley, H., Dix, G., Oxenbridge, S., 2005. *Inside the Workplace: First Findings from the 2004 Workplace Employment Relations Survey (WERS 2004).*

Leat, M., 1998. Human Resource Issues of the European Union, Financial Times Pitman Publishing, London.

Marchington, M., 1988. The Four Faces of Employee Consultation. Personnel Management, May, 44–47.

Marchington, M. and Wilkinson, A., 1996. *Core Personnel and Development.* IPD, London.

Marchington, M., *et al.*, 1992. *Recent Developments in Employee Involvement.* Employment Department Research Series No. 1, HMSO, London.

Purcell, J., 1989. How to manage decentralised collective bargaining. *Personnel Management*, May, 53–55.

Salamon, M., 1992. *Industrial Relations: Theory and Practice*, 2nd Edition. Prentice Hall, Englewood Cliffs, NJ.

Strauss, G., 1979. Workers participation: symposium introduction. *Industrial Relations* 18: 247–261.

Walker, K.F., 1974. Workers' participation in management: problems, practice and prospects. *Bulletin of the International Institute for Labour Studies* 12: 3–35.

Chapter 10

Negotiating

Introduction

We noted in the first chapter of this text that, in certain perspectives, the employment contract is characterized by conflict, employees and employers have different interests and these have to be reconciled with each other. We also noted that this reconciliation of the different interests results in an individual contract that has legal force but that this legal contract is also accompanied by a psychological contract in which are located the parties expectations of each other and what they hope to gain from their ongoing relationship. These expectations and the outcomes of the reconciliation of interests are both affected by the relative bargaining power of the parties.

Reconciliation of the different interests can be brought about through a number of different processes and these can be both individual and collective. Individual employees enter into an agreement when agreeing to become an employee of the employer and it may be that the terms and conditions of the employment contract entered into are the product of discussions and agreements between themselves and the employer individually. However, the terms of the agreement may well be the product of collective agreements arrived at between employers (or groups of employers) and representatives of the employees, most commonly these will be representatives of the trades unions which the employees have formed or joined in order to enhance their bargaining power in the process of reconciliation with a view to obtaining enhanced terms and conditions of employment.

It is important that we do not forget that the values and attitudes of people towards work and the employment relationship vary from country to country and we must therefore expect variations in the approach adopted to reconciling these conflicts of interest inherent in the relationship between employers and employees. Indeed, perceptions of whether the conflict is inherent are likely to vary along with attitudes towards each other and perceptions of the appropriateness of particular processes and the behaviour of the parties.

One of the characteristics of the employment relationship is the mutual dependence of the parties, both employee and employer need each other and generally this need is an ongoing one. It is possible to buy labour by the hour or day on a once and for all basis but in this text we have been interested in employment relationships that are to some extent ongoing, they may not be permanent or full time but are nevertheless ongoing. This mutual dependence and ongoing nature of the relationship is likely also to influence the way in which conflicts are reconciled and the terms of that reconciliation.

In this chapter we examine different approaches to resolving conflict between people, the influence that different work related values and cultural attributes may have for these approaches and then we focus on the process known as negotiating, the process which is inherent to effective collective bargaining. In **Chapter 9** we examined collective bargaining as a process for resolving conflicts of interest between employers and employees and through which employees collectively can participate in determining the terms and conditions upon which they are employed.

Learning objectives

After studying this chapter you will able to:

- Identify and differentiate between different approaches to resolving conflict.
- Understand and explain the advantages and disadvantages of the different approaches.
- When confronted by conflict yourself use this model to choose an appropriate approach.
- Understand that some approaches to resolving conflict are more or less consistent with particular national cultures.

- Understand that there are different stages in the negotiating process.
- Appreciate the skill mix required for successful negotiating.
- Engage more successfully in negotiating activities.

Handling/resolving conflict

Conflicts, defined as differences of interest, at work are common. They can occur between individual employees, between managers, between individual employees and their manager as well as between employees, both individually and collectively, and their employer. In this text we are particularly concerned with the latter of these but the different approaches that may be adopted when confronted by conflict, the skills involved and the advice given about how to negotiate apply generally.

In this chapter we use a model of five different approaches that may be adopted when confronted by conflict and in certain circumstances each of the approaches may be the appropriate one to use, though as noted above we focus later on one of them, the compromising or negotiating approach.

The five approaches

Avoiding

This approach consists of choosing not to address the issue, so that the conflict remains unresolved. There may be circumstances in which this is an appropriate response, for example, the issue may be unimportant to one of the parties, something that they are not concerned about, something which they have no interest in resolving. Avoiding is an approach to dealing with conflict but it is not an approach which is likely to result in the conflict being resolved. Choosing to avoid because the issue is unimportant to you is not the same as avoiding out of weakness or because you cannot face the confrontation, in these latter circumstances avoiding may be an inappropriate approach.

Competing

This may be an appropriate approach when the issue is of paramount importance to you, where you can accept no solution other than the one you propose, or where there is no time to use one of the other approaches such as collaborating or compromising. If decisions and action have to be taken and there is only one acceptable solution to you then adopting a competitive approach may be your only effective choice, though it is important to bear in mind that you need to have the bargaining power to enforce or impose your preferred solution. However, while you may win it is important that you appreciate that this approach involves the other party losing and this may well have undesirable consequences. For example, unless absolutely necessary this would be an unwise approach to adopt if the parties need each other or if the relationship between them is an ongoing one, such as between employees and their employer. Losing may well also involve losing face with those you represent and bargaining power has a habit of changing over time, use of the competitive approach runs the risk that it may be used effectively against you at some point in the future. Nevertheless, despite the risks there are times and issues over which it is the appropriate approach to employ.

Accommodating

This approach involves allowing the conflict to be resolved on the other party's terms. It may be that the issue is of relatively little importance to you or you may acknowledge that it is very important that the other party's interests are accommodated on this occasion. If the issue is of importance to you then this is not an approach to use since it effectively means that the other party's interests are satisfied and not yours. However, sometimes it is worth accommodating the other party's interests and in the process build-up credit for the future so that when there is an issue of importance to you, you may expect a similar accommodation in return. This approach is different from the avoiding approach above, since in this case the conflict is being resolved but on party's terms or in their favour, whereas with avoiding the conflict is not addressed or resolved.

Collaborating

Here the conflict is resolved to the full satisfaction of both parties. This is an approach that is only likely to be used and indeed to be successful when the parties trust each other, where they are able to divulge information to each other and where they can work together to create a solution. Often this approach can be detected in the creation of joint working parties to examine a problem and propose solutions. Creative solutions are the intended outcomes of this approach, solutions which enable both parties to satisfy their interests. This approach is often characterized as one which has as its outcome an increase in the size of the cake to be divided between the parties, whereas the other approaches all to some extent are concerned to divide the existing cake between them. For example, a joint working party which finds ways of increasing labour productivity with little or no additional cost may provide the opportunity for both employer and employees interests to be satisfied fully, the employer may get the enhanced labour flexibility and competitiveness that they want and at the same time employees may be able to obtain the pay increase that they want.

Compromising or negotiating

This approach involves the parties compromising their demands and expectations so that both parties to the conflict can each satisfy some of their concerns and interests even if they are unable to satisfy them all. It is an approach which is often characterized as one intended to produce half or part wins for both parties. As with collaborating above this approach takes time and, therefore, if quick solutions are necessary it may not be appropriate. However, where the relationship between the parties is an ongoing one and where conflict between the interests of the parties is also ongoing then this is an appropriate approach resulting in agreements which resolve the conflict for a period of time and thereby providing a basis for the relationship to continue. Compromising in this context is not weakness but a realistic approach to resolving the issues and maintaining the relationship.

As noted earlier this is the approach at the heart of collective bargaining and it is the process which we focus on in the latter part of the chapter.

Before leaving this section it is important that you realize that these five approaches represent a range of choice. When confronted by conflict people have a choice as to which approach to adopt and the choice should be based on a realistic appraisal of the circumstances including an assessment of how important the issue is to you and to the other party, whether the relationship is likely to be an ongoing one and the relative strengths of the parties.

It is often argued that as individuals we are likely to have our own natural preference for dealing with conflict, some people will naturally seek to avoid it whereas others will always be competitive trying to win at all costs and on every occasion. However, whatever your natural approach may be, in the context of handling work related conflict it is important that you are aware that; there are different approaches, each approach may be appropriate in particular circumstances, you do have a choice and you should make that choice in the light of a realistic appraisal of the circumstances. There are also skills that can be learned to make it easier for you to use the various alternatives successfully and in the latter part of this chapter we identify some of these skills in the particular context of negotiating.

In this text we are concerned with the employment relationship and therefore in this chapter we are examining handling conflict and negotiating in that context. In the latter part of the chapter we examine the stages and skills involved in the somewhat stylized and frequently team-based negotiation of terms and conditions of employment. However, negotiations occur in everyday life as well and while not stylized, staged or team based, many of the skills and advice emphasized in this chapter are also relevant to the negotiations that we may have on a daily basis with suppliers of goods and services, with our workmates or with our friends and family.

The relevance of culture

This same model of approaches can also be used to demonstrate the relevance of some dimensions of national culture which influence preferred ways of dealing with conflict resolution. There are several well-known models for measuring differences in national culture with those of Hofstede (1980) and Trompenaars (1993) being probably the best known.

Here we focus on a couple of the dimensions identified by Hofstede in order to illustrate the influence that national cultures can have.

The dimensions are Hofstede's Power Distance and Individualism.

Power Distance is a measure of the extent to which people expect and accept that power is unequally divided in society, including the workplace. In countries where there is high power distance this means that there is an expectation that, and acceptance of, power will be distributed unequally. In the workplace employees expect to be closely supervised, they expect management to make the decisions and to do so in either an autocratic or paternalistic manner, they are often afraid to disagree with their boss and would not expect to be involved in decision making, in fact attempts by management to involve them in any form of decision making might be perceived negatively and as a sign of weakness. In countries where the power distance is low, there is likely to be a much greater expectation of, and emphasis upon, cooperation and joint decision making. Here management are much more likely to engage with employees in decision making and employees are much more likely to be willing to become involved, they will also be much less afraid of disagreeing with their boss.

Using the model of approaches that has been outlined above, we might then reasonably expect employees to use avoiding or accommodating approaches in high power distance scenarios and to seek compromise or collaborative outcomes where power distance is low. Management are also likely to pursue compromising or collaborative approaches where power distance is low and to be competitive in high power distance environments as they perceive their authority to be challenged.

Hofstede's individualism dimension measures the extent to which people perceive themselves to be primarily individuals or members of a group. Where individualism is high people are concerned predominantly with their own interests and looking after themselves and their immediate family, where individualism is low people are much more likely to see themselves as part of a group with a responsibility to look after the interests of the group rather than their own. Again we can trace the implications for approaches to resolving conflict. Where individualism is high we might expect there to be an emphasis upon either competitive or avoiding approaches, where the issue is important to the individual it is likely that the competitive approach will be adopted, however, where the issue is unimportant then we can expect the individual to decline to even address the conflict. On the other hand where individualism is low and members perceive themselves primarily as a member of a group, group interests, including their workmates and the organization for which they work, are important and we might expect either collaborative or accommodating approaches to be used. Where the issue is relatively unimportant to employees we would expect them to defer to the interests of the organization and accommodate them, where the issue is important we would expect management and employees to pursue collaborative approaches in the interests of all members of the group.

In addition to influencing approaches to addressing conflict and its resolution, dimensions of national culture are also likely to influence perceptions of what is important and the behaviour of the parties in any particular attempts to jointly resolve differences. Examples of cultural dimensions that exert influence in this context include:

- the relative importance of the task versus relationships,
- attitudes towards time,
- the relevance of context,
- attitudes towards the expression of emotion.

In some cultures it is considered important that you develop an ongoing relationship and that you consider the interests of the other party, whereas in other cultures it is the task, and only the task, that matters. Where relationships are considered to be important conflict resolution is likely to incorporate concession and face saving, whereas an emphasis upon the task is likely to encourage a much more assertive style involving few if any concessions and probably also an emphasis upon speed, getting the job done. Where the conflict resolution is cross cultural and these two different sets of values meet one side are likely to make concessions which are not reciprocated by the other side and the side that emphasizes relationships is likely to frustrate the other by placing little emphasis upon speed and coming to a conclusion.

Attitudes towards time have been classified as either monochronic or polychronic (Hall, 1960). In some cultures time is seen as a valuable resource which is limited and which therefore should be used sparingly, time is money and meetings should start on time and time should not be wasted. This is referred to as time being seen as monochronic and tends to encourage approaches to dealing with issues in a sequential and linear fashion. So, for example, in monochronic cultures not only is time important but this also tends to influence approaches towards dealing with agenda items – one at a time and in sequence – and also attitudes towards the order in which people speak and whether people should speak one at a time. In polychronic cultures time is seen to be expendable and of relatively little importance, so meetings starting on time, time not being wasted, the sequence in which items are dealt with and people only speaking one at a time are all considered to be unimportant. Again when people from such different cultures meet to resolve conflicts additional conflicts can be occasioned as a result of these different attitudes.

Hall and Hall (1990) distinguish between low and high context cultures, in low context cultures there is an expectation that people will be explicit, that they will say what they mean and positions will be expressed clearly and directly. Whereas in high context cultures there is much less emphasis upon being clear and direct and a much greater willingness to read between the lines and a greater emphasis upon body language and its interpretation.

Trompenaars distinguished between affective and neutral approaches, in some cultures the expression of emotion is frowned upon and often perceived to be embarrassing and people from such a culture will approach the resolution of conflict in a reserved and unemotional manner. On the other hand people from an affective culture will willingly express frustration and anger and meetings to resolve conflict may be highly charged emotional events.

Cultures, then, differ and these differences are likely to influence both the approach to resolving conflict and the behaviour and expectations of the parties involved in conflict resolution.

We now move on to examine the process of compromising known as negotiation. We examine this in a predominantly UK context.

Negotiating

A definition

Negotiation is a process through which parties with different interests come together to reach a mutually acceptable and agreed resolution of the differences between them.

Gennard and Judge (2002) suggest that the process involves the use of both purposeful persuasion and constructive compromise. Each party will try to persuade the other of the merits of its case but must be willing to compromise on some of their demands or desires in order to enable an agreement to be reached. Agreement is only possible if there is some common ground between the parties and the agreed outcome is likely to be within this area of common ground. The precise terms of the agreement will depend on a number of factors including both the relative bargaining power of the parties and the skill with which the negotiations are conducted by the respective participants.

Stages

Negotiations can be seen to go through a number of common stages. There are a number of different models or typologies of stages but in this text we use a simple fourfold model:

1   Preparation
2   Presentation
3   Proposing and exploring
4   Trading and agreeing.

Preparation

Almost certainly the most important stage in the negotiating process there are a number of distinct elements to preparing for negotiating. These can be summarized as including:

- the collection and analysis of relevant data;
- the determination of objectives;
- the determination of strategy and tactics;
- the allocation of work and negotiating team roles.

The collection and analysis of data

The nature of the information required will vary according to the subject matter of the negotiations. For example, if the subject matter is a pay claim and you are on the receiving end as management you will need to collect and analyse data facilitating comparison with other claims and awards in the industry, in the company, in similar jobs, in the local labour market; you will need to be able to cost various outcomes; you may need to examine these in the context of the current and future business environment and in the context of the profitability of the organization; you may need to be able to demonstrate the implications of various outcomes for prices to be charged for the product and the impact price increases may have upon demand; you may want to ascertain how an increase might be paid for, how and where efficiencies can be gained, what kind of flexibilities and their value that you might seek in return.

Other subject matter may not require the same data to be collected and analysed but it is likely that there will be similar requirements and this must be done prior to the negotiations starting. No experienced negotiator will willingly enter into negotiations feeling that they do not know the answers and that they are unable to fully explain and cost both the demands from the other party but also their own proposals.

These data collection and analysis requirements have significant implications for the knowledge and skills required on the team responsible for the preparation and for the negotiations themselves.

Objectives

These are crucial, you need to know what you want to achieve, what outcomes you would like and which ones you can live with. A useful technique is to think of objectives in terms of your ideal outcome, the outcome you think realistic or likely and the minimum outcomes you could accept, this latter is sometimes also referred to as your fall-back position. In addition to identifying these for your own side you also need to try and envisage the same three sets of outcomes for the other party and this will provide an indication of whether there is sufficient common ground for an agreement to be possible as well as indicating the area in which agreement may be likely. When negotiations are taking place over a range of different items it is important that this objective setting activity is undertaken in relation to each item. Undertaking this activity should enable you to identify the issues on which you and your opponents may be willing to compromise as well as the extent of that possible compromise, in effect you identify the scope for bargaining or trading.

A simple example illustrates the importance of this activity. Again we take the example of a pay increase, if as employee representatives your ideal outcome is a pay rise of £10 per week but you could accept an increase of £4 per week and you estimate that management's ideal outcome is a pay increase of £2 per week but you think their fall-back position is a pay increase of £6 (in this case this is the most that management will agree to) then there is an overlap between the two fall-back positions indicating that agreement should be achievable between £4 and £6. If on the other hand you estimate management's fall-back position, the most they will agree to, is only £3 then this would indicate that agreement is unlikely.

Figure 10.1 demonstrates this in diagrammatic form and the overlap between the fall-back positions is sometimes referred to as the bargaining range.

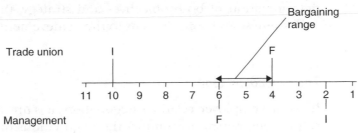

Figure 10.1
Bargaining parameters and bargaining range.

It may be that both parties are unwilling to compromise at all on particular items and the prospect for agreement then shifts to whether there are any items on which both parties are willing to compromise and whether there is any common ground on those items. Undertaking this activity not only enables you to assess the range of likely outcomes but also provides you with information that you can use to determine your strategy and the tactics you employ to achieve the best outcome you can.

Strategy and tactics

In the main this involves identifying and anticipating the arguments and case that the other side is likely to put forward and how you intend to counter them, similarly you should try and identify how the other side is likely to respond to your arguments and case so that you anticipate their responses and again have explanations or counter arguments ready. Other issues that fall into this category might be the order in which items are dealt with, it may be that you want to leave a particular topic till last because you feel that is where the most resistance is likely to be and that if agreement has been achieved on all the other items this will put additional pressure on the other party to compromise more on the last item. In complex negotiations agreeing the agenda can be as difficult as any of the subsequent negotiations on items on that agenda and as noted earlier attitudes towards time are likely to influence this, where the attitude is monochronic, the agenda is likely to have greater significance than where the attitude is polychronic.

The use of adjournments is another issue on which you might want to decide your strategy beforehand, are you going to use them, if so in what circumstances and are you going to deliberately delay returning to the negotiating table once you have decided to have an adjournment.

If the negotiations are to be conducted by a team representing an interest it is important that all members of the team are involved in the determination of both objectives and strategy, this helps build team cohesiveness and commitment to the achievement of those objectives.

The negotiating team

In formal employee relations negotiations it is unwise for either party to rely on one person to conduct the negotiations on their behalf, there is too much to be done by one person. It is important that the parties pay particular attention to the skills and roles of team members. As has already been implied above, the team needs someone who is capable of undertaking the data analysis necessary both before and during the negotiations, it is by no means unusual for new material or new and different interpretations of data to be presented during the negotiations and it is important that someone on the team is able to understand and analyse the data.

The team needs a leader and spokesperson who has effective interpersonal and persuasive skills, good judgement and who can hold the team together if the going gets tough or if there are disagreements between team members. There is a tendency to think that all members of a negotiating team have the same interests and agenda and while this may be true up to a point it is by no means unusual for differences to surface as the negotiations proceed. An example might be between a full-time trade union official and the lay representatives of the employees who are the subject of the negotiations. The lay representative is likely to be interested predominantly in the outcome for his or her members whereas the full-time official is also likely to have a national policy agenda to consider and what might be acceptable to the lay representative may be inconsistent with the Union's policy. In such circumstances it is important that any lack of unity within the team does not become apparent to the other side, experienced negotiators may well be able to take advantage of any public indication of dissent or differences within the opposing negotiating team. The leader must be able to hold the team together and if necessary enforce team discipline, though any enforcing of discipline should not take place in front of the other side. Generally you should expect the team leader to be the sole spokesperson, but it may be that expert input from one or more of the other team members may be required at times and when this is the case that team member should only speak when invited to do so by the team leader and only if this has been agreed beforehand as part of the agreement of strategy and tactics.

It is also very useful to have on the team someone who listens and watches for signals and signs of movement and also someone who takes notes of what is said and in particular what might be agreed. It is possible that one person can combine these roles but if the negotiations are complex or of extended duration it is probably wise to separate them.

The listening and watching role is often undervalued and many negotiating teams leave this to be undertaken by team members on an ad hoc basis. Ideally the team needs someone who is experienced not only in listening to and interpreting the spoken word but who also has some expertise in interpreting body language. In everyday life, and negotiations are no different in this respect, substantial proportions of interpersonal communication are via looks, facial expressions and body movements and posture and a negotiating team needs someone able to identify and interpret this body language, the words may be communicating one message but the body may be communicating a message that is substantially different.

An accurate record of what has been said, offers that might have been made and what has been agreed is crucial at times, especially prior to taking an adjournment and at the end of the negotiations when a careful recording of the terms of the agreement reached should be undertaken and confirmed by both the parties.

In addition to identifying and allocating the roles to be performed by team members it is also very important that the team members exercise self-discipline and stick to the roles that they have been allocated, the last thing any team needs is someone who is not the spokesperson interrupting or otherwise intervening at a crucial point when your spokesperson is seeking to elicit important information, is in the process of extracting a concession or stating your sides position. Obviously situations will arise where the team members need to communicate with one another once the negotiations have started and this should be done via whatever mechanism has been agreed beforehand, commonly this is through the passage of notes but other signals or mechanisms can be agreed. If a member of the team feels that something has been misunderstood or a signal has been missed the answer is not to interrupt or intervene directly themselves but to indicate to the team leader the need for a recess or adjournment so that the team can speak together in private. Adjournments should not be seen as sign of indecision or weakness but as a positive forum in which positions can be reappraised following developments in the negotiations and in which any need for a reinforcement of team discipline can be achieved.

Presentation

Presentation is what tends to characterize the first face-to-face meeting of the sides. Sometimes written submissions will have been made by either or both sides prior to this first meeting but even where this has happened the first meeting tends to be where both sides go through their case and it is where the parties are likely to outline their ideal position or outcome. It is important that the parties indicate at this stage all the issues that they wish to discuss so that at the end of this stage both parties know the agenda for the negotiations. Some negotiators use the tactic of keeping something up their sleeve at this stage, believing that it will be to their advantage to have a new issue to introduce into the negotiations at a later date, for example for when they wish to divert attention from a weakness in their argument on other issues or because they feel that having secured agreement on all other issues it will be easier for them to secure agreement on the hidden issue right at the last minute. This is a dangerous tactic to employ, it might work once but is likely to harm the trust between the parties and may well rebound on the party using this tactic in subsequent negotiations. One of the contextual characteristics influencing negotiations on employee relations issues is that the relationship between the parties is likely to be an ongoing one and it is always important to bear this in mind when devising tactics since what you do this time round may rebound on you in the future. Remember that the motive for trying to resolve differences on employment relationship matters through negotiation leading to agreement is the mutual dependence of the parties.

It is not at all uncommon for these initial sessions to be fairly emotional with allegations and counter allegations being made about the perceived conduct of the parties and claims being argued aggressively. Ideally, of course everyone remains calm but the reality at this stage is sometimes that one or more of the parties find this difficult. While emotions should not be allowed to get out of hand, presentations in which parties demonstrate their strength of feeling and resolve may well have a cathartic effect and may also provide invaluable insight into one or other side's priorities and the issues and claims that may not be negotiable.

At this stage it is important that the parties understand the other's opening position and it is advisable for each side to ensure this through careful questioning where positions and meanings are at all unclear. The purpose of the questioning should be to seek clarification and this can be checked by each side summarizing its understanding of the other side's position. At this first stage the questioning should not be geared towards establishing areas of potential movement or common ground, this comes in the next stage.

Where there are a range of issues now on the agenda it is likely that the first face-to-face meeting will end at this point with a further meeting arranged at which the parties will begin exploring for indications of a willingness to move or compromise, searching for areas of common ground. However, where the agenda is relatively simple with perhaps only one or two issues it may be that the parties decide to continue into the second stage at this first meeting, though it is always advisable for the parties to take some time considering what they have just heard and planning their response and this can be done through an adjournment.

Proposing and exploring

This is the stage at which the parties should be exploring for signs of movement, seeking to identify the issues which are negotiable and which not and the direction and extent of any movement that be available. To some extent this can be achieved through careful questioning but also through seeking responses to hypothetical proposals. This stage is sometimes referred to as the 'If-then' stage. Parties explore for signs of movement or common ground through making hypothetical proposals and listening very carefully to the responses. The skills of listening and questioning are important in all the stages that we have so far identified but none more so than this third stage.

The sort of proposals made are likely to take the form of saying that you might be able to move in one area in return for movement by the other parting that or some other area. So, for example management might say 'If your members were willing to begin the process of multiskilling then we might be able to look again at your request for additional days of annual leave'. In reply the employees side might say 'As it is my members are not prepared to discuss multiskilling but if management were willing to change shift patterns as we have requested then it might be possible to begin discussions on the introduction of some limited multiskilling'. In effect each party is beginning to make proposals in the form of conditional offers.

Exchanges of this kind may proceed for some time as each side seeks to test the other side's priorities and the items on the agenda which are negotiable, on which the parties might be willing to trade. As the process continues the areas of potential agreement should become clearer and the gap between the parties gradually narrows as common ground is identified.

It is important at this stage that the parties concern themselves with seeking agreement in principle before beginning to discuss the details of the trade. Depending on the complexities it might even be that having established agreement in principle on the items to be traded a joint working party is established to investigate the detail and formulate recommendations to both sides which then form the basis for further negotiations and eventual agreement between the parties.

Eventually of course the proposing and exploring has to stop and trading begins. However, it is a mistake to think that negotiations proceed calmly through each of these stages in turn and it is quite likely that there will be some toing and froing between the stages with, for example, the exploring phase being interrupted by further periods for preparation as new positions or facts emerge, or even after some trading has taken place there may be a return to proposing and exploring on remaining issues.

It should be apparent from this brief discussion that in addition to the communication and persuasive skills of the leader the process places considerable demands upon the team members in their roles as analyst, listener and note taker and summarizer. Proposals need to be formulated with care, the consequences need to be analysed, signals need to be picked up by the listener and the note taker needs to have an accurate record of both proposal and response as well as being to summarize where the parties are at any given time. Additional skills often mentioned as being crucial to the success of negotiations are timing and judgement as well as effective interpersonal skills which may well be imperative in order to prevent negotiations breaking down.

Trading and agreeing

As noted above the proposing and exploring for common ground eventually stops and an agreement is either concluded or it is not. The basis of the agreement will be a trade between the parties, one party giving something in order to obtain something it wants from the other side. If we return to the earlier example management might agree to an additional 2 days extra paid annual leave in return for a limited introduction of multiskilling, or if the employees agree to a more extensive introduction of multiskilling they might agree to both an increase in annual leave and a revision of the shift patterns.

As a general rule parties should seek to trade something which is relatively cheap for them to give in return for something which is valuable to them to receive.

It is also important that parties who come under pressure to conclude an agreement quickly do not allow themselves to be rushed. It is always difficult to judge when final offers or positions have been reached and if you allow yourself to be rushed into an agreement it is quite likely that you accept an offer or position from the other side that was not their final offer, in other words you do not get the best deal that you could have obtained. Parties often say that something is their final offer, take it or leave it, when it is not and often this assertion is used as a means of trying to exert pressure to come to an agreement quickly. You should always be wary when your opponents use this tactic and you should generally resist the pressure to accept. Final offers like all others should be carefully considered before they are accepted. Negotiators should also be wary of using this final offer tactic unless they really mean it, since if the opposing side call your bluff and refuse to accept the final offer you will find yourself in a difficult position confronted either by a failure to reach agreement or having to concede more in order to obtain agreement. Once your bluff has been called in this way the other side will always distrust your assertions that you can give no more and this may well make future agreements more difficult to achieve. The general rule again is that you should say what you mean and mean what you say.

Another general rule at the trading stage is not to give anything unless you receive something in return, as noted above you should try to give things that are relatively cheap for you to give in return for something which is valuable for you to receive. In this context also it is unwise to start the negotiations adopting an unrealistic position, experienced negotiators on the other side are likely to realize this, not take it seriously and reject it. Then you are left with the choice of the negotiations either not starting at all or alternatively you have to improve your offer or concede on your opening demands and receive nothing in return, this gives the other side the upper hand at the outset of the negotiations and it is difficult to regain the initiative once this has happened. Once you concede something or improve your offer but receive nothing in return the other side quite reasonably will try and make you do it again and again.

You should also be wary of what is often referred to as the concession close, this is where one of the parties voluntarily makes a concession, receiving nothing in return, in order to reach an agreement. The concern in such cases should be that if they are willing to give something for nothing you might actually have been able to obtain more than you have.

Once agreement has been reached it is absolutely crucial that the parties take time to agree what has been agreed. Often in the euphoria of reaching agreement negotiators forget or do not bother to do this and commonly this failure results in misunderstandings and disputes over what was agreed. The note takers should ensure that an accurate written record is made of the terms of the agreement and the parties should take time to study this record, satisfy themselves that this is indeed what they understood had been agreed and the written agreement should then be signed by both parties confirming it as an accurate record. Time taken doing this will make misunderstandings and difficulties over interpretation both less likely and easier to resolve. It is of course important that the wording of the agreement is unambiguous and that meanings are clear.

It should be remembered that in many countries collective agreements arrived at through negotiation between the parties do have legal effect and it is therefore very important that the written agreement does accurately reflect both what the parties intended and thought had been agreed.

Summary

In this chapter we have examined different approaches to resolving conflict and discussed the circumstances in which each might be the appropriate approach to use. It is possible for individuals to choose the approach which they adopt, even though they might have a natural preference it is possible to learn to use other approaches and to switch approach as circumstances dictate.

We also examined the relevance of national culture and particular cultural dimensions for the approach adopted to conflict resolution and also to the behaviour and expectations of the parties.

Negotiating is only one of these approaches but it is the approach which in the UK has characterized the joint resolution of conflicts between employees and their employers. The parties to the employment relationship have a mutual dependence and it is this which encourages the willingness of the parties to enter into joint decision making using negotiating. The intended outcome of negotiating is a joint agreement. Negotiating is the essence of collective bargaining.

There are a number of identifiable stages to negotiating, each of which is important but arguably the preparation stage is the most important. There are a range of roles relevant to negotiating and these each require particular skills and there are also a range of good negotiating practices and guidelines.

The objective is agreement and it is crucial that once agreement is achieved it is accurately and clearly written down and agreed by the parties.

Activities to test understanding

Activity 1

It is sometimes argued that conflicts between buyers and sellers of labour and their representatives are distinctive in that there is a mutual dependence between the parties and the relationship between them is an ongoing one. How might this influence the choice of approach to resolving the conflict?

Activity 2

In many cultures conflict is an emotive term, without going back to read the text, how have we defined conflict for the purposes of this chapter?

Activity 3

Having examined the implications of each of the cultural dimensions individually, see whether you can work out the probable implications of the following combinations.

1 High power distance combined with high individualism.
2 Low power distance with low individualism.

Activity 4

Without going back to look at the text try and distinguish mono-chronic from polychronic attitudes towards time and their respective implications for conflict resolving approaches and behaviour.

Activity 5

1 What distinguishes negotiating from the other approaches to resolving conflict?
2 What determines whether agreement is possible?

Activity 6

In the preparatory stage of negotiations how can you establish whether agreement is possible?

Activity 7

What qualities, skills and attributes would you look for in the leader of a negotiating team?

Activity 8

What signals or messages might the listener derive from this exchange?

Activity 9

In the section on trading and agreeing we mentioned a number of general rules that should be followed, what are they?

References

Gennard, J. and Judge, G., 2002. *Employee Relations*. IPD, London.

Hall, E.T., 1960. The silent language of overseas business. *Harvard Business Review* May/June, 38(3): 87–95.

Hall, E.T. and Hall, M.R., 1990. *Understanding Cultural Differences*. Intercultural Press, Yarmouth, ME.

Hofstede, G., 1980. *Cultures Consequences*. Sage, Beverley Hills.

Trompenaars, F., 1993. *Riding the Waves of Culture*. Nicholas Brealey, London.

Chapter 11

Employee relations procedures

Introduction

In this section we examine the procedural dimension of employee relations, why organizations have procedures, the sorts of areas in which they
do, and where appropriate, the legal requirements for procedures. These
procedures constitute outcomes of the interaction between the parties to
the employment relationship which then also become part of the context
within which that interaction takes place and impose constraints upon it.

Much of this chapter is taken up with advice on how particular issues
should be dealt with and the rights and obligations of the interested parties. In some instances, these rights and obligations are imposed through
legislative means; in others, they are the product of agreements between
the parties. Precise legal constraints vary from one country to another
but it can be argued that there is also a set of best practice principles
that should apply irrespective of the country in which the operations
occur and irrespective of whether there is a legislative requirement.

In the main, these matters are likely to be dealt with at the level of the
employing organization; though in countries and industries characterized

by multiemployer bargaining, it may be that the procedural arrangements provide for stages in the procedure that are outside the firm, for example at a regional or national level. It is also common, where there are legislatively imposed rights and obligations and where individuals feel that one or more of these rights have been infringed, for there to be mechanisms for the employee to seek redress outside the firm through processes of conciliation and/or arbitration or through the appropriate legal mechanisms, tribunals or courts. The mechanisms for conciliation or arbitration may also be state funded, or they may be provided through the industry or national procedures agreed through multiemployer-trade union bargaining. The variety of practices and requirements can be detected from the exhibit in which are outlined procedural and legal rights and obligations in respect of fair and unfair dismissals in a range of different countries.

Exhibit

Conditions under which individual dismissals are fair or unfair[a]

	Legal provisions	Score (scale 0–3)
Australia	**Fair:** If justified on the basis of capacity or conduct, subject to whether it is harsh, unjust or unreasonable as well as for economic redundancy ("retrenchment"). **Unfair:** When process of an employee dismissal is 'harsh, unjust or unreasonable'. Factors are whether there was a valid reason for the termination related to the capacity/conduct of the employee or operational requirements of business, whether employee notified of reason, whether employee given opportunity to response, whether warned of unsatisfactory performance if that is the ground of termination, degree to which employers business affects procedures, degree to which absence of dedicated HR people impacts on employers procedures. Also dismissals on grounds of race, colour, sex, sexual preference, age, physical or mental disability, marital status, family responsibilities, pregnancy, religion, political views and union membership opinion, national extraction or social origin.	0
France	**Fair:** Dismissal for real and serious cause: for personal characteristics such as non-performance or lack of competence, or for economic reasons. In case of dismissal for economic reason, the employer must take account of certain criteria (such as social characteristics, family responsibilities, professional qualification). During one year after dismissal the employee is given a priority when rehiring. **Unfair:** Dismissal without serious cause. In case of dismissal for medical or economic reasons, obligation for the employer to consider	2

(Continued)

	Legal provisions	Score (scale 0–3)
	alternative solution (reclassement). Null: Dismissals for reasons relating to the private life of the employee, based on discrimination or following moral or sexual harassment.	
Germany	**Fair:** Dismissals based on factors inherent in the personal characteristics or behaviour of the employee (such as insufficient skill or capability), or business needs and compelling operational reasons. **Unfair:** Dismissals where the employee can be retained in another capacity within the same establishment or enterprise, and redundancy dismissals where due account has not been taken of "social considerations" (e.g seniority, age, family situation). Rehabilitation must already have been attempted before the dismissal, or the dismissal is considered unfair.	2
Ireland	**Fair:** Dismissals for lack of ability, competence or qualifications, or redundancy. **Unfair:** Dismissals reflecting discrimination on grounds of race, religion, age, gender, etc. including when these factors bias selection during redundancies. Exercise or proposed exercise of rights under Carer's Leave or minimum wage legislation.	0
Italy	**Fair:** Termination of contract only possible for "just cause" or "just motive" including significant non-performance of the employee, and compelling business reasons. **Unfair:** Dismissals reflecting discrimination on grounds of race, religion, gender, trade union activity, etc.	0
Japan	**Fair:** Dismissals for 'reasonable cause': incompetence of the employee or break of disciplinary rules. Redundancy dismissals require urgent business reasons for reducing the number of staff: reasonableness of selection criteria and reasonableness of procedures. **Unfair:** Dismissal for reason of nationality, gender, belief or social status, of workers on sick leave, child birth and maternity leave, and when conditions on fair dismissal have not been satisfied.	1
Mexico	**Fair:** Dismissals are fair only when the employer can demonstrate the worker's lack of integrity or actions prejudicial to the company's interests (such as negligence, imprudence, or disobedience). Redundancy or poor performance are normally not legal grounds for dismissal.	3
The Netherlands	**Fair:** Dismissals on grounds of employee conduct or unsuitability, and for economic redundancy. In the latter case, data on the financial state of the company and proof that alternatives to redundancy have been considered must be given, and the selection of dismissed employees be justified ("last in – first out" principle, or age/sex balance of the workforce, for example). **Unfair:** Unfair are "obviously unreasonable" terminations, and dismissals of pregnant women, the disabled, new mothers and works council members.	1.5

(Continued)

	Legal provisions	Score (scale 0–3)
Norway	**Fair:** Dismissals on "objective grounds", i.e. economic redundancy (rationalization measures, etc.) and personal circumstances (disloyalty, persistent absenteeism, etc.). **Unfair:** Dismissals for economic reasons are unfair if the employee could have been retained in another capacity. Dismissals for reasons of age (under the age of 70), for trade union activities, military service, pregnancy and of recent mothers and employees on sick leave are also unfair.	2.5
Portugal	**Fair:** Dismissals for disciplinary causes, economic grounds and for lack of professional or technical capability. Dismissals for individual redundancy must be based on urgent needs and must not involve posts also manned by people on fixed-term contracts. Dismissals for lack of competence are only possible after introduction of new technology or change to job functions. **Unfair:** Dismissals where employees could have been, reasonably, in view of their skills and abilities, transferred and retrained.	2
Spain	**Fair:** Dismissal for "objective" causes (worker's incompetence, lack of adaptation to the job post, absenteeism, lack of adaptation to organization changes if a training course of 3 months has been offered – not compulsory); dismissal for "justifiable" causes (economic, technological, organizational, due to changes in cyclical demand, due to lack of financing for public programs carried out by the public administration or other non-profit organization); dismissal for "disciplinary" causes. **Unfair:** Dismissal based on discrimination on grounds of gender, race, religion, social condition, political ideas, trade union activity, and any dismissal violating an employee's constitutional and civil rights, as well as rights related to maternity. Rehabilitation must already have been attempted before the dismissal, or the dismissal is considered unfair.	2
Sweden	**Fair:** Dismissals on "objective grounds", i.e. economic redundancy and personal circumstances, including lack of competence. In cases of redundancy, selection of workers to be dismissed has to be justified (mainly based on last-in, first-out principle). **Unfair:** Objective grounds are deemed not to exist if an employee could reasonably have been transferred to another work, or if dismissal is based on events that happened over two months ago.	2
United Kingdom	**Fair:** Dismissals relating to the capability, qualifications or conduct of the employee; because of economic redundancy; because continued employment would be illegal; or some other "substantial reason". One year tenure generally necessary for being able to file for unfair dismissal. **Unfair:** Dismissals related to a range of reasons including trade union activity, health and safety whistle blowing, pregnancy or maternity, and the national minimum wage. No qualifying service required for complaints for these reasons.	0

(Continued)

	Legal provisions	Score (scale 0–3)
United States	**Fair:** With the exception of the public sector, it is generally fair to terminate an open-ended employment relationship without justification or explanation ("employment-at-will" principle) unless the parties have placed specific restrictions on terminations. **Unfair:** Dismissals based on breach of Equal Employment Opportunity principles (i.e. national origin, race, sex, etc.) and dismissal of employees with physical or mental impairment if work could be performed through appropriate workplace adjustment. In addition, there are increasing numbers of cases where employees pursue wrongful termination claims by alleging that dismissal was based on an "implied contract" for continued employment.	0

(a) For scoring methodology, see *OECD Employment Outlook* (2004), Chapter 2, Annex 2.1. Table 2A1.1 – item 5.

Adapted from OECD. A detailed description of employment protection regulation in force in 2003. Background material for the 2004 edition of the *OECD Employment Outlook*.

While we are not able to examine all of the possible procedural areas in great depth, however in this chapter we do examine procedures for managing and handling discipline and grievances, in both cases focusing on the legal requirements in the UK but as noted above the general principles for dealing with these issues are not nation specific and do therefore have a wider relevance. First, however, we examine what the procedures are and what they do and then we identify the reasons for having procedures.

Learning objectives

After studying this chapter you will be able to:

- discuss the reasons for having employee relations procedures, their implications for managerial prerogative and the relevance of fairness and justice;
- identify and discuss criteria against which the effectiveness of procedures may be assessed;
- identify and discuss the principles of natural justice;
- identify and discuss issues and elements of good practice in the devising and drafting of disciplinary procedures;
- explain the difference between a grievance and a dispute;

- identify and discuss issues and elements of good practice in the devising and drafting of grievance procedures;
- advise on some of the dos and don'ts, skills and aptitudes needed to manage discipline and handle grievances effectively;
- understand the legal requirements regarding disciplinary and grievance procedures in the UK including the legal status of the Code of Practice on Disciplinary and Grievance procedures;
- examine grievance and disciplinary procedures against the requirements of good practice.

Procedures – what they are and why they are needed?

It was noted in **Chapter 1** that among the outcomes of the industrial relations system (Dunlop, 1958) are both substantive and procedural rules. The procedural outcomes tend to govern the relationship between the parties to the employment relationship, how they deal with each other and with particular issues and situations. In a sense, the procedures provide the constitution, the set of principles and rules, within and by which the employment relationship should be conducted, but they are also operational mechanisms used by the parties in the day-to-day handling of issues. For example, as we see later in this chapter, a disciplinary procedure should inform and guide the parties as to the rights and obligations of both employee and management, the sanctions and options available to both parties as well as how a particular situation should be handled.

The industrial relations system of Dunlop (1958) tended to assume that these procedures would be the product of joint decision making through the process of collective bargaining. However, they may equally well be the product of unilateral decision making by management and/or the response to a legal requirement.

In advocating the joint determination of procedures, Hawkins (1979) argued that agreed procedures can be seen as a voluntary code of behaviour encompassing restraints upon the use by the parties of their respective power, though it must be remembered that the parties are likely to have used this power in reaching the procedural agreement.

There is a considerable range of issues and eventualities in the arena of employee relations which may be governed by formal procedures. It is generally likely that organizational size will be one of the influences upon the existence of formal procedural arrangements with larger organizations being more likely to have a wider range of formal arrangements and smaller organizations tending to rely more on the informal approach and on a narrower range of subject matter.

It is not so unusual for a large organization to have a set of procedures that encompass most if not all of the following areas of subject matter and circumstances:

- trade union recognition, individual representation, negotiating and dispute resolution procedures;
- joint consultative procedures and arrangements;
- grievance procedures;
- redundancy procedures;
- discipline and/or dismissal procedures;
- performance appraisal procedures;
- the implementation and operation of payment systems;
- job evaluation procedures;
- promotion and transfer procedures;
- equality of treatment, access and harassment;
- procedures governing the introduction of new technology and working practices.

In many countries, there are legal requirements that procedures exist, though it is unlikely that legislation would apply in all of the above cases. In some instances, the legislation also spells out what the minimum procedures should be. Member states of the EU, for example, are required by legislation at the EU level to ensure that employing organizations have procedures concerning:

- the formation of health and safety committees and the procedural and consultation rights of the safety representative;
- the consultation of employee representatives in the event of collective redundancies and/or a transfer of undertaking;
- the information and consultation of employee representatives at both a European and national level concerning a wide range of specified organizational issues and circumstances;
- the prevention of discrimination on a range of different grounds including gender, nationality, race or ethnic origin, religion, sexual orientation and age.

In addition, in the UK there is legislation requiring employing organizations to have procedures regarding the treatment of disciplinary issues, and in particular, dismissal, as well as the handling of employee grievances. There is also legislation requiring employers to recognize trade unions for collective bargaining purposes if certain conditions regarding levels of union membership or support are met, and again, certain minimum procedures can be imposed.

In all of these cases, the parties are encouraged to come to their own procedural agreements and to introduce and implement procedures consistent with their own circumstances and preferences as long as the legislative minimums are complied with. The legislative imposition of procedural arrangements is only likely where management refuses to enter into negotiations designed to produce agreement or where the parties within the organization try but fail to reach agreement.

However, before looking at specific procedural areas, we should examine why it is a good idea for organizations and the respective parties to devise, develop and implement procedural rules. We need also to ask what the criteria are for the success of procedures.

Marchington and Wilkinson (1996) identify a number of reasons why employers implement procedures in the area of employee relations:

1   They help to clarify the relationship between the parties within the organization.
2   They should focus conflict within the agreed mechanisms and thereby help with its resolution, they can create a framework for good employee relations. Note that there are similarities here with the pluralist approach to the question of what constitutes good employee/industrial relations (see earlier discussion of this in **Chapter 1**).
3   They provide a mechanism for conflict resolution by identifying the position or person that has the responsibility to deal with the issue in the first instance and also what the subsequent procedures may be: who deals with appeals against the original decision? how many stages there are to be? etc.
4   They act as a safety valve and provide time during which the heat in a situation can be diffused.
5   They help ensure that employees are treated consistently throughout the organization no matter who their first line manager may be and no matter which part of the organization they work in.
6   They tend to lead to more adequate record keeping because of the formality of the procedure, because the parties know that their performance is likely to be judged against the requirements of the procedure, so there is an incentive for records to be kept.
7   Procedures that are jointly agreed may yield benefits in terms of the working relationship between the parties to the process of negotiation; it may even be that this process takes the form of joint problem solving and is more cooperative/collaborative in nature.

The majority of these points can be viewed as reasons for management to want to have procedures and are, in that sense, of advantage to management.

From the employees' viewpoint, an advantage often claimed for devising and implementing procedures is that they provide a foundation for the achievement of fairness and equity in the treatment of employees and it is interesting that Marchington and Wilkinson (1996) do not include equity of treatment as a specific 'reason' in their list above. Consistency may be more important to managers and it may be argued that equity is achieved through consistent treatment. It was noted in **Chapter 1** that equity of treatment may be an important expectation of employees and that it often forms an essential element of the psychological contract between employee and employer.

We need also to bear in mind that agreed procedures do represent a further incursion into what would otherwise be an area of managerial prerogative. Therefore, the process of agreeing the procedures itself yields benefits to employees and their representatives, reinforcing the legitimacy of their participation in managerial decision making within the organization.

While the list above contains a number of benefits to management, we must not assume that all managements and all levels of management within an organization are going to share these views of the usefulness of procedures. It has been suggested earlier that globalization, the increasing pressures for deregulation of labour markets, the exporting of much manufacturing employment to the developing world and a decline in the membership and influence of trades unions, have all contributed to an enhanced bargaining power for managements and that they have felt more able to voice their criticisms and uncertainties about the advantages of such procedural arrangements. Perhaps particularly, we have seen managers, and indeed governments, arguing that procedures introduce rigidity as well as constituting a brake upon their autonomy. It has been argued that the emphasis upon procedures acts as a brake upon the business need to be more flexible and responsive to changes in customer tastes and to the threats of global competition. Managers have criticized procedures for leading to long drawn-out decision-making processes which are no longer appropriate; sometimes hard decisions have to be taken and they have to be taken quickly if the organization is to survive and prosper.

Other criticisms tend to come from the lower levels of line management who often see procedures, especially if they are the product of agreement with the trade unions, as a direct attack upon their right and ability to manage their own particular group of employees effectively. The provision of rights for employees to appeal against or raise grievances against first line supervision is perceived as a direct threat to their autonomy and also often as a weakening of support from more senior levels of management. The personnel function, which tends to be involved in devising and agreeing the procedures, is often the subject of criticism from other managerial functions for its role in the formulation of these rules and their nature.

Other criticisms of the procedural and collective approach emerge from the new emphasis upon individualism, individual contract, linking pay and individual performance and the future, compared with the perceived procedural emphasis upon the past and precedent, consistency and equity. Many managers do not appreciate that there may be a relationship between equitable treatment and employee commitment, another of the much discussed 'new' objectives of management in the EI era, and employees may perceive flexibility as simply another word for arbitrary treatment.

We must also bear in mind that having a procedure does not necessarily mean that it will be used or implemented properly. There is commonly a degree of difference between the espoused policies and procedures in an organization and what actually happens in practice on the ground and there are many reasons why this may be so. Relationships at work can become very emotional, and in such circumstances, agreed procedures can be forgotten very easily. Sometimes decisions do have to be taken on the spot and quickly and it may well be that there just is no time to progress an issue through the agreed procedures, though this may say more about the organization and design of work and the appropriateness of the procedures than anything else. Sometimes you will find that procedures are not followed because the parties at ground level are not sure of what they are and what they mean. There may be failings in the process by which they are communicated and it may be that the organization has not invested in the appropriate training for managers in how to implement them. It is also possible that non-adherence is deliberate on the part of either party.

One common event is for stages in procedures to be missed out or deliberately bypassed. Commonly, first line supervisors are missed out as a stage in the procedures, either because it is their action that is the subject of the procedural complaint or because it has been realized that they do not have the power to make a decision and going through that procedural stage is simply a waste of time. This kind of bypassing is, of course, only possible if more senior management allows it to happen. To prevent it, managers need to say 'no', and they often find this difficult when at the same time they claim to operate an open-door policy or have emphasized open communications.

When it comes to assessing the effectiveness of procedures, there are obviously criteria that one can apply in the assessment but, looking back at the above, maybe the main criterion is or should be whether they are used or not, the implication being that, if the parties actually use the procedures, it is likely to be because their experience leads them to the conclusion that they work because:

- they contain or provide a mechanism for the resolution of conflict;
- they do lead to greater consistency and equity;
- they do ensure that the organization does not become liable for legal action to be taken against it.

Many years ago, Marsh and McCarthy (1968) suggested that there were two main criteria for assessing the effectiveness or adequacy of procedures and these were *acceptability* and *appropriateness*.

Disciplinary procedures

When labour is employed, its contribution to the product or service needs to be directed, coordinated and controlled and in order for the organizational objectives to be achieved, the labour needs to be capable of the task and appropriate standards of performance and conduct need to be achieved. It is in the context of these requirements that management may need to discipline employees in order to achieve improvements in performance or conduct; capability issues may require remedies that extend beyond the disciplinary arena.

However, in exercising discipline to achieve its objectives, management should bear in mind the expectations of employees that they should be treated fairly. There are relatively few organizations in the developed world in which management can manage successfully through coercion; much more commonly management needs employee cooperation or commitment in order for the organization's potential and objectives to be achieved and this requires that employees' expectations are also met. Employees will generally accept that there are circumstances in which employees may need to be punished, and even that this punishment may appropriately take the form of dismissal, but they expect both the process and the punishment to be fair.

Disciplinary rules and procedures therefore need to be designed to enable management to have effective means at their disposal to pursue improvement and, where appropriate to punish, but the standards and process, as stated above, should also be perceived to be fair. Implicit in this is a moral imperative, but business effectiveness is also likely to be undermined if employees feel that their expectations are not being met.

In many ways, the best way to ensure that employee expectations are met is to involve them in the drafting of the rules and procedures and, in many organizations, this is achieved through negotiations with the appropriate trade unions or staff or works council. In some countries in Europe, there is a legal requirement that employee representatives are at least consulted on the rules and procedures and they may also have to be consulted before management can actually take disciplinary action; neither of these is a requirement in the UK.

Disciplinary procedures are not necessarily dismissal procedures; often these two concepts are used interchangeably and they should not be. One form of disciplinary action may be dismissal, but this should normally be an action of last resort, being taken and implemented only when other options have been exhausted. There are also, of course, reasons for dismissal that have absolutely nothing at all to do with issues of discipline.

Bearing the above in mind, it is possible to identify a range of best practice principles and guidance that should govern the disciplinary rules and procedures devised within an organization and how these issues are dealt with.

Rules

The first issue that management needs to deal with concerns the rules; these should specify as clearly as possible the standards of behaviour expected of employees, so that employees and management know what is acceptable and what is not, and so that the risk of misinterpretation is reduced to the minimum possible. The rules should be written and specific to the organization, its circumstances and requirements, and ideally each employee should either have a copy or have easy access to a copy. It has to be recognized that not every eventuality is foreseeable and the rules therefore are unlikely to ever be totally comprehensive; nevertheless, management should try to achieve as comprehensive a set of rules as possible and should try to indicate how serious a breach of the rules or standards might be.

In all organizations, some rules or standards of behaviour will be considered to be more serious or important than others and in that respect appropriate action taken in respect of a breach or failure is likely to vary. For example, poor timekeeping may merit a first warning whereas drunkenness or assault may merit dismissal even as a first offence or instance. Generally, it is advisable for managements to try to be as specific as possible about the failures falling into this latter category of meriting dismissal. When devising the rules, management should concentrate on the requirements in their organization or workplace and, while no doubt ideas and guidance may be derived from studying the rules established in other organizations, it is generally not a good idea simply to borrow a set of rules from somewhere else. The rules required are likely to vary with the type of work, working conditions and size of establishment. Managements should always have in the forefront of their minds the need for the rules to be perceived by employees as fair and reasonable. Quite apart from any other reason, where employees consider the rules to be fair, they are more likely to comply. They are also more likely to exert peer pressure on others to comply and to accept disciplinary action against one of their fellows as fair.

Examples of areas of behaviour or conduct where it is commonly necessary to have clear written standards include theft, physical and verbal assault, fraud, dishonesty, timekeeping, attendance, being under the influence of drink or drugs, discrimination and harassment, complying with instructions, and health and safety.

Procedure

When it comes to devising the procedural arrangements to be applied in the workplace, there are basic principles that should be followed if the objectives of fairness and justice are to be achieved. In much of the literature on this subject, reference is made to *the principles of natural justice* and disciplinary procedures should comply with these as a minimum requirement.

The principles of natural justice would normally be considered to include the right to be:

- informed of the complaint against you;
- given the opportunity to state your case before a decision is reached;
- accompanied by a friend, trade union or legal representative;
- given the outcome of the hearing in writing;
- provided with and informed of a right of appeal.

In addition to these basic principles and the advice on rules above, best practice guidance also suggests that:

- the procedures should be in writing and specify to whom they apply;
- the procedures should ensure that employees are not normally dismissed for a first offence, unless the offence is considered to be very serious; in the UK the term gross misconduct is often used to signify the seriousness of certain failures or offences;
- the procedures should provide for matters to be dealt with quickly;
- there should be a clear indication of the actions that may be taken;
- the procedures should specify clearly those members of management with the authority to dismiss;
- the allegations are carefully investigated before any action is taken;
- the procedures apply to all employees with no discrimination between them;
- any period of suspension for the purposes of investigation is with pay unless the contract of employment specifically provides otherwise.

Generally, the actions taken should be appropriate to the circumstances and action should not be taken against an individual unless management feels that, on the balance of probability, the employee did commit the alleged offence.

Even where the above advice is complied with as regards the disciplinary rules and procedures there remains a range of issues and decisions that need to be addressed.

Stages and warnings, number and type

Decisions always need to be made about these issues, and once again the task of those devising the procedures should be to try and achieve procedural arrangements consistent with the size and circumstances of the organization at the same time as complying with the advice above, the need to be fair and reasonable and any specific legal requirements.

We have already noted that the procedure needs to provide for the right of appeal and generally this should be to a person not involved in the original decision, implying at least a two-stage process, though this may be difficult in small organizations.

In addition, decisions need to be made about the range of penalties that may be imposed upon those found not to have met the standards of conduct specified, and most procedures are likely to distinguish between offences, depending upon their seriousness, so that where the offence is considered to be very serious, it may be appropriate to dismiss the employee even where it is a first offence. However, for less serious matters, there should be a range of sanctions that may be imposed including warnings, disciplinary suspension and demotion.

It is common to have a series of warnings, the purpose being twofold, to let the individual know that they are not achieving the required standards at the same time as seeking to achieve improvement. It is necessary to decide how many warnings a person may receive before they progress to the point of dismissal, whether they are to be written or oral warnings and how long a warning is to be live in terms of being taken into account in the event of further action being necessary.

The length of time during which the warning or other action is to remain live is also an issue to be decided. Commonly, the more serious the offence or failure, the longer will be the period of time during which the warning remains live, so that, for example for relatively minor issues, it might be decided that the warning is to be live for 3 months. Whereas for fairly serious matters, and if you are at the final warning stage, then it might be decided that the appropriate live period should be 12 months.

The best advice is to make sure that, once formal disciplinary action is a possible outcome, decisions are put in writing and this applies to warnings. Formal warnings should be written and clearly specify the offence, the precise improvements in conduct required, how long the warning is to be regarded as live, and what is likely to happen if there is the need for further disciplinary action during this live period. Commonly, employees are likely to receive at least one written and formal warning and a final written and formal warning before dismissal, dismissal therefore being the third stage. Some organizations provide for even more written warnings than this but it is debateable whether much is achieved by further stages if employees have not taken the message of both a first and a final warning and improved their conduct to the point of it being satisfactory.

When devising the procedure, it is necessary to balance the need to be fair and just with the need also for the organization to be effective and efficient. Prolonged procedures with many stages are unlikely to achieve either of these objectives. Depending upon the seriousness of the case, the procedure might start at any stage and, as noted above, in cases of very serious (gross) misconduct, the first action taken may be the final stage of dismissal.

Many procedures provide for counselling and oral warnings as stages in the formal procedure; there have been debates about this and it seems as if the best advice is to regard such action as informal, before and outside the formal procedure; otherwise there arises the slightly ludicrous position of having to put in writing the fact that an employee has received an oral warning, how long it is to be live for, what will happen if.... Obviously if the relevant legal system specifies that this should form part of the procedure then it must be done but it really seems to make little sense.

Records

Allied to the above is the question of what happens to the records of disciplinary action once created and, perhaps even more important, what is done with them once they have been effectively spent. There are obvious concerns that if the record of the warning or other action remains on the employee's personal file it will be taken into account even if the live period has passed. At the same time, managements tend to be very reluctant to destroy records and often what happens is that records of spent action are removed from personal files and relocated in a file specifically for this purpose. As long as this composite file is not accessed by those hearing the case, then it is close to being the best practice.

Preparing for and conducting the hearing

As noted above, disciplinary action should never be taken without employees against whom allegations are made being given the chance to put their side of the story at a hearing. Management should make sure that employees know and understand the disciplinary procedure and what the possible outcomes are if the allegations or complaints are well founded. Employees should have the right to be told of the allegations and this needs to be as specific as possible so that they can prepare a defence, be invited to the hearing and given the chance to collect evidence on their own behalf and to be accompanied. It is also preferable for the manager who is going to have to make the decision to be accompanied at the hearing so that there can be corroboration of what was said in the event of an appeal or allegation of unfairness. Prior to this management should conduct a thorough investigation in order to establish the facts and obtain witness statements where appropriate. Guilt should not be assumed.

At the beginning of the hearing management should check again that employees understand what the allegations are and how the process will work. The hearing should be conducted as calmly as is possible, though it needs to be recognized that there can be a lot of emotion on both sides and so this may not be easy. It may well be an idea to adjourn the meeting if the proceedings become heated. Witnesses should be invited to the hearing and employees should be given the opportunity to cross-examine or question them. Decisions should not be made instantly and it is often wise to avoid making a decision there and then; a period of reflection can be beneficial. When considering the evidence and before making a decision, management should take into account individuals' work and disciplinary records and any mitigating circumstances offered by employees should be taken into account. Many managers think that they must slavishly follow precedent, but this should not be done; they should make the decision which results as far as possible in fairness and justice being achieved given all the circumstances of the case.

If this advice is followed, there is a greater likelihood that the matter will be dealt with fairly and reasonably and it should make it easier for management to rebut any allegations that it did not act fairly and reasonably.

Disciplinary procedures and the law in the UK

Until recently, the scale and nature of legislative intervention regarding both disciplinary and grievance procedures was quite limited. Employers were required to give employees certain information in a statement of the main particulars of their employment, including the disciplinary rules and the identity or description of the person to whom they could go if they had a grievance or were dissatisfied with a disciplinary decision (Employment Rights Act, 1996). But there was no absolute requirement for employers to have a disciplinary procedure. This has been changed by the Employment Act of 2002 which for the first time imposes a legal obligation upon employers to have a disciplinary procedure and to include details in the Employee Statement.

The notion of legally fair and unfair dismissal was introduced into legislation in the UK via the Industrial Relations Act of 1971 and it was this legislation that introduced the opportunity for employees to allege that a dismissal had been unfair. The courts and employment tribunals were required to apply the test of fairness and reasonableness in all the circumstances to the dismissal. This test applied both to the substantive reason for the dismissal and to the way in which it had been handled, and a dismissal could be found to be unfair on either or both grounds. There have been many cases since in which the courts concluded that while the reason for a dismissal was fair, the way in which proceedings had been handled, or not, rendered the dismissal unfair.

The need to determine procedural fairness prompted the publication in 1976 of the *ACAS Code of Practice on Disciplinary Practice and Procedures*. There have been several revisions to this document and the most recent version, applicable from October 2004, updates the code to take account of changes introduced in both the Employment Act of 2002 and Employment Relations Act of 2004. The Code of Practice also now contains a section dealing with grievance procedures and handling (see next section). This document effectively spells out the minimum requirements for a disciplinary procedure to be regarded by the Tribunals and Courts as fair. The Code itself is not legally binding; it has a kind of quasi-legal status in that it can be taken into account by the relevant legal authorities when trying to judge whether a dismissal was fair. Over the years as the tribunals and courts have done this, and through the device known as case law, the code has acquired an authority that to all intents and purposes means: 'comply with the code or run the risk of the dismissal being found unfair'. Remember that the Code is concerned with discipline, not only dismissals.

Over the years since 1977 and prior to the Employment Act of 2002 (see later), the tribunals and courts utilizing the law and the Code of Practice had arrived at a point where a dismissal could be ruled to be unfair on procedural grounds for any one of three reasons:

- the absence of a disciplinary procedure;
- the existence of an inadequate one, in comparison with the advice in the Code of Practice;
- the mis-application of an otherwise fair procedure.

In deciding whether a procedure was adequate or fair and/or whether an employer had acted reasonably from a procedural perspective, there would appear to be a set of core principles of reasonable behaviour, derived from the code, that should be complied with.

- Use procedures primarily to help and encourage employees to improve rather than just as a way of imposing a punishment.
- Inform employees of the complaint against them, and provide them with an opportunity to state their case before decisions are reached.

- Allow employees to be accompanied at disciplinary meetings.
- Make sure that disciplinary action is not taken until the facts of the case have been established and that the action is reasonable in the circumstances.
- Never dismiss an employee for a first disciplinary offence, unless it is a case of gross misconduct.
- Give employees a written explanation for any disciplinary action taken and make sure they know what improvement is expected.
- Give employees an opportunity to appeal.
- Deal with issues as thoroughly and promptly as possible.
- Act consistently.

The Employment Relations Act of 1999 introduced a Right of Accompaniment for workers (not only employees) in both grievance and disciplinary hearings or meetings. All workers now have a statutory right to be able to choose a fellow worker or trade union representative to accompany them to and in any disciplinary (and grievance) hearing or interview. More detail is given on this right in a later section 'Grievance Procedures and the Law in the UK'.

The 1999 Act prescribed a somewhat limited role for individuals accompanying workers and specified that they can address the hearing and confer with the worker but not answer questions on the worker's behalf.

There was considerable concern about the limited nature of the role prescribed and amendments were made in Sections 37 and 38 of the Employment Relations Act of 2004. These are explained in the following quote from the DTI guidance document on the new legislation:

> Under the amended law, the employer must allow the companion to address the hearing to put the worker's case; to sum up that case; and to respond on the worker's behalf to any view expressed at the hearing. The companion may still confer with the worker during the hearing. The companion will therefore normally be able to address the hearing both at the beginning and end of the hearing and will also have the opportunity to respond to views expressed.
>
> The amended law also provides that the employer is not required to permit the companion to answer questions on the worker's behalf, address the hearing if the worker indicates that he does not wish the companion to do so, or use the powers in away that prevents the employer from explaining his case or any other person making his contribution.
>
> Section 37 also amends section 12 of the 1999 Act to make it clear that where a worker attends a hearing as the companion of another worker, he is protected against detriment and dismissal not only in respect of the act of accompanying the worker but also for addressing or seeking to address the hearing.

We noted above that the Employment Act of 2002 introduced for the first time a legal requirement that employing organizations should have both disciplinary and grievance procedures. The Act sets out what are referred to as statutory procedures in both areas and it is clear that these are intended to constitute minimum requirements applicable to all employers, irrespective of size. In the case of the statutory procedure relating to disciplinary action, it applies if the employer is contemplating dismissing an employee or imposing some other disciplinary penalty that is not a suspension on full pay or a warning. In other words, the statutory procedure is intended primarily to apply to disciplinary action resulting in dismissal.

If an employee is dismissed without the employer following this statutory procedure, and he or she makes a claim to an employment tribunal, the dismissal will automatically be ruled unfair. The statutory procedure is a minimum requirement and even where the relevant procedure is followed the dismissal may still be unfair if the employer has not acted reasonably in all the circumstances.

However, in the context of determining whether a dismissal is fair or unfair, the Act seems intent on varying the legal status quo in that it goes on to state that, provided the minimum standards set out in the Act are met and the dismissal is otherwise fair, procedural shortcomings can be disregarded. Employers will always have to follow the basic procedures, but will no longer be penalized for irrelevant procedural mistakes beyond that – provided the dismissal would otherwise be fair. This means that the dismissal must have been for a fair reason and the employer must have acted reasonably in treating it as a reason for dismissing the employee. The legislation applies only to employees and not to all workers (we elaborate upon this distinction in a later section 'Grievance Procedures and the Law in the UK').

2002 Employment Act Standard Disciplinary procedure

- Employer must set out complaint in writing and send copy to employee and invite employee to meeting.
- Employee to be given reasonable time prior to meeting to consider response.
- The employer should take no disciplinary action, other than suspension, prior to meeting.
- Employee must make every effort to attend meeting.
- Employee to be informed of decision and where appropriate of right to appeal.
- If the employee decides to appeal he/she must inform employer.
- Employer must call another meeting to consider appeal.
- Employee to have right to be informed of appeal outcome.
- Disciplinary action does not have to wait for appeal to be held.

The 2002 Act provisions regarding both disciplinary and grievance procedures were implemented in 2004 and it will be some time before we see how they affect the handling of disciplinary issues in practice. As noted above they are clearly considered to be minimum requirements and it is as yet unclear how they will interact with the existing standards of best practice which are the subject of the Code of Practice and which are generally consistent with the advice given in the earlier sections of this chapter (see **Figure 11.1**).

The Code of Practice also contains advice on some particular cases and issues such as dealing with absence and the particular problems of disciplinary action against a trade union official and dealing with employees charged with or convicted of a criminal offence.

In the UK a distinction is drawn between misconduct and gross misconduct. Gross misconduct is the type of conduct which may warrant summary dismissal (i.e. dismissal without notice). Summary is not

Figure 11.1
ACAS best practice guidance.
(*Source*: ACAS Code of Practice on Disciplinary and Grievance Procedures).

At a glance
Drawing up disciplinary rules and procedures
- Involve management, employees and their representatives where appropriate (Paragraph 52).
- Make rules are clear and brief and explain their purpose (Paragraph 53).
- Explain rules and procedures to employees and make sure they have a copy or ready access to a copy of them (Paragraph 55).

Operating disciplinary procedures
- Establish facts before taking action (Paragraph 8).
- Deal with cases of minor misconduct or unsatisfactory performance informally (Paragraphs 11 and 12).
- For more serious cases, follow formal procedures, including informing the employee of the alleged misconduct or unsatisfactory performance (Paragraph 13).
- Invite the employee to a meeting and inform them of the right to be accompanied (Paragraphs 14–16).
- Where performance is unsatisfactory explain to the employee the improvement required, the support that will be given and when and how performance will be reviewed (Paragraphs 19 and 20).
- If giving a warning, tell the employee why and how they need to change, the consequences of failing to improve and that they have a right to appeal (Paragraphs 21 and 22).
- If dismissing an employee, tell them why, when their contract will end and that they can appeal (Paragraph 25).
- Before dismissing or taking disciplinary action other than issuing a warning, always follow the statutory dismissal and disciplinary procedure (Paragraphs 26–32).
- When dealing with absences from work, find out the reasons for the absence before deciding on what action to take (Paragraph 37).

Holding appeals
- If the employee wishes to appeal invite them to a meeting and inform the employee of their right to be accompanied (Paragraphs 44–48).
- Where possible, arrange for the appeal to be dealt with by a more senior manager not involved with the earlier decision (Paragraph 46).
- Inform the employee about the appeal decision and the reasons for it (Paragraph 48).

Records
- Keep written records for future reference (Paragraph 49).

necessarily synonymous with instant, and it is arguable that instant dismissal cannot be fair since it implies that even the minimum procedural requirements are not complied with. Incidents of gross misconduct will usually still need to be investigated as part of a formal procedure. Acts which constitute gross misconduct are those resulting in a serious breach of contractual terms and are for organizations to decide in light of their own particular circumstances. However, the Code suggests that they might include the following:

(i)   theft, fraud and deliberate falsification of records;
(ii) physical violence;
(iii) serious bullying or harassment;
(iv) deliberate damage to property;
(v)   serious insubordination;
(vi) misuse of an organization's property or name;
(vii) bringing the employer into serious disrepute;
(viii) serious incapability whilst on duty brought on by alcohol or illegal drugs;
(ix) serious negligence which causes or might cause unacceptable loss, damage or injury;
(x)   serious infringement of health and safety rules;
(xi) serious breach of confidence (subject to the Public Interest (Disclosure) Act of 1998).

In the UK also there are both fair and automatically unfair reasons for dismissal. Fair reasons include: Capability or qualifications, conduct, redundancy, breach of a statutory provision such as may occur if employees are required to drive and they lose their licence, and 'some other substantial reason' which by its nature is difficult to define and which must pass the reasonable testing that the courts will assess whether it was reasonable of the employer in the circumstances to treat the reason as sufficient for dismissal. Automatically unfair reasons include dismissal which is discriminatory where, for example, the principal reason for the dismissal is sex, pregnancy, race or disability. It is also automatically unfair to dismiss employees because of union membership or because they take part in union activities not including industrial action.

See **Figure 11.2** for an example of a disciplinary procedure.

Figure 11.2
An example of a disciplinary procedure
(Source: Adapted from one produced for an NHS Trust).

1 PURPOSE AND SCOPE

This procedure is designed to help and encourage all employees to achieve and maintain the highest possible standards of conduct, attendance and job performance. The aim is to ensure consistent fair treatment for all.

2 PRINCIPLES

2.1   No disciplinary action will be taken against an employee until the case has been fully investigated by an independent Manager not in direct line management of the individual concerned. There are three categories of misconduct – Minor Misconduct, Serious Misconduct and Gross Misconduct (for examples of Gross Misconduct, see paragraph 4).

2.2   At the onset of disciplinary proceedings a copy of Rights Of Staff (Appendix 1) will be given to the individual concerned. The employee will be advised at every stage in the procedure of the nature of the complaint and will be given the opportunity to state his/her case before any decision is made. All relevant information should be made available to the individual concerned prior to the hearing.

2.3   At all stages the employee will have the right to be accompanied by a trade union representative or work colleague not acting in a legal capacity during the disciplinary interview.

2.4   No employee will be dismissed for a first breach of discipline except in the case of gross misconduct, when the penalty will be dismissal without notice or payment in lieu of notice.

2.5   An employee will have the right to appeal against any disciplinary penalty imposed.

2.6   The procedure may be implemented at any stage if the employee's alleged misconduct warrants such action.

3 PROCEDURE

Minor faults will be dealt with informally, to identify the problem and to resolve it, but where the matter is more serious, the following procedure will be used:

Stage 1 – Spoken warning

If conduct or performance does not meet acceptable standards, the employee will normally be given a formal SPOKEN WARNING. He/she will be advised of the reason for the warning; that it is the first stage of the disciplinary procedure; and that he/she has a right of appeal. A brief note of the spoken warning will be filed but will be removed after a period of between 1 and 3 months defined at the starting date and subject to satisfactory conduct and performance

Stage 2 – Written warning

If the offence is a serious one, or if a further offence of a like nature occurs, a WRITTEN WARNING will be given to the employee. This will give details of the complaint, the improvement required and the timescale. It will warn that action under Stage 3 will be considered if there is no satisfactory improvement and will advise of the right of appeal. A copy of this written warning will be kept but it will be disregarded for disciplinary purposes after a period of between 3 and 6 months defined at the starting date and subject to satisfactory conduct and performance.

Stage 3 – Final written warning

If there is still a failure to improve conduct or performance is still unsatisfactory, or if the misconduct is sufficiently serious to warrant only one written warning, (in effect both first and final written warning) but insufficiently serious to justify dismissal, a FINAL WRITTEN WARNING will normally be given to the employee. This will give details of the complaint, will warn that dismissal will result if there is no satisfactory improvement and will advise of the right of appeal. A copy of this final written warning will be kept but it will be spent after a period of between 6 and 12 months (the period may be longer in exceptional cases) defined at the start date and subject to satisfactory conduct and performance.

Stage 4 – Dismissal

If conduct or performance is still unsatisfactory and the employee still fails to reach the prescribed standards, DISMISSAL will normally result. The employee will be provided with written reasons for dismissal, the date on which employment will terminate and the right of appeal.

4 GROSS MISCONDUCT

The following list provides examples of offences which would be regarded as gross misconduct:

- theft; fraud; deliberate falsification of records;
- physical assault or threatening behaviour on another person;

Figure 11.2
(*Continued*)

- sexual harassment;
- deliberate damage to Trust property;
- incapability due to being under the influence of alcohol or drugs;
- negligence which causes unacceptable loss, damage or injury;
- serious act of insubordination.

If you are accused of an act of gross misconduct, you may be suspended by your Manager from work on full pay (normally for not more than 10 working days), while the Trust investigates the alleged offence.

5 APPEALS

An employee who wishes to appeal against a disciplinary decision should inform the Manager who made the decision within 14 working days. The Senior Manager (the next level of management from the Manager concerned) will hear the appeal and his/her decision is final on behalf of the Trust.

Appendix 1
To Disciplinary Procedure

RIGHTS OF STAFF

In disciplinary matters, each member of staff has the right:

1 to be represented by an accredited trade union representative or a colleague in the Disciplinary Procedures from the outset, when sufficient time shall be allowed for the representative to advise the member and to prepare the case. Management will give the maximum assistance in securing this representation promptly so that the matter may be resolved without unnecessary delay, and will make arrangements for the release from normal duties of accredited staff representatives.
2 to professional legal representation but this may only be employed at the appeal stage subject to the Trust being notified 3 working days prior to the hearing.
3 to be advised of the details of the alleged misconduct.
4 to look at the records of any disciplinary action which are retained on his/her personal file.
5 to be informed in writing of his/her right of appeal in matters involving Serious and/or Gross Misconduct.
6 to be informed in writing on whose authority he/she may be dismissed.

Figure 11.2
(Continued)

Grievance procedures and handling

We have already noted in the previous sections that the way in which employers handle employee grievances may be legally regulated and that some minimum legislative rights and requirements have recently been introduced into the UK. However, once again the primary focus of this section is not upon complying with the legislation but upon good practice from an employee relations perspective and again it should be noted that employees have expectations concerning the way in which management deals with any grievances that they may have, fairly and with an outcome that they perceive to be just. It is in management's interest to deal with employee grievances quickly and fairly. Managements should want to know if their employees have grievances since unresolved grievances are likely to contribute to dissatisfaction and thereby to poor performance, absenteeism and labour turnover.

Before we go any further, we need to define what a grievance is in this context and to distinguish it from what we might refer to as a dispute.

Definition

A *grievance* is an expression of dissatisfaction or a complaint by an individual that usually concerns the application, interpretation, implementation of or change to a statutory right or existing procedure, rule, custom, working practice or agreement. It may be that the complaint or dissatisfaction is concerned with the consistency of implementation, interpretation, with the failure to apply, or with the application in inappropriate circumstances of one or more of what are often referred to as rights, rights not necessarily in terms of legislative rights but in the context of the agreement, procedure or custom and practice. Many grievances are occasioned by management introducing change to existing working arrangements and methods.

Commonly, individuals allege that management is not treating them fairly, not giving them their due or that they have been disadvantaged in some way or other, often in comparison with the way that it is perceived management has treated someone else. Another of the distinguishing features of a grievance is that it is commonly a complaint against a member of management, often the immediate supervisor.

Grievances are not exclusively individual; they can be felt by a group, but this is a more unusual occurrence.

Disputes, on the other hand, tend to be collective and concern rates of pay or some other substantive element of the terms and conditions of employment. Commonly, a dispute concerns dissatisfaction with the terms and conditions status quo, the existing situation, rather than the employees' rights under existing rules and regulations and tends to surface as a request to improve, or in some other way amend, the status quo. The most obvious example is a dispute concerning the employees' request for an increase in pay. A dispute concerning the recognition of a trade union for collective bargaining purposes, where employees are collectively seeking such recognition, may not be substantive in the traditional and accepted sense but it is certainly about change to the existing situation, the status quo, rather than the interpretation, etc. of an existing rule or custom and it is change that is being initiated by employees rather than by management. The dividing line between the two is sometimes blurred and it is not uncommon for something that starts off as an individual grievance to escalate into a collective dispute.

Issues and considerations

As noted already, grievances should be dealt with by management fairly, expeditiously and constructively. It is easy for management to become defensive about grievances since they are often expressions of employee dissatisfaction with something that management either has done or said or indeed has not done.

Many of the imperatives that should inform the drawing up of grievance procedures are the same as those informing disciplinary procedures and some of the issues to be decided are similar.

The *objectives* of a grievance procedure then should be:

- to provide employees with a mechanism for raising and having a grievance redressed;
- to ensure that this can be done promptly and constructively;
- to ensure that employees are treated fairly and consistently and with dignity;
- to reduce the possibility of unpredictable action and an escalation of a grievance into a dispute.

The prompt, fair and constructive resolution of grievances is of interest to both management and employees and it is common for these procedures to be jointly determined and agreed. There is advantage to management in involving employees and/or their representatives in this process since the procedures then have a legitimacy within the organization that they may well not otherwise have.

Subject matter coverage/jurisdiction of the procedure

Management, or the parties to an agreed procedure, might not want a comprehensive list of the kinds of grievances that can be dealt with via the procedure, but they would need to decide whether some issues are to be excluded and dealt with differently or separately; examples of such might include appeals against disciplinary action, allegations of sexual harassment and other discrimination, and whistle blowing.

An individual might well feel that the existing disciplinary procedure has been applied inappropriately or unfairly and this might constitute a legitimate grievance in the terms of the definition above, something that could arguably be dealt with within the grievance procedure. However, the disciplinary procedure should contain provision for the individual on the receiving end of the action to appeal against that action and in such circumstances it might be advisable, in order to reduce uncertainty and support the authority of the disciplinary as well as the grievance procedure, to stipulate explicitly that such matters cannot be dealt with in the grievance procedure.

The issue of sexual harassment and its relationship to the grievance procedure is different in nature but still important in that grievances are generally perceived as complaints against management about the way in which management has treated an employee. An allegation of sexual harassment can fall into this category but it may also have nothing to do with management directly and the allegation may well be that the harassment was committed by another employee or employees. In these circumstances, it might lead to confusion as to the purpose of the grievance procedure if such matters were dealt with in that way. It might seem appropriate to deal with issues of sexual harassment in a completely separate procedure which provides for informality and counselling in the early stages as well as providing mechanisms through which the matter can be resolved and the harassment stopped.

Distinct procedures can sometimes be usefully linked at certain points and an example of this would be the linking of harassment and disciplinary procedures at the point at which the harassment constitutes a disciplinary offence, though a personal view would be that the integrity of procedures is best preserved by keeping them separate and distinct from each other.

Information and representation

Irrespective of any legislative requirements (see later) employees need to know that there is a grievance procedure and they need to understand how it works, what their rights are and, perhaps particularly, who they should take the matter up with in the first instance.

Additionally, they need to know whether they have to take the matter up on their own or whether they can be accompanied and if so by whom. In the interests of fairness it is essential that employees do have the opportunity to be accompanied. Many employees will be reluctant to take up a grievance on their own and, while this might have an initial appeal to management, unresolved grievances tend to fester and can easily lead to significantly greater problems in the future.

Ideally employees are given a copy of the procedure and it is explained to them so that they understand what kind of issues might constitute a grievance, what they should do if they do feel aggrieved about something within the jurisdiction of the procedure and what their rights are within the procedure.

Stages

As with disciplinary procedures, decisions have to be made about how many stages there are to be and who is to preside at each of these stages. To some extent these issues will be dependent upon the size and structure of the organization and also whether there are bargaining structures within the industry which extend beyond the level of the firm. For example, in a small firm there may only be room for one or two stages internally, whereas in the National Health Service in the UK where there are still some national negotiations on terms and conditions of employment as well as nationally agreed procedural arrangements, then it would not be surprising if the procedure allowed for more stages to ensure consistency of treatment across the service and that some of these stages were outside the particular Trust or health unit.

There is no right number of stages but generally the advice would be that there should be more than one and that the final stage should be at a level that does facilitate consistency and fairness of treatment across the organization. It is also important that the first stage should involve the person about whom the allegation is made, the individual who is the subject of the grievance. Often such a first stage may not result in resolution but it is important that the subject of the grievance is not bypassed in the procedure, he or she should be given the opportunity to reconsider the way in which they have interpreted a particular rule or procedural provision. One of the problems that commonly occurs at this first stage is that the line manager does not have the authority to resolve the grievance and, in order for the first stage of the procedure to be effective, line managers need to be given as much authority to take decisions and resolve grievances as possible. Where line managers do not have the authority, there will be a tendency for the first stage to fall into disrepute and for employees and their representatives to bypass this stage and take the grievance to a higher level of management. This should be resisted by the higher levels of management, since the line manager's authority is undermined in this way. It will also damage their ability to manage on a daily basis and it may reduce their motivation to manage their staff. Line managers should be involved in dealing with grievances as well as discipline.

As organizational structures have been flattened and de-layered in recent years, many existing grievance procedures have had to be altered to fit the new structure. The reduction in the number of layers in the organizational structure and hierarchy has sometimes meant that restructuring has encouraged the shortening of grievance procedures.

One of the questions often raised is whether the final stage in the procedure should be within or external to the organization. Is management's decision to be final or is there to be recourse to an organization like ACAS for conciliation or arbitration? As noted in **Chapter 5**, conciliation is a process that seeks to obtain an agreed solution to a problem whereas arbitration is more judicial in nature, a process whereby the power of decision is given to a third party. Some people argue that agreeing to go to arbitration is a dereliction of management's responsibility and duty to manage and runs too many risks in terms of an outcome that is not consistent with other decisions taken within the organization and that it may create more problems than it solves. Conciliation, on the other hand, may be a much more acceptable option given that the parties retain the decision-making power and can accept or reject any suggested solution or outcome.

Time limits

It is fair to try and deal with a grievance within a reasonable period of time and certainly employees should not be left wondering just how long it is going to take for their grievance to be dealt with. These pressures have often led organizations to introduce into grievance procedures time limits on the holding of a grievance hearing after the lodging of the grievance, the giving of an answer, the advising of intent to appeal and progression to the next stage. The most important advice on this issue is that the limits, if necessary, should be realistic and not too optimistic, they should also be fair to both sides and they should be adhered to. Where a procedure contains time limits to the various stages, it is common for these to lengthen as the grievance is processed through the stages. Speed should not be at the expense of fairness and the ability to deal with the issue raised in a constructive manner. All too often organizations have devised procedures with time limits that cannot be kept and the danger is that, because the time limits are not adhered to, the whole procedure falls into disrepute and other means are taken to secure resolution of the grievance.

Grievance handling

Negotiation

There is a temptation for managers to think that in dealing with a grievance they can preserve their managerial prerogative, their unilateral right to manage, to decide issues. However, the reality is that grievance hearings are usually characterized, at the end if not at the beginning, by a process of searching for compromise, for a solution that sufficiently meets the needs and interests of both parties to be acceptable to both. It is relatively rare for right to all be on one side and often the process of dealing with a grievance yields evidence that there are other problems which need to be resolved and again these are often to be resolved through the process of negotiation (see **Chapter 10**). A reasonably common example would be the realization that existing rules are not fair or sufficiently precisely drafted or that there are inconsistencies within or between them which need to be ironed out and which may result in the formation of some form of joint working party or problem solving group.

The hearing/interview

In most grievance procedures, there is provision for a hearing or an interview in which the complainant outlines the grievance, its nature and the circumstances in which it occurred and in which the manager about whom the complaint is made will also have the opportunity to explain the decision made or action taken. As noted above, the first of these should normally be with the employee's immediate supervisor, who is quite likely also to be the individual who is the subject of the allegation. As also noted above, it is advisable that there is at least one further stage, which may be regarded as an appeal stage since it is only

Figure 11.3
The grievance
interview.
Adapted from
Gennard and Judge
(1997), pp. 211–12.

Listen
Keep an open mind
Question
Collect facts: keep in mind the 5 'Ws'
    What
    When
    Where
    Who
    Why
Check understanding with employee

likely if the first raising of the grievance results in a failure to agree to a satisfactory outcome.

Whatever the precise format and however many people attend, it would be normal for the hearing to be conducted by management even though it has been initiated by an employee.

The importance of preparation and conducting as full an investigation as possible, allowing the employee to put his or her case, considering this input, trying to ensure that all the parties remain calm, and being consistent and fair is just as great as it is in the case of disciplinary hearings.

Figure 11.3 contains some simple but important guidelines on conducting a grievance interview.

It is important that the parties to the hearing remain calm, that they keep as open a mind as possible, that they listen and question when they do not understand something, and that efforts are made to establish the facts where this is possible.

Nevertheless a grievance hearing is very different from a disciplinary hearing in that, at the end of the day, management is being asked to conclude that a member of its own ranks made a mistake or deliberately did something that occasioned the employee to feel aggrieved that rights were being infringed or violated. In this context, there is obviously the danger that management will require a great deal of convincing before it is prepared to acknowledge the grievance to be genuine; there may well be a natural desire to side with a management colleague. In these circumstances, a scrupulously open and fair approach is even more of a necessity if an acceptable solution is to be found.

Records

Ideally, records are kept of each stage in the grievance procedure and these form part of the evidence taken into account at the next stage. The record should spell out the nature of the grievance, who raised it, what the management response was and whether any action was taken.

Wherever possible, the record should be signed by both parties and their representatives to indicate agreement that it is an accurate record and this is particularly important at the agreement stage, as in any set of negotiations it is important at the end that the parties agree on what has been agreed. The written record also facilitates the monitoring of grievances and the establishment of whether there have been precedents and how particular rules or agreements have been interpreted in the past.

It should be borne in mind that managers will often regard the requirement to keep a record as both irksome and intrusive and, given that management is often on the defensive in the case of a grievance and that keeping a record may effectively mean keeping a record of a management mistake, it may be necessary for the HR specialist or more senior management to ensure that lower levels of management actually do keep the records required.

Grievance Procedures and the Law in the UK

The Employment Rights Act of 1996 specifies that employees generally have a legal right to be informed of the person or officer of the organization to whom they can take a grievance and this should be included in the statement of particulars given to the employee. Where the organization has a grievance procedure, the statement should also include, or refer to a document which lays down further steps in the procedure. At the time of that legislation, there was no legal requirement for organizations to have a grievance procedure but, as with disciplinary procedures, the Employment Act of 2002 has introduced a legal requirement and specifies a minimum or standard procedure (see later).

As has been noted earlier, the 1999 Employment Relations Act has provided all workers with the right of accompaniment and the right in respect of grievances is the same as for disciplinary hearings. It was felt that this new right would put greater pressure upon employers and managers to deal with worker grievances fairly and reasonably and that it might indeed lead to some initial increase in the raising of grievances as workers realize that they no longer need to be quite so afraid of raising a grievance as perhaps they had been in the past.

However, the right is very much a limited one and applies only in the event of a worker wanting to raise a grievance concerning:

'grievance hearings which concern the performance of a duty by an employer in relation to a worker'.

The Code of Practice on Disciplinary and Grievance Procedures of 2004 points out that this means a legal duty arising from statute or common law (e.g. contractual commitments). Ultimately, only the courts can decide what sort of grievances fall within the statutory definition but the individual circumstances of each case will always be relevant.

The Code then gives some explanatory examples of when a worker grievance might be covered by the legislation and when not. For instance, it suggests that an individual's request for a pay rise is unlikely to fall within the definition unless specifically provided for in the contract, whereas a grievance about equal pay would be included as this is covered by a statutory duty imposed on employers. Another example might concern car parking facilities; generally employers are not under a legal obligation to provide car parking facilities but if the worker is disabled then there might be a legal obligation. It is undoubtedly going to be some time before a body of case law develops which will clarify the implications of this new right in the context of grievances.

The legislation states that the person who is to accompany the worker, at the grievance (or disciplinary) hearing can be a single companion who is either:

- a fellow worker, i.e. another of the employer's workers, or
- a full-time official employed by a trade union; or a lay trade union official, so long as they have been reasonably certified in writing by their union as having experience of, or as having received training in, acting as a worker's companion at disciplinary or grievance hearings.

Workers are free to choose an official from any trade union to accompany them at a disciplinary or grievance hearing regardless of whether the union is recognized or not. However, the Code recommends that, where a trade union is recognized in a workplace, it is good practice for an official from that union to accompany the worker at a hearing. It also points out there is no duty on a fellow worker or trade union official to accept a request to accompany a worker and suggests that no pressure should be brought to bear on people if they do not wish to act as a companion.

We noted earlier in the section 'Disciplinary Procedures and the Law in the UK' that the person accompanying the worker has certain legally specified rights to participate and that these have been amended by the Employment Relations Act of 2004 but are still limited. The Code gives the same advice in the context of grievance hearings as for disciplinary hearings and suggests that the person accompanying should be allowed to participate in the hearing as fully as possible.

The Code does not only deal with the legal rights and obligations of the parties and, as with Discipline, also contains sections giving general best practice advice to employers on how to deal with grievances. This advice is summarized in **Figure 11.4**. The contents of the Code with respect to grievances have the same legal status as for Discipline, that is that it is not itself legally binding but will be taken into account by Employment Tribunals and the Courts.

Figure 11.4
ACAS best practice
guidance.
(*Source*: ACAS Code
of Practice on
Disciplinary and
Grievance
procedures).

At a glance
Drawing up grievance procedures
- Involve management, employees and their representatives where appropriate (Paragraph 90).
- Explain procedures to employees and make sure they have a copy or ready access to a copy of them (Paragraph 94).

Operating grievance procedures
- Many grievances can be settled informally with line managers (Paragraph 67).
- Employees should raise formal grievances with management (Paragraph 73).
- Invite the employee to a meeting and inform them about the right to be accompanied (Paragraph 77).
- Give the employee an opportunity to have their say at the meeting (Paragraph 78).
- Write with a response within a reasonable time and inform the employee of their right to appeal (Paragraph 81).

Appeals
- If possible, a more senior manager should handle the appeal (Paragraph 82).
- Tell the employee they have the right to be accompanied (Paragraph 82).
- The senior manager should respond to the grievance in writing after the appeal and tell the employee if it is the final stage in the grievance procedure (Paragraph 83).

Records
- Written records should be kept for future reference (Paragraph 87).

As with Discipline, the Employment Act of 2002 includes provisions regarding a minimum and Standard Grievance procedure, so that now all employers should operate a grievance procedure that at least complies with the requirements of the legislation. This specifies that:

- the employee must give employer a written statement of grievance;
- the employer should call a meeting to discuss the grievance, but the meeting should not take place until the employee has told the employer the grounds for the grievance and the employer has had the time to consider their response;
- the employee must make every effort to attend the meeting;
- the employee has the right to be informed of the decision and of the right to appeal;
- the employee has the right to appeal against the decision and if he or she decides to do so then the employer must be informed;
- there should be another meeting to deal with the appeal, again the employee should make every effort to attend and the employee has right to be informed of the outcome of the appeal.

As with the statutory standard disciplinary procedure, the legislative requirements were implemented late in 2004 and it will therefore be some time before it is possible to judge the impact that it has upon the handling of employee grievances and the resolution of disputes within organizations.

Evidence on the incidence of disciplinary and grievance procedures in the UK

The WERS (2004) obtained information on the incidence of formal grievance and disciplinary procedures and also explored how many workplaces have arrangements in place which apparently meet the statutory procedural requirements of the Employment Act of 2002. The survey also explored compliance with the new statutory right to be accompanied.

Formal procedures existed in the vast majority of workplaces, 88 per cent for handling grievances and 91 per cent for dealing with disciplinary issues or dismissals (excluding redundancies). There was no change in the incidence of grievance procedures since 1998, but there was an increase in the incidence of disciplinary procedures (85 per cent in 1998).

In both instances, formal procedures were less likely in smaller workplaces, the private sector and in workplaces without a recognized trade union.

The new legislation requires a three-step procedure in both cases; putting the matter in writing, employees having the right to attend a formal meeting, and employees having the right of appeal. The survey data revealed that of those claiming to have formal procedures, by no means all reported the presence of each of the three components. Conversely, less than 2 per cent of workplaces reported having none of the three elements.

The single most widespread feature was the right for employees to appeal against decisions, 94 per cent for grievances and 95 per cent for disciplinary actions. The use of formal meetings was similarly widespread for both disciplines, 95 per cent, and grievance procedures, 92 per cent. The requirement to put matters in writing in disciplinary situations was marginally less widespread (91 per cent) but was considerably less common for grievance procedures at 76 per cent.

In handling grievances raised by individuals, 43 per cent of workplaces reported that all three elements applied. The incidence of workplaces with arrangements which matched the three-step procedure in relation to disciplinary action was higher: 71 per cent of workplaces had each step in place.

Arrangements matching the 'three-step procedure' were more prevalent in larger workplaces, in the public sector and in workplaces with a recognized trade union.

Of the workplaces reporting that a formal meeting was part of their procedural arrangements, almost all allowed employees to be accompanied. Interestingly, managers in many workplaces indicated that they allowed the companion to answer questions and respond on the employee's behalf, a right not included in legislation, 47 per cent at grievance meetings and 49 per cent in the case of disciplinary meetings. It would seem therefore that many employers allow the companion to perform a wider role than is actually required by the legislation. As noted earlier the amendments to the role of the companion enacted in the Employment Relations Act of 2004 do not require employers to allow the companion to answer questions on the employee's behalf.

Summary

In this chapter we have examined both disciplinary and grievance procedures and how to handle both types of issue. The emphasis of the chapter has been upon the provision of practical advice rather than focusing upon legal requirements, though it was noted that in many countries there are specific legislative rights and constraints applying in both areas. The practical advice focuses upon the expectations of fairness and justice that employees are likely to have as part of their psychological contract with their employer and which, from the employer's point of view, is likely to contribute to a positive employee relations climate within the organization.

There is a potentially wide range of procedural outcomes and they tend to provide the parties to the employment relationship with a constitution as well being operational mechanisms. Procedures may be the product of joint decision making between the employee's representatives and management or they may be the outcome of unilateral decisions by management. Some procedures are required by law. There are several reasons why it is a good idea to have a comprehensive portfolio of procedures and these include clarifying the relationships between the parties, focusing and resolving conflict, encouraging consistency and equity in the treatment of staff, encouraging a more collaborative approach and relationship between the parties, and providing a safety valve and additional means by which managerial prerogative may be curtailed.

The tests for the effectiveness of procedures are that they are used and that they are accepted and appropriate.

Disciplinary procedures in the UK have been significantly influenced by the publication in 1976 of the Code of Practice which has acted as a template of best practice. The Code's notion of fairness rests upon the principles of natural justice, reasonableness, clarity and transparency.

We have distinguished a grievance from a dispute and you have been made aware of some of the procedural issues that must be resolved in devising and drafting both disciplinary and grievance procedures. We have also examined the legal situation in the UK with regard to both Disciplinary and Grievance procedures.

In the latter part of the chapter we have emphasized the importance of seeing a grievance hearing and the quest for a solution in terms of negotiating and achieving compromise, rather than simply asserting management's prerogative, and we have pointed out the importance of certain interpersonal and communication skills along with keeping an open mind and establishing the facts.

In the final part of the chapter we examined the WERS 2004 data on both the incidence of grievance and disciplinary procedures in the UK and the extent to which they appear to comply with the new statutory requirements for a minimum three-stage procedure.

Activities to test understanding

Activity 1

Devise lists of the advantages and disadvantages to both management and employees of having effective employee relations procedures.

Activity 2

The ACAS Code of Practice rests upon the principles of natural justice. What are they? Think of the rights of someone suspected of a criminal offence, and if this does not help, think of the rights you would want to have if the person charged with the criminal offence was you.

Activity 3

Examine the copy of a disciplinary procedure in **Figure 11.2** and assess it against the best practice guidance given in the chapter and, if appropriate, the legislative requirements in the UK.

Your task is to identify areas in which the procedure might be considered deficient. Look at it from the viewpoint of management as well as from the viewpoint of whether you are going to be legally safe.

Activity 4

Short answer questions:

1 Identify some of the criticisms of the procedural approach that have been expressed more freely in recent years.
2 Which of the various alternatives would you choose to use as a measure of the effectiveness of procedures and why?
3 Explain the legal status and relevance of the Code of Practice on Disciplinary and Grievance Procedures.

Activity 5

1 Explain the difference between a grievance and a dispute.
2 Outline the main points of difference between managing discipline and managing grievances.

Activity 6

Examine the grievance procedure displayed in **Figure 11.5** and identify and discuss the ways in which the procedure might be amended in order to comply both with best practice and the legislative requirements in the UK.

GRIEVANCE PROCEDURE

INTRODUCTION

1 Every employee has the right to seek redress for grievances relating to his/her employment, and it is important that every individual should understand the correct procedure for doing this.
2 It is very important that grievances are settled fairly, promptly, and as near as possible to the point of origin.

Procedure

Stage 1: The employee with the grievance must first raise it with his/her immediate Team Leader/Manager.

Stage 2: If the matter has not been satisfactorily resolved during Stage 1, then arrangements will be made for the employee to see the next level of management.

Stage 3: If the grievance remains unresolved after the above meeting, then arrangements will be made for the employee to attend an interview with the Head of Department and, if necessary, the Company Personnel Manager.

Stage 4: If the grievance is still unresolved then a meeting will be called to give the employee an opportunity to discuss his/her grievance with a Director of the Company. In attendance will be the Senior Manager responsible in the department and the Company Personnel Manager.

Notes:

1 Up to and including Stage 2, the grievance may be verbal or written, but should it not be resolved during Stage 2, then the employee will be asked to put his/her grievance in writing before Stage 3.

   In addition to this, the level of management involved at Stage 2 will be required to put in writing the points discussed and the decision made so far, if any.

   These 2 documents should be passed to the Company Personnel Manager who will arrange for Stage 3 of the procedure.
2 If the grievance is not resolved at Stage 1, then the employee may, if he or she so wishes, request that a colleague be present at any subsequent meetings held under Stages 2, 3 or 4.
3 Stage 4 represents the Appeal Stage.

Figure 11.5
Various stages of a grievance procedure.

References

Advisory Conciliation and Arbitration Service, 1976. *Code of Practice 1 on Disciplinary Practice and Procedures.* HMSO, London.

Advisory Conciliation and Arbitration Service, 2004. *Code of Practice on Disciplinary and Grievance Procedures.* HMSO, London.

Dunlop, J.T., 1958. *Industrial Relations Systems.* Holt, New York.

Gennard, J. and Judge, G., 1997. *Employee Relations.* IPD, London.

Hawkins, K., 1979. *A Handbook of Industrial Relations Practice.* Kogan Page, London.

Kersley, B., Alpin, C., Forth, J., Bryson, A., Bewley, H., Dix, G., Oxenbridge, S., 2006. *Inside the Workplace. First Findings from the 2004 Workplace Employment Relations Survey (WERS 2004).* Routledge, London.

Marchington, M. and Wilkinson, A., 1996. *Core Personnel and Development.* IPD, London.

Marsh, A.I. and McCarthy, W.J., 1968. *Disputes Procedures in Britain.* Donovan Commission Research Paper No.2 Part 2. HMSO, London.

Bibliography

Advisory Conciliation and Arbitration Service, 1976. *Code of Practice 1 on Disciplinary Practice and Procedures.* HMSO, London.

Advisory Conciliation and Arbitration Service, 2004. *Code of Practice on Disciplinary and Grievance Procedures* for 2004.

ACAS, 2006. Annual Report for 2005–6.

ACAS, 2004. Annual Report.

Annual Reports of the Certification Officer.

Armstrong, M., 1995. *Personnel Management Practice*, 5th Edition. Kogan Page, London.

Atkinson, J., 1984. Manpower strategies for the flexible organization. *Personnel Management* August, 28–31.

Banker, R., Field, J., Schroeder, R. and Sinha, K., 1996. Impact of work teams on manufacturing performance: a longitudinal field study. *Academy of Management Journal* 39(4): 867–890.

Barrell, R. and Pain, N., 1997. 'EU: an attractive investment. Being part of the EU is good for FDI and being out of EMU may be bad'. *New Economy* 4(1).

Bartlett, C.A. and Ghoshal, S., 1989. *Managing Across Borders: the Transnational Solution.* Harvard Business School Press. Boston, Mass.

Batstone, E. and Gourley, S., 1986. *Unions, Unemployment and Innovation.* Blackwell, Oxford.

Beatson, M., 1995. *Labour Market Flexibility.* Employment Department, Research Series No. 48.

Becker, G., 1957. *The Economics of Discrimination.* The University of Chicago Press, Chicago, IL.

Beer, M., Spector, B., Lawrence, P.R., Quinn Mills, D. and Walton, R., 1984. *Managing Human Assets.* Free Press, New York.

Black, J. and Upchurch, M., 1999. Public sector employment. In Hollinshead, G., Nicholls, P. and Tailby, S., (eds), *Employee Relations.* Financial Times Pitman Publishing, London.

Blyton, P. and Turnbull, P., 1994. *The Dynamics of Employee Relations*. Macmillan, Basingstoke.

Blyton, P. and Turnbull, P., 1998. *The Dynamics of Employee Relations*, 2nd Edition. Macmillan, Basingstoke.

Blyton, P. and Turnbull, P., 2004. *The Dynamics of Employee Relations*, 3rd Edition. Macmillan, Basingstoke.

Braverman, H., 1974. *Labour and Monopoly Capital*. Monthly Review Press, New York.

Brewster, C. and Hegewisch, A. (eds), 1994. *Policy and Practice in European Human Resource Management*. Price Waterhouse/Cranfield Survey, Routledge, London.

Brewster C., Mayrhofer, W. and Morley, M., (eds), 2000. *New Challenges for European Human Resource Management*. Palgrave Macmillan, Basingstoke.

Burchell, B., Day, D., Hudson, M., Lapido, D., Mankelow, R., Nolan, J., Reed, H., Wichert, I., and Wilkinson, F., 1999. *Job Insecurity and Work Intensification*. Joseph Rowntree Foundation, London.

Burniaux, J-M., Duval, R., and Jaumotte, F., OECD 2004. *Coping with ageing: a dynamic approach to quantify the impact of alternative policy options on future labour supply in oecd countries*. Economics Department Working Papers No. 371.

Claydon, T., 1996. Union derecognition: a re-examination. In Beardwell, I. (ed.), *Contemporary Industrial Relations: A Critical Analysis*. OUP, Oxford.

Crouch, C., 1982. *The Politics of Industrial Relations*, 2nd Edition. Fontana, London.

Cully, M., Woodland, S., O'Reilly, A. and Dix, G., 1999. Britain at Work, As Depicted by the *1998 Workplace Employee Relations Survey*. Routledge, London.

Cully, M., O'Reilly, A., Millward, N., Forth, J., Woodland, S., Dix, G. and Bryson, A., 1998. *The Workplace Employee Relations Survey: First Findings*. DTI, ACAS, ESRC, PSI.

Dickens, L. and Hall, M., 1995. The state: labour law and industrial relations. In Edwards, P. (ed), 1995. Industrial and Relations: Theory and Practice in Britain. Blackwell, Oxford.

Donovan Commission Report, 1968. *The Report of the Royal Commission on Trade Unions and Employers Associations*. Command 3623, HMSO, London.

Dowling, P. and Schuler, R., 1990. *International Dimensions of Human Resource Management*. PWS, Kent.

Dowling, P., Welch, D. and Schuler, R., 1999. *International Human Resource Management*. South Case Western, Cincinnati.

Dunlop, J.T., 1958. *An Industrial Relations System*.

Eaton, J., 2000. *Comparative Employment Relations*. Polity Press, Cambridge.

Edwards, T., Rees, C. and Coller, X., 1999. Structure, Politics and the Diffusion of Employment Practices in Multinationals. *European Journal of Industrial Relations* 5(3). November, 286–306.

Edwards, P., 1995. The employment relationship. In Edwards, P. (ed.), *Industrial Relations: Theory and Practice in Britain*. Blackwell, Oxford.

Edwards, P., Marginson, P., Armstrong, P., and Purcell, J., 1996. Towards the transnational company? The global structure and organization of multinational firms. In Crompton, R., Gallie, D. and Purcell, K., (eds), *Changing Forms of Employment*. Routledge.

Etzioni, A. 1975. *A Comparative Analysis of Complex Organizations.* Free Press, New York.

European Commission, 1999. *Employment in Europe*, 1998.

European Commission, 2005. *Employment in Europe*, 2004.

European Commission, 2004. Report on Equality and Non-Discrimination.

European Commission, 2004. Gender Equality: Slow Progress in Closing Gender Gap Hampering EU Competitiveness.

European Industrial Relations Observatory, 2004. Developments in European Works Councils.

European Industrial Relations Observatory, 2004. Working Time – Developments in EU and National Regulation.

EIRO Online, 2004. Trade Union Membership 1993–2003.

Farnham, D. and Pimlott, J., 1995. *Understanding Industrial Relations*, 5th Edition. Cassell, London.

Felstead, A., Burchall. B. and Green, F., 1998. Insecurity at work. *New Economy.* 5(3): 180–184.

Flanders, A., 1970. *Management and Unions.* Faber, London.

Flanders, A., 1974. The tradition of Voluntarism. *British Journal of Industrial Relations.* 12(3): 352–70.

Fox, A., 1966. *Industrial Sociology and Industrial Relations.* Royal Commission Research Paper No. 3. HMSO, London.

Fox, A., 1974. *Beyond Contract.* Faber and Faber, London.

Freeman, R. and Medoff, J., 1984. *What do Trade Unions Do?* Basic Books, New York.

Gallie, D. and White, M., 1998. *Restructuring the Employment Relationship.* Oxford University Press, Oxford p. 316.

Geary, J., 2003. New forms of work organisation: still limited, still controlled, but still welcome? In Edwards, P. (ed.), *Industrial Relations; Theory and Practice*, 2nd Edition. Blackwell, Oxford, pp. 338–678.

Geary, J.F., 1995. Work practices: the structure of work. In Edwards, P. (ed.), *Industrial Relations: Theory and Practice in Britain.* Blackwell, Oxford.

Gennard, J. and Judge, G., 1997. *Employee Relations.* IPD, London.

Gennard, J. and Judge, G., 2002. *Employee Relations.* CIPD, London.

Ghertman, M. and Allen, M., 1984. *An Introduction to the Multinationals.* Macmillan, Basingstoke.

Gold, M. 1993. Overview of the social dimension. In Gold, M., (ed.), *The Social Dimension – Employment Policy in the European Community.* Macmillan, Basingstoke.

Gospel, H. and Palmer, G., 1993. *British Industrial Relations*, 2nd Edition. Routledge, London.

Grainger, H., 2006. *Trade Union Membership 2005.* DTI.

Greenberg, J. and Baron, R.A., 1996. *Behavior in Organizations: Understanding and Managing the Human Side of Work*, 6th Edition. Prentice-Hall, New Jersey.

Guest, D., 1987. Human resource management and industrial relations. *Journal of Management Studies* 24(5): 503–521.

Guest, D., 1989. Human Resource Management: its implications for industrial relations and trade unions. In Storey, J. (ed.), *New Perspectives on Human Resource Management.* Routledge, London.

Guest, D. and Hoque, K., 1994. The good, the bad and the ugly: employment relations in new non-union workplaces. *Human Resource Management Journal* 5(1): 1–14.

Guest D., 1995. Human Resource Management, trade unions and industrial relations. In Storey J., (ed.), *Human Resource Management: A Critical Text*. Routledge, London.

Guest. D. and Conway N., 1999. *Fairness at Work and the Psychological Contract*. IPD, London.

Hall, E.T. and Hall, M.R., 1990. *Understanding Cultural Differences*. Intercultural Press, Yarmouth, ME.

Hall, E.T., 1960. The silent language of overseas business. *Harvard Business Review* May/June, 38(3): 87–95.

Hall, M., 1994. Industrial Relations and the Social Dimension of European Integration: Before and after Maastricht. In Hyman, R. and Ferner, A., (eds), *New Frontiers in European Industrial Relations*. Blackwell, Oxford.

Hall, P.A. and Soskice, D., 2001. *Varieties of Capitalism: The Institutional Foundations of Comparative Advantage*. Oxford University Press, Oxford.

Hamill, J., 1983. The labour relations practices of foreign owned and indigenous firms. *Employee Relations* 5(1): 14–16.

Hancke, B., 2000. European Works Councils and the Industrial Restructuring in the European Motor Industry. *European Journal of Industrial Relations*. 6(1): 35–59.

Hawkins, K., 1979. *A Handbook of Industrial Relations Practice*. Kogan Page.

Hayes, N., 1997. *Successful Team Management*. International Thomson Business Press, London.

Heery, E. and Salmon, J. (eds), 2000. *The Insecure Workforce*. Routledge, London.

Hendry, C., 1994. *Human Resource Strategies for International Growth*. Routledge, London.

Herzberg, F., 1966. *Work and the Nature of Man*. World Publishing, Cleveland, Ohio.

Hofstede, G., 1980. *Cultures Consequences*. Sage, Beverley Hills.

Hofstede, G., 1991. *Cultures and Organisations. Software of the Mind*. McGraw Hill, London.

Hofstede, G., 1997. *Cultures and Organisations: Software of the Mind*. McGraw Hill, London.

Hollinshead, G. and Leat, M., 1995. *Human Resource Management: An International and Comparative Perspective*. Pitman, London.

Hyman, R., 1999. National industrial relations systems and transitional challenges: an essay in review. *European Journal of Industrial Relations* 5(1): 90–110.

Hyman, R., 2000. Editorial. *European Journal of Industrial Relations* 6(1): 5–7.

Ietto-Gillies, G., 1997. Working with the big guys: hostility to transnationals must be replaced by co-operation. *New Economy* 4(1): 12–16.

Keller, B.K., 1991. The role of the state as corporate actor in industrial relations systems. In Adams, R.J., (ed.), *Comparative Industrial Relations, Contemporary Research and Theory*. Harper Collins, New York. p. 83.

Kennedy, T., 1980. *European Labour Relations*. Lexington Books, Mass.

Kersley, B., Alpin, C., Forth, J., Bryson, A., Bewley, H., Dix, G. and Oxenbridge, S., 2005. *Inside the Workplace First Findings from the 2004 Workplace Employment Relations Survey (WERS 2004)*.

Kochan, T.A., Katz, H.C. and McKersie, R.B., 1986. *The Transformation of American Industrial Relations*. Basic Books, New York.

Leat, M., 1998. Human Resource Issues of the European Union. Financial Times Pitman Publishing, London.

Leat, M., 1999. Multi-nationals and employee relations. In Hollinshead, G., Nicholls, P. and Tailby, S. (eds), *Employee Relations*. Financial Times Pitman Publishing, London.

Legge, K., 1989. Human Resource Management: a critical analysis. In Storey, J. (ed.), *New Perspectives on Human Resource Management*. Routledge, London.

Legge, K., 1995. *Human Resource Management: Rhetorics and Realities*. Macmillan, Basingstoke.

Marchington, M., 1988. The four faces of employee consultation. Personnel Management, May, 44–47.

Marchington, M. *et al.*, 1992. Recent Developments in Employee Involvement, Employment Department Research Series No. 1. HMSO, London.

Marchington, M. and Wilkinson, A., 1996. *Core Personnel and Development*. IPD, London.

Marginson, P., Hall, M., Hoffmann, A. and Müller, T., 2004. The Impact of European Works Councils on Management Decision-Making in UK and US-based Multinationals: a case study comparison. *British Journal of Industrial Relations* 42(2): 209–234.

Marsh, A.I. and McCarthy, W.J., 1968. *Disputes Procedures in Britain*. Donovan Commission Research Paper No. 2, Part 2. HMSO, London.

Maslow, A., 1943. A theory of human motivation. *Psychological Review* 50: 370–396.

Maurice, M., Silvestre, J.-J. and Sellier, F., 1980. Societal differences in organizing manufacturing units: a comparison of France, West Germany and Great Britain. *Organizational Studies* 1: 59–86.

McGregor, D., 1960. *The Human Side of Enterprise*. McGraw Hill, New York.

McIlroy, J., 1995. *Trades Unions in Britain Today*. Manchester University Press, Manchester.

McLoughlin, I. and Gourlay, S., 1994. *Enterprise Without Unions*. OUP, Oxford.

Milne, S., 1991. Germany 37, Britain 39, *The Guardian*, 25 October.

Michels, R., 1966. *Political Parties*. Free Press, New York.

Moore, S., McKay, S. and Bewley, H., 2005. The content of new voluntary Trade union recognition agreements 1998–2002. Volume two – Findings from the survey of employers. *Employment Relations Research Series*. No. 43. DTI.

Mowday, R.T., Steers, R.M. and Porter, L.W., 1982. *Employee–Organization Linkages: The Psychology of Commitment, Absenteeism and Turnover*. Academic Press, New York.

Mueller, F. and Purcell, J., 1992. The Europeanisation of manufacturing and the decentralisation of bargaining: multinational management strategies in the European automobile industry. *International Journal of Human Resource Management* 3(1).

Mueller, F., Procter S. and Buchanan, D., 2000. Team working in its context: antecedents, nature and dimensions. *Human relations* 53(11): 1387–1424.

Needle, D., 2000. *Business in Context*, 3rd Edition. Thomson Learning, London.

Nicholls, P., 1999. Context and theory in employee relations. In Hollinshead, G., Nicholls, P. and Tailby, S. (eds), *Employee Relations.* Financial Times, Pitman, London.

OECD, 1999. Annual Employment Outlook 1999.

OECD, 2002. OECD in Figures.

OECD, 2004. Annual Employment Outlook.

OECD *Factbook 2006 – Economic, Environmental and Social Statistics.*

OECD. *Employment outlook* 2005.

OECD. *Employment outlook* 2006.

O'Hagan, E., Gunnigle, P. and Morley, M., 2005. Issues in the management of industrial relations in international firms. In Scullion, H. and Linehan, M. (eds), *International Human Resource Management – A critical text.* Palgrave Macmillan, Basingstoke.

Ohmae, K., 1990. *The Borderless World: Power and Strategy in the Interlinked Economy.* Harper, New York.

Perlmutter, H., 1969. The tortuous evolution of the multi-national corporation. *Columbus Journal of World Business* 4(1): 9–18.

Pollert, A., 1988. The flexible firm: fixation or fact. *Work, Employment and Society* 2(3): 281–306.

Poole, M. and Mansfield, R., 1992. Managers' attitudes to Human Resource Management: rhetoric and reality. In Blyton, P. and Turnbull, P. (eds), *Reassessing Human Resource Management.* Sage, London.

Prahalad, C.K. and Doz, Y.L., 1987. *The Multinational Mission.* Free Press, New York.

Purcell, J. and Ahlstrand, B., 1989. The impact of corporate strategy and the management of employee relations in the multi-divisional company. *British Journal of Industrial Relations* 27(3): 397–417.

Purcell, J. and Ahlstrand, B., 1994. *Human Resource Management in the Multi-Divisional Company,* Oxford.

Purcell, J. and Gray, A., 1986. Corporate personnel departments and the management of industrial relations: two case studies in the management of ambiguity. *Journal of Management Studies* 23(2).

Purcell, J. and Sisson, K., 1983. Strategies and practice in the management of industrial relations. In Bain, G.S. (ed.), *Industrial Relations in Britain.* Blackwell, Oxford.

Purcell, J., 1989. How to manage decentralised collective bargaining. *Personnel Management* May, 53–55.

Regini, M., 1995. Firms and institutions: the demand for skills and their social production in Europe. *European Journal of Industrial Relations* 1(2): 191–202.

Roethlisberger, F.J. and Dickson, W.J., 1939. *Management and the Worker.* Harvard University Press, Cambridge, Mass.

Salamon, M., 1992. *Industrial Relations: Theory and Practice,* 2nd Edition. Prentice Hall, Englewood Cliffs, NJ.

Schein, E., 1988. *Organizational Psychology.* Prentice Hall, Englewood Cliffs, NJ.

Schregle, J., 1981. Comparative industrial relations: pitfalls and potential. *International Labour Review* 120(1).

Schuler, R., Budwhar, P. and Florkowski, G., 2002. International Human Resource management: review and critique. *International Journal of Management Reviews* 4(1): 41–70.

Schulten, T., 1996. European Works Councils: prospects of a new system of European industrial relations. *European Journal of Industrial Relations* 2(3): 303–324.

Storey, J., 1987. *Developments in the management of human resources: an interim report.* Warwick Papers In Industrial Relations No. 17, IRRU, School of Industrial and Business Studies, University of Warwick, November.

Storey, J. (ed.), 1989. *New Perspectives on Human Resource Management.* Routledge, London.

Storey, J., 1992. Developments in the Management of Human Resources Blackwell, Oxford.

Storey, J. (ed.), 2001. *Human Resource Management; A Critical Text.* 2nd Edition. Thomson Learning, London.

Strauss, G., 1979. Workers participation: symposium introduction. *Industrial Relations* 18: 247–261.

Supiot, A., 2001. *Beyond Employment-Changes in Work and the Future of Labour Law in Europe.* Oxford University Press, Oxford.

Taylor, F.W., 1911. *Principles of Scientific Management.* Harper, New York.

Taylor, R., 2002. *Britain's World of Work – Myths and Realities.* ESRC, Swindon.

Teague, P., 1989. *The European Community: The Social Dimension.* Kogan Page, London.

Torrington, D., 1989. HRM and the personnel function. In Storey, J. (ed.), *New Perspectives on Human Resource Management.* Routledge, London.

Traxler, F. and Woitech, B., 2000. Transnational Investment and National Labour Market Regimes: A case of regime shopping. *European Journal of Industrial Relations* 6(2): July, 141–159.

Trompenaars, F., 1993. *Riding the Waves of Culture – Understanding Cultural Diversity In Business.* Economist Books, London.

TUC, 1995. General Council Report for 1995.

TUC, 1999. British Trade Unionism – the Millennial Challenge.

TUC, 2003. Trade Union Trends Recognition Survey 2003.

TUC, 2005. Trade Union Trends Recognition Survey 2004–2005.

Turner, H.A., 1962. *Trade Union Growth, Structure and Policy.* Allen and Unwin, London.

Turner, L., 1996. The Europeanization of labour: structure before action. *European Journal of Industrial Relations* 2(3): 325–344.

UNCTAD, 1999. UNCTAD Report on World Investment 1998.

UNCTAD, 2004. World Investment Report 2003. New York, United Nations.

UNCTAD, 2005. World Investment Report for 2004. Overview. New York, United Nations.

Undy, R. and Kessler, I., 1995. The changing nature of the employment relationship. *Presentation to the IPD National Conference.*

Waddington, J. and Whitston, C., 1995. Trade unions: growth, structure and policy. In Edwards, P. (ed.), *Industrial Relations Theory and Practice in Britain.* Blackwell, Oxford, pp. 151–202.

Waddington, J. and Whitston, C., 1997. Why do people join trade unions in a period of membership decline? *British Journal of Industrial Relations* December.

Wakelin, K., Girma, S. and Greenaway, D., 1999. *Wages, Productivity and Foreign Ownership in UK Manufacturing.* Centre for Research on Globalization and

Labour Markets. University of Nottingham: Centre for Research on Globalisation and Labour Markets.

Walker, K.F., 1974. Workers' participation in management: problems, practice and prospects. *Bulletin of the International Institute for Labour Studies* 12: 3–35.

Walters, M., 1995. *Globalisation.* Routledge, London.

Whitston, C. and Waddington, J., 1994. Why join a union? *New Statesman and Society* 18 November, pp. 36–38.

Wilkins, M., 1970. *The Emergence of the Multinational Enterprise.* Cambridge University Press, Cambridge.

Willey, B. and Morris, H., 2003. Regulating the Employment Relationship. In Hollinshead, G., Nicholls, P. and Tailby, S., (eds), *Employee Relations.* Financial Times, Pitman, London.

Womack, J., Jones, D. and Roos, D., 1990. *The Machine that Changed the World.* Rawson Associates, New York.

Index

and p...
context of w...
Saxon England; ... Flan...
Vietnam; from the war... ...erday to the war...

JON STALLWORTHY is a poet and a Fellow of the ...
Academy. Formerly Professor of English Literature at Wolfson
College, Oxford, he is the author of prize-winning biographies
of Wilfred Owen and Louis MacNeice, the editor of Owen's
Complete Poems and Fragments and of *The Oxford Book of War
Poetry*. He has published many volumes of poems, works of literary
criticism, anthologies of poetry, and a memoir, *Singing School: The
Making of a Poet*.

SURVIVORS' SON

from Maldon to the Somme

JON STALLWORTHY

CAMBRIDGE
UNIVERSITY PRESS

CAMBRIDGE UNIVERSITY PRESS

ɔrk, Melbourne, Madrid, Cape Town, Singapore, São Paulo, Delhi

Cambridge University Press
The Edinburgh Building, Cambridge CB2 8RU, UK

ned in the United States of America by Cambridge University Press, New York

www.cambridge.org
Information on this title: www.cambridge.org/9780521727891

First published 2008

Printed in the United Kingdom at the University Press, Cambridge

A catalogue record for this publication is available from the British Library

ISBN 978-0-521-89906-2 hardback
ISBN 978-0-521-72789-1 paperback

WITH A POPPY
for Macnair Jon Stallworthy
11.11.01—

What was it for,
that War to End Wars?
It was for us.
It was for you and yours.

Contents

Voice over

When W. H. Auden, acknowledging the powerlessness of the unacknowledged legislator to alter the events of 1 September 1939, wrote 'All I have is a voice', he articulated a general truth about his calling, his mystery. All any poet has is a voice. Apart from the finger-print, the human voice-print is arguably our most distinctive feature and one that alters less than most from youth to age. Some voices do not then fall silent but continue, from age to age, speaking to an ever-increasing audience 'Of what is past or passing or to come'.

By 1939, Auden had lost his belief in the poet's voice as an agent of effective political change: 'poetry makes nothing happen', his elegy 'In Memory of W. B. Yeats' declared. He would not have dared say that to the living Yeats, who saw painters, poets, playwrights, sculptors as the architects of civilization, generally, and in his own time and place, specifically, those who made the 1916 Easter Rising 'happen', 'When Pearse summoned Cuchulain to his side'.

History suggests that the voices of Auden and Yeats each articulate a truth. In the short term, 'poetry makes nothing happen'. British, French, Spanish, German, and Italian poets of Auden's 'low dishonest decade' could not avert the Spanish Civil War or the Second World War. In the longer term, however, the writers of the Irish Renaissance can be credited with educating and energizing the freedom-fighters

of 1916 and after; much as the poets of the First World War –
the principal subject of the essays in this book – can be
credited with kindling the anti-war fury that blazed through
the streets of London in February 2003.

I have spent many of the most rewarding hours of my life
listening to the voices of absent friends – Thomas Hardy,
William Yeats, Wilfred Owen, David Jones, Wystan Auden,
Keith Douglas, and Old Uncle Tom Eliot and all – singing

> of human unsuccess
> In a rapture of distress;

and I think of the essays in this book as thank-you letters
expressing gratitude in terms that, I hope, may lead other
readers to *listen* to their voices and hear in them what I have
heard.

Good poets are survivors – even if, like Keats and Owen,
they die at twenty-five – and it pleases me to remember a poem
I learnt as a boy, one of the few to break the sound-barrier of
translation, William Cory's version of Callimachus's 2,000-
year-old epigram:

> They told me, Heraclitus, they told me you were dead,
> They brought me bitter news to hear and bitter tears to shed.
> I wept as I remembered how often you and I
> Had tired the sun with talking and sent him down the sky.

> And now that thou art lying, my dear old Carian guest,
> A handful of grey ashes, long, long ago at rest,
> Still are thy pleasant voices, thy nightingales, awake;
> For Death, he taketh all away, but them he cannot take.

Wolfson College,
Oxford

Acknowledgements

I am indebted to many friends who, over many years, have helped in many ways with the preparation of this book: in particular, the late Mr John Bell, Dr Sarita Cargas, Dr Santanu Das, Dr Christopher Dowling, Ms Angela Godwin, Mrs Sue Hales, Professor Seamus Heaney, Dr Dominic Hibberd, Mrs Jenny Houlsby, the late Professor Gwyn Jones, the late Sir Geoffrey Keynes, Dr Stuti Khanna, Dr Nancy Macky (my hawk-eyed editor), Dr Jane Potter, Mrs Gail Purkis, Mr Michael Ramsbotham, Dr Kay Ryan, Dr Maartje Scheltens, Professor Vincent Sherry, Mr Dennis Silk, Ms Jennifer Speak (my exemplary indexer), Ms Sue Usher, and those others whose work is acknowledged in my notes.

I also wish to thank the ever-obliging staff of the following institutions: Bodleian Library, British Museum, Britten–Pears Library (Aldeburgh), English Faculty Library (Oxford), Humanities Research Center (University of Texas at Austin), Imperial War Museum, Kings College (Cambridge) Library and Wolfson College (Oxford) Library.

Some of the essays collected here have been revised since their first appearance in the following publications:

'The Death of the Hero' in my *Oxford Book of War Poetry* (Oxford University Press, 1984);

'Survivors' Songs' in my Gwyn Jones Lecture, *Survivors' Songs in Welsh Poetry* (University College Cardiff Press, 1982);

'England's Epic?' in *Slightly Foxed*, 15 (autumn 2007);
'Who was Rupert Brooke?' in *Critical Survey*, 2, 2 (autumn 1990);
'Owen's Afterlife' in my selection of Wilfred Owen's *Poems* (London: Faber and Faber, 2004);
'Henry Reed and the Great Good Place' in Henry Reed's *Collected Poems* (Oxford University Press, 1991, and Manchester: Carcanet Press Ltd, 2007); and
'The Fury and the Mire' in my Laurie Lee Memorial Lecture, *War and Poetry* (Cheltenham: The Cyder Press, 2005).

I am grateful to the editor and publishers of these; also for permission to reproduce copyright materials from the following sources:

W.H. Auden: 'The Shield of Achilles', from *Collected Poems*. Copyright © 1952 by W.H. Auden. Used by permission of Random House, Inc., and of Faber and Faber Ltd.

John Balaban: 'In Celebration of Spring', from *Locusts at the Edge of Summer: New and Selected Poems*. Copyright © 1997 by John Balaban. Reprinted with the permission of Copper Canyon Press, www.coppercanyonpress.org.

Rupert Brooke: quotations from *The Letters of Rupert Brooke*, ed. Geoffrey Keynes (Faber and Faber Ltd, 1968). Copyright © 1968 by The Rupert Brooke Trustees; and poems from *The Poetical Works*, ed. Geoffrey Keynes (Faber and Faber Ltd, 1946).

James Dickey: 'The Firebombing', from *Poems 1957–1967*. Copyright © 1967 by James Dickey. Reprinted by permission of Wesleyan University Press.

James Fenton: 'Dead Soldiers', from *The Memory of War and Children in Exile: Poems 1968–1983*. Copyright © 1983 by James Fenton. Reprinted by permission of PFD on behalf of James Fenton.

Anthony Hecht: 'More Light! More Light!', from *Collected Earlier Poems*. Copyright © 1990 by Anthony E. Hecht. Reprinted by permission of Alfred A. Knopf, a division of Random House, Inc., and Carcanet Press Ltd.

Ted Hughes: 'Snake Hymn', from *Collected Poems*. Copyright © 2003 by The Estate of Ted Hughes. Reprinted by permission of Faber and Faber Ltd and Farrar, Straus and Giroux, LLC.

Randall Jarrell: 'The Death of the Ball Turret Gunner', from *The Complete Poems*. Copyright © 1969, renewed 1997 by Mary von S. Jarrell. Reprinted by permission of Farrar, Straus and Giroux, LLC, and Faber and Faber Ltd.

Robert Lowell: 'Women, Children, Babies, Cow, Cats' and 'Fall 1961', from *Collected Poems*, ed. Frank Bidart and David Gewanter. Copyright © 2003 by Harriet Lowell and Sheridan Lowell. Reprinted by permission of Farrar, Straus and Giroux, LLC, and Faber and Faber Ltd.

Wilfred Owen: quotations from *The Collected Letters*, ed. Harold Owen and John Bell (Oxford University Press, 1967). Copyright © Oxford University Press 1967; and poems from *The Complete Poems and Fragments*, ed. Jon Stallworthy (Chatto & Windus, The Hogarth Press and Oxford University Press, 1983). Copyright © The Executors of Harold Owen's Estate 1963 and 1983.

Siegfried Sassoon: 'Glory of Women', from *Collected Poems of Siegfried Sassoon*. Copyright 1918, 1920 by E.P. Dutton. Copyright 1936, 1946, 1947, 1948 by Siegfried Sassoon. Reprinted by permission of the Estate of George Sassoon, and of Viking Penguin, a division of Penguin Group (USA) Inc.

Louis Simpson: 'The Heroes', from *Selected Poems*. Copyright © 1966 by Louis Simpson.

CHAPTER I

The death of the hero

'Poetry', Wordsworth reminds us, 'is the spontaneous over-flow of powerful feelings', and there can be no area of human experience that has generated a wider range of powerful feelings than war: hope and fear; exhilaration and humiliation; hatred – not only for the enemy, but also for generals, politicians, and war-profiteers; love – for fellow soldiers, for women and children left behind, for country (often) and cause (occasionally).

Man's early war-songs and love-songs were generally exhortations to action, or celebrations of action, in one or other field, but no such similarity exists between what we now more broadly define as love poetry and war poetry. Whereas most love poems have been in favour of love, much – and most recent – war poetry has been implicitly, if not explicitly, anti-war. So long as warrior met warrior in equal combat with sword and lance, poets could celebrate their courage and chivalry, but as technology put ever-increasing distance between combatants and, then, ceased to distinguish between combatant and civilian, poets more and more responded to 'man's inhumanity to man'. Not that heroic societies were oblivious to the domestic consequences of their heroes' 'brain-spattering, windpipe-slitting art'. *The Iliad* ends with Andromache watching from the walls of Troy, as her husband's broken body is dragged away behind his killer's chariot: 'she mourned, and the women wailed in answer'.[1] Similarly, as the hero's funeral pyre is lit at the close of the Old English epic, written 1,500 years later,

> A Geat woman too sang out in grief;
> with hair bound up, she unburdened herself
> of her worst fears, a wild litany
> of nightmare and lament: her nation invaded,
> enemies on the rampage, bodies in piles,
> slavery and abasement. Heaven swallowed the smoke.[2]

Hers, however, is not the last word. That is spoken by Beowulf's warriors:

> So the Geat people, his hearth-companions,
> sorrowed for the lord who had been laid low.
> They said that of all the kings upon the earth
> he was the man most gracious and fair-minded,
> kindest to his people and keenest to win fame.[3]

Such societies recognized the cost of warfare, but the code to which they subscribed counted it a necessary price for the pursuit of fame, honour, renown. This was to be acquired by generosity in peace, mighty deeds in war, loyalty to the living and loyalty to the dead.

    That heroic tradition died, and another was transplanted to English soil, when King Harold's foot-soldiers were cut down on a ridge above Hastings by the cavalry of William, Duke of Normandy. Less than a hundred years before, one of the last Old English poets had chanted or declaimed in a Saxon hall the poem we know as 'The Battle of Maldon'.[4] And three hundred years after Harold and his housecarls had gone the way of Byrhtnoth and his thanes, cut down on the shore of the Blackwater estuary, the first new English poet introduced to a more cultivated audience

A knight [...] a worthy man,
That fro the time that he first bigan
To ridden out, he loved chivalry [...]⁵

The intervening years had seen Duke William's son Henry, in the words of the Anglo-Saxon Chronicle, 'dubbed a rider', married to a Saxon girl, and the two peoples and the two languages fused and intermingled. Under the influence of the troubadours, the Church, and the new learning out of Italy, *chivalry* had come to mean more than *cavalry*, that other derivative of the Latin *caballarius*, a horseman. The descendant of Duke William's superbly efficient but hardly sophisticated *chevalier* could, like Chaucer's Squire,

Wel [...] sitte on hors, and faire ride;
He coude songes make, and wel endite,
Juste and eek daunce, and wel purtreye and write.

The Universities of Oxford and Cambridge had been founded before Chaucer was born, and in his lifetime the first of the so-called 'public schools', Winchester, opened its doors to the sons of noblemen and gentlemen. By 1440, when Eton was founded, the word *gentleman* had come to denote a clearly defined social status, inferior to nobility and superior to the yeomanry, but not necessarily dependent on ancestry. These schools and those others later modelled on them grafted the 'classical learning of the monastic schools upon the chivalric training in honour, in sport, in military exercise, in social intercourse, in courtesy and generosity, in reverence and devotion, of the schools of Christian knighthood'.⁶

Chaucer had seen military service – had been captured and ransomed – in France, where two centuries later fought and was wounded Henry Howard, Earl of Surrey, who returned to translate Books III and IV of the *Aeneid* into blank verse. Raleigh served in the Huguenot army at Jarnac and Moncoutour; Gascoigne saw military service in Holland; Donne took part in the Earl of Essex's two expeditions to Cadiz; Davenant was knighted by Charles I at the siege of Gloucester; Lovelace served in the Scottish expeditions of 1639; and the Earl of Rochester showed conspicuous courage in the Second Dutch War of 1665–6.

The chivalric tradition, transmuted into the courtly tradition of the High Renaissance, required proficiency in the arts of war as well as in such peaceable arts as music and poetry. The courtier–poet was expected to serve his king in much the same way as the Anglo-Saxon *scop* took his place in the shield-wall with his lord. The Earl of Surrey left a moving elegy to his Squire;[7] Gascoigne, a rueful account of his capture and ransom;[8] and Donne condensed his experience of Cadiz into an epigram.[9] Considering how many courtier–poets had experience of battle, however, the reader in a later century – when war poems are commonly written by those who have never seen a battlefield – may be surprised by how rarely Renaissance poets write of war. Conventions had changed. Love had become the subject proper to a poet. On the rare occasion when the blast of war blows through a poem, it is likely to be the carefully orchestrated overture to a protestation of devotion, such as Lovelace, the dashing Cavalier, offers 'To Lucasta, Going to the Wars'.[10] Paradoxically, the convention that proclaimed the subject of warfare too gross for the polite art of poetry sanctioned, and indeed required, a select use of military terminology in the imagery of the love lyric. Cupid is an archer. The besieging lover, having no shield proof against his darts, can only hope that his Beloved in a spirit of Christian compassion will surrender.

During the eighteenth century, soldiering reached the low place in British society that it was to hold until the Great

War, an occupation despised by the middle and working classes as a disgrace hardly less than prison. If an eighteenth-century poet wrote of war – which he seldom did – it was as a remote phenomenon. So John Scott of Amwell declares:

> I hate that drum's discordant sound,
> Parading round, and round, and round:
> To me it talks of ravaged plains,
> And burning towns, and ruined swains,
> And mangled limbs, and dying groans,
> And widows' tears, and orphans' moans;
> And all that Misery's hand bestows,
> To fill the catalogue of human woes.[11]

As the French Revolution made its contribution to that catalogue, warfare once more became a subject of interest to British poets. The Napoleonic wars moved Sir Walter Scott and Thomas Campbell to patriotic outpourings.[12] Coleridge and Wordsworth, on the other hand, 'hailed the rising orb of liberty'. Both were subsequently disillusioned, and in Book 4 of *The Prelude* Wordsworth writes movingly of his meeting with a battered veteran of Wellington's armies. No poet of the Romantic period, however, was more alive to the horrors of war than Byron; alive not only to sufferings of the combatants but to the domestic consequences. The eyes of the dying Gladiator in *Childe Harold* are

> with his heart and that was far away;
> He reck'd not of the life he lost nor prize,
> But where his rude hut by the Danube lay
> *There* were his young barbarians all at play,
> *There* was their Dacian mother – he, their sire,
> Butcher'd to make a Roman holiday [...][13]

Byron, as a schoolboy at Harrow, had been steeped in the classics. He visited Greece in 1809 and 1810 and the first two

cantos of *Childe Harold*, based on his experiences, launched a
tidal wave of literary philhellenism.

By the time of the Greek Revolution in 1821, the educated public in
Europe had been deeply immersed in three attractive ideas – that
Ancient Greece had been a paradise inhabited by supermen; that the
Modern Greeks were the true descendants of the Ancient Greeks; and
that a war against the Turks could somehow 'regenerate' the Modern
Greeks and restore the former glories.[14]

Invoking the example of Leonidas and his three hundred
Spartans, commemorated in Simonides' epigram,[15] Byron
sounded the call to arms:

> Must *we* but weep o'er days more blest?
>   Must *we* but blush? – Our fathers bled.
> Earth! Render back from out thy breast
>   A remnant of our Spartan dead!
> Of the three hundred grant but three,
> To make a new Thermopylae.[16]

His love for the land of Pericles and Homer proving stronger
than his hatred of war, he set off for Greece with half a dozen
military uniforms and a couple of helmets, gilded, crested,
and bearing the family motto: 'Crede Byron'.

Like every other philhellene who took that road, he was to
learn how unrelated were the reality and the dream. Those
more fortunate, who returned with their lives, brought tales
of betrayal and brutality, squalor and needless suffering, that
anticipate the war correspondents' revelations from the Crimea
thirty years later. The philanthropic spirit of the age that
urged Florence Nightingale to the hospitals of Scutari found
expression in anti-war poems by Thackeray[17] and others,
but these were counterbalanced by many sounding a savage
note, and the one poem from the Crimean War to have
survived in the popular memory celebrates a heroic exploit.
Significantly, since Tennyson's imagination had long been

engaged with the chivalric world of King Arthur and his knights, it was the *cavalry* charge of the Light Brigade in 1854 that spurred him into song.[18]

It is one thing to 'Honour the charge' of professional cavalrymen of one's own country against foreign gunners thousands of miles away, but quite another to watch one's own countrymen – many of them boy civilians in uniform – killing and maiming each other. Walt Whitman was drawn into the American Civil War by a brother, wounded in the Battle of Fredericksburg, who was in need of nursing. He remained, long after his brother was better, a non-combatant witness to the horrors of war, tending his wounded:

> Bearing the bandages, water and sponge,
> Straight and swift to my wounded I go [...][19]

He regards them as '*my* wounded', seeing the results of cavalry action from a markedly *un*-Tennysonian perspective:

The neck of the cavalry-man with the bullet through and through I examine,
Hard the breathing rattles, quite glazed already the eye, yet life struggles hard,
(Come sweet death! Be persuaded O beautiful death!
In mercy come quickly.)

His eyes unclouded by the chivalric vision, his tongue untrammelled by the chivalric diction and rhetoric, he perceives 'in camp in the daybreak grey and dim' what Siegfried Sassoon and Wilfred Owen were to perceive in the trenches of the Western Front:

Young man I think I know you – I think this face is the face
of the Christ himself,
Dead and divine and brother of all, and here again he lies.[20]

While America was forging a new society in the fires of civil war, Britain was making one of those cautious

adjustments to the old society by which she had avoided civil
strife for three hundred years. Thomas Arnold, as headmaster of Rugby from 1827 to 1842, had revitalized the
public-school system. Perceiving that the country and the
empire needed more – and more efficient – civil servants and
managers than the aristocracy and landed gentry could
supply, he and the headmasters of the many Anglican boarding schools that opened their gates in the 1850s sought to
make 'Christian gentlemen' of the sons of the middle classes.
The ethos of these schools was essentially chivalric. As
readers of *Tom Brown's Schooldays* will remember, schoolboy fights were elevated into gentlemanly duels, and on the
playing fields the same code of etiquette called for 'fair play'
and 'the team spirit'. Each school was dominated by its
chapel, which suited the philistine respectability of the
devout bourgeois, and the curriculum was dominated by
Latin, and to a lesser extent, Greek. In 1884 there were
twenty-eight classics masters at Eton, six mathematics masters, one historian, no modern-language teachers, and no
scientists. As late as 1905, classics masters still formed more
than half the teaching staff.

The poet–spokesman for the public schools at the end of
the nineteenth century was Henry Newbolt. The title of his
poem 'Clifton Chapel' acknowledges a debt to Matthew
Arnold's 'Rugby Chapel', but whereas the headmaster's
son addressed his father and 'the noble and great who are
gone', Newbolt exhorts a new generation of imperialists:

> To set the cause above renown,
>   To love the game beyond the prize,
> To honour, while you strike him down,
>   The foe that comes with fearless eyes;
> To count the life of battle good,
>   And dear the land that gave you birth,

And dearer yet the brotherhood
That binds the brave of all the earth.
[...]

God send you fortune, yet be sure,
Among the lights that gleam and pass,
You'll live to follow none more pure
Than that which glows on yonder brass:
'*Qui procul hinc,*' the legend's writ, –
The frontier-grave is far away –
'*Qui ante diem periit:*
Sed miles, sed pro patria.'[21]

In a more famous or notorious poem, 'Vitaï Lampada' – a title taken from Lucretius, meaning '[They pass on] the Torch of Life' – he envisaged the public-school ethic at work on a frontier far away:

The river of death has brimmed his banks,
And England's far, and Honour a name,
But the voice of a schoolboy rallies the ranks:
'Play up! play up! and play the game!'[22]

Newbolt's repeated celebration of the imperialist officer and gentleman, carrying to his country's battlefields a sporting code acquired on the playing fields of his public school, parallels a poetic reappraisal of the private soldier initiated by Kipling's *Barrack-room Ballads* and sustained by Housman's *A Shropshire Lad*.

Requirements for a commission in the army had altered radically since the 1850s. 'In place of the old patronage system came, first, limited competition – examination for the select few whom the authorities had personally nominated – and then, in 1870, open competition.'[23] The year 1870, of course, saw the outbreak of the Franco-Prussian War that inaugurated the era of violence in international politics, precipitating further army reforms, the rapid mechanization of warfare, and the growth of imperialist ideologies. Malvern van Wyk Smith has shown how in Britain, at the start of the Boer War, militarist and pacifist doctrines were clearly defined and opposed; and how, because the Education Acts of 1870 and 1876 had made the army that sailed for South Africa the first literate army in history, the British Tommy sent home letters and poems that anticipate those his sons were to send back from the Western Front.[24]

These factual and often bitter accounts of combat, to say nothing of the greater poems by Thomas Hardy,[25] had been forgotten by 1914 when that War we still – many wars later – know by the adjective Great was greeted in some quarters with a curious gaiety and exhilaration. Rupert Brooke captured the mood of that moment in a sonnet to which he gave the paradoxical title of 'Peace'.[26] His first line 'Now, God be thanked Who has matched us with His hour' – and the 'hand' and the 'hearts' that follow reveal one of his sources: the hymn, and ironically it is a hymn translated from the German, beginning

> Now thank we all our God
> With heart, and hands, and voices [...]

Shortly before Brooke's death, the Dean of St Paul's read aloud in a sermon from the Cathedral pulpit another of his 'war sonnets', 'The Soldier'.[27] So the soldier-poet was canonized by the Church, and many other poets – civilians and soldiers alike – found inspiration for their battle-hymns, elegies, exhortations, in the well-thumbed pages of *Hymns Ancient and Modern*.

Most of the British poets we associate with the years 1914 and 1915 had a public-school education and this, more than any other factor, distinguishes them from those we associate with the later phases of the war. The early poems return again and again to the appallingly anachronistic concept of war as a game, a concept most clearly articulated by E. B. Osborn, in the introduction to his bestselling anthology *The Muse in Arms*, published in 1917. He wrote:

> Modern battles are so vast and so extended in both space and time that composed battle-pieces, such as have come down to us from the far-off centuries of archery and ballad-making, may no longer be looked for. The thread on which all such pictures are strung – the new impressions such as 'The Assault' [a poem by Robert Nichols] and old ballads such as 'Agincourt, or the English Bowman's Glory' – is the insular conception of fighting as the greatest of all great games, that which is the most shrewdly spiced with deadly danger. The Germans, and even our allies, cannot understand why this stout old nation persists in thinking of war as a sport; they do not know that sportsmanship is our new homely name, derived from a racial predilection for comparing great things with small, for the *chevalerie* of the Middle Ages. In 'The English Bowman's Glory', written before any of our co-operative pastimes were thought of, the fine idea is veiled in this homely term:
>
> > Agincourt, Agincourt!
> > Know ye not Agincourt?
> > Oh, it was noble sport!
> >   Then did we owe men;
> > Men, who a victory won us
> > 'Gainst any odds among us:
> >   Such were our bowmen.
>
> Light is thrown on this phase of the British Soldier's mentality by the verse [...] he writes in honour of the games and the field-sports in which he acquired the basal elements of all true discipline – confidence in his companions and readiness to sacrifice the desire for personal distinction to the common interest of his team, which is, of course, a mimic army in being.[28]

The legacy of the public-school classroom was as significant for the poets as that of the playing field. Paul Fussell rightly points out in his stimulating book, *The Great War and Modern Memory*, that the British soldier tended to look at the war through literary spectacles. He evidences the popularity of Quiller-Couch's *Oxford Book of English Verse*, but surprisingly overlooks the extent to which the public-school poets' attitude to war was conditioned by their years of immersion in the works of Caesar, Virgil, Horace, and Homer. A reading of these authors would leave no intelligent boy in any doubt that war was a brutal business, but by setting 'The Kaiser's War' in a long and, dare one say, a time-honoured tradition, the classics encouraged a detached perspective – quite apart from offering the soldier, by analogy, the intoxicating prospect of a place in history and literature. In the poems of 1914 and the first half of 1915, there are countless references to sword and legion, not a few to chariot and oriflamme, but almost none to gun and platoon. Siegfried Sassoon writes, in a poem of 1916, 'We are the happy legion'; while Herbert Asquith begins his elegy 'The Volunteer':

> Here lies a clerk who half his life had spent
> Toiling at ledgers in a city grey,
> Thinking that so his days would drift away
> With no lance broken in life's tournament.
> Yet ever 'twixt the books and his bright eyes
> The gleaming eagles of the legions came,
> And horsemen, charging under phantom skies,
> Went thundering past beneath the oriflamme.[29]

A similar vision prompted Rupert Brooke, under orders for the Dardanelles, to write to Asquith's sister, Violet:

Do you think *perhaps* the fort on the Asiatic corner will want quelling, and we'll land and come at it from behind and they'll make a sortie and meet us on the plains of Troy? [...]

I've never been quite so happy in my life, I think. Not quite so *pervasively* happy; like a stream flowing entirely to one end. I suddenly realize that the ambition of my life has been – since I was two – to go on a military expedition against Constantinople.[30]

On the troopship, he and his friends read Homer to each other, and in a verse-letter from the trenches, Charles Hamilton Sorley remembers how Homer sang

> Tales of great war and strong hearts wrung,
> Of clash of arms, of council's brawl,
> Of beauty that must early fall,
> Of battle hate and battle joy
> By the old windy walls of Troy.
> [...]
> And now the fight begins again,
> The old war-joy, the old war-pain.
> Sons of one school across the sea
> We have no fear to fight [...][31]

The poems of these young men move us, as human documents, more than many better poems. They illustrate the hypnotic power of a long cultural tradition; the tragic outcome of educating a generation to face not the future but the past. By the end of 1915, Brooke, Sorley, and many lesser public-school poets were dead. Sassoon, it is true, survived to follow Sorley's lead and break the code of his upbringing – and all honour to him. By publicly protesting in 1917 against the continuance of the war, and by lashing the leaders of Church and State and the Armed Forces in his poems, he rejected the obedience to authority that is one of the prime tenets of the public-school system. The poets who followed him – Owen, Rosenberg, Gurney – had no such conventions to reject. They went to war, as Whitman had done, with no Homeric expectations, and set themselves to expose what Owen called

The old Lie: Dulce et decorum est
Pro patria mori.[32]

One, indeed, had Whitman in mind. 'When I think of "Drum
Taps"', wrote Rosenberg three months before he was killed,
'[*my* poems] are absurd.'[33]

It is often assumed that chivalry died with the cavalry,
scythed by machine guns, in the Battle of the Somme. Auden,
characterizing the past in his poem 'Spain 1937', wrote:

Yesterday the belief in the absolute value of Greek;
The fall of the curtain upon the death of a hero [...][34]

The curtain may have fallen, but it was to rise and fall again.
It is a commonplace that traditions die hard, and none die
harder than military ones. Leaving Oxford in 1940 to join a
cavalry regiment, Keith Douglas embellished a photograph
of himself in uniform – humorously, it must be said – with
the scrolled caption 'Dulce et decorum est pro patria mori'.
Two years later, chafing at his enforced inactivity behind the
lines while his regiment was engaging Rommel's tanks in the
Western Desert, Douglas drove off – in a two-ton truck and
direct disobedience of orders – to join them; earning thereby
his batman's commendation: 'I like you, sir. You're shit or
bust!' His subsequent achievement as a poet was to celebrate
the last stand of the chivalric hero,

the doomed boy, the fool
whose perfectly mannered flesh fell
in opening the door for a shell
as he had learnt to do at school.[35]

In 1915, on the Western Front, Julian Grenfell had written of
the cavalryman that

In dreary, doubtful waiting hours,
Before the brazen frenzy starts,

> The horses show him nobler powers;
> O patient eyes, courageous hearts![36]

So Douglas, in his fine elegy, 'Aristocrats',[37] takes the horse as the natural symbol for his anachronistic hero, and in its last line we seem to hear the last echo from the Pass at Roncesvalles: 'It is not gunfire I hear but a hunting horn.' That poem succeeds where most poems of 1914 and 1915 fail. It is sharply focused, acknowledging both the stupidity and the chivalry, the folly and the glamour of cavalrymen on mechanical mounts duelling in the desert. Douglas's language, finely responsive to his theme, fuses ancient and modern: his heroes are 'gentle' – like Chaucer's 'verray parfit gentil knight' – and at the same time 'obsolescent'.

Sidney Keyes was killed on his first patrol in North Africa, but in such poems of 1942 as 'Orestes and the Furies' and 'Rome Remember' he sees the Gorgon-head reflected in the classical shield he had acquired at a public school. He wrote:

> I am the man who groped for words and found
> An arrow in my hand.[38]

Not a rifle, but an arrow. Henry Reed celebrated the rifle in the first of his 'Lessons of the War',[39] but the ironic detachment of these superb meditations on war and peace owes something to Horace, whose lines, saucily emended, stand as epigraph to the sequence and cunningly announce and encapsulate the theme of his Lessons.[40]

By no means all British poets of the Second World War came from public schools, and many more spoke a language that had more in common with Owen and Rosenberg. None, however, offers so sharp a contrast to the work of Douglas and Keyes as the American infantryman-poets, Louis Simpson and Lincoln Kirstein. Simpson tells us that after the war he suffered from amnesia, eventually broken by

dreams of battle that – as with Owen – released his poems.
He has, indeed, other resemblances to Owen – admiration
for the soldier's endurance, compassion for his suffering, of
which he writes with something of the same reverberant
simplicity:

> Most clearly of that battle I remember
> The tiredness in eyes, how hands looked thin
> Around a cigarette, and the bright ember
> Would pulse with all the life there was within.[41]

In his long poem 'The Runner', Simpson's college-boy anti-
hero Dodd is humiliated by the rest of his platoon for a
momentary act of cowardice; although like the Youth in *The
Red Badge of Courage* he redeems himself subsequently.
Cowardice, a taboo subject to poets in the chivalric tradition,
is a theme of Kirstein's *Rhymes of a PFC*, the first poem of
which ends:

> The rage of armies is the shame of boys;
>   A hero's panic or a coward's whim
> Is triggered by nerve or nervousness.
>   We wish to sink. We do not choose to swim.[42]

Where Douglas had asked, in 'Gallantry', 'Was George fond
of little boys?' and had answered

> who will say: since George was hit
> We never mention our surmise[43]

Kirstein writes openly and tenderly of homosexual love.
Similarly, he and Simpson share – and show in their poems –
what Simpson has described as 'the dog-face's suspicion of
the officer class, with their abstract language and indifference
to individual, human suffering'.[44] It is interesting that
Simpson identifies the general infantryman with the animal
that used to run beside the huntsman-cavalryman's horse.

Simpson and Kirstein speak for the civilian stuffed into uniform not very tidily and against his will. They write of a wider range of military experience – not excluding coward-ice and homosexuality – because they write as men rather than as soldiers conscious of soldierly tradition.

What may be termed the anti-heroic tradition is at least as old as Falstaff. It makes sporadic appearances in eighteenth-century English poetry, but does not oust its older rival until transplanted to America in the next century. A civil war fought by large numbers of conscripted civilians, a high proportion of them literate (but few versed in classical literature), was a new kind of conflict, and America's pro-duced a new kind of poetry. Its principal poets, Whitman and Melville, were civilians and they established a perspec-tive and a tone that would be adopted by those that followed them, combatant and civilian alike: so James Dickey, veteran of a hundred combat missions, begins 'The Firebombing': 'Homeowners unite'.[45] That, surely, is the one hope for the human race. Only if the poets' perception that we are all civilians gains universal acceptance will we be spared the fulfilment of Peter Porter's dark prophecy, 'Your Attention Please':

> The Polar DEW has just warned that
> A nuclear rocket strike of
> At least one thousand megatons
> Has been launched by the enemy
> Directly at our major cities.
> [...]
> All flags are flying fully dressed
> On Government buildings – the sun is shining.
> Death is the least we have to fear.
> We are all in the hands of God,
> Whatever happens happens by His Will.
> Now go quickly to your shelters.[46]

CHAPTER 2

Survivors' songs

One of the first poets from these islands to raise a lasting elegy for companions killed in a battle he himself survived was Aneirin, sixth-century author of a sequence of elegies known as *Y* [*The*] *Gododdin*.

> Of three hundred champions who charged on Catraeth,
> It is tragic, but one man came back.[1]

This brings to mind another text, one perhaps known to Aneirin:

And there came a messenger unto Job, and said, The oxen were plowing, and the asses feeding beside them:

And the Sabeans fell upon them, and took them away; yea, they have slain the servants with the edge of the sword; and I only am escaped to tell thee. [...]

While he was yet speaking, there came also another, and said, the Chaldeans made out three bands, and fell upon the camels, and have carried them away, yea, and slain the servants with the edge of the sword; and I only am escaped to tell thee.[2]

Whether Aneirin intended it or not, the double coincidence of the three hundred – elsewhere in *The Gododdin* defined as three bands – and the one survivor, adds a tragic resonance to his poem. Not that it is a narrative, although a narrative emerges from the elegies with which the poet celebrates the exploits of those who fell at Catraeth – or *some* of those who fell at Catraeth. For Aneirin, as a man of rank, extols the officers and gentlemen but makes no mention of the 'other ranks', the infantry, whom scholars assume to have accompanied each mounted knight. He extols them not as an obituarist or war-correspondent, but as kinsman and friend:

In a shining array they fed together round the wine-vessel. My heart has become full of grief for the feast of Mynyddog, I have lost too many of my true kinsmen. Out of three hundred wearing gold torques who hastened to Catraeth, alas, none escaped but for one man.[3]

We hear that Cibno, before 'the uproar of battle', took communion, but the three hundred seem bound together by the secular sacrament of the mead cup. Over this they utter not prayers but boasts, pledging themselves to deeds of valour, which they are thereby obliged to perform or to perish in the attempt.

On the night before they set off for Catraeth, we can imagine one of the company in the hall of Mynyddog, who drinks from the cup but does not join in the boasting. Instead, he sings. Perhaps, as David Jones says in the Preface to *In Parenthesis*,[4] 'He is instructed to sing [...] the song of the Battle of Camlann' – the song, now lost, that lies behind Malory's *Morte Darthur* 'This tale Sir Bedivere, a Knight of the Table Round, made it to be written', Sir Bedivere, who left the battlefield echoing Job's messenger: 'I only am escaped to tell thee.'

Perhaps Aneirin sang on the field of Catraeth – as Taillefer was to sing the *Chanson de Roland* riding in front of the Normans at Hastings, tossing his sword in the air. At all events, we know how Aneirin left the battlefield:

Aeron's two war-hounds and tough Cynon,
And myself, soaked in blood, for my song's sake.[5]

His escape indicates no act of cowardice. That blood testifies to an active role in the battle, but a poet of the heroic age was not primarily a warrior. His function was to ensure that his friends did not die unsung. He must escape that he may *tell*; bear witness that what was promised in the hall was performed on the field. 'Bleiddig son of Eli was a wild boar for fierceness'; 'the son of Nwython slew a hundred princes wearing gold torques so that he might be celebrated'; 'the son of Sywno (the soothsayer foreknew it) sold his life that his glory might be told forth [...] because of his pledge [...], he charged forwards in the forefront of the men of Gwynedd.'

Aneirin, of course, was neither the first not the last Welsh poet to bear such witness. Taliesin told *his* listeners:

> There was many a corpse beside Argoed Llwyfain;
> From warriors ravens grew red,
> And with their leader a host attacked.
> For a whole year I shall sing their triumph.
>
> And when I'm grown old, with death hard upon me,
> I'll not be happy save to praise Urien.[6]

In the twelfth century, Cynddelw Brydydd Mawr praised his patron, Owain Gwynedd, in similar terms; and in the fifteenth, Llywelyn ab y Moel told of the Battle of Waun Gaseg – with less pride in his calling than Aneirin displayed after the Battle of Catraeth:

> For me – ah! poor pre-eminence –
> The sole advantage I had thence
> Was but that with surpassing haste
> I ran, my fellows far-outpaced,
> Across the gorge in full view
> Of foes who knew me – too well they knew!
> Dull fool is he who in white coat strays,
> Courting ill hap, on the mountain ways.[7]

There are survivors' songs also in Old English: most notably 'The Battle of Maldon', of all Anglo-Saxon poems the closest in tone to *The Gododdin*. Its unknown poet knows and names his warriors, distinguishing their weapons, reporting their speeches, persuading us that he too had his place in their shield-wall. But if he did, and if Bryhtnoth's hearth-companions were true to their boasts that they would not leave their leader's body, how did the poem come to be written? I see him at the last, taking leave of his companions and escaping, like Aneirin, soaked in blood, for his song's sake.

Almost one thousand years later, in 1919, there was published a new translation of the *Chanson de Roland*.[8] Made by Charles Scott Moncrieff, it was dedicated

To three men
scholars, poets, soldiers
who came to their Roncesvals
in September, October, and November
nineteen hundred and eighteen
I dedicate my part in a book
of which their friendship
quickened the beginning
their example has
justified the continuing

Philip Bainbridge
Wilfred Owen
Ian Mackenzie

The translator had been a close friend of Wilfred Owen, among whose papers an earlier form of dedication is to be found:

To Mr W.O.

To you, my master in assonance, I dedicate my part in this assonant poem: that you may cover the faults in my handiwork with the protection of your name [...] At this time lessons are to be found in the Song of Roland that all of us may profitably learn. To pursue chivalry, to avoid and punish treachery and to fight uncomplaining when support is withheld from us; to live, in fine, honourably and to die gallantly. So I have worked and written that the song our Saxon forbears heard our Norman forbears shout at Hastings – may not be altogether unheard in their children's armies.[9]

The accompanying manuscript draft of Moncrieff's first 179 lines confirms that Owen was familiar with *The Song of Roland*, and we are left with the problem of whether the dedication was altered simply because he was dead, or whether – as I prefer to think – he had expressed himself unhappy to be associated with the chivalric tradition. Before he died, however, he had testified in the tradition of his Welsh forbears:

> It seemed that out of battle I escaped
> Down some profound dull tunnel, long since scooped
> Through granites which titanic wars had groined.[10]

'I only am escaped to tell thee.' But what he tells us is not what Aneirin tells us, testifying to the heroic exploits of his friends. Though Owen also speaks of a friend, it is of a 'strange friend' who tells him:

> I am the enemy you killed, my friend.
> I knew you in the dark: for so you frowned
> Yesterday through me as you jabbed and killed.
> I parried; but my hands were loath and cold.
> Let us sleep now ...

Much of the force of this derives from the Christian subversion of the pagan heroic terms; a subversion proclaimed by another Welsh poet of the Great War, David Jones, in his Dedication to *In Parenthesis*:

THIS WRITING IS FOR MY FRIENDS
IN MIND OF ALL COMMON & HIDDEN
MEN AND OF THE SECRET PRINCES
AND TO THE MEMORY OF THOSE
WITH ME IN THE COVERT AND IN
THE OPEN [...]
AND TO THE ENEMY
FRONT-FIGHTERS WHO SHARED OUR
PAINS AGAINST WHOM WE FOUND
OURSELVES BY MISADVENTURE

Jones, like Owen, accords the enemy the status of honorary friends.

Unlike Owen, however, he was able to reflect on the experience of the trenches for almost twenty years before putting pen to paper, and by then had come to see that experience in a wider historical context. His Preface speaks, in terms of which Charles Scott Moncrieff would have approved, of 'the intimate, continuing, domestic life of small contingents of men, within whose structure Roland could find, and, for a reasonable while, enjoy, his Oliver'.[11] Echoes of the *Chanson de Roland* reverberate throughout *In Parenthesis*. John Ball has a friend, the signaller Olivier, of whom we are reminded when the poet numbers among the dead

> Taillefer the maker,[12]
> and on the same day,
> thirty thousand other ranks.
> And in the country of Béarn – Oliver
> and all the rest – so many without memento
> beneath the tumuli on the high hills
> and under the harvest places.

At the end of *In Parenthesis*, Jones gives Turold, the maker of the *Chanson de Roland*, the honour of the last word:

The geste says this and the man who was on the field ... and who
wrote the book ... the man who does not know this has not understood anything.[13]

In Parenthesis is a difficult work. Jones called it a 'writing',
at once acknowledging and dodging his reader's first question: 'Is it poetry or prose?' Having read it, we know the
answer is 'both'. It has the narrative structure we associate
with the novel, but its language at many points takes on
the allusiveness, density, and momentum of poetry. This
blending of categories, like its blending of matter ancient
and modern, unsettles the reader – as, clearly, Jones meant
us to be unsettled – and leaves us with the problem of how
'this writing' is to be read. Some of its most attentive readers
have come to different conclusions. Herbert Read found it
'as near a great epic of the war as ever the war generation will
reach';[14] a judgement John H. Johnston endorsed,[15] though
neither, I think, has satisfactorily explained how the reader's
epic expectations are manipulated, confirmed, and denied by
Jones's modernist variations of his form. Paul Fussell, who
holds that the Great War 'will not be understood in traditional terms', finds *In Parenthesis* 'curiously ambiguous
and indecisive' and 'a deeply conservative work which uses
the past not, as it often pretends to do, to shame the present,
but really to ennoble it'.[16] In Fussell's view, the book is
an 'honourable miscarriage' by a 'turgid allusionist'.[17] I
disagree with him, but his criticisms raise crucial questions,
which bear on how 'this writing' is to be read; and that
problem I should now like to consider.

Setting aside for the moment Jones's Preface, in which he
speaks frankly and informally, as author to reader, we are
introduced in the Dedication to the more hieratic intonation
of the poet. Its opening words proclaim it part of the work –
THIS WRITING IS FOR MY FRIENDS. Printed in capital

letters and without punctuation, it looks like a war memorial and sounds like a poem. The Dedication states the theme, which is the commemoration of the dead – friends and enemies who shared the same pains. Dedication is followed by Prologue, by the title of Part I and its epigraph – three quotations, three chords if you like, extending and developing the echoes of the Dedication. In the Prologue, quoting from Lady Charlotte Guest's translation of *The Mabinogion*, David Jones speaks through the lips of the teller of the tale of Branwen the Daughter of Llŷr:

Evil betide me if I do not open the door to know if that is true which is said concerning it. So he opened the door ... and when they had looked, they were conscious of all the evils they had ever sustained, and of all the friends and companions they had lost ... and because of their perturbation they could not rest.

The same recognition of friends and companions lost, the same perturbation preventing rest, are transmitted by the title of Part I: 'THE MANY MEN SO BEAUTIFUL'. On the white page below or in the silence that follows, we can imagine the rest of Coleridge's stanza taking shape:

> And they all dead did lie:
> And a thousand thousand slimy things
> Lived on; and so did I.[18]

So with the epigraph to Part I, in which another lone survivor, sufferer of a similar loss and a similar perturbation, speaks:

> Men marched, they kept equal step ...
> Men marched, they had been nurtured together.[19]

Even a Welsh reader might not recognize the source of these lines as *The Gododdin*, but neither will an Irish reader recognize the source of every quotation in Joyce's *Ulysses*.

Modernist writers, however, have taught their readers how
to respond to this strategy and, if the author of *In Parenthesis*
is a 'turgid allusionist', as Fussell charges, the authors of
Ulysses, 'Hugh Selwyn Mauberly', and *The Waste Land* must
stand indicted of the same offence – and to a greater degree, in
that their allusions are culled from wider fields of reference.

Jones, unlike Joyce, assists his reader with notes, so there
can be no mistaking the one message of his three preliminary
quotations. They introduce the action like the voice of the
chorus in Greek tragedy, and the descendants of those who
died at Catraeth once again keep 'equal step':

> '49 Wyatt, 01549 Wyatt.
> Coming sergeant.
> Pick 'em up, pick 'em up – I'll stalk within yer chamber.
> Private Leg ... sick.
> Private Ball ... absent.[20]

The shift of tone – from tragic poetry to comic prose – is
bold and brilliantly successful. One must not overlook the
jokes: that at the expense of the most famous poem by Sir
Thomas Wyatt, whose book, *Certayne Psalms*, was published
in 1549 – '01549 Wyatt' – and, more important, Jones's pun
on his hero's name. Fussell misses two thirds of the point
when he says that John Ball is 'named after the priest who led
the Peasants' Revolt in 1381'. Our Private Ball, who follows
Private Leg in the sergeant's roster, is sacerdotal, surely, but
also ballistic and – it must be said – anatomical. When finally
he comes on parade, 'that silence peculiar to parade grounds
and to refectories' is broken – but broken liturgically:

Captain Gwyn does not turn or move or give any sign.
> Have that man's name taken if you please, Mr. Jenkins.
> Take that man's name, Sergeant Snell.
> Take his name, corporal.

Take his name take his number – charge him –late on parade – the Battalion being paraded for overseas – warn him for Company Office.
Have you got his name Corporal Quilter.
Temporary unpaid Lance-Corporal Aneirin Merddyn Lewis had somewhere in his Welsh depths a remembrance of the nature of man, of how a lance-corporal's stripe is but held vicariously and from on high, is of one texture with an eternal economy. He brings in a manner, baptism, and metaphysical order to the bankruptcy of the occasion.
'o1 Ball is it – there was a man in Bethesda late for the last bloody judgment.
Corporal Quilter on the other hand knew nothing of these things.21

The narrator, like his Lance-Corporal, brings a metaphysical order to the bankruptcy of the occasion. A prosaic manner is appropriate to an age all-but-bankrupt in terms of heroic and religious values, but we are reminded that some hierarchies are still observed. Lance-Corporal Aneirin – named, no doubt, after the poet – holds his stripe vicariously (like a vicar) and from on high, and his joke has a prophetic ring: ''o1 Ball is it – there was a man in Bethesda late for the last bloody judgment.' Ball, the survivor, will be late for the last bloody judgment attended by the rest of his platoon. The Welshman has in his depths a remembrance, but the English Corporal Quilter on the other hand 'knew nothing of these things'.

The Lance-Corporal's bardic namesake had celebrated the high-ranking heroes of *The Gododdin* in a high style. The low-ranking celebrant of a more democratic age suits his style to his lower-ranking heroes, though his ear is marvellously attuned to social distinctions. As befits a poet whose first memory 'was of a thing of great marvel – a troop of horses moving in a column to the *tarantara* of bugles', and who thereupon resolved 'some day I shall ride on horse-back',22 his mounted officers are generally presented in chivalric terms. Mr. Jenkins, in keeping with his lower station, is presented in gentlemanly terms – 'The Squire from the Rout of San Romano smokes Melachrino No. 9' – and presented affectionately:

> Mr. Jenkins got his full lieutenancy on his twenty-first birthday, and a parcel from Fortnum and Mason; he grieved for his friend, Talbot Rhys (killed and left hanging on the wire), and felt an indifference to the spring offensive – and why was non-conforming Captain Gwyn so stuffy about the trebled whisky chits.[23]

With the exception of 'that shit Major Lillywhite' and one other officer, all the characters in *In Parenthesis* are presented sympathetically, including 'the enemy front-fighters' and those who pray for them behind the lines:

> But all the old women in Bavaria are busy with their novenas, you bet your life, and don't sleep lest the watch should fail, nor weave for the wire might trip his darling feet and the dead Karl might not come home.[24]

Jones has his indignation, but it is reserved for a certain category of non-combatants first referred to in Part 2. Entitled 'CHAMBERS GO OFF, CORPORALS STAY', this opens with the troops being lectured 'in the barn, with its great roof, sprung, upreaching, humane, and redolent of a vanished order'.[25] There are lectures on hygiene by the medical officer, 'whose heroism and humanity reached toward sanctity'.[26] Like the great roof of the barn, *upreaching, humane*, he speaks of a vanished order; as, in a sense, does the Adjutant when he addresses them on the history of the Regiment. But 'The old order changeth, yielding place to new', and Jones portrays the representative of the new less kindly:

> the Bombing Officer [...] told them lightly of the efficacy of his trade; he predicted an important future for the new Mills Mk. IV

grenade, just on the market; he discussed the improvised jam-tins of the veterans, of the bombs of after the Marne, grenades of Loos and Lavantie – he compared these elementary, amateurish, inefficiencies with the compact and supremely satisfactory invention of this Mr. Mills, to whom his country was so greatly indebted.[27]

Long before the Bombing Officer takes his leave 'like a departing commercial traveller', Jones's scornful irony has told us that he is no gentleman and has no understanding of history, heroism, or humanity. This theme is developed further at the end of Part 2, when the 'Chambers Go Off' and our hero is introduced to the supremely satisfactory invention of someone in Mr. Mills's line of trade:

John Ball would have followed, but stood fixed and alone in the little yard – his senses highly alert, his body incapable of movement or response. The exact disposition of small things – the precise shapes of trees, the lilt of a bucket, the movement of a straw, the disappearing right boot of Sergeant Snell – all minute noises, separate and distinct, in a stillness charged through with some approaching violence – registered not by the ear nor any single faculty – an on-rushing pervasion, saturating all existence; with exactitude, logarithmic, dial-timed, millesimal – of calculated velocity, some mean chemist's contrivance, a stinking physicist's destroying toy.[28]

The indictment of the scientist, delivered with all the explosive force of that rhetorical suspension, is delivered more coolly and more searchingly in the Preface:

We feel a rubicon has been passed between striking with a hand weapon as men used to do and loosing poison from the sky as we do ourselves. We doubt the decency of our own inventions [...][29]

Not everyone would feel the same about the *decency* of 'striking with a hand weapon', but Jones's use of the word is revealing. *Decency* is the distinguishing characteristic of the gentleman, that nineteenth-century mutation of the mediaeval knight. The traditions of the gentleman were chivalric, humanistic, and tended to produce a deep distrust of science. The subject of *In Parenthesis* is the destruction of an old order – still recognizably chivalric – by a new *dis*order, here represented by 'some mean chemist's contrivance, a stinking physicist's destroying toy'.

The imminence of that destruction reinforces the tragic dignity with which Mr. Jenkins's platoon prepares for what the reader senses will be its last battle. Two moments of preparation, in particular, evoke the rituals of the old order, and at both the narrator adopts the shorter line, the higher style of poetry. As Cibno took communion and his comrades drank together before setting off for Catraeth, so the men of No. 1 section receive the sacrament – 'one-third part of a loaf' and a share of the 'half mess-tin of rum':

Come off it Moses – dole out the issue.
Dispense salvation,
strictly apportion it,
let us taste and see,
let us be renewed,
for christ's sake let us be warm.
[...]
    Each one in turn, and humbly, receives his meagre benefit. This lance-jack sustains them from his iron spoon; and this is thank-worthy.[30]

The sacrament of Last Supper is followed – as the mead-drinking in the hall of Mynyddog was followed – by the boast. Dai Great-coat

        articulates his English with an alien care.
            My fathers were with the Black Prinse of Wales
        at the passion of
        the blind Bohemian king.
        They served in these fields [...][31]

Dai's boast, modelled on Taliesin's in *The Mabinogion*, asserts that he was present at all the major moments in the history of the 'hand weapon', from the primal war in Heaven to the Crucifixion, from Roncesvalles to Camlann. That history begins its last chapter with Part 7 of *In Parenthesis*, entitled 'THE FIVE UNMISTAKABLE MARKS'.[32] The allusion to the five wounds of the crucified Christ is balanced by the secular epigraph:

> Gododdin I demand thy support.
> It is our duty to sing: a meeting
> place has been found.[33]

Invoking Aneirin's aid, in Aneirin's words, Jones procedes to discharge his duty as a poet: he *sings* – there is more poetry in Part 7 than in any other – of the meeting at Mametz Wood in July 1916. As the platoon waits to go over the top on 'the place of a skull', the first of the comrades is killed:

> No one to care there for Aneirin Lewis spilled there
> who worshipped his ancestors like a Chink
> who sleeps in Arthur's lap [...][34]

His elegist apportions blame, but not to the enemy:

>   Properly organized chemists can let make more riving power
> than ever Twrch Trwyth;
> more blistered he is than painted Troy Towers
> and unwholer, limb from limb, than any of them fallen at Catraeth
> [...][35]

At zero hour, 'Mr Jenkins takes them over' and almost at once

> Lurched over, jerked iron saucer over tilted brow,
> clampt unkindly over lip and chin
> nor no ventaille to this darkening
> and masked face lifts to grope the air [...][36]

Ventaille – the Old French word for a helmet's movable visor – reminds us that it is the Squire from the Rout of San Romano who has fallen. But the Disciplines of the Wars are maintained 'and Sergeant T. Quilter takes over'. One by one, however, the 'family' – Jones's word – is cut down until Private Ball finds himself, first, 'alone in a denseness of hazel-brush', and then shot in the legs. He crawls away, encumbered by his rifle:

Slung so, it swings its full weight. With you going blindly on all paws, it slews its whole length, to hang at your bowed neck like the Mariner's white oblation.
[...]
Hung so about, you make [...] your close escape.[37]

Once again we hear the voice of the survivor: 'I only am *escaped* to tell thee.' But his elegy for his friends is not yet finished, and we share the wounded man's pastoral hallucination of the Queen of the Woods dispensing garlands to the dead:

She plaits torques of equal splendour for Mr. Jenkins and Billy Crower.
   Hansel with Gronwy share dog-violets for a palm, where they lie in serious embrace beneath the twisted tripod.[38]

The modern poet makes no distinction between officer and private soldier; they receive 'torques of equal splendour' – we remember the gold torques of *The Gododdin* – and German and Welshman, friend and so-called enemy, embrace. At the last, the survivor disengages himself from his rifle, as the Ancient Mariner (with whom he had earlier identified himself) had disengaged himself from his albatross. I think we are meant to infer that he, too, has expiated his guilt as a killer and, having *escaped*, must *tell*. His message, however, is not that of Aneirin and Turold: the celebration of the heroic dead, that their names may live and their example be followed. David Jones bears witness to the death of friends who never saw the men that killed them.

When Fussell calls *In Parenthesis* a work 'which uses the past not, as it often pretends to do, to shame the present, but really to ennoble it',[39] he fails to recognize that Jones's present is a battlefield on which past and future clash in unequal combat. The poet celebrates the traditional humanity his heroes show to one another, their courage in the face of almost certain death, as he execrates the inhumanity of the mechanistic forces brought against them.

Twenty-seven years after Private Jones of the Royal Welch Fusiliers escaped from that stricken field, Lieutenant Alun Lewis of the South Wales Borderers lay on an operating table in an Indian hospital. Afterwards he wrote: 'I surrendered to what Edward Thomas foresaw – the land he must enter and leave alone.'[40] He also wrote a poem, 'Burma Casualty'. In this, a wounded survivor escapes death a second time – on the operating table:

> He went alone: knew nothing: and returned
> Retching and blind with pain, and yet alive.
>
> IV
> Mending, with books and papers and a fan
> Sunlight on parquet floors and bowls of flame
> He heard quite casually that his friends were dead.
> His regiment too butchered to reform.
> And he lay in the lightness of the ward
> Thinking of all the lads the dark enfolds
> So secretly.
> And yet a man may walk
> Into and through it, and return alive.[41]

The tone is Owen's: the disarming adverb 'casually' setting up the reader for the shock of what follows: first, the general news 'that his friends were dead'; then the more specific information that, in Owen's phrase, they had died 'as cattle' – 'His regiment too *butchered* to reform'.

In another of Lewis's poems, 'The Run-In', a soldier on a landing craft is contemplating this question against the enemy, and thinking

Always when I awake there is a little wind on my skin and
I sweat and cannot find any consolation and cannot tell
What point in the universe I am. There is no retention.
Life transfers itself; the dead have friendships with the living,
And the living often hold their profoundest loyalties with the dead.
And most of us owe something both to the dead and the living, and
move almost unconsciously between worlds.[42]

Aneirin, Owen, Jones, and Lewis come to us – as the four messengers came to Job – saying in turn: 'I only am escaped to tell thee.' They come to tell the living of the dead and, hearing them bear witness to how they lived and how they died, we become aware of the paradox that it is the song and not the singer that escapes. As Auden reminds us:

The words of a dead man
Are modified in the guts of the living.[43]

All our words were once the property of the dead. In the Preface to *In Parenthesis*, Jones says: 'I did not intend this as a "War Book" – it happens to be concerned with war.'[44] The message of the so-called 'war poet' is essentially the same as that of his fellow poet in times of so-called 'peace'. He pays his dues to the living in the currency of the dead. Over and over again we see a poet's appetite for life sharpened by an awareness of how it tasted on the tongue, sounded on the tongue, of the dead. Knowing himself a survivor – one who lives above (*super vivere*) as well as beyond the dead – he tells his listener, as the Ancient Mariner the wedding-guest: 'I only am escaped to tell thee.'

CHAPTER 3

England's epic?

Beowulf (a Scandinavian saga, albeit one brilliantly translated from Anglo-Saxon by an Irish bard)?[1] Malory's *Morte Darthur*? Tennyson's *Idylls of the King*? Doughty's *The Dawn in Britain*? No. None can compare with Homer's *Iliad* or Virgil's *Aeneid* as England's foundational epic. Let me propose another and, to my mind, stronger candidate: *The Golden Warrior* by Hope Muntz.

Published in 1948, this was reprinted three times in its first year and twice more before its reissue in paperback in 1966. Its all-too-brief bestsellerdom was the result of fortunate timing and virtues justly celebrated in a Foreword by the doyen of British historians, G. M. Trevelyan, that begins:

I regard it as an honour to be asked to introduce to the public this remarkable book. The author [...] has a deep knowledge and love of the island she has twice seen threatened with invasion. This is the story of the successful invasion of England long ago.

It is not an ordinary historical novel, for the historical novel usually avoids the great personages and the famous scenes, and fills its canvas with imaginary characters. But this book is a Saga of Harold and William. The other personages, English and European, are historical portraits; they are subordinate to the two protagonists, but each of them stands as a clear-cut figure in the tapestry.[2]

The Golden Warrior is not 'an ordinary historical novel' in any sense. These, and even extraordinary historical novels like Tolstoy's *War and Peace*, tend to be written by novelists after a period of historical research. Hope Muntz (1897–1981), however, was a historian, Fellow of both the Society of Antiquaries and the Royal Historical Society, and co-editor of a volume in the Oxford Mediaeval Texts. Having lived more than half her imaginative life with Earl Harold Godwinson and Duke William the Bastard, she astonished those expecting a scholarly monograph by producing a magnificent novel.

When Trevelyan speaks of the book's 'historical portraits', each standing 'as a clear-cut figure in the tapestry', his metaphor is at once accurate, suggestive in its allusion to the Bayeux Tapestry, and at the same time misleading. Nothing could be further from the immobility of a portrait or the two-dimensional comic/tragic strip of a mediaeval tapestry than the breathing figures in Muntz's story. Her narrative has an epic shape, a variant form of the traditional quest, as her protagonists seek and compete for 'an heirloom fashioned like the Wessex Dragon, a golden arm-ring [...] the royal ring, which all the Kings [of the English Royal House] had borne'.[3] A serpentine coil rather than a simple circlet, this has an envenomed reputation as 'a thing accursed'.[4] Two of its royal owners have been murdered before Muntz's narrative begins and when Earl Harold, receiving his father's inheritance, 'saw the royal ring, the Golden Dragon of Wessex, lying on blood-red silk',[5] the omens become audible. Resisting ambition (a key-word in the book), Harold sends the royal ring to Edgar Atheling, heir to Edward the Confessor's throne, and only after the Atheling's premature death ('coughing blood') does Harold agree to wear it.

The land symbolized by the Wessex Dragon is the prize for which the English Hector and Norman Achilles compete. Both are master strategists on the battlefield and in the political arena at home and abroad. Well matched in physical strength and raw courage, their differences are significant and skilfully delineated. Harold, the Golden Warrior, is said to have hair 'like shining bronze',[6] while William's is 'black as coal',[7] and their styles of leadership are as different as day and night. Harold's radiant charisma inspires love and loyalty in both men and women, whereas William's dark power generates awe and fear. Both find sexual fulfilment outside the ordinances of the Church: Harold is raising a family with a much-loved handfast wife, Edith Swan-neck, until obliged to weld the halves of his kingdom together by marriage with a daughter of the northern House of Leofric; William entering into a marriage banned by the Holy See. Ever the cynical strategist, he subsequently negotiates atonement and a papal blessing on his imperial ambitions against England.

Women – mothers, wives, daughters – play major roles in Muntz's narrative, and it is as much a love story as a war story. Nothing so vividly shows the crucial difference between the protagonists as their leave-taking of their women before their final battle: William, coldly and with self-deceiving self-justification;[8] Harold, tenderly,

his voice far off and low: 'Do you remember the mown meadow, Edith, and St. John's Eve; the dancing round the baal-fire and the songs, and then we two alone under the apple-trees? If it were sin, yet surely we loved much.'

She did not answer. [...]

They were long silent. The King lay with his eyes closed. At last his hand that held hers loosed its hold. Edith sat unmoving. The candles guttered and went out. The fire was ashes. When she looked down, she could not see his face.

King Harold rode from Nazeing after Midnight. Edith stood with the boy Harold in her arms and the old nurse beside her. They watched until the torches vanished in the deep forest.[9]

In 1064, Harold had been shipwrecked on the coast of
Normandy, imprisoned by the Count of Panthieu, but
ransomed by Duke William. For a time they became
friends, each recognizing the other's strengths and, more
importantly, the one recognizing the other's weakness: 'In
mighty matters and in small,' says William, 'his heart will
sway him.'[10] The recognition comes to him witnessing
Harold risk his life to rescue two common soldiers from
a quicksand. 'William asked him: "Why did you do it?"
"I could not bear to hear them yell," said Harold.'[11] His
compassion is a manifestation of a humanity reinforced by
strong religious belief. Bishop Wulfstan 'was the Earl's
confessor and his dearest friend'.[12] We hear nothing of
the Duke's confessor. Had he wanted one (which may
seem unlikely), that role would no doubt have been taken
by his brother, Bishop Odo, a monster of avarice and
brutality. Wulfstan, by contrast, was a good shepherd in
his Master's image, a compassionate man of simple tastes
and strong faith. When Harold's life was threatened by a
mysterious illness, he asked Wulfstan whether he should
visit the shrine in the Bishop's cathedral and there make
prayers and offerings. The Bishop wrote back: 'Look
higher than this place, dear son, as God shall teach you.'[13]
With his letter he sent an illuminated manuscript book
of Old English poems. That night Edith leant over the
stricken Earl. 'She wore a little golden cross, his gift on
the first night. It swung between them like a star.'[14] The
star supplies the answer to Wulfstan's riddling injunction:
Waltham Holy Cross, the young lovers' forest church,
where 'many poor folk had found healing'.[15] Harold orders
his men to take gifts to the humble shrine and there offer
Masses for his recovery. Then, opening Wulfstan's book at
the Bishop's marker, he reads in 'The Dream of the Rood':

On me the Son of God   suffered for a space;
Wherefore now I rise   glorious beneath the heavens,
And I can heal   all who fear me.[16]

His faith rewarded, Harold recovers and, in due course,
receives the royal ring from the hand of the dying King
Edward. When Duke William contests his claim, the scrupu-
lous historian's reader already understands the complex interaction of ambition, chance, rights and wrongs, in each
claimant's case. Both men are heroes of Shakespearean stature,
heroes to their peoples and to each other. Both have flaws; the
difference being that Harold's is a tragic flaw, long recognized
by his adversary. He is undone by his most admirable qualities: compassion, sensitivity, self-knowledge. He will not
allow himself to take the Holy Cross as the emblem on his
standard, because he had earlier violated an oath sworn, under
duress, on holy relics. His courage is heroic but, like Beowulf
(hero of a poem he knows), he takes risks appropriate in a
warrior, inappropriate in a king; and with the same tragic
outcome. He fights his final battles under a standard, embroi-
dered by his mother, bearing the image of a golden warrior;
and when some of his men desert, there is at least an implication that they might have stood firm under the Holy Cross.
The battles of Stamford Bridge and Hastings are set-pieces
that will stand comparison with Stendhal's Waterloo and
Tolstoy's Borodino.[17] After the King has fallen and the
Duke has taken possession of 'an arm-ring wet with blood',
the last of Harold's Housecarles wield their axes, chanting the
words of the 'The Battle of Maldon':

I am grown grey-hair'd;   go hence I will not,
But I here abiding   with my bread-giver,
By so loved a man   look to perish.[18]

The braided themes of love and war are united after dark, as
Edith searches among the stripped bodies for that of her lord.

She finds him and he is buried at dawn with her cross in his cold hand.

The Golden Warrior has a grand and intricate narrative, coiled like an arm-ring, but that alone would not make it a great novel. As with other great novels, its distinction lies in an ideal marriage of language and structure: they are one flesh. 'Ordinary historical novels' are all too often as clearly a product of their author's period as of their subject's: eighteenth-century props – crinolines and cutlasses – at variance with twentieth-century psychology and turns of phrase. Not so *The Golden Warrior*. Hope Muntz had studied the Anglo-Saxon Chronicle longer than a London clubman *The Times*, and has given us a composite, brilliantly fleshed-out, 'translation' of non-existent Anglo-Saxon and Norman chronicles of the years 1051–66. Her chapter titles set the tone: 'Of Harold's Heirship-ale', 'Of Duke William's Marriage', 'Of the Atheling'. Heirship-ale and Atheling are not 'explained' (any more than Landfather or Wayfaring Bread). Context makes the meaning clear. Muntz's sentences are short, simple and declarative, in the manner of eleventh-century chronicles. They make little use of metaphor or simile, but her speakers have a gift for the apt proverb: 'Let him slay the bear […] before he sell the bearskin'; 'There is little for the rake after the besom'; 'Small fish are better than no fish.'[19] The master-stroke that makes the masterpiece, however, will already be apparent from my quotations: the scarcity of words with a Greek or Latinate root, particularly in the mouths of Old English speakers. Muntz paints her great canvas from a sombre Anglo-Saxon palette, her rare touches of bright colour frequently symbolic – as in the 'blood-red silk' cushioning the royal ring, or the phoenix-like image at the book's end:

Odo spoke again. His words were given in the English tongue. The warriors shouted anew. The clarions and the trumpets rang.

A third time the Bishop spoke, thundering his words: 'Hail your deliverer, men of England. King William comes to make you free.'

The trumpet-calls and shouts rang out unanswered. Then a man cried aloud in English. The people stirred and murmured, their faces changed.

'What does he say?' said the Duke.

'Sire,' said Malet, 'he says their King cannot be slain, that he will come to save them.'

Odo said to Duke William: 'Have the fellow seized. You will not win this people with fair words.'

'Let him go,' said William. 'Let them all depart.'

He turned his horse and rode at a foot-pace towards the camp. His Barons and his captains followed. The dawn wind struck cold to their wounds; weariness beyond telling was upon them.

William turned his head and looked across the sea. The sun rose up in splendour and the day grew bright. He saw far out the sails of warships, coming from Normandy.[20]

Hope Muntz's Godwinsaga is an epic in everything but the texture of its telling. Herbert Read called David Jones's prose poem, *In Parenthesis*, 'as near a great epic of the [Great] war as ever the war generation will reach'.[21] In the same way, and by the same standard, *The Golden Warrior* may be called as near a great epic of the Norman Conquest as any generation will reach. That said, it is tempting to imagine the national epic England *might* have had if Thomas Hardy had taken Harold and William, rather than Wellington and Napoleon, as the protagonists of *The Dynasts/An Epic-Drama*. Perhaps Yeats, author himself of a would-be national epic, *The Wanderings of Oisin*, should have the last word:

> Though the great song return no more
> There's keen delight in what we have:
> The rattle of pebbles on the shore
> Under the receding wave.[22]

CHAPTER 4

Who was Rupert Brooke?

This was a question asked by the poet's oldest friend forty years after his death. Geoffrey Keynes, having selected and edited his letters, had just sent a set of proofs to each of his fellow literary trustees and to a few of Brooke's other friends. To his consternation, several responded with horror, saying in effect: 'The letters to me show the *real* Rupert, but his posturing in the others distorts the portrait out of all recognition.' In vain did Keynes point out that they each regarded the letters to him or to her (Frances Cornford was one of those most troubled) as expressing the *real* Rupert and shook their heads over the rest. In vain did he remind them of Brooke's undergraduate letter to *him* saying 'I attempt to be "all things to all men"; rather "cultured" among the cultured, faintly athletic among athletes, a little blasphemous among blasphemers, slightly insincere to myself ...'[1] So strong was the feeling among the poet's friends that Keynes's selection misrepresented him that the book was put on ice, and Christopher Hassall was commissioned to write a biography that would reveal the *real* Rupert Brooke.

What is interesting here is not that he adopted a different tone in writing to different people – we all do that – but that they cared so passionately that the world should know the *real* Rupert, *their* Rupert. It is worth remembering, too, who they were, these friends who valued him so highly; friends that included the Asquiths, the Cornfords, Hugh Dalton, E. M. Forster, David Garnett, Edmund Gosse, Henry James, Geoffrey and Maynard Keynes, Cathleen Nesbitt, Stanley Spencer, Edward Thomas, and Virginia Woolf.

Looking for an answer to the question, 'Who was Rupert Brooke?' I went back to the testimony of his friends and found a common denominator that had hitherto escaped my attention – and the attention of most who never met him. Geoffrey and Margaret Keynes used to say how funny he was, and in a letter of 1905 Rupert asks Geoffrey, 'Have I not often made you laugh?'[2] Frances Cornford wrote, in a poem entitled 'Rupert Brooke':

> Perhaps
> A thousand years ago some Greek boy died,
> So lovely-bodied, so adored, so young,
> Like us they grieved and treasured little things
> (And laughed with tears remembering his laughter).[3]

David Garnett remembered him as 'tall and well built, loosely put together, with a careless animal grace and a face made for smiling and sudden laughter':[4] while A. C. Benson recalled him laughing 'rather huddled, in his chair'.[5] Sybil Pye wrote: 'His gay unembarrassed laugh of pleasure still rings in one's head – one knew so well the sound of it.'[6]

Brooke himself set great store by laughter, writing to Jacques Raverat from the South Seas:

laughter is the very garland on the head of friendship. I will not love, and I will not be loved. But I will have friends round me continually, all the days of my life, and in whatever lands I may be. So we shall laugh and eat and sing and go great journeys [...][7]

Returning to England in 1914, he was introduced to Lascelles Abercrombie and reported to Ka Cox: 'He laughs very well.'[8] There is much talk of laughter in Brooke's letters and much occasion for it. It is hard not to warm to the Rugby schoolboy who, suffering from pink-eye, explains that 'The disease comes of gazing too often on Butterfield's architecture';[9] or to the dying man who, informed that Dean Inge had read his sonnet 'The Soldier' aloud in St Paul's, praising it but saying 'it fell somewhat short of Isaiah's vision', responded that 'he was sorry Inge did not think him quite as good as Isaiah'.[10] I suspect a fear that this Brooke – the laughing Brooke – would be overshadowed by the tormented lover may have been a factor in the adverse reaction to Keynes's original *Selected Letters*. The figure to emerge from Hassall's biography (1964) and Keynes's edition of *The Letters* (1968) was much more complicated, confused, and credible than the 'young Apollo' of Marsh's Memoir in the *Collected Poems* (1918). Most critical attention since has tended to concentrate on the tormented lover of 1911–13, losing sight of the happier man who, in the years before and after, wrote the poems by which he is today remembered.

The quality Brooke looked for in his friends he celebrated in a review of the 1912 edition of his favourite poet:

as Donne saw everything through his intellect, it follows, in some degree, that he could see everything humorously. He could see it the other way, too. But humour was always at his command. It was part of his realism; especially in the bulk of his work, his poems dealing with love. There is no true lover but has sometimes laughed at his mistress, and often at himself. But you would not guess that from the love-songs of many poets. Their poems run the risk of looking a little flat. They are unreal by the side of Donne. For while his passion enabled him to see the face of love, his humour allowed him to look at it from the other side. So we behold his affairs in the round.

But it must not appear that his humour, or his wit, and his passion, alternated. The other two are his passion's handmaids. It should not be forgotten that Donne was one of the first great English satirists, and the

most typical and prominent figure of a satirical age. Satire comes with
the Bible of truth in one hand and sword of laughter in the other.'¹

In an earlier essay, Brooke had quoted the remark of Hugo
to Baudelaire, 'You have created a new shudder', and went
on to suggest that one might say of Ernest Dowson, 'He has
created a new sigh.'¹² Similarly, one might say of Brooke that
he created a new laugh. Laughter is audible in no less than a
third of the poems and fragments in Keynes's edition, a statistic
doubly surprising given the nature of his central subject. This
emerges in one of his earliest poems, 'It Is Well',¹³ written
when he was sixteen. It begins:

> Nay, love, I weep not, but laugh o'er my dead,
> My dreams long perished; though I forfeited
> To save thee sorrow, joy unutterable –
> I would not have it otherwise; 'twas well.

I suspect *that* laughter was meant to sound despairing, but it
is possible to hear it also as self-mocking in wry acknowledgement of the nineties' archaic diction, the dreams and
sorrow borrowed from Yeats and others. The laughter and
death, life and death, juxtaposed in the first line re-emerge in
the poem's last stanza:

> And, when our Death dawns pale, and we must go,
> Though infinite space may part us, this I know;
> If, looking upward through the bars of Hell,
> I see that face in Heaven, it will be well.

We notice, however, that the vision is conditional: '*If* looking upward'. The speaker may not – or may not be able to –
look upward.

Two years later, flaunting the fashionable nihilism of the
decadent poets of the nineties, Brooke addresses one of their
favourite themes in his poem 'Man':

> Time drew towards its ending: every where
> Bent with their little sorrows and old pain,
> Men cried to God.

As Apocalypse approaches, the poet records that cry:

> Why are we vexed with yearning? Surely it is
> Enough for us to crouch about the fire
> And laugh the irretrievable hours away,
> Heedless of what may wait us in the gloom,
> The muttering night beyond? Yet though we strive
> So to live in the present and forget,
> Ever the voice returning wakes again
> The old insatiate yearning in our hearts,
> Whispering words incomprehensible,
> Infinity, Eternity, and – God.

Man's lament ends with a call to the incomprehensible Godhead for an incomprehensibly 'eternal End'. Brooke's letters of this time play with eschatological themes: 'With advancing years I find one's thoughts turn increasingly towards the Hereafter and the Serious Things of Life.'[14] And again: 'I love to think of myself as seated on the greyness of Lethe's banks, and showering ghosts of epigrams and shadowy paradoxes upon the assembled wan-eyed dead.'[15] A sonnet of 1905, beginning 'When on my night of life the Dawn shall break', shows him playing once again with just such a fantasy. The beloved is more sharply imagined than in the earlier dawn of 'It Is Well'. She now has a 'brave smile', 'bright swift eyes', and a Yeatsian, Pre-Raphaelite, 'pale cloud of [...] tossing hair', but the earlier conditional ('If, looking upward ... / I see that face in Heaven') reappears reformulated:

> Only – I fear me that I may not find
> That brave smile [...]

The death of God is a recurrent theme of Brooke's early poems, but the Great Incomprehensible (and His Mother) return in a sonnet in 1907, 'My Song', to preside over another vision of the last dawn, another version of the beloved's entry into the Hereafter:

> Yes, in the wonder of the last day-break,
> God's Mother, on the threshold of His house,
>   Shall welcome in your white and perfect soul,
> Kissing your brown hair softly for my sake;
>   And God's own hand will lay, as aureole,
> My song, a flame of scarlet, on your brows.

We are not told whether the poet is to be present at the investiture, but he is certainly and centrally present in the final retake of this scene, a sonnet written in April 1909:

> Oh! Death will find me, long before I tire
>   Of watching you; and swing me suddenly
> Into the shade and loneliness and mire
>   Of the last land! There, waiting patiently,
>
> One day, I think, I'll feel the cool wind blowing,
>   See a slow light across the Stygian tide,
> And hear the Dead about me stir, unknowing,
>   And tremble. And *I* shall know that you have died,
>
> And watch you, a broad-browed and smiling dream,
>   Pass, light as ever, through the lightless host,
> Quietly ponder, start, and sway, and gleam –
>   Most individual and bewildering ghost! –
>
> And turn, and toss your brown delightful head
> Amusedly, among the ancient Dead.

This is a dramatic advance on anything Brooke had written before – a fact he recognised by putting it first in his first book of poems. The voice is a relaxed voice of 1909 rather than a literary voice of the 1890s. The speaker is now at the centre of the poem, and the solemnity of the occasion – a solemnity that had made the earlier poems portentous – is held in check by the good-humoured tone and the fact that the *ghost* is good-humoured, a 'smiling dream'. Seen first as a 'a slow light' in the shade of the last land, she passes 'light as ever, through the lightless host', her light and lightness lightly re-emphasized when he sees her

> turn, and toss your brown delightful head
> Amusedly, among the ancient Dead.

Amusedly – the key word – is quintessential Brooke, as is the ironic counterpoint on which the poem comes to rest. Alliteration links that adverb to 'the ancient Dead' (just as the new ghost is linked to the old), but the fact that she views them *amusedly* mocks and calls in question their ancient authority.

Brooke himself continually questioned, and increasingly denied, the ancient and modern authorities, positing the existence of an afterlife. His handling of this theme takes on the character of a debate. 'The Hill', a sonnet of 1910, rejects the comforting mythology of 'Oh! Death will find me'. The setting is *this* world, which the poet endows with the splendour ascribed by others to the *next*:

> 'And when we die
> All's over that is ours; and life burns on
> Through other lovers, other lips,' said I,
> 'Heart of my heart, our heaven is now, is won!'
>
> 'We are Earth's best, that learnt her lesson here.
> Life is our cry. We have kept the faith!' we said;
> 'We shall go down with unreluctant tread
> Rose-crowned into the darkness!' ... Proud we were,
> And laughed, that had such brave true things to say.
> – And then you suddenly cried, and turned away.

Brooke's rhetoric here gets the better of him, and the turn from laughter to tears is markedly less successful than the earlier sonnet's turn from solemnity to amusement.

It is generally agreed that his best period was his *Wanderjahr* in the South Seas, and finishing a poem 'Mutability' begun in London, he puts both sides of the debate. The ancient Dead are quoted first:

> They say there's a high windless world and strange,
>   Out of the wash of days and temporal tide,
>   Where Faith and Good, Wisdom and Truth abide,
> *Æterna corpora*, subject to no change.

The counter-argument, however, carries the day and, as in so many of Brooke's other poems, *laugh* seems synonymous with *life*:

> Dear, we know only that we sigh, kiss, smile;
>   Each kiss lasts but the kissing; and grief goes over;
>   Love has no habitation but the heart.
> Poor straws! on the dark flood we catch awhile,
>   Cling, and are borne into the night apart.
>   The laugh dies with the lips, 'Love' with the lover.

The debate continues in two other sonnets of 1913. 'Suggested by some of the Proceedings of the Society for Psychical Research' and 'Clouds' both appear to reject the idea of a remote heaven but settle for an intermediate state not perhaps so very different. In the sestet of 'Clouds', the ancient Dead and the speaker seem to agree:

> They say that the Dead die not, but remain
>   Near to the rich heirs of their grief and mirth.
>   I think they ride the calm mid-heaven, as these,
> In wise majestic melancholy train,
>   And watch the moon, and the still-raging seas,
>   And men, coming and going on the earth.

The authorities, the ancient Dead, are cited again in the poem 'Heaven', only now it is not '*They* say' but '*Fish* say':

> Oh! never fly conceals a hook,
> Fish say, in the Eternal Brook,
> But more than mundane weeds are there,
> And mud, celestially fair;
> Fat caterpillars drift around,
> And Paradisal grubs are found;
> Unfading moths, immortal flies,
> And the worm that never dies.
> And in that Heaven of all their wish,
> There shall be no more land, say fish.

This is a more cunning version of the debate than any hitherto, in that the authorities seem to have the floor to themselves, but of course their testimony is invalidated by the speaker's satiric voice. The targets of his satire are generally taken to be Platonism and Christianity, but there is I think another target: that signalled by 'the Eternal Brook', the poet so attracted to representations of an after-life. This poem is not only a more cunning but also a more successful version of the Eternal Brooke's eternal debate, partly as a result of his switch to the shorter line. The slow march of the iambic pentameter encouraged his tendency to indulge in what, with characteristic self-mockery, he described as 'the purest Nineteenth Century grandiose thoughts, about the Destiny of Man, the Irresistibility of Fate, the Doom of Nations, the fact that Death awaits us All, and so forth. Wordsworth Redivivus. Oh dear! oh dear!'[16]

He continued to have such grandiose thoughts, but in his best poems he engages them with 'the sword of laughter'. Both the tone and the rhetorical structure of 'Tiare Tahiti' owe something to Marvell's 'To His Coy Mistress'. Brooke's mistress, the Mamua of his poem, was not coy so he does not

have to persuade her to surrender to his advances, but he
opens with another playful vision of a Platonic eternity:

> Mamua, when our laughter ends,
> And hearts and bodies, brown as white,
> Are dust about the doors of friends,
> Or scent a-blowing down the night,
> Then, oh! then, the wise agree,
> Comes our immortality.
> Mamua, there waits a land
> Hard for us to understand.
> Out of time, beyond the sun,
> All are one in Paradise,
> You and Pupure are one,
> And Taü, and the ungainly wise.
> There the Eternals are, and there
> The Good, the Lovely, and the True,
> And Types, whose earthly copies were
> The foolish broken things we knew;
> There is the Face, whose ghosts we are;
> The real, the never-setting Star;
> And the Flower, of which we love
> Faint and fading shadows here;
> Never a tear, but only Grief;
> Dance, but not the limbs that move;
> Songs in Song shall disappear;
> Instead of lovers, Love shall be;
> For hearts, Immutability;
> And there, on the Ideal Reef,
> Thunders the Everlasting Sea!

The first movement of the poem puts the arguments of 'the
wise' but simultaneously undermines them. Its conclusion:

> And there's an end, I think, of kissing,
> When our mouths are one with Mouth ...

is at once more light-hearted and more tender than the comparable conclusion of Marvell's first movement:

> The grave's a fine and private place,
> But none, I think, do there embrace.

The wise had celebrated

> Types, whose earthly copies were
> The foolish broken things we knew;

but in the poem's second movement Brooke introduces a
re-evaluation of their terms. Their wisdom is the 'foolishness'
to be washed away 'in the water's soft caress', the Pacific tide
that hears and answers 'the calling of the moon', unlike 'the
Everlasting Sea' of the Platonic realm where 'moons are lost in
endless Day'. The poem earns its conclusion – 'There's little
comfort in the wise' – and convinces us (I doubt if Mamua
needed convincing) that there is more than comfort in those
'foolish things' that time will break.

    'Tiare Tahiti' is dated February 1914. Brooke left Tahiti in
April, writing to Cathleen Nesbitt:

It was only yesterday, when I knew that the Southern Cross had left
me, that I suddenly realised that I'd left behind those lovely places
and lovely people, perhaps for ever. I reflected that there was surely
nothing else like them in this world and very probably nothing in the
next [...][17]

Four months later, the outbreak of war prompted a general
resurgence of 'grandiose thoughts about the Destiny of Man,
the Irresistibility of Fate, the Doom of Nations, the fact that
Death awaits us All, and so forth'. In South Africa, Isaac
Rosenberg, envisioning an exhausted civilization rejuvenated
by conflict, ended his poem 'On Receiving News of the War':

> O! ancient crimson curse!
> Corrode, consume.
> Give back this universe
> Its pristine bloom.[18]

In France, Wilfred Owen used the same word at the same time to develop a similar natural image in the sestet of his sonnet '1914':

> For after Spring had bloomed in early Greece,
> And Summer blazed her glory out with Rome,
> An Autumn softly fell, a harvest home,
> A slow grand age, and rich with all increase.
> But now, for us, wild Winter, and the need
> Of sowings for new Spring, and blood for seed.[19]

In England, Brooke began work on the first of the 1914 sonnets that were to make his name. Paradoxically entitled 'Peace', it celebrates the discovery of a cause, a vision resembling Owen's and Rosenberg's: the regeneration of 'a world grown old and cold and weary'. The solemnity of the occasion prompted grandiose thoughts and, forsaking Marvellian tetrameters for Tennysonian pentameters, Brooke yielded to the temptations of a high style that in his better poems he had resisted. Despite the change of style, however, his subject remains the same: the place of life and laughter after death. His fourth sonnet, 'The Dead', comes to the same conclusion as 'Tiare Tahiti':

> These had seen movement, and heard music; known
>   Slumber and waking; loved; gone proudly friended;
> Felt the quick stir of wonder; sat alone;
>   Touched flowers and furs and cheeks. All this is ended.
>
> There are waters blown by changing winds to laughter
> And lit by the rich skies, all day. And after,
>   Frost, with a gesture, stays the waves that dance
> And wandering loveliness. He leaves a white
>   Unbroken glory, a gathered radiance,
> A width, a shining peace, under the night.

What is new in this is the closing metaphor's implication that human laughter has returned to its natural source, is now a part of nature. Although 'Frost, with a gesture, stays the waves that dance', sun and moon will in time release them and the changing winds blow them to laughter once again.

Brooke's fifth and most famous sonnet reverts, in its sestet, to the Platonic position he had so often mocked:

> And think, this heart, all evil shed away,
>   A pulse in the eternal mind, no less
>   Gives somewhere back the thoughts by England given [...]

'The Soldier' would not have had the success it has had if it were not, in its way, a good poem, but I wonder whether some of the unease that over the years has crept into its readers' response may not be related to a lack of conviction on the part of its author as he tried to convince himself of the existence of an afterlife in which he did not believe. The irony is, of course, that whether or not Brooke *is* now 'A pulse in the eternal mind', he *does* give back, in the best of his poems:

>   the thoughts by England given;
> Her sights and sounds; dreams happy as her day;
> And laughter, learnt of friends; and gentleness,
>   In hearts at peace, under an English heaven.

Rupert Brooke is not a War Poet. He is a poet of peace, a celebrant of friendship, love, and laughter.

CHAPTER 5

Christ and the soldier

Siegfried Sassoon is commonly called a 'War Poet' – hardly a satisfactory label at the best of times, and more than usually unsatisfactory in Sassoon's case. But if he is not simply a War Poet, what is he? Late in life, he wrote to Dame Felicitas Corrigan, the nun who had guided him into the Roman Catholic Church: 'almost all [the critics] have ignored the fact that I am a religious poet'.[1]

A review of the evidence for such a claim must start with biography, especially in the case of a poet whose autobiographical writings are a necessary complement to his poems. Surviving the war, Sassoon recovered quickly from his wounds, but the psychological damage war had inflicted took much longer to heal. By 1926, however, he was able to begin work on the obsessive autobiographical enterprise which was to occupy the rest of his life. The first three volumes (later collected under the title, *The Complete Memoirs of George Sherston*) were *Memoirs of a Fox-Hunting Man* (1928), *Memoirs of an Infantry Officer* (1930), and *Sherston's Progress* (1936). This trilogy was followed by two volumes covering his early life: *The Old Century and Seven More Years* (1938) and *The Weald of Youth* (1942). A final volume, *Siegfried's Journey* (1945), dealt with his literary activity during the Great War and after – a subject almost totally omitted from the Sherston trilogy. Other subjects totally omitted have since emerged with the publication of his diaries and the biographies by Moorcroft Wilson, Roberts, and Egremont: a long period of tormented homosexuality, a marriage, the birth of a son, and the breakdown of his marriage. In 1957 he became a Roman Catholic and in 1967, at the age of eighty, he died.

Paul Fussell sums up Sassoon's career: 'Exactly half his life he had spent plowing and re-plowing the earlier half, motivated by what – dichotomizing to the end – he calls "my queer craving to revisit the past and give the modern world the slip". The life he cared to consider ran from 1895 to 1920 only.'[2] Sassoon's diaries show he cared that his successors – though not his contemporaries – *should* consider his life beyond 1920. Fussell is right, however, about Sassoon's dichotomizing; what he calls his 'binary vision'. The last of the memoirs published in his lifetime, *Siegfried's Journey*, ends with a long shot of its hero: 'Picturing him in the clear afternoon light, in his New York straw hat, with the National Gallery in the background, I can almost believe that I have been looking at a faded photograph.'[3] The Prelude to Sassoon's *Diaries 1920–1922* opens: 'Writing the last words of a book, more than four years ago, I left a man – young for his age, though nearly thirty-four – standing in Trafalgar Square, vaguely conscious that his career had reached a point where he must begin it all over again.'[4] The careful splicing of that film calls attention to its double image – he and I – and, when the soldier–poet makes his choice at the crossroads (appropriately commemorating a battle), he takes with him a troubling sense of doubleness. The Prelude ends: 'Inconsistency – double life – as usual – trying to be serious about life and work – buying a horse and dreaming of winning the Vale of the White Horse point-to-point.' The way in which this binary vision operates, ordering

memory and imagination into structural polarities, becomes
clear as we follow him in his ploughing and re-ploughing.

At the start of *Memoirs of a Fox-Hunting Man*, we are told:
'My father and mother died before I was capable of remembering them.'[5] Having removed them from the scene – perhaps
because he was embarrassed to speak of their separation – he
replaces them with surrogate parents, Aunt Evelyn and Dixon,
her groom; *he* determined to make a man of Master George, *she*
fearful that he will break his neck on one of the ponies – and
then horses – to which Dixon introduces him. Deprived of
parental love, and '[a]s a consequence of my loneliness', he says,
'I created in my childish day-dreams an ideal companion who
became much more of a reality than such unfriendly boys as I
encountered at Christmas parties.'[6] The search for that ideal
companion leads – by way of a succession of friendships with
admired figures – ultimately, I believe, to his religious conversion, the union with God.

Fussell says that four-fifths of *Memoirs of a Fox-Hunting
Man* is pastoral romance, adding perceptively that

The reader sensitive to the thematic architecture of the book will do
his own remembering [...] of the numerous prewar 'stand-to's',
delighted anticipatory dawn-watches, of young Sherston back in
Kent. One is especially memorable, on the morning of his triumphant
performance at the Flower-Show Cricket Match, on a day destined to
bring him nothing but joy:

> I loved the early morning; it was luxurious to lie there, half-
> awake, and half-aware that there was a pleasantly eventful
> day in front of me. ... Soon I was up and staring at the
> tree-tops which loomed motionless against a flushed and
> brightening sky. ... There was no sound except the first
> chirruping of the sparrows in the ivy. [Downstairs] there
> was the familiar photograph of 'Love and Death', by Watts,
> with its secret meaning which I could never quite formulate in
> a thought, though it often touched me with a vague emotion

of pathos. When I unlocked the door into the garden the early
morning air met me with its cold purity [...] How little I knew
of the enormous world beyond the valley and those low green
hills.[7]

In the final two chapters of the book, we follow George
Sherston out of the valley, from hunting field to battlefield
where he will begin to learn the meaning of Love and Death.
The polarities are starkly contrasted, but we perceive numerous cunning connections between these disparate spheres.
George had grown up in a society conscious of its imperial
and martial past. There was General FitzAlan – 'He'd been
in the Indian Mutiny' – and Jack Barchard – 'recently
returned from the Boer War'. George acquires on the hunting field the courage he will display so conspicuously on the
battlefield. We overhear a Master of Foxhounds urging an
audience of hunt supporters 'to do everything in their power
to eliminate the most dangerous enemy of the hunting-
man' – he meant 'barbed wire'. In the final chapter, barbed
wire appears as an enemy of the fighting man. A telegram
informs George that his boyhood friend Stephen has been
killed. He shows it to his latest friend, Dick, and shortly
afterwards Dick is killed – on a wiring-party. Sassoon's fox-
hunting man becomes a Boche-hunting one, as George goes
out on patrol determined to take revenge. The polarities are
cunningly juxtaposed as we leave him, 'staring across at the
enemy I'd never seen. Somewhere out of sight beyond the
splintered tree-tops of Hidden Wood a bird had begun to
sing. Without knowing why, I remembered that it was
Easter Sunday. Standing in that dismal ditch, I could find
no consolation in the thought that Christ was risen.'[8]

Christ was risen, but Dick has fallen. George, at this stage,
has no belief in a Christian afterlife and is consistently critical
of the role of the Established Church: 'The Brigade chaplain',

he wrote, 'did not exhort us to love our enemies. He was content to lead off with the hymn "How sweet the name of Jesus sounds"!'[9]

The dynamics of Sassoon's *Memoirs of an Infantry Officer* are, as Fussell says, 'penetration and withdrawal: repeated entrances into the center of trench experience, repeated returns to the world of "home"'. The grotesque disparity between these worlds, and the fact that they were so close, make this the dominant polarity of the book. In Spring 1916, Sherston leaves the trenches, and what he calls 'my personal grievance against the Germans', to go on a course behind the lines. Returning, he plays a courageous part in a disastrous raid, wins the Military Cross, and is granted seven days' leave, which he spends in pastoral Kent. Back, then, to watch in the worst day's fighting of the war, the opening of the Battle of the Somme, from a ridge some five hundred yards behind the British trenches. Between 9 o'clock in the morning and 3.30 in the afternoon of 1 July 1916, the British Army lost 19,000 men killed and 38,000 wounded. On 3 July, Sassoon was himself involved in heavy fighting but, shortly after, was invalided home for seven months with what was diagnosed as enteritis but was probably typhoid. Returning to the Front in April 1917, he was shot through the shoulder and invalided once more. 'At Charing Cross a woman handed me a bunch of flowers and a leaflet by the Bishop of London who earnestly advised me to lead a clean life and attend Holy Communion.'[10] Such bitter ironies, such wilful ignorance at home of the horrors of the Front, lead Sherston to a momentous decision. 'It was', he says, 'a case of direct inspiration; I had, so to speak, received the call, and the editor of the *Unconservative Weekly* [H.W. Massingham, editor of the *Nation*] seemed the most likely man to put me on the shortest road to martyrdom.'[11] The religious

phraseology of 'call' and 'martyrdom' – for all its defensive
irony – is revealing. He makes the public protest that he
expects, and perhaps hopes, will lead to a well-publicized
court-martial, but the book's final irony is the futility and
ultimate failure of that protest.

In case anyone should miss the allusion in the title of the
last volume in the trilogy, *Sherston's Progress*, Sassoon adds
an epigraph from *Pilgrim's Progress*: 'I told him I was a
Pilgrim going to the Celestial City.' The next step on that
road was the shell-shock hospital, Craiglockhart, to which he
had been committed by the military medical authorities. He
arrived there, he says,

> still inclined to regard myself in the role of a 'ripe man of martyr-
> dom.' But the unhistoric part of my mind remembered that the
> neurologist member of my medical board had mentioned someone
> called Rivers. 'Rivers will look after you when you get there.' [...]
> Rivers was evidently some sort of great man: anyhow his name had
> obvious free associations with pleasant landscapes and unruffled
> estuaries.[12]

W.H.R. Rivers, a distinguished neurologist, becomes
over the five months of Sassoon's stay at the hospital the
most important of his ideal companions,[13] a substitute for the
father he never knew. Another companion crucial to his
development was Wilfred Owen, a genuine shell-shock
case (as Sassoon was not). He is not mentioned in *Sherston's
Progress* – though he is in *Siegfried's Journey* – but it is hard to
believe that Owen, with his strong religious background and
beliefs, did not take the would-be martyr further along the
road to the Celestial City. At all events, Sherston/Sassoon
comes to believe that a different form of martyrdom is
required of him. He must return to his men and, if necessary,
give his life for them. Dichotomizing still, he concludes that
'going back to the War as soon as possible was my only

chance of peace'. He returns to the Front, again is shot, again survives, and again has failed to make himself a martyr. Rivers visits him in hospital, and *Sherston's Progress* ends with the wisdom that he brings: 'He did not tell me that I had done my best to justify his belief in me. He merely made me feel that he took all that for granted, and now we must go on to something better still. And this was the beginning of the new life toward which he had shown me the way.'[14] The veiled religious phraseology – 'the new life', 'the way' – is the more interesting in that it would be another twenty years before Sassoon would come within sight of the Celestial City and, entering the Roman Catholic Church, would have his last lesson in the secret meaning of Love and Death.

The trilogy, focusing on the man of action, makes virtually no mention of the poet or his poems, though even the fox-hunting boy had been as committed to his writing as to his riding. His mother had introduced her son to Eddie Marsh, Winston Churchill's private secretary, friend and patron of the poets whose work he was to include in the *Georgian Poetry* anthologies (the first of them published in 1912). Marsh introduced Sassoon to a number of their contributors, among them Rupert Brooke, and his initial reaction – as reported in *The Weald of Youth* – is revealing:

The unromantic and provocative character of Brooke's 1911 volume had produced a vividly disturbing effect on my mind. Slow to recognize its abundant graces, I was prevented – by my prejudice against what I designated 'modern ugliness' – from perceiving his lovely and never prettified work as it really was.[15]

Sassoon was a true Georgian, never a modernist. In 1922, he 'looked at a few pages of James Joyce's new and enormous novel and found it repellent', and though happy to have T.S. Eliot as his publisher, he never cared for his poetry.

The title of his first 'war poem', 'Absolution',[16] written in mid-1915, leads one to expect a religious theme, but far from having anything to do with the forgiveness of sins, it involves the freeing of the eyes – to see what? 'Beauty shines in all that we can see.' In confusing contradiction, the speaker acknowledges

> Horror of wounds and anger at the foe,
> And loss of things desired [...]

(hardly a prophetic reckoning of the cost of the years 1914–18) but, he consoles himself, 'all these must pass'. In the meantime, 'We are the happy legion' – an echo of the public-school classroom – and 'What need we more, my comrades and my brothers?' When his own brother, Hamo, was killed at Gallipoli, his elegy ended with a similarly optimistic and, it must be said, confused blending of pagan classical and Christian:

> Your lot is with the ghosts of soldiers dead,
> And I am in the field where men must fight.
> But in the gloom I see your laurell'd head
> And through your victory I shall win the light.[17]

The title of his first poem to be written from experience of the front line, 'The Redeemer',[18] again seems to promise a Christian theme, an expectation not fulfilled by the first, scene-setting stanza:

> Darkness: the rain sluiced down; the mire was deep;
> It was past twelve on a mid-winter night,
> When peaceful folk in beds lay snug asleep;
> There, with much work to do before the light,
> We lugged our clay-sucked boots as best we might
> Along the trench; sometimes a bullet sang,
> And droning shells burst with a hollow bang;
> We were soaked, chilled and wretched, every one;
> Darkness; the distant wink of a huge gun.

The graphic realism of this – much more down-to-earth than Rupert Brooke's 'modern ugliness' – disguises the underlying dichotomy of darkness and light, a dichotomy dramatically brought into prominence in the stanzas that follow:

> I turned in the black ditch, loathing the storm;
> A rocket fizzed and burned with blanching flare,
> And lit the face of what had been a form
> Floundering in mirk. He stood before me there;
> I say that He was Christ; stiff in the glare;
> And leaning forward from His burdening task,
> Both arms supporting it; His eyes on mine
> Stared from the woeful head that seemed a mask
> Of mortal pain in Hell's unholy shine.
>
> No thorny crown, only a woollen cap
> He wore – an English soldier [...]

This is a powerful image, but the longer we look at it, the less convincing it becomes. Like countless other representations of the infantryman as Christ laying down his life for his friends – representations not only in poems but in sermons and leading articles – the similarity dissolves as we remember that infantrymen carry more than planks, and that Christ endorsed the commandment 'Thou shalt not kill.' We sense some suppressed recognition of this when, in the last stanza, Sassoon's speaker repeats his assertion. He seems to protest too much:

> I say that He was Christ, who wrought to bless
> All groping things with freedom bright as air,
> And with His mercy washed and made them fair.
> Then the flame sank, and all grew black as pitch,
> While we began to struggle along the ditch;
> And someone flung his burden in the muck,
> Mumbling: 'O Christ Almighty, now I'm stuck!'

For all its bad theology, the poem does have a certain dramatic force – much of it derived from the explosive colloquialism of the last line. This use of direct speech, learnt from Sassoon's reading of his admired Thomas Hardy in 1914, brings us literally down to earth, whereas the ending of 'Absolution' had left us uncomfortably in the air.

The theological and stylistic limitations of 'The Redeemer', written before the Battle of the Somme, stand out more sharply if it is compared with 'Christ and the Soldier',[19] written a month after Sassoon's experience of that terrible first of July. It begins:

> The straggled soldier halted – stared at Him –
> Then clumsily dumped down upon his knees,
> Gasping, 'O blessed crucifix, I'm beat!'
> And Christ, still sentried by the seraphim,
> Near the front-line, between two splintered trees,
> Spoke him: 'My son, behold these hands and feet.'
>
> The soldier eyed Him upward, limb by limb,
> Paused at the Face; then muttered, 'Wounds like these
> Would shift a bloke to Blighty just a treat!'
> Christ, gazing downward, grieving and ungrim,
> Whispered, 'I made for you the mysteries,
> Beyond all the battles moves the Paraclete.'

This is incomparably more dramatic than anything he had written before. The figure on the Crucifix is seen through the eyes of the astonished soldier, 'sentried by the seraphim', and the immeasurable distance between the two speakers is brilliantly, satirically, captured by their two dictions:

>   'Wounds like these
> Would shift a bloke to Blighty just a treat!'
> Christ, gazing downward, grieving and ungrim,
> Whispered, 'I made for you the mysteries,
> Beyond all the battles moves the Paraclete.'

Christ should have known that the soldier would not have known a Paraclete from a Paradox.

In the second part of the poem, when the soldier says: 'O Christ Almighty, stop this bleeding fight!'

> Christ asked all pitying, 'Can you put no trust
> In my known word that shrives each faithful head?
> Am I not resurrection, life and light?'

In part three, at the third time of asking, the soldier says:

> 'But be you for both sides? I'm paid to kill
> And if I shoot a man his mother grieves.
> Does that come into what your teaching tells?'

Not surprisingly, the figure on the Cross is silent and the soldier has the last word:

> 'Lord Jesus, ain't you got no more to say?'
> Bowed hung that head below the crown of thorns.
> The soldier shifted, and picked up his pack,
> And slung his gun, and stumbled on his way.
> 'O God,' he groaned, 'why ever was I born?' ...
> The battle boomed, and no reply came back.

The indignation that, like an electrical current, generates the spark between the positive and negative poles of this poem provides the power behind most of Sassoon's better poems of the war years. Almost all are structured around a central dichotomy, and frequently this involves the juxtaposition of innocent Young and guilty Old: the boys and the Bishop in the scathingly anti-clerical 'They'; the boys and the General in the anti-High-Command 'The General'; the corpses and the chorus girls in the anti-Home-Front 'Blighters'; or that other variant of the same polarization of men and women, 'Glory of Women':[20]

> You love us when we're heroes, home on leave,
> Or wounded in a mentionable place.
> You worship decorations; you believe

That chivalry redeems the war's disgrace.
You make us shells. You listen with delight,
By tales of dirt and danger fondly thrilled.
You crown our distant ardours while we fight,
And mourn our laurelled memories when we're killed.
You can't believe that British troops 'retire'
When hell's last horror breaks them, and they run,
Trampling the terrible corpses – blind with blood.
    O German mother dreaming by the fire,
While you are knitting socks to send your son
His face is trodden deeper in the mud.

Like many of Sassoon's later war poems, this is launched at the
reader like a grenade. The sudden switch from British women
to German mother detonates the brutal irony of the last
sentence, whereby the one mother is knitting socks for a son
already trodden into mud by the feet of those presumably
wearing socks knitted by the other mothers. The German
mother is presented ambiguously: we sense that the speaker
both pities her and blames her for the reasons that he blames
the British women. He blames them for believing 'That
chivalry redeems the war's disgrace', but who invented chivalry, celebrated it, and taught women to celebrate it? Men.
Sassoon may present the German mother ambiguously, but no
such ambiguity attends his presentation of German sons. In
'Christ and the Soldier', the soldier had asked the Son of God:
'be you for both sides?' He had received no answer, but
Sassoon leaves us in no doubt that *he* is for both sides: his
concern, his tenderness, is for the young victims of the old
men on both sides. Like Charles Sorley before him, Wilfred
Owen and David Jones after him, he stresses the similarities
rather than the differences of the front-line soldiers who face
each other in their trenches. In 'A Night Attack',[21] he makes
this point in characteristically dichtomizing fashion. A group
of British soldiers are talking:

One says 'The bloody Bosche has got the knock;
And soon they'll crumple up and chuck their games.
We've got the beggars on the run at last!'
    Then I remembered someone that I'd seen
Dead in a squalid, miserable ditch,
Heedless of toiling feet that trod him down.
He was a Prussian with a decent face,
Young, fresh, and pleasant, so I dare to say.
No doubt he loathed the war and longed for peace,
And cursed our souls because we'd killed his friends.

Robert Graves, attempting to explain Sassoon's sympathy for such victims, once wrote with brutal frankness that, as a homosexual, he felt about a battlefield strewn with dead men much as he, Graves, would feel about a battlefield strewn with dead women. There may be truth in this, but it fails to acknowledge the emotions of pity, caritas, and respect for human dignity displayed throughout Sassoon's poetry and prose. It would seem that, in a sense, the pressures and challenges of the war held the divided warrior together, but that when he had taken off his Sam Browne belt for the last time, he felt his selves to be coming apart. One dreamt of writing a Proustian masterpiece, but the other, a puritanical censor, forbade that. In due course, he retired – in both civilian and the military senses of that verb – to live the life of a reclusive, eighteenth-century country gentleman.

In 1957, he made what he called his 'unconditional surrender' to God and, if the devotional poems of his last years lack the vitality and power of those written during – and, later, about – the Great War, that is because he was, by nature, a poet of polarity and protest rather than of union and acceptance. Whatever one thinks of his last poems, however, his war poems surely justify his claim to be a religious poet.

CHAPTER 6

Owen's afterlife

When, on New Year's Eve 1917, Wilfred Owen proudly told his mother 'I am a poet's poet',[1] he spoke more truly than he knew. He meant, as he wrote, that he was 'held peer by the Georgians', poets associated with the *Georgian Poetry* anthologies edited by Edward Marsh. His work had been praised first (and for him most importantly) by Siegfried Sassoon, and then by Robert Graves and Harold Monro.

We can see him now as 'a poet's poet' in two other senses, only one of which he would have recognized. As a boy, he had bound himself apprentice to a Master, John Keats, and by close study and emulation grafted his own early work onto the Romantic tradition. It was a fortunate – not to say inspired – choice, because he and Keats had more in common, in terms of temperament and talent, than he could have known. Owen warmed to the sensuality and musicality of the older poet, and Keats's physicality (heightened by his study of anatomy and experience of illness) accorded with his apprentice's own precocious awareness of the human body. Owen's earliest extant poem, 'To Poesy' (written in 1909–10),[2] owes much to the theme and diction of Keats's 'The Fall of Hyperion' and speaks of arms, face, eyes, hands, heart, tongue, brow, brain. 'Uriconium' (written in 1913) anticipates even more clearly the tender physicality of Owen's mature work. Porphyro, in Keats's 'Eve of St Agnes', had 'set / A table'

with delicacies for the sleeping Madeline. This would seem
to be subconsciously recalled by the twenty-year-old Owen
contemplating the excavated ruins of the Roman city of
Uriconium, which, with its inhabitants (his guidebook told
him), 'perished by fire and sword':

> For here lie remnants from a banquet-table,
> – Oysters and marrow-bones, and seeds of grape –
> The statement of whose age must sound a fable;
> And Samian jars, whose sheen and flawless shape
>   Look fresh from potter's mould.
> Plasters with Roman finger-marks impressed;
> Bracelets, that from the warm Italian arm
>   Might seem to be scarce cold;
> And spears – the same that pushed the Cymry west,
> Unblunted yet [...]

Owen's compassionate awareness of the victims' *bodies* – so
prominent a feature of his later and greater poems – enables
him to feel those

> Plasters with Roman *finger-marks* impressed;
> Bracelets, that from the *warm Italian arm*
>   Might seem to be *scarce cold*;

and it sharpens his perceptions of the weapons that killed
them – 'spears [...] / *Unblunted* yet'.

A priggish and self-centred child had, by 1913, grown into
a compassionate young man; a transformation encouraged
by a second apprenticeship to a second Romantic poet. Two
years earlier, while working as a lay assistant to the Vicar of
Dunsden, Owen had come upon the poems of Shelley and
soon discovered, as he delightedly told his sister,

Shelley lived at a cottage within easy cycling distance from here. And
I was very surprised (tho' really I don't know why) to find that he
used to 'visit the sick in their beds; kept a regular list of the

industrious poor whom he assisted to make up their accounts'; and
for a time walked the hospitals in order to be more useful to the poor
he visited! I *knew* the lives of men who produced such marvellous
verse could not be otherwise than lovely, and I am being confirmed
in this continually.[3]

Owen's devout and devoted mother hoped that her son's
experience of Dunsden might lead to a career in the Church.
He was to help the Vicar with his parish duties, in return for
free board and lodging and some tuition to prepare him for
the university entrance exam. The arrangement was not a
success. The Vicar had no interest in literature, and Owen
soon lost interest in theology, the only topic offered for
tuition. Disillusioned, too, by what he called 'The Vicar's
Strong Conservation', he was forced to recognize that literature meant more to him than evangelical religion. This had to
be explained to the Vicar. They quarrelled and, in February
1913, Owen left Dunsden on the verge of a nervous breakdown. That summer he sat a scholarship exam for University
College, Reading, but failed, and in mid-September crossed
the Channel to take up a part-time post teaching English at the
Berlitz School in Bordeaux. Over the next two years, he grew
to love France, its language and its literature, and had reached
perhaps the highest point of happiness that life would offer
him, tutoring an eleven-year-old French girl in her parents'
Pyrenean villa, when, on 4 August 1914, Germany invaded
Belgium and war was declared.

   The same month, he wrote to his mother:

I feel my own life all the more precious and more dear in the presence
of this deflowering of Europe. While it is true that the guns will effect
a little useful weeding, I am furious with chagrin to think that the
Minds which were to have excelled the civilization of ten thousand
years, are being annihilated – and bodies, the product of aeons of
Natural Selection, melted down to pay for political statues.[4]

Those sentiments and the insensitive imagery of *deflowering, weeding, melted down* show a reversion to Owen's earlier self-regarding priggishness, but a visit to a hospital for the wounded soon brought him to his senses. A September letter to his brother Harold reveals the compassionate concern for the bodies of victims evidenced in his poem 'Uriconium':

One poor devil had his shin-bone crushed by a gun-carriage wheel, and the doctor had to twist it about and push it like a piston to get out the pus. Another had a hole right through the knee [...][5]

For a year, Owen debated with himself whether or not to risk the 'melting down' of his own body. He considered joining the French Army; then contemplated applying for a Commission in the (British) Artists' Rifles; then thought he would 'like to join the Italian Cavalry; for reasons both aesthetic and practical'.[6] His delayed decision indicates an understandable reluctance to go to war, but at no point do his letters speak of any principled aversion to fighting. 'Do you know what would hold me together on a battlefield?' he asked his mother. 'The sense that I was perpetuating the language in which Keats and the rest of them wrote!'[7] Finally, returning to England with two boys he had been tutoring in Mérignac, near Bordeaux, he said goodbye to his family and, on 21 October 1915, enlisted in the Artists' Rifles.

The following June, Owen was commissioned into the 5th Battalion of the Manchester Regiment, which in January 1917 was thrown into the Battle of the Somme. He was engaged in fierce fighting until May, when he was found to be suffering from shell-shock and invalided back to Craiglockhart War Hospital, on the outskirts of Edinburgh. There he met Sassoon and, with his advice and encouragement, began writing the poems that would constitute his own powerful contribution to 'the language in which Keats and the rest of them wrote'. Discharged from Craiglockhart in November 1917, he returned to France in August 1918. He won the Military Cross in a successful assault on the Germans' Beaurevoir-Fonsomme line, but was killed on 4 November, attempting to lead his company across the Sambre and Oise Canal. A week later, the Armistice bells were ringing in Shrewsbury when his parents' front-door bell sounded its small chime, heralding the telegram they had dreaded for two years.

There is a second sense in which Owen is 'a poet's poet'. W. H. Auden, in his great elegy 'In Memory of W. B. Yeats', wrote:

> The words of a dead man
> Are modified in the guts of the living.

And surely no aspect of Owen's afterlife would have pleased him more than the way his words have been modified in the guts of living poets and contributed to the poetry that came after him. Siegfried Sassoon and Edith Sitwell edited the first edition of his poems that appeared in 1920. More influential was Edmund Blunden's edition of 1931 – influential, in that it was this edition that was read, marked, learnt, and inwardly digested by the next generation of poets, those who would be known as 'the Poets of the Thirties'.

The first to respond in print to Owen was almost certainly Auden, who ended a poem of 1933:

> The Priory clock chimes briefly and I recollect
> I am expected to return alive
> My will effective and my nerves in order
>   To my situation.
> 'The poetry is in the pity', Wilfred said,
> And Kathy in her journal, 'To be rooted in life,
>   That's what I want.'
> These moods give no permission to be idle,

For men are changed by what they do;
And through loss and anger the hands of the unlucky
   Love one another.[8]

There are two quotations from Owen here: the first, his assurance (to his mother) of 4 October 1918, 'My nerves are in perfect order'; the second, a famous statement from the draft Preface to his poems that would be repeated over the years like a mantra, a passage of scripture: 'The poetry is in the pity.'

It was clearly Owen's example – the poet as witness to the horrors of war – that led to Auden's decision trumpeted in a banner headline of the *Daily Worker* on 12 January 1937: 'FAMOUS POET TO DRIVE AMBULANCE IN SPAIN'. Explaining his decision to a friend, Auden wrote: 'I shall probably be a bloody bad soldier but how can I speak to/ for them without becoming one?'[9] This echoes a letter of Owen's to his mother: 'I came out in order to help these boys – directly by leading them as well as an officer can; indirectly, by watching their sufferings that I may speak of them as well as a pleader can.'[10] In the event, Auden did not stay long in Spain. He was horrified by what he saw, particularly the burnt-out churches, and the one poem he wrote, overtly, about the Spanish Civil War owes nothing to Owen.

Stephen Spender was more impressionable. His critical book, *The Destructive Element* (1935), shows him to be deeply influenced by Owen. He repeats 'The poetry is in the pity' twice and compares Owen's poems with those of Yeats and Eliot – to the younger poet's advantage. Spender also went to Spain, where he helped the Republicans with radio propaganda and wrote poems such as 'The Coward' and 'The Deserter', which each owe something to Owen's 'S.I.W.', as does his 'Ultima Ratio Regum' to Owen's 'Disabled'.

Rupert John Cornford was named after his mother's friend Rupert Brooke but when, unlike Auden and Spender, he went

to fight in the Spanish Civil War, it was Owen who influenced
his most famous poem, 'A Letter from Aragon'.[11] Cornford
was dead but the Spanish Civil War still in progress when, in
1937, Yeats's *Oxford Book of Modern Verse* was published. No
poem of Owen's was included and, in his Introduction, Yeats
spent more time justifying his exclusion than the inclusion of
most other poets:

I have a distaste for certain poems written in the midst of the great
war [...] The writers of these poems were invariably officers of
exceptional courage and capacity, one a man constantly selected for
dangerous work, all, I think, had the Military Cross; their letters
are vivid and humorous, they were not without joy – for all skill is
joyful – but felt bound, in the words of the best known, to plead the
suffering of their men. In poems that had for a time considerable
fame, written in the first person, they made that suffering their own.
I have rejected these poems for the same reason that made Arnold
withdraw his *Empedocles on Etna* from circulation; passive suffering
is not a theme for poetry.

Some of Yeats's inclusions – Grenfell's 'Into Battle', and
seventeen poems by Oliver St John Gogarty (praised for his
'heroic song') – reveal his belief that the poet was one of the
principal architects of civilization; his task, the representation
of the great pagan images of love and war, passion and
courage. The draft Preface to Owen's poems would, therefore,
have seemed to him pernicious heresy, an abdication of the
poet's traditional 'responsibility'. In the light of the furious
debate prompted by Yeats's statement that 'passive suffering is
not a theme for poetry', Owen's exclusion from the *Oxford
Book* probably benefited – rather than harmed – his reputation.

It was Edmund Blunden, editor of the second edition of
Owen's poems, who the following year introduced them to
Keith Douglas, one of his undergraduates at Merton College,
Oxford. That introduction was to play a part in shaping,

arguably, the finest British poet of the Second World War. Temperamentally, Douglas was as unlike Owen as it was possible to be. The son of a decorated veteran of the Great War, he had long had a romantic interest in warfare and, enlisting in a cavalry regiment in 1940, enscrolled a photograph of himself in uniform with the words 'Dulce et decorum est pro patria mori'. Yeats would have approved of his *sprezzatura* and surely considered 'heroic song' Douglas's poem 'Gallantry', which begins:

> The Colonel in a casual voice
> spoke into the microphone a joke
> which through a hundred earphones broke
> into the ears of a doomed race.
>
> Into the ears of the doomed boy, the fool
> whose perfectly mannered flesh fell
> in opening the door for a shell
> as he had learnt to do at school.[12]

One wonders what Owen – who wrote that his book was 'not about heroes' – would have made of this poem about 'three heroes'; its echo of his 'Doomed Youth'; its use of the pararhyme he pioneered (fool/fell); its thematic and linguistic links with his own poem 'The Last Laugh'. Douglas was not the first poet of the Second World War to echo Owen. On the other side of the Atlantic, Weldon Kees introduced his poem 'June 1940' with two epigraphs

> Yet these elegies are to this generation in no sense consolatory. They may be to the next. All a poet can do today is warn.
>
> The old Lie: Dulce et Decorum est
> Pro patria mori.[13]

The voice of Wilfred Owen has continued to inspire his successors not only in time of war. Ted Hughes grew up in a

Yorkshire household darkened by his father's reminiscences
of Gallipoli and his uncle Walter's of the Somme. In the 1950s,
he wrote 'Wilfred Owen's Photographs', but a closer engagement with Owen emerges in one of his posthumous *Birthday
Letters*, 'A Picture of Otto'. At a 'Strange Meeting' in hell (or
hell on earth) with the ghost of Otto Plath, his wife Sylvia's
father, Hughes echoes Owen's Preface – 'if the spirit of [this
book] survives – survives Prussia –' when he says:

> A big shock for so much of your Prussian backbone
> As can be conjured into poetry
> To find yourself so tangled with me –
> Rising from your coffin, a big shock
>
> To meet me face to face in the dark adit [...]

As in Owen's 'Strange Meeting', friend and enemy are
conflated:

> This underworld, my friend, is her heart's home.
> Inseparable, here we must remain,
>
> Everything forgiven and in common –
> Not that I see her behind you, where I face you,
> But like Owen, after his dark poem,
> Under the battle, in the catacomb,
>
> Sleeping with his German as if alone.

So much for the published evidence of the imaginative
impact of Owen, the 'poet's poet', on the work of his
successors. Its subconscious or subterranean impact is harder
to determine, but Seamus Heaney gives us a rare glimpse of
it in his lecture, 'Sixth Sense, Seventh Heaven':

By the time I wrote 'Bogland', I had been lecturing for a couple of
years in Queen's University, and spoke every week to the students in
First Arts English on the subject of modern poetry. One of the set
books I most enjoyed teaching was Wilfred Owen's *Collected Poems*

and one of the Owen poems I liked to focus on was 'Miners', which I myself had first encountered as a sixth former. It had come up as an unseen poem, an exercise in 'critical analysis and appreciation', and it made an unforgettable impression on me. Many things come together in it. The poet's comfort by a coal fire, for example, leads him to remember all those who, like coalminers and front-line soldiers, toil comfortlessly at the bottom of the social pyramid, carry its weight, are exploited by it, crushed by it, but still suffer in silence and retain their dignity. What makes the poem a real imaginative feat is the fact that Owen's moral indignation doesn't peel away from his sensuous language: the poet in him and the protester feel their way down the same intuitive paths, and while the burning coal shifts in the grate, these paths lead from a domestic interior to a geological and evolutionary panorama where all things are in a state of vegetal, even arcadian, bliss [...]

Harold Bloom's phrase 'the anxiety of influence', has had a great airing in the past couple of decades, but it is probably not the right way to describe how a poet feels about his or her susceptibility to another earlier poet's work. For example, when I remembered in the course of preparing this lecture that Owen's poem had been in my mind when I wrote 'Bogland', what I felt was closer to gratitude than anxiety. 'Miners' wasn't being imitated by me, but 'Bogland' was affected by the way 'Miners' shifted itself forward, its combination of free association and internal logic, its floating levels of earth and time. The movement and method of Owen's poem worked like a moving stair under my own, and are likely to have been more important than the archaeological data and bits of local boglore that made up much of the content.[14]

Why have so many poets – not to mention so many general readers – responded so deeply to the work of a poet who, dying at twenty-five, saw only five of his poems in print and left many others to be re/constructed from manuscript by his editors? At the most superficial level, there is the romance of an early death that has come to seem emblematic of all the tragedies of the Great War. Young poets are often (in T.S. Eliot's phrase) 'much possessed by death'. I was myself, but never read Owen's poems with any care until I was in my thirties and came to them by a curiously circuitous route. I was then 'much possessed' by Yeats and, invited to write an essay for a volume to be published in his centenary year, I encountered the problem of why he omitted – and so disapproved of – Owen's work. The answer to this question quickened my interest in the younger poet.[15]

Although Owen's Preface insists that his book 'is not about heroes', there is also the manifest heroism of a reluctant and vulnerable young officer, who led his 'boys' as well as a leader can and spoke of their sufferings as well as a pleader can. The power of his pleading challenges the validity of Yeats's pontifical dictum that 'passive suffering is not a theme for poetry'. Milton's sonnet on his blindness and many elegies speak of passive suffering, but are unquestionably poetry of the highest order. Moreover, as in the case of Milton's sonnet and elegies that similarly offer consolation, Owen's poems tend to make an active response to the suffering of which they speak. He is a classic example of what would become a quintessentially twentieth-century figure: the poet as witness – and not a passive witness. Most of his later and greater poems are fuelled by indignation. Introduced by Sassoon to the genre of the 'protest poem', he soon outgrew the two-dimensional poster-poem (such as 'The Dead-Beat') and tapped deeper and richer imaginative levels than ever Sassoon would reach.

The subject of his protest is often indicated by a title which the poem will subvert – 'The Parable of the Old Man and the Young', 'Smile, Smile, Smile', and 'Dulce et Decorum Est'. A similar strategy appears in his subversion of the literary epigraphs chosen for 'The Show', 'S.I.W.', and 'The Next War'; and the indignant response to other texts that kick-start 'Anthem for Doomed Youth', 'Dulce et

Decorum Est', and the fragment 'Cramped in that funnelled hole'.[16]

Owen's readiness to express his feelings – of grief, tenderness, delight, as well as indignation – is a significant part of his appeal. Readers are often moved by the immediacy of his work before they appreciate the subtle density of its literary allusion. So with its music. In February 1918, he told Leslie Gunston: 'I suppose I am doing in poetry what the advanced composers are doing in music.'[17] Apprenticed to Keats and Shelley, he had absorbed the traditions of harmony and rhetoric they inherited and extended. The harmonic tradition he himself extended with his pioneering use of 'pararhymes': escaped/scooped, groined/groaned. In 'Strange Meeting', from which these examples are taken, the second rhyme is usually lower in pitch than the first, giving the couplet 'a dying fall' that musically reinforces the poem's meaning; the tragedy of the German poet (one manuscript reads 'I was a German conscript, and your friend'), his life cut short by the British poet whom he meets in Hell. In the poem 'Miners', the pitch of the pararhymes rises and falls as the sense moves from grief to happiness and back to grief again:

> The centuries will burn rich loads
>   With which we groaned,
> Whose warmth shall lull their dreaming lids,
>   While songs are crooned;
> But they will not dream of us poor lads,
>   Left in the ground.

The same poem offers an example of another of Owen's harmonic innovations – the punning internal rhyme of 'wry [...] writhing', found also in the 'Men [...] Many' of 'Dulce and Decorum Est'.

What finally sets him apart from all but his most major contemporaries, however, is a breadth and depth of vision

that in 'Futility', for example, can hold – as it were in the
palm of a hand – the grand and the granular together:

> Move him into the sun –
> Gently its touch awoke him once,
> At home, whispering of fields half-sown.
> Always it woke him, even in France,
> Until this morning and this snow.
> If anything might rouse him now
> The kind old sun will know.
>
> Think how it wakes the seeds –
> Woke once the clays of a cold star.
> Are limbs, so dear achieved, are sides
> Full-nerved, still warm, too hard to stir?
> Was it for this the clay grew tall?
> – O what made fatuous sunbeams toil
> To break earth's sleep at all?

So, in the larger meditative structure of 'Insensibility', Owen
can move with no loss of tension from the colloquial to the
cosmic, from 'poets' tearful fooling' to 'the eternal reciprocity
of tears', a phrase that even Shakespeare might have envied.

CHAPTER 7

Owen and his editors

There is yet another sense in which Wilfred Owen, proclaiming himself 'a poet's poet',[1] wrote more prophetically than he knew. The four substantive editions of his poems have been edited by five poets: Sassoon and Edith Sitwell (1920), Blunden (1931), Day Lewis (1963), and Stallworthy (1983).

He died having seen only five of his poems in print: 'Song of Songs' in *The Hydra/Journal of the Craiglockhart War Hospital* and *The Bookman*; 'The Next War' in *The Hydra*; and 'Miners', 'Futility', and 'Hospital Barge' in the *Nation*. In June 1918, two and a half months before Owen's return to France for the last time, Edith and Osbert Sitwell encouraged him to submit poems for the 1918 edition of their anthology, *Wheels*. He sent them eight,[2] but it seems likely that they arrived too late for inclusion. After his death his mother sent a further selection, and *Wheels* (1919), edited by Edith Sitwell, was dedicated 'TO THE MEMORY/OF/WILFRED OWEN, M.C.'. It contained seven of his poems: 'The Show', 'Strange Meeting', 'À Terre', 'The Sentry', 'Disabled', 'The Dead-Beat', and 'The Chances'.

It was almost certainly Edith's enthusiasm for these that prompted the first edition of Owen's *Poems* published by Chatto & Windus in 1920. Sassoon has been credited with its editing because, as Owen's friend and better-known fellow

soldier, he agreed to write the Introduction. This was rushed
and unrevealing as, he wrote to Dennis Welland, 'the whole
business was utterly painful to me'.[3] It must have been more
painful still when, after publication, studying Owen's manuscripts for the first time, he began to recognize the inaccuracy
of the texts Edith Sitwell had printed. For example, from the
early pages of her edition:

p. 6,   'The Show', *line 5 reads* fitted *for* pitted
p. 8,   'Mental Cases', *line 7 reads* hand *for* hands'
p. 9,   'Parable of the Old Men [sic] and the Young',

> *lines 12–15 read*
> Neither do anything to him. Behold,
> A ram caught in a thicket by its horns;
> Offer the Ram of Pride instead of him.
> But the old man would not so, but slew his son ....
> *for*
> Neither do anything to him, thy son.
> Behold! Caught in a thicket by its horns,
> A Ram. Offer the Ram of Pride instead.
> But the old man would not so, but slew his son,
> And half the seed of Europe, one by one.

p. 10, 'Arms and the Boy', *line 5 reads* bullet-heads *for*
        bullet-leads

> *and lines 7–8 read*
> Or give him cartridges of fine zinc teeth,
> Sharp with the sharpness of grief and death.
> *for*
> Or give him cartridges whose fine zinc teeth
> Are sharp with sharpness of grief and death.[4]

The reviews and sales of this first edition justified a reprint in
1921.[5] One poem was added – 'The End' ('After the blast
of lightning from the east'), appropriately at the end of the

book – and a few errors were corrected, but none of those listed above.

As the 1920s advanced and Owen's reputation grew, the need for a fuller and better edition became clear, and Sassoon persuaded his friend and fellow soldier-poet, Edmund Blunden, to undertake it.[6] An experienced biographer, critic, and editor (as Sassoon and Sitwell were not), he was an excellent choice, and his commitment to the work of a younger soldier-poet was apparent in every aspect of the second edition of *The Poems* (1931). It began with a comprehensive Memoir (though he and Owen never met). When he sent Susan Owen his judicious, sympathetic, and elegant handwritten draft of this, she – like Rupert Brooke's mother before her – required certain changes to burnish the halo of her Saint-and-Martyr son. To the twenty-four poems printed in the 1921 reissue of the first edition, all reprinted by Blunden, he added a further thirty-seven,[7] though two were halves of the same poem ('The Calls') and another, printed as a fragment ('It is not death'), he failed to recognize as the concluding stanzas of another fragment ('Has your soul sipped') quoted in the Memoir. Though far from perfect – as all editions of Owen's poems have been – Blunden's is a marked improvement on Sassoon and Sitwell's. For example, he corrects the errors noted in 'The Show' and 'Mental Cases' on p. 82 above but not all of those in 'Arms and the Boy' and 'The Parable of the Old Men [sic] and the Young'.

Blunden's 1931 edition helped to consolidate Owen's reputation and elevate him to the iconic status he was to hold for poets and readers of poetry in the 1930s and after. The book contributed to the success of a public appeal for money – orchestrated by Blunden and Sassoon – with which to purchase from Owen's family his manuscripts for the nation. Fair copies of a number of poems had been included in his letters to his mother and these, naturally, she had kept. Most of his other manuscripts (apart from a sackful she had burnt on his instructions)[8] had been held in his desk at 'Mahim', the family's Shrewsbury home. Blunden and Sassoon selected fair copies, final and near-final drafts of the more important poems, and Sassoon had them mounted in two handsome volumes, bound in scarlet morocco. The success of their campaign was announced on 16 April 1934, when *The Times* reported the British Museum's acquisition of an autograph collection of Owen's poems as a gift from the Friends of the National Libraries, 'the first manuscript of a modern author to be bought by the Friends for presentation to a library'.

Later in the 1930s, Wilfred Owen's poems went to war in Spain, and in the 1940s to war in Europe and North Africa;[9] but it was not until after the Second World War that his reputation crossed the frontiers of English-speaking countries to become truly international. Making that journey, Owen travelled not on his own passport but that of Benjamin Britten. On 16 February 1961, Britten wrote to Dietrich Fischer-Dieskau:

Please forgive me for writing to such a busy man as yourself [...] Coventry Cathedral, like so many wonderful buildings in Europe, was destroyed in the last war. It has now been rebuilt in a very remarkable fashion, and for the reconsecration of the new building they are holding a big Festival at the end of May and beginning of June next year. I have been asked to write a new work for what is to us all a most significant occasion.

I am writing what I think will be one of my most important works. It is a full-scale Requiem Mass for chorus and orchestra (in memory of those of all nations who died in the last war), and I am interspersing the Latin text with many poems of a great English poet, Wilfred Owen, who was killed in the First World War. These magnificent poems, full of the hate of destruction, are a kind of commentary on the Mass; they are, of course, in English. These poems will be set for tenor and baritone, with an accompaniment of chamber orchestra, placed in the middle of the other forces. They will need singing with the utmost beauty, intensity and sincerity.

Peter Pears has agreed to sing the tenor part, and with great temerity I am asking you whether you would sing the baritone.[10]

The answer of course was yes. Britten's *War Requiem* was first performed at the reconsecration of the Cathedral on 30 May 1962. Afterwards, the composer wrote to his friend, the poet William Plomer:

'dear Heather Harper did splendidly;[11] and weren't the two chaps marvellous? Poor F-Dieskau was so upset at the end that Peter couldn't get him out of the choir-stalls! It was that wonderful "Strange Meeting"' – the setting, which concludes the *War Requiem*, of Owen's poem in which a dead British soldier meets the German he has killed. Fischer-Dieskau confirms this in his memoirs: 'I was completely undone; I did not know where to hide my face. Dead friends and past suffering arose in my mind.' The playwright Peter Shaffer, reviewing the performance for *Time & Tide*, was equally moved: 'I believe it to be the most impressive and moving piece of sacred music ever to be composed in this country [...] the most profound and moving thing which this most committed of geniuses has so far achieved. It makes criticism impertinent.'[12]

Britten's respect for Owen showed in his treatment of the poems. He let them speak for themselves without distortion or orchestral competition. The *War Requiem* caught the public imagination more than any other musical event of 1962. Concert-goers and radio-listeners in the British Isles and beyond asked themselves: 'Who is this Wilfred Owen?' Sales of his poems soared and his publishers, Chatto & Windus (who now owned their copyright), commissioned a new edition from the poet Cecil Day Lewis, a member of their editorial staff. This appeared in 1963, a year in which Decca sold 200,000 copies of their two-disc set of the *War*

Requiem 'in a striking black box with white lettering, of the recording that Britten had directed'.[13] The third edition, [mis]called *The Collected Poems*, contained all those printed in the first and second editions, with the two halves of 'Has your soul sipped' and 'The Calls' reunited, and seven poems and fragments added from the substantial body of unpublished material. Day Lewis improved Blunden's texts at a number of points: for example, he corrected the errors in 'Arms and the Boy' and that in the title of 'The Parable of the Old Man and the Young'.[14] He followed Blunden's reading of lines 12–15 of the latter, but printed what would prove Owen's later revision in a footnote. In this and other such notes, Day Lewis offered a simple (and sometimes incomplete) list of a poem's drafts, their whereabouts, and some variant readings. As he admitted, however, in a critical Introduction complementing Blunden's biographical Memoir, which he printed as an appendix,

> it is not always possible to determine the order in which these drafts were composed. [... And since] it is not possible to date a great number of these poems, I have arranged them in a non-chronological order. Part One gives all the completed poems which are directly concerned with the war [...] In Part Two I have placed poems on other subjects, or not primarily concerned with the war, together with some fragments. Part Three offers a selection of Owen's juvenilia and minor poems [...][15]

This, effectively, reverses their order of composition and gives a misleading impression of the poet's development.

My own engagement with Owen began in the 1960s. Invited to contribute to a volume of essays marking the centenary of Yeats's birth in 1865, I immersed myself in the Clarendon Press file of his *Oxford Book of Modern Verse* (1936) and wrote a piece on 'Yeats as Anthologist'.[16] His brilliant polemical Introduction to the *Oxford Book* introduced me to my favourite poet's *un*favourite poet, and prompted me to open – for the first time – *The Collected Poems of Wilfred Owen*. When I asked myself why the Old Man, celebrant of conflict and heroism, should have so detested the work of the Young, the answer was inescapable: they represented competing value-systems – Ancient and Modern, Homeric and humane – and in the 1930s, let alone the 1960s, there could be no competition.[17]

My essay was read by Dame Helen Gardner, who had earlier persuaded the Delegates of Oxford University Press to publish my book, *Between the Lines: W.B. Yeats's Poetry in the Making* (1963), and now persuaded colleagues in the British Academy to invite me to give their annual Chatterton Lecture on an English Poet. I chose Wilfred Owen as my Chattertonian poet, and was introduced to his brother Harold by my colleague John Bell, who had edited his trilogy, *Journey from Obscurity: Memoirs of the Owen Family* (1963, 1964, 1965). Harold kindly gave me access to his family's manuscript holdings, which proved more extensive and more interesting than a statement of Day Lewis's had suggested: 'The bulk of Wilfred Owen's autograph poems are in the British Museum.'[18] My lecture, on Owen's poetic development, was written in a seaside cottage some miles north-east of the Cape of Good Hope, with a driftwood fire crackling at my back and an October gale laying down a barrage beyond my quaking window. When I came to bombard the British Academy,[19] Harold Owen was in the front line, and afterwards asked if I would write a biography of his brother and edit a comprehensive edition of the poems and fragments. I said yes.

The biography was to be written first, to generate a larger audience for an edition expensive to produce and expensive to buy, but this made better publishing sense than scholarly sense. Day Lewis had identified a major problem with his edition, as with his predecessors', and with all the secondary literature on Owen and his work: 'it is not possible to date a great number of these poems'. I would have written a better biography had I edited the poems first and, in so doing, solved the major problem. My predecessors had tended to assume that Owen's fair copies – where they existed – reflected his final intentions but, as I worked on the biography, it seemed to me there were often literary-critical arguments indicating that some heavily corrected draft post-dated the fair copy. So, how to proceed?

A curious feature of the manuscripts, I had noticed, was that many carried a watermark: I could distinguish twenty-four in the 600-plus surviving folios carrying Owen's poems and fragments, and guessed that, being poor, he tended to buy small quantities of good-quality paper. Matching the watermarks solved a few of the dating problems: where a watermarked folio could be detected, it seemed reasonable to assume that others with the same watermark came from the same period. However, not until after the biography was published in 1974 did it occur to me that Owen's letters are dated and, if written on the same paper as his poems, one could arrive at an approximate dating of at least the water-marked folios. The letters had been sold to the Humanities Research Center at Austin, Texas (for £9,000, having been offered first to the Bodleian for £3,000), so with Harold Owen's blessing I packed up the family's manuscripts and bought two air-tickets to Texas.

My wife and I had an uneventful flight until, an hour out of Atlanta, turbulence struck. The aircraft responded like a bronco released from a rodeo stall, bucking and rearing until it seemed its spine must snap. Then it plunged and oxygen masks dropped like oranges from their overhead compartments. I pressed mine to my stiff upper lip and inhaled. Nothing came through and, glancing down the aisle, I could see other passengers having the same trouble. My ears were beginning to ache. It was a moment for Last Thoughts: 'The *children*'? No. 'The *manuscripts*'! Under the seat in front of me, an orange ruck-sack – a blue ruck-sack under the seat in front of my wife – crouched imperturbably, as if they contained climbing gear rather than half the surviving verse manuscripts of Wilfred Owen. Had they survived gunfire and gas on the Western Front, a gas-chamber at the Cornell University Library (to rid them of their British bacilli), only to be incinerated in a Texas plane-crash? And what about us? '*Was it for this the clay grew tall?*' Striving for a small immortality as editor of Owen's poems, I should be remembered only as the man who fed them to the flames.

Suddenly, it all made sense. I was a Literary Resurrection Man, and the first manuscripts I had exhumed were those of Yeats, who wrote:

> Accursed who brings to light to day
> The writings I have cast away!

Yeats had thought Owen 'unworthy of the poet's corner of a country newspaper', and I had incurred his curse. Clearly, it was about to be fulfilled.

An ashen-faced stewardess inched down the aisle, gripping the shoulders of the seats to left and right, whispering to their occupants. ... She said: 'There's no cause for alarm. We're not at the altitude at which oxygen is supplied to the masks. I'm sorry about your ears. Would you like a sweet?' Yeats had let me off with a caution.

When I unpacked my rucksacks in the Humanities Research Center and matched the watermarks of the verse

manuscripts with those of the letters, the results were gratify-
ing. The two sets of papers had sixteen watermarks in
common, and since the letters with a particular watermark
seldom dated from more – and frequently from less – than a
couple of consecutive months, one could be reasonably sure
that verse manuscripts with the same watermark dated from
roughly the same period. Those sixteen watermarks and the
matching of papers, inks and pencil made possible for the
first time a detailed chronology of individual drafts of many
poems. They confirmed my hypothesis that scribbled drafts
were often later than tidy fair copies, but solving some
problems, they presented others. How, for example, should
poems finished and unfinished be differentiated and
arranged: by presumed date of earliest draft or latest?

Chatto & Windus, with courage and vision worthy of
their author, had commissioned an edition of *The Complete
Poems and Fragments* more elaborate than any previously
undertaken for a twentieth-century poet in the English language. When so many of an author's texts are, of necessity,
editorial constructions, a sceptical reader needs to see the
raw material from which they are constructed. The new
edition was to be in two volumes, enabling readers to have
text, notes, and manuscript material before them at the same
time. Poems and fragments would be numbered in chrono-
logical sequence and ordered by date of final revision rather
than first composition. Since the text in each case should
reflect Owen's latest intentions, it would have been misleading to place the poems and fragments in a chronology
determined by his earliest intentions. The successive stages
of composition were to be detailed and dated in a footnote
to each poem, followed by any information relevant to
its biographical, historical, and literary context. The first
volume would contain plain texts of all finished poems,

each with its accompanying note; and the second volume, supporting manuscript material – in the form of typeset facsimile – for 110 poems that could be called finished and 67 fragments. Together, these would more than double the 79 poems and fragments in the 1963 *Collected Poems*. The second volume was to conclude with Appendixes presenting Owen's draft Preface for his poems; his draft Lists of Contents; and a table detailing the paper sizes and water-marks of his manuscripts. Information contained in the last of these would explain the rationale behind the dating or re-dating of drafts and the consequent need to revise previously published texts.

During the inevitably incomplete reconstruction of Owen's manuscript mosaic, in which I was assisted by Dr Dominic Hibberd, some re-dating was found to have more than textual significance. The date of his discovery or rediscovery of the pararhyme (as Blunden called it) is a case in point. Blunden's Memoir states:[20]

In July 1914 Owen, like most of his contemporaries, was intent upon the brighter side of experience, and that month he wrote the ingenious and fresh verses beginning

> Leaves
>   Murmuring by myriads in the shimmering trees
> Lives
>   Wakening with wonder in the Pyrenees.
> Birds
>   Cheerily chirping in the early day.
> Bards
>   Singing of summer scything thro' the hay.

Day Lewis accepts Blunden's dating and calls 'From My Diary, July 1914' 'the earliest finished example of Owen's use of consonantal rhyming'.[21] D.S.R. Welland is slightly more cautious:

the earliest dated poem in which he tries out the new device is 'From My Diary, July 1914', a poem which, if the date of its title is the date of composition, was written in France in the year following the publication of [Jules Romains's] *Odes et prières*.[22]

The only manuscript of this poem carries a POMPEIAN/ PARCHMENT watermark to be found in letters dating from 5 November 1917 and 24 January 1918 and several poems of that period. So far as is known, Owen was keeping no diary in 1914 and, in fact, did not reach his hosts' Villa Lorenzo in the Pyrenees until 31 July. He presumably dated his 'diary entry' July, rather than August, to suggest the last days of peace, and his poem becomes much more poignant when one imagines him trying to recover his mental equilibrium, thinking himself back to a life 'Wakening with wonder', a wonder all too soon to be eclipsed by the horrors of the Somme.

'From My Diary, July 1914' was almost certainly not his first poem in pararhyme: 'Song of Songs' was written between late June and mid-August 1917, and 'Has your soul sipped' between July and August that year. The origin of this form of 'consonantal rhyming' has been much debated:

Critics have suggested many sources for it, from ancient Welsh verse to recent French experiments, but no fully pararhymed poem earlier than Wilfred's has yet been discovered. Robert Graves believed Wilfred had got the idea from him, and there certainly is a partly pararhymed poem in Graves's first book. However, there is no evidence Wilfred had read any Graves before writing 'Song of Songs'. He may well have worked out the system for himself, having been interested in musical effects ever since Bordeaux.[23]

An earlier pararhymed poem *has* now been discovered, William Barnes's 'On the Road':[24]

Still green on the limbs of the oak were the leaves,
Where the sloe daily *grew*, with its skin-bloom of *grey*,
Though in fields, summer-*burnt*, stood the *bent*-grass, well brown'd,

And the stubble of *wheat* fields was withering *white*,
While sooner the sunlight now sank from the sight,
And *longer* now *linger'd* the dim-roaded night.

But bright was the daylight that dried up the dew,
As the foam-water fill'd the wide pool in its fall,
And as I came to climb, by the chalk of the cliff,
The white road full *steep* to the wayfaring *step*,
Where along by the hill, with a high-beating breast,
Went the girl or the man to the feast in their best.

There the horse pranced along, with his neck a high bow,
And uptoss'd his broad *nose* over outspringing *knees*;
And the ox, with sleek *hide*, and with low-swinging *head*;
And the sheep, little *knee'd*, with a quick-dipping *nod*;
And a girl, with her head carried on in a proud
Gait of walking, as smooth as an air-swimming cloud.   [My italics]

This poem has elements in common with Owen's: skin-bloom/bloom; summer-burnt/summer; daylight/day; dew/dews; foam-water/waterbrooks; pool/pond; a girl/A maid. The similarities may be no more than a curious coincidence. Owen did not own a copy of Barnes's *Poems*, but if he and Sassoon had spoken of Hardy – and it is hard to believe they did not – Sassoon might have prompted him to look at Barnes.

Watermarks also facilitated the re-dating of 'Exposure', which, as Blunden noted, 'Owen dates [...] February 1916, but I take that to be a slip of the pen for 1917.' Day Lewis agreed. The earliest page of rough working, however, carries a HIERATICA/BOND/BRITISH MAKE/JS & Co Ltd watermark found in letters dated 25 November 1917 and 3 December 1917; while one page of a heavily corrected draft carries a SOCIETY BOND/JW & Co watermark found in letters dating from late January to 28 February 1918. The (necessarily later) heavily corrected fair copy appears to be dated 'Feb 1916', suggesting that Owen's '6' is either a mistake or, more likely, an incomplete '8'. This dating is confirmed by the fact that the poem beginning 'Cramped in that funnelled hole', brilliantly reconstructed by Blunden, can be dated late-1917; and carries an early form of line 16 of 'Exposure'.

The texts of Owen's three poems published in the *Nation* presented different problems. Sitwell and Sassoon, Blunden, and Day Lewis all seemed unaware that there was a printed text of 'Hospital Barge' that they could follow, adopting instead a corrected fair copy inferior in its punctuation and, in line 9, printing 'One reading by that sunset raised his eyes' rather than the *Nation*'s version: 'One reading by that calm bank shaded eyes'. Again, all earlier editors appear to have overlooked the printed text of 'Futility', following instead a corrected fair copy with inferior punctuation and one substantive variation from the final form of line 3: 'whispering of fields unsown' for the *Nation*'s 'whispering of fields half-sown'. The third poem published in that magazine, 'Miners', does follow the printed text, but in my view should not. The one manuscript, a corrected fair copy, has a curious feature not noticed by its earlier editors. Three of its 'corrections' are, in fact demurely bracketed *alternatives* in Sassoon's unmistakable hand above, beside, or below Owen's uncancelled words. I print Sassoon's alternatives in italics:

> *(For many hearts with coal are charred)*,
> Line 19.   Many the muscled bodies charred
> 21.   *I (*And*)* thought of some who worked dark pits
> 34.   Left in the ground.
> *(Lost)*

I suspect that Owen, hero-worshipping Sassoon, allowed the senior poet's alternatives to take precedence (against his better judgement) over his own uncancelled words. Consequently – and perhaps questionably – I follow the uncancelled manuscript rather than the printed text.

The Complete Poems and Fragments departs from earlier editions at hundreds of less contentious points in the texts they have in common, and the typeset facsimiles of volume II offer justification for such changes. Is the *CP&F*, then, completely accurate? Of course not. I am aware of some twenty errors – all minor – that would call for correction in the unlikely event of a reprint being affordable; and no doubt there are errors of which I am not aware. Is the *CP&F* a complete compendium of all Owen's surviving poems and fragments? To the best of my knowledge, I would say yes – with one interesting exception. I have long known that Harold Owen gave the occasional manuscript to a deserving friend, and believed I had traced them all. Ten years after *CP&F* was published, however, I learnt of the most important such gift: the second of six surviving drafts of 'Anthem for Doomed Youth', given to Benjamin Britten in gratitude for his setting of that and other of Owen's poems in the *War Requiem*. Since it does not appear in *CP&F*, I give a transcript here (ink in Roman type, pencil in italics):[25]

Anthem for Dead Youth

What passing bells for you who die in herds?
       ~~sullen~~ monstrous
Only the ~~monstrous~~ anger of the guns!
       long monotony
Only the stuttering rifles' rattled words
   Can patter out your hasty orisons.   *low*
    wreaths   *or* ~~pomps~~   *balms no ~~sweet-voiced~~*
No ~~chants~~ for you, ~~nor balms~~, nor ~~chanting~~ choirs,
         { cry   ~~dole~~
    wailful { ~~griefs~~ but –
   Nor any ~~voice of grief~~ – save ~~walful~~ shells.
And   ~~grief [?] save~~ shrill
~~Our~~ bugles calling ~~sadly~~ but save wailful

for you from ~~sad~~ shires
your
~~Leave a deep silence by the village wells.~~
{ T
Saddening the twilight: { these are our farewells ~~farewells~~.
boys
What candles may ~~we~~ hold to speed you all?
{ ir   ~~sweetly~~ *hollow*.
Not in { the   hands ~~of boys~~, but in their eyes
~~lights long~~ *the* your
quiet   ~~gleams~~
Shall Shine the ~~holy gleams~~ of ~~your~~ goodbyes.
quivering flowers   of
~~The pall.~~   The pallor of girls' brows must be your pall.
~~Pale are girls' brows; and they must be your pall.~~
dying
Your flowers: the tenderness of ~~comradly~~ minds
~~comrade's~~
mortal
And each slow dusk a drawing down of blinds.

Like other of Owen's poems,[26] 'Anthem for Doomed Youth' appears to have been triggered by a strong adverse reaction to another text, in this case *Poems of Today: an Anthology* (1916), of which he owned the December 1916 reprint. The anonymous Prefatory Note to this declared:

This book has been compiled in order that *boys* and *girls* already perhaps familiar with the great classics of the English speech may also know something of the newer poetry of their own day. Most of the writers are living, and the rest are still vivid memories among us, while one of the youngest almost as these words are written, has gone singing to lay down his life for his country's cause [...] there is no arbitrary isolation of one theme from another; they mingle and interpenetrate throughout, to the music of Pan's flute, and of Love's viol, and the *bugle-call* of Endeavour, and the *passing-bell* of Death. [*My italics*]

Owen's angry question, 'What passing bells ...?' invites the answer, None: 'no prayers nor bells', but the bells invoked in his 'Anthem' have tolled across the century since it was composed. And since 1962 they have tolled more loudly, more insistently, thanks to Benjamin Britten. Harold Owen could not have chosen a more deserving recipient for the manuscript, nor provided a more salutary reminder of the fallibility of editors.

CHAPTER 8

The legacy of the Somme

If you look at a British coin, what do you see? On one side, the realistic profile of a real Queen, and on the other, an imaginative representation of Britannia ruling the waves (until her proposed dethronement), a heraldic thistle or a heraldic rose. Here are two ways of looking at history: the one realistic, the other symbolic – but symbolic of what? Something other, older, and larger than the monarchy.

Historians are engaged in a search for the real – what really happened. They require imagination in reading the evidence and assessing probability where there is a gap in the evidence, but they require it less often and to a lesser degree than imaginative writers, dramatists, novelists, and poets. Historical evidence, historical writing, however, cannot alone account for the perception of historic events in a country's cultural history. Take, for example, the sack of two cities: Constantinople in 1453, and Troy in the Bronze Age. Two historical events: the first, of greater historical importance; the second, of greater cultural importance. Homer gave us Troy in a poem more often and more widely translated than any other book apart from the Bible; a poem that has inspired other poems, plays, paintings, sculpture, operas, novels, films. Why? Because Troy has come to stand for, to symbolize, more than itself. Homer's account contains all the archetypes of heroic literature, decked out in the primary colours of romance: Love, Lust, Ambition, Courage, Cruelty, Cunning. By contrast, the sack of Constantinople has no such cultural, symbolic, accretions – at least in English.

Again, take the Battles of Stamford Bridge and Hastings: the second more historically important than the first, but would Hastings feature so prominently in our cultural history were it not for its artistic accretions: the Bayeux tapestry, two novels successful in their day – Bulwer-Lytton's *Harold* (1848) and Hope Muntz's *The Golden Warrior* (1948)[1] – and, last but not least, Sellar and Yeatman's *1066 and All That?* These contribute to our understanding that the Battle of Hastings stands for more than the archetypal Gallant British Defeat. It symbolizes the merging of Norman and Saxon, the confluence of two languages that gave the English-speaking peoples the English they speak.

Now, crossing the Channel, let me pause in my slow march to the Somme at the battlefields of Crécy and Agincourt, the latter eclipsing the former in Our Island Story thanks to Shakespeare's *Henry V* and Laurence Olivier's film of that play. Why did the British Government commission and subsidize Olivier's film in the 1940s? For propaganda: Agincourt as precedent for a great victory won – against overwhelming odds – by an army symbolizing a united kingdom, represented by the English Bardolph, Nym and Pistol; the Welsh Fluellen; the Irish MacMorris; and the Scottish Jamy.

So at last I come to the Somme and the question that has engaged revisionist historians since the 1980s: why has one bloody battle come to overshadow the winning of the war? There were few (if any) professional writers among the professional soldiers of the British Expeditionary Force, who bore the brunt of the battles of 1914 and 1915. Sub-Lieutenant Brooke was horrified by the sight of refugees fleeing from Antwerp, but wrote of his horror only in letters.

Captain Grenfell's obituary appeared in *The Times* only a month after Brooke's, and with it his death-and-glory poem 'Into Battle', for a time as famous as Brooke's sonnet 'The Soldier'. Captain Sorley fought at Loos and, after his death in 1915, there was found in his kit-bag the manuscript of perhaps the first poem of the Great War to get the numbers right and strike the anti-heroic note. It begins:

> When you see millions of the mouthless dead
> Across your dreams in pale battalions go,
> Say not soft things as other men have said,
> That you'll remember. For you need not so.
> Give them not praise. For, deaf, how should they know
> It is not curses heaped on each gashed head?
> Nor tears. Their blind eyes see not your tears flow.
> Nor honour. It is easy to be dead.

Private Ledwidge fought at Gallipoli and 2nd Lieutenant Hodgson at Loos. Both wrote fine poems. Both were killed on the Western Front. None of these poets lived to write an autobiography, nor after the war was there a prose account of Gallipoli or the other battles of 1914–15 that made an impact comparable to those of 1916–17.

By contrast, however, with the relative scarcity of literary testimony to the battles of 1914–15, probably no battle in world history was witnessed by more writers than were present at the Somme. They include (and this is by no means a comprehensive roll-call of even the British ones): Richard Aldington, Mary Borden, Edmund Blunden, Charles Carrington, Ford Madox Ford, Gilbert Frankau, Robert Graves, Ivor Gurney, Basil Liddell Hart, David Jones, Frederic Manning, John Masefield, Wilfred Owen, Herbert Read, Isaac Rosenberg, Siegfried Sassoon, Geoffrey Studdert Kennedy, John Ronald Tolkien, Arthur Graeme West, and Henry Williamson. None of these was a professional soldier. All were civilians in uniform, all were intelligent, all educated – even if (like Rosenberg) largely self-educated.

In an important and influential lecture on 'A Military Historian's View of the Great War',[2] Corelli Barnett made a frontal attack on 'the war writers' for propagating a distorted view of the war that would later unbalance public opinion and encourage appeasement when the country should have been arming itself against Hitler. He claimed that

with the exception of Manning and Rosenberg they came from the sheltered, well-off, upper or upper-middle classes. They had had an absurd upbringing at home and at their public schools which gave them no knowledge or understanding of the real world of their time, but instead a set of ludicrously romantic attitudes, most famously expressed in Rupert Brooke's excruciating poem 'Now God be Thanked'. They were in fact the repositories of the liberalism and romanticism of Victorian England. They all lived at Howards End, having delicate emotional responses to the aesthetic stimulus of landscape, and cherishing a knightly idealism.

Barnett has a case, but in the way of powerful polemicists, he overstates it. Of the twenty writers I have named as present at the Somme only seven went to a public school, and only three or four could be said to have lived at Forster's 'Howards End'.

Ninety Julys after the opening of the battle, how should we view their alleged distortions? Barnett and other historians criticize the imaginative writers' over-emphasis on casualties, and cite comparable numbers killed in the Napoleonic wars and the American Civil War. Sassoon was no historian, but one of his childhood neighbours was Jack Barchard, 'recently returned from the Boer War'. Young Siegfried would have heard of defeats that rocked the nation: Colenso (143 Britons killed) and Spion Kop (243 killed). When, on 1 July 1916, he

found himself the survivor of a day that saw more than *twice*
the number of British soldiers killed by enemy action (19,000)
than were killed by enemy action in the *entire* Boer War
(7,774), is it surprising that he should have thought casualties
worthy of emphasis? *The Memoirs of George Sherston* are
largely transcribed from Sassoon's diaries, and all but five
days of the front-line action he describes is on the Somme. His
memoirs are memoirs of that battle, not of the war. The same
is true of Graves's *Goodbye to All That*, David Jones's *In
Parenthesis*, the poems of Ivor Gurney and Isaac Rosenberg,
and all but a handful of Owen's. Far from *over*-emphasizing
the casualties of the Somme, John Masefield *under*-emphasized
them in *The Old Front Line or The Beginning of the Battle of the
Somme*, a book subsidized by the government propaganda
bureau at Wellington House. In an autumn 1916 letter to his
wife, he wrote:

We went into a wood, which we will call Chunk-of-Corpse-Wood,
for its main features were chunks of corpse, partly human, partly
trees. There was a cat eating a man's brain, & such a wreck of war as I
never did see, & the wounded coming by, dripping blood on the
track, & one walked on blood or rotten flesh, & saw bags of men
being carried to the grave. They were shovelling parts of men into
blankets.[3]

Nothing so graphic found its way into his book, which
has more of the pastoral than the charnel about it; and not
one dead body to be seen in its sixteen photographs of the
battlefield.

A second distortion for which these 'sensitive intellectuals'
have been held responsible is their holding the generals
responsible for avoidable casualties. Certainly, school-children
who study the war will encounter Sassoon's poems 'The
General', 'The March-Past', and 'Base Details', but they
will find no criticism of the General Staff in his 1917 protest,

little in his prose, or in the trench memoirs of Blunden and Graves, or in the letters of Owen and Rosenberg. Brian Bond finds 'Sassoon's failure to address the complex issues of military strategy, foreign policy and diplomacy in 1917 [...] understandable'.[4] I think anyone would. The view from the trench periscope is, of course, restricted – that is its limitation – but when the viewer's life depends on what he sees, its sharp focus is its strength. The combatant poets called attention to the casualties, but they left it to their readers and reviewers to draw their own conclusions. Historians rightly speak of the generals' 'learning curve' at the Somme, but given some of their tactical misjudgements in that battle, one might have expected more criticism – rather than less – from the trench memoirs and poems of 1916.

A third alleged distortion of the so-called 'sensitive intellectuals' is said by some to be their over-emphasis on the uncongenial conditions of trench life. Corelli Barnett offers a useful corrective to the myth of the golden Edwardian afternoon when he reminds us that

Nearly a third of the British population lived their entire lives in [squalid] conditions. Descriptions of contemporary British slums remarkably echo those of the trenches Thus

> Two rooms, seven inmates [...] Dirty flock bedding in living-room placed on box and two chairs. Smell of dirt and bad air unbearable [...]

Or:

> There is no water supply in the house, the eight families having to share one water-tap with eight other families.[5]

Thus, Barnett concludes, 'it is hardly surprising that the rank and file did not take things so hard as the war writers.

Many of them were better off in the army than in peacetime life.' No doubt the war writers were sometimes guilty of over-statement in their passionate reminiscences. Most of us are sometimes guilty of over-statement when our passions are aroused: even historians. I wonder about the seven inmates of those two rooms: a husband, wife and five children perhaps? Might not such a husband prefer to spend his nights with his family, his days in a farmyard, shop, or mill, than with other men huddled in a wet trench? I wonder, too, what Wilfred Owen (unpaid assistant to the vicar of a poverty-stricken rural parish) or Isaac Rosenberg ('chained', as he put it, 'to a fiendish mangling engraving machine' in the East End of London) would think of Barnett's assertion that 'The social, aesthetic, intellectual, and moral world in which the war writers lived before the war was in fact almost as unreal as the pastoral play-acting of the French royal court before the Revolution.'[6]

The British public, of course (or 25–35 million of them: more than half the total population of the country), were not introduced to the Somme by those unrealists, but by the most popular news film of the war, *The Battle of the Somme*. More graphic than Masefield's despatches from that Front,

The film concentrated on the scale of the offensive bombardment and presented the battle as a clear British victory, but to an audience unused to such images it was a shocking introduction to what the Western Front looked like, and how men appeared when they returned from combat. At the emotional climax of the film, as British troops went over the top and advanced into the smoke, the piano accompaniment ceased. The dramatic silence was filled with screams from the audience as they saw men fall.[7]

As in the American Civil War and the Boer War, the photographic image reinforced the printed word in bringing home to the public some (but not all) of the horrors of the Front.

Ironically, while many newspapers published the appalling casualty lists in full, editors were prevented by government edict from printing photographs of British dead. As the war progressed, the official War Artists Scheme sent painters of the calibre of Percy Wyndham Lewis, Paul Nash, John Singer Sargent, and Stanley Spencer to one or other battle-zone, and some of their pictures – notably Singer Sargent's 'Gassed' – further contributed to the emerging belief that the Somme 'spelt the end of innocence'.[8] As Private David Jones, painter and poet, wrote in the Preface to *In Parenthesis*:

[July 1916] roughly marks a change in the character of our lives in the Infantry on the West Front. From then onward things hardened into a more relentless, mechanical affair, took on a more sinister aspect. The wholesale slaughter of the later years, the conscripted levies filling the gaps in every file of four, knocked the bottom out of the intimate, continuing, domestic life of small contingents of men, within whose structure Roland could find, and, for a reasonable while, enjoy, his Oliver.[9]

In recent decades, military historians have countered the myth of the 'lions led by donkeys', showing that 'the Somme was the muddy grave of the German field army'[10] and made possible the final 'Forgotten Victory'.[11] Few who survived the Somme wrote about its aftermath. Two who did were Wilfred Owen and R. C. Sherriff. Owen, far from anticipating victory on his return to the Front in August 1918, there completed his last three poems – 'The Sentry', 'Smile, Smile, Smile', and 'Spring Offensive' – all focused on the death of 'comrades that went under'. A good deal of ink has been wasted trying to square the action and the language of *Journey's End*, set in March 1918, with Sherriff's later view of it as 'a war play in which not a word was spoken against the war, in which no word of condemnation was uttered by any of its characters'.[12] He was forgetting the word 'murder', twice used (on pp. 87–8) to describe a raid the company commander calls 'absurd' (p. 75) and the Colonel says he would 'give anything to cancel'. It does prove to be murder, and we are left in no doubt that the end of the company's journey is under an artillery barrage. Sherriff's curious misreading of his play's unambiguous message is understandable in psychological terms: his loyalty towards the 'simple, unquestioning men' (as distinct from insufficiently questioning staff officers) with whom he had been proud to serve. Literary critics have long known to distrust the singer, not the song.

For almost a decade after the Armistice, all was quiet on – and from – the Western Front, as veterans and their families and the families of the bereaved tried to forget their pain and rebuild broken lives. Then came the Return of the Repressed. In 1926, six books of personal trench reminiscence were published; in 1927, fifteen; and in 1928, the tsunami crested with the publication of Sassoon's *Memoirs of a Fox-Hunting Man* and Blunden's *Undertones of War*. Their success was followed – and in some cases exceeded – in 1929 by that of Graves's *Goodbye to All That*,[13] Remarque's *All Quiet on the Western Front*, Sherriff's *Journey's End*, and Aldington's *Death of a Hero*. The memoirs of the three poets were set on the Somme, as their poems (like Gurney's, Owen's, and Rosenberg's) had been, and as Aldington's novel also was. Last, but by no means least, of the great imaginative writings about that battle was David Jones's *In Parenthesis* (1937).[14]

A second phase of major literature centred on the Somme began, like the first, with the work of a poet: Ted Hughes. Three poems in his first book, *The Hawk in the Rain* (1957), derive from his uncle Walter's accounts of the battle: 'Bayonet Charge', 'Griefs for Dead Soldiers', and 'Six Young Men'.[15]

A similar family memory would give Michael Longley his 'Wounds', beginning:

> Here are two pictures from my father's head –
> I have kept them like secrets until now:
> First, the Ulster Division at the Somme
> Going over the top with 'Fuck the Pope!'
> 'No Surrender!': a boy about to die,
> Screaming 'Give 'em one for the Shankill!'[16]

The exploits of the Ulster Division on 1 July 1916 have a mythic resonance for Irish Protestants, that day being the anniversary of the Battle of the Boyne in 1690. At the end of Frank McGuinness's play *Observe the Sons of Ulster Marching Towards the Somme* (1986), the Ulstermen exchange their Orange sashes and the Younger Pyper prays:

God in heaven, if you hear the words of man [...] Let this day at the Somme be as glorious in the memory of Ulster as that day at the Boyne, when you scattered our enemies. Lead us back from this exile. [...] Let us fight bravely. Let us win gloriously. Lord, look down on us. Spare us. I love – . Observe the sons of Ulster marching towards the Somme.

Something of the order of 750 books on the Great War were published between 1939 and 1987.[17] This second tsunami, far from diminishing, crested in the 1990s with a succession of bestselling novels centred on the Somme. They followed Susan Hill's *Strange Meeting* (1971), a novel that took its title from Owen's most famous poem and explored the relationship between two front-line soldiers with a delicacy worthy of the poet.[18] Central to Pat Barker's *Regeneration Trilogy*[19] is the relationship between Owen and Sassoon, for which she drew heavily on their writings and on the books about them. Again, the title of Sebastian Faulks's *Birdsong* (1993), the most recent and most successful of Somme novels, suggests the influence of Sassoon's lines: 'O, but Everyone / Was a bird; and the song was wordless; the singing will never be done.'[20] In a new Introduction to the paperback edition of *Birdsong*, Faulks writes: 'As an epigraph, I took the line from Rabindranath Tagore that Wilfred Owen had quoted in his final letter to his mother before his return to the Front, where he was killed in November 1918.' Tagore wrote: 'When I go from hence, let this be my parting word, that what I have seen is unsurpassable.'

The shades of Owen and Sassoon, if not directly invoked as here, can be sensed in the hellscape of these and other novels. In their poems, letters and memoirs, the poets of the Somme gave our culture its defining symbolic image of the Great War: the trench mouth as the mouth of Hell. The sumptuous brochure of Martin Randall, 'Travel Company of the Year', offers tours to such cultural sites as 'Ancient Egypt', 'Russian Palaces and Gardens', and 'Poets and the Somme'. Numbered among the 'poets whose works are included' are Charles Sorley (who died at Loos), Edward Thomas (who died at Arras), and several who never saw the Western Front at all.

Due to its cultural accretions, the Somme – like Troy, Hastings, and Agincourt – has come to stand for, to symbolize, something other and larger than itself: nothing less than the First World War, specifically, and modern mechanized warfare, generally. Much as I applaud the work of military historians in setting the 1916–18 record straight, the cultural historian in me believes that, unless a bestselling novel and film can rescue the Battle of Amiens from anonymity, whenever you spin the Somme coin outside a conference of military historians, it will come down symbol side up.

CHAPTER 9

The iconography of the Waste Land

T.S. Eliot's *Waste Land* records a journey through hell: an inner hell lit by the flames, haunted by the flickering images, of an outer hellscape from which Western Europe was only then beginning to emerge. Shaw, in his 1919 Preface to *Heartbreak House*, had said that 'the earth is still bursting with the dead bodies of the victors'' and the speaker of 'The Burial of the Dead' cries out:

> 'Stetson!
> 'You who were with me in the ships at Mylae!
> 'That corpse you planted last year in your garden,
> 'Has it begun to sprout? Will it bloom this year?'[2]

What makes that at once so horrible and so memorable is the unexpected superimposition of a corpse on a garden. This is a miniature example of the theme, the territory, I mean to explore.

In 1918, Wilfred Owen wrote to a friend:

For 14 hours yesterday I was at work — teaching Christ to lift his cross by numbers, and how to adjust his crown; and not to imagine he thirst till after the last halt; I attended his Supper to see that there were no complaints; and inspected his feet to see that they should be worthy of the nails. I see to it that he is dumb and stands to attention before his accusers. With a piece of silver I buy him every day, and with maps I make him familiar with the topography of Golgotha.[3]

My subject is the topography of Golgotha. Owen was a believing Christian, as Sassoon in 1918 was not, but from the very first the older man's writings about the war were steeped in Christian imagery. His first war poem was called 'Absolution', his second 'The Redeemer' and, early in 1916, he wrote 'Golgotha' and 'Stand-to: Good Friday Morning'.[4] In the middle of the latter sketch of the trenches, three lines are typographically indented:

> Dawn was misty; the skies were still;
> Larks were singing, discordant, shrill;
> *They* seemed happy; but *I* felt ill.

The same polarities are as cunningly juxtaposed at the end of *Memoirs of a Fox-Hunting Man*:

Somewhere out of sight beyond the splinters of tree-tops of Hidden Wood a bird had begun to sing. Without knowing why, I remembered that it was Easter Sunday. Standing in that dismal ditch, I could find no consolation in the thought that Christ was risen.[5]

With the trenches suggestive of graves, those splintered trees suggestive of crosses are the dominant images of the hell-scape of the Western Front. We see them again in 'Christ and the Soldier':[6]

> The straggled soldier halted – stared at Him –
> Then clumsily dumped down upon his knees,
> Gasping, 'O blessed crucifix, I'm beat!'
> And Christ, still sentried by the seraphim,
> Near the front-line, between two splintered trees,
> Spoke him: 'My Son, behold these hands and feet.'

The conjunction, the conflation, of Christ and soldier is as old as St Paul's Epistle to the Ephesians (6:11–17), and Sassoon's icon has a significant resemblance to the Anglo-Saxon 'Dream of the Rood'. In this, the Tree climbed by 'the young warrior' says:

'Now, I desire thee,   my dear son,
that thou reveal   this vision to men,
declare in plain words   that it is the Cross of Glory,
which Almighty God   agonised upon
for the manifold   sins of mankind,
and for the ancient   offence of Adam.'[7]

This alludes to the tradition encapsulated by Donne:

We think that Paradise and Calvary,
     Christ's cross, and Adam's tree, stood in one Place [...][8]

It is customary to give Eliot the credit for the vision of a post-war world as the Waste Land named and traversed by Malory, re-traversed by Tennyson, but we should not forget the earlier version of his great contemporary: Yeats's 'The Second Coming'. 'The Dream of the Rood' has given place to nightmare. If 'somewhere in sands of the desert' a rough beast 'Slouches towards Bethlehem', might it not also be slouching towards Golgotha? Yeats's poem may or may not have influenced Eliot's, but we know that Conrad's vision of the Heart of Darkness did, because its original epigraph was a quotation from that novel:

Did he live his life again in every detail of desire, temptation, and surrender during that supreme moment of complete knowledge? He cried in a whisper at some image, at some vision, – he cried out twice, a cry that was not more than a breath –
                              'The horror! The horror!'[9]

Marlow's quest had led him down 'a mighty big river, [...] resembling an immense snake' not to the primal garden, but to a house in the primal forest flanked by

a dozen slim posts [...] roughly trimmed, and with their upper ends ornamented with round curved balls [...] Then I went carefully from post to post with my glass, and I saw my mistake. These round knobs

were not ornamental but symbolic [...] I returned deliberately to the
first I had seen – and there it was, black, dried, sunken, with closed
eyelids – a head that seemed to sleep at the top of that pole, and, with
the shrunken dry lips showing a narrow white line of the teeth, was
smiling too, smiling continuously at some endless and jocose dream
of that eternal slumber.[10]

Although Eliot in 1922 was no closer to being a Christian
than Conrad, Sassoon, or Yeats, his *Waste Land* shows
topographical features resembling theirs. He looks back to
a vanishing Eden, a world of pastoral all but passed:

> The river's tent is broken; the last fingers of leaf
> Clutch and sink into the wet bank. The wind
> Crosses the brown land unheard. The nymphs are departed.[11]

The quester's route across the Waste Land goes by way of
Golgotha:

> After the agony in stony places
> The shouting and the crying
> Prison and palace and reverberation
> Of thunder of spring over distant mountains
> He who was living is now dead [...][12]

I approach the iconography of the Waste Land by way of
three pairs of more recent texts: first, a pair of poems. In
1934, Geoffrey Grigson canvassed contemporary poets on
the state of their art and, in response to his question 'Do you
think there can now be a use for narrative poetry?' David
Gascoyne replied:

What might be useful now would be a poem expressing the ever-
rising feeling of crisis, anxiety and panic; a poem that would treat this
feeling in a loose, universal and epic sort of way. I mean a poem
narrating the contemporary Zeitgeist of Europe, or even of the
World.[13]

Some years later, Gascoyne followed his own prescription, albeit with a lyric rather than an epic. His poem 'Ecce Homo' begins:

> Whose is this horrifying face,
> This putrid flesh, discoloured, flayed,
> Fed on by flies, scorched by the sun?
> Whose are these hollow red-filmed eyes
> And thorn-spiked head and spear-stuck side?
> Behold the Man: He is Man's Son [...]

> And on his either side hang dead
> A labourer and a factory hand,
> Or one is maybe a lynched Jew
> And one a Negro or a Red,
> Coolie or Ethiopian, Irishman,
> Spaniard or German democrat.[14]

This Christ re-crucified is on 'the tree of human pain', that tree proclaiming its descent from the Tree of Life, and behind it lies the Waste Land located between Eden and Golgotha:

> Besieged by drifting sands
> And clefted landslides our about-to-be
> Bombed and abandoned cities stand.

In the wake of the Second World War prophetically envisioned in that poem, Auden wrote 'The Shield of Achilles',[15] a title directing the reader to Book 18 of *The Iliad*, a condensed version of which his poem offers, albeit a version as modernized as Gascoyne's revision of the Gospels' account of the Crucifixion. Homer's description of the shield Hephaestos makes for Achilles highlights the antithesis between peace and war, an antithesis that Auden develops further. We see the armourer at work through the eyes of the hero's mother, Thetis, who hopes for a prophecy of good fortune for her son:

> She looked over his shoulder
>   For vines and olive trees,
> Marble well-governed cities
>   And ships upon untamed seas [...]

As so often in depictions of pastoral or a golden age, this is
counterbalanced by a harsher and darker alternative:

> But there on the shining metal
>   His hands had put instead
> An artificial wilderness
>   And a sky like lead.

In place of the natural vines and olive trees of pre-Christian
pastoral, she sees an artificial – that is to say unnatural –
wilderness made by the arts of man. The antithetical structure of the poem is developed by its alternating stanza forms:
the two buoyant ballad-like quatrains of that opening suggest a mythic past far removed from the slower, flatter
movement of the rhyme royal that follows with its vision
of a modern Waste Land:

> A plain without a feature, bare and brown.
>   No blade of grass, no sign of neighbourhood,
> Nothing to eat and nowhere to sit down,
>   Yet, congregated on its blankness, stood
>   An unintelligible multitude,
> A million eyes, a million boots in line,
> Without expression, waiting for a sign.

Looking for positives and peace, Thetis can see only neg-
atives and the outbreak of war:

> Column by column in a cloud of dust
> They marched away enduring a belief
> Whose logic brought them, somewhere else, to grief.

She looks again, hoping for the happier omen of a scene that
Auden borrows from Keats's 'Ode on a Grecian Urn':[16]

> She looked over his shoulder
>> For ritual pieties,
> White flower-garlanded heifers,
>> Libation and sacrifice,
> But there on the shining metal
>> Where the altar should have been,
> She saw by his flickering forge-light
>> Quite another scene.

The light of the ancient forge reveals modern barbed wire, and in place of ritual pieties she witnesses the ultimate impiety: the sacrifice not of heifers but of the Lamb of God:

> three pale figures were led forth and bound
> To three posts driven upright in the ground.

The posts – reminiscent of those flanking Mister Kurtz's hut – are reminders also of the vines and olive trees of the alternate world of pastoral. The pagan goddess, having been granted this vision of the death of a later God, fails to understand the implications of that 'libation and sacrifice' and turns to the next panel on the armourer's shield:

> She looked over his shoulder
>> For athletes at their games,
> Men and women in a dance
>> Moving their sweet limbs
> Quick, quick, to music,
>> But there on the shining shield
> His hands had set no dancing-floor
>> But a weed-choked field.

Far from seeing men and women moving together in harmony, a dance proleptic of a closer movement of 'their sweet limbs', she witnesses disharmony, alienation, man murderously out of tune with nature and his own kind:

> A ragged urchin, aimless and alone,
>   Loitered about that vacancy; a bird
> Flew up to safety from his well-aimed stone:
>   That girls are raped, that two boys knife a third,
>   Were axioms to him, who'd never heard
> Of any world where promises were kept,
> Or one could weep because another wept.

Only now does Thetis 'of the shining breasts' (emblematic of love, fecundity, and her eternal life) understand, at least in part, the prophecy of the shield. Auden's juxtaposition of idealized golden age with a recognizably modern leaden age in which Christ is crucified, or re-crucified, posits a Christian era as brutal and sterile as that in which 'man-slaying Achilles [...] would not live long'.

The spatial constraints of the lyric form restrict these representations of the Waste Land to the status of peopled landscapes, but two twentieth-century novels are concerned with process rather than stasis: the journey from Eden to Golgotha. The first, William Golding's *Lord of the Flies* (1954), is set in the closest modern equivalent of the primal garden, a South Sea (one can hardly say Pacific) island. The reader's first view of this is directed to a 'long scar smashed into the jungle'.[17] Right at the outset, man has wounded nature: a plane has crashed, the victim of an attack, and somewhere else, we learn, an atom bomb has exploded. Golding's depiction of the Waste Land, like Auden's and others from the decade of the 1950s that I will be discussing later, is clearly prompted by the Second World War, as was Eliot's poem by the First.

In his opening pages, Golding gives notice that he is re-working an older fable. One of the survivors 'undid the snake-clasp of his belt, lugged off his shorts and pants, and stood there naked'.[18] The snake is not native to the island.

The boys bring it with them. They expect it to be there. Later, one of the younger boys will claim to have seen 'A snake-thing. Ever so big.' He will be reassured by Ralph, whose belt had the snake-clasp: 'You couldn't have a beastie, a snake-thing, on an island this size [...] You only get them in big countries like Africa, or India.'[19] We are also reminded of the older fable when 'the fat boy', delighted by the rich variety of fruit, says: 'I expect we'll want to know all their names.'[20] This variation of Adam's naming of the beasts is developed when the boy confesses to his own animal nickname: Piggy. Although he and Ralph of the snake-clasp subsequently display less animal behaviour than most of the other survivors, Golding's point is clear: not only is man an animal, but a predatory animal. Armed with their spears, the boys single out a sow 'sunk in deep maternal bliss'.[21] Not one is moved – as, clearly, the reader is meant to be moved – by the fact that 'the great bladder of her belly was fringed with a row of piglets that slept or burrowed and squeaked'.[22] After her ferocious killing, one of the hunters giggles while the others smear their faces with her blood.

Just as Auden highlights the horror of his Waste Land by contrasting it with a pastoral alternative, Golding emphasizes the horror of his island story by contrasting it with an earlier classic of the genre, R.M. Ballantyne's *The Coral Island*. In this novel of the *1850s*, the castaways Jack, Ralph, and Peterkin rise to the occasion as decent, courageous, and resourceful young Britons were supposed to. They live an idyllic life on their island – interrupted, it is true, by black cannibals and white pirates, but the cannibals are converted to Christianity and the pirates deservedly destroyed. Golding takes over the names Jack and Ralph and, by converting Peterkin to Simon, announces the religious significance of his central figure. He has said in an interview:

I intended a Christ figure in the novel, because Christ figures occur in humanity, really, but I couldn't have the full picture, or as near as full a possible picture of human potentiality, unless one was potentially a Christ figure. So Simon is the little boy who goes off into the bushes to pray. He is the only one to take any notice of the little 'uns – who actually hands them food, gets food from places where they can't reach it and hands it down to them. He is the one who is tempted of the devil: he has this interview with the pig's head on the stick, with Beelzebub, or Satan, the devil, whatever you'd like to call it, and the devil says, 'Clear off, you're not wanted. Just go back to the others. We'll forget the whole thing.'[23]

Beelzebub is the Greek form of a Hebrew word meaning 'lord of insects', but the devil who tempts Simon in the wilderness is, of course, an emblem, a projection, of the evil that the boys bring with them. This Lord of the Flies is the severed head of the maternal sow, set on a stick sharpened at both ends like the heads outside Kurtz's house; and, like other twentieth-century depictions of the Waste Land, Golding at one point appears to acknowledge his debt to *Heart of Darkness*. At the end of this scene, 'Simon found he was looking into a vast mouth. There was blackness within, a blackness that spread [...] Simon was within the mouth' much as Marlow saw the dying Kurtz 'open his mouth wide – it gave him a weirdly voracious aspect, as though he wanted to swallow all the air, all the earth, all the men before him'.[24]

Simon resists the temptation to 'forget the whole thing', climbs the mountain, and there finds another Lord of the Flies, the corpse of the parachutist still held upright by his harness. With Christ-like compassion, we are told,

he took the lines in hands; he freed them from the rocks and the figure from the wind's indignity [...]

The beast was harmless and horrible; and the news must reach the others as soon as possible. He started down the mountain [...][25]

He descends to the accompaniment of thunder and the hunters' choric chant – '*Kill the beast! Cut his throat! Spill his blood!*'[26] – reminiscent of an earlier refrain: 'Crucify him!' Simon's death, like Christ's, is marked by a cosmic convulsion, one that mirrors and magnifies the book's opening image of the scar: 'The dark sky was shattered by a blue-white scar [...] The blue-white scar was constant, the noise unendurable. Simon was crying out something about a dead man on a hill.'[27]

Patrick White's *Voss* (1957) was published three years after *The Lord of the Flies*. It opens with the arrival of its eponymous hero at the house of Mr Bonner, sponsor of his projected expedition across the Australian desert. He is received by Bonner's niece, Laura Trevelyan, who says: 'You must see the garden [...] Uncle has made it his hobby. Even at the Botanic Gardens I doubt there is such a collection of shrubs.'[28] Once again we embark on a journey from fertility to sterility, Eden to Golgotha, albeit with a hint of redemption and resurrection beyond. On the eve of the expedition's departure, the Bonners give a party at which Voss and Laura, meeting by chance in the luxuriant garden, have a curious conversation:

'You are so vast and ugly,' Laura Trevelyan was repeating the words; 'I can imagine some desert, with rocks, rocks of prejudice, and, yes, even hatred. You are so isolated. That is why you are fascinated by the prospect of desert places, in which you will find your own situation taken for granted, or more than that, exalted. You sometimes scatter kind words or bits of poetry to people, who soon realise the extent of their illusion. Everything is for yourself. Human emotions, when you have them, are quite flattering to you. If those emotions strike sparks from others, that also is flattering. But most flattering, I think, when you experience it, is the hatred, or even the mere irritation of weaker characters.'

'Do you hate me, perhaps?' asked Voss, in darkness.

'I am fascinated by you,' laughed Laura Trevelyan, with such candour that her admission did not seem immodest. '*You* are *my* desert!'[29]

Gradually it emerges that he in his pride and she in her humility complement each other. As Carolyn Bliss puts it:

Voss's purposes require him to renounce all gentler emotions, avoid all human relationships, and utterly repudiate the comforts of the flesh. This side of life he condemns as weakness, identifies with the feminine in general and Laura in particular, and rejects as inappropriate to incipient deity. Thus when we meet Voss he is already fragmented, having denied so much of his full self. As Laura knows, man's nature partakes of both the human and the divine. If he is to reclaim his wholeness, he must do justice to the godlike in himself by embracing the human, or that which Laura represents and encourages. It is this crucial failure, this surrender of Voss to the whole self, which the novel traces.[30]

En route to the desert the expedition pauses to refresh itself in an Edenic valley known as Rhine Towers. Sanderson, the owner of this property, 'tended his flocks and herds like any other Christian [...] and both he and his wife would wash their servants' feet in many thoughtful and imperceptible ways'.[31] Moved by their loving relationship, Voss writes to propose marriage to Laura, whose letter of acceptance introduces a familiar feature of the landscape of the Waste Land:

I do truthfully believe that you are always lurking somewhere on the fringes of my dreams, though I seldom see your face, and cannot even distinguish your form. I only know it is you, I *know*, just as I have sat beside you beneath certain trees, although I could not describe their shape, nor recite their Latin names. I have touched their bark, however.[32]

I think we know their shape.

Voss and Laura never meet again in the body, but spiritually they cross the desert together and, at the moment of his death, she breaks free from what was thought to be a fatal fever to echo the words of Christ on the Cross: "'O God,' cried the girl, at last, tearing it out. "It is over. It is over."'[33] On the other side of the continent, an exhausted Voss has been awaiting death at the hands of aborigines alarmed by the appearance beside the Southern Cross of a comet they see as a snake. Voss, too, in his new-found humility and humanity is frightened, we are told,

of the arms, or sticks, reaching down from the eternal tree, and tears of blood, and candle-wax. Of the great legend becoming truth [...]
So the explorer waited. He did not fear tortures of the body, for little enough of that remained. It was some final torment of the spirit that he might not have the strength to endure. For a long time that night he did not dare raise his eyes towards the sky. When he did, at last, there were the nails of the Cross still eating into it, but the Comet, he saw, was gone.[34]

Eventually decapitated, like one of Kurtz's victims or the Lord of the Flies, Voss is not a traditional Christ-figure. Rather, he exemplifies Laura's statement that 'When man is truly humbled, when he has learned that he is not God, then he is nearest to becoming so. In the end he may ascend.'[35]

I pass now from a modernist to a post-modernist Waste Land: '*A country road. A tree*'.[36] The scene, stripped of all features but these, is Beckett's, though the road has been travelled by many: some I have already mentioned, and others include Oedipus, Christian, and Charlie Chaplin. Estragon and Vladimir, descendants of the last of these, are waiting for Godot: 'He said by the tree.'[37] What species of tree is unspecified. 'What is it?' asks Estragon. 'I don't know.' Vladimir replies: 'A willow.' We remember the unidentified trees whose bark White's Laura had touched. Whether or not Beckett's tree is a willow, it is certainly a tree of weeping: its tears being those of both the first Adam (Estragon tells Pozzo his name is Adam) and the second.

VLADIMIR: (*Silence. Estragon looks attentively at the tree.*)
             What do we do now?
ESTRAGON: Wait.
VLADIMIR: Yes, but while waiting.
ESTRAGON: What about hanging ourselves?
VLADIMIR: Hmm. It'd give us an erection.
ESTRAGON: (*highly excited*). An erection! […]
             Let's hang ourselves immediately![38]

This is potentially a tree both of sterile sexuality and suicide, a tree of life and death. The second aspect is more empha-sized in Act I where the talk turns to 'Two thieves, crucified at the same time as our Saviour'.[39] Bert States, one of Beckett's more enlightening critics, comments:

I've wondered if there isn't a possible connection between Didi and Gogo and Dysmas and Gestas, the names given to the two thieves in the Middle Ages (see the apocryphal *Acts of Pilate*) […] Dysmas (crucified to Christ's right) was the repentant thief. He entered heaven with a cross on his shoulders, the first mortal redeemed by Christ's death. But which tramp should have the honor? Didi seems the logical beneficiary, given his preoccupation with repentance and crucifixion throughout the play; and at the end he does speak the words, 'Christ have mercy upon us.' Unfortunately, this would con-sign Gogo to a fate worse than death and that is hardly what the play has in mind. But if the reader finds the idea far-fetched, consider one propounded by Beckett himself on Estragon's chances: 'One of Estragon's feet is blessed, and the other damned. The boot won't go on the foot that is damned; and it will go on the foot that is not. It is like the two thieves on the cross' (Harold Hobson, 'Samuel Beckett,' p. 153). I simply don't know what to make of this: it seems to be carrying thievery to the limit of subtlety (Should one presume, or despair?). Perhaps we should call it a stand-off: Estragon gets at least one foot in the gate, which is more than we can clearly say for Vladimir.[40]

As Act I draws to a close, a stage direction announces: *'The light suddenly fails. In a moment it is night.'* We remember St Luke (23:43); 'There was a darkness over all the earth until the ninth hour.' In Beckett's darkness, Estragon decides to abandon his boots, prompting the play's most savage exchange:

VLADIMIR: But you can't go barefoot!
ESTRAGON: Christ did.
VLADIMIR: Christ! What has Christ got to do with
it? You're not going to compare yourself
to Christ!
ESTRAGON: All my life I've compared myself to him.
VALDIMIR: But where he lived it was warm, it was dry!
ESTRAGON: Yes. And they crucified quick.[41]

Act II, we are told, takes place *'Next day. Same Time. Same Place.'* The landscape, however, has changed: *'The tree has four or five leaves.'* Estragon exclaims: 'It must be the Spring.' But no sooner are we lulled into thinking that the tree of death may have turned back into the tree of life, than we learn that disaster has struck Pozzo and Lucky. Finally, confirming how little progress they have made across the Waste Land,

Estragon draws Vladimir towards the tree. They stand motionless before it. Silence.

ESTRAGON: Why don't we hang ourselves?[42]

Beckett's God may be busy elsewhere, exiled, resting, or dead, but the playwright has re-made Man in His image; and we find much the same situation – as well as the same black comedy – in Ted Hughes's *Crow*. He has said of this cycle of poems,

My main concern was to produce something with the minimum cultural accretions of the museum sort – something autochthonous and complete in itself, as it might be invented after the holocaust and demolition of all libraries, where essential things spring again – if at all – only from their seeds in nature – and are not lugged around or hoarded as preserved harvests from the past. So the comparative religion/mythology background was irrelevant to me, except as I could forget it.[43]

He cannot of course forget it. Keith Sagar says that 'Crow has a distinguished lineage in mythology',[44] but the Waste Land over which it flies seems more familiar than Hughes or Sagar allow. God the Father may be sleeping in several of these poems, outwitted by Crow in others, but the mythology they inhabit is predominantly Christian. It is rendered as a montage of fragments, somewhat in the manner of Eliot's *Waste Land*, which it echoes at a number of points. This is hardly surprising since Hughes's work, even more than Eliot's, is a response to domestic disaster projected on to a cosmic screen. Confronted, not simply with 'The horror! The horror!' but more specifically with 'the horror of Creation', he attacks the Creator by attempting to re-write the Old and New Testaments. In the darkness – rather than the light – of his experience, he parodies God's promise,

> a black rainbow
> Bent in emptiness
>   over emptiness[45]

and revises the primal myth: 'In the beginning was the Scream'. The 'Lineage', with which this opens, leads to a God

> Who begat Nothing
> Who begat Never
> Never Never Never
>
> Who begat Crow [.][46]

The echo of Lear's anguished cry over Cordelia, 'Never, never, never, never, never', is significant in a work dedicated to the memory of a tragic mother and her child. Crow 'is stronger than death', the survivor in a Waste Land more grotesque than Lear's heath, a battlefield like that imaged in Eliot's poem: 'he took the battle of the Somme in one hand'.[47] 'Crow's Account of the Battle' describes 'legs in a treetop', a tree sprung surely from a seed of the Tree in the Garden where Crow played 'A Childish Prank':

> Crow laughed.
> He bit the Worm, God's only son,
> Into two writhing halves.
>
> He stuffed into man the tail half
> With the wounded end hanging out.
>
> He stuffed the head half headfirst into woman
> And it crept in deeper and up
> To peer out through her eyes
> Calling its tail-half to join up quickly, quickly
> Because O it was painful.[48]

As in the phantasmagoria of Eliot's *Waste Land*, sex is the root of the problem; and the serpent rears its cobra-head again in the poem 'Apple Tragedy',[49] another Hughesian variation of the Genesis story, that ends with Adam trying 'to hang himself in the orchard'. There is no such *Godot*-like solution to the problem more conventionally – and I think more movingly – presented in the book's final treatment of this theme:

Snake Hymn

> The snake in the garden
> If it was not God
> It was the gliding
> And push of Adam's blood.

The blood in Adam's body
That slid into Eve
Was the everlasting thing
Adam swore was love.

The blood in Eve's body
That slid from her womb –
Knotted on the cross
It had no name.

Nothing else has happened.
The love that cannot die
Sheds the million faces
And skin of agony

To hang, an empty husk.
Still no suffering
Darkens the garden
Or the snake's song.[50]

I take this to mean that Fall and Crucifixion are endlessly re-enacted; that the body on the Cross has no *one* name; and that lovers in the Garden, seduced by the snake's song, hear no cries from Golgotha until they hear their own.

These crossings of the Waste Land seem, despite their differences of genre and tonality, remarkable for their similarities. And what are we to infer from the persistence of their iconography? Firstly, that far from being an image of exclusively twentieth-century alienation and despair, the Waste Land is perceived as a timeless image of the human condition, the nightmare of history, that has no end this side of Golgotha. However, the persistent representation of the trees marking the extremities of that terrain – and particularly their representation by non-Christians – indicates the archetypal power of the Christian story. Lastly, I am led by the example of Sassoon and Eliot, who made their crossings without the shield of faith, to wonder whether the icons themselves might not sometimes be stepping-stones across the Slough of Despond; whether representations of some stage of the journey from the Garden to Golgotha – musical, pictorial, sculptural, as well as textual representations – might not be catalysts in the experience of conversion.

CHAPTER 10

War and peace

Central to British mythology of the First World War is the figure of the poet who descends like Orpheus into the Underworld, like Dante into the Inferno, and comes back singing of what he has seen. Several of the poets also wrote immensely successful prose accounts – sometimes lightly fictionalized – of their underworldly experience, with the result that British novels of the war have tended to be over-shadowed by those memoirs and by translations of such foreign masterpieces as Henri Barbusse's *Le Feu* (published in English as *Under Fire*, 1917) and Erich Maria Remarque's *Im Westen Nichts Neues* (published in English as *All Quiet on the Western Front*, 1939.) Sometimes, too, the often lethal legacy of the war in novels written after it – novels in which the violence has already occurred, as in Greek tragedy, off-stage – tends to be obscured by other events.

Virginia Woolf's *Mrs Dalloway* (1925) opens in

the middle of June. The War was over, except for someone like Mrs Foxcroft at the Embassy last night eating her heart out because that nice boy was killed and now the old Manor House must go to a cousin; or Lady Bexborough who opened a bazaar, they said, with the telegram in her hand, John, her favourite killed; but it was over; thank Heaven – over.[1]

'The War was over, *except* …' At the centre of the novel, at the centre of Clarissa Dalloway's world, of Virginia Woolf's world, are the exceptions that show in a very real sense that the war was not over. More will be heard of Lady Bexborough, a figure based on Lady Desborough, mother of Julian Grenfell, whose poem 'Into Battle' had been printed in *The Times* on 24 April 1915, the same day as his obituary.

Richard Dalloway, walking home, reflects:

Really it was a miracle thinking of the war, and thousands of poor chaps, with all their lives before them, shovelled together, already half forgotten; it was a miracle. Here he was walking across London to say to Clarissa in so many words that he loved her.[2]

He may have half forgotten those poor chaps, but it is the tragedy of Septimus Warren Smith that he cannot forget Evans, his officer, killed just before the Armistice. Woolf's own experience of mental disturbance admits her to the horrors of Septimus Warren Smith's shell-shocked hallucinations: 'A voice spoke from behind the screen. Evans was speaking. The dead were with him. "Evans, Evans!" he cried.'[3] The dead are with him more palpably than the living, but finally it is the ignorance and insensitivity of the doctor who refuses to acknowledge this that drives him to his suicide. Septimus had been decorated for bravery in the war, but when he hurls himself from the window, 'down on to Mrs Filmer's area railings', the doctor exclaims 'The coward!' So at last the war intrudes on Mrs Dalloway's party and her consciousness: 'The clock began striking. The young man had killed himself.'[4] That sentence tolls in her head like a refrain, like Big Ben striking the hour. 'The War was over, except ...

Two years later, Woolf muses in her diary:

I luxuriate most in a whole day alone [...] slipping tranquilly off into the deep water of my own thoughts navigating the underworld [...] I am making up 'To the Lighthouse' – the sea is to be heard all

through it. I have an idea that I will invent a new name for my books
to supplant 'novel'. A new – by Virginia Woolf. But what? Elegy?[5]

To the Lighthouse is an elegy for her parents, for the world of
her childhood, a world destroyed by the Great War. The
elegy commemorates, but also questions. Mrs Ramsay is
aware 'that her daughters – Prue, Nancy, Rose – could
sport with infidel ideas [...] there was in all their minds a
mute questioning of deference and chivalry'.[6] Half a lifetime
and millions of lives later, Julia Stephen's daughter Virginia
(no longer mute) can be heard questioning deference and
chivalry as she depicts Mr Ramsay terrifying Lily Briscoe:

Indeed, he almost knocked her easel over, coming down upon her
with his hands waving, shouting out 'Boldly we rode and well', but,
mercifully, he turned sharp, and rode off, to die gloriously she
supposed upon the heights of Balaclava. Never was anybody at
once so ridiculous and so alarming.[7]

'The Charge of the Light Brigade' is Mr Ramsay's theme-
song, intoned over and over in Part I of the novel. It celebrates
a military episode far removed from that of which we hear in a
documentary aside in Part II: '[A shell exploded. Twenty or
thirty young men were blown up in France, among them
Andrew Ramsay, whose death, mercifully, was instantane-
ous.]'[8] Was it twenty, or was it thirty? One might think it
important, but when the casualty figures are in thousands or in
tens of thousands, who cares whether it was twenty or thirty?
So much for Andrew's father's fantasies of chivalric death and
glory.

   The Great War is, in every sense, at the centre of *To the
Lighthouse*, although we only hear it off-stage in the 'Time
Passes' section. When we emerge from that dark tunnel, the
world has changed; and we are surely meant to understand that
it has been changed in part by the awful result of those male

fantasies of death and glory represented by Mr Ramsay's *pre-war* favourite poem. In Part III he intones not Tennyson's 'Charge of the Light Brigade' but Cowper's 'The Castaway'; death and glory having been replaced by death without glory, fantasy by the reality of a depressive widower:

> No voice divine the storm allayed,
>   No light propitious shone,
> When, snatched from all effectual aid,
>   We perished, each alone;
> But I beneath a rougher sea,
> And whelmed in deeper gulfs than he.

One of the most searching examinations in fiction of post-war England and the English was, in fact, started before the war. In 1912, the year D.H. Lawrence met and fell in love with Frieda Weekley, he began a novel he planned to call 'The Sisters'. It was to be a more searching examination of the nature of love than he had previously attempted, but was set aside in 1914. The first half of what he retitled *The Wedding Ring* (a novel rejected by Methuen in 1914) became *The Rainbow*, which was attacked by reviewers for its overt sexuality, then withdrawn from sale and, finally, banned for obscenity in November 1915. Disillusioned with England and hating the war, Lawrence retreated to Cornwall and the following spring started revising the second half of 'The Sisters' manuscript. After rewriting it twice, he had a finished version of what had become *Women in Love* twelve months after the banning of *The Rainbow*. This again was rejected by publishers, and only in 1921 did the final version appear.

Lawrence's experience of love had deepened during the painfully protracted gestation of his novel, and his view of England and the English had darkened. The book's original title survives in that of its opening chapter, 'Sisters', where the 'flame'-like Ursula and the 'cold' Gudrun meet their

matching men, Rupert Birkin and Gerald Crich. To Gudrun,
Gerald looked

> pure as an arctic thing. Perhaps he was thirty years old, perhaps
> more. His gleaming beauty, maleness, like a young, good-humoured
> smiling wolf, did not blind her to the significant, sinister stillness in
> his bearing, the lurking danger of his unsubdued temper. 'His totem
> is the wolf,' she repeated to herself.[9]

Gudrun's first impression is confirmed as his portrait
emerges under Lawrence's hand: 'Gerald was Cain, if anybody. [...] Gerald as a boy had accidentally killed his
brother.'[10] His old nurse's testimony seems to call into
question the nature of that accident: 'that Gerald was a
demon if ever there was one, a proper demon, ay, at six
months old'.[11] The narrator tells us that 'During his childhood and his boyhood [Gerald] had wanted a sort of savagedom. The days of Homer were his ideal, when a man was
chief of an army of heroes.'[12] He sounds like Julian Grenfell
and any number of other public schoolboys with a classical
education. 'School had been torture to him', we learn. 'Yet
he had not questioned whether one should go through this
torture.'[13] Confirming the law that 'Those to whom evil is
done / Do evil in return',[14] Gerald as a boy 'was filled with
the wildest excitement and delight' when soldiers came to
break a strike at his mine-owner father's pit-head. 'He
longed to go with the soldiers to shoot the men.'[15]

Leaving school, he refused to go to Oxford and was then
offered an opportunity to indulge the appetite for savagedom
that the miners' strike had not assuaged: 'he must try war'.[16]
We are told nothing of his wartime experience; only that
when it was over he resigned his commission.[17] One might
expect someone who had survived 'the torture of lying
machinally shelled'[18] at Gallipoli or on the Western Front

to question the social benefits of the new machines. Not so Gerald Crich, 'soldier, [...] explorer and a Napoleon of industry',[19] as he became on his return home, assuming managerial responsibility in his father's firm.

'Now he had a vision of power':[20] the power of machines to enforce the managerial will and extend its reach.

He was the God of the machine. [...]
  And it was his will to subjugate Matter to his own ends. The subjugation itself was the point, the *fight* was the be-all, the fruits of *victory* were mere results. [...] His will was now, to take the coal out of the earth, profitably. The profit was merely the condition of *victory*, but the *victory* itself lay in the feat achieved. He vibrated with zest before the *challenge*. Every day he was in the mines, examining, testing, he consulted experts, he gradually gathered the whole situation into his mind, as *a general grasps the plan of his campaign*. [My italics][21]

Gerald's use of *subjugate/subjugation* indicates an unconscious belief in industrialization as a continuation of war by other means, and his military imagery contrasts brutally with the Christian idiom clothing his father's confused philanthropy:

He wanted to be a pure Christian, one and equal with all men. He even wanted to give away all he had, to the poor. Yet he was a great promoter of industry, and he knew perfectly that he must keep his goods and keep his authority.[22]

To Gerald, 'The whole Christian attitude of love and self-sacrifice was old hat.' Not the least of the novel's ironies is the 'arctic' warrior's suicide (a prohibited perversion of Christian self-sacrifice) on the snow-slope. Lawrence would seem to imply that, but for the war, Gerald's life, the lives of his work-force and their families – and, by extension, the society they represent – might have followed a more life-enhancing trajectory. His double portrait of Victorian father and Edwardian soldier son stands at the centre of a nation altered forever by the Great War.

The war is again all but invisibly at the centre of L.P. Hartley's fine novel, *The Go-Between* (1953), another study of martial fantasy, sex, and death in a divided nation. Hartley announces a debt to Proust in his opening sentence: 'The past is a foreign country: they do things differently there.' And the sixty-year-old narrator (seven years younger than the novelist) revisits that country to exhume the secret buried by a traumatized subconscious in his diary for the year 1900. Opening that book – for the first time in almost fifty years – he sees

round the year thus confidently heralded, the first year of the century, winged with hope, clustered the signs of the zodiac, each somehow contriving to suggest a plenitude of life and power, each glorious, though differing from the others in glory. [...]

In my zodiacal fantasies there was one jarring note, to which, when I indulged them, I tried not to listen, for it flawed the experience. This was my own role in it. [...]

I was between twelve and thirteen, and I wanted to think of myself as a man.

There were only two candidates, the Archer and the Water-carrier [...] I leaned to the Archer as the more romantic, and because the idea of shooting appealed to me.[23]

The boy's martial fantasies of glory are encouraged by his admiration for an aristocratic veteran of the Boer War (then in progress) whom he meets when spending the long hot summer of 1900 at a school friend's country house. As the drama unfolds, the boy becomes neither Archer nor Water-carrier, but instead a Go-between, carrying messages between the aristocratic veteran (the Archer), a tenant farmer (the Water-Carrier), and the daughter of the Big House (the Virgin of the zodiac), for whose favours the two men are competing.

The Boer War – and again the conflict is off-stage – plays at once a literal and a metaphorical role in the book. When the owners and guests of the Big House field a cricket team to play the village, the twelve-year-old narrator sees the match in military terms:

> it crossed my mind that perhaps the village team were like the Boers, who did not have much in the way of equipment by our standards, but could give a good account of themselves, none the less [...]
>
> [...] disasters followed. [...] These Boers in their motley raiment, triumphantly throwing the ball into the air after each kill, how I disliked them! The spectators disposed along the boundary, standing, sitting, lying, or propped against trees, I imagined to be animated by a revolutionary spirit, and revelling in the downfall of their betters.[24]

Hartley's subject is the boy's fall from innocence into traumatic experience; that action set in the sunlit garden of late-Victorian England, where the snake is already at work. A divided and corrupted society is moving towards its own expulsion from the garden into the traumatic experience of the trenches. Far from realizing the dream of glory offered by his diary's constellation of zodiacal signs, the boy is forced to betray his exploitative friends, Virgin and Water-carrier, and witness their love-making. His unwilling betrayal results in – causes, it must seem to him – the Water-carrier's self-inflicted death by gunshot. And so the martial dream turns to nightmare. From this he escapes into neurasthenic amnesia, such as Louis Simpson would suffer in the wake of the Second World War; a form of forgetting that Wilfred Owen might have preferred to nightmares of a sentry he had positioned and for whose subsequent blinding he felt responsible: 'I try not to remember these things now', he wrote, but when he tries to forget them, he finds 'Eyeballs, huge-bulged like squids', / Watch my dreams still.'[25]

Chronologically, the Great War is at the centre of *The Go-Between* in much the same way as it is at the centre of *To the Lighthouse*, although Hartley's narrator only mentions it once. Having confronted – and, one must hope, exorcised – the horrors that caused his amnesia, he looks back on his life as a bachelor librarian:

the life of facts proved no bad substitute for the facts of life. It did not let me down; on the contrary, it upheld me and probably saved my life; for when the first war came, my skill in marshalling facts was held to be more important than any service I was likely to perform on the field. So I missed that experience, along with many others, spooning among them.[26]

The Big House of Hartley's novel, with its elaborate hierarchy of family, guests, and servants, is an emblem of late-Victorian society. Called Brandham Hall, it does *brand them all*. It is another Heartbreak House, and in Bernard Shaw's Preface to the play of that title, he excoriates the selfish indolence of the owners of Heartbreak House and Horseback Hall.

They hated politics. They did not wish to realise Utopia for the common people: they wished to realise their favourite fictions and poems in their own lives; and, when they could, they lived without scruple on incomes which they did nothing to earn. [...] They took the only part of our society in which there was leisure for high culture, and made it an economic, political, and, as far as practicable, a moral vacuum.[27]

Unlike the non-combatants, Woolf, Lawrence, and Hartley, Ford Madox Ford enlisted at forty-one and saw action in the Battle of the Somme, not from a front-line trench but close enough to be blown up and gassed. Severely concussed by an exploding shell, he lost his memory like the Go-between and Louis Simpson, and for some days was unable to remember even his own name. He survived that descent into the underworld of trenches and, in 1918, published a book of survivors' songs, *On Heaven and Poems Written on Active Service*. These have little of the vision, precision, or lyrical intensity of his younger contemporaries, Blunden, Owen, Rosenberg, and Sassoon, but the eye and ear of the poet Ford Madox Hueffer were to play their part in creating the modernist masterpiece of the novelist Ford Madox Ford (who changed his name in 1919), the quartet now known as *Parade's End*. This consists of *Some Do Not* (1924), *No More Parades* (1925), *A Man Could Stand Up* (1926), and *Last Post* (1928), and their action is played out against the indolent background of Heartbreak House and Horseback Hall. Unlike the war memoirs of his fellow poets, Ford's fictional quartet is both centred on the war and as concerned as the novels of Woolf, Lawrence, and Hartley with the painful transition from pre-war to post-war England.

The story of Christopher Tietjens began to take shape in his imagination shortly after he had been invalided home from the Western Front. His memory was haunted by the dead and, increasingly, by one dead man in particular. Arthur Marwood had been the son of a well-known Yorkshire family, a brilliant mathematician in the government office of statistics, and Ford's associate in publishing the *English Review*. 'He possessed', said Ford, 'the clear, eighteenth century English mind which has disappeared from the earth, leaving the earth very much the poorer.'[28] Tuberculosis forced him into inactive retirement, but he re-emerged from his friend's imagination metamorphosed into Christopher Tietjens.

I seemed [said Ford] to see him stand in some high place in France during the period of hostilities taking in not only what was visible but all the causes and all the motive powers of infinitely distant places. And I seemed to hear his infinitely scornful comment on those places. It was as if he lived again.[29]

Ford made the hero of his tetralogy a good deal more attractive than he makes Marwood sound. In Christopher Tietjens, the half-German novelist created a German Romantic's idealization of an English gentleman. More 'bohemian' than 'gentleman' himself, Ford had studied the type with an artist's eye and loaded him with history. Like other artists with a strong sense of tradition – Tennyson dreaming of Camelot, Yeats of an eighteenth-century 'Romantic Ireland' – he endowed his hero with a past that never existed. Ford's imagination was rooted in an eighteenth-century 'Romantic England' of pastoral patriarchy: a High Tory earth under a High Tory heaven, in which Tietjens can picture the Almighty

as, on a colossal scale, a great English Landowner, benevolently awful, a colossal duke who never left his study and was thus invisible, but knowing all about the estate down to the last hind at the home farm and the last oak; Christ, an almost too benevolent Land Steward, son of the Owner, knowing all about the estate down to the last child at the porter's lodge, apt to be got round by the more detrimental tenants; the Third Person of the Trinity, the spirit of the estate [...][30]

Satirical as this may seem, it illustrates a serious theme. *Christ*opher *Teach*-ens, younger son of an English Landowner, is presented as a Christ-like figure.[31] 'He wants', says his awful, adulterous wife Sylvia, 'to play the part of Jesus Christ';[32] and again, 'Our Lord was a gentleman ... Christopher is playing at being our Lord calling on the woman taken in adultery.'[33] He gives to the poor; has remarkable prophetic and telepathic power; is said to have a 'mania for sacrificing himself';[34] and

on four occasions in the last volume his saintliness is mentioned. This identification may have been suggested or reinforced by the image, popular in the early years of the war, of
the soldier as a type of Christ. Commonly used in the press
and the pulpit, it also found its way into poems such as Owen's
'Greater Love' ('Greater love hath no man than this, that a
man lay down his life for his friends')[35] and Sassoon's 'The
Redeemer'.[36]

Tietjens's story begins in time of peace. *Some Do Not* opens
with an image of comfort, tranquillity, and good order:

> they were of the English public official class – sat in the perfectly
> appointed railway carriage. The leather straps to the windows were
> of virgin newness; the mirrors beneath the new luggage racks
> immaculate as if they had reflected very little; the bulging upholstery
> in its luxuriant, regulated curves was scarlet and yellow in an
> intricate, minute dragon pattern, the design of a geometrician in
> Cologne. The compartment smelt faintly, hygienically of admirable
> varnish; the train ran as smoothly – Tietjens remembered thinking –
> as British gilt-edged securities.[37]

The carriage may be 'perfectly appointed', but the fact that
its mirrors look as if they 'had reflected very little' might be
thought to suggest something about 'the English public
official class'. The train may have run 'as smoothly [...] as
British gilt-edged securities', but in fact it was not running
from London to Rye as its passengers supposed. It was
running instead from the past into the future, into the
Waste Land of the war, where Tietjens will find himself
preparing to send a draft of Canadian troops 'up the line to
death'. But where are they? Held up somewhere by a train
crash. So what will happen to the men they are supposed to
relieve? Now the Canadians have been found. And now the
original orders have been found. But now the original orders
have been countermanded.

All that may still be in the future, but Tietjens, the brilliant statistician, can foresee the future. He had prophesied

that about the time grouse-shooting began, in 1914, a European conflagration would take place which would shut up half the houses in Mayfair and beggar their inhabitants. He had patiently supported his prophecy with financial statistics as to the approaching bankruptcy of various European powers and the growingly acquisitive skill and rapacity of the inhabitants of Great Britain.[38]

In one of the time-shifts characteristic of Ford's narrative strategy, we see Tietjens (in a flash-forward) returned from the war and greatly changed. Sylvia asks him

'What really happened to you in France? What is really the matter with your memory? Or your brain, is it?'
He said carefully:
'It's half of it, an irregular piece of it, dead. Or rather pale. Without a proper blood supply.... So a great portion of it, in the shape of memory, has gone.' [...]
[He] had at last convinced her that he had not been, for the last four months, acting hypochondriacal or merely lying to obtain sympathy or extended sick leave. Amongst Sylvia's friends a wangle known as shell-shock was cynically laughed at and quite approved of.[39]

Tietjens is made of tougher stuff than Woolf's shell-shocked Septimus Warren Smith. He reloads his memory by reading the *Encyclopedia Britannica* and prepares to return to the trenches.

Time-shifts like this – juxtaposing peacetime with wartime – point up the cruelty and moral chaos they have in common. Sylvia betrays her husband, runs off with another man and, when she runs back, delights to torment him with the possibility that he may not be the father of her son. His banker dishonours Tietjens's cheques so that he will be disgraced and (his banker hopes) divorced by Sylvia whom *he* wishes to marry. Any last doubt we may have that their society is rotten is removed when Tietjens's false friend Macmaster is knighted for work that Tietjens did for him; the dishonest stay-at-home elevated, the honest patriot ruined. All this Tietjens stoically endures in a manner reminiscent of the Old Testament prophecy of Christ: 'as a sheep before her shearers is dumb, so he opened not his mouth'.[40] His decency, goodness, generosity compound his problems. These qualities serve as a reproach to others and lead them to treat him worse.

The second volume of the tetralogy, *No More Parades* (a phrase repeated again and again until it comes to have the force of a refrain), brings us to within range of the front. Enter then Captain McKechnie, whose wife has betrayed him, with an Egyptologist, and a private soldier, O Nine Morgan, whose wife has betrayed him with a prize-fighter. Tietjens has just rejected the private's application for compassionate leave (having been advised that the prize-fighter would probably kill him) when a shell saves the prize-fighter that effort. The scene will haunt Tietjens's memory as Wilfred Owen was haunted by the eyes of his blinded sentry. At such moments Tietjens is sustained by the talismanic thought of the poet George Herbert, on a hill above his country parsonage, composing the lines:

> Sweet day, so cool, so calm, so bright,
> The bridal of the earth and sky [...][41]

The poem offers a vision of sanity and serenity, reminding him of a natural order in which – despite the unnatural disorder surrounding him – he still believes. If he can hold on to that, perhaps he will survive to see peace again: peace – when a man could stand up on a hill.

The third volume takes its title from this phrase: *A Man Could Stand Up*. It opens on Armistice Day 1918 with a telephone call telling us that Tietjens has survived, has come home, but has apparently lost his mind. A time-shift then takes us back to a day in the trenches where Tietjens is in command of his regiment, its over-taxed Colonel having slid into drunkenness. This extended flashback is presented mainly as impressionistic interior monologue. A modernist *tour de force*, it reaches its climax when a shell falls, burying Tietjens, young Lieutenant Aranjuez, and Lance-Corporal Duckett. Tietjens, as always, is victim; in keeping with his Christ-like role, we never see him shooting or injuring anybody. On this occasion, he crawls out of the sucking mud and sets to work rescuing Aranjuez. 'If Tietjens's heroism takes the form of salvation,' Max Saunders reminds us, 'his attempts to save are themselves ambiguous. Lance-Corporal Duckett is already dead. Aranjuez gets shot in the eye while Tietjens is carrying him, which causes Tietjens to feel that far from saving him he has actually been responsible for injuring him.'[42] Such failures do not invalidate the Christ-like parallel. Tietjens is not a miracle-worker, but Christ saved neither himself nor those crucified with him; and the salvation he promised his disciples did not always preclude martyrdom. Tietjens is not martyred. Here, fighting for his sanity, he seizes on peaceable analogies and takes strength from the talismanic vision of what peace means: standing up on a hill, 'On the moors above Groby. April sunlight. Lots of sunlight and larks.'[43] No sooner has he extricated the boy, than he has to face another hazard, an inspecting General, who explodes with fury at his filthy appearance and relieves him of his command.

With that ironic twist, the war ends for Christopher Tietjens. Another time-shift returns us to Armistice Day, when he and the young woman he loves, Valentine Wannop, are reunited in his empty London house; she quoting to herself the biblical Song of Solomon (symbolic of Christ's marriage to his Church). But then, just as the war scenes were interrupted with memories of peacetime, so now the lovers' reunion is interrupted with reminders of war. The mad officer McKechnie knocks at Tietjens's door. Shell-shocked, he has lost his mind. Then Aranjuez turns up – he has lost an eye – and, after him, an officer who has lost an arm. The books ends with a wild party and a dance parodic of the marriage dance that ends so many comedies on the stage:

They were prancing. The whole world round them was yelling and prancing round. They were the centre of unending roaring circles. The man with the eye-glass had stuck a half-crown in his other eye.[44]

This offers a bitter contrast to Sassoon's better-known response to the Armistice:

> Everyone's voice was suddenly lifted;
> And beauty came like the setting sun:
> My heart was shaken with tears; and horror
> Drifted away ... O, but Everyone
> Was a bird; and the song was wordless; the
>   singing will never be done.[45]

A reader of Ford's twentieth-century *War and Peace* might expect that, with the return of peace, the modernist fragmentation so well suited to the wartime narrative might give place to the traditional linear progression of the pre-war narrative. That, however, would imply a new peace resembling the old; order succeeding the anarchic disorder of war, which both the structure and texture of *Last Post* show it has not. Robie Macauley defines its dark structure with an illuminating analogy:

Christopher Tietjens is present physically for only one moment at the end of the book and yet he is the most central being in it. The system of the book might be thought of as a temporarily eclipsed sun with a number of visible satellite consciousnesses surrounding and defining its position. There are nine relative and interconnected interior monologues representing several people in the general vicinity of the cottage to which Christopher and Valentine and [Christopher's older brother] Mark and his long-time French mistress (now his wife) have gone after the war.[46]

In the midst of battle, Tietjens had clung to a pastoral vision of 'the moors above Groby', the family's country house. Peace found his vision translated into rural (rather than pastoral) reality. The rise of the monied middle class at the expense of the landed gentry – apparent in the aristocratic Archer's leasing of Brandham Hall to the middle-class Virgin's father in *The Go-Between* – has necessitated the lease of Groby Hall to tenants with no feeling for Tietjens family tradition. As Mark Tietjens, head of the family, is dying in a crowded cottage, he hears that the ancestral Groby Great Tree has been felled:

Christopher was at the foot of his bed. Holding a bicycle and a lump of wood. Aromatic wood, a chunk sawn from a tree. His face was white; his eyes stuck out. Blue pebbles. He gazed at his brother and said:
'Half Groby wall is down. Your bedroom's wrecked. I found your case of sea-birds thrown on a rubble heap.'[47]

Before Mark dies, however, holding the hand of his brother's new wife Valentine, he breaks a long silence to speak of the child shortly to be born to her and Christopher. Many people see the Last Word of Ford's tetralogy as that of its title, which echoes a prophecy of the adjutant at the disbanding of the battalion:

'the adjutant saying *There will be no more parades* ... For there won't. There won't, there damn well won't. ... No more Hope, no more Glory, no more parades for you and me any more. Nor for the country ... nor for the world, I dare say ... None ... Gone ... Na poo, finny!'[48]

In its context, this is offered as bad news, but at the end of a war that had claimed millions of lives and ruined many more, it strikes a more optimistic note. This is confirmed by the fact that Christopher and Valentine are in love; in renewed contact with the earth, living on what their hands can grow; and about to have a child to inherit their values and help form a society saner than that shattered by the Great War. For *Parade's End*, as for *Women in Love*, the war is over and life-renewing peace a possibility unimaginable in the No Man's Landscape of Jones's *In Parenthesis*, Blunden's *Undertones of War*, and many other memoirs of the Western Front.

CHAPTER 11

The fire from heaven

The image of the trench is so ubiquitous in writings about the First World War that one can forget it was fought in the air as well as on the ground. Yeats had eulogized and elegized 'An Irish Airman', Major Robert Gregory, RFC, MC, Legion of Honour, killed on the Italian Front in January 1918. And just as the trench had its mythic dimension as the mouth of hell, so 'the daring young men in their flying machines' were to enter popular mythology as heirs to the wings of Daedalus and Icarus. The aviator as hero becomes a common figure in the literature of the 1930s. At the hopeful start of that decade, Cecil Day Lewis begins a poem 'Come out in the sun, for a man is born today!' and prophesies:

> Now shall the airman vertically banking
> Out of the blue write a new sky-sign [...][1]

When he wants to celebrate his *literary* hero, Auden, he elevates him to the skies: 'Look west, Wystan, lone flyer, birdman, my bully boy!' And in *A Time to Dance* (1935), his modern mini-*Odyssey* begins:

> Sing we the two lieutenants, Parer and M'Intosh,
> After the War wishing to hie them home to Australia,
> Planned they would take a high way, a hazardous crazy air-way:
> Death their foregone conclusion, a flight headlong to failure,

We said. For no silver posh
Plane was their pigeon, no dandy dancer quick-stepping through
    heaven,
But a craft of obsolete design, a condemned D. H. nine;
Sold for a song it was, patched up though to write an heroic
Line across the world as it reeled on its obstinate stoic
Course to that southern haven.[2]

As the decade advanced and darkened, however, the image
of the aviator began to acquire other associations. At the start
of Yeats's poem 'Lapis Lazuli', written in the last months of
the Spanish Civil War, hysterical women say:

> everybody knows or else should know
> That if nothing drastic is done
> Aeroplane and Zeppelin will come out,
> Pitch like King Billy bomb-balls in
> Until the town lie beaten flat.[3]

After the indiscriminate killing of civilians in a bombing raid —
by German aircraft — on the Spanish town of Guernica in 1937,
everybody knew or else should have known that the emblem
of the Next War would be the bomb, the fire from heaven.

So it proved. On 1 September 1939, Germany, in pursuit
of imperial ambitions and without warning, launched a
savage attack on Poland by land and air. Two days later,
Britain and France declared war on Germany. By the end of
the month, Germany and her ally Russia had between them
defeated and partitioned Poland. It was then Russia's turn
to attack Finland and, in April 1940, Germany invaded
Denmark and Norway. For Britain and France, the period
of inactivity that came to be known as "The Phoney
War" ended in May, when the German Army overran
Luxembourg, invaded the Netherlands and Belgium, and
their armoured columns raced for the English Channel.
Cut off, the British forces were evacuated by sea, with

heavy losses, from Dunkirk and, in June, France signed an armistice with Germany. In August, as prelude to an invasion, the German Air Force, the Luftwaffe, attacked England. Over the months that followed, the fighter pilots of the Royal Air Force challenged the enemy bombers' nightly Blitz of London and other major cities. The Battle of Britain, as it came to be called, cost the Luftwaffe 2,300 planes, the RAF 900. And the heroes of that battle were the fighter pilots who, in their bullet-riddled Spitfires and Hurricanes, eventually caused the Germans to abandon their plans for invasion. One of those pilots, Richard Hillary, wrote a memoir in the tradition of the *Bildungsroman* (the novel of education) that was highly influential in helping to crystallize and complicate the image of the aviator as hero.

His book, *The Last Enemy* (published in 1942), begins with a Proem, or preamble, which introduces us to 603 Squadron as it takes off to engage the German raiders. When the narrator confesses to 'the usual sick feeling in the pit of the stomach, as though I was about to row a race', one wonders whether this signals a return to the War-as-Sport theme so common in literature of the First World War. It does. But first we see him shot down – 'thinking "So this is it!" and putting both hands to [his] eyes' (a detail of some significance in the light of what follows).[4] He is rescued from the English Channel, horribly burned, and the Proem ends: 'The foundations of an experience of which this crash was, if not the climax, at least the turning point were laid in Oxford before the war.'[5]

Book One goes back in time to Hillary's life at university, of which he says:

Perhaps as good a cross-section of opinion and sentiment as any at Oxford was to be found in Trinity, the college where I spent those two years rowing a great deal, flying a little – I was a member of the University Air Squadron – and reading somewhat.[6]

He describes a community of well-to-do and snobbish young men, radiating an 'alert Philistinism', and reports a conversation with a pacifist friend about what they would do in the event of war:

I told him [...] I should of course join the Air Force. 'In the first place,' I said, 'I shall get paid and have good food. Secondly, I have none of your sentiments about killing, much as I admire them. In a fighter plane, I believe, we have found a way to return to war as it ought to be, war which is individual combat between two people, in which one either kills or is killed. It's exciting, it's individual, and it's disinterested. I shan't be sitting behind a long-range gun working out how to kill people sixty miles away. I shan't get maimed: either I shall get killed or I shall get a few pleasant putty medals and enjoy being stared at in a night club. Your unfortunate convictions, worthy as they are, will get you at best a few white feathers, and at worst locked up.'

'Thank god,' said David, 'that I at least have the courage of my convictions.'[7]

We know from the Proem that the narrator was to be badly burned, and so sense an irony in the statement 'I shan't get maimed', though the full and bitter force of that irony will only be revealed later.

In July 1938, Hillary was one of a group of Oxford oarsmen who went to row in a German regatta for what had been known as the Kaiser Fours, but had recently become General Goering's Prize Fours. Looking back at that race from 1942, he finds it

a surprisingly accurate pointer to the course of the war. We were quite untrained, lacked any form of organization and were really quite hopelessly casual. We even arrived late at the start, where all five German crews were lined up, eager to go.[8]

At the half-way mark they were five lengths behind, but as they passed under a bridge somebody spat at them.

It was a tactical error. Sammy Stockton, who was stroking the boat, took us up the next half of the course as though pursued by all the fiends in hell and we won the race by two-fifths of a second. General Goering had to surrender his cup and we took it back with us to England. It was a gold shell-case mounted with the German eagle and disgraced our rooms in Oxford for nearly a year until we could stand it no longer and sent it back through the German Embassy.[9]

Hillary admits that, for purely selfish reasons, he welcomed the war. It 'solved all problems of a career, and promised a chance of self-realization that would normally take years to achieve.'[10] He imagined himself, as a would-be writer, acquiring the imaginative capital on which he would draw once the war was over. Embarking on what one might call his 'higher education', he has no awareness of human suffering. His first feeling after his first kill was

of the essential rightness of it all […] I realized in that moment just how lucky a fighter pilot is. He has none of the personalized emotions of the soldier, handed a rifle and bayonet and told to charge. He does not even have to share the dangerous emotions of the bomber pilot who night after night must experience that childhood longing for smashing things. The fighter pilot's emotions are those of the duellist – cool, precise, impersonal.[11]

But, he adds, 'From this flight Broody Benson did not return', introducing what shortly comes to have the force of a refrain: 'From this flight [Larry Cunningham/Bubble Waterston] did not return.'

From one such mission he himself returns burned almost beyond recognition. There follows a painful account of plastic surgery undergone in a medical unit known as 'the Beauty Shop', where he is fitted with new eyelids. All this he endures – if one can trust the evidence of his book – with stoical courage and with no sign of bitterness towards the enemy or Fate or others more lucky than himself. In this, he abides by the duellist's code he had earlier articulated, but one does begin to sense that his vaunted impersonality is beginning to be eroded by a visit from the lifeboat crew who had rescued him; by the plight of his fellow patients; and (most of all) by the support of a friend's fiancée after his friend is killed. These prepare for the subsequent crisis – and the book clearly has a place in the long tradition of crisis-autobiography that extends from St Augustine's *Confessions* to Joyce's *Portrait of the Artist* and beyond – but it is from another woman, a stranger, that he learns his final lesson.

One evening in 1941 he is out of hospital and walking through London in an air-raid. He takes shelter in a pub, only to have it collapse about him from a direct hit. With his half-healed hands he helps to drag the masonry from a buried mother and child.

Finally we made a gap wide enough for the bed to be drawn out. The woman who lay there looked middle-aged. She lay on her back and her eyes were closed. Her face, through the dirt and streaked blood, was the face of a thousand working women; her body under the cotton night-dress was heavy. The nightdress was drawn up to her knees and one leg was twisted under her. There was no dignity about that figure.[12]

We realize that Hillary cares about dignity, and we remember the similar perception in John Cornford's 'Letter from Aragon': 'Death was not dignified.'[13] But this woman was not dead. She opens her eyes and, looking into his, with their grafted eyelids, says: 'I see they got you too.'[14] The man who had earlier imagined himself bemedalled, and enjoying 'being stared at in a night club', finds the reality very different and himself, for the first time, afraid:

I wanted to run, to run anywhere away from that scene, from myself, from the terror that was inside me, the terror of something that was about to happen and which I had not the power to stop.

It started small, small but insistent deep inside of me, sharp as a needle, then welling up uncontrollable, spurting, flowing over, choking me. I was drowning, helpless in a rage that caught and twisted and hurled me on, mouthing in a blind unthinking frenzy. I heard myself cursing, the words pouring out, shrill, meaningless, and as my mind cleared a little I knew that it was the woman I cursed. Yes, the women that I reviled, hating her that she should die like that for me to see, loathing that silly bloody twisted face that had said those words: 'I see they got you too.' That she should have spoken to me, why, oh Christ, to me? Could she not have died the next night, ten minutes later, or in the next street? Could she not have died without speaking, without raising those cow eyes to mine?

'I see they got you too.' All humanity had been in those few words, and I had cursed her. Slowly the frenzy died in me, the rage oozed out of me, leaving me cold, shivering, and bitterly ashamed. I had cursed her, cursed her, I realized as I grew calmer, for she had been the one thing that my rage surging uncontrollably had had to fasten on, the one thing to which my mind, overwhelmed by the sense of something so huge and beyond the range of thought, could cling. Her death was unjust, a crime, an outrage, a sin against mankind – weak inadequate words which even as they passed through my mind mocked me with their futility.

That that woman should so die was an enormity so great that it was terrifying in its implications, in its lifting of the veil on possibilities of thought so far beyond the grasp of the human mind. It was not just the German bombs, or the German Air Force, or even the German mentality, but a feeling of the very essence of anti-life that no words could convey. This was what I had been cursing – in part, for I had recognized in that moment what it was that Peter and the others had instantly recognized as evil and to be destroyed utterly. I saw now that it was not crime; it was Evil itself – something of which until then I had not even sensed the existence. And it was in the end, at bottom, myself against which I had raged, myself I had cursed. With awful clarity I was myself suddenly as I was. Great God, that I could have been so arrogant!'[15]

The unknown woman's opened eyes had opened his – those eyes over which he had put his hands in the blazing cockpit.

What finally brings him through his crisis is the recognition that he can make atonement by writing of what he has learnt:

I would write of these men [his fellow fighter pilots …] I would write for them and would write with them. They would be at my side. And to whom would I address this book, to whom would I be speaking when I spoke of these men? And that, too, I knew. To Humanity, for Humanity must be the public of any book. Yes, that despised Humanity which I had so scorned and ridiculed […][16]

If this seems unsubtle – in the same way, and for the same reason, that the coda to Cornford's 'Letter from Aragon' was unsubtle – we must remember the urgency of the occasion. Hillary was twenty-one when he wrote the book, and it is clear that he wrote it in the spirit of Wilfred Owen's Preface to his poems: 'All a poet can do today is warn. That is why the true Poets must be truthful.'

Hillary's intention was also to warn but, unlike Owen, he did not offer 'the whole truth and nothing but the truth'. His biographer, Sebastian Faulks, reveals that the final chapter of *The Last Enemy*, 'I See They Got You Too', was invented. 'He did change,' Faulks adds, 'but the process was slow.'[17] It cannot have been very slow, since Hillary was shot down in September 1940; appears to have begun writing in summer 1941; and had proofs of his book by October of that year. His change of heart about 'war as it ought to be' was evidently more gradual than the Pauline conversion he describes, but there seems no reason to doubt its authenticity, and it gives his narrative the dramatic climax a crisis-autobiography requires. The woman in the rubble may have been a fiction, but it is surely significant that so macho a 'duellist' should have shown himself converted by a woman.

Women had no need of conversion to 'that despised Humanity', and they made their voices heard in the poetry of those sulphurous days: Edith Sitwell with 'Still Falls the Rain: the Raids, 1940', and H.D. [Hilda Doolittle] with *The Walls do not Fall* (1944). At the same time, Eliot and MacNeice were both fire-watchers: Eliot taking his turn with the stirrup-pump and the sand-bucket on the roof of Faber and Faber. Embarking on the last of his *Four Quartets* in 1942, that experience provided an image for the trials through which the quester must pass on his way to the Chapel Perilous. *Little Gidding* completes the *Four Quartets*, and can also be seen as completing the larger quest whose first movement, *The Waste Land*, was undertaken in the wake of an earlier war. With the second section of *Little Gidding*, the reader moves from the English countryside to the fire-bombed city of MacNeice's 'Brother Fire' and 'The Streets of Laredo':[18]

> O early one morning I walked out like Agag,
> Early one morning to walk through the fire
> Dodging the pythons that leaked on the pavements
> With tinkle of glasses and tangle of wire;
>
> When grimed to the eyebrows I met an old fireman
> Who looked at me wryly and thus did he say:
> 'The streets of Laredo are closed to all traffic,
> We won't never master this joker today.
>
> 'O hold the branch tightly and wield the axe brightly,
> The bank is in powder, the banker's in hell,
> But loot is still free on the streets of Laredo
> And when we drive home we drive home on the bell.'

Eliot and H.D. were both American, as were two of the most powerful poetic witnesses to the war in the air. The first, Randall Jarrell enlisted in the US Army Air Corps at the age of twenty-eight, failed to qualify as a pilot, and served as a control-tower operator, working with B-29 bomber crews. His war poems are to be found in two books, *Little Friend, Little Friend* (1945) and *Losses* (1948).

The epigraph for the first is taken from an exchange between a bomber and its fighter escort. 'Then I heard the bomber call me in: "Little Friend, Little Friend, I got two engines on fire. Can you see me, Little Friend?" I said "I'm crossing right over you. Let's go home."' *Losses* was the stock euphemism for casualties – as in "Our losses were light today" – and both titles suggest Jarrell's concern with victims. His most famous victim was the subject of his poem, 'The Death of the Ball Turret Gunner':

> From my mother's sleep I fell into the State,
> And I hunched in its belly till my wet fur froze.
> Six miles from earth, loosed from its dream of life,
> I woke to black flak and nightmare fighters.
> When I died they washed me out of the turret with a hose.[19]

To get the full force of this, one has to know that a ball turret was a plexiglass sphere set into the belly of a bomber and contained two machine guns and one small man – he had to be small. When this gunner tracked with his machine gun a fighter attacking his bomber from below, he revolved with the turret. Hunched upside down in his little sphere, he looked like a foetus in a womb. Jarrell gives us a life compressed into five lines; the first of them recalling the Book of Genesis: 'And the Lord God caused a deep sleep to fall upon Adam, and he slept: and he took one of his ribs, and closed up the flesh instead thereof; And the rib, which the Lord God had taken from man, made he a woman.'[20] Eve was born into the state of innocence, from which she and Adam subsequently fell, which gives an ironic vibration to the Ball Turret Gunner's statement: 'From my mother's sleep I fell into the State' – both the nation-state and the state of experience – one brilliantly metamorphosed into metaphor: 'And I hunched in its belly till my wet fur froze.' That fur, the fleece lining of the airman's jacket and helmet, reminds us that man is one of the more savage members of the animal kingdom. This man wakens from a dream of life to the reality of death, 'to black flak and the nightmare fighters'. 'When I died they washed me out of the turret with a hose.' The euphemism of the first half of that sentence – 'When I died' (not 'When I was torn apart by shrapnel') – and the gentle verb 'washed' leave us quite unprepared for what follows. Only with the last word – 'hose' (and it would have been a *steam* hose) – does the full force of the abortion metaphor hit us. Aeroplanes and steam hoses are machines, and airmen are more dependent on machines than infantrymen. It is not, therefore, surprising that machines, and their murderous inhumanity, play a larger role in writings about the war in the air than in writings about the war on the ground.

James Dickey was a bomber pilot in the Pacific, and is forced to relive that experience – rather like Coleridge's Ancient Mariner – in his poem 'The Firebombing'.[21] This has two epigraphs. The first is from the German of Gunter Eich:

> *Denke daran, dass nacht den grossen Zerstörungen*
> *Jedermann beweisen wird, dass er unschuldig war.*[22]

The second, from the biblical Book of Job – 'Or hast thou an arm like God?'[23] – is echoed early in the poem as its suburbanite speaker remembers, twenty years before,

> some technical-minded stranger with my hands
> Is sitting in a glass treasure-hole of blue light,
> Having potential fire under the undeodorized arms
> Of his wings, on thin bomb-shackles,
> The 'tear-drop-shaped' 300-gallon drop-tanks
> Filled with napalm and gasoline.

Like some sort of mythological god, he takes off for Japan
and, in his recollection, obeys Gunter Eich's injunction –
'*Denke*':

Think of this   think of this

I did not think of my house
But think of my house now

Where the lawn mower rests on its laurels
Where the diet exists
For my own good   where I try to drop
Twenty years, eating figs in the pantry
Blinded by each and all
Of the eye-catching cans that gladly have caught my wife's eye
Until I cannot say
Where the screwdriver is   where the children
Get off the bus   where the new
Scoutmaster lives   where the fly
Hones his front legs   where the hammock folds
Its erotic daydreams   where the Sunday
School text for the day has been put   where the fire
Wood is [...]

He cannot now escape from thoughts of fire any more than
his victims then could escape from the reality:

Fire hangs   not yet fire
In the air above Beppu
For I am fulfilling

An 'anti-morale' raid upon it.
All leashes of dogs
Break under the first bomb, around those
In bed, or late in the public baths: around those
Who inch forward on their hands
Into medicinal waters.
Their heads come up with a roar
Of Chicago fire:
Come up with the carp pond showing

The bathhouse upside down,
Standing stiller to show it more
As I sail artistically over
The resort town followed by farms,
Singing and twisting
All the handles in heaven kicking
The small cattle off their feet
In a red costly blast
Flinging jelly over the walls
As in a chemical war-
fare field demonstration.
With fire of mine like a cat

Holding onto another man's walls,
My hat should crawl on my head
In streetcars, thinking of it,
The fat on my body should pale.

The poet recognizes the pilot's 'anti-morale' raid for what it was – Orwellian Newspeak for 'murder' – and hearing himself 'sail artistically over' the harmless civilian target, delivers a double indictment. He condemns the pilot for his self-congratulatory detachment then, the poet for his artistic detachment now, and goes on to make that implicit accusation explicit:

One is cool and enthralled in the cockpit,
Turned blue by the power of beauty,
In a pale treasure-hole of soft light
Deep in aesthetic contemplation,
Seeing the ponds catch fire
[…]
It is this detachment,
The honoured aesthetic evil,
The greatest sense of power in one's life,
That must be shed in bars, or by whatever
Means, by starvation
Visions in well-stocked pantries:

The moment when the moon sails in between
The tail-booms   the rudders nod   I swing
Over   directly over the heart
The *heart* of the fire.

The poet is honest enough to question the nature and form of
this confession, to question his motives in making an art-
object out of a murderous act. Would silence be better?
Wilfred Owen provided an answer when, in his Preface, he
wrote: 'All a poet can do today in warn. That is why the true
Poets must be truthful.' James Dickey persuades this reader, at
least, that 'The Firebombing' is essentially truthful.

Having completed his 'anti-morale' raid, the poet–pilot
heads for home and returns from past to present:

All this, and I am still hungry,
Still twenty years overweight, still unable
To get down there or see
What really happened.
                            But it may be that I could not,
If I tried, say to any
Who lived there, deep in my flames: say, in cold
Grinning sweat, as to another
Of these homeowners who are always curving
Near me down the different-grassed street: say
As though to the neighbor
I borrowed the hedge-clippers from
On the darker-grassed side of the two,
Come in, my house is yours, come in
If you can, if you
Can pass this unfired door. It is that I can imagine
At the threshold nothing
With its ears crackling off
Like powdery leaves,
Nothing with children of ashes, nothing not
Amiable, gentle, well-meaning,
A little nervous for no
Reason   a little worried   a little too loud

> Or too easygoing   nothing I haven't lived with
> For twenty years, still nothing not as
> American as I am, and proud of it.

> Absolution? Sentence? No matter;
> The thing itself is in that.

'I can imagine', he says, but what he imagines is then cancelled by the five-fold repetition of 'nothing'. His imagination, his poem, is not equal to its task. So has his confession earned him 'Absolution? Sentence?' Self-convicted, self-sentenced, he is condemned to repeat his confession every time 'The Firebombing' is read. Like the Ancient Mariner,

> The man hath penance done
> And penance more will do.

These and the other (relatively few) poems about the war in the air tend to be structurally less traditional – which is not to suggest they are better or worse – than the ground-war poems of Louis Simpson,[24] Lincoln Kirstein, Keith Douglas,[25] or Alun Lewis,[26] many of which show the influence of First World War trench poetry. In much the same way, the major novels of the war in the air, Joseph Heller's *Catch 22* (1961) and Kurt Vonnegut's *Slaughterhouse-Five* (1969), are structurally less traditional, more innovative, than such major novels of the war on the ground as Norman Mailer's *The Naked and the Dead* (1948) and Evelyn Waugh's *Sword of Honour* trilogy (1965).

These comparisons lend support to the hypothesis that, despite triumphant modernist examples of battlefield poetry and prose, David Jones's *In Parenthesis*[27] and Ford Madox Ford's *Parade's End* tetralogy, later writings about traditional warfare on the ground tend themselves to be traditional, whereas writings about the new war in the air tend to take new forms. Poetry and prose fiction, however, have proved unequal to the task of recording the dominant image of that war in its final form, the mushroom cloud. No imaginative writing has matched the power of the photographic image, though the absence of a towering cloud from the apocalyptic climax of J.G. Ballard's novel, *Empire of the Sun* (1984), an absence requiring us to imagine its presence elsewhere, contributes to the restrained intensity of that scene:

A flash of light filled the stadium, flaring over the stands in the south-west corner of the football field, as if an immense American bomb had exploded somewhere to the north-east of Shanghai. The sentry hesitated, looking over his shoulder as the light behind him grew more intense. It faded within the stadium, the looted furniture in the stands, the cars behind the goal posts, the prisoners on the grass. They were sitting on the floor of a furnace heated by a second sun.

Jim stared at his white hands and knees, and at the pinched face of the Japanese soldier, who seemed disconcerted by the light. Both of them were waiting for the rumble of sound that followed the bomb-flashes, but an unbroken silence lay over the stadium and the surrounding land, as if the sun had blinked, losing heart for a few seconds. Jim smiled at the Japanese, wishing that he could tell him that the light was a premonition of his death, the sight of his small soul joining the larger soul of the dying world.[28]

CHAPTER 12

Henry Reed and the Great Good Place

The author of 'Naming of Parts', probably the most anthologized English poem of the Second World War, has too often been held to be that and that only. Like Julian Grenfell, author of 'Into Battle', he is seen as the saddest freak of the literary fairground: the one-poem poet. His *Collected Poems* give the lie to that gross misperception.[1]

Henry Reed was born, in Birmingham, on 22 February 1914 and named after his father, a master bricklayer and foreman in charge of forcing at Nocks' Brickworks. Henry senior was nothing if not forceful, a serious drinker and womanizer, who as well as his legitimate children fathered an illegitimate son who died during the Second World War. In this, he may have been following ancestral precedent: family legend had it that the Reeds were descended from a bastard son of an eighteenth- or nineteenth-century Earl of Dudley. Henry senior's other enthusiasms included reading, but the literary abilities of his son Henry junior seem, paradoxically, to have been inherited from a mother who was illiterate. Born Mary Ann Ball, the eldest child of a large family that had migrated from Tipton to Birmingham, she could not be spared from her labours at home during what should have been her schooldays, and when, in her late middle age, her granddaughter tried, unsuccessfully, to teach her to read, she wept with frustration and shame. Mary Ann

Reed had a remarkable memory, however, and a well-stocked repertoire of fairy stories – told with great verve – and songs to enchant her children and grandchild.

A daughter, Gladys, born in 1908, was encouraged to make the most of the schooling her mother had not had. She was a good student and in due course became a good teacher, discovering her vocation in teaching her younger brother. Gladys played a crucial role in the education of Henry (or Hal, as he was known in the family, a name perhaps borrowed from Shakespeare's hero) and was to become and remain the most important woman in his life. He was not an easy child. On one occasion dismembering his teddy bear, he buried its head, limbs, and torso around the garden and went howling to his mother. She was obliged to exhume the scattered parts, wash, and reassemble them for the little tyrant. At the state primary school in Erdington, he clashed with a hated teacher who pronounced him educationally subnormal. A psychiatrist was called in and, having examined the child, claimed to have detected promise of mathematical genius.

Moving on to King Edward VI Grammar School in Aston, Reed specialized in Classics. Since Greek was not taught, he taught himself, and went on to win the Temperley Latin prize and a scholarship to Birmingham University. There he was taught and befriended – as were his Birmingham contemporaries Walter Allen and Reggie Smith – by a young Lecturer in the Classics Department, Louis MacNeice. Reed had a remarkable speaking voice and a gift for mimicry (and for assuming the accents of a class not his own), and, as an undergraduate, he acted in and produced plays, which may have led to his career in radio; in any case, for the rest of his life he delighted in the company of actors – partly perhaps because he was acting a part himself: that of the debonair, even aristocratic, literary man about town.

He gained a first-class degree at Birmingham in 1934 and wrote a notable thesis on Thomas Hardy, leaving the University two years later as its youngest MA. Like most of his Birmingham contemporaries, he had so far lived at home, but was not a happy member of the household. Hal was ashamed of his parents, or so they felt, and only his sister Gladys had much sympathy for the elegant butterfly struggling to break free from the Brummagem chrysalis. There was another factor, though how much Reed's parents knew of this is uncertain: he had had his first sexual, homosexual, experience when he was nineteen, and later had a tormented affair with a boy who developed paranoia. It was clearly time for him to leave home.

Like many other writers of the 1930s, he tried teaching – at his old school – and, again like most of them, hated it and left to make his way as a freelance writer and critic. He began the research for a full-scale life of Thomas Hardy, and his father financed a first trip to Italy. There he was taken to the ample bosom of a Neapolitan family he found more congenial than his own and would later celebrate in a radio play, *Return to Naples* (1950). Before he could himself return, Mussolini had to be overthrown, and in the summer of 1941 a Hal much less heroic than Shakespeare's was conscripted into the Royal Army Ordnance Corps. On 10 July, he wrote to his sister (now Mrs Winfield and mother of a daughter, Jane):

We have begun our departmental training – which means that army training has to be concentrated into $\frac{5}{8}$ of the day, and is therefore increasing in savagery. This blitztraining is, to my mind, absurd. The RAOC lost 10% of its personnel in Belgium, through being non-combatant. They aim, therefore, at making us combatant, in 9 weeks; at the end of that time we are expected to be able to shoot accurately, to manage a bren gun, an anti-tank gun & various other kinds, to use a bayonet, to throw hand-grenades & whatnot and to fire at aircraft. I do not think the management of a tank is included in the course, but pretty well everything else is.

Our departmental training, some of which is an official secret, known only to the British & German armies, has consisted mainly of learning the strategic disposition of the RAOC in the field: this is based, not, as I feared, on the Boer War, but on the Franco-Prussian War of 1871. It is taught by lecturers who rarely manage to conceal their dubiety at what they are teaching. But it is restful after the other things, & we are allowed to attend in PT 'kit'. This is nicely balanced by the fact that we attend PT wearing *all* our 'kit', except blankets. (I will never call a child of mine Christopher).

The same letter gives, incidentally, a clear view of the left-wing political position that Reed, for all his aristocratic fantasies, was never to abandon: 'I hope', he wrote, 'a good deal from Russia, of course, but rather joylessly: the scale of it all is beyond my grasp, & it is terrible to see a country which, with all its faults, has been alone in working to give the fruits of labour to the people who have earned them, thus attacked [...]'

Reed served – 'or rather *studied*', as he preferred to put it – in the Ordnance Corps until 1942 when, following a serious bout of pneumonia and a prolonged convalescence, he was transferred to the Government Code and Cypher School at Bletchley. At first he was employed as a cryptographer in the Italian Section, but was subsequently moved to the Japanese Section, where he learned the language and worked as a translator. In the evenings he wrote much of his first radio play, *Moby Dick*, and many of the poems later to be published in *A Map of Verona*. It was not a life he would have chosen, but it had its compensations: security, time for his own work, and the start of an important – perhaps his most important – homosexual relationship.

Michael Ramsbotham was also a writer, five years younger than Henry Reed, and from a more privileged background.

After Charterhouse, from which he was expelled, he went up
to King's College, Cambridge. At the end of his second year,
in June 1940, he was called up and given a commission in the
RNVR. His active service ended in September 1941, when he
was posted to the Italian Section of Naval Intelligence at
Bletchley. In 1943, he and Reed would sometimes escape the
monotony of the canteen for a civilian lunch in Leighton
Buzzard. The following year, they went on leave together
twice to Charlestown, a little fishing harbour near St Austell
in Cornwall. Reed by this time had lost all trace of his
Birmingham accent and acquired a somewhat Sitwellian manner. A quick wit and a staggering memory – especially for
Shakespeare – made him an engaging companion.

On VJ Day 1945, he was demobbed. A few weeks earlier,
Ramsbotham had suffered a nervous breakdown and went
absent without leave, taking himself off to North Cornwall
where, after a month or two, Reed joined him. Later both
men were recalled to the Service. Reed, adopting Nelson's
tactics, declined to see the signal, and the Navy let the matter
drop. Ramsbotham was posted to the Staff of the
Commander-in-Chief, Portsmouth, and during the following autumn and winter commuted, whenever he was off
duty, from Portsmouth to Dorchester where Reed was living
at the Antelope Hotel, continuing his research for the Hardy
biography.

In April 1946, Ramsbotham was demobbed and they
celebrated with a holiday in Ireland, the highlight of which
was a happy fortnight as guests of Elizabeth Bowen at
Bowen's Court. Returning to England in July, they briefly
rented a house in Charlestown, but soon moved to another
rented house, Lovells Farm, in Marnhull, Dorset – Hardy's
Marlot – where Ramsbotham worked on a novel while Reed
reviewed fiction and poetry for the *Listener* and the *New*

Statesman and worked on Hardy. His first and only collection of poems, *A Map of Verona*, dedicated to Ramsbotham, was published in London that year (1946) by Jonathan Cape, and in New York the following year by Reynal & Hitchcock. In January 1947, the two-hour radio adaptation of Melville's novel *Moby Dick* was produced by the BBC, and published the same year, again by Cape.

By February 1948, however, the atmosphere at Lovells Farm had become too emotionally claustrophobic for Ramsbotham and he walked out – leaving a note – but by April had returned, and the two set off for a long holiday in Cyprus. The following February, Reed rented Gable Court, a large sixteenth-century house with Victorian additions in the Dorset village of Yetminster, where he continued his research for the life of Hardy and wrote two fine verse plays about another poet whose work he was translating and with whom he identified strongly, Giacomo Leopardi: *The Unblest* (1949) and *The Monument* (1950). The year at Gable Court, for Reed the best of times, was followed by the worst of times. In February 1950 the couple split up, Reed leaving his Eden (as it would, increasingly, seem to him) for London, where he was to live for the rest of his life, apart from terms as a Visiting Professor of Poetry at the University of Washington, Seattle, in 1964, 1965–6, and 1967, and occasional trips to Europe.

Perhaps in search of an earlier happiness, Reed had returned to Italy in July 1951, heading for Verona, 'the small strange city' lovingly imagined in the title-poem of his first book:

> one day I shall go.
>
> The train will bring me perhaps in utter darkness
> And drop me where you are blooming, unaware

That a stranger has entered your gates, and a new devotion
Is about to attend and haunt you everywhere.²

A letter to his parents suggests that his prophecy had been
fulfilled: 'It is a most lovely city,' he wrote, 'small enough for
me to walk right across it in less than an hour; I had a letter of
introduction to a friend of a friend & was in consequence
well looked after & made much fuss of. My arrival was even
announced on the radio, I learned with much delight later
on.' It was a successful holiday and resulted in one of the best
of Reed's radio plays on Italian themes, *The Streets of
Pompeii*, awarded an Italia Prize in 1951. Much of his work
for the BBC Features Department was commissioned and
produced by Douglas Cleverdon, who wrote of him in his
obituary (*Independent*, 11 December 1986):

In these Italian pieces Henry Reed revealed his instinctive mastery of
the art of radio. All his creative powers were brought into play. For
he was not only a poet of great sensibility; he had also a lively sense of
comedy and of the absurd, and a remarkable gift for dramatic
invention. He could be extremely witty, both in his social life and
in his radio writing; and the wit could overflow into satire and
occasionally malice. Yet, though homosexual by nature, he had an
extraordinary sympathy with women's most profound emotions, and
could portray them with tenderness and understanding [...]
    His scripts were rarely completed more than a day or two before
rehearsals began, but he particularly relished the affectionate esteem in
which he was held by the group of players who usually formed the
nucleus of his cast. As he usually attended all rehearsals, this affection
was enhanced during the later stages of his radio career, when the poetic
content of his work was gradually overtaken by the hilariously satirical.

In the mid-1950s, Reed made a major liberating decision:
he abandoned the biography of Hardy, which for years had
burdened him with guilt like the Ancient Mariner's albatross.
That failed quest – perhaps related to the failure of his earlier

quest for lasting love – played out a dominant theme of his radio plays:[3] from failure as a biographer, he turned to triumphant success in a radio play about a nervous young biographer, Herbert Reeve, engaged on just such quest as he had himself abandoned. Reed's hero (whose name owes something to that of Herbert Read, the poet and critic, with whom he was tired of being confused) assembles a mass of conflicting testimony about his author, the novelist Richard Shewin. His witnesses include a waspish brother, his wife, two spinsters of uncertain virtue, and (the finest comic role he was to create for radio) the 12-tone composeress Hilda Tablet. The success of *A Very Great Man Indeed* (1953) prompted six sequels, the best of them *The Private Life of Hilda Tablet* (1954), in which Reeve is browbeaten into switching the subject of his biography from the dumb dead to the exuberantly vocal living composeress.

The modest income that Reed's work for radio brought him he supplemented with the still more modest rewards of book-reviewing and translation. The reviewing was to result in a British Council booklet, *The Novel since 1939* (1946), and his published translations include Ugo Betti's *Three Plays* (1956) and *Crime on Goat Island* (1961), Balzac's *Père Goriot* (1962) and *Eugénie Grandet* (1964), and Natalia Ginzburg's *The Advertisement* (1969). Several of his translations found their way into the theatre, and in the autumn of 1955 there were London premières of no less than three. His own poems and translations of those by Leopardi continued for a time to appear, usually in the pages of the *Listener*. Douglas Cleverdon published a limited Clover Hill Edition of five *Lessons of the War* in 1970, and *The Streets of Pompeii and Other Plays for Radio* and *Hilda Tablet and Others: Four Pieces for Radio* were issued together by the BBC in 1971. In 1975, the BBC broadcast his anthology of Leopardi's poems in his own translations; a last relinquishing of work long pondered over resulted in 1974–5 in the publication of a handful of his poems in the *Listener*, with the elegiac love poem *'Bocca di Magra'*, perhaps written in the 1950s, as a final word. Over the years he had worked on (and seemingly completed two acts of) a three-act verse play about the false Dimitry; a long poem called variously 'Matthew' and 'In Black and White', perhaps set during the American Civil War; a dramatic monologue, 'Clytemnestra', possibly as a pendant to his Sophoclean 'Triptych' in *A Map*; and a commissioned translation of the *Ajax* of Sophocles. He had drafted and all but finished polishing a translation of Montale's haunting *Motetti*. Reed's *Who's Who* entry for 1977 listed *The Auction Sale and Other Poems* among his publications, but no such collection ever appeared. Talk even at the end of the 1970s of a collected edition came to nothing. As a perfectionist, he could not bring himself to release what he must have recognized would be his last book until it was as good as he could make it, and it never was.

Reed greatly enjoyed his fifteen years with the BBC, his membership of the Savile Club, his London life and his frequent journeys to Italy (often on a BBC commission). But in his last decade, drink and self-neglect (his staple diet was Complan) increasingly undermined his always fragile health. His notebooks record a continuing and courageous struggle. At one point, he conducts an experiment:

> I wonder if the difficulty of writing
> could be solved by drink alone
>
> Now how much better am I writing?
>
> Now how much better am I writing? Not
> much, it seems. But oh, for freedom from
> these adventitious aids.

Again, on 10 March 1985 he notes:

After the horrors and the reliefs of the last terrible weeks I have 'resumed' what seemed like a period of hopeful convalescence (though God knows it is very painful to move about & eyesight is at rock-bottom). The Income Tax, and my all but paralysed will about it, stand in the way. Yet prowling round the three or four poems from the 50s I still want to finish occasional jerks forward do occur.

He became increasingly incapacitated and reclusive, but devoted friends never ceased to visit him in the Upper Montagu Street flat he continued to occupy, thanks to the generosity of a long-suffering landlady, until, removed to hospital, he died on 8 December 1986.

Reed's poems of the 1930s — particularly the earlier sections of 'The Desert' — owe something of their use of the *paysage moralisé* to the landscapes of Eliot and Auden. In 'South', the traveller of 1938 hears an unexpected voice:

'But look more closely', the landscape suddenly told him,
    'What do you see?'
And he saw his life. He saw it, and turned away,
And wept hot tears down the rock's hard cheek, and kissed
Its wrinkled mouths with the kiss of passion, crying,
    'Where is my love? [...]

This landscape of desire is, in every sense, unsatisfactory — not least because the nature of that desire is obscured by symbolic fog.

Very different is the landscape of 1942:

Japonica
Glistens like coral in all of the neighbouring gardens,
And today we have naming of parts.

The homely word 'neighbouring' disguises the fact that this is an extension of another symbolic landscape, the archetypal landscape of desire, that garden in which Adam *named* the animals. The presence of desire is felt the more strongly here for being shown hovering at the edge of consciousness, as the speaker himself hovers at the edge of the weapon-training squad. A second difference between the two poems is that of tone – the humour that now disguises the gravity of the subject. Reed had 'studied' to good effect during his basic training in the RAOC, and would later entertain his friends with a comic imitation of a sergeant instructing his recruits. After a few performances, he noticed that the words of the weapon-training instructor, couched in the style of the military manual, fell into certain rhythmic patterns which fascinated him and eventually provided the structure of 'Naming of Parts'. In this and two subsequent 'Lessons of the War', the military voice is wittily counter-pointed by the inner voice – more civilized and still civilian – of a listening recruit with his mind on other matters.

Countless poems of the First World War had carried titles and/or epigraphs in Latin. Reed followed Wilfred Owen, who in 'Dulce et Decorum Est' had challenged and subverted that tradition, when he chose – and emended – a Horatian epigraph for his sequence. Horace wrote (*Odes*, 3: 26.1-2):

> Vixi puellis nuper idoneus
> Et militavi non sine gloria

which can be roughly translated: 'Lately I've lived among girls, creditably enough, and have soldiered not without glory.' Slyly, Reed turns upside down the *p* of *puellis* (girls), to give *duellis* (battles). In this way exchanging *girls* for *battles*, he cunningly encapsulates in his epigraph the theme of the Lessons that follow.

A third difference between the two poems is the dramatic element that in 'Naming of Parts' counterpoints the two voices. At approximately the same point in each of the first four stanzas, the recruit's attention wanders from the instructor's lesson in the unnatural art of handling a lethal weapon, back to the natural world: branches, blossom, life as opposed to death. Plucked by the Army from gardens where, at this season, he should have been enjoying the company of his Eve, he sees the bees 'assaulting and fumbling the flowers': the military and sexual associations of those verbs reflecting the confusion in his mind. The hint of corruption, Innocence yielding to Experience, is confirmed by the *double entendres*, the rueful ironies, of the final stanza.

The dialectical opposition of two voices, two views of a landscape, is a strategy refined in two remarkable poems of Reed's middle years. 'The Changeling' must have been written either shortly before or shortly after his expulsion from the Eden of Gable Court. A brilliantly condensed autobiography, it uses the changeling figure (from his mother's fairy stories) and the family legend of noble descent to articulate a troubling sense of doubleness: true self and false self. Bright landscapes darken until, as in all the best fairy stories,

> Love takes him by his hand,
> And the child to exile bred
> Comes to his native land.
>
> And comes, at last, to stand
> On his scented evening lawn
> Under his flowering limes,
> Where dim in the dusk and high,
> His mansion is proudly set,
> And the single light burns
> In the room where his sweet young wife
> Waits in his ancient bed.

The possessive pronoun, 'proudly set' to every item in this catalogue of Paradise Regained, begins to sound disturbingly over-insistent when extended to 'his summer sky, [...] his first pale stars'. He protests too much, masking a doubt that finally turns to desolate certainty:

> All this is false. And I
> Am an interloper here.

Reed's most ambitious exploration of the landscape of desire occurs in 'The Auction Sale'. A Forsterian or Hardyesque short story, set in the Hardy country he had recently left, it is told in a voice as flat as if the speaker were reading from a country newspaper:

> Within the great grey flapping tent
> The damp crowd stood or stamped about;
> And some came in, and some went out
> To drink the moist November air [...]

After the auctioneer has rattled off the opening lots, he turns to something different, announcing '*There's a reserve upon this number.*' A shrouded object is unveiled, revealing

> The prospect of a great gold frame
> Which through the reluctant leaden air
> Flashed a mature unsullied grace
> Into the faces of the crowd.
> And there was silence in that place.

As the ordinary field of 'Judging Distances' had been succeeded by one where

> the sun and the shadows bestow
> Vestments of purple and gold [,]

in the grey tent and leaden air of the auction sale there blazes a scene as different as the language in which it is described:

> *Effulgent in the Paduan air,*
> *Ardent to yield the Venus lay*
> *Naked upon the sunwarmed earth.*

The inner voice that, in the English silence, proceeds to detail so lovingly the Italian landscape of mythologized desire can be understood to be that of the young man who now bids against the London dealers. As the figures mount, the grey voice and the golden contrapuntally compete:

> *Ardent to yield* the nods resumed
> *Venus upon the sunwarmed* nods
> *Abandoned Cupids danced* and nodded
> *His mouth towards her* bid four thousand
> Four thousand, any advance upon,
> *And still beyond* four thousand fifty
> *Unrolled towards the* nodding *sun.*

When, finally, the young man drops out of the bidding, he takes leave of his Paradise Lost with an unvoiced elegy, and is later seen – like Masaccio's Adam, but more tragic for being alone –

> in the dusk,
> Not walking on the road at all,
> But striding beneath the sodden trees ...
> Crying. That was what she said.
>
> Bitterly, she later added.
>
> Crying bitterly, she said.

This fine poem was to prove prophetic. When in the 1970s the author of *A Map of Verona* again sought out his 'city of a long-held dream', it was too late. 'The Town Itself' is a love poem addressed to 'my darling', but Verona has other things on her mind, and the lover is unrequited:

> I shall never be accepted as a citizen:
> I am still, and shall always be, a stranger here.

Reed never abandoned his quest for the Great Good Place, and his late manuscript poems provide a poignant record of dreams and mirages encountered in the Waste Land. When he comes to 'The Château', echoes of the 23rd Psalm tell us he comes from the valley of the shadow of death. Standing outside 'the great grey mansion' ('in my father's house are many mansions'), he feels, not as the Changeling felt outside *his* mansion, that he was about to come into his own, but that his life has been going on elsewhere and otherwise:

> surely beyond that great façade my life is being lived?
> Lived, loved and filled with gaiety and ardour [...]

To reach it and take his place at 'the starry feast', he has only to cross the last threshold, a step his imagination takes with an intensity of vision that will stand comparison with the close of *Little Gidding*:[4]

> Surely there will be a signal? Inconspicuously,
> One of the giant roses in the gardens around us
> Will perhaps explode on to the autumn grass:
> Something like that, perhaps. I know I shall know the moment.
>
> And surely (and almost now) it will happen, and tell me
> That now I must rise and with firm footsteps tread
> Across the enormous flagstones, reach, find and know
> My own and veritable door;
> I shall open it, enter and learn
> That in all this hungry time I have never wanted,
> But have, elsewhere, on honey and milk been fed,
> Have in green pastures somewhere lain, and in the mornings,
> Somewhere beside still waters have
> Mysteriously, ecstatically, been led.

Italy, the setting of most of the late manuscript poems was, after Gable Court, the closest he could come to the Great Good Place on earth, but to both he comes as a stranger or

'Intruder'. The poem of that title described his return (a charged word in Reed's lexicon) in a double capacity: an earlier self and his own 'noonday ghost', whose presence falls like a shadow between the speaker and the companion he has just embraced. The spectre is said to be seeking

> Something I dared not say,
> And bent in distress beside me
> Ashen and anguished and lonely.

What he is seeking and why a *noonday* ghost should have 'an *agèd* face' we can infer when the speaker

> saw he was visiting again this place
> A quarter-century hence
> And pausing and hoping and sighing,
> Recapturing a half or a third
> Of what we were saying there now,
> As though what we said had mattered,
> There by the base of the fountain
> Or at that pause on the hill-side
> Where we always said our goodbyes [...]

Such goodbyes are clearly far from final, but this cunning interweaving of time past, time present, and time future ends – as a good ghost story should – with a leave-taking of another kind. After so many sunlit Italian landscapes, the wintry English cityscape of 'L'Envoi', the manuscript poem in which Reed takes leave of his reader, makes a contrast the more poignant for the genial tone of the fable's telling.

Randall Jarrell wrote that 'A good poet is someone who manages in a lifetime of standing out in thunderstorms to be struck by lightning five or six times: a dozen and he is great.' By this criterion, or any other, Henry Reed is a poet who can now, at overlong last, take his rightful place at 'the starry feast'.

CHAPTER 13

The fury and the mire

'My subject is War, and the pity of War. The Poetry is in the pity.' That was Wilfred Owen in 1918.[1] *My* subject, many wars later, is War and the fury of War. The Poetry is in the fury.

Poetry is notoriously difficult to define. 'Of the many definitions', said W.H. Auden, 'the simplest is still the best: 'memorable speech.'[2] To be worth writing, and reading, it must be memorable – as so much so-called poetry is not. And what do we mean by War Poetry? Logically, this category – to my mind, this unsatisfactory category – should embrace any poem about any aspect of war: it should include Eliot's *Waste Land* and *Little Gidding*; it should include Yeats's 'The Second Coming'. Each has a World War at its centre, and in the field – the battlefield – of poetry it is hard to think of speech more memorable. But when we speak of War Poetry we normally mean battlefield poems, and my subject in this chapter is the controlled fury of battlefield poems. These, too, can be difficult to define, but we know them when we see – and hear – them: Owen's 'Dulce et Decorum Est',[3] for example. What does that poem do? First of all, it persuades us that it is true; secondly, that its truth is shocking; and thirdly, that we should do something about it. Owen offers us what a mediaeval rhetorician would call an *exemplum*, an example, an illustration of a man choking to death on poison-gas; that followed by a *moralitas*, a moral coda of passionate indignation.

If in some smothering dreams you too could pace
Behind the wagon that we flung him in,
And watch the white eyes writhing in his face,
His hanging face, like a devil's sick of sin;
If you could hear, at every jolt, the blood
Come gargling from the froth-corrupted lungs,
Obscene as cancer, bitter as the cud
Of vile, incurable sores on innocent tongues, –
My friend, you would not tell with such high zest
To children ardent for some desperate glory,
The old Lie: Dulce et decorum est
Pro patria mori.

The victim's fate is pitiful, but to my ear the Poetry is in the controlled fury of the final twelve-line sentence, rather than in the pity.

Almost twenty years later, a young Cambridge Communist, John Cornford, set off for the Spanish Civil War, carrying the pistol his father had carried through the Great War and, in his head, Owen's 'Dulce et Decorum Est'. We know that because his 'Letter from Aragon'[4] takes its structure from Owen's poem: first, the *exemplum* (or, to be exact, three *exempla*):

This is a quiet sector of a quiet front.

We buried Ruiz in a new pine coffin,
But the shroud was too small and his washed feet stuck out.
The stink of his corpse came through the clean pine boards
And some of the bearers wrapped handkerchiefs round their faces.
Death was not dignified.
We hacked a ragged grave in the unfriendly earth
And fired a ragged volley over the grave.
You could tell from our listlessness, no one much missed him.

This is a quiet sector of a quiet front.
There is no poison gas and no H.E.[5]

But when they shelled the other end of the village
And the streets were choked with dust
Women came screaming out of the crumbling houses,
Clutched under one arm the naked rump of an infant.
I thought: how ugly fear is.

This is a quiet sector of a quiet front.
Our nerves are steady; we all sleep soundly.

In the clean hospital bed, my eyes were so heavy
Sleep easily blotted out one ugly picture,
A wounded militiaman moaning on a stretcher,
Now out of danger, but still crying for water,
Strong against death, but unprepared for such pain.

This on a quiet front.

Cornford's 'Letter from Aragon', like Owen's memory of the Somme, persuades us that it is true, shocking, and a call for action. The soldier's fury builds in his refrain, the repeated echo of the Great War's most famous book-title, *All Quiet on the Western Front*,[6] and the reference to poison gas offers another link to Owen's poem. Cornford's coda, his *moralitas*, is again a direct address to his reader:

> But when I shook hands to leave, an Anarchist worker
> Said: 'Tell the workers of England
> This was a war not of our own making
> We did not seek it.
> But if ever the Fascists again rule Barcelona
> It will be as a heap of ruins with us workers beneath it.'

Cornford did not leave Spain. He was killed on his twenty-first birthday, or the day after, in the battle for Madrid.

As many people had forseen, the Spanish Civil War proved to be the curtain-raiser for a second World War. 'It is a truth universally acknowledged', as Jane Austen would say, that unlike the First World War, the Second produced no poetry of importance. This truth is no more truth-ful than the one mocked by Austen or that attacked by Owen as 'the old Lie'. There are wonderful, terrible poems of the later war, too little known on this side of the Atlantic because half are American; too little known in America because half are British.

To illustrate this point, my third *exemplum* is an American poem as strong – as pity-ful, as furious – as any by Owen or Sassoon: Louis Simpson's 'The Heroes'.[7] Simpson served with a glider-infantry regiment of the 101st Airborne Division in France, Holland, Belgium, and Germany. In combat he was a runner. He carried messages. In Holland he was wounded by a shell, and at Bastogne his feet were frost-bitten; but he survived. After the war, however, he had a nervous breakdown and was taken into hospital suffering from amnesia. The war was blacked out in his mind, as were episodes in his life *before* the war. When he was discharged from hospital, he found he could hardly read or write. In a contributor's note to an anthology, Simpson says:

Before the war I had written a few poems and some prose. Now I found that poetry was the only kind of writing in which I could express my thoughts. Through poems, I could release the irrational, grotesque images I had accumulated during the war; and imposing order on those images enabled me to recover my identity. In 1948, when I was living in Paris, one night I dreamed that I was lying on the bank of a canal, under machine-gun and mortar fire. The next morning I wrote it out in the poem 'Carentan O Carentan', and as I wrote I realized that it wasn't a dream, but the memory of my first time under fire.[8]

Simpson's experience bears a striking resemblance to Wilfred Owen's: both suffered from neurasthenia, or shell-shock. Owen never lost his memory, but only after he was forced to relive the horrors of battle in those dreams that are a principal symptom of shell-shock was he able to write about the Western Front.

Simpson's first dream poem, 'Carentan O Carentan', appeared in his first book, *The Arrivists* (1949), and has a dreamlike distance from experience. The poems of his second book, *Good News of Death* (1955), show reality emerging from the dream:

The Heroes

I dreamed of war-heroes, of wounded war-heroes
With just enough of their charms shot away
To make them more handsome. The women moved nearer
To touch their brave wounds and their hair streaked with gray.

I saw them in long ranks ascending the gang-planks;
The girls with the doughnuts were cheerful and gay.
They minded their manners and muttered their thanks;
The Chaplain advised them to watch and to pray.

They shipped these rapscallions, these sea-sick battalions
To a patriotic and picturesque spot;
They gave them new bibles and marksmen's medallions,
Compasses, maps and committed the lot.

A fine dust has settled on all that scrap metal.
The heroes were packaged and sent home in parts
To pluck at a poppy and sew on a petal
And count the long night by the stroke of their hearts.

The title signals a line of descent from a poem of the previous war, Sassoon's 'The Hero',[9] which begins:

'Jack fell as he'd have wished,' the Mother said,
And folded up the letter that she'd read.
'The Colonel writes so nicely.'

Simpson follows Sassoon in contrasting civilian illusion with military reality, as revealed in their two linguistic registers (the civilian's 'patriotic and picturesque spot' unspoilt by the military, 'scrap metal'). The Heroes' 'brave wounds' echoes the Mother's consolation that her son had been 'so brave', and prepares for the chilling irony of the poems' concluding stanzas. Sassoon's Hero, 'cold-footed useless swine', had tried

> To get sent home, and [...] died,
> Blown to small bits.

Simpson's Heroes are, arguably, more fortunate – 'packaged and sent home in parts', albeit not to a Heroes' Welcome but a workbench at which to assemble poppies, like the veterans of the previous war. The Sassoon template, like Simpson's savagely ironic choice of comic rhymes (*rapscallions/battalions*) in a tragic context, deepens the fury that gives his poem its propellant power.

No one, I think, would deny that these are powerful war poems, but of course most (like most poems) are less potent, and many are altogether impotent. To demonstrate the qualitative range of poems prompted by warfare – and to suggest why many fail – I propose to move on to a brief case-study of the poetry of the Vietnam War.[10] This falls, more starkly than the poems of any earlier conflict, into two principal categories: those written by so-called 'Stateside' poets, who never left America, and those of the 'Vets', the veterans, who did.

The Stateside poems can themselves be divided into two categories: first, the poetry of first-hand witness to the moral and other effects of the war on *America* – poems by Allen Ginsberg, for example; second, the poetry of second-hand witness to the war in *Vietnam* – too much of it like this:

Women, Children, Babies, Cows, Cats[11]

'It was at My Lai or Sonmy or something,
it was this afternoon. ... We had these orders,

we had all night to think about it –
we was to burn and kill, then there'd be nothing
standing, women, children, babies, cows, cats. ...
As soon as we hopped the choppers, we started shooting.
I remember ... as we was coming up upon one area
in Pinkville, a man with a gun ... running – this lady ...
Lieutenant LaGuerre said, "Shoot her." I said,
"You shoot her, I don't want to shoot no lady."
She had one foot in the door. ... When I turned her,
there was this little one-month-year-old baby
I thought was her gun. It kind of cracked me up.'

This was written by a great poet – Robert Lowell – but I cannot be alone in thinking it is not a great poem. In fact, I think it embarrassing in its blend of black demotic ("I don't want to shoot no lady") with the literary ('we hopped the choppers', and the coy 'Lieutenant LaGuerre'). The speaker does not persuade me he mistook the baby (so neatly foreshadowed in his orders) for a gun; or that 'It kind of cracked [him] up'. Certainly, the poem does not crack *me* up. It would tell us – even if we did not know that Lowell never served in Vietnam – that his testimony is second-hand. In this, it is strikingly unlike his poignant and powerful poem 'Fall 1961',[12] which bears first-hand witness to a father's fear in the midst of the Cuban missile crisis:

> All autumn, the chafe and jar
> of nuclear war;
> we have talked our extinction to death.
> I swim like a minnow
> behind my studio window.
>
> Our end drifts nearer,
> the moon lifts,
> radiant with terror.
> [...]

> A father's no shield
> for his child. […]

If, like me, you feel more for the American father and his child than for the Vietnamese mother and baby, it might be that the poet felt more. Few parents can feel as much pity and terror for a mother and baby seen in a newspaper or a television screen as for a threatened child of their own.

It does not follow, however, that a poem of first-hand witness will necessarily be better – more moving because more focused – than one of second-hand witness. Tennyson did not see the Charge of the Light Brigade other than with his mind's eye, but his lifelong absorption in Arthurian legend and chivalry enabled him to take his place, imaginatively, with the 'Noble six hundred'. He feels – and enables us to feel – fury, and horror, and pity, and amazed admiration:

> Cannon to right of them,
> Cannon to left of them,
> Cannon behind them
>   Volleyed and thundered;
> Stormed at with shot and shell,
> While horse and hero fell,
> They that had fought so well
> Came through the jaws of Death,
> Back from the mouth of Hell,
> All that was left of them,
>   Left of six hundred.[13]

Thomas Hardy did not see the Boer War burial party 'throw in Drummer Hodge, to rest / Uncoffined – just as found', but his lifelong absorption in the little world of Wessex enabled him to take his place, imaginatively, at the boy's graveside:

> Young Hodge the Drummer never knew –
> Fresh from his Wessex home –
> The meaning of the broad Karoo,
>   The Bush, the dusty loam,
> And why uprose to nightly view
>   Strange stars amid the gloam.[14]

There is no fury in Hardy's poem, but only profound pity and sadness – as for the son he never had. These poems of second-hand witness have an immediacy and power equal to any of first-hand witness, being the work of great poets, each with a lifelong imaginative investment in his subject. But such poems are rare. The second-hand testimony of lesser poets, lacking such investment, is seldom impressive and sometimes embarrassing.

For demographic and social-historical reasons, the ratio of poets to other servicemen and women serving in Vietnam was less than in either World War. Most American intellectuals disapproved of the Vietnam War, and men of military age – particularly white men of military age – could avoid conscription by signing up for university education. And many did. The ratio of Stateside poets to battlefield poets was, therefore, greater than in either World War. There were hundreds of armchair poets pretending, like Lowell, to first-hand witness and/or degrees of moral commitment to which they were not entitled. Few were as good as Lowell, and collectively they deserved the savage rebuke offered by a front-line veteran of the Second World War, Anthony Hecht. He wrote of one such (fortunately unidentified) armchair poet:

> Here lies fierce Strephon, whose poetic rage
> Lashed out on Vietnam from page and stage;
> Whereby from basements of Bohemia he
> Rose to the lofts of sweet celebrity,

Being, by Fortune, (our Eternal Whore)
One of the few to profit by that war,
A fate he shared – it bears much thinking on –
With certain persons at the Pentagon.[15]

The knock-out punch of the last line should not blind us to the
lightning jab of the first: 'Here *lies* fierce Strephon'. Is he lying
in the grave or telling lies, or both? The fury driving this
poem is directed, I assume, not at a Stateside poet bearing true
witness to the impact of the war on America, but one pretending to first-hand witness of combat in Vietnam.

Hecht's rebuke comes with the moral authority of a poet
burdened with the responsibility of bearing witness to the
ultimate brutality of the Second World War. He served with
the Infantry Division that discovered Flossenburg, an annex
of Buchenwald.

When we arrived [he writes], the SS personnel had, of course, fled.
Prisoners were dying at the rate of 500 a day from typhus. Since I had
the rudiments of French and German, I was appointed to speak, in the
hope of securing evidence against those who ran the camp. Later,
when some of these were captured, I presented them with the charges
levelled against them, translating their denials or defences back into
French for the sake of their accusers, in an attempt to get to the
bottom of what was done and who was responsible. The place, the
suffering, the prisoners' accounts were beyond comprehension. For
years after I would wake shrieking. I must add an important point:
after the war I read widely in Holocaust literature, and I can no
longer separate my anger and revulsion at what I really saw from
what I later came to learn.[16]

After the war, his Jewish imagination seared with what he
had seen and read, Hecht discharged his responsibility to the
dead, to history, in one of the war's most powerful poems,
'More Light! More Light!' (supposedly the last words of the
poet Goethe as he lay dying in Weimar).[17] This opens with a
graphic account of a sixteenth-century atrocity, committed

in the name of religion: a Christian martyr's burning at the stake. The smoke from his pyre mingles with that from a later and greater atrocity committed not in the name of religion, but against an entire religious community:

> We move now to outside a German wood.
> Three men are there commanded to dig a hole
> In which the two Jews are ordered to lie down
> And be buried alive by the third, who is a Pole.
>
> Not light from the shrine at Weimar beyond the hill
> Nor light from heaven appeared. But he did refuse.
> A Lüger settled back deeply in its glove.
> He was ordered to change places with the Jews.
>
> Much casual death had drained away their souls.
> The thick dirt mounted toward the quivering chin.
> When only the head was exposed the order came
> To dig him out again and to get back in.
>
> No light, no light in the blue Polish eye.
> When he finished a riding boot packed down the earth.
> The Lüger hovered lightly in its glove.
> He was shot in the belly and in three hours bled to death.
>
> No prayers or incense rose up in those hours
> Which grew to be years, and every day came mute
> Ghosts from the ovens, sifting through crisp air,
> And settled upon his eyes in a black soot.

There can be no immediate first-hand experience here, but what Hecht had seen and heard in Flossenburg galvanized his imagination with a shock of such high voltage that his poem passes it on to its readers. Obviously the voltage is reduced when it reaches us – as it must be in 'Dulce et Decorum Est' and any such poem – but 'More Light! More Light!' shocks an exposed nerve. This is its function and its value and, in this, it has something in common with the reporting of a first-class war-correspondent like Robert Fisk. The difference – a crucial difference – is that we can hold 'Dulce et Decorum Est' and 'More Light! More Light!' in our memory, as we cannot retain the front-line journalism of a Fisk – or, for that matter, the front-line letters of an Owen.

The charge against a poem like Lowell's 'Women, Children, Babies, Cows, Cats' is that, far from shocking an exposed nerve, it has the numbing effect of second-hand journalism, thereby contributing to the insensitive apathy that enables us to turn, unmoved, from our newspaper's coverage of disaster to that of a football match. Hecht's rebuke to 'fierce Strephon' points up the further disturbing fact that many of those protesting against the war made money from appearances on 'page and stage'.

The situation and the poetry of the combatant 'Vets' could not have been more different. Their poems of first-hand experience often have a raw power, but I know of none that lives in the memory like 'More Light! More Light!' A problem for many American poets then aspiring to be War Poets was that, rightly perceiving it to be an unjust war, they could not participate as servicemen or women; and lacking first-hand experience, could not write convincingly of the war 'on the ground'.

Given some of their trumpeted expressions of moral commitment to the anti war cause, it is perhaps surprising that none of them felt strongly enough to follow the example of W.H. Auden who, in January 1937, prompted a banner headline of the *Daily Worker*: 'FAMOUS POET TO DRIVE AMBULANCE IN SPAIN.' Explaining his decision to a friend, he wrote: 'I shall probably be a bloody bad soldier but how can I speak to/for them without becoming one?'[18]

One American poet *did* follow Auden's example. John Balaban went to Vietnam, but not as an ambulance-driver. He went as a Conscientious Objector to work in an orphanage (for children orphaned by his country's war), learnt Vietnamese, and stayed after the war to teach in a Vietnamese university. His poems of those years have a fine grain, a specificity of detail, rare in the many poems bearing first-hand witness to an armchair reading of newspapers or the watching of television news. As with the war poems of earlier wars, many of Balaban's best were written after the guns had fallen silent, for example:

In Celebration of Spring[19]

Our Asian war is over; others have begun.
Our elders, who tried to mortgage lies,
are disgraced, or dead, and already
the brokers are picking their pockets
for the keys and the credit cards.

In delta swamp in a united Vietnam,
a Marine with a bullfrog for a face,
rots in equatorial heat. An eel
slides through the cage of his bared ribs.
At night, on the old battlefield, ghosts,
like patches of fog, lurk into villages
to maunder on doorsills of cratered homes,
while all across the U.S.A.
the wounded walk about and wonder where to go.

And today, in the simmer of lyric sunlight,
the chrysalis pulses in its mushy cocoon,
under the bark on a gnarled root of an elm.
In the brilliant creek, a minnow flashes
delirious with gnats. The turtle's heart
quickens its raps in the warm bank sludge.
As she chases a frisbee spinning in sunlight,
a girl's breasts bounce full and strong;
a boy's stomach, as he turns, is flat and strong.

Balaban's opening has disturbing vibrations for readers in 2008: 'Our Asian war is over; others have begun.' As for

Owen and Sassoon, the guilty men are the old men who sacrificed the young – 'Our elders who tried to mortgage lies'. Scavenging vermin in America – 'the brokers' – anticipate the somehow more attractive scavengers in Vietnam – the bullfrog and the eel. The controlled fury of the speaker's first stanza is followed by pity for the dead of both sides, and for the living dead. There is not much celebration 'on the old battlefield' or 'across the U.S.A.' but, with the third stanza, Spring returns and the natural cycle of generation begins again: the 'chrysalis *pulses*' … 'a minnow *flashes*' … ' the turtle's heart / *quickens*'. And not only the turtle's heart:

> a girl's breasts bounce full and strong;
> a boy's stomach, as he turns, is flat and strong.

Adam and Eve are in their garden again. Finally, as at the end of Owen's 'Dulce et Decorum Est' and Cornford's 'Letter from Aragon', Balaban turns from his *exempla* to address his reader directly:

> Swear by the locust, by dragonflies on ferns,
> by the minnow's flash, the tremble of a breast,
> by the new earth spongy under our feet;
> that as we grow old, we will not grow evil,
> that although our garden seeps with sewage,
> and our elders think it's up for auction – swear
> by this dazzle that does not wish to leave us –
> that we will be keepers of a garden, nonetheless.

A garden not a battlefield.

Balaban spoke of 'Our Asian war' and, of course, it *was* an American war, but not all its poets were American. Britain had its 'Stateside' contingent of armchair witnesses, and one – so far as I am aware, only one – poet-witness to the war on the ground: James Fenton. In the 1970s, he was a freelance

reporter in Indo-China and a foreign correspondent in
Germany for the *Guardian*. Like Hecht a poet of the
School of Auden, his German experience fuelled one of the
great English-language poems of the holocaust, *A German
Requiem*.[20] This was published in 1981, the same year as
one of the great English-language poems of the south-east
Asian wars, his 'Dead Soldiers'.[21] The power and poignancy
of each derives from Fenton's first-hand experience of
human suffering, but the poignancy is sharpened by his
deployment of grimly comic detail and a refusal to lapse
into mawkish solemnity. The seeming solemnity of his
poem's title is subverted by what follows:

Dead Soldiers

When His Excellency Prince Norodom Chantaraingsey
Invited me to lunch on the battlefield
I was glad of my white suit for the first time that day.
They lived well, the mad Norodoms, they had style.
The brandy and the soda arrived in crates.
Bricks of ice, tied around with raffia,
Dripped from the orderlies' handlebars.

And I remember the dazzling tablecloth
As the APCs fanned out along the road,[22]
The dishes piled high with frogs' legs,
Pregnant turtles, their eggs boiled in the carapace,
Marsh irises in fish sauce
And inflorescence of a banana salad.

On every bottle, Napoleon Bonaparte
Pleaded for the authenticity of the spirit.
They called the empties Dead Soldiers
And rejoiced to see them pile up at our feet.

Each diner was attended by one of the other ranks
Whirling a table-napkin to keep off the flies.
It was like eating between rows of morris dancers –
Only they didn't kick.

This most curious of war poems begins on a battlefield
but, as in Greek tragedy, the violence takes place off-stage.
Instead of bloodstained battledress, we see a white suit, a
dazzling (presumably white) tablecloth, and whirling (presumably white) napkins. A poet who has seen a battlefield
gives his poem a narrator who remembers the menu rather
than the body-count.

> '[...] one eats well there', I remark.
> 'So one should,' says the Jockey Cap:
> 'The tiger always eats well,
> It eats the raw flesh of the deer,
> And Chantaraingsey was born in the year of the tiger.
> So, did they show you the things they do
> With the young refugee girls?'

The casual brutality of this passes with no more comment
from the narrator than his earlier report on the only casualties he notices:

> They called the empties Dead Soldiers
> And rejoiced to see them pile up at our feet.

The insensitive speaker has none of Fenton's own knowledge of Cambodian politics, and depends for his information
on a dubious source (one hesitates to call 'intelligence'). Pol
Pot's brother

> tells me how he will one day give me the gen.
> He will tell me how the prince financed the casino
> And how the casino brought Lon Nol to power.
> He will tell me this.
> He will tell me all these things.
> All I must do is drink and listen.

He drank, listened, predicted, and was 'always wrong'. He is
no wiser now:

I have been told that the prince is still fighting
Somewhere in the Cardamoms or the Elephant Mountains.
But I doubt that the Jockey Cap would have survived his good
    connections.
I think the lunches would have done for him –
Either the lunches or the dead soldiers.

And so the poem comes full-circle – back to its title. But at this (their third) appearance, the dead soldiers are no longer capitalized, metaphorical, but actual dead soldiers.

What do these and other war poems achieve? In that their subject is tragedy, they can – when made with passion and precision – move us (as Aristotle said) to pity and terror; also, I suggest, to a measure of fury. And just as we go to a performance of Shakespeare's *King Lear* or Britten's *War Requiem* for pleasure, we return (or at least I return) to 'Dulce et Decorum Est' or 'The Heroes' for the wonder and pleasurable satisfaction a masterpiece affords.

In the short term, I doubt whether the poems about Vietnam had any significant effect on the course of the war. Certainly the (much better) poems of 1914–18 and 1939–45 had no significant effect on the course of the two World Wars. In the longer term, however, war poems *have* through history had a significant effect in shaping their societies' attitudes to warfare. The epics of heroic ages – *The Iliad, Beowulf* – encouraged the pursuit of glory with their celebration of courage and skilful swordplay. Over the centuries, all that changed. More British poems of the First World War confirmed 'The Old Lie: Dulce et decorum est / Pro patria mori' than challenged it; but, with few exceptions, they have been relegated to the dustbin of history. The poets whose work has survived sing a very different song: one that has played a significant part in introducing subsequent generations to the realities of modern warfare.

The poems of the Second World War have had less impact – not because they were less good, but because the reading public has become increasingly attuned to prose, and because the Word (prose as well as verse) has increasingly lost ground to the Image. Today, our knowledge of the war in Iraq probably derives as much from newspaper and television images as from the spoken or written word. I have yet to see a poem about 'our [latest] Asian War' that is worth the paper it is written on, but all the precedents suggest we should not expect to see one yet. As and when we do, I think it is more likely to come from the hand of a doctor or war-correspondent than from an armchair witness or a serving soldier. And while there may be poetry in the pity, I would bet there will be more in the fury.

Notes

1. THE DEATH OF THE HERO

1. See Jon Stallworthy (ed.), *The Oxford Book of War Poetry* (Oxford University Press, 1984), p. 9.
2. Seamus Heaney (trans.), *Beowulf* (London: Faber and Faber, 1998), p. 98.
3. *Ibid.*, p. 99.
4. Stallworthy (ed.), *Oxford Book of War Poetry*, pp. 23–31.
5. Geoffrey Chaucer, General Prologue to *The Canterbury Tales*, lines 43–5.
6. F. J. C. Hearnshaw, 'Chivalry and its Place in History', in Edgar Prestage (ed.), *Chivalry* (London: Kegan Paul, 1928), p. 22.
7. 'Norfolk sprang thee, Lambeth holds thee dead'. Stallworthy (ed.), *Oxford Book of War Poetry*, p. 44.
8. 'The Fruits of War'. Stallworthy (ed.), *Oxford Book of War Poetry*, pp. 45–8.
9. 'A Burnt Ship'. Stallworthy (ed.), *Oxford Book of War Poetry*, p. 49.
10. Stallworthy (ed.), *Oxford Book of War Poetry*, p. 50.
11. 'The Drum'. Stallworthy (ed.), *Oxford Book of War Poetry*, pp. 68–9.
12. 'Ye Mariners of England'. Stallworthy (ed.), *Oxford Book of War Poetry*, pp. 69–70.
13. Lord Byron, *Childe Harold's Pilgrimage*, Canto IV, lines 1262–7.
14. William St Clair, *That Greece Might Still Be Free* (London: Oxford University Press, 1972), p. 19.
15. 'Thermopylae'. Stallworthy (ed.), *Oxford Book of War Poetry*, p. 9.
16. Lord Byron, *Don Juan*, III, lines 725–30.
17. 'The Due of the Dead'. Stallworthy (ed.), *Oxford Book of War Poetry*, pp. 119–20.

18. Stallworthy (ed.), *Oxford Book of War Poetry*, pp. 115–16.
19. 'The Wound-Dresser'. Stallworthy (ed.), *Oxford Book of War Poetry*, pp. 125–7.
20. 'A Sight in Camp in the Day-Break Grey and Dim'.
21. 'He who lies far from this place […] died before daybreak: but he was a soldier and he died for his country.'
22. Stallworthy (ed.), *Oxford Book of War Poetry*, p. 146.
23. Rupert Wilkinson, *The Prefects* (London: Oxford University Press, 1964), p. 10.
24. *Drummer Hodge: The Poetry of the Anglo-Boer War* (Oxford: Clarendon Press, 1978).
25. Stallworthy (ed.), *Oxford Book of War Poetry*, pp. 147–51.
26. Stallworthy (ed.), *Oxford Book of War Poetry*, p. 162.
27. *Ibid.*, p. 163.
28. E.B. Osborn (ed.), *The Muse in Arms* (London: John Murray, 1917), pp. vi–vii.
29. Stallworthy (ed.), *Oxford Book of War Poetry*, p. 163.
30. Geoffrey Keynes (ed.), *The Letters of Rupert Brooke* (London: Faber and Faber, 1968), pp. 662–3.
31. Jean Moorcroft Wilson (ed.), *The Collected Poems of Charles Hamilton Sorley* (London: Cecil Woolf, 1985), pp. 130–1.
32. 'Dulce et Decorum Est'. Stallworthy (ed.), *Oxford Book of War Poetry*, pp. 188 9.
33. Ian Parsons (ed.), *The Collected Works of Isaac Rosenberg* (London: Chatto & Windus, 1979), p. 267.
34. Stallworthy (ed.), *Oxford Book of War Poetry*, pp. 236–9.
35. 'Gallantry'. Stallworthy (ed.), *Oxford Book of War Poetry*, p. 267.
36. 'Into Battle'. Stallworthy (ed.), *Oxford Book of War Poetry*, pp. 164–5.
37. Stallworthy (ed.), *Oxford Book of War Poetry*, pp. 268–9.
38. 'War Poet'. Michael Meyer (ed.), *The Collected Poems of Sidney Keyes* (London: Routledge & Kegan Paul, 1945), p. 82.
39. 'Naming of Parts'. Stallworthy (ed.), *Oxford Book of War Poetry*, pp. 254–5.
40. See p. 172 below.
41. 'The Battle'. Stallworthy (ed.), *Oxford Book of War Poetry*, pp. 282–3.

42. 'Fall In'. Lincoln Kirstein, *Rhymes of a PFC* (New York: New Directions, 1964), pp. 3–4.
43. Stallworthy (ed.), *Oxford Book of War Poetry*, p. 267.
44. Ian Hamilton (ed.), *The Poetry of War, 1939–45* (London: Alan Ross, 1965), p. 172.
45. Stallworthy (ed.), *Oxford Book of War Poetry*, p. 290.
46. Stallworthy (ed.), *Oxford Book of War Poetry*, pp. 338–9.

2. SURVIVORS' SONGS

1. Joseph Clancy (trans.), *Y Gododdin*, quoted in Gwyn Jones (ed.), *The Oxford Book of Welsh Verse in English* (Oxford University Press, 1977), p. 6.
2. The Book of Job, 1: 14–17. (This and subsequent quotations from the Bible are taken from the King James version.)
3. Kenneth Hurstone Jackson (trans.), *The Gododdin: The Oldest Scottish Poem* (Edinburgh University Press, 1969), p. 106. Subsequent quotations from *The Gododdin* are from Jackson's translation, unless specified to the contrary.
4. David Jones, *In Parenthesis* (London: Faber and Faber, 1937), p. xiii.
5. Clancy (trans.), *Y Gododdin*, quoted in Jones (ed.), *Oxford Book of Welsh Verse*, p. 3.
6. 'The Battle of Argoed Llwyfain', trans. Anthony Conran, quoted in Jones (ed.), *Oxford Book of Welsh Verse*, where will also be found translations of the poems by Cynddelw Brydydd Mawr and Llywelyn ab y Moel.
7. Jones (ed.), *Oxford Book of Welsh Verse*, p. 60.
8. Charles Scott Moncrieff (trans.), *Song of Roland* (London: Chapman & Hall, 1919).
9. English Faculty Library, Oxford. The Owen Collection, 409.
10. Wilfred Owen, 'Strange Meeting', lines 1–3.
11. Jones, *In Parenthesis*, p. ix.
12. *Ibid.*, p. 163. Taillefer was a minstrel in the army of William the Conqueror, who at the Battle of Hastings reputedly encouraged the Normans by singing of the deeds of Roland. See p. 19.
13. Jones, *In Parenthesis*, p. 187.
14. 'A Malory of the Trenches', *London Mercury*, 36 (July 1937), 304–5.

15. John H. Johnston, 'The Heroic Vision: David Jones', *English Poetry of the First World War* (Princeton University Press, 1964), pp. 284–340.
16. Paul Fussell, *The Great War and Modern Memory* (New York and London: Oxford University Press, 1975), pp. 146–7.
17. *Ibid.*, p. 144.
18. S. T. Coleridge, 'The Rime of the Ancient Mariner', lines 236–9.
19. Jones, *In Parenthesis*, p. xxi. Here, as in subsequent epigraphs from *The Gododdin*, Jones unites separate quotations from the translation by Professor Edward Anwyl that appeared in *Transactions of the Honourable Society of Cymmrodorion, Session 1909–10*, 1911, pp. 120–36.
20. Jones, *In Parenthesis*, p. 1.
21. *Ibid.*, pp. 1–2.
22. David Jones, 'Fragment of an Autobiographical Writing', *Agenda*, 12, 4/13, 1 (Winter–Spring 1975), p. 98.
23. Jones, *In Parenthesis*, p. 107.
24. *Ibid.*, p. 149.
25. *Ibid.*, p. 13.
26. *Ibid.*
27. *Ibid.*
28. *Ibid.*, p. 24.
29. *Ibid.*, p. xiv.
30. *Ibid.*, p. 73.
31. *Ibid.*, p. 79.
32. *Ibid.*, p. 151. Mischievously, Jones's note gives only the literal source of this quotation: Carroll's *Hunting of the Snark*, Fit the 2nd, verse 15.
33. Jones, *In Parenthesis*, p. 151. Lines translated from *Y Gododdin*.
34. Jones, *In Parenthesis*, p. 155.
35. *Ibid.*
36. *Ibid.*, p. 166.
37. *Ibid.*, pp. 184–5.
38. *Ibid.*, p. 185.
39. Fussell, *Great War*, p. 147.
40. Quoted in Ian Hamilton (ed.), *Alun Lewis: Selected Poetry and Prose* (London: George Allen & Unwin, 1966), p. 52.
41. *Ibid.*, p. 122.

42. *Ibid.*, p. 132.
43. 'In Memory of W.B. Yeats', lines 22–3.
44. Jones, *In Parenthesis*, p. xii.

3. ENGLAND'S EPIC?

1. Heaney (trans.), *Beowulf* (London: Faber and Faber, 1999).
2. Hope Muntz, *The Golden Warrior: The Story of Harold and William*, paperback edition (London: Chatto & Windus, 1966), p. v.
3. *Ibid.*, pp. 9–10.
4. *Ibid.*, p. 10.
5. *Ibid.*, p. 32.
6. *Ibid.*, p. 37.
7. *Ibid.*, p. 4.
8. *Ibid.*, p. 261.
9. *Ibid.*, pp. 326–7.
10. *Ibid.*, p. 155.
11. *Ibid.*, p. 147.
12. *Ibid.*, p. 47.
13. *Ibid.*, p. 59.
14. *Ibid.*, p. 60.
15. *Ibid.*, p. 61.
16. *Ibid.*
17. See Stendhal, *La Chartreuse de Parme* (1839), chapter 3, and Tolstoy, *War and Peace* (1865–9), Book X.
18. Muntz, *Golden Warrior*, p. 387.
19. *Ibid.*, pp. 225, 229, 234.
20. *Ibid.*, pp. 399–400.
21. 'A Malory of the Trenches', *London Mercury*, 36 (July 1937), 304–5.
22. W.B. Yeats, 'The Nineteenth Century and After'.

4. WHO WAS RUPERT BROOKE?

1. Geoffrey Keynes (ed.), *Letters of Rupert Brooke* (London: Faber and Faber, 1968), p. 73.
2. *Ibid.*, p. 18.
3. Frances Cornford and Virginia Woolf, *Rupert Brooke* (Burford: Cygnet Press, 1978), unnumbered pages.

4. Quoted in Christopher Hassall, *Rupert Brooke: A Biography* (London: Faber and Faber, 1964), p. 190.
5. Quoted in Hassall, *Rupert Brooke*, p. 242.
6. Quoted in John Lehmann, *Rupert Brooke: His Life and His Legend* (London: Weidenfeld & Nicolson, 1980), p. 18.
7. Keynes (ed.) *Letters of Rupert Brooke*, p. 539.
8. Quoted in Hassall, *Rupert Brooke*, p. 449.
9. Quoted in *ibid.*, p. 81.
10. Quoted in *ibid.*, p. 507.
11. *Poetry and Drama*, 1, 2 (June 1913), 187.
12. Hassall, *Rupert Brooke*, p. 94.
13. This and other of Brooke's poems cited or quoted in this chapter may be found in Geoffrey Keynes (ed.), *Rupert Brooke: The Poetical Works* (London: Faber and Faber, 1970).
14. Keynes (ed.), *Letters of Rupert Brooke*, p. 27.
15. Quoted in Hassall, *Rupert Brooke*, p. 65.
16. Keynes (ed.), *Letters of Rupert Brooke*, p. 491.
17. *Ibid.*, p. 570.
18. Vivien Noakes (ed.), *The Poems and Plays of Isaac Rosenberg* (Oxford University Press, 2004), p. 84.
19. Jon Stallworthy (ed.), *Wilfred Owen: The War Poems* (London: Chatto & Windus, 1994), p. 16.

5. CHRIST AND THE SOLDIER

1. Letter quoted in Dennis Silk, *Siegfried Sassoon* (Tisbury: Compton Russell, 1975), p. 26.
2. Fussell, *Great War*, p. 92.
3. Siegfried Sassoon, *Siegfried's Journey, 1916–1920* (London: Faber and Faber, 1945), p. 224.
4. Rupert Hart-Davis (ed.), *Siegfried Sassoon: Diaries, 1920–1922* (London and Boston: Faber and Faber, 1981), p. 15.
5. Siegfried Sassoon, *The Complete Memoirs of George Sherston*, new edition (London and Boston: Faber and Faber, 1972), p. 9.
6. *Ibid.*, p. 10.
7. Fussell, *Great War*, pp. 94–5.
8. Sassoon, *Complete Memoirs*, p. 282.

9. *Ibid.*, p. 274.
10. *Ibid.*, p. 449.
11. *Ibid.*, p. 476.
12. *Ibid.*, p. 517.
13. 'He [Rivers] is an absolute dear and has been a most delightful companion in our evening talks about literature etc.' Sassoon, letter of 10 August 1917 to Robert Graves, quoted in Max Egremont, *Siegfried Sassoon: A Biography* (London: Picador, 2005), p. 164.
14. Sassoon, *Complete Memoirs*, p. 656.
15. Siegfried Sassoon, *The Weald of Youth* (London: Faber and Faber, 1983), p. 221.
16. Rupert Hart-Davis (ed.) *The War Poems of Siegfried Sassoon* (London: Faber and Faber, 1983), p. 15.
17. *Ibid.*, p. 18.
18. *Ibid.*, pp. 16–17.
19. *Ibid.*, pp. 45–7.
20. *Ibid.*, p. 100.
21. *Ibid.*, pp. 42–3.

6. OWEN'S AFTERLIFE

1. Harold Owen and John Bell (eds.), *Wilfred Owen: Collected Letters* (London: Oxford University Press, 1967), p. 521.
2. Jon Stallworthy (ed.), *Wilfred Owen: The Complete Poems and Fragments, Volume I* (London: Chatto & Windus and Oxford University Press, 1983), pp. 3–6.
3. Owen and Bell (eds.), *Wilfred Owen*, p. 106.
4. *Ibid.*, p. 282.
5. *Ibid.*, p. 285.
6. *Ibid.*, p. 347.
7. *Ibid.*, p. 300.
8. Edward Mendelson (ed.), *The English Auden: Poems, Essays, and Dramatic Writings, 1927–1939* (London: Faber and Faber, 1977), p. 144.
9. Quoted in E.R. Dodds, *Missing Persons: An Autobiography* (Oxford: Clarendon Press, 1977), p. 133.
10. Owen and Bell (eds.), *Wilfred Owen*, p. 580.
11. Stallworthy (ed.), *Oxford Book of War Poetry*, p. 229.

12. *Ibid.*, p. 267.
13. Donald Justice (ed.), *The Collected Poems of Weldon Kees* (Lincoln: University of Nebraska Press, 1960), p. 17.
14. Seamus Heaney, 'Sixth Sense, Seventh Heaven', Lecture delivered in Wolfson College, Oxford, on 29 January 2002.
15. See below, pp. 86–7.
16. Stallworthy (ed.), *Wilfred Owen: Poems and Fragments, Volume I*, pp. 99–100, 140–1, *Volume II*, pp. 511–13.
17. Owen and Bell (eds.), *Wilfred Owen*, p. 531.

7. OWEN AND HIS EDITORS

1. Owen and Bell (eds.), *Wilfred Owen*, p. 521.
2. 'Mental Cases', 'Disabled', 'Parable of the Old Men [sic] and the Young', 'The Last Laugh', 'The Last Word', 'Soldiers Dreams' [sic], 'Arms and the Boy', and the untitled early poem beginning 'Long Ages Past'. '"The Last Laugh" and "The Last Word" are very similar versions of the same [...] poem.' Osbert Sitwell, *Noble Essences or Courteous Revelations* (London: Macmillan, 1950), p. 107.
3. Dennis Welland, 'Sassoon on Owen', *TLS*, 31 May 1974, p. 589.
4. Typeset facsimiles of the manuscripts of these and Owen's other poems can be found in Stallworthy (ed.) *Wilfred Owen: Poems and Fragments, Volume II*.
5. In a 1948 radio broadcast, Sassoon gave the total number of copies printed as 2,250, of which 750 went to the United States.
6. Sassoon to H.M. Tomlinson, 17 August 1953. (Humanities Research Center, University of Austin, Texas). See also Welland, 'Sassoon on Owen', *TLS*, 31 May 1974, p. 590.
7. Two of them, printed in full, appeared in his notes: 'Bold Horatius' (a mistitling of 'Schoolmistress') and the fragment 'Beauty'.
8. Memoir, in Edmund Blunden (ed.), *The Poems of Wilfred Owen* (London: Chatto & Windus, 1931), p. 3.
9. See above, p. 75.
10. Quoted in Humphrey Carpenter, *Benjamin Britten: A Biography* (London: Faber and Faber, 1992), pp. 404–5.
11. She sang the soprano part, written for Galina Vishnevskaya, wife of Mstislav Rostropovich, who had been prevented from accepting Britten's invitation. 'Ekaterina Furtseva, the [Russian]

minister of culture asked her: "How can you, a Soviet woman, stand next to a German and an Englishman and perform a political work?"' Carpenter, *Benjamin Britten*, p. 410.

12. *Ibid.*

13. *Ibid.*, p. 411.

14. See above, p. 82.

15. C. Day-Lewis (ed.), *The Collected Poems of Wilfred Owen* (London: Chatto & Windus, 1963), pp. 28–9.

16. In A. Norman Jeffares and K.G.W. Cross (eds.), *In Excited Reverie: A Centenary Tribute, W.B. Yeats 1865–1939* (London: Macmillan, 1965), pp. 171–92.

17. See above, p. 74.

18. Day-Lewis (ed.), *Collected Poems of Wilfred Owen*, p. 28.

19. On 1 November 1970, four days before the fifty-second anniversary of Owen's death.

20. Blunden (ed.), *Poems of Wilfred Owen*, p. 9.

21. Day-Lewis (ed.), *Collected Poems of Wilfred Owen*, pp. 25, 117.

22. D. S. R. Welland, *Wilfred Owen: A Critical Study* (London: Chatto & Windus, 1960), p. 110.

23. Dominic Hibberd, *Wilfred Owen: A New Biography* (London: Weidenfeld & Nicolson, 2002), pp. 257–8.

24. I am indebted to Christopher Ricks for calling my attention to this poem, published in 1879 and now to be found in Bernard Jones (ed.), *The Poems of William Barnes, Volume II* (Carbondale: Southern Illinois University Press, 1962), p. 825.

25. This manuscript was first reproduced in typeset facsimile in Jon Stallworthy, 'A Slowly Evolving Elegy', *Daily Telegraph*, 7 November 1998.

26. 'Dulce et Decorum Est' and 'Cramped in that funnelled hole', for example.

8. THE LEGACY OF THE SOMME

1. See above, pp. 35–41.

2. Boldly delivered to the Royal Society of Literature (of which he is himself a Fellow) on 24 April 1969. Mary Stocks (ed.), *Essays by Divers Hands*, New series 36 (London: Oxford University Press, 1970), 1–18.

3. Quoted in Dan Todman, *The Great War: Myth and Memory* (London: Hambledon and London, 2005), p. 2.
4. 'British "Anti-War" Writers and Their Critics', Hugh Cecil and Peter H. Liddle (eds.), *Facing Armageddon: The First World War Experienced* (London: Leo Cooper, 1996), p. 819.
5. 'The Western Front Experience as Interpreted through Literature', *RUSI Journal*, December 2003, 53.
6. 'A Military Historian's View of the Great War', p. 8.
7. Todman, *Great War*, p. 15.
8. David Stephenson, *1914–1918: The History of the First World War* (London: Penguin Books, 2004), p. 273.
9. Jones, *In Parenthesis*, p. ix.
10. Captain von Hentig of the Guard Reserve Division, quoted in Gary Sheffield, *The Somme* (London: Cassell, 2003), p. 155.
11. See Gary Sheffield, *Forgotten Victory* (London: Hodder Headline, 2002).
12. R.C. Sherriff, *No Leading Lady: An Autobiography* (London: Gollancz, 1968), pp. 72–3.
13. Perhaps ironically echoed in Sellar and Yeatman, *1066 and All That*.
14. See above, pp. 19–34.
15. See also 'A Picture of Otto' in Hughes's *Birthday Letters* (1998), discussed on p. 76 above.
16. Michael Longley, 'Wounds', in *An Exploded View: Poems 1968–72* (London: Gollancz, 1973), p. 40.
17. Todman, *Great War*, p. 237, note 80.
18. As with so many second-generation writers about the Somme, Susan Hill had a familial connection with the battle. This she describes in the Introduction to the 1984 reprint of *Strange Meeting*. As a child she would visit her maternal grandmother and her sister. They were two of nine children, with one brother

> cherished and idolised by them all, of course. When he was eighteen, he went to war – the Great War, as they called it, the 1914–1918 War. On his nineteenth birthday, he was killed, like so many other thousands of young men, at the Battle of the Somme.
>
> I don't think the family was ever the same again.

They had a photograph of him in his uniform, and I used to take it down and look at it. He had such a young face, even I could see that, as a child, he was not much more than a child himself. His ears stuck out, I remember, and his hair was cut very, very short under his cap. His Christian name was Sidney, and the family surname was Owen. It is coincidence of course, but the long arm of *that*, as they say, is a long one, and I am a believer in these small signs and symbols, as important parts of one's life.

19. *Regeneration* (1991), *The Eye in the Door* (1993), and *The Ghost Road* (1995). *The Regeneration Trilogy* was first published in 1996.
20. 'Everyone Sang'. Hart-Davis (ed.), *War Poems of Siegfried Sassoon*, p. 144.

9. THE ICONOGRAPHY OF THE WASTE LAND

1. Bernard Shaw, *Heartbreak House*, 1919 (New York: Penguin, 1964), p. 12.
2. T.S. Eliot, *The Complete Poems and Plays, 1909–1950* (San Diego: Harcourt Brace Jovanovich, 1971), p. 39.
3. Owen and Bell (eds.), *Wilfred Owen*, p. 562.
4. Hart-Davis (ed.), *War Poems of Siegfried Sassoon*, pp. 15–17, 24, 28.
5. Sassoon, *Complete Memoirs*, p. 282.
6. Hart-Davis (ed.), *War Poems of Siegfried Sassoon*, pp. 45–7.
7. Harold F. Brooks (trans.), *The Dream of the Rood* (Dublin: The Sign of the Three Candles, 1942), [p. 4].
8. Helen Gardner (ed.), *John Donne: The Divine Poems* (Oxford: Clarendon Press, 1952), p. 50.
9. Valerie Eliot (ed.), *The Waste Land: A Facsimile and Transcript of the Original Drafts Including the Annotations of Ezra Pound* (London: Faber and Faber, 1971), p. 23.
10. Joseph Conrad, *Heart of Darkness, with the Congo Diary* (London: Penguin, 1995), p. 94.
11. Eliot, *Complete Poems and Plays*, p. 42.
12. *Ibid.*, p. 47.
13. David Gascoyne, 'Answers to an Enquiry', *New Verse*, 11 (October 1934), 12.

14. Robin Skelton (ed.), *David Gascoyne: Collected Poems* (London: Oxford University Press, 1965), pp. 44–5.
15. Edward Mendelson (ed.), *W.H.Auden: Collected Poems* (New York: Random House, 1976), pp. 454–5.
16.   Who are these coming to the sacrifice?
              To what green altar, O mysterious priest,
           Lead'st thou that heifer lowing at the skies,
              And all her silken flanks with garlands dressed?

    John Barnard (ed.), *John Keats: The Complete Poems* (Middlesex: Penguin, 1973), p. 345.
17. William Golding, *Lord of the Flies* (London: Faber and Faber, 1954), p. 11.
18. *Ibid.*, p. 15.
19. *Ibid.*, p. 47.
20. *Ibid.*, p. 16.
21. *Ibid.*, p. 166.
22. *Ibid.*
23. Source unidentified.
24. Golding, *Lord of the Flies*, p. 178; Conrad, *Heart of Darkness*, p. 97.
25. Golding, *Lord of the Flies*, p. 181.
26. *Ibid.*, p. 187.
27. *Ibid.*, p. 188.
28. Patrick White, *Voss* (Aylesbury: Eyre and Spottiswoode, 1957), p 17.
29. White, *Voss*, p. 94.
30. Carolyn Bliss, *Patrick White's Fiction: The Paradox of Fortunate Failure* (Hampshire: Macmillan Press, 1986), p. 65.
31. White, *Voss*, p. 135.
32. *Ibid.*, p. 255.
33. *Ibid.*, p. 420.
34. *Ibid.*, p. 415–16.
35. *Ibid.*, p. 411.
36. Samuel Beckett, *Waiting for Godot: A Tragicomedy in Two Acts*, 2nd edition (London: Faber and Faber, 1965), p. 1.
37. Beckett, *Godot*, p. 6.
38. *Ibid.*, p. 9.

208 Notes to pages 122–32

39. *Ibid.*, p. 4.
40. Bert O. States, *The Shape of Paradox: An Essay on 'Waiting for Godot'* (Berkeley: University of California Press, 1978), pp. 17–18.
41. Beckett, *Godot*, p. 46.
42. *Ibid.*, p. 86.
43. Keith Sagar, *The Art of Ted Hughes*, 2nd edition (Cambridge University Press, 1978), p. 107.
44. *Ibid.*, p. 106.
45. 'Crow Alights' and 'Two Legends'. Ted Hughes, *Crow: From the Life and Songs of the Crow* (London: Faber and Faber, 1970), pp. 9, 17.
46. Hughes, *Crow*, p. 10.
47. 'Examination at the Womb-Door' and 'Crow Improvises'. Hughes, *Crow*, pp. 11, 53.
48. Hughes, *Crow*, p. 15.
49. *Ibid.*, p. 66.
50. *Ibid.*, p. 73.

10. WAR AND PEACE

1. Virginia Woolf, *Mrs Dalloway*, new edition (London: Hogarth Press, 1947), pp. 6–7.
2. *Ibid.*, p. 127.
3. *Ibid.*, p. 103.
4. *Ibid.*, p. 204.
5. Anne Olivier Bell and Andrew McNeillie (eds.), *The Diary of Virginia Woolf, Volume III* (London: Hogarth Press, 1980) pp. 33–4.
6. Virginia Woolf, *To the Lighthouse*, special edition (London: Hogarth Press, 1943), p. 16.
7. *Ibid.*, p. 32.
8. *Ibid.*, p. 207.
9. D.H. Lawrence, *Women in Love*, Phoenix edition (London: Heinemann, 1954), p. 9.
10. *Ibid.*, p. 20.
11. *Ibid.*, p. 204.
12. *Ibid.*, p. 213.
13. *Ibid.*, p. 197.
14. W.H. Auden, 'September 1, 1939', lines 21–2.

15. Lawrence, *Women in Love*, p. 218.
16. *Ibid.*, p. 214.
17. *Ibid.*, p. 57.
18. Wilfred Owen, 'S.I.W.', line 19.
19. Lawrence, *Women in Love*, p. 56.
20. *Ibid.*, p. 214.
21. *Ibid.*, pp. 215–16.
22. *Ibid.*, p. 219.
23. L.P. Hartley, *The Go-Between* (London: Hamish Hamilton, 1953), pp. 5–7.
24. *Ibid.*, pp. 136–41.
25. Wilfred Owen, 'The Sentry', lines 22–3.
26. Hartley, *Go-Between*, pp. 293–4.
27. Dan H. Lawrence and Daniel J. Leary (eds.), *Bernard Shaw: The Complete Prefaces* (London: Penguin, 1995), pp. 2, 319.
28. Ford Madox Ford, *Return to Yesterday* (London: Gollancz, 1931), p. 373.
29. Ford Madox Ford, *It was the Nightingale* (London: Heinemann, 1934), p. 202.
30. Ford Madox Ford, *Parade's End* (New York: Vintage Books, 1979), pp. 365–6.
31. 'Critics have made much of the religious symbolism of the series – usually too much, rather than what the novels will support.' Max Saunders, *Ford Madox Ford: A Dual Life, Volume II* (Oxford University Press, 1996), p. 223. At several points in his biography, Saunders judiciously explores the sources and implications of this symbolism, a central theme of the series. See pp. 208, 223, 243–6, 256, and 269–70.
32. Ford, *Parade's End*, p. 379.
33. *Ibid.*, p. 380.
34. *Ibid.*, p. 460.
35. St John, 15:13.
36. See above, pp. 62–4.
37. Ford, *Parade's End*, p. 3.
38. *Ibid.*, p. 155.
39. *Ibid.*, pp. 167–8.
40. Isaiah, 53: 5.
41. George Herbert, 'Virtue', lines 1–2.

42. Saunders, *Ford Madox Ford, Volume II*, p. 223.
43. Ford, *Parade's End*, p. 639.
44. *Ibid.*, p. 674.
45. Siegfried Sassoon, 'Everyone Sang', lines 6–10. Hart-Davis (ed.), *War Poems of Siegfried Sassoon*, p. 144.
46. Robie Macauley, Introduction to Ford, *Parade's End*, p. xvii.
47. Ford, *Parade's End*, p. 835.
48. *Ibid.*, pp. 306–7.

11. THE FIRE FROM HEAVEN

1. 'From Feathers to Iron', 29, C. Day Lewis, *Collected Poems* (London: Jonathan Cape with the Hogarth Press, 1954), p. 75.
2. Day Lewis, *Collected Poems*, p. 142. 'D.H. nine': aeroplane made by the De Havilland Aircraft Company.
3. Richard J. Finneran (ed.), *W.B. Yeats: The Poems* (New York: Macmillan, 1983), p. 294.
4. Richard Hillary, *The Last Enemy*, new edition (London: Macmillan, 1950), p. 4.
5. *Ibid.*, p. 8.
6. *Ibid.*, p. 10.
7. *Ibid.*, p. 16.
8. *Ibid.*, p. 21.
9. *Ibid.*, p. 22.
10. *Ibid.*, p. 29.
11. *Ibid.*, pp. 121–2.
12. *Ibid.*, p. 213.
13. Galassi (ed.), *Understand the Weapon, Understand the Wound*, p. 41.
14. Hillary, *Last Enemy*, p. 214.
15. *Ibid.*, p. 214–16.
16. *Ibid.*, p. 221.
17. Sebastian Faulks, *The Fatal Englishman* (London: Vintage, 1997), p. 161.
18. Peter McDonald (ed.), *Louis MacNeice: Collected Poems* (London: Faber and Faber, 2007), p. 253.
19. Randall Jarrell, *The Complete Poems* (London: Faber and Faber, 1971), p. 144.

20. Genesis, 2:21–2.
21. James Dickey, *Poems 1957–1967* (New York: Collier Books, 1968), pp. 181–8.
22. 'Think, how everyone will show that he had no hand in the great destruction.'
23. Job, 40:9.
24. See above, pp. 15–17, and below, pp. 181–3.
25. See above, pp. 15–17.
26. See above, pp. 33–4.
27. See above, pp. 19–34.
28. J.G. Ballard, *Empire of the Sun* (London: Victor Gollancz, 1984), pp. 207–8.

12. HENRY REED AND THE GREAT GOOD PLACE

1. I am indebted to the poet's niece, Jane Reed, and his friend, Michael Ramsbotham, for much of the biographical information in this Introduction to Reed's *Collected Poems* (Oxford University Press, 2007).
2. This and all other poems cited or quoted in this chapter can be found in the *Collected Poems*.
3. See Roger Savage's excellent article, 'The Radio Plays of Henry Reed', in John Drakakis, ed., *British Radio Drama* (1981).
4. The last of Eliot's *Four Quartets* may have been kindled in June 1941 by a spark from Reed's incendiary satire, 'Chard Whitlow', published on 10 May 1941.

13. THE FURY AND THE MIRE

1. Stallworthy (ed.), *Wilfred Owen: Complete Poems and Fragments, Volume II*, p. 535.
2. Edward Mendelson (ed.), *W.H. Auden: Prose, 1926–1938* (London: Faber and Faber, 1996), p. 105.
3. Stallworthy (ed.), *Wilfred Owen: Complete Poems and Fragments, Volume I*, p. 140.
4. Galassi (ed.), *Understand the Weapon, Understand the Wound*, p. 41.
5. H[igh] E[xplosive].

6. Erich Maria Remarque, *In Westen Nichts Neues*, trans. A. W. Wheen as *All Quiet on the Western Front* (London: G.P. Putnam's Sons, 1929).

7. Louis Simpson, *Selected Poems* (London: Oxford University Press, 1966), p. 20.

8. Louis Simpson in Ian Hamilton (ed.), *The Poetry of War: 1939– 1945* (London: Alan Ross, 1965), pp. 171–2.

9. Hart-Davis (ed.), *War Poems of Siegfried Sassoon*, p. 49.

10. For a comprehensive critical and contextual study, see Subarno Chattarji, *Memories of a Lost War: American Poetic Responses to the Vietnam War* (Oxford: Clarendon Press, 2001).

11. Frank Bidart and David Gewanter (eds.) *Robert Lowell: Collected Poems* (London: Faber and Faber, 2003), p. 596.

12. *Ibid.*, p. 329.

13. Christopher Ricks (ed.), *The Poems of Tennyson, Volume II*, 2nd edition (London: Longmans, Green, 1987) pp. 510–13.

14. 'Drummer Hodge', James Gibson (ed.), *Thomas Hardy: The Complete Poems* (London: Macmillan, 1976), pp. 90–1.

15. Anthony Hecht, *Anthony Hecht in Conversation with Philip Hoy* (Oxford: Between the Lines, 1999), p. 77.

16. *Ibid.*, p. 24.

17. Anthony Hecht, *Collected Earlier Poems* (New York: Alfred A. Knopf, 1990), pp. 64–5.

18. W.H. Auden, quoted in Dodds, *Missing Persons*, p. 133.

19. John Balaban, *Locusts at the Edge of Summer: New and Selected Poems* (Washington: Copper Canyon Press, 1997), pp. 108–9.

20. James Fenton, *The Memory of War* (Edinburgh: The Salamander Press, 1982), pp. 9–19.

21. *Ibid.*, pp. 26–8.

22. A[rmoured] P[ersonnel] C[arriers].

Index

Shaw, George Bernard: Preface to
Heartbreak House 109, 136
Sheffield, Gary: *Forgotten Victory* 105
Shelley, Percy Bysshe: Owen and
69–70, 79
Sherriff, R. C.: *Journey's End* 105–6
Sherston's Progress (Sassoon) 55, 60, 61
'The Shield of Achilles' (Auden) 113–16
'The Show' (Owen) 78, 81, 82, 83
A Shropshire Lad (Housman) 9
Siegfried's Journey (Sassoon) 55, 56, 60
Simonides: epigram on Spartans 6
Simpson, Louis 16–17, 160; amnesia
suffered by 15, 135, 181; and Owen
15–16; writes as civilian in uniform
16–17; *The Arrivists* 182; 'The
Battle' 16; 'Carentan O Carentan'
181, 182; *Good News of Death* 182;
'The Heroes' 181, 182–3, 194; 'The
Runner' 16
'Sing we the two lieutenants ...' (Day
Lewis) 146–7
Sitwell, Edith: edition of Owen's poems
72, 81–3, 94; 'Still Falls the Rain'
154; *Wheels* 81
Sitwell, Osbert 81
'S.I.W.' (Owen) 73, 78
'Six Young Men' (Hughes) 106
Slaughterhouse-Five (Vonnegut) 160
'Smile, Smile, Smile' (Owen) 78, 105
Smith, Malvern van Wyk 10
Smith, Reggie: befriended by
MacNeice 163
'Snake Hymn' (Hughes) 125–6
'The Soldier' (Brooke) 10, 44, 54, 100
soldiering: commissions 9; status of 4–5
Some Do Not (Ford) 137, 139
Somme, Battle of the 71; casualties at 59,
101–2; cavalry at 14; film of 104;
in literature 106–8; media
presentation of 104–5; military
strategy at 103; in national cultural
history 99, 105, 108; Ulster Division
at 107; writers present at 100–1
'Song of Songs' (Owen) 81, 92
Sophocles: *Ajax* translated by Reed 170

Sorley, Charles Hamilton 108; on
similarities between foes 66;
verse-letter from trenches 13;
'When you see millions ...' 100
'South' (Reed) 171
Spanish Civil War ix, 73, 74, 147,
179, 189
Spencer, Stanley: as friend of Rupert
Brooke 43; as official war artist 105
Spender, Stephen: 'The Coward' 73;
'The Deserter' 73; *The Destructive
Element* 73; influenced by Owen
73; in Spanish Civil War 73;
'Ultima Ratio Regum' 73
Spion Kop: casualties at 101
'Spring Offensive' (Owen) 105
Stallworthy, Jon: *Between the Lines*
87; biography of Owen 87–8;
Chatterton Lecture on Owen 87;
and dating of Owen's poems 88–94;
discovers Owen 77–8, 87; edition
of Owen's poems 81, 86, 87, 90–5;
on Texas-bound aircraft 88–9;
and Yeats 78, 86; 'Yeats as
Anthologist' 86
Stamford Bridge, Battle of 39, 99
'Stand-to: Good Friday Morning'
(Sassoon) 110
States, Bert: on *Waiting for Godot* 122
Strange Meeting (Hill) 107
'Strange Meeting' (Owen) 22, 76, 79,
81, 85
'The Streets of Laredo' (MacNeice) 154
The Streets of Pompeii (Reed) 168, 169
'Suggested by some of the Proceedings
of the Society for Psychical
Research' (Brooke) 49
Surrey, Henry Howard, Earl of: elegy
on his Squire 4; military service
of 3; translation of *Aeneid* 3
survivors: as witnesses 18–20, 21, 32, 34
The Sword of Honour (Waugh) 160

Tagore, Rabindranath: quoted by Owen
108
Taillefer 19, 23

LAST
LIGHT

· · · · ·

Alex Scarrow

First published in Great Britain in 2007 by Orion,
an imprint of the Orion Publishing Group Ltd.

A CIP catalogue record for this book is
available from the British Library.

ISBN: (hardback) 978 0 7528 8614 5
(trade paperback) 978 0 7528 8615 2

Typeset by Deltatype Ltd,
Birkenhead, Merseyside

Set in Monotype Times New Roman

Printed in Great Britain at
Mackays of Chatham plc, Chatham, Kent

The Orion Publishing Group's policy is to use papers
that are natural, renewable and recyclable products and made
from wood grown in sustainable forests. The logging and
manufacturing processes are expected to conform to the
environmental regulations of the country of origin.

The Orion Publishing Group Ltd
Orion House
5 Upper Saint Martin's Lane
London WC2H 9EA
An Hachette Livre UK Company

www.orionbooks.co.uk

For my son Jacob, smart, imaginative …
and maybe one day, competition. I love you man.

For Jacob's eyes only:
VQ BMJJN RJXB GR ZWB BDWCB RNBADC FADNSRMPR
OQXL CGN JRMP NO RWZTDUZWC

Acknowledgements

There's a small list of people that deserve a mention for the help they gave me in putting together this book. There's no particular order in which I want to do this, so I'll dive right on in.

Robin Carter for extensive proofing and valuable comments. Yes ... his name does appear in the book as you, dear reader, will soon see. Obviously for legal reasons, I need to say something about this being utterly coincidental and any resemblance ... blah, blah, blah. A damn good character name that. I also want to thank Andy Canty for his proof reading and comments as well, and again ... that's another Christian name that has turned up in the book! Funny old world.

My thanks also go out to someone I can't name for security reasons, who gave me some useful 'on the streets' details of life in Iraq. He knows I'm thanking him anonymously like this, and that's how it needs to be.

I want to thank my wife, Frances, for reading the first draft. I must extend my apologies for making her cry with the second draft. Her comments were many and varied; you'll never truly know how valuable her feedback is. Dad, Tony, and brother, Simon, thanks you two for your encouragement. Additional thanks go to Jerry Stutters for some background military details.

Finally, a thank you to my editor, Jon Wood, and agent, Eugenie Furniss, for working with me on this and helping me to finesse the story and take it up to the next level.

December 1999

Room 204

She stared at the door of room 204.

Like every other door along the corridor, it was a rich dark wood with the room number and handle in gold plate.

A *bloody* expensive hotel, that's what Dad had said.

'*Enjoy it guys ... we'll probably never stay in another as expensive as this one.*'

He'd made a joke to Mum about sneaking out the bathrobes and selling them at some place called 'eee-bay'.

The corridor was silent, leaving the lift her footsteps were hushed by the thick carpet – not even the muted noise of quiet conversations or a TV on low, coming from any of the rooms, the doors were so thick and heavy.

Now it was decision time ... and she *knew* this would happen on the way up from the foyer, where she'd left Mum waiting impatiently. She knew she was going to forget the number in the lift going up   way too busy thinking about what she was going to buy with the spends Dad had given her for the trip.

204? It is 204 isn't it? ... Or was it 202?

Leona wondered if Dad's business was all done now, or if he was still waiting for his mystery visitor. He'd been a little nervous and jumpy when he had shoo-ed her and Mum out to go window-shopping; snappy, tense, just like Leona remembered being on her first day at big school earlier that year.

Nervous – *exactly* like that.

Mum was pretty sure he must have finished his meeting by now. Since he'd bundled them out a couple of hours ago, they'd both visited a big department store glistening with Christmas displays, and grabbed a coffee and a Danish in a bustling coffee shop that overlooked the busy streets surrounding Times Square. And Dad had assured them his *very important* business meeting would be over quickly.

Leona hoped maybe he would be able to join them; to come back down with her now that the 'work' part of their family trip to New York was over.

It wasn't the same without him. But either way she *really* needed to pick up that beanie-bag of hers with all her spends in. There were just too many things she'd seen in the last two hours that she desperately *needed* to buy.

She decided it was room 204 they were staying in, not 202, after all. She placed her hand on the old-fashioned brass door-handle. She noticed a flicker of light through the keyhole beneath.

Dad nervously pacing the room? Or maybe his meeting had started already? She was about to hunker down and spy through the keyhole to be sure she wasn't going to interrupt his business, but her grasp of the door-handle was heavy enough that, with a click, the latch disengaged and the door swung in heavily.

The three men stared at her, their conversation frozen in time. They stood at the end of the emperor-sized bed; three men, old men, very smart men, looking down at her. She noticed a fourth, younger, dark-haired man standing to one side, a deferential distance away from the others. He broke the moment, starting to move swiftly towards her, his hand reaching into a pocket.

'No,' whispered one of the three. That stopped him dead, although his hand remained inside his smart jacket.

The one who spoke turned towards Leona, stooping down slightly. 'I think you've come into the wrong room my dear,' he said, his voice pleasant and disarming, like a doting grandfather.

He smiled warmly at her, 'I think your room is next door.'

'I'm really s-sorry,' Leona replied awkwardly, taking a contrite step backwards out of the room and into the corridor, pulling the door after her.

The door closed gently with a click of the latch and there was a long silence before one of the two older men who had remained silent, turned to the others.

'She saw all three of us. We were seen together.'

A pause.

'Is this going to pose a problem?'

'Don't worry. She doesn't know who we are. She doesn't know why we're here.'

'Our anonymity is everything … as it has always been, since—'

'She's a little girl. A few years from now, the only thing she'll remember will be whatever she got for Christmas and the Millennium Eve fireworks. Not three boring old men in a room.'

The Present

Monday

CHAPTER I

. . . .

8.05 a.m. GMT

BBC, Shepherd's Bush, London

'He's lost some weight,' said Cameron.

'Really? I think he's put some on.'

Cameron studied the monitors lined above the mixing desk. On them, Sean Tillman and his co-anchor, Nanette Madeley, were exchanging a few improvised witticisms between items.

'No, you can see it in Sean's face. It's less jowly.'

His assistant producer, Sally, wrinkled her nose in judgement. 'I don't think he's lost any weight. Do you suppose he's feeling threatened by the younger news team over on Sky?'

'Christ, yes. Can't blame him though,' Cameron replied. 'Let's be honest, if you've just woken up and you're channel-hopping first thing in the morning, whose face would you want yapping the news at you? Flabby old Sean Tillman, or someone who looks like Robbie Williams' younger, sexier brother?'

'Hmmm, tough call,' said Sally casting a casual glance across to their news-feed screen.

The domestic feed, a horizontal, news text bar, was scrolling some dull story on a farmers' dispute in Norfolk whilst the Reuters' feed was streaming results on an election in Indonesia. Pretty uninteresting stuff all round.

Cameron cast a glance up at the monitor to see Sean Tillman checking himself in a small hand-mirror. 'I know Sean's also worried about the *chin* factor.'

Sally snorted with amusement.

'Yuh, that's what he calls it. He's really pissed off about the studio floor being re-covered last month with a lighter linoleum. I heard him having a good old moan to Karl in make-up that the floor's deflecting the studio lights. That he's getting lit from underneath.'

Cameron leant forward and studied the monitor, watching both Sean and Nanette preparing for the hand-back from Diarmid. 'He's got a point though. He's really coming off worse there. Nanette actually looks better, more radiant since they changed the—'

'Cameron,' muttered Sally.

'—floor covering. Poor Sean though. It sort of makes the flesh under his chin glow. And there is a fair bit of it wobbling away under his—'

'Cam!' Sally said, this time more insistently.

'What?'

She pointed to the Reuters' news feed.

As the words scrolled slowly across the display bar, he read them one after the other, gradually making sense of the text he was reading.

'Shit!' he said, turning to Sally. 'We're going to need a whole bunch of graphics. This is going to hog the news all day.'

'It's not *that* big a deal, is it?'

'You're kidding me, right?'

Sally shrugged. 'Another bomb. I mean we get a dozen of those every day in Ira—?'

'But it's *not* Iraq, is it?' Cameron snapped at her. She flinched at the tone of his voice, and despite the sensation of growing urgency and the first prickling of a migraine, he felt she deserved a word or two more from him. 'Trust me, this story's going to grow very quickly, and we don't want to be left chasing it. Let's get ahead of the game and get all the assets we're going to need. Okay?'

Sally nodded. 'Sure, I'll get on to it.'

'Thanks,' he muttered as he watched her disappear out of the control room. He shot another glance at the Reuters' feed, more detail on the story was already coming in.

There were a couple of other control-room staff in there with him and they stared silently at him, waiting for orders. Normally he fed his input through Sally to them. But with her gone and chasing down the things they were going to need, it was just them.

'Okay Tim, patch me through to Sean and Nanette. I suppose I'd better let them in on this.'

CHAPTER 2

. . . .

8.19 a.m. GMT

Shepherd's Bush, London

Jennifer Sutherland hopped awkwardly across the cold tiles of the kitchen floor, whilst she struggled to zip up the back of her skirt and tame her hair with the straighteners, all at the same time. Too many things to do, too few hands, too little time. That bloody little travel alarm clock had let her down again.

Jenny checked her watch; she had ten minutes until the cab was due; time enough for a gulped coffee. She slapped the kettle's switch on.

Today, if all things went well, was going to be the beginning of a new chapter; the beginning of a *brand new* chapter to follow the last one, a long and heartachingly sad one – twenty years long. She had a train to catch from Euston station taking her up to Manchester, and an interview for a job she dearly wanted; needed, in fact.

So this was it.

If they offered her the job, she could be on her way out of what had become a painful mess for her and Andy. This whole situation was hurting him a lot more than it was her. She was the one who was leaving and she knew when the dust settled, and both his and her parents performed a post-mortem on this marriage, the blame would fall squarely on her shoulders.

'*Jenny got bored of him. She put herself before their kids, put herself before Andy.*'

And the rest ...

'*You know she had an affair, don't you? A little fling at work. He found out, and he forgave her, and this is how she repays him.*'

The kettle boiled and she reached into the cupboard above it pulling out the last mug. The rest were packed away in one of the many cardboard boxes littered throughout the house, each box marked either with 'Jenny' or 'Andy'. Jennifer had been busy over the last week, since Andy had gone off on his latest job, sorting out two decades of stuff into *his* and *hers* piles.

The house was now on the market, something they both agreed they might as well get on and do now that they were going to go their separate ways. Living together under the same roof, after both tearfully conceding it was all over, had been horrible: passing each other wordlessly in the hallway, waiting for the other to leave a room before feeling comfortable enough to enter it, cooking meals for one and then eating alone.

Not a lot of fun.

Dr Andy Sutherland, the geeky geology student from New Zealand she had met twenty years ago, who had loved The Smiths and The Cure, who could quote from virtually every original episode of *Star Trek*, who could do a brilliant Ben Elton impersonation, whom she had once loved, whom she had married at just nineteen years of age; that same Andy had somehow become an awkward and unwanted stranger in her life.

She tipped in a spoon of decaf granules and poured some boiling water into her mug.

But it wasn't all her fault. Andy was partly to blame.

His work, his work … always his bloody work.

Only it wasn't *work*, as such, was it? It was something else. It was an obsession he'd fallen into, an obsession that had begun with the report he'd been contracted to write, the special one he couldn't talk about, the big earner that had bought this house and paid for a lot more besides. And of course, the rather nice family trip to New York to hand it over in person. He'd earned a lot of money for that, but ultimately, it had cost them their marriage.

The walls of his study were filled with diagrams, charts, geological maps. He had become one-dimensional over that damned fixation of his. It had eroded the funny, complex, charming person that he had once been, and now it seemed that anything that he could be bothered to say to her, in some oblique way, linked back to this self-destructive, doom-laden fascination of his with the end of the world.

And she remembered, it had all started with a report he'd been commissioned to write.

When he'd first stumbled upon … *it* … and breathlessly talked her through it – what they should do to prepare, should it happen – she had been terrified and so worried for their children. They had taken a long hard look at their urban lifestyle and realised they'd be thoroughly screwed, just like everyone else, if they didn't prepare. In the early days they had looked together for remote properties hidden away in acres of woodland or tucked away in the valleys of Wales. He had even nearly talked her into moving to New Zealand; anything to get away from the centres of population, anything to get away from people. But, inevitably, life – earning a crust, paying the bills, getting the kids into the *right* school – all those things had got in the way. For Jenny, the spectre of this impending disaster had faded after a while.

For Andy, it had grown like a tumour.

Jenny gulped her coffee as she finished fighting with her coarse tawny hair and turned the straighteners off.

Sod it. Good enough for now. She could do her make-up on the train.

The interview was at one o'clock. She was surprised at the shudder of nerves she felt at the prospect of sitting before a couple of strangers and selling herself to them in just a few hours' time. If they gave that job to her she would have to pull Jacob out of his prep school; the very same school she had fought hard to get him into in the first place. Jake would be going up north to Manchester with her. Leona on the other hand, had just started at the University of East Anglia; home for her was a campus now, as it would be for another two years.

Jenny hated the fact that she was being instrumental in breaking her family up, but she couldn't go on like this with Andy. She was going to make a new home for herself and Jake, and there would always be a bed for Leona – wherever it was that Jenny eventually found for them to live.

The worst task lay ahead of course. Neither of the kids knew how far things had gone, and that she and Andy had made the decision to go their separate ways. Leona perhaps had an inkling of what was on the cards, but for young Jake, only eight, whose focus was on much more important matters such as his next major Yu-Gi-Oh deck-trade, this was going to be coming right out of nowhere.

Outside she heard a car horn, the taxi. She drained the rest of the coffee and grabbed her handbag, heading out into the hallway. She opened the front door, but then hesitated, looking back inside the house as the taxi waited outside.

Although she planned to be back in a couple of days to begin tidying up all the loose ends that were left for now flapping loosely, it felt like she was walking out for the last time; it felt like this was the moment that she was actually saying goodbye to their family home.

And goodbye to Andy.

CHAPTER 3

. . . .

8.31 a.m. GMT

University of East Anglia (UEA), Norwich

Leona stirred, slowly waking by inches. And then still half-asleep, she remembered who was sharing her bed. She shuddered with a smug, secret pleasure, as if she were holding a million pound prize-winning lottery ticket but had yet to tell anyone.

Danny moved sleepily in the bed next to her. She sat up and looked down at him. He was breathing evenly and deeply, still very much lost in the land of slumber, a content half-smile spread across his lips.

Daniel Boynan.

He looked even more lovely with his eyes closed, his lips pursed, and not pulling any stupid faces to make her laugh. Totally angelic. His mop of dark hair was piled around him on the pillow, and his dark eyebrows momentarily knit as his mind randomly skipped through a dream. Leona had spotted him on the first day, registration day, queuing like her to get his Student Union card and his campus ID.

Donnie Darko, she thought. That's who he had reminded her of.

And throughout most of the first term Leona had pursued him, discreetly of course. Never appearing too interested, though, just enough that he got the message, eventually.

God, boys can be so flippin' blind – he hadn't noticed Leona had been eyeing him up for the last eight weeks.

And then it sort of happened last night. What should have been Step Five of her Ten Step Plan to conquer the heart of Dan Boynan, had turned into a rapid tiptoe through Six, Seven, Eight, Nine ...

And Step Ten had been just about perfect.

She watched him breathe easily, and pushed a lock of hair away from his porcelain face. Here he was, Daniel, gorgeous normally – doubly-so asleep. A brass ankh pendant, dangled down from his neck, the fine leather thong draped over his collar-bone, the small looped cross nestled in a hollow at the base of his throat. That's what she liked about him – with any other lad, that would have been a big chunk of *bling* on a thick silver chain.

Outside her room, she could hear the others stirring in the kitchen. The dinky little portable TV was on, and she could hear the tinkle of spoons on mugs as someone was making a brew.

Beside her, the radio alarm clock switched on quietly and she heard the nattering, way-too-cheerful voice of Larry Ferdinand bantering with one of his studio sidekicks. Leona smiled, Mum listened to him too. If you asked Mum, she would swear blind that it was *her* who turned on to him first, and then got Leona listening to him, which was, of course, rubbish.

She turned the volume down slightly, not wanting Daniel to be woken up, well, not yet anyway, and then slid gently out of bed. She picked up Daniel's burgundy coloured FCUK hoodie, discarded by the side of the bed, and slipped it on. It was so big on her, it hung down almost to her knees.

Daniel said he loved her Kiwi accent. Leona didn't think she had even a trace of Dad's clipped vowels. For the most part she thought she sounded like everyone else: same ol' Home Counties' blandness. But there you go.

It was odd though, it's not like she had been particularly close to Dad, not for the last four or five years, anyway. In fact, she hardly ever saw him. He was always either off on some contract abroad, or distracted with some freelance work in his study. But perhaps from earlier years, when he'd had the time for her and Mum and Jake, that's where the faint echo of his New Zealand accent had been picked up.

Still who cares, Danny loves it. Bonus.

On the radio she heard Larry Ferdinand hand over to the newsreader.

Daniel stirred in his sleep, mumbling something that sounded like 'take my other d-d-dog ...'

He had the slightest stutter, just very slight. Leona found it charming. It made him seem just a little vulnerable, and when he was cracking a joke, somehow that little hitch in his delivery seemed to make the punch line that much more amusing.

She smiled as she looked down at him. *Love* seemed too strong a word right now – way too early to be throwing around a word like that. But she certainly felt she was more than just *in lust* with him. And sure as hell she wasn't going to let Daniel in on that little secret.

Play it cool, Lee.

Yup, that was what she was going to do, especially after she had let him get his cookies last night.

'... now this could mean a very serious shortfall in oil supplies ...'

Leona cocked her head and listened to the faint voice coming from the radio.

'... if the situation is allowed to get much worse. As it is, it's early days, and it's unclear exactly what has happened over there. But this much is certain: it will have an immediate knock-on effect on oil prices ...'

She sighed. Oil ... terrorists ... bombs – that's all news seemed to be these days; angry mobs, guns being fired into the sky, faces full of hatred. The news reminded her of the tired old doom 'n' gloom Dad tended to spout after a glass or two of red wine.

'It'll happen quickly when it happens ... one thing after another, going down like dominoes. And no one will be ready for it, not even us, and Christ, we're in the minority that know about it ...'

Shit. Dad could be really wearing when he got going on his pet hobby-horse; rattling on about stuff like Hubbert's Peak, petro-dollars, hydrocarbon footprints ... it was his special party piece, the thing he talked about when he couldn't think of anything else interesting to say. Which, to be honest, was most of the time. God, he just wouldn't shut up about it when he got going, especially when he thought he had an interested audience.

Leona reached over and snapped the radio off.

She knew Mum was getting to the point where she'd had enough, to put it bluntly; she wondered if Mum was getting bored of Dad. She could feel something brewing at home, there was an atmosphere. Leona was just glad to be away at uni, and glad her little brother, Jacob, was at his prep school. It gave her parents some room and an opportunity to sort out whatever they needed to sort out.

She padded lightly across the floor of her room, stepping over the trail of clothes both her and Daniel had shed behind them as they'd worked their way briskly from first base to last, the night before.

She opened the door of her room and headed into the kitchen where a pile of pots, plates and pans encrusted with beans and ravioli were waiting in vain to be washed up, and a couple of her campus floor-mates were watching *Big Brother Live* through a haze of cigarette smoke on the TV nestled in the space above the fridge.

CHAPTER 4

· · · ·

11.44 a.m. local time

Pump station IT-1B

Ninety-five miles
north-east of Al-Bayji, Iraq

Andy Sutherland reached into the back seat of the Toyota Land Cruiser and grabbed hold of a large bottle of water. It had been sitting in the sun back there, and although he had pulled it out of the freezer that morning a solid bottle-shaped block of ice, it was now almost as hot as a freshly brewed cup of tea. He gulped a few mouthfuls and then poured a little across his face, washing away the dust and the mild salt-sting of his own sweat.

He turned around to look at Farid, standing a few feet away from him.

'You want some?'

Farid smiled and nodded, 'Thank you.'

He held out the bottle to him and then shot another glance at the burned-out remains of pump station IT-1B.

There was nothing worth salvaging, just a shell of breeze blocks and twisted piping that would need to be pulled down before a replacement could be built. IT-1B, along with three other sibling stations, serviced the north-south pipeline leading to Turkey. The whole thing, pipeline, connection nodes, pretty much everything, was screwed-up beyond belief in so many places.

Utterly fubar.

Farid handed the bottle of water back. Andy noticed the old man had only taken a small amount of water, just a few sips.

'Have some more if you want,' he said, miming washing his face. After all, the old translator was just as covered with dust and dried-on sweat as anyone else.

Farid shook his head. 'Not know when you will need the water only for drink,' he replied in the weak, cracked, high-pitched voice of an elderly man. His command of English was pretty good, better than the last translator, who had just decided to vanish without warning a few days ago.

'Okay,' Andy nodded. That was a fair point. Finding regular clean water was still an ongoing concern for many Iraqis. Water scarcity was what they had grown accustomed to over the last few years.

Parked up nearby, in a rough approximation of a defensive laager, was another Land Cruiser, used by the other civilian contractors, and three modified Nissan pick-up trucks manned by a dozen men from the Iraqi Police Service, who were warily scanning the irregular horizon of building carcasses around them.

The caution was well placed; the militia had been this way only a few days ago – not to destroy the pumping station, that was old damage – but instead to make an example of some of the men at the local police station. Four men had been taken from outside the police building the day before yesterday, friends and colleagues of the men standing guard. Their bodies had yet to be discovered, but undoubtedly right now, they were lying out in the afternoon sun at some roadside waiting to be found.

According to Farid, for now, they were relatively safe. The militia had been, done their work and moved on. They'd be back again of course, but not for a while. There were so many other places that needed their special attention.

Andy picked up his hat; a well-worn, sun-bleached turquoise fishing cap, that he wouldn't dare don in public back in England, but over here it cast merciful shade over his head, face and neck. His pale scalp, inadequately protected by a sandy-coloured mop of hair, was beginning to burn as he pulled on his cap and tugged it firmly down.

He wandered across the densely packed, sun-baked clay ground towards the other engineers surveying the remains of IT-1B. He approached the engineer he had shared the Land Cruiser with on the way up, a big, round-shouldered American with a dense black beard called Mike. He reminded Andy of a bigger, less cuddlier version of Bob Hoskins.

'It's totally fucked,' Mike offered analytically as Andy drew up beside him.

Andy nodded. 'I don't see anyone getting much out of the Kirkuk fields until this mess is sorted out.'

Mike shrugged. 'That isn't going to happen for a while.'

Too true.

As they all well knew, it really didn't take much to trash an overland pipeline; hundreds of miles of thin metal casing riding across the ground. It only took one small improvised explosive device placed anywhere along its length, and that would be a done deal until the damage could be repaired. In a country like Iraq, you could forget about using overland pipelines, especially up here in the Salah Ad Din region where every single mile of pipeline would need to be guarded day-in, day-out. Of course it had been a different story thirty or forty years ago when most of the pipelines were laid down. Iraq had been an ordered, prosperous country back then.

'Who're you working for?' asked Mike.

'A small risk assessment consultancy in the UK. But it's Chevroil-Exxo who's paying them. What about you?'

'I'm freelancing for Texana-Amocon.'

Andy smiled. They all seemed to be hyphenated now, the oil companies. It was a sign of the times; struggling companies merging their dwindling reserves, all of them desperately consolidating their assets for the end-game.

'They want to know how long it's going to be before we can get something out of this damned country,' the American added. 'I mean, what the hell do you tell them?'

Andy half-smiled and cast a glance at the darkened shell of the building in front of them.

'Not for years.'

Mike nodded. 'It's sure looking that way. So,' he turned to look at Andy, 'we haven't done full names yet. I'm Mike Kenrick.'

They'd spoken only briefly this morning as the convoy of vehicles had taken several hours picking their way north-east along the road out of Al-Hadithah. They had talked about the crappy hotel they were both staying in, a dark maze of cold empty rooms, tall ceilings sprouting loose electrical cables, and sporadic power and running water.

'Dr Sutherland, call me Andy though,' he replied offering the American a hand.

'So Andy, where you from anyway?'

'Originally a Kiwi. But I guess home is England now. I've been living there on and off for nineteen years,' replied Andy. 'It doesn't much feel like a home right now,' he added as an afterthought.

'Problems?'

'Yeah ... problems.'

The American seemed to understand that Andy wasn't in the mood to elaborate. 'Shit, this kind of job does that,' he added gruffly after a moment's reflection. 'Time away from home can bust up even the strongest of marriages.'

'What about you?'

'Austin, Texas.'

Andy fleetingly recalled seeing this bloke strutting around the hotel the day before yesterday wearing his 'Nobody Fucks with Texas' T-shirt and some white Y-fronts.

Nice.

There were two other civilian contractors currently poking through the remains of the building and photographing it with digital camcorders. Andy had seen them around the compound, but not spoken to them yet. One was Dutch or French, the other Ukrainian, or so he'd been told. They had kept themselves to themselves, as had Andy.

In fact, the only person he'd really spoken to since coming out earlier this week was Farid, their new translator. The four-man field party had been assigned a translator along with the two Toyota Land Cruisers and the two drivers. They didn't get to choose them or vet them, they just inherited them.

'You been out here before?' asked Mike.

'Yeah, a couple of times, but down south – Majnun, Halfaya. Different story down there.'

The American nodded. 'But that's changing as well.'

They heard a disturbance coming from one of the Iraqi police trucks. Andy turned to look. One of the policemen was talking on his cell phone, and then turning to the others, relaying something to them. The others initially looked sceptical, but then within a moment, there were half-a-dozen raised voices, all speaking at the same time. The policeman on the phone quickly raised his hand to hush them, and they quietened down.

Andy turned to Farid and beckoned him over.

'What's all that about?' asked Mike.

'I find out,' the translator replied and went directly over to the policemen to inquire. Andy watched the older man as he spoke calmly to them, and in turn listened to the policeman holding the mobile phone. And then Farid said something, gesturing towards the driver's cabin. One of the policemen rapped his knuckles loudly on the roof and shouted something to the man dozing inside. He lurched in his seat and craned his neck out the driver-side, presumably to ask who the fuck had woken him up.

The guy holding the mobile phone repeated what he'd heard, Farid contributed something, and the driver's expression changed. He pulled back inside, reached to the dashboard and flipped on the radio. There was music which he quickly spun away from, through a wall of crackles and bad signals, finally landing on a clear station and the sound of an authoritative voice; a newsreader.

'Something's happened,' muttered Andy.

The policemen were all silent now, as was Farid. All of them listening intently to the radio. Then out of the blue the American's Immarsat satellite phone bleeped. Mike jumped a little and looked at Andy, one of his dark eyebrows arched in surprise as he opened up the little hip-case it came in. He walked a few steps away to answer it privately.

Andy instinctively checked to see if his mobile phone was on – it was, but no one was calling him.

Andy, growing impatient, caught Farid's eye and spread out his palms, *what's going on?*

The translator nodded and held up a finger, asking him to wait a moment longer, as he craned his neck to listen to the news crackling out of the radio.

He turned back to Mike, who was frowning as he listened to what he was being told over his phone.

'For fuck's sake, what is it?' asked Andy, exasperated that he seemed to be the only person left in the dark.

A moment later, Farid stepped away from the police truck and wandered over to Andy, his face a puzzle ... as if he was trying to work out exactly what he'd just heard.

'Farid?'

Mike snapped the case on his Sat phone shut just as the Iraqi translator came to a halt before them. The American and the Arab looked at each other for a moment.

Andy cracked. 'Is somebody going to tell me what the fuck's going on?'

CHAPTER 5

. . . .

8.45 a.m. GMT

He took off from JFK at just after ten at night. Not a popular time to take a flight so there were plenty of seats in business class. He had checked in effortlessly using his Mr Ash identity. The passport paperwork was good, impeccable. It always was.

Ash.

A good enough name for this particular errand. It was fun anyway, assuming a stolen identity, trying to imagine what the real *Mr G. J. Ash* was like, to get a feel for the person who had lived in this particular skin for the last thirty-seven years. Not that it mattered greatly.

For the duration of this task, *he* was Mr Ash, no one else was, not even the real Mr G. J. Ash, whose identity had been temporarily cloned for the job. *Ash* was the name he imprinted on himself in his mind. Until this job was done, *Ash* was the only name he'd answer to.

There was a sense of urgency to this job. Time was going to work against him this time round. Things were going to start happening very soon, if they hadn't already. When law and order began to unravel, and it would do so rapidly, it would get theoretically very difficult for him to find his given target. So he was going to have to work as quickly as possible.

Ash looked out of the window at the grey Atlantic below.

Leona Sutherland. Eighteen. Occupation: student. Current residence: University of East Anglia campus.

He had no problem with this target. She was a girl, just a child still. But far more important than that, she was a security risk. A very big risk, certainly right now, with what was going on.

Quickly in and quickly out.

He'd make sure she died quickly and painlessly, he could at least do that;

after all it wasn't her fault she was a security risk. Leona Sutherland had made a simple mistake, adding a 'PS' to an email, that's all – half-a-dozen words tagged on to a chatty email to her father ... words it seemed, she hadn't set out to write but had popped into her head at the last moment.

Unfortunately, those few words were going to be her death sentence.

Ash sighed.

How careless people are with what they say, blurting out things – intentionally, unintentionally – that are best left unsaid. He often thought most of the pain and death and misery in the world was caused by people unable to keep inside them, what should rightly stay there.

This wasn't going to be his finest hour though, killing an innocent child, but it was necessary. It was a lesser evil for a greater good.

He was clearing up a few loose ends which to be honest, he should have been allowed to do years ago. Those foolish old men had let the little girl walk out of that hotel room alive.

That's why they needed people like him; to tidy up after them.

CHAPTER 6

. . . .

12.35 p.m. GMT

Manchester

Jenny stepped out of the swing-doors on to Deansgate and took a deep, deep breath.

'I've got it!' she whispered to herself, clutching her hand into a fist and discreetly punching the air when she was sure no one was looking.

The interview had been so much easier than she expected it would be. She had made them laugh a couple of times, everyone's body language seemed to be relaxed and open. She felt she had been on to a winning ticket from the moment she walked into the interview room. It was just one of those things, they all *clicked*.

The give-away, or so she felt, was towards the end when one of the lads asked her how much notice she would need to serve out with her current employer.

'I've got it,' she muttered to herself again, as she walked down Deansgate towards a café bar she'd spotted on the way to the interview.

Of course they couldn't say to her 'you've got it'. There were several more applicants they had to see that afternoon. It would be improper, unprofessional even, to do that. But in every other way – how they had said goodbye, the way they shook hands, nodded and made eye-contact screamed to her *we'll be in touch*.

She grinned in a way she hadn't for a long time. It felt like one giant leap away from the mess in London. There was much to do of course, and the very first thing on the list would be sorting Jake out. Her poor little boy was going to be bewildered by all of this, but once they got settled in Manchester, Jenny was going to spoil him rotten for a bit. Make a real fuss of him. And most importantly, get him into various activity groups and clubs. She knew he liked those little Games Workshop characters. He spent ages painting them and then playing with them. Well, they had one of those shops up here, and they did Saturday and Sunday clubs which she'd take him along to, positive that he'd make a few friends there in no time at all.

Jenny arrived outside the café bar, pulled the door open and stepped inside.

She ordered a hot chocolate with a small mountain of cream – the type Andy referred to as shaving foam – and a Danish pastry and went and picked a seat in the window. The combined plate and mug count was probably close to a thousand calories, but stuff it, she'd played a blinder back there, and put one in the back of the net, so to speak.

She deserved a 'well done' present from herself.

She sat down at a window seat, her mind still running through the mental tick-list of things she needed to do. In the background a TV behind the counter babbled away to itself.

'... spreading chaos over there. News has just come in that senior members of the Saudi royal family have been flown out from the King Khalid International airport in Riyadh. Although no official confirmation has been given on this, it's clear that unrest has spread to the capital and there was a perceived threat to them ...'

She'd have to give them a month's notice down in London. But then Jenny knew they owed her a couple of weeks' leave, so she could work out two of those weeks, and take the last two off. Andy would have to take charge of selling the house though. Mind you, there's not a lot he'd have to do, just make sure he was around to let in the estate agent.

'... it's clear now that the rapid escalation of events in Saudi Arabia was triggered this morning by the bombing of the Sunni holy mosques in Mecca and Medina. Although nobody has come forward claiming responsibility for the bomb, Shi'a Muslims and mosques across the country have been targeted by the majority Sunnis and Wahhabis in what appears to be the beginning of a very bloody and dangerous civil war in the country ...'

And there's all that furniture, the bric-à-brac of twenty years to get rid of. Jenny really didn't want to cart all of that stuff up with her. They could probably shift a lot of it on eBay, or maybe try something like a garage sale. She drew the line though at taking herself down to a whole load of car-boot sales as a vendor, their stuff was worth more than the penny prices they could expect to get.

'... on Wall Street this morning, share prices took a major tumble as oil prices rocketed to over $100 a barrel. There are some murmurings that the worsening Saudi situation will trigger what is known in some obscure corners of the oil and gas industry as an artificial Peak Oil scenario ...'

Jenny turned towards the TV.

The phrase cut through her meandering this-and-that planning, like a hot knife through butter.

'Peak Oil'.

That was one of Andy's pet phrases; a pair of words that had become conjoined together like Siamese twins in their household. It was a phrase that she had grown utterly sick of hearing over the last few years. And now on the TV, on daytime news, for the first time, she'd heard *someone else* use that term. The words sounded odd and a little disconcerting coming from some-one other than Andy. But not just some fellow petro-geologist, or some other frothy-mouthed conspiracy-nut that Andy had struck up a relationship with courtesy of his website; no ... a newsreader, on the BBC, on the lunchtime news had used the phrase.

The barman behind the counter had finished serving the customer, and once more picked up the remote control and deftly flicked through a few channels before settling on one showing a football match; Manchester City versus someone or other.

Jenny almost called out for him to turn it back. She looked around, half expecting several other customers to join her in calling out for the news to be put back on, but none of the little packs of students, nor any of the other customers hurrying in for a hasty lunch-break sandwich, had taken any notice of the news. Everyone seemed too busy to care.

Just like her, too busy with the minutiae of life: earning a crust, paying the bills, getting the kids off to school ... getting a new job.

Her mind went back to the news. Someone else, other than Andy, had just muttered the phrase 'Peak Oil'.

All of a sudden, the sense of euphoria she'd felt walking out of that inter-view began to evaporate.

CHAPTER 7

3.37 p.m. local time

Desert, Salah Ad Din Region, Iraq

'**W**here the hell are they going?' yelled Mike.

The Iraqi police vehicle ahead of them had suddenly lurched to the right off the bumpy road heading south-west back to Al-Bayji.

Andy watched the vehicle rattle away across the rough terrain and then on to a small tributary road. The other two police trucks followed suit, pulling out of their convoy and heading off after the lead truck, away from them.

'Shit. What do we do? Do we follow them?' asked Mike.

Andy shrugged, 'I don't know, that's taking us in the wrong direction.' He watched the three vehicles recede amidst a plume of dust.

'They have other business,' Farid offered from the front seat. The old man pointed to the radio recessed into the dashboard, 'Al-Tariq, the radio station, say Sunni Shi'a unrest in Saudi has spreading over here. They have much explosions, a lot of fighting in Baghdad.'

Mike looked at Andy, 'That's just great.'

Farid frowned uncertainly, not getting the irony. 'The police now go and fight for their side,' he added.

'Sunnis?'

The old man nodded.

Andy bit his lip and took a deep breath. They were dangerously exposed now. With no escort they were going to be a very tempting soft target. There was, of course, their driver, a young man called Amal, and in the other Land Cruiser there was another driver called Salim. Both drivers had on them AK47 assault rifles. How prepared they were to use them in a stand-up fight, he wasn't so sure. The truth was he couldn't expect Farid, Amal or Salim to lay down their lives to protect him or the other three westerners. Shit, if the roles were reversed and they came across an American patrol looking for some likely looking ragheads to play around with, it's not like he, Mike and the other two contractors would level those same guns at the Americans to protect them.

They just had to hope the road back into town was open, and everyone with a gun and a chip on his shoulder would be too busy laying into each other to worry about jacking them.

He looked out of the window at the passing scrub and dusty ground, the occasional cluster of date palm trees, and wondered just what was going on this morning. Mike said his phone call had been from his head office in Austin, Texas, to tell him what they were hearing from Reuters; that all hell had broken loose in Saudi Arabia after some mosques had been blown up, with many casualties. That country was ripe for this; a tinderbox waiting to go up. Understandably, with the situation so volatile in Iraq, things were predictably going to flare up in sympathy, and the same was probably going to happen in other vulnerable Arabic nations: Kuwait, United Arab Emirates, Oman.

Andy could imagine the focus of world news right now was on events in Riyadh as they unfolded hour by hour, and he guessed that experts on Arabic culture and Islamic affairs were being rushed into television studios across the globe to pontificate on what was going on. But he wondered who was taking a look at the bigger picture.

As of this morning, with the troubles rapidly destabilising Saudi Arabia, the world had just lost the regular supply of somewhere between a quarter and a third of its daily oil needs.

He reached into a pocket and pulled out his mobile.

'Who're you calling?' asked Mike.

'I'm phoning home,' Andy replied, flipping it open and hitting the quick-dial button. There was a long pause before he finally heard a flat tone. 'Shit, can't get a signal.'

'It's hit and miss, some cells work better than others,' said Mike. 'We're on the move, so try again in a minute.'

Farid turned round in his seat to talk to them. 'Maybe bad driving into Al-Bayji. Riots, fighting.'

'Shit, well what else do you suggest we do?' snapped Mike. 'We can't stay out here.'

Andy looked up. 'I think we could skirt the town, and head on for K-2. It's another hour or so.'

K-2 was an airstrip extensively upgraded by the Americans and a pivotal supply and extraction point for forces deployed in the north of the country.

'You want to leave Iraq?' asked Mike.

'Yeah, I want to leave Iraq. I see this getting a lot worse.'

Andy tried the home number again, and this time he got a tone. Several rings later he got their answerphone, his own voice coming back at him. 'Shit.'

Do I try her mobile?

She was likely to hang up on him. He wanted the kids back at home, not at school or university, and he wanted Jenny to go down to their local Tesco and buy up enough food and water for a few weeks.

Christ, am I being paranoid?

Maybe. But then if he was over-reacting, so what? It's only food, it would get eaten, eventually. But right now he suspected Jenny would just tell him to piss off, and that she wasn't going to mess the kids around just because he was having some sort of panic attack.

Or maybe she would just be more concerned about him, being over here whilst this was all kicking off. Not thinking for one moment that what was happening in Saudi Arabia would have the slightest effect on her cosy life in Shepherd's Bush, London.

He tried Jenny's number anyway, and got a 'this phone may be switched off' message.

'No luck?' asked Mike.

'Nope.'

Andy wondered whether he should just bypass her for now. He could see this getting a lot worse. If he was right about things, they were going to know about it in two, three or maybe four days. That's how quickly he suspected the impact of a sudden oil strangulation would be felt. Even now he suspected emergency oil conservation measures were being discussed in Downing Street, and would be announced by the Prime Minister sometime before the end of the day. And when that happened, the penny would drop for everyone else and all hell would break loose.

Sod it. I'll give her a call.

Andy called the only other mobile number he had on quick-dial.

CHAPTER 8

. . . .

12.38 p.m. GMT

UEA, Norwich

Leona was walking out of the lecture theatre and heading towards the student union bar across a courtyard busy with students criss-crossing it to use the various on-campus shops, when the phone trembled in her breast pocket.

She reached in and pulled it out, expecting it to be Daniel wondering where the hell she was. Things had overrun somewhat, which was fine with her. She didn't want to turn up before him, or worse still, exactly on time. Leona was still firmly in the let's-appear-to-be-cool-about-things phase.

She quickly read the display to see who was calling her. At first glance the number was unfamiliar, but she answered anyway.

'Yuh?'

'Leona? It's Dad.'

'Dad!' she replied, the pitch of her voice shooting up with surprise.

He rarely called her. If it was a call from home, it was Mum, and Dad might pick up the other handset and say 'hi', ask how things were going, and if she needed anything. But that was it. Mum was the one who got all the gory details. She wondered if something bad had happened to her.

'Is Mum okay?'

'What? Oh yeah, she's fine.'

The signal was awful, crackling and dropping.

'Are you okay Dad?' she asked.

There was a momentary delay suggesting the call was from abroad.

'Yeah, yeah I'm fine, love.'

'Are you still out of the country?' she asked.

'Yeah, I'm still over here. I'm coming back very soon though.'

'Oh, okay. Cool.' But that wasn't why he'd called. She could hear that in his voice clearly. 'So is that why you rang?'

'No. Listen Leona, did you watch the news this morning?'

'No, not really.'

'There are serious problems over here. There was a bomb in Saudi—'

'Oh yeah, I heard about that on the radio. Riots or something.'

A pause, or maybe it was the signal dropping, it was hard to tell.

'I'm worried about this, Leona. I think it's going to affect everyone.'

Oh not this. Not the big oil lecture. Why now?

'Dad, look, if it was serious there'd be an announcement on the campus of some sort. Don't worry about us,' she replied with a weary sigh. Then it occurred to her that *he* might be in some danger. 'How are things over there for you?'

'I'm okay right now. But I'm planning to get a plane out tonight if I can, honey. I think it's going to get very nasty here. But listen, this is really important, Leona.'

She reached the student union bar and pulled the door open. Inside she could see Daniel sitting in a window seat, watching for her. He waved.

'Dad, I've got to go.'

'No! Listen. Leona …?'

She halted, nodded at Daniel and put a finger up to indicate she'd be with him in a minute. And then let the door swing to, shutting out the noise coming from inside.

'What is it?'

'Where's Mum?'

'She said something about going up to Manchester for something … to visit some friends, I think. She's up there until the end of the week.'

Leona heard him curse under his breath.

'Listen sweetheart, I'd like you to go home to London, right now.'

'What?'

'I'd like you to pick up Jake from his school, go to the supermarket and spend as much as you can on food, water and—'

'Dad! I can't do that!'

'Leona … I'm asking you!' he replied, his voice beginning to develop *that* tone; the one that ultimately led to a bollocking if you pushed him hard enough.

'No, you can't ask me to do that. I can't bail out of uni before the end of term—'

He surprised her when his voice softened, 'Please, Leona. I know you're all fed up hearing about crap like this. I'm not stupid. I know I've bored you

• 31 •

with all those oil things. But I think this situation is going to get bad enough that you need to be prepared for it. I have to know you're all okay.'

'We're fine! Okay? We're absolutely fine.'

'Leona, you know I'm not go—'

The call disconnected suddenly and left her with the soft purr of a dial tone. She pulled the phone away from her ear and looked down at it as if it was some kind of alien life form.

My God, that was strange. Really strange.

She waited a moment for the phone to tremble again, and after hanging on patiently for a minute, she tucked it away into her jacket pocket, pulled the door open and entered the bar. Daniel was still sitting in his seat, same posture, but with a quizzical look on his face.

As she sat down beside him she said, 'Don't ask. It was my dad being really weird.'

'What's wrong with him?'

'Oh God, it would take too long.'

He smiled and shrugged. 'Fair enough. What do you want?'

'Half a lager.'

Daniel got up and squeezed past her, placing a hand on her thigh and pinching gently – a little gesture that he was thinking about last night – and then wandered over to the bar.

But her mind was elsewhere. On the call from Dad, and also on those short sound-bites she'd heard on the radio that morning, only what ... four or five hours ago? Surely things hadn't changed that much in such a short time.

CHAPTER 9

. . . .

6.42 p.m. local time

Road leading to Al-Bayji, Iraq

'I don't know for sure. They look like ours.'

Andy squinted at the line of vehicles in the weakening light of the early evening. They were motionless, none of them with their lights on. The only light was a muted, flickering torch coming from beneath the bonnet of the front vehicle. They looked like Land Rovers to him, at least the silhouettes did.

'British,' muttered Farid.

'Brits?' echoed Mike. 'Yeah, probably. Those definitely aren't Hummers.'

Andy watched as the torchlight flickered around, catching the movement of several men standing outside the front vehicle.

So why are they sitting around like that, lights off?

'Bloody suspicious,' Andy offered after a while.

'What? Like us?'

As the light had begun to fail, they had elected to drive on with the lights of their two vehicles off. With the police escort's sudden departure earlier in the day, they had felt dangerously exposed, and as the shadows of the late afternoon had lengthened and given way to twilight, they had decided not to advertise their presence any more than they had to.

The engine of their Land Cruiser idled with a steady rumble as Andy took a couple of steps away from the open door and studied the short column of vehicles, three – four hundred yards away.

Mike climbed out and followed him. 'You know, if we can see them—'

'They can see us. I know.'

And we're sitting here with our lights off.

Andy found himself hoping they were British, and not a trigger-happy US patrol. Over the last year, it had been the American troops that had policed the worst of the growing chaos the Iraqi government still refused to call a 'civil war'. There were a lot of battle-weary and frightened young US ground troops out there carrying some very powerful weapons and ready to fire at any vehicle that moved, especially at night, especially if its lights were off.

'I think you're right,' said Mike, clearly guessing what Andy was thinking. He nodded towards them, 'I know our boys are pretty strung-out right now, and liable to loose off first, and apologise after. Maybe we should stick our lights on and hope they're British.'

Andy nodded. 'Yeah.' He turned to Farid. 'Let's put 'em on.'

And hope for the best.

Farid nodded silently, and spoke in whispered Arabic to Amal. A moment later their headlights flicked on and cast twin fans of light along the pitted tarmac road towards the parked convoy of vehicles.

Immediately Andy could see they were army vehicles. Not American, not the fledgling Iraqi army, but were, as they suspected, British troops.

They watched as a section was issued a barked order, and began to approach them warily in two flanking groups of four – spreading out as they closed the distance, their weapons raised and aimed.

Andy cupped his hands and called out, 'We're civilian contractors!'

A reply came out of the gloom from one of them. 'Don't bloody care! Everyone out of the vehicles where we can see you!'

Andy turned to nod at Farid, Amal and to the second car where the other two contractors had already begun to climb out. He wanted to assure their old translator that the worst of the day was over and they were now safe. But watching the eight young lads approach, caught in the glare of their headlights, meeting their eyes along the barrels of their weapons and through their weapon sights, Andy wondered how much trigger weight was already being applied to their SA80s.

'That's it. Outside, all of you!' one of them shouted.

Andy kept his eyes on the nearest of the soldiers. The lad closed the last few yards alone, whilst the rest of his section held their position in a spread-out semi-circle. The young soldier – a lance corporal, Andy noticed by the stripes and scrawled name and rank on the front of his combat body armour – lowered his gun slightly, and after a moment spent silently studying them, offered a relieved grin.

'Sorry about that gents, we've had one fucking shit day today.'

'It's gone absolutely bloody crazy out there,' said Lieutenant Robin Carter shaking his head. 'I woke up this morning ready for another *normal* day in this place, and … well, since then things have gone a bit haywire.'

Erich, the French contractor, spoke for the first time today with heavily accented English. 'What is going on?'

Lieutenant Carter looked surprised. 'You don't know?'

'We heard a little about some bombs in Saudi, and some riots,' added Mike.

'Oh boy, are there riots. It started with bombs in Mecca, Medina and Riyadh this morning. Someone blew up the Ka'bah, or at least detonated somewhere near it. If you wanted to start a holy war, that's the way to do it. It's spread right across Saudi Arabia, a full-scale civil war; Wahhabis, Sunnis and Shi'as. And it's spreading like bloody bird flu. There are riots in Kuwait, Oman, the Emirates.'

'All this over one bombing?' asked Mike.

Carter shook his head. 'The Holy Mosque in Mecca? You couldn't pick a worse place in the world to target. It's the centre of the Muslim universe. It seems like some radical group of Shi'as immediately announced they were behind it.' The officer shook his head. 'If you want to trigger a global Sunni verses Shi'a civil war … I guess that's how you'd go about doing it. From what I've heard, Riyadh is a slaughterhouse, Saudi's a mess, there are explosions, pitched battles, riots everywhere, and it's spreading like wildfire right across the Middle East.'

Andy nodded. This was one of the things he'd written about eight years ago, in that report. A brief chapter on how easily religious sensibilities could be used as a tool to destabilise the region; a small act of leverage … damaging or destroying somewhere sacred, like the Holy Mosque, the Ka'bah, yielding maximum impact – civil war.

'Jesus,' muttered Mike.

'Yup. And of course Iraq was one of the first countries to get into the spirit of things. It's seriously screwed up out here,' the lieutenant replied. 'There have been multiple contacts going on all day in virtually every town and city. The Iraqi police and the army are joining in the bloodletting, of course. God knows how many casualties we've had in the battalion. Our boys have been caught out all over the place.'

Andy nodded towards the Rover at the head of the six-vehicle convoy. 'You got a problem?'

Carter nodded. 'Yup. It's looking like we've got a sheared drive-shaft.' The officer cast a glance out at the flat arid plain, dotted with the darker shapes of date palms, clustered in twos and threes. 'We put out a call a few hours ago for a vehicle recovery team to pick us up. No bloody sign of it yet.'

He looked at Andy. 'To be honest, I don't think they'll send out a recce-mech tonight. Not into the shit that's going on out there.'

Lieutenant Robin Carter looked to be in his mid-twenties.

Christ, he's only half-a-dozen years older than Leona.

'Take a look over there.' Robin Carter pointed to the horizon in a south-westerly direction. The sky, finally robbed of the last afterglow of the sun, was showing the faintest orange-red stain.

'Al-Bayji. I guess there's some buildings on fire over there. I'm sure the locals right now are tearing into each other. Our boys are all hunkered down in battalion HQ, the other side of the Tigris. The only way to us by road is via the bridge at Al-Bayji. So I'm guessing nobody's coming out for us tonight.'

Mike looked at Andy. 'Great.'

'You're staying out here tonight?' Andy asked. He studied the officer, biting his bottom lip for a moment, weighing up God knows how many factors.

'That Rover's going nowhere without a lift. And frankly, I don't fancy driving through Al-Bayji, or any other town, this evening. I think we'll be better holding up here until first light, and then make a go of it in the early hours. Hopefully things will have died down by then, and we can sneak back home under the cover of dark.'

'Do you mind if we hook up with you?' asked Mike. 'Our goddamned IPS escort bailed on us.'

'You'd be stupid not to.' Lieutenant Carter offered a lopsided grin. 'Anyway, the more pairs of eyes and hands the better.' He cast a glance at Farid and the two young Iraqis. 'Do I need to spend men watching them?'

Andy shook his head. He didn't think so. After all, they had stayed on course when the police had decided to casually break off and abandon them. But the gesture was lost in the gloom. It was Mike who answered aloud.

'You probably want to relieve them of their guns, Lieutenant. They're carrying AKs in the drivers' compartments.'

Carter considered that for a moment and then nodded. 'Yes, maybe that's a prudent measure, for now.'

Andy turned round to look at Farid, who shook his head almost imper-ceptibly, before turning to the two young drivers and explaining to them in Arabic that they were going to have to surrender their weapons.

Lieutenant Carter summoned over a lance corporal and instructed him to retrieve the assault rifles from the drivers of the two Land Cruisers.

Andy studied the reactions of the three Iraqis. The drivers, both much younger men, answered Farid in an animated, yet wary tone. Clearly they were unhappy at having to hand over their guns, casting frequent and anxious glances at the British soldiers gathered at the roadside beside the stationary convoy of vehicles. Farid carried an expression of caution in his manner, speaking softly, seemingly offering them some kind of reassurance.

'All right,' said Lieutenant Carter, clearing his throat and raising his voice for the benefit of the platoon as well as the four internationals before him, 'let's pull these Rovers round into a defensive circle – those two Cruisers as well. Sergeant Bolton?'

A hoarse voice – with a northern accent Andy couldn't quite place – barked a reply out of the darkness.

'Sir?'

'See to that will you? Post some men to stand watch and establish a vehicle control point down the road. Everyone else can stand down and get some rest. We'll be moving out again at 05.00. There's another two hours' drive ahead of us. We should get back to battalion HQ just in time to catch the first trays of scrambled egg.'

None of the men laughed, Andy noticed.

He's new to these men. He sensed the jury was still out amongst Carter's platoon.

CHAPTER 10

· · · ·

9.21 p.m. local time

Road leading to Al-Bayji, Iraq

Andy squeezed the last of the meal around in its flexible foil pouch. After a dozen or so mouthfuls of tepid chicken and mushroom pasta he decided his hunger had been more than sated. In the same way of the all-too-common roadside burger van, the smell of the field rations stewing in boiling water over their small hexamine field stoves had been about a hundred times more appetising than the actual taste.

In the dark interior of their Land Cruiser, Andy, Mike and the French engineer, Erich, ate in silence; the only noise the rustling of their foil food pouches. Outside, the full moon cast a worryingly bright light down on the quiet road and the surrounding flat terrain. In the last three hours they had seen no more than a dozen vehicles pass by. Each one had been stopped by the hastily established vehicle control point, and then waved on after a cursory inspection by flashlight. All of the vehicles passing were heavily laden with possessions and people on the move, presumably away from the growing unrest in the larger towns. Out here, with only the moon and the stars and the gentle hiss of a light breeze for company, Andy conceded you could be excused for thinking it was a quiet and uneventful night for all of the country – except for the distant and disturbing orange glow of Al-Bayji on the horizon – you could think that.

From the snippets they were picking up from the BBC World Service and the more detailed reports coming from local stations, and translated for them by Farid, it seemed as if the unrest that had started first thing this morning in Riyadh had spread right across the Arabian peninsula like a tidal wave.

'They've gone insane,' said Mike, breaking the silence.

In the darkness Andy nodded in agreement, although the American wouldn't have been able to see the gesture. 'I just can't believe how quickly this seems to be spreading,' he replied after a moment.

'There's no working these crazy assholes out. First they're turning on us because we kicked out their tinpot dictator, now all of a sudden they're turning on each other. Do you think they just got bored with blowing up foreigners?'

Andy sucked in a breath and let it go. He had sat through so many conversations that started like this back in London, around the dinner table in the company of Jenny's friends and their husbands. Invariably the hubbies rarely strayed beyond talking about *Top Gear*, football, property prices and very occasionally, politics, and even then only in a superficial 'that's how I'd sort things' kind of way.

Erich sat in silence for a moment before murmuring something in French that suggested he agreed with the Texan. He ended his sentence with a solitary English word, 'savages'.

The driver-side door opened and a cool flurry of wind blew in a cloud of grit and dust. Farid climbed in, his *shemagh* fluttering around his face. He quickly pulled the door closed.

'The others okay?' asked Andy.

Farid nodded. 'Amal and Salim sleeping. The other engineer, U-u ...'

'Ustov,' said Erich.

Farid nodded politely, 'Ustov sleeping too.'

The silence was uncomfortable until Mike decided to break it in his own blundering way.

'So why are all you people fucking well ripping the crap out of each other?'

The old Iraqi man turned to Mike, 'Is not *all* of us. Many, like me, we want just peace.'

'Yeah? Well every time another roadside mine blows a hole in one of our convoys, there's one hell of a lot of you out there on the streets jumping up and down and firing your guns in the air.'

'That is not *everyone*.'

'And now you're doing it to each other,' Mike said, almost laughing with exasperation, 'I mean ... I don't get it ... why?'

'I do not expect you to understand.'

'But you're all brothers aren't you? ... All Muslims? *We're* supposed to be the *big bad guys* aren't we?'

'Would you ask me to try understand why so many Christian brothers died in your American Civil War?'

There was a lull in the car that Andy suspected might precede an enraged outburst from Mike. But to his credit he replied in a measured manner. 'No, I suppose you wouldn't understand if you're not from a southern state. Shit, of course you wouldn't.'

Andy turned in his seat to face both Mike and Farid. 'Why don't we leave off politics for now, huh?'

'I just want to understand what makes these people tick,' said Mike. 'We came in and kicked out Saddam, we've tried rebuilding this country, fixing the power stations, the sewage systems, the water supplies, the hospitals. Rebuilding the schools so all the little boys and girls—'

'You rebuild our country, yes ... but in *your* image!' Farid replied, his soft voice raised ever so slightly in pitch. It was the first time Andy had seen the normally placid old man raise his voice in anger. Under the stress, his very good English began to fracture a little.

'We not wanting our girls go to school, to learn how to become business lady, to dance around undressed in exercise gym before other men, to do power lunch, make big business deals. We do not want to buy McDonald burgers, or Coke, or Pepsi, or cowboy boots.'

Farid came to an abrupt halt, ground his teeth in silence and stared out of the window at the moonlit desert. 'It still our country. Only Iraqi people can know how to make fixed again, like a puzzle. We know what all the pieces is ... are, and how they going together. You Americans don't even know what picture is on the jigsaw!'

Mike laughed. 'Oh Jesus, what a load of crap. I tell you this – I know you ain't got your goddamned *pieces* right when you have women and children blown to bloody shreds in the market-places every day. The best chance you had of rebuilding this shit-pit piece of desert you call a country, was when we rolled in and knocked over Saddam's statue. And you threw that chance right back in our faces. And frankly all we've *ever* wanted to do since, is get the fuck out again.'

Farid shook his head. 'Everyone know why America comes here.'

'Let's just leave it there,' said Andy addressing both men. 'We don't need—'

'Shit! Who are you? My mom?' snapped Mike.

'I'm just saying we can do without this right now.'

'Yeah right, this is bullshit,' his deep voice rumbled. He opened the back door and stepped out, slamming the door behind him.

They watched his large frame, a dark silhouette against the glowing, pale blue moonlit ground, fade quickly into the night. A moment later they saw the flare of a match, and then a glowing orange tip move up and down every so often.

'He just like every American,' Farid muttered.

'Farid, enough of this for one night, okay?' said Andy quietly looking sternly at the old man. 'They,' he said nodding towards Mike, 'want to get out of here just as much as you want them out. It's not your oil they're here for.'

The translator looked less than convinced by that assurance, but he offered no reply. After a moment's silence listening to the gritty dust tinkle against the windows, blown across by a lively breeze, he stirred.

'I get rest now,' he said before bidding goodnight to Andy and Erich and leaving their Land Cruiser for the other one.

Andy shook his head at those words.

It's not your oil they're here for.

If only it were that simple. Anyone who had a fair understanding of Iraq's complete incapacity to pump and export oil knew that. Anyone who'd taken the time to look at the much bigger picture knew that. Anyone who took the time to research the long-term game-plan knew that. If Andy was asked *why* the Americans were over here and was only allowed to give one straight and clear reason, just to make this complex scenario simple and digestible, he knew what answer he would give.

They're here to keep the Saudis in line.

The Gulf War, the second one at least, wasn't about hunting down Al-Qaeda, it hadn't been about finding weapons of mass destruction, nor about removing a dictator. It had been about placing a permanent and very visible military presence right in the middle of all of these oil-producing nations. A crystal clear warning to all of them, particularly the Saudis, that they better just keep on playing ball with America.

And now it looked like things had all gone wrong.

He suspected the focus for US forces would be damage limitation, a desperate attempt to guard and preserve the oil facilities in Saudi, and for that matter in Kuwait, Oman and the other big producers. He wondered, however, if they'd be able to put a lid on this thing before every other refinery and pump station in this part of the world ended up looking like IT-1B, the burned-out shell they'd been picking over this morning.

Christ, if all of the Arabian oil producers head that way …?

This was a scenario, one of many, he had imagined *could* happen. And that's all it would take to start things tumbling down, a few months, shit … a few weeks, maybe even a single week without a regular flow of the stuff, would do it.

He had imagined something like this might eventually happen. One might even use the word ... *predicted.*

Andy pulled out his mobile phone once again, checked for a signal and cursed.

CHAPTER II

• • • •

8.33 p.m. GMT

UEA, Norwich

Ash looked around the room. It was as messy as he would have imagined; discarded clothes lay in a pile on the end of the bed, a small mountain of shoes lay at the foot of it. Beneath the small sash window, there was a modest desk, cluttered with cheap cosmetics and text books and folders. From the look of them she was studying something to do with movies.

But it looked like good news. Leona Sutherland may have decided to go out tonight, but her study books and papers were all here. She'd be back, if not tonight, then first thing tomorrow morning, to collect them before going in to study.

He spotted a packet of photos on the table and leafed through them. A collection of fresh-faced kids squished together into a tent, pulling faces at the camera. He spotted Leona in only one of them; she would have been taking the pictures.

Her hair was darker in this picture, darker than in the picture he'd been given, and a little longer. She also looked somewhat older. The picture they had secured of her was not as recent as they had assured him it was. No matter, he would recognise her easily. Ash was particularly good with faces.

He smiled – *as good as young Leona here.*

She had been so silly with that email of hers. But then that was perhaps a harsh judgement; she had no reason to think that was a foolish thing to do. And hers wasn't a life lived in shadows and under pseudonyms. Her mind wasn't, by default, switched to checking every room she entered for bugs, checking windows for line-of-sight trajectories with some building across the street.

She wasn't to blame for attracting her death sentence.

There was nothing else here that was going to help him track down where she was right now; no phone books, no hastily scribbled notes or 'don't forget' memos to herself. He decided it was time to go talk to her flat-mate.

He stepped out of her room into the communal kitchen and squatted down beside the girl, taped up to one of the kitchen stools, and gagged with a strip of tape across her mouth.

'I'm going to remove the tape,' he said gently. 'Don't tense your lips when I do it, or it'll rip some of the skin off. Ready?'

She nodded.

Ash grabbed one corner and pulled it quickly. The girl flinched.

'Right then, to work,' he said with a tired shrug. 'Let's start with an easy one. What's your name?'

'A-Alison ... Alison Derby.'

He nodded. 'Alison's good enough for now. Thank you. You can call me Ash. So then, here's another easy one for you. Do you know where Leona has gone this evening?'

Alison shook her head. 'No ... n-no, I d-don't. She-she never told m-me,' she replied, her voice trembling uncontrollably.

Ash placed a hand lightly on her shoulder. 'Okay,' he laughed gently, 'okay, I believe you. I know what you kids are like. Spur of the moment and so on.'

Alison nodded again.

He looked around the kitchen, it adjoined the lounge – clearly the one main communal space for them. 'How many of you share this place?'

'S-six of us.'

'And where's everyone else?'

'Th-they've gone, f-for a reading week.'

'Skiving?' smiled Ash.

She nodded.

'So you're telling me, it's just you and Leona here this week.'

She nodded.

'Well that's good. No one's going to come barging in on us then. Very good.'

Alison looked up at him – direct eye contact for the first time. 'P-please d-don't rape me ... I—'

'Rape you?' his eyebrows knotted with a look of incredulity. 'I'm not going to rape you, Alison. What kind of animal do you think I am?'

'I ... I'm sorry, I ... but ... I just—'

'Don't worry,' he said in little more than a soothing paternal whisper, 'no raping, Alison. Just some questions is all.'

'O-okay.'

'So then, let me see, who is she with?'

'Dan. Th-that's her boyfriend.'

'Dan huh? You know where he lives?' he asked.

She shook her head.

'Hummm ... do you think they'll come back here tonight?'

She shook her head again. 'I don't th-think so.'

'Why's that?'

'She said she was s-staying at h-his tonight.'

Ash stroked his chin. 'Hmmm. I'd dearly like her to come back here tonight. Call her.'

She shook her head. 'I c-can't.'

'And why's that?'

'I d-don't know her number.'

'You live together, but you don't know her number? That's not a very good lie, Alison.'

'I'm not lying!' she whimpered. 'She replaced her phone a couple of weeks ago.'

'But you would know her number by now.'

'I d-don't! Honest! I just ... I hardly ever call her, I don't need to, we see each other all the time.'

He looked down at her, placed a finger under her chin and lifted her face up so that she met his eyes again. That seemed to be the truth. There were no deceitful micro-tics in her expression; no involuntary looking upwards as her mind hastily constructed a piece of fiction.

'Tell me, what do you think would make her come back here tonight?'

Alison shook her head, 'I-I don't ... k-know.'

He smiled cheerfully, 'You know what? I think I've got an idea. And you can help.'

CHAPTER 12

· · · ·

11.55 p.m. GMT

Whitehall, London

'T hose figures have to be incorrect, surely?' he said looking around at the men and women sitting at the table with him. 'Surely?' he asked again.

'I'm sorry, those are the figures, that's our best approximation.'

The Prime Minister looked down at his legal pad. He had scribbled only a few hasty notes, but the last three words he had written down were the ones he found most disturbing.

Two weeks' reserves.

'Two weeks? That's *all* we have in our strategic reserves?'

'Our *strategic* reserves actually only contain about a week's worth of oil at normal everyday consumption rates,' replied Malcolm Jones, the Prime Minister's Strategic Advisor, and confidante.

'However, within the distribution chain throughout the country, terminals, depots, petrol stations, there's perhaps another week's worth of supply at the normal consumption rate. If we locked down any further selling of petrol, right across the country, right now we would have a reserve that might last our armed forces and key government installations six to nine months.'

The Prime Minister stared silently at him for a moment before finally responding.

'You're telling me that in order to supply the army and the government with the oil it needs to keep operating for the next few months, we'd have to suck every corner petrol station dry?'

Malcolm nodded, 'Until, of course, normality returns and shipments of crude from the Gulf resume.'

'And the week's worth of oil in our strategic reserves?'

'If restricted only to the armed forces and government agencies,' the civil servant replied, 'we could perhaps make it last three or four months.'

The Prime Minister jotted that down on his pad and then looked up at the assembled members of his personal staff. He had his Principal Private Secretary, his Director of Communications, Malcolm, his Chief Advisor on Strategy and Malcolm's assistant. These were the people he worked with daily, these were the small band of colleagues he trusted. None of them were party members, none of them politicians, none of them secretly jostling for his job. He'd long ago learned that his smartest and most effective decision-making was done here, in this office, with these people, and not around the long mahogany table with his cabinet. The cabinet meetings were where policy was *announced*, not *decided*.

'So,' he began calmly, 'how the hell did we let ourselves get so bloody exposed?'

He directed that towards Malcolm. 'How did we let this happen?'

Malcolm stirred uneasily, but retained that dignified calm that seemed to stay with him always. 'We've not been able to buy in enough surplus oil to maintain, let alone build up, our reserves. In fact, we've not been able to do that for the last few years,' he replied. 'It's been a gradual process of attrition, Charles. It's not that we let it happen, we've had no choice.'

Charles nodded.

'And we're not the only ones,' added Malcolm. 'The increasing demand for oil from China and India, combined with Iraq being a damned basket-case and Iran's continued oil embargo; all of that has made it difficult for *anyone* to build up a surplus. We're all over a barrel.'

'What about the Americans? Can they help us out?'

Malcolm shrugged. 'They have significant reserves, but whether they'll share it with us, I'm not sure.'

The Prime Minister cast a glance across the table towards his Private Secretary. 'Well then let's ask. It's the least they can do after all the support we've been giving them since ... well, since 9/11.'

His secretary scribbled that action point down.

'So, what do we do right now?'

Malcolm nodded to his assistant, Jane. She consulted some papers she had brought along to the meeting. 'There's a trickle of oil coming in from other smaller oil producers; Nigeria, Qatar, Mexico, Norway ...'

'What about Venezuela?' asked the Prime Minister. 'I know their preferred client is China, but surely during this temporary crisis they'll negotiate some short arrangement with us? I mean they'll screw us on price, but surely ...'

'Prime Minister, this came in an hour ago,' said Jane. She read from an intelligence bulletin. 'An explosion at the Paraguaná refinery, Venezuela. Fires still burning, damage yet to be assessed, casualties unknown.'

'Venezuela has loads of crude,' said Charles, 'loads of it. And yeah ... they might well have been happy to cover our short-term problems, but it's heavy. It's not fit for purpose until it's been through a refinery specifically configured to deal with that particular blend. And Paraguaná was it.'

'How long will this Paraguaná refinery be out of action then?'

Malcolm shrugged. 'Who knows? This is all we have on this so far.'

'Well then what about the Tengiz oilfields in the Caspian? There's a lot of oil coming out of that area, isn't there?'

Jane nodded. 'Yes Prime Minister, we can hope to share some of what's coming through Georgia, but then so will every other country in Europe. With all the major Gulf producers out of the loop, that's sixty to seventy per cent of the supply chain gone. We're all now feeding on the last thirty per cent. With regard to Tengiz oil, we're right at the end of the supply chain.'

'You can be sure that our European cousins, along the way, will all want their share,' added Malcolm.

The Prime Minister looked around the people assembled in the conference room. 'Then what? What are you telling me? We're screwed? That we've only got the oil that's sitting in our reserves, depots and petrol stations around the country, and that's it?'

Jane looked down at her crib sheet again, 'There's also a residual drip-feed of oil still coming in from the North Sea.'

'But not enough to bail us out of this ... right?'

'Not even close.'

He looked down again at his legal pad. He'd written nothing there that was going to help him. The only information that stood out on the legal pad were those three words: *two weeks' reserves*.

'Okay so we've got a big problem with oil. That means for the next couple of weeks no one's going to be driving. What about power generation? We're okay on that front, aren't we?'

'The good news, Charles, is that we don't make much power from oil. It's mostly gas and coal as you know. The bad news is, we import most of our gas and coal,' said Malcolm.

Jane consulted some notes. 'Thirty-six per cent of capacity from gas, thirty-eight from coal.'

Charles, looked from one to the other, he could see where they were going. 'And our usual suppliers, Russia, for the gas ...?'

'Australia, Colombia, South Africa, Indonesia for the coal,' responded Jane.

Malcolm looked at him. 'I imagine they'll want to hold up on exporting to cover their energy gap.'

'Shit. What about nuclear?'

'We produce less than five per cent of our needs from that, right now. You know this yourself, the old stations are mostly being mothballed, and the new ones ... well they've only just started building them. If this had happened in a couple of years' time ...'

Malcolm gestured at Jane to be silent. 'Charles, this has really caught us on the hop.'

'So what, if our regular gas and coal suppliers decide to get twitchy, we're down to five per cent of our normal capacity?'

'Eight per cent if we count renewables,' said Jane.

'Christ.' Charles loosened his tie. It was getting stuffy in the conference room.

'We will have to put into place some kind of immediate rationing of power. Whether we share it out on a rota basis, or whether we concentrate it on some nominated areas.'

'Fan-fucking-tastic,' he grunted and looked down silently at his legal pad.

'Charles?' said Malcolm quietly.

'What is it?'

'We have another time-critical decision to make. Our boys in Iraq.'

He was right.

The Americans were pulling most, if not all, of their men out of Iraq and deploying them in Saudi, Kuwait, Oman, overnight. It was already happening. During the day, a lot of damage had been done to the Saudi pipeline network, and many installations had been damaged and destroyed in the rioting. There were still significant oil assets that could be protected if they moved quickly. But that meant a drastically reduced military presence left behind in Iraq; soldiers who would be dangerously exposed.

'We have to decide what to do with our forces out there,' prompted Malcolm. 'And quickly.'

'And your suggestion?'

'We have to pull them out. We can't leave them on their own in Iraq. As soon as the insurgents there realise the Americans have gone ...'

It didn't need saying. With US military might focused elsewhere, the seven or eight thousand troops they had committed to regions in the north and the south of Iraq, some of them in small battalion-sized garrisons, would be overrun within days.

'The decision is whether we help the Americans to guard what's still intact over there. Or, we pull them out and bring them home,' said Malcolm. 'If we leave them there and this crisis lasts much longer …'

They could be stranded there.

Charles looked at them. 'We're going to want them to come home, aren't we?'

Malcolm and Jane shot a glance at each other and nodded.

'This is going to be a tough one to ride out. Before this week's finished, I think we're going to need to have troops on the streets, Prime Minister,' Jane added.

'My God, this has happened so quickly,' Charles muttered, reaching up unconsciously to undo the top button of his shirt. 'I got up this morning with nothing more serious to worry about than looking good at an informal sixth form college Q and A.'

The small trusted band before him offered a muted nervous chuckle.

'And now I'm facing some kind of end-of-days scenario. Shit.'

Malcolm leaned over and patted his shoulder, 'We'll get through this.'

He then turned to Jane and nodded. The young woman pulled out a slim folder from beneath her crib sheet. 'Prime Minister, if I may, we do have some emergency protocols drawn up within the Cassandra Report for this kind of situation,' she said, opening the folder and flipping forward through pages of text and charts.

Charles nodded. He vaguely recalled an approval being passed during the previous government's tenure for a committee of experts to discreetly go away and worry about all manner of oil and energy emergency scenarios, and then to write up their findings.

'This report was compiled three years ago, after the road hauliers strike back in 2004. If you recall it was a handful of depots blockaded by less than a hundred or so truck drivers that nearly brought this country to a standstill after only three days.'

'I know, go on.'

'There were some recommendations for dealing with an intermediate oil shut-off scenario.'

'Intermediate?'

'Intermediate … defined as between two and eight weeks.' Jane cleared her throat before continuing. 'I'll cut to the recommendations.'

Jane continued. 'Action point one: sale of any oil fuel products should cease immediately. Petrol and diesel will then be rationed to key civilian personnel such as doctors or technicians. Point two: food supplies should be rationed. Vendors and distributors of food products should be forced to limit the sales of food products to customers to minimum sustenance levels until a proper rationing card or book system can be put in place—'

'Christ! Rationing food? At this stage?'

'Yes sir,' Jane looked up from the report. 'The earlier we do that, the better.'

'I can understand telling people they can't fill up their cars ... but—'

'Charles, think about it,' Malcolm interrupted. 'The vast majority of the food we eat in this country comes from abroad. As a matter of fact, we produce only a tiny fraction of what we consume, and even then it tends to be niche food items like ... I don't know ... crap like Marmite, mayonnaise. Your basic food stocks like wheat, grains, root crops, meat – most of those things come from overseas suppliers. We don't grow that kind of stuff over here any more. With a suspension of oil supplies across the world, one of the very first things to be affected is going to be the transportation of goods ... food.'

The Prime Minister buried his face in his hands for a moment, trying to massage away the stress-induced migraine he knew was well on its way.

'So now we also have to worry about a strategic food reserve?'

'Which we don't have, Prime Minister. We have only the food that exists in the domestic distribution chain.'

'In other words, what's currently sitting on the shelf in my local supermarket down the road?'

Jane shrugged apologetically, 'In a manner of speaking ... yes.'

Malcolm gestured towards the report, 'Carry on, Jane.'

'Point three: immediate application of martial law, and a curfew, enforced by armed police and military units deployed in every major city. Point four: cessation of all inter-city travel services—'

Charles raised a hand to stop her. 'This is over the top. If I get on breakfast TV tomorrow morning and announce measures like these, they'll be rioting in the streets by lunchtime!'

He got up from the table and walked towards the bay window, pulling it up a few inches to allow a gentle breeze into the room. The window overlooked the modest rear gardens of Number 10.

'This is day one of the crisis ... *day one*! I can't dive in with measures like this. It'll cause more harm than good. And this thing in the Gulf may blow itself out in a few weeks. Okay, so we'll need to tighten our belts until then, of course, but these action points will come across as a panic reaction.'

Malcolm got up and walked over to the Prime Minister standing by the window staring out at the garden, illuminated by half-a-dozen security floodlights.

'What if it doesn't blow itself out in a few weeks? What if this situation escalates? What if we have China and Russia fighting over the Tengiz oil reserves?' Malcolm gestured towards the report.

'Charles, you need to read that thing. I've been reading through it this afternoon. There's an analogy they use in it to describe what's happening,' Malcolm closed his eyes for a moment, trying to remember the wording.

'The world is an old man with a weak heart, and oil is the blood supply.'

He opened his eyes again and gazed down at the garden as he continued. 'It needs only a single blocked artery to throw him into a seizure, and if it lasts long enough, the organs start dying, Charles, one by one.'

Malcolm turned to look the Prime Minister in the eye. 'Even if the blockage clears and blood starts flowing again – once those organs start failing, there's really no way back.'

He looked out at the garden. 'It's a very fragile world Charles, very fragile, built on very vulnerable interdependencies. And something like this ... what's been happening today, really could bring the whole lot down.'

Tuesday

CHAPTER 13

. . . .

5 a.m. local time

Road leading to Al-Bayji, Iraq

Andy was aware he was dreaming, no, not dreaming – replaying that memory, as he dozed on the front seat.

A gentle tap on the door. And then it opens. A man enters the hotel room. Andy can only see his silhouette. As per the instructions they sent him, the main light in the room is turned out, the thick velvet curtains are drawn. The man closes the door, and now the room is lit only by the pale ambient glow of daylight stealing in beneath the curtains.

'I advise you to look away as well, Dr Sutherland. If we are certain you can't identify us, then we shall all feel happier.'

Andy does as he's told, turning in his seat to face away from the man.

'The report's on the end of the bed,' he says.

'One copy only? Handwritten?'

'Yes.'

Andy hears the rustle of movement, and paper as the man picks it up. The flicker of a pen light. A few moments of silence, as the man inspects the first pages.

'Whilst I can't tell you who commissioned this report, I can say that your work will certainly help make the world a safer place. They are grateful.'

'I wasn't aware of quite how ... fragile the world was until I started working on that,' Andy says.

'Yes it is fragile.'

'I hope what's in there will convince somebody at the top – whoever – that we need to come off our oil dependency before it's too late,' Andy adds. 'Something like that is going to happen one day.'

The man says nothing at first. 'Perhaps it will.'

Andy wonders about that response. Perhaps it will convince someone? Or something like that is going to happen one day?

He hears the man moving towards the door, then, he stops before opening it.

'The balance will be transferred this morning to the account you specified.'

'Thank you.'

'A final reminder. You are not to talk about the contents of this report to anyone, ever. We will trust you on this, but also … we will be listening.'

'Don't worry,' Andy smiles nervously, 'you've spooked me enough already.'

He hears a gentle laugh. 'Good.'

A pause. The man is still there.

'You know, I did this for the money at first,' says Andy quickly. 'But having written it … you know, it's scary stuff. I really hope it makes a difference.'

'It will.'

Another silence, just a few moments.

'Please remain here for ten minutes before leaving your room. Do you understand?'

Andy nods. 'Yes.'

'Goodbye.' Andy hears the door open, and light from the corridor floods in, then it's dark, and he hears it click shut behind the man.

It's silent, except for the muted rumble of traffic and bustle outside. Several minutes pass, he wishes he'd set his stopwatch to countdown ten minutes, just to be sure.

Then he hears a knocking on the door …

The persistent knocking roused Andy from the past.

He opened his eyes and saw Sergeant Bolton rapping his knuckles heavily on the passenger-side window. Andy lowered the window letting in a cool blast of air.

'Wakey, wakey little lambkins, we're moving out in five minutes,' muttered the NCO quietly, a small plume of steamy breath quickly dispersed in the chilly early morning air. He casually rapped once more on the roof of their Cruiser and then headed over to the second one to wake up Farid and the two drivers.

Andy blinked the sleep out of his eyes as he watched the occasional flicker of torchlight illuminate the soldiers climbing aboard five of the six Land Rovers. The army Rover that had broken down had been stripped of anything useful.

It was still dark outside, although the sky was just beginning to lighten. He wondered if Lieutenant Carter had left things just a little bit late. They still had about another two hours' drive time to get them back to the battalion headquarters beyond Al-Bayji. It would be approaching seven in the morning as they rumbled through the narrow streets of the town. It would be broad daylight, and there was no knowing if those streets were going to be obstructed with the results of last night's anarchy. He guessed Carter was banking on the people in Al-Bayji stirring later than normal after such a busy night.

Andy leaned over the back of his seat to give the others a prod. 'Wake up guys, we're on the move.'

Mike, Erich and Ustov stirred silently, as Andy opened the door and stepped out into the cool early morning to stretch his legs.

He realised for the first time how nervous he was. This wasn't the normal, ever-present always-check-over-your-shoulder wariness that one experienced as a westerner in Iraq.

This was a whole new order of scary.

Their only way back to the relative safety of a friendly camp was over a bridge and through a town that, only a few hours ago, had been tearing itself apart – a majority of Sunnis versus a minority of Shi'as. If that was still going on, any white faces turning up were going to be a viable target for both sides. He hoped to God things had died down and they were all tucked up in their homes getting some sleep as Carter's recon platoon rolled discreetly through.

What was most frustrating for him, though, was knowing so little about what was happening on a wider scale. The situation in Saudi had stirred things up in Iraq, but then to be fair, it didn't take a lot to agitate the constant state of civil war in this country. But had it spread? Or had it run its course?

Lieutenant Carter approached Andy with a friendly nod. 'A couple of my boys are going to need a lift in your vehicles. We're down one Rover as you know.'

Andy nodded. 'That's okay. We've got space enough for another two at a pinch, in each car.'

'Good. I'd like at least one armed effective in each vehicle. It might help if you and your colleagues also armed yourselves with those AKs we took off your drivers.'

'I uh ... I've never held a gun. I'd probably end up shooting myself in the foot.'

Carter looked surprised. 'Didn't your employer provide you with some kind of basic firearms training?'

'No.'

'Oh great. What about the others?'

'I don't know. But I'd guess Mike probably has.'

'The American?'

Andy nodded.

'Right, well we'll issue him with one I suppose, and you can decide amongst you who'll have the other one.'

'All right.'

Andy noticed the young officer nervously balling his trembling hands into fists. 'How long have you been out here?'

Carter looked at him and smiled. 'It shows does it?'

'Just a little,' Andy lied.

'I only got commissioned this year, and they sent me out here last month. The lads lost their platoon commander a few weeks ago. I think he was caught out by a mortar attack. Those bastards are getting more and more accurate with those damned things,' the Lieutenant put his idle hands to use and tightened the straps of his webbing. 'So anyway, that sort of makes me the new boy, as it were.'

Andy offered a wan smile.

Wonderful.

The convoy headed along the south-west heading road. They passed through a small village in the dark without incident. Making good progress, they reached the outskirts of Al-Bayji at about ten to seven in the morning. Lieutenant Carter was in the front Rover, on top cover, standing up in the back of the vehicle between the bars of the roll cage with another soldier, both of them holding their SA80 assault rifles ready and cocked. The soldier on top cover in the following Rover had the platoon's Minimi, a belt-fed light machine-gun, mounted on a barrel-fitted bipod. Following that, were the two Toyota Land Cruisers.

Andy was in the first, with Mike, Farid, the young driver Amal, and a chatty lance corporal from Newcastle who just wouldn't shut up, called Tim Westley. Mike was holding Amal's AK. Andy noticed the young Iraqi casting a resentful glance over his shoulder at the American. Apparently, the two young drivers actually *owned* these weapons. Farid explained that possessing their own assault rifle had been one of the prerequisites for the job; as well as being able to drive, that is. Andy could understand the lad's rancour, an AK cost a month's salary.

In the following Cruiser was Erich carrying the other AK, Ustov the Ukrainian contractor, the second driver Salim, and two more men from

Carter's platoon. Bringing up the rear were the other three Land Rovers, with Sergeant Bolton on top cover in the last of them.

Lance Corporal Westley was in full flow, as he had been pretty much since they set off at five that morning.

'—and the other fuckin' idiots in second platoon like, was wearin' them *shemaghs* thinkin' they was right ally with it man,' continued Tim Westley's stream-of-consciousness one-way conversation. Mike listened and nodded politely at all the right moments, but from his expression Andy could see the Texan couldn't understand a single word he was hearing.

'—an' it's right naff, man. Aye, was all right first time round, like – Desert Storm an' all, but right fuckin' daft now, mind. Only the TA scallys wear 'em now. You can spot those soft wallys a mile off . . .'

The convoy slowed down to a halt, and with that, Lance Corporal Westley finally shut up as he wound down the window and stuck his head out to take a look-see.

Up front, Andy could see Lieutenant Carter had raised his hand; a gesture to his platoon to hold up there for a moment. Beyond the leading Rover he could see a swathe of coarse grass and reeds leading down a shallow slope towards the River Tigris, and over this a single-lane bridge that led across the small fertile river valley into the town of Al-Bayji beyond. On the far side of the bridge, some 500 metres away, he could see the first dusty, low, whitewashed buildings topped with drab corrugated iron roofs. Beyond them, taller two and three-storey, flat-roofed buildings clustered and bisected randomly with the sporadic bristling of TV aerials, satellite dishes and phone masts along the rooftops.

With his bare eyes he could see no movement except for a mangy-looking, tan dog that was wandering slowly across the bridge into the town, and several goats grazing on the meagre pickings of refuse, dumped in a mouldering pile that had slewed down the far slope of the small valley into the river. He spotted several dozen pillars of smoke, dotted across the town skyline, snaking lazily up into the pallid morning sky. The columns of smoke seemed to be more densely grouped towards the centre of the town.

'It looks like they had a lot of fun last night,' muttered Mike.

Andy could see Lieutenant Carter had pulled out some binoculars and was slowly scanning the scene ahead.

'We should just go for it,' said Mike quickly checking his watch. 'It's almost seven already.'

Andy nodded in agreement. Through the town was the only way, flanked as it was by fields lined with deep and impassable irrigation ditches.

If they put their foot down and just went full tilt, they'd be out the far side and heading down open road towards the British encampment before anyone could do anything about it.

Come on, come on.

But then, what if there was an obstruction, a burned-out vehicle, or a deliberately constructed roadblock? They'd find themselves stuck. Andy decided, on reflection, that the young officer's caution was well-placed. But time was against them, the sun was breaching the horizon now, and even from this side of the bridge, he could sense Al-Bayji was beginning to stir, perhaps readying itself to face a second day of sectarian carnage.

Lieutenant Carter raised his arm once again, balled his fist and stuck a thumb upwards.

'All clear ahead,' said Westley, translating the hand signal for them.

And then the officer patted the top of his helmet with the palm of his gloved hand.

'Follow me.'

Carter's vehicle lurched gently forward with a puff of exhaust, off down the pitted tarmac road towards the bridge, and one by one the convoy of vehicles revved up and followed on.

'Here goes,' said Mike, winding his window down and racking his AK, ready for action. The American looked comfortable with the assault rifle in both hands. But then, Andy reflected, Mike was probably the kind of guy that had a display-case back home in Texas full of interesting firearms.

Andy noticed a look of unease, perhaps anger, flashing across the face of Amal, and a subtle gesture from Farid, placing a calming hand on the lad's arm.

CHAPTER 14

. . . .

6.57 a.m. local time

Al-Bayji, Iraq

Lieutenant Carter's Land Rover rolled off the end of the bridge and into the outskirts of the town, with the convoy following tightly behind.

Up close, the signs of yesterday's chaos were apparent. Splashed across the side of the road, Andy spotted a dark, almost black, pool of congealed blood and a long smear leading away from it towards the doorway of a nearby building; no doubt the body of some poor unfortunate dragged back home to be mourned in private.

The lead Rover picked up speed as it rumbled down a relatively wide, but scarred, road, flanked with a few single-storey buildings. They approached an open area that Andy recalled passing through about this time yesterday, a market square full of traders preparing their stalls for the day ahead. This morning it was deserted.

Travelling through this open and exposed part of the town, he felt they were a little less vulnerable. The doorways, the windows, the roof terraces from which an opportunistic ambush might be launched, were far enough away from them, beyond the area of the market-place, that most of the shots would go wide, and they'd have a chance to react. However, up ahead the road that they were cruising along at a fair clip, punishing the suspension of each vehicle with every pot-hole, carried on towards the centre of town, and vanilla-hued buildings, one or two storeys high, encroached on either side. To Andy's inexperienced eye, the way ahead looked dangerously constricted and overlooked.

'Keep yer eyes peeled lads,' said Westley, his cocky demeanour now subdued and replaced with a flinty wariness.

Mike exchanged a glance with Andy.

'Rooftops an' garden walls,' he added. 'They don't like firing off from *inside* the buildings, like … it leaves 'em vulnerable to being bottled up.'

Mike seemed to understand that. 'Gotcha,' he replied.

Lieutenant Carter's Rover led them into the shaded alley, and as the sun flickered and disappeared behind the rooftops overlooking them, it felt disturbingly like driving into the gaping jaws of some menacing beast.

'Shit,' muttered Andy.

Let's do this quickly.

The road bent round to the right, a tight corner that had them slowing down to a crawl as they weaved their way past a van parked inconveniently on the bend.

And then Carter's Rover came to an abrupt halt.

Amal responded quickly enough so that they slewed to a halt only a foot from the Rover in front.

'What's going on?' asked Mike. The van and the corner were obscuring Carter's vehicle from view.

Westley put a hand to the ear of his PRR – personal role radio – headset. 'CO says the road round the corner's blocked. We've got to fuckin' well back up and find another way through.'

Andy turned in his seat, and saw the rear-most Rover, with Sergeant Bolton up top, reversing already.

And that's when he heard the first crack of gunfire.

'Ahh shit, someone's firing already,' growled Mike.

Turning to face forward again, he saw a flicker of movement from the balcony of a building directly ahead and above them. The squaddie on top cover in the Rover just in front of them spotted the same movement, and swung the Minimi machine-gun swiftly round on its mount, aiming upwards at the chipped and flaking waist-high balcony wall.

Instantly a string of white puffs of plaster powder erupted along the length of it and the man dropped down out of sight.

'Ah smeg, tha's really gonna wake 'em all up now!' shouted Westley.

Amal, meanwhile, was reversing their Cruiser following the other vehicles backing up along the narrow road.

They had passed a right-hand turn fifty yards up, just a few moments earlier, which would take them more or less in the direction they wanted to go. It was another narrow street, overlooked by tall buildings with balconies, but maybe it wasn't blocked.

Andy spotted movement now in the windows of several other buildings: the fleeting faces of some children and their mother, in another an old man wearing a white *dishdash* staring out curiously from the darkened interior of his home.

The rear of Lieutenant Carter's vehicle now appeared, reversing around the corner, the young officer and the soldier beside him double-tapping – firing two or three-round bursts – at the balcony to keep the man up there down on the ground and out of trouble.

The convoy moved backwards slowly, with no further shots being fired at them. That single shot seemed to have been all there was; and even then, Andy wasn't sure it had been a gunshot. It could well have been a vehicle misfiring in a nearby street for all he knew.

Still, the damage was done. The Minimi burst, and the subsequent bursts from Lieutenant Carter's Land Rover must surely have roused the locals.

They pulled past the right-hand turning, going back several dozen more yards to allow the two vehicles in front to back up past it. Then, with a squeal of tyres and a shower of gravel spat out from beneath it, Carter's Rover spun right into the narrow street, and the rest of the convoy swiftly followed suit.

'Let's go!' Mike urged Amal, banging repeatedly with his fist on the back of the driver's seat.

The short exchange of gunfire had definitely stirred the townsfolk. They spotted many more faces peering from darkened windows and doorways down the narrow street and on the balconies above them. Andy, looking up, could only see a narrow strip of blue sky criss-crossed with electrical cables and dangling laundry. This street was even narrower than the one they had just backed out of.

We're going to get trapped.

To him that seemed bloody obvious; a foregone conclusion the way things seemed to be going already. They were getting tightly boxed in here. If there was an obstruction this way, things could get hairy.

Up ahead, the convoy approached another corner, this time turning left. The lead Rover spun round it quickly dislodging a cloud of dust in its wake, and the others followed swiftly.

To everyone's relief, the street widened out, and opened on to a much wider stretch of road; a dual lane, with some semblance of paving on either side and a grass-tufted island running down the middle. There were only one or two vehicles parked on either side, and along the central, weed-encrusted island, several withered old date palms were dotted, giving the street the notional appearance of a once pleasant boulevard gone to seed. Andy noticed, though, that there were quite a few pedestrians out and about, gathered in clusters. Whether they were about their normal business, or roused by the short burst of gunfire and curious, he wasn't sure.

Lieutenant Carter's Rover came to a halt, and the rest of them followed his lead.

'Why's he stopping?' asked Mike.

Andy leaned his head out to get a better look at what was happening ahead, and saw that the far end of the boulevard was packed with a gathering of men; some kind of town meeting in a building that had spilled out on to the road. The people were blocking the road ahead.

'Shit, we can't get through, the road's blocked. That's why he's stopped.'

Westley cursed under his breath. 'Shit. We could just push through, like. You know?'

Farid cast a glance over his shoulder at the soldier in the back seat. 'You want we run over them?'

'Yeah, smeg it. If they won't move out of the way.'

'I agree,' Mike said to the young squaddie, 'anyway, if we fire off some warning shots first, they'll move aside. And if they don't ... well that's their look out.'

'I am thinking they will not move,' Farid countered sternly.

'So what? We just sit here and let them swarm us?' Mike snapped back at the old man.

'It is *haram* to just drive into them. That is murder. Bad.'

'Them or us?' added Westley, 'Fuck, I say us.'

Farid turned to Amal and spoke to him quickly in Arabic.

'What the fuck are you telling him?' shouted Mike angrily.

Farid turned in his seat to face him. 'I ask him if he know another way around. Amal have family in Al-Bayji. He knows the town.'

Andy, ignoring the debate, was watching the distant milling crowd. There were many faces now turned towards them, and hands pointing. The convoy of vehicles nestling discreetly in the shadow of the side-street had finally been noticed by the crowd.

'Ahh shit!' said Westley, listening in on his PRR headset. 'CO says he sees some RPGs and other weapons amongst them.'

Andy nearly asked what an RPG was, but stopped himself. Even little Jacob knew what those three letters stood for: rocket-propelled grenade.

The crowd began to move slowly towards them, and as they spread out, Andy could see for himself that they had a fair distribution of weapons of various types amongst them.

Whatever we do, we better bloody do it now.

As if in answer to his thought, he noticed one of the crowd stopping, kneeling down and swinging a long tube round and up to an aiming position.

The next second he saw a momentary flash and a puff of smoke, and a small black projectile weaving up the road towards them.

'RPG! Shit!' shouted Westley.

It whistled by the convoy easily missing them by a dozen yards, but close enough that they heard the angry hum of displaced air. It thudded against the wall of a building fifty yards behind them, dislodging a large patch of plaster, but failing to explode.

Lieutenant Carter had apparently decided enough was enough and gestured to the soldier manning the Minimi in the Rover behind to lay down some suppressing fire.

The machine-gun began chattering loudly, and Andy watched with horror as half a dozen of the men leading the advancing crowd seemed to disintegrate as pink clouds of blood and tissue erupted from chests and heads. In response, every armed man in the crowd decided to open fire at pretty much the exact same moment and the hot air just outside their Land Cruiser seemed to pulsate with shots whistling past.

Carter's vehicle swung erratically to the left, and Andy could see the officer gesturing wildly with one hand towards a two-storey pink building with a high-walled compound in front of it. There was a sturdy iron gate in the middle of the wall that was closed and appeared to be padlocked. His vehicle cannoned towards it, bouncing up on to the kerb and a moment later crashing heavily into the gate. The gate rattled violently on its hinges as it swung inwards.

'Go, go, go!' shouted Westley. Amal instinctively spun the wheel round and slammed his foot down, pulling out from behind the Rover with the Minimi towards the building. The Rover in front of them remained stationary, the machine-gun still chattering suppressing fire at the crowd, keeping them from advancing any closer.

Andy realised something must have happened to it, and as they pulled past and swung left, he saw the windshield had gone and the driver was slumped forward on the dash. There were three other men in the Rover; two had climbed out of the back and were kneeling down using the rear of the car as cover, the third was still standing up through the roll bars and firing the Minimi in a series of long bursts that were rapidly eating up the belted ammo. All three were in danger of being left behind.

Amal drove towards the pink building, bumpily mounting the kerb as the lead Rover had done, everyone inside banging their heads on the roof as they rode over it and through the now open gates into the compound beyond.

Their Cruiser slid to a halt amidst a cloud of dust, and in quick succession, the second Cruiser entered, followed by the remaining three Rovers.

Through the fog of dust Andy could see that Lieutenant Carter was already dismounted, running across the compound towards the open gate and shouting orders to his men who began piling out of their vehicles. Carter took cover behind the wall, beside the gate, leaning out quickly several times to check on his three lads trapped in the middle of the street.

CHAPTER 15

. . . .

7.21 a.m. local time

Al-Bayji, Iraq

'This is bloody mad,' Lieutenant Carter whispered breathlessly to himself.

Sergeant Bolton jogged over and joined him leaning against the wall beside the gate, catching his breath in short gasps, and tightening the straps on his Kevlar helmet.

'All right sir?' he grunted.

Carter nodded. 'I'm fine. It's those poor bastards outside I'm worried about.'

They could hear the Minimi continuing to fire in short disciplined, regular bursts. But they were becoming shorter and the pauses between them longer.

'Whatever we do sir, it's got to be quick.'

Carter nodded. 'Sergeant, I don't know their call-sign, I haven't learned yet who's—'

'Those lads are part of Yankee-two-two, sir.'

The young officer nodded. 'Okay, okay. Right.' He looked anxiously around the compound as he bit his bottom lip, thinking.

'Sir, we've got to do something now,' barked Sergeant Bolton impatiently.

Carter peeked around the wall at the three men. The man on top cover was still firing. The other two were offering sporadic double-taps from the rear of the Rover, whilst the ground around them danced with plumes of dust and sparks that sprayed off the pock-marked, bullet-dented metal of the vehicle.

He touched the push-to-talk button of his radio and did his best to speak calmly into the throat mic. 'Yankee-two-two ... this is Yankee-two-zero.

You've got to make a run for it lads. We'll give you covering fire from the gate and the wall.'

'Fucking make it quick, sir!' the crackling response came back from one of the three men.

Carter turned to Bolton. 'Sergeant, get some of our boys up on the wall.' He looked around and saw there was a stacked pile of wooden pallets in the corner of the compound. 'Use those to stand on. And rally a section over here by the gate. We'll assemble some firepower here, all right?'

Sergeant Bolton nodded and began issuing voice commands on a separate channel.

'And Sergeant, I want a man watching those three Iraqi gents we have with us.'

Bolton acknowledged that, and then jogged across the compound with a confidence and an aura of invincibility that Carter would have given anything to possess.

A few moments later, eight men of his platoon, including a burly-looking Fijian, were shifting the pallets across the ground to the base of the seven-foot cinder-block and plaster wall and stacking them high enough to allow them to see over.

The chatty Geordie lance corporal – Westley – scrambled over and slumped against the wall beside Carter, followed by a section of twelve men, who all followed his lead and fell in against the rough cinder blocks. Carter turned to see a line of anxious young faces studying him intently and waiting anxiously for their CO to formulate a way out of this mess for them.

'All right lads, first thing we're doing is getting Yankee-two-two out of that fix and in here with us. Then ... then we'll deal with the next thing on the list. Okay?'

Shit Robin ... never bloody well ask them if an order's 'okay'.

'So, that's what we're doing boys,' he hastily added. 'On my command take half this section out through the gate and break right. There's a truck you and your men can use for cover. I'll take the other half, and we'll cover your move from the gateway. When you're settled in we'll come out break left, and we'll all give those lads out there covering fire. Hopefully that'll give them enough time to scarper over here. You got it?'

'Aye sir,' nodded Westley.

'All right, take up your position on the other side of this gateway. Let's get ready.'

Outside Carter could hear that the Minimi's chattering bursts were diminishing in length and frequency. The bloke firing it – damn, he wished he'd had a little more time to learn their names – was clearly doing his best to conserve the last of his ammo, yet keep firing often enough to hold the crowd back.

Westley slapped six of his comrades on the shoulder and led them in a loping dash across the open gateway to the wall on the other side of the compound's entrance, where they squatted in a row, ready to go.

No time to waste. Do it.

'Yankee-two-two,' said Carter over the radio, 'we're coming out to give you covering fire. On my command just get the fuck out of there and get over here.'

He looked over his shoulder to see that Sergeant Bolton had some men hunkered down on top of the pallets and ready to give covering fire over the top of the wall. He nodded to Bolton and then turned back to face Lance Corporal Westley on the far side of the gate.

He raised his hand so that both Bolton and Westley could see it and then counted down.

Three ... two ... one.

He pulled his hand into a fist as he jumped to his feet, leading his men round the iron gate and into the opening of the gateway. All seven of them dropped down to their knees and let loose a barrage of fire on the crowd that now was almost upon the stranded Rover. Meanwhile, Westley led his men out through the gate, breaking right across half-a-dozen yards of uneven paving towards a rusting truck parked with two tyres up on the kerb. There, they quickly found covered positions, and placed a withering barrage of suppressing fire down the boulevard. The advancing crowd had, as one, dropped to the ground to avoid the opening salvo of gunfire.

'Yankee-two-two ... Go!' Carter shouted into his throat mic.

The squaddie who had been doing an excellent job of top cover with the Minimi, instantly ducked down through the roll cage and began to scramble towards the back of the Rover. The other two men, meanwhile, leapt out from the meagre cover provided by the rear of the vehicle and started across the thirty feet of open ground towards the pink-walled compound, weaving to and fro in the hope of throwing off anyone attempting to draw a bead on them.

The third man still in the Rover suddenly stopped, and was hesitating, like some piss-head wondering whether he'd left his wallet back in the pub. Then Carter saw him reach up through the roll cage bars to retrieve the machine-gun.

He was tempted to shout out an order to the man to forget about it. But the Minimi was such an effective support weapon, to have it would make a real difference to the platoon's chances of holding this position. They had plenty more belts of ammo for it in the other Rovers.

'Come on, come on,' he found himself muttering as he and his men continued to offer staccato bursts of covering fire, which for now was keeping most of the heads down out in the street.

The soldier in the vehicle managed to pull the awkwardly shaped weapon, with its extended bipod, down through the bars of the roll cage, and then out of the back of the Rover, tumbling out on to the ground with it in the process.

'Smeggin' hell move it, Shirley, you lazy bastard!' Carter heard the Geordie lance corporal shout over the platoon channel, completely dispensing with formal call-sign protocol.

Over the shared channel, he heard the laboured breathing of the man, as he struggled with the gun and made ready to cross the open ground towards the entrance.

'Fuck off Westley, you girl's blouse,' he heard the man reply.

'Yankee-two-two ... Dammit! ... *Shirley!*' barked Carter, making a mental note to ask him how he got that nickname. 'Get over here now!'

The man shouldered the weapon, took a moment to steady his nerves, and then lurched out into the open, adopting the same weaving pattern as his two comrades had, but dangerously slowed down by the bulk and weight of the machine-gun.

The suppressing fire coming from Carter's men, Sergeant Bolton's position over the top of the compound wall and Lance Corporal Westley's men was breaking down as magazines began to empty. At least half the men in all three sections were now somewhere in the process of ejecting a spent magazine, pulling a new one out of their pouches and slamming it home.

The armed militia amongst the crowd were beginning to be encouraged by the faltering volley of gunfire and several of them emerged from places of cover across the boulevard and tapped short bursts in the direction of the lone soldier, desperately scrambling across the road.

Inevitably, a shot landed home.

A puff of crimson exploded from the man's leg and he clattered to the ground still some yards from the kerb.

'Get off your fuckin' arse, you twat!' bellowed Bolton from the top of the wall, his booming voice carrying over the din of gunfire.

The intensity of the fire suddenly increased as the militia-led mob were further encouraged. The cinder-block wall beside Carter and his men began to explode with bullet impacts, showering them all with a cascade of plaster dust and stinging splinters of cement.

Carter heard a hard wet smack and glanced to his left to see that the squaddie who had been kneeling next to him had been thrown backwards by a shot dead centre to his face. There was nothing he could recognise above the chin and below his ginger eyebrows – just a crater of mangled tissue.

Shit, shit, shit.

The lad was gone, dead already, despite the drumming of his boots on the kerb.

And there was the soldier in the road with the leg wound; he was screaming in agony, rolling around on the ground clasping his thigh.

Carter knew he had to pull his men back inside before he lost any more.

'Everyone inside, now!' he screamed over the radio.

Lance Corporal Westley's men moved swiftly back towards the gate in well-practised fire-and-manoeuvre pairs. But Westley hovered by the truck he'd been using for cover.

Carter caught his eye as he gestured for his section to fall back inside. 'Get inside! NOW!' he bellowed to him. The Geordie hesitated a moment longer before reluctantly sprinting full tilt for the gateway.

Carter grimaced. *We're leaving that poor sod out there, still alive.*

He brought up the rear, emptying his clip in one long wildly sprayed burst before turning round and diving for the open gateway.

With all of them inside, the iron rail gates were closed, clattering noisily as they slammed together. Sergeant Bolton had some men ready with more wooden pallets and other detritus found in the compound and swiftly piled it against the gates.

Carter clambered up the pallets stacked against the wall and then, waiting for a slack moment in the firing, chanced a quick glance over the top.

The soldier, Shirley, with the Minimi, had taken another couple of hits, by the look of his shredded combat fatigues, darkened from the blood of several wounds, the poor young lad was on his way out. Then, mercifully, perhaps, a shot knocked his head back and dislodged his helmet.

He was dead.

Shirley ... he'd wanted to know where the fuck that daft name had come from ... but of course, he was never going to find out now.

CHAPTER 16

. . . .

8 a.m. GMT

Manchester

'**O**h come on!' cried Jenny impatiently.

The digital tune playing over and over as she sat on hold was very quickly driving her insane. The bleeping melody was broken periodically with a recorded announcement that she was on hold to On Track Rail Customer Services, and would be answered by an operator shortly.

Jenny was still in bed, in the Piccadilly Marriot Hotel. The plan had been to take a detour up to Leeds to see some old friends and then home again to begin sorting her life out.

But, with all these worrying things going on thousands of miles away, it didn't seem like such a good idea any more. All of a sudden, a piss-up with some old, old school friends – ones she had only recently got back in contact with courtesy of Friends Reunited – had lost its appeal. She'd probably go through the motions, buy drinks, get pissed, reminisce, but her mind would be on other things; including Andy, stuck out there, and from what she was picking up on the news, possibly in a dangerous situation.

Jenny wasn't really that news-savvy generally. She probably put more time into watching soaps and reality shows than she did keeping an eye on current affairs. But, yesterday, in that café bar, she had heard one or two phrases – no more than soundbites – that had sent a shiver down her spine.

At his most obsessive, perhaps a year ago, Andy had warned her that only those who were listening for it, the *Big Collapse*, listening for the tell-tale signs, would get the crucial head start. The advance warning would come through on the news in phrases that were like a code, encrypted for the few that knew what to listen out for. They would be the ones who would have a chance to prepare before widespread panic kicked in.

Yesterday, watching the news, she felt she had heard something very much like that coded warning.

Peak Oil.

She felt stupid at first, of course. Walking out after her coffee, shopping in the Arndale Centre, having some dinner and coming back to the hotel, she had almost managed to dismiss the nagging notion that maybe she had better get a move on back to London and do an extra-large grocery shop.

Then this morning, having slept on it, and rehashed all those doom and gloom predictions of Andy's that had so worn her down over the last few years, she realised she'd heard the warning.

And she'd climbed out of bed.

Her friends could wait for another time.

And if she was panicking, over-reacting, so what? Better to be back home sitting on more cans of food than they'd normally keep in the kitchen, than be caught out. It would eventually get eaten anyway.

What about Leona and Jacob?

At least if she was back in London and things did look like they were going to get worse, she could nip across and pick Jacob up easily enough. Heading up to Leeds for a pissed-up reunion? ... Well, she just wasn't going to enjoy herself if she was distracted with niggling concerns.

The digital tune was interrupted by the voice of a *real* person.

'On Track Rail Customer Services,' answered a man.

'Ahh, about time! I had a ticket booked to London at the end of the week. And I wondered if I can change it for one going back down from Manchester today?'

'I'm sorry, inter-city rail services have been suspended this morning.'

'What? For how long?'

'I've not been given a time. All we know is that they are currently suspended.'

'Why?'

'I'm sorry, that's all we know ... services are suspended until we hear otherwise.'

'Well, how am I supposed to get back home?' she asked angrily.

'I ... uhh ... I'm sorry madam,' the man replied awkwardly, and then disconnected the call.

'Great,' she hissed, 'flipping great.'

She picked up the remote from her bedside table and turned on the small TV which was perched on a bracket in a corner of the room. Flipping across the meagre selection of five channels, all of them had a news programme of one sort or another, and every single one of them was talking over some new development of the troubles. She turned up the volume.

'... the incident in Georgia. Early reports are that the explosions at the Baku refineries near the Tengiz oilfield may be the result of an accident caused by a sudden increase in demand and production, coupled with the ageing Soviet-era oil infrastructure and machinery. However, there are conflicting reports that the explosions may have been caused by a deliberate act of sabotage ...'

Jenny flipped over to another channel.

'... sources from the Pentagon say that additional troops may be re-deployed from the Gulf to guard the other refineries and pipelines in the Caspian region. However, it's clear that US forces already out there are being stretched dangerously thin, to the point that command control and supply routes to the men could possibly begin to become a problem. Commentators in Washington are suggesting that the President may be forced to announce some kind of draft to cover the additional manpower needed in the immediate future. But even then, things are happening very swiftly and troops are required now to ...'

And another.

'... unclear what happened to the Amoco Dahlia this morning. The explosion ripped the super-tanker's hull open just as the vessel entered the main shipping lane through the Straits of Hormuz. The Amoco Dahlia has shed many millions of gallons of oil, and is still burning. It's unknown whether the super-tanker hit a mine, or perhaps more likely, was targeted by a fast-moving terrorist boat rigged with explosives ...'

And another.

'... this morning. The Prime Minister's press secretary said that an announcement would be later today. Traders in the City of London will, of course, be trying to anticipate what he's going to announce. The obvious thing to be looking out for would be a temporary relaxing of duty on petrol and diesel. With prices per barrel this morning rocketing past the $100 barrier and still rising, it's clear that short-term measures to counter immediate damage to the already fragile economy will be at the forefront of his mind ...'

Jenny looked down at the mobile phone, still in her hand and realised that, for the first time in a long while, she wished Andy was right there, and telling her what she needed to do.

CHAPTER 17

. . . .

11 a.m. local time

Al-Bayji, Iraq

Andy ducked back inside the pink building as Sergeant Bolton bellowed a warning. A moment later the mortar shell they had heard launching from nearby dropped into the compound with a dull thump, but no explosion – another dud.

He heaved a sigh of relief. The armed insurgents amongst the gathering crowd outside had launched half-a-dozen mortars at the compound, only two had landed on target, and neither had exploded.

The sporadic gunfire was beginning to die down again.

Throughout the morning, the pattern had been consistent; sustained and intense periods of gunfire coming from nearly every rooftop along the boulevard and outside along the street itself, punctuated by interludes of peace and quiet.

The crowd outside had grown in size, presumably as word had spread across the town that a small patrol of coalition forces had been run to ground.

Andy was surprised at how bold they were. Surely the people out there had to be aware that a relief force would be combing the area looking for Carter's patrol? The battalion HQ was only thirty minutes away, they'd be sending someone, surely?

Or perhaps they know something we don't?

The comms system installed in Lieutenant Carter's Rover had taken several hits from gunfire as the vehicle had swerved across the road towards the pink building. And now they had no reliable means of getting in touch with the battalion.

The only other way they had of contacting the battalion HQ was, believe it or not, via mobile phone. Out in the wilderness, it was down to luck. But in a place like Al-Bayji, the coverage was pretty thorough.

In the last hour, once it became apparent that there was no imminent threat of being overrun, and that for now, they could hold the compound, Lieutenant Carter had set about trying to get a call through to somebody, *anybody*, at battalion HQ. Eventually he managed to get through to a Quartermaster Sergeant, a buddy of Bolton's, and through him to Major Henmarsh.

Carter had made the call well away from where any of the lads in his platoon could hear, but for some reason, he had allowed Andy to be within earshot. Andy had heard the news, and it wasn't good.

The battalion had abandoned their permanent camp south-west of the town and pulled back to K2, the region's main airstrip, where they were holding a defensive perimeter as a steady stream of Hercules C130s were landing and evacuating the British army from this region of Iraq, one company at a time.

Carter had said that the Major was looking into putting together a relief effort of some sort to bail them out, but from the grim look on the young man's face, Andy guessed the officer had been told this was going to be a very long shot.

'You okay?' asked Andy.

'Why the hell are they leaving?'

Andy shook his head. 'This situation must have got worse.'

A lot worse if the British army was pulling out.

'I just don't get it. Surely they'd be sending more troops here to help calm this thing down.' Lieutenant Carter wiped dust, sweat and grime from his face with his *shemagh*. 'Things have just gone crazy.'

'I've got a feeling there's much more going on than we know about,' Andy said quietly. 'We know it started with a series of explosions in Saudi designed, by *someone*, to provoke widespread rage.'

'Someone? You mean like Al-Qaeda?'

Andy shrugged, 'Possibly, they're the obvious candidates. This does feel ... *orchestrated*, doesn't it?'

Carter nodded absent-mindedly, distracted with more immediate concerns.

'Listen,' he said after a while, 'I'm not sure they can spare the men to come after us. It sounded like they were stretched thin and getting a lot of contacts around K2.' He bit his lip again, and then added, 'We might have to make our own way out of this mess.'

'Oh Christ,' replied Andy.

'But don't tell anyone. Don't tell my men. Okay?'

'Sure.'

Carter squatted down on his haunches and leant against the pink wall, burying his face in his hands.

'Shit, I don't know what to do,' he muttered.

Andy looked around and noticed some of the platoon looking uncertainly at the officer from their stations around the compound wall. He kneeled down beside him.

'Your men are watching you,' he whispered quietly.

The young officer immediately straightened up and sucked in a deep breath. 'You're right,' he replied with a nod and a grim smile. 'I'll work something out.'

Andy nodded, 'Sure.' He wanted to give the lad a reassuring pat on the shoulder, but with those squaddies intently studying their CO, he knew they probably shouldn't witness that. No matter how screwed up the young Lieutenant thought the situation was, as far as the lads were concerned, this had to look like a momentary operational glitch, that things were in hand and a remedy already on its way. Lieutenant Carter had to look upbeat.

Andy didn't envy him having to brass it out like that. He stood up and made his way across the compound to where Mike, Erich and Ustov sat in the shade of the parked vehicles and, a few yards away, Farid and the two young drivers sat, watched over by a soldier.

Mike nodded in the direction of the Lieutenant. 'What's the news then?'

'We're not the only ones with problems.'

'And what fuck is that meaning?' asked Erich.

Andy felt he had to support Carter and throw some sort of a positive spin on things, but it felt crap lying to them. 'It means it might take them a little while to get round to helping us out. But they will.'

Mike offered a wry smile. 'Sure.'

Andy's mobile phone began to ring. He looked down at it with some surprise and checked the number of the incoming call.

'It's the wife,' he muttered with a bemused look, which triggered a snort of laughter from both Mike and Erich, whilst Ustov simply looked confused.

'I told you honey, never call me at work,' quipped Mike.

Andy smiled and then answered the call. 'Jenny?'

'Andy?' she replied. The signal was astonishingly clear. 'Oh God. Are you all right over there?'

Andy was tempted to reply with some dry humourless sarcasm; after all, the last time they'd spoken, as he'd packed his bags preparing to leave for this particular job five days ago, it had been somewhat less than cordial.

'I'm okay.'

'I was worried. They're saying on the news that the whole of the Middle East is in a right mess.'

'What the hell's going on, Jenny? What do you know?'

'I don't know, it seems like things are happening everywhere. There've been bombs and explosions in ... in central Asia somewhere.'

'Georgia, near the Tengiz fields?'

'Yes, that's right. They mentioned that place on the news ... Tengiz. They're talking about oil shortages, Andy. Just like ... you know, just like—'

'Yes,' he finished for her, 'I know.'

'And then this morning there was one of those huge oil-tankers blown up in—'

'The Straits of Hormuz?'

'Yes. You heard about it? Apparently it's blocked off the Straits to all the ships that had oil and could have delivered it.'

Andy felt something ice-cold run down his spine. 'Yes ... yes, I heard that from somewhere.'

The Tengiz refineries hit, Hormuz blocked, pan-Arabian unrest triggered by an attack on something like the Ka'bah – all these events within twenty-four hours of each other. Exactly as described.

'Andy, I'm scared. The trains aren't running. They've stopped the trains, and there's going to be some big announcement made by the Prime Minister. The radio, the TV ... they're all talking about problems right across the world.'

The only edge Jenny and the kids had right now over most of the other people around them was the few hours' advance warning he could give her. She had to sort herself out right now.

'Jenny, listen to me. If they announce the sort of measures I think they might at lunchtime, the shops will be stripped bare within hours. It's going to be fucking bedlam. You've got to get the kids home, and go and buy in as much food—'

'I can't! I'm stuck up in Manchester.'

Damn! He remembered she'd arranged some bloody job interview up there. Part of her whole *screw-you-I-can-do-just-fine-on-my-own* strategy.

'Is there no way you can get home?' he asked.

'No. No trains, no coaches. It looks like they've stopped everything.'

'Then get Leona to make her way down from Norwich, pick up Jake, take him home and buy in as much as she can!'

A pause.

'Jenny,' continued Andy, 'she won't listen to me. I spoke to her yesterday.

I think she thinks I'm just being an over-anxious wimp or something. She'll listen to you. After all, you were always the big sceptic.'

He heard laboured breathing on the end of the phone; Jenny was crying. 'Yes, yes okay. Oh God, this is serious isn't it?'

'Yes, I think it will be. But listen, you need to do this now. Do you understand? Don't take 'no' for an answer from her.'

She can be so bloody wilful and stubborn.

'Of course I won't,' she replied, her voice faltering.

'And then you've got to find a way to get down to London to be with them,' Andy added.

'I know ... I know.'

'Any way you can, and as quickly as possible.'

Jenny didn't respond, but he could hear her there, on the end of the line.

'Andy,' she said eventually, 'this is really it, isn't it – you know ... what you've been—'

'Please, Jenny. Just get our kids safely home,' he replied.

CHAPTER 18

. . . .

11.18 a.m. local time

Al-Bayji, Iraq

Sergeant Bolton joined Private Tajican standing on the stack of pallets and keeping a watch on events outside in the street.

'What is it?' he asked the Fijian.

'Movement, Sergeant. Something going on.'

Bolton looked up at the soldier who dwarfed him both in height and width. Tajican pointed towards some activity down at the far end of the boulevard. 'There, sir.'

He squinted against the dazzling mid-morning sunlight; even though the normally blue sky was veiled by a coating of featureless white cloud, the diffuse light leaking from behind made it hard not to screw up his eyes. A crowd of men were gathered around a truck parked in the entrance to a side street, they were doing *something* with it, but it was hard to make out exactly what.

'What are you buggers up to?' Sergeant Bolton murmured to himself.

'No good?'

Bolton grinned and nodded. 'S'right lad, up to no bloody good.' He spoke quietly into his throat mic on the command channel. 'Lieutenant? I think we might need to get ready for another contact.'

Across the compound, Carter stirred to life, walking swiftly across the dirt, doing his best to look relaxed and in control. He weaved through the vehicles parked in the middle of the compound over to where Bolton and Tajican were standing on the pallets stacked against the wall.

'What is it, Sergeant?'

Bolton ducked down behind the wall and turned to face his CO. 'Well, sir, looks to me like they're rigging something up on a truck.'

'More specifically?'

Bolton shot a glance at the big Fijian. 'I think they're loading some ordnance, some sort of improvised explosive device.'

Tajican looked at the Sergeant and then nodded in agreement, 'Reckon so, chief, an IED.'

Carter sighed. He climbed up on to the stack to join them, studied the activity for a few seconds, before ducking down and turning to the two men.

'Well, it's obvious isn't it? They'll drive the bloody thing over here, probably park by the gate and then set it off.'

Sergeant Bolton nodded. 'Yup.'

'So, we've got to stop it getting over here. What have we got in the platoon that's meaty enough to disable it?'

'The Minimi might have done it,' replied Bolton. 'We've got a couple of SA80s with grenade launchers ... USGs.'

'Have we got anyone good enough with their aim to drop a grenade into the back of that truck?'

'Lance Corporal Westley, the Geordie lad, he's pretty fit with it, but not at this range, sir. We'll need it to be closer. Maybe we can catch it on the approach.'

'Wait till it's a moving target? That's a pretty crap idea, Sergeant.'

'Or we can try sending some of our boys out to nobble it before they get going, sir?'

Lieutenant Carter thought about it for a moment, and then shook his head. 'No, they'd be dead before they got fifty yards – they've got guns on every damned roof.'

The options weren't great, or varied. He balled his fists and tapped them together a few times as he weighed one against the other.

'Okay, let's go with your first crappy idea, Sergeant. We'll put every gun we have on it, and the two USGs too if ... when, it starts heading towards us. Maybe we'll get lucky and something will hit the explosives they've loaded in the back.'

Carter took another peek over the wall. It looked like they'd just about finished loading whatever it was, and some activity was going on amongst the crowd towards the front of the truck.

Looking for a volunteer to drive, eh? That was something they seemed to have an endless supply of over here in this land of martyrs; young men ready to die.

Andy watched Mike as he got up and wandered over to the three Iraqis huddled anxiously together in the shadow of one of the Land Cruisers, a soldier a few yards away watching them. Mike squatted down in front of them, studying them silently for a moment as he held the AK47 loosely – not aimed, but not exactly swung away either.

'What are you doing here?'

Farid shrugged, 'I'm not understand.'

'It's simple, why the hell are you in here, and not out there with your buddies? I mean, if you're such a good little brother like you said, and you think our shitty western ways stink, why aren't you out there with them, taking pot-shots at us?'

'I am a Muslim, is wrong for me to take your life, even though you are an infidel – even though you are nothing.'

Mike screwed his face up in disgust. 'Oh we're *nothing* are we? We've sacrificed several thousand young American lives so you savages can have a democracy; a chance to fucking well vote.'

'And we will replace with Shari'ah as soon as you Americans gone,' replied Farid defiantly. 'Your ways are not ours.'

Andy could see the exchange between the two men was going to escalate quickly, particularly given how strung out they all were. He pulled himself up to his feet and walked over, uneasily, wondering how he was going to calm him down.

'Mike,' he interrupted quietly. 'Calm down. I don't think he means "nothing" in the same way we'd mean it. It's a language thing.'

'Yeah, right,' he smiled dryly. 'Tell you what, why don't I just hand over this gun to him, or one of his little buddies? You heard him ... we're nothing to him, just vermin. You think that's a good idea? Think your little old friend here will stand shoulder to shoulder with you?'

'Look,' Andy replied, 'this isn't helping anyone, Mike. Like it or not, Farid and these two boys are in this mess alongside us. They're here because they're just as big a target as we are. Think about it! They're LECs – locally employed civilians. If the insurgents out there get hold of them, they'll be made an example of. You can bet on that.'

Mike looked at him. 'You trust them?'

Andy shrugged. He wasn't sure what answer he could honestly give; trust them or not, they were all in the same boat right now.

CHAPTER 19

. . . .

8.21 a.m. GMT

UEA, Norwich

Leona smiled.

Two nights in a row now.

It was definitely looking very promising. She had half-expected Dan to make up some excuse yesterday, about not being able to get together again last night. Most lads his age were like that.

Break the glass, grab the goodies and run.

But it seemed not Dan. She hated leaving him this morning, dashing out whilst he was still stretched out and dozy in his messy bed. Staying over at his place hadn't exactly been planned, and now she had to scurry over to her rooms on campus to get her books before today's first lecture. It was only halfway back up the Watton Road entrance to the UEA grounds that she remembered she had left her phone switched off.

It rang as soon as she switched it on.

'Leona?'

'Dad?'

'For crying out loud, Mum and me have been trying to get hold of you all morning. Are you all right?'

'I'm fine.'

'Listen, your mum and I have talked. We both want you to go get Jake and go home.'

'You mean because of those riots?'

'Yes.' He sounded tired and stressed.

Leona ground her teeth with frustration.

Not now. Please, not now.

'Dad, I'm right in the middle of some *really* important assignments,' she replied.

And I've finally landed Daniel, don't let's forget that.

'Leona, I'm not going to argue with you, love.'

Love. Leona rolled her eyes. God that was irritating, Dad only called her that when he was about to blow off steam, like some flipping primeval volcano; annoying actually, rather than intimidating.

'Look Dad, I'm not—'

'SHUT THE FUCK UP AND LISTEN!' his voice barked furiously.

Leona recoiled. The phone nearly slipped out of her hand on to the ground.

'YOU WILL do as Mum said. Leave now, pick up Jake, go home, and get as much tinned food as you can.'

Leona was stunned into silence. Now, all of a sudden, sensing things had become serious.

'Are we going to have riots over here?' she asked. 'I heard something on the radio yesterday about—'

'Yeah, it may happen. Food shortages, power shortages, all sorts.'

His voice sounded stretched and thin, and worried – frightened even. She had heard that sort of fear in his voice once before, years ago.

'Dad, did you get my email?'

'What?'

'My email. I sent it on Friday?'

'What? Yeah … yeah I got it, but what's—'

'I saw one of those men on TV, Dad. One of those men I saw in New York.'

There was a pause, although she could hear a lot of noise in the background. Voices shouting and banging like someone hitting a nail with a hammer.

'I'm not sure we should talk about this, Leona. Not over the phone.'

'Why?'

Another long pause.

'Leona, please just get your brother, and go home. Buy as much food and water as you can.'

In the background she heard voices rising in timbre; several of them, loud, insistent.

'Dad? What's going on?'

And then she heard the staccato sound of hammering again, more of it joining in.

'Leona!' Dad shouted, his voice distorted by the noise. 'Leona! I've got to go now!'

She'd never heard him sound like that, not ever. Angry a few times, but never like that.

'Dad! What's going on?' she replied, her voice beginning to wobble, sown with the first seeds of panic. She heard a man in the background, close by, as if he was standing next to Dad. It was the sort of voice she guessed was normally very deep, but was now raised, almost shrill with panic – God, it was frightening. Something was going on.

She heard Dad one last time. 'Please! DO AS I ASK! I've got to—'

And then they were disconnected.

The call left her trembling. The voice in the background had sounded foreign, American perhaps. But if truth be told, it wasn't the shrillness of his timbre, but the words she had heard this man shout that had set the hairs on her forearms standing.

'Here they come.'

The memory came back to her five minutes later, as she was playing over and over the last few seconds of that bizarre phone call. It was the tone of Dad's voice though, that had brought the memory to the surface – fear, not for himself of course, fear for her ...

Dad seems so on edge. He sits her down on the bed, and looks at her intently.

'You saw nothing important Leona. Do you understand? Nothing important,' he says, speaking loudly, clearly ... almost as if he's speaking to someone else, someone on the other side of the room.

'But who were those men Daddy?'

'No one you need to concern yourself with. Just a bunch of boring old business men, nothing to worry about, okay?'

Leona knows that's a brush-off. Those men were the 'mystery men' Dad was meant to meet. They're the reason Dad's been so distracted, short-tempered, nervous these last few days. But she knows by the way he's staring at her, by the tremble in his voice, that she should do as he says and forget about them.

Leona smiles reassuringly at him. 'Okay.'

'It happens, sweetheart, wrong room. I've done that before. No harm done.'

Leona nods.

'Good girl. Let's just forget about this now, huh? Just a silly little secret between you and me?'

'Okay.'

'Good. Remember Leona: our secret. Come on, I'm going to buy you that Beanie Doll you're after ... what's her name?'

'Sally Beanie.'

'Sally Beanie, that's right. And maybe, if you're good, we'll get the pony-riding set too?'

Leona finds herself grinning, the men in the room next door forgotten for now.

The memory, from when she was ten – that family trip to New York – had all but faded. She had almost forgotten wandering into that wrong room, then the right room, walking in on Dad, sitting in the dark. And then telling him what had just happened.

But seeing that old man's face again on the TV recently had been unsettling, and hearing that fear again in Dad's voice – the memory had come tumbling out from a dark and dusty corner, as clear as day. She wondered for a second time, if she *should* have emailed Dad about it. There'd been something so intense about him – the day he made her promise to forget.

He hadn't been frightened, he'd been terrified.

CHAPTER 20

. . . .

11.22 a.m. local time

Al-Bayji, Iraq

Lieutenant Carter watched the approaching truck. It chugged up the boulevard towards them, belching a cloud of exhaust behind it, and complaining loudly as the gears crunched and it gathered speed.

'Move your fucking arses,' shouted Sergeant Bolton as he waved the last of the platoon forward into firing positions up along the wall and beside the barricade of detritus covering the iron gate.

Lance Corporal Westley waited beside Carter, the SA80 with the grenade launcher fitted beneath the barrel in his hands. He pulled the stock against his shoulder and prepared to fire.

'Easy,' he said, 'not yet, let it get closer.'

'Aye, sir.'

Following in the wake of the slowly moving truck, a respectful distance behind, he could see a large group of armed men and boys jogging to keep up. They were using the truck for cover to get closer. Carter could see their game-plan as clear as day. The truck would roll up to the compound, or crash through the iron gate, and then the explosives in the back would detonate. The armed men running behind the truck would storm through the open gateway seconds after the explosion and clean up quickly and easily.

Simple and sensible.

Westley was their best bet to set the bastard off before it hit them, but only if he could drop a grenade somewhere in the back of the flatbed truck. In their favour, the vehicle looked as if it was on its last legs and struggling to build up any significant speed. It rumbled closer, and with a shuddering clatter it bounced up on to the island running down the centre of the boulevard. The armed crowd jogging behind the truck were beginning to lag behind as the truck finally seemed to find its legs and began to pick up some speed.

'Okay,' muttered Carter, 'when you're ready.'

Westley nodded and then lined the approaching truck up through his weapon sight. He raised the barrel, calculating the drop as best he could.

With a thud and a puff of acrid smoke he launched a grenade.

It arced through the air tumbling erratically as it went, coming down and bouncing up high off the ground several yards in front of the advancing truck. It exploded, shattering the windshield and ripping the hood of the truck off, exposing a grime-encrusted and rusty engine that shuddered violently on its ancient mountings.

'Shit. Get the other USG, quick!' ordered Lieutenant Carter.

Westley picked up the second SA80 fitted with the grenade launcher, and lined up his second and final attempt.

The truck bounced off the near side of the central island on to the road, amidst a cloud of dust and flecks of rust thrown and shaken loose.

He hunkered down, aimed and then raised the gun upwards, once more allowing for the drop.

A second thud and a puff of smoke exploded from the stubby and wide barrel of the launcher. The grenade arced upwards again, a steeper angle and much higher than the first, tumbling in the air and then finally dropping down.

With only about twenty yards between the truck and the gate, Sergeant Bolton gave the order to fire. Every gun in the platoon, plus Mike and Erich both issued with the AKs, let rip. The front of the truck seemed to explode amidst a shower of sparks that reminded Carter of a Catherine wheel.

Fifteen yards ...

The truck's driver flopped back in his seat, shredded by the volley and only vaguely recognisable as having once been a human being. Carter watched Westley's grenade continue to drop. It landed on the back of the truck and then bounced high again, off the back of the flatbed area ... and then detonated.

The blast pushed both of them back off their stack of pallets down on to the floor of the compound. Carter landed heavily and lay on the ground, temporarily winded – but bizarrely, looking up at the blue sky and enjoying the slow-motion cascade of a million comets of debris trailing ribbons of black smoke.

And it was silent.

He'd expected the detonation to be loud, but the only noise he could hear was the dull rush of blood in his ears, like the roar of waves crashing on a rocky shoreline. Really quite pleasant.

He sensed movement around him, and slowly the reassuring rumble of distant ocean waves receded, to be replaced with the sound of voices screaming, impact, gunfire. He pulled himself up on to his elbows, still struggling to get his breath and looked around.

The momentum of the truck had done its job and the shattered and burning chassis had managed to smash through the gateway. The immense blast seemed to have knocked everyone to the ground, and he watched as his platoon picked themselves up. Two of the Land Rovers and one of the two Cruisers nearest the gate had caught some of the blast and were burning fiercely.

And there were some casualties; a couple of the lads who had been standing closest to the gateway were lying still – one of them in several pieces.

Through a curtain of flames in the gap that had once been occupied by an iron gate, he could see the armed insurgents gathering. They were savvy enough to know their attack needed to follow in quick succession to take advantage of the shock and disorientation of the blast. And even as he pulled himself to his feet and fumbled for his weapon, the first and most foolhardy of them were scrambling through the burning debris strewn around the compound entrance.

As the last of the debris from the truck rained down around them, Andy stuck his head up over the bonnet of their Land Cruiser.

'Shit, they've broken through!' he shouted.

He spotted the prone forms of a couple of British soldiers, the others were scrambling for cover, ready for the insurgents to stream in through the gateway.

Mike reached for his AK. 'I'm going to help them,' he said.

Andy took a look at the situation.

Lieutenant Carter was rallying men behind some scattered pallets to the left of the gateway; he had about six or seven men with him, and Andy watched as they settled in and trained their rifles on the opening either side of the burning chassis of the truck.

Sergeant Bolton, meanwhile, had called the rest of the platoon to him. Andy counted only another half-a-dozen men. They took up position around and behind the burning vehicles in front of the gateway. He was impressed at the speed with which they had gathered their wits and found effective covering positions; Andy's head was still spinning from the noise and shock wave of the blast.

There were a couple of weapons spare, lying on the ground beside two young men caught in the blast. He could rush out and grab one, if he was quick. But Andy could see the shimmering forms of men through the blaze, and one or two un-aimed shots whistled through the flames and smoke towards them. He didn't fancy running out from behind the cover of their Cruiser to retrieve one of the guns.

Mike turned to him. 'You better stay here,' he shot a glance at Farid, and the two Iraqi lads, 'keep an eye on them.'

Andy nodded. It made sense. He didn't have a gun to fire, and if he did, he suspected he'd be more of a liability than a help.

Several rounds thudded into the side of the Land Cruiser they were cowering behind. The gathered mob outside began to grow impatient waiting for the flames to die down and fired indiscriminately through the curtain of flames at the smouldering vehicles inside.

Mike shook his head in disgust. 'No fucking way I'm dying here in this shitty town,' he muttered to himself. 'I've got more important shit to attend to.'

It was then that young Amal made a dash away from the soldier who was meant to be watching over him, but was now distracted – focusing on the threatening press of enemy bodies beyond the diminishing flames.

'Hey!' shouted Mike. 'The bastard's making a break for it!'

The Texan raised the AK in his hands and drew a bead on the young lad as he raced two dozen yards across open space towards the gateway. As he pulled the trigger Andy knocked the rifle upwards, and three rapidly fired rounds whistled harmlessly up into the sky.

'Are you fucking crazy!'

Amal wasn't trying to escape from them.

The young man slid to the ground dislodging a cloud of dust as he reached the nearest of the two bodies, and the dead man's rifle. The ground around the body suddenly exploded with several puffs of dirt, as the insurgents zeroed in on the movement inside the compound. Amal waited, lying as flat as he could behind the body of the British soldier, using it as cover as several more bullets thudded into the side of it.

'He's going for the guns.'

Mike said nothing in reply, as he watched the Iraqi lad cowering nervously, with the rifle lying flat across his chest.

The gunfire diminished momentarily and Amal flipped himself over on to his belly, ready to leap to his feet at a moment's notice.

Mike hunkered down and aimed down the barrel towards the young man.

'Jesus! I said he's going for the guns!' shouted Andy.

'Shut up!' grunted Mike. 'I'm giving him a hand.'

He fired off half-a-dozen well-aimed rounds towards the mob on the far side of the truck. One of them threw his arms up and went down; the others ducked instinctively.

'Amal! Go! *Yallah*!' shouted Andy realising Mike was offering covering fire.

The young man sprang to his feet and lurched another dozen yards across the compound, and then hit the dirt as he arrived beside the second dismembered body and reached out for the gun there.

It was at this point that the first and most courageous of the mob outside decided to pick their way through the smoking and scattered debris, and enter the compound with their guns firing.

Lieutenant Carter's and Sergeant Bolton's men both opened up at the same time, releasing a criss-crossing lattice of bullets that quickly cut them down. Several more of them filed in from behind, dropping down behind the bodies of their comrades, using them for cover, and firing back with surprisingly cool heads.

Amal remained where he was, trapped by the incoming and outgoing gunfire zipping past only inches above his prone form. The intense exchange lasted for only about ten seconds, and then a shared lull occurred as both sides reloaded.

Amal took his chance then, pulled himself to his feet, clutching both of the SA80s in his arms and began to scramble back across the compound towards the Land Cruiser.

'Oh shit, come on!' Andy yelled. Farid had joined them and was yelling something, probably very similar, in Arabic.

Amal's luck lasted most of the way across, but a well-aimed burst coming from one of the half-dozen men that had gone to ground and established a toe-hold inside the compound, brought the lad down. He fell forward as a shot punched him squarely between the shoulders, and the two assault rifles spilled out on to the ground beside him.

Mike thrust his AK into Andy's hands, and then leapt out from behind the Rover. He loped across twenty feet of open ground towards the two valuable weapons, frustratingly close to being retrieved.

Sergeant Bolton's men were firing again, having reloaded. They were managing to keep the heads of the men inside the compound down. Even so, more of them were stepping through the steaming, smoking debris and firing towards the American, attracted by the sudden burst of movement.

Mike dropped to his knees as he reached the two weapons. He grabbed the strap of one of them, and slung the gun over his shoulder. Then, he reached down and grabbed both of Amal's hands.

The lad was light, and Mike dragged him roughly across the ground, like an empty sleeping-bag, as bullets threw divots of dirt up around him.

Sergeant Bolton spoke over his radio on the command frequency to Lieutenant Carter.

'Sir, we need to throw these bastards back out – now.'

'Yes I know,' the Lieutenant's voice crackled back.

Bolton counted about half-a-dozen men that had managed to make their way into the compound and find secure, hardcover positions amidst the scattered mess of debris inside. From there, those buggers were doing a good job of holding the door open for the mob outside. He had some grudging respect for them. Those men were seasoned fighters, perhaps having cut their teeth in Afghanistan; the hardcore few that one seemed to find at the centre of every contact that seemed to exist in the midst of every street riot. And they were prepared to die, happy to die, longed to die. In Sergeant Bolton's experience, a mindset like that, having no fear of death, was more than a match for any type of cutting-edge battlefield technology they could counter them with.

The mob outside was gaining confidence, and the first few were picking their way through the gateway, given covering fire by those hardcore bastards. Bolton decided they couldn't wait any longer. This was the moment that would swing things either way. They needed to push hard right now, and dislodge their toe-hold on the compound, before numbers overwhelmed them.

'Right lads,' he said, turning to the six men sheltering with him behind the two unharmed Rovers. 'We've got to kick those raggys out, or ...'

Or this'll be all over in the next minute.

'Or we'll be well on the way to being buggered,' he added.

One of the lads, Lamby, nodded towards the dug-in enemy gunmen. 'How do we do that? They got a fucking good position.'

'If we sit here they have,' replied Bolton grinning, 'but if we take them by surprise and charge them – they'll bolt like rabbits.'

Actually, he doubted very much that they would. He hit the press-to-talk button on his PRR. 'Sir, we're going to charge over and barrel-shoot the bastards.'

Lieutenant Carter's reply was hesitant. 'Okay, in that case we'll give you covering fire Sergeant. Give me your shout and we'll try and keep their heads down.'

'Yes sir,' he replied as he refreshed his magazine and then turned to the others. 'Check your ammo, lads. On my command we're going over there and giving those shits a good kicking. The other boys will give us covering. You ready?'

The six young men nodded in unison as they clambered to their feet, keeping low, but ready to charge on their Sergeant's command.

Bolton smiled.

Good lads, all of them.

'All right then.'

He spoke into his throat mic. 'Sir, we're ready to go.'

'We're ready to cover you.'

'On "one" then sir?'

'Understood.'

Bolton counted down loudly, 'Three ... two ... ONE!'

He leapt out from behind the parked Rovers, his rifle held at the hip, and without a moment's hesitation the six men with him followed suit. Simultaneously, Lieutenant Carter's men opened fire on the dug-in militia and as sparks flew around them, they all hunkered down.

Sergeant Bolton found himself laughing breathlessly as he screamed encouragement at his men. They scrambled across thirty feet of open ground with gunfire whistling past them inaccurately from the mob outside.

As they reached the smouldering tangle that had not so long ago been a truck, the men dug in there were largely caught out, looking up at the screaming, enraged faces of the British squaddies with only a scant moment to try and swing their AKs up in response.

Bolton stumbled upon an old man who looked old enough to be his grandfather; a tanned face rich with laughter lines and framed with a white-and-grey beard, and big blue eyes opened wide with surprise. As he pulled the trigger and destroyed that face, he oddly found himself thinking in the heat of the moment that the man had looked a little like Santa Claus.

His section made quick work of the other half a dozen; firing down at the prone forms quickly and ruthlessly. He saw one of them drop his gun as if it were red-hot and quickly raise his hands. But the soldier standing over him made a snap decision to ignore that and fired a dozen rounds into his chest and head.

Bolton nodded approvingly, this wasn't the kind of exchange where prisoners could be taken.

Lieutenant Carter led his men out from their position behind the stacked pallets and emerged into the open, dropping smartly into a firing stance. They unleashed a sustained volley at the mob that had begun to press forward through the wreckage to reclaim their toe-hold. As the first few of them dropped to the ground, the others quickly fell back and within little more than a dozen seconds Carter's men had pushed them back out of the compound and on to the kerb outside, where a sense of panic swept through the crowd like wildfire, and the mob began to waiver, then disperse. They turned on their heels and beat a retreat back across the boulevard to the shelter and safety of the buildings and walled gardens on the far side.

The ground around the gateway was littered with the bodies of many of them. Only a couple of the prone forms were still moving.

Lieutenant Carter waved his arm. 'All right, cease firing!' he shouted. He knew the section's wind was up, but they desperately needed to conserve the ammo they had left.

He turned round to look for Sergeant Bolton, firstly to congratulate him on having the bottle to pull that charge off, and secondly to issue orders to seal that gateway somehow. They'd probably need to push one or two of the blast-damaged Rovers over to plug the gap. That would be enough of an obstruction for now.

And then he saw Bolton standing amidst the wreckage holding both hands to his pelvis and looking down at the spreading dark stain and the ragged hole in his tunic.

'Bollocks.' Bolton groaned angrily before dropping to his knees.

CHAPTER 21

. . . .

8.55 a.m.

UEA, Norwich

Ash stepped silently over the stiffening corpse of Alison Derby. The blood that had gushed from her carotid artery last night was now a dry pool of dark brown gel on the linoleum floor. She was dead within two minutes of him slipping the narrow blade of his knife into the side of her neck – unconscious after only a minute. He had decided he couldn't afford to be distracted by her shuffling and whimpering.

A shame; she had been nice, courteous and helpful.

But he needed it to be quiet inside, so he'd hear when Leona Sutherland came up the stairs and approached the door. He had waited all through the night, sitting on the stool in the kitchen, in the dark, patiently waiting. It seemed likely, after midnight, that the girl was staying over with her boyfriend. But he couldn't afford to be asleep just in case she did turn up.

He'd had the dark hours alone, to sort through his thoughts.

We could have closed the door on the little girl, when she entered. I could have finished her there.

But no, that would have been needlessly reckless. Processing a body in an exclusive hotel, in the middle of Manhattan, would have been difficult. Yet, what she had seen was dangerous; three of The Twelve. Worse still, the three of them together in the same room.

He knelt down beside Alison Derby, her face was grey, her lips a bluey-purple, her eyes still open, dull and not quite focused on anything. Ash could kill a ten-year-old girl just as easily as an eighteen year old. The end always justified the means. And in any case perhaps it was a kindness. The next few weeks were going to be truly apocalyptic. A young girl like Alison, with no advance knowledge of what was coming, unprepared, no stocks of food, or water … reduced to living like a cave-dweller and at the mercy of a very brutal form of Darwinism? She'd not have lasted long. She almost certainly would have been one of those who failed to make it out the other side.

Ash passed several hours confessing to Alison everything he knew about the *plan*, and why *they* were doing it. Why it needed to be done. And then he told her all about himself. How lonely it was to live only within the shadows, to move from one pseudonym to the next.

She was a great listener. The dead usually were.

Dawn arrived early, a clear sky, a strong sun and Ash listened to the campus slowly wake up, the noises drifting in through the open kitchen window; an alarm radio snapping on, a kettle boiling, the laughter and to-and-fro from a couple of girls on the floor above, the thud of a dance track from someone's stereo.

And then he heard footsteps on the stairwell outside. It could be her, could be someone else. Either way, he should be ready to pull her in and quickly deal with her as soon as that door opened.

Leona took the stairs up to the second floor of her accommodation block fogged with worry and jumbled thoughts. In the foyer she stood with the keys jangling in her hands. Coming down the stairs from the floor above she could hear someone's stereo pumping out a baseline that made the stairwell window vibrate subtly.

Everyone seemed to be calmly going about their business.

'… *it'll catch everyone by surprise, no one will know what's happened until all of a sudden there are soldiers stationed around every petrol station and food shop* …'

Dad's words sent a shiver down her.

'… *you don't want to be the last person to react to this* …'

'Shit, I really have to go home,' she muttered quietly to herself.

But there were a few things she needed to get: some clothes, the house keys, her iPod; and then she'd have to see what time the first available train down to Liverpool Street station was. She shuffled through her keys and found the one for their door, hoping that Alison had the kettle on so she could grab a quick cup of tea before packing her bag to go home.

Of course, Alison was going to want to know why the hell she was going home all of a sudden, instead of sticking around for reading week like she'd promised. Leona wasn't sure she was quite ready to come out with something like, 'Oh I'm heading home because my Dad said the end of the world's about to happen. He knows about that kind of stuff.' Alison was pretty cool though. Unlike the four other girls they shared with, who spent most of their time talking *Big Brother*, she was quite switched on.

She was about to slide the key into the door lock when her phone rang.

CHAPTER 22

• • • •

It made her jump.

She looked at the number on the display, it was Dad again.

'Dad, you okay? It sounded like something was going on over th—?'

'Leona, listen to me. I haven't got much charge on my phone. I ...'

'Dad, I was so worried about—'

'LISTEN!'

She shut up.

'Do *not* go to our home. It's not safe! Do you understand?'

'What? Why?'

'I haven't got time to explain. It's going crazy here, my phone could cut off at any time. Look, I might be wrong. I probably am, but just to be safe ... get Jake, get some food and water, you know what kind of food. Tins. And then go to Jill's.'

Jill was a friend of Mum's, she lived alone three houses down on the opposite side of their leafy little street.

'Jill's? Why?'

'Just do that will you? Stay away from home. Go to Jill's instead.'

'But why Dad?'

'I haven't got the time. Where are you right now?'

'I'm just letting myself into my digs, I was going to pack some—'

'Oh for Christ's ... Leona, get the hell away from there!'

'What?'

'Please, do me a favour and leave right now.'

'Dad? What's going on ? You're scaring me.'

'Leona, leave RIGHT NOW—'

The call disconnected.

She stared at the door in front of her for a moment, suddenly very wary of what might be inside. Her key had been poised inches from the lock when the phone rang. It was still hovering inches away now. There was no ambiguity there. Dad said to 'get the hell away' from her digs. If he'd said that in any other way; a nagging, hectoring tone, a snotty irritable voice, his softly-softly *do it for me* voice, she would probably have decided to tune him out.

But he'd said it in just the right way to scare the shit out of her.

Leona put the key back in her pocket, turned as quietly as she could on her heels and took the stairs quickly down to the front door of the building.

He was still splayed out on his bed, dead to the world, fast asleep.

She crossed the room and knelt down beside him. 'Dan. Wake up, Dan,' she said quietly.

He stirred almost immediately, stretching, squawking out a strangled yawn and then rubbed his big blue eyes with the backs of his hands.

Baby eyes.

Leona had to ask him a favour. She had to try. Walking briskly back across the centre of town she had tried the Virgin ticket line only to find out that for some unspecified reason, there were no trains down to London. She'd had the same luck with Express coaches. Oh God, she hated that she had to ask such a big favour, with them only being an item for what ... no more than 24 hours? Not that they were officially an item yet. It's not like any of it was *official* – they were both sort of still finding their way through whatever it was they had going together.

'Dan?'

'Yeah,' he muttered sleepily, reaching out with one hand and cupping her small chin in it. 'Ask me anything you want, sexy babee,' he added.

'Dan, I need a favour. A really big favour.'

Oh crap, here goes. And if he says 'NO' you know you can't really blame him.

'Could you drive me to London?' she blurted, wrinkling her face in antici-pation of his answer. It really was unfair to ask him like this, and she really did feel like a selfish, needy cow for—

'Sure,' he muttered sleepily.

They drove the first half an hour in silence, some music blaring from the van's cheap stereo. Leona wasn't really listening to it; instead she was wondering how she was going to explain this sudden, desperate need to head home, without sounding like a total doomsday propeller-head, like Dad.

Daniel drove on quite happily nodding his head to the music, trundling un-certainly along in the slow lane as his van, an ancient-looking rust-encrusted

Ford given to him by his mum, struggled doggedly to achieve a steady sixty miles per hour.

As the A11 merged into the M11, they managed to overtake a surprisingly long convoy of army trucks. Daniel counted twenty of them, all of them full of soldiers, some of who had spotted Leona in the passenger seat as they passed by and waved, grinned and made some crude and suggestive gestures towards her. She stared rigidly ahead, determined to ignore them.

It wasn't until they eventually hit the M25 and the outskirts of London that either his patience finally ran out, or the idea occurred to him to actually ask. He turned the music down.

'Why *are* we going to London anyway?'

Leona sighed. 'Dan, you're going to think I'm a bit mad.'

He smirked, 'I know you're mad.'

So, she wondered, *how do I begin?*

'Have you seen the news?'

Daniel shook his head, smiling goofily. 'Uh ... no, not recently. It's all ugly old members of the government humping office staff, and losing lots of money, isn't it?'

Leona ignored his joke. 'Well, give me an idea of the last news you saw or heard?'

He was silent for a moment, giving the question serious consideration. 'Last time I was home, I guess,' he pursed his lips, counting silently, 'yeah ... about five weeks ago, I saw some.'

Leona shook her head. 'My God, we could be facing the end of the world, and you wouldn't have the first idea, would you?'

Daniel thought about that for a moment, before turning to look at her, still smiling. 'Are we?' he asked.

Leona shrugged. 'I don't know. I really don't know.'

The last track on the CD came to an end, and he reached out to restart it.

'Can we put the radio on?'

'Sure,' he said, 'I s'pose I better find out if the world is ending, huh?'

As they began to negotiate the increasing traffic heading west across the north of London, Leona hopped from radio station to radio station, dialling through inner-city urban stations pumping out R&B without a care in the world. They caught several news bulletins on Radio 1, and then she tuned to Radio 4, a station she wouldn't normally touch with a barge-pole, except today. They had some experts in the studio talking with great solemnity and concern about the developing global crisis and more specifically, about the lunchtime announcement the Prime Minister was scheduled to make.

Leona's navigation left a lot to be desired and they struggled to find the correct way off the M25 to head down to North Finchley, where Jake's prep school was located, doubling back on to the ring road several times before they found the right junction to come off at.

'So, what ... we're suddenly going to run out of electricity or something?' asked Daniel, after listening to a heated exchange between a couple of guests on the programme they were listening to.

'Yeah,' she replied, 'I think that's what'll happen.'

He hunched his shoulders, 'Oh, okay. Not so bad then, I suppose. I thought we were—'

She looked at him in astonishment. 'You've gotta be kidding me?'

Go easy on him, Dan's not had the five-year oil paranoia crash course, that you have.

'Uh no, I'm not kidding ... am I?'

'Dan, running out of electricity is just one thing. Do you know what else it really means – running out of oil?'

He thought about that for a moment. 'Hospitals and stuff? Shit, UEA would have to close as well, right?'

She gestured towards a road sign. 'There, left at the traffic lights. That takes us south towards North Finchley. Anyway, no it means much more than the university closing. God, much more.'

'What do you mean?'

'No oil means so much more than no petrol for your car, or power for your ... for your guitar amp.'

With a sudden realisation it occurred to her that she sounded so much like Dad. Even her barely detectable inherited accent was coming through more strongly.

'Dan,' she continued, 'it means no bloody food, no water—'

'Uh! No food? No water? How's that then? It's always pissing down in England, there's water everywhere! And food, shit, there's loads of it around.'

'Yeah?'

'Yeah. I mean, it's all farms and fields out there, once you get out in the countryside. That's all food isn't it?'

'*Some* of it is food. But not nearly enough.'

Daniel laughed out loud. 'What's this all about? There's some, like, riots on the other side of the world and suddenly you're telling me we're all going to be starving over here?'

Leona said nothing and looked at him.

Daniel laughed some more, and then turned to look at her. His smile slipped quickly away when he saw how intense she looked.

'Oh come on,' he said after a while.

'Daniel, my dad's an oil engineer. And for the last few years, you know what? All he's talked to me and Mum about, is how one day the oil might suddenly be stopped from flowing. At first it was a little frightening. He'd be telling us this stuff, how easily, you know, *society* would fall apart, what could start it all happening ... the warning signs. And he was so paranoid too, Dan. Talking about all this crap and then saying we should keep it to ourselves.'

Leona laughed. 'As if I was going to spout that stuff to my mates at a party. He was so secretive about it all, he ...'

'It's our little secret, Leona. Forget about those boring old men ...'

'Well anyway, it all started getting very boring. And for the last couple of years I started to think of Dad as a tediously paranoid dick.'

She looked out of the window at the street, clogged with cars nudging slowly forward amidst a soup of exhaust fumes shimmering in the mid-morning warmth, pedestrians passing by seemingly without a care in the world and enjoying the sun, the shop fronts on either side full of goodies at bargain-basement prices ... an electronics store, with several forty-inch plasma screen TVs in the window all showing some monster trucks racing around a dirt track.

'And this morning I discovered, after all this time ... that maybe he wasn't.'

CHAPTER 23

. . . .

9.41 a.m. GMT

Manchester

The taxi-cab controller stared at her with a look of disbelief spreading across his face.

'Yes, that's right,' said Jenny, 'London. How much?'

He shook his head. 'You're taking the piss.'

Jenny sighed. 'I'm not taking the piss. I really *need* to get home. So, come on, how much?'

The controller pointed out of the window towards the road leading down from Whitworth Street to the station. 'Get a train, love.'

'I can't get a bloody train,' Jenny snapped, 'because the trains are not running for some reason.'

A customer who had been waiting in line behind Jenny stepped forward. 'Yeah, I just discovered that too,' he said leaning on the cab controller's counter beside Jenny. 'Apparently there was some terrorist threat received this morning. That's the rumour I heard, some sort of bomb threat.'

Jenny turned back to the controller. 'There, see? That's why I need a flippin' cab. Did you know the coaches are out too?'

'And the airports,' added the man standing next to her. 'There've been security alerts everywhere, it seems. There were tanks rolling up outside Heathrow I heard.'

The controller shook his head again. 'Well, whatever. We only do a local service, love.'

'Okay,' replied Jenny digging into her bag to produce her purse, 'how much then? A couple of hundred?'

'No, look sorry, sweetheart, we can't take you down to London.'

'Would five hundred cover it?' said the other man.

The controller looked at him with a sceptical frown. 'You'll pay five hundred pounds?'

He nodded. 'Yup, I've got a meeting this afternoon I can't afford to miss. I'll pay five hundred.'

The controller scratched his head. 'O-o-okay, your money. I'll see if we have a taker then,' he muttered shaking his head with bemusement. He began talking over the radio.

Jenny turned to the man behind her. 'Could we possibly share? I can pay half.'

The man, tall, slim, wearing a dark blue suit, the jacket carefully draped over one arm and the top button of his striped, office shirt unbuttoned, turned to look at her. She guessed he was in his mid-thirties, sensibly short dark hair, and glasses that looked as if they were at the cheaper end of the scale. Jenny thought he wouldn't have looked out of place holding a mug of coffee and a doughnut in either a teachers' common room, or standing, Magic Marker in hand, before a flip-pad in some ad agency's creative mush-pit.

He pursed his lips as he considered the offer. 'I need the cab to get me to Clapham. I'm not sure if—'

'That's fine,' she replied quickly, 'just as long as I can get to any tube station. I can get where I'm going from there.'

He tipped his head slightly, 'Well I suppose so then, if you're going to cover half.'

Jenny felt a small surge of relief. 'Yes, I will. Thanks, I was beginning to wonder if I'd have to walk home,' she added with a nervous chuckle.

'You're in a big hurry too?'

Jenny nodded. 'I just … well, with things the way they are, I want to be home.'

He seemed confused by that. 'The way *what* is?'

'You know? The news. The riots.'

'The riots? Do you mean that Middle East thing?'

She nodded.

'Oh right. Yes, I suppose that's a little worrying, especially if we're now getting bomb threats over here. It's really screwed up travelling today. But you know, hopefully it'll all be back to normal again tomorrow, business as usual.'

The controller thanked the driver he'd been talking to and turned to them. 'Yeah, all right I've got a driver who'll do it later on this morning. But he wants the five hundred in cash, and wants to see it in your hand before he'll take you.'

'Oh God, thank you!' Jenny sighed with relief. 'Thank you.'

The controller shrugged. 'It's your money, love. Me, I'd spend the money on a nice hotel tonight and try my luck with the trains tomorrow.'

Trains tomorrow? Anything at all running tomorrow?

She wondered if she should just come out and say something like that. But then, she didn't want to scare off the man standing beside her by sounding like some kind of nut.

'I'm just in a really big hurry, all right?' she said.

UEA, Norwich

He listened to the call connect, then a short electronic warbling as the digital encryption filter kicked in, then a voice, masked with a pitch filter answered.

'Yes.'

'I nearly had the target. But someone warned her at the last moment.'

'Yes. We know this. She received a call from her father. He now suspects we may be after her.'

'That makes things a little more difficult.'

'Yes. The father gave her instructions to go to another location. He called it "Jill's" place.'

'Jill?'

'Possibly a member of the family or a close friend. The target can be reacquired there.'

'Were there any other details?'

'No. We just have the name "Jill".'

'There'll be something at the target's home to identify this "Jill".'

'That is what we think too.'

'Understood.'

'Proceed quickly. Things will begin to disintegrate soon, you may lose her.'

The call disconnected.

Ash pocketed his phone and cast one last glance around the room. He had been tempted to set fire to the place, so that his tracks would be covered for a while. The body of the girl would be discovered, and a good forensic pathologist might discern that she was dead before she was burned. Under normal circumstances that would be a sensible tactical move. But given how things were going to be in a few days' time, he was confident he'd not have to worry about the police following in his footsteps.

They were going to be far too busy to worry about one dead student.

As he stepped out into the stairwell, a young man passed by, casting a suspicious glance back at him as he descended the stairs.

Ash knew his appearance was incongruous. He looked completely wrong for this environment; too old, too smart, clearly not a student, and clearly with no business being here. The young man would undoubtedly tell somebody this morning, and someone would come knocking to see if everything was okay.

He let the lad go on his way.

Again, leaving a trail was of no concern to Ash. Right now his immediate priority was working out where Leona Sutherland was headed.

Next stop then, the Sutherland's home in Shepherd's Bush. He knew the address off by heart – 25 St Stephen's Avenue. Perhaps he might even catch her there, if she was silly enough to chance a quick visit to grab a change of clothes.

CHAPTER 25

· · · ·

11.37 a.m. GMT

North Finchley, London

Leona instantly recognised the tree-lined gravel driveway that led up to the main school building, a stately stone structure that had, once upon a time in a previous century, been built amidst smoothly rolling green acres, but was now hedged in on all sides by suburbia. Tall, mature conifers kept the world outside from peeking in at the dozen or so acres of manicured grounds, sports fields and tennis courts.

Leona had come with her dad a few times to drop Jake off. His school tended to return a week or so before college, and Jake usually begged for Leona to come along too. She wasn't sure whether that was because he wanted to spend as much time with her as possible, or because he enjoyed showing off his older sister to the lecherous and spotty boys in the years above.

'Wow,' said Daniel, 'this is sort of like Hogwarts.'

'Yup, and very expensive,' she replied looking out of the window at the boys taking turns to volley over the net on the tennis courts to their left. The tennis coach shot a disapproving glance at the scruffy little Ford van as it coughed and crunched up the gravel drive.

'You sure it's okay for us to be here?' he asked uneasily. 'I mean school's in session, aren't we trespassing or something?'

Leona shrugged. 'Don't care. Dad asked me to get Jake out.'

Daniel parked the van in a visitor's slot beside the imposing main entrance, sheltered by a grand-looking portico supported on two stone pillars. The last time she had seen Jake was six weeks ago, helping Dad to drag his trunk up the stairs and in through that entrance. The little monkey-boy had been doing his level best to look cool in front of all the other boys arriving in their parents' lumbering Chelsea tractors. She knew he was holding the tears back and would probably blubber once Dad had placed the trunk at the end of his dormitory bed and was giving him a final goodbye hug.

Mum never came along when it was time to take Jake back; she'd be in tears, sniffling and beating herself up with self-reproach and parental guilt all the way up from Shepherd's Bush, and then embarrass the hell out of Jake when it came time for hugs and kisses. Ironic really, Mum was the one who had worked the hardest to get him into this school, and yet was totally unable to deliver him come the start of each new term.

'So what now?'

'I'll go in and see if I can find his housemaster,' she replied. She turned to look at Daniel, dressed in his ripped jeans, and his FCUK T-shirt. 'You're probably best waiting here, okay?'

Daniel smiled with some relief. 'Sure.'

After asking directions from a confounded and harried-looking young boy, who was clearly late for a class and flushed crimson as he spoke to her whilst staring, transfixed, at her pierced navel, exposed above the low waistline of her jeans, she eventually found the housemaster's study. She knocked on the door, and hearing a muffled acknowledgement coming from within, opened the thick, heavy wooden door and stepped inside.

A man in a scruffy brown suit jacket and dark trousers that were scuffed with chalk dust was standing over an untidy desk shuffling through a tray of papers.

'Yes?' he grunted, without looking up.

'You're Mr North, the housemaster?' she asked.

Mr North looked up, and did a double take. 'I'm sorry, who are you?'

'Leona Sutherland. My brother's in your house.'

'Uhh, right well, you do know family visits are limited to specific week-ends, don't you?'

Leona nodded. 'Of course. But I'm not really visiting.'

He stopped shuffling through his tray. 'So then, how can I help you?'

'I'm here to collect Jacob and take him home.'

Mr North frowned. 'I don't know anything about this. When was this arranged? Because I've not received any written approval from the Head. At least I don't think I have. Let me just check my in-tray.' He leant across his desk and started rummaging through another tray, full to overflowing with papers and envelopes yet to be opened.

Leona wondered whether she could take advantage of his apparent inability to keep abreast of his paperwork, and lie to him – make out that it'd been approved and he'd simply lost the paperwork.

'I mean it's possible that I just missed it,' he continued, slightly flustered as he sorted through the haphazardly piled envelopes and notes, 'and the approval's in here somewhere. When did your parents write to me about this?'

Decision time … oh shit, I'm crap at lying.

'They didn't.'

Mr North looked up, a momentary confusion written across his face.

'They decided this morning to take Jake out, and they sent me to collect him,' Leona added.

The housemaster frowned and then shook his head. 'No. I'm sorry. It doesn't work that way. We need a written request from a pupil's parents or legal guardians, and a very good reason given before we allow them to be taken out in the middle of a term.'

'They have a very good reason, Mr North,' replied Leona. 'They both think the world's about to come to an end.'

That sounded pretty bloody silly, well done.

Mr North stopped shuffling through his in-tray and looked up at her. 'The riots?'

Leona nodded.

He came around from behind the desk and took a few steps towards her. 'Your mum and dad aren't the only ones.' He lowered his voice ever so slightly. 'I've already had two other parents call me this morning to ask if their sons could be taken out.'

'And can they?'

He shook his head, 'Only with written consent, and approval from the headmaster.'

'Please, I really need to get my brother.'

The housemaster studied her silently for a moment. 'I was watching the news last night. It does look very worrying. It does seem like the world went a little mad yesterday. I do wonder if there'll be more going on today.'

'I don't know. But my dad's in the oil business, and he's the one who's panicking.'

'Why haven't your parents come for him?'

'Dad's stuck in Iraq, and Mum's stuck up in Manchester. They've stopped the trains and coaches.'

Mr North looked surprised. 'Stopped the—?'

'They didn't say why. So it's just me, and I need to get him.'

He nodded silently, deep in thought. 'Look, I have to get to my lesson, I'm already late.'

Leona took a step forward. 'Please!'

He studied her silently for a while, a long silence, punctuated by the sound of a clock ticking from the mantelpiece above a decorated Victorian fireplace. 'Maybe your father's right,' he said quietly. 'You can see the way this could possibly go.'

Leona nodded. 'My dad thinks we're going to be in really big trouble.'

'I see.'

She offered him a wan smile. 'That's why I've got to get my brother.'

Mr North nodded. 'Hmmm. It *does* seem really quite worrying.'

'Please,' she said, 'I have to get him. I'm in a hurry.'

He looked at her silently for a moment. 'I can't give you my permission to just walk in and take him without prior written consent. But,' he said, 'I can't really stop you if I don't know about it, can I?'

She understood and nodded a thank you.

'Who's your brother?'

'Sutherland. Jacob Sutherland.'

'Ahh yes, junior year two. I think you'll find his class in C block, that's the language wing.'

'Thank you Mr North.'

'You go and get him. And the first I'll know about this is when we do our afternoon assembly roll call. Which means we haven't met, all right?'

She nodded and then turned to go.

'So,' he said as she reached out and opened the door, 'what advice do you think your dad would give us here at the school?' he asked. 'What advice do you think he would give me?'

Leona turned round. 'Leave now. Get out of London before everyone else wakes up to this.'

'I see.'

'Goodbye,' she said. And then as an afterthought, 'Good luck.'

He smiled politely as she closed the door on him.

Leona looked up and down the wood-panelled corridor, and decided she might need Dan's help.

'No, see, this isn't right Leona. I'm sure this is basically illegal.'

'No it isn't, he's my brother,' she replied, craning her neck to look surreptitiously through the small window in the classroom door. Inside she could see a class of boys who looked a couple of years older than Jacob. 'Shit, not in this one either.'

Daniel cast a wary glance up and down the hallway between the classrooms. 'Look, it's abduction isn't it? Taking a minor like this?' he muttered.

'It's not, we're getting him on my mum and dad's instructions. Come on,' she waved him on, and they paced down the hallway towards the next pair of classroom doors.

'Look, even if you find him, they won't let you take him right out of the classroom.'

She stopped and looked at him, and smiled. 'Which is sort of where you come in.'

'What? How?'

'If one of the staff stands in the way ...'

'What, you want me to knock 'em down?'

She nodded, 'Well maybe not punch them or anything, just sort of push them aside.'

Daniel shook his head. 'Look Leona, I think I've been pretty good so far this morning, driving you here and—'

She grabbed his wrist. 'God, please Dan, just this last favour. I have to get him home.'

He spread his palms. 'Because here ... what? He's *not* safe?'

She led him up to another window, looked in briefly and saw instantly that they weren't Jake's age.

'Look in,' she said.

Dan shrugged and did as she asked. The boys inside were wearing head-phones and repeating French phrases in unison.

'So?'

'So, you've been listening to the radio this morning. The trains and coaches have been quietly stopped and the army is coming home from abroad, and there's no more oil coming in. And they,' she gestured at the classroom door, 'are still doing stupid French oral.'

Which seemed to strike him as pretty dumb, once put in that context.

'Dad was right. Everyone's standing around with their heads in the sand, just like he said they would, you know, if something like this happened,' she added, trying to keep her voice down as it started to thicken with a mixture of anxiety and anger.

She jogged across the hallway to look through a door window on the far side. 'Okay,' he said following her across. 'Just this last thing, then I'm head-ing back to—'

'That's Jake!' she hissed, looking through the window. Without a second's hesitation, she grabbed the handle and flung open the door.

The heads of thirty seven-year-old boys and the teacher, a lady who looked a few years younger than her mum, spun round to look at them.

The silence was broken by the teacher, 'Yes?'

'Jacob,' she said ignoring her, 'you have to come with me.'

Beneath his mop of curly blond hair, and behind the milk-bottle glasses, Jacob's round eyes darted towards his teacher then back to Leona, whilst his jaw slowly dropped.

'I'm sorry,' said the teacher, 'you can't just burst in here and take one of my students.'

Leona continued to ignore her. She flashed a warning glance at Jake. 'Now!' she barked.

Jacob obediently began to rise from his seat.

'It's all right Jacob,' said the teacher gesturing for him to take his seat again, 'sit back down, there's a good boy.'

'JAKE!' Leona barked as she smacked her fist on the corner of the desk next to her, it hurt – but it also got everyone's attention. 'Mum and Dad want you home, RIGHT NOW!'

He rose uncertainly out of his seat again.

The woman advanced toward Leona. 'You're his sister?'

Leona nodded.

'Well, look, you'll have to leave. I'm in the middle of a lesson. If his parents need him home then you need to tell them that they should contact the headmaster.'

Leona turned to her, acknowledging the teacher for the first time. 'He's coming with me right now,' she said calmly and then nodded her head at Daniel standing just behind her, 'and you better not get in our way, all right?'

Daniel puffed himself up slightly and attempted a menacing frown.

'Jake, get over here now!' shouted Leona taking a few steps across the classroom towards her brother. Daniel filed in behind keeping a wary eye on the teacher and balling his fists in what he hoped was a vaguely intimidating way.

Jake did as he was told, standing up and starting to pack his exercise books and stationery back into his shoulder bag.

'Oh for God's sake, leave that Jake! We've got to go right now!'

He looked confused, placing his things back down on the desk. 'Why am I going?'

'Questions later, okay? We're in a hurry.'

The woman stirred. 'Yes, why? Can you at least tell me that? I can't let him go without knowing why—'

'Because the world's about to end,' Daniel offered uncertainly with a shrug.

'What?' the woman replied, frowning with disbelief.

Leona reached out for Jacob's small hand, and led him towards the classroom door before turning back towards the teacher. 'He's right. In a few days' time, we're all going to be hungry, and people are going to get mad, and fight. And these boys,' she gestured with her free hand at the pupils who had watched in silent and rigid disbelief at the surprise intrusion, 'should all be sent home to their families, before it's too late.'

Leona led Jacob out of the classroom and Daniel backed out after them.

'You know I'll have to notify the school security guard,' the teacher called out. 'And the police!'

In the hallway outside Leona turned to Daniel. She was trembling.

'Oh my God, we're going to be in so much trouble if Dad's wrong,' she said.

Jacob looked up at Daniel and pointed a finger at him. 'Who is he? Is he your boyfriend? Where are we going?'

She knelt down in front of him. He was tiny for his age. 'Jake, I'll explain everything later. Right now, we just need to get home, okay?'

He thought about it for about three seconds, then nodded and saluted like a trooper. 'Roger, roger.'

All of a sudden, they heard the deafening ring of what sounded very much like a fire-alarm bell.

Daniel cupped his mouth, 'I think we should run!' he shouted.

CHAPTER 26

. . . .

12.30 p.m. GMT

Whitehall, London

He stared at his reflection in the mirror above the basin as he washed his hands. Caught in the downward glare of the little recessed spotlight above him, every bump, groove and crevice on his face stood out with merciless clarity. He looked ten years older standing here – fifty-five instead of forty-five.

It occurred to him that what he was doing was a job much better suited to a younger man. It was the arrogance and confidence of youth that carried you through this kind of undertaking. Doubting, second-guessing, checking the dark corners ... those debilitating habits came with *maturity* ... shit, who was he kidding ... *old age.*

His passport might say he was forty-five, but the tread-marks on his face spoke of a man much older. The wear and tear of staying at the top of the game had made its indelible mark on him. And now there was *this.*

He heard knuckles rapping against the wooden door to the gentlemen's wash-room.

'They're ready in the press room, Prime Minister.'

Charles nodded. 'Just give me a few minutes.'

His press secretary was still outside, Charles could see the twin shadows of his legs punctuating the strip of light coming through under the door.

'Sir, we are running short of time. Your broadcast is rescheduled for 1.30, and the TV people need you down in the press room to put some make-up on and do their lighting.'

For Christ's sake ...

'I said I'll be along in a minute!' he shouted irritably.

The twin shadows shuffled beneath the door for a moment, and then vanished.

He splashed some water on his face and let out a ragged sigh. With only an hour to go, he had yet to fully decide what exactly he was going to announce.

How honest should I be?

That was the question.

During the night most of the Cassandra recommendations had been discreetly put into action. Internal travel arteries had been locked down. The terror threat cover story was being pushed hard, and all airports, sea ports and rail stations had been successfully closed. But the cover story wasn't going to last for long.

Throughout the morning the process of blocking the main motorways had begun. Each blockage explained as either a severe traffic accident, or some truck losing its load across all four lanes. Again, those cover stories were only going to last a few hours at best; if they were lucky, until tomorrow morning.

Most of the main oil storage depots had, by now, been garrisoned with soldiers. The oil out there in the wider distribution system; the tankers, the bigger petrol stations – all of them would need to be requisitioned at some point, but that was a very visible process, and could only be done at the last possible moment.

The trick here was going to be not to spook the general population. Malcolm's advice had been that they had to keep *them* doing whatever they normally do, for as long as possible. That was his job, the Prime Minister's job, to keep everyone happy and calm for as long as he could. Malcolm had wryly quipped that Charles' role now was to be nothing more than the string quartet on the promenade deck of the *Titanic*.

Just keep them happy with your reassuring smile, and words of encouragement.

In the meantime, for as long as the public could be fooled, they had to get as many of their boys as they could back from Iraq and guarding key assets in the time they had. They had to get their hands on as much of the oil and food as was spread out there in warehouses and oil terminals.

It meant doing what he did best – bullshit the public for as long as possible.

Time was running out.

The travel lock-down was going to be explained as a 'large-scale unspecified threat' picked up by their secret services. That would also help to explain the higher than normal military traffic that people would undoubtedly have already noticed. There would be questions about the worsening situation in the Middle East, and whether that and the cessation of oil production from the region had anything to do with these 'security' measures.

And here he'd have to deliver the Big Lie, and he'd better do it convincingly.

'No,' muttered Charles aloud, staring at his reflection, knitting his dark eyebrows and narrowing his photogenic eyes; producing a very believable expression of sincere concern which he projected exclusively at the listener in the mirror. He backed it up with a reassuring nod as he continued.

'There's no link other than a general heightened security level. We have a healthy strategic reserve of crude oil to see us through this temporary upset. Potential choke points in oil supply, particularly from an unstable region like the Middle East, is something we have prepared for long in advance, and there is certainly no need for anyone to panic.'

His secretary was back, shuffling uncomfortably just outside the door once more. Charles could visualise him with his fist raised and knuckles hovering inches from the wooden door, agonising over whether to knock again, but knowing that he must.

'It's all right,' shouted Charles, loosening his tie ever so slightly and undoing the top button of his shirt to affect that tousled 'I've-just-been-dragged-away-from-my-desk-to-tell-you-how-I'm-fixing-things' look. He rolled up his sleeves for good measure. It was all about appearances. The right tone of voice, the right facial expression, the right look for the occasion. He'd learned a lot of that watching Tony Blair, a brilliant performer during moments of crisis.

Charles nodded at the reflection. He looked like a man who'd been working hard through the night but now, had a firm handle on things.

'I'm ready.'

CHAPTER 27

. . . .

3.42 p.m. local time

Al-Bayji, Iraq

Mike stared down at the corpse of the young man.

Amal had died quickly, only perhaps a minute or two after being dragged to safety behind the Land Cruiser. The bullet that had knocked him to the ground had also ripped a lung to shreds on its way through. Amal had died gurgling blood and struggling desperately for air in Mike's arms. His shirt, a Manchester United football shirt, was almost black with blood that was already congealing, drying in the heat of the afternoon.

Mike chugged a mouthful from his water bottle. The platoon medic had circulated some of the bottled water around the men half an hour earlier, and now that the situation outside had calmed down, he realised how dehydrated he'd become through the morning.

Farid squatted in the shade of the vehicle a few feet from him. He said nothing and stared at the body of the young lad, but Mike sensed the old man was actually studying him, wordlessly coming to some kind of conclusion about him. It felt uncomfortable being silently judged, appraised like that and he decided to break the silence.

'I dragged his ass back here because he had the goddamned car keys in his pocket,' Mike grunted coolly.

Farid nodded silently.

'He had the keys in his pocket, and I didn't want those fuckers outside getting hold of them,' he added for clarity.

Farid finally looked up at the Texan. 'But you have not take keys from Amal.'

Mike shrugged.

'Keys still in his pocket.'

'I'll get them when I'm good and ready.'

Farid's eyes narrowed as he looked at Mike. 'You not get him for the keys,' he said quietly.

Mike rolled his eyes tiredly. 'All right, you win, okay? I didn't get him because he had the keys. You happy now?'

Farid shook his head. 'Why?'

'Why did I go get him?'

The old man nodded in response.

Mike opened his mouth to speak before really knowing what sort of answer he was going to give. 'Shit, I don't know. Maybe because the kid had the balls to go out there and grab those guns, whilst the rest of us pussies were sitting back here sucking our thumbs.'

It took the Iraqi a moment to translate and understand what he'd said. 'You get him, because Amal was brave?'

Mike shrugged again. 'Yeah, so maybe I did, okay? That was a pretty fucking gutsy thing for the kid to do. And really shit luck that he didn't make it all the way back.'

Farid smiled and nodded. 'Allah smile upon you for your courage.'

Mike laughed. 'Yeah? If Allah sent me out to rescue the kid, why the hell did he allow him to die?'

The old man shrugged. 'His will. Is not for man to understand.'

'Yeah,' sniffed the American, 'that's what I figured, the usual religious rationale. Basically bullshit.'

'Not bullshit. But beyond our understanding.'

'Yeah see, though, that's the same old crap every goddamn fanatical imam or suicide bomber uses. *It is God's will* and who are we to question it, or try to understand it? Kind of open to a little abuse, isn't it?'

Farid nodded. 'Yes. Bad men do this. Imams who teach violence against others. That is bad, that is *haram*. As are those men who kill with terror bomb, or gun ... or tank, and helicopter. To kill in Allah's name is *worst* sin of all.'

Mike looked up at the old man, surprised to hear him say that. 'That's the first time I've heard one of your lot say that.'

Farid shook his head wearily. 'There are many who say this. But, picture of brothers burning American flag, or firing gun in the air, and the sinful ones, calling for Jihad and war and death, those things are what is make the news on TV, uh?'

The American pursed his lips in consideration. 'Maybe.'

'The Qu'ran teaches peace above all.'

Andy squatted against the wall a dozen yards away and tried dialling

Leona's number again, but the screen on his mobile winked out halfway through. That was it, the bloody thing was run flat. He pushed it back in his pocket and cursed to himself.

He had no idea if Leona had *really* understood not to go home. Yes, he'd told her that, but if they'd had a few more moments to talk, he could have explained why.

They were watching him. He had always half suspected that might be the case, but never fully convinced himself that they – whoever *they* were – would go to quite that much trouble.

And who the hell were they anyway? For a long time after that trip to New York, Andy had suspected he'd actually done business with some shady section of the CIA. He had read enough about them over the years to be more than a little spooked. And to know you don't mess them around.

Now he found himself wondering *did I really deal with the CIA?*

If not, who the fuck was it in that hotel room next door?

Andy cast his mind back to Saturday, just two days ago, sitting in his room in Haditha, using the PC there to log on and pick up his mail. He'd been pleasantly surprised at seeing one from Leona. It had been chatty but short, typical of her – Jenny got the long ones – no mention of any mysterious faces though. And Christ, he would have remembered *that* if he'd read it in her mail.

No doubt about it. The realisation had hit him as soon as she'd mentioned *who* she had seen during the earlier call this morning.

They're tapping my mail.

Leona's mail had been edited. Andy wished he could have quizzed Leona further over the phone, wished he'd asked her where she'd seen him, in whose company, in what setting?

What else had they intercepted? He looked down at his dead phone.

Oh shit.

Andy felt a surge of panic.

I said don't go home. I said go to Jill's. But I didn't say who Jill was, did I? I didn't say where Jill was, did I?

He was sure he hadn't. Of course not, because Leona knew Jill well.

Can they find out who she is? Is she in our phone book?

Probably not … no, definitely not. She was Jenny's mate. Jenny knew her number, it was in her head, in the quick-dial list on her phone. The phone book was for family, casual friends, people you sent the cheaper Christmas cards to.

Leona and Jake will be safe there for now. Jill will look after them.

As long as Leona did as she was told. As long as she stayed clear of their house, she and Jake would be safe, in theory. But, as far as he was concerned, the sooner he could get to them the better. Every hour, every minute that passed, with him stuck out here was an hour, a minute, too long.

Andy looked up at the situation around him. Smoke still billowing from the wreckage around the entrance, the British troops just a bunch of frightened young lads and Lieutenant Carter on his own, out of his depth and terrified.

I've got to find a way home, somehow.

He walked across the compound towards the young officer. Closer, he could see the young man was trembling, clearly shaken by the recent encounter. He looked up at Andy.

'They nearly h-had us. Fucking nearly broke in.'

Andy nodded, and squatted down. 'But you got us through it.'

He shook his head. 'Bolton got us through it.'

Andy looked around for the sergeant. Without the NCO, these men would be truly lost. He saw that Bolton was being treated by the platoon medic, Corporal Denwood. Bolton was smacking his fist on the ground angrily and cursing the medic loudly, as the wound was being dressed.

Somehow that seemed encouraging.

Andy saw that many of the lads in the platoon had noticed Carter slumped down; sensed the desperation in his body language.

'You know, they're watching you,' he said quietly.

Carter looked up at his men, grouped in weary, gasping clusters, sheltering behind the compound walls and several smouldering, tangled mounds that had not so long ago been vehicles. He could see the whites of eyes amidst soot-smudged faces, pairs of eyes that darted elsewhere as he met their gaze.

'You're right.'

'If you lose it, we're all dead.'

'We're all dead anyway. They're not going to send a relief force for us.'

'You managed to get through to your battalion again?' Andy asked.

Carter nodded. 'Through again to Henmarsh in the battalion ops room. They've already evacuated half the men holding position around K2. Their perimeter is beginning to get stretched thin. It sounds like they're getting a lot of contacts over there.' Carter stifled a grim, guttural laugh, 'The militia are smelling our blood. They know the army's leaving. It's party time for them. The best he said they could do was send a Chinook to wait for us outside the town.'

Andy grinned. 'Fuck, there we go then. That's our way home!'

'You're kidding me, right?' sighed Carter.

Andy looked up at the only way out of the compound. The entrance gate was twisted and welded into the carcass of the truck. There was no way they were going to shift that obstruction enough to drive out in the remaining vehicles.

'We leave here, we're doing it on foot,' muttered Carter, 'and they'll cut us down before we get twenty yards from the wall.'

Andy leant forward, his face suddenly pulled back into a snarl. 'There's no way I'm bloody well sitting here like a lemon,' he hissed.

Carter shook his head. 'You want to go? Fine, take my gun if you want. There's the exit. You'll be dead inside thirty seconds.'

'And we're dead if we stay.'

Carter shrugged, 'Pretty crappy deal, isn't it?'

'Shit! That isn't fucking good enough, mate. I can't afford to just give up like this. I've *got* to get home.'

'We all want to go home, *mate*.'

Andy spat grime out of his mouth on to the ground, and then looked up at the walls for a moment. 'So where will they send this Chinook if we want it?'

'Anywhere outside the town.'

'How about back over the Tigris, the way we came in this morning?'

Lieutenant Carter nodded wearily.

'How much longer are they holding their position around K2?'

'I don't know. As long as it takes to complete the battalion's evac.'

'Tonight?'

Lieutenant Carter nodded. 'Maybe.'

'We'd stand half a chance at night at least, wouldn't we? I mean,' Andy picked up Carter's SA80, 'these have got those night-vision things, right?'

Carter looked at him and nodded. For the first time today Andy saw the faintest flicker of a smile spread across the young man's mouth.

'Yeah ... and theirs haven't.'

CHAPTER 28

· · · ·

12.57 p.m. GMT

Hammersmith, London

'**O**h no we're going shopping? Why?' Jacob whined.

Leona led the way into the supermarket, pushing a trolley and dragging her brother along by the hand. Daniel obediently followed, trying to control two more trolleys simultaneously.

'Because we are, all right?' she snipped tersely. 'Mum and Dad want me to stock up our cupboards.' Jacob sagged.

'So we're doing a Big Shop?'

'Yes, Jake, we're doing a Big Shop. Now just shut up a moment and let me think.'

She looked around. It was busy with the sort of customers she'd expect to see midweek at lunchtime – people popping in for a sandwich, a snackpot, a pasty, and perhaps something convenient and microwave-able for this evening.

'So where do you want to start?' asked Daniel.

Leona pursed her lips as she decided.

She remembered a few years back when Dad had been momentarily distracted from his Peak Oil ramblings by the threat of bird flu. After the first case of human-contracted disease, he, like everyone else in the country, had hit the panic button and flocked to the supermarket to stock up on essentials.

He had returned home a few hours later with a car full of tinned pilchards in tomato sauce and, it seemed like, a hundred bottles of still water.

Tinned goods because they'll last longer. Pilchards because that's a very high protein meal.

That was how he explained only buying just the one type of food. Of course it made sense, very practical. But when a month or so later, bird flu turned out like SARS to be yet another media-hyped non-event, they'd been stuck with their own little tin-can mountain of pilchards in ketchup to work their way through. After a couple of months of stepping round the damned tins of fish, and trying to conjure up some inventive family meals that could use a couple of tins, Mum finally had enough and donated the lot to a nearby hospice.

But that was then, a long time ago now. And now here she was, in the exact same situation as Dad had been, having to decide what to buy, and how much of it.

Daniel started up the first aisle: Fruit and Veg.

'Potatoes are good,' he said picking one up and inspecting it. 'I'm sure you could keep a small family going on one of these for weeks.'

Leona sighed, plucked it out of his hand and tossed it back onto the shelf. 'Dan ... are you making fun of me?'

Daniel instinctively shook his head, but a moment later the slightest smile leaked on to his face.

'I'm sorry ... this just seems, I dunno. It's just getting a little *intense*. So far this has turned out to be a really ... funny day.'

'Funny?'

'Wrong word, sorry. I guess I'm—'

'Shit Dan, I can't do this with you taking the piss out of me. I can't do this on my own. I know this time Dad's right; that we're in for a whole load of trouble. But I can't do this on my own.'

Jacob cocked his head. 'Who's in trouble?'

They both ignored him, staring at each other intently.

'I apologise for dragging you along, Dan. I really do. But I'm glad you're here with me. And if this goes the way Dad says it will then I think you'll be glad you came with me.'

He had no family to go home to, to worry about. He had a biological mother out there somewhere in Sheffield that he'd looked up once and who'd made it clear he wasn't that welcome. She had an all-new family, with all-new kids and a husband who was keeping her how she wanted to be kept. They had met just the once, and never would again, he had stoically assured her.

Daniel nodded silently. 'I ... look, I'm sorry Lee, I guess that whole abduction scene at your brother's school has got me a bit, like, freaked. I sort of laugh and take the piss a bit, when I get nervous. It's just me being a dick, okay?'

She stood on tiptoes and kissed his cheek. 'You're no dick. And you were great back there. Thank you.'

Jacob curled his lips in disgust. 'Oh gross! That's puke-making.'

Leona rolled her eyes and let Daniel go. 'Come on,' she said patting his arm, 'work to do.'

'So where do we want to go?' he asked.

'Tinned stuff. I know just what to get.'

She led the way past aisles of chocolate treats and salty snacks, with Dan following, pushing one trolley, and Jake doing his best to steer the third one.

'What about stuff like rice and pasta?' called out Dan. 'That stuff keeps well doesn't it?'

Leona looked back at him. 'And how do you cook it when the power finally runs out?' she replied. 'We may only have a few more days of it.'

A woman passing by them with a trolley full of frozen pizzas and a variety of Meal-in-a-Minute TV dinners, glanced curiously at them – she'd obviously heard her.

Leona smiled awkwardly back.

As they entered the tinned goods aisle, Leona was aware that it was noticeably busier than the other areas in the supermarket they had walked through; half-a-dozen shoppers, like herself, warily eyeing each other up, whilst filling their trolleys with canned goods. As she, Dan and Jacob wheeled their trolleys down towards them, there was a moment of shared communication, eyes meeting, and barely perceptible nods of acknowledgement.

My God, they're here for the same reason.

Somehow, the thought that there were other people out there who had begun to see beyond the news soundbites to something more disturbing, made the bizarre situation she was in right now feel that much more real.

They had that same look as Dad; a slightly rumpled, dishevelled appearance, unburdened with any fashion sense; a couple of them vaguely reminded her of lecturers she'd had back at UEA. They were unmistakably from the same ... *tribe* as Dad; nerdish, the type that subscribed to obscure academic periodicals, took rock hammers on their holidays, the type who would never, in a month of Sundays, know who was still hanging in there on *Celebrity Big Brother.*

'So what are we getting?' Daniel asked quietly. She could tell he sensed it too, that they were amongst that tiny minority of *those who know.* Leona could see that these few people alone had already cleared the shelves of several ranges of product in this aisle.

My God. There's only six of them at it, and already the shelves in this aisle are beginning to empty.

She shuddered at the thought of what it was going to be like in this supermarket, and every other one around the country, when the penny finally dropped for everyone else.

'I know what we need,' she muttered in response, scanning the stock that was left in the aisle for tins of pilchards.

She looked at her watch. It was nearly half past one. She knew the Prime Minister was due to make some sort of big announcement around about now. Obviously it was to do with the strife her Dad was caught up in abroad – God, she hoped he was all right – and the impact it was going to have over here. She just hoped they were all done here in the supermarket before the hordes inevitably descended.

'Let's get a move on,' she said out of the side of her mouth.

CHAPTER 29

. . . .

1.30 p.m. GMT

Whitehall, London

Jesus, you better make this good.

Charles walked briskly into the press room, accompanied by the Deputy Prime Minister, and Malcolm. The room was full, as it often was, but today there were so many people crammed into it that they were standing along the back wall and on either side of the rows of seats arranged in front of the small podium. It was stuffy and hot. The air conditioning in the room was struggling with both the increasing warmth of the day and such a high body count.

The small, well-lit auditorium flickered with camera flashlights going off as Malcolm and the Deputy took seats to one side of the podium and Charles stepped on to it. He felt uncomfortably like a condemned man climbing a scaffold. He placed the small deck of index cards on the stand before him, each one with a simple bullet-point he wanted to get across.

A deep breath. A moment to shoo away the butterflies.

Make this good, Charlie.

He also remembered Malcolm's last words of advice, muttered quietly and accompanied by a friendly pat on his back.

Keep the focus away from oil.

'Okay,' he began. 'Good afternoon, and thanks for attending at such short notice. There's a lot to get through, so I'll just get started,' he said, and then cleared his throat before continuing. 'I'm sure you're all aware that we've got some problems to deal with. I'm going to start off by telling you what we know about the situation in Saudi Arabia, and the various other hot spots. Yesterday morning, during morning prayers in Riyadh, the first of many bombs exploded in the Holy Mosques of Mecca and Medina, and in several more mosques in Riyadh. A radical Shi'ite group, shortly after, sent a message to Al Jazeera that they were responsible for the devices. This inevitably triggered a response among the Sunni majority in Saudi Arabia. At the same time, or very shortly afterwards, similar explosions occurred in several other cities in Saudi Arabia, Kuwait, Oman and Iraq. Each one of these incidents has added to the problem. Throughout yesterday, a state of, well – not to put too fine a point on it – civil war has erupted across most of the Arabian peninsula. The situation has continued to escalate today, and because of the potential danger this poses to our remaining troops in Iraq, after consultation with Arab leaders, a decision was taken last night to pull them out of the region until this particular problem has corrected itself.'

Good start.

'Because of the highly charged nature of this *sectarian* problem, there are security implications for virtually every country in the world. We are aware that, over here, emotions will be running high amongst various communities. And that there will be a tiny minority amongst them who will feel compelled to bring this civil war to our streets. For this reason, and lessons have been learned as a result of the appalling number of people who lost their lives on the seventh of July 2005, I have decided to act swiftly and concisely on this matter. Because the threat level has risen, all air and rail traffic has been temporarily suspended. Other potentially vulnerable terror targets around the country, such as our nuclear power stations and natural gas storage facilities, are now being guarded by members of the armed forces. And finally, because of the instability and uncertainty this situation is causing amongst the markets, I have also decided to close the stock exchange for today. Now, these are all temporary measures which will be reviewed throughout the rest of today. These are short-term measures ... let me stress that ... *short-term* ... measures to ensure that we aren't caught out.'

'It's my firm belief that the dreadful situation in the Middle East will blow itself out in a matter of days, that common sense will prevail amongst these troubled people. I ask that you,' Charles gestured towards the gathered members of the press and the media, 'help me by not sensationalising current events.'

He aimed a reproachful gaze towards a row of seats in the middle, reserved for journalists from the various popular red-tops.

'One thing I really don't want to see are racial and religious differences being stirred up with inflammatory headlines. We're a responsible, liberal, tolerant nation, which is why we will *not* see the sort of things we've seen on the news in the last twenty-four hours occurring on the streets of Bradford or London or Birmingham.'

He paused for effect.

'Okay, I'll take one or two questions, no more.'

The press room was instantly a chaotic stew of noise and movement, as hands and voices were raised across the auditorium.

Charles looked for, and found, the face of *News Stand*'s correspondent, Desmond Hamlin. Desmond was one of the good guys. Malcolm and Desmond had some sort of history together. Malcolm had made sure the journalist had got a seat near the front, where his voice would be easily picked up by the boom and podium mics.

'Yes?'

Come on Desmond, give me one I can put in the back of the net.

'Desmond Hamlin, political correspondent for *News Stand*.'

Charles nodded and smiled.

'Prime Minister, the withdrawal of the remaining brigades in Iraq – our rapid reaction force – will, I'm sure, be applauded by our readers. We want those boys back home, and it's good to see you've acted quickly there. My question is about the troops we have stationed out in Afghanistan. We've heard they're being mobilised to come home as well. Can you comment on this?'

Charles nodded. 'Yes, of course.'

This was one he needed to handle deftly. Yes, the 20,000 troops they had committed to that country were coming home as fast as they could be shuttled out. It was the *why* he was going to have to be careful about. On the surface, an *unreasonable risk* to our armed forces came across as a weak but well-intentioned motive. In truth, Charles had been briefed that they were facing the very real prospect of several months of instability at home. Malcolm's comment that the riots in Paris not so long ago were going to be what they could be looking at, or worse, had had a sobering effect on the Prime Minister. They were going to need the manpower to enforce some sort of martial law.

'What's happening in Saudi Arabia, Iraq and the other states in the region, has already started to spread to Afghanistan. Military assessment on the ground is that it could ...' *a deep breath, inject some heartfelt remorse,* '... regrettably, become as bad there. Make no mistake ladies and gentlemen. The bombs that went off yesterday, damaging the Holy Mosque in Mecca, killing a hundred and fifty Muslim pilgrims, have stirred some very powerful emotions throughout the Islamic world. The anguish, the rage is, I think, very difficult for us in the west to truly quantify. It would be prudent to pull our boys out for now, until this situation calms down, which is why I'm asking for you all to be measured in how you report this.'

Charles was happy with that. He had put the issue of a global religious schism right in front of these people, centre stage, and carefully shunted to one side the question of whether all our armed forces really needed to be brought back home quite so quickly. It was a good opening question.

Well placed, Malcolm.

The other good guy Malcolm had told him to pick out was also close to the front and centre, the correspondent for *News 24*. He couldn't remember her name, but the face was familiar. As he nodded towards her he wondered what question Malcolm had primed her with. It was Malcolm's suggestion that he keep the exact wording from him, otherwise the answer he came back with might sound too rehearsed. It didn't matter. Malcolm was good at playing this game.

Charles trusted him.

'Janet Corby, *News 24*,' she announced loudly and clearly. 'The unfolding riots in Saudi Arabia and Iraq seem to have eclipsed several other events in the last thirty-six hours, Prime Minister. I'm referring, of course, to the tanker that was damaged in the Straits of Hormuz. I believe the ship shed most of its full load, it's still burning and will do for some time. There are rumours that the ship was damaged by a mine placed in the middle of the shipping lane.'

Charles felt his cheeks flush ever so slightly.

'Effectively that closes down the world's busiest shipping choke point,' said Janet Corby. 'Then there was the explosion at the refinery in Venezuela, the Paraguaná refinery. And several other pipeline explosions in and around the refineries based in Baku, Kazakhstan ...'

Oh Christ, I can see where this is going.

'All these things within a few hours of each other—'

'Yes, we're aware of these other isolated events, and the details are hazy on what's happened there,' Charles cut in, 'but I think the unrest spreading across the Middle East deserves our focus right now. This is where we—'

Ms Corby wasn't going to let it rest. 'Prime Minister, these *isolated* events, as well as the spreading unrest, are all going to be part of the same overriding issue for us here.'

Shit shit shit, she's pulling this where we don't want to go.

'The overriding issue right now, is ensuring that the fear and anger and rage that is ripping the Middle East apart doesn't spread to the Muslim community in *our* country. There are over two million—'

'Prime Minister, the *big* issue has nothing to do with religion, or what British Muslims will or won't do ...'

Cut her off and move along.

'I'm sorry, I'll have to give someone else a go,' he said, smiling apologetically at her. He turned from her to survey the other journalists, most with their hands raised, and made a big gesture of deciding who to point to next. He settled on a familiar face, Louis Sergeant, political correspondent for *News Review*, BBC2.

'Louis?' he said.

'Thank you, Prime Minister. I'd like to echo the line of questioning my colleague from *News 24* was pursuing.'

Oh fuck.

'These events don't actually feel like isolated incidents. In fact, it feels like a concerted attempt at disrupting the global oil supply chain. My question is what is our exposure here?'

Charles stared at the BBC journalist, realising he was utterly trapped by the question, realising it wasn't one he could dodge by looking for someone else to pick. They were all of them, smelling something. If he tried to dodge it, it was going to look bad, very bad. Still, he needed a few more seconds to think how best to answer the man.

'I'm sorry,' he said, 'could you repeat your question?'

'Prime Minister, there's a real prospect of our oil supply being cut off. What's our exposure to this?'

CHAPTER 30

. . . .

1.32 p.m. GMT

Whitehall, London

'**W**hat's our exposure?' The Prime Minister asked, repeating the question and buying himself only a handful of seconds to pull together an answer.

He shook his head wearily, hoping that he looked like a man who was becoming tired of having to deal with a complete non-issue. The first prickling beads of sweat were starting to dampen his forehead.

Jesus, it's so hot in here.

'Listen,' replied Charles, 'of course there's a knock-on effect with what's going on. Of course there is. Which is why, for example, trading in the City has been suspended. The unnatural spike in the price per barrel that this is causing could be very damaging to the economic—'

'I'm not talking about the price of the stuff. I'm talking about the availability,' the journalist pressed him.

'Well naturally, whilst this problem is playing itself out, supply of oil from the region is going to be reduced. That is, of course, entirely predictable, and whilst the big Middle East suppliers are dealing with their problems, we are simply sourcing our needs from other places.'

A voice from the back of the room broke into the pause that Charles had deployed for effect.

'And what other places are these?'

Watch it. You're losing control of this.

The journalist continued, 'Caspian oil has been cut off with the bomb blasts in and around Baku. The remaining east-flowing pipelines are going to be contested by Russian, Chinese and Indian interests. Are you also aware of several minor explosions in Nigeria effectively disabling the refineries at Alesa-Eleme, Warri and Kaduna?'

Charles nodded, he was. He'd been hoping that the big Middle East story would have eclipsed a detail like that. There'd been few reported casualties, the explosions had been minor; but of course, they'd been large enough to ensure all three refinery complexes were effectively neutralised.

'My question is this; where exactly is the oil we need *tomorrow* coming from, Prime Minister?'

'Well yes, you're right, there's not a lot coming into the UK at this moment in time ...'

Here we go.

Charles shot another glance at Malcolm, who calmly nodded, again, almost imperceptibly.

'But we have reserves in this country that will see us through this ... blip.'

Inside he cringed at using the word 'blip'. He wondered if that was a soundbite that was going to come back and bite him somewhere down the line.

'And how long is this *blip* going to last?' called out another journalist in the audience.

'How long will our reserves last?' called out yet another.

It was obvious to Charles, the whole religious war spin was being pushed roughly aside. The bastards were smelling blood, and like a pack of hunting dogs they were going for the kill. The room became suddenly silent, everyone leaning forward, keenly interested in an answer to the last shouted-out question. Charles realised a point had been reached. He could bullshit them and have a go at trying to pull this press conference back on script, or he could take on the question and actually answer it

They'll find out it's all about oil by the end of today ... if not in the next few hours.

All of a sudden, Charles realised the best tactical move was an outburst of honesty. At the very least, he might buy himself the tiniest bit of political kudos; best-case scenario – an impassioned, heartfelt plea for calm and co-operation aimed squarely at the general public, might just mean the emergency measures they were putting into effect would keep this crisis manageable.

He took a deep breath. 'We have reserves that'll last us some months. But obviously, we will have to deploy some good old-fashioned common sense in how we use what we have.'

Janet Corby from *News 24*, stood up. 'Are the airport closures and the shutdown of railway lines linked to the oil issue?'

Before he could answer, another question was shouted from the back of the small room. 'Prime Minister, there are rumours that several large oil distribution points have been taken over by the army. Is this the first step towards controlled distribution? Petrol rationing?'

'Uhh, well, there will have to be some degree of rationing, of course,' he replied quickly. 'It's only common sense at this stage that we—'

'What about power supplies?' shouted another. 'Can we expect black-outs?'

Charles shook his head, 'It's too early for us to worry about shortages in power, food—'

Oh shit.

Several in the audience jumped on that.

'Will there be an effect on the supply of food?'

'What about the transportation of food supplies? Imports?'

He knew that he had to nail this down quickly. He raised his hands to quieten them down, before speaking. The chorus of voices in the room amongst the assembled journalists took a long while to settle down to a rustling hubbub that he could be heard clearly over.

'There is no need for anyone to panic here. *No one* needs to panic. There has been a lot of planning, a lot of forward thinking about a scenario like this, a scenario in which there's a temporary log-jam in the global distribution of crude oil—'

'Is the army being brought back from Iraq to keep order?' someone shouted out.

That comment left the room in near silence; a silence that Charles quickly realised he'd allowed to last one or two seconds too long.

They know that keep-the-boys-safe shtick was bullshit.

'Yes,' he replied, 'we will require the army to help keep order.'

'Does this mean we will be facing some form of martial law in Britain?'

He realised now that too much of the truth was out there. They had done as much as they could during the last eighteen hours under the veil of mis-direction and various cover stories that, frankly, they were lucky to have not been vigorously challenged before. Perhaps this was the only opportunity, possibly the last opportunity, he would have to call upon the general public to keep calm, to pull together and not lose their heads.

There was a gesture he had once seen in a film, he couldn't remember which film it was, but it had starred someone like Morgan Freeman play-ing the President of the United States. He remembered it being a powerful gesture, something, during the last three troublesome years in office, he had fantasised about doing himself. Well, here was the best opportunity he was ever going to get to do it. And at an instinctive level, he knew it was the right thing to do.

It was what the people of this country needed to see right now; something visual, something strong, something powerful – not just another politician puffing more hot air. Charles picked up the index cards from the speaker's stand in front of him and silently ripped them up, tossing the shreds of card over his shoulder.

'Okay, that's probably enough crap for one day. You people deserve better than that.'

Once more the room was brought to an instant standstill. A droplet of sweat rolled down the side of his face.

'Yes,' he continued, 'all right, the truth is we *are* in a bit of trouble. Whilst this mess is sorting itself out, we're going to have to make do on the resources we have. We do have enough oil and we do have enough food to last us until normality returns. All right, it's not stockpiled in some giant, secret government warehouse, but spread out across every city, every town, every street. Our corner shops, our supermarkets, our local grocers, our nearest petrol stations … all these places contain the reserves we're going to need to draw upon to ride this thing out. I am asking all of you to work together with me. We are going to need to ration the food we have, restrict the sale of petrol and diesel to key personnel, in short, pull together, like we did once before, sixty years ago during the Second World War.'

And that was it. Charles realised he'd dried up. That was all he had to offer. The silence that followed was truly terrifying.

Oh God, what the fuck have I done?

In that moment he realised he'd been too bloody candid. Instead of inspiring the nation to dig deep and find within it some inner reserve of Dunkirk spirit, to pull together as once they had, and ride this thing out, he had effectively incited every person in the country to make a mad dash to the nearest shop before it was too late.

The press room once more erupted with a deafening chorus of voices. Charles found himself staring in shock at the sea of cameras and faces. Everyone was on their feet now, hands raised. He turned away from the lectern a little too quickly, realising what that would look like on this evening's news.

Running away.

He shot a glance at Malcolm as he strode towards the door. He expected him to be shaking his head grimly, realising too that Charles had really screwed things up, but instead, there was the slightest hint of a smile on the man's face.

CHAPTER 31

. . . .

2.15 p.m. GMT

Hammersmith, London

Wheeling the trolleys out across the supermarket car-park towards Daniel's van, Leona noticed the first of many, many cars turning into the parking area from the high street. One after another, a steady procession, stopped only when a pedestrian light further up the street turned red.

Dan noticed too. 'It's getting busy.'

'Yeah.'

'Are we going home now?' asked Jacob. 'Or are you taking me back to school?'

'Home,' she replied, distracted as she watched a woman slew her car carelessly into a parking slot, scramble out quickly and run across the tarmac towards the supermarket's entrance. She watched as another driver did the same, this time coming in too quickly, and bumping another parked car, which set off its alarm. The driver climbed out oblivious to this, hastily zapping his car with the key-lock, and sprinted away from it towards a trolley station.

There were more and more cars coming in.

'Let's hurry up,' she said to Daniel.

He nodded, unlocked the back door of his van and started hastily shovelling in the mountain of tinned goods and bottled water they'd managed to buy, emptying Leona's bank account in the process. Leona joined him, tossing in what she had in her trolley.

I think they're beginning to realise.

She had hoped they would make it home safe and sound, triple-lock the front door, and be able to heave a sigh of relief before things started to get panicky. But it looked like it was starting already.

Maybe someone's made an announcement?

Yes, there was the Prime Minister. He was due to be on the telly at lunchtime, wasn't he?

A hefty 4x4 swung around into their row in the car-park and with a screech of tyres lurched forward towards the empty slot next to them. The woman behind the wheel spun it around into the parking space at the last moment, clipping one of their trolleys and knocking it over, spraying the last few dozen cans across the ground.

She climbed out quickly, locking the vehicle after her husband had emerged from the passenger side, and stepping over the scattered cans. 'Go get a trolley, Billy!' she shouted, as she began to make her way past, Daniel and Jacob staring at her in dismayed silence.

Leona stood in her way. 'Look what you just did,' she said icily.

The woman, a hard-faced bottle-blonde with an orange tan, barely registered her. 'Out of the way, love.'

'Hey, you just sent our stuff flying!'

The woman didn't respond, and simply pushed Leona back against the van, and stepped past.

Leona grabbed her wrist. 'Excuse me?'

The woman acknowledged her presence now, of course. 'Fuck off!' she snarled.

'But you just—'

'Let go or I'll fucking break your nose.'

Leona recoiled instantly, and released her grip. At which point Daniel stepped in.

'Hey! That's out of order,' he said walking around the other two, nearly empty, trolleys to join Leona.

The woman glanced at him with undisguised contempt. And then called out to her husband. 'Billy!'

The man, thickset with middle-age flab beginning to cover a muscular frame beneath, and equally orange in colour, stained with the blue of fading tatoos on each forearm, turned round and immediately began striding towards them.

'You better get out of my fucking way, you little prick,' said the woman.

Daniel stayed where he was, but Leona could see he was trembling like a yappy dog left tethered outside a pub.

'Just let her pass, Dan. It's not worth it. We need to just go.'

Daniel took another look at Billy, and then reluctantly stepped back out of the woman's way, allowing her to get past.

The woman hurried towards her husband, not even bothering to look back at them; jabbing her fingers towards the trolley station. The man, however, aimed one long menacing glare towards them, before turning around to go grab one of the few trolleys left. Leona figured if they weren't in such a big rush, ol' Billy-Boy would quite happily have slapped Daniel enough times to leave a spattered blood and snot trail down the side of his scruffy little van.

Daniel wheezed with relief. 'Shit, I thought he was going to have me. I really did.'

'Oh God, so did I.'

She surveyed the car-park. Whereas thirty minutes ago it was half full, now it was jam-packed, with cars, and people on foot, flooding in. She could see several minor altercations occurring in different places, as people squabbled over shopping trolleys, or jostled in the entrance to get inside against the flow of shoppers coming out.

'Let's get out of here as quickly as we can.'

'Okay,' said Dan, scooping up the last of the cans off the floor.

This is just the start of it. What are people going to be like tomorrow? Or in a week's time?

'This is how Dad said it was going to be,' muttered Leona anxiously, as she resumed loading the last of their cans into the back of the van.

Dan wasn't sure he understood what she meant by that. 'What are you talking about?'

She nodded towards the 4x4 couple, now jogging with a trolley towards the entrance of the supermarket and finally shouldering their way through the customers surging out with groceries piled high.

'Law of the jungle.'

Goldhawk Road, leading away from the bustling green at the centre of Shepherd's Bush towards the quieter, more suburban end, was normally quite sedate in the middle of the afternoon on a weekday. Right now it was as busy as Leona had ever seen it. The pavements on either side were packed with people laden with plastic grocery bags, pushing trolleys and wheelie baskets. Traffic along the road was crawling, log-jammed with vehicles. Occasionally it got this bad during the morning rush-hour, or when there was a match on at the nearby White City football ground.

She looked at her watch, it was only three in the afternoon.

'Everyone's going home early,' said Dan, 'to get what they need from the shops.'

She noticed a news-stand outside a convenience store that had so many customers, a queue was beginning to form outside on the street. She saw a headline hastily scrawled across it, beneath the *Evening Standard* banner, '"Please Don't Panic" – PM'.

Another stand next to it had another early edition headline, 'Oil and Food Will Run Out!'

Leona pointed them out to Daniel. 'That's it then. Everyone knows now.'

Daniel looked at her. 'Is it really going to get as bad as you say?'

'I'm just telling you what my dad's been telling me these last few years.'

She studied the desperate faces on the pavements either side of them. Most of the pedestrians were heading towards the Green or towards Hammersmith where the big supermarkets were. She wondered if there was still food on the shelves, or if they'd already been emptied.

'Look at all these people Dan. How many of them do you think know how to do something as simple as grow a tomato plant?'

'What?'

'When they've finished stripping the shops clean, and they've eaten what they took home, they're all going to starve.'

Daniel shook his head. 'It's not going to get that bad Leona, trust me.'

'Yeah? So where's all the food going to come from then, if the oil problem continues?'

Jacob leaned through the front seats. 'Leona,' he said, 'is the world going to end?'

'No, don't be silly Jake,' she replied, 'but things are going to be a little difficult for a while.'

She hated the dismissive way she'd said that, because, in truth, it was going to be a lot worse than just 'difficult for a while'. However, right now, she couldn't face the twenty or thirty million questions she was going to be bombarded with if she'd answered him more truthfully.

Just then they heard a police siren, and a moment later a police van nudged its way through the traffic, as the cars on the road obediently pulled over. As the van passed by she looked up, through the rear windows, and saw the grim faces of the officers inside. She could see the thin black stalks of what looked to her like gun barrels poking up from below. She suspected they were attempting to keep the guns out of sight as best they could. But failing ... or maybe that was deliberate.

'The police have got guns,' she said quietly, as the van whisked by.

Jacob piped up cheerfully. 'Oh cool!'

CHAPTER 32

. . . .

2.45 p.m. GMT

M1 motorway, north of Birmingham

The roadblock was only a dozen or so vehicles ahead of them; a row of orange cones placed evenly across all three lanes and the hard shoulder. Behind this meagre barrier, three traffic police Rovers were parked end to end. The six police officers that had arrived in them to set up the roadblock were now having to deal with a growing crowd of drivers who had climbed out of their vehicles to find out why the hell the motorway was being closed like this.

Jenny turned round to look out of the rear window of the taxi. Behind them, the traffic had backed up very quickly. They were wedged in a river of inert trucks, vans and cars that stretched into the distance as far as she could see.

'We're going nowhere,' said Paul Davies, the man Jenny had met only hours ago, and who she was sharing the taxi with.

'It looks like that, doesn't it?' she replied.

Paul looked up at a driver who passed by them on foot to join the gathering crowd up ahead. 'I'm going to find out what's up.' He opened the door and stepped on to the road.

'I'm coming too,' said Jenny, equally anxious to find out.

Jenny walked single file behind Paul as he made his way forward, weaving through the parked cars and trucks, finally reaching a knot of bewildered drivers remonstrating with the policemen.

'Can't fucking well block it like this!' a truck driver was shouting, 'I've got a fucking load I need to deliver this afternoon.'

A traffic cop standing opposite him, behind the thin line of cones, shook his head sympathetically. 'Sorry mate, the way's closed until further notice. There's nothing we can do about it.'

'This is to do with that lunchtime press conference,' a man standing beside Jenny said.

She turned to him. 'What's that?'

'Did you not hear it?' he replied with a look of surprise.

'No, what happened?'

'The PM? You don't know about that?'

She shook her head.

'It looks like we're going to be totally screwed. He said they're going to ration petrol and everything else.'

Jenny could see the people around her were beginning to catch on to how serious the situation was getting. These weren't just angry people, she could actually sense an undercurrent of growing panic, like a low charge of static electricity floating amongst them. Not good.

'I got a feeling this is going to get pretty nasty,' the man added in a hushed voice looking at her. 'Somebody on the telly was saying we could all be starving by the end of the week.'

One of the policemen pulled out a dash-mounted radio handset from inside one of the Rovers. 'Everyone, please return to your vehicles!' he said, his voice crackling over the loudspeakers on the roof of his car. 'This motorway will not be re-opened. You will all need to go back the way you came!'

A burly man at the front lost his temper and angrily kicked one of the cones aside. He stepped towards the policemen. 'You have got to be fucking kidding!' he said throwing a hand back to point at the jam behind him, 'I've got eighteen wheels of articulated back there with a full fucking load. How the fuck do I turn that around, you stupid—'

'Step back behind the barrier!' shouted one of the policemen.

'Or what?' he shouted, his face inches away from the nearest officer. 'This is bullshit!'

Several other drivers advanced behind the trucker through the gap in the cones, as if that was an open door.

'Everyone please step back!' shouted the policeman on the microphone. 'This is an official police line!'

Jenny could see the truck driver continuing to shout, his words lost in the growing cacophony of angry voices. He raised a hand, balled into a fist and shook it near the officer's face. It seemed the traffic cop decided that that was enough to be interpreted as a threatening gesture. He reached out for it and began twisting the truck driver's arm into an arrest hold. The trucker's other hand swung around, clasped into another fist and smashed into the officer's chin, dropping him effortlessly. Jenny watched with growing alarm, as three of the other policemen rushed to the aid of their fallen colleague, whilst the vanguard of angry people that had surged through the gap in the cones increased in number.

Paul turned to her. 'Jesus, this is getting out of hand!'

People surged past Jenny as she watched the policemen wrestle with the truck driver on the ground. A young woman started picking the traffic cones up and moving them to the central aisle, whilst a portly middle-aged man wearing an expensive-looking suit decided that someone needed to take the initiative and back the police Rovers out of the way so they could all pass. He opened the driver-side door of the nearest one and climbed in, started the engine and began reversing it slowly across the motorway to the hard shoulder to clear the way forward.

The policeman holding the microphone barked an order, 'Stop the vehicle immediately and get out!'

What happened next seemed to occur too quickly; all in a matter of seconds.

One of the traffic police, pulled out of the struggling scrum of bodies, stepped smartly to the back of his Land Rover, opened a door and swiftly produced what appeared to be a firearm. For the briefest moment she thought, assumed, hoped, that everyone had seen the weapon; the brawl would instantly break up, and the person behind the wheel of the police car would stop, and sheepishly step out.

He has a gun ... a traffic copper with a gun. Jenny thought that would be enough to bring everyone to their senses, instantly.

But that didn't happen.

The policeman levelled the gun at the moving police car and fired. One of the headlights exploded. The sound of the gunshot stopped everyone in their tracks; the squirming trucker on the ground, the three policemen holding him down, the young woman collecting cones, and everyone else milling around nearby – they all froze as if someone had just hit a magic *pause* button.

The man with the smart suit inside the police Rover raised his hands.

'Get out of the vehicle!' shouted the traffic cop on the microphone.

He stepped out of the Rover, his hands timidly raised above his head.

And that really should have been the conclusion to the little drama. But it wasn't.

The gun went off a second time.

The man in the expensive-looking suit staggered backwards as his nice, smart, crisp, white business shirt exploded with a shower of dark crimson. For a moment Jenny couldn't believe what she was seeing, for a moment thinking someone in the crowd had inexplicably decided to shoot the man with a paintball gun.

He slumped back against the car and then slid down to the ground.

The traffic cop holding the gun looked like he had gone into shock, his jaw hung open, his face ashen. Jenny could see this wasn't meant to have happened. It was an accident; he'd been holding the gun in a way he shouldn't – finger resting too heavily on the trigger, the weapon not aimed down at the ground as it should have been. These men weren't trained to use firearms, that was obvious, they were out of their depth, these guys were panicking.

'Shit. I didn't mean to ...' the policeman with the gun cried loudly, staring at the body in disbelief.

One of the crowd of drivers standing near to him, a big man, recovered his senses and broke the static tableau, he reached for the gun and snatched it out of the policeman's hand.

Replaying this in her mind later, Jenny suspected this big man, was removing the gun from the policeman in shock, not to use it on anyone, merely to take a dangerous element out of the equation.

But in the highly charged atmosphere of the moment, the gesture was misinterpreted.

The policeman with the microphone, whipped a second gun out of his car and aimed it at the man. Amidst the noise of people crying out and shouting, Jenny wasn't sure whether a warning was called out before the traffic cop fired. His shot clipped the man, who dropped to his knees clutching his upper arm.

The crowd that had been surging forward began to scatter in all directions. Paul grabbed Jenny by the arm and led her back towards their taxi, the driver standing beside the vehicle craning his neck to see what was going on.

'Come on!' he said. 'This is going to get worse.'

Jenny looked back at the blockade. The other traffic police had pulled back to their vehicles and produced their guns and were, thankfully, firing shots in the air to scatter the crowd, and not aiming at them instead.

This is Britain still, right? Not apartheid-era South Africa, or Tiananmen Square? Jenny's racing mind asked in disbelief as she and Paul hastily made their way back from the police line.

They're just trying to disperse the crowd, that's all.

But then she heard the loud growl of a diesel engine beside her, and a large container truck lurched forward, effortlessly shunting aside the cars in front of it. As the truck pushed forwards towards the blockade, the traffic cops trained their weapons towards it, and they all fired.

'Fuck this!' said Paul changing direction and heading towards the metal barrier beyond the hard shoulder. She watched him go and then, as the truck crashed into the blockade of police cars, she turned back to watch as the policemen peppered the truck with shots as it rolled past.

'Are you coming or what?' said Paul, swinging his other leg over and dropping down on his haunches on the other side of the barrier. She heard another burst of gunfire behind her.

Oh shit.

She followed him across the hard shoulder, lifted her light cotton skirt up and swung her legs over the barrier. On the other side, a grass verge descended down towards a field. She dropped down to a crouch beside him, and together, stooping low to keep their heads below the corrugated aluminium barrier they stumbled down the verge, away from the motorway, towards the lumpy, uneven field of waist-high rape-seed.

Behind her, she heard the rumble of several other trucks starting up, and the crunch of other vehicles being pushed forward. The sound of gunfire intensified.

She wondered if any of this would have happened if properly trained armed response units had been manning the roadblock. Maybe, maybe not. It was all so sudden, the escalation from an unintended shot to this.

'Where are we going?' she gasped.

'I don't know, but I don't want to stumble across any more highly strung, untrained cops carrying guns they can't handle. Do you?'

'No.'

They stumbled across the uneven, muddy field of rape-seed, Jenny stopping once or twice to look back with disbelief at the roadblock behind them, wondering if that really did happen, or whether she was going mad.

CHAPTER 33

. . . .

10 p.m. local time
Al-Bayji, Iraq

Andy watched as Lieutenant Carter put a hand to his ear and silently listened to the communication coming in on his headset. Eventually he whispered an acknowledgement and then turned to the fourteen men left of his platoon, gathered in a silent group in front of him. He had a man up on the front wall keeping an eye on the street, and three more were outside the compound, scanning the route they were going to have to take – they'd gone over the wall a few minutes earlier. The route they were planning to take back out of town was the one they had taken that morning. Andy suspected that in the dark, the twists and turns of these little streets could lose some of them.

'And try and remember the way we came this morning,' whispered Carter.

'If you get lost lads, just keep heading north-east,' added Andy quickly. 'You'll hit the river eventually.'

Carter nodded. 'S'right. And hopefully you'll be able to see the bridge from wherever you emerge.'

The young officer took a few deep breaths, looking around at the men in front of him.

Andy looked at his watch anxiously. 'We've got less than an hour.'

Carter nodded, 'Yeah you're right. No point messing around then. We've got an hour to make it a mile across town and over that bridge. Our ride's arriving at eleven, and they won't be hanging around for us for long.'

The men nodded.

'Okay, you all know what groups you're in. You all know where we're headed, and how long you've got. Five minutes between each group. If you lose your way, like he says,' said Carter, nodding towards Andy, 'just keep heading north-east, you'll hit the edge of town.'

The young squaddies nodded.

'Right then. First group ready?'

The platoon medic, Corporal Denwood, stood up, and marshalled the men that would be with him; five soldiers, the Ukrainian engineer, Ustov, and the young Iraqi driver, Salim.

'We'll dispense with this platoon's usual call-sign protocol, Corporal, since we're all mixed up with civvies. For the next hour, you're call-sign Zulu, understand?'

'Yes, sir.'

'Okay then, off you go. We'll see you on the other side of the bridge.'

Denwood beckoned for Ustov and Salim to join his men. Ustov clasped hands with Erich, Mike and Andy muttering a farewell, whilst Farid patted the young Iraqi lad on the back.

Denwood climbed up on to the wall, swung his legs over and was gone. The other men followed suit and within a minute call-sign Zulu had departed.

Carter started his stopwatch. 'Five minutes, then your group are up next, Private Tajican.'

The Fijian acknowledged that and gathered the men in his group to him.

To Andy it seemed the next five minutes passed unbearably slowly. And then with a nod from Lieutenant Carter, the next group, call-sign Yankee, which consisted of Tajican, five other soldiers and Erich, went quietly over the wall.

Carter once more started timing.

The next few minutes seemed to take an eternity, and then the young officer nodded at Lance Corporal Westley, to take his group over.

'You're X-ray. I'll see you at the bridge,' he said slapping Westley on the back.

'Aye, sir,' he replied.

Mike turned to Andy and held out a hand. 'Good luck.'

Andy grabbed his hand. 'See you in an hour.'

Westley waited until the two soldiers in his group along with Mike and Farid had climbed over the wall, before following them. His call-sign were going to pick up the other three men already waiting quietly in the dark outside the compound.

And now there was Andy, Sergeant Bolton, Lieutenant Carter, two more men, both bandaged from minor wounds, and another man on watch up on the wall, whom Carter quietly ordered over the radio, to join them.

Andy looked at Sergeant Bolton, holding one hand protectively against his dressed wound, and in the other, a cigarette. 'You know those things'll kill you,' he said.

Bolton's face creased with a wry smile. 'Ha bloody ha.'

Carter looked at his Sergeant. 'You going to be okay?'

Bolton grunted as he pulled himself up on to his haunches and stubbed out the cigarette. 'Just fine, sir.'

'Okay, good. Mind your footing. Denwood said that dressing can only take so much.'

The man who had been up on the wall, keeping watch over the boulevard, loped across the compound, the equipment on his webbing jangling in the silence. He squatted down beside Lieutenant Carter, and made a quick report.

'Nothing going on out there, sir. It's like a ghost-town. No lights, no noise. Nothing'

'All right, time to go.'

Carter went over the top first, and then with Andy and one of the other men helping from within the compound, they got Sergeant Bolton over and down on to the pavement on the other side managing, so far, not to unravel his field dressing, loosen the clamp and open the wound. He knelt down in silence, struggling with his breath, clearly in a lot of pain, and holding both of his hands over the wound.

Crouching at the base of the wall, Carter looked through the scope on his SA80; a bulky attachment on the top of the rifle, above the magazine – called the SUSAT – that allowed limited night vision. He swept it around, quickly scanning the cluster of narrow street openings ahead. He squinted at the grainy green image he was seeing through the small circular lens.

'You men see anything?' he whispered.

The other two soldiers, hunched over their weapons, staring keenly through their scopes and panning hastily left and right, were quick to answer that they could see no immediate threat.

'All right, then. We're heading up that street ahead of us. You see the one with the big old-style satellite dish sticking out on the first floor?'

'Yeah,' grunted one of the soldiers.

'That's the one we came down this morning. Let's go.'

Mike studied the grainy, glowing forms of the men in his group, through his weapon's night scope. Lance Corporal Westley was squatting against the corner of the wall looking out on to the junction. This was the wide road they had entered Al-Bayji on. Right would take them into town, left would take them to the outskirts of town, through the market-place and to the single lane bridge over the Tigris.

The other men were scanning the rooftops and both sides of the road, left and right, for activity.

He could see Farid resting against the wall, staring up at the sky, the scope making his eyes glow a devilish lurid green, flickering every now and then as he blinked.

Westley had put Mike in charge of the Iraqi man. The Lance Corporal didn't trust the translator, but didn't want to waste one of his men on the task of watching him.

Westley rose to his feet, and with a beckoning gesture, led them out into the wider road, turning left, heading roughly north-east towards their rendez-vous. In the distance Mike could see the taller buildings giving way to single storey, and the opening out that signalled the market area.

And then there was a flicker of light up ahead.

He saw Lance Corporal Westley stop and suddenly place a hand to his ear, an instinctive reaction. There was radio traffic coming in. He heard the young man's rasping whisper.

'Shit!'

Westley listened to some more, and then turned round to his men.

'There's a search-party up ahead coming down this road. Big mob, torches, guns. They're almost upon Zulu.'

They heard the sound of gunfire – a distant rattling and popping. Mike pulled the gun scope to his eye and aimed up the road. He could see sporadic flickerings of light, and a tracer lancing upwards into the sky. Then he spotted an amorphous glowing blob of light in the middle of the road that undulated like some cellular life form growing and dividing, growing and dividing.

'Bollocks!' hissed Westley. 'There's the bastards comin' down this way!'

Dropping his gun down, and looking with his bare eyes, Mike could see a large group cautiously advancing down the road towards them, a dozen beams of torchlight dancing from one side of the road to the other ahead of them. Meanwhile, beyond them in the market area, the fire-fight seemed to have intensified. It looked like the mob had found Zulu, and the poor bastards were having to fight their way out of it.

'Shit. What now?' whispered one of the other soldiers.

Westley looked anxiously around. They were walking alongside a long tall, flat wall with no places to hide nearby. Further up ahead of them on the left was another side-street. But that would take them closer to those advancing torch beams, and they were bound to be spotted making a run forward towards it. Opposite, across the wide road, was a garden wall, chest high.

Westley gestured with one gloved hand towards it. 'Over that wall, now!'

The five British soldiers sprinted desperately across the four lanes of open street, with Mike grabbing Farid's arm and leading the old man after them. As they stumbled across, he prayed that the approaching torch beams dancing from one side of the thoroughfare to the other, hadn't picked out the movement.

Mike thudded against the garden wall, catching his breath for a moment before turning to the old man.

'Get over the wall,' he said to Farid.

Farid didn't hesitate, pulling himself up and over. And Mike swiftly followed, dropping down inside the garden where Westley and his four comrades were waiting.

The veil of cloud in the sky was beginning to break, and a full moon shone down between the fleeting gaps.

'Shit, that doesn't help matters,' muttered Westley.

In the undulating moonlight Mike could see them hunched down in a semi-circle, he could hear their chorus of laboured and ragged breathing during the sporadic pauses between distant bursts of gunfire.

CHAPTER 34

. . . .

7.23 p.m. GMT

Between Manchester and Birmingham

Jenny walked silently beside Paul for several hours, trying to digest what she'd recently witnessed on the motorway. They steered away from the main roads, spotting on several occasions in the distance convoys of army trucks and police wagons rumbling along the deserted tarmac, unhindered by traffic.

She found her shoes, with only a modest heel, were impractical for the fields they crossed, and the tufted grass verges they were keeping to. She was beginning to wish she'd packed more practical clothing in her overnight bag. But then yesterday morning, she couldn't have imagined she'd be travelling cross-country with a man she knew nothing about.

She tried her phone several times as they made their way, roughly heading south she guessed by the position of the waning sun. There was no signal on several attempts, and when she did pick up a signal, she received a message that the service was experiencing difficulties dealing with an abnormally large volume of traffic.

As the warm evening sun was beginning to dip below the tops of the trees ahead of them, Paul steered them towards a small wood.

'This way,' he said staring down at the glowing screen of his palm pilot. 'We'll be able to rejoin the M1 on the other side of it.' He had some sort of GPS functionality built into the gadget.

She looked at the woods; densely grouped mature trees that cast an impenetrable shadow on the undergrowth below. She had never been a big fan of that kind of thing – quiet, spooky woods and forests. It was always in places like that, certainly in fairy-tales, that nasty things happened to the carefree and innocent. It didn't help that Andy had taken her along to see *The Blair Witch Project* many years ago.

'Do we have to go through?' she said. 'I'm not exactly kitted out for this kind of off-road rambling.'

'It's half a mile through it, according to this. Or about five to ten miles to skirt around it. Look, I can see you're a little spooked, but trust me okay? We'll be quickly through it.'

Jenny looked at him.

'I'm knackered, okay?' he smiled apologetically, 'I just want to hit some flat, sturdy road as quickly as possible. Just half a mile through this and we're back to civilisation.'

She looked up at the trees, and the orange sun, bleeding through the leaves at the top, and the shadows lengthening across the field they had just crossed in long forbidding purple strips.

'The longer we leave it, the darker it'll get in there.'

'All right,' she said unhappily, 'let's go through as quickly as we can, okay?'

He smiled, 'Of course.'

He led the way, stooping through a barbed wire fence. He held the wire up for her as she doubled down and squeezed through the gap. Her blouse caught on the back, somewhere between her shoulder blades.

'Ouch,' she whimpered.

'I've got it,' said Paul, unhooking her deftly.

'Thanks,' she muttered.

The ground was overgrown with nettles and brambles, and fallen branches, all apparently competing to snag her skirt, scratch her calves or sting her ankles.

They made very slow progress. Half a mile began to seem like a lot more than she remembered it being. They spent almost as much time fighting through the undergrowth as they did traversing any noticeable distance.

Paul stopped. 'I need a rest. How about you?'

I'd rather get the hell out of here.

'No, I'm good,' she replied.

He sat down on a log anyway. 'Sorry, need to just catch my breath. We've been walking for hours.'

'Okay.' She looked around for somewhere else to sit – there was nowhere, so she squatted down against the base of a tree.

They sat in silence for a couple of minutes, he scowling down at his palm pilot, she trying her phone again and again. She was getting a signal, but the service was giving her that damned message. The mobile networks had to be overloaded with anxious people trying to get in touch with loved ones.

It was Paul that broke the silence. 'So, crazy fucking day or what, eh?'

She nodded. It was that all right.

'I can't believe that traffic policeman shot a guy dead,' he said, shaking his head.

'No, neither can I.'

'You just don't expect that kind of thing, you know, here in good ol' Britain.'

'No ... I suppose not.'

He turned his palm pilot off. 'I can't get the GPS signal in here. And the charge is running down.'

Jenny looked up at him urgently. 'We're not lost are we?'

He grinned. 'Nope, I know where we are. Don't need it now. Like I say, it's just a little way through the woods, and then we're right on the M1 again.'

'Oh, thank God for that. I don't think I could cope being stuck in here after dark.'

'You ever camped out in a wood at night?'

'Never. I don't ever plan to either.'

'I did a paintball weekend with my work mates last year. Night-time sessions with those cool night sights and everything. Very hardcore, very intense. As much fun as you can possibly have in a wood at night.'

Jenny nodded unenthusiastically.

'So, did you say you got kids or something?' he asked.

She nodded. 'They're at home in London, on their own. I just want to get back to them as quickly as possible.'

'No dad to look after them then?'

Why is he fishing for details?

Jenny felt uncomfortable with that, stuck out here, alone with him. She sure as hell wasn't going to tell this guy that she had recently split from her husband of eighteen years. He'd probably take that as some sort of encouragement.

That's not fair. Has he given you any reason to think of him like that?

She looked at him – he hadn't.

To be honest, there were many other blokes she'd worked alongside in the past, whom she would not trust for a moment in a situation like this. This guy, Paul, so far had kept his eyes, his hands and any sexually charged innuendoes, to himself. He'd shown his little gadget more interest than her.

But you never know, do you?

Oh come on, she countered herself, if he was *that* kind of bloke, right here … right now would be the moment he'd start getting just a little bit too familiar, probing the lay of the land, so to speak and … and asking questions like 'no dad to look after them', perhaps?

Maybe he's just making conversation?

Yeah? And maybe the next thing he'll ask is, 'you got a fella out there worried about you?', or how about, 'you're looking a bit cold, it is getting a little fresh. Come on, why don't you sit over here next—'

'Come on,' said Paul, getting up off the log. 'I can see this place is giving you the heebie-jeebies. Let's press on and hit the road whilst we've still light to see.'

She smiled gratefully. 'Yeah, good idea.'

They managed to beat a path through undergrowth that seemed intent on preventing them getting any closer to the motorway. As the sun began to merge with the horizon, dipping behind a row of distant wind-turbines on the brow of a hill, they emerged from the wood and descended down a steep grass bank on to the motorway.

They both surveyed the six empty lanes, stretching as far as the eye could see in both directions, without a single vehicle to be seen.

'That's just such a weird sight,' said Paul.

They turned right, heading southbound, enjoying the firm flat surface beneath their feet.

'I'm really thirsty,' said Jenny.

'Yeah, me too. I bet we'll find somewhere along here soon. This part of the M1 is loaded with service stations and stop-overs.'

'You sure? I don't fancy walking all through the night without something to drink.'

'Christ, I've driven this section enough times to know. Got to admit though, I don't believe I've ever walked it.'

She smiled.

'If we get really desperate I might even consider going into a Little Chef.'

She managed a small laugh.

It felt good to do that. It wasn't exactly a funny joke, wasn't exactly a joke, but it was good to hear a little levity, especially after everything she'd seen and heard today.

'We'd have to be really desperate though,' she quipped. 'I mean, really desperate, and I'm still some way from that yet.'

Paul chuckled and nodded.

CHAPTER 35

. . . .

10.24 p.m. local time

Al-Bayji, Iraq

'**S**hit, they're heading our way,' hissed Carter.

Andy looked up and down the narrow street. There was nowhere for them to hide, it was no more than four or five feet wide, and cluttered with a few small boxes and bins; nothing large enough to hide behind. Any second now the large group of militia the lieutenant had just spotted would be turning into it, and their flashlights would pick them out in a heartbeat.

Andy spotted a small side-door recessed in the flaking plaster of the wall to their left. 'Try the door,' he muttered to Derry, the young soldier next to him.

Lieutenant Carter nodded. 'Go on.'

The soldier tried the handle of the door and twisted it. It was locked, or stuck. It rattled as he pulled and pushed desperately on it.

'For fuck's sake Derry, you girl's blouse, kick it in!' growled Sergeant Bolton, leaning waxen-faced against the wall beside it.

Private Derry, took a step back, raised a booted foot, and kicked hard at the rusting metal door. A shower of rusty flakes fell to the ground and it clanged and rattled noisily in its frame, but the lock held. Behind them, out on the main thoroughfare they heard raised voices, and several beams of torchlight fell on the mouth of their side-street, dancing and bobbing as they began to run towards it. They'd heard the noise and were coming to investigate.

Private Derry swung his foot at the door right next to the lock the second time, and on impact, it swung in, with a clattering sound of a lock shattering inside.

'In, in, in!' shouted Carter desperately. Derry led the way and Andy followed in his wake. One of the other two privates and Carter hauled Sergeant

Bolton up on to his feet and carried him through, whilst the last man fired off a dozen shots of covering fire, then dived in after them.

Inside, the darkness was complete, and once more Andy found himself having to fumble his way whilst the others picked out at least some detail through their weapon scopes. There were concrete stairs leading upwards, and walls that felt like rough breeze-blocks, scraping the skin from his fingertips as he held his hand out for guidance.

They had turned a corner, for a second flight of concrete steps, when it sounded like someone had taken a jackhammer to the rusty metal door. The dark stairwell below, suddenly strobed with sparks as a dozen or so rounds punched jagged holes through the door.

'Fuck, move it!' Andy heard one of the squaddies shout behind him.

They sprinted up the second flight of stairs in darkness, and then a door opened up ahead. Andy could see the glow of moonlight through the opening.

Down below, the metal door was kicked open again. He could hear footsteps and see the dancing flash of torchlight coming up the stairwell after them. The soldier behind him, gave Andy a hefty shove forward towards the open door, then turned round to face down the stairs.

The gunfire was deafening in the contained area, piercing, sharp, painful and punctuated by a cry from below as at least one shot found a target.

Andy tumbled forwards up the last few steps and out through the open door, his ears ringing. They were on a long balcony that overlooked a wide road. Andy recognised it as the road they had driven into town on this morning.

Beneath them, only fifteen or twenty feet below, Andy could see several dozen armed men and boys in loose clusters across the broad thoroughfare, torch beams arcing up and down the street, desperately trying to find them.

Oh shit. Please don't look up.

Ahead, Carter, Bolton, Derry and the other squaddie had dropped down low as they made their way along the balcony – a waist-high wall of breeze-blocks, crumbling, pitted and scarred, was keeping them from being seen. Behind him, through the open door to the stairwell, Andy could hear a concentrated barrage of fire as the last man in their group endeavoured to hold the mob back on the stairs.

Andy kept pace with the others, desperately trying to avoid the clutter of wicker chairs, children's toys, potted shrubs that were parked in front of a succession of front doors. Small windows looked out on to the balcony, and through several he passed by, grimy and fogged with dust, he could see the frightened faces of women and children cowering inside.

The gunfire in the stairwell suddenly stopped. Andy turned to look back along the balcony, hoping to see their man emerge from the doorway.

A single shot rung out from the stairwell.

One to the head to be certain. Our lad's down.

They'd be emerging through that doorway in the next few seconds. 'Fuckin' move it,' Andy found himself shouting at the men up ahead, slowed down by trying to drag Bolton along with them. 'They're right behind us!'

A second later he heard the door to the balcony swing open and a burst of gunfire behind him. Half-a-dozen shots whistled past him as he dived to the floor, tangling his legs with a discarded wicker chair.

'Down here!' Carter shouted back at them.

Andy got to his feet, and sprinted forward to join them. He caught up with Derry, kneeling and firing spurts of two and three rounds back at the doorway, and Carter struggling to manoeuvre Bolton down a narrow flight of stairs.

'Gimme a gun,' said Andy to Lieutenant Carter, 'I can help Derry slow them down.'

Carter unslung Bolton's SA80 and chucked it up at Andy. 'Know how to use it?'

Andy shrugged, 'Got a vague idea.'

'God 'elp us,' drawled Bolton.

Andy shouldered the weapon, feeling its reassuring weight in his hands. He swung the barrel around with his finger on the trigger; both Bolton and Carter cringed.

'Safety's off by the way,' Bolton grunted, pointing at the weapon, as Carter pulled him clumsily down the stairs.

Andy grinned sheepishly. 'Shit, sorry.'

He turned round, took half-a-dozen steps up to join Derry on the balcony.

Derry fired then ducked, as a long volley chipped, then shattered a large earthen pot beside him. 'Fucking fuck!' he yelled as he sprawled to the ground beside Andy. He looked up at him, surprised to see an assault rifle cradled in his hands.

'Yeah, I get to have one now,' Andy muttered. He then leaned out and fired a long burst down the length of the balcony, that had the pursuing militia picking their way forwards, needlessly diving for cover as the volley pulled the barrel up and his shots peppered the floor of the balcony above.

Derry used the bought seconds to squeeze past Andy, off the balcony and down on to the stairs. 'Short bursts,' he shouted.

'Right.'

Andy jabbed again at the trigger and fired a short burst, more accurately this time.

'I'm completely out,' said Derry, 'not exactly the world's greatest fucking rearguard action.'

'Go then,' said Andy, 'I'll hold here a few more seconds.'

Derry nodded, slapped Andy on the back and staggered down the stairs.

Oh Jesus, what the hell am I doing?

He wondered what Jenny would make of this if she could see him now, doing his best Bruce Willis impersonation.

He fired a few shots into the open doorway, whilst Derry made it down to the bottom. Almost immediately two heads popped out from the darkness, and a couple of AKs fired a volley in response. He felt the puff of displaced air on his cheek as a shot whistled past his head only an inch away, whilst another glanced off the wall just behind his head.

'Okay, screw this,' he muttered, getting to his feet and scrambling down the stairwell after Derry. He fired another un-aimed burst into the air to deter them from following too closcly, hopefully buying them a few more precious seconds.

Call-sign Whisky were reunited at the bottom of the stairs, in a small, rubbish-filled opening that led out on to a three-foot wide rat-run, strewn with a *mélange* of discarded furniture and bric-à-brac, rotting vegetation and a central sewage gully down which a clotted stream of faeces flowed.

'This way, I think,' said Carter pointing upwards.

'Yeah,' Andy replied, gasping and breathless, 'right or wrong though, we had better fucking run.'

CHAPTER 36

. . . .

7.40 p.m. GMT

Shepherd's Bush, London

'This is it,' said Leona, 'turn left here.'

Dan swung his van out of the almost static river of traffic on Uxbridge Road into St Stephen's Avenue, a narrow tree-lined road, flanked on either side by a row of comfortable-looking Edwardian terraced houses.

'Home!' cheered Jacob from the back of the van.

Leona twisted in her seat. 'Jake, we're going to be staying at Jill's place.'

'Uh?'

Dan looked at her, 'Yeah ... *uh?* I thought I was taking you home?'

'She lives three doors down from our place, she's a good friend of the family.'

'Why aren't we going home?' asked Jacob

To be entirely honest she had no idea why, only that Dad had been really insistent that they go to Jill's and not home. There had been the sound of fear in his voice, implied danger. And deep down, she knew it had something to do with the man she saw. None of this was going to make sense to Dan or Jacob, nor to Jill of course.

'Dad said for us to go there, so Jill can mind us until Mum or he can get home.'

'Aren't you a bit big for a babysitter?' said Dan.

'You saw what it was like in Hammersmith.'

Dan nodded. 'Yeah, I see what you mean.'

They drove slowly down the narrow avenue, squeezing around the large family vehicles parked half on, half off the pavement. Passing number twenty-five on their left, Leona looked out at their home. None of the lights were on. It looked lifeless.

'We live there,' Jacob informed Dan as they drove slowly past.

Leona pointed to a house ahead of them, on the right. 'Number thirty. That's Jill's house.'

Her car, a Lexus RX, was parked on the pavement outside, but there were no lights on. Dan parked up next to her car, and Leona quickly climbed out. She opened the garden gate and headed up the short path through her front yard – little more than a few square yards of shrivelled potted plants embedded in gravel – to the front door. She could see junk mail was piling up in the post-box, and knew that Jill must be abroad on one of her conferences.

'Damn!'

'What's up?' said Dan, joining her with several shopping bags in each hand.

'She's gone away.'

'Ah.'

Jacob staggered up the path with a solitary bag full of tins. 'Heavy,' he grunted like a martyr.

'So, back to yours then?' said Dan.

Leona looked over her shoulder at their house, thirty yards away on the other side of the avenue. 'I suppose we've got no choice, if Jill's gone on one of her visits.'

Dan nodded, 'Okay.' He turned and headed down the path.

Do NOT go home ... it's not safe.

There was no mistaking the urgency in Dad's voice. There was something he knew – didn't have time to tell her. The limited time he had on the phone was taken up with one thing; making sure she understood not to go home. That was it, explanations would no doubt come later.

'Wait!' she called out. Dan and Jacob stopped.

She looked around uncomfortably before picking up a stone from the front yard and quickly smashing the frosted narrow glass panel in the middle of the front door. The glass clattered down inside, as she reached through and fumbled with the latch.

'Oh boy,' said Jacob, 'that's against the law.'

Jill never double-locked her front door, even when she was going away. Instead she relied on the timed lights in her house, and the always on radio in the kitchen to convince would-be burglars that elsewhere would be a better prospect. She was a little ditzy that way.

The door cracked open and she pushed it wide, spreading the junk mail across the wooden floor in the hallway.

Dan looked at her. 'Uh, Leona, you're breaking and entering.'

'She's a friend. She wouldn't press charges. Now let's get our stuff inside as quickly as possible.'

She headed out to the van to grab a load when she spotted the DiMarcios, two doors down, on the other side of the avenue. Mum was on pretty good terms with them, particularly Mrs DiMarcio.

'Leona!' she called across to her.

'Hi, Mrs DiMarcio,' she said offering a little wave.

The woman was slim and elegant, in her early forties – yet, as Mum often said of her, she could easily pass as someone ten years younger.

'Leona! What you do home?' she asked, her English clipped with a Portuguese accent.

'I ... er ... my mum and dad said I had to,' she replied.

'This thing? This thing we see on the news?' she asked.

'Yeah.'

'Pffft ... this is terrible, hmm? This Mr Smith, your Prime Minister, he say we will have rations?'

'Rationing, that's right. That's what Dad was saying too. This could be quite bad.'

She looked over Leona's shoulder at Dan and Jacob carrying another load of shopping bags between them. 'You buy rations?'

She nodded. 'We went to Tesco, bought in some tinned goods and bottled water.'

Mrs DiMarcio looked at her with eyes that slowly widened. She knew about Dad's preoccupation with Peak Oil; he'd bored both her and Mr DiMarcio with it over dinner one night, after he'd had a couple of glasses of red.

'Your father? He tell you this could be bad?'

'Yeah.'

'Is this the thing, what he call it, Peak thing?'

'Peak Oil?'

'Yuh, that's it. Is this ...?'

'I don't know. But Dad said I had to come back, collect Jake, get some supplies in and stay over at Jill's house.'

Her hand covered her mouth. '*Oh, meu Deus, o teu pai estava certo!*'

'You know, you should hurry if you want to get some things,' said Leona. 'When we left, people were going mad in the supermarket, it was really quite scary.'

'I wonder, we maybe leave?' Mrs DiMarcio said, more to herself than Leona. She was thinking aloud. 'Is city,' she said gesturing with her hands at the avenue, 'this is a city ... I remember your father he say city is a bad place to be in a ... a ...'

'In a crisis?'

The woman nodded.

Leona was surprised at how much they'd taken in. Perhaps they had been listening after all when Dad had gone off on his anti-oil diatribe.

'I will talk with my husband when he comes in.'

'Maybe it's a good idea to leave if you can,' said Leona. 'Find somewhere out of town to stay.'

'We take you and Jacob with us, if we go?' she offered. 'We have spaces in car.'

Leona shook her head. 'Thanks, but I've got my orders to sit tight inside,' she said nodding at her home. 'And wait for Mum and Dad to get home.'

Mrs DiMarcio nodded. 'I understand. I talk with my husband. We stay? We go? We will talk about this.'

'Okay. Look, I better help with the shopping,' said Leona.

She reached out with her hands, grasped Leona's shoulders and smiled. 'You are good girl, very sensible girl. Jenny and Andy I think very proud of you.'

Leona shrugged awkwardly.

'I go. Maybe I ring Eduardo on his mobile,' she said, thinking aloud. With that she turned and headed hastily back to her house.

Up and down the normally quiet, leafy, avenue, Leona noticed more activity than normal; a man was busy un-loading bags of goods from his car, whilst talking animatedly on his phone. A few houses up, a woman emerged from her home, running; she hopped into her people carrier and started it up. Leona stepped out of the road to allow her to pass, as she drove down St Stephen's Avenue, at a guess heading towards the busy end of Shepherd's Bush to do some panic-buying.

You're probably too late, already.

The thought sent a chill down her spine.

She heard a car door slam, and another car engine start up with a throaty cough; it felt like the whole avenue was beginning to stir to life.

Leona reached into the van and grabbed an armful of bags and began to help the two boys get their supplies inside.

They stumbled noisily down the back-street, picking their way through small stacks of rubbish, wooden crates of rotting vegetables, trying to avoid stepping in the sewage gully running down the middle.

Andy and the others were no longer worrying about keeping quiet. They scrambled through the mess and the crap as quickly as they could, doing their best not to lose their footing or tangle with the obstacles in their way.

Behind them, Andy could see the bouncing and flickering of torches as they were being chased, their pursuers having an equally difficult time with the terrain. Sergeant Bolton, however, was slowing them down.

The militia-men were closing the gap on them.

Lieutenant Carter and Private Peters, still carrying Bolton, stumbled and fell to the ground, splashing into the sewage gully; a tangle of shit-soaked limbs.

'Ah fucking hell!' Bolton cursed angrily. 'The bloody dressing's come off!'

'Hold still!' hissed Carter. In the dark the officer fumbled to find the surgical band amongst the river of faeces.

'It's bloody pouring out,' said Bolton.

Andy turned to look back down the narrow passage. The flashlights were getting closer. He aimed the Sergeant's assault rifle towards them spraying a long burst that had the torches lancing wildly around as they dived for cover.

'Short bursts, you twat,' cursed Bolton, 'it's not a bloody water pistol!'

Andy waited a moment before letting loose another three-round volley. This was only going to buy them time whilst the gun had rounds in the clip.

'All right, sod this for a laugh. Give me the friggin' gun and piss off.'

'No,' snapped Carter. 'We're not leaving you behind.'

'Yes you are. Because I'm bleeding like a bastard.'

Derry leant over, and placed a hand on Bolton's arm. 'You're a shithead if you think we're leaving you, sir.'

'Shut up Derry,' Bolton wheezed painfully, 'you'll all be dead if you carry on dragging me. Just give me a bloody gun and fuck off, all right?'

Andy looked at Carter, Peters and Derry. They were all thinking the same thing – Sergeant Bolton was right – but none of them wanted to be the one to say it.

There's no time for this macho crap.

'He's right,' said Andy. 'He can buy us the time we're going to need.' He pointed up the rat-run. There was a flickering glow in the distance, perhaps a couple of hundred yards away. 'That's the market-place up there.'

Carter struggled with the decision for a while, whilst back along the way they had come, the torches were on the move again, cautiously drawing nearer.

'All right Bolton,' said Carter, wearily resigned. 'Your way then. Give him a rifle.'

'Sir, we can't leave!' protested Derry.

'Shut it! And do as the officer says!' grunted Bolton.

Derry reluctantly handed him his rifle. 'It's out sir.'

Bolton took the gun, pulled a clip out from a pouch on his webbing and slammed it home with a grunt of pain. 'Good to go.'

Andy checked his watch. 'It's quarter to eleven. We have to go.'

'Bolton,' said Carter, 'keep those bastards off our tail.'

'Uh-huh,' he groaned, shifting painfully into a prone position behind a pile of rotting household rubbish.

Andy reached out for the Sergeant's leg holster and pulled out his service pistol. He placed it on the ground beside Bolton. 'Don't let them take you alive,' he said quietly. 'Understand?'

Bolton nodded. 'No fucking chance. Now you lot better piss off.'

The men shared a glance, there was no room for any words. Bolton racked the gun and stared down the barrel, through the scope at the flickering shapes moving swiftly up the side-street towards them.

They started off towards the flickering glow in the distance.

Sergeant Bolton watched the torch-beams slowly approaching him. They were taking their time, cautiously sweeping the way ahead before advancing.

Very sensible. This little alleyway was a jumble of rubbish and boxes, discarded furniture and tufts of weeds. Nightmare terrain to be advancing through, especially at night.

Just a little closer and then he'd pop off a few rounds at the nearest git holding a flashlight. Sooner would be better than later. He could feel himself slipping. In fact, it felt a little like being pissed. Like having a pint mid-morning after a heavy session the night before – hair of the dog.

Slipping, and it was happening quite quickly.

He'd been leaking blood slowly for twenty minutes, and now he'd lost enough that things were beginning to shut down on him.

Bollocks.

He wanted to drop a few of them before he went under. Just a couple would do.

'Come on you fuckers!' he shouted out, realising with some amusement that he sounded like some drunken bastard at closing time brazenly taking on half-a-dozen coppers.

There was a flicker of reaction. The torch beams swept up the alley towards him, and then across the mound of detritus he was nicely hidden behind.

Yeah, yeah, yeah ... can't see me, fuckers.

Slipping.

He decided it was time. He squeezed the trigger, aiming at one of the torches.

It spun into the air and dropped.

Score one.

Slipping further. He'd felt this pissed a couple of times before; once at his wedding, once when England caned the Aussies at Twickenham.

Fuckin' all right.

Vision was blurring, spinning. But he was lying down already. Good. He'd look a right twat if he was trying to stay on his feet.

The torches all winked out instantly, and half a second later he saw three or four muzzle flashes picking out the alley in stark relief. And the stinking pile of rubbish in front of him began to dance with the impact of bullets, and the air either side of his head was humming.

He felt his shoulder being punched. Just like a hearty pinch and a punch, first of the month.

Didn't bloody well hurt, so fuck you.

He fired again at the swirling, flickering muzzle flashes, pretty certain he was probably aiming at phantoms now.

Another punch, and another. Neither hurt.

Struggling to make sense now of the swirling light-show, he squeezed the trigger and held, firing until the magazine emptied.

Jesus, that was fun. Surely hit something down there.

And then with some effort he reached out for the pistol Andy had placed on the ground beside him. His arm seemed to have no strength in it, like pins and needles. He found the pistol's butt, fumbled at it with useless fingers, and then managed to get some semblance of a grip on it.

The rubbish was dancing again, the air humming ... and he felt another punch in one of his legs.

Big ... fucking ... deal.

He fumbled for the pistol on the ground beside him.

But then another of those flailing, wimpy, pussy-punches landed home.

CHAPTER 38

· · · ·

7.46 p.m. GMT

Shepherd's Bush, London

You can tell so much about a family from their kitchen corkboard, or the mementoes, Post-it Notes and silly clutter that they'll stick to their fridge with little fruit-shaped magnets. Ash had a theory, one of many little theories he'd accumulated over the years, observing as he did, life – normal life, that is – from afar. This one went along the lines of, 'the more cluttered the family fridge, the happier they are', and it was a theory he'd just come up with.

The Sutherland fridge was bare. No photos, memos, notes or shopping lists.

And it was as clear as anything that this was a home in which things had pretty much come to a dismal conclusion. In the kitchen boxes were stacked in the corner, full of crockery and utensils, in the lounge there were boxes of CDs, DVDs and books; in the hallway, lined against one wall, boxes containing wellingtons, scarves and anoraks – on all of these boxes, scrawled with a Magic Marker, was written either 'Jenny' or 'Andy'.

The Sutherlands, as a family unit, were disintegrating.

Ash had hoped to find Mrs Sutherland home, in the hope that she might be able to help him find out who exactly 'Jill' was, and more importantly, where she lived. But alas, an empty house.

The study, Dr A. Sutherland's study, he'd hoped might yield something. Turning the PC on, he checked through the email addresses in Outlook Express's contact book, to no avail. There was no Rolodex, or equivalent, on the desk either.

In the lounge though, he found a tiny black phone book. It listed a small number of people, some friends, some family; not a huge number of friends, which was convenient. Ash could see no one called 'Jill' here either, nor anyone with 'J' as an initial.

But there was a sister in London. A sister, as opposed to a friend, because it was on the same page as 'Mum and Dad', written in the unmistakably round handwriting of a woman. Beside the tidy entry was scrawled 'Auntie'; the carefree scrawl of a child. Mrs Sutherland's sister, and obviously they were quite close, because as well as an address and a home phone number, there was a mobile number.

Sisters who probably get together quite often, who share the banal little details of everyday life. He looked down at the page.

Kate.

Yes, he was pretty sure Kate Marsh (née Marsh?) might have an idea who 'Jill' was. Obviously it was someone close enough to the family that Dad would entrust his kids to them during this period of crisis; someone who must have, at one time or another, been casually mentioned by Jenny whilst nattering with Kate over coffee and biscuits.

That was all he had to go on. Not brilliant.

He combed through the rest of the house, finally ending up in Leona's room.

Although there were still posters of boy bands on the wall, and a small mountain of soft toys piled on a chair by the window, it was clearly on its way to becoming a guest room. The child that had grown up in this space was gone now; *flown the coop*, to use a tired aphorism.

Standing well back from the window, away from the warm glow of the evening sun, he gazed out at the cosy suburban street below. In every house opposite he could see the flickering blue glow of television screens; most people, it seemed, glued to the news and no doubt beginning to wonder how an across-the-board fuck up like this could have been allowed to happen.

He watched as several more cars started up and weaved their way down to the end of the avenue – no doubt in a last-minute bid to see what they could still pick up at their local supermarket – and outside, several houses up, he could see a young couple and their little boy, busily unloading bags of shopping from the boot of their van.

Ash shook his head, feeling something almost akin to pity for all these people so unprepared for what was lying ahead of them.

CHAPTER 39

. . . .

10.50 p.m. local time

Al-Bayji, Iraq

Andy, Carter and the other men looked out at the market-place from the darkness of the rat-run.

'That's it, they've blocked us off,' Carter groaned.

In the middle of the market-place was a large bonfire; an oil drum, piled with broken-up wooden pallets that illuminated the whole area with a flickering amber glow. Surrounding it, enjoying the warmth and chattering animatedly was at least thirty militia. Beyond them, beyond the market-place, was the road out of town, and just visible, the bridge over the Tigris.

'What do you think?' asked Andy.

Carter was silent for a moment before replying. Andy noticed the young officer biting down on his bottom lip, a nervous gesture he'd been aware of back in the compound. But now it seemed a little more pronounced; the young man's head shook a little too, just the slightest tic that suggested to Andy that Carter was beginning to fracture inside.

'I d-don't know. There's a lot of those bastards out there, and a lot of distance for us to run across. Maybe if it wasn't for that bloody bonfire, we might have been able to sneak across to the bridge. But this, this isn't so good.'

Andy looked down at his watch. 'Shit, we've only got nine minutes left. We have to do something!'

Carter shook his head. 'We ... we won't make it through.'

'Fuck it!' Andy hissed at him. 'We can't stay here either. They'll be coming up behind us in a minute. We've got to go—'

They heard the throaty rumble of a vehicle approaching – it sounded like it was coming down the main road, from the centre of town, and fast, very fast.

A moment later, Andy noticed the men out in the market-place reacting, turning towards the source of the approaching noise. They weren't readying their guns yet, perhaps thinking the approaching vehicle was bringing more militia up to help them block off this end of town.

And then the truck rolled into view, rumbling down the main road, flanked on either side by the rows of empty market stalls. Without warning, it slewed to a halt. And from the back of the truck Andy saw several dark forms sitting up.

Carter's hand went up to his earpiece. 'Those are our boys ... their PRR just came into range. They're chattering like a bunch of fishwives.'

'Who is it?' asked Andy, 'Westley's lot?'

'That might be Corporal Westley's lot,' whispered Carter, 'or the Fijian bloke's.'

Andy counted the heads on the back of the truck. 'Or maybe both.'

The truck came to a halt, on the edge of the perimeter clearly illuminated by the bonfire. The militia-men gathered round the fire, turned to look at the truck. From their casual demeanor, Andy guessed they assumed the men on the back of the truck were theirs.

'I think they're waiting for us,' he whispered to Carter. 'They've slowed down for us, but they can't stay for long.'

Lieutenant Carter nodded. 'Maybe.'

Carter studied the edge of the market-place.

'No sign of Zulu then.'

Andy shook his head. 'None.'

Carter cursed under his breath.

Andy looked out at the market-place. 'We've got to go!'

'They'll see us the moment we step out.'

Andy looked back down the rat-run. Bolton's gun had stopped chattering a minute ago, and he could see the flashlight beams bobbing towards them. 'We can't bloody stay!'

Derry and Peters looked uncertainly at their CO. 'Sir?'

Carter shook his head. 'It's too open, too far.'

Andy grabbed the officer's arm. 'Fuck it. This is it. This is our last chance. I'm peggin' it.'

He pulled himself to his feet, crouched low, ready to sprint out into the open.

'All right,' said Carter, 'we all go. Fire and manoeuvre in twos. Okay?'

Westley spotted them as soon as they emerged from the shadowy mouth of a small alleyway – four of them moving in pairs into the open. The first two dropped to the ground and started firing into the crowd of militia gathered around the fire, the second two taking advantage of the confusion and sprinting towards the truck.

'Friendlies coming in from our left lads! Give the bastards some covering fire!'

Almost immediately the dozen men on the back of the truck let rip, firing into the scattering shapes of the militia. The short volley took down about a dozen men and was initially uncontested as they scrambled for positions, but very quickly return fire forced the men on the truck to duck back down.

Westley waited a few seconds before sticking his head up to scan the situation. All the miltia had gone to ground. There was a paucity of cover for them; the meagre planks and rusty tube-metal frames of the empty market stalls weren't going to stop anything. Some were firing back towards the truck, and the occasional rattle and spark against the thick side of the truck's bed was a testament to the fact that some of them had recovered from the surprise opening volley to be aiming their shots well.

'... we go. Got to move now!' Tajican's voice crackled over the radio, half the sentence lost amidst white noise and a whining, piercing feedback.

The incoming fire was intensifying now that the militia had recovered their senses. Not for the first time, Westley acknowledged that amongst the mob, there were definitely men who knew how to fight.

'Okay, but slow ... we've got friendlies coming in!'

The truck began to roll forward with a roar of complaint from the diesel engine and a cloud of acrid smoke that burst out of the exhaust pipe and billowed around the back of the truck.

Westley watched as the four men came in closer, racing recklessly past the prone militia towards the truck – the fire and manoeuvre routine now already abandoned. They sprinted the last fifty yards towards the truck like children chasing desperately after an ice-cream van on a hot day.

'Come on move it, you wankers!' he shouted getting up and climbing over the back of the truck, leaning out and standing precariously on the rear bumper.

The truck was moving along a little too quickly.

'Taj, you got to slow down for 'em.'

There was no answer, just a popping and hissing. Maybe Tajican had heard and was replying, maybe he hadn't. PRR could be inconsistent sometimes.

The men were successfully closing the distance to thirty ... twenty yards. But the truck was beginning to pick up speed and he could see they were beginning to flag.

'For fuck's sake Taj ... slow down!' he shouted into his radio.

Shit. Taj isn't hearing me.

Westley tossed his SA80 up into the truck and then leant out towards the running men, stretching his arm out towards them. It was then that, catching a glimpse of their faces he registered *who* the four were.

Lieutenant Carter, Derry, Peters ... and that civilian ... Andy.

Sergeant Bolton's gone then. Shit.

'Come on!' he shouted.

The nearest was Peters. He grabbed Westley's hand, then quickly got a hold of the tailgate and pulled himself up. Derry was next, with the truck beginning to find some pace after grinding into second gear. Westley had to give his arm a viciously hard tug to pull him close enough that he could make a grab for the back of the truck. With a grunt of complete exhaustion he managed to get himself up and roll over the lip on to the rough bed, where he gasped like an asthmatic.

It was just Lieutenant Carter now and Andy, the Kiwi bloke. He could see both of them had blown whatever strength they had left in them whilst sprinting the last thirty yards, and were just about managing to keep pace, but that wasn't going to last for much longer. It was sheer terror that was keeping these two poor bastards swinging their spent legs now, nothing more.

Westley leant out as far as he could, stretching his hand so that his gloved fingers almost seemed to brush their faces.

Grab it! For fuck's sake, grab it!

He heard the truck clatter and complain loudly as Tajican slammed it up another gear. He turned round and shouted to one of the men near the back of the truck to go forward, bang on the roof of the cab and get Tajican's attention ... and slow the fuck down. But his hoarse shout was lost against the rumble of the truck, and the staccato of the final retaliatory shots being fired out the back towards the militia in the market-place, who had now got to their feet and were pursuing *en masse*.

And then he felt his hand being grabbed.

One of them had done it; found enough left over to make a final lunge for his hand. The other? The other just wasn't going to make it. The truck was now picking up speed.

He spun round to see who it was – who was probably going to be the last man up.

CHAPTER 40

• • • •

7.52 p.m. GMT

Shepherd's Bush, London

Leona looked out of the lounge window at St Stephen's Avenue. Diagonally opposite, one house up, was the DiMarcio's house. She could see the silhouette of their heads through the lounge window, both staring at their TV. In the house directly opposite, was another couple with a baby; she could see activity in their lounge, the woman striding up and down, feeding her baby, the man standing, watching TV as well.

Leona craned her neck, looking through the venetian blind to see her house, number 25. She could just about see it through the foliage of the stunted birch tree opposite.

Dark, still, lifeless.

Like Jacob, she'd much rather be settled in over there, amongst familiar surroundings, amongst her things.

She looked up at her bedroom window – and thought she saw something tall and dark against the back wall of her room. Motionless, like her, studying the gathering madness outside ... the shape of a person.

'What ...?' she mouthed silently.

A gentle breeze caused the birch to sway slightly and she lost sight of her bedroom window amidst the swirling of leaves. A few seconds passed, the breeze lapsed, the tree settled once more. For a long minute she struggled to peer into the gathering gloom of her bedroom, but it was made difficult with the fading evening light and the sheen of a reflected golden sun balancing on the rooftops.

She could see nothing now.

Don't go home.

Leona shuddered and turned away from the window to join Daniel sitting on the sofa in front of Jill's luxurious plasma screen TV, like everyone else in the world, watching the news. They sat in silence, whilst Jacob lay on the floor in front of them, sorting meticulously through his Yu-Gi-Oh cards.

'... spreading across the country, in every city. In most cases the flash point of each riot has been centred around the big supermarkets, the larger petrol stations. In many of the bigger cities, there simply isn't any sense of order or control. The police have been armed, and the armed forces have been mobilised and stationed around key government installations and supply depots, but beyond that, there simply are no uniforms to be seen ...'

The reporter on screen had a face that Leona recognised; he usually reported on business things, from the City. But now here he was on the rooftop or balcony of some building looking down on a street thick with black smoke from a burning car, and people running erratically. His usually well-groomed appearance, the smartly side-parted hair, the navy-blue suit and tie had been replaced with the look of someone who had been roused from sleep after an all-night vigil.

'Law and order has apparently vanished from the streets of this country in the last six hours, since the Prime Minister's disastrous lunchtime press conference. Amongst the chaos down there, below us, we have distinctly heard the sound of gunfire several times in the last few minutes,' the reporter continued, gazing down on the smoky scene below.

Leona, shuddered anxiously.

My God, he's really frightened.

'There have been unconfirmed reports of military personnel guarding key locations, using live rounds on civilians. There have been hundreds of eye-witness reports describing fights over food, killings in many cases. This is a truly horrifying scenario, Sean, being played out on every street in every major town and city in the country ...'

The image cut back to the studio.

'Diarmid, is there no sign at all of the police or the army out there? I mean, we're looking at Oxford Street right now, aren't we?'

'That's right, Sean. Wholly unrecognisable right now, but yes, this is Oxford Street. This particular disturbance began at about three in the afternoon around a Metro-Stop supermarket, when the staff attempted to close the store and pull down the shutters. This triggered a riot, which quickly led to the store being rushed and the stock completely looted. I saw people emerging from it hours ago pushing trolleys full of food, and then several fights breaking out on the street as other people attempted to lift goods from these trolleys. This particular riot then spread to the other stores up and down the street, with people, quite unbelievably, storming a sports clothes retailer nearby, and next to that, an electrical goods store. Looking down on this now Sean, one is reminded of some of the scenes we saw during the LA riots in 1992, and also in the aftermath of Katrina in New Orleans. But to answer your question Sean, I have seen absolutely no police or army since we arrived here.'

The image on screen cut back to the studio.

'Thank you for that report, Diarmid,' Sean said, looking down at a sheaf of papers in his hands. 'Those scenes of the rioting currently going on in central London.'

Sean Tillman took a long steadying breath, and then looked up again to camera; the trademark early morning smile that Leona found irritating, but frankly would have loved to have seen now, replaced with a chilling portrayal of grim resignation.

'There has still been no further comment from the Government since the lunchtime press conference. We have been informed though that the emergency committee, code-named "Cobra", with full legal authority, is in effect now governing the country. Whether the Prime Minister is steering that committee, or some other minister is, as yet, unclear.'

Leona turned to Daniel. 'Oh God, Dan, this is so scary,' she whispered.

Daniel nodded silently.

'Reports have been coming in from foreign correspondents throughout the afternoon. A similar pattern of events seems to be occurring in many other countries. In Paris, unrest that started in the suburb of Clichy-sous-Bois, has spread across the city, with many buildings now on fire, and reports of many hundreds of deaths amongst the rioters. In New York, the announcement of a city-wide emergency food rationing ordinance was met with demonstrations on the streets that quickly escalated to a full-scale riot.'

Daniel got up. 'Can I use your phone? I want to try my mum again.'

Leona nodded. 'Sure.'

As he headed out of the lounge to the hall phone table, Jacob stirred. 'Lee, are we having a big war?' he asked casually.

'What? No, of course not!' she snapped at him irritably. And then noticed from the worried scowl on his small face that even Jake was aware that all was not well with the world. 'No Jake, we're not having a war. But things have gone … wrong, and people are getting a bit panicky.'

Jacob nodded as he digested that, and then looked up at her again. 'I want Mum. Where is she?'

Leona smiled, she hoped reassuringly.

I want Mum too.

Daniel returned. 'There's no tone on the telephone line. It's, like, dead.'

'Dead?'

'Not a thing.'

'Who's dead?' asked Jake, his lips were beginning to quiver unhappily.

Leona could do without him whimpering right now. 'No one Jake. No one's dead. Just play with your cards right now, okay?'

Jacob nodded, but instead of returning to his cards and continuing to sort them into monster and spell decks, he looked up at the TV and watched the flickering montage of flaming cars, and smoke-smudged skylines. He listened to the words, with cocked head, not entirely understanding what was being said, but instinctively knowing that none of it was good.

'You want to use my mobile?' asked Leona.

'Yeah, please,' replied Daniel.

'... in Saudi Arabia, Iraq and Afghanistan particularly. From what we know, the evacuation of troops from the region is continuing apace, with a steady procession of Hercules transport planes depositing troops at several RAF bases, including ...'

On the TV screen Sean Tillman suddenly disappeared. The only thing left on screen was the *News 24* logo in the top left corner and the scrolling news feed along the bottom.

'It appears,' his voice announced, 'we have lost some lighting in the studio. I'm sure this will be rectified short—'

And then there was a chaotic blizzard of snow on the TV and a hiss.

'What happened to the TV man?' asked Jake.

Daniel, holding Leona's phone in his hand, looked up at her. 'Oh shit. What's going on now?'

She shook her head.

And then the lights in the lounge went out and the TV winked off.

'Whuh—?'

The amber-hued streetlights outside along the avenue, which had only minutes ago flickered on, went out.

'The power's gone,' she whispered in the dark.

Jacob began to panic. 'It's all dark! Can't see!' he whimpered.

'Relax Jake, you can see. It's not dark, it's just gloomy,' she said as calmly as she could manage, feeling the leading edge of a growing wave of panic preparing to steal up on her too.

Jacob started crying.

'Shhh Jake. Come up here and sit with us.'

He got up from the floor and squeezed on to Jill's leather Chesterfield sofa between Leona and Dan. 'There,' she said, 'nothing scary's going to happen, we're just going to sit here and—'

Then her phone rang and all three of them jumped.

CHAPTER 41

· · · ·

7.53 p.m. GMT

Between Manchester
and Birmingham

'Leona?' cried Jenny with relief, 'Is that you?'

'Mum?'

'Yes. I've been trying to get hold of you all day. Are you all right love?' she replied quickly, not daring to waste a second of precious phone time. God knew how much longer the mobile phone system was going to last. 'Did you pick up Jacob?'

'Yes, he's here.'

'Are you at home?'

She heard Leona pause, a moment's hesitation was all.

'Mum,' Leona started, 'Dad told me to go to Jill's house.'

'Jill's place? Why?'

Another, even longer, pause. 'Dad just thought we'd be safer here in Jill's house.'

Jenny wondered what the hell Andy was thinking about. She'd be much happier knowing they were settled in safely at home. Anyway, she remembered Jill was away this week, on one of her sales team's get-togethers abroad.

'How did you get in to—?'

She could hear Leona crying.

'Doesn't matter, I'm sure Jill won't mind. Do you two have food?'

The question prompted a gasp from her daughter. 'Oh my God, it was horrible Mum. It was just ...'

Jenny could hear the tears tumbling in the timbre of her daughter's voice.

'... at the supermarket, as we came out, things began to go really bad. We were nearly in a fight. And we've been watching the news, and it's …'

Jenny interrupted. 'I know love, I know.'

Oh Christ do I know.

Jenny had seen things in the last few hours that she never imagined she would see in a country like this; a civilised, prosperous country, with the exception of the odd gang of youths on the roughest of estates, it was a place where one largely felt safe.

'I know,' she replied falteringly. She could hear her own voice beginning to wobble too.

Be strong for her.

'Oh God, Mum. It's just how Dad said it would be, isn't it? It's all falling apart.'

Jenny wondered what was best for her children now. Denial? A blank-minded reassurance that everything was going to be as right as rain in a day or two? Was that what Leona needed to hear from her? Because that *wasn't* the truth, was it? If she now, finally, had come round to trusting Andy's prophetic wisdom; if her worn-down tolerance and weary cynicism was to be a thing of the past and she was now ready to fully take onboard his warnings … then she had to concede this wasn't going to sort itself out in a couple of days.

Things were going to get a lot worse. Andy had foreseen that. Andy had warned her, Christ, Andy had bored her to death with it, and now, finally, here it was.

'Leona, my love. Have you got food?' Jenny asked, swiftly wiping away the first tear to roll down her cheek as if somehow her daughter might catch sight of it.

'Y-yes, Mum. We got a load of tinned things from the supermarket.'

'Good girl Leona. Can I speak to Jacob?'

Jenny heard a muffled exchange in the background, and then her son was on the phone.

'Mummy?'

'Jake,' she replied, the trembling in her voice becoming too difficult to hide.

'Mum? Are you okay?'

'Oh I'm just fine, love.'

'You sound sad.'

'I'm not sad.'

'When are you coming home?'

'As soon as I can get home. I'm trying … really,' replied Jenny looking across at the face of the man she'd been walking beside for the last four hours. Paul. She didn't know him from Adam really. As much a stranger as the other dozen or so people sitting on the orange, plastic chairs around the burger van on the lay-by.

'Okay. Leona and Daniel are looking after me until you come home.'

'Who's Daniel?'

'He's a man. He's Leona's friend.'

A man?

'Jacob, let me speak to Leona.'

Jenny heard the rustle of the phone changing hands again.

'Mum?'

'Who the *hell* is Daniel?' asked Jenny. 'Jacob said it's a *man.*'

'It's all right Mum, he's a mate from uni. He drove us home. He helped us get the food.'

Jenny puffed a sigh of relief. This Daniel was just another kid then, no doubt her current boyfriend. Jenny had lost track of who was who on the list of names Leona casually ran through when she got her daughter's weekly social update over the phone. Jenny found that comforting, there was a lad there looking out for her, and Jake.

'Okay.'

'Have you heard from Dad?' asked Leona. 'I've not spoken to him since early this morning.'

'No love, that was when I last spoke to him.'

'Oh God, I hope he's okay.'

Jenny realised how much she hoped that as well. In the space of a day, she had found herself rewriting recent personal history; the last five years of seeing him as a tiresome mole digging his own little lonely, paranoid tunnel to nowhere. That was all different now. Andy had been seeing *this* ... she looked around at the frightened people beside her, the empty motorway, the dark night sky no longer stained a muted orange by light pollution from the cities beneath it ... he had actually been seeing this with his own eyes. All he'd been trying to do was warn them, that's all.

'He'll be fine Leona, I'm sure he's doing okay.'

Leona started crying.

'Listen sweetheart, you have to be strong now—'

There was shrill warbling on the line, followed by crackling and static.

'Leona!'

The crackling continued.

'Leona!' Jenny cried again desperately.

'Mum?'

'Oh God, I thought the phone system had gone down.'

'Mum, please get home as quick as you can. The power went just before you called. It's getting dark now and we're all scared, and there's these noises outside in the stree—'

Then the line went dead.

'Leona!'

This time there was nothing, not even the crackling. Jenny looked across at Paul, who was hungrily devouring some of the stale buns the small group had managed to find inside the locked-up burger van parked in the lay-by.

'The phones aren't working now,' she whispered, feeling her scalp run cold and realising that this was it; her children were on their own just as things in London – as no doubt they were in every other city in the country, perhaps the world – were about to go to hell.

Paul took a swig from a can of Tango. Several twenty-four packs of fizzy sugary drinks and a dozen large catering packs of buns were all the small gathering of people, travelling on foot, had been able to liberate from the burger van. Some of these people, sitting silently on the bucket chairs outside the van, had been among the mob that had pushed past the police blockade. One or two others had joined them, emerging from the flat, featureless farmlands and drab industrial estates beyond the motorway, down the grass bankings lined with stunted, monoxide-withered saplings, as the light of the afternoon had slipped away.

'You better eat something,' Paul said quietly, handing her half-a-dozen buns.

Jenny stared down at the food in front of her.

'I can't eat. I'm not hungry.'

'You should. There's no knowing where we'll find our next meal.'

She tore a bun off from the rest and took a bite out of it, chewing the stale bread with little enthusiasm.

The children are home, they have food. They're safe inside.

That was all that mattered. Jenny knew it might take three or four days walking down the M1 on foot before she could be there for them. But they had food.

Andy's warning, his advance warning ... the one they should have heeded a little earlier than this, had sort of paid off, kind of. Of course, if she'd listened to him four or five years ago, they'd be living in some secluded valley in Wales, with an established vegetable garden, a water well, some chickens maybe, a generator and a turbine. Sitting pretty.

Instead, it seemed her kids had only *just* managed to beat the rest of the population, *the blinkered masses* – that used to be one of Andy's pet phrases – to the draw.

Sitting pretty.

Maybe not. They might have had their secluded, self-sufficient smallhold-ing, but, she wondered, how long would they have been able to keep hold of it? Especially once the looted supermarket food ran out and hunger began to bite. Those people, the blinkered masses, would come looking, foraging.

Jenny shook her head.

Andy wasn't the kind of guy who could defend himself, his family. He was a pacifist. She struggled to imagine him guarding their little survival fortress, with an assault rifle slung over one shoulder and his face dappled with that camouflage make-up the boys liked so much.

He could plan, but he wasn't a fighter.

CHAPTER 42

. . . .

10.53 p.m. local time

Al-Bayji, Iraq

Westley yanked Andy forward with a savage jerk of his arm, almost pulling him off his feet. With his other hand, Andy managed to grab hold of the truck's tailgate, and together with the Lance Corporal grabbing hold of his sweat-soaked shirt, pulling him up, he found himself lying in the back of the truck, looking up at the flitting moonlit clouds.

With a crunch and a loose rattle of worn metal, the truck finally found third gear, and lurched forward.

Westley was screaming at Lieutenant Carter to get a move on. This truck was *not* going to slow down for him.

Andy sat up and looked over the rim at the back of the truck's bed to see the young officer falling behind them. Beyond, a hundred yards back, the mob were furiously pursuing.

'Come on, fuckin' move it, sir!' he shouted.

Lieutenant Carter ditched his webbing and his gun, and pounded the ground hard with his boots, his face a snarl of effort. His arms pumped hard, and to Andy's amazement, his pace had picked up enough that he began to close the gap. Andy climbed over the rim and joined Westley leaning out of the back of the truck, one arm fully extended. Carter was so exhausted he would need both of them to pull him up, there was no way he was going to have anything left over to get himself up. Once they grabbed hold of him he was going to be dead weight.

'That's it!' shouted Andy. 'Come on!'

Carter increased his pace, and raised one arm out towards the back of the truck, his fingers brushed Andy's.

A puff of crimson suddenly erupted from his torso; the young man lurched and fell forward.

'No!'

Carter shrank as the truck rumbled on and left him behind. He'd taken a hit. Andy could see him scrambling drunkenly to his feet again, clutching at his chest. It was over for him. He could see that on the young man's face. The gunshot wound looked bad.

'Oh shit! Oh shit! He's fucking dead.'

Carter collapsed to his knees, but stayed upright. Andy could see clearly the mob were going to get to him long before the wound did its job.

'Oh this is fucked up,' groaned Westley.

Andy quickly pulled himself back up and reached out for one of the SA80s in the truck. He steadied himself as best he could in the lurching rear of the vehicle as it rattled on to the bridge.

'What are you—?' Westley had time to say before Andy emptied the magazine.

The dirt around Carter danced. Most of Andy's shots missed, but mercifully, a couple landed home, knocking Carter to the ground, where, to Andy's relief, he appeared to lay still.

One of the soldiers up at the front of the truck shouted, 'Hang on! Blockade!' A moment later the truck careered into the flimsy burned-out shell of a small car, knocking it effortlessly aside amidst a shower of sparks and a cloud of soot, smoke and baked flecks of paint.

The truck roared past a dozen or so more militia, most of them diving out of the way of the truck and the tumbling chassis of the car. The truck rattled noisily across the bridge and Andy watched as the blockade, the dark, lifeless town and the enraged mob of people, dwindled behind them. The last he could vaguely pick out through the night-sight was the darkening mass of people, silhouetted against the distant bonfire, gathering around the body of Lieutenant Carter.

Already his mind was ready with the slow-motion playback.

He felt a slap on his shoulder, and turned to see Mike sitting behind. He nodded. 'You did good,' he said.

Andy looked at his watch. It was half past eleven and there was nothing at all to be seen, or, more importantly, heard, in the night sky.

Andy nodded. 'I guess they're not coming then.'

'Are you sure Lieutenant Carter said they were coming here?' asked Mike. 'At eleven?'

'I'm sure.'

There were any number of reasons why the Chinook hadn't turned up; perhaps it had tried to make the rendezvous but had been beaten back, or even brought down, by a surface-to-air missile? Or perhaps they'd simply been considered too high a risk and left to it? It didn't matter now. They were royally screwed.

'Those boys back there are wondering what the hell we're going to do next,' said Mike, 'they've lost both their commanding officers and they're scared shitless.'

Mike was right. The lads gathered in the back of the truck were just that, boys; nineteen, twenty, twenty-one … most of them. Andy was thirty-nine, old enough to be a dad to some. They were looking at him right now, two rows of eyes staring at him from the back of the truck, wanting to know what happens now.

Mike spoke to him quietly. 'They're looking to *you*, you know that don't you?'

Andy nodded. 'Yeah,' he said reluctantly.

'So we need to think what we're going to do now.'

'No shit. We can't drive south-west to the K-2 airstrip. We'd have to go back through Al-Bayji,' he muttered, thinking aloud. He looked once more at the night sky, clear now, and sparkling with stars. There was only one thing they could do. He looked toward the north. 'How far do you reckon?' asked Andy.

'How far to where?' Mike replied.

'Turkey.'

Mike's eyes widened, his thick eyebrows arching above them. 'Excuse me?'

'If we go north, we can drive out of Iraq and make our way home via Syria or Turkey.'

'You plan to drive all the way home?'

Andy turned to look at him, 'Yeah. I've got two kids and a wife who need me. I want to go home.'

'Hmmm. I guess there's not much we can do.'

'No. It's not like we got a shit-load of choice here,' said Andy. 'Anyway, we might get lucky and run into some troops … yours or ours. Who knows?'

Mike nodded. 'I guess it's about 150 miles to the border with Turkey.'

Andy pursed his lips. 'As the crow flies. More like 200 if we want to avoid any more big towns and stay off the main northbound road.'

'Then what?'

Andy shrugged. 'Then we drive through Turkey I guess.'

'That's the plan?'

'That's the plan.'

Mike grinned, his white teeth framed by his dark beard. 'You're a fucking tenacious hard-ass bastard Andy, I think I like that about you.'

Andy shrugged. 'If we make it home and you meet my wife, you tell her what a big *hard-ass* I am, okay Mike? Right now she thinks I'm just a dick.'

He slapped Andy's back. 'It's a deal.'

Andy smiled weakly in response.

'You got a family to get home to,' added Mike.

Andy's smile faded. 'Every minute that ticks by that I'm out here is another minute my kids are all alone.'

Mike nodded and looked back at the truck. 'So you better go tell those boys then,' he said, 'I get the feeling they've put you in charge.'

'Ah bollocks, I'm not sure I'm up to it. I can't even bloody well fire a gun straight.'

Mike shook his head and laughed. 'There you see, you ruined it. For a moment, you were almost sounding like a true alpha-male.'

Wednesday

CHAPTER 43

. . . .

5 a.m. GMT

Between Manchester and Birmingham

Jenny stirred, and realised that she had actually managed to fall asleep in the plastic bucket seat for at least a couple of hours. The first light of dawn had penetrated the surreal, complete darkness of night, and as the steel-grey early morning hours passed, she studied the empty motorway across the narrow grass verge that separated it from the lay by.

An empty motorway.

Such a strange and unsettling sight, she decided. At least, it was in this country. An empty motorway with weeds pushing up between the cracks in the tarmac – that was one of those iconic images of a long-dead society, a post-apocalyptic world. Well, they were halfway there, the weeds would come soon enough.

Looking around, she could see that five or six of the dozen or so people that had converged last night on the burger van, had set off during the night. There was nothing left to plunder here; the fizzy drinks and burger buns were all gone. She decided they should make a move too.

Paul stirred not long after Jenny.

He stretched a little, nodded silently at her and then with a discreet jerk of his head towards the M1, he suggested they might as well make a start whilst the going was good.

As she picked up her overnight bag, buttoned her jacket and turned up the collar against the cool morning breeze, one of the other travellers slumbering in the plastic chairs stirred.

'Is it okay if I come along with you?' she asked quietly.

Jenny could see why the woman was keen to come along. The other people, still sleeping, were all men of varying ages. They stared at each other silently, both sharing the same thought.

Today, and tomorrow, and for God knows how long … you don't want to be a woman on your own.

'Sure,' muttered Jenny, pleased to make their number three.

The woman, dark haired, in her early thirties Jenny guessed, wore a navy-blue business trouser-suit that was doing a reasonable job of hiding forty or fifty pounds of surplus weight. She picked up her handbag and weaved her way through the occupied plastic chairs careful not to bump the snoring, wheezing occupants.

She put a hand out towards Jenny, 'I'm Ruth,' she muttered with a broad, no nonsense, tell-it-how-it-is Brummie accent.

'Jenny,' she replied, 'and this is Paul.'

'Hi,' he grunted, with a perfunctory glance towards her.

Jenny shook Ruth's extended hand with a tired smile.

'Let's go then,' said Paul, turning to head up the lay-by leading on to the motorway, heading south.

'So where are you two trying to get to?' Ruth asked Jenny, as they started after him.

'London.'

'I want to get to Coventry.'

'Okay, well that's on the way then.'

They walked down the fast lane alongside the central barrier most of the time, subconsciously keeping a wary distance from the hard shoulder, and the occasional clusters of bushes and exhaust-poisoned and atrophied trees that grew along the motorway banking. The sky was clear and the morning soon warmed up as the sun breached the horizon.

They walked in silence, each of them lost in their own thoughts and worries, but also aware of how strangely silent it was. No planes, no distant rumble of traffic, nothing at all on the motorway, not even military traffic, something Jenny had thought they might see a lot of. Eventually, it was Ruth who broke the silence.

'Are you two married or something?'

Jenny stepped in quickly, 'Oh God no! We just sort of ended up sharing a taxi that got caught up in a blockade on the M1. We're both heading for London, made sense to travel together,' she replied. And then added, 'I've got family in London, children I have to get to.'

'And I had a meeting,' said Paul, 'an important bloody meeting to close a deal. I had a lot of money riding on that one. I suppose that's all fucking history now,' he muttered. 'Now I just want to get back to my flat before some snotty little bastards see it's empty, break in and clear me out.'

'What about you?' Jenny asked, looking at Ruth.

'I'm an account manager. I was doing my rounds when this ... thing started. I want to get home to my hubby. He's useless without me.'

'Not so far for you then.'

'Far enough on foot. This is ridiculous – closing the motorways like this. I mean what the hell was the bloody government thinking?'

Reduce population migration from the cities. That's what Andy would have dryly answered, thought Jenny. It was the first step in disaster management – you have to control the movement of people as quickly as possible.

'I can't believe what's happened in the last day,' continued Ruth. 'You just don't expect this sort of thing in this country. Do you know what I mean?'

'That's what I thought,' said Paul. 'I think this isn't as bad as it seems.'

Jenny looked at him. 'What do you mean?'

'Well, I think what's happened is that the government panicked, they overdid the measures, and *that's* what's caused all the rioting and disorder – classic fucking overkill cock-up. I mean blocking the motorways? Stopping the trains and coaches? What the hell was that all about? Of course, doing that, it's made everyone think the end of the world is nigh. So what does that make them do? They start panic buying, you end up with food running out in the shops, people getting even more worked up. Christ, they couldn't have screwed this up more if they'd tried.'

'There's been a whole load of riots, I heard that on the news earlier,' said Ruth.

'And this is going to easily last another couple of days before everyone wakes up and realises we're not in as bad a state as we thought we were. Until then though, I'd rather get home and off the street.'

Ruth look appalled. 'This is England for God's sake! Surely we can look after ourselves for a week without acting like a bunch of savages going mad?'

'Who says this is going to be all over in a week?' said Jenny.

The other two looked at her.

'I'm just saying.'

Paul shook his head. 'This'll be over in a few days, once the rioting calms down in the Middle East, and then we'll look back at our own riots in disgust. And guess what? There'll be a whole load of voyeuristic CCTV reality programmes showing the thuggish idiots that took part. And hopefully the bastards will be arrested.'

'And what happens if things don't calm down in the Middle East? What happens if we continue into a second week, or a third week without oil and regular shipments of food from all over the world?' said Jenny.

'Oh, Paul's right. It'll sort itself out before then, I'm sure,' said Ruth.

'But what if it *doesn't*? This is the third day. Already I've seen someone killed with my own eyes! What am I going to see on day five? Or day seven? Let alone in two or three weeks?'

'Calm down,' said Paul, 'things have a way of being anti-climactic in this country. Remember the SARS scare, the bird flu scare? There were experts all over the TV telling us how millions would die and the economy would spiral out of control. This'll pass.'

They walked along the motorway until mid-morning, spotting no one except one group of people on the opposite side of the motorway heading north. As they passed each other, there was no exchange of news, just a politely exchanged 'good morning'.

Shortly after they saw a sign advertising Beauford Motorway Services five miles ahead, and as it turned midday they veered off the motorway on to the slip-road leading up to it.

They were all very thirsty. Paul had a notion that the facilities would most probably be closed up and the staff sent home until this unrest had played itself out. They could help themselves to a few bottles of water and a few sandwiches; even if they did end up being recorded on CCTV. He said he was thirsty and hungry enough to accept the risk of getting a rap on the knuckles and a fine several months from now.

They walked across the car-park, which was empty except for a small area reserved for staff, where a solitary car was parked snugly beside a delivery truck. The service station consisted of a Chevco petrol station, a glass-fronted pavilion with a billboard announcing that inside they'd find a Burger King, a KFC, an amusement arcade, a TQ Sports outlet, a Dillon's Newsagent and toilets.

Jenny looked at the pavilion, and through the smoky-brown tinted glass she could see movement. There were people inside, looking warily out at them.

'It's not empty,' she said.

'I know, I see them too,' Paul replied. 'Well, I've got some money on me. I'll buy us some water and sandwiches.'

They crossed the car-park, and as they approached the wide revolving glass door at the entrance, a lean man in his mid-fifties, with a receding hairline and small metal-rimmed glasses emerged from the gloom inside. He pushed against a glass panel of the motionless, revolving door, heaving it sluggishly round until he stood outside, in front of them.

He planted his legs firmly apart, straightened up, and produced a child's cricket bat, which he swung casually from side to side. It looked like his best attempt to appear threatening. His slight, marathon runner's frame, narrow shoulders, and nerdy short-sleeved office shirt topped with a lawn-green tie and matching green plastic name-tag wasn't helping him.

'We're closed,' he announced curtly, slapping the cricket bat into the palm of one bony hand for effect. 'We've had enough trouble already this morning.'

Jenny noticed some cracks for the first time, scrapes and scuff marks on the thick, reinforced glass at the front of the services pavilion, and scattered across the deserted parking lot; dislodged paving tiles, broken – presumably picked up and dropped – to produce handy fist-sized projectiles. Clearly there had been something going on.

'Bloody pack of yobs were here last night, trying to break in and help themselves,' the man continued.

'Look,' said Jenny, 'we've been walking since yesterday lunchtime. We're thirsty and hungry. We've got money. We just wanted to buy a bottle or two of water, and maybe a few sandwiches.'

The man shook his head disdainfully. 'Money? Money doesn't mean anything right now.'

Jenny could see he was nervous, twitchy.

'Are you in charge here?'

He nodded. 'I'm the shift manager,' he replied.

'And the others?'

He cast a glance over his shoulder at the people inside, looking warily out through the smoky glass to see how their boss was handling the situation.

'What's left of yesterday's shift,' he replied. 'They're the ones who get the bus in. Those who had cars buggered off, leaving these poor sods behind. They're mostly immigrants, speak very little English and they're frightened and confused by what's going on.' He shrugged. 'They're better off here with me, whilst things are like this. And anyway, we've got power here – an auxiliary generator.'

'That's good.'

'And they're helping guard the stock,' he added. 'We had some little bastards tried to force their way in last night, before we'd managed to lock up the front entrance. They beat up Julia, my deputy shift manager, when she tried to stop them.'

'*Little bastards?* Do you mean kids?' asked Paul.

'Kids – no. Most of them were teenagers. You know the kind, townies, hoodies, chavs, pikies, neds ... I'm sure you know the type I mean.'

Townies. Jenny knew what those were. That was the term Leona used to describe the sort of mouthy little buggers who gathered in surly, hooded groups on street corners.

Ruth craned her neck around the manager to look at his staff peering out through the glass. 'Is she okay?'

'Of course she's not. They broke her arm, and her face is a mess.'

'I'm a nurse, let me have a look at her,' said Ruth.

Jenny and Paul turned to look at her. 'You said you were a—'

'I was a nurse first.'

The manager looked at Ruth. 'Oh blimey, would you? I just don't know what to do for her. She's in a lot of pain. She's been screaming, crying all morning, disturbing the other members of staff.'

'Can we all come in?' asked Paul.

The manager looked them over quickly. 'Well I suppose so.'

CHAPTER 44

. . . .

11.31 a.m. GMT

Shepherd's Bush, London

Leona looked out of the lounge window, across Jill's small front garden, on to the leafy avenue outside, lined with parked cars, mostly very nice ones. Last night she had sat up in bed, terrified, unable to sleep, listening to the noises outside.

Several groups of kids, mostly lads judging by their voices, had been up and down the street in their cars, the bass from their music systems pounding so loud the bedroom window had rattled. She heard them running around kicking over bins, having a lot of fun by the sound of it.

They were drunk. She heard the clinking of carrier-bags full of booty, and the shatter of empty bottles casually tossed on to the pavement. Leona guessed they had been to Ashid's Off-licence at the top of their road, and swept the shelves clean. They were making the most of it, celebrating the total black-out, and the total absence of police.

What she found most disturbing was the sense of ownership these lads – there'd been teenagers and young men among them too – had of the street. It was all *their* playground now that it was clear the police weren't likely to come calling any time soon.

Leona wondered how long the novelty of messing around up and down the narrow avenue would last, though. She wondered when they'd decide that the houses on either side of it were a part of their playground too. She shuddered at the thought that the only reason they hadn't broken into any of the houses down St Stephen's Avenue last night was that the idea simply hadn't occurred to them yet.

They'd been having too much fun drag-racing up and down, messing around with the wheelie bins, smashing up some of the sillier garden orna-ments and uprooting someone's willow saplings.

They hadn't worked out yet that in fact they could do *anything* they wanted right now.

Anything.

Until, that is, the police got a grip on things again – whenever that was likely to happen.

Leona noticed Daniel had managed to sleep beside her through most of it. But then he was a little more used to this kind of ruckus, coming as he had, from various foster homes in Southend, overlooking the sea, and the parking strip used most nights by joyriders showing off their PlayStation-honed driving skills.

Jake had somehow managed to get some sleep as well.

The noises had continued until the first grey rays of dawn had stained the sky, and then it had gradually quietened down, and the last thing she'd heard – as her watch showed half past five – was one of them, left behind by the others, heaving up his guts in someone's garden and groaning loudly, several dozen yards up the street.

At about nine, both Daniel and Jacob rose tiredly and padded barefoot downstairs to join her in the kitchen. Leona had found a wind-up radio in Jill's study, and had quickly found several stations still busily broadcasting.

'Is the power back on?' asked Daniel hopefully as he entered.

Leona shook her head and held up the radio for him to see. 'You wind it up for power.'

'Oh,' he replied, disappointed.

Jacob looked around. 'I want some cereal.'

'There's the BBC World Service still doing its thing. And Capital FM, and one or two others.'

Daniel offered her a hopeful shrug, 'So maybe it's not so bad out there then?'

She turned to look at him. 'Listen to it Dan, it's horrible ... the things that are happening.'

'Can I have some cereal?' piped Jacob again.

Leona turned irritably on him. 'No!'

'Why not?'

'There's no milk in the fridge. If you want cereal, you'll just have to have it dry, without milk.'

'I want milk on it,' Jacob answered.

She turned the radio up. 'Just listen to it, Dan. God, we're in a real mess.'

'... burning across the city. It looks like Beirut, or no, more like Baghdad the day after the fall of Saddam's regime. I've never seen anything like this in Britain, the riots last night, the total lawlessness. I have heard there were isolated areas of order, and in some smaller towns we've heard the fire service was still functioning, and the police were seen, although largely unable to intervene. There has been no further comment from the Prime Minister or any senior government representatives, however the provisional crisis authority, "Cobra", has continued to broadcast a general call for calm ...'

'Can I have some toast then, Lee?'

'... amongst the population, reassuring everyone that measures have been taken to ensure order will be returned during the course of the day. Last night's widespread power-outs across the country, which helped fuel the panic and the riots, were described as a transitory event with authority for the distribution and allocation of power being switched from the utility companies to regional emergency authorities. A spokesman for Cobra confirmed that, for the next few days, there was going to be a lot less power available with France no longer able to export a surplus, and Russia temporarily suspending exports of natural gas whilst the crisis is ongoing. A rationed system of distribution is being put into effect with most regions, we've been assured, receiving power for a short period every day. In addition, we're being told that supplies of food and bottled water have been secured and stockpiled and a rationing system will be announced shortly. Meanwhile, I've been hearing broadcasts from other countries in Europe and across the world. This has hit everyone equally badly it seems. In France, rioting in the southern ...'

'Leona, can I have some toas—'

'Shut up!' snapped Leona. 'Can't you see I'm trying to listen?'

'But I'm hungry. I want some toast!'

'And how the fuck am I supposed to make you some toast, Jacob? Hmmm?'

Jacob's mouth hung open. 'You said the "F" word.'

'Yes I did, didn't I?' she replied. 'I'm sorry.'

Jacob shrugged, 'S'okay, I won't tell Mum or Dad, or anything.'

Leona felt a pang of guilt for lashing out at him like that. She knelt down beside him. 'No, I'm really sorry for shouting at you monkey-boy. It's just that things are ... well, I just can't make any toast right now.'

'Because the power's all gone away?'

'That's right, Jakey. Because the power's gone away, and it might not come back again for a bit.'

Jacob nodded silently, his eyebrows knitted in concentration as he absorbed that concept for a moment.

'So,' he continued, 'if the power's gone away, how will Mum and Dad come home? They need power to come home.'

Leona suddenly felt tears fighting their way up; tears of panic and grief.

They were both out there in this horrible mess, both of them alone. There was no way of knowing what sort of trouble they might be in, if they were hurt, or worse.

Jesus, don't even think like that.

'They'll find a way home, Jacob,' she said offering him a quick reassuring smile. 'They'll be home sometime soon. And all we've got to do is sit tight here and wait for them, okay?'

Jacob nodded. But he knew in some way, that his big sister was telling him a white lie.

A good lie.

That's what Mum called white lies; the ones you tell to cheer people up.

'Okay,' he said, 'no toast then.'

Leona stood up, sniffed and wiped at her eyes. 'How do you fancy some baked beans for breakfast?'

Jacob nodded.

'Cold, like we have them in the summer sometimes?'

CHAPTER 45

. . . .

12.15 p.m. GMT

Beauford Service Station

'**W**e've got, let me see ...' said the shift manager. He hadn't thought to introduce himself, instead Jenny had noticed the name on his plastic tag: Mr Stewart. She noticed all the other members of staff had only their first names printed on their tags; a privilege of rank she guessed, to be known by your surname.

'We've got a load of confectionery and snacks,' he repeated pointing towards the racks of chocolate bars, crisps, sweets and canned drinks in the newsagents, Dillon's. 'And then burgers, chicken, potato fries, we have in the freezers over there,' he said pointing towards the two fast food counters sitting side by side. 'We've got an auxiliary generator that kicks in if there's a power failure, and that'll keep going for about a week at most, and then of course the frozen stuff will start to go off. So we'll munch our way through that stock first. That's my plan.'

'So you're sorted for a while then?' said Paul.

Mr Stewart nodded eagerly. 'We'll be just fine here until things right themselves once more.'

Jenny looked out at the scuffed and damaged glass wall at the front of the pavilion. It had taken a pounding. It didn't look pretty any more, but it wasn't going to give any time soon.

'How did they manage to get in and assault your assistant manager?' Jenny asked.

'That was unlocked,' said Stewart pointing to the large revolving door in the middle of the front wall. 'I'd just sent Julia to bring in the ice-cream signs and other bits and pieces we have outside, when they turned up.'

He turned to face them with a confident smile, 'It's locked now, that's for bloody sure.'

'You think they'll be back?' asked Jenny.

'They might,' he answered quickly, 'and they can prat around out there and hurl as much abuse as they like, those little bastards won't be able to get in. Just you see.'

They heard the sound of someone moaning in pain.

'Ah, that's poor Julia. I better go and see how your friend is getting on with her.'

Mr Stewart turned smartly away and walked with an echoing click of heels across the foyer towards the manager's office. He passed by a huddle of his staff sat amongst the tables in the open-plan eating area and offered them a way-too-cheery smile.

'Cheer up!' he called out as he breezed past.

His staff, a worried and weary-looking group of eastern European women and a couple of young lads, nodded mutely and then returned to whispering quietly amongst themselves.

'I can't stay here any longer, Paul,' she said quietly. 'Every minute I'm sitting here, is another minute away from my kids. I've got to go.'

Paul looked at her. 'Listen to me. The smart thing to do, the clever thing to do, is to sit tight. Just for another day, and see how things are.'

'What?' she whispered. 'I can't stay! I have to get home!'

He nodded, thinking about that. 'I'd like to get home too. But you know ... look, yesterday afternoon, at that roadblock was pretty scary, wasn't it?'

She nodded.

'Well, I think it's going to be even worse out there today and worse still tomorrow. You don't want to be out there walking the roads whilst things are so unstable.'

'My kids, I have to get home to them.'

'You said your kids were tucked up safely at your friend's home? And they got in a whole load of food? That's the last thing you heard right?'

Jenny nodded.

'Then, right now, they're probably a lot better off than everyone else.'

Jenny thought about that for a moment, and realised that Paul might well be right. Sitting tight in Jill's modest terraced house; one anonymous house amongst many identical houses in a sedate suburban back road, riding this thing out quietly, not drawing anybody's attention ... Leona and Jacob were doing exactly the right thing.

'You won't be doing them any favours heading out there today,' said Paul. 'Not whilst it's one big lawless playtime for the kiddies. Hang on a day or two, let the worst of it pass. The police *will* get a grip on things later on today or tomorrow, mark my words. Then, shit, I'll come with you. I want to get home too.'

Jenny decided that he might have a point. On her own, today or tomorrow, out there on the road, anything could happen.

Oh bugger, Andy, what do I do? Our kids ... are they really okay? Are they really safe at home?

Jenny would have happily sold her soul for five minutes on a mobile phone that worked right now. Just to know the kids were still okay, just to know that Andy was okay, and perhaps tell him that – you know what? – maybe she'd been a little hasty. Maybe she did still love him after all.

'You go wandering out there today, and well ... your kids'll fair a lot better *with* a mum than *without.*'

Jenny looked uncertainly through the scuffed plastic.

'Hang on for today, okay? I promise you, we'll see police cars out there tomorrow.'

Jenny nodded. 'Okay, just today then.'

They heard the door to the manager's office open. Ruth and Stewart emerged and walked over towards Jenny and Paul.

'They broke her nose and dislocated her shoulder, and her jaw's swollen. I'm going to pop her shoulder back, but it's going to really hurt her. I've given her a load of painkillers,' she looked at her watch, 'which should kick-in in about ten minutes.'

Mr Stewart muttered angrily. 'Those vicious little bastards. What I wouldn't give to catch one of them and give him a damn good hiding.'

'Is there anything I can do to help?' asked Jenny.

Ruth nodded. 'Yeah, thanks. You may need to hold her for me. It won't be nice.'

Jenny grimaced, 'I can handle it.'

Ruth looked at Mr Stewart. 'Is there any booze in this place?'

'Uh ... yes,' he answered awkwardly, 'there's ahh ... a bottle of brandy in my office.'

'Good, I need a nip, you might want to have one too,' she said to Jenny, 'and I'm sure poor old Julia might want a slurp too.'

Mr Stewart nodded, a tad reluctantly. 'Help yourselves.'

'Ta. Come on.'

Jenny looked at Paul, 'You going to give us a hand?'

But Paul was studying the glass front to the pavilion; his mind was elsewhere. 'So, you think those lads will be coming back?'

The shift manager nodded and smiled grimly. 'Oh yes. They said they'd be back sometime soon. And promised me that once they got in they would ...

what was the phrase? Oh yes, "happy slap me 'til I were a shit-stain on the floor".'

'Nice.'

'Oh, I'm not worried. In fact I think I'd like it if they *did* come back. It'll be fun to watch those violent little shits getting hungry outside our nice big window. They can watch me serve up burgers and fries to my staff.'

'Yeah, that'll be great fun, better than TV,' he smiled uncertainly back at Mr Stewart.

CHAPTER 46

. . . .

2 p.m. GMT

Shepherd's Bush, London

'Come on, let's see how things are,' said Dan. 'Maybe we'll find some policemen out there. There's gotta be someone cleaning things up, sorting things out.'

Leona said nothing.

'Come on, just to get some fresh air.'

'Not too far, okay? Just a quick look around.'

'Sure,' Dan nodded.

'All right.' She turned to Jacob. 'You stay inside Jake, okay?'

'Can't I come?'

'No. You stay inside and … I don't know, play with your toys. We won't be long.'

Leona decided Dan was right. They needed to find out, after yesterday's sudden and violent release of chaos, if the worst was now over. And finding a policeman, or a fireman, in fact anybody in uniform, out on the street making a start on clearing things up, was the sort of reassurance she needed right now.

She headed down the hallway to the front door, Dan beside her, unbolted and opened it. She turned back round to Jacob.

'You stay inside. Do you understand me?'

Jake nodded.

They stepped out on to the short path that led up Jill's scruffy, rarely tended front garden to the gate, and the avenue beyond. It was sunny, pleasant, T-shirt 'n' shorts warm.

'It's quiet,' said Dan. They could hear some birds in a nearby tree, but there was no hum of traffic coming from Uxbridge Road; no car woofers pounding out a thudding bass line, or the distant warble of a police siren wafting over the rooftops.

Leona looked up and down. The kids last night had left something of a mess. Many of the parked cars, SUVs, 4x4s, had had one or more of their windows smashed. Glass granules littered the pavement all the way up and down on both sides. It looked like there'd been a hailstorm. She noticed discarded cans and bottles, dropped on the pavement and tossed into the front gardens.

'What a mess they made.'

Dan shrugged, 'Looks just like my mum's street.'

They walked up the avenue towards the junction with Uxbridge Road. As they passed by her home, Leona fought an urge to glance up at her bedroom, worried that she might again see the outline of someone staring out of the window. She had convinced herself since that the fleeting dark form she thought she'd seen had been nothing more than a trick of the evening light and an over-active imagination.

Uxbridge Road was the main thoroughfare for Shepherd's Bush. If there were going to be any police out, they'd be up there, where all the shops were; where the police station was.

As they reached the top, she looked up and down the main road.

'Oh ... my ... God,' she muttered.

On either side, every shop window was gone, and the goods spilled out on to the street; washing machines, TVs, clothes, newspapers and magazines, spread across from pavement to pavement. It seemed most of the damage and mess was focused around the many grocers, Halal mini-markets and takeaways. A hundred yards down, she could see the pale squat block that was the police station for Shepherd's Bush.

'You know, I haven't seen anyone yet,' said Dan. 'Where'd they all go?'

He was right – she'd not seen a single soul either.

'I don't know,' she replied, 'maybe everyone's too scared to come out.'

They picked their way down the street, stepping past the sooty carcass of a car that was still smouldering, and past puddles of mushed food that could have been something stolen from a takeaway nearby, or perhaps was merely someone's vomit.

'Let's try the police station,' said Leona, 'somebody's got to be there.'

The police station was set back from the road, up three steps from the mess on the street that was already beginning to smell, heated to a tepid stew by the midday sun.

The double frosted-glass doorway leading to the front desk swung easily inwards. Inside it was dimly lit by a single strip light fizzing and humming above the counter that normally would have had a desk sergeant manning it.

'Well *they've* got some electric,' snorted Dan, 'it's all right for some.'

'They probably have one of those back-up generators.'

Leona leaned against the desk. 'Hello?'

Her voice echoed ominously around inside.

'Is anyone on duty?' she called again. But there was no answer.

She turned to look at him. 'There must be someone manning this place, even if they're down to a skeleton crew. Surely?'

Dan shrugged. 'Dunno, it looks kind of deserted to me. I'll have a look.'

He lifted up a foldable section of the front counter, stepped through and looked around the office space on the far side of the counter. 'Shit, it's a bit of a mess back here, papers and stuff all over the place.'

He wandered through towards the rear of the area, towards a frosted-glass door, beside which was a keypad that kept it locked.

Leona could see from where she was standing that the frosted glass was cracked, and the door had been forced. 'Looks like someone's already been through this place and trashed it,' she called out after him.

Danny nodded. 'Yeah.'

'Just be careful.'

'Okay.' He pushed the door inwards and Leona heard his feet crunch on broken glass.

'Anyone around?' he called out as he poked his head into the room beyond. 'Any police?'

Leona watched as he stepped inside the room, the frosted-glass door swung to behind him, and all she could see was the foggy outline of his form moving beyond.

'Don't go too far Dan!' she called out, and she heard his muted voice beyond say, 'Okay'.

It was so eerily quiet. She looked back out at the street through the double doors they came in through. Uxbridge Road should have been humming with traffic, the pavements thick with pedestrians and groceries, fruit 'n' veg, laid out on benches and tables, alongside cheap mobile phone covers and dodgy SIM cards. But instead it was like some western ghost town. She half expected tumbleweed to come rolling past.

Dad had once told her about a hurricane that hit London in '87, and emerging early for work to find the streets deserted and covered in flotsam and jetsam. She imagined it must have looked something like this, but surely not quite as bad.

So quiet.

She hadn't heard any movement from Dan for a while. 'Dan?'

No answer.

'Dan? You okay in there?' she called out again.

Nothing, for a moment, then the sound of something scraping in there.

'Dan?'

She saw something through the frosted glass, a dark outline, swaying slightly.

'Dan, is that you?'

It hesitated for a moment, froze. And then she saw it moving again, a hand reaching out for the door.

The door swung open and she saw Dan, his face expressionless, pale.

'Oh my God, are you all right?' she asked.

Dan nodded slowly, as he made his way back across the office towards the counter. 'Let's go,' he said quietly. 'Now. Let's just get out of here.'

'What's up? Did you see something?'

He joined her on the far side of the counter and grabbed her hand. 'Let's just go.'

'Any sign of the police?'

He nodded again and swallowed uncomfortably. 'Yeah, I saw one.'

They headed outside, screwing up their eyes against the bright sunlight as they stepped through the double doors. 'I think we should head back,' said Dan, 'I've seen enough for now.'

Leona pointed to her left. 'There's a supermarket just there, do you see? Maybe we'll find police guarding it?'

'Maybe, but why don't we just go home, Lee?'

Leona grabbed his arm and looked at him. 'I really want to find a policeman, Dan. I just want to hear from someone in charge what we're supposed to do.'

'Okay, okay,' he said, 'the supermarket then home.'

CHAPTER 47

. . . .

2.01 p.m. GMT

Hammersmith, London

T he motorbike across the road from him would be ideal, Ash decided. The man sitting on it was merely an inconvenience he would quickly dispense with. He picked his way across the junction, cluttered with some shopping baskets and about a million sheets of printer paper spread out across the silent road like snow, fluttering in the light afternoon breeze.

The man on the bike was a policeman, and he was busy surveying the junction. On any other day at this time, it would be locked to a standstill with traffic. Today it was deserted. Ash noticed a few dozen other people in the vicinity, picking through the fall-out of last night.

The policeman quickly became aware of Ash approaching in a direct line.

'Can you stay back please, sir,' he said in an even tone.

Ash slowed down, but didn't stop. 'I need some help,' he replied. 'I need an ambulance,' he added, in his mind quickly throwing together some story that needed to only hold together for another twenty seconds, another ten yards.

'What's the problem?' the policeman asked.

Ash continued forward. 'My wife, she needs a hospital, badly.'

The policeman held out an arm, 'Please stay where you are, sir. What's wrong with her?'

Ash slowed his pace right down, but kept closing the gap. His face crumpled with anguish. 'Oh God, I think she's dying! I can't ... I can't ...'

The policeman's hand drifted to the saddlebag where Ash could see the butt of a firearm sticking out of it. 'I said, stay where you are!'

He almost stopped.

Five yards ... just a little bit closer.

The policeman studied Ash, sobbing uncontrollably in front of him. 'There's nothing I can do right now, sir. I can call it in, but the service is stretched as it is. What's wrong with her?'

Ash took another tentative step forward.

Good enough.

'Stay where you are!'

Ash produced his thin blade and lunged forward, sliding into the policeman's stomach as he fumbled for his gun. He tugged it upwards with a sawing action the way you'd fillet a fish, knowing the catastrophic damage the blade was doing inside. With his other hand he grabbed one of the policeman's wrists and held it firmly. The policeman's unrestrained hand reached around to where the blade had gone in, fumbling and slapping ineffectually at it, trying to pull it out.

'Shhhh,' said Ash. 'Easy does it,' he whispered, his face close to the man's, almost intimate. 'It'll all be over in a second my friend.' Ash lifted him off the motorbike and laid him gently down on the pavement, his mouth flapping open and closed, producing only an unhappy gurgling sound.

Ash climbed on to the bike. A few of the people nearby seemed to have noticed and stared slack-jawed at him as he kick-started the bike.

Epsom.

He'd spent last night by candle-light, studying the Sutherland's *London A to Z*. Provided the roads were clear and there weren't any roadblocks, he estimated he could find his way there sometime this afternoon. And hopefully find this sister, Kate, was in.

He spun the bike round, heading around the Hammersmith circular, and turning south, down Fulham Palace Road. Most of the shop windows were gone along this road as well.

He was surprised at how little it had taken to rip apart the veneer of law and order; at least within central London. No one was starving yet, probably not even hungry. But the mere *mention* of food rationing by that moronic Prime Minister had driven them all into a state of panic, further exacerbated by the hysterical way the media had responded and then the nationwide power-out last night – sudden, without any warning.

He smiled.

They had handled that very well over here, perfectly in fact; orchestrated complete disintegration within a couple of days.

CHAPTER 48

· · · ·

2.05 p.m. GMT

Shepherd's Bush, London

Leona led the way another hundred yards up Uxbridge Road. It was only as they crossed the debris-strewn road that they noticed someone else, the first sign of life so far. She could see about five people, an Asian family, picking through the mess of a jewellery shop, making a tentative start at clearing the mess up. She felt encouraged by that. It seemed like a good sign.

Ahead of them was a small shopping precinct, above it a multi-storey car-park. Normally, night and day, the precinct was awash with neon lights, backlit billboards, and thousands of little shopping mall spotlights embedded in the precinct's relatively low ceiling. Right now, despite being a sunny afternoon, it looked quite dark inside.

'The supermarket's just a little way inside,' said Leona. She might have turned back at this point, but seeing that family not so far away, making a start on fixing up their shop, there was a pervading sense that the worst of this might actually be over.

'Can't see any police down there,' said Dan.

'Let's take a quick look. And if there's no police inside, we might be able to pick up a few extra supplies in the supermarket.'

Dan didn't look so keen.

'A quick look, then we'll come out again.'

She led the way, heading into the precinct.

Out of the sunlight it felt cooler. Their footfall against the smooth, well-polished floor, echoed loudly inside. She was taken aback at how lifeless it looked, so used to the place always being busy and noisy with the sound of shopping muzak, squealing packs of teeny-boppers, and the clatter of heels and shopping trolleys and mums pushing baby buggies.

Every store-front window had been smashed.

At the far end of the precinct she could see the long and wide windows of the supermarket. From where they were, it was clear it had been looted; windows were smashed, shopping trolleys and hand baskets were tangled everywhere and the ground was covered with discarded packaging, cardboard boxes, spilled, crushed and spoiled food.

They approached a smashed window and looked inside. It was dark. No power. The shelves were uniformly empty, the floor space between littered with more debris from the orgy of looting that must have happened here yesterday afternoon and evening.

'It's been totally cleared out,' said Dan quietly. 'This is so-o-o like that New Orleans Katrina thing. I remember that on the news. It just … just looked like this.'

Leona nodded. 'I know. You just don't think that would happen here, you know, until it does.'

'We should head back now,' he said, 'we've left Jake long enough.'

Leona smiled and reached for his hand, 'You'd make a good older brother.'

They heard the scrape of a foot on glass shards behind them and both spun round.

'You got a fag, mate?'

CHAPTER 49

. . . .

5 p.m. local time

Northern Iraq

Andy watched Tajican, Westley and Derry as they busily worked on siphoning the fuel from the damaged vehicles across the road – three Humvees and a truck. The small convoy had quite clearly been halted by an explosive device by the side of the road; the first Hummer was little more than a blackened and twisted carcass. Behind it, the other three vehicles were pockmarked with bullet-holes. Clearly, the halted convoy had subsequently been ambushed by gunmen from the cover of the sand berms either side of the road. Brass bullet-cases littered the ground around the vehicles, there had obviously been a sustained fire-fight, and from the dark smudges in the sand, and on the seared tarmac of the road, it was clear there had been a number of casualties.

There were bodies, barely recognisable as such, in the first vehicle, and a dozen more to be found in a ditch several dozen yards away from the road. The bodies were all those of American soldiers. To Andy it looked as if they had made their last stand here; fire coming from all sides, their vehicles providing inadequate cover, they must have bailed out and beat a retreat across the road towards the ditch, and the fight had finished there.

Whilst they were siphoning fuel out of the vehicles, Andy had asked Westley to post some look-outs. Four of the platoon, with Peters in charge, were a hundred yards up the road keeping a look-out, another four men under Benford, were back down the road keeping tabs on the other direction. It was another two or three hours before sundown and as far as Andy was concerned the cover of darkness couldn't come soon enough.

Mike studied the bodies in the ditch. 'Those boys were engineers, not frontline combat,' his voice rumbled angrily.

'Looks like this went down sometime on Monday,' said Andy, 'you know ... judging by the state of the bodies.'

Mike nodded. 'Poor bastards.' He turned to Farid. 'These boys were probably on their way to repair or build something for *your* people, when this shit happened.'

Farid met his gaze. 'It is unfortunate.'

Mike laughed dryly and shook his head. 'Yeah see, I just don't get you people. Why? I mean why the fuck do you people not want your bridges fixed, your water treatment plants repaired? Why the hell don't you want this friggin' country repaired?'

Farid shrugged. 'Iraqi people want water, want bridges, Mike. We just not want America made here in this country.'

'We're not trying to rebuild America here, we're just trying to fix up your goddamn infrastructure—'

'Which I believe was intact and working just fine before we arrived,' said Andy. 'I think it's probably worth mentioning that.'

Mike stopped, and then to his credit nodded. 'Just pisses me off though. We get rid of your dictator, who I'm sure your people all agree, was a nasty piece of shit, and then give you the chance to create a fair and democratic nation here—'

'We not want that,' said Farid calmly. 'We tell you this, many times. But America not listens. We not want this democracy, it is rule of man by man. We want for rule of man by Allah.'

'I don't get that,' replied Mike.

'I've got to say I don't get that either, Farid,' said Andy. 'At least with the ability to vote, to decide who gets to run things, you can kick out the guys at the top if they turn out to be bad. What's so wrong with that?'

Farid shook his head. 'This put man in charge. It mean man decide things. Look what happen in your country when it is men in charge. They steal money, they make huge wars, they lie to people. And then, you have vote ... yes? Then you have new man in your ... White House, and then *he* steal money too, and make the same wars. No difference. Shari'ah law is God's law. It not be changed or ... inter—'

'Interpreted?'

Farid nodded. 'Because man always will change things to suit his need. Always this happen.'

'You're saying Shari'ah law is incorruptible,' prompted Andy.

'Yes, that is what I try and say. Is *incorruptible*. Never change.'

'That's a load of crap,' muttered Mike. 'The men at the top, the imams, they play fast and loose with Islam. They make it say whatever they damn well want.'

'Those who do this, are not good Muslims,' cautioned the old man. 'Saddam say he was a good Muslim. He was not.'

Andy could see his point. Perhaps, in theory, the simple laws of God, as defined in the Qur'an were a viable way for a society to live. Like communism, it worked on paper, but once you introduced a few self-serving bastards into the equation, it began to come unravelled. Perhaps though, there was something to be said for the simple code of Islam; the egalitarianism, the strong emphasis on charity, on family. If they could strip out the God bit, and the lopsided take on the woman's role in life, he wondered if it was something he could possibly embrace.

'Answer me this Farid,' said Mike, 'and I want you to be honest.'

The old man looked at him.

'What is it that you guys really want?'

Farid smiled disarmingly. 'You know what every good Muslim want?'

'What?'

'Islamic world. All of us, brothers together.'

Mike shook his head. 'See that's what I always suspected. There's no room for infidels like me, like Andy, like Israel. Secretly – and most of the time you guys are real careful what you say in public secretly, you want us gone, you want us wiped—'

'No!' Farid cut in angrily. 'No! I want world of Islam with *all my heart*. But, I would not agree to the death of even *one* person, one *infidel* to do this.'

Mike studied him silently.

'Jihad not mean war, Mike. Jihad mean ... *struggle*. I wish for you to accept Allah into heart. You as well, Andy. That is my struggle, my *Jihad*. But Allah can only be *accepted* ... you understand? Not with gun, or bomb, or fear. He can only be *accepted*.'

Andy turned to the old man. 'You know something Farid, I'm never going to believe in a God. You know that, don't you? I consider religion, all of it, to be little more than mindless superstition.'

Mike shrugged. 'Me neither. Christian, Jewish or Islamic, ain't gonna happen. And I'll probably burn in hell for saying that.'

Farid offered them a broad smile. 'God accept in Heaven, believer and non-believer. If you are good man, there is room.'

'It's only the real assholes he doesn't let in?' said Andy.

Farid laughed and nodded. 'That is right.'

Mike nodded. 'I guess I can go with that.'

CHAPTER 50

. . . .

2.30 p.m. GMT

Cabinet Office Briefing Room A (COBRA), London

The Prime Minister had buckled under pressure as Malcolm thought he might. Charles was exhibiting the signs of an approaching nervous breakdown. Which was understandable really. His appalling naivety yesterday, in attempting to appeal to some nebulous notion of a nascent Dunkirk spirit, had successfully thrown the country into a premature state of chaos. Making the job of mobilising the army and police to secure key assets around the country a hell of a lot easier.

Charles' well-intentioned gamble to try and get everyone on-side and pulling together had, in fact, worked wonderfully well for *them*. Certainly in Britain, it was all going to schedule. Social collapse had occurred far more quickly than they had predicted – all credit to Charles' contribution. Now, with all the key assets under guard, and a steady flow of troops coming back home to bolster their hold on things, the situation was pretty much manageable, and measurable.

Malcolm and his colleagues had firm control of COBRA, the civil contingencies authority. There were eight in this ruling committee, five of them were insiders – members of the One Hundred and Sixty. And now as it appeared that all the little pieces were sliding into the right places, it was time to carefully apply the pressure – to nudge the process along, little by little.

And they needed to do this very carefully.

Nearly a decade ago, when the need for an event like this was first discussed, there were those who had cautioned that it could spiral out of their control. Malcolm had been amongst them. Which was why this thing needed to be handled here in this country, and everywhere else, with surgical precision.

One foot on the accelerator ... and one foot hovering just above the brakes.

There was a target, a goal to aim for. The danger would be in *overshooting* that, letting this whole process build up its own uncontrollable momentum and run away from them.

Malcolm looked down at the executive orders he had drafted ready to put in front of his fellow COBRA attendees. Four of the committee would pass these orders without even a murmur. They knew exactly why these things had to be done. The other three would no doubt blanch with horror and ask why the distribution of power was being so ruthlessly limited, why water supplies to large areas of the country were to be turned off.

And Malcolm would calmly justify it to them. Something along the lines of: *'This crisis could last for months, gentlemen. We have entered into an unknown, unpredictable and dangerously unstable period. The free flow of oil is the one thing, the ONE thing that sustains this interconnected, inter-dependent world. It's the scaffolding that holds this global house of cards up, and somebody, somewhere, God know's why, decided to pull it away. We're an island of sixty-five million people and very limited resources. It's our duty to ensure we preserve a pool of supplies that will sustain, if not the entire population, then at least a significant portion of it, through this period, through the aftershock, and through the recovery. Power, water and food are the three things we must now take complete responsibility for controlling, rationing and distributing ...'*

And if those three members didn't go along with that line of hogwash, so be it, it really didn't matter. Five votes to three would sideline their opinion anyway.

Malcolm sighed. How tempting it would be to just come right out into the open and explain what he and his colleagues were up to. They would see the sense of it, he was sure. They would see the bigger picture. They would see that this needed to be done for *everyone's* benefit. They would see what would one day happen, the frightening future scenarios, if something as unpleasant as this wasn't orchestrated now.

But to do that, to talk openly of the *goal* to these three uninitiated commit-tee members, would mean to hint at the controlling hand behind these events, the One Hundred and Sixty and the Twelve.

And, knowing of these things, they would, of course, have to die.

Shepherd's Bush, London

Leona turned round to see three of them standing right behind them. She was surprised that they had managed to get so close without making a sound.

Unless they were trying to, of course.

'You got a fag mate?' said the one in the middle, who was black, shorter than the other two; a scrawnier version of 50 Cent. He was flanked on either side by two taller lads, both lean, white, wearing baggy tracksuit trousers that hung like full nappies. They called students that dressed like that 'wiggers' at uni – morons who pretended they were gangsters, homeboys; white kids who desperately yearned to be black, and did their faltering best to sound like they'd been brought up on the bad streets of L.A. She hated the term, almost as much as the one it was derived from, but it did a good job of summing them up.

'Uh, I don't smoke, mate,' replied Dan with a friendly but uncertain smile. 'Well I sort of do a little stuff, at parties and ... and ... but no, right now I don't have any smokes on me.'

The kid who looked like 50 Cent turned to address Leona. 'What about you, love?'

Leona already knew this wasn't about scrounging a cigarette. 'I don't smoke either. But I bet you'll find hundreds of cartons inside there,' she replied, pointing through the broken window behind them.

'Shit, yeah ... maybe looksee,' replied 50 Cent, shooting a glance at the window, then back to her. 'You wanna go flicc with us, girl?'

Leona shook her head. She was pretty sure 'flicc' meant 'hang around' and not something worse, but she could guess that might be where this was headed, what he was thinking about.

'No thanks, I'm going home now with my boyfriend.'

Dan nodded. 'Yeah, we're all done here … just … just heading back home now.'

'It's jungle time now, not *urban* jungle no more,' said 50 Cent. 'Police are gone away. It's fuckin' mad out here.'

One of his two wingmen, his wigger homeboys, laughed and nodded. Leona guessed he must have been about seventeen, his baby-smooth skin pockmarked with spots around his eyebrows – one of which was shaved into little dashes.

'Yeah, we noticed,' said Dan. 'So, we're gonna make tracks—'

'Yo, man. Ain't talkin' to you,' said the kid with the dashed eyebrow. 'Fuckin' twat,' he added.

Leona squeezed Dan's hand gently to shut him up. There was probably a way for them to excuse themselves and be about their business, but only coming from *her* mouth; something clever, laddish, funny might just do it, make 'em laugh and move on. Anything coming from him was going to be considered a challenge.

'It's mad all right,' said Leona. 'Yeah … really fuckin' buzzin' man. Buff ain't it?'

The three youths nodded and smiled. She guessed they liked her saying that, or maybe they were just laughing at her unconvincing *sister*-talk.

Dan took a step to the left, his feet noisily shuffling glass and clutter across the concrete.

'Fuck you goin'?' said 50 Cent.

'We're just going, okay?' said Dan. 'We don't want any trouble, we're just going to—'

'You goin' nowhere.'

Dan nodded obediently. 'Sure, okay. I'll just sit down or something,' he mumbled submissively stooping down with his hands reaching out for the ground. Leona knew, then and there, he was going to do something.

With a flick of both hands he flung a cloud of dust and shards of glass up at the three youths standing in front of them.

They flinched, covering their faces. Leona took the opportunity to scoop up a crushed and twisted can of pineapple segments and throw it at the nearest of them. It bounced off the forehead of the kid with the dashy-eyebrow just as he'd dropped his hands from protecting his face. Leona was about to grab another can when Dan turned to her and hissed, 'Run!'

She turned to her left, and started to sprint, hoping he was following, hoping Dan was right behind her. She ran for twenty or thirty yards along the front of the supermarket, weaving through the discarded shopping trolleys, before she dared to turn round and check that that was the case.

But he wasn't right there as she hoped, expected ... behind her. She couldn't see him anywhere.

She could see two of the three youths sprinting up the concourse she and Dan had been walking down a minute or so earlier. It led outside on to Uxbridge Road. Dan must have shot off that way – attempting to draw them away from her. Two of them had gone after him, but the white youth who'd called Dan a 'twat', 'Dasher', was chasing after her, kicking the trolleys out of his way as he hurtled towards her. In the split second that she looked at him, she could see a splash of crimson on his pale spotty forehead.

He was the one she'd got with the tin.

Leona turned back round, continuing to run another twenty yards, until she remembered this section of the precinct was a dead end – it went nowhere. There was a Boots chemist at the end of it, a newsagent and a Woolworths, but no access back on to the street.

She pushed past the last of the trolleys, swinging it round behind her to be sure it would lie in her wake and hopefully slow down the bastard behind her as he kicked it out of the way. Up ahead, emerging out of the gloom, Leona saw the dead end. Her only hope of avoiding him was through one of the stores on either side; a choice between Boots and Woolworths. Both of them were big outlets, large enough that she stood a chance of losing him inside, and big enough, she knew, that they had other street entrances – both of them opening on to Uxbridge Road and Goldhawk Road.

She swung towards Woolworths, she could see one of the automatic doors had either powered-down in the open position, or been yanked open by somebody; either way it decided the matter for her.

She could hear his trainers smacking against the ground, and the clatter and rattle as the last of the trolleys was kicked out of the way.

'Come 'ere you cu-u-u-n-n-t!' she heard him shout, his voice reverberating around the concourse behind her.

She ran in through the open door, not prepared for how dark it was going to be inside with the power gone. Even being a sunny day outside, the light filtering in from the doorway, and the long tall windows along the front of the store either side of the entrance, did little to illuminate the low-ceilinged, floor space ahead of her, criss-crossed with aisles and counters.

Here, as everywhere else, looters had been in and made a mess. Around the Pick 'n' Mix sweet stand, and the shelves near the tills, where twenty-four hours earlier Mars Bars, Twixes and KitKats had been stacked, was where most of the desperate scrabbling for things had occurred.

As she squeezed past a till-aisle, half-blocked by a trolley on its side, chocolate bars spilled from it across the floor and trampled to a sticky brown sludge, she turned to check his progress again.

Dasher hesitated for just a few moments in the open automatic doorway, either, smartly, allowing a few seconds for his eyes to adjust, or briefly intimidated by the gloomy labyrinth ahead of him.

'You bitch,' she heard his cold adolescent voice snarl. 'I'm going to fuckin' bitch-slap you, then I'll shag you senseless!'

Leona ducked down on the other side of the trolley, and crawled on all fours across the scuffed linoleum floor towards the nearest of the product aisles. She placed one of her feet on a packet of crisps, and the foil packet crinkled noisily in the silence.

It was enough of an invitation for him. She heard movement, a clatter of things falling to the floor, and then the slap-slap of his trainers.

'Where are you?' he called out, striding swiftly along the top of the aisles, just beyond the tills, looking down each one in turn, trying to find her.

She got to her feet, but still crouching low, began to jog as quietly as she could down the aisle she was in, before he could get to hers.

But she was too slow. Just as she reached the end of the aisle – still stocked with soft toys, untouched by yesterday's chaos – she heard him.

'I see you!'

Oh fuck.

She turned at the end, headed right, taking her towards the Music, DVDs and Games section. She skidded on her heels and dived in between two large racks of PlayStation games. Behind her, the sound of those bloody trainers slapping the floor, and now ... she could hear his breathing. He was gaining on her.

She didn't stop. He was way too close to have been thrown off by that little manoeuvre. She needed somewhere in the shop she could really lose herself, somewhere—

'Fuckin' stop,' he called out again. 'I just want to talk!' he added breathlessly twenty yards behind.

Yeah right.

She reached the end of the games racks. Ahead she could make out a centre store lay-out of tables stacked with jumpers and fleeces, and jackets on garment rails; the children's clothing section.

She leapt forward, throwing herself almost immediately to the ground beneath a four-sided, rotating garment rail, from which long winter school coats were dangling.

Only three or four seconds later, she heard his slapping trainers, that suddenly hushed as his feet passed on to the plain, cord carpet that marked this section, clothing, from the rest of the store. In the dark she could only see the pale grey of daylight filtering across the low tiled ceiling, everything else now was black and formless.

She listened intently as he moved around, the only sound now the swishing of clothes, and jangling of plastic coat-hangers as he passed impatiently.

'Come on,' he hissed with frustration. 'I just want to fucking talk ... I just ...'

Dasher was struggling to keep the rage out of his voice ... and the excitement. Leona shuddered at what awful fantasies were running through that shaved little bullet-head of his.

'Come on!' he pleaded, sounding for a moment like a child begging his mum for a tenner. 'I just want to ...' his voice tailed off.

I know what you 'just want to'. You dirty shit.

Even though it was stifling, hidden as she was amongst the dangling winter coats, she shuddered violently as she imagined what he and his two buddies would do if they got hold of her.

Oh God, he's just a kid.

He was, really, just a snotty seventeen year old, surely no older than that, all bullet-head and big ears beneath that stupid baseball cap. But he was certainly strong enough to do what he wanted to do. And this was surely a game to him, just a game.

Find her – slap her – shag her – leave her, heh heh.

That's how his little game was going to be wrapped up. And he'd walk away from it, pulling up his pants and his baggy trousers, with a cocky 'I got mine' grin on his face, whilst she would be left on the floor, bruised and bleeding, and struggling to find the ragged remains of the clothes he'd torn off her.

'Come on, I thought you was after some fun!' he said again, this time terrifyingly close to her. 'Shit, it's like fuckin' Disneyland out there.'

He had to be only a dozen feet away. Leona held her breath.

'Everythin' for the takin'. It's fuckin' mad, man.'

He's getting closer.

'And no fuckin' pigs either. All gone, fucked off somewhere. Apart from that one we found, stupid tosser. It's playtime now. Playtime for the kiddies, yeah.'

She felt the gentlest breeze of displaced air waft over her skin as he walked by, only feet away from her.

'So come on,' he said in that whiny voice again, 'I'm beggin' you love. I won't hurt you or nuffing, we'll just have a bit of a laugh.'

Leona felt the stiff wire of a coat-hanger beneath her hand. She followed the curved hook with her fingers. It descended into a plastic base; the shoulders were plastic, but the hook was wire.

He was quiet for a moment, but she could hear him breathing as he stood there, above her, almost on top of her. He was breathing loudly, noisily, the run had winded him. On the other hand, she was still holding her breath and wasn't going to be able to hold it for much longer.

Please, please move away.

She needed to breathe, but knew the breath she let out would be deafening in the silence. Her hands worked on the metal wire of the coat-hanger, pulling the hook out into a straightened spike. A lousy weapon to be sure, but it was something she could lash out with.

'Oh fuck this,' Dasher growled angrily, 'I can fuckin' hear you anyway. You're round here somewhere, I can hear you fiddling about.'

All of a sudden, the coats above her moved, with a *swish* from the rail above. His hands groped through the layers of thick cloth.

'I'm gonna fuckin' have you!' he whispered, knowing she was right there, 'Then so are me mates, and then we're really gonna—'

Leona, grabbing the plastic shoulders of the coat-hanger with both hands, wire facing outwards, shoved it up hard, roughly where she guessed his face would be.

It jolted as it came into contact with something, the plastic shoulders broke off in her hands as it did so. She briefly heard something wet and viscous give before she heard him scream.

CHAPTER 52

. . . .

3.47 p.m. GMT

Shepherd's Bush, London

Leona scrambled out from beneath the school coats, as the young man's shrill and protracted scream filled her ears. In the gloom she could see him staggering clumsily around with both of his hands to his face.

'My fuckin' eye! My fuckin' eye! You've popped it!'

She got to her feet and started for the glow of daylight on the far side of the shop. It would have been tempting to hang around, find something long, hard and heavy and beat him with it, but she was frightened his screams would attract the other two.

Best to quit whilst she was ahead.

She made her way out of the clothing section, her heels clacking on linoleum once more as she headed out past aisles of greeting cards, undisturbed, like the soft toys and the PlayStation games, by yesterday's looting spree, and towards the wide shop windows and the automatic glass doors leading out on to Goldhawk Road. All the while, the tall gangly youth behind her, Dasher, continued to scream in agony.

The automatic doors were closed. She tried to prise them open with her hands, but they weren't going to budge any time soon.

'Shit,' she whispered to herself.

Someone had had a go at one of the display windows to the right of the doors, the glass was cracked in several places. She decided to finish the job. Pulling a fire extinguisher from the wall nearby she hefted it in both hands and threw it towards the cracked glass. The window shattered easily and noisily and exploded out on to the pavement, all the while, that idiot chav was wailing like a banshee in the background.

She stepped out on to the pavement, warily looking up and down Goldhawk

Road for the two other lads that had been with him and given chase after Dan. There was no sign of them.

More importantly, she looked around for Dan. There was no sign of him either. She hoped he would have headed home, rather than come looking for her. She was now getting worried about Jacob, and was having visions of him wandering around Shepherd's Bush trying to find her.

Jake was dumb enough to do that.

Leona noticed a few more people. The Asian family were still trying to make a start on tidying up their shop, she noted several other storekeepers picking over the debris of their business, strewn outside on the pavement. They had stared at her and Dan earlier, suspiciously, no doubt wondering if they were out trawling for something to loot. She noticed one or two other *explorers*, like Dan and her, wandering about with a dazed expression on their faces. But nobody in uniform. No police, firemen, paramedics.

No one in authority.

No Dan.

Though there were a few people around, and that made her feel a little safer, she wondered if she were accosted right now, pulled to the ground by 50 Cent or Dasher or the other kid, in plain sight of them, whether *anyone* would dare come to her aid.

She decided to head back home the way they had come earlier, along Uxbridge Road, jogging back most of the way, looking from side to side for a sign of Dan. She counted about three dozen people in total, milling around on the streets, or rifling through the interiors of shops, but no Dan.

Walking down their avenue, she passed several neighbours she recognised by sight and nodded to them. They were in their small front gardens, tidying away the discarded beer cans and broken bottles.

They think this is all over.

Clearly that's what they were thinking, that this was now the clear-up phase, that the hurricane had been and gone. She guessed that they and those shopkeepers were expecting the power to come back on sometime this afternoon, the police and the army to arrive shortly after to supervise the clearing up. And to be honest, Leona allowed herself to hope that might be the case too.

She picked up the pace down towards their end of St Stephen's Avenue, guessing that Dan was already back at Jill's with Jacob and no doubt fretting about her. As she approached their house, she noticed the people opposite – she didn't know them by name – were out in their front garden nailing sheets of plywood over their downstairs windows.

She walked up the path to Jill's home and knocked on the front door, expecting it to open almost immediately. But it didn't.

'Dan? Jake?' she called through the letterbox.

She heard shuffling coming from inside, then a pair of legs came warily into view. A moment later she heard the bolt slide and the door opened. Jacob stood there, hugging a soft fluffy spotty dog he must have found lying around Jill's place. His eyes were puffy from crying, his bottom lip quivered.

'I thought you left me for ever,' he managed to whimper.

'Did Dan not come back?'

He shook his head silently.

CHAPTER 53

. . . .

8.51 p.m. GMT

South of London

Ash made slow progress south, out of London; the roads were cluttered with abandoned vehicles and the mess left by last night's rioting. On several occasions he'd had to make an off-road diversion to avoid police and army roadblocks, knowing that driving a police motorbike, he was asking for trouble if he got too close.

Leaving the city behind and driving through into the suburbs he noticed that conditions seemed to fluctuate; some areas had been hit badly by last night's rampaging, others looked largely untouched. He drove down a high street in a well-to-do area, not noticing a single broken shop window. It was quiet of course, everyone tucked inside their homes – and he spotted many a curtain twitching as he passed through – but to all intents and purposes it could have been tea time on any given weekday evening.

He also noticed that the power-outage, which had swept across the country last night, was not as complete as he had thought it would be. He drove through a dozen or so areas that demonstrated at least an intermittent supply of electricity; neon shop-signs still steadfastly glowing, and street lights – their timing mechanisms knocked out of sync by the chaos of the last twenty-four hours – casting down unnecessary pools of flickering amber light during the daylight hours.

Ash had assumed the emergency authority would have cut *all* power, *everywhere*. But then, he wasn't privvy to how the *details* were being handled in this country – that was for others to know. Each had their own responsibility, their own way of doing things. The bigger picture ... that was the thing.

He finally managed to emerge from the extended suburban carpet around London, as the evening light began to falter.

Along the A road, heading south-west out of London, he came across clusters of pedestrians walking along the hard shoulder, most of them heading away from London. Ash presumed they were people who commuted into London to work and had been caught out by the suddenness of events, now wearily trying to make their way home. There were also a few who seemed to be heading into the capital.

I wouldn't recommend that folks.

But then, they too were probably making for home – where else would they be going?

That's where you long to be in a time of crisis, isn't it? Home.

He found himself wondering again about the whereabouts of the Sutherland girl. This family friend 'Jill', this good family friend, a friend who could be trusted to look after Mr and Mrs Sutherland's children, would she not live close by? Close enough to drop in regularly?

Probably.

But unless he had an address …

What if the girl decides to go home to get something? What if this 'Jill' decides she'll quickly drop in to pick up some changes of clothes for the kids … a favourite toy for the younger one?

Ash was momentarily unsettled with doubt. Perhaps he should have just stayed put there and waited?

No. He could be waiting there indefinitely. Time was everything. He had an address. His hunter's instinct told him this Kate would know who Jill was. Better to follow his nose, than sit in the dark at 25 St Stephen's Avenue doing nothing.

Along the road, he found a cluster of abandoned cars, left in an orderly bonnet-to-bumper queue along a slip-road leading into a petrol station. He presumed, sometime yesterday, the petrol station had run dry, or more likely the army had swept in to appropriate what was below ground in the storage tanks. The fuel gauge on his bike told him he was running low. With some effort, a little cursing, and too much wasted time, he managed to siphon off what was left in the discarded cars. He winced at the thought of the bottom of the barrel sludge he was putting through the bike's engine.

It was gone ten o'clock as his bike entered a place called Guildford. It was dark and quiet.

He found the address quickly enough.

The woman lived in one of a row of apartments overlooking a busy high street. One of those yuppie developments that young professional singles and couples like so much.

No kids then. Pity. They were so handy as leverage in a getting-some-information type scenario.

Ash didn't bother with the buzzer. It probably wasn't working anyway. He kicked in the front door of the apartment complex and entered the plush, carpetted foyer and took the steps up to the first floor.

He found her apartment door with no trouble. A swift kick near the handle and the door swung inwards. He stepped quickly inside.

'Kate?' he called out.

There was no answer. No one home. She lived alone, that much was obvious, there was no sign of the live-in presence of a man. The apartment was tidy, no one had been in and rifled through this place. For a few moments he had a concern that maybe this Kate had gone away, perhaps abroad this week. But then on the answerphone, he picked up a message from someone called Ron, presumably a boyfriend.

'Kate? You there? Pick up ... pick up ... oh shit. You must be caught up at work in London still. Give me a call when you get back home, okay? I'm worried.'

Ash winced with frustration. So Kate had gone to work as normal on Tuesday morning, and then found herself marooned in the capital. He had passed by many people walking out on foot, along the hard shoulder of the A roads he had been on – most probably driving right past her.

So, he would imagine a single woman like Kate, would probably hole up at her place of work, probably with dozens of other colleagues, and wait for the worst of the rioting to subside, and the police to promptly reclaim the streets before considering a return home.

But how long would she wait?

A day? Two?

There was no way of guessing that. Ash decided he could give it a day. He found some food in the kitchen, and a well-stocked fridge that was still cool inside despite the power being off. He could eat, get some rest and take a view tomorrow. There were, after all, other people in the Sutherland's address book he could go calling on. But that said, his gut reaction was to hang on at least for one night for this Kate.

CHAPTER 54

· · · ·

11.57 p.m. local time

Northern Iraq

Andy Sutherland sat at the front of the truck's open bed leaning against the roof of the driver's cab and studying the flat moonlit terrain ahead. The truck rumbled along the north road, a steady drone in the night. The others, as far as he could see, were asleep, rocking and bumping limply as the truck found the occasional pot-hole.

He could only think of one thing, now that there was time enough to spare a thought that was anything other than the basic next step to survive. Last night's desperate scramble through that town, the fire-fight, and watching that young lieutenant dying on the road leading out of town … all of that had, through necessity, sucked his thoughts away from those he cared about.

God, I hope she did as I told her. I hope Jill's looking after them for me.

He'd tried his phone several dozen times since then, in the vain hope that the mobile system out in Iraq was still up and running. Not a thing, no signal. And the local radio stations still running in the country were no longer broadcasting news that could be considered reliable, instead it was a mishmash of religious sermons, calls to arms and incitement to sectarian violence.

They had managed to pick up some moments of the BBC World Service earlier in the day, and it made for grim listening; riots and looting in every city in the country, an emergency ruling authority, and nothing from the Prime Minister or government now for a while.

It was all as Andy thought it would be – a fucking mess.

But somehow, he'd retained a residual hope that things might have held together in the UK just a little longer. They were Brits right? The blitz spirit an' all that? Whilst the rest of the world might have descended to looting and pillaging, he'd hoped the Brits would have at least resorted to some sort of vigorous queuing for a while.

With more time to think, and having heard even more snippets of news, Andy was certain now that in some contributory way, his work of eight years ago had led to this. In that report he had focused on eleven specific nodes in the global oil distribution web; nodes that were vulnerable to the sort of hit-and-run tactics favoured by terrorist groups. So far he'd heard news of seven of those nodes being hit. That alone was suspicious, but the fact that they'd been hit within twenty-four hours of each other ... that was the clincher. Because that was the very point he had made near the end of the report ...

If all eleven of these highest risk distribution chokepoints were to be hit within a twenty-four hour period, the global distribution of oil would be completely shut off.

Recalling those words – he shuddered.

This is my report being actually fucking realised by someone.

It meant that once upon a time he had briefly dealt directly with the people who were responsible. But far worse – Leona had seen them. She could identify one or more of them. He wondered whose face she had recognised on the TV. Someone in the public eye, someone newsworthy? His mind paraded possibilities – a politician, a national leader? A pivotal member of Al-Qaeda? The spokesperson of some kind of hardcore eco-pressure group? An industrialist or an oil baron? Some eccentric billionaire?

Who the fuck would actually want something like this to happen? Who the hell benefits?

He had a fleeting vision of some stereotypical Bond bad guy, complete with an evil chuckle and a long-haired Persian cat perched on his lap. He was reminded of all the weird and wonderful 9/11 conspiracy theories he'd allowed himself to get sucked into for a while after the event. The kookiest one he'd heard was that an alien craft had crashed into the Pentagon and the US authorities had smothered it with the terrorist cover story so they could research all the lovely alien technology at their leisure.

He shook his head and laughed quietly to himself. People will believe any old crap if you show 'em a fuzzy photograph, or some shaky CCTV footage.

'What is make you laugh?'

Andy looked across the truck at Farid who seemed to be awake, studying him intently.

'Oh nothing, just a little wool-gathering.'

'Wool-gath ...?'

Andy shook his head, 'Never mind. It's a saying. Look I wanted to talk to you … we'll be over the northern border into Turkey soon.'

Farid nodded, still gazing out at the desert. 'Yes.'

'So, what do you want to do?'

Farid turned to look at him. 'What you mean?'

'I mean, do you want us to put you down some place inside Iraq, before we go over the border line?'

Andy saw the Iraqi's tired half-smile by the silvery light of the stars and the moon. 'You drop me up here? Amongst the Kurds? I last only five minutes.'

'I'm sorry Farid. This whole fucking mess has screwed everyone up, left a lot of people hopelessly stranded.'

'Yes. Anyway,' the old man replied, 'borders no longer, it all gone for now.'

Andy nodded, he wasn't wrong. It was unlikely there would be anyone manning the roadside barrier, on either side of the border. The Turkish police, just like civil law enforcement in every other country in the world, would no doubt be fighting a losing battle to maintain order amongst their own people.

'Now there nothing left in Iraq for me,' added Farid, after a while.

'No family?'

'No. Not any more.'

He sensed the tone in the old man's voice revealed more than those few words.

'I lose son to militia and wife to American bomb.'

Andy studied the man and realised, at an instinctive or a subconscious level, that he had known that the old man carried a burden of sadness with him. He was a quiet man, not like the two younger drivers. He was reflective, thoughtful, the grief he carried with him so carefully locked away.

He wondered if the old man would open up to him.

'What happened to your family, Farid. Do you want to tell me?'

He nodded. 'I not talk about it much. It is my sadness alone.'

'I understand. I'm sorry for asking.'

'Is okay. I tell,' replied Farid, shuffling a little closer to Andy so as to be able to talk more quietly against the rattling drone of the engine. 'My son work for IPS … police. One day he and other men in station surrounded by militia. They take away police at gunpoint. His mother know he is dead, but I say he will be return. A good Muslim boy, they will let him go. He join police not for money, but for to … ahhh … rec … con …'

'Reconstruction?'

Farid nodded, 'Yes help recon … ah … rebuild Iraq.' The old man remained silent for a good few moments. Andy sensed he wanted to continue, but was composing himself, working hard to keep something painful inside carefully boxed up where he clearly wanted it to remain, and only let out the little bit he was prepared to share.

'We hearing three day later, they find bodies outside police building. My son was one of them. He was *officer* in IPS, the other men ... below him, not officer. My son was in charge. So they make special example of him.'

Farid paused again.

'They cut throat of all the men. But my son, they torture for two day, then cut his eyes out. Then cut his throat.'

Andy stopped himself from blurting out something useless and inadequate. Instead he reached across and placed a hand on the old man's arm.

'My son's eyes they send to me in package later with message from leader that say, "Your son's eyes have seen the work of God." I know these men not doing Allah's will. I know these men evil. They film what they do with camera, and I know it is seen by many like them on Internet, and they cheer as my son scream.'

Andy nodded, wishing he could think of something, anything to say, that wouldn't sound blithe and clichéd. To lose a child is the end of things, to lose a child like that is beyond comprehension.

'My wife, she die a week later when American bomb is drop on our town to kill this leader of these militia. They drop bomb they know will destroy many house in street. My wife visiting with her sister, they living in house nearby, all dead. They did not kill this leader, but they kill my wife, and twenty other people. The Americans find out this, they take away all the bodies and they say only two or three die. They took my wife body six month ago, I never see her again I know. She is gone. I will never see body.'

'That's a pretty shit deal,' grunted Mike.

Andy thought the American had been asleep. Farid turned to look at him, and for a moment he thought the Iraqi would take Mike's comment the wrong way. He wouldn't blame him if he did, it was a clumsy intrusion on their private conversation.

'Pretty shit deal,' didn't even come close.

'*Both* your people and my people take from me all that I love. I have nothing left here.'

They rode in silence for a while, the rumble of the truck's diesel engine producing a steady, reassuring drone.

'Between us all we really fucked over this country pretty bad, didn't we?' said Mike.

Andy nodded. 'It probably could have been handled better.'

'Stupid, careless American soldiers and evil men who say they fight for Allah, but they are *haram*, outside of God ... they *all* fuck my country.'

Mike sat forward. 'Tell me Farid, how the hell do you still believe in God after all this shit has happened to you? And this stuff that's happening now, Muslims killing Muslims ... all of this crap in the name of God. How the hell do you make sense of all of that?'

'I have the Qur'an. It is complete, it is correct. It is God's word. What is happen now, what we see ... is bad work of man, not of Allah.'

'Maybe you're right,' Mike sighed. 'Us humans seem pretty good at screwing most things up.'

Andy turned to look at the American. That seemed like an interesting step for someone like him to take.

'So Farid,' said Andy, 'where do you want to go?'

'I have brother who go to Great Britain many year back. He is all my family now. I join him.'

Andy reached over again and rested a hand on his arm. 'We'll get you there old man, I promise you that.'

He looked around the truck. The lads were all asleep. And there was Erich, watching quietly. He nodded courteously.

CHAPTER 55

· · · ·

10.03 p.m. GMT

Shepherd's Bush, London

It was dark.

Oh God, where the hell are you Danny?

She'd put Jacob to bed as early as she could, after sharing another un-appetising meal of cold pilchards in tomato sauce and a slice of buttered bread. When she had tried to pour them each a glass of water, nothing had come out of the tap. It rattled and gurgled noisily, and produced nothing but a few drips. She realised that from now on they would have to start using their bottled water.

It was another hot evening, stuffy inside again. She opened some of the upstairs windows whilst keeping all of the ones downstairs firmly closed and locked. She patiently reassured Jacob that all was going to turn out well, that Dan, whom it seemed Jacob quite openly hero-worshipped, would be back soon and then by torchlight, she found a Harry Potter book on Jill's bedside table and began to read that to him.

But it was all done in a distracted, worried stupor, one ear constantly cocked and listening out for Dan, whom she expected at any time to come rapping on the front door to be let in. Even though she had, in effect, taken charge of things since they'd left university in Dan's van, she hadn't realised how much she had been relying on him for support.

Just me and Jake now?

Already, she could feel herself beginning to come apart, sitting downstairs in the lounge, in the dark, waiting and listening. She knew she couldn't do this on her own for much longer.

The noises started just before eleven.

The gang of youths were back again. She watched them from the lounge window, concealed as she was, behind the blind. There were twenty, maybe thirty of them, some looked as young as fourteen or fifteen, others somewhere in their mid-twenties. There were one or two girls amongst them. Leona thought they looked a couple of years younger than her. The gang arrived in small groups, gradually amassing in the narrow street outside, over an hour, as if it had been some loosely agreed rendezvous made the night before.

A car turned up, bathing St Stephen's Avenue with the glare of its head-lights, and the sound of a pummelling bass that had the lounge windows vibrating in sympathy. They were drinking again, presumably more of their haul taken from the nearby off-licence. Their voices grew louder as the evening advanced, and by midnight she could hear and see that most of them were pissed out of their skulls. One of them staggered into the front garden, tripped over a paving stone and fell on to Jill's small, poorly tended flower-bed. He lay there, quite content to look up at the stars for a while before turning to his side and retching.

There was a fight between two of the lads. She watched it brewing, it was over one of the girls; one of the 'smurfettes', as she'd decided to call them. She couldn't hear exactly what was being said, but from the gestures she could guess that the older-looking one wanted some squeeze-time with one of the girls, and the younger one wasn't too happy about it. The girl in question, of course, wasn't exactly being consulted about this. Leona had seen countless fights like this brewing outside the pubs and clubs she'd been used to frequenting in Norwich. Always the same pattern to them, a lot of shouting, chest beating, finally pushing and shoving and then the first punch is thrown.

This fight, though, seemed to escalate far more quickly. She watched in horror as it progressed from punches being exchanged, to a knife being pro-duced by the younger-looking lad. It was hard to make out what was going on amidst the frantic movements of both of them, but caught in the glare of the headlight, she soon saw a bright crimson stain on the crisp white T-shirt of the older boy. They thrashed around together some more, until, suddenly, she saw the younger lad spasm violently. Some of the youths gathered round the fighting emitted a drunken howl of support. She noticed a lot of the others were silent, as they watched the younger one shuddering on the ground in front of the car.

One of the girls screamed.

Leona pulled back from the window, shaking as she sat in an armchair and stared instead at the undulating light from outside flickering across the lounge ceiling, as the gang gathered around in front of the car's headlights to study the body.

The party didn't break up though. It continued. The drinking went on, the music got louder. The party migrated up the avenue a little way and at about a quarter to midnight, she heard someone hammering on something repeatedly. She knew it was the door to one of the houses when she heard the splintering of wood, the sound of it rattling on its hinges and a roar of approval from the mob of lads gathered outside.

Then what she heard shortly after made her blood run cold, and her scalp tingle.

The house being ransacked, many things breaking, glass shattering ... and the screams of a woman.

Oh shit, oh shit, oh shit.

Leona raced to the window again and peeped out through the blind. She could only see at an oblique angle what was going on; a lot of movement, the pale flash of many white trainers and baseball caps picked out by those headlights and the less distinct muddy colours of T-shirts and bare torsos. They were milling around the front of the house, in and out the front door. On any other, normal, night, it could have passed, at this distance anyway, as some kid's house-party getting out of control.

But Leona looked at the body of the teenager, now dead for a half hour or so, lying forgotten in front of the car.

This is how it goes, like Dad said ... like a jungle now.

Thursday

CHAPTER 56

· · · ·

7 a.m. local time

The Turkey/Iraq border

Driving north-west took them well clear of Mosul. They drove across the Ninawa region, a desolate and empty portion of northern Iraq. They passed between Sinjar and Tall Afar, two smaller rural towns, again managing to skirt them widely and avoid any unwanted contact. The arid desert swiftly gave way to irrigated farmland as they swung north through the second night, passing at one point within only a few miles of the Syrian border as they swung north-east crossing the Bachuk river and heading towards the border with Turkey.

From Al-Bayji they had traversed nearly 200 miles over two successive nights, and three siphoned refills. The truck, despite the dreadful noises it was making, hadn't let them down as Andy had feared it might, but he suspected they were asking too much to expect it to get them across a second country.

They passed through the border control point into Turkey without incident. The barriers were unmanned and left open. The truck rolled over a fading red paint line across the tarmac and they were now officially in Turkey.

To one side of a cluster of low concrete buildings was a fenced compound containing a collection of various parked vehicles; trucks, a couple of coaches, some small vans, impounded for various reasons.

Private Tajican was on driving duty, he shouted out of the driver-side window to Andy, who was leaning across the roof of the cab.

'We could take one of those for our new ride, chief.'

Andy looked across at the vehicles. This was probably the best opportunity they were going to get for a while to change their vehicle and perhaps scavenge for extra fuel, water, food; particularly water. In this heat they had quickly gone through the little water they'd brought with them.

'Okay, pull into the compound,' he shouted down.

Tajican steered the truck off the road and through a gap in the wire fencing on to the forecourt where the vehicles were parked up.

They dismounted quickly.

Lance Corporal Westley came over to Andy looking to him for orders he could parcel out to his men.

'Right then,' said Andy looking around, conscious of the fact their eyes were all on him, hoping he had some clear and concise instructions for them to carry out. 'We need someone to check over those vehicles for petrol we can siphon off, and which one we should take. Taj is right, we can't rely on that crappy old truck getting us much further, so we'll need a new ride. And whilst we're here, we should take a look inside those buildings see if we can pick up some water and food. Westley?'

'Sir?'

'Whilst we're checking this place out, let's have some men on look-out duty too, okay?'

'Right-o,' said Westley and turned smartly around to bellow some orders to the eleven other soldiers of the platoon.

Andy smiled. *I sounded pretty convincing just then.*

He caught Mike's eye. The American grinned and nodded.

Westley put Tajican in charge of checking over the vehicles and sent six men off to help with that. He sent three of them out on the road to set up an improvised vehicle control point and keep an eye open for anyone approaching in either direction.

'You want to take a butcher's inside then?' asked Westley nodding towards the building nearby.

Andy nodded. 'Yeah. Let's see if there's anything inside we can grab.'

The young Lance Corporal turned to the two remaining men, Derry and Peters, who had both put down their rifles and were preparing to unstrap their webbing. 'Come on, off your arses you fuckin' numpties. This isn't a bloody sit-down tea-party. We're going to sweep the buildings.'

'Hey Wes, go easy mate,' muttered Derry.

Westley cuffed the back of Derry's head as he sauntered past them. 'Any more shit from you Dezza, and I'll rip yer fucking cock off. Come on, get off your crap-'oles and follow me.'

They both groaned wearily as they got to their feet and headed dutifully after Westley. Mike, following in their wake, nudged Andy as he passed. 'You just need to pick up a little of that colourful language Andy, and you'll fit right in.'

Andy shrugged. Jenny might get a little buzz of excitement if she could see her nerdy husband playing – quite convincingly actually – at being a big tough soldier. He wasn't too sure she'd be thrilled if he brought the locker-room language home though.

CHAPTER 57

• • • •

10 a.m. GMT

Beauford Service Station

A bump woke Jenny up; somebody had squeezed past the two plastic chairs she'd been lying across in the eating area, but accidentally knocked heavily against them. She was awake in an instant and sat up.

The staff at the service station were being served a cooked breakfast; quarter-pounder burgers, fried chicken, fried eggs, milk – basically all the refrigerated items ... made sense.

Mr Stewart was overseeing the distribution of this, carefully pouring the milk and counting out the helpings to ensure everyone was getting their fair share.

He spotted Jenny sitting up.

'Good morning. We're serving up breakfast,' he called out cheerfully. 'Join the queue.'

She had to admit it smelled pretty good. She dutifully stood at the back of the short, shuffling line, and very soon was receiving her rations from Mr Stewart, who beamed with what he must have supposed was a morale-boosting smile.

Or maybe he just gets off on this sort of thing. She wondered if, outside of office hours, he was a Cub Scout leader or something.

'Thanks,' she said and wandered over to a table at which Paul and Ruth were sitting.

'Load of bollocks, that really is,' Paul was saying as Jenny sat down beside Ruth.

'What is?'

'Oh, according to this *Mirror*-reading moron here,' he said jerking a thumb at Ruth, 'this whole oil mess is the work of the Americans.'

Ruth shook her head and tutted, 'I didn't say that. I just said the whole thing seems to have been co-ordinated somehow. And surely the only country with enough clout across the world is America?'

Jenny thought about that. 'But what do they gain by disrupting the oil like this? Surely they need it more than anyone?'

'Maybe they have enough stockpiled to ride this out?'

'I heard they had riots in New York, just like we had in London,' said Jenny. 'It sounds like they're having just as tough a time of it.'

'Exactly,' scoffed Paul, 'what a load of crap. I suppose you're one of those nutters that think Bush and his cronies were behind the Trade Towers thing.'

'Well, there's a lot of stuff that didn't add up there. I always thought the whole thing was very fishy,' said Ruth. 'It was all very convenient, wasn't it?'

'Oh you'd get on well with my husband then,' murmured Jenny.

'Lemme guess, they knocked the Towers down just so's they'd have an excuse to go in and steal Saddam's oil ... is that what you were going to say?'

Ruth nodded, 'Yup.'

'You know that just really fucking irritates me, that. That stupid conspiracy crap. You can't just accept that something happened the way it appeared, can you? There's always some gullible idiots, that being you by the way,' Paul smiled at Ruth, 'who have to think there's some big evil bogeyman behind it. Well yeah, okay, in this case there was ... that Bin Laden bloke. But oh no! That's not interesting enough is it?. No. Of course it would be far more interesting if say ... the President is behind it.'

'Well he was.'

'Let me guess ... you think Princess Diana was assassinated by MI5 too, love?'

Ruth's face hardened, and her lips tightened. 'You're taking the piss out of me, aren't you?'

Paul sighed. 'I think the truth is a bunch of bloody Arabs got a little too excited with the idea of knocking seven shades of shit out of each other. It's incapacitated the world's biggest supplier at a time when we could have really done with their oil, and we've allowed ourselves to, rather stupidly, become so reliant on it, that we've all been caught with our pants down. Add to that a bloody government that couldn't organise a shit in a bucket, and didn't plan for anything like this. I don't see any conspiracy there, I see a lot of stupidity is all.'

Jenny nodded in agreement with some of that – the stupidity. 'We've been very short-sighted.' She took a bite out of a burger, savouring the juicy fatty flavour, but instinctively begrudging the calories. 'Really stupid,' she continued, 'for allowing ourselves to rely so much on stuff that comes through just half-a-dozen pipelines from around the world.'

'How long do you reckon this'll last?' asked Ruth.

'I'd say a few more days,' said Paul. 'Our dickhead of a Prime Minister was caught off guard and put the fear of God into everyone on Tuesday. It's no wonder there were riots in every bloody town. But the police will get a grip on things soon enough.'

Ruth shook her head. 'Where are the police though? I haven't seen one since Tuesday.'

Paul shrugged.

'See that's what worries me so much,' said Ruth, 'not having the police around. And how long is it going to be before we see another? Meantime,' Ruth pointed towards the two fast food counters, 'places like this, where there's still food and drink, pumping out nice yummy smells are going to become a target when everyone's tummies start rumbling.'

Paul flashed an uncomfortable glance at the wide, empty, car-park outside.

Jenny followed his gaze. It was empty now, but she imagined it full and a crowd of starving people surging forward, their faces and hands pressed against the perspex front wall, begging for a handout.

Only they probably won't be begging.

CHAPTER 58

• • • •

9.12 p.m. local time

Southern Turkey

In the darkness of the coach he could study Andy Sutherland more discreetly. It was an old tour coach; thirty rows of threadbare seats and air conditioning that didn't work. The men were spread out, legs and arms draped over neighbouring seats, and arm-rests that wouldn't budge.

He sat diagonally opposite Andy. The engineer was staring out at the evening sky, whilst everyone else, exhausted from the frantic activity of the last few days, slept.

What's on your mind, Dr Sutherland?

He wondered if this man from New Zealand was thinking about global events. Having been with him since the weekend, one thing was for certain. He was not on the inside. He was not one of them. This had genuinely taken him by surprise. In any case, Sutherland wouldn't have been stupid enough to be stuck out in the middle of Iraq if he'd known what was going to happen this week.

The big question, the really big one, was – *just how much does he know about them?*

They had used him years ago; falsely recruited his expertise to help them hard-focus their plans. If Sutherland had known *who* he was dealing with, if Sutherland had *any* way of identifying them, he would have been dealt with years before now.

So, unfortunately, it would seem … because he was still alive, he knew nothing about them; certainly nothing that *they* would consider dangerously revealing.

And he certainly wasn't one of *them*.

I could always take the direct approach. Pull him to one side, come right out with it and tell him who I am, who I work for, and pump him for any details that could help us.

It was an idea. If he could only get through to his people, that's what he'd suggest; to confront this man, but there was no way to do that right now.

Sutherland could be the key. He had dealt with them directly, he might have *seen* one of them, might even be able to identify one of them. This might be a golden opportunity to glimpse through that almost impenetrable veil of secrecy around them.

They had scraped together some scant details about them over the years; just enough to realise how little they knew. There was a larger group who referred to themselves as the One Hundred and Sixty, and a much smaller group referred to as the Twelve. A classic power pyramid – the Twelve decided policy, the One Hundred and Sixty enacted it. The secrecy surrounding them was complete ... truly impressive. In the many years his people had devoted entirely to unearthing the truth, there had only been one of them prepared to talk.

And he had, but only briefly. Two meetings, held in absolute darkness, in a basement of an abandoned building, in a nondescript industrial town in the middle of Germany. Two meetings that lasted only a few minutes, with the man's voice trembling like that of a condemned man on the scaffold. He revealed about himself that he was a banking man ... and that he was merely one of the One Hundred and Sixty.

A week after the second meeting, a man who was the largest private shareholder of one of the bigger merchant banks based in Frankfurt, a member of the ECB Advisory Committee, and a senior director of the Deutsche Bundesbank, apparently committed suicide by hurling himself from the rooftop of his penthouse apartment. The man was merely one of their foot soldiers.

By comparison, the Twelve, whose true identities were unknown even to the One Hundred and Sixty, were untouchable. And yet eight years ago, this man, Dr Sutherland – if the rumours they had unearthed were to be trusted – might have actually met one of them. That was why they had begun tapping his phone twelve months ago. He wondered, however, whether Dr Sutherland should just be directly approached now, and debriefed by his people.

Until then, the potential goldmine of what Sutherland might be able to remember of his dealings with them ... was invaluable. He needed to stay alive.

CHAPTER 59

. . . .

6 p.m. GMT

Beauford Service Station

Jenny was walking the perimeter at the back of the service station where it was slightly cooler, darker, away from the glare of the evening sun shining in through the front. It was like sitting in a greenhouse up at the front in the eating area.

She'd pulled out her phone, turned it on and tried once more to see if there was a signal. Of course there wasn't, and there was precious little charge left on her phone. She turned it off quickly to conserve what juice was left.

She self-consciously looked around to check that she was alone and not being observed before clasping her hands together.

'Oh God, please, please be looking after my kids,' she whispered, 'I know I'm not a believer or anything, but please ... if you, you know, exist, please keep them safe.'

What the hell am I doing?

Jenny had never believed. *Never.* And that was something else she'd had in common with Andy: another proud atheist. They had even once gone into school together – Leona's primary school – to complain about the excessive religious content being rammed down the pupils' throats. An atheist household, they always had been, and now, here she was, praying, for Chrissakes.

I don't care. I'll bloody pray if I want to.

There was always an outside chance, a remote possibility, that there was a kernel of truth to all this God nonsense.

Anyway, when it comes to your kids, you'll do anything, right? You'd sell your soul to the Devil ... if, of course, such a thing existed.

'You didn't strike me as the God-squad type.'

Jenny jerked her hands down, embarrassed. She looked around and saw Paul standing in a dark alcove lined with arcade machines.

'I'm not,' she replied defensively. 'I'm just ... you know, just desperate I suppose.'

'Yeah, of course, you've got kids, haven't you?' said Paul, running his hands along the back of a plastic rally-car driver's seat. 'I don't, so it makes things a little easier for me.'

Jenny nodded. 'Yeah, it does. So what are you doing back here?'

He turned towards the arcade machine, stroking the padded vinyl of the seat. 'I noticed they had a Toca Rally 2 machine. When I was a teenager I used to play that a lot. I put a lot of money in these over the years,' he said wistfully. 'Classic driving game. It's old now. Booth like this is a bit of a collector's item.'

Jenny nodded politely, listening, but not listening.

He sighed and patted it. 'You know I can't imagine a world without electricity ... power. There's so many things we take for granted, aren't there? Losing it for a few days like this ... and look at us.' He smiled. 'Living like cavemen. When things get back to normal, I'll—'

'Who says things *will* go back to normal?'

'Of course they will,' he replied, 'things always right themselves.'

'I think things will be different after this.'

'Yeah? How do you mean?'

'I don't know ... I just think ... well, there's something my husband Andy used to say.'

Paul cocked his head, interested, 'Go on.'

'He said oil was like the twentieth-century version of the Roman slave economy. We've grown used to having it. It does everything for us. It makes power, it's used to fertilise crops, in pesticides, to make medicines, every kind of plastic ... basically we use oil in absolutely everything. But I remember this one thing he said. He said some economist once calculated the ways in which oil helps us live and translated that into slave power. He compared the oil economy to the Roman slave economy.'

'Sorry, I don't understand.'

'Well, say you've come home from work and you want to wash your office shirt for tomorrow. You'd shove it in your washing machine, and then put it on a fast spin-dry afterwards, wouldn't you? And maybe you want a cup of tea whilst you're waiting, maybe put on the TV, and throw a frozen dinner in the microwave. Well in slave terms, that would have required a slave to take your shirt, chop wood to make a fire, to heat the water, to wash it. You'd probably need another slave to go hunt or gather the food for your dinner, another to chop wood and build a cooking fire, to boil the water for your tea, and cook the food that the hunter-slave brought in. Still more slaves to entertain you in place of a TV set. And let's not forget the four or five slaves that carried you home from work on their backs, instead of the car you drive home in. Anyway, you get the point right? So, this economist calculated that the average American or Western European would require ninety-six slaves tending to him night and day, to maintain this lifestyle we've all grown accustomed to.'

'Ninety-six slaves?'

'Ninety-six oil-slaves. Even the poorest person in this country, *the poorest*, has his own team of oil-slaves tending to him; a TV set, electric heating, hot water, a kettle, levels of luxury that only the richest aristocrats from the previous century could dream about.'

Jenny gestured towards Mr Stewart and his staff, sitting together in the sunlight. 'Look at them, look at us, everyone in fact ... we've just had our slaves taken away from us. We're all like those pampered aristocrats after the French Revolution, seeking refuge without their servants to tend them, incapable even of tying their own shoelaces.'

'Hardly,' Paul scoffed.

'Yeah? Who here knows how to do the basic things to survive? How to grow their own food? Plan an allotment to provide enough sustenance all year round? How to locate drinkable water? How to sterilise a small cut so it doesn't become infected? How to make a loaf of bread?'

Paul smiled. 'You make it sound like some kind of on the edge of apocalypse thing. The oil will get flowing again. This is just a blip.'

'God, I hope you're right. But this little blip has only been going four days. Can you imagine what it's going to be like if it lasts a couple of weeks?'

Paul's smile faded a little.

'Or a month even?'

'What are you looking at?' asked Jenny.

Ruth stirred and pointed at the single car parked alongside the truck in the staff section on the other side of the car-park.

'Those,' she said.

'Why, what's up with them?'

Ruth turned to her. 'Mr Stewart's wonderful perspex wall might stand up to some bricks being thrown at it, but I'm not too sure how it would flippin' well cope with a car, or even that truck being driven into it.'

'Oh my God, you're right.'

'Where's that wally anyway?'

They both turned to look around, and saw the shift manager officiously overseeing the distribution of cups of tea, carefully pouring it from a large, steaming metal urn into Styrofoam cups. Ruth snorted, amused.

'What's so funny?' asked Jenny.

'You know who he reminds me of?'

Jenny shook her head.

'Remember *Dad's Army*? I used to love watching that. He reminds me of Captain Mainwaring – a real busybody who loves being the heroic little *organiser*.'

Jenny cocked her head slightly, not convinced.

'Remember that episode where they all end up marooned on the end of the pier overnight?' Ruth persisted, 'And Captain Mainwaring takes charge of distributing their rations – a small bag of humbugs?'

Jenny managed a wan smile. 'Yeah, I see it now.'

'Don't you just get the feeling he's loving it? Loving the idea of leading his little *troops* through this crisis? Controlling the *rations*, and deciding how much everyone gets. A real flippin' power trip.'

Jenny could see how pompous and ridiculous he looked, but a small voice of reason inside her head chipped in.

Maybe, but he's doing the smart thing though, isn't he?

Carefully rationing from the very beginning ... because ...

That's right, because who knows how long this situation will last.

He was finished pouring for his staff and approached them holding his large steaming teapot and two cups.

'Tea?'

Ruth and Jenny nodded, and he poured them a cup each.

'Do you think those lads will be back again? The ones that beat up Julia?'

Mr Stewart nodded. 'Yes, I think they probably will.'

Ruth gestured towards the front of the pavilion. 'Your nice shiny perspex frontage may well hold out to another night of pelting with paving stones and rubble. But I'm not sure it'll stand up to a truck being driven into it.'

The manager looked out at the large vehicle parked out there in plain view ... and blanched.

'Yup,' continued Ruth, 'I'm sure that'll occur to at least one of them nonces out there, eventually. And I'm also pretty sure at least one of the little buggers will know how to hotwire the car, or even that truck.'

Stewart nodded, his eyes widened anxiously. Some of the smug, irritating self-assurance he'd been coasting around on, had slipped away. 'Uh ... m-maybe someone could go out there and immobilise them somehow?'

Ruth cocked an eyebrow, 'Yeah? Just *nip* out there and *quickly* disable them both, huh? You going to volunteer?'

Mr Stewart replied, flustered. 'Of course I ... I ... but then, s-someone has to uh ... look after my staff.'

'Uh-huh, pretty much what I thought you'd say,' sneered Ruth.

Jenny had an idea. 'We could drive that truck over here, and park it right before the front wall. I think the truck's probably just about as long as the wall is wide?'

Mr Stewart nodded. 'Yes ... yes I think you're right.'

'And that'll be good enough to stop them using that car, or any others lying around.'

'Yes, a very good idea,' replied the shift manager, shaking his head vigorously. 'So ... uh ... who's going to go out there and drive it over though?'

'More importantly,' said Ruth, 'who knows how to drive a rig like that? I've never driven anything bigger than my little car.'

'And we don't have the keys anyway,' said Paul joining them in the middle of the foyer, 'unless someone here knows how to jack a truck. I'm sure there's a bit more to it than smashing the steering column and holding two wires together.'

'I have the keys,' said Mr Stewart. 'They're hanging up in my office. That's Big Ron's rig. He's one of our regulars. The night before last he'd had one too many drinks in the back of that cab of his and was planning to carry on with his run. I took the keys off him.'

'He's here?' asked Jenny.

'No, I don't know where he is. Probably took a room in the Lodge, a mile down the road. I've not seen him since this all started.'

Paul turned to look out at the front. 'Well, we should get on and do this now, before they turn up again for an evening of fun and games.'

Mr Stewart nodded. 'I'll go get the keys for you.'

'What?' said Paul shaking his head awkwardly. 'I uh ... I can't drive.'

Jenny, Ruth and Mr Stewart stared at him

He shrugged. 'I never got round to learning. I cycle. I take taxis, I take trains – never needed to learn.'

Ruth looked at Paul through narrowed eyes, and shook her head. 'I'd go do it if I knew how to flippin' well drive one. I'd probably flatten the building if I got behind the wheel.' She aimed her words at Paul. '*I'm* not afraid to go out there.'

'What? Neither am I.'

All eyes turned on Mr Stewart. His eyes widened. 'Well I would ... but, someone has to look after—'

'The staff. Yeah, we know,' said Ruth flatly.

'I'll do it,' said Jenny reluctantly. 'I've got a tiny bit of experience with trucks.'

It took Mr Stewart a little while to find the keys, and ten minutes later Jenny was walking quickly across the tarmac, warmed by the evening sun, towards the truck, anxiously scanning the periphery of the car-park for signs of any gathering people. She swung the cricket bat Mr Stewart had given her in one hand, slapping it into the palm of the other, hoping the gesture was enough to deter any spotty young thug who might be lurking nearby from confronting her.

The sense of stillness outside was unsettling. The only sound she could hear was the chattering of some birds nestling in the stunted saplings along the edge of the car-park, and the caw of a crow, circling high up in the clear evening sky.

Idyllic ... if it wasn't so damned unnatural – none of that ever-present rumble of passing traffic. It was just so strange, unsettling.

She quickened her pace, turning briefly to look back at the large window-wall at the front of the service station pavilion and seeing a row of pale ovals staring back out at her, waving her on.

Finally she reached the truck, unlocked the driver's door, yanked it open and then pulled herself up into the cab. Inside it was stifling. As the clouds had cleared throughout today, the sun had had ample opportunity this afternoon to flood in through the wide windscreen.

It smelled in here too. It reeked of body odour, cigarette smoke and stale doner kebabs. In fact it smelled exactly as she imagined the inside of a long distance truck-driver's cab would smell.

It smelled of *bloke*.

She looked around the dashboard in front of her, completely unfamiliar with the lay-out. Jenny had driven a small truck once, a long, long time ago, some place in India in her backpacking days – but that experience wasn't going to help her a great deal. It had just meant that of those inside, she was marginally more qualified to try and give it a go at driving it over.

'Come on, where the hell's the ignition?' she muttered impatiently.

She finally located it.

She was about to insert the key when she heard a thud against the door beside her. It made her jump. She looked out of the window and saw below a group of about a dozen people; a random mixture of age and gender; they could well have been the first dozen pedestrians you passed on any pavement, in any city.

'Hello love? Open up, will ya?' a man called out.

Jenny wound the driver's window down, at the same time feeling a surge of nervous adrenaline welling up.

'Yeah? What d'ya want?' she grunted in a voice she hoped made her sound like she might just, plausibly be the legitimate driver of this truck.

'That your rig, love?' asked the man. He looked to be in his early thirties and graced with a fading tattoo on his upper left arm; one of those swirling Celtic patterns that Andy had once, almost, decided to have. Until, that is, he'd spotted David Beckham sporting one on a TV commercial that had him dressed, for whatever reason, as some sort of gladiator.

'Yeah, it's mine. I'm pissin' off,' she grunted, inwardly cringing at her lame impersonation of a tough bitch trucker.

'The roads are all blocked off, love,' said the man. 'The fuckin' army and police have blocked everything off. You're better just sittin' tight, love.'

Jenny shrugged. 'Yeah? Well I'm goin' to try me luck. There's nothin' here. Just that bollocks service station over there, and they won't let me in.'

The man cast a glance towards it. 'Yeah. Selfish bastards inside won't open up. Water's stopped running now, and we're all getting fuckin' thirsty. Shit ... I mean some people, eh?'

Jenny nodded. 'Yeah. And there's no way in. It's all locked up tight. Pretty solid too. Bastards.'

'We came up night before last askin' for some food. There's no fuckin' food at all now on our estate. Just one corner shop selling fags and sweets, and that's all cleaned out now.'

She offered a grim supportive smile. 'Yeah. It's crazy. What's going on?'

The man nodded. 'Just fuckin' unbelievable. One minute it's all normal, the next minute everyone's going crazy. And now there's no fuckin' food anywhere, because the selfish bastards who got in first are hoardin' every-thing what they took.'

'I guess it's the same everywhere, not just here,' she replied.

'Yeah, s'pose. Anyway. We sort of formed a co-operative, over on the Runston housin' estate. There's old 'uns and a lot of mums and kids that're gettin' hungry over there,' said the man. He turned and pointed towards the pavilion. 'There's a shit-load of food in there they should be sharin' out with us. But the fuckin' manager of this place won't give us a thing.'

'Yeah, selfish bloody bastards,' Jenny said, shaking her head disdainfully. 'Look, good luck anyway mate. I hope you have better luck than I did.' She began to wind the window up.

'Hang on love,' said the man, placing his hand over the rising rim of glass.

She stopped winding it up. 'Yeah?'

'You can help us out.'

'I don't see how. They wouldn't let me in, so I guess I'll see if there's somewhere else—'

'Listen love. You could just smack their front wall in. It's only fuckin' plastic. We thought it was glass last time we was here, it wouldn't break. Things just kept fuckin' well bouncing off it.' The man pointed towards the pavilion. 'You could just run your truck into the front, beside the entrance. Wouldn't need to do it too hard neither, you could just reverse it in really. It wouldn't do your rig any damage.'

Jenny made a big show of giving it some thought as the man warily kept his hand over the rim of the window. Behind him, the other people looked up at her hopefully; a cluster of very normal and very worried people, very much at odds with Mr Stewart's description of the 'gang of yobbos that had terrorised us' earlier. Perhaps they had been kids that were passing through, or perhaps kids from the same housing estate as these people? Either way, *these* were just ordinary people trying to survive, no different to the lucky few inside who'd been working the evening shift here when things started to unravel.

Jenny wondered what right Mr Stewart had to decide who should receive and who shouldn't, and why he'd been willing to let her, Paul and Ruth in, and yet not prepared to help these people.

It was all down to our appearance, wasn't it? Ruth in her dark business trouser-suit, my smart interview clothes, Paul's tidy, expensive looking casuals. Not a single tattoo between us, no sportswear, no trouble.

That's what it boiled down to she supposed, at least to someone like Mr Stewart.

Those nice, smart-looking people can come in. But those bloody oiks from the estate? Let 'em starve.

Jenny looked up. She could see many, many more people emerging from the line of stunted saplings, coming down the slip-road and gathering in loose clusters and groups across the car-park. If there had been tattered piles of neatly ordered bric-à-brac on the ground and a row of sensibly parked Ford Escorts behind them, it would have looked like the early stages of a car-boot sale.

'What do you reckon?' prompted the man.

Jenny shifted uncomfortably. These people deserved to share what was in there, just as much as those inside. But, there were just too many of them – perhaps a hundred now, and, she suspected, there would be more to come. She could imagine the scale of this little siege growing quickly, as word spread to the various estates and villages around this nondescript piece of A road in the middle of nowhere.

Maybe Mr Stewart let us in simply because it was just the three of us, on our own?

Jenny looked around. In a matter of hours this car-park could be full of people pressed against the wall, hammering on it, pleading for food and water, and seeing them inside drinking tea and enjoying fried burgers ... and that frustration quickly turning to anger, rage.

And if they found a way to smash in the front?

Jenny shook her head. 'Look, sorry mate.' She resumed winding up the window and stuck the key into the ignition.

'Fuckin' hell, love,' shouted the man through the glass, his matey, we're-in-this-together demeanour quickly replaced with a flash of aggression. 'Just askin' for a little fuckin' help!' he shouted over the throaty rumble of the truck's diesel engine, idling noisily. Jenny stabbed the accelerator and the truck growled deafeningly and belched smoke.

'Sorry!' she shouted apologetically back, and with an awkward backward lurch that almost pulled the man's tattooed arm out of its socket as he hung on to the driver's side door-handle, she reversed away from the knot of people that had gathered at the front.

The truck bunny-hopped manically, rocking alarmingly on its suspension as she struggled to get a feel for the peddles. The clusters of people that had gathered in the car-park had to quickly leap out of the way.

She guessed her crude bluff that she was the regular driver of this particular rig was well and truly blown now. Not that she had any illusions that the tattoo guy had been convinced in the first place.

Clear now of anything, or anyone, she might hit, she spun the large steering-wheel and swung the truck round towards the service station. Almost immediately, above the loud rattle of the engine, she heard a chorus of voices cheering her on.

They think I'm going to ram it for them.

The pavilion was only about seventy-five yards ahead of her. She drove slowly towards it, unsure how well she could control the vehicle – how quickly this monstrous bugger would come to a halt after she'd applied the brakes. It would be the definition of bloody irony if she *accidentally* rolled through that wall. Jenny needed to park it parallel to it, and as snugly close to it as she dared.

Thirty yards away she swung the truck to the right, taking it off course for a few moments, before turning it sharply left, back towards the entrance, swinging it round in a large loop so that now it was coming in at a tangent towards the front of the pavilion. Seconds later, the wheels beneath the cab rode the curb surrounding a stubby bush planted out front, then knocked aside an uninspiring children's little wooden climbing-frame and some picnic benches before riding up on to a small paved pedestrian area in front of the pavilion.

Jenny slowed the truck right down, gently rolling forward until the cab, and the trailer behind it – carrying a freight container – more or less covered the entire front wall of the pavilion. She then jabbed the brakes which spat and hissed loudly like a giant serpent. She swung open the driver-side door.

It thudded heavily against the front of the pavilion, scuffing the perspex and only half-opening – not quite enough to squeeze through.

Oh great.

She realised she'd done too bloody good a job of parking snugly against the front of the pavilion.

CHAPTER 60

. . . .

6.11 p.m. GMT

Beauford Service Station

Jenny turned round to look over her shoulder, out through the passenger-side window at the car-park. Those people were coming this way; many of them walking swiftly, some jogging. She sensed there was some confusion amongst them over whether the truck had managed to knock a hole through, or was preparing to reverse and try again ... or something else. Either way, people were gravitating towards it, curious to see what was going on.

They were going to be upon her in less than a minute, perhaps that tattoo man would be amongst the first to arrive, and she was sure he'd be mighty pissed off with her, when he sussed her intention had been to blockade the front with the articulated truck.

She guessed there was just about enough time to climb out of the passenger-side door, run around the front of the truck, squeeze into the narrow two or three foot gap between the side of the truck and the front wall, and hope to God the revolving door – which protruded a little – wasn't blocked, or obstructed by the truck in any way.

You've got to immobilise the truck.

Shit, yes she had to. It was a fair bet there was someone out there who'd know how to get this thing going without the need of the ignition key.

The approaching crowd was converging. Many of them now jogging towards her, perhaps hoping she'd broken through. She could see still more people emerging from the distant tree line around the edge of the car-park, and coming down the slip-road. It was as if some jungle drums, playing on a frequency beyond her hearing, was summoning the thirsty and the hungry for miles around.

Oh Jesus ... get a move on girl!

She grabbed the steering-wheel lock-bar off the passenger seat and fumbled with it, trying to work out how it fitted on to the steering-wheel. She looked up again.

They were running, sprinting towards her now – only forty or fifty yards away. She spotted the tattooed man leading the charge. Clearly he *had* twigged that she'd fooled him, that she was on of *those bastards inside* ... one of the *selfish bastards*.

He was going to beat the crap out of her for sure.

'Oh shit! Come on!'

Jenny had used a locking-bar on her little Peugeot many years ago; a dinky little bar that, to be honest, could have been jimmied loose and opened with a two pence piece and a little patience. It looked nothing like this heavy-duty thing that looked like it belonged in a gym. But, she could see a groove cut into the thick side of the bar, where obviously it was designed to rest across the wheel. Placing the groove against the steering-wheel, everything quickly fell into place, and she could see how it closed and locked. With a reassuring click, the bar secured around it, and protruded two feet out, preventing the wheel turning more than halfway round. One might be able to turn the truck around with many backward and forward steps, with this lock still attached but it would have to do.

She clambered across both seats, cursing her calf-length cotton skirt as it caught momentarily on the gear stick, and then, pushed open the passenger-side door, just as the first of those people – the tattooed man amongst them – were bearing down on her, no more than a dozen yards away. His face was stony, rigid with anger, she thought she could hear him calling her all sorts. Jenny knew she was in big trouble if they got a hold of her.

She jumped down to the ground and immediately dropped to her hands and knees and began to crawl under the truck; it seemed the quickest way. Behind her she could hear the thud of trainers against tarmac, and the frustrated bellow of a winded voice.

'You fucking bitch!'

As she crawled on her belly beneath the lumpy grime and oil-encrusted chassis, she felt her ankle suddenly being squeezed by a vice. Looking back down, she could see a hand wrapped around it and the start of a tanned and muscular forearm. Then *his* face dipped down into view; tattoo-man.

'Fucking cow! You're with those bastards inside,' he snarled as he pulled hard on her leg. She felt the coarse pebbly paving slabs grate painfully against her stomach and chest as she was being dragged out roughly from beneath the truck.

'No!' she screamed. 'No please!'

Jenny wrapped her forearm around a support strut on the side of the chassis and held as tightly as she could. The man tightened his grip on her leg and redoubled his effort to pull her out.

'Come on out, bitch!'

Jenny could now see several pairs of legs had joined those of Mr Tattoo. She felt another pair of hands on her shin, and as they settled into a rhythmic jerking action, she felt her grip weakening with each successive pull.

'No, please!' she screamed pointlessly.

Another hard pull and Jenny found her armlock on the strut had been broken. She flailed around for something else to grab, once again feeling the rough paving slabs scrape away at her skin as her body was being pulled out into the open.

And then he was standing over her, flanked on one side by a short squat man who looked to be ten years older, and on the other, by a woman, perhaps the same age as Jenny, her platinum-blonde hair pulled back tightly away from a hard, lean, humourless face, into a ponytail.

Tattoo shook his head. 'Fuckin' selfish bastards like you always seem to do all right when things turn to shit,' he muttered angrily.

'Look, I'm sorry,' Jenny whimpered, 'I was just –'

'Yeah. I thought you was talking a load of *pony*. Bloody truck driver, my arse.'

Jenny tried again, 'I was just –'

'Yeah, we know what you was just doing, love,' said the woman. 'I've got three fuckin' kids and a baby at home all crying because I can't find anything to fuckin' feed them. And there's you, you stuck-up bitch, making sure you and those selfish bastards in there get to keep it all for yourselves.'

Oh God, they're really going to hurt me.

'Fuckin' do this bitch, Tom,' said the platinum blonde. 'I can't stand stuck-up cows like this – think they're better than everyone else.'

Tattoo looked down at her. 'I bet people like *you* are doin' all right. People like *you* who got the spare money to have extra food hidden away, to make sure you come out all right. Whilst us poor bastards are left on our own to fuckin' starve.'

'It's only been a couple of d-days,' Jenny muttered, her voice wobbling, 'n-nobody's s-starving yet.'

'Yeah? You think? My kids are!' screamed the blonde. 'There's nothin' where we live ... nothin'. And no one's come to fuckin' help us.'

I've got to keep them talking.

'But they will,' replied Jenny. 'It's j-just like that New Orleans thing. Help will arrive. The p-police will be back.'

The woman leaned down and slapped Jenny across the face. 'Just shut up! SHUT UP!'

Tattoo shook his head. 'Police aren't fuckin' coming, 'cause they're too busy guarding important shit. It's just us. And we've got to look after ourselves.'

Jenny wiped the blood from her lip. 'You're right, we need to work tog –'

The blonde slapped her again. 'SHUT IT!' she screamed.

'Let's do her!' said the woman, 'Show those bastards inside that we mean business.'

Tattoo looked around at the growing pack of people. There was a knot of perhaps twenty or thirty gathered around Jenny looking down at her, and more were joining the crowd with every second. She could see they were all emotionally strung out – frightened, hungry, thirsty – desperate for someone to take the lead and point the way forward. She could see there were some who just wanted a share of what was inside – no violence please – just a fair share.

And there were some who wanted to rip her to shreds.

She knew it was those of the latter kind who tended to make the biggest noise, the *hidden sociopaths*, the ones who cried loudest and longest for a lynching when some paedophile, benefit-defrauding immigrant, or disgraced minor celebrity was being outed by the red-top press.

The witch burners.

'Pull her out where those shits inside can see her. Then let's do her!' goaded the blonde again. Voices in the crowd shouted approval at that.

Tattoo-man perhaps hadn't intended to take things that far, but Jenny could see him looking around at the crowd, the blonde bitch was baying for blood, and that was swaying the crowd.

'Okay!' he shouted above the noise. 'We'll do her where they can see!'

She saw a flicker of metal, a penknife in someone's hand.

Oh no, please no.

Jenny flushed cold, and her bladder loosened. She closed her eyes with shame.

She heard a younger man shout, 'Hey! She's pissed herself! Look!'

And then she felt hands all over her, on her arms and legs, and where they didn't need to be … pulling her roughly off the ground.

The fear of the knife she had seen pushed every other thought out of her mind.

Don't cut me, don't cut me, don't cut me.

CHAPTER 61

6.15 p.m. GMT

Beauford Service Station

'STOP RIGHT NOW!'

It was such a loud voice.

'WHAT THE *HELL* DO YOU THINK YOU'RE FLIPPIN' WELL DOING?'

A deafening, parade-ground loud voice that cut over the jeering and shouting of the crowd like a gunshot. Tattoo-man, the hard-faced platinum blonde and the dozen or so other people who were manhandling Jenny, stopped. They didn't put her down mind, but for the moment they hesitated.

'WHAT THE *HELL* IS GOING ON?'

It was Ruth's voice Jenny could hear; that no crap taken, tell it how I see it, call a spade a spade, Birmingham accent.

'IS THIS HOW GROWN-UPS ARE MEANT TO BEHAVE?' Ruth continued like a secondary school teacher chastising a classroom of unruly teenagers.

Jenny felt some of the hands that were holding her, begin to loosen, temporarily shamed. She was lowered back down to the ground. She looked up, squinting at the setting sun, melting against the horizon. Ruth stood beside the front of the truck, standing firmly with her legs planted apart, her hands held behind her back. In her dark business trouser-suit, she looked a little like a policewoman, a prison guard perhaps.

'That's right, put her down!' she barked again, a little less deafening, now the crowd had quietened down. 'What the bloody hell were you people thinking of?'

Tattoo-man was the first to regain his voice. 'Fuckin' bitch is with those bastards inside!'

Jenny looked across at Ruth, and realised.

They think Ruth's one of them?

Perhaps in the confusion they hadn't seen her emerge from behind the truck? Jenny made eye contact with her, and Ruth seemed to nod back, almost imperceptibly.

She's picked up on that too.

'Yeah? Well maybe she is, but this is no bloody way to behave! Absolutely disgraceful. We're not a bunch of flippin' savages are we?'

Ruth's chastising approach seemed to be working for now. Maybe somehow at an instinctive level she was tapping into that inner-child thing everyone has. The baying mob right now looked like a class of thirteen year olds being read the riot act by their deputy head.

'But those selfish bastards inside are sitting on all that food, and we're all fuckin' hungry!' replied the platinum blonde, still holding Jenny's arm in a tight, painful grip.

'We're thirsty too. There's no running water,' someone in the crowd called out.

Ruth took a few tentative steps forward towards Jenny. 'Well that's as maybe. I'll talk to them,' she announced. 'I'll make 'em see reason. But right now, let this poor young lady go,' she looked pointedly at the platinum blonde, 'there's a good girl.'

The mood of the crowd of people around Jenny seemed uncertain, wavering. She sensed even more than water or food, they wanted someone to step forward and be in charge, and this sturdy-looking lady with a foghorn voice and a reassuring line of common sense seemed to be filling that void.

Oh my God ... she's going to get me out of this!

Tattoo-man loosened his grip on Jenny.

But platinum blonde still had one sinewy hand wrapped tightly around Jenny's upper arm, her long nails digging painfully into her skin.

Ruth now focused her stern gaze solely on the blonde.

'Listen love,' said Ruth taking another couple of steps forward until she was a mere yard away, and staring powerfully down at the whippet-thin woman. Ruth's generous figure, not inconsiderable height, and that dark business suit – all those subtle things were helping to sway the delicate situation in her favour.

'I'll talk to them, just as soon as you've let her go. We're Brits for Christ's sake! We are NOT going to behave like a bunch of flippin' Third-World savages. Do you understand, love?'

Ruth took another step forward and reached a hand out for Jenny, the other hand still tucked behind her back.

The blonde eyed her suspiciously, tightening her grasp on Jenny's arm. 'Yeah? And how you gonna get them to share out that food? Huh? And anyway, who fuckin' well put you in charge?'

Ruth's face hardened, she pursed her lips and her eyes narrowed. 'You re-e-e-ally don't want to tangle with someone like me darlin', you really don't. I eat little slappers like you for breakfast.'

Oh God, thought Jenny, sensing she was nearly home and dry ... *she's truly terrifying.*

The blonde studied Ruth silently for a moment. 'Hang on, you're not from our fuckin' estate anyway. I know everyone's face. I don't know yours.'

Jenny's eyes flickered towards Ruth.

You've been rumbled.

'So flippin' what? I come from Burnside, fucking toughest estate in Birmingham. Doesn't mean shit really does it?'

Jenny heard it. That meant everyone else had heard it too; a slight wavering in Ruth's voice.

The blonde smiled, knowing the tide was swaying her way again.

'You're one of 'em wankers from inside aren't cha?' She turned to address the crowd. 'She's not from our estate, she's not one of us!'

There was a moment's lag. Clearly they would have preferred Ruth as a leader, but the unspoken agreement was that their neighbourhood was their *tribe*. They had to stick together, because it looked like no one else was going to come and help them out. When things turn to shit, you stick with your own.

Ruth took advantage of the moment.

With surprising speed for her size, she whipped her other hand out from behind her back and held it inches away from the face of the blonde. Jenny could see she was holding something small and blue, a can of something.

It hissed and sprayed something into her face.

The blonde screamed in agony and dropped to the floor where she clawed at her face with her hands. Ruth roughly jerked Jenny forward.

'RUN!' she bellowed, pointing towards the front of the truck. 'There's space to squeeze round!'

Jenny staggered forward, rushing past Ruth.

Ruth held her ground a moment longer, keeping her arm aloft.

'It's mace! Take a step closer and I'll flippin' well burn your face off with this stuff!' she yelled at the crowd of people in front of her.

As Jenny rounded the front of the truck, she spotted the squeeze-gap between the truck and the pavilion's perspex front. She shot a glance back at Ruth, who was now backing up one step at a time, with the can of mace held in front of her like a gun.

Some of the crowd were keeping pace with her, some more had spread out either side. Jenny could see Ruth's steady retreat was in danger of being cut off by some of these people. She needed to turn and run right now.

'Ruth!' she cried, 'Come on!'

'I'm coming!' Ruth called back, not daring to look away from the people in front of her. She took another couple of retreating steps, and then she began to turn.

But something lanced through the air towards her; a brick, a piece of loose paving … it hit her on the back of the head and she lost her footing and tumbled to the ground.

'Ruth!' Jenny screamed.

The crowd from the estate were upon her almost immediately and before the mob closed around Ruth's prone form, Jenny spotted the platinum blonde kneeling down over her, tears streaming from bloodshot eyes, punching Ruth's face repeatedly with a balled, bony fist.

'Oh my God!' she whispered, rooted to the spot.

'Jenny. For fuck's sake come inside!' hissed Paul, standing in the space between the truck and the pavilion.

She turned to look at him. 'We've got to help her! They'll kill her!'

Jenny turned back to look at the crowd. There seemed to be some amongst them who were reluctant to take part, there were even some who were desperately trying to pull others back off Ruth.

'Come on, inside!' Paul grabbed her by the arm and pulled her into the gap. 'There's nothing we can do for Ruth now.' He led her to the revolving door, pushed her ahead into the open segment and leant hard against the plastic door to turn it – looking anxiously over his shoulder, as the door slowly moved.

Without power turning it, he had to work hard to budge it.

Jenny emerged from the segment into the greenhouse heat of the foyer, just as Paul dived into the next open segment. She saw the first of the mob squeeze around the front of the truck, and along the pavilion wall towards the door, hammering their fists on the thick plastic to intimidate them.

'Come on Paul!' she screamed, and reached out to grab a panel as it swung round in front of her. She threw her weight against it, and the door turned a little faster.

Paul emerged just as the first of them entered an open segment. He quickly grabbed a bucket seat from nearby and wedged it into the closing gap. The door shuddered, and through the thick glass she could hear them outside jeering angrily.

Inside, she could hear a pin drop. Mr Stewart's staff, uncertain what was being shouted at them through the plastic, but clearly understanding the intent behind the jeering and taunting, stared in horrified silence at the pale, enraged, faces outside.

One of Stewart's older ladies, a Nigerian, started crying, repeating something over and over.

A prayer?

Jenny's blood run cold. 'They killed her,' she muttered to herself. 'They killed Ruth.'

And we're going to be next.

CHAPTER 62

· · · ·

9.51 p.m. GMT

Shepherd's Bush, London

If this had been a normal night, like, for example, this time last year, they would have been out in their tiny backyard. Perhaps Dad would have barbecued some kebabs, and Mum would have rustled up some salad and spoon-bread. She would almost certainly have invited over the neighbours from across the street, the DiMarcios, because they made Mum laugh. Dad probably would have kept to himself though, he just wasn't that good with Mum's crowd.

The point is, being so warm now that the predictable early June clouds had gone away, they would have been outside, enjoying it – getting tipsy on sangria.

Instead she was trapped inside someone else's home, an unfamiliar environment, looking out at the last light of a warm summer evening.

Leona looked out of the front-room window – the blind drawn across to hide her – on to the avenue. She saw the net curtains twitch upstairs at the DiMarcio's house. They must still be there then; hiding like her and Jake, and hoping nothing about the outside of their hiding place would attract the attention of the gang tonight.

Last night had been truly terrifying, hearing the sounds of them breaking in to someone's home, just thirty or so yards up St Stephen's Avenue. Leona had heard a lot of voices; cheering, shouting, laughing. In and amongst that cacophony, she swore she heard someone screaming somewhere in that house.

She wished she hadn't.

'Are the Bad Boys back again?' asked Jacob anxiously, looking up from the deck of cards he had spread out on the lounge floor.

'Not yet, Jake. They won't come out until it's gone dark.'

Jacob nodded. It was still light now, light enough to be able to read the numbers on his Yu-Gi-Oh cards – just, and whilst there was daylight, they were safe.

Jacob wished Dan would come back. Leona said he'd decided to go home and look after his mum. Jake knew she was lying though. She lied bad, just like every other girl … lots of 'ummms' and 'ahhhs'. Jake on the other hand could tell huge porkers all day long without batting an eyelid.

Dan hadn't gone to look after his mum.

He'd dumped Leona. That's what he reckoned had happened. That's why she'd been doing that crying today when she thought he wasn't looking.

He'd teased her last time she'd split up with a boyfriend, Steve. Jacob hadn't liked him anyway. He was always looking in mirrors, and shiny surfaces, playing with his hair. And the one time he'd bothered to play with Jacob – whilst waiting for Leona to do *girl stuff* in the bathroom – he'd just been pretending, not re-e-eally playing with him … just trying to impress Leona, and look good in front of Mum and Dad.

Dan, on the other hand, was cool. Dan knew how to play. He missed Dan.

Leona did too.

And with him around, he'd felt a little safer too. He suspected the Bad Boys were scared of Dan, that's why they had been left alone, that's why they had stayed out in the street. But now he was gone, the Bad Boys might not be frightened any more.

He wondered if Dan had decided to be a Bad Boy too and make a nuisance outside long after bed time. Maybe he'd got bored of sitting in the lounge, eating those gross tins of pilchards in that yucky ketchup – which tasted nothing like proper ketchup – bored of playing Yu-Gi-Oh with him?

Probably.

He looked up at the lounge window. The sky was getting dark now. *They* would be coming soon, coming out to play.

'Lee?'

Leona stirred, let the blind drop back into place and turned to him, wiping her cheek quickly. 'Yes Jake?'

'Can I sleep with you tonight?'

'I … I stay down here. I don't sleep in any of the upstairs rooms.'

'Can I stay down here with you then?'

Leona thought about it for a moment. 'Okay, go get a quilt and pillow and you can sleep on the sofa down here.'

Jacob got up and made for the stairs, and then had a thought. He came over and planted a clumsy kiss on her cheek. It was damp – she'd been doing some more of her secret crying.

'Nevermind,' he said hoping it was the right thing to say, 'I bet you'll have another boyfriend soon.'

She turned away to look out of the window again. 'Just get your things, there's a good boy.'

Jacob ran up the stairs quickly. It was too dark up here for his liking, so he made quick work of grabbing a quilt and pillow from the nearest bed. He entered the lounge to find Leona staring at him, a finger raised to her lips, the sadness that had been spread all over her face like chocolate after an éclair, was gone.

She looked scared now.

'Shhh … they're back,' she whispered.

Jacob tiptoed quietly over to her, dropping his bedding on the floor, and then joined her by the window. Directly outside their house a car was parked, headlights lighting up the street, the doors open and the sound of bass-heavy music thumping from within. He saw movement inside the car.

The Bad Boys were back.

CHAPTER 63

. . . .

11.43 p.m. GMT

Beauford Service Station

The truck parked hard up against the front of the pavilion obscured most of what was going on outside. But standing over on the right-hand side, Jenny could see round the front of the truck. There was a bonfire out in the middle of the car-park. They had amassed a pile of rubbish and set it alight. And now it was burning ferociously, bathing the place in a flickering amber glow.

Jenny stared out at it, and the mass of people that had gathered around it. It seemed in the last couple of hours, since ...

... since I was nearly beaten to a pulp ... and Ruth was ...

... since then the number of people out there had doubled. She guessed there must be a couple of hundred of them milling around outside.

Ruth.

She'd hardly got to know her really. They had spoken a bit this morning, and yesterday walking along the hard shoulder, but she knew very little about her. She'd perhaps learned more about her in those last moments outside, when Ruth had held a mob at bay for a couple of minutes with nothing but the force of her personality.

She was probably not the sort of person Jenny would have mixed with, done lunch with, back in normal times, but right now Jenny would have traded in every last one of her upwardly mobile friends, past and present, to have someone as Bolshie, loudmouthed and downright ballsy as Ruth, by her side.

She looked out at the Dante-esque scene before her. It looked like some sort of satanic cult gathering. She expected to see hooded and robed figures calling things to order, and some young virgin, raised on an inverted crucifix over the fire.

Of course, it was the dancing flames coming from the fire that lent the scene such a disturbing aura. She reminded herself they were normal people, just very frustrated and hungry normal people.

She looked around at Mr Stewart's staff. She could see they were frightened; staring at the scene outside and exchanging muted comments in Polish, Romanian, Cantonese, she realised that for them – unable to understand a lot of what had been going on over the last few days, and knowing they were so obviously *outsiders* – this must have been even more terrifying.

Paul wandered over to stand beside her. 'That doesn't look good,' said Paul. 'When you get the mob starting to light fires, it doesn't take long for buildings to start burning down.'

'They won't try and set this place on fire, surely? It would destroy all the food and water they're after.'

Paul shook his head. 'I don't know. Maybe they're too pissed off to care about that now. Maybe thirst is driving them a bit loopy.'

Yes, they had to be bloody thirsty out there.

It had been a very warm week since Monday; hot even, at times. And now, there was no longer any running tap-water. She had noticed earlier this afternoon when she'd tried to flush the toilet. They had to be getting thirsty outside, and other than tap-water, cans or bottles, what else could they drink? She'd not noticed any nearby rivers or reservoirs. And anyway, the state of most waterways these days, thick with foam and floating condoms – you'd need to be bloody desperate first.

Meanwhile, inside the pavilion, they had fridge-cold bottled water, hundreds of cans of Pepsi and Fanta glistening with dew-drops of condensation, cartons of fruit juice, even tubs of Ben and Jerry's ice-cream, for crying out loud.

'Yup,' said Paul quietly, 'thirst makes people do a whole load of crazy things.'

Jenny looked at him, wishing he hadn't said that. She looked back out again, at the milling crowd around the bonfire and then noticed that someone was standing on something, and addressing them. Jenny watched the person gesturing, shouting. Although she couldn't make out what was being said, she could guess.

She could just make out the raised voice drifting across the crowded car-park towards them. It had that unmistakable, shrill, humourless tone – it was the platinum-blonde woman. That skinny, hard-faced bitch, in her vest top and tracksuit bottoms, those long nails … and those thin lips stretched across those snarling teeth.

Platinum Blonde seemed to have won over the people out there. Not good.

She was sure many of those people simply wanted to break in, grab some food and water and go home, that's all. But the blonde, she'd want to make an example of someone.

Me probably.

'They're going to get in here tonight. Aren't they?'

Paul looked out at the crowd. 'Yeah. I don't think they're going to be satisfied just throwing a few bricks and stones at this place. They need to get in tonight … they're getting desperate.'

'What if we throw some water out to them?'

A wry smile spread across his mouth. 'Yeah, I'm sure that'll placate them. And off they'll trot back home.'

Jenny ignored his sarcasm. 'So what do you suggest we do?'

He looked furtively over his shoulder before speaking. 'I suggest we leave before it all kicks off. As in, pretty bloody soon.'

She glanced at the staff, huddled together anxiously in the foyer, talking in hushed, frightened tones. Mr Stewart, meanwhile, was nowhere to be seen. He had retired to his office a couple of hours earlier. She hadn't seen him since.

'What? We can't abandon them. Look at the state of them.'

'And? They're not my responsibility, nor are they yours. I want to get home, and I don't particularly want to get caught up in this fucking mess.'

'It was your bloody idea to stay!'

'Yeah, well, guess what? I got that wrong. This is looking nasty and I suggest we sneak out whilst there's a chance.'

'And leave them?' she nodded towards the others.

'It sounds pretty shitty, but yeah.'

Jenny shook her head. 'I'm guessing you're a bit of a selfish bastard in normal life, aren't you?'

He shrugged. 'Call me selfish, but I just don't want to be lynched by the mob, all right?' he said. 'I just know we can't take on all these poor sods. They have to look after themselves. We have to put ourselves first. That's how things are now, I'm afraid. Who do you want to save? These strangers, these people who you've known for five minutes? Or your family?'

Jenny watched the silhouette of Platinum Blonde as she stirred up the crowd milling around the burning car.

'It all came undone so quickly. Just a few days,' she gestured towards those outside, 'and look at us.'

Paul nodded as he watched the people outside. 'I suppose, when the rules go, no matter which country you live in, we're all the same. We're just a few square meals, a power-cut, a sip of water away from doing things we never dreamed we would, from being a bunch of cavemen.'

Outside something was beginning to happen. Platinum Blonde had finished saying her piece and had stepped down off her box and merged with the milling crowd.

'Shit, I think they're about to do whatever it is they've been planning,' muttered Paul. 'We need to find a way out now.'

The thought of that woman breaking in to the service station and finding her sent a chill through Jenny. Paul was right, they had to think of themselves right now. Guilt, self-reproach, introspection – that could come later when there was time.

'Find a way out? Where? How?'

He turned away from the perspex wall, looking back at the dimly lit interior of the pavilion. The emergency generators still running the food freezers were also supplying power to a few muted emergency wall lamps towards the back of the area. 'My guess is there'll be a trade entrance at the rear somewhere, maybe we'll get lucky and no one's thought to watch the back of this place.'

The crowd outside began to approach them. Jenny noticed some were carrying containers; buckets, bottles. She backed away from the perspex wall as they came round the front of the truck and squeezed into the gap between the truck and the wall. They peered through the scuffed surface, shouting angrily as they made their way along the narrow space towards the locked revolving door. The first to get there was holding a two-litre plastic bottle of pop. There was a three or four inch gap between the revolving door's frame, and the door panel of one of the segments. He pushed his arm through the gap and poured something out of the bottle on to the floor inside.

The smell wafted through almost instantly.

'Petrol,' said Paul. 'They're going to burn the doorway down. That won't take long to melt. Let's stop dicking around and go.'

Jenny looked once more at the frightened huddle of staff. Paul grabbed her arm.

'No!' he said quietly. 'If you tell them we're going out the back, they'll all get up and follow us. Those people outside will see that and suss what's going on.'

He started towards the rear of the pavilion, pulling her arm. 'Come on.'

She reluctantly followed him, looking back over her shoulder at the doorway. Several more of the crowd had squeezed their arms through the gap and poured the contents of their containers into that segment. The reek of petrol was that much stronger.

Then she saw Platinum Blonde standing at the front of the truck holding a burning stick in one hand, and peering through the scuffed perspex wall, her face pushed up against it.

She's looking for me.

Jenny felt an even greater surge of fear take hold of her. For some reason, that woman had focused on her, as if Jenny personified somehow the desperate predicament they were all in.

I really ... really, don't want her to get hold of me.

She turned back to look at Paul. 'Okay, okay, let's go.'

CHAPTER 64

11.46 p.m. GMT

Beauford Service Station

Paul led her back into the dimly lit rear of the pavilion, past the amusement arcade, past the closed door to Mr Stewart's office. She wondered what he was doing in there. His staff, mostly older women, confused and frightened, needed him out there in the foyer, not hiding away like this.

There was a row of doors ahead of them. Three of them were toilets, the fourth was simply marked up as being for 'Staff Only'.

Paul pushed the door open to reveal a narrow passageway, lit by a red bulb dangling from a socket in the low ceiling. The passage was only about three or four feet wide and was cluttered with cardboard boxes and crates stacked untidily against the right-hand wall; stock and supplies for the shop and the non-perishables for the fast food counters. No food of course, just the useless crap you'd expect to pick up at a service station; *Rock Classics For The Road* – 48 x CD, 'Beauford Services Souvenir Mugs' – pack of 24, 'Celebrity Head Wobblers' – assorted characters, 24 units.

Paul led the way down the hallway, struggling in places to squeeze past the stacks of boxes.

'If this is where they've dumped their stock, I'd guess the delivery door is somewhere back here.'

She stopped beside a stack of boxes: Evian – 1 litre x 36. She tore open the top flap of the box and pulled out half-a-dozen bottles.

At the sound of the box being ripped open, Paul stopped and turned round. 'Yeah, maybe a good idea.' He left her and carried on down the passage. Jenny cradled the bottles in her arms and followed on.

'Here we go,' he said pointing. 'That looks like a delivery gate.'

The passageway ended with a four-feet wide, floor to ceiling, corrugated metal shutter that looked like it slid from left to right. It was padlocked.

'Oh, there we go then, locked,' she muttered.

'It's okay,' replied Paul pulling out a bunch of keys from his trouser pocket. 'I lifted these off of Mr Stewart's desk a little earlier.'

'He didn't notice?'

'Not really. He was pissed, finished off that medicinal brandy of his.'

Paul sorted through the keys, inconveniently, none of them were marked or tagged.

Jenny sniffed the air. 'Oh shit! Can you smell that?'

Paul stopped what he was doing and inhaled. 'Burning plastic?'

'Yes. They've started on the front door already. You better hurry.'

'I'm going as fast as I can,' he muttered trying key after key in the padlock.

Jenny turned and looked up the narrow, dimly lit passageway, and listened intently to the muted noises that were coming down it. She could hear some of the staff in the main area of the pavilion crying and pleading to be left alone, either in pidgin English or their own tongue. Their voices sounded shrill, taut and wretched with panic and fear. Beyond that she could hear the distant taunting calls and jeers from the people trying to get in.

'Come on! Which one of you bastards is it?' Paul hissed with frustration, as he fumbled with the keys.

A thought occurred to Jenny. 'What if they're waiting for us just outside this door?'

Paul paused for a moment. 'Screw it, I don't know. They probably haven't thought that far ahead anyway. We'll just have to hope they're all around the front.'

Jenny nodded doubtfully, that wasn't the reassuring answer she'd been hoping for.

The smell of burning plastic was getting stronger and she could now hear some banging, it sounded like someone was kicking at the door panels, testing them to see if the perspex had softened enough to give.

'Oh Christ, please hurry!' she cried.

'I'm going as fast as I can.'

She heard him jangle the keys again and this time after a moment's frustrated jiggling around, she heard a *click*.

'That's it. Got it!'

He removed the padlock and tossed it aside, then reached for the handle of the sliding delivery door.

'Please open it quietly,' she whispered.

Paul nodded and then pulled gently on the handle. The door grated noisily, metal casters scraping in the runners along the top and bottom. He slid the door to the side by only an inch and Jenny saw a hairline vertical crack of deep blue light – a clear night's sky.

He waited a moment, hoping the scraping sound hadn't attracted any unwanted attention, and then slowly pushed the delivery door a little further to the side.

There was a thud and the corrugated door rattled, and then with a roar from the little metal castors, the door was yanked to the right, clattering noisily against the frame. Silhouetted against the evening sky, and dimly lit by the red emergency light back up the passageway, she saw about a dozen of them standing outside. From what she could make out they were mostly men, a couple of women, some young, some middle-aged; people from the estate.

'Please … don't hurt us!' she pleaded with them, feeling the cold grasp of fear suck the air from her lungs and the strength from her legs.

One of them stepped forward; a young man with a skinhead, his shirt tied around his waist, exposing a lean, taut and muscular torso, decorated down one side with those popular Celtic swirls. Jenny stared at him, his face hot and blotchy, aggressively thrust forward, close to hers. He looked hard, angry, ready to lash out at her.

He pointed at the bottles of water she held in her arms.

'Could I 'ave a drink of one of those? I'm fuckin' parched.'

Jenny was taken aback. 'Yeah … uh … sure,' she replied handing him a bottle. He took it and nodded.

'Thanks.'

'There's a load more back there,' said Paul. 'A stack of boxes on the right, go help yourself.'

The rest of the group of people surged quickly past the lad, some of them muttering a 'thank you' as they stepped by.

Jenny watched the lad gulping the Evian. He was desperately thirsty, his Adam's apple bobbing up and down as he made quick work of it. She turned and jerked her head toward the passageway. 'You better go after those others and get yourself some of that water before it's all gone.'

He nodded, handing back the nearly empty plastic bottle and wiping his mouth with the back of his hand.

'Yeah. Cheers for that,' he said and jogged down the narrow walkway after the others, weaving around the stacks of boxes.

Jenny turned to Paul. 'I thought he was going to tear me to pieces.'

Paul appeared equally surprised. 'A polite chav,' he replied shaking his head in disbelief. 'Come on, let's get out of here while the going's good.'

They both stepped outside.

The night was warm still. Under different circumstances, it would have been a lovely evening to sit out. Paul looked both ways up and down the back of the building. He saw the dark forms of another group of people jogging along the back of the building towards them, attracted by the red glow of light spilling out from the open delivery entrance.

Paul grabbed her arm and whispered. 'These ones might not be so polite. Pretend to be one of them.'

As the group approached them, Paul called out, 'The delivery door's open, there's loads of stuff inside.'

'Cheers mate,' a voice called out from the dark.

Another asked, 'Any water in there?'

'Yeah, but you want to get in there quick,' Paul replied.

The group passed by without further comment, and picked their pace up to a jog as they neared the delivery entrance.

Paul and Jenny rounded the corner of the pavilion, and from there they could see the car-park and the bonfire still burning, now all but deserted. Jenny assumed everyone who had been milling around it earlier on, must now be piling inside the service station at the front, helping themselves to whatever they could find. She could hear a lot of noise filtering out from inside; shouting, the clatter of goods being spilled and knocked over, but with an almost overwhelming sense of relief, she could hear no screaming – no sounds of violence, no pleas for mercy.

'What are we going to do now?' she whispered.

'That car,' he replied, 'it's Mr Stewart's. I grabbed his car keys as well.'

'Oh right. God I hope they haven't trashed it.'

'Come on.'

Paul started across the car-park, walking swiftly towards the staff-reserved area on the far side. Jenny set off after him, looking anxiously over her shoulder at the pavilion. The truck across the front was blocking most of the front to the building, but every now and then she could see the flickering beams of torches playing around the inside of the foyer and the amber glow of flames coming from the revolving door. The fire they'd used to weaken the entrance looked like it had begun to take hold and she was certain by morning the service station would be nothing more than a smouldering ruin.

Paul pulled out the bunch of keys from his pocket, and she heard them jangling again as he went through them.

'Ah, that feels like a car fob,' she heard him say in the dark, and a second later the car squawked and the hazard lights on it flashed a couple of times. They both headed for it. It looked like the vehicle had been untouched; no dents, scrapes, the tyres weren't flat. She allowed herself to hope they were going to get out of this mess.

They jumped in, anxious to take possession of the vehicle and be off before anyone else had noticed. Jenny dumped her armful of Evian bottles on the floor inside the car.

'Be nice if Mr Stewart thought to fill her up,' said Paul, jamming the key in the ignition. He turned it, and the lights on the dash came on.

'Thank fuck,' he sighed. 'Half a tank, fair enough. Better than nothing.'

'I thought you said you couldn't drive?'

Paul smiled sheepishly as he spun the car round. 'Okay, I lied – so shoot me.'

Jenny twisted in her seat and studied the pavilion anxiously, half-expecting a swarm of people to suddenly emerge from it and charge them down, hell-bent on pulling them out of the car and ripping their throats out.

My God, doesn't this feel just like that ... Like one of those crazy zombie movies?

This whole situation was like some post-apocalyptic scenario; the glimmering firelight from the bonfire, the debris and detritus strewn across the tarmac, the flickering torchlight and the frantically scrabbling crowd inside the building, the noise, the chaos.

Paul drove across the car-park towards the exit leading on to the slip-road that led out to the motorway and headed south once more.

She watched the service station in the wing mirror until it disappeared from view.

My God, this is how it is after only four days.

Friday

CHAPTER 65

• • • •

3 a.m. local time

Southern Turkey

*Y*ou've got to think they're all okay. You know they're okay ... okay?

Andy fidgeted uncomfortably in the coach seat. It was an old coach and most of the seats were lumpy and uncomfortable, some with springs poking through the tattered and frayed covers. He'd tried sleeping, God knows he needed some. He had been awake since Monday morning; he had possibly managed to steal an hour of sleep here and there, but he wasn't aware of having been able to do that. During the events of the last few days, in the periods when things had been quiet enough to try for some rest, his mind wouldn't turn off, wouldn't stop thinking about the kids and Jenny.

You know they're okay.

Running the same things over and over; the last two or three telephone conversations ... he'd given Leona and Jenny an early warning. They'd had time to get in the essentials and get home and lie low. That's all they had to do now, just lie low and let this thing play out.

Leona was a sensible, clever girl. Even though he'd not had time to put into crystal-clear words why she was in danger, why she couldn't go home, Andy was sure she'd do as she was told. But the possible pursuit of some shadowy men from God knows where was only *half* the equation.

He wondered how things were in London; a big city, a lot of people – it didn't take a genius to work out how nasty things could get if the British authorities had been caught on the hop by the oil cut-off. And knowing how useless the government in his adopted country could be at preparing for anything out of the ordinary – unseasonably heavy rain, too many leaves on the track, a drier than average summer – the prognosis wasn't great.

He conjured up an image of Jenny and the kids at Jill's house. Jill, a loudmouth with a big personality – a woman who quite honestly grated on his nerves, would be looking after them. He could visualise them huddled together in front of the radio, or her expensive plasma TV, hanging on every word from the newsreaders, eating tinned peaches and worrying ... maybe even about him.

They're fine Andy, ol' mate. Just you concentrate on getting home.

Private Peters, who was on driving duty, stirred.

'Headlights up ahead,' he called out over his shoulder to Andy, spread out across the row of seats behind.

That roused him instantly. His eyes snapped open. He shook away the muddy-headed drowsiness and once more swept thoughts and worries for his family to one side.

'Kill our lights and stop!'

Peters turned the coach's lights off, brought the vehicle to a standstill and quickly turned off the engine. It was then that Andy realised he'd made a really stupid call. He was reminded of the first time he and the other engineers had encountered Carter's platoon, stranded out in the desert – and how lucky they'd been that time, not to have been shot at.

Whoever those lights belonged to had almost certainly seen them as well.

The lights on the road up ahead winked off in response. That wasn't good.

Shit.

He saw half-a-dozen muzzle flashes, and a moment later the windshield of the coach exploded. Peters jerked violently in the driver's seat – a pale blizzard of seating foam blew out of the back of his seat and fluttered down like snowflakes. He flopped forward on to the steering-wheel.

He heard Westley's voice, bellowing coarsely from a seat two rows further back. 'This is a fuckin' kill box! Everyone out!'

The firing from up the road continued, shots whistling in through the exploded windshield, down the middle of the coach as the men squeezed out of their seats and converged in the central aisle. The soldier beside Andy, scrambling towards the steps beside the driver's seat, was thrown off his feet. He heard the exhaled 'oof' of the man, winded by the chest impact, the jangle of his equipment and webbing and the crumpled thud as he hit the floor.

'Shit! They're covering the exit!' yelled Westley.

Andy, squatting on his haunches behind the ineffectual cover of the seat in front of him, looked around. They were sitting ducks in the coach.

'Out of the windows!' he shouted hoarsely.

Westley picked up on that and echoed the order with a much louder bark as he smashed the nearest window to him with the butt of his rifle.

'Come on! Fuckin' move your arses!'

Windows all along the length of the coach shattered, and the men tumbled out of the coach and landed heavily on the road outside.

Andy, being right at the front, just behind the prone form of Peters was trapped. He needed to get to his feet in order to roll out over the open frame of the window beside him, but the shots were still whistling down the coach, every now and then thudding into the head-rest beside him, blasting away another chunk of his meagre cover.

He recognised the deeper chatter of a heavy machine-gun being fired from somewhere ahead, not dissimilar to the Minimi this platoon had used to suppress the mob back in Al-Bayji to great effect. He realised he might as well be cowering behind a wet paper bag. Those high calibre rounds were having no trouble shredding their way through the coach.

He just needed a second's pause in the firing to stand half a chance.

Outside on the road, he heard the lighter clatter of the platoon's SA80s, zeroing in on the muzzle flashes up the road.

And that bought him his pause.

Shit, here we go.

Andy stood up and hurled himself out of the open frame into the darkness of the night outside. He covered his head and neck with his arms, suspecting that if a single high calibre round didn't tear the top of his head off, he would undoubtedly smash his skull out on the concrete below.

He landed on his back, instantly winded, and stunned by the impact. The flickering lights, and tracer streaks in the air just above his face, were a blurred and beautiful kaleidoscope. If his lungs hadn't been struggling so desperately to get some air back in them, this would have been a beautiful moment. He felt a hand fumble clumsily across his face and chin until it found the collar of his jacket and began to pull on it, dragging him roughly across the pitted and jagged surface of the road. By the flickering light of the muzzle flashes coming from the lads, he looked up and saw the bearded face of Mike, grimacing with the exertion, and beside him, Lance Corporal Westley calmly squirting short bursts of covering fire.

In that dreamy, stoned, moment he felt like drunkenly announcing to both of them they were his *bestest bloody mates ever … no really, you guys are just the best*.

Another of the lads tumbled out from the coach above him, almost landing right on top of him.

'For fuck's sake Warren, you fucking clumsy ape!' shouted Westley, still firing.

Mike continued to drag Andy, and as they rounded the back of the coach, he felt the fog of concussion beginning to clear.

Thud!

Mike's jacket exploded with a puff of cotton lining. Andy felt a light spray of warmth on his cheeks.

'Fucking bitch!' the Texan yelled as he dropped to his knees and clutched his side.

Andy, almost match fit again, scrambled to his feet, and pushed Mike round the corner of the coach. 'Are you hit?' he shouted.

Mike looked at him with incredulity. 'Of course I'm fucking hit!'

Andy squatted down and pulled aside Mike's jacket, lifted up his 'Nobody Fucks with Texas' T-shirt, bloodied and tattered as if a chainsaw had been rammed through it. By the wan light of the moon, he could see nothing.

'Here, I have torch,' said Erich leaning against the rear of the coach beside them. He flicked on a penlight and handed it to him.

Andy studied the wound. There was no entry hole, just a deep gash along the side of his waist. The shot had glanced down his side.

'Ah, you're bloody lucky, it's nothing, Mike.'

Mike's eyes widened. 'Nothing? Try being on the goddamned receiving end of *nothing*.'

They heard Westley bellow an order from around the corner of the coach. 'Fuck this! Pull back lads! Round the back! Now!'

A moment later, the small area of shelter which Mike, Andy and the soldier all but filled, was inundated with the rest of the platoon, rolling, diving, flopping into the narrow space; a tangle of panting, adrenaline-fried bodies.

'Jesus-effing-Christ, those cunts up the road have got us cold,' one of the men grunted between gasps.

The deep rattle of the heavy machine-gun up ahead of them ceased, as did the lighter chatter of several assault rifles.

Silence, except for the sound of laboured breathing all around him.

'Hell this is fun. We should do it again sometime,' muttered Mike.

Andy looked at Westley. 'What will they do now?'

'Shit, I don't—'

'Well, what would *you* do?'

'Outflank,' the Lance Corporal replied quickly, automatically.

Andy nodded. 'Then that's why they've gone quiet.' He looked around at them. 'We're all jammed together on top of each other. We're dead if we stay here. We've got to make a run for it. How are you fellas for ammo?'

'I'm out,' replied a voice in the dark.

'Me too,' said another, several more of them echoed that.

'Just what's in me clip,' Westley added.

'Couple of rounds left,' said Derry, 'after that, all I got is colourful language.'

'Great,' muttered Andy.

They heard a voice calling out. It was unclear, garbled by the distance and the echo bouncing back off distant rocky peaks either side of the road.

'Shhh, hear that?' muttered the Lance Corporal. 'Anyone hear that?'

Silence, except for a gentle breeze that rustled through the shrivelled, dried trees above them on the slopes. Then they heard the faint voice calling out again, a bit clearer this time.

'That sounded English,' said Derry.

There was another long silence that settled about them, broken only by the rasping sound of their breathing, fluttering with tension.

'Hey! You guys behind the coach! Hold up!'

Andy heard one of the boys whispering, 'Is that a Yank?'

The voice again. 'You guys! You American? You British?'

Westley turned to Andy, 'For fuck's sake. They're Yanks!'

Andy cupped his hands. 'We're British! Hold your fire!'

There was no reply for a few seconds, then they heard the same man shout, 'Come out in the open where we can see you, drop your guns!'

Westley turned to Andy. 'You reckon they're pukka?'

'I don't think we've got a choice anyway. I'll go first.'

Andy took a deep breath and stood up, then with hands raised, he walked out from behind the coach, his face screwed up in anticipation of a shot slamming home. But no one fired.

He heard Westley mutter behind him, 'The fight's over lads. Come on.'

The Lance Corporal and the others emerged reluctantly, one by one, their hands raised, and their empty weapons left behind.

To Andy it felt like an eternity, exposed like that, knowing that even in the dark, whoever was out there had their cross-hairs trained on them, fingers resting lightly on triggers and watching them silently.

After a few moments, he heard the unmistakable clump of army boots walking down the road towards him. A torch snapped on, into Andy's face.

'You're British, huh?' said a deep, gravelly American voice.

'Yes.'

'How many?'

'Fuck knows. There *were* fifteen of us, before you started firing, mate,' snapped Andy.

'Shit,' said the voice behind the torch. 'Real sorry about that.'

Peters had died instantly. The opening volley hit him in the head, the throat and the chest. He was dead even before he'd slid forward on to the wheel. Private Owen on the other hand, who had been hit in the aisle inside the coach, right next to Andy, had obviously lasted a few moments longer, having pulled himself up some way towards the front, leaving a snail-trail of already drying blood behind him.

Two others were killed on the road beside the coach, Private Craig and the platoon medic, Benford.

Westley saw to them, collecting their dog-tags after Benford's opposite number in the US platoon had briefly looked them over and pronounced all four of them dead. He and the other squaddies picked them up and laid them out side by side at the edge of the road.

Andy, meanwhile, realised Mike was nowhere to be seen. He finally found the American at the back of the coach, holding Farid. The old man had taken a hit in the stomach. His pale checked shirt was almost black with blood. On his belly, a small, perfectly round hole slowly oozed blood that looked as dark as oil by torchlight. But beneath him, the pooling blood, and shreds of expelled tissue, spoke of a much larger exit wound.

Mike looked up at Andy, silently shaking his head. 'Not good,' he said quietly.

Farid stared up at Mike with glassy eyes. He spoke, but in Arabic; private words, not for either of them. He spoke in short bursts, punctuated by painful spasms that caught his breath and made him screw up his eyes and grimace.

A US soldier approached down the aisle. He pointed his torch down on to the old man's face. 'Who's the—'

'Our translator,' interrupted Andy. He didn't want to know what euphemism the young American sergeant was about to use.

'Our friend,' added Mike, looking up pointedly at him.

The sergeant seemed to have the sense not to say anything, and nodded silently. He turned round and shouted up the aisle, 'Get the medic! We got a live one here!'

Mike stroked the old man's face. 'Hey, we got some help coming. You hang in there.'

Farid focused on him and managed a faint smile. 'I know you are good man. Good man inside.'

'Just a normal guy, that's all,' said Mike. 'Save it for later, okay?'

Farid placed a bloodied hand on his arm. 'God is open door to all good men.'

The medic squeezed past Andy and crouched down to look at the old man. His examination was brief, and after gently easing the old man over and inspecting the rear wound he looked up at his sergeant, barely shook his head before saying, 'I can hit him with morphine, but that's really all I can do.'

'Do it then,' said the sergeant.

The drug had an almost instant effect, and Farid sagged, no longer tensing and flexing with the pain. He smiled. 'I see my family soon. My son ...' the rest he muttered in Arabic.

'You go see your son, and your wife,' said Mike quietly.

CHAPTER 66

• • • •

3.25 a.m. local time

Southern Turkey

'**Y**ou're kidding? How far away from here?' asked Andy outside.

The sergeant nodded, 'No, I'm not kidding. It's not far, just a few miles. The landing strip's not big enough for the large transport planes, shit ... nowhere near long enough. But we're getting a steady stream of C130s down on it okay.'

'You guys can get us out?'

'Fuck, I don't know. We got a lot of stragglers like you, American, British, some UN troops from all over. We got planes coming in and going out like a goddamn taxi rank. It's bedlam, man. Absolute fuckin' bedlam. And then we got all sorts crowding outside the strip, civilians – Turks, Kurds, Iraqis – all wanting us to fly 'em all over the place, thinking things ain't so bad elsewhere.'

'How *are* things elsewhere? We haven't heard anything much since Tuesday.'

The sergeant looked at him with incredulity. 'You don't know?'

Andy shook his head.

'The answer is ... shit. We got food riots back home. My home state's under martial law. Fuckin' internment camps everywhere. And I'm pretty sure we're doin' better back home, than most places.'

'Hear anything about Britain?'

The sergeant shook his head. 'Not much, but I heard enough to know you guys have got it pretty bad over there. It's all very fucked up.'

'Jesus.'

'Anyway listen, you guys get back in your coach, and I'll have one of my boys guide you there. You don't want to waste any time. We're holding that strip for just a while longer, maybe until tomorrow afternoon, then that's it, we're bailing out of here.'

Andy turned to head back inside the coach.

'Listen fella,' called out the American. 'I'm sorry about the ... we just. We've had hostiles taking pot-shots at us all week, you know? My boys're all strung out.'

Andy nodded but didn't say anything. 'Sorry' fixed nothing. It didn't bring back to life the four young men lying beside the road, or an old Iraqi translator.

He turned back to the truck. Westley and Derry had lifted out Farid's body from inside the coach and placed him alongside the four young squaddies, shoulder to shoulder with them. Maybe they'd not done that consciously, or maybe they had, but it said something about these boys that made Andy feel proud to have struggled out of Iraq alongside of them.

Well done lads.

He approached Westley. 'You okay?'

Westley nodded. 'Bad enough losin' your mates in a contact with the enemy ...'

He left that unfinished but Andy knew what he wanted to say.

But it really stinks when you lose them to friendly fire.

'Get the boys back inside. The Yanks are going to lead us to an airstrip nearby.'

Westley looked up. 'Seriously?'

Andy offered him a tired smile. 'Yeah. It looks like we're out of here.'

CHAPTER 67

. . . .

4 a.m. local time

Southern Turkey

Half an hour later, they took a turning off the main road, down a smaller road – a single lane in both directions. As they approached the airstrip it became clogged with civilians, mostly on foot, many carrying a meagre bundle of possessions on their backs or dragging it behind them.

Tajican honked the coach's horn, and slowly the vehicle edged its way through the thickening river of people towards a hastily erected spool-wire perimeter lit every few hundred yards by powerful floodlights. Behind the curls of razor wire, US marines stood, evenly spaced, guns ready and coolly regarding the growing mass of people only a few yards away from them.

The American soldier sitting beside Private Tajican urged the Fijian to keep the vehicle moving and not let it come to a complete standstill.

'They'll overrun us in seconds,' he muttered warily eyeing the surging crowd ahead and either side of them.

Andy was impressed at how Tajican calmly kept a steady forward momentum, his face locked with concentration, whilst all around him palms and fists thumped noisily against the side and front of the coach.

Something suddenly flew into the coach through the open, glassless front; a stone, a rock ... whatever it was, it glanced off Tajican's head, and he clasped a hand to the gash it had caused. Blood rolled down the back of his hand, his arm and soaked into his sleeve.

But he continued calmly driving forward.

When another projectile arced through from the front into the coach, the American soldier sitting at Tajican's side decided he'd had enough. He swung his assault rifle down and fired a long burst over the heads of the people outside.

The effect was instant. The road ahead cleared.

'Hit the fuckin' gas!' the American shouted. Tajican did just that, and the coach sped up towards the perimeter fence ahead and the entrance gate – a Humvee, parked lengthways across a twelve-foot wide gap in the razor wire. The Humvee rolled out of the way at the very last moment, allowing the coach through, and then immediately rolled back to prevent the thick gathering of people surging through in its wake.

Andy was unprepared for the level of chaos he could see around him. He had seen the inside of several US and UK army bases since he'd started doing field-work in Iraq; always a hive of activity – chaos to the untrained eye. But the disarray he witnessed before him bore no resemblance to any military camp he had seen.

The sky was still dark, but showing the first pale stain of the coming dawn. The airfield was lit by dozens of floodlights erected on tripods and deployed along the main strip. From what he could see, it was an airfield that had been mothballed in recent years, but, in the space of the last forty-eight hours, had been hurriedly revived and adapted to meet immediate needs. There was a control tower to one side of the strip. Clearly the building had, at some point in the past, been gutted of all its electronic equipment, but was now being used in an *ad hoc* way. At its base a communications truck was parked, whilst several men stood up in the observation tower monitoring the steady stream of transport planes coming in and taking off, they were using laptops that trailed thick cables out through the tower's rusty old window-frames down to the truck below.

Along the airstrip Andy could see hundreds of men, clustered in groups, most of them lying down; a patchwork quilt of exhausted soldiers, each group awaiting its turn to board a plane.

On the strip, Andy watched a Hercules C130 coming in to land at one end, whilst at the other, another plane was awaiting its chance to take off. Halfway along the strip, on a tarmac turn-off, a plane was being hurriedly loaded up with a group of men who had been roused from their slumber and herded at the double towards the boarding ramp.

The American soldier who had guided their coach in, led Andy, Mike, Erich, Westley and his men towards a tent in the middle of the airfield. A flap was pulled to one side. The clinical blue glow of half-a-dozen halogen strip lights swinging from the tent support frame amidst drooping coils of electrical flex, spilled out through the opening into the pre-dawn gloom.

They entered the tent. Standing inside, looking harried, tired, and more than ready to grab some bunk time, was a Marine colonel; a short squat man with greying crew-cut hair and leathery skin pulled tight around a pair of narrowed eyes.

'Colonel Ellory, sir. We picked these guys up on the border road. They're Brits, sir.'

Ellory turned to look at them. His eyes ran quickly across Andy and the other two civilians, and then towards Westley, looking for rank insignia. 'Okay son, where's your CO?'

Westley saluted awkwardly. 'We lost him, also our senior platoon NCO. I'm highest rank here, sir. Lance Corporal Westley.'

Colonel Ellory frowned as he worked to make sense of Westley's Geordie accent. 'You're in charge, son?'

'Yessir.'

He turned to the others, 'And you are?'

'I'm a civilian contractor, Andy Sutherland.'

'Mike Kenrick, I'm a contractor too.'

'Erich Feillebois, engineer with Ceneco Oil.'

Ellory nodded. 'Okay guys. This is how it is. We're trying to get as many of our boys home as quickly as possible. There's a limited number of planes, a limited amount of fuel. Not everyone's getting home. Priority goes to military personnel, and amongst them, priority goes to *our* boys. That's the deal, I'm afraid. I know it sounds shitty, but … well, that's how we're doing it.'

'Have you got any other British troops?' asked Andy.

'Yeah, there's a few around. We've had some stragglers rolling in over the border road. A bunch of army vehicle retrieval engineers, quite a few independent security contractors, all goddamn nationalities. A mixed bunch out there. You'll just have to take your chances with them. The Brits and the other internationals are in two separate groups down the other end of the strip.'

Colonel Ellory looked like he was pretty much done with the conversation and ready to turn his attention elsewhere.

Andy stepped in quickly. 'How long are you planning on keeping this strip open?'

Ellory sighed. 'I'd like to say, as long as it takes. But we'll keep it going until I get orders to pull the plug and get out.'

'How bad is it out there?' asked Mike.

'Out where? You mean the Middle East? Or home?'

Mike shrugged. 'We've been out of the loop.'

Ellory ran a hand through his coarse grey crew-cut. 'The Middle East is a goddamn write-off. We sent our boys into Saudi to try and save what they could. The crazy Moslem sons of bitches made for the refineries first. Pretty much destroyed most of them before we could get in there.' Ellory looked at them. 'And that's pretty fucking smart if you ask me. There's multiple redundancy in those pipelines and the wells. Not the case with their refineries. Those sons of bitches targeted exactly the right things. And it's the same deal in Kuwait and the Emirates. You ask me, this wasn't a fucking spontaneous outbreak of religious civil war. It was a goddamned organised operation. Some serious military-level planning went into this shit. They hit Venezuela, they hit the refineries in Baku. These motherfuckers knew exactly what they were doing.'

'Who? Which motherfuckers?' asked Mike.

'Shit. You kidding me?'

'Don't tell me you think it was Al-Qaeda,' Mike laughed, 'because if you—'

'Do I look like a dumbass?' Ellory shook his head. 'Of course I don't think it's Al-Qaeda. They couldn't organise a piss in a bucket. Fuck ... they're just a bunch of phantoms anyway. No. I can make an educated guess as to who's behind this shit though,' said Ellory, placing his hands on the desk in front of him and arching a stiff and tired back. 'Those sons of bitches in Iran.'

Andy nodded. It was a possibility. Perhaps they were the ones behind all of this. They had the wherewithal to pull off something on this kind of scale. And motive too.

'Yeah, I could believe they're behind this,' said Mike. 'I mean, we stalled their nuclear programme. But this ... this has worked better than God knows how many nukes would have done.'

'Exactly,' said Ellory 'They know goddamn well they can hurt the world far more this way, by hitting the most vulnerable oil chokepoints. And shit, they got us all. But I'll say this. When we get this crap fixed-up again, and mark my words, we will, they'd better run for shelter in Tehran, because we are going to bomb those fuckers back to the Jurassic.'

Andy wondered whether plans were already being drawn up to deliver some payback, or whether the US government, like every other government, was focusing on damage limitation right now. If Iran really had been behind this, Andy reflected, they'd better bloody well hope the world wasn't going to recover enough to focus its attention on them and bring some retribution to bear. Proof of their involvement, or no proof.

'Shit, we should've seen this coming.' Ellory shook his head. 'Anyway, I haven't got time to talk this crap through with you guys.' He pointed towards Andy, Westley and his men standing just outside the tent. 'You guys'll have to take your chances with the other Brits assembled at the end of the strip,'

He pointed to Erich, 'And you need to get yourself down and join the international group.'

He pointed to Mike. 'You, on the other hand, you'll need to make your way over to where we've put all our civilian contractors, US nationals, defence contractors.'

Mike looked across at Andy. 'These guys have been through a lot Colonel, they—'

'I do not have the fucking time to argue the point! If we have the time and the planes, we'll get them out, but American nationals and personnel are to go first. Now if you wouldn't mind getting your ass out of my tent, I've got a million and one things to attend to,' Colonel Ellory said, offering a formal nod and then turning towards a sergeant who had entered brandishing a clipboard.

Andy turned to Westley, 'Okay then, I guess we do as the man says, and go find the other Brits.'

They walked out of the tent into the half-light, towards Wesley's platoon gathered in a loose and weary-looking huddle beneath the glow of a floodlight several dozen yards away. Erich shook hands with Andy and Mike.

'I go now,' he said quietly. 'See if I find any other French here. You stay safe, eh?'

Andy nodded, 'Safe journey, mate.'

They watched him walk away along the edge of the airstrip, past silent islands of soldiers, sitting, resting, some smoking, some sleeping.

Lance Corporal Westley walked over towards his men and got them on their feet. He left Mike and Andy standing watching the planes come and go, listening to the roar of propeller engines turning, and the distant cries and chants of the civilians massing outside the perimeter of razor wire.

'Well I guess this is where we part company, Dr Sutherland,' said Mike.

'Yeah, we'll have to get together and do this again next year.'

Mike laughed.

Andy stuck out a hand. 'I'd give you my email address, but I'm not sure there'll be an Internet when we get back home.'

'No, you're probably right,' said Mike, grabbing the offered hand and shaking it.

'But look, if it turns out this isn't actually the end of the world,' Andy continued, 'you can always get me through my website – PeakOilWatch. co.uk.'

Mike nodded. 'I'll make a point of looking you up.' He watched Westley's men preparing to move off. 'You know, for a guy that's never handled a gun before,' he said pointing towards the remnants of the platoon, 'you did a good job leading those boys out of trouble.'

Andy shook his head. 'Not good enough. Telling Peters to turn off our lights—'

'Shit like that happens, Andy. But you got the rest of these boys through, that's what counts,' said Mike, a grin flashing from his dark beard. 'You did good.'

They shared an awkward silence, not really sure what came next, but knowing there was more to be said.

'We went through a lot of stuff, these last few days, didn't we?' said Mike.

'Yes. I'm sure we should be talking it out or something, Dr Phil style.'

'There never seems to be time enough to talk. It seems like all we've done in the last three days is fight, run and drive.'

'Yeah. Anyway,' said Andy, 'I'm not sure I want to revisit any of it right now. I've got a wife and two kids to get home to.'

Mike nodded. 'If they're half as resourceful as you, they'll be just fine, Andy. Trust me.'

He shrugged. 'What about you, Mike? You must have family you're worried about.'

'Nope,' said Mike shaking his head, 'it's just me. The job always seemed to come first.'

'I guess that makes things easier.'

'A lot.'

Andy caught sight of a smear of dry blood on the American's forearm. 'I'm sorry about Farid. I'd have liked him to have made it.'

'Yeah. He made some sense, didn't he?'

'I think he did.'

'And we lost some good men back there. Lieutenant Carter, Sergeant Bolton ...'

Andy nodded.

'Good soldiers,' said Mike casting a glance at Westley and his men who were beginning to head wearily down towards the end of the strip, 'all of them, good men. You Brits can put up a good fight.'

Andy smiled, 'Ahh, except I'm not a Brit.'

'You Kiwis too,' Mike replied, slapping him on the shoulder.

'Take care Mike. I hope things aren't as fucked up for you back home as I suspect they are for us.'

'This mess will right itself eventually.'

'I'm not so confident.'

CHAPTER 68

. . . .

4.05 a.m. GMT

Paul drove for several hours down the M1, bypassing Birmingham in the dark, marked not by city lights or the ever-present amber-tinged glow of urban light pollution bouncing off the night sky, but by the sporadic intervals of buildings on fire and the flickering movement of people around them.

Parts of Coventry, on the other hand, seemed to have power; they drove along a deserted section of dual carriageway that was fully lit by the arc sodium lights along the central island. To Jenny's eyes the distribution of power seemed almost haphazard, as if some central switchboard had been overrun by monkeys who were now randomly punching the shiny buttons in front of them. She'd thought there might have been an even-handed distribution of powered time-slots, or if not that, then certain 'safe' regions – a little unfairly maybe – which would be allocated a constant supply of power to the detriment of the lost-cause big cities.

But no. There seemed to be no discernible pattern at all to it.

South of Coventry, the lights along the dual carriageway went out and they once again adjusted to the pitch-black of night. Paul spotted a sign for a Travelodge ahead and swung Mr Stewart's car down the slip-road as it came up.

'What are you doing?' asked Jenny.

'I need to sleep. I've not slept since Monday night. It would be stupid if having made our escape earlier, we end up wrapping ourselves around the central barrier on the motorway.'

Jenny nodded. It made sense.

'Let's give it a look. If it's surrounded by a baying mob, then we'll push on, all right?'

They drove off the slip-road into an empty car-park in front of the motel. There were tell-tale signs that similar things had happened here as at Beauford Service Station; bits and pieces scattered across the parking area, some broken windows in the lobby at the front of the building, but that was all. The Little Chef next door to it on the other hand, looked like it had been more thoroughly seen to, every window smashed and a trail of detritus and trampled goods strewn in front of it.

'Well, seems like whatever happened here has been and gone,' said Paul.

'I suppose everywhere that can be looted for food and drink has been emptied by now,' said Jenny. 'I wonder when all that's been gobbled up, what people will do for food?'

'I'm sure we'll start seeing troops or police on the streets sometime today. It's got to happen today,' he said with less conviction than the last time he'd bullishly asserted things would right themselves quickly. He swung the car round and parked it just outside the entrance to the motel.

'It seems okay to me.'

Jenny looked up at the two floors of dark little curtained windows. It would be nice to have a bed to sleep on, and the chance of stumbling across any wandering bands of thirst-maddened crazies here appeared to be acceptably remote.

There was no sign of anyone here and she wondered where exactly everyone was. Sixty-four million people on such a small island and since leaving Beauford Services, she'd seen hardly any.

They're all tucked away in their homes waiting this out. Only fools like us and those with bad intentions are outside, roaming around.

Paul climbed out of the car and led the way inside. It was dark, of course. Pitch-black inside, with no ambient light from any source at all coming in through the cracked smoked-glass at the front.

'Hang on,' she heard him murmur, and a moment later, a pale square of light lit the foyer up dimly.

'What's that?' she asked.

'My organiser.'

'Clever.'

In the absence of any other light, it was surprisingly bright.

'Okay ... stairs,' said Paul. She watched the pale square of light float across in front of the reception desk towards a doorway, 'Over here,' she heard him say.

She followed him through, up one flight of stairs, through another door, and then they were standing in a corridor.

'You seem to know your way around this one,' she said.

'They're all very similar. And I use them quite a lot. Right then, first floor rooms. You choose.'

Jenny walked down the corridor, passing a door that was open. Jagged splinters of wood jutting out from the door-frame told her the door had been forced. She didn't want to sleep in a room that had been picked over by someone. That just somehow felt ... *clammy*. The next door along had also been kicked in, and the next. Finally towards the end of the corridor, she found a door that remained intact, locked. 'I'll have this one,' she said.

'You're okay being alone? I spotted another locked one on the other side, up the far end. I can take that one.'

Jenny stopped to think about that. She wasn't entirely sure she wanted to spend the night sleeping in the same room as this guy, but then ... being alone down one end of the corridor, in a deserted motel.

'Okay, maybe we should share this one.'

'I think that makes sense,' said Paul.

He lifted his organiser up towards the door to read the room number. 'How does Room 23 sound?'

With one well-aimed kick at the swipe-card door lock, the door swung in and banged off the wall inside, the noise echoed disturbingly down the empty corridor.

Inside, it was how she hoped she'd find it, undisturbed, cleaned, bed made for the next customer. She opened the curtain and the blind behind it, then swung open the window. The room was hot, and a faint breeze wafted in.

In the sky the grey light of dawn was beginning to provide enough natural light for them to find their way around. Paul quickly turned his organiser off and pocketed it.

'Okay then, sleep,' said Jenny, sitting down on the bed; a double bed.

Paul pulled open a cabinet door to reveal a drinks fridge. 'A-hah. We're in luck.' Inside he found it decently stocked. 'There's several cans of Coke, ginger beer, tonic water, and a pleasing range of mini-liquors: vodka, gin, rum, whisky. Some beer even.'

Jenny smiled in the pale grey gloom of dawn. After the recent hours, the last few days, a single stiff rum and Coke would be absolutely what the doctor ordered, even if it was going to be warm and without ice.

'I'll have a rum and Coke, please.'

'Good choice, Ma'am,' said Paul. She heard the pop and hiss of the Coke can, the click of a lid being twisted off and the gurgle of the rum being poured.

'Here.'

The first one was a strong one. The second drink she asked for she wanted weak, but Paul's definition of 'weak' didn't seem to square with hers.

'So, you mentioned something a while back,' said Paul, 'about your hubby *predicting* this?'

'Well, sort of. He wrote a report a while back ... lemme see, yeah it was back in 1999, because that was the year we did Christmas in New York. It was an academic paper really, he wrote most of it when he was at university in the States, but then when he got commissioned to write it again, he did some new research and updated chunks of it with new data he'd managed to track down.'

'And it was about this whole thing?'

'Well, sort of I suppose. Andy was very secretive about it, client confidentiality kind of thing. But I know it had something to with Peak Oil, and our growing reliance on fewer and fewer major oil reserves, and how that made us much more vulnerable to someone needing only to disable a few places around the world to hold us all to ransom. He described how it could be done ... which were the most vulnerable places ... that sort of thing.'

And that's where Andy's obsession had truly began. Wasn't it?

The people who'd commissioned his work had paid him good money for that. Very good money – enough that they bought that house of theirs outright, and money left over that they were able to put both kids through fee-paying schools.

'But after doing that job, you know ... he started changing. Became I guess ... edgy, very serious. He spent too much time obsessing about the whole Peak Oil thing. And a little paranoid too. Just silly little things like worrying about viruses on his computer that might be spying on him, noises on the phone line. Daft really. I don't know, he used to be so much fun. Great company. And then, like I say, he changed after New York. And it's been a slow steady roll downhill ever since. So much so, in fact, I was actually in the middle of organising our big split-up when this happened.'

'That's too bad,' said Paul. 'So, where is he now?'

'Somewhere in Iraq. He's been getting regular assignments there for the last few years. He was over there when this started. And my kids are alone in London.'

Jenny's voice caught.

Shit, I should know by now drink does this to me.

'You okay?' Paul asked, placing a hand on her shoulder and squeezing gently.

'Of course I'm not. I just want to get home. They need me.'

His arm slid across one shoulder, across her neck to the other. 'Don't worry Jen, I'll get you home safe and sound. I've got you this far haven't I?'

She felt the tips of his fingers slide under her chin, lifting her face up to look at him, and it was then that she knew where this was going.

'Look, I ... errr ... I think I've had enough to drink.'

'You're kidding right? There's loads more, and Christ we deserve it after the shit we've been through together. What do you say?'

'I think we've probably both had too much. We need to keep our wits about us, right? Who knows what might happen tomorrow?'

Jenny swung her legs off the bed. 'And you know what? I might try one of the other rooms—'

A hand wrapped around her forearm. 'Why? What's up?'

It was a tight, urgent grip, and it hurt a little.

'Look, I just think it's a good idea, okay?'

'What? Come on. We're just talking here. No harm done.'

'Can you let go please?'

His grip remained firm. 'I've been looking out for you these last few days. It's not too much to bloody ask is it? A little ... conversation?'

She could hear the slightest slur in his voice. He wasn't pissed as such, just a little tipsy. No worse than the couple of come-ons she'd fended off at the last office Christmas party she'd been to; harmless enough somewhere crowded, but a little disconcerting, alone like this.

'I've been looking out for you,' said Paul again. 'Not asking much, for Chrissakes.'

'I think Ruth looked out for me a little more than you did,' she replied, and almost immediately wished she hadn't.

'Fuck you,' he snarled.

'Would you mind letting go please?'

He let her go, and she headed for the door. 'I'll see you in a few hours, when you've sobered up.'

She stepped out into the corridor, and strode through the darkness of it, the only light, the faintest pre-dawn grey coming in through a window at the far end. She picked a doorway halfway down on the right. It was a door that had been forced by someone, and as she stepped in, she could see that the room had been hunted through and the drinks cabinet emptied.

Good, hopefully all the other cabinets in this place are empty too.

She'd hate to see what Paul was like when he was fully loaded.

Jenny pushed the door shut behind her. And as an afterthought, she pulled the armchair in the corner of the room across the doorway. Not that she thought it was entirely necessary. Paul was like the other office Romeos; emboldened a little by the booze, but still essentially a coward. A sharp 'no', or a 'piss off', did the trick for the likes of them ... most of the time.

No ... he'd probably drink himself into a stupor and fall asleep trying to whack himself off.

She lay down on the bed and then felt the tears coming – worried about Jacob and Leona, and Andy too, realising she'd been so wrong in the way she had treated him. She wished the robust, no-shit-taken Ruth was here with her right now, talking some good plain common sense, probably making her laugh too. If Ruth were here, they'd probably be raiding the drinks cabinet together right now and shamelessly taking the mickey out of Paul.

Jenny closed her eyes and was asleep within a minute.

CHAPTER 69

. . . .

6.29 a.m. GMT

It was lighter when she opened her eyes again, fully daylight now. Jenny guessed she must have managed to get a few hours sleep. A shard of sunlight streamed through the gap in the curtain, across the bed and on to the carpet.

Her head ached slightly, the mildest of hangovers, and more probably attributable to her general fatigue than the two generous rum and Cokes she'd had earlier. Paul would be feeling a lot worse this morning, deservedly. She was going to have to drive this morning instead.

The smell of alcohol on her breath seemed to be strong, very strong. There must have been a hell of a lot of rum in that drink for it to still be on her breath like that. She decided she was fit enough to get up and start rousing Paul. That was probably going to take a little time.

She started to sit up, and then saw him.

He was standing beside the bed, silently staring down at her.

'What the—'

'Took me ages to find you,' he said, his voice thick and slurred. He was swaying slightly. 'Thought you'd gone up a floor, didn't I? But here you were all along, just down the way from me.'

He was pissed out of his skull. He must have found another cabinet full of booze.

'What are you doing in here?'

He reached a hand out and grabbed her. 'For fuck's sake! Why d'you have to be such a stuffy bitch!'

Jenny pulled his hand off of her shoulder, his fingernails raking across her skin. 'We were havin' a nice drink, we're both grown-up. There's no bloody law against you and me, you know ...'

'Paul. Look, I'm grateful for you finding a way out of that service station

'... but it doesn't mean I want to sleep with you, okay?' said Jenny, shifting slowly past him towards the end of the bed.

Paul watched her moving, his head slowly turning, one hand reaching out for a wall to steady himself. 'Well what about what I *deserve*? I've been good ... looked after you. Could've jumped you anytime ... but I didn't. Been a perfect bloody gentleman, actch-erley.'

'Yes, you have,' Jenny replied slowly, beginning to rise from the bed. 'And you don't want to ruin that good behaviour now, do you?'

'Just want a shag ... that such a big fucking crime?' he announced loudly, angrily.

'It is a crime Paul, if the person you want to *shag*, doesn't want to shag *you*.'

He nodded and laughed. 'Oh ... see what you mean.' He took a couple of steps towards her, successfully blocking the doorway out of the room. 'So, what's so wrong with me? I'm what? Five or six years younger than you? I got all my hair,' he paused for a moment, gathering his thoughts, and reaching out again for a wall to steady him, 'not a fat bastard like most blokes ... wear nice clothes. Shit, I'm top salesman at Medi-Tech Supplies UK ... meaning I'm a rich bastard.' He looked at her, arching his eyebrows curiously. 'None of that good enough for you then?'

'No. Because right now, sex is the last thing on my mind.'

He recoiled, hurt, irritated. 'Guess you *are* ... a stuck-up bitch, then. Thought you were a sport ... stupid me,' he said, taking a step forward. 'You know, it's been a lo-o-o-ong time ... for me, a long time. My ex was a fuckin' tease, ripping me off, spending my money, never let me near her though. Bitch. I thought you were different. Not another fuckin' tease.'

Jenny, pulled herself back on to the bed, there was no room to step past him. 'Rape's a crime, Paul,' she said, knowing full well she wasn't going to be able to reason with him. 'Even now, whilst everything's a mess out there, it's still a crime.'

Paul giggled. 'Oh, right ... well you know what? I think this week in particular ... maybe the *normal rules* don't apply. I think, that's what everyone else has figured out too. Know what I'm saying?'

Jenny shook her head.

'That's why everyone's behaving so *un-British*. Eh?' He giggled again. 'No rules this week, ladies and gents ... so you'll have to amuse yourselves 'til normal service can be resumed.'

'Come on. Let's forget about this. You go lie down and sleep it off. And then we'll get going down to London, when you're feeling fit enough to travel.'

He pursed his lips, thinking about that for a moment.

Jenny realised how silly she'd been to allow herself to wind up in this situation; alone with a man who was essentially a stranger, who was drunk, during a chaotic and lawless time like this. She should have guessed that at some point travelling with him, there would end up being a moment like this.

'Sorry love ... need a shag ... you'll fucking well do.'

He took another step towards her. Jenny kept her distance, retreating back across the bed, putting her feet on the floor on the far side.

'Think what you're doing,' she said. She hated the wavering, shrill sound creeping into her voice; it was a pleading, begging tone. To his ears that was going to sound like submission.

He smiled as he started to unbuckle his belt. 'Maybe a fucking crime, love, but who's going to know now, eh?'

He put a foot on the bed and stepped up on to it, wobbling precariously. 'Here's Jo-o-o-n-n-y!!' he announced excitedly peeling his shirt off.

Sod this.

Jenny leant forward and slapped him hard across the face. It was more a punch than a slap. Her hand had been balled up into a fist. He fell backwards, rolling off the bed on to the floor with a heavy thump.

Not waiting around to see if that was a K.O., or merely going to buy her a few seconds, she ran around the end of the bed and out of the room into the corridor.

What now?

She had decked him. But now she could hear him struggling to his feet. 'You fucking bitch!' she heard him shouting inside the room. 'I'm going to bloody well get you!'

'Who's going to know now ... eh?'

Those words chilled her. It meant the bastard had crossed a line. He was beginning to realise what every other potential rapist ... bully ... abuser ... *murderer* ... must be aware of. Here was a window of time in which he could do whatever he wanted, indulge *any* fantasy, certain in the knowledge that when – if – order was restored again, evidence of his deed would be untraceable; lost amidst the chaotic aftermath.

And I'd be that evidence ...

She could imagine ... her body stuffed in a cupboard somewhere in this motel, perhaps never to be discovered, or maybe chanced upon months from now when the clear-up operation began in earnest.

Paul? He'd do something like that?

Possibly. She didn't really know him at all.

She heard him stumbling across her room, into that armchair, cursing.

What now, come on ... what now?

Jenny decided to go for the car and leave him behind. She really couldn't trust him now, not even if he got down on his knees this instant and pleaded for her forgiveness, and swore he'd never even look sideways at her again.

Up the corridor for the stairs down –

'Shit, the keys,' she whispered.

Paul had them in his room, and she knew exactly where they were; sitting on the little writing-desk, next to the television. She remembered seeing him tossing them on there when they entered the room, by the light of his palm pilot.

She ran down the corridor to the open door of his room, 23. Behind her, he staggered out, calling after her, every name he could drunkenly think of.

She stepped into the room, over to the writing-desk. They weren't there.

'No ... no,' she muttered, a desperate panic beginning to get a hold of her. She could hear him lurching up the corridor towards her, weaving from side to side, pissed out of his tiny little mind. Jenny decided she could probably take him on. He was all over the place, his judgement and reaction time shot to hell. But he had the ace card, as all men do over women – brute strength. If he got a good grip on her, it wouldn't matter how much faster she could move. It wouldn't matter one bit – brute strength was everything.

'Come on, come on!' she hissed. 'Where are they?'

She looked all over the desk, trying both of the drawers, before finally spotting them on the floor. He must have knocked them off during the last few hours, during his binge. She scooped the keys up into one hand and was turning to leave just as he appeared in the doorway.

'A-ha!' he grinned and wagged a finger at her. 'I got you!' he cheerfully announced in a sing-song voice as if they were playing a game of playground tag.

'Paul,' she tried a scolding tone, 'this is unacceptable.'

He laughed. 'What are you? ... My mum?'

He started towards her. Jenny realised this might be the last opportunity left to her, to catch him off guard. She ducked down low and charged towards him, crashing into him like a battering-ram, sending them both out through the doorway into the corridor, sprawling on to the floor together.

He was winded, but he still managed to grunt, 'Bitch, bitch, bitch', his hands scrabbling to get a firm hold of both of her arms, which she was frantically flailing, landing soft ineffectual blows on his face; slaps, scratches and punches that were achieving nothing.

He swung a leg over hers, instantly trapping them both in a vice-like grip on the floor.

Oh God, he's getting hold of me.

She kept her hands and arms moving, but he managed to grab one wrist, and then very quickly the other. He rolled over, moving his body weight on top of hers, his face – stinking of every different liquor that could be found in the cabinet – was close to hers; close enough that the tip of his nose was touching her cheek.

'Why the fuck ... was this ... such a big problem, eh?' he whispered.

She struggled. There was no answer she could give that he'd understand.

'Eh? I just wanted a one-night stand. You'd have ... had a good time too. Now ... look at us.'

Jenny realised she had one last chance.

She turned her head towards him, towards that breath, towards that face of his; a face at any other time, under different circumstances, from a distance, she might have even thought was vaguely attractive, but instead was now a vicious, snarling mask – one hundred per cent frustrated testosterone. Fighting to keep the sense of revulsion and anger inside; struggling to pro-duce something that was almost impossible right now ...

She managed to smile.

'All right then, let's do it,' she whispered.

As if she'd uttered a magic password, the effect was almost instant. The thigh-hold he had on her legs loosened.

'You sure about that?' he muttered, his voice suddenly changed, the anger gone and now, in its place the considerate tone of a gentleman seeking con-sent.

Jenny struggled to keep the solicitous smile on her face and nodded.

He let go of one of her wrists, his hand travelling down to the zip on his trousers.

Her loose hand could punch him right now, scratch him, jab at one of his eyes. But she decided that just wasn't going to be enough. She needed to really incapacitate him with something much more effective.

She head-butted him. Her forehead smacked hard against the bridge of his nose and she heard it crunch and crackle.

He rolled off her, both hands now on his face, blood instantly beginning to stream down over his lips on to his chin. Jenny was up on her feet and running before the shock of the blow had subsided enough for Paul to let loose the first enraged howl of pain.

Two-thirds of the way down the corridor was the entrance to the stairs. She flew down them, out into the foyer, through the doorway into the morning light and was heading towards Mr Stewart's car before she allowed herself to believe that she had actually managed to escape him.

The car fob made it easy to single out the key from the rest on the key-ring. The headlights flashed and the car squawked as she unlocked it and quickly hopped inside.

She wasn't going to scramble to insert the ignition key as danger raced towards her, as she'd seen in countless teen slasher movies. No. She sensibly locked the car first; all four doors responded simultaneously, securing themselves with a reassuring *thock!*

Through the windscreen she suddenly saw Paul, emerging from the foyer of the hotel, a crimson stream of blood down his nice, expensive shirt, one hand cradling his broken nose, the other waving frantically at her to stop.

She started the engine.

He rushed over to the car. If he'd had a bat or a brick in his hand, she would have thrown the car into reverse and got the hell out of there before he could even try and smash his way in. But he didn't. All he had were his two, soft, office-hands – good for tapping out emails on a Blackberry organiser, or shaking on a big deal – but not quite so good for smashing, bare-knuckled, through a windscreen.

He splayed his hand out on the driver-side window. 'Jesus! I'm sorry Jenny. I'm really, really sorry!' The thick slur was gone now, the adrenaline rush had instantly sobered him up. His snarling manner, now one of genuine regret.

She looked at him through the glass, and shook her head

'Please! I ... it was the drink,' he pleaded, 'I'm ... I've worked it off now! I don't know what the hell came over me!'

His splayed hand was leaving blood smears on the window.

'Come on Jen ... we've got to stick together ... you and I. It's a ... it's a jungle out there!'

That's right.

She felt a pang of guilt as she threw the car into reverse and pulled out of the parking slot. He stumbled after her. She could hear him calling, pleading, bleating, over the whine of the engine and the sound of her crunching the gears into first. But there was no way she could feel safe again with him – booze or no booze. She spun the steering-wheel round and headed towards a sign pointing towards the slip-road that led on to the M1, southbound.

CHAPTER 70

. . . .

12.31 a.m. EST

New York, USA

The line connected. There was a solitary ring before it was answered by a male voice.

'Cornell and Watson Financial Services, how can I help you?'

'I want to book an appointment,' he replied quickly.

'I'm afraid we're booked up for the foreseeable future, sir.'

'How about Christmas Day?'

A pause. 'What time sir?'

He sighed. 'A minute past midnight.'

'One minute.'

It was a necessary ritual. They were as much at risk of being exposed and destroyed by *them*; more so in fact, since their resources were dwarfed by those of their quarry. The agency was small, tiny in fact ... a staff of no more than about thirty agents operating out of the rear offices of a discreet back-street firm in New York. The firm, seemingly, offered walk-in financial services, but never quite seemed to be able to fit an appointment in to anyone who might actually walk in off the street.

He heard a male voice. 'Jesus! We thought you were dead! We've been trying to contact you since Tuesday!'

'If you must know, Jim, I've been through a shitting war zone. My—'

'No names remember.'

'My fucking sat' phone got blown to pieces on Tuesday, and I've been shot at God knows how many times since—'

'We've had a breakthrough. A huge goddamn solid gold breakthrough.'

'—this whole crazy thing ... Breakthrough? What are you talking about?'

'Our target, the one you're with right now ... he's not who we want.'

'Well I'm not with him right now, not any more. We got separated. I'm waiting for the military to find me space on a flight out of Turkey right now.'

'It's his *daughter*. It's the target's daughter.'

'What? What the hell are you talking about?'

'We think she could be able to identify one or more of *them*.'

He suddenly found his pulse racing. 'You're shitting me. What's happened?'

'She called him on his cell, Tuesday morning. Christ, you might have even seen him take the call.'

He tried to think back. Tuesday morning, they'd been fighting for their lives in that pink compound, all hell breaking loose. He couldn't specifically remember Sutherland taking any calls, but then that whole day was a jumble of blurred, panic-stricken memories.

'And listen, we think she saw *several* of *them*.'

'Several? Several of the One Hundred and Sixty?'

'No, better than that … several of the Twelve.'

'My God!' He looked anxiously around the communications tent. No one was close enough to hear him talking, no one was even watching. The soldiers were all too busy holding the razor-wire perimeter or hustling. He spoke more quietly all the same. 'We have to find her.'

'I know, we have to re-deploy very quickly. *They* may know what we know. They might even be closing in on her as we speak.'

'We've got to try.'

'Yes.'

'She's in England?'

'That's right, London.'

'I can try and swing the next plane out of here heading that way. I'll do it somehow. Can you get some more assets on the ground over there?'

'It'll be difficult under current circumstances. We might be able to fly a couple of men in to help you.'

'Do it. Do it now.'

'We will.'

Mike was about to hang up; the Marine colonel had said he had just a couple of minutes, no more.

'What's it like there?'

'Here? New York? It's shit. The place is falling apart, just like everywhere else. We get power for a couple of hours a day, and there are riots everywhere. Not good.'

CHAPTER 71

• • • •

7.31 a.m. GMT

Guildford

Ash was awake with the first light of dawn. The thought of spending an-other twenty-four hours in Kate's apartment, waiting for her to show up, was an agonising prospect. He had the patience of a saint, if he was waiting on a certainty, but this was a long shot. This woman might never return.

But she would try, wouldn't she? It's the homing instinct. In a time of crisis, that's exactly where everyone tries to get – home.

And the delay could be quite legitimately rationalised. Tuesday afternoon things went pear-shaped. Kate would have decided after seeing the riots, and finding out the trains weren't running, to camp out at work overnight. Wednesday came – she'd have been hoping the police had restored order, and perhaps a limited train service had returned. But there'd been no sign of that. There's a canteen at work maybe? So another night camping there, basic food and drink laid on. Thursday, same thing again. Only by then the canteen would be running low on food, and everyone would be getting very anxious to return home. There'd still be no news on the radio, and no sign of police retaking the streets. Friday, it'd be obvious to her and her colleagues they couldn't stay there forever, the rioting must have died down once everything that could be looted, had been looted.

At some point today, Ash decided, she'll set off for home, walking with other wary pedestrians along the main arteries out of London. It'll take her four, five maybe six hours on foot? Provided nothing stops or delays her.

She'll arrive sometime today.

That sounded very much like wishful thinking to Ash. But there was not a lot else he could consider doing. Perhaps, he could return to the Sutherland's house and wait there? Pointless ... Sutherland had warned her to stay well away. There were many other names in the phone book he could try, one by one. But most of the places – he'd looked them up on a road map he had found by Kate's telephone table – were a long way out of London.

He decided the best course of action would be to hang on until tomorrow. And then if she still hadn't turned up, he would camp out at the Sutherland home. Sutherland's daughter, or his wife, or even the man himself might come by, just to pick up one or two essentials … that ol' homing instinct was very, very strong.

Yes, that would do then. First thing tomorrow morning, Ash decided he'd head back up.

CHAPTER 72

· · · ·

7.51 a.m. GMT

Shepherd's Bush, London

'Please don't go outside Lee!' Jacob whimpered, putting down his knife and fork heavily. They clattered noisily against the plate, and on to the dining-table. He hopped off his chair, scurried round the table and held on to her arm. 'Please don't go!'

She looked down at her little brother, his face crumpled with worry.

'Look Jakey, it's safe right now. They only come out at night, the Bad Boys. We're perfectly safe in the daytime,' she said, not entirely convinced by her own assurance.

'But last time you went out, you were gone for ever. I thought ... I thought you were ... dead.'

'I'll be fine, Jake. I'm just going to check on our neighbours, that's all. You can watch me out of the window of Jill's bedroom, okay? Keep an eye on me as I do the rounds.'

Jacob stared at her silently. His face looked unhealthily pale and unnaturally older; skin rumpled with the bumps, grooves and lines of unceasing worry. She wondered if he had a suspicion of what had happened to Dan. If he'd guessed that he must be lying dead down some back-street ...

Don't do this Leona, think about something, anything, else.

Now really wouldn't be a good time to fold and start sobbing, not whilst she was trying to settle down Jake's jangling nerves.

'I'll be fine. Now, let's both finish our pilchards, okay?'

She wanted to check on the DiMarcio's house, a few doors up. The DiMarcio's next-door neighbours had been broken into last night. Leona had heard the noises; very unsettling, chilling noises. It had all proved too much for her and she had scooped Jacob up and taken him into the back room to sleep, where the sounds of the house being ransacked were, at least, muted.

Shortly after they had finished their breakfast she stepped out of the front door, and her heart skipped a beat; she spotted gouge-marks in the green paint on the front door, around the lock. Someone had been working on it, trying to jimmy the door quietly. She wondered if it had been one or two of the gang members discretely hoping to break into a house on their own, whilst their colleagues were busy elsewhere? Or someone else?

Either way, it suggested their turn was approaching, if not next, then soon. The thought of them, all of them, the bad boys, streaming into the house, raucous shouts, smashing, grabbing ... and finding Jacob, and finding her ...?

Time was running out.

She desperately wanted to locate some other people they could group together with. She'd be more than ready to share the tinned food and bottles of water they had left. It wouldn't last them quite so long, but she would happily trade a week's sustenance for some others that she could feel safe with; preferably adults, older adults.

Leona found herself remembering a childhood fantasy she'd once had: living in a world populated only by teenagers – the beautiful people, young, alive, energetic and fun. It was an essay she'd written at school. A world that was one long party, nobody to boss them around, no parents to tell them what time the party had to end, or to turn the music down, or how much they were allowed to drink, or getting them up early the next morning so they wouldn't be late for school or college.

She laughed weakly. Well, that was it, she'd witnessed that little fantasy of hers being played out in the avenue over the last few nights. But it was no fantasy – it was a nightmare, and it reminded her of a book on the required reading list for her English Literature A-level.

Lord of the Flies.

She headed down the short path, out through the gate and on to St Stephen's Avenue. The casually discarded refuse was beginning to build up now. Not just discarded bottles and cans, but broken pieces of furniture, smashed crockery. A mattress lay in the middle of the street, stained with drink, some blood, and other things she didn't want to think about.

It was their sex-pit.

That's where they were doing it, with their gang girls, their Smurfettes.

The house to the right of the DiMarcio's had been 'done' by the gang; that much she knew already. She'd seen them breaking into it last night. But her heart sank as she approached the DiMarcio's home. They had been paid a visit as well. Leona had been hoping to hook up with them. She liked Mr and

Mrs DiMarcio, trusted them even. Mr DiMarcio, Eduardo, was a cab-driver, a big round man originally from southern Portugal, whose laugh was loud and infectious. He was fun. But she also knew he could handle himself. Last year he'd caught a couple of lads trying to break into a car parked down this street; boys from the rough White City estate nearby who'd spotted this avenue as a soft target and started to prey on it. Mr DiMarcio had handed out a hiding to them both. She vaguely recalled the boys had tried to press assault charges, but she wasn't sure it had got anywhere close to going to court. By contrast, Mrs DiMarcio was slim, always well-groomed and came across as very cultured, well-educated. Leona wished she'd accepted their offer to take her and Jacob away from all this on Tuesday, even though it might have meant the chance of missing Mum or Dad coming home.

The DiMarcio's front door had been smashed open.

She knew they hadn't been away. Leona had seen the curtain twitching on Wednesday.

She wondered whether they had managed to escape; perhaps when the house next door was being ransacked they had decided the smart thing to do was to leave their house, to creep out, hopefully to find someone further up the street who would take them in. If they'd come knocking on her door, she would have opened it to them in a heartbeat.

She looked round, diagonally across the avenue back towards Jill's house. Upstairs she could see the little blonde tuft of Jacob's head looking out at her. He waved. She waved back and then stepped up the DiMarcio's path and in through the open front door.

The mess inside was horrendous. The floor was strewn with broken things; plates, dishes, expensive-looking crockery, Mrs DiMarcio's beloved china cats. The walls were gouged, scratched and scuffed, ragged strips of their lovely expensive wallpaper had been torn away, graffiti sprayed here and there.

In their kitchen, it was obvious the room had been stripped clean of anything remotely edible or drinkable. The Bad Boys had been through it like a horde of locusts.

Leona was relieved not to have found any signs of violence done to the family, so far. She quickly checked through their lounge and dining-room which opened on to a conservatory and a small area of decking beyond that. Everything was dislodged, moved, overturned or broken.

With a growing sense of relief that they had vacated before the Bad Boys had arrived, she decided she had to at least take a quick look upstairs. She needed to know that they'd got out okay. She took the stairs quickly, not wanting to spook herself by taking one at a time and cringing with each creak.

She jogged up to the top of the stairs. Only to find Mr DiMarcio's thick, rounded legs sticking out of the doorway to their bedroom.

'Oh God, no,' Leona whimpered. She took a few quick steps across the landing towards his body and saw the rest of him lying in the doorway. His head was battered and bruised. His face almost unrecognisable with swellings and bumps and abrasions. But he had probably died of blood loss from the stab wounds. There were several of them on his chest, his lower arms, his hands.

He was fighting them off with his fists.

She could imagine him doing that, throwing big hard punches at them, flailing at them furiously, shouting curses at them in Portuguese. But they'd brought him down with their knives; slashing at him, like a pack of dogs bringing down a bear.

'Oh, Mr DiMarcio,' she whispered.

She knew he would have only fought like that to defend his wife. With a heavy heart she could guess what she was going to find in the bedroom if she stepped over his body and looked inside. She resolved not to go in, but looking up at the wall opposite the doorway, she caught sight of Mrs DiMarcio's bare legs in a cracked mirror on a chest of drawers. Her bare legs, scratched and bruised, and blood, dark and dried on the bed-sheet beneath.

She felt a momentary rush of nausea. It passed quickly, swept aside by an overpowering surge of rage.

'You fucking bastards!' she found herself hissing angrily. She knew if she had a gun in her hand now, and one of those evil little shits was cowering in front of her, she'd be able to pull the trigger.

'You fucking bastards!' she screamed angrily. Her voice bounced back at her off the walls, and then it was silent.

Except it wasn't.

She heard movement. Someone was upstairs with her, and, probably startled by her cry, had been thrown off balance and kicked something by accident that rolled noisily across the parquet floor in the next room and came to a rest.

Oh shit, oh God, oh fuck.

Run? Yes.

She turned quickly, stepping across Mr DiMarcio's feet and heading for the top of the stairs. She bounded down them, nearly losing her footing and taking a tumble. At the bottom of the stairs she chanced a look back up but saw nothing, and heard nothing either. She headed towards the open front door and out into the morning sunlight.

She sprinted across the street, weaving around the broken furniture towards

Jill's house. As she reached the gate, she chanced another look back, and saw a curtain upstairs twitch ever so slightly.

Oh my God, someone was in there with me.

She hammered on the door with the palm of her hand, and a moment later heard the bolt slide and it creaked open.

'W-what happened Lee?' asked Jacob.

She looked at him and realised the time had come to start levelling with her little brother.

'We're going to have to defend ourselves Jake.'

He said nothing.

'Okay ... okay,' she gasped, her mind racing. 'You saw that film, *Home Alone*, right?'

He nodded.

'Well like that, booby traps and stuff, okay? Just like the film ... just in case the Bad Boys try coming in here.'

'They won't, will they?'

Leona found she was too tired and too frightened to even try putting an optimistic spin on this. If they were coming tonight, Jacob needed to know.

'Tonight they might.'

He didn't go into hysterics as she thought he might. He simply nodded and said quietly, 'Okay, let's get ready for them.'

CHAPTER 73

. . . .

4.23 p.m. GMT

Outskirts of London

South of Coventry there had been a roadblock on the M1 which had forced Jenny to take a roundabout route along some A roads clogged with abandoned cars, coaches and container trucks, and one or two B roads – some plugged with discarded vehicles and utterly impassable. She'd got lost at least twice before eventually finding her way back on to the motorway heading into London. She had wasted most of the day, cursing and crying with frustration as time ticked by and she seemed not to be getting any closer to her children. The arrow on the fuel of Mr Stewart's car had been wobbling uncertainly over 'empty' for the last hour. Finding the M1 again cheered her up and seeing the distant sprawl of London ahead, lifted her spirits further ... until she came across yet another roadblock.

Jenny slowed down as soon as she saw it; a barrier across the M1 and the slip-roads leading on to the M25. It was comprised of triangular blocks of concrete laid side by side, designed to prevent any kind of vehicle smashing through. Behind that was a barrier of barbed wire. And behind that, several dozen soldiers watched her approaching slowly.

She came to a halt in front of the concrete blocks, and climbed out.

'You can't come through. I'm sorry, love,' shouted one of the soldiers across the barricade.

Jenny felt her shoulders wilt with fatigue and despair. 'Why not?' she called out.

'Orders.'

'Oh come on,' she cried, 'what orders?'

'We're not to let anyone through, either way, in or out of London,' the soldier replied.

'Why?'

The soldier shrugged. 'Those are our orders, love.'

She felt anger welling up inside her. It erupted so quickly it caught her by surprise. 'For fuck's sake! You idiots are sitting here with your thumbs up your arses, and out there,' she pointed back up the motorway, 'people are killing each other for water and food.'

The soldier said nothing, his face impassive.

'It's like the end of the world out there! Women being raped, people fighting, killing. And you're doing nothing! Just sitting here!'

The soldier continued to stare silently at her, but then finally, perhaps feeling she deserved some kind of response, he said, 'I know it's rough, love. My advice ... just go back home, sit tight, and wait for this situation to work itself out.'

'I'm trying to bloody well do that!' She pointed to the city skyline behind them. 'I live there! I just want to get home to my children. Please let me through ... please,' Jenny pleaded, her voice beginning to break.

She took a few steps forward, until she was almost upon the razor wire, only a yard away from the soldier who had bothered to reply.

'Please,' she whispered.

The soldier looked around, left and right, then spoke quietly. 'Look love, we can't let your car through, and don't even think of trying any other roadways in. They're all like this, blockaded.' He lowered his voice still further, 'But ... there's plenty of ways in on foot ... all right?'

Jenny looked around. He was right. She could abandon the car somewhere on the hard shoulder, leave the motorway and walk in. The soldiers might have blocked all the roads, but of course London was a porous urban spread not just accessible by roads – there were cycle lanes, paths, kerbs, alleyways, unused scraps of rubbish-encrusted ground.

She nodded and thanked him quietly for the suggestion. She climbed into the car, turned it around and headed on back up the M1. She drove far enough away that she was sure they could no longer see her and then pulled over to the hard shoulder.

'So, I'm going to walk across north London then, no problem,' she spoke to herself. 'How far is that? A day's walking?'

A day, if nothing holds me up.

She had managed to come this far. Home was just fifteen or so miles away now. Not so far. She decided nothing was going to stop her now. She climbed out of the car and looked across the industrial estate beyond the hard shoulder. It was deserted. There was little sign that anything was amiss there ...

Other than the fact that on any other Friday afternoon there would be half-

a-dozen people outside the delivery bay of that sheet-metal works, having a mug of tea and a fag break; there would be smoke coming from the chimney of that ceramic tile factory; there'd be a lifter moving those pallets of goods outside that distribution warehouse ...

Jenny surveyed the lifeless landscape. Beyond the industrial park, looking south-west towards central London, the direction she had to head, she could see scattered pillars of smoke here and there, not from factories though, but from the shells of cars, homes, shops, where rioting had occurred over the last week.

There was activity in there, people there.

My children are in there.

She picked up the last couple of bottles of water and put them in her shoulder-bag. She slammed the car door and walked across the hard shoulder, swinging a leg over the waist-high metal barrier and stepped on to the grass verge. It sloped down towards the back lot of the deserted industrial estate.

'Okay, then,' she muttered to herself.

On Tuesday, or Wednesday, she doubted she would have dared to head into this kind of landscape alone, unarmed. But today was Friday. The last two days in that service station and overnight in that Travelodge, had changed her. She realised if the need came, she could handle herself, she could do what was needed to survive.

She spotted a short length of metal piping lying outside the sheet-metal works. She bent down and picked it up, hefted it in one hand, then in both, and swung it a couple of times, feeling mildly comforted by the *swishing* sound it made through the air.

It'll do for now.

If she came across any young buck who fancied trying out his luck on her, she decided she would probably just swing first and ask questions later.

She checked her watch. It was just approaching half past; she guessed she had another four hours before the sun hit the horizon. That would be a good time to find some safe, dark corner to huddle up in, and let the crazies, the gangs – whoever it was at the top of the predatory food chain – have their night-time fun.

Nearly home.

Tomorrow, some time in the morning, she was finally going to get home.

And Leona and Jacob will be there, no doubt frightened, but alive, well.

She swished the metal pipe once more into the palm of her hand with a satisfying smack.

'Okay then,' she said loudly, her voice echoing back off the corrugated iron wall of the nearest industrial unit.

CHAPTER 74

. . . .

10.27 p.m. local time

Over Europe

Andy looked out of the window of the 727. It was a civilian plane, one of the fleet belonging to GoJet; one of the bigger budget airlines flying the various European holiday runs. They were over Hungary right now, not far off Bucharest. Outside though, it was pitch-black. No faint strings of orange pinpricks to mark out major roadways, nor mini constellations of amber-coloured stars marking out a town or a village – just pitch-black.

The airliner was packed to capacity, every single seat taken, the vast majority of them filled with soldiers from various mixed, jumbled-up units, all of them stripped of their bulky kit, their webbing and weapons. Amongst them, a handful of civilians, contractors like Andy caught in the chaos, but lucky enough to have been scooped up in this hastily scrambled repatriation effort.

Westley was sitting beside him, the rest of the platoon – just six men – in the two three-seat rows behind them. They were all fast asleep.

'Can't believe we're on our way home, like,' said the Lance Corporal. He nodded towards the window. 'What've you seen outside?'

'Nothing, not a single thing,' Andy turned to look at him, 'I haven't seen a single light since we took off.'

'That's not so good then, is it?'

'No.'

'You think it'll be as bad back home, you know ... as it was back *there*?' Westley cocked his head, gesturing behind them.

'I don't know. I think it'll be pretty desperate. It's been almost a week now without oil. I don't know how they'll be coping. I wish there was some news.'

'A lad from one of the other units says there's good bits and bad bits. Some places, like London, where it's a fuckin' mess, and other places, like, where it's okay.'

Andy nodded. He could quite clearly imagine what London was like. It wouldn't be an easy place to maintain order. It was too large, too many people. He would guess there would be many smaller towns, perhaps the dormitory towns of various military bases or barracks, and areas around key installations, resource depots and storage centres where some semblance of order had been maintained. But the rest of the country, particularly the large urban conglomerations, he surmised, was being left to its own devices. He could see farmers dusting off their old shotguns and changing the birdshot for something a little stronger, jealously guarding their modest crops, and cornershop owners – those that had yet to have their stores stripped bare – barricading themselves in, armed with baseball bats and butcher's knives.

And how long would that state of affairs last?

His best guess was a month, perhaps two. That's how long it might take to repair the damaged oil infrastructure; the sabotaged refineries, the blown pipelines.

And it might be some time after that before commercial freight ships and aeroplanes were flying once more, loaded up with oranges from South Africa, lamb from New Zealand, Brussels sprouts from Romania.

Oil companies . . . big business interests . . . they were the first culprits that had sprung to mind. But as far as Andy could see, this had devastated the oil market, irreparably. And when the world recovered . . . *if* the world recovered, it would be hypersensitive to oil dependencies, and the dwindling reserves that were left. There was simply no economic motive – for anyone – that he could see behind what had been happening. There were no winners.

The only way one could work out who might have been behind it all would be to look back in a few months' time – or perhaps a few years' time – and see who got hurt the least, or who benefited the most from this chaos. All Andy could see now was that millions, perhaps hundreds of millions of people, billions even, were struggling to survive, simply because somebody had temporarily grabbed hold of the world's oil drip-feed, and squeezed tightly.

How fragile the world is, how very fragile.

There was that metaphor he had used in the report, one he'd been very proud of and thought quite clearly illustrated the tenuous situation of this interdependent modern world. Stopping the continual flow of oil, even for a very short time, was akin to an embolism or stroke a sick man might suffer. And that's exactly what this oil strangulation had turned out to be – a global, economic heart attack.

His eyes grew heavy. The soothing rumble and hiss of the jet engines, carrying them over an unlit Europe, was as good as any sedative. A week of stolen sleep finally caught up on him with a vengeance, and as his chin drooped to his chest, his last conscious thought was that Jenny and the kids had probably fared better than most this week.

CHAPTER 75

. . . .

10.05 p.m. GMT

Shepherd's Bush, London

The Bad Boys turned up as they had on the previous three nights, appearing, as they did, in surly twos and threes, just after the last glow of dusk had gone from the sky, and the darkness of night was complete. They were not so boisterous tonight she noticed, no catcalling, no wolf-whistling amongst them.

She sensed, for them, tonight wasn't going to be about recreation. It was going to be about necessity; quenching their thirst and hunger. This little avenue was their *larder*. It had provided them with rich pickings since Tuesday. They were going to keep coming back until every last house had been plundered, and then, and only then, would they move on to somewhere else.

She had been in and out of the house this afternoon, using the few tools Jill kept in the cupboard under the sink to fashion the crudest and most basic of weapons and traps. Hopefully they would prove dissuasive enough to the gang tonight, that they might pick on someone else.

Just one more night.

Leona was certain Mum or Dad would come for them tomorrow. Instinct? Or wishful thinking? Or maybe the alternative, that they were gone for ever, was simply unthinkable.

After finding Mr and Mrs DiMarcio this morning, and worried about the chances of being broken into tonight, she had taken a count of the houses down St Stephen's Avenue, and how many had already been looted. There were twenty-seven homes along the short leafy avenue. Fifteen had been done over by the gang, including their home. Leona had been tempted to wander inside, but remembered Dad's warning and steered clear of it. She was pretty sure six of the houses had been entered during the course of last night. It seemed like the gang of boys weren't rationing themselves at all; just breaking and entering until they'd had enough. All of the six homes hit last night had been roughly in the middle, too close for comfort. Jill's house and a couple of others, remained prominently untouched amidst the gutted shells of the other homes; they stuck out like a sore thumb.

She watched them as they gathered right outside the gate to Jill's garden.

Their behaviour was noticeably different from previous nights. Not quite so full of cocky attitude, not so noisy. She sensed the seriousness of the situation had finally become apparent to them. This was no longer about having a *larrrf* in the absence of the law; things were becoming serious for them now. It was about getting their hands on what they needed to survive; drink, food. The plunder of Tuesday night – what they'd taken from the off-licence – had obviously been consumed very quickly. The subsequent nights of ransacking had yielded barely enough to keep all of them going. Finding enough to keep them all fit and well was going to become increasingly hard for them. Soon she imagined, after the last house had been plundered, they would turn on each other, as the stakes for survival increased.

From what she could see through the slats of the blind, tonight they all looked sober, thirsty, hungry ... and for the first time, a little frightened. Perhaps the hierarchy amongst their group was already beginning to fragment.

'They're back, already?' asked Jacob, seeing the look on her face.

'They're back.'

His face turned ashen.

Leona forced a smile. 'Don't worry Jake. We've got our special secret weapons. We'll be fine. Just remember how well that little boy in *Home Alone* did, eh? He showed them, didn't he?'

Jacob nodded, trying to match his sister's bravado.

Outside the pack of Bad Boys grew. She noticed the Smurfettes were no longer with them. What did that mean? That they had been left at what this gang considered their HQ to keep them safe? Because this was *men's* work – the hunting and gathering, and *their* job was simply to lay down and provide gratification for the boys?

Or worse, the novelty factor had been exhausted and they'd been *dispensed* with?

She spotted the older boy, the one who had stabbed to death the other lad the night before last. He stood in the middle of the street, wearing a vest top sporting the Nike swoosh. She could see him talking animatedly, his hands swooping and flickering around in front of him in that *street* way. He had clearly assumed the mantle of leadership; the others, younger, shorter and less self-assured, nodded with his every instruction.

And then she knew why he seemed so familiar. She had seen him up close before.

50 Cent.

One of the three who had accosted her and Dan on Wednesday. She leaned closer to the window, trying to get a better look.

Yes. It's him.

He and one of his Wigger protégés had chased after Dan and – she was almost certain now – killed him.

His wrist suddenly flicked towards Leona, and their heads all turned as one to look in her direction.

Shit.

She pulled back from the window, hoping they hadn't seen her staring out at them. 50 Cent then gestured towards the house opposite, and they looked that way in unison.

They're deciding which house to go for first. Eeny-meeny-miney-mo …

That's what they were doing.

She reached out for her weapon; a rounders bat, with several six-inch nails hammered through it. She had been too eager to cram the end of it with nails, and the wood at the end of the bat had begun to split. So she'd had to wrap sellotape around the end of it to stop the thing splintering and falling apart. She really wasn't sure whether it would disintegrate the first time she swung it at something, but it was all she had.

Jacob held a plastic Swingball bat in one hand. Leona had knocked a few short nails through the holes of the grid in the middle. She thought it looked like it could do some harm if Jacob managed to swat at someone's face with it. During the afternoon he had swished it around a few times, getting some practice. Although she was more worried the clumsy little sod would swat himself with it, and she'd end up having to bandage his face up.

They could have left this afternoon – just grabbed some bottles of water and run for it. But to where? No, she'd decided to stay. This is the only place Dad and Mum would know to come to. If they left, then the pair of them would be well and truly on their own.

He held it tightly in one hand now, and whether or not it was going to be an effective weapon, she could see it was giving him a little confidence – that *tooled-up* feeling. It was going to be his comfort blanket tonight.

50 Cent, the gang's unassailable leader, the one who she'd seen stab that younger lad the night before, had stopped talking, and now in silence,

looked towards Leona, then at the house opposite. He was the one making the decision.

Please no … no.

He nodded towards the other house and Leona let out a gasp of relief. The Bad Boys turned their backs on Jill's and headed *en masse* towards the front door of the house opposite. Leona saw a curtain twitch inside, and in that moment, the name of the family who lived there – the McAllisters, came to her. They had only recently moved in, six months ago. She remembered Mum briefly mentioning them, 'a nice young couple, with a toddler and a baby'.

She could imagine Mr McAllister inside, just behind the front door and ready with whatever household weapon he'd managed to crudely fashion, trembling so violently his heels would be tapping the floor, but driven by something deep down to fight to the very last for his young family, as Eduardo DiMarcio had done for his wife.

The gang began to smash against the front door, taking turns to kick at it around the handle.

She shot a glance towards their front door, buried behind a barricade of heavy furniture they had hauled across during the afternoon. The barricade would slow the gang down a little. It wasn't going to stop them though, not if they were determined to get in here tonight.

The McAllister's front door cracked with the next kick. The next blow caused it to splinter around the handle. A final blow sent it swinging inwards. Last night the Bad Boys had cheered when each front door had caved in, in the same way patrons of a crowded pub might raucously cheer at the sound of a pint-pot being accidentally dropped. Not so tonight. They were less rowdy. More single-minded, more determined.

She saw them stream into the dark interior.

'Cover your ears Jake,' she said. He did so obediently.

And then came the chilling, muted noises she had expected to hear – Mr McAllister's last stand.

It took them an hour to finish what they were doing inside the house. All two dozen of them had pushed their way in. This time there had been no spill out on to the street, no furniture being dragged out and smashed up. No sense of a house-party out of control. It had been much quieter … after the screaming coming from inside had stopped, that is.

The light was completely gone from the sky now. When she saw the flickering beams of several flashlights emerge from the front door, she knew it was now their turn.

'Jacob, go upstairs to our hiding place,' she whispered.

'I don't want to go alone.'

'Go! Now!'

She could hear his shuddering breath in the dark, or was it hers?

'Go!' she hissed.

Leona felt one of his arms reach out and fumble for her, wrapping itself around her waist. 'Please don't die.'

'Shit! I'm not going to … die, okay? Please … go.'

The arms unwrapped, and she heard his footfall towards the stairs.

Outside, the narrow street was filling up again, as the gang members emerged single file from the house opposite. 50 Cent and several others seemed to be nursing minor wounds. She could hear one or two of them crying out intermittently from the pain of their injuries.

A vague hope crossed her mind that the young father opposite, Mr McAllister, had knocked some of the fight out of them before going down. But after only a few moments, and a few words of discussion, she saw the gate to Jill's garden being pushed open and a party of half a dozen of them walking up the path towards the front door.

Her grasp tightened on the bat.

The first blow came quickly and sounded deafening, a heavy thud that made the barricade of furniture stacked against the inside of the front door rattle worryingly. She heard a sharp crack after the second blow.

If only Dan was here.

Several more hard and focused blows landed against the door, and all of a sudden she could see a shaft of torchlight piercing through the tangle of stacked furniture. They'd managed to knock a hole through the flimsy wood of the front door. She turned her torch on and shone it towards the door. She could see a face peering through a jagged hole in the bottom door-panel.

'Go away!' she screamed frantically.

The face, momentarily startled, disappeared. She heard voices outside, not whispering, just conferring quietly. Then one of them kneeled down and shouted through the hole. It was 50 Cent.

'Come on, open the door!'

'Please, go away!' she whimpered. 'We've got nothing in here. Nothing!'

'Yeah right,' he replied. 'Don't fuck with me. Just open up or we'll kick it in eventually.'

She said nothing.

The voice coming through the hole tried a different tack. 'Look, you open up, see, and share out what you got in there, and we let you go.'

She wanted to answer him, to ask if he really meant that. But she knew that he was making an empty promise.

His face appeared at the ragged hole in the front door again. She shone her torch on him and he squinted.

'What you lookin' like?' he said, and then produced his torch and aimed it through the hole at her. The light lingered on her face, and then travelled down her body and then up again. 'Oh ... I know you. You the bitch I see up in the precinc', innit.' He laughed, a friendly, cheeky laugh, or at least it might have sounded friendly in another context.

'You *my* honey when we get in,' he grinned. He pushed his hand through the hole in the door, and then panned the torch he was holding around at the barricade stacked against the door. 'You think this is going to stop us?' he said laughing. His face disappeared from the hole and then she heard him talking quietly to the others.

They're going to try another way in.

The lounge windows were the obvious alternative.

She raced back into the lounge from the hall, just as the first brick flew in, sending a shower of jagged shards into the room.

The first of the gang was already pulling himself cautiously in through the window-frame, when his foot found the plank on the window-sill; the plank she had hammered a row of nails into earlier this afternoon.

'Ouch shit! Fuckin' something, fuckin' ... shit!' he yelled, pulling his leg back out.

Another of them squeezed in through the window-frame, two hands feeling cautiously for the plank. They found it, and pulled the thing out and flung it across the garden.

'The tricky little bitch,' she heard one of them say outside.

The window-frame was full once more with the hunched-over form of another of them trying to climb in, and this time she realised she had to swing.

The bat came down on top of his head, several nails piercing the baseball hat perched on his head, and punching through the skull beneath with a sickening crunch. The boy jerked violently, one of his hands reaching up curiously fumbling to discover what was attached to his head.

Leona yanked hard on the rounders bat to pull it lose. It came out with a grating sound, and the boy flopped back out of the window on to the ground outside.

She heard several of them gasp. 'Fuck! Bitch killed Steve. She killed Steve.'

A second window smashed, beside the first. She waited with the bat raised, but nothing came through for a few seconds. Then she saw something large filling the second window-frame. It blocked the light coming from the torches outside. It squeezed in through the frame. She switched on her torch and saw it was the bulging form of a bed mattress being pushed through; a makeshift shield, behind which they would be waiting to surge through.

She swung her bat at it, hoping to dislodge it from the grip of those behind. The nails tore through the material exposing the white foamy stuffing inside.

'Go away, go away!' she screamed several times, her voice growing shrill and ragged.

'Here we co-ome!' someone outside called in a teasing singsong way.

Run to the hiding place. Now!

Leona had failed to pay attention to where she was standing as she'd swung ferociously at the bulging mattress. Her back was to the other open window. All of a sudden, she felt a pair of hands grab hold of her left wrist, and another hand snaked up her shoulder and tangled with her hair. She screamed in agony as the hand pulled hard, almost ripping her hair out by the roots.

Oh my God, they've got me!

Her head banged heavily against the window-frame as the hands struggled to pull her out over the jagged shards of glass still stuck in the frame into the front garden.

Then he appeared out of nowhere, out of the darkness in the lounge, an ice-white face, eyes wide like porcelain marbles behind the rim of his spectacles, his mouth a dark yawning oval of rage. She felt the swish of air, and saw a pale-blue plastic blur.

The Swingball bat smacked the forearm of the hand that had hold of her hair.

'Let go of my sister!' screamed Jacob like a banshee. He pulled the bat back off the arm, revealing half-a-dozen gouges, and then swung it down again on the forearm. The hand instantly let go and retreated taking the Swingball bat with it, still firmly attached.

Leona ducked down and sank her teeth into the hands around her wrist. They too swiftly let go.

The mattress was almost wholly inside the lounge now, and she sensed she and Jacob had already lost the initiative. They were coming in regardless.

She turned to Jacob, grabbing him by the hand, she turned on her heels, leading him out of the lounge, into the hall, and towards the bottom of the stairs.

London

When the sky had started to darken she knew she had only a little daylight left to make use of. Jenny decided it was dangerous to be walking out in the streets on her own. The length of pipe she had picked up earlier today had felt like an all-powerful mace capable of dealing out death with one blow. But that had been back when it was in the middle of the afternoon. She'd felt a lot braver then. Now it was dark, and every shadow promised to be the poised form of some starving ghoul, waiting for her to get just a little bit closer before leaping out at her.

Her big metal pipe, right now, felt about as effective and menacing as one of those long twisty party balloons you can make a poodle out of.

Her feet were tired and blistered. She must have walked ten or fifteen miles from Watford.

Along the way she had counted the number of people she had spotted; 47, that was all. Most of them through windows, behind curtains and blinds, picking through piles of discarded plunder in the doorways of stores, or cowering in the dim shells of their homes.

As she had passed through the outskirts of north-west London, entering Kenton, and started seeing bodies, pushed to the kerbside, half-buried down rubbish-strewn alleyways, tucked behind wheelie bins, she'd decided to count them too.

She gave up at 100.

As she passed north-east of Wembley and spotted the unmistakable archway of the stadium in the distance, she entered Edgware. It had gone ten in the evening when she decided the prudent thing would be to find somewhere discreet to curl up and hide until the morning, even though Shepherd's Bush was now only a few miles away. It would be the cruellest irony if only three or four miles from home she was jumped by someone.

She found a furniture store that had been broken into and some of the stock dragged out and carried away. She was bemused by that, that someone would decide *now* was a good time to get their hands on that lusted-after leather couch. She felt confident that no one would be lurking inside though. There was no food or water to be had here. That meant it was relatively safe.

She found a comfy couch near the front of the shop, where she could look out of the still intact display window on to the high street, yet she was shielded from view by the high back and the over-large cushions. Safe-ish, comfortable, a good enough place to quietly curl up, watch the sky darken and wait for dawn to come. She finished off her last bottle of water.

She awoke with a start. It was fully dark. The glow-hands on her watch showed it was 10.31 p.m. Something had prodded her awake. A sound? She could hear nothing right now.

It was pitch-black inside.

Outside, on the other hand, was faintly discernible, lit by the pallid glow from the moon. There was nothing she could see in detail, just the outlines of the buildings opposite. There was no movement of any kind. But something had awoken her from a very deep sleep. Something had jabbed her sharply to pull her out of that.

And then she sensed it wasn't anything outside on the high street. It wasn't anything inside the furniture shop either. It was within her. An alarm going off; a shrill, terrifying shriek warning her at an intuitive level, that something was happening *right now*, to her children.

'Oh no,' she whispered to herself.

Her adult mind chided her.

Just a nightmare, Jenny. God knows you're due one after everything you've been through this week.

Yes ... a nightmare. That was it. But the sensation was strong; an over-powering sense of being hunted, chased, fleeing from certain death.

Classic nightmare material is all this is, Jen. This really isn't what you think it is.

Isn't what? Maternal instinct? Of course not. She reminded herself that that was the sort of nonsense that belonged in those silly agony aunt columns, or tales from the heart short stories you'd find somewhere in the middle of those glossy Moronic Mummy Mags, tales of mothers *sensing* their child calling out to them for help.

But it felt so intense, so real, that Jenny found herself sitting up, and clasping a hand to her chest. It hurt, something in her was hurting, like a stomach ulcer that had gravitated up into her chest.

'Please ... please,' she cried, as huge rolling tears coursed down her face in the absolute darkness, her hand kneading her breastbone.

She desperately wanted to rush out into the street and start running towards home. She was maybe as little as what ... five or six miles away? She could be home in the space of an hour. But it was dark out there, in which direction would she run? She might start running in the dark, and end up in the morning further away, lost amidst some anonymous suburban warren in Finchley.

Your kids need you to be smart, Jenny. Not stupid. It was a bloody nightmare. Lie down. Get some rest. Just a nightmare ... just a nightmare. You'll see the kids tomorrow.

Jenny did as she was told. She lay down. She couldn't sleep though.

CHAPTER 77

. . . .

10.11 p.m. GMT

Shepherd's Bush, London

Leona dragged Jacob up the stairs.

At the top, they crossed the small landing and dived into Jill's guest bed-room. In the corner of the room was a wash-basin. It wasn't plumbed in, that was something she had yet to arrange – '*you know how it is, you can never find a good plumber in London*'.

The basin had been built into a recess in the wall, and the space beneath it, where, one day, plumbing and pipes would descend to the floor, had been boxed in with plywood panels and a little access hatch to make it presentable and flush with the bedroom wall.

Leona knew there was space in there for both of them, they'd tried it out this afternoon. And, as an afterthought, Leona had pulled one of Jill's chintzy tea-towels out from beneath the kitchen sink, and with thumbtacks, attached it so that it draped down over the hatch. She hoped none of the Bad Boys would think to lift the tea-towel and pull on the small brass handle beneath.

Well at least that's what she hoped.

She lifted the corner of the towel up and opened the hatch. 'In you go.'

Jacob scrambled inside. She climbed in after him, curling up with her knees jammed under her chin and her arms wrapped tightly around them; curled up snugly, foetus-like, she just about managed to squeeze into the space beside him. She pulled the hatch to, hoping that the towel hadn't caught on the handle and had flopped down smoothly, concealing their hiding place.

'Are we safe Lee?' whispered Jacob.

'We're safe. But you have to be very quiet now, okay?'

She felt him trembling as he nodded silently.

The noises coming from downstairs indicated that several of them were inside the house now. She could hear the furniture barricade being pulled aside in the hallway, the clatter of furniture being yanked at angrily and thrown across the hall. She could hear footfalls along the hallway, kitchen unit doors being opened and slammed as the first of the gang to make it inside hunted for the most important thing ... something to drink, alcoholic or not. Quenching the thirst came above all else.

She knew they were going to easily find all those two-litre bottles of water stacked in the broom cupboard and it would all be quickly consumed by the gang.

There seemed to be a lot of movement in the kitchen. She heard several voices raised angrily, the sound of a scuffle, a fight amongst them. It seemed that although 50 Cent might be nominally in charge, there was no firmly established pecking order or agreement on how the spoils were to be distributed amongst them. It was just a free-for-all.

The noises from the kitchen died down after a few minutes ... thirsts had been quenched.

That's all our water gone.

Under any other circumstances that would have been a frightening realisation; to know the next drink they managed to find would probably come from the Thames, or the putrid, microbe-infested offerings of someone's roof storage-tank, festering in the heat of the last few days.

But her thoughts were on right now, her focus was on remaining undiscovered for the next ten, twenty, thirty minutes. That would surely be more than enough time for the Bad Boys to find all of their carefully stored rations of food and water; enough time to completely clean them out and then collectively decide who was the next lucky household to be paid a night-time visit.

But that's not everything they want, is it?

She shuddered at the thought, her arms and knees twitching violently.

'What's up?' Jacob whispered.

'Shhhh.'

It wasn't just food and water they were after, was it? They'd be looking for a replacement Smurfette, a gang sex-slave. If she was unlucky, she'd end up like Mrs DiMarcio.

We should have run.

Leona realised they had made a big mistake staying here. They should have run during the afternoon. Those boys downstairs – no, *boys* was the wrong word – Leona realised she had stopped thinking of them as such, some time over the last couple of days. She saw them as feral creatures now; wild things, ogres, trolls, hobgoblins. They reminded her of a pack of baboons she had once seen on a family trip to the zoo many years ago, simple-minded creatures with a basic set of overpowering drives: thirst, hunger, anger ... rape.

Oh God, we should have gone this afternoon.

She heard footsteps coming up the stairs, so many of them, a dozen or more coming upstairs to hunt her down. Because they knew she was somewhere inside still. They knew it, and they were coming for their cookies.

Leona realised if she'd been smarter, she would have left the back door open, suggesting that they had bolted out into the night. But of course, she hadn't thought ahead, she hadn't been smart, and now they *knew* she was still here, somewhere inside. This was going to be another playground game for them to have fun with; hide and seek ... with the special prize going to the first of them to find her and drag her out kicking and screaming.

The door to the guest bedroom swung in and she heard four or five of them enter. They were giggling. Now that the pressing need to quench their thirst had been dealt with, it was fun and games time. The anticipation, the excitement, the thrill of the hunt and the promise of the fun they'd have as soon as they found her, and raped her, was making them giggle like little boys sharing a guilty secret, an in-joke.

She could feel Jacob's little frog-like arms quivering against her in shuddering waves that ebbed and flowed. His breathing fluttered in and out. If those boys weren't making so much noise, they'd hear that so easily.

'Tch ... tch ... tch ... Here pussy! Here pussy!' one of them called as if trying to coax out a household pet. The others laughed.

Leona flinched as a narrow shard of light swept across her hand. A flashlight was being panned about the room, a slither of it had found a narrow crack or a seam in the panelling.

That giggling again ... Beavis and Butt-head giggling. She used to find that cartoon funny. She used to find the sniggering they used to do hilarious, for some unfathomable reason. Right now, that sound was as terrifying as the metallic rasp of a blade sliding from its sheath.

Her throat constricted with fear, the breath she'd held for far too long, now had to come out. Exhaling, she let out the slightest strangled whimper.

'Hear that?'

'She's in here?'

'Shit, yeah.'

She heard them spreading out, pulling open the wardrobe doors, opening a closet ... then the sound of a hand brushing aside the tea-towel and fumbling at the brass handle for the hatch.

Oh God this is it.

Leona leant over and kissed the top of Jacob's head, she knew this was going to be her very last opportunity to do that.

'Be brave Jakey,' she whispered into his ear.

A shout from downstairs.

Another frantic shout and then a scream.

'What's up?' she heard the voice just outside, beyond the panel, utter.

'Fuck, dunno.'

Leona could hear something crashing around downstairs, as if a bull had somehow found its way inside and was struggling to find a way back out again.

A single gunshot!

The scream of one of the lads.

Then about a dozen more shots.

A voice downstairs screaming, 'Fuckin' Boomers! Wankers!'

More crashing and thumping.

The boys in the room were spooked. 'Shit, Boomers. They got fuckin' pieces!'

'Shit, we're dead if they catch us!'

Leona heard their feet on the bedroom floor, then the rumble of a dozen or so of them charging down the stairs. The noise coming from downstairs continued for about five minutes; shouting, screaming, the crash of young men throwing each other around, and the sporadic pop of a gun.

And then it diminished as the fighting migrated out of the house into the avenue.

She heard the fighting continue for another couple of minutes, diminishing still further as it moved up the street.

And then eventually, silence.

'Have the Bad Boys gone, Lee?' whispered Jacob.

'I think they have,' she replied.

'Should we get out now?'

Leona wasn't ready to climb out of their little hidey-hole just yet. It was uncomfortable, insufferably stuffy and she was getting terrible cramp in her legs, but right now, she'd rather be tucked in here than anywhere else on the planet.

'Why don't we stay in here for a while longer, okay?'

'Sure,' said Jacob.

CHAPTER 78

· · · ·

11.59 p.m. GMT

Guildford

His wishful thinking paid off. He heard the tentative shuffling of feet outside in the hallway, and a moment later he heard a key in the door. Ash moved quickly, from the first sound of footsteps outside to the door creaking open had only been a few seconds, but enough time for him to rouse himself and be ready to deal with any travelling companion she might have brought with her.

As it happened, she entered alone, and almost immediately sensed, even though it was pitch-black, that something was not quite right.

Before she could turn and go, he was upon her, an arm around her neck, his blade tickling her left cheek, and his mouth close to her ear.

'Kate, I've been waiting *ages* for you.'

She let out a scream, and his hand quickly stifled it.

'I thought you were never going to come home, Kate.'

She struggled in his firm grasp.

'Easy, let's not wiggle about too much. I might pop your eye out with this thing.'

Kate's eyes rolled down at the glinting object beside her face, and she stopped struggling.

'That's better. Now, I need to have a quick chat, Kate. So let's both sit down. We'll get a little candle-light going so I can see what I'm doing, okay?'

Five minutes later he had a scented candle from the kitchen glowing prettily in a saucer. Kate sat on the floor, her hands taped up behind her back and Ash squatted over her, swinging his blade like a pendulum in front of her.

And he realised he could have handled this a little more cleverly.

'Please! Please,' she whimpered, her eyes locked on to the blade of his knife, as it moved from side to side in front of her face.

Ash had screwed this up. It just goes to show, he mused; you think you're at the top of your game, and then you find you can still make mistakes.

His error was in letting Kate realise that he was after the Sutherland girl. He could have ... *should have* made out he was after Jill – Kate of course didn't care much about her sister's friend. She said she'd met her once or twice, had heard Jenny prattle on about Jill from time to time ... but she clearly wouldn't lay down her life to protect this woman.

It seemed though, she was prepared to go quite a long way toward protecting her sister's kids.

'I ... I d-don't know where she lives ... please ...'

'Does she live *close* to them?'

There was a flicker of reaction on her face. One of those involuntary micro-ticks difficult to control, and the sort of thing a trained interrogator, a hostage negotiator ... or even a big business deal-closer looks out for; better, much better, than a blip on a polygraph.

'Ahh, so she *does* live nearby then?' he said smiling.

Kate shook her head.

'Too late, Kate. Your very expressive and very pretty face just told me, you know. Now, I suppose I could go look up all the *J. Harriotts* in the phone book, and pick out any that live nearby your sister's place. But that sounds to me like a bit of a chore. And you know what? I'm a little pressed for time. Far easier if you just tell me, hmm?'

Kate shook her head.

Ash sighed. 'Oh dear.' He gently prodded her left cheek, just below the eye, with the tip of his knife. 'How shall we do this? Fingers? Or perhaps I could start on your face. What do you think?'

'P-please ... please don't h-hurt me,' she whispered.

He stroked the bristles on his chin – a normally well-trimmed goatee, that after the last two days of neglect was just beginning to look the slightest bit untidy. 'You do have a very pretty face, Kate. It would be horrible, wouldn't it, to no longer have a nose? Or perhaps be missing a bottom lip?'

'Oh ... G-god, no!' she gasped.

He smiled and looked at his knife. 'This little blade has seen plenty of action, Kate, over the years. I've actually popped this little sucker into some quite important people ... you might even have heard of one or two of them, if you read around the Sunday papers enough. So you're going to be in good company.'

Kate stifled a whimper.

'It's a very sharp blade. I really wouldn't have to apply too much pressure for it to slide through the skin and gristle of that very nice nose of yours.'

She shuddered, and a tear rolled down her cheek. Ash tenderly brushed it away. 'I think you're ready to tell me now, aren't you?'

She nodded.

'Okay then, let's have it.'

'What w-will you d-do to my niece?' Kate whispered.

He decided a little white lie would keep things rolling along nicely. 'We just want to talk to her, Kate. That's all. It's something to do with her daddy's work.'

'Y-you won't h-hurt her?'

Ash shook his head. 'She's just a child. What sort of person –?' he snapped, scowling at her. 'Look, I have a sister her age, for Chrissakes. No, Kate, I won't hurt her. But I need to talk to her, quickly.'

Kate glanced again at the knife, still only a few inches away from her face.

'Who are you?' she asked.

Ash's eyes widened with surprise. 'Oh, *you're* asking the questions now, are you?' He laughed. She smiled anxiously, hoping that was helping her somehow.

'Since you ask, I'm with the secret services, I can't tell you which branch of course. But I'm on very important government business.'

He knew that sounded hooky, but frightened and wanting to believe it, she might just.

She nodded. 'I ... but you don't s-sound British,' she whispered sceptically.

Ah well, worth a try.

Ash smiled. 'You're right, I'm not. But believe me when I say I will mutilate you badly if you don't tell me what I need to know, right now.'

'Jill lives in the same street as them,' Kate blurted quickly.

Ash grimaced. *I knew it.*

'Where exactly?'

'A ... a few doors d-down, on the o-other side.'

You saw her, you fucking idiot. You saw her, didn't you? Unloading that van ... and then later on, looking out of the window of that house, looking straight at you.

He cursed under his breath. That could have been her. On both occasions he hadn't been close enough to get a clear look at her face, but yes, thinking back, it was the girl in the photo – a different hair colour, and maybe a little slimmer than the girl in the picture he had. He even recalled thinking there was a passing resemblance, but for crying out loud, who would be so stupid as to go into hiding a mere fifty yards from home?

Shit.

He could have had her yesterday.

Kate looked intently at him, wary of the flickering signs of distraction and anger on his face. 'What are you g-going to do with m—?'

'Oh shut up!' he snapped irritably, swiping the blade quickly across her throat, and stepping smartly back as blood arced out in front of her and pitter-pattered on to the spotless cream carpet in front of her.

He wiped the blade clean as she recovered from the shock and realised what had just happened. She wriggled around on the floor, trying to work her hands free. Why exactly, Ash didn't know; holding her hands to her gaping neck wasn't going help her much now.

He looked down at her and offered her a smile. 'It's not personal, Kate. As a rule I prefer to leave bodies behind me, instead of yapping mouths.'

She tried to gurgle something to him and then slumped forward on to her knees, her forehead pressed against the carpet. The blood splattered out as the wound across her neck opened wider.

'That's a good girl, that'll speed things up for you.' He stepped towards her front door. 'I'll let myself out then.'

Saturday

CHAPTER 79

. . . .

4.21 a.m. GMT

Heathrow, London

They landed at Heathrow Airport at a few minutes after four a.m.

Andy had awoken from a deep sleep twenty minutes before they were due to land. He guessed his body had sensed the change in air pressure, or been awoken by the increase in chatter and excitement around him. Looking out of the window, as the plane made several stepped drops in altitude, he saw the same pitch-black nothing, the same absence of any sign of human activity that they'd seen earlier across Europe.

On the final approach to Heathrow he finally spotted a string of lights marking out the landing strip, and, in the sky, the strobing navigation lights of a dozen other planes that were either coming in to land, or had recently taken off.

There were no announcements from the airliner's captain. It had been an oddly silent trip. They landed heavily with a bump and a bounce, and taxied swiftly off the main runway, following the tail of a military truck instead of the usual CAA follow-me buggy.

At last, as the plane rolled towards its slot amidst a mixed assortment of military planes, C130 Hercules transports, Tristars and various passenger jets, Andy heard the pilot speak for the first time.

'Uh ... this is your pilot speaking. My name's Captain Andrew Melton. And this is a GoJet plane flying under military jurisdiction right now. So, we're home again, back in the United Kingdom,' his tired voice announced over the cabin-speakers. There was a muted cheer from some of the soldiers up and down the cabin.

'But ... uh ... as you may have guessed, things have changed a lot back here in the UK over the last week. I've just been told by air traffic control that Heathrow Airport is under military control at the moment, and has been for the last two days.'

Through the window Andy watched passengers emerge from a neighbouring plane, an EasyJet 727. They looked to be mostly military personnel, but he thought he spotted amongst them some civilians, a few women and one or two children.

Very, very lucky holiday-makers.

The order of priority for getting British nationals home had been military first. That's what this huge effort had been all about, not for civilians stranded abroad whilst on holiday, but to get troops back home. Given the state of things right now, Andy could see that made perfect sense.

'I've been told that all military passengers aboard are going to be processed off this plane first. Then the civilian passengers will be processed,' said the captain. 'I'm not really sure what they mean by "processed" folks, but that's the word they're asking me to use.'

Westley gave Andy a nod. 'Looks like this is where we part company, like.'

'Yeah.'

They both stared out of the window at the floodlit scene. They could see lines of people from recently arrived planes, snaking across the tarmac towards the terminal ahead. Watching over them, directing the disembarked passengers, were armed soldiers looking to all intents and purposes like prison guards overseeing a shuffling chain-gang.

The pilot came on again. 'I'm not sure how much you people are aware of. Since this crisis started on Monday an emergency authority has taken over control and we are effectively under some sort of martial law. I'm not sure what that means in terms of what we can and can't do, but obviously things are different ... uh ... one second.'

The cabin-speakers clicked as the pilot switched channels and now all they could hear was a hiss.

'Right,' the pilot's voice returned over the speakers. 'There's a stairway locking on now. When the doors open, can we have military personnel disembarking first please?'

Andy could hear the mobile stairs as they gently nudged the plane. A moment later the plane's hatches opened with a clunk. Immediately the noise from outside roared in; the whine of jet engines from the planes parked either side, the distant roar of a jet getting ready to take off, and the rumble of another touching down.

Westley unbuckled his belt and stood up in the central aisle between the rows of seats, stretching tiredly and looking down at the few remaining members of his platoon.

'Shake a leg lads,' he said. 'Hey, Derry, wake up you soft lad.'

The aisle filled with soldiers, most of them stripped down to their olive T-shirts, their desert camouflage shirts tied around their waists or slung over one arm. Andy looked around, there were about twenty people still seated – civilians, contractors like himself, mostly.

At the front of the plane an officer appeared in the aisle. 'All right lads, let's go. Down the stairs, there's a truck waiting for you,' he called out loudly.

Westley turned to Andy and held out a hand. 'This is it then,' he said.

Andy grabbed his hand. 'Yup. You look after yourself, okay? We've been through way too much shit for you to get knocked over by a baggage trolley now.'

Westley laughed. 'Right-o, sir.'

'You know what? I might even let you call me Andy instead of "Sir".'

The lance corporal smiled. 'Sorry, force of habit.'

'Take care of yourself Westley.'

He shrugged. 'Ahh, we've been through the worst of it, eh? Can't be any bloody worse here.'

Andy nodded. 'Yeah, you're right.'

'When things get better, we'll meet up, yeah?'

'Beers are on me; you and the platoon,' said Andy.

Westley laughed. 'You'll probably regret that.' He let go of his hand. 'Take care Sutherland.'

'You too.'

Westley nodded and smiled and then shuffled awkwardly. They'd said all that needed to be said. He then turned to face his men. 'Come on lads, let's do as the officer says, and get a move on!' he barked. The lads of the platoon shuffled past Westley, each nodding a goodbye towards Andy as they went.

'Good luck lads,' said Andy, watching them make their way down towards the front of the plane.

Westley was about to follow on after them but he stopped and turned round, and leant forward over the seat in front of Andy. 'Oh, by the way, I left you a pressie,' he whispered, 'you might need it.' He winked at Andy and then turned to join his men. Andy watched him go before looking down at the seat to his right; there was nothing he could see there. He then looked at the pouch on the back of the seat in front and saw that the sick-bag bulged with something.

Andy could guess what it was. He let the last of the soldiers squeeze past in the narrow aisle before pulling the paper bag out of the pouch and looking inside it.

Yup.

He took the service pistol and the two spare clips out and tucked them into the thigh pocket of his shorts.

CHAPTER 80

· · · ·

10.03 a.m. GMT

Shepherd's Bush, London

Leona stirred in the complete darkness. For a second she wondered where she was, and then remembered. She tried to move her arms and legs, but they were numb, and when she did finally manage to coax some movement out of them, she felt an explosion of pins and needles in all four limbs.

She pushed the hatch open, and a pale morning glow flooded into their hidey-hole. She realised she must have actually managed to fall asleep in there.

'C'mon Jakey,' she said to her little brother. He stirred quickly, his yawn no more than a tired squeak.

She climbed out, helped Jacob scramble out, and then, wary that there might still be members of the gang hanging around, they stepped lightly across the room to the hallway.

She glanced into each room. There was no one. The rooms had all been ransacked, of course.

They tiptoed down the stairs and quickly came across the results of last night's ruckus on the ground floor.

The lounge, the kitchen, Jill's study, were completely trashed. It looked like the entire house had been gently lifted a couple of yards off the ground, and then dropped. She noticed a row of shallow craters along the lounge wall, and realised they were bullet-holes. And she noticed a fair amount of blood splattered along the skirting-boards, and smeared across the smooth parquet floor of the entrance hall, as if a body had been dragged, or someone badly hurt had tried to drag himself away.

The barricade built from the stacked kitchen chairs, table, and a couple of heavy chests had been pushed to one side and the front door was dangling from one last screw holding the top hinge to the door-frame. It swung with a gentle creak.

She found two bodies in the kitchen. They both looked younger than her, perhaps fifteen, sixteen; smooth, young, porcelain faces, eyes closed as if sleeping – they looked almost angelic lying side by side amidst a dark, almost black pool of blood that had spread during the night across most of the kitchen floor. Several of the MDF kitchen units sported jagged splintered bullet-holes. Under foot, shards of glass crackled and popped against the tile floor.

Jacob wandered in before she could stop him.

'Oh,' he said.

'Jake, out ... go on.'

Jacob didn't budge, fascinated by the two corpses, 'They're dead aren't they?' a hint of awe in his voice.

'Yes, Jake, they're dead.'

'Did someone shoot them?'

'Yup.' She counted a dozen jagged holes around the kitchen. Someone had fired off a lot of bullets in here. One of the dead boys was clutching a kitchen knife, beside the other one she spotted a baseball bat.

Hardly an even fight.

She recognised both of them as being members of the gang that had been preying on the avenue these last few nights. She had guessed that the fight last night must have been between the Bad Boys and some other group – perhaps a rival gang from White City.

But these other ones had guns.

She led Jacob out of the kitchen, literally dragging him away from the bodies, which he studied with an intense fascination.

And then she saw him, through the open front door, lying amongst the weeds in Jill's front garden; caught the slightest movement.

'Go into the lounge and stay there,' she commanded Jacob.

'Why?'

'I'm just going to take a peek outside.'

Jake nodded. 'Be careful, Lee,' he whispered as he padded across the hallway and sat down in front of the shattered screen of Jill's extravagant TV set and stared at it, willing it to come on.

She stepped out of the house, cautiously advancing on the body writhing slowly on the ground.

She recognised him.

50 Cent.

Closer now, she could see he'd been shot in the shoulder, his crisp white

Nike shirt was almost entirely coloured a rich, dark sepia, and he lay on a bed of pebbles now glued together by a sticky bond of drying blood. He looked weak, he had lost too much blood during the night to last for very much longer. She would have thought the underlings in his gang would have returned for their leader.

Apparently not.

So much for the notion of gang loyalty – not so much this lifelong brotherly bond, as she'd heard many a rapper say of his homies – instead, more like a group of feral creatures, co-operating under the intimidating gaze of the pack alpha. When it came to it, they'd all scurried off, leaving the little shit bleeding out on the gravel.

In one hand he held a pistol, which he tried desperately to raise off the ground and aim at her, but he had only the strength to shuffle it around on the ground.

He looked up at her, recognised her face and smiled. 'My honey,' he grunted with some effort. 'Help me.'

Leona knelt down beside him and reached out for the gun. He hung on to it, but she managed to prise it loose from his fingers with little effort.

'I need help,' he said again, his voice was no more than a gummy rattle.

This was probably an opportune moment.

'You recognised me last night, didn't you? You were the one who asked me for a fag up at the mall.'

The boy said nothing.

'What did you do to my boyfriend?'

50 Cent shook his head almost imperceptibly. 'He ran.'

And then she noticed the ankh pendant nestling amongst the stained folds of his T-shirt.

Dan's pendant.

Leona knew right then that she didn't need to hear the lie in his voice to know what had happened to Dan. With a movement so swift that there was no room for any internal debate, she aimed the gun at his head, closed her eyes and pulled the trigger.

There was an overpowering stench that hung in the warm midday air; a mixture of rotting cabbage and burning rubber. She noticed several thin whispy columns of dark smoke on the horizon. London wasn't exactly ablaze, just smouldering in one or two far-off places. But that burning smell certainly carried. After a while, Leona decided she'd rather breathe just through her mouth.

They walked up Uxbridge Road, which was even more cluttered with detritus than it had been on Wednesday, the last time she had been out. She noticed one or two bundles of clothing amongst the piles of rubbish that turned out to be bodies. She made a point of distracting Jacob as they walked past the closest of them. He didn't need to see any more stuff like that, not so up-close anyway. They walked past Shepherd's Bush Green, over the large roundabout, which was normally surrounded by a moat of stationary cars, vans and trucks beeping, honking, getting nowhere fast, but was now just an isolated island of grass with a large, pointless, blue thermometer sculpture in the middle. On the top of it, a row of crows patiently sat and watched them.

Where did all the pigeons go?

She wondered whether the bird world mirrored the human world. The crows were the gangs, and the pigeons were nervously hiding away some-where else.

'I'm scared,' muttered Jacob.

'Don't be, we've got this now,' she replied calmly, lifting her shirt an inch or two to reveal the gun stuffed into the waist of her jeans.

'Can I fire it?'

'No.'

'You had a go,' he complained.

'It went off when I picked it up,' she lied, feeling the slightest unpleasant twinge; the thin end of something she knew was going to inhabit her dreams for years to come.

'Can I hold it then?'

'No.'

They walked over the roundabout towards Holland Park where the homes came with an extra zero to their price tag, and looked a good deal grander than their humble terraced house. Here, she noticed, there had been less rioting and looting. The road, although still cluttered with some debris, was a lot clearer than it was back over the roundabout in Shepherd's Bush. Leona guessed the people there had so much less need to loot. There'd be well-stocked larders in every home, and the chavs and hoodies who normally populated the cor-ners round here, were probably up in those grand three-storey town houses helping mother and father work their way through the wine collection.

'I'm sure we'll find something to drink and eat round here,' she said. 'It looks much less messed up than back home.'

'This is where the really rich people live,' he said.

She nodded, 'Yeah, and they always seem to do all right when there's a problem.'

Five minutes later they spotted a small convenience store tucked down a cul-de-sac, lined with hanging baskets of flowers; very *villagey*, very pretty and largely untouched by the last week's chaos. Metal roller-shutters had come down, probably at the first sign of trouble, and apart from a couple of dents in them where someone had tried their luck smashing through, and one of the large windows behind had been cracked but not shattered, it looked like the store had yet to be looted.

'Is there food in there?' asked Jacob.

Leona nodded. 'I think as much as we need. Stand back.'

She aimed the pistol at a sturdy looking padlock at the bottom of the shutter, and grimaced as she slowly squeezed the trigger.

Jacob yelped with excitement, hopping up and down as the gun cracked loudly. The padlock fragmented into several jagged parts and the glass door behind the shutter shattered.

'Yeah!' shouted Jacob, as the smoke cleared and the glass finished falling. 'Wicked!'

'Stay out here,' she said.

She pushed the shutter up and stepped inside the shop, holding the gun up in front of her, shakily panning it around the gloomy interior.

'Okay,' she called out to Jacob. 'Looks clear.'

He joined her inside.

It was a small convenience store, a baker's and delicatessen. The meat was spoiled, she could smell that and a few blue spots of mould had blossomed on most of the bread. There was, however, a heartening array of tinned produce on the shelves, and two large fridges full of bottles and cans, all of them of course warm, but that didn't matter.

She pulled out a bottle of water and gulped it, then handed it to Jacob. He shook his head.

'Not thirsty?'

'Yeah, but I want Coke,' he replied, reaching into the fridge on tiptoes and pulling out a litre bottle.

'Mum would have a fit if she saw you drinking that. It's just sugar and chemicals.'

Jacob shrugged as he twisted the cap off and slurped from the bottle.

'I can't believe this,' she said, with a big grin spreading across her face. 'We've struck a gold-mine.'

'No more pilchards,' added Jacob, wiping his mouth with the back of his hand and belching.

Leona looked back at the open shutter. 'Let's grab what we need quickly. Other people may have heard the bang.'

They found a tartan wheelie bag nearby, one of those shabby things that only old blue-rinsed ladies seem to favour, and filled it with as many tins and bottles of drink as they could squeeze in. Leona found some wire hand-baskets and filled those with some more tins and bottles. She gave a couple of lighter basket-loads to Jacob to struggle home with, filled the wheelie bag, and stacked another couple of baskets full of supplies on top of it.

As they emerged out of the convenience store on to the cul-de-sac, they saw several people warily approaching the entrance, presumably lured by the sound of the padlock being shot off and the glass shattering. The nearest to them, an old couple, eyed the pair of them cautiously.

'Is the shop uh ... open now?' the old man asked.

Jacob, grinning, piped up. 'Yup, open for business.'

The old couple nodded gratefully and quickly disappeared inside.

'We should go,' said Leona, 'it's going to get busy here.'

They headed out of the cul-de-sac and turned right on to Holland Park Avenue, towards the Shepherd's Bush roundabout. They passed a few people along the way, who eyed their plunder with interest, and hurried along swiftly in the direction they had come from.

'We need to be careful,' she said, 'when we get closer to home, there might be some who will try and take what we have.' She patted the bulge on her hip, the heavy, cold lump of metal there felt reassuring.

Heading back past the grand town houses, Leona saw dozens of people curiously emerging on to their balconies and the twitching of countless curtains and blinds. The streets might have been all but deserted, but there seemed to still be plenty of people around, hidden away in their homes. At least here there were.

They approached the roundabout, the crows still sitting atop the big blue thermometer in the middle, watching events with idle interest. Leona spotted someone in the middle of the road up ahead, walking around the central island briskly.

A woman in a white, cheesecloth skirt, holding her shoes in one hand, her back to them as she rounded the grassy island and began to disappear from view.

Her hair, her movement, it was all so very familiar.

'Mum?' she called out, but not loudly enough. The woman carried on, leaving them behind. Leona could only see her head bobbing around the far side of the roundabout's island.

'Mum!' she shouted, her voice breaking. The cry echoed off the tall buildings either side of the road and the woman on the far side of the roundabout stopped dead.

She turned round, and looked back.

Even 200 yards away, her face just a distant pale oval, Leona recognised her.

'MUM!'

The woman looked around, uncertain where the cry had come from. Leona let go of the wheelie bag and waved frantically. The movement caught the woman's eye, and a second later, Leona heard what sounded very much like her mother's voice; a mixture of surprise, shock, joy and tears.

'Leona?' she heard the woman ask more than say.

'Oh my God! ... It *is* Mum, Jake! It's Mum.'

Jacob dropped his basket as well, some of the tins and bottles bounced out on to the road – unimportant to them now. She grabbed her brother's hand and ran forward down the road towards the roundabout, completely unaware that her face had crumpled up like a baby's and she was crying a river of tears, just like her little brother.

They collided into each other's arms a moment later, a three-way scrum of flailing arms and buried faces.

'Oh God, oh God!' sobbed Jenny, squeezing them both as hard as she could. 'Thank God you're all right!'

Leona struggled to reply, but her words were an unintelligible syrupy mewl.

'Mummy!' cried Jacob, 'I missed you, I missed you.'

'God, I missed you too, sweetheart. I was so frightened for both of you.'

'We've been in a battle,' said Jacob. 'It was frightening.'

Jenny looked into Leona's face, and her daughter nodded, her lips curled, tears streaming down her cheeks.

'Leona? Honey?'

She swept a sleeve across her face. 'Yeah, they attacked the house. We nearly ... we nearly ...'

'We nearly died Mum,' Jacob finished helpfully. 'But we've got a real gun now,' he added brightly.

CHAPTER 81

. . . .

11.35 a.m. GMT

Heathrow, London

It could almost have been any normal midsummer's morning there in Terminal 3's departure lounge, thought Andy. It looked unchanged since last time he came through here two weeks ago, on his way out to Iraq to make that assessment on the northern pipeline and pumping stations. However, this time round, the shops and places to eat were closed, the metal shutters pulled down, and beyond the large floor-to-ceiling viewing windows, the tarmac was a hive of activity.

He could see soldiers streaming wearily out of military and civilian jets; a jumbled mess of units, some in desert khakis, some wearing the temperate green camo version. With so many men in uniform, looking lost, weary and confused, it was what the ports along the south coast of England must have looked like on the morning after Dunkirk.

In the departure lounge with him, Andy guessed there were about 200 people; civilians – mostly men, a few women and a handful of children. They were mainly businessmen caught out by events and some holidaymakers; a mishmash of the lucky few British nationals abroad who had managed to stumble upon the various efforts being made to repatriate military personnel. Most of them looked exhausted, dehydrated, and many of them lay stretched out and sleeping on the long, blue couches.

They had been kept waiting in the lounge for several hours without any information. If they weren't all so exhausted, he suspected a ruckus would have been kicked up before now. They had been promised that someone would come and talk to them, and tell them what would happen next.

Finally some people arrived; a woman, accompanied by a couple of armed policeman, and a young man carrying a clipboard. She wore a radio on her belt, and had an official-looking badge pinned to her chest.

'Excuse me!' she called out. 'Excuse me!'

The people in the departure lounge, including Andy, quickly roused themselves and gathered round her.

'We're sorry for keeping you all waiting so long.' She looked harried, flustered and almost as exhausted as the anxious people surrounding her. 'We're going to be moving all of you to a safe zone where we can supply you with food and water rations whilst the current situation continues.'

'What's going on out there?' asked someone behind Andy.

The woman, he could see from her name badge, was an emergency manager with the Civil Emergency Response Agency. She shook her head. 'I'm afraid things are a bit of a mess out there, across the country. The emergency authorities have been establishing several safe zones where we can control things more easily and sensibly distribute rations. Outside of those, it's ... ' she shook her head again,' ... well, it's not good.'

'Where are these "safe zones"? How many, how big?'

Her head spun round to face the direction from which the query had come. 'I don't know how many exactly. But in the capital, the Millennium Dome is being used as an emergency mustering point and supply centre. We have another major supply and distribution safety zone based in Battersea and another at Leatherhead. These zones are being guarded by the police and the army to ensure ...'

'Guarded? From who?' Andy raised his voice from the back.

She turned to face him, and took a moment to think before answering. 'We have supplies in the safe zones to keep some of the population going for the foreseeable future. But I'm afraid not all.'

The crowd stirred, he heard voices murmuring, whispered concern amongst them.

'Are people dying out there?'

That's a stupid bloody question, thought Andy.

She nodded. 'There's a lot of instability, riots, chaos. The water system stopped functioning several days ago. People are drinking unclean water, they're becoming sick, and yes ... some will eventually die. We're seeing what we've seen on the telly in the aftermath of disasters like the tsunami; infectious diseases, spoiled food and water ... those sorts of things. Until the oil flows again, supplies of sterile water and food are the critical issues.'

'When will the oil flow again?' shouted another in the crowd.

She shrugged. 'I don't have the answer to that.' She put on a reassuring smile for them. 'But when it does ... we'll be on our way out of this situation. And every effort will be made to distribute medicines and emergency supplies of food and water to those who need it most. In the meantime, we're working hard to ensure we can help as many people as possible ride this out in, like I say, these safe zones.'

She gestured towards the young man standing beside her with the clipboard. 'We need to take all of your names, a few particulars, look at your passports if you have them ... and then when we're done, there's a couple of army trucks which will be taking you to either the Leatherhead or the Battersea safe zone. So if you can form an orderly line here, we'll get started.'

The crowd of people around her shuffled compliantly into a long queue, and the young man pulled up a seat to sit on and another stool to use as a makeshift desk. The two armed policemen, wearing Kevlar vests and casually cradling their machine-guns, took a step back, perhaps sensing this crowd was too beaten and tired to pose any sort of security risk.

The woman, meanwhile, disengaged from the process and found a quiet space between two large potted plastic plants and, ignoring the sign on the wall behind her, lit up a cigarette.

Andy wandered over towards her. Closer, he could see how tired and drawn she was; there were bags beneath her eyes, and a nervous tremor shook the hand that held the cigarette shakily to her lips.

Her eyes fixed on him as he closed the last few yards. She almost bothered to put her 'we've-got-it-all-under-control' smile back on for him ... but clearly decided it was too much trouble.

'Help you?' she asked, blowing smoke out of her nose.

'Do I get a choice?'

'Sorry?'

'Do I get a choice? I mean, if I don't want to be taken into one of these safe zones?'

'You don't?' She was genuinely surprised. 'Why the hell would you not?' she said, and then took another long pull on her cigarette.

'I need to get home to my family.'

She shrugged, 'I can understand that.'

Andy turned round. 'These people,' he said gesturing at the queue that had formed in the middle of the departure lounge, 'are going to die in your safe zones. You know that, don't you?'

'Excuse me?'

'How many people have you rounded up at Battersea, Leatherhead, the Dome?'

'Look, I don't know off hand ... I'm just a sub-regional co-ordinator.'

'Guess.'

'Shit, I don't know,' she shook her head, too tired and strung-out to want to get sucked into this kind of conversation.

'A hundred thousand? A million?'

She nodded. 'Yeah, maybe half a million around London, and in other places too. Look, we're doing our best—'

'I don't doubt you are. But do you have enough food and water to feed them for six months? Nine months? Maybe even a year?'

'What?' she said, her eyebrows knotted with confusion. She blew out a veil of smoke. 'What the hell are you talking about?'

'Recovery.'

'Listen,' she said flicking ash into one of the pots beside her and glancing casually at the 'No Smoking' sign on a wall nearby, 'it's not going to take a year for the oil to get flowing again. Some pipelines got blown, some oil refineries got damaged, right? That's what happened.'

Andy nodded.

'So how long does it take to fix that? I'm sure there're people out there working on it right now. We'll have oil again in a couple of weeks, okay? So look, why don't you give me a break, join the queue and let me have a fag in peace?' She offered him an apologetic shrug. 'It's been a really long, fucking day.'

Andy took a step closer and lowered his voice. 'Somebody up there, in charge of things, is being very naive if they think it's all going to be hunky-dory again within a few weeks.'

'So ... what? You want us to let you go?'

Andy nodded, 'Yup. I'll take my chances outside one of your safe zones.'

She stubbed her cigarette out and tossed it into one of the pots. 'Okay then, your funeral. I'll have one of our lads escort you out of the perimeter.' She pulled the radio off her belt and talked quickly and quietly into it. 'Somebody will be along shortly to take you out,' she said to him.

'Thanks,' said Andy and then turned to go and sit down again.

'Wait,' said the woman.

He turned back to face her.

'You really think this is going to go on that long? Six months?'

'Sure. The oil might start gushing again next week, but where's our food going to come from? The Brazilian farmer growing our coffee beans, the Ukrainian farmer growing our spuds, the Spanish farmer growing our apples ... think about it. Is his little business still functioning? Is he still alive, or is he injured, or sick? Or how about this ... has his crop spoiled in the ground, uncollected because he didn't have fuel to operate his tractor? And what about all those crop-buyers, packagers, processors, distributors ... all the links in the chain that get food out of the soil around the world and into the supermarket up the road? Can those companies still function? Do they still exist, or are their factories looted, burned down? And what about their workforce? Are they alive still? Or lying in their homes puking their guts up because they've been drinking the same water that they're shitting into?'

The woman was silent.

'Just a few questions off the top of my head that somebody up the chain of command needs to be asking right now,' said Andy dryly. 'It's not just a case of handing out water bottles and high-energy protein bars for the next fortnight. The oil being stopped ... even for just this week, has well and truly fucked everything up.'

'It can't be that bad,' she replied.

'System-wide failure. It's all stalled. The world was never designed to reboot after something like that.'

'And you'd rather take your chances out there? There's no food, nothing. Whatever there was to loot has been taken by now. Do you not think you're being a bit stupid?'

'Six months from now, the Millennium Dome and all those other safe zones? They'll be death camps.'

The woman looked at him incredulously. 'Oh come on.'

Andy noticed a couple of armed police officers enter the departure lounge and walk towards them.

'Ah,' she said, 'here they are.' She reached a hand out and placed it on his arm. 'Look, why don't you join the queue like the others? I can send them away. It's dangerous in London right now.'

He could see her plea was a genuine act of compassion. She meant well.

'Thanks, but right now I'd rather find my family and get as far as I can from *anyone* else. The last place I'd want to be in six months' time is crammed into a holding-pen with thousands of other people.'

The police escort arrived, and the woman instructed them to guide him out of the building and through the guarded security perimeter around the terminal.

She wished him good luck as they parted.

CHAPTER 82

2.32 p.m. GMT

Shepherd's Bush, London

'**W**hy?' Jenny asked, looking at her daughter. 'Why is it so important that we don't go back to our house?'

Leona shook her head. 'It's what Dad said.'

'I know it's what he said, but he thought Jill was going to be here to look after you. I thought that's why he said to come here.'

Jenny stared at the two bodies in the kitchen, at the pool of blood and splatter streaks on the walls and cupboards. 'We can't stay here. I don't want Jacob having to see any more of this than he has alread—'

'We *have* to stay away, Mum,' said Leona. 'We can't go home.'

Jenny grabbed her shoulders and turned her round. 'Why?'

Leona shook her head. Jenny could see there was something she wanted to say.

'Come on. We can't talk in here,' said Jenny looking down at the corpses. She led her children through to the conservatory at the back of the house, where things were a little less topsy-turvy. She sat Leona down in a wicker chair, and pulled up another. Jacob climbed on to Jenny's lap, holding her tightly. She rocked him without even thinking about it.

'Come on Lee, this isn't making any sense.'

Leona was silent for a while, watching Jacob. His eyes quickly grew heavy, and after a couple of minutes the even sound of his breathing told them both that he was fast asleep.

'It's dangerous at ours,' said Leona, in a hushed voice.

'What?' Jenny shook her head, confused. 'It's no more dangerous than here.'

'Mum,' Leona looked up at her, 'I think Dad tried to tell me on the phone ... tried to tell me someone's after me.'

'What?'

'A man, or men – I'm not sure.'

'What the hell are you talking about?'

Leona slumped in the chair. 'You remember our trip to New York?'

Jenny nodded. 'Of course, who could forget such an extravagant Christmas?'

'It was a business trip for Dad, as well as a treat for us, wasn't it?'

'Yes, of course.'

'Dad had written something important, and was giving it to someone very important.'

Jenny nodded. She'd known there was an issue of confidentiality surrounding the work, and that had definitely put Andy on edge throughout their trip. She remembered thinking that there was perhaps something about this business that was ... somewhat *unusual*.

'I think it had something to do with *that*,' Leona said, gesturing with both hands, 'what's been going on.'

Jenny shook her head again. Jacob murmured, disturbed by the movement. She wanted to say that was crazy. But something stopped her. What Leona was suggesting sounded ridiculous ... and yet, so many things over the last eight years began to make some sort of sense, if what she said was true. Andy's paranoia – if she thought about it, yes – it did really start with New York; his obsession with Peak Oil, with privacy, his gradual detachment from the world ... it all began then.

And let's not forget his very special area of expertise, Jenny, it's always been specifically THIS – the choking of global oil ... what's happening right now.

'Mum,' said Leona. 'Dad was never meant to *see* the important men he was dealing with, it was that big a deal. That's what he told me.'

'*That's what he told you*? Why didn't he tell *me* any of this? Why the hell am I finding out about this now?'

'Because it wasn't Dad who saw them ... it was me.'

'What?'

'In that really posh hotel? Remember I went up to get something? I walked into the wrong room, the one next door. I saw some men. And I knew even then they were important, like ... running-countries kind of important.'

'Oh my God.'

'And now this whole oil thing is happening, I think they ...' Leona's voice quivered, 'I think they might need me to be dead.'

CHAPTER 83

· · · ·

9 p.m. GMT

Cabinet Office Briefing Room A (COBRA), London

Malcolm looked at the other two members of the COBRA committee. 'I think we're in danger of losing control of this situation.'

The other two looked at him sternly.

'The longer this situation persists, the harder it's going to be to pick up the pieces afterwards.'

'This situation will persist Malcolm, for as long as they say it needs to,' said Sir Jeremy Bosworth. 'We don't have a choice on this.'

Malcolm sighed. 'I know, I understand that we're all in this together, but the level of attrition this situation is causing isn't evenly spread, gentlemen. It's hitting us much, much harder than others. I'm a little concerned that by the time the satisfactory conditions are met, there'll be nothing left to salvage in this country.'

'You're exaggerating Malcolm,' replied the other man, Howard Campbell. 'We all need to remain calm whilst this is going on.'

'Exaggerating? I wonder. You *are* aware of conditions out there aren't you?'

'Of course, it's not pretty,' said Sir Jeremy.

'The safe zones we established to concentrate resources and manpower, are not forming up as we'd hoped. We simply don't have enough manpower to maintain them; we don't have enough troops on the ground.'

'The troops are mostly back from our various commitments overseas, aren't they?'

'There are still significant numbers stranded abroad. And even if we had managed to get them all back home, we just wouldn't have the numbers we need to do this properly.'

'We have large numbers of territorials we can draw on don't we?'

Malcolm nodded, 'But hardly any have turned up for duty, and of the few thousand that have, many have already abandoned their posts. I might add, we're also losing a lot of police officers.'

'It's understandable,' said Jeremy. 'People want to be with their families.'

Malcolm looked at him 'Does that not concern you, though?'

Sir Jeremy nodded. 'It's a concern, of course it is. But we have to continue looking at the bigger picture. That's what this has always been about, the bigger picture.'

'Look, I'll be honest. I'm worried that once they are happy that the goal has been met, the time it will take to get things running again will be too long.'

'Now is not the time to start being squeamish, Malcolm,' said Howard.

'I'm not being bloody squeamish, Howard. I simply would like to have something left that's governable once we're done with this!'

'Come on, Malcolm, let's not squabble liked politicians. We're better than that.'

Malcolm nodded, 'You're right.' He smiled at them. 'I'm merely suggesting that we need to start thinking about applying the brakes to this thing. It's picked up a lot more momentum than I think any of us really expected.'

Jeremy shrugged. 'I must admit, I was a little surprised at the riots on Tuesday. Your man, Charles, did a superb job frightening everyone.'

Howard looked from one to the other. 'You know we can't do that. We can't effect any sort of recovery until we receive word. You are *bound*.'

Malcolm sensed the veiled threat behind that one word. They did not readily forgive colleagues who acted alone.

'It's not starting a recovery procedure I'm talking about. I just believe we've perhaps been a little … over-zealous this week. We've achieved the required result far more quickly than our colleagues have elsewhere. I take the blame for that. I underestimated the fragility of this country.'

Howard leant forward and placed a gentle, supportive hand on Malcolm's arm. 'This was never going to be easy, we all accepted that. Future generations will no doubt judge us harsh, ruthless, cruel. But they will understand, Malcom, they *will* understand.'

CHAPTER 84

• • • •

9.15 p.m. GMT

London

Hammersmith without a single light? It was the proverbial ghost-town. On a normal Saturday evening, this place would be buzzing with people streaming out of the tube station, through the mall and out on to the pavement, ready to try and cross the busy ring road. The pubs would already be full and spilling merry twenty-somethings outside to discuss where they were going next.

It shouldn't be like this; the tall buildings dark and lifeless, the opening into the mall, a gloomy entrance to a forbidding chasm.

There was a constant smell too. A smell he'd started to register on his way north-east from Heathrow, passing through Hounslow. It was the smell of bin-bags ripped open by an urban fox and left to fester in the sun for a few too many days. Walking through Kew, he noticed there was more to the odour than that; the faintest whiff of decay – the first smells of the dead. Andy had spotted only a dozen bodies. That was, perhaps, encouraging. In anticipation of what London would be like in this exact scenario, he'd painted a mental image of the dead and dying filling the streets. He'd imagined the gutters awash with the jettisoned fluids of those who might have drunk, in desperation, from the Thames, from the drip trays of air-conditioning units, or worse.

By the time he'd made his way into Hammersmith, there was a suggestion of the smell of human shit, added to all the other odours.

Of course, there aren't any flushing toilets. There'll be several days of that lying around.

Nice.

Andy had seen about fifty people since leaving the guarded perimeter around Heathrow's Terminal 3. They had all looked very unwell, bearing the symptoms of food poisoning, having no doubt eaten things that had spoiled, or consumed tainted water.

The sun had gone down. And now only the day's afterglow dimly stained the cloudless sky.

His foot kicked a tin can that clattered across the empty road, startling him and a cluster of birds nearby that took off with an urgent flutter and rustle of flapping wings.

He pulled the gun out, the gift from Lance Corporal Westley. He had to admit, it felt bloody good in his hands. That was something he never thought he'd feel and so whole-heartedly appreciate – the righteous power of a loaded firearm.

'Thanks Westley,' he muttered quietly.

It was getting dark, but he was so nearly home now, just two or three miles away. He walked up Shepherd's Bush Road, towards the Green, passing a Tesco supermarket on his left. By the last of the light, he spotted about half-a-dozen people picking through a small mound of detritus in the supermarket's car-park, like seagulls on a landfill site.

A few minutes later he was looking out across the triangular area of Shepherd's Bush Green, and the dark row of shops bordering it. This was his neighbourhood, so nearly home now.

He had allowed himself to nurture a foolhardy hope that when he finally made it here, he'd discover an enclave in Greater London that had got its act together, blocked the roads in, and was sharing out the pooled essentials amongst the locals. After all, this area was home to the BBC. For every rough housing estate in the area, there were rows and rows of supposedly sensible middle-class, middle-management types and media-moppets – the *Guardian* sold just as well as the *Sunday Sport* round here.

But then, that was clearly a silly supposition; blue collar or white collar, if you're starving enough, you'll do anything to survive; middle-class, lower-class, tabloid or broadsheet reader. You scratch the surface and we're all the same underneath.

He walked up past the Green and turned left on to Uxbridge Road, seeing what he expected to see; the mess strewn across the road, every shop window broken ... one or two bodies.

All of a sudden he found himself breaking into a run, the fatigue of walking the last fifteen miles forgotten now that he was less than five minutes from home. His heart was beginning to pound with a growing fear of what he'd find when he finally pushed open the front door of Jill's home.

'Oh God, please let them be okay,' he whispered.

His footsteps echoed down the empty street as his jog escalated in pace to a run, and he repeated that hypocritical, atheist's prayer under his breath.

Let them be okay, let them be okay, let them be okay . . .

As he turned left off Uxbridge Road into St Stephen's Avenue, his run was a sprint, and his heart was in his throat.

And that's when he saw them, standing ahead of him, blocking the road. Three people; three men, by the shape of their dark outlines. They were standing there, almost as if they'd been waiting all along for him, expecting him.

Andy whipped out his pistol and held it in front of him in both hands. 'I've got a gun, so back the fuck up and let me past!' he shouted at them.

There was no response. The three dark forms were motionless. The one in the middle then slowly moved towards him. Andy racked the pistol noisily and aimed it. 'Another fucking step and I'll blow your fucking brains out, mate.'

The dark form stopped in his tracks. 'Dr Andrew Sutherland?'

CHAPTER 85

. . . .

9.51 p.m. GMT

Shepherd's Bush, London

Jenny sat at the top of the stairs, the gun that Leona had managed to get hold of resting in her lap. After some resistance from them both, she had convinced them to go and get some sleep upstairs. They were exhausted and needed some rest. Only when she had assured them that she would stand guard at the top of the stairs would either of them leave her side.

She was tired too, but there was much on her mind. There was no way she was going to sleep. Leona's confession earlier on was the problem.

On the one hand, it introduced a whole new level of fear to the equation – the thought that some shady characters might just be out there looking for her daughter, with one intention only. To kill her. On the other hand, she was angry that Andy's business affairs had jeopardised their daughter's life, their family. She was angry that he had never confided in her that their paths might have briefly crossed with those of some very dangerous people. She was angry that he'd sworn his daughter to secrecy.

And finally, she was sad that he'd been living with that kind of unsettling, nagging anxiety alone, for so long. It explained so much … it even put into context all those little tics Andy had developed in the last few years; his irritating habit of checking the tone on the house phone immediately after ending a call, the ritual tour of the downstairs windows and doors before bedtime. Jenny had even begun to suspect he was developing a minor case of obsessive compulsive disorder.

And now she knew why.

Christ.

It made her shudder. Rampaging chavs were one thing, Big Brother watching you, that was quite another.

'Dr Andrew Sutherland?' the dark form in front of him asked again in a quiet voice.

'I said stay where you are, or I'll put a bloody great hole in your head!'

Andy wished Westley had decided to leave him one of those SA80 night-scopes. Right now the edge of those silhouettes were fast merging with the darkening night sky and, for all he knew, they were watching him through scopes of their own and lining up cross-hairs on his forehead.

'Just take it easy, Andy.'

The voice was familiar – very familiar.

'Who's that? I know you.'

'Hi, Andy, it's me.'

Mike? It sounded like the American.

'Mike? Is that you?'

'It's me. How're you doing?'

'What ... what are you doing here?' he asked, and then looked at the other two forms. 'And who's that you're with?'

The form in the middle, the one he guessed was Mike, took another step forward and Andy felt the weight of a hand rest on his gun, pushing it gently down until he was pointing it at the ground.

'We have to talk Andy, and we have to talk very quickly about your family.'

Those words chilled him to the core.

'Oh God. What is it? What's happened? Are they okay?'

Mike hesitated to reply. 'We don't know. It's your daughter Andy, Leona. That's who we're really worried about. That's who we need to talk to.'

Andy studied the dark form in front of him.

Oh God, he's with them!

Andy raised his gun. 'Stay back! Or I'll shoot. I mean it.'

Mike advanced slowly. 'Andy my friend, I'm sorry, but I've got a gun trained on your head right now. And,' Mike laughed, 'I also know how bloody awful your aim is. Lower your gun or I'm afraid I'm going to have to put most of your brains out on the road.'

Andy suspected the other two men were aiming at him as well. He lowered his gun.

Mike addressed the other two sharply. 'Get him inside.'

They disarmed him, grabbed him forcefully by the arms and dragged him across the narrow street, through the gate of a small front garden and into a house that had clearly been ransacked and looted by someone in the last few days. They dropped him unceremoniously into an armchair.

He could see nothing, it was so dark. He felt someone brush past his legs, and then a moment later a small lantern popped on – a handheld sodium arc strip light, that glowed a dim, pallid cyan. Mike was kneeling before him, his gun still held in one hand, not aimed at him, but not exactly put away either.

'Andy,' he said, 'you ever seen that film with Keanu Reeves and Laurence Fishburne ... *The Matrix*?'

Andy nodded silently.

'You remember the blue pill?'

He nodded – the moment in the movie when one character, the one played by Keanu Reeves, was being asked to forget everything he knows and prepare himself for a new reality. The blue pill had been the visual metaphor.

'Yeah, okay ... the blue pill, so?'

'Well, I guess this is going to be *your* blue pill moment.'

Jenny heard it distinctly; in the dark, somewhere downstairs in the hall, the unmistakable rasp of cloth against cloth, the faintest *whiff* of friction, some-one or something moving.

She held her breath, and listened.

A moment later she heard another faint rasp, followed by the slightest creak of one of the parquet slats in the hallway.

She reached for the gun in her lap and aimed it down at the bottom of the stairs.

'I can hear you,' she said quietly, almost a whisper, yet sounding so loud in the absolute stillness of the night.

The creaking, the rasping, stopped instantly. Even more frightening for Jenny, it was confirmation that someone *was* down there, and not just a phantom of her imagination.

'I-I've got a gun, and I'm aiming it right now,' she whispered again.

That was met with silence, again.

Then she sensed something on the bottom step. 'Stop!' she hissed, 'or I'll shoot.'

'Mrs Sutherland?' a soft voice, a man's voice.

Hearing her name emerging from the darkness like that rattled her.

'Who's that? Who are you?'

'Who I am really doesn't matter,' the voice replied. 'I'm here for a reason. I'm here because a hundred yards away are men who have come to kill your daughter.'

'What?' she gasped.

'They're coming for her, you know, we've only got a few seconds before they arrive.'

'Who the fuck are you?'

'Like I've said, who I am doesn't matter. I have to get your daughter out of here before it's too late.'

'I think you suspect some of this already, Andy,' said Mike. 'The things that are going on in the world, hmm?'

Andy nodded. 'My work, it's based on my work.'

Mike smiled, 'Yes, your report. And you must have been wondering who it was you handed it over to all those years ago. You were doing a lot of thinking in the back of that truck in Iraq, Andy, weren't you?'

Andy stared at the gun, only a few inches away from him. Was he fast enough?

'Well, you gave that report to the right sort of people. What did they tell you when you were first approached? That they were security experts working for several anonymous clients in the oil industry?'

Andy nodded, 'Yes, pretty much those words.'

'It never occurred to you that they might have been terrorists? Or middlemen for some rogue foreign power?'

'I wouldn't have handed it over if I did.'

Mike nodded. 'No, I suspect you wouldn't, despite the money. It was quite a lot, wasn't it?'

Andy shrugged.

'These people value their anonymity. That's very important to them, particularly now that they've done this thing; brought the world to its knees. You know, millions will starve. There will be hundreds of small-scale wars in which many more will die. Old scores settled, old rivalries emerging, whilst the world deals with this temporary instability. Now is really not a good time for them to be publicly named. And here's the problem they have,' Mike said, 'your daughter could do just that.'

Andy looked at Mike. 'You're with *Them* aren't you?'

'Come on Mrs Sutherland, put the gun down. We don't have time for this.'

'So w-who's out there?' she asked.

'People, bad people – those that are behind the disaster. It's all tied up you see, it's all one thing.'

'And what about you?' she asked the voice at the bottom of the stairs.

'Me? The less you know the better. Let's just say I'm a hired hand, hmm?'

'Hired to ... what?'

'Find your daughter and protect her, of course. Look, now isn't the time for this,' he continued. 'You keep hold of your gun, just as long as you know how to slide the safety on. Let's get her out of here, let's get her safe and then you can slide the safety back off, turn your gun on me, and ask as many questions as you like.'

That sounded convincing. God knows, she wanted the voice down there to be that of a saviour, and not her daughter's executioner.

'Can I trust you?' she asked.

'What do you expect me to say, Mrs Sutherland? No? A stupid question given the situation, given we really don't have much time left.'

It was stupid.

'Mrs Sutherland? Can I come up and get your daughter now?'

She heard a stair creak under his weight. 'Stay where you are!' she hissed.

'Okay,' the voice replied. 'I'm right here, not going anywhere.'

Oh God she wanted to trust him.

He said I could keep hold of my gun, didn't he? He said that. If he meant to harm Leona, why would he allow me to keep hold of it?

She was about to lower her weapon and cautiously accept his help when a thought occurred to her.

'How did you know Leona was here, not at her home?'

Mike looked at Andy. 'You're kidding me, right?'

They heard three rounds being fired in quick succession.

Fuck it.

Andy reached out, grabbed the lamp and hurled it across the room against the wall. It smashed and the room was thrown into darkness. As the three men recoiled in surprise, Andy was already on his feet. He shoved hard against Mike, knocking him on to his back, and cannoned into another of the men on his way out of the room, into the hallway, and out through the open front door, on to the moonlit street.

His feet pounded the tarmac as he weaved around a mattress, the broken remains of chairs and a table, and other household bric-à-brac strewn across the avenue.

He shot a glance at their home on the left as he sprinted past it. It had been broken into like all the other houses, the front door wide open and their things smashed and discarded in the front garden.

Up ahead on his right, was Jill's house.

He kicked the gate aside, and raced up the garden path in a couple of seconds. The front door was shut. He could see that it had been damaged, a large ragged hole had been kicked through the wooden panelling. He charged the door with his shoulder without breaking stride. The last hinge gave way, and the door clattered loudly on to the hallway floor.

'JENNY!' he shouted, his voice echoed around inside. There was no response, just a silence that had his blood running cold and the dawning realisation that he had so nearly made it home in time to save his family.

He'd heard the executioner's shots; one for his wife, one for each of his children, and it was all over.

Then he heard it, faintly, the sound of sobbing coming from the top of the stairs. He could see absolutely nothing, but it grew louder and more distinct as it migrated down the stairs, and then, it was beside him. In the wan glow of the moon, he saw two pale white hands reach out for him.

'Oh God, Andy!' Jenny cried, grasping him tightly and burying her head into his shoulder. 'Andy! Andy!' she sobbed uncontrollably.

'Jenny,' he had to ask, 'Jenny … the kids?'

She looked up at him, 'They're both all right.'

'I heard gunshots.'

She was about to answer, when a beam of torchlight fell across them, and they heard the sound of footsteps pounding down the avenue towards them.

'Oh God!' she gasped, breaking her hold on Andy and producing a gun.

'Give it to me,' he said. She handed it to him and he trained it on a space above the nearest bobbing torch.

'Who are they?' she whispered, as the torch's motion slowed to a halt and the sound of footfalls ceased.

'I don't know yet.'

'Andy!' Mike called out from the darkness just beyond the garden gate. 'Don't be stupid, there's three of us, and one of you. Lower the gun.'

Andy wasn't ready to surrender. In the last minute, he had gone from absolute certainty that his family had been murdered, to finding out they were unharmed and now, quite possibly, were about to fall victim to these men.

'Who the fuck are you, Mike?' his voice rasped.

'We're the good guys Andy, the good guys, trust me,' the American replied, sounding short of breath, recovering from the pursuit.

'He said there were men outside after our daughter,' said Jenny.

'He?' replied Mike. 'Who?'

Andy looked at her.

'He was here moments ago, on the stairs. He said he'd come to protect Leona. I told him to stay where he was …' her voice faltered, '… but he didn't listen … I fired … and then he ran away.'

'Andy,' said Mike. '*They* are here, they know where she is. You've got to trust me now.'

Andy kept the gun levelled.

'Look, if we wanted your daughter dead, I wouldn't be talking with you right now – we'd already be stepping over your bodies and on our way inside. Think about it.'

From the top of the stairs, Andy heard Jacob calling out.

'Is Daddy home?'

They sat together in the ransacked lounge, illuminated only by a couple of scented candles Jenny had found in a kitchen drawer. Andy and his family were gathered together on Jill's leather sofa, slashed and stained, and Mike sat opposite them on the one wooden kitchen chair that hadn't been smashed to pieces.

'There's some fresh blood at the bottom of the stairs. I think you hit something,' he said.

'He just kept coming closer,' whispered Jenny.

'You did the right thing,' Mike replied. 'If you had let him come another step closer you and your children would be ...' he looked at Jacob's wide-eyed expression, 'well, he would have acquired his target.'

'Me?' muttered Leona.

Mike nodded.

Andy shook his head. 'Look Mike, if that's really your name—'

The American smiled, 'Mike's my first name, yeah.'

'I really don't know who the hell you are now; I thought I did, back in Iraq ... but I haven't got a clue now. All I know is that some very powerful bastards want my girl. Who are they Mike? And for that matter where do you,' he shot a glance at one of Mike's men standing guard in the hallway, 'and your sidekicks, fit into all of this?'

'I can tell you a lot more about us than I can about them,' he replied. 'Which is why your daughter is so important to us.'

'Let's start with you then.'

Mike shrugged. 'I work for an ... let's call it an *agency*. A small operation, once upon a time part of the FBI, that was a long time ago. Now we're privately funded, which allows us to stay off the radar. We do one thing in this agency Andy, just one thing ... we try to find *them*.' He stroked his beard as he considered how to continue.

'They ... *they* ... don't even have a name; they're that smart. They don't have a logo, or a motto, they don't have a headquarters, they don't reside in any particular country, they don't have any political allegiance, or ideology; they are just wealth and influence. They're a club. We ... my little agency was set up forty years ago Andy, in 1963 to be precise, after this club decided they'd put the wrong man in the White House.'

'My God ... Kennedy?'

Mike nodded. 'It was his brother, Robert, that put us together in the aftermath. And that's why the bastards nailed him too. And we've had to operate off the grid since then.'

'Shit,' Andy whispered.

'Yeah. Eight years ago you did some work for a bunch of very dangerous and powerful people. Breaking through the secrecy around them has been virtually impossible. In forty years we've learned little more than they number 160 members, twelve of whom make the big decisions.'

'You must have an idea who these people are, right?'

'We can guess. That's pretty much all we've been able to do. We've only ever had one informant; if you're up on European politics you'd probably recognise the name ... he talked to us twice, briefly, before they got to him.' He looked briefly from Andy to Leona.

'And then we come to you two,' he sighed. 'Andy, you did business with *Them* – you actually dealt directly with the Twelve. Did you have any idea what you were dealing with?'

Andy shrugged, 'I guessed they were oil execs.'

Mike chuckled. 'The world's a pyramid of power. Everyone makes the mistake of thinking the apex of the pyramid is government. That's the big mistake. *Governments* are merely a tool for them to use. You have corporations, and they're owned by bigger corporations, who in turn are owned by even bigger corporations. The bigger they get, the less familiar people are with the corporate names. Ultimately these huge corporations are owned by banks that in turn are controlled by bigger banks, again, with names that aren't commonly known ... and ultimately these bigger banks are owned by shareholders; very rich, very reclusive shareholders. If I was to hazard a guess at who the Twelve members are, I'd start there.'

'But, it seems,' he smiled at Leona, 'you actually saw some of them. More importantly, you recognised one of their faces; someone who was on the television just before things went screwy, right?'

Leona nodded. 'I don't know who he is though, I don't know the name.'

'It doesn't matter. Because what we're going to do is get you out of here to somewhere safe, and then we'll show you a whole bunch of photographs, and all you've got to do is say which ones you saw.'

He turned back to Andy. 'Your daughter has in her head, right now, the most important nugget of information in the world. And that makes her very precious to us, and dangerous to them.'

'What about the man who was here?' asked Jenny. 'He was one of them then?'

Mike was cautious. 'He's gone, but maybe not too far. We'll sit tight until we've got daylight.'

'What if he comes back?' asked Andy.

'I've got my men covering the front and back doors. They're well-equipped and well-trained; they're packing night scopes and body armour, both very capable men.'

Jenny shook her head. 'You know I almost let him up. He was so believable.'

'And he's lethal too,' cut in Mike. 'I think he's someone we know of. Well, at least, we know of his work. He's their best field-operative, I'm certain they've used this same man many times before. He works on his own, completely autonomously. I've never seen him but I've seen his handiwork.' He stopped himself. 'Not nice. I just wish we had more information on him.'

Jenny turned to Andy, 'We're safe aren't we? I mean the kids ... you and me?'

Andy squeezed her hand, 'I think we are now,' he replied tiredly. 'We've survived the worst of it, Jen.'

Mike got up and patted Andy on the shoulder. 'Your husband turned out to be a real alpha-male back in Iraq, a sharp thinker – a good field-man,' he said. 'If you still don't think you can trust me, you can certainly trust him.'

Jenny nodded and looked up at her husband. 'I do,' she said. 'I'm so sorry that I didn't, you know, before this.'

'You guys might want to get some sleep, if you can. We're all leaving here at first light,' said Mike. 'We'll take you somewhere safe.'

'Okay. We'll sleep down here, if that's okay?'

'Fine. That's nice and close where I can keep an eye on you,' he said with a reassuring nod. 'Get some sleep. I'll go and check on my fellas.'

Mike stepped out of the room, and left them to snuggle down together on the sofa. There were a couple of sleepy questions from Jacob that neither Andy nor Jenny could answer adequately. Then they curled up together, and after a few more whispered words, and some more shared tears of relief, Jenny, Leona and Jacob were fast asleep.

Andy felt a week of fatigue creeping up on him quickly. The chorus of rustling, even untroubled breathing of his family asleep, and the distant murmur of Mike conferring with his colleagues outside, was comforting enough that he finally allowed himself to join them.

CHAPTER 87

11.36 p.m. GMT

Shepherd's Bush, London

The lucky bitch had caught him with one of those three shots. It cracked his collarbone on the way in and tore a bloody exit wound from the rear of his shoulder on the way out.

He would have carried on up the stairs, finished her off with a quick swipe of his blade, and gutted the two children in two blinks of an eye. But he knew the sound of the gun would have those men outside running.

He would have been trapped upstairs with nowhere to go.

Ash beat a retreat out through the front door and crouched amongst the clutter on the avenue. The father, Sutherland, passed within a few feet of him and then those three men, seconds later. None of them saw him squatting down in the middle of the avenue, visible amongst the mess to anyone who bothered to look closely enough. He remained absolutely motionless, knowing movement would draw someone's eye, and watched them from the darkness.

When finally the big American man, *Mike*, had won over Mrs Sutherland, they went inside ... and he could move. He let himself into the house opposite, pulled some clothing out of a wardrobe and ripped a length of material to use as a bandage. He bound it diagonally and tightly round his neck and down under his left armpit, grimacing with every movement of his left arm. It wasn't going to stop the bleeding, but the compression would slow it.

The bullet had sheered some nerves or tendons in his left shoulder, and he found his arm dangling uselessly by his side. If it had been the other side, his knife arm, that might have presented a bit of a problem.

Sitting in the darkness of the house, he assessed the situation.

Three on one.

They were all packing guns with night scopes and wearing vests, whilst he had a knife.

Ash smiled; they didn't stand a chance.

He knew they were nervous, they'd be jumping at shadows. Ash's reputation had a habit of preceding him, and he knew these men were well aware of his work. That always worked in his favour; their nerves would get the better of them. He knew what they would do – they would stay there until daylight, rather than risk moving out into the dark. There'd be a man posted at the rear of the house in that sun lounge, watching the back garden, and another guarding the front door.

They know I'm wounded. There'd be fresh blood on the floor. That might make them a little more confident … *a little foolhardy perhaps?*

He smiled. Even with the use of only one arm, they were going to be putty in his hands. He suspected that they – knowing he was wounded – might even be foolish enough to attempt to trap him, to capture him alive, if an opportunity presented itself.

That's how they'd come unstuck, he realised. These boys were jumpy and keen to bag him as quickly as possible, of that he had no doubt.

He knew what to do.

'It's got to be the same guy that they're using,' Mike murmured quietly to the man standing beside him in the doorway. 'I wish we had more on this sonofabitch.'

He scanned the street silently; the only noise the gentle murmur of a light breeze through the branches that arched over the avenue.

'You think this guy's coming back?' asked Blaine in a hushed voice, sweeping the road outside through the scope on his pistol.

'Of course he will. Come on, you know who we're dealing with.'

'Yeah, I guess I was hoping maybe they'd used someone else this time.'

'Too much at stake, Blaine. They were only ever going to send this guy to clean up.'

Blaine nodded, and licked his lips nervously.

'Just relax. The bottom line is, no matter how good he is, he's only human.'

'Sometimes I wonder.'

'What?'

'If he *is* just human,' Blaine grinned sheepishly. 'I mean in our dossier, somebody nicknamed this guy "the ghost".'

'Whoever decided to come up with that was a moron. He's just a good freelancer who's managed to stay lucky so far. Well, up to now that is. Andy's wife got him at least once. My biggest worry is the bastard has scampered off and died somewhere out there. It would have been good to get a hold of him. God knows how much *he* knows about *them*.'

'Kind of embarrassing that, eh? In the end it's an untrained civilian, a woman at that, who finally nailed the ghost.'

'Blaine, you call him that again, and I'll shoot you dead,' whispered Mike, not entirely joking. 'Now shut up and concentrate.'

'Right.'

They stood in silence for a full minute before Blaine opened his mouth to ask another question.

'Shhh … less talk, more watching,' whispered Mike.

'Okay boss.'

It was then that Mike thought he saw a flicker of movement in the upstairs window of the house opposite. He tapped Blaine on the shoulder.

'Straight ahead, first floor window on the left.'

The man raised the line of his night scope. 'Shit, yeah … I saw something move.'

Mike had to evaluate quickly.

He's upstairs in that house. He's trapped, stairs the only way down – that or out the window with the chance of breaking a leg. He's already been wounded, perhaps two or three hits. We've got a good chance of nailing this cocksucker tonight. Catch him alive, we might even get him to talk. Bonus.

'We can trap him if we move right now.'

Blaine nodded, 'Fuck it, you're right.'

'Cover!' hissed Mike. He headed across the avenue, scooting through the rubbish, whilst Blaine kept his weapon trained on the window. Mike signalled for Blaine to join him against the wall beside the open front door. The man scrambled over quickly and quietly, and presently squatted down beside him.

'There's still movement up in that room. He's up to something in there.'

'Right, standard room-by-room procedure … only we know downstairs is clear. I'll take point.'

Blaine nodded.

Mike entered first, his pistol and scope aimed up the narrow stairs to the first floor.

These houses are all built the same; small bathroom at the top, landing doubles round, three bedroom doors in a row on the left, boiler cupboard at the far end.

He took the first few steps and then paused, listening for any sound of movement from up above. It was silent, except for the occasional gust of wind coursing through the broken windows of the house, moaning gently. He waved to Blaine, who climbed the stairs quietly, squeezed past Mike and went another half a dozen beyond him – nearly to the top.

They waited to see if they'd been detected, for some sort of reaction. However, it remained silent, except for the rustling of paper and plastic bags being teased gently across the avenue.

Mike overtook his man. Reaching the top of the stairs he whipped his gun one way then the other, staring intently through the scope.

If this was the ghost ... then he was a very slippery sonofabitch. They knew painfully little about him, except he favoured a long thin knife, and had been described by the few people who had encountered him – and lived – as looking Middle Eastern. He had no name, and a million names; using a new alias on every job. And he was used exclusively by *them*. Mike knew of three jobs that had his unique signature on them. There was the fireman from Ladder 57 who claimed to have discovered un-detonated demolition charges amidst the rubble at Ground Zero and had died as the result of a *supposed* street stabbing. The minister in Saddam Hussein's government who had a *world shattering* revelation to make, and then was supposed to have slit his own throat. And there was that Russian banker championing the sale of Tengiz oil in euros instead of dollars – all of them victims of a never-recovered, narrow-bladed knife. All of them victims, Mike was certain, of this guy.

He waved Blaine up and pointed to the bathroom at the top of the stairs. The man squeezed past him. And after silently counting to three, he lent deftly in to check the bathroom was clear.

'It's clear,' he whispered.

Mike decided playing quiet was pointless. This man undoubtedly knew they were inside the house with him.

'We know who you are,' said Mike. 'We know your work.'

There was no reply.

'You're *their* man, you only work for *them*. We've been watching you.'

Silence.

'We will take you, and that will probably mean killing you in the process. If you come out unarmed, then we can at least talk.'

The only sound was the flapping of a curtain coming from a front room. *Damn.*

Mike had hoped they could bag this guy alive. He was too dangerous to fuck around with. If they were going to *take* him, then they'd have to go in hard, and go for a quick kill.

He signalled to Blaine that he would take the next room. Again they counted down, he kicked the door, and stepped in, sweeping his gun frantically one way then the other. It was clear.

Blaine took the next, again nothing.

So by a process of elimination … the last room.

'I'll take this one,' whispered Mike. 'Watch my back, I want you right behind me as we go in.'

The man nodded. 'Got it, Mike.'

He took a deep breath, counted down from five silently, sticking his hand up so that Blaine, crouched behind him, could see the fingers folding down one after the other.

Three … two … one …

Mike kicked the door, and barged into the front bedroom, rolling to a stop against the opposite wall. He whipped his gun around, left then right – scoping the room with rapid jerking movements. His aim was drawn almost instantly towards something moving near the bedroom's window. It was a bed sheet, draped over what looked like a floor-standing lamp, the breeze was toying with it, fluttering the corners of cotton. That's what they'd seen through the window from the front door of the Sutherland's house.

'Shit!' muttered Mike. 'It's clear,' he called out.

It was obvious they'd been played with. The bastard had lured them out.

'Blaine! Back to the fucking house! RUN!'

Mike turned on his heels to head out of the room. Out on the landing, at the top of the stairs he saw Blaine's body, stretched out like he was taking a nap.

And that's when he felt a vicious punch to his kidneys. There was an explosion of pain and his first thought was that the well-aimed punch had hit a vulnerable nerve-cluster. But reaching to grab his side, he felt a protruding shaft, and a wetness on his fingers.

'Oh fuck,' he grunted. Something had found the three-inch gap between the front and rear plates of his vest.

'Yes,' whispered a voice in his ear, 'it's fatal. You have no more than five minutes to live. If you lie still, maybe a minute or two longer.'

Mike felt his legs buckle, and as he slumped down, he felt the knife come out, and a hand grabbed him under each armpit. He felt himself being gently lowered to the ground.

CHAPTER 88

· · · ·

11.54 p.m. GMT

Shepherd's Bush, London

Ash kneeled over him. He snapped on a torch and checked the man's wound. The blood was jetting out in rhythmic spurts.

'Understand,' said Ash gently, 'this will be a relatively easy death. The painful bit is over. Bleeding out will be relatively quick. I apologise for not making it instant,' he said with a hint of regret.

The dying man stared up at him, expressions of bewilderment and anger flickering across his face. Ash could empathize with the anger; to be caught off guard like that ... lured out and skewered.

'You must be Mike, I'm guessing by deduction,' he said. 'Yes, just a silly trick. The sheet, over the lamp, and the help of a light breeze.'

'Fucking shit trick,' groaned Mike.

'Let me ask you. Do you believe in God?'

Mike laughed defiantly and winced. 'No I fucking don't.'

'Maybe now's a good a time as any to find some faith, eh? Hedge your bets.'

'You know ... a friend of mine assured me ... God accepts non-believers too ... it's just assholes he doesn't let in.'

That was quite funny, he liked this American's defiance in the face of death. It was admirable.

Mike grunted something, his voice warbling and weakening.

'You're asking about your other colleague in the house? Yes, I'm afraid he's dead too. I did him first. You probably didn't hear him drop did you? Too busy chatting away at the front.'

Mike grasped one of his hands. 'Let the ... family ... go,' he struggled between gasps to get the words out.

'Sorry, they're on my "to do" list,' he replied and then smiled down at him, with a shred of sympathy it seemed, as the American struggled to draw air in. 'We know you've been out there watching us for a long time – your humble agency. The funny thing is, we've been trying to track you down as well.'

They … they had known of it, and hunted for this persistent nuisance, whilst this microdot of an agency, in turn, had been doing the same; two predators blindly stalking each other over four decades, their subtle tracks imprinted on recent history.

To be fair, the agency was no real match for the people Ash kept things tidy for. The resources of a couple of dozen field and desk agents and the black budget that kept them ticking over, versus the sort of wealth, power and influence that decided world leaders, initiated and concluded wars, timed and controlled global economic cycles. No real match there, a proverbial David and Goliath.

This man's agency though, had done well, identifying and homing in on the only weak link in their chain, the traitor … the son-in-law and heir-apparent to one of the highest echelon – one of the Twelve; the young man, a banker, a member of the lower order, who had suddenly got cold feet – he had given this agency just enough to zero in on Dr A. Sutherland.

Of course all of this unpleasantness now, chasing around this shitty little country, could have been avoided if they'd let him finish that girl in the hotel room, back in New York.

Hypocrites.

They were preparing to orchestrate events that were ultimately going to lead to the deaths of hundreds of millions, and yet they didn't have the stomach to witness the death firsthand of one solitary child. He realised, in some ways, he had more in common with this man before him, than the privileged and pampered elite that he worked for.

'You nearly exposed them. You nearly won, my friend. The girl could have identified three of the Twelve for you.'

Ash knew then that he alone had a unique status … knowing more than any of the members of the lower order; he had been entrusted with an almost sacred confidentiality because he was their personal watchdog. He knew these twelve men, and they were not brave men; they were weak.

Knowing the identity of just one of them would be enough for this determined, tenacious little agency. They'd find a way to get to an identified member, they'd find a way to get him to talk, that wouldn't be so hard.

'You came so close,' Ash said.

'Fuck you,' grunted Mike. 'We know all about you shit-heads.'

Mike tried to move, to reach out towards his gun, dropped on the landing just a few feet away. Ash kicked it casually across the floor and out of reach.

'Stay still,' he cautioned Mike, 'or you'll bleed out faster. I want you to know my friend, because, well ... because you've *earned* it.'

The American could do little but nod weakly.

'Know *all* about us?' Ash laughed. 'You don't know anything. What you know is just the little bit you've managed to scratch off the surface. You think a group of fat industrialists in expensive suits are behind this, don't you? It goes much higher. You can trace the reins of power up through banks that own banks that own banks to just a dozen names.'

Mike frowned, struggling through the growing fogginess to comprehend what he was hearing.

'The world is owned by a dozen families headed by a dozen men, some of whom have surnames that even the mindless sheep on the streets would recognise, and other names that have always remained hidden.'

'And believe me when I say their influence, even before recent years, was pretty damn impressive.' He leant over Mike, moving closer to his face. It looked like the American's pupils were beginning to dilate, as he started his inevitable slide into unconsciousness.

'These people I work for ... you can see their fingerprints everywhere in history, Mike, fingerprints smeared everywhere, like a crime scene. Take the Second World War for instance ...'

Mike's breathing caught.

'Oh yeah,' Ash grinned, 'that was their ill-conceived attempt to stifle the further spread of communism. They've never liked popular uprisings. They *made* Hitler, they paved the way for him ... so long as he did what he was told, he was unassailable. But then, of course, he went *off script*, and the rest, as they say, is history.'

'The war ...?'

'Yes, of course, it was orchestrated by them.'

Mike tried to gurgle something.

'Did you know the American Civil War was a power struggle amongst members of the lower order? That war was just a squabble between two groups of business men. What about your War of Independence? That was *them* struggling to keep a hold of the colonies, via England. Of course, they lost that war. But then, instead, down the road they *bought* the country, through investment.'

Ash laughed gently. 'Your history Mike, American history ... don't you see? It was written by a cartel of European families. The wars, the hundreds of thousands of dead young American boys, the poverty and hardship, the great depression, two world wars … ultimately nothing more than a board-room struggle amongst the ruling elite; the growing pains, my friend, of their influence.'

Mike struggled to talk. A small trickle of black-as-oil blood trickled from the side of his mouth and ran down into his beard.

'Why … this?'

'What's happening now?' Ash cut in. The dying man nodded, but it was nothing but the weakest twitch of his head. Ash looked down at the blade in his hand, it needed cleaning. He wiped it along the length of Mike's shirt-sleeve.

'They decided it, Mike, it was something that needed to be done; a correc-tion, an adjustment, a little bit of house cleaning.'

Ash paused.

'It's running out, you know?' he said. 'There's a lot less of it than people think … oil. Yes, a lot less than the publicly stated reserves. They decided there were simply too many of us all expecting our oil-rich luxuries, all expecting our big cars, big homes, and an endless supply of power and oil to feed them. It wasn't going to last for much longer. They knew that fact long before anyone else. And they knew that there were going to be wars, horrific wars, most probably with a few nukes being thrown around … for the last of that oil. And you don't want that – nukes being thrown around. They knew economic necessity, oil-hunger, would drive us to destroy ourselves. And I suppose you can see it from their point of view, after struggling so hard for … well, one could say, since the Middle Ages, they didn't want to see it all thrown away. You can see how annoying that might be, can't you?'

He slid his blade back into his ankle sheath.

'So they made the decision at a gathering back in 1999. A decision to lance the boil, if you'll excuse such a crude euphemism. They chose to cull mankind, before we went too far down that road. You see Mike, these people I work for, they're like … I don't know … they're like caretakers, quietly steering things, balancing things, keeping those big old cogs turning. They did this for the sake of us all … because it needed to be done.'

He studied the face of the dying American. There still seemed to be life in those glazed eyes, Mike was still hearing this, he was sure.

'So, the decision was made back in '99, right at the end of that year,' Ash laughed gently, 'as the sheep all prepared to celebrate an exciting new century and got all worked up about that millennium bug, and had their big, big parties, and nursed sore heads the morning after. It was decided that things needed to be put in place for this; to get everything ready to turn the taps off.'

Ash nudged Mike. 'You see, that's the great thing about oil, it really *is* our oxygen, our life's blood ... it's the *perfect controlling mechanism*. If you turn the tap up, the world gets really busy; you turn it down enough, things grind to a halt. It's like the throttle on a motorbike – a perfect device.'

The American let out a bubbling gasp of air, a noise Ash recognised as a man's final gasp.

'It's taken them some time to organise this, a very big project you see. And you know, everything since '99 ...' he looked down at Mike. His pupils had completely dilated now and gazed sightlessly up at the ceiling. He wasn't hearing him any more.

'Everything, I mean, *everything* – all starting with two passenger jets crashing into New York – *everything* since then, my friend, has been about one thing; getting the world ready for this ... the culling.'

The American was dead.

'Pity,' said Ash, and listened for a moment to the breeze, whistling along the landing and down the stairs. He'd wanted this dying man to hear it all, to understand why it had to happen, perhaps even to agree with him that it was a measure that had to be taken, for mankind's benefit. But most probably a good portion of what he'd said had made no sense in the man's dying mind.

'Pity.'

He closed the American's eyes and got to his feet, grunting with pain. Sutherland's wife had hit him in the collarbone, and even though he'd bound the wound up efficiently, he knew all was not well – he was bleeding internally.

He felt a little light-headed.

Not good.

There were still some loose ends to tidy up.

Sunday

CHAPTER 89

· · · ·

12.01 a.m. GMT

Shepherd's Bush, London

Andy awoke. Something had disturbed him; a noise, one of the kids stirring? His eyes opened and he let them adjust to the dark whilst he sat still, listening.

Just the breeze outside. Mike and his colleagues were silent; there was no quiet, wary murmuring as there had been earlier.

That's worrying.

He eased himself out of the tangle of limbs on the sofa and walked quietly across to the door that opened on to the hallway. He looked to his left and saw the weak light of the moon casting flickering half-shadows of branches and leaves through the open front door on to the smooth parquet floor.

Where's Mike?

He turned to the right. The hallway led to the rear of the house and Jill's sun lounge. He wondered if they were gathered back there. If they were he'd be bloody worried – leaving the front door unguarded like that?

A dozen light, soundless steps down the hall and he stood in the doorway. His eyes, now more accustomed to the dark, couldn't pick out any shape that might be someone standing guard.

'Hello?' he whispered. 'Anyone awake?'

There was no reply and, with a shudder of realisation, he knew something must have happened. His hand reached for the gun tucked into his trousers. He felt some small comfort sensing the rough carbon grip of the handle.

Then he sensed the draught of movement behind him.

He whipped round, the gun raised and ready to fire.

'Shit Dad! It's me!' Leona whimpered.

He exhaled. 'Christ, Lee, I nearly blew a hole in your head.'

She smiled and shrugged. 'Sorry,' she whispered. 'What are you doing up, anyway?'

'I can't find Mike and his guys.'

Her mouth dropped and her eyes widened. 'Oh God!' she cried a little too loudly.

He raised a finger to his mouth to hush her.

There can't have been a fight. Surely any shots fired would have awoken us all? They're out in the front garden, checking something out, maybe?

He took a step into the hall again and his foot slipped in something. He looked down and noticed a dark mat on the floor.

'You bring a torch?' he whispered.

Leona nodded.

'Shine it on the floor.'

She switched it on, and instantly recoiled at the bright red pool at their feet.

'Oh shit!' she hissed.

Andy grabbed the torch from her and panned it around the sun lounge. The beam picked out one of Mike's men curled in a foetal position behind the wicker armchair beside them.

They're here!

'Get behind me!' he whispered into her ear. He snapped off the torch, turned and headed up the hallway again, towards the lounge; slow, cautious steps, his gun arm extended, sweeping with quick jerks from one side to the other.

Andy knew there was only one course of action to take. Grab Jenny and Jacob, get out of the house, and run, and run ... and keep running. He swung his aim up the stairs, a dark abyss that could be hiding anything.

They reached the open doorway to the lounge. He could hear Jacob stirring, no longer the even rasp of rest, but short tremulous gasps.

'Jenny we have to leave now,' he said, quietly snapping on the torch again.

The halo of light fell on Jacob, standing. A dark forearm was wrapped across his narrow shoulders, and above the tuft of blond hair he saw the dark face of a man, smiling mischievously. The tip of a long, thin-bladed knife was pressed into his son's pale neck, creating a dimple that threatened to burst blood if another gram of pressure was applied to it.

Jenny was on her knees, on the floor, rocking, too frightened to cry, too frightened even to breathe.

'Lose the gun, Andy Sutherland,' the man said calmly.

Andy kept the weapon trained on him.

You drop the gun and that's it for bargaining.

'I won't do that, mate,' Andy said.

Jenny turned to look at him. 'What? Andy! For fuck's sake! Drop the gun!'

He hushed her with a wave of his hand. 'I can't do that Jenny. If I do that, we die.'

The man smiled. 'Your husband's being quite sensible under the circumstances, Mrs Sutherland.'

He looked up at Andy. 'We can talk for a bit anyway. I think I'd like that. You can call me Ash, by the way.'

He's in no hurry. That means ...

'The others?' Andy nodded towards the front door. 'They're out there somewhere ... dead?'

Ash nodded. 'Just a little too keen to try and take me alive.'

'So, this is all about what my daughter thought she saw, right?'

'What we *know* she saw. You see, this lovely young lady,' he said gesturing with his knife-hand, a flick of the wrist that took the blade away from Jacob's throat for a moment, 'knows enough to be very dangerous. When things start sorting themselves out again—'

'You are mightily fucking mistaken,' Andy sneered, 'if you think things are going to sort themselves out.'

Ash cocked an eyebrow.

'What? You thought it would?' he asked, genuinely incredulous.

'They will ensure the oil flows again, when the time's right.'

Andy shook his head and sighed. 'It doesn't work that way. I thought I made that patently bloody clear in my report. It's a zero sum thing. You don't just bounce back from something like this. I don't know what fucking morons you work for, but they've seriously screwed things up.'

The blade returned to Jacob's neck. 'Whatever. You're the *big expert.*'

Andy nodded. 'Yeah ... yeah, you got that right. I've spent enough time thinking about it over the years.'

'Nonetheless, I have my objective,' his blade-hand flicked away again from Jacob's neck, the tip pointing towards Leona, ' ... her.'

Leona sobbed. 'Oh, please ...'

Ash shrugged, pouting a lip with sympathy. 'I'm afraid so, my dear. However we resolve this situation, I can't let you walk away. I can, however, make it quick and painless.'

'Oh Christ! Oh God! Andy, don't let him. DON'T LET HIM!' Jenny cried.

'I really don't see how you can stop me,' said Ash.

Andy noticed a blood-soaked bandage of material wrapped tightly around his shoulder.

Is he losing blood slowly? Can I stall him until he drops?

'Look, it's over. It's out of control. Whoever you're working for isn't going to be able to make things right again. They're screwed, we're screwed, even you ... you're screwed too. It really doesn't matter what my daughter saw,' said Andy, 'not any more. Because once things shut down at the scale that they have done, there's no going back.'

'I think you're talking shit.'

'Am I? How long will it take for the Saudi refineries to come on tap? How long will it take to get the Baku refineries, the Paraguaná refinery? Months is my best guess. And that's plenty of time for things to get worse; for the likes of China and Russia to see an opportunity, for every simmering border dispute to flare up, for the US economy to drop into free fall. Don't forget, that's an economy that's remained afloat for the last thirty years on the value of trillions of petro-dollars. That's been wiped out.'

'And so I should just let your little girl walk away?'

Oh fuck, am I convincing him?

'You know, maybe the world needed something like this,' said Andy.

Ash eyed him warily.

'We're a planet that was only ever capable of supporting what? Two? Three billion? We were well on our way towards eight billion before this happened,' Andy continued. 'I don't know who's behind this, and I don't know why they've done this. But ... maybe something like this needed to happen?'

Ash nodded. 'Of course it did,' he said, his voice sounded thick and lazy.

Make it sound good Andy.

'So, listen. Maybe I agree with the people you work for? Hmm? Okay it's not nice. But at least this has been a global sacrifice; everyone has paid the price, right? Not just ... say, the Third World.'

Ash nodded again.

'I can see now, this needed to happen. Even if we knew, we're not about to go and tell the world *who* made it happen,' he turned to Leona, 'are we honey?'

Leona shook her head vigorously, 'No, n-no.'

'Please ... she doesn't *need* to die.'

Ash swayed slightly. 'Almost convincing. But I have my contract.'

'Contract?' Andy shook his head. 'You do realise the money you're being paid, if it isn't already worthless, this time next week it will be.'

Ash frowned, irritated by that. 'It's not about fucking money,' he snapped.

Andy noticed he was beginning to slur his words.

'Well, what is it about, for Christ's sake? Why does my girl have to die?'

Ash sighed, his grip loosened and the point of his knife dropped away again from the scored skin on Jacob's neck. He pursed his lips with thought. 'You see, it's about professional pride, I guess. It's about finishing the job.'

Oh Christ. This isn't about money, or conviction . . .

'There's a reason why I know their identities . . . The Twelve, the most powerful men in the world. It's because I'm reliable. It's because I *always* finish the job, I always come through. I'm the best freelancer. The best there is. That means something –'

This is about pride. I won't be able to reason with him . . .

'– to me. It's what I am. I've become the best there is. I've earned that. So you see, I really don't give a shit about her life. I've killed much younger, much more innocent victims, believe me. It's water off a duck's back.'

Ash swayed enough that he staggered slightly.

'I'm not that interested in hearing any more impassioned pleas for mercy, that's not going to help you one little bit. Oh fuck it . . . you know what?'

Ash was expecting him to answer.

'What?'

'I'm now getting a little bored with this.'

Shit, is he weakening? Is this the wound talking?

'So, here's how it goes. Drop your gun, and you can have Tiny Tim back unharmed, and in return, I'll have your daughter, please.'

'Oh God, no, don't . . . !' cried Jenny.

'Shut up!' Ash spat, his calm, softly spoken voice, raised for the first time. 'The alternative is – I'll finish him in a blink, and be upon you, Sutherland, gutting you before you know it. And then, of course, I'll be able to take all the time in the world with your wife and your daughter. So how's that sound to you?'

Ash swayed again, ever so slightly. 'Decision time. I'll give you, let me see . . . yeah, let's say, five seconds. Five . . .'

Leona grabbed hold of Andy, she began screaming. 'Dad! Please! Don't let him kill me!'

'Four . . .'

Jacob's eyes were swollen with fear.

'Three . . .'

Jenny sobbed uncontrollably on the floor, and Leona collapsed to her knees.

'Two . . .'

Andy realised he'd now run out of options.

CHAPTER 90

He fired.

The shot missed his son by inches and punched a hole in Ash's chest, knocking him back against the wall. He pulled Jacob back with him, tumbling with him to the floor, the blade still held to his son's throat. Andy charged across the lounge, knowing in the three long strides it would take to reach them, this man could sink the blade in with one convulsive twitch of his hand.

Somewhere across the small room, his hand let go of the torch and it dropped to the floor, the beam of light bouncing and flailing around.

He hurled himself at where the man had gone down, and landed heavily on top of Jacob's writhing body. In the dark, Andy's hands fumbled around, desperately seeking the knife before it was pushed home and extinguished his son's life.

Jenny could hear both men struggling in the dark and Jacob's muffled voice, crying, presumably tangled up with them, sandwiched in between them, that blade still, presumably, inches away from his throat or his face. She reached out for the torch on the floor and swung it around.

By the light of the torch, she could see the man's and Andy's legs kicking and swinging around. She could see one of Jacob's little arms emerging from between both men's writhing torsos, it flapped around raining small ineffectual un-aimed blows on both the man and Andy.

She could hear both men grunting with effort, and then she saw the glint of the knife amidst the confused tangle of limbs. Andy had a hold of the man's long knife by the blade. It was lacerating his fingers, and dots and splatters of Andy's blood flew up against the lounge wall.

The man lurched to one side, pulling Andy over with him. And then Jenny saw Jacob manage to wriggle some way out. She stepped toward him, reached out and grabbed Jacob's extended hand and pulled as hard as she could. He tumbled on to the floor with her, freed from the two men.

'Shoot him Andy!' she screamed, now that Jacob was safely out of the way. 'SHOOT HIM!'

The men rolled across the floor, behind the sofa, and now all she could see in the dancing light of the torch, were two pairs of legs, kicking, scissoring, flailing ... and more blood flicking up on to the wall.

'Oh God, Mum!' howled Leona. 'He's gonna kill Dad! He's going to KILL DAD!'

Jenny looked around the floor, hoping that the gun might have been dropped and kicked clear in the struggle.

And then the room flickered as if a firecracker had gone off, and simultaneously they heard the bang of the gun.

Both pairs of legs ceased moving. Jenny studied them for a moment, unable to move, not daring to look behind the back of the sofa.

'Andy?' she whispered.

Then the man's – Ash's – legs began to move, a short, jerking, twitching movement. Andy's legs remained still.

'Andy?' she cried.

Ash's legs stopped moving.

'Oh shit!'

Andy's voice.

'Oh, shit!' Andy grunted again.

'Dad, are you all right?' cried Leona, her voice trembling.

'Ah, jeeez, that's just bloody disgusting,' sighed Andy.

Jenny watched his legs kick at the body as he emerged from beneath it, and a moment later she saw his bloodied and torn hands on the back of the sofa.

'Don't let the kids come round the back, Jenny,' he muttered. 'I've got most of this guy's brains down the front of my shirt.'

His face appeared and he pulled himself up, wincing as he looked down at the thick dark slick across his chest.

'Daddy won,' whispered Jacob, the hint of awe in his voice unmistakable. 'He beat the baddie.'

'Oh my God, Andy,' Jenny uttered. And that was all she could say for the moment. The 'God I Love You's ... were all going to have to come later. For now the only thing that Jenny could do was sob with relief.

Andy looked up from the splattered debris of Ash's head on his shirt and offered his family a goofy grin.

'Should've changed my bloody shirt first. I liked this one.'

Leona and Jenny both managed to push a smile through the tears. Jacob grinned proudly at his father, then studied with a mixture of revulsion and fascination, the bloody mess.

'What's that?' Jake asked, pointing at another rapidly expanding crimson stain lower down the shirt.

Andy looked down, and saw the small, slim handle jutting out from his lower abdomen.

'Oh, just great,' he managed to mutter before collapsing.

Epilogue

It's been eighteen months now. Eighteen months since the world collapsed.

I miss Andy. I miss him so much. And his children miss him.

I don't know how we've survived, how we managed to keep going. It's been a blur to me, just moving from one day into the next. I know we left London soon after that night. I remember Leona had to drag me out of our house, away from our bedroom, where we left Andy.

Leona's been a tower of strength. I was useless for a long time. She got us out of London, and then we finally found a community in the countryside willing to take us in.

Very kind people, very different – historical re-enactors; the sort of people you would see at those big English Heritage events where they replayed battles from the English Civil War. Normal people with jobs and mortgages (back before the collapse), but with this other parallel life, attempting to revive, to learn the everyday skills of a time long before we had oil doing everything for us. Very different people, unlike any I've met before; they had already mastered so many of those skills of survival, the basics like ... how to make soap, how to make bread from grain. You know? The simple things.

And there's so much to do, we're kept busy, which is just as well.

We have several wind-up radios in the community, and from time to time there are broadcasts from the BBC World Service. For a time, just after the first week, it looked like a recovery might be on the cards. Oil lines were being fixed and a trickle of oil was getting through. But things were too broken, too messed up. We heard horror stories coming from the two dozen or so 'safe areas' the government had established. The supplies ran out at the end of the second month, and the people crammed inside turned on each other. And the same thing, so we hear, has happened in other countries around the world. America, I think, has been hit particularly badly.

In the months that followed, there was a worrying time ... there was a limited war between China, India and Russia over the Tengiz oilfields. It started with tanks and infantry, and escalated to a few nuclear bombs. Then very quickly it blew itself out. Perhaps some sanity broke out at the last moment, or perhaps their troops decided to stop fighting. Or maybe they simply ran out of the oil they needed to continue fighting.

Often, in the evenings, when the community gathers together, we discuss who was behind it all. Because, you see, it's obvious to everyone now that there was someone behind this. The theories are many and varied. The most-voiced opinions are that it was either a Muslim plot to destroy the decadent western lifestyle, or, alternatively, an attempt by America to destabilise all her economic rivals in one go ... but somehow it went wrong for them too.

I'm not convinced by either theory, but I don't know enough about politics to offer a better suggestion. Andy would have known. He knew all about that kind of thing.

We're being kept very busy right now, as I was saying. There's a lot to do, crops to grow, tend, cultivate or pick. We're digging a well, down to the clean water-table below us, and we have animals that need looking after. Jake's landed the main role as chicken tender; feeding them, collecting the eggs. When he's a little older, he'll also have to cope with killing them on occasion, plucking them, gutting them.

Leona's struggling a bit now. She was strong for me when I needed her. Now, she's finding it hard to cope. I know she misses her father, and I know some of the things that happened before I got home really traumatised her. There's a lot of crying.

Jacob misses Andy terribly too. But he's also so proud of his dad, and tells anyone who'll listen that his dad was a superhero. I love that he thinks that about Andy.

Anyway, we're alive, and my kids will mend eventually. And things will eventually knit themselves back together again. All those empty cities, full of burned-out homes, and looted shops ... one day people will migrate back to them. When it all eventually comes back together again, I think it's going to be very different.

To use one of Andy's pet phrases ... the oil age is over.

Just like all those other ages; the Stone Age, the Bronze Age, the Steam Age ... it's been and gone. Hopefully what replaces it will be a world less greedy, less obsessed with having things; trinkets and baubles, gadgets and bling. I wonder what my children's children will make of the weathered and faded mail order catalogues they'll undoubtedly come across, everything lavishly powered by electricity; giant American-style fridge freezers, those extravagant patio heaters, electric sonic-pulse hi-spin toothbrushes, automatic can-openers.

God, did we really get that lazy?

That's something Andy would have said, isn't it? Christ, I miss him.

I need to say something though, out loud.

I'm pretty sure you won't hear this Andy, you're gone. There's none of that looking down from heaven nonsense, is there? You're gone, that's it. But all the same, I need to say this even if it's just for my own ears ...

I'm sorry. I did always love you, I just forgot that for a while. You came back for us, and you saved us. Our son and our daughter will always, always remember you as a hero.

And so will I.

Love you, Andy.

Author's Note

Last Light started out four years ago as a result of my stumbling across a phrase being repeated over and over by two posters for a forum. They were hotly debating a geological issue and this phrase kept cropping up: Peak Oil. Being capitalized like that suggested that this was some sort of technical term in common use by those in the know. Curious, I Googled it.

And so, to indulge in an appalling cliché, a journey of discovery followed. Out there in internet-land are hundreds, perhaps thousands, of websites devoted to Peak Oil. I should perhaps explain what the term means before going any further. Simply put, it refers to the point at which all the easy-to-extract oil has been sucked out of the ground leaving only the really hard to get to, very expensive to refine, stuff. Now, there is a great deal of debate amongst geologists and petro-industry experts about how much oil there is left in the ground. It ranges from either a doom 'n' gloom scenario that we've already 'peaked' and it's rapidly running out, to a naively optimistic view that we have another fifty or sixty years of untapped oil. I'm not going to make a call on that debate here. But what no one disagrees on is how utterly reliant we are on the stuff. If you're reading this, having read the book, you don't need me to reiterate here the warnings Andy offered his family. The fact is, with *globalism* having run its course, the world is now inextricably linked as one large, interlocked set of dependencies; we get our sausages from *this* far flung country, our trainers from *that* far flung country, our plasma TVs from yet another far flung country ... and so on.

Whether we're about to run out of oil, or whether the world is approaching a clash of religious ideologies or an economic – possibly military – showdown between the new economic superpowers and the old; whether the world's climate is on the cusp of a dramatic change that could imperil billions and lead to mass migration; whichever one of these scenarios lies ahead of us, to be so completely dependent – as we are here in the UK – on produce grown, packaged and manufactured on the other side of the world ... well, that's simply asking for trouble.

Last Light is the book I've wanted to, no, *needed* to write since ... well, since 9/11. It's not really a book about Peak Oil – that was merely the starting point for me. No, it's a book about how lazy and vulnerable we've allowed ourselves to become. How reliant on the system we are. How little responsibility we are prepared to take for our actions, for ourselves, for our children. Somewhere along the way, in the last two or three decades, we *broke* this society of ours; whether it was during Blair's tenure of power, or Thatcher's, I'm not sure. But somehow it got broken.

And here we are, the ghastly events of 7/7; the increasing prevalence of gang related gun crime in London; legions of disaffected kids packing blades to go to school; a media that night and day pumps out the message – *screw everyone else, just get what's yours*; reality TV that celebrates effortless transitory fame over something as old-fashioned as 'achievement'; corporations that rip off their employees' pension funds; a Prime Minister deceiving us into entering an ill-conceived war; and politicians of all flavours putting themselves and their benefits first. All these things, I suspect, are the visible hairline cracks of our broken society that hint at the deeper, very dangerous, fault lines beneath. And all it'll take is some event, some catalyst, for the whole thing to come tumbling down.

Damn ... this has turned into something of a rant, hasn't it? That wasn't my intention. Ah well sod it, 'author's notes' is my one opportunity to get things off my chest without having to worry about plot, character and pacing.

Anyway, I'd like to think that a whiff of *Last Light* will remain with you once you snap the cover shut. I'm hoping Andy Sutherland achieved something; that the world looks slightly different to you now – more fragile, more vulnerable. After all, to be aware is to be better prepared.

I dunno ... is it just me? Or do you get that feeling too? That something's coming, something on the horizon ... a *correction* of some sort?